Dictionary of Medieval Civilization

Dictionary of

Medieval Civilization

Joseph Dahmus

MACMILLAN PUBLISHING COMPANY
NEW YORK
Collier Macmillan Publishers
London

Macmillan Publishing Company
866 Third Avenue, New York, NY 10022

Collier Macmillan Canada, Inc.

Library of Congress Catalog Card Number: 83-25583

Printed in the United States of America

printing number
1 2 3 4 5 6 7 8 9 10

Library of Congress Cataloging in Publication Data
Main entry under title:
Dahmus, Joseph Henry, 1909–
    Dictionary of medieval civilization.
    1. Civilization, Medieval—Dictionaries.   I. Title.
CB351.D24   1984   909.07′03′21   83-25583
ISBN 0-02-907870-9

Editorial and Production Staff

Charles E. Smith, *Publisher*
Elly Dickason, *Project Editor*
Morton I. Rosenberg, *Production Manager*
Joan Greenfield, *Designer*

Contents

Preface

A few words to the reader are in order regarding the purpose and peculiar value of the *Dictionary of Medieval Civilization*. As the title suggests, the volume presumes to be inclusive. Historical people and events appear, and so do books, monasteries and universities, countries, tribes, and cities, terms as strange as puzzle-jug and misericord, alongside the more useful feudalism, guild, scholasticism, and Magna Carta.

Despite its pretensions, the work does not replace such multi-volume encyclopedias as the *Britannica, Der Grosse Brockhaus, New Catholic Encyclopedia,* and *La Grande Encyclopédie.* These four sets aggregate some eighty volumes. For the most minor figures and esoteric terms, as well as for an extended discussion of persons, events, and things, the reader will continue to turn to these encyclopedias or to more specialized studies such as Planche's *Cyclopaedia of Costume* or Apel's *Dictionary of Music.* But the reader, the student, even the specialist, will in all probability find in this handy one-volume reference work concerning the Middle Ages all the information required for ordinary purposes.

No attempt has been made to introduce original analyses in the preparation of the entries, and identifications will, I hope, strike the informed reader as conventional. Since this is necessarily a work of selection and compilation, the most likely area of criticism will be the borderline that separates terms that must be included from those which limitations of space exclude. The first limiting factor, that of time, is easiest to justify. The startingpoint is generally the fourth century, although names of Christians from the time of Christ have been introduced where these appear with some frequency in medieval learning, literature, or art. Even though the Middle Ages closed on 31 December 1500, room has been furnished for those individuals who lived beyond this point but who contributed something of significance before that moment. In justifying what individuals, terms, and places deserved mention within these chronological limits I selected those that in my judgment would suffice for the great majority of readers.

With some exceptions, the entries follow alphabetically. Where a name such as *John* introduced a series of entries, first place went to popes, second to emperors (Byzantine), third to kings, after which the other *Johns* followed alphabetically.

Variant spellings pose a problem since many names may be "correctly" spelled a number of ways. Where several spellings appear in medieval sources or in their modern transliterations, these have been included within limits. No one would insist upon seeing the more than thirty variants of Wyclif's name. Still, does one write Roger Bacon or Bacon, Roger; William Lorris or Guillaume de Lorris; William Tell or Wilhelm Tell? A purist will write the Abbey of Sankt Gallen, but will he also use Köln for Cologne? And what does the person who wants all entries Anglicized do with Walther von der Vogelweide? Does this poet's name become Walter of the Bird Meadow? Is it Strassburg or Strasbourg, Presburg or Bratislava; Averroës or Ibn Rushd? Where usage has established a particular spelling that has been given preference, thus Strasbourg, Presburg, and Averroës. In the spelling of cities Shepherd's *Historical Atlas* has usually served as the guide.

I wish to acknowledge the financial assistance given me by the Institute for the Arts and Humanistic Studies of the Pennsylvania State University toward the completion of this volume.

Dictionary of Medieval Civilization

AACHEN (Aix-la-Chapelle), city located about 45 miles southwest of Cologne which Charlemagne (d. 814) preferred as his residence, partly because of the warm spring in the vicinity. The Romans had erected baths there by the close of the first century, and it was from these waters and the shrine which Charlemagne built there, that Aachen derived its French name, Aix-la-Chapelle. Charlemagne erected a splendid palace and cathedral at Aachen and through his efforts made it a center of Western culture and learning during the ninth century. Aachen served as capital of the Frankish kingdom under Charlemagne and Louis the Pious (d. 840) and as the coronation site of German kings from Otto I (936) until 1531.

AACHEN CATHEDRAL, the most famous church of the Carolingian era. It originated with the royal chapel erected by Charlemagne and was dedicated by Pope Leo III in 805. The church reveals Byzantine influences, in design notably that of San Vitale in Ravenna, from which city came some of the granite and marble columns used for the gallery around the first story. The central structure, which consisted of a sixteen-sided polygon covered with an octagonal dome, greatly impressed both men of the time and those of later centuries. Charlemagne intended the chapel to serve as his tomb, and tradition has him buried there. A Gothic choir was added to the east end of the structure in the fourteenth and fifteenth centuries.

AAGESEN, SVEND, fl. 1185, Danish historian, a clerk in the service of Absalon, archbishop of Lund. With that prelate's encouragement he prepared a brief history of the early Danish kings. He is also the probable author of a Latin translation of the military laws of Canute the Great (d. 1035).

AARGAU, a Swiss canton first identified in 763. It had been under Roman rule for 400 years before falling to the Alemanni. In the sixth century it became part of the Frankish empire. In 1415 the Swiss Confederation took it from the Hapsburgs.

ABA, SAMUEL, king of Hungary, 1040–4, brother-in-law of Stephen I. He expelled Stephen's successor King Peter (Orseolo), but failed to make good his seizure of power and was slain in the battle of Menfö.

ABAD, Arabic term meaning time in an absolute sense. In more specific usage it might signify the eternal or incorruptible.

ABAILLARD. *See* ABELARD.

ABAN IBN 'ABD AL-HAMID AL-LAHIKI (also known as al-Rakashi), d. c. 815, poet at the court of Harun al-Rashid who composed panegyrics in praise of the caliph and of the Barmecides who patronized him. He also engaged in heated poetical exchanges with other court poets including the more illustrious Abu Nuwas.

ABANO, PETER OF (Pietro d'), d. 1316?, philosopher and physician of Padua, founder of the Paduan school of medical dialectics. In his *Conciliator Differentiarum* he sought to harmonize Averroism with Christianity. He was accused of magic and heresy and tried by the Inquisition. He died in prison.

ABARBANEL, ISAAC. *See* ABRABANEL, ISAAC.

ABBA, Aramaic term for father which Christ and the early Christians used when speaking of God. From it was derived the title abbot which was held by superiors of monasteries.

ABBADIDS (Abbadides, Abbadites), Moslem dynasty that ruled from Seville from 1023 to 1091. It was established by Abbad I (Abúl-Qasim Mohammed) following the disintegration of the caliphate of Córdoba. Under his son, Abbad II, Seville became the most powerful state in Spain. His grandson, Abbad III, a poet and patron of the arts, appealed to the Almoravids of Morocco for help against Alfonso VI of Castile. They answered his appeal, but then deposed him and took over his rule.

ABBA MARI, French rabbi of the early fourteenth century who attacked the writings of Jewish philosophers and those of Moses Maimonides in particular for what he judged to be their baleful influence upon Jewish theology.

ABBAN, name of several Irish saints, the best known of them Abban of Magheranoidhe (modern Adamstown), d. 620, the son of Cormac, king of Leinster. He is credited with establishing a large number of churches and monasteries.

ABBAS, d. c. 653, wealthy merchant of Mecca, uncle of Mohammed (half-brother of his father), and ancestor of the Abbasids. Despite the protests of his Abbasid apologists who came to his defense, it appears that he was a tardy supporter of the Prophet and joined him only when he came marching on Mecca in 630 with an army.

ABBASIDS, the most celebrated Islamic dynasty. It was established by Abu-l-Abbas as-Saffah (750–4) who brought an end to Omayyad rule in 750. The dynasty which survived until 1258 based its claim to leadership of Islam on descent from Abbas, an uncle of Mohammed. It found its principal support in the Persian province of Khurasan but also enjoyed the adherence of the Shiites, followers of Ali, the son-in-law of the Prophet, and the more numerous Mawali (non-Arab converts who suffered discrimination). The establishment of a new capital at Baghdad in 762 by the second Abbasid caliph Mansur announced the triumph of Persian influence and ushered in the most brilliant era in the history of Islamic culture. This reached its height during the reigns of Harun al-Rashid (786–809) and his son Al-Ma'mun (813–33). The military power of the Abbasids proved incapable, however, of maintaining control of the far-flung Islamic empire. Spain was lost in 756 while more and more provincial governors were declaring themselves autonomous from the middle of the ninth century on. Marked decline set in during the reign of Al-Muqtadir (908–32), after which real power rested usually with the military leaders (sultans) of the Buwayhids (a Persian house) and the Seljuk Turks. In 1258 the Mongol chieftain Hulagu destroyed Baghdad and slew Al-Musta'sim, the last Abbasid caliph. A branch of the dynasty retained a position of religious leadership in Egypt until 1538.

ABBESS, the female superior of a community of nuns whose position corresponded to that of the abbot. Female monastic communities appeared as early as the fourth century and the earliest known use of the title abbess dates from 514. Abbesses of great houses ranked with abbots as feudal lords and might occupy seats in Parliament.

ABBEVILLE, town located near the mouth of the Somme. It was the principal city of Ponthieu and a thriving commercial center from the twelfth century on. It derived its name from its possession by the abbot of St. Richier (*Abbatis villa*). In 1184 it received a charter. Here in 1259 Henry III concluded a treaty with Louis IX by which he surrendered claims to English possessions north of the Loire but retained English rights in Aquitaine.

ABBEY, a monastic community of either monks

or nuns whose superior bore the title of abbot or abbess. [*See* MONASTERY.]

ABBO OF CERNUUS, d. after 921, a Benedictine monk who wrote a description in Latin verse of the siege of Paris by the Normans (855–6) and of subsequent events to 896. He was an eyewitness of the siege.

ABBO OF FLEURY, ST., d. 1004, abbot of the Benedictine monastery of Saint-Benoît-sur-Loire (Fleury) from 988. Abbo, who studied at Paris, Reims, and Fleury, was distinguished for his learning and sanctity. He took an active part in the Cluniac reform movement and proved himself a staunch defender of the rights of the church. He was slain at the priory of La Réale in Gascony in a revolt which broke out when he brought in a group of his own reformed monks. He left writings on logic, mathematics, astronomy, and an epitome of the lives of the popes.

ABBOT, title borne by the superior of a monastic community of monks. The term, derived from *abba,* the Aramaic word for father, was first used by Egyptian anchorites of the fourth century to designate their spiritual father. St. Benedict (d. c. 547) ordered its use in his *Rule.* He also provided that the monks of the community should elect the abbot who would then rule with a paternalistic authority although under obligation to consult at least the more mature members of the household on important matters. Until the early ninth century the abbot might be a layman and for several centuries he would owe his position to the king or local lord. [*See* INVESTITURE CONTROVERSY.] Such secular interference in the election of the abbot followed from the fact that the monastery which the abbot directed often possessed extensive lands. This put the abbot in the position of a feudal lord and imposed upon him many of the traditional feudal obligations to his overlord (king).

ABBREVIATOR, member of the papal chancery who prepared the first draft of a document or letter which would later be given a polished form. The number of such clerks increased from the fourteenth century as the business of the Curia expanded. The abbreviator received his name from the large number of abbreviations he employed.

ABCEDARII, name given to students in medieval schools who were just beginning to read.

ABCEDARIUM, schoolbook suggestive of the ABC's, the medieval ancestor of the spelling book. The word is also associated with law books of the late Middle Ages whose contents were alphabetically arranged.

ABD, Arabic word for slave and often part of an Arab's name: e.g., Abd al-Rahman, that is, "the slave of the Merciful."

ABD-ALLAH (Abdullah), d. c. 570, father of Mohammed who died shortly before his son's birth, probably about the age of 25. Little is known about him.

ABDALLAH IBN 'ALI, d. 764, uncle of the first two Abbasid caliphs, who captured Damascus and conquered Palestine. He then served as governor of Syria, but was later removed for his pretensions to the throne and eventually murdered.

ABDALLAH IBN JASIN (Abdullah ibn Yasin), d. 1058, founder of the Almoravid dynasty. He inspired a religious reform movement among the Moslem Berbers of the Atlas mountains, then delegated the forceful spread of his movement to a warrior by the name of Jusuf ibn Tashfin. He and his followers were marked for their puritanical intolerance.

ABD-AL-LATIF, d. 1231, Arabic scholar who lived for a time at the court of Saladin in Egypt. He earned great fame for his knowledge of medicine, alchemy, geography, philosophy, and mathematics. His numerous writings attest to the breadth of his learning.

ABD-AL-MALIK (Abdu-l-Malik), Omayyad caliph, 685–705, son of Marwan I. He restored

Islam's rule over Arabia and Iraq, made Arabic the official language in the conduct of financial affairs, improved postal facilities, and minted the first gold dinars. These replaced the Byzantine coins that had been in use in the Islamic world up to that time.

ABD-AL-MUMIN (Abdu-l-Mumin), able statesman and general who assumed the military leadership of the religious reform movement sponsored by Ibn Tumart among the Almoravids. He had been Tumart's favorite companion. He overthrew the Almoravids, conquered their territories in north Africa and Spain, and ruled as the first caliph (1140–63) of the Almohad dynasty. He fitted out several ports, notably Rabat, for his fleet. The Almohads are also known as Muwahhids.

ABD AL-RAHMAN (Abd er-Rachman, Abdu-r-Rahman, Abd ar-Rahman), name held by five Omayyad rulers of Spain. The most important of these was Abd al-Rahman I (756–88), the only member of the Omayyad dynasty to escape death at the hands of the triumphant Abbasids. He managed to make his escape to Spain, there defeated the emir of Córdoba and took over his country, later extended his rule over the greater part of Spain. During the reign of Abd al-Rahman III (912–61), Islamic Spain attained the height of its power, prosperity, and cultural brilliance, and Córdoba became one of the greatest cities in the west. Abd al-Rahman III was the first Omayyad ruler to assume the title caliph.

ABD AL-RAHMAN (Abdu-r-Rahman), d. 732, Moslem governor of Spain, invaded France and won a victory at Toulouse, but then suffered a decisive defeat at the hands of Charles Martel and the Franks at the battle of Tours in 732. Tours marked the fartherest penetration of the Moors in western Europe.

ABD-AL-WADID DYNASTY, ruling family of a loosely defined Berber state in northwestern Africa which controlled the greater part of Maghreb (not including Morocco) from 1239 to 1554. It was then overwhelmed by the Ottoman Turks from Algiers. It had its capital at Tlemcen.

ABDAST (*Wudu*), minor ritual ablution involving the washing of hands which Moslems observed preparatory to praying.

ABDIAS OF BABYLON, ST., an apocryphal and semilegendary writer said to have been one of Christ's 72 disciples. The Apostles Simon and Jude are said to have appointed him the first bishop of Babylon.

ABDINGHOF, ABBEY OF, Benedictine monastery founded in Westphalia in 1015 by Meinwerk, bishop of Paderborn. It was recognized as an important cultural center during the eleventh and twelfth centuries.

ABDISHO BAR BERIKA (Ebedjesu), d. 1318, Nestorian metropolitan of Nisibis and Armenia, the author of letters, numerous theological and exegetical works, and translations into Syriac of the writings of Greek and Syrian church fathers.

ABDULLAH. *See* ABD-ALLAH.

À BECKET, THOMAS, ST. *See* BECKET, THOMAS, ST.

ABEL, second son of Adam and Eve. In the Middle Ages Abel was regarded as a type of Christ because of the purity of his life, his sacrifice, and his violent death.

ABELARD (Abaelard, Abaillard), PETER, d. 1142, leading scholastic of the twelfth century, a native of Brittany, studied under Roscelin of Compiègne, William of Champeaux, and Anselm of Laon. His intellectual arrogance led him to set up his own school in Melun (near Paris), although in time his ecclesiastical superiors recognized his genuine brilliance of mind and appointed him to teach dialectic and theology at the cathedral school of Notre Dame. Here a love affair with Heloise, niece of a canon of the cathedral, almost ended his career. Heloise became a nun, Abelard a monk, but his troubles continued. In 1121 a council at Soissons condemned his writings on the Trinity, a condemnation which St. Bernard of Clairvaux and a council at Sens repeated some 20 years later. Abelard started for Rome in the hope of convincing the pope of his orthodoxy, but he permitted himself to be persuaded by Peter of Cluny to make his peace with the church. He died in a Cluniac priory near Chalon-sur-Saône.

Abelard's principal contribution to scholasticism was the compromise he proposed concerning the problem of universals called conceptualism, essentially the moderate realism later accepted by St. Thomas Aquinas. His purpose in the *Sic et Non* in which he introduced conflicting statements from the church fathers in support of and opposed to a suggested thesis was not to sow doubt among Christians but to stimulate independent thought. What might be considered his principal contribution to theology and ethics was the emphasis he placed upon intent in judging the morality of an act. Scholars dispute his influence upon the evolution of the scholastic method. Abelard left sermons, letters, and some verse. [*See* UNIVERSALS.]

ABELITES (Abelians, Abelonians), small sect in north Africa who lived celibate lives after the presumed example of Abel. Only St. Augustine furnishes any information concerning them.

ABENCERRAGES, Moorish nobility of Granada whose military exploits in wars with the Christians during the late Middle Ages became the theme of Spanish romantic poets.

ABERCIUS, INSCRIPTION OF, actually the epitaph of Bishop Abercius of Hieropolis in Syria who died in the late second or early third century. The inscription is important for the information it provides concerning early Christianity, particularly in regard to the devotion to the Eucharist of which it furnishes the first testimony. The *Life of Abercius,* which incorporates the text of the inscription, is probably of the late fourth century.

ABERDEEN, city in Scotland situated on the North Sea some 130 miles northeast of Edinburgh, whose history dates back to c. 1179 when William the Lion granted it a charter. It supported Robert the Bruce in his struggle for the throne. In the twelfth century it became an episcopal see. In 1338 the English burned the burgh. The university of Aberdeen was chartered in 1495 by Pope Alexander VI upon the request of William Elphinstone, bishop of Aberdeen.

ABERGAVENNY, English town on the Welsh border, the Roman Gobannium, a fortress which guarded the river Usk. Ruins of the eleventh-century Norman castle built by Hamelin de Ballon (or Baludin) remain today. The town was frequently involved in border warfare during the twelfth and thirteenth centuries and in 1404 was burned by Owen Glendower.

ABGAR, name of several rulers of Edessa from 132 B.C. to A.D. 214. Eusebius writes that King Abgar V (4 B.C. to A.D. 50), called Uchama (the Black), corresponded with Christ who had cleansed him of an incurable disease.

ABHDISHO BAR BERIKHA. *See* ABDISHO BAR BERIKA.

ABINGDON, ABBEY OF, Benedictine house in Berkshire, England, founded c. 675. It was destroyed by the Danes but rebuilt c. 954, after which it became an important center of monastic revival. That it owed the Norman kings the service of 30 knights suggests the extensiveness of its holdings. The abbot controlled the town and it was not until 1556 that the townspeople gained the right to manage local affairs. The abbey was dissolved in 1538.

ABJURATION, a renunciation under oath of heresy or error contrary to Christian faith by a Christian who wished to be reconciled with the church.

ABNER OF BURGOS, d. c. 1346, Jewish rabbi and physician of Valladolid who became a Christian (baptized Alfonso). His theological writing (in Spanish) provoked attack from Jewish scholars.

ABONDANCE, MONASTERY OF, house of Canons Regular of St. Augustine in Savoy, probably founded in 1080. By the thirteenth century it had become the leading abbey in the diocese of Geneva and had founded a number of abbeys and priories in the region.

ABRABANEL (Abravanel, Abarbanel), ISAAC BEN-JUDAH, d. 1508, learned Jewish exegete and philosopher who served Alfonso V of Portugal as minister of finance, then Ferdinand and Isabella of Spain. He subsequently took service with the governments of Naples, Sicily, and Venice after his banishment from Spain, along with other Jews, in 1492. He authored many exegetical and philosophical works, upheld the validity of miracles against the rationalism of Maimonides, translated a treatise of St. Thomas Aquinas into Hebrew, and looked to the establishment of a Jewish state in the Holy Land.

ABRACADABRA, magic formula used by the Gnostics in the second century to invoke the aid of benevolent spirits to ward off evil. It was often engraved on amulets which then served as protective charms.

ABRAHAM BEN DAVID, d. 1198, Jewish philosopher, a critic of Maimonides, and one of the first Jewish thinkers to incline to mysticism. Contemporaries honored him as both a scholar and a saint.

ABRAHAM, BOSOM OF, a Biblical expression symbolizing the blissful abode of the righteous dead, a favorite subject of medieval artists who usually portrayed the patriarch as seated and having several small figures on his lap.

ABRAHAM IBN DAUD, d. c. 1180, Jewish philosopher of Toledo and author of a chronicle to the year 1161. He died a martyr at the hands of the Moors.

ABRAHAMITES, a Syrian sect of the ninth century that denied the divinity of Christ. It was named after its founder, Abraham of Antioch.

ABRAHAM OF CLERMONT, ST., d. c. 480, man of Persian origin who was driven to flee from Persia to France in order to escape persecution. He first lived as a hermit near Clermont, then became abbot of a religious community composed of men whom the fame of his sanctity had attracted.

ABRAHAM OF EPHESUS, ST., d. 553, bishop of Ephesus and founder of a monastery of Abrahamites in Constantinople. His homilies throw light on early Christian liturgical practices.

ABRAHAM, TESTAMENT OF, an apocryphal Greek legend concerning the death of Abraham, probably written in the second century A.D. The story, which tells how the Archangel Michael took the patriarch to heaven where he showed him the two roads, one leading to heaven, the other to hell, found its way into many ancient languages. The legend was of either Jewish or Christian origin.

ABRAKADABRA. *See* ABRACADABRA.

ABRAXAS (Abrasax), name given by Gnostics to the supreme deity. The term, which may also have possessed some mystical or magical significance, is found on ancient and medieval amulets. Gnostics, particularly the Basilidians (Basilides), appear to have used such amulets.

ABROGANS, the name of a late Latin wordlist which was translated into German about 765. It is considered the oldest example of learned writing to appear in the German language.

ABSALON, d. 1201, archbishop of Lund (1177), administrator, statesman, and warrior who enjoyed considerable influence with Waldemar I and Canute VI of Denmark. He used force against the pagan Wends in order to extend Christianity east of the Baltic, in the course of which he built the castle where Copenhagen had its origin. Danish supremacy in northern Germany had its beginnings in his military successes. The archbishop was a patron of Svend Aagesen and of Saxo Grammaticus.

ABU, Arabic word meaning father when followed by a personal name.

ABUBACER. *See* IBN TUFAIL.

ABU BAKR (Bekr), first caliph, the successor of Mohammed. He had been one of the very first Arabs to accept Mohammed as Prophet and was also the father of Aishah, Mohammed's favorite wife. During his short caliphate of two years (632–4), the Riddah wars were successfully fought to keep the Islamic state intact and to force back into submission Arab tribes that had renounced Meccan lordship following the death of Mohammed.

ABU DAWUD, d. 888, Arabic theologian and author of one of the major collections of Islamic traditions (*hadith*) called *Sunan*.

ABU FIRAS, d. 968, Arab poet of Aleppo who composed a poetical diary of his times and of his own turbulent life. He had several times been a prisoner of the Byzantine empire.

ABU HANIFA, d. 767, Islamic theologian and jurist who founded and gave his name to one of the four orthodox schools of jurisprudence (Hanafite) in Islam. His was the most tolerant of the four schools.

ABU KHASIM (Abulcasis), fl. 11th century, Arab physician, author of an important text (*Tasrif*) on medicine and surgery. It was translated into Latin and other languages.

ABU-L-ABBAS (Abu-l-Abbas as-Saffah), first Abbasid caliph (750–4), whose ruthless extermination of the members of the Omayyad dynasty won him the title of "al-Saffah," meaning the "Bloodshedder." He established his capital at al-Anbar in north Iraq on the Euphrates.

ABUL-L-AL-MA'ARRI, d. 1057, blind Syrian poet who spent some years in Baghdad as a member of its famous learned and literary circle. The pessimism and skepticism expressed in his verse is supposed to have reflected the growing social and political decay of his times. His two collections of verse are among the most outstanding of the Golden Age of Arabic literature.

ABU-L-ATAHIYA, d. c. 828, Arab composer of religious poems and love songs. Some of his verse attacked the frivolous life of Baghdad and the caliph's court although he showed himself ready to accept a large annual stipend from his patron, Harun al-Rashid. He has been called the father of Arabic sacred poetry.

ABU-L-BARAKAT, d. 1324, Coptic priest of Cairo and court secretary, author of a dictionary, sermons, and of a particularly valuable theological encyclopedia. He collaborated on a history of Islam that extended to 1325.

ABU-L-FARAJ 'ABDALLAH IBN ATTAYYIB, d. 1043, Christian monk and ecclesiastical administrator, physician of Baghdad, and author of commentaries on Aristotle and of treatises dealing with medicine, canon law, and Scripture.

ABU-L-FARAJ AL-ISBAHANI (Isfahan), d. 967, Arab writer whose *Kitab al-Aghani* (*Book of Songs*) constitutes a major source for the history of early Islamic culture. The work which earned him 1000 gold pieces from his patron, included 100 songs.

ABU-L-FIDA (Abulfeda), d. 1331, Christian Arab prince, historian, geographer, patron of men of letters, and governor of Hama in Syria during the closing period of the Crusades. He wrote a universal history that became a valuable source for Arab history for the years 700 to 1200.

ABU-L-WAFA (Wefa), d. 998, a Persian, one of Islam's greatest mathematicians and astronomers.

ABU MA'SHAR (Abu Ma'sar Dscha 'far al-Balchi), d. 886, a leading Islamic astrologer whom the West referred to as Albumasar (Albumazar). His works, which were translated into Latin, exerted great influence upon Western thought.

ABU MOHAMMED IBN TUMART, Berber theologian who called himself Al-Mahdi, that is, the prophet who was to reform Islam. Following his return from Baghdad where he had been instructed by Al-Ghazali, he gained many supporters, chief among them the warrior Abd-Al-Mumin, who brought an end to the Almoravid (Murabit) regime and established the Almohad (Muwahhid) c. 1140.

ABU MUSLIM, d. 755, Persian freedman, political and religious agitator who helped organize opposition to the Omayyads and whose military talents contributed significantly to the success of the Abbasid revolt. Although appointed governor of Khurasan, he was subsequently murdered on orders of the caliph Al-Mansur who feared him.

ABUNA (from the Arabic for father), title of a priest among the Syrian Christians and the patriarch of the Ethiopian church.

ABUNDIUS OF COMO, ST., d. c. 468, bishop of Como whom Pope Leo I sent with others to examine the orthodoxy of the patriarch Anatolius of Constantinople. The patriarch had been charged with Nestorianism.

ABU NUWAS HASSAN, d. c. 815, popular Arab poet at the court of Harun al-Rashid who sang of the pleasures of wine, women, and the hunt, in addition to composing panegyrics in honor of the caliph and the Barmecides. His sensuous verse reflected the license which Harun al-Rashid permitted at his court.

ABU SAID IBN ABD-L-KHAIR, d. 1049, Persian poet, a Sufi and dervish, who was the first to write *rubaiyat* in the manner that Omar Khayyam employed.

ABU TALIB, paternal uncle of Mohammed who took the boy under his care when he was eight years old. When Abu Talib died in 619, Mohammed's position in Mecca grew precarious, leading to his decision to flee to Medina (622). Abu Talib never accepted his nephew as the Prophet.

ABU TAMMAM, d. 845, Arab court poet in Baghdad and author of a popular anthology entitled *Hamasa*. He is best known for his military verse.

ABYSSINIA. *See* ETHIOPIA.

ACACIAN SCHISM, schism between Rome and Constantinople which continued from 484 until 519. It was precipitated when Acacius, patriarch of Constantinople, endorsed the *Henoticon* promulgated by Emperor Zeno in 482 and approved the consecration of the Monophysite Peter Mongus as patriarch of Alexandria. This action led Pope Felix III to excommunicate Acacius, and Acacius in turn to repudiate papal authority. The schism endured until the accession of Emperor Justin I.

ACACIUS, d. after 365, bishop of Caesarea in Palestine, an eloquent, influential, and politically adroit principal in the Arian controversy. He was an Arian under Emperor Constantius, later shifted to orthodoxy under Jovian, then back to Arianism under Valens. His followers, known as Acacians, represented a distinct and important theological party between 357 and 461.

ACACIUS, patriarch of Constantinople. [*See* ACACIAN SCHISM.]

ACACIUS OF BEROEA (Aleppo), d. after 433, bishop of Beroea in Syria who took an active part in the Christological controversies of the period. Although he opposed Arianism and Nestorianism, he intrigued with other churchmen to effect the exile of the orthodox St. John Chrysostom.

ACANTHUS, any species of the genus *Acanthus*, perennial plant native to the Mediterranean region. In Christian art the acanthus symbolized heaven.

ACATHISTUS, title of a hymn to the Mother of God which was inspired by the destruction of the Persian and Avar fleets before Constantinople in 626. The faithful credited the Byzantine victory to the intervention of Mary. During the singing of the hymn, the faithful stood rather than sat, whence the derivation of its title which means "not sitting."

ACCA, ST., d. 740, bishop of Hexham, England, who encouraged the liturgical reform after the Roman usage. He persuaded Bede to write his history.

ACCENTUS ECCLESIASTICUS, in early church music a part of the liturgy, including the collect, epistle, and gospel, that was ordinarily sung by the priest or a single cleric, as opposed to the *concentus,* a portion of the Mass, such as the psalms, sung by the choir.

ACCIAIOLI (Acciaiuli, Acciajuoli), aristocratic family of Florence, prominent in trade, banking, politics, and the arts from the twelfth century. The fame of Niccolo A. (d. 1365) prepared the way for members of the family to rule as dukes of Athens, Corinth, Sparta, and Thebes. Angelo A. (d. 1408), archbishop of Florence and cardinal, served as regent for the young king of Naples and supported the popes at Rome during the Western Schism. Donato A. (d. 1478) was a humanist, philosopher, poet, and historian.

ACCIDENT, in medieval philosophy, an attribute or quality that was not essential, an entity whose essential nature was to inhere in another entity as a subject. Medieval scholastics appealed to this term and the principle involved to explain the miracle of transubstantiation, when the accidents, e.g., the color of the bread, remained the same after the words of consecration had changed the substance of the bread into the body (and blood) of Christ.

ACCIDIE, from the Greek word meaning negli-gence or indifference and employed in the context of Christian asceticism to signify a state of restlessness and inability either to work or to pray. It was identified with sloth as one of the Seven Deadly Sins.

ACCLAMATION, vocal approval by a group, crowd, or legally constituted body of the election of a high official, most commonly that of a bishop or pope, e.g., the election of St. Ambrose as bishop of Milan in 374. The term also applied more narrowly to the musical salutation given a Byzantine emperor when he made a public appearance at the Hippodrome in Constantinople, or to a patriarch or other high Byzantine dignitary.

ACCOLADE, an embrace used in the early feudal period to welcome knights, later a blow on the shoulder given with the flat side of a sword as part of the knighting ceremony.

ACCOLTI, BENEDETTO, d. 1466?, Italian humanist, lawyer, and historian. His most important work was a history of the First Crusade. Tasso is supposed to have drawn the idea of *Jerusalem Delivered* from this book.

ACCOLTI, BERNARDO (Unico Aretino), d. 1535, son of Benedetto Accolti, Florentine exile, for a time apostolic abbreviator in the Roman Curia, and author of a comedy. He was famed for his ability to recite extemporaneous poetry.

ACCURSIUS, FRANCISCUS, d. 1263, Italian jurist, professor of Roman law at Bologna, who prepared a compilation of the commentaries made by all Bolognese glossators on the *Corpus Juris Civilis*. Dante placed his son Francesco (Franciscus) in hell (*Inferno,* XV, 110).

ACEPHALI, that is, without a head, name given the Eutychians who in 482 repudiated Peter Mongus, patriarch of Alexandria, when he proposed a compromise creed in an effort to conciliate the orthodox. They preferred to be without any head, whence their name.

ACHARD OF SAINT-VICTOR, d. c. 1172, abbot, bishop of Avranches, and author of an authoritative work on the Trinity, of learned sermons, and a treatise on spiritual psychology.

ACHILLINI, ALESSANDRO, d. 1512, Italian scientist who taught medicine and philosophy at Bologna and Padua. He is best known for his writings on anatomy.

ACOEMETAE, from the Latinized form of the Greek word meaning "sleepless ones," a name given to monks of the Byzantine monastery at Irenaion (Asiatic shore of the Bosporus) because they never ceased the singing of the divine office, neither day or night. The monastery was founded c. 400 by Abbot Alexander. The monks practiced absolute poverty, did no manual work, but pursued a zealous missionary vocation. In their anxiety to combat Monophysitism, they became tainted with Nestorianism and in 534 were excommunicated by Pope John II.

ACOLYTE, a cleric who had received the fourth and highest of the minor orders in the Latin church. His duties included the lighting of the candles on the altar and attendance upon the celebrant at Mass.

ACOMINATUS, MICHAEL. *See* CHONIATES, MICHAEL.

ACOMINATUS, NICETAS. *See* CHONIATES, NICETAS.

ACRE, ancient Syrian seaport of considerable commercial and military importance, the best harbor on the Palestine coast, taken by the Arabs in 638. It changed hands several times during the period of the Crusades and from 1190 to 1291 was held by the Knights Hospitalers, whence its French name. Its fall to the Moslems (of Egypt) in 1291 led to the rapid extinction of the remaining Christian possessions along the coast.

ACROPOLITES (Acropolita), GEORGE, d. 1282, Byzantine scholar, historian, grand logothete, imperial representative at the Council of Lyons (1274), and author of a valuable chronicle covering the years 1203 to 1261.

ACROSTIC, a poem in which one or more sets of letters, usually the initial or final ones, when taken in order, formed a word (phrase, sentence). Because of their symbolic and didactic value, the use of acrostics was popular in the Middle Ages.

ACTA PILATI, also known as the *Gospel of Nicodemus,* an apocryphal work probably of the fourth century which embellished the biblical account of Christ's crucifixion with semilegendary information including the story of Veronica and her veil.

ACTA SANCTORUM, collection of lives of the saints which the Jesuit priest John Bolland (Bollandus) initiated in 1643 and which Bollandists have continued to publish. The lives are arranged in the order of their feasts in the ecclesiastical year. It is the aim of the Bollandists to eliminate all matter of a legendary character.

ACTON, a form of gambeson, a quilted coat worn under the mailshirt for added protection.

ACTS OF THE APOSTLES, one of the books of the New Testament, traditionally ascribed to St. Luke. It covers events and the actions of the Apostles, principally those of St. Paul, dealing with early Christianity to c. 90.

ACTS OF THE MARTYRS, records of early Christian martyrdoms, a few contemporary and based on eyewitness accounts, others embellished with hearsay information and legend. Eusebius of Caesarea (d. c. 340) may have been the first Christian writer to produce a collection of "Acts of Martyrs." His is no longer extant.

ADAHAND MANUSCRIPT, one of the finest examples of illuminated manuscripts from the Carolingian period. It consists of a luxuriously copied gospel made about 800 for the Abbess Ada who, according to tradition, was a sister of Charlemagne.

ADALARD, ST., d. 826, grandson of Charles Martel, abbot of the monastery at Corbie, and a leading figure in the Carolingian renaissance. He served as adviser to Louis the Pious in ecclesiastical affairs.

ADALBERO I, bishop of Metz, d. 962, took an active part in French-German politics and was also a vigorous supporter of monastic reform. He chiefly was responsible for reforming Gorze Abbey and for preparing it to assume the direction of an important monastic reform movement in Lorraine.

ADALBERO OF AUGSBURG, BL., d. 909, was largely responsible for establishing the high level of spiritual and intellectual life that was maintained in the monastery of Lorsch. He later served as tutor and adviser to Louis the Child.

ADALBERO (Ascelin) OF LAON, d. 1030, bishop of Laon who supported the cause of Hugh Capet against Charles of Lorraine for the French throne. He led the Gallic episcopacy in their opposition to the reform movement sponsored by the monastery of Cluny. He left some verse.

ADALBERO (Adalberon) OF REIMS, d. 989, abbot of the monastery at Gorze, later archbishop of Reims (969). He supported the candidacy of Hugh Capet and crowned him at Reims. He encouraged monastic reform and placed the famous scholar Gerbert in charge of the cathedral school at Reims.

ADALBERO OF WÜRZBURG, ST., d. 1090, bishop of Würzburg, supported Henry IV in his contest with Pope Gregory VII over investiture until the king proclaimed the pope's deposition. Henry subsequently forced him into exile.

ADALBERT, d. 1072, archbishop of Hamburg-Bremen (from 1043), member of a noble Saxon family, the most brilliant of the prince-bishops of Bremen. His ambition to establish a powerful ecclesiastical state, a "Patriarchate of the North," from which to carry Christianity to the Slavs and Scandinavians was blocked by German political rivals as well as by the rulers of Scandinavia who preferred bishops of their own. He served as adviser to Henry III and from 1064 until 1066 as regent for the youthful Henry IV. He greatly expanded Bremen's commerce and made it the "market of the northern peoples."

ADALBERT, archbishop of Mainz, d. 1137, chancellor of Henry V of Germany whose investiture claims he pressed against Pope Paschal II. As archbishop he supported the pope, spent three years in a dungeon to which Henry had consigned him, then upon the death of Henry helped arrange the election of Lothair II. He is credited with establishing the foundations of the ecclesiastical state of Mainz.

ADALBERT OF PRAGUE, ST., d. 997, bishop of Prague, the first Czech to occupy the see, was twice expelled from his diocese because of opposition to his reforming efforts. During his exile he took up the life of a Benedictine monk, served for a time as adviser to Otto III, then labored as a missionary among the Hungarians and Poles and, finally, among the Prussians who martyred him.

ADALBERT, ST., monk, worked as a missionary-bishop among the Russians, later returned to Germany when Otto I appointed him first archbishop of Magdeburg. As metropolitan of the Slavs he established a number of bishoprics including those of Brandenburg and Posen. Earlier, as bishop of Weissenburg in Alsace, he continued the chronicle of Regino of Prüm to 967.

ADALDAG, ST., d. 988, chancellor of Otto I who had him elected archbishop of Hamburg-Bremen. As archbishop he organized new bishoprics to the north and east including Schleswig and Odense, sent missionaries among the Slavs and Danes, and preserved the ecclesiastical independence of his own see against the ambitions of Cologne.

ADALGIS (Adelgis) OF NOVARA, ST., d. c. 850, bishop of Novara who enjoyed considerable prominence in both church and Italian political circles during the last fifteen years of his life.

ADAMANTIUS, early fourth-century anti-Gnostic writer, whose *De Recta in Deum Fide* takes the form of a dialogue between himself and adherents of Gnosticism. The pagan arbitrator gave the victory to Adamantius in the end.

ADAM DE LA HALLE (Adam le Bossou), d. 1288?, called the "hunchback of Arras," composer of motets, love lyrics, ballads, dramatic pieces, and, perhaps, the earliest comic opera. His is an important name in the history of music.

ADAM EASTON, d. 1397, English Benedictine monk and cardinal (1381) who spent most of his life in Rome. His writings reveal him to have been one of the leading biblical scholars of the fourteenth century. He is also noteworthy for a refutation he prepared attacking the views of John Wyclif and Marsilius of Padua concerning papal authority.

ADAMITES, name assigned to a variety of sects, the first appearing as early as the fourth century. Many Adamites conducted the worship of God while naked, either as a reminder of the innocence of man in Paradise or for the sake of mortification. Members of the Waldensian, Taborite, and Beghard groups have been identified as Adamites.

ADAMNAN (Eunan, Adomnan) OF IONA, ST., d. 704, was educated at Iona where he later became abbot. He was among the greatest scholars to come out of Iona. He urged the Irish to accept the Roman liturgy and calendar. The Synod of Tara (697) which he convened forbade women and children to be made prisoners of war. His most important work was a biography of St. Columba. He is no longer considered the author

of *Adamnan's Vision,* an Irish composition of the tenth or eleventh century.

ADAM OF BREMEN, d. c. 1081, probably of East Franconia, a monk of Corvey, who came to Bremen upon the invitation of Archbishop Adalbert. His valuable history of the bishops of Hamburg-Bremen, notably of the career of Adalbert, provides a general survey of the history, geography, and civilization of northwestern Europe. In addition to describing Russia, the Baltic regions, Scandinavia, Iceland, and Greenland, the author makes the earliest known reference to Vinland, that part of North America discovered by Leif Ericsson.

ADAM OF EBRACH, BL., d. 1161, Cistercian monk. As abbot of Morimond abbey he established a number of monasteries including that of Ebrach (near Mannheim) which he served as abbot. His correspondence with the mystic Hildegarde of Bingen has survived.

ADAM OF FULDA, d. 1505, Benedictine monk, one of the most learned and influential musicians and musical theorists of his age. He composed a mass, motets, hymns, and several secular songs.

ADAM (OF) MARSH (de Marisco), d. 1258, an English Franciscan theologian who studied under Robert Grosseteste, later taught theology at Oxford, the first Franciscan to do so, and served as an adviser to Henry III. He exercised great influence in English political and social circles. His letters are of great importance, while his unusual learning earned him the title of "Doctor Illustris."

ADAM OF ORLETON, d. 1345, studied law at Oxford and served as bishop of several sees including that of Winchester. Although a principal figure in forcing Edward II to abdicate in favor of Isabella and Mortimer, he was able to continue an active career under Edward III who banished Isabella from the court and had Mortimer executed.

ADAM OF PERSEIGNE, d. 1221, Cistercian monk, abbot of Perseigne (near Alençon), was known for his learning and sanctity. Respected alike for his piety and wisdom, he attempted on occasion to arbitrate the disputes between Philip II Augustus of France and John of England.

ADAM OF ST. VICTOR, d. between 1177 and 1192, monk in the monastery of Saint-Victor in Paris and considered by many scholars the leading, surely the most prolific, medieval composer of hymns and sequences. He is credited with having brought the sequence to perfection. His theological views reveal his Augustinianism.

ADAM OF USK, d. 1430, English chronicler of the late fourteenth century (1377–1421). He took an active part in the political events that led to the abdication of Richard II and the accession of Henry IV.

ADAM SCOTUS (Adam of Dryburgh), d. c. 1212, Premonstratensian monk and theologian, abbot of the monastery of Dryburgh (Scotland), who spent his last years in a Carthusian monastery in Wiltham (England). He produced a number of mystical treatises and numerous sermons.

ADDAI, according to tradition the founder of the Church at Edessa. Syriac tradition made him one of the 72 disciples of Christ (Luke 10:1). [See ADDAI, THE DOCTRINE OF.]

ADDAI AND MARI (Addeus and Maris), LITURGY OF, the Syriac liturgy that continues to be the ordinary rite of Nestorian Christians. It probably dates from c. 200 and was used in the Syriac-speaking Church at Edessa which honored Addai and his disciple Mari as its founders.

ADDAI, DOCTRINE OF, a Syriac work, probably written c. 400, which tells how King Abgar was brought into communication with Christ and how Addai was sent to Edessa to convert him.

ADELAIDE (Adelheid, Euphraxia, Praxedia), d. 1109, daughter of the grand prince of Kiev,

consort of Henry IV of Germany. Later imprisoned on the charge of adultery, she escaped to the court of Countess Matilda of Tuscany and subsequently returned to Kiev where she entered a convent.

ADELAIDE (Adelheid), ST., d. 999, widow of Lothair, king of Italy, appealed to Otto I of Germany against Berengar, margrave of Ivrea, who had seized the crown for himself and put her in prison. Otto came to her rescue and married her (his second wife). When Otto died in 973, Adelaide remained in the counsel of her son Otto II until the ascendancy of his Byzantine wife Theophano. Again for a time, following the death of Theophano, she served as regent for her grandson Otto III. Adelaide lived an ascetic life and took an active hand in monastic reform.

ADELAIDE OF TURIN, d. 1091, thrice-widowed daughter of the count of Turin who ruled the March of Turin as regent for her son. Her daughter Bertha married Henry IV of Germany. As Henry's mother-in-law she worked with Countess Matilda of Tuscany to effect a reconciliation between the king and Pope Gregory VII at Canossa.

ADELANTADO, highest provincial official in medieval Spain. He exercised both military and juridical authority over a district.

ADELARD OF BATH, d. c. 1145, English Benedictine of the twelfth century who was among the first Western scholars to translate Greek and Arabic scientific and mathematical writings into Latin and to urge the value of scientific research. He traveled widely in the eastern Mediterranean world, Spain, and southern Italy. It was Adelard who introduced the West to such ancient scientific theories as that of Democritus concerning atoms. In his principal philosophical work entitled *De Eodem et Diverso,* he attempted to resolve the problems of nominalism and realism.

ADELE (Adela), d. 1137, daughter of William I (the Conqueror) and mother of Stephen of Blois who later reigned as Stephen I of England. She took an active hand in the administration of Blois and served as regent there during the minority of her son. She sometimes assumed the role of mediator in disputes between lay rulers and reforming church leaders, principally in the matter of lay investiture.

ADELELM OF BURGOS (Lesmes), ST., d. 1097, Benedictine abbot of Castile who was distinguished for his asceticism and for his ability to work miracles. He usually performed these in the cure of the sick.

ADELHEID. See ADELAIDE.

ADELMANNUS (Almannus), d. c. 1061, student of Fulbert of Chartres, later a teacher of theology at Liège and Speyer. He composed an acrostic poem about the leading scholars at Chartres.

ADEMAR (Adhemar) OF CHABANNES, d. 1034, Benedictine monk of Limoges, author of sermons, liturgical writings, and a valuable chronicle of Aquitaine.

ADEMAR OF PUY. See ADHEMAR OF PUY.

ADENET, ADAM, d. after 1297, called le Roi, a French court poet and musician whose poems consisted largely of reworkings of epic materials from the Carolingian period. He served as principal minstrel in the service of the count of Flanders.

ADENULF OF ANAGNI, d. 1289, studied and taught at Paris and left sermons and several philosophical and theological writings. Of his wealth he supported students and arranged for the transcription of manuscripts. He was an avid collector of manuscripts long before Petrarch and his humanist friends took up that avocation.

ADEODATUS I. See DEUSDEDIT I, Pope.

ADEODATUS (Deusdedit) II, Pope, 672–76, a Roman, was active in monastic reform and in the suppression of the Monothelite heresy. He initiated the papal practice of dating events from the year of a pope's pontificate.

ADEODATUS, d. 388, natural son of St. Augustine of Hippo, was baptized with his father after his mother had returned to Carthage. The boy, who is said to have been unusually intelligent, died in his sixteenth year.

ADHAN, call of the muezzin to prayer, made five times daily and for public worship on Friday.

ADHEMAR DE CHABANNES. See ADEMAR OF CHABANNES.

ADHEMAR OF PUY (of Monteil), d. 1098, bishop of Le Puy and appointed by Pope Urban II to serve as papal legate and deputy on the First Crusade (1096–99). Although he offered some military counsel, his major role was that of mediating differences arising among the leaders of the Crusade and between them and the Byzantine emperor. He died on the Crusade.

ADJUTOR, ST., d. 1131, Norman knight who took part in the first Crusade, was captured by the Moslems but later escaped. Upon his return to France he became a monk in the Benedictine Abbey of Tiron; he later lived as a hermit near the monastery.

AD LIMINA VISIT (Visitatio ad limina apostolorum), a practice perhaps from the early centuries for bishops to make periodic visits to Rome in order to give evidence of their acceptance of the authority of the bishop of Rome. The visit included a visit to the tombs of SS. Peter and Paul. The practice originated in the decree of a Roman synod (743) which enjoined such visits on all bishops consecrated in Rome. From the thirteenth century such visits were required of all bishops.

ADMINISTRATOR, APOSTOLIC, vicar appointed by the pope to administer a diocese during the vacancy of the see.

ADMONT, ABBEY OF, Benedictine abbey in Styria whose origins as a cloister may go back to the mid-ninth century. During the twelfth century it enjoyed considerable renown for its ascetic spirit and for the beautiful illuminations and script of its scriptorium. It maintained a hospital for the poor and for lepers.

ADOLF I, archbishop of Cologne, d. 1220, helped effect the release of Richard I (Lion-Heart), king of England, from his prison in Austria. He actively supported the candidacy of Otto of Brunswick as king of Germany in the contest over the throne following the death of Henry VI in 1197. Because he subsequently threw his support to the rival Hohenstaufen Philip of Swabia, Pope Innocent III deprived him of his archdiocese, although he did not actually lose it until the death of Philip in 1208 and the accession of Otto IV.

ADOLF OF NASSAU, succeeded Rudolf of Hapsburg as king of Germany in 1292 when the German princes passed over Rudolf's son Albert for fear that the Hapsburgs had grown too powerful. In return for a handsome subsidy, he became the ally of Edward I of England against Philip IV of France. In 1298 Adolf fell in battle with Albert who then succeeded to the throne.

ADO, MARTYROLOGY OF, martyrology compiled in 858 by St. Ado (d. 875), archbishop of Vienne. Subsequent martyrologies adopted the plan and arrangement of this martyrology.

ADO (Adon) OF VIENNE, ST., d. 875, disciple of Lupus of Ferrières, later archbishop of Vienne when he advanced the cause of church reform and stoutly opposed Lothair II of Lorraine in his attempt to divorce his wife. His writings include a martyrology and a useful chronicle of the world to A.D. 869.

ADOPTIONISM, the doctrine that Christ as man is the adoptive son of God, but as divine is the natural son of God. Although the origins of this belief go back to Theodotus of Byzantium (c. 190) and, more important, to Paul of Samosata (d. 268), it came to be formally preached only in the late eighth century in Spain when Elipandus, the archbishop of Toledo, subscribed to it. Charlemagne summoned a council to Frankfort in 794 which accepted Pope Adrian I's condemnation of the heresy. In 798 Pope Leo III convened a council in Rome which repeated the condemnation. A modified form of the heresy reappeared in the twelfth century in the views of Abelard, Gilbert de la Porrée, and other scholastics.

ADORO TE DEVOTE, hymn addressed to Christ in the Blessed Sacrament. The traditional view that St. Thomas Aquinas was its composer is now being disputed.

ADOUBEMENT, the ceremony in which the knight was invested with the arms and weapons befitting his new station in life.

AD PERENNIS VITAE FONTEM, first line of the *De Gaudio Paradisi,* a hymn often attributed to Peter Damian (d. 1072). The poem's theme is death, judgment, and eternity.

AD REGIAS AGNI DAPES, Ambrosian hymn of unknown authorship which sings the praise of the redeeming Christ who invites the faithful to his feast.

ADRIAN (Hadrian) I, Pope, 772–95, member of the Roman aristocracy, acclaimed pope while only a deacon. He persuaded Charlemagne to come down to Italy to protect Rome from Desiderius, king of the Lombards. Charlemagne destroyed the kingdom of the Lombards, then confirmed the pope in his possession of the territories which Pepin III, Charlemagne's father, had transferred to the papacy. [*See* DONATION OF PEPIN.] Adrian requested the Byzantine Empress Irene to summon the Second Council of Nicaea (787) which condemned iconoclasm. He also worked for the suppression of Adoptionism, a heresy most widespread in Spain.

ADRIAN (Hadrian) II, Pope, 867–72, whose pontificate revealed a significant decline in papal power from that enjoyed by his predecessor Nicholas I (858–67). His dispute with Lothair II of Lorraine who wished to put away his wife and marry his mistress, only terminated with Lothair's death in 869. He also had difficulties with Hincmar, the powerful bishop of Reims, who sought to defend his metropolitan authority against the interference of the papacy. Charles the Bald and Louis the German ignored Adrian's protests when they divided the kingdom of Lorraine between themselves (Treaty of Mersen in 870). Adrian did succeed in appointing Methodius archbishop of Pannonia and he also deserves credit for authorizing the use of Old Slavonic in the liturgy of the south Slavs. His legates took part in the Eighth Ecumenical Council (869–70) which ordered Photius deposed, and he accepted the twenty-first canon of this council which ranked the authority of the patriarch of Constantinople second only to that of the pope.

ADRIAN (Hadrian) III, St., Pope, 884–5, whose brief pontificate was cursed with factional strife in Rome. He died on his way to the Diet of Worms to which Charles the Fat had summoned him to help settle the problem of imperial succession.

ADRIAN (Hadrian) IV, Pope, 1154–59, Augustinian canon and abbot, cardinal, and the only Englishman (Nicholas Breakspear) to attain the papacy. In 1152 he went to Scandinavia as papal legate to reorganize the hierarchy of that region. He initially cooperated with Frederick I Barbarossa of Germany in destroying the Roman "republic" set up by Arnold of Brescia, then broke with him and joined Milan and other cities of north Italy to block the emperor in his ambition to extend his rule south of the Alps. Adrian was obliged to acknowledge William I as king of Sicily and southern Italy, although he secured from William recognition of his position as suzerain. Toward Henry II of England he pursued a benevolent policy, and he appears to

have granted him possession of Ireland with his bull *Laudabiliter*.

ADRIAN (Hadrian) V, Pope, July 11, 1276, to August 18, 1276, appointed cardinal by his uncle Innocent IV, went to England as papal legate in 1265 to seek a reconciliation between Henry III and his barons. Elected pope, he died before he was ordained to the priesthood.

ADRIANOPLE, city of Thrace, scene of a disastrous defeat of the Roman army by the Visigoths in 378. It was captured successively by Avars, Bulgars, and Crusaders (1204), then in 1362 fell to the Turks. It served as the capital of Turkey from 1365 until the fall of Constantinople to the Turks in 1453.

ADRIANOPLE, BATTLE OF, battle fought in 378 between the Visigoths and the Roman army which resulted in the destruction of the imperial forces and the death of the emperor Valens. In 376 Valens had permitted the Visigoths to move across the Danube into Roman territory in order to escape the advancing Huns. Because of ill treatment at the hands of Roman agents, they revolted and in the battle the Visigothic cavalry proved the decisive factor in gaining them the victory. Although Rome recovered from this disaster, the battle marked the beginning of the rapid decline of the empire. From now on Rome's armies became progressively more non-Roman in character.

ADSO OF MONTIER-IN-DER, d. 992, monk of Luxeuil, friend of Gerbert and himself a leading scholar of the period. He served as abbot of the monastery of Montier-en-Der, later of Saint-Bénigne at Dijon. He composed lives of a number of saints.

ADVENT, period before Christmas consisting of approximately four weeks, beginning with the Sunday closest to the feast of St. Andrew (November 30). During this period the Christian faithful were exhorted to prayer and self-denial in preparation for the coming birth of Christ.

The origins of the practice are obscure, but it appears to have been established in the West in the sixth century and in the Greek Church in the eighth.

ADVOCATUS ECCLESIAE, lay person, generally of aristocratic birth, who served as agent for a church or monastery to defend it judicially in the courts. He might even be called upon to defend it militarily against its enemies.

ADVOWSON, in England the right of patronage of a church or ecclesiastical benefice. The patron had the right to nominate a person to such a church or benefice, who, if found acceptable to the bishop, would then be instituted to that office. Advowson was an incorporeal hereditament.

AEDESIUS, d. c. 355, neo-Platonist philosopher of Cappadocia, a pupil of Iamblichus of Syria, who taught at Pergamum.

AEGIDIUS ROMANUS. *See* GILES OF ROME.

AEGIDIUS, ST. *See* GILES, ST.

A.E.I.O.U., letters inscribed here and there by Frederick III, king of Germany (1440–93), which he declared spelled the great future fortune had in store for Austria. The letters stood for the Latin "Austriae est imperare orbi universo" or the German "Alles Erdreich ist Österreich Untertan." Both statements meant the same, namely, that the entire world is subject to Austria.

AELFRIC GRAMMATICUS (the Grammarian), d. c. 1020, first abbot of the Benedictine monastery of Eynsham (near Oxford), who received his education in the Benedictine monastery at Winchester under Ethelwold (Aethelwold). He is recognized as the leading Anglo-Saxon author of the tenth and eleventh centuries and the most distinguished and prolific literary personality of England in his day. His writings include numerous homilies which he hoped would aid the clergy in being orthodox in their sermons. He also left exegetical works, lives of the saints, all in Anglo-Saxon, the *Heptateuch,* a free translation of the first seven books of the Bible, and a Latin grammar. This last work gave him his title of "the Grammarian." His writings reveal a scholar well versed in the knowledge of patristic literature and later theological and canonical writings. Many of his works continued to be copied and used throughout the Middle Ages.

AELFRIC OF CANTERBURY, ST., d. 1005, abbot of St. Albans, bishop of Ramsbury and Wilton, who was elevated to Canterbury in 995. He may have been the archbishop who replaced the secular clergy at Canterbury with monks.

AENEAS OF GAZA, d. 518, Christian neo-Platonist who in his *Theophrastus* rejected tenets of Platonism that conflicted with orthodox Christian doctrine: e.g., the preexistence of the soul and the eternity of the world.

AENEAS SILVIUS PICCOLOMINI. *See* PIUS II.

AENGUS (The Culdee), ST., d. 824, was educated in the monastic school in Cleonengh, Ireland, lived as a hermit for some years, then entered a monastery near Dublin where he collaborated with Maelruain in composing prose lives of the Irish saints. These include the oldest of the Irish martyrologies.

AËRIUS OF PONTUS, initially a friend of Eustathius, bishop of Sebaste (d. 380). He later attacked that prelate, then went on to deny the sacred character of the clergy, the usefulness of prayers for the dead, the observance of Easter which he held was a Jewish superstition, and fasting and abstinence. His sect was largely limited to Sebaste and to his own lifetime.

AESTII, tribes located along the Baltic who were mentioned by Tacitus, Jordanes, Cassiodorus, and Einhard. The origin of the name and the extensiveness of the tribes are matters of dispute. Some scholars link them with the Prussians and with other Baltic peoples.

AETERNA CAELI GLORIA, hymn once attributed to Pope Gregory the Great (590–604) in which appeal is made to Christ for an increase of faith, hope, and love.

AETERNA CHRISTI MUNERA, hymn composed by St. Ambrose (d. 397) and intended for liturgical use on days dedicated to martyrs.

AETERNE RERUM CONDITOR, hymn composed by St. Ambrose (d. 397) in which he presents mystical interpretations of the crowing of the cock. Caesarius of Arles (d. 542) recommended the hymn to his monks.

AETERNE REX ALTISSIME, opening words of three hymns of unknown authorship, two of which glorify the crown of thorns. The third hymn, and the earliest, may have been composed by St. Ambrose (d. 397). It hails Christ's victory over death.

AETHELBALD. *See* ETHELBALD.

AETHELBERT. *See* ETHELBERT.

AETHELBURGA. *See* ETHELBURGA.

AETHELRED. *See* ETHELRED.

AETHELREDA. *See* ETHELREDA.

AETHELSTAN. *See* ATHELSTAN.

AETHELWOLD. *See* ETHELWOLD.

AETHELWULF. *See* ETHELWULF.

AETIUS, d. c. 370, Arian sophist of Alexandria, made a bishop by his Arian adherents, apparently with the approval of the emperor Julian. He and his followers, notably Eunomius, his secretary, maintained the total unlikeness of the Father and Son. They were known as Anomoeans.

AETIUS FLAVIUS, d. 454, son of Gaudentius, master of the cavalry, the last great general of the Roman empire in the west. As a youth he spent some time as a hostage of Alaric, King of the Visigoths, then later as a hostage of the Huns.

He directed the Roman army in putting down revolts in Gaul and driving back the German invaders. In 436 at Worms, he crushed the Burgundian kingdom with the aid of Hunnish auxiliaries. (This battle furnished part of the theme of the *Nibelungenlied*.) Between 437 and 439 he defeated the Visigoths in Toulouse. His greatest and most decisive victory was gained over Attila the Hun at Chalons in 451. This he accomplished with the aid of the Visigoths and other German tribes who felt equally menaced by the approach of the Huns. Aetius was the de facto ruler of the western empire during the reign of the weak Valentinian III from 433 to 454. In 454 Valentinian had him murdered lest he take over the imperial throne. Aetius's officers avenged his death by murdering Valentinian in 455, after which no western Roman emperor even pretended to question the will of his Germanic general.

AFFLIGEM, ABBEY OF, Benedictine monastery in Brabant, founded by six thieving knights in the late eleventh century where they lived as monks to atone for their earlier misdeeds. St. Bernard of Clairvaux among others praised the piety of the monks.

AFONSO, kings of Portugal. [*See* ALFONSO.]

AFRICANUS, SEXTUS JULIUS, Christian historian of the early third century, a resident of Palestine, and author of a universal history to 221 which Eusebius used.

AGAPE, a funeral feast in ancient times which was adopted by the Jews and passed on to the Christians. With Christians it usually lost its funereal associations and might take on the character of a eucharistic service, a fraternal feast, or a benefit for the poor. While never a universal or mandatory practice, it tended to disappear after the fourth century. As a Greek word used by early Christians, *agape* expressed the love of God or Christ or the love of one Christian for another. It was usually translated into the Latin word *caritas,* meaning charity.

AGAPE, SS., name of several martyrs: a) one Agape, believed martyred during the reign of Hadrian (117–138); b) A. of Thessalonica, martyred with her sisters Chionia and Irene in 304; c) A., martyred at Antioch in 411; d) A. of Terni, beheaded under Aurelian in 273.

AGAPETAE, Christian virgins whose material needs were taken care of by laymen, often celibate themselves, an arrangement which freed the women to dedicate themselves more fully to the service of God. The practice led to early abuse and scandal and suffered condemnation by several church councils of the fourth century.

AGAPETUS, deacon of the church of Hagia Sophia, reputed to have been the tutor of the emperor Justinian I (527–65) to whom he addressed a series of exhortations concerning his spiritual and civil responsibilities. Humanists of the late Middle Ages held his letters in high esteem.

AGAPETUS I, ST., Pope, 535–6, priest of Rome, went to Constantinople upon the direction of the Ostrogothic King Theodahad to dissuade the emperor Justinian I from proceeding with his plans to conquer Italy. While in Constantinople, Agapetus secured the removal of the Monophysite patriarch Anthimus and his replacement by Mennas.

AGAPETUS II, Pope, 946–55, asked Otto I of Germany to come to Rome to restore law and order. He gave Otto wide control over the monasteries in Germany and, through the archbishop of Hamburg-Bremen, over the bishops of Denmark.

AGAPIOS OF HIERAPOLIS, tenth-century Syrian bishop who composed a world history extending from Adam to 941–2. It contains some valuable history concerning the metropolitans of the Eastern church.

AGATHA, ST., d. 250, virgin martyr of Catania, Sicily, who was executed during the persecution of Decius. People of the area appealed to her intercession against eruptions of Mt. Etna, and elsewhere, especially in south Germany, against the danger of fire and lightning. Her name is listed among the saints in the canon of the Roman Mass. Two early churches in Rome were dedicated to her.

AGATHIAS, d. c. 582, Greek lawyer, historian, and poet. He composed erotic verse, epigrams, and a valuable history of the reign of the Byzantine emperor Justinian I for the years 552 to 558. It is doubtful that he was a Christian.

AGATHO, ST., Pope, 678–81, monk of Sicily who was elected pope when already far advanced in years. His writings attacking Monothelitism led to its condemnation by the Council of Constantinople III in 681. The council accepted his definition of the two wills in Christ. He urged the English and Celtic churches to adopt the Roman liturgy.

AGDE, COUNCIL OF, council held at Agde in southern France in 506 under the direction of St. Caesarius of Arles. Forty-seven genuine canons have been preserved. These include a number dealing with clerical celibacy, the canonical age for ordination, public peace, and church property.

AGERE SEQUITUR ESSE, the scholastic principle meaning *to act follows to be,* since to act presupposes being and one cannot take place or exist without the other.

AGHLABIDS, an Arab dynasty that established its independence in north Africa (Tunis) from Abbasid rule in 800, conquered Sicily in 827, later lost the island to the Normans, and was itself overwhelmed by the Fatimids of Egypt in 909.

AGILES (Aguilers), RAYMOND D', accompanied the count of Toulose on the First Crusade (1096–99), served as chaplain to Adhemar, the papal deputy, and left an uncritical chronicle of the expedition.

AGILOLFINGS (Agilulfings), old Bavarian noble family first noted c. 550. Its last duke, Tassilo III, was deposed by Charlemagne in 788.

AGINCOURT, BATTLE OF, battle fought in Artois on October 25, 1415, when Henry V of England, with a smaller but better organized army, won an overwhelming victory over the French. The English longbow proved a critical factor in Henry's victory. The victory led shortly to an Anglo-Burgundian alliance and the Treaty of Troyes (1420) which made Henry regent for the insane Charles VI of France and designated him to succeed Charles as king of France.

AGIOS O THEOS (O Holy God), opening words of a Greek invocation or doxology. In the Latin church the Greek phrase survived among the *Reproaches (Improperia)* of the Good Friday liturgy.

AGNELLI, GUGLIELMO, FRA, d. c. 1313, Dominican lay brother, sculptor, architect, pupil, and co-worker of Nicolo Pisano. The marble reliefs on the tomb of St. Dominic in Bologna are his best known works.

AGNELLUS, ANDREAS, d. c. 846, historian of Ravenna whose *Liber Pontificalis Ecclesiae Ravennatis* traces the history of the see from St. Apollinaris (first-second century) to his own day. It contains much useful information, particularly about customs and buildings in Ravenna.

AGNELLUS OF PISA, BL., d. 1232, companion of St. Francis, founder of the Franciscan province in England and the first minister provincial. He established a school for the friars at Oxford and induced Robert Grosseteste to serve there as teacher. He may, accordingly, be credited with helping establish Oxford's repute as a center of scientific studies.

AGNES OF ASSISI, ST., d. 1253, younger sister of St. Clare who, with the encouragement of St. Francis, worked with her and other noble women to organize the Poor Ladies of St. Damian's later known as the Poor Clares. Agnes

subsequently established convents near Florence and in other cities in north Italy.

AGNES OF BOHEMIA (Prague), BL., d. c. 1282, daughter of Ottocar I, king of Bohemia, who is said to have rejected the proposal that she marry Henry III of England or Frederick II of Germany, instead entered the convent of St. Clare in Prague which she had founded. She later became its abbess.

AGNES OF POITOU, d. 1077, daughter of William, duke of Aquitaine, second wife of Henry III, king of Germany, and regent until 1062 for her son Henry IV. She spent her last years in a cloister in Italy where she encouraged monastic reform.

AGNES OF ROME, ST., one of the most highly regarded virgin-martyrs of the early church despite the obscurity that shrouds her life. St. Ambrose and Prudentius, among others, sounded her praises. According to one story, she was executed at Rome during the reign of Diocletian in 304 when only twelve years old. Some time before 349, Constantina, daughter of Constantine I, erected a basilica over her tomb in Rome. Her name was listed in the canon of the Roman Mass. In art she is represented as a lamb, no doubt because of the similarity between her name and *agnus*, the Latin word for lamb. On her feastday, two lambs were blessed and pallia made from their wool. The pope sent the pallia to archbishops whose consecration he had approved.

AGNES SOREL, d. 1450, mistress of Charles VII of France and mother of four of his daughters. She came to the French court in 1442 where she enjoyed considerable influence.

AGNOETAE, a Monophysite sect that attributed ignorance to the human nature (soul) of Christ. It was founded by Themistius, a sixth-century deacon of Alexandria, whence the name of Themistians by which his followers were also known.

Pope Gregory I (590–604) condemned their teaching as heretical.

AGNUS DEI: a) Latin for Lamb of God, a phrase first used prophetically in Isaiah 53:7, then by John the Baptist in referring to Christ (John 1:29). The formula made its way into the liturgical service and may have become an official part of the Mass by order of Pope Sergius I (687–701). The response to the thrice-repeated salutation remained *Miserere nobis* until the tenth or eleventh century when *Dona nobis pacem* came to be substituted for the third response; b) a wax medallion with the figure of a lamb which the pope blessed in the first year of his pontificate and every seventh year afterward.

AGOBARD OF LYONS, d. 840, archbishop of Lyons (816) who became involved in the political turmoil that cursed the reign of Louis the Pious (814–40) and who spent some time in exile in Italy. He attacked the Adoptionist heresy and Jews in his writings, and throughout his life he fought courageously for the reform of the church and for its independence from secular interference. He also attacked such practices as trial by ordeal, belief in witchcraft, and the excessive veneration of images. His writings included works on liturgical, juridical, and political subjects.

AGOSTINO DI DUCCIO, d. 1481, one of the leading Florentine marble sculptors of the fifteenth century. His work reveals the influence of his teacher Luca della Robbia. His relief work makes no effort to introduce illusionism or rounded figures. Although he worked in a number of Italian cities, his name is associated principally with the wealth of sculptural decoration in the Templo Malatestiano at Rimini. His reliefs on the façade of the cathedral at Modena are well known.

AGOSTINO DI GIOVANNI, Italian sculptor of the early fourteenth century, probably of Siena, whose name and career were so closely linked with those of his co-sculptor Agnolo di Ventura

that it is difficult to differentiate their work. They were also active as architects in Siena where they designed the church of St. Francis and other famous buildings.

AGOSTINO NOVELLO, BL., late thirteenth-century jurist and counselor of Manfred, king of Sicily. Left for dead on the battlefield where Manfred was slain (1266), Agostino recovered, joined the order of St. Augustine, became general of the order, confessor of Pope Nicholas IV, and later retired to devote himself to prayer and the care of the sick and aged.

AGRAPHA, that is, unwritten, referring to words presumably spoken by Christ but not recorded in the Gospels. They were found in ancient Christian writings or on papyri. Few have been positively proved authentic.

AGRICOLA, ALEXANDER, d. 1506, one of the leading composers of the later Burgundian school who wrote masses, motets, and *chansons*. He spent some time at the court of Archduke Philip of Austria in Brussels, and earlier in Italy in the palace of Lorenzo de' Medici. In 1500 he became chaplain and chanter for Philip the Fair of Spain.

AGRICOLA, RUDOLFUS (Huusman, Huysman), d. 1485, Dutch humanist, a man of many talents, philosopher, theologian, musician, and painter. As one of the first of the German humanists, he proved an inspiration to later humanists in northern Europe. He knew Greek and Hebrew and possessed an elegant Latin style. His writings include an oration in praise of philosophy and a life of Petrarch.

AGRICULTURE, MEDIEVAL. *See* SERF; MANORIALISM; TWO-, THREE-, OPEN-FIELD SYSTEM.

A. H., abbreviation for *Anno Hegirae,* that is, the year of the Hejira. The date of the Hejira, Mohammed's flight to Medina, was 622. That event marked the base year in the Islamic calendar.

AHL AL-KITAB, Arabic for People of the Book,

referring to Jews, Christians, and Sabians because they possessed sacred writings based upon divine revelation, as opposed to pagans who did not. Mohammed made an exception of the People of the Book. They were not to be exterminated.

AHMADI, TADJ AL-DIN IBRAHIM B. KHIDR, leading Turkish poet of the fourteenth century. His poetry includes panegyrics, a romance, a poem about good health, and another on the use of medicine.

AHMED AL-BADAWI, d. 1276, greatest Moslem saint and wonder-worker of Egypt whose disciples, members of the Order of Ahmedija which he founded, identified themselves by wearing a red turban.

AHMED JESEWI, d. 1166, a Sufi who was honored as a saint in western Turkestan. His writings provide some of the earliest examples of Turkish-Islamic literature.

AHRIMAN, god of evil, identified with the physical and the sensual, who was engaged in eternal conflict with Ahura Mazda, the god of light, of goodness, and of wisdom. These two spirits appeared in the dualistic doctrine of Zoroaster and in earlier Iranian mythology.

AHURA MAZDA, old Iranian form of the name of the highest god, the Wise Lord, as he appears in the teaching of Zoroaster. The struggle which he carries on for all eternity against Ahriman, the god of evil, appears both in the world in general as well as in the thoughts and actions of the individual person. This dualistic doctrine found some echo in Christian times in the Manichaean sect and in later Catharism.

AID, FEUDAL, type of feudal dues which the vassal paid his lord. The most traditional aids were three: those paid on the occasion of the knighting of the lord's eldest son, the marriage of his eldest daughter, and the ransoming of the lord himself should he be held captive. In general the vassal paid his lord an aid when the latter had need for assistance, namely, when building a castle. The term aid in broader usage might refer to the tax a manorial lord demanded from the peasantry living on his land, as well as that which a king might levy on his subjects. [See FEUDALISM; TAILLE; TALLAGE.]

AIDAN, ST., d. 651, monk of Iona, bishop of Lindisfarne, founder of a number of churches and monasteries in Northumbria. Bede praised him for his piety, his learning, and his humility. Despite the efforts of British reformers, he observed the date of Easter as practiced by the Celtic church.

AIGUANI (Anguani, Angriani), MICHELE, d. 1400, a Carmelite, also known as Michael of Bologna, prior general of the order, teacher of theology in Bologna, and author of numerous theological works. He was caught up in the controversies of the Western Schism.

AIGUES-MORTES, seaport on the western fringe of the Rhône river delta which Louis IX (d. 1270) fortified and used as a port of embarkation for his two Crusades. It proved an impregnable fortress. The name of the seaport is derived from the "dead waters" (aquae mortuae) of the surrounding marshy plain. Its ramparts as well as a fortified tower remain, but the harbor has silted up.

AILETTE, a kind of epaulette, of iron or steel, and worn at the base of the neck to protect the shoulders of the knight.

AILLY, PIERRE D', d. 1420, French cardinal and scholar, doctor of theology, chancellor of the university of Paris, and teacher of John Gerson. He was a conciliarist, that is, one who advocated the superiority of the general church council to the pope as the only realistic manner of going about ending the Western Schism. (There were two popes from 1378, one at Rome, the other at Avignon, neither willing to resign or convene a church council to resolve the issue of who was the legitimate pope.) D'Ailly took an active part in the Council of Pisa in 1409 which further complicated the schism by adding a third pope, whose successor, John XXIII, made D'Ailly a cardinal. D'Ailly next labored for the convening of still another council, this one materializing in the Council of Constance (1414–18) which finally ended the schism with the emergence of Martin V as the one and only pope. In philosophy D'Ailly accepted the principles of Ockhamite nominalism. He left writings on conciliarism, theology, philosophy, cosmography, even some religious verse in French. His *Image of the World* served to encourage Columbus to sail westward in order to reach India.

AILRED, ST., d. 1167, Cistercian monk, the "Bernard of the North," abbot of Rievaulx (1147). His extensive spiritual writings show marked similarity of interest and spirit with those of St. Bernard of Clairvaux. He composed his first important work, the *Speculum Caritatis,* upon Bernard's request. His devotion was characterized by a strong attachment to the suffering humanity of Christ. Included with his works is a life of Edward the Confessor and a Christian adaptation of Cicero's *De Amicitia.*

AIMERIC OF ANGOULÊME, eleventh-century Latin poet, probably a monk, author of a scholarly treatise on quantity and accent in Latin words which he intended for use in the instruction of pupils in the art of public speaking. Aimeric reveals acquaintance with an astonishing number of ancient writers.

AIMERIC OF PIACENZA, d. 1327, a Dominican, master general of his order, who taught for 24 years at Bologna. It appears he resigned his post as master general rather than proceed with the suppression of the Knights Templars in Leon and Castile as he had been instructed to do by Pope Clement V. He believed them innocent of the charges that had been brought against them by Philip IV of France.

AIMOIN, d. 889, monk of Saint-Germain-des-Prés, author of a work concerning the miracles of St. Germanus which is also a valuable source for the history of the period.

AIMOIN, d. after 1010, Benedictine monk of Fleury and author of a popular chronicle of the Franks (to 654). The continuation of this chronicle constitutes the first volume in the *Grandes Chroniques de France* which dates from 1274. He is also the author of several books about St. Benedict.

AIN JALUT, BATTLE OF, decisive victory won by the Mamluks of Egypt under Baibars in 1260 which effectively checked the advance of Mongol power southward toward Egypt.

AIOL, name of a Middle Dutch romance of the thirteenth century concerning the adventures of the Frankish hero Aiol in Persia. Only fragments of the story are extant.

AISHAH (A'isha), d. 678, daughter of Abu Bakr and Mohammed's third and favorite wife. She remained unmarried when widowed at the age of 18. After the failure of her efforts to block the succession of Ali, the cousin and son-in-law of the Prophet, as caliph — she had actually led an army against him — she went into retirement. She was an authority on the life and sayings of the Prophet.

AISTULF, king of the Lombards, 749–56, overran the exarchate of Ravenna in 751 but was twice prevented from seizing Rome by Pepin III (the Short), king of the Franks, who came to the city's defense upon the urgent pleas of Pope Stephen II. Pepin forced Aistulf to surrender the conquered lands and turn them over to the papacy. [*See* DONATION OF PEPIN.]

AIX-LA-CHAPELLE. *See* AACHEN.

AKHTAL, AL- (Ghiyath Ibn Harith), d. 710, Christian Arab poet of the Omayyad period whose poetry was noted for the perfection of form.

AKSCHAM (Achscham), the evening prayer, one of the five daily prayers required of Moslems.

ALADDIN (Alaeddin) OF THE WONDERFUL LAMP, an Oriental tale usually associated with the *Thousand And One Nights*. When the lamp was rubbed, a spirit appeared who was willing and capable of carrying out any wish the owner might voice. The story found its way into many languages.

ALAIN DE LILLE. *See* ALAN OF LILLE.

ALAMANNI. *See* ALEMANNI.

ALAN DE LA ROCHE (Alanus de Rupe), d. 1475, a Dominican, probably from Brittany, who became a distinguished theologian and teacher at several Dominican convents. He is credited with giving the rosary its modern arrangement and the Hail Mary its traditional form.

ALANI. *See* ALANS.

ALAN OF LILLE (Alain de Lille, Alanus Ab Insulis), d. 1202, Cistercian lay brother, an encyclopedic scholar, preacher, theologian, canonist, scientist, philosopher, and poet. He studied and taught in Paris, then entered the abbey of Citeaux. His writings include a compendium of theology (his chief work), a treatise on preaching, sermons, allegorical poems, attacks on heretics, Moslems, and Jews, a dictionary of biblical terms accompanied with literal, moral, and allegorical interpretations, and the first medieval manual for confessors. Contemporaries called him the "universal doctor."

ALAN OF TEWKESBURY, d. 1202, Benedictine prior at Canterbury who supported Thomas Becket in his quarrel with Henry II. Extant is his life of Thomas Becket and his correspondence with Henry II concerning the archbishop's body.

ALANS, Iranian steppe people, related to the Sarmatians, who were located in the area of the Black Sea north of the Caucasus. When the Huns overwhelmed them c. 350, a group of them made its way into Pannonia and from there in the early fifth century, in company with the Vandals and Suevi, to Spain. From Spain many of them crossed over to Africa with the Vandals. Most of the Alans remained north of the Caucasus until the thirteenth century when they were driven out by the Mongols, after which some settled in Hungary.

ALANUS AB (DE) INSULIS. *See* ALAN OF LILLE.

ALANUS ANGLICUS, learned Welsh canonist of the early thirteenth century and a distinguished lecturer at Bologna. He left a collection of decretals and glosses on the *Decretum*. As was true of many canonists of the period, he shifted his position from one supporting the respective independence of church and state to the theocratic one later given expression by Pope Boniface VIII in his bull *Unam Sanctam* (1302).

ALARIC I, d. 410, king of the Visigoths from 395 when he assumed leadership of that nation following the death of the Roman emperor Theodosius. He took his people on a pillaging march through Thrace, Macedonia, and Greece, then into Italy after the death of Stilicho who had blocked his earlier attempts to cross the Alps. (Emperor Honorius in the west had come to distrust his general Stilicho and had him executed.) After negotiating for several days before Rome, Alaric entered the city (410) and sacked it, then moved south with the intention of crossing over to Africa. When a storm destroyed the ships they had gathered, Alaric and his people turned north, but Alaric died and was buried in the bed of the Busento river. His brother-in-law Ataulf succeeded him and led his people to southwestern Gaul. Alaric's sack of Rome furnished St. Augustine with his explanation for writing his famous *City of God*.

ALARIC II, king of the Visigoths, 484–507, ruler of Spain exclusive of Galicia and of southwestern France. He had a law book prepared, entitled *Breviarium Alaricianum (Breviary of Alaric)*, based principally upon Roman laws, for use by his Roman subjects. He died in a battle near Poitiers with Clovis, king of the Franks.

ALB, a white linen vestment with tight-fitting sleeves that reached to the ankles. The priest or deacon put it on prior to robing for divine service. It was probably a modification of the ordinary Roman tunic of secular attire. By the ninth century, if not earlier, its use had become liturgically mandatory. The alb was then taken to symbolize purity.

ALBA (Aubade, Alborado, Tagelied, dawn song), a branch of troubadour poetry dealing with the lament of lovers who must part because the dawn had broken. They were often warned by a sympathetic watcher, or perhaps a nightingale, of the approach of dawn.

ALBAN, ST., by tradition Britain's first martyr, a pagan soldier in the Roman army, stationed near the present city of St. Albans, who had given shelter to a fugitive priest. When the Roman governor sent for the priest, Alban disguised himself as the priest, and was subsequently beheaded (c. 303 or perhaps c. 309). Some of the legendary materials linked with Alban's martyrdom appear in Bede's *History*. The famous monastery of St. Albans was erected on what was believed to have been the site of his martyrdom.

ALBANIA, small country on the eastern shore of the Adriatic, in Roman times included in the prefecture of Illyricum. It was occupied by the Visigoths in the fifth century, but again brought under Roman (Byzantine) rule by Justinian I in 535. Because of its mountainous character and the cities along the coast which could be served by a fleet, no one ruler was able to control the entire country during the Middle Ages. Serbs and Bulgars occupied much of the inland, Venice and Amalfi such seaports as Scutari and Durazzo. In 1272 Charles I of Naples was proclaimed king of Albania, but Serbs conquered the greater part of the country in the fourteenth century. In the late fifteenth century the national hero Scanderbeg, with help from Venice and Naples, managed to hold out against the overwhelming might of the Turks until 1478 when all the country, with the exception of Durazzo, passed under Ottoman rule. Durazzo held out against the Turks until 1501.

ALBAR OF CÓRDOBA, Spanish nobleman of the ninth century whose letters reveal a man with deep interest in, and knowledge of, both law and theology. His writings include a devotional manual on confession and an attack on the religious beliefs of Islam.

ALBELDA, ABBEY OF, Benedictine monastery and center of learning founded in 924 near Saragossa. The quality of its illuminated manuscripts attests to the deserved fame of its scriptorium. A chronicle of Albelda extends to 883.

ALBERGATI, NICCOLÒ, BL., d. 1443, Carthusian monk, prior, bishop of Bologna, cardinal, grand penitentiary, and *camerlengo*. He attended the Council of Basel as the pope's legate, later participated in discussions with the Greeks at the Council of Ferrara-Florence over ending the schism between the Latin and Greek churches. He also employed his diplomatic talents in bringing Charles VII of France and Philip the Good of Burgundy to accept the Peace of Arras (1435).

ALBERIC (Elberich), a dwarf who appears in the *Nibelungenlied* where he is worsted by Siegfried who took from him the magic cloak of invincibility.

ALBERIC I, d. c. 925, duke of Spoleto, a Lombard noble who married Marozia, daughter of Theophylact. This alliance gave him control of Rome and later of the duchy of Spoleto. In 915 he helped expel the Saracens from Rome.

ALBERIC II, d. 954, duke of Spoleto, son of Alberic I and Marozia, imprisoned his mother and Pope John XI, his half-brother, then ruled Rome and the papacy from 932 until his death. His generally peaceful reign of some 20 years attests to his considerable ability as a statesman. His interference in spiritual matters was not excessive, and he gave his support to monastic reform.

ALBERIC DE BESANÇON, French poet of the early twelfth century who is credited with preparing the first Western rendition of the Alexander epic.

ALBERIC OF MONTE CASSINO, d. c. 1105, Benedictine monk and rhetorician who supported Pope Gregory VII in his efforts to reform the church. He authored lives of the saints, hymns, and treatises on theological and political subjects.

ALBERIC OF OSTIA, d. 1148, monk of Cluny, abbot, bishop of Ostia, and cardinal. He served as papal legate in England, Scotland, and Antioch, opposed Albigensianism in southern France, and cooperated with St. Bernard of Clairvaux in preaching the Second Crusade.

ALBERIC OF ROSATE, d. 1360, Italian jurist and author of several learned legal studies who took an active part in the political affairs of Bergamo. He authored an excellent treatise on private international law and the first satisfactory lexicon of civil and common law.

ALBERIC OF UTRECHT, ST., d. 784, Benedictine monk who labored as a missionary among the Frisians, then joined the circle of scholars at Aachen, later served as bishop of Utrecht.

ALBERO (Adalbero) OF MONTREUIL, d. 1152, zealous, reforming archbishop of Trier, papal legate to Germany, and a man of great influence in political affairs. He helped arrange the election of Conrad III against the ambitions of Henry the Proud, duke of Bavaria.

ALBERT I, king of Germany, 1298–1308, eldest son of Rudolf of Hapsburg, whom the electors passed over in favor of Adolf of Nassau in 1291 when his father died because of the formidable position the Hapsburgs had acquired in south Germany. Then in 1297 the electors deposed the aggressive Adolf who had moved into Thuringia, and chose Albert, who defeated Adolf and assumed the crown (1298). His own ambitions to acquire Bohemia and Thuringia were cut short when his disgruntled nephew John, duke of Swabia, later known as the "Parricide," murdered him.

ALBERT II, king of Germany, 1438–9, also elected king of Hungary and of Bohemia in 1438. As duke of Austria he had married Elizabeth, daughter of Emperor Sigismund, thereby uniting the two richest and most powerful dynasties in Germany, the Hapsburg and the Luxemburg. He died before his coronation.

ALBERT III (the Pious), duke of Bavaria, 1438–60, proved himself a capable ruler and earned acclaim as a saint for his efforts in the cause of monastic reform. In 1440 he rejected the crown of Bohemia which the nobles of that country had voted to offer him.

ALBERT IV (the Wise), duke of Bavaria, 1460–1508, made his court the center of a cultural awakening through his patronage of the arts. He also established the principle of primogeniture for his duchy.

ALBERT II, archbishop of Mageburg, 1205–32, first supported the candidacy of Philip of Swabia following the death of Henry VI of Germany in 1197, then that of Otto of Brunswick, finally that of Frederick (II), king of Sicily, when Pope Innocent III repudiated Otto. Frederick appointed him ruler of Romagna.

ALBERT I, bishop of Riga, d. 1229, extended Christianity and German power into the area of Livonia by means of a crusade. There he founded the city of Riga in 1201 and became its first bishop. In time he encountered great difficulties with the Livonian Knights of the Sword who had earlier supported his efforts, and with the papacy because of the high favor he enjoyed with Frederick II of Germany.

ALBERT II, bishop of Riga, d. 1273, first nominated as bishop of Livonia only to have the chapter refuse to elect him. In 1240 the pope appointed him archbishop of Armagh. In 1246 when he was appointed archbishop of Prussia, Livonia, and Esthonia, local opposition prevented him from occupying the see. In 1253 he was finally elected bishop of Riga.

ALBERT III ACHILLES, margrave of Brandenburg, 1470–86, a major prop for the unstable throne of Frederick III of Germany, opposed Charles the Bold of Burgundy and drew up a fundamental law *(Dispositio Achillea)* which established the principle of primogeniture for Brandenburg. This assured in the end the succession of the house of Hohenzollern.

ALBERT BEHAIM, d. c. 1260, deacon of the cathedral of Passau, member of the papal Curia under Innocent III and Honorius III, later a leader of the papal party in Germany opposed first to Frederick II, then to his son Conrad IV. When expelled from Germany in 1241, he found refuge with the pope, returning to Germany after the death of Frederick (1250). His letters constitute a valuable source for the history of the period.

ALBERT HALBERSTADT, learned priest of the early thirteenth century who composed a poem closely imitative of Ovid's *Metamorphoses.* His was the first work to appear in German, directly based upon a Latin classic and not made from an earlier French translation.

ALBERTI, name of two important families of medieval Italy. Members of the Tuscan feudal family of the Alberti are noted as counts from the tenth century when they were numbered with the most powerful lords of the country around Florence. The family made its submission to Florence in 1200. The Alberti del Giudice were among the wealthiest merchant bankers of Florence in the later Middle Ages. They engaged in extensive international trade and had a leading role in the financial transactions of the papacy. In 1402 they lost out to the Albizzi, their chief political rivals, and did not

recover their position until the fall of this family in 1434.

ALBERTI, LEONE BATTISTA, d. 1472, a leading Italian humanist, musician, philosopher, sculptor, and architect who spent some time in the service of the pope. The treatises he composed concerning the theories and principles of art greatly influenced architectural design of the period. The single-nave interior of the church of St. Andrea in Mantua which he designed proved a popular model for several centuries.

ALBERT OF AIX, fl. c. 1130, canon of the church of Aachen, author of a history of the First Crusade (1096–9) and of the Latin kingdom of Jerusalem (to 1121). William of Tyre used this work in the preparation of his own history of the kingdom of Jerusalem. Despite considerable second-hand information which he incorporated in his work, his history remains one of the principal sources for the history of this crusade.

ALBERT OF EYB, d. 1475, jurist, humanist, and papal chamberlain. He translated several of the plays of Plautus into German and worked for the improvement of German prose, using classical Latin as his model.

ALBERT OF JERUSALEM, ST., d. 1214, bishop of Bobbio, papal legate who displayed great skill in his negotiations with Frederick I Barbarossa and the north Italian cities. His diplomatic talents, as well as his piety, led to his appointment as patriarch of Jerusalem. Since the Moslems held the city he made his home in Acre, and while there he drew up a rigorous rule for the hermits of Mount Carmel.

ALBERT OF JOHANSDORF, a minnesinger of the late twelfth, early thirteenth century who was in the service of the bishop of Passau. The themes of both piety and chivalry find place in his verse.

ALBERT OF SAXONY (Albert of Helmstedt), d. 1390, nominalist philosopher and scientist, taught at Paris and rector there. Later he became first rector of the University of Vienna and bishop of Halberstadt. He left numerous writings on logic, natural philosophy, mathematics, and ethics. Several of his mathematical treatises were used extensively as textbooks. Later scholastic logicians adopted such terminological distinctions of his as *a priori* and *a posteriori*.

ALBERT, ST. *See* ALBERT THE GREAT.

ALBERT I THE BEAR, d. 1170, count of Ballenstedt, established the foundations of Brandenburg (he called himself margrave of Brandenburg), founded Berlin, and invited Dutch, Flemish, and Germans from the Rhine country to settle there. The expansion of German influence and power to the east of the Elbe during this period came as a result of his efforts, those of Henry the Lion of Saxony, and the missionary zeal of the Premonstratensians.

ALBERT THE BRAVE, duke of Saxony, 1464–1500, ruled Saxony with his brother until 1485 when the brothers divided the duchy. Albert, who became the founder of the Albertine line of the house of Wettin, led the imperial armies of Frederick III against Charles the Bold of Burgundy and Matthew Corvinus of Hungary.

ALBERT THE GREAT (Albertus Magnus), d. 1280, a Dominican, studied at Paris, taught there and at Cologne where he had St. Thomas Aquinas as a disciple. In 1260 he became bishop of Regensburg, but two years later he returned to his teaching in Cologne. In 1277 he went to Paris in an attempt to avert the condemnation of the Aristotelian views held by himself and by Aquinas. His voluminous writings include letters, sermons, and treatises on logic, natural science, metaphysics, ethics, Scripture, and theology. Although Albert retained the substance of the Augustinian tradition in his philosophical-theological writings, he incorporated much Aristotelian thought, the fruit of his own intensive study of the works of the Greek philosopher. Albert's scientific studies, which contributed significantly to the growth of medieval science,

revealed an independence of mind and a constant appeal to experimentation and observation. Perhaps his greatest contribution to learning was that of putting Aristotle into the good graces of the ecclesiastical authorities.

ALBERTUS MAGNUS. *See* ALBERT THE GREAT.

ALBI, city in Languedoc, an episcopal see from the fifth century and ruled by its bishop from the late twelfth century to the French Revolution. It became a stronghold of Catharism and gave its name to the Albigenses. In 1254 Louis IX of France summoned a church council to meet there for the purpose of suppressing the last vestiges of the heresy. The city's huge red brick Gothic cathedral (thirteenth-fourteenth century) resembles a fortress more than it does a church.

ALBICUS, SIGISMUND, d. 1427, studied medicine at Prague, law at Padua, later taught medicine at Prague. For four years he served as archbishop of Prague, then resigned. He left a number of treatises on medical subjects.

ALBIGENSES (Albigensians), a branch of the Cathari that took its name from Albi, where the sect was especially strong in the twelfth and early thirteenth centuries. (Cathari could also be found in some number in north Italy and in parts of the Balkan peninsula.) While the sect accepted the fundamental principle of two supreme beings, one good, the other evil, which can be traced to the Manichaeism of the early Christian era, variety and confusion of its beliefs and practices suggest the impact of diverse influences, including persecution, during the centuries intervening. The Cathari held flesh to be evil and salvation essentially emancipation from the needs of the body. Their leaders, the Perfect, attempted to approach the goal of a completely spiritual existence by leading most austere lives. One day the same renunciation of the desires of the flesh would be expected of the rank and file, the Believers. Since there was no hell but only transmigration until purification had been achieved on earth, the moral laxity of the masses proved as typical of the movement as the sanctity of the Perfect. Contributing to the spread of the movement were the laxity of the Christian clergy and the cupidity of the aristocracy. The aristocracy expected to be the principal beneficiaries from the confiscation of church property that the Cathari preached. The Albigenses were condemned by several church councils, notably by the Fourth Lateran Council of 1215 which defined orthodox Christian doctrine with special reference to their heresy. [See ALBIGENSIAN CRUSADE.]

ALBIGENSIAN CRUSADE, 1208–29, was proclaimed by Pope Innocent III against the Albigenses following the murder of his legate, Peter of Castelnau, by agents of Count Raymond VI of Toulouse, and after several years of fruitless efforts to suppress the heresy through preaching and diplomacy. Philip II Augustus of France took no direct part in the crusade although he permitted his northern vassals to do so, chief among them Simon de Montfort who was the principal leader until his death in 1218. Before Simon died, he gained a decisive victory at Muret over the combined forces of Raymond and Peter II of Aragon, after which Raymond sued for peace. It was, however, not until the direct intervention of Louis VIII who in 1226 captured Avignon, the last stronghold of the Albigenses, that the strength of the heresy was finally broken. Unfortunately, the bitter fighting and ruthless destruction that marked the crusade brought an end to the cultural brilliance of Languedoc. In 1233 Gregory IX established the Court of the Inquisition for the purpose of eradicating heresy, including what traces remained in southern France of Albigensianism.

ALBION, ancient, possibly pre-Celtic, name for Britain.

ALBIZZI (Albizi), an old Italian family first noted in 1199 prominent in Florentine politics from the thirteenth century until it fell to the superior power of the Medici in the mid-fifteenth.

ALBO, JOSEPH (José), d. c. 1440, Jewish scholar, polemicist, and philosopher. His best known work, *Sefer ha-Ikkarim,* constituted a complete system of Jewish theology and was intended to set forth the essential beliefs of Judaism in order to aid in its defense. The influence of Maimonides is evident in the work.

ALBOIN (Albuin), king of the Lombards, 565–72, destroyed the Gepids in 567 with the help of the Avars, married Rosamund, the daughter of the Gepid king who had been slain, then overran the greater part of northern Italy. He was murdered by a paramour of his wife. He had mortally offended her by having her drink wine from a goblet fashioned out of her father's skull.

ALBORNOZ, GIL ÁLVAREZ CARRILLO DE, d. 1367, archbishop of Toledo, royal chancellor of Alfonso of Castile, and primate of Spain. He worked with Alfonso in the unification of Castile and distinguished himself in fighting against the Moors. He fled to Avignon when he fell out with Alfonso's successor, Peter I. Innocent VI made him a cardinal and entrusted him with the restoration of papal authority in the Papal States. He entered Rome with Cola di Rienzo who had at one time been in control of the city, then succeeded by means of diplomacy and military force to restore papal authority in the Marches and Romagna. Later as papal legate, he founded a college for Spanish students in Bologna which still exists.

ALBRECHT. *See* ALBERT.

ALBRET, French family celebrated in French history that took its name from Labrit, a small village in Gascony. As the lords of Albret acquired more and more seigneuries, they grew ever more influential, and in 1494, through marriage, they became kings of Navarre. Members of the family took an active part in the Hundred Years' War. One of the members of the family, Alain d'Albret (1440–1516), became a leading magnate of France and was called Alain the Great.

ALBUIN OF SÄBEN-BRIXEN, ST., d. c. 1006, bishop of Säben in the Tyrol who moved the episcopal residence to Brixen. Its location on the principal route between Italy and Germany, together with Albuin's own talents, enabled him to exercise much influence upon Otto II and Henry II.

ALBUMAZAR. *See* ABU MA'SHAR.

ALBUS, a German silver coin used in Trier since 1362, whence its use spread throughout the Rhineland area and west Germany.

ALCABALA, a Spanish sales tax introduced in the twelfth century.

ALCAFORAGO, FRANCIS, Portuguese navigator who is credited with exploring Madeira c. 1419.

ALCÁNTARA, ORDER OF, one of the three major knightly orders of Spain, founded in 1156 or 1166, for the purpose of opposing Moorish arms in Spain. Alfonso IX of Leon granted the order the walled town of Alcántara which became its headquarters. The crown held the dignity of grandmaster after 1494.

ALCÁZABA, name frequently given to Moorish fortresses in Spain, as, for example, the military part of the Alhambra.

ALCÁZAR, a Spanish castle or strong-walled palace, erected during the centuries of Moorish domination. It might serve as a fortress or simply as a defensible residence. The name Alcázar may be also given to places: Alcázar de San Juan.

ALCHEMY, ancient art or pseudo-science whose origins may reach back into early Egypt or China, more immediately to Hellenistic Alexandria. Wherever its roots, the principal aim of alchemists has generally been the same, namely, to transmute base metals into gold by some chemical means. More extraordinary goals, such as the discovery of an elixir that would restore a man's youth, together with the use of symbolic languages and signs to conceal their activities, have earned alchemists the suspicion of most ages, including that of the Middle Ages. Almost as old as alchemy has been the division of its devotees between those interested in the practical uses to which chemical processes might be applied, and those concerned with more mystical and superstitious objectives. Alchemy came to western Europe in the twelfth and thirteenth centuries principally through the writings of Arabic scholars. The most influential Westerner to write on the subject was a Spanish alchemist of the fourteenth century who may have used the name Geber in order to give his work wider acceptance. (Geber or Jabir ibn Hayyan was considered the most authoritative of Islamic alchemists.) Despite the superstitions that hampered progress from within and the persecution of a hostile society from without, the alchemist contributed a significant measure of valuable knowledge for the use of future chemists: e.g., distillation, sublimation, stills, and furnaces.

ALCHER OF CLAIRVAUX, obscure Cistercian monk of the middle and late twelfth century who is believed to have been the author of an influential treatise, *De Spiritu et Anima,* on the subject of mysticism. He drew heavily upon St. Augustine, also on Boethius, Cassiodorus, and Hugh of Saint Victor, for his ideas.

ALCOBAÇA, ABBEY OF, Cistercian abbey founded by King Alfonso I of Portugal in 1153 in the district of Leiria. It was rebuilt in the thirteenth century and became the leading monastery of Portugal in the fourteenth, actually rivaling in size and wealth the greatest abbeys of the Middle Ages. It assumed an important role in both the cultural and the economic development of the country. It furnished Portugal with its first public college, pharmacy, and printing press. The early kings of Portugal are buried in the abbey.

ALCOCK, JOHN, d. 1500, bishop of Rochester, Worcester, and Ely, privy councillor under Richard III and Henry VII, and keeper of the great seal. He was distinguished for his piety as well as for his knowledge of law and architecture. He left a number of sermons and treatises on mysticism, and was founder of Jesus College at Cambridge.

ALCUIN (Albinus), d. 804, learned monk of York and head of the school there, whom Charlemagne invited to Aachen where he graced the palace school for 14 years as its most respected scholar and teacher. At Aachen he also served as Charlemagne's private teacher and as his counselor in ecclesiastical, cultural, and political matters. At Aachen, too, he busied himself with the preparation of treatises on theological subjects, manuals for use in the schools, with emending St. Jerome's *Vulgate,* purifying liturgical practices, and composing some poetry and 18 votive Masses. Charlemagne rewarded him with the abbacy of the monastery of Tours (796) where he set up a library and school and encouraged the work of the monks in developing the beautiful script known as the Carolingian minuscule. The more than 300 letters which Alcuin left possess great historical importance.

ALDA (Aude), the sister of Oliver and the betrothed of Roland in the *Chanson de Roland.*

ALDEBERT AND CLEMENT, priests of the first half of the eighth century, Clement the Irish disciple of Aldebert. Clement claimed to have visions and to be able to work miracles. Although a synod at Soissons, under urging of St. Boniface, condemned the two men as frauds, many people continued to revere them as saints.

ALDEGUNDIS, ST., d. c. 700, abbess of the Benedictine monastery at Maubeuge, France, which she founded. People invoked her intercession for the cure of eye and childhood diseases.

ALDFRITH, king of Northumbria, 685–704, a patron of literature and responsible for the flour-

ishing of scholarship in that northern province. He was educated for the priesthood but succeeded to the throne when his brother was slain. Bede and Alcuin praised his learning.

ALDHELM, ST., d. 709, disciple of Hadrian who became abbot of Malmesbury and later also served as first bishop of Sherborne (from 705). He founded several churches and monasteries. Contemporaries recognized him as a leading scholar, and he was well known both in England and on the Continent for his treatises on secular and religious learning, for his letters, and his religious poems. Some of these were in Latin, others in Anglo-Saxon. His turgid Latin style reveals Irish influence.

ALDINE PRESS. *See* MANUTIUS, ALDUS.

ALDRED, d. 1069, monk of Winchester, abbot of Tavistock, bishop of Worcester, and archbishop of York (1060). He stood high in the counsels of Edward the Confessor and it was he who had the honor of crowning William the Conqueror in 1066. (He may also have crowned Harold.) Aldred was the first English bishop to visit Jerusalem.

ALDRIC OF LE MANS, BL., d. 856, who spent several years as a youth at the court of Charlemagne at Aachen, was later ordained a priest and placed in charge of the cathedral school at Metz. He subsequently served Louis the Pious as confessor and was consecrated bishop of Le Mans.

ALDUS MANUTIUS. *See* MANUTIUS, ALDUS.

ALEMANNI (Alamanni, Alemans), German tribe closely associated with the Sueves, first noted in the early third century when they were located on the upper Main. After the death of Aetius in 454, they spilled over into the Roman empire in the area of Switzerland. In 495 Clovis, king of the Franks, defeated them and might have destroyed the tribe had it not been for the intervention of Theodoric, king of the Ostrogoths. They were eventually absorbed into the Frankish kingdom of the Carolingians, but reappeared later in the duchy of Swabia. They remained pagan until the first half of the eighth century.

ALEPPO (Alep), ancient city of northwest Syria on the chief caravan route across Syria to Baghdad. The city fell to the Arabs in the seventh century, was recovered by Byzantium in the tenth, and taken by the Seljuk Turks late in the eleventh. The Crusaders failed in their attempt to capture the city, but it fell to Saladin in 1183. The Mongols captured the city in 1260 and massacred its inhabitants, but it recovered, only to fall to the Mongol Timur the Lame in 1401. Shortly after this, it returned to Turkish control. It enjoyed de facto independence during the greater part of the tenth and eleventh centuries, during which period its trade and wealth reached their peak.

ALESSANDRIA, city southeast of Milan which the Lombard League converted into a powerful fortress in order to block the advance southward of Frederick I Barbarossa, king of Germany. It was given the name Alessandria in recognition of the assistance given the League by Pope Alexander III (1159–81). The city was at first a free commune, then in 1348 passed to the duchy of Milan.

ALEXANDER I, ST., Pope, c. 107–c. 116, is listed as the fifth successor of St. Peter. Almost nothing is known about this bishop of Rome.

ALEXANDER II, Pope, 1061–73, a disciple of Lanfranc of Bec, became bishop of Lucca and was the first pope to be chosen following the proclamation of the Papal Electoral Law of 1059. (Henry IV of Germany supported the antipope Honorius II.) Alexander who kept Hildebrand as one of his advisers, vigorously supported the reform program of his predecessors. With the view of strengthening papal leadership, he sent legates to Lombardy, France, Spain, and England, and held four synods at Rome. He compiled a collection of canons which proved highly influential in the investiture controversy

and which were later incorporated into Gratian's *Decretum*. [See GREGORY VII.]

ALEXANDER III, Pope, 1159–81, professor of canon law at Bologna, cardinal, and papal chancellor. Frederick I Barbarossa, king of Germany, refused to recognize him as the successor of Adrian IV, drove him from Rome where he installed his own pope Victor IV, then Paschal III when Victor died. During the schism Alexander spent most of his time in France where he made the acquaintance of Thomas Becket, the exiled archbishop of Canterbury. After the defeat of Frederick at Legnano (1176) which the Lombard League accomplished with the assistance of Alexander, the pope negotiated a settlement with Frederick at Venice in 1177. Because of his difficulties with Frederick, Alexander felt it prudent to adopt a temporizing policy in the controversy between Henry II of England and Thomas Becket. Alexander convened the important Third Lateran Council in 1179. His most scholarly work was a commentary on the *Decretum* of Gratian.

ALEXANDER IV, Pope, 1254–61, continued the policy of his predecessors against the Hohenstaufens. For this reason he was driven from Rome by Manfred, king of Sicily, the son of Frederick II, although he was able to bring about the fall of Ezzelino da Romano, the son-in-law of Frederick. His efforts to unite Europe against the threat of the Mongols who had overrun Hungary proved unsuccessful.

ALEXANDER V, Pope, 1409–10, a Franciscan, lecturer in theology at Paris, archbishop of Milan, and cardinal, was elected pope by the cardinals who had assembled at Pisa in 1409 in the hope of ending the Western Schism. In electing Alexander, the cardinals aggravated the schism by adding a third pope to the two who already claimed to be canonically elected. Alexander V is identified as the first of the Pisan popes. He died 10 months after his election.

ALEXANDER VI, Pope, 1492–1503, a Spaniard, born Rodrigo Borgia about 1431 in Valencia. As nephew of Pope Callistus III, he became richly beneficed, a cardinal at the age of 25, bishop of Valencia two years later, after which he served several popes as vice chancellor. Despite a low moral reputation — Pius II had felt obliged to rebuke him for his immorality — he was elected pope in 1492, probably with the help of bribery. As pope he pursued an active political role, first in alliance with Spain against France, after 1498 as an ally of France. French occupation of Florence four years earlier (1494) precipitated Alexander's difficulties with the Dominican reformer Girolamo Savonarola which terminated with the friar's execution in 1498. In 1493 Alexander granted to Spain all lands to the west and south in the Atlantic that were not held by another Christian power (Line of Demarcation). His son Cesare (Caesar) reestablished Alexander's authority in the papal territories.

ALEXANDER, Byzantine emperor (912–3), third son of Basil I of the Macedonian dynasty, a vicious, irresponsible ruler, whose actions caused great dissension in both ecclesiastical and political circles. His refusal to pay the annual tribute to the Bulgars in accord with the treaty of 896 led to war with the great Bulgar leader Simeon. His early death left the empire in danger both internally and externally.

ALEXANDER I, king of Scotland, 1107–24, son of Malcolm III and Margaret of Scotland (St.). He put down a revolt in northern Scotland, encouraged conformity with the ecclesiastical usages (Roman) in England (Celtic traditions still prevailed in Scotland), and established several monasteries, including the abbeys at Inchcolm and Scone. He may have ruled as a vassal of Henry I of England whose illegitimate daughter Sibylla he married.

ALEXANDER II, king of Scotland, 1214–49, successor of William the Lion, joined the barons against King John and repudiated England's claim to suzerainty over Scotland. He later mar-

ried the sister of Henry III and paid homage to Henry, although friction between the two kings continued principally over the northern counties which both men claimed. A significant growth in the number of religious houses took place in Scotland during his reign.

ALEXANDER III, king of Scotland, 1249–86, married the daughter of Henry III, but denied him homage although he later paid homage to Henry's son, Edward I, but only for his English estates. Edward hoped to annex Scotland by arranging a marriage between his son Edward (II) and Alexander's granddaughter Margaret (Maid of Norway), but the girl died, a death that brought the Scottish ruling dynasty to an end and precipitated a struggle over the succession. Alexander gained the Isle of Man and Hebrides (Western Isles) from Magnus VI of Norway in return for a down payment and an annual rent. (Magnus's predecessor, Haakon IV, had failed in his efforts to drive the Scots off the Hebrides.)

ALEXANDER NECKHAM, d. 1217, English scholar who studied at Paris and Oxford, became an Augustinian canon, later abbot of Cirencester. His extensive writings reveal him to have been a man of encyclopedic learning, especially in the field of the natural sciences. There is found in his writings the earliest European reference to the use of the compass as a guide to seamen.

ALEXANDER NEVILLE, d. 1392, consecrated archbishop of York in 1374, was convicted of treason by the "Merciless Parliament" in 1388, his property confiscated and he himself banished. He spent his last years in exile in Louvain.

ALEXANDER NEVSKI, d. 1263, prince of Novgorod who was able to repel the invasions of the Swedes, Lithuanians, and Teutonic Knights. He later felt obliged to recognize the suzerainty of the Golden Horde. The Mongols had overrun all of Russia with the exception of Novgorod which was protected by marshes. In 1246, upon the death of the grand prince of Vladimir and Kiev, Alexander visited the court of the Great Khan in Mongolia and eventually received Mongol approval for his assuming that post for himself. The Greek Orthodox Church canonized him in 1380, and he has been honored as one of the great national heroes of Russia.

ALEXANDER OF HALES, d. 1245, English Franciscan, studied at Paris and later occupied a chair of theology at that university. He introduced the practice of lecturing on the *Sentences* of Peter Lombard rather than on the Bible directly, thus giving the study of theology a new approach which it then followed for the balance of the Middle Ages. He is regarded as the founder of the Franciscan school of theology. Alexander was among the first scholastics to incorporate a measure of Aristotelianism into the Augustinian school of thought which prevailed at that time. That he is listed among medieval encyclopedists of science suggests the wide range of his learning. His views influenced the thought of St. Thomas Aquinas.

ALEXANDER OF ROES, canon of the cathedral of Cologne and political theorist of the late thirteenth century. He accorded control of the church (*sacerdotium*) to the papacy and Rome, that of the state (*imperium*) to Germany, while leadership in the field of learning he gave to France.

ALEXANDER OF VILLA DEI, d. c. 1250, canon of the cathedral of Avranches, taught at Paris and was the author of a favorite Latin grammar in hexameter verse which retained its popularity in medieval scholarly circles until the triumph of humanism.

ALEXANDER, ROMANCE OF, one of the cycles of courtly romances that glorified the deeds, most legendary, of Alexander the Great. They usually portrayed him as the epitome of knightly chivalry. Tales about Alexander appeared in Old English as early as the reign of Alfred the Great (d. 899), later in Middle Irish, Middle High German, and French. The period of their greatest popularity came in the twelfth century, highlighted by the French epic of the *Roman d'Alexandre*. In addition to poems and prose tales about Alexander in the vernacular, versions in Latin also made their appearance.

ALEXANDER, ST., d. 328, patriarch of Alexandria (313), vigorously opposed the views of Arius, one of his presbyters, concerning the divinity of Christ. After two synods in Alexandria had condemned but not silenced Arius, Alexander and Hosius, bishop of Córdoba, Emperor Constantine's episcopal adviser and the leading theologian of the West, persuaded him to convene a general council at Nicaea (325) in which Alexander played a major role. Alexander was ably assisted at the council by his deacon Athanasius who later succeeded him as patriarch.

ALEXANDRIA, leading city of Egypt in Roman times. The establishment of Christianity there has been traditionally credited to St. Mark. The Council of Nicaea assigned the see of Alexandria a place of honor second only to Rome. The rise of Constantinople served to eclipse the eminence of Alexandria by the close of the fifth century, but what proved most injurious to its high position in the Christian world was its adherence to Monophysitism. Though its population and prosperity had declined with that of the empire, the real break in its political and commercial history came in 646 when it fell to the Arabs who moved the capital to what is now Cairo. The silting of the Nile in the fourteenth century contributed to the city's further decline. What proved a more severe blow was the discovery in 1498 of an all-water route via the Cape of Good Hope to the Indies.

ALEXANDRIA, PATRIARCHATE OF. *See* ALEXANDRIA

ALEXANDRIA, SCHOOL OF, catechetical and theological center at Alexandria that might date from the city's earliest bishops. (The catechetical and theological schools were not actually identical although their associations were close and most scholars were members of both.) As a center of Christian learning, Alexandria rivaled Rome and Constantinople. Among its eminent representatives were Clement, Origen, whose influence has been called overwhelming, Athanasius, and Cyril. The theology of the early church at Alexandria was markedly influenced by the Platonic tradition of philosophy. The school gave special emphasis to the divinity of Christ and also favored an allegorical, mystical interpretation of Scripture as against the literal-historical preference of the school of Antioch. In their opposition to the tendency of the theologians at Antioch to exalt Christ's humanity, both Monophysitism and Monothelitism found many adherents in Alexandria.

ALEXANDRIAN RITE, LITURGY OF, the oldest of the Egyptian rites and one traditionally linked with the name of St. Mark the Evangelist. It is the source from which other Egyptian rites, including the Coptic, had their origin.

ALEXANDRINE, a measure consisting of 12 iambic syllables, with the caesura coming after the sixth syllable. Its name derived from the fact that certain French poems of the twelfth and thirteenth centuries concerning Alexander the Great were composed in that meter.

ALEXIAN BROTHERS (Alexians or Cellites), an order of laymen particularly active in Flanders and the Rhineland during the period of the Black Death (1348–50) when the organization was established. The members dedicated themselves to the care of the sick, the burial of the dead, and, later, to the education of children. While members of the order were occasionally arraigned on charges of heresy, as was the case in England where they were confused with Lollards, they consistently enjoyed papal protection.

ALEXIAN NUNS, a religious community that appeared in the fifteenth century and was affiliated with the Alexian Brothers. The nuns engaged in activities similar to those of the Brothers.

ALEXIUS I (Comnenus), Byzantine emperor, 1081–1118, overthrew Nicephorus III in 1081, drove the Petchenegs away from Constantinople (1091) with the aid of the Cumans, and in 1095 repulsed the Cumans who had turned against him. In 1094 he appealed to Pope Urban II for assistance against the Seljuk Turks, an appeal that culminated in the First Crusade (1096–9). He managed to persuade most of the different leaders of the Crusade to promise to restore to him all lands they should recapture, a promise they did not honor. By means of diplomacy, his own military efforts, and an alliance with Venice and Pisa, he succeeded in thwarting Robert Guiscard and his Normans in their ambition to conquer Greece, and he reestablished Byzantine authority over a large part of Asia Minor. Alexius proved himself one of the last Byzantine emperors able to maintain the military and political prestige of Byzantium.

ALEXIUS II, Byzantine emperor, 1180–3, son and successor of Manuel I. His mother, who served as regent for him, alienated the Greek population of Constantinople by favoring the Latins. In 1183 Alexius's cousin Andronicus stormed the city, which had revolted, became joint emperor with Alexius, but shortly after had him strangled.

ALEXIUS III (Angelus), Byzantine emperor, 1195–1203 seized the Byzantine throne from his brother Isaac II in 1195, was overthrown in 1203 by his nephew Alexius (IV) with the help of Crusaders (Fourth Crusade), and died a prisoner of his son-in-law Theodore Laskaris in Nicaea in 1210.

ALEXIUS IV (Angelus), Byzantine emperor, 1203–4, son of Isaac II and brother-in-law of Philip of Swabia, was able to secure momentary control of Constantinople in 1203 with the help of Venice and Crusaders (Fourth Crusade), only to be slain the following year in the course of a popular uprising.

ALEXIUS V (Ducas Murtzuphlus), d. 1204, son-in-law of Alexius III Angelus. When the Greeks revolted against Isaac II and his son Alexius IV, Alexius V came to power, but was shortly after driven from the city, then captured by Crusaders (Fourth Crusade), and beheaded.

ALEXIUS, SONG OF, an Old Norman French legend about St. Alexius (semilegendary saint of the fifth century) in verse which appeared in the middle of the eleventh century.

AL-FARABI. *See* FARABI, AL-.

AL-FASI, Isaac ben Jacob ha-Kohen, d. 1103, Jewish Talmudic scholar, author of *Halachoth,* a codification of the Talmud which contains a simplified exposition of difficult Talmudic passages. His collection of *Responsa* was initially written in Arabic before being translated into Hebrew.

ALFONSIAN (Alfonsine, Alphonsine) TABLES, astronomical charts drawn up c. 1272 on order of Alfonso X, king of Castile and Leon. The *Tables,* which accepted a solar system based upon the theories of Ptolemy but improved and revised, noted the spatial relationships of sun, moon, and planets. They were principally the work of two Jewish scholars, Jehuda Ben Moses and Isaak Ben Sid.

ALFONSO I (the Warrior), king of Aragon, 1104–34, a better fighter than he was diplomat, took Saragossa from the Moors and made it his capital. His marriage to the heiress of Castile which he hoped would unite the two countries, itself failed and the union did not materialize. His subjects did not honor his will which bequeathed his kingdom to the Templars and Hospitallers. His life was spent in continuous warfare.

ALFONSO II (the Chaste), king of Aragon, 1162–96, united Barcelona and Aragon under his own rule, drove the Moors southward almost to Valencia, and by inheritance added Rousillon and Provençe to his domain. He was a patron of troubadours and composed some of his own Provençal verse.

ALFONSO III, king of Aragon and count of Barcelona, 1285–91, successor of Peter III, weakened his position by extending wide privileges to his nobility. He first supported, then opposed, his brother James's claim to Sicily against that of Charles II of Naples.

ALFONSO IV, King of Aragon and count of Barcelona, 1327–36, son and successor of James II. A revolt in Sardinia which he had conquered before his accession, involved him in a war with Genoa.

ALFONSO V (the Magnanimous), king of Aragon, 1416–58, also ruler of Naples and Sicily following his conquest of Naples in 1422. He left his wife to administer his Spanish posssessions, while he spent the rest of his life in Naples. There he proved himself a patron of humanism —he founded the first Italian humanist academy—, maintained a splendid court and beautified the city, but in political affairs enjoyed but modest success.

ALFONSO III (the Great), king of Castile and Leon, 886–910, expanded his domain at the expense of the Moors and also reduced the power of his aristocracy. His sons who forced him to abdicate in 910 ruled Castile and Leon as separate countries. Alfonso died two years later.

ALFONSO VI, king of Castile and Leon, 1072–1109, inherited Leon from his father and succeeded to the throne of Castile after the assassination of his brother Sancho II. In 1073 he took Galicia from his brother Garcia, thus becoming the most powerful Christian ruler in Spain. With the assistance of Rodrigo Dias de Vivar (the Cid), he captured Toledo in 1085, but against the invading Almoravids he fared poorly. His court at Toledo became a center of cultural relations between Moslems and Christians in Spain.

ALFONSO VII, king of Castile and Leon, 1126–57, seized Aragon upon the death of his stepfather Alfonso I of Aragon, but achieved little permanent success against the Almohads. When he died, Castile and Leon again went their separate ways.

ALFONSO VIII, king of Castile, 1158–1214, though at first at war with his Christian neighbors of Navarre, Aragon, and Leon, he gained a decisive victory over the Moors in 1212 with their assistance at the battle of Las Navas de Tolosa. The Moors were never again able to regain their ascendancy after this defeat. Alfonso founded the first university in Spain at Palencia (1212 or 1214). He married Eleanor, daughter of Henry II of England, and their daughter, Blanche of Castile, married Louis VIII of France and became the mother of the future Louis IX.

ALFONSO IX, king of Leon, 1188–1230, whose marriage to the daughter of Alfonso VIII of Castile led to the unification of Castile and Leon under his son Ferdinand III.

ALFONSO X (the Wise), king of Castile and Leon, 1252–84, took Cadiz from the Moors and later was elected antiking in Germany although he never visited that country. His promotion of learning; founding of schools; sponsorship of the first general history of Spain, the *Alfonsian Tables* in astronomy, and the translation of many Arabic books on astronomy into Latin; the composition of a number of songs; and the codification of laws (*Siete Partidas*) gained him recognition as the most learned prince of the century. He displayed weakness in dealing with his nobles and he debased the coinage.

ALFONSO XI, king of Castile and Leon, 1312–50, lost Gibraltar to the Moors (1333) but later, in 1340, with the aid of Portugal, Aragon, and Navarre, won a great victory over them at Tarif (Salado). In 1344, with an army including many knights-errant from other countries, he took Algeciras, and he died while laying siege to Gibraltar. He strengthened the royal power at the expense of the aristocracy and the cities.

ALFONSO I (the Conqueror), first king of Portugal (his father was Henry of Burgundy, his mother, Theresia of Castile), assumed the title of king in 1139 after defeating the Moors at Ourique. He then declared his country independent of Castile and Leon. In 1147, with the assistance of English, Flemish, and German crusaders (Second Crusade, 1147–9), he drove the Moors from Lisbon and made that city his capital. He died in 1185.

ALFONSO II (the Fat), king of Portugal, 1211–23, spent his reign quarreling with the Church and with his brothers and sisters to whom his father, Sancho I, had left many of his estates. His army helped win the decisive battle of Las Navas de Tolosa against the Moors in 1212.

ALFONSO III, king of Portugal, 1248–79, successor of Sancho II from whom he had taken most of Portugal before the latter's death, reconquered what parts of Portugal remained in Moorish hands. He was involved in a long struggle with the Church over lands he had seized. In 1254 he convened the first Portuguese Cortes that included commoners. [*See* CORTES.] He also introduced reforms in the government and encouraged the growth of cities and of commerce. Partly due to his patronage, his reign witnessed a good measure of intellectual and cultural activity.

ALFONSO IV, king of Portugal, 1325–57, son and successor of Diniz and of St. Elizabeth (Isabel), had difficulties with his father against whom he had revolted. He first fought a fruitless war against Alfonso XI of Castile, then joined him in winning the great victory of Tarifa over the Moors. He is best remembered for contenancing the murder of his son's mistress (or wife), Inés de Castro, the most romantic figure in Portuguese history and literature.

ALFONSO V (the African), king of Portugal, 1438–81, continued the explorations of his uncle Prince Henry the Navigator and seized Alcázar, Tangier, and Arzila from the Moors. He laid the foundation of Portugal's colonial empire.

ALFRED OF SARESHEL (Alfredus Anglicus), an English scholar of the early thirteenth century, prepared translations of several of Aristotle's works, also of a number of scientific treatises from the Arabic. His study of Galen and other writers on medicine served to advance interest in that subject and in physiology.

ALFRED THE GREAT, king of England, 871–99, ruler of Wessex, subsequently extended his authority over the greater part of central and southern England and forced the Danes to limit themselves to the northeastern third of the country (the Danelaw)) Although the Danes had initially driven Alfred into hiding in the Somerset fens, his reorganization of the fyrd and the construction of ships superior to those the enemy possessed enabled him to gain the upper hand. Alfred devoted much effort to reviving Christianity and learning, and to that end encouraged monastic reform and the translation of what he considered particularly valuable books, including Pope Gregory I's *Pastoral Rule,* the *Consolation of Philosophy* of Boethius, and Orosius's historical writings. Some of the translations — they were freely done — include interpolations made by Alfred himself. To Alfred are traced the beginnings of Old English prose.

AL-GAZEL. *See* GHAZALI, AL-.

ALGEBRA, the branch of mathematics concerned with calculation with variables (not simply the numbers of arithmetic) and the solution of polynomial equations. The study of algebra in the Middle Ages reached back through the Greeks to the ancient Babylonians, while the principal link between the Greeks and the medieval West was furnished by Arab mathematicians who prepared commentaries on what the Greeks had written. The most influential of these Arabic scholars was al-Khwarizmi (d. 850) whose book on equations (*Kitab al jabr w'al-muqabala*) gave its name to algebra.

ALGECIRAS, seaport of southernmost Spain, just west of Gibraltar, may have been a Roman city but was refounded by the Moors in 713. Its name is from the Arabic meaning island. It remained in Moorish hands until Alfonso XI of Castile captured it in 1344 after a famous siege of 20 months.

ALGERIA, country of north Africa, part of the Roman empire and still a thriving area, economically and culturally, when Christianity came to prevail in the fourth century. Its leading scholar and theologian, St. Augustine of Hippo (d. 430), already witnessed the ending of this great era which terminated when the Vandals overran the country (430–1). Justinian I (d. 565) was able to recover the region for Rome (Byzantium), but the old culture did not revive, and in the early seventh century what little remained was almost completely obliterated by the Moslem Arabs. Because their civilization was closer to that of the native Berbers of the region than had been the case with earlier conquerors, Arabic culture took root and most of the population accepted the Arabic language and became Moslems. Still the country remained in a state of political confusion with dynasties rising and falling, including those of the Almoravids and Almohads. For a time these were successful in erecting extensive empires that included Morocco and spilled over into Spain. In 1518 the country fell to the Ottoman Turks.

ALGER OF LIÈGE (Alger of Cluny, Algerus Magister), d. c. 1132, cathedral canon, monk of Cluny, whose writings include commentaries on the church fathers, theological treatises, and an attack on Berengar's views concerning the Eucharist, a subject to which he gave much thought. He placed emphasis upon the individual's faith and his intention when receiving the Eucharist as opposed to external action in appraising the spiritual value of the sacrament.

ALGIRDAS (Polish Olgierd), d. 1377, grand prince of Lithuania, 1345–77, when Lithuania was one of the largest states in Europe. He managed to block further expansion of the Teutonic Knights at Lithuania's expense and through marriage acquired a number of Russian principalities. His defeat of the Tatars in 1362 gave him control of the steppes north of the Black Sea to the Dnieper in the east. In 1363 he annexed the principality of Kiev. He was three times involved in wars with the princes of Muscovy and for a short time in 1370 occupied Moscow. He remained a pagan although he showed himself tolerant in matters of religion.

ALHAMBRA, palace and fortress of the Moorish rulers of Granada, the greater part of whose construction took place between 1248 and 1354. It remains one of the most striking of the architectural monuments of Islamic Spain. Though suffering some destruction when the Moors were forced out in 1492, most of the damage has been repaired. Parts of the citadel, the palace of the kings, halls and chambers surrounding the open courts, including the Court of Lions, together with magnificent specimens of honeycomb and stalactite vaulting and among the most exquisitely done arabesques found in the entire Islamic world still exist.

ALHAZEN (Abu- 'Ali al-Hasan ibn al-Haytham), d. after 1039, Arab mathematician, wrote on scientific and geometrical subjects but was especially famous for his treatise on optics. His work on this subject constituted the first major advance since Ptolemy (second century A.D.).

ALI 'ABBAS (Ali ibn al-'Abbas), d. 994, physi-cian of Persia and author of a learned medical handbook which presented a discussion of the art of healing based upon the most authoritative Greek and Islamic writers.

ALI BABA AND THE FORTY THIEVES, tale generally included with the *Thousand And One Nights* which told of a poor woodcutter who happened upon a treasure that forty thieves had stored in a cave. He eventually secured possession of the hoard by using the magical "Open Sesame" to gain entrance.

ALIDS, the followers of Ali. *See* ALI IBN ABI TALIB.

ALI IBN ABI TALIB, caliph, 656–61, son of Abu Talib, the uncle of Mohammed, and the husband of Fatima, the Prophet's daughter. During the caliphate of Othman (655–6), Ali's predecessor, opposition to his leadership of Islam developed among the Legitimists who insisted that the succession should have gone to Ali on the grounds of blood relationship. When Othman was assassinated, Ali succeeded, but Mu'awiya, head of the Omayyad clan of which Othman had been a member, refused to recognize him, and civil war ensued. Ali was murdered, and ever since Islam has been divided between the two communities of Sunnites and Shiites (Ali's followers). Ali was the father of Al-Hassan and Al-Husain, the only grandsons of the Prophet to grow to adulthood.

ALIPIUS (Alypius), ST., d. after 429, close friend of St. Augustine and baptized with him by St. Ambrose. As bishop of Tagaste, Alipius fought the Pelagians and Donatists. He organized the clergy of his diocese after the monastic system Augustine had established for his diocese of Hippo.

ALISCANS, Old French epic of the late twelfth century, a branch of the William of Orange cycle, whose theme centers on the battle William was said to have fought with the Saracens.

ALJAMIAD LITERATURE, works of Spanish Moslems living under Christian rule who used Arabic letters in their Spanish writings.

AL-KHOWARIZMI. *See* KHWARIZMI, AL-.

AL-KINDI. *See* KINDI, AL-.

ALLAH, the one God of the Moslems whose attributes resembled those of the Hebrew Jehovah and the Christian God. Arabs worshipped Allah in pre-Islamic times, but only from the time of Mohammed identified him as the one and only god.

ALLAT, goddess worshipped by Arabs during the pre-Islamic period. Her worship was especially popular in Ta'if.

ALLELUIA (Halleluia, Hallelujah), an expression of religious joy in praise of God that is derived from ancient Judaism. The word appears throughout the Christian liturgy in the Middle Ages, notably in the West and there with greatest frequency during Eastertide. Pope Damasus (366–84) may have introduced the word into the Mass.

ALLOD, a nonfeudal holding held in full ownership through gift, inheritance, or purchase. From the time of William the Conqueror (1066–87), there were no allodial holdings in England since he claimed all the country as his own, and few in France as well since that country observed the principle *Nulle Terre sans Seigneur* (there is no land without its lord). The owners of allods owed none of the traditional feudal obligations to a suzerain. Their number tended to grow smaller as landowners sought protection by turning their holdings over to more powerful lords and receiving them back as fiefs.

ALL SAINTS, FEAST OF, a day set aside by the church for the special veneration of all the saints. As a liturgical feast it appeared first in the fourth century when only martyrs were venerated. Pope Gregory III (731–41) ordered all saints to be included in the feast and assigned November 1 as its date although the formal Feast of All Saints

was probably not celebrated until the ninth century. It was observed as a day when all Christians were required to hear Mass. In countries where Celtic influence was strong, the vigil of All Saints (October 31), Halloween, was associated with customs peculiar to that night.

ALL SAINTS (Allerheiligen), MONASTERY OF, a Premonstratensian monastery in the Black Forest of Bavaria founded by the Duchess Uta of Schauenburg in 1196.

ALL SOULS COLLEGE, college at Oxford founded by Henry VI in 1437 and endowed by Archbishop Chichele in 1438.

ALL SOULS, FEAST OF, liturgical feast which appeared in the tenth century as a day dedicated to a general commemoration of the dead. The selection of November 2 for the feast has been attributed to St. Odilo (d. 1048), abbot of Cluny, who introduced it for his community, whence the practice was later extended to the entire Christian world.

ALMAGEST, Arabic name (*The Great Treatise*) given to Ptolemy's encyclopedic work concerning the astronomical knowledge of the ancient world. Upon this work rested the Ptolemaic system which men accepted until the time of Copernicus (d. 1543). The first Latin translation of Ptolemy's work directly from the Greek may have anticipated by a dozen years that made by Gerard of Cremona from the Arabic in 1175.

AL-MAMUN. *See* MA'MUN, AL-.

ALMANZOR (Al-Mansur) MOHAMMED IBN ABI AMIR, d. 1002, viceroy of the Spanish caliph Hischam II and virtual ruler of Omayyad-held Spain, who succeeded in recovering territories the Christians had retaken following Moslem conquest of the greater part of the peninsula in the eighth century. He was a patron of the arts.

ALMA REDEMPTORIS MATER, one of the four Marian antiphons honoring the Virgin incorporated into the Divine Office. On doubtful evidence, both the words and the music have traditionally been attributed to Hermannus Contractus (d. 1054).

ALMOHADS (Almohades), also known as Mu-wahhids, A Berber sect founded by the Moslem theologian Abu Mohammed ibn Tumart. Tumart called himself the Mahdi (Deliverer) and preached (c. 1120) a regeneration of Islam placing major emphasis upon the doctrine of the oneness of God. His disciple and successor, Abd al-Mu'min, changed his movement into a military crusade and overthrew the Almoravid empire in Morocco (the capital Marrakesh fell to him in 1147), then overran the Spanish peninsula as far as Toledo. Almohad power declined rapidly after its defeat at the battle of Las Navas de Tolosa in 1212 at the hands of the Spanish and Portuguese. In Morocco their rule gave way in 1269 to that of the Marinids.

ALMONER, member of a religious order who dispensed alms either for a church or a secular ruler. Such a person might also attend a nobleman and serve as his confessor. Several almoners were in attendance at the French court in the fifteenth century. One of these, the grand almoner, exercised considerable influence. The almoner appeared at the English court in 1236 where he was often a bishop.

ALMORAVIDS (Almoravides), also known as Murabits, name given to the rulers of northwest Africa and a large part of Spain in the eleventh and twelfth centuries. The initial force that produced this dynasty was a religious revival among the Moslem Berbers inspired by a theologian named Abdullah Ibn Yasin. A warrior, Yusuf ibn Tashfin, undertook to spread Yasin's ideas, conquered north Africa west of Tunis, then crossed into Spain in 1086 at the invitation of Moorish princes who were being threatened by Alfonso VI of Castile and Leon. He defeated Alfonso (1086), then subdued the local Moslem rulers and added their territories to his own in Morocco. In 1147 Almohads replaced the Al-moravid regime in Spain and a few years later took over what remained of their empire in Morocco.

ALP ARSLAN, d. 1072, became sultan of the Seljuk Turks in 1064 upon the death of his uncle Tughril Beg. He overran Turkestan, Georgia, Iran, and Armenia, and opened the way for Turkish conquest of the greater part of Asia Minor by destroying the Byzantine army under Emperor Romanus IV at Manzikert in 1071. His son Malik Shah inherited his well-organized state.

ALPETRAGIUS. See BITRUDJI, NUR AL-DIN ABU ISHAK AL-.

ALPHA AND OMEGA, the first and last letters of the Greek alphabet, often used in conjunction with Christian medieval art to symbolize the eternity and infinitude of God.

ALPHANUS OF SALERNO, d. 1085, taught at Salerno where later as archbishop he encouraged the study of medicine. He spent some time as a monk in the Benedictine monastery at Monte Cassino. He earned fame as a theologian, hagiographer, Latin versifier (hymns), and humanist.

ALPHEGE OF CANTERBURY, ST., d. 1012, monk, hermit, abbot, bishop of Winchester, and archbishop of Canterbury (1006). He was captured by Danish invaders. Refusing to permit himself to be ransomed at the expense of his poor tenants, he was executed.

ALPHONSE I, d. 1148, count of Toulouse, son of the Crusading count Raymond IV, was born in Lebanon. In 1112 he succeeded to the county of Toulouse and the marquisate of Provence, but was obliged to fight the duke of Aquitaine, the ruler of Barcelona, and even Louis VII of France in order to retain possession of them. He encouraged the growth of towns, curbed the power of the aristocracy, and founded Montauban (1144). In 1146 he took up the cross but was poisoned in Caesarea.

ALPHONSE II, count of Poitiers and Toulouse, d. 1270, fifth son of Louis VIII and brother of Louis IX, acquired Toulouse through his wife, the daughter of Raymond VII of Toulouse, thereby paving the way for the assimilation of that county into the royal domain. He did much to repair the destruction caused in Toulouse by the Albigensian crusade. He accompanied his brother on both his Crusades and died on his way home from the second.

ALPHONSINE TABLES. *See* ALFONSIAN TABLES.

ALPHONSO. *See* ALFONSO.

ALSACE, province on the west bank of the upper Rhine which Germans had occupied by the first century B.C. Alemanni overran the area in the early fifth century, while Clovis conquered it in 496. The Treaty of Verdun (843) assigned Alsace to Lothair, and the Treaty of Mersen (870) gave the territory to the East Franks. Later in 925 it became a part of the duchy of Swabia. Alsace constituted the center of imperial power during the Hohenstaufen period. In the thirteenth century the major cities of Alsace gained their virtual independence as free imperial cities. They were successful in blocking the ambition of Charles the Bold, duke of Burgundy, who hoped to absorb them into his domain.

ALTAR, raised platform used for sacred purposes in a place of worship. In Christian usage it originated as a table, from the table of the Lord's Last Supper. The first eucharistic tables were often of stone with the remains of martyrs buried beneath. Because of the difficulty of making or moving stone altars, the requirement that they be of stone was modified in time to that of a simple square slab of stone containing relics and located in the middle of the altar where the sacred vessels and host rested. Side altars soon appeared in the larger churches to meet the demands of a number of resident priests. Toward the close of the Middle Ages, altars might be adorned with tabernacles of metal or stone which were intended for the reservation of the Eucharist.

ALTARPIECE, also known as retable, a structure above the altar table adorned with paintings, sculptures, and/or wood carvings of saints or biblical subjects. The practice of erecting such structures reaches back to at least the eleventh century. A famous altarpiece which may be from that century is the triptych of the *Savior Between the Virgin and St. John* in the cathedral of Tivoli. Outside Italy the use of painted altarpieces was rare prior to the fifteenth century.

ALTENBURG, town in Thuringia which grew up near a fortress erected there by Otto I (936–73). Because of its location on the road between Leipzig and Nuremberg, it developed into an important grain and timber center. It also served as the royal residence of Frederick I Barbarossa (1152–90) who founded an Augustinian monastery there. In 1329 it passed to the house of Wettin and later became the capital of Saxe-Altenburg. The Hussites burned the city in 1430 but the tower of the monastery still stands.

ALTHING, parliament of Iceland, the oldest in Europe, which met at Thingvellir in southwestern Iceland in 930.

ALTICHIERO DA ZEVIO, d. c. 1395, Italian painter of Verona and Padua who continued the tradition of Giotto. Among his famous works are the frescoes in the chapel of S. Felice in the church of S. Antonio in Padua.

ALTMANN OF PASSAU, ST., d. 1091, bishop of Passau, a vigorous monastic reformer and courageous opponent of Henry IV, king of Germany, in the latter's struggle with Pope Gregory VII over lay investiture. He died in exile.

ALTSWERT, MASTER, of Alsace, a late fourteenth-century composer of love allegories (e.g., *Das Alte Schwert*).

ALTZELLE (Altenzelle, Altzella), a Cistercian monastery in Saxony founded about 1162 which served as burial ground for members of the Wettin family. It was known for the excellence of its abbey school and its library.

ALUMNO DI DOMENICO, fl. late fifteenth, early sixteenth century, painter and illustrator of Florence. He was a disciple of Ghirlandaio.

ALUMNO, NICCOLÒ, d. 1502, noted Umbrian painter of altarpieces and holy pictures. His work reveals the influence of his teacher Gozzoli.

ÁLVAREZ OF CÓRDOBA, BL., d. 1430, Dominican friar who preached in Andalusia and Italy and was also active in politics. He was instrumental in securing the election of John II as king of Castile in 1406. The tableaux which he erected on the priory grounds of Scala Coeli which he had founded and to which he retired, proved forerunners of the Stations of the Cross.

ALVARO PELAYO (Alvarus Pelagius), d. 1350, Spanish Franciscan who served as grand penitentiary to Pope John XXII and was later consecrated bishop of Silves (Portugal). In his writings he attacked the views of Marsilius of Padua and maintained that papal authority was the source of all secular authority. He urged Alfonso XI, king of Castile and Leon, to extend his conquests into Morocco which he insisted belonged rightfully to Christians.

ALVASTRA, ABBEY OF, the oldest and most important Cistercian monastery in Sweden. It was founded in 1143 by King Sverker and staffed with monks whom St. Bernard sent from Clairvaux.

ALYPIUS, a Greek student of music who lived in Alexandria c. 350. His treatises on the subject are the source of most of our knowledge of Greek music.

AMA (Amma), a Semitic term meaning female slave which the Copts employed as a title of respect for the religious and for ladies of high rank. The term in Christian usage might also refer to a vessel in which the people offered the wine to be used in the eucharistic service.

AMADEUS OF LAUSANNE, ST., d. 1159, French nobleman who became a Cistercian monk upon the urging of St. Bernard of Clairvaux. Bernard later persuaded him to pursue an active career in political and church affairs. Amadeus is the author of a number of homilies honoring the Virgin.

AMADEUS V OF SAVOY (the Great), d. 1323, supported the Italian campaign of Henry VII of Germany, established the unity of Savoy, then assured its stability by introducing the rule of primogeniture.

AMADEUS VIII OF SAVOY, d. 1451, received the ducal honor from Emperor Sigismund in 1416, retired in 1433, then in 1440, although a layman, was elected pope (Felix V) by the cardinals at Basel who had repudiated Pope Eugenius IV. Amadeus who was recognized as pope only in Germany, was the last antipope. He resigned his papal office in 1449 and accepted the dignity of cardinal bishop and the post of papal vicar and legate in Savoy.

AMADIS OF GAUL, a famous and popular romance of chivalry which idealized knighthood. It was first composed in Spain or Portugal in the fourteenth century and probably drew from French sources.

AMALARIC, d. 531, king of the Visigoths, son of Alaric II, who assumed full royal power in 526 over Spain and a part of Languedoc. He married Clotilde, the daughter of Clovis, but was defeated and slain in 531 when the Franks invaded his country.

AMALARIUS OF METZ, d. c. 850, pupil of Alcuin, taught at Aachen, later became archbishop of Trier. His writings on the liturgy, principally his *De Ecclesiasticis Officiis*, proved influential in the evolution of the liturgy used in the Latin church. One of his objectives in writing the book was to facilitate the fusion of Roman and Gallican practices.

AMALASUNTHA (Amalaswintha), d. 535, daughter of Theodoric, king of the Ostrogoths, who succeeded him in 526 as regent for her son Athalarich. Upon the death of her son in 534, she offered the title king to her cousin Theodahad—who was one of the bitterest opponents of her pro-Byzantine policy. Theodahad accepted, then had her murdered. Her death provided Justinian I, the Byzantine emperor, some justification for undertaking the conquest of Italy.

AMALFI, city on the north shore of the Gulf of Salerno, founded in the fourth century. In the ninth century it became the first maritime republic in Italy. As a duchy in 953, it was a rival of Pisa, Venice, and Genoa in wealth and power. The Normans took the city in 1131, while Pisa sacked it in both 1135 and 1137. Then in 1343 the sea swept away part of the city. The tenth-century cathedral, built in Sicilian-Arabic style with its fine bronze doors, continues to grace the city.

AMALRIC (Amaury) I, king of Jerusalem, d. 1174, succeeded his elder brother Baldwin III in 1163 and brought his kingdom to the height of its power and prestige. For some years he even sought control of Egypt but eventually lost out to Saladin. He continued an active alliance with Byzantium, as much to strengthen his own position in his kingdom as to advance his ambitions in Egypt. He adopted a commercial and maritime code and secured the adoption of assizes which strengthened his position as ruler. He was succeeded by his son Baldwin IV.

AMALRIC OF BÈNE (Bèna) (Amaury de Chartres), d. c. 1207, mystic and pantheist, taught theology for a time at Paris, later was obliged to retract certain of his views which had been condemned as heretical. The Amalricians, the sect composed of his followers, suffered condemnation in 1210. The heresy was responsi-

ble for a temporary ban on the study of Aristotle at the university of Paris.

AMALRICIANS, a sect that found its inspiration in the views of Amalric of Bène, who was actually not so extreme as his followers. The Amalricians professed pantheistic views of the universe, attacked the sacraments, and questioned the distinction between good and evil. The sect was suppressed early in the thirteenth century.

AMALS (Amal), ruling family of the Ostrogoths which may have attained its position of prominence in the fourth century. The most famous member of the dynasty was Theodoric, king of Italy (493–526). The family appears as the Amelings in German sagas.

AMANDUS, ST., d. after 676, a native of Aquitaine, became a monk and labored as missionary-bishop in northern France. He is known as the Apostle of Flanders. His zeal carried him in time as far as the North Sea where he appears to have accepted the post of bishop of Tongeren-Maastricht.

AMATI, name of an Italian family of Cremona, first noted in the early eleventh century, which became famous for its production of fiddles.

AMATUS OF MONTE CASSINO, d. before 1105, perhaps a bishop before becoming a monk at Monte Cassino where he wrote a valuable history of the Normans and composed some religious verse.

AMAURY. See AMALRIC.

AMBO, the desk or pulpit in early Christian churches from which the gradual was sung and the epistle and gospel were read to the faithful. In the course of the fourteenth century the pulpit came to replace the ambo.

AMBOISE, city on the Loire east of Tours, from the tenth century the seat of a powerful aristocratic family that produced more than its share of statesmen, generals, and bishops in the late Middle Ages. After 1431, when the French recovered the city from the English, it served as the favorite residence of the French kings. Its celebrated castle, which served as a royal residence and is mostly in late Gothic style with Renaissance additions, overlooks the city.

AMBOISE, GEORGES D', d. 1510, almoner of Louis XI, archbishop of Narbonne and Rouen, minister of Louis XIII and actual director of the court, cardinal, and papal legate. His principal achievement, the *Ordonnances* of 1499, significantly improved the administration of justice. He was most generous in his patronage of artists and writers.

AMBROISE (Ambrose), d. 1190, Norman poet and minstrel, accompanied Richard I of England on the Third Crusade. His account of this Crusade is preserved in the *Estoire de la guerre sainte,* which is an adaptation of his work. It has little literary value but is of considerable importance as a historical source for the Third Crusade (1189–92).

AMBROSE, ST., d. 397, son of the praetorian prefect of Gaul and himself governor of two provinces in north Italy. While still only a catechumen, he was chosen bishop of Milan by popular acclaim in 374. As bishop he acquired fame as a preacher, instructed and baptized St. Augustine, successfully opposed Arianism and resurgent paganism, and for the first time affirmed the principle that in matters of faith and morals, all men, including the emperor himself, were subject to the authority of the church. Of his writings, which concern themselves with Christian living rather than with theological definition, the most important was the *De Officiis Ministrorum.* Because of the hymns which he composed and the encouragement he gave for the use of hymns in the liturgy, he has been called the father of Western hymnody. His birth and talents assured him a dominant voice in the Latin church and enabled him to exert considerable influence upon Emperor Theodosius I (d. 395).

AMBROSE TRAVERSARI, BL., d. 1439, learned Camaldolese monk of Florence whose fame as a classical scholar and a student of philosophy and patristic literature attracted humanists to his cell. He translated much Greek patristic literature into Latin and at the Council of Ferrara-Florence (1438–39) worked earnestly for the reunion of the Latin and Greek churches.

AMBROSIAN CHANT, the chant sung in the diocese of Milan and in areas influenced by Milan, e.g., Switzerland and Bavaria. It was probably introduced by Auxentius, bishop of Milan (353–74), who was originally from Cappadocia, hence the Syriac elements in the chant. While no manuscripts containing Ambrosian chant prior to the twelfth century have survived, it is believed that the entire congregation participated in the singing and that this singing included hymns, antiphons, and responsories. Because St. Ambrose (d. 397) introduced the antiphonal (alternate) mode of singing, his name has been associated with this chant.

AMBROSIAN HYMN OF PRAISE. *See* TE DEUM.

AMBROSIAN LITURGY (Rite), a liturgy used in Milan which in the eighth century came to be associated with the name of St. Ambrose (d. 397). It differed from the Roman in a number of minor points such as the Offertory coming before the Creed rather than after.

AMBROSIANS, name given to several religious congregations who honored St. Ambrose as their patron: a) a group in Milan in the ninth century; b) a community approved by Pope Gregory XI (1370–78) which engaged in preaching and works of charity; c) a community of pious women in Lombardy in the early fifteenth century who led cloistered lives.

AMBROSIASTER, name which Erasmus gave to the author of a scholarly commentary on the Epistles of St. Paul that had been mistakenly attributed to St. Ambrose in the Middle Ages. The author remains a mystery although he probably lived in the fourth century. St. Augustine ascribed the work to Hilary of Poitiers.

AMBRY (Aumbry, Armarium), niche in early Christian churches that served as a place for storing sacred vessels, holy oils, relics, even the Eucharist; also a cupboard for books, or a library.

AMBULATORY, a cloister, gallery, or sheltered place where monks walked for exercise; also a passageway in a large church or cathedral around the high altar along the wall of the apse.

AMEN, a word expressing approval ("verily") which the Christian liturgy took over unchanged from the Hebrew. Christ used the word in the sense of "truly."

AMERBACH, JOHN, d. 1513, famous printer of Basel who published the writings of many church fathers, including those of St. Ambrose and St. Augustine, as well as the Bible and the *Corpus Juris Canonici*.

AMERCEMENT, in English law an arbitrary penalty, usually a fine, given an offender by the peers of the party amerced. It represented a commutation of a sentence of forfeiture of goods. Articles 20 to 22 of Magna Carta regulated the assessment of amercements.

AMESBURY, town in Wiltshire, England, site of a meeting of the *witenagemot* in 932, a royal manor in 1086, and a market and fair in 1317. It is the Almesbury of Arthurian legend. Stonehenge, Britain's famous monument from the megalithic period, is nearby.

AMFORTAS (Anfortas), the king of the Grail and the uncle of Parsival in the account of Wolfram von Eschenbach and his successors. Parsival saved the king's life when he had been struck by a pagan's poisonous arrow.

AMIATINUS. *See* CODEX AMIATINUS.

AMICE, a short, linen cloth, rectangular in shape, worn by the priest about the shoulders when engaged in liturgical service. Its first use was apparently that of a scarf to protect the outer liturgical garments from being soiled about the neck and face.

AMICUS AND AMELIUS, according to a medieval saga, two friends, similar in figure and disposition, who died in battle fighting with Charlemagne against the Lombards. The theme of the two close friends which was of Oriental origin became popular all over Europe.

AMIENS, city located on the Somme, the principal city of Picardy, whose origins go back to pre-Roman times. The Franks destroyed the city in 409, the Northmen again in 859. The city's Christian origins are linked with a St. Firmin who, according to tradition, was martyred there c. 303. He was considered the founder of the city and its first bishop.

AMIENS CATHEDRAL, famous Gothic church which was erected between 1220 and c. 1247 to replace an earlier one which had been destroyed by fire. It is the largest and one of the most imposing Gothic structures in the world. The nave, which is 149 feet high, is noted for its splendid vertical lines. Other noteworthy features include a richly decorated façade flanked by two towers, the rose window (sixteenth century), and the recessed portals.

AMIR. *See* EMIR.

AMIR KHUSRAU, d. 1325, Persian poet and historian, lived most of his life in India and in his historical epics dealt with the rulers, peoples, and events of that country. He composed idylls, odes, and lyrics, some history in prose, and a large collection of elegant compositions and letters.

AMIS ET AMILES, Old French epic written c. 1200 about two close friends, one of whom kills his own children to enable his friend, who has leprosy, to be healed by bathing in their blood. The children are then miraculously restored to life. The poem is one of the finest of the Carolingian epics. Its theme appeared in most European literatures. In England there is the Middle English metrical romance of *Amis and Amiloun* (Amiles) whose theme is that of the self-sacrificing love of two brothers.

AMLODI, the ancient Nordic name of the Danish hero Hamlet. The principal source of the Hamlet story is the *Gesta Danorum* of Saxo Grammaticus.

AMMANATI DE' PICCOLOMINI, JACOPO, d. 1479, student of the classics and a patron of the arts whom Pope Pius II adopted into the Piccolomini family and gave a curial post. He later became bishop of Pavia and a cardinal.

AMMIANUS MARCELLINUS, d. c. 400, a Greek soldier who wrote a sober and generally accurate history of Rome, continuing where Tacitus had left off and, he hoped, after the manner of that distinguished historian. Of the history, which is in Latin, only the books covering the years 353 to 378 remain extant. Though a pagan and an admirer of the emperor Julian (361–3) who had reintroduced the persecution of Christians, he was quite fair in his treatment of Christianity.

AMMON, ST., a late fourth-, early fifth-century hermit of Egypt who retired to the desert after 18 years of celibate life with his wife. The fame of his sanctity attracted many ascetics whom he organized into monastic communities upon the advice of St. Anthony. He is mentioned by St. Athanasius in his life of St. Anthony.

AMMONIAN SECTIONS, divisions on the margins of most Latin and Greek manuscripts of the Gospels, their purpose being to illustrate parallelism between corresponding passages in the different Gospels. They were once attributed to Ammonius Saccas, but are now judged to have been the probable work of Eusebius of Caesarea.

AMMONIUS SACCAS, d. c. 242, a Christian who became a pagan, a celebrated teacher in Alexandria who is reputed to have been the founder of neo-Platonism. He may have influenced Plo-

tinus. He left no writings, and his students were pledged not to reveal anything about the content of his teaching.

AMORBACH, MONASTERY OF, a Benedictine house in Bavaria founded c. 700 by St. Pirmin which served as a missionary center in the conversion of the Saxons.

AMORIAN DYNASTY, the ruling family of the Byzantine empire from the accession of Michael II (820–9) to the death of Michael III (842–67). The family hailed from Amorium in Anatolia.

AMPHILOCHIUS OF ICONIUM, d. after 394, a lawyer, then monk and member of St. Basil's monastic community at Caesarea. He later became bishop of Iconium and a militant and learned champion of the doctrine of the Trinity against the attacks of such heretical groups as the Messalians. Church councils of the fifth century made appeal to his writings as those of an authority on patristic doctrines.

AMPLONIAN LIBRARY, library at Erfurt which took its name from Amplonius Ratinck de Berka (d. 1435), a physician, who endowed a college at the university of Erfurt and donated his library of approximately one thousand volumes.

AMPULLA, small glass or clay bottle used by Romans for perfume, oil, and wine. The word is applied to flasks carried by travelers in the Middle Ages and to containers holding oils for coronation ceremonies and for liturgical purposes. The most famous is the *Saint Ampoule* which a dove is said to have brought for the baptism of Clovis, king of the Franks, in 496. It was kept at Reims and used in the coronation of French kings. The ampullae found in the catacombs have remained a matter of dispute. It has been suggested that they may have served as containers of oil used to anoint the dead or for lamps left burning before the shrines of martyrs buried there.

AMRA, name given to certain ancient Irish elegies or panegyrics about native saints such as the Amra of Coluimb Cille.

AMR IBN AL- 'As, d. 664, Arab general in the service of the caliph Omar who conquered Egypt (634–44) and later ruled there as governor (658–64). He was among the early supporters of Mu'awiya. He founded the garrison-city of Fostat (Fustat) which proved to be the origin of Cairo.

AMRU-L-KAIS, sixth-century Arabic poet whose verse, like that of pre-Islamic poets, was subjective and formally quite perfect. He was esteemed as the model of erotic poets and for many years was in high favor at the imperial court in Constantinople.

AMSTERDAM, city of Holland on the Zuider Zee, a fishing town as late as the thirteenth century when it first came to view. Its rapid growth during the fourteenth and fifteenth centuries has been attributed to its association with the Hanseatic League and to the expansion of its trade in the Baltic.

ANACLETUS (Cletus), ST., Pope, c. 79–92, died a martyr during the reign of Domitian. He may have been the Cletus referred to in early patristic writings.

ANACLETUS II, Pope (antipope), 1130–38, member of the powerful Pierleoni family, monk of Cluny, and cardinal deacon who was entrusted by several popes with important assignments. He received a majority of the votes cast following the death of Pope Honorius II, although other cardinals and St. Bernard of Clairvaux opposed him and gave their support to Innocent II who is generally considered the legitimate pope. Anacletus remained in control of Rome and the greater part of Italy during his pontificate.

ANADOLU HISARI, a fortress constructed in 1396 by the Turkish sultan Bayazid I on the Asiatic side of the Bosphorus at its narrowest point for the purpose of disrupting communications between Constantinople and the Black Sea. It lost its importance with the fall of the city in 1453.

ANAGNI, ancient city of central Italy, besieged by the Saracens in 877. Its best known families in the medieval period were the Conti and the Gaetani. Four popes hailed from Anagni, among them Innocent III and Boniface VIII.

ANAGNI, CRIME OF, the humiliation Pope Boniface VIII suffered at the hands of William de Nogaret and Sciarra Colonna in September 1303 at Anagni. [See BONIFACE VIII, Pope.]

ANAMNESIS, the commemoration of the Passion, Resurrection, and Ascension of Christ which in most liturgies is included in the part of the canon immediately following the consecration.

ANAN BEN DAVID, late eighth-century Jewish theologian and first literary figure of the Karaite sect which rejected the rabbinical traditions preserved in the Talmud. He united into one organization scattered groups whose common rejection of the authoritarian practice of Talmudic law recommended their union.

ANANIAS, member of the early Christian community in Jerusalem who with his wife Sapphira was rebuked by St. Peter for his deception and attempted fraud. He fell dead at the apostle's feet (Acts 5:1–11).

ANANITES. See KARAITES.

ANAPHORA, a liturgical term in the Greek rite which referred to that part of the service that corresponded to the canon in the Latin Mass. It may also have referred more specifically to the offering of the eucharistic bread.

ANASTASIA, ST., Christian woman martyred at Sirmium in Pannonia during the persecution of Diocletian (c. 304). A basilica erected in her honor in Rome in the fourth century served the

Palatine and imperial palace. Her name appeared in the canon of the Latin Mass.

ANASTASIS, the Greek for resurrection and pertaining to the resurrection of both Christ and of mankind in general. Early churches in Jerusalem and Constantinople were dedicated to the Anastasis of Christ.

ANASTASIUS I, ST., Pope, 399–401, a Roman by birth who earned the commendation of St. Jerome for the sanctity of his life. He condemned several Origenist writings and objected to the translation of Origen's works into Latin. He encouraged African bishops in their efforts to suppress Donatism.

ANASTASIUS II, Pope, 496–8, controversial figure whose anxiety to resolve the Acacian schism [See ACACIAN SCHISM] led him to endorse a heretical doctrine in the judgment of some Western theologians. Dante placed him among the heretics in hell (*Inferno* XI: 3).

ANASTASIUS III, Pope, 911–3, shortlived pope whose public acts were largely governed by Theophylact and his wife Theodora who were in control of Rome.

ANASTASIUS IV, Pope, 1153–4, restored the Pantheon and extended special privileges to the Order of the Hospitalers of St. John. Sweden's payment of Peter's Pence dates from his pontificate.

ANASTASIUS I, Byzantine emperor, 491–518, drove the Isaurians who had supported his predecessor Zeno from the city, reorganized Byzantine finances, and strengthened the fortifications to the west of Constantinople with a long wall that reached from the Sea of Marmora to the Black Sea. His policy favoring Monophysitism pleased Syria and Egypt but antagonized many in the European part of his empire, in particular Rome and Western theologians.

ANASTASIUS II, Byzantine emperor, 713–5, rescinded the Monothelite decrees of his prede-cessor Philippicus and accepted Rome's position, namely, that there existed two wills in Christ, a divine and a human will. He defended Syria from the Arabs and sent a formidable naval force to relieve Rhodes which they had under attack. Disaffection in the army led to a revolt. He was defeated, fled to Nicaea where he abdicated, and became a monk. A subsequent attempt to recover his throne led to his execution.

ANASTASIUS, ST., d. c. 1039, German disciple of Adalbert, the bishop of Prague. He served as abbot of two monasteries that Adalbert had founded, one near Prague, the other in Poland, then headed a monastery in Hungary which Stephen I had established. He died as archbishop of Esztergom. His name is important in the conversion of Hungary.

ANASTASIUS, ST., patriarch of Antioch, d. c. 599, learned theologian who opposed Emperor Justinian's decree endorsing Aphthartodoce-tism, later suffered exile during the reign of Justin II because of his Christological views. His writings greatly influenced later Greek theologians.

ANASTASIUS THE LIBRARIAN (*Bibliothecarius*), d. c. 878, cardinal priest, scholar, and classicist. For a few days in 855 he maintained that he was the pope, but then submitted, faithfully served three popes, later became abbot of S. Maria in Trastevere and librarian of the Roman church. He authored hagiographical writings and also translated Greek works, chiefly those that were historical and biographical in character.

ANASTASIUS SINAITA, ST., d. c. 700, monk, later abbot of the monastery of St. Catherine on Mt. Sinai, exegete, theologian, and bitter opponent of Monophysitism. His most important work, the *Hodegos* (Guide), represents an attack on that heresy.

ANATHEMA, a condemnation, usually of heretics, which came into regular use soon after the Council of Elvira (c. 306) had anathematized a number of dissidents. In medieval times it did not entail death as prescribed by Mosaic law although it carried complete exclusion from Christian society. In this respect it was more severe than minor excommunication which involved only exclusion from the worship and the sacraments of the church and similar to major excommunication. [*See* EXCOMMUNICATION.]

ANATHEMAS OF CYRIL, a summary of 12 divisions of the position taken by Cyril of Alexandria in his attack of Nestorius. The name derived from the manner in which Cyril presented his views, namely, that anyone who would refuse to accept any of them was to be judged anathematized.

ANATOLIUS OF CONSTANTINOPLE, d. 458, patriarch of Constantinople, a disciple of Cyril of Alexandria who sent him to the Byzantine capital. He helped secure the condemnation of Dioscurus, the Monophysite patriarch of Alexandria, by the Council of Chalcedon (451) and worked to convince Illyrian and Egyptian bishops of the orthodoxy of Pope Leo I's *Tome*.

ANATOLIUS OF LAODICEA, ST., d. c. 282, bishop of Laodicea (Syria), a philosopher, man of great erudition, and theologian, author of a treatise concerning the date of Easter, also of a manual of arithmetic in ten books.

ANCHARANO, PETRUS DE, d. 1416, taught at Bologna and other universities, occupied civil posts in Bologna and Venice, took part in the Council of Pisa (1409), and authored an important commentary on papal decretals.

ANCHORESS, a woman who withdrew from society to live a solitary life of prayer and mortification, usually in a strictly defined place such as a cell.

ANCHORITE, a hermit, one who withdrew from society, usually to the desert or similarly isolated region, in order to lead a more spiritual life.

ANCILLA DEI, a title given to a deceased woman in early Christian inscriptions but later restricted to nuns by order of Pope Gregory I (590–604).

ANCONA, port city of central Italy on the Adriatic, attacked by Goths, Lombards, and Saracens, recovered its importance in the ninth century when it became a semi-independent republic under the nominal rule of the papacy.

ANCONA, CIRIACO D', d. c. 1455, Italian antiquarian who enjoyed the patronage of Cosimo de' Medici and Pope Eugenius IV in his search for ancient inscriptions, manuscripts, and similar antiquities.

ANCREN(E) RIWLE (Wisee), an early thirteenth-century code or rule in Middle English governing the lives of anchoresses (recluses). It was originally intended for three sisters, not nuns, who had decided to take up a life of prayer and penance. The author of the work, as well as the identity of the sisters, is not known. It represents one of the few extant examples of early Middle English prose.

ANCYRA. *See* ANGORA.

ANDALUSIA, province covering all of southern Spain and included in the ancient Roman province of Bactria. The Visigoths occupied it in the fifth century, but part of it was recovered by Justinian's army in the sixth century. In 711 Moors overran the region and made it the center of the emirate of Córdoba. It remained under Moorish rule until the thirteenth century when most of it was reconquered by the kings of Castile. The last part of it, Granada, fell to Ferdinand and Isabella in 1492. Andalusia attained the height of its prosperity during the period of Moorish rule when agriculture, mining, trades, and industries in such commodities as textiles, pottery, and leather flourished and when its principal cities, Córdoba, Seville, and Granada, were famed as centers of culture, science, and the arts.

ANDEIRO, JOÃO FERNANDES, d. 1383, count of Ourém, statesman of Portugal, who fled that country for England when Portuguese forces suffered defeat at the hands of the king of Castile. In England he sought to advance the candidacy of John of Gaunt, duke of Lancaster, to the throne of Castile. In the course of treaty negotiations, he served as intermediary between the English and Portuguese courts. He returned to Portugal in 1381 and was made count of Ourém.

ANDORRA, state in the Pyrenees which, tradition had it, Charlemagne and Louis the Pious gave to the Spanish bishop of Urgel. Andorra succeeded in fighting off the attempts of the counts of Foix to annex it and in 1278 had its independence confirmed. The bishop was to serve as joint suzerain with its count.

ANDRÉ (Andreas), BERNARD, d. after 1521, Augustinian canon, a student of law, poet, and humanist, who served as poet laureate and historiographer at the court of Henry VII of England. He directed the education of the crown prince Arthur.

ANDREA DA FIRENZE, Florentine painter of the second half of the fourteenth century who is known for his fresco in the Spanish chapel of the church of Santa Maria Novella in Florence.

ANDREAS CAPELLANUS (André Le Chapelain), a chaplain, possibly at the French court or that of Marie, countess of Champagne, and author of a treatise entitled *De Amore* which he composed c. 1186. The treatise consists of a long Latin prose discussion of love modeled after Ovid's *Art of Love*. Some scholars have taken its description of courts of love seriously, others consider it an actual exposition of courtly love. Historians dismiss it as purely imaginative literature.

ANDRELINI, PUBLIO FAUSTO, d. 1518, humanist, court poet at Paris, and poet laureate in Rome. Vulgarity and mediocrity characterize much of his verse.

ANDREW II, king of Hungary, 1205–35, son of Bela III, succeeded to the throne of Hungary after a long struggle with his brother Emerich which he won by making generous grants of crown lands to his aristocratic supporters. He further weakened the crown when, following the failure of his crusade in Syria, his magnates forced him to issue a Golden Bull (1222) which extended valuable privileges to the nobility. He did expel the Teutonic Knights from Transylvania. He was the father of St. Elizabeth of Hungary.

ANDREW, d. 1174, grand prince of Vladimir, the most powerful Russian ruler of the century. His state was located in the region of the upper Volga. He fortified and beautified his capital city of Vladimir and built a number of churches including the magnificent cathedral of Our Lady. He invited peasants and craftsmen from other regions to settle in his realm. In 1169 he stormed Kiev and eventually placed a prince of his choice in control of Novgorod. A revolt triggered by his ambition to rule absolutely led to his murder.

ANDREW ABELLON, BL., d. 1450, French Dominican who taught philosophy and theology in a number of priories, for a time preached in southern France, then served as prior in several convents. He was a reformer, also a painter of spiritual subjects.

ANDREW, ACTS OF ST., an apocryphal book that tells of the Apostle's imprisonment at Patras in Greece. *The Martyrdom of St. Andrew* which is drawn from the *Acts,* describes the saint's crucifixion but makes no mention of "St. Andrew's Cross." [*See* ANDREW, ST.]

ANDREW CACCIOLI, BL., d. 1254, a Franciscan, companion of St. Francis of Assisi, experienced difficulties with Elias of Cortona, the superior who succeeded Francis, and twice suffered imprisonment. Andrew may have been the first priest to join the order. All others had been laymen.

ANDREW CORSINI, ST., d. 1373, native of Florence, a Carmelite who was active in Tuscany in succoring those attacked by the plague (Black Death) and in reviving spiritual life among the laity as well as among the clergy. As bishop of Fiesole he encouraged devotion to the Trinity.

ANDREW DE COMITIBUS, BL., d. 1302, Franciscan brother who was distinguished for his humility and for the miracles his contemporaries attributed to him. Pope Boniface VIII (1294–1303), among others, was convinced of Andrew's sanctity.

ANDREW OF CRETE, ST., d. 740, monk of Jerusalem, popular preacher and composer of hymns, later archbishop of Gortyna in Crete. He took part in contemporary controversies over Monothelitism and iconoclasm and influenced the evolution of Byzantine liturgical practices.

ANDREW OF LONGJUMEAU (Lonjumel), d. c. 1270, Dominican missionary whom Louis IX of France sent to visit the Great Khan in Mongolia in 1249 in the hope of converting him to Christianity. (Andrew had acquired a proficiency in several Oriental languages.) The first of two trips that Andrew made to Mongolia was as a member of a missionary group which Pope Innocent IV had sent out in 1245.

ANDREW OF RHODES, d. 1440, theologian who abjured the Greek Orthodox Church and accepted Latin Christianity. He became a Dominican and archbishop of Rhodes, and took an active part in the discussions of the Councils of Basel and Ferrara-Florence where he urged the Greeks to accept the primacy of the pope.

ANDREW OF SAINT-VICTOR, d. 1175, canon regular, exegete, a student of Hugh of Saint-Victor in Paris, later abbot of Wigmore in Herefordshire, England. He was the first Western scholar who systematically studied Jewish texts in his exposition of the Old Testament.

ANDREW, ST., one of the twelve Apostles, the brother of Simon Peter. He is the patron of Russia and Scotland. Tradition has it that he labored as a missionary in Asia Minor, Macedonia, and southern Russia and suffered martyrdom in Greece. The X-shaped cross on which he was supposed to have been crucified is a tradition that cannot be traced back earlier than the thirteenth century.

ANDRIA, ancient city in southeastern Italy whose recorded history in the medieval period dates from the coming of the Normans in the eleventh century. The city became a favorite home of Frederick II of Germany (d. 1250) who built a massive octagonal Gothic structure that boasted of plumbing installations unknown in that day. Several Renaissance palaces grace the city, together with a restored tenth-century cathedral.

ANDRONICUS I (Comnenus), Byzantine emperor, 1183–5, dissolute uncle of Alexius II whom he murdered, then married his widow, after which he instituted a reign of terror which ended with his death at the hands of an infuriated populace. His administration of the provinces was firm but just since he protected the peasantry from their greedy landlords and powerful aristocratic neighbors.

ANDRONICUS II (Palaeologus), Byzantine emperor, 1282–1328, son of Michael VIII, an intellectual and patron of the arts rather than a statesman. Religious strife vexed his long reign, while externally he was losing almost the whole of Asia Minor to the Ottoman Turks. In the hope of strengthening his frontiers against pressure exerted by the Serbs, Bulgars, and Turks, he involved his country still deeper in the rivalry between Venice and Genoa, to the ultimate loss of Byzantine economic independence. When his grandson Andronicus III seized the throne in 1328, he retired to a monastery where he died in 1332.

ANDRONICUS III (Palaeologus), Byzantine emperor, 1328–41, deposed his grandfather Andronicus II after several years of civil war, then ruled with commendable ability although his reign witnessed the loss of what remained of

Byzantine possessions in Asia Minor to the Turks. He also lost parts of Albania and Macedonia to the Serbs. He did manage to recover the islands of Lesbos, Chios, and Phocaea from Genoa and to reestablish Byzantine authority in Epirus and Thessaly.

ANDVARI, dwarf in Nordic mythology whom Loki forced to surrender the ring by which he could make gold (the ring of the Nibelungs).

ANEURIN, Welsh bard, possibly the son of the chronicler Gildas (d. 570), said to be the author of *Gododin,* a poem about the defeat of the Britons by the Saxons. The poem is one of the oldest pieces of Welsh literature.

ANFREDUS (Alfredus, Aufredus) CONTERI, Franciscan theologian of France of the early fourteenth century and a disciple of Duns Scotus. His writings reveal both the influence of Duns Scotus and, curiously, that of the anti-Scotist Henry of Harclay.

ANGEL, one of an order of spiritual beings already enjoying the blessings of God's presence in heaven. Angels usually ranked lowest among the nine choirs. The hierarchy of angels in three choirs appears in the early Christian era. The classes are seraphim, cherubim, thrones, dominations (dominions), virtues, powers, principalities, archangels, and angels. The cult of the Guardian Angel was especially popular in the Middle Ages.

ANGELA OF FOLIGNO, BL., d. 1309, a member of the Third Order of St. Francis, left an account (by dictation) of her visions and of her spiritual regeneration from the sinful life she had lived as a young woman. The account, entitled *Book of Visions,* describes the 20 penitential steps she took before reaching the threshold of the mystical life. Typically Franciscan was the emphasis she placed upon poverty and the love of the crucified Christ as necessary prerequisites to a more spiritual life.

ANGELICA, name of an herb commonly used as a remedy for the plague in the late Middle Ages. In medieval art, where it appears as early as the ninth century, it is presented as the flower of the Trinity.

ANGELIC DOCTOR. Honorific title of St. Thomas Aquinas.

ANGELIC HYMN. *See* GLORIA IN EXCELSIS DEO.

ANGELICO, FRA (Giovanni da Fiesole), d. 1455, Dominican friar and probably an accomplished artist (miniaturist) when he entered the order in 1407. A renowned artist of the Florentine school, he treated only religious subjects and in his work combined naturalism with deep spirituality. A remarkable idealistic unity permeates his paintings and frescoes. Among other works for which he is famous are the frescoes he painted in the convent of S. Marco in Florence (*Crucifixion with St. Dominic, Crucifixion*), and the frescoes and altarpieces and small reliquaries for the churches and convents of Fiesole. In 1445 Pope Eugenius IV summoned him to Rome where his frescoes in the chapel of Pope Nicholas V in the Vatican are particularly celebrated.

ANGELINA OF MARSCIANO, BL., d. 1435, became a Franciscan tertiary as a young widow and turned her castle in the Abruzzi into a community for members of the Third Order. When the king of Naples exiled the community, it moved to Assisi, then to Foligno where, under her guidance as abbess, it adopted a more rigorous rule.

ANGELINA, ST., d. c. 1510, daughter of a Serbian prince who ruled the principality of Zeta after her husband's death and managed to preserve its independence from the Turks. The Serbs honored her as the mother and queen of Montenegro.

ANGELO CARLETTI DI CHIVASSO, d. 1495, Franciscan theologian and canonist, turned his back on a career in political life and became instead vicar general of his order. He preached against the Waldensians in north Italy and promoted the use of *Montes Pietatis.* He is best known for his scholarly writings on the subject of moral theology.

ANGELOT (Angel, Ange d'Or), name of two gold coins, one a French-English piece minted from 1427 to 1467 with an angel on the French side, an English shield on the other; the second was an English coin first minted in 1470 and bearing the images of St. Michael and a dragon.

ANGELRAM, d. 1045, scholar and poet, monk of the Benedictine abbey of Saint Riquier, later abbot of the community. He was famed for his knowledge of music, grammar, and dialectic.

ANGELUS, name of three emperors who occupied the Byzantine throne from 1185 to 1204 (Isaac II, Alexius III, Alexius IV).

ANGELUS, a prayer dedicated to the mother of God and commemorative of the Annunciation and birth of Christ, aspects of which devotion date from the ninth century. By the close of the Middle Ages, the Angelus was being recited three times a day, at six in the morning, at noon, and at six in the evening, and usually at the signal of a church bell. The bell was sounded three times for each Ave and nine times for the concluding prayer.

ANGELUS CLARENUS, d. 1337, a Spiritual Franciscan who was imprisoned for his views, then released and reconciled with the church. He became co-founder of the Celestines (Clareni) but continued to suffer harassment until his death. His *Apologia,* written c. 1331, prompted inquisitorial proceedings to be instituted against him, but he died before any action could be taken.

ANGERS, city of Celtic origin on a tributary of the lower Loire, a bishop's seat in 372 and capital city of the county of Anjou. In Frankish times it served as a major fortress against the Bretons. A fine cathedral from the twelfth and thirteenth centuries and a castle from the latter century survive, together with many tapestries from the fourteenth century.

ANGERS, UNIVERSITY OF, emerged from the distinguished cathedral school of Angers, probably received a major impetus upon the dispersion of scholars from Paris in 1229. In 1337 it was recognized as a *studium generale* and in 1364 given a charter by Charles V.

ANGEVIN, name of two medieval dynasties that originated in France. The older house traced its origin to Fulk who became count of Anjou in the tenth century. Fulk V, count of Anjou, became king of Jerusalem (1131–43), as did his younger son and his descendants until the dynasty became extinct in 1186. Fulk's elder son Geoffrey (Plantagenet) inherited Anjou, conquered Normandy, and married Matilda, daughter of Henry I of England. Their son Henry (II) became king of England in 1154, the first of the Angevin or Plantagenet kings of that country. They held the throne until 1399 when Richard II abdicated, after which the line divided into the two houses of Lancaster and York. The cadet house traced its origin to Charles, younger brother of Louis IX of France, who was made count of Anjou, acquired Provence by marriage, and the throne of Naples in 1266 as Charles I. When Joanna I was deposed in 1381, the descendants of Charles struggled over the succession.

ANGHIERA, PIETRO MARTIRE D', d. 1526, Italian geographer and historian who moved to Spain in 1487. There he became acquainted with Columbus, Vespucci, Magellan, and other navigators and explorers.

ANGILBERT, ST., d. 814, friend and counselor of Charlemagne and father of Nithard, the chronicler, by the emperor's daughter Bertha. Angilbert, who acquired great skill as a Latin versifier, was later appointed lay abbot of the monastery of Saint-Riquier. He made its library one of the largest of the period.

ANGILRAMNUS OF METZ, d. 791, principal chaplain at Charlemagne's court at Aachen, later abbot of the monastery of Sens, still later bishop of Metz. He was mistakenly believed to have been the author of part of the Pseudo-Isidorian decretals known as *Capitula Angilramni*. {*See* PSEUDO-ISIDORIAN DECRETALS.}

ANGIOLIERI, CECCO, d. c. 1312, best known of Italian "comic" poets, was born at Siena. His 150 sonnets featured humor, satire, puns, also the traditional themes of wine, women, and song of Goliardic poets who may have influenced him. These were largely new to Italian literature.

ANGLES, German tribe first mentioned by Tacitus (d. 117?), located in the area of Holstein, which along with the Saxons and Jutes invaded Britain in the fifth and sixth centuries.

ANGLESEY (Anglesea), island off the northwest coast of Wales, known as Mona to the Romans, and open to a stream of invaders including Irish pirates, Saxons, Vikings, and Norman adventurers. It was finally conquered from the Welsh by Edward I (1272–1307). The island was important as a route to Ireland, a fact apparently known to Celtic missionaries, remains of whose churches date from the very early period of Celtic Christianity. The best known of the Celtic monastic foundations were those of St. Gybi on Holy Island and St. Seiriol at Penmon.

ANGLESEY (Anglesea), PRIORY OF, religious community in northwestern Wales perhaps founded by Henry I (1100–35). It first served as a hospital but c. 1212 was refounded as a house of Canons Regular of St. Augustine. During the thirteenth century it undertook many chantry services.

ANGLO-NORMAN (Anglo-French), dialect spoken in Normandy and brought by the Normans to England in 1066. It became the language of the court and of formal literature and remained so during most of the thirteenth century although undergoing a measure of alteration. It

continued in use in the government and courts up into the fifteenth century.

ANGLO-SAXON CHRONICLE, historical narrative in Old English which covered the history of England from the fifth to the twelfth century. It was compiled by monks at Winchester, Canterbury, and Peterborough, and probably at other monasteries as well. The first part of the account to the year 892 may have owed its appearance to the encouragement of Alfred the Great (d. 899). While its quality as historical evidence varies, it is most valuable from the reign of Edward the Confessor (1042–66) to 1154 when the chronicle lapses.

ANGLO-SAXON LITERATURE. The earliest Anglo-Saxon poems, although recorded after the native Britons had accepted Christianity, reveal a strong undercurrent of Germanic paganism. Such is the case with the epic poem *Beowulf* and such shorter poems as *Widsith* and *Deor*, the last being the earliest English lyric poem. Religious poetry in Anglo-Saxon began with the hymns of Caedmon who is introduced by the Venerable Bede (d. 735). The work of Cynewulf and his followers include stories about the saints as well as homilies. Especially noteworthy for its spirit and religious vigor is the *Dream of the Rood*. The heroic spirit of Anglo-Saxons in wartime is best reflected in *The Battle of Maldon* and *The Battle of Brunanburh*. Literary prose in Anglo-Saxon dates from the reign of Alfred the Great (d. 899) who had several "great" books, such as Pope Gregory the Great's *Pastoral Care*, translated from the Latin. The *Anglo-Saxon Chronicle* may date from his reign. The best original prose may be found in the homilies of Aelfric and of Wulfstan, bishop of Worcester and archbishop of York.

ANGLO-SAXONS, collective term applied to the Germans who invaded England in the fifth and sixth centuries and conquered the greater part of the country from its Celtic (Britons) occupants. The Angles who may have come from the region of Holstein and Schleswig settled in the eastern, central, and northern parts of the country where they laid the foundations of East Anglia, Mercia, and Northumbria. The Saxons who were continental neighbors of the angles furnished the foundations of Sussex, Wessex, and Essex. The Jutes, a third nation usually introduced with the Anglo-Saxon invaders of Britain, hailed from the region about the mouth of the Rhine. They settled in Kent and on the Isle of Wight.

ANGORA (Ancyra), the modern city of Ankara, ancient city of Ancyra, capital of the Roman province of Galatia. First mention of the Christian church appeared in 192. The city came under attack on a number of occasions during the course of the Middle Ages, by Chosroes II, king of the Sassanid Persians (590–628), by Arabs in the seventh and again in the eighth century, and by the Seljuk Turks in 1073 who held the city until 1101 when the Crusader Raymond of Toulouse took it from them. About the year 1150 the Seljuks recovered control of the city and in 1360 it fell to the Ottoman Turks.

ANGORA, BATTLE OF, decisive battle fought in 1402 between the Turks under their sultan Bayazid I and Timur the Lame, leader of the Mongols. The Mongols destroyed the Turkish army and took Bayazid captive. The disaster suffered by the Turks at Angora provided the city of Constantinople a respite of fifty years before its eventual capture.

ANGOULÊME, city of west-central France, an episcopal see in the fifth century and in the ninth the residence of the counts who administered the region as vassals of the duke of Aquitaine. In 1372 the city fell to the French in the course of the Hundred Years' War, and the English never regained possession.

ANGOULÊME, COUNTY OF, feudal principality that became part of Aquitaine in the seventh century. The Romans had established it as an administrative district (*civitas*) in the fourth

century, while in the fifth it became a Christian diocese. In 508 the Franks under Clovis conquered it from the Visigoths. It passed under English control during the reign of Henry II (1154–89) through his wife, Eleanor of Aquitaine, a vassal of the king of France. In 1373 France acquired complete control of the county.

ANGUS, eastern county of Scotland, inhabited by Picts in Roman times, later subjected to invasions by Angles and Vikings. During the twelfth century Flemish immigrants moved into the region and established linen and woolen industries.

ANGUS, EARLS OF. Angus was originally one of the seven provinces of Pictish Scotland. The Celtic line of earls ended with Matilda (d. c. 1267), but her marriage in 1243 to a Norman introduced a series of four Norman earls, the last dying in 1381. Meanwhile a new line of Scottish earls had been created inasmuch as these Norman earls had supported England. The first of the Scottish earls was John Stewart (d. 1331). In 1389 George Douglas was created earl. His great-grandson Archibald Douglas (d. c. 1514), the fifth Douglas in the Douglas line, was known as the Great Earl.

ANIANE, ABBEY OF, Benedictine abbey in lower Languedoc founded in 782, received patronage from Charlemagne and developed into a leading monastic center in the ninth century. The Council of Aachen in 817 established the monastic customs of Aniane for all monasteries of the Carolingian empire.

ANIANUS OF ORLÉANS, ST., d. c. 453, bishop of Orléans who, according to Gregory of Tours, helped save the city from Attila by rallying the people to resistance and by reorganizing the city's physical defenses.

ANICETUS, ST., Pope, c. 155–66, died a martyr. Little is known about his pontificate except the persistence of the perennial problem concerning the date of Easter. Polycarp is said to have come to Rome to confer with him about that matter.

ANIMA CHRISTI, a prayer dating from the early fourteenth century to which Pope John XXII (1316–34) attached rich indulgences. He may have been its author. The prayer became popular and appeared frequently in devotional books of the fifteenth century.

ANJOU, powerful county in west-central France which gave its name to the extensive Angevin (from Anjou) empire of Henry II of England (1154–89). It became independent of the Capetians in the tenth century and shortly after conquered Touraine and Main. About this time it came into the possession of the first line of counts of Anjou. Fulk (d. 1143) had his son Geoffrey, the first of the counts to bear the name Plantagenet, marry Matilda, daughter of Henry I of England. It was their son Henry (II) who was the first English king to rule the county. In 1204 Philip II of France seized Anjou and in 1246 Louis IX gave it in appanage to his brother Charles, count of Provence, later to become king of Sicily and Naples. In 1360 John II made Anjou a duchy and gave it to his son Louis. When Louis's grandson René died in 1480, Louis XI returned it to the royal domain.

ANNA (Anne), according to early Christian tradition, the wife of Joachim and the mother of Mary who became the mother of Christ. The legend of her life appears in the second-century *Protevangelium of James*.

ANNA COMNENA, d. 1150, daughter of Alexius I Comnenus who sought to depose her brother but was defeated, whereupon she retired to a convent. She is the author of a long epic poem entitled *Alexiad* which eulogized the achievement of her father. The poem is an important source for the history of the First Crusade (1096–9).

ANNALS, written accounts of events set down in chronological order without benefit of further organization, analysis, or elaboration. As sources of medieval history they preceded in time the more informative and literary chronicles although some cannot be easily distinguished from the other. Their greatest period extended from c. 650 to 1100. [*See* CHRONICLE.]

ANNATES, payment to an ecclesiastical superior or institution of the revenue (or a percentage thereof) realized from an ecclesiastical benefice by the newly instituted incumbent during the first year of his occupancy. Such payments appeared in the eleventh century but were made only to bishops and abbots until the fourteenth when popes began to collect them.

ANNE. *See* ANNA.

ANNE DE BEAUJEU, d. 1522, daughter of Louis XI of France, who with her husband, Pierre de Beaujeu, duc de Bourbon, acted as regent for her brother Charles VIII in 1483 when her father died. She possessed a large measure of administrative ability and political acumen and was successful in preserving the royal domain against France's rebellious nobles. In 1491 she arranged the marriage of Charles VIII to Anne of Brittany, after which time her influence rapidly declined.

ANNE OF BOHEMIA, d. 1394, queen consort of Richard II of England, daughter of Emperor Charles IV, and sister of Emperor Wenceslaus. She married Richard in 1382 and proved a steadying influence on her husband in the cause of clemency and moderation. Her death occasioned Richard great grief and, according to some historians, contributed to the "tyranny" of the king's last years.

ANNE OF BRITTANY, d. 1514, inherited Brittany from her father Francis II in 1488. A number of powerful suitors had their eyes on her duchy. She first married Maximilian of Germany by proxy, then had that marriage annulled and married Charles VIII of France. When Charles died in 1498, she married his successor Louis

XII. Her marriage to Charles brought Brittany into the French royal domain.

ANNIUS, JOHN (Nanni), d. 1502, Italian humanist, theologian, historian, preacher, and student of Oriental languages. His seventeen-volume collection of excerpts from the works of ancient writers elicited justifiable criticism from contemporary scholars who questioned the authenticity of some of their contents.

ANNO DOMINI, from the Latin, "in the year of the Lord." The current system of reckoning years is based upon the study of Dionysius Exiguus (d. c. 550). The accuracy of his calculations has been denied and the actual birth of Christ is believed to have taken place several years earlier, some time between 7 and 4 B.C. Some authorities prefer the year A.D. 6.

ANNONA, land tax levied by the Roman imperial government and collected in kind, e.g., grain, wine, olive oil.

ANNO (Hanno) OF COLOGNE, ST., d. 1075, archbishop of Cologne, imperial chancellor and confessor of Henry III, served for a time as regent during the minority of Henry IV. His zealous efforts in the cause of monastic reform earned him his reputation as a saint. Probably his principal contribution to the church was that of securing the recognition of Alexander II as pope at the Council of Mantua (1064) against the pretensions of his rival Honorius.

ANNO SONG, an epic poem in Middle High German composed some time before 1105 in order to advance the canonization of Archbishop Anno of Cologne. This was the first hagiographical work to appear in the German language.

ANNUNCIATION, FEAST OF THE, liturgical feast commemorating the appearance of the Angel Gabriel to Mary to announce the birth of Christ (Luke 1:26–38). It made its way into the liturgical calendar some time between the fifth and seventh centuries and was assigned the date of March 25, that is, nine months before Christmas when Christ was born.

ANOMOEANS, a religious sect of the fourth century, its leaders Aetius and Eunomius, who maintained a doctrine akin to extreme Arianism. They maintained that whereas God had always existed, Christ had been created, and thus God and Christ could not be alike.

ANONYMUS BELAE REGIS NOTARIUS, an unknown notary of King Bela III of Hungary (1173–96) who was the author of the chronicle *Gesta Hungarorum.*

ANONYMOUS OF YORK, name given to the author(s) of 31 tractates drawn up presumably in York in the early twelfth century which in general defended royal claims against those advanced by the champions of papal authority. The tractates probably had little influence on contemporary thought although they are of interest to historians concerned with relations between church and state.

ANSAR, name given to the "helpers," those inhabitants of Medina who accepted and protected Mohammed upon his arrival from Mecca, as opposed to the Muhadschirun or "emigrants" who had accompanied him.

ANSBACH, city in western Bavaria that grew up around an eighth-century Benedictine abbey. In 1331 it became the residence of the Franconian branch of the Hohenzollern family.

ANSEGIS (Ansegisus), ST., d. 833, monk and adviser to Benedict of Aniane who was as distinguished for his learning as for his piety. He became abbot of Luxeuil which he reorganized, then of Fontenelle whose library he made one of the finest in western Europe. He prepared a valuable collection of Frankish capitularies.

ANSEGISEL (Ansigisil, Adalgisil), d. 685, son of Arnulf of Metz, mayor of the palace under Sigibert II of Austrasia, and father of Pepin of

Heristal. He was, accordingly, an ancestor of the Carolingians.

ANSELM OF BEC (Canterbury), ST., d. 1109, the father of scholasticism, as a young man left Italy and made his way to the Benedictine monastery of Bec, became a monk, then abbot, then in 1093 archbishop of Canterbury. He was one of the first original thinkers of the medieval West and among the first Christian scholars who insisted that theology must seek support in reason whenever this was possible; in fact, he more than any other scholastic convinced the church of the value of dialectic to faith. On the other hand, he was sharp in his criticism of dialecticians such as Roscelin of Compiègne who would have permitted reason to limit their faith. Anselm's best known works, the *Monologion* and *Proslogion,* present arguments for the existence of God. Anselm drew heavily upon St. Augustine for the substance of his thought. When Anselm went to Rome in 1097 against the wishes of William II to receive the pallium from the pope's own hands, the king seized the temporalities of Canterbury, so Anselm remained in exile until 1100 when Henry I succeeded. In 1106 he agreed to a settlement of the investiture controversy with Henry known as the Compromise of Bec. [*See* BEC, COMPROMISE OF.]

ANSELM OF HAVELBERG, d. 1158, Premonstratensian canon and bishop of Havelberg (1129) who twice visited Constantinople to discuss the termination of the schism dividing the Greek and Latin churches. The emperor Frederick I Barbarossa held him in high regard and made him archbishop and exarch of Ravenna.

ANSELM OF LAON, d. 1117, scholastic at the cathedral school of Laon, pupil of Anselm of Bec and teacher of Abelard. Together with William of Champeaux, the leading teacher at Paris, he endorsed the doctrine of realism in the controversy over universals, a position that later drew attack from Abelard. He was among the first Christian scholars to attempt with his *Sentences* a

systematic treatment of scholastic theology based upon the Bible.

ANSELM OF LIEGE, d. after 1056, chronicler, attended the cathedral school at Liège where he became a canon, then dean. His chronicle contains biographies of some 25 bishops of Liège.

ANSELM OF LUCCA. *See* ALEXANDER II, Pope.

ANSELM OF LUCCA, ST., d. 1086, nephew of Pope Alexander II (1061–73) who was invested with the see of Lucca by Henry IV in 1071. He later repented his investiture by a lay ruler, resigned his see, and retired to a Cluniac monastery near Mantua (at Polirone). Upon the insistence of Pope Gregory VII, he returned to Lucca but his strictness in enforcing discipline led to his expulsion by the emperor and antipope Guibert (c. 1080). He prepared an important collection of canons which were subsequently incorporated in Gratian's *Decretum.*

ANSELM OF NONANTOLA, ST., d. 803, turned his back on his duchy (Friuli), became a Benedictine monk, and established a number of hospices for the care of the aged and poor. For the last 50 years of his life he served as abbot of the monastery of Nonantola which he had founded.

ANSGAR (Anschar, Anskar), ST., d. 865, monk of Corbie and teacher at Corvey, who earned the title of the Apostle of the North because of his extensive missionary work in Denmark and Sweden. He served as abbot of Corvey, then first bishop of Hamburg, and when that city was destroyed, as first archbishop of the see of Hamburg-Bremen. It was as archbishop of this see that he converted King Haarik of Denmark and King Olaf of Sweden.

ANSUERUS, ST., d. 1066, scholarly abbot of the Benedictine monastery of St. George in Ratzeburg, later missionary among the Slavs. He suffered martyrdom at the hands of the Wends.

ANTELAMI, BENEDETTO, leading north Italian Romanesque sculptor of the late twelfth and early thirteenth centuries. His later sculptures reveal evidence of contacts with the early Gothic sculpture of the Ile-de-France. An excellent example of his relief work that shows influences from southern France is that of Christ as judge in the baptistery at Parma.

ANTE-NICENE AND POST-NICENE FATHERS, church fathers who wrote from apostolic times to the Council of Nicaea (325) as distinguished from those whose period of activity extended from this council to roughly the death of Pope Gregory I (d. 604).

ANTEPENDIUM, a hanging, usually richly ornamented, that covered the front part of the altar. From the thirteenth century the color of the antependium varied with the color of the vestments used at Mass that day.

ANTERUS (Anteros, Antherus), ST., Pope, 21 November 235 to 3 January 236, probably a Greek, the tradition of whose martyrdom may be in error.

ANTES, large division of Slavs located between the Carpathians and the Donets in the sixth century, to be distinguished from the Sclaveni who lived north of the middle and lower Danube.

ANTHELM OF CHIGNIN, ST., d. 1178, Carthusian monk, later prior of La Grande Chartreuse, first minister general of the order, and bishop of Belley (France). Frederick I Barbarossa granted him and his successors the title of Prince of the Holy Roman Empire.

ANTHEMIUS, d. 472, Western Roman emperor, 467–72. He had been a prominent dignitary at the imperial court in Constantinople whom Leo I, Eastern Roman emperor, appointed with the approval of Ricimer, German chieftain, who was virtual ruler of Rome. When Anthemius attempted to free himself from the domination of Ricimer, he was captured and beheaded.

ANTHEMIUS, praetorian prefect under Arcadius, Eastern Roman emperor (395–408), who was of great assistance to that emperor and his successor Theodosius II, in handling the problems of imperial administration.

ANTHEMIUS OF TRALLES, sixth-century Greek mathematician, sculptor, and architect who collaborated with Isidore of Miletus in designing Justinian's famous church of Hagia Sophia in Constantinople.

ANTHIMUS OF TREBIZOND, patriarch of Constantinople, 535–6, earlier bishop of Trebizond, who was made patriarch largely at the wish of the empress Theodora. He was later deposed when Pope Agapetus objected to his Monophysite views. For political reasons the emperor Justinian carried out the pope's order to have him removed.

ANTHONY III, patriarch of Constantinople, 974–9, called the Studite, was appointed patriarch by John I Tzimisces but was removed by Basil II because of Anthony's support of Bardas Sclerus who had opposed the emperor.

ANTHONY IV, patriarch of Constantinople, 1389–90, 1391–7, insisted upon his right as patriarch of Constantinople to exercise authority over the other patriarchs of the East. He worked earnestly to preserve Byzantine sovereignty which was being threatened by the Turks.

ANTHONY (Antony) OF EGYPT, ST., d. 356, father of monasticism, gave up his wealth and for 80 years lived as a hermit in the desert east of the Nile. There, according to tradition, the devil failed in all his wiles to tempt Anthony to sin. For many of the years that Anthony spent as a hermit, he gave spiritual guidance to other ascetics who had been attracted by the fame of his sanctity. Despite his preference for solitude, he used his influence to support the Nicene position in the Arian controversy. It was this interest that brought him into association with St. Athanasius who wrote a biography of the hermit; it proved one of the most influential hagiographical works ever written. Anthony was the patron of herdsmen. His intercession was also sought in cases of erysipelas.

ANTHONY OF PADUA, ST., d. 1231, was born at Lisbon, became a canon regular of St. Augustine, later a Franciscan. He taught at Bologna, Montpellier, and Toulouse, preached against the Albigenses in southern France, and gained renown for his eloquence. St. Francis of Assisi appointed him to teach theology to his fellow Franciscans. In a vision he was said to have held the child Jesus in his arms, whence his portrayal in that pose in medieval art.

ANTHONY PAVONIUS, BL., d. 1374, Dominican prior of the monastic community at Savigliano (Piedmont), later served as inquisitor general in northern Italy where he was murdered by Waldensians.

ANTHONY'S FIRE, ST., a medieval disease, probably a kind of gangrene, which the faithful believed might be cured through the intercession of St. Anthony.

ANTICHRIST, a spiritual being, the incarnation of evil, who was expected to be born again and work much evil before finally being overthrown by Christ. The subject of the antichrist proved a popular one in evil times.

ANTIDORON, what was left of the bread used for consecration in the Mass. This was then blessed and distributed after Mass to the faithful. This practice of the early church continued on in churches of the Greek rite.

ANTILEGOMENA, writings whose canonicity and right to be included in the New Testament were disputed, as opposed to *Homologumena,* which were accepted. The designation was given such works by Eusebius of Caesarea (d. c. 339).

ANTINOMIANISM, a doctrine maintained by several early Gnostic communities that Christians, inasmuch as they had been bought by the pre-

cious blood of Christ and were justified by their faith, were exempt from the obligations of the moral law.

ANTIOCH, ancient city of south Turkey, the third city of the Roman empire, where the followers of Christ were first called Christians (Acts 11:26). In 538 Antioch fell to the Persians, in 637 to the Arabs who held it until 969 when Nicephorus II recovered it for Byzantium. Then in 1085 it fell to the Seljuk Turks but was stormed by Bohemond and a crusading army in 1097 during the First Crusade. It remained in Christian hands until 1268 when it fell to Baibars I, the Mamluk sultan of Egypt. In 1401 Timur the Lame, the Mongol conqueror, sacked the city and left little but ruins to remind travelers of its former greatness.

ANTIOCH, COUNCIL OF, council held in 341 on the occasion of the consecration of Constantine's Golden Church. Four different creeds were proposed at this council as replacements for that adopted at Nicaea in 325.

ANTIOCH, PATRIARCHATE OF, ancient see which tradition had it was founded by St. Peter. It was one of the three oldest Christian patriarchates. After the destruction of Jerusalem in A.D. 70, Antioch assumed a position of leadership in the Christian world. From the fifth century, Antioch tended to lose some of its influence with the rise to prominence of the patriarchate of Constantinople.

ANTIOCH, PRINCIPALITY OF, Christian state established by the crusaders (First Crusade) in 1098 and claimed by Bohemond. It allied itself with the Mongols in 1260, but in 1268 was captured by Baibars, general of the Mamluk sultan of Egypt, who massacred and enslaved its population.

ANTIOCH, SCHOOL OF, the catechetical center (not a formal school) in Antioch composed of theologians who tended to accept a grammatical-historical exegesis as opposed to an allegorical, which was popular in Alexandria. Theologians in Antioch also objected, when involved in Christological controversies, to any sharp distinction being drawn between Christ's divine and human natures.

ANTIOCHENE LITURGY, a liturgy such as the Syrian liturgy of St. James used in ancient times in the patriarchate of Antioch. The usage of Antioch, as modified at Jerusalem, served as the model for most Eastern rites.

ANTIPHON, verse or sentence from Scripture that served to introduce, often to express, the thought of the psalm that followed. At the conclusion of the psalm the antiphon was repeated. The antiphon might also refer to a psalm or hymn sung or chanted in responsive, alternating parts. The Introit, Offertory, and Communion of the Mass were originally antiphons but were later used independently. In a class all their own are the four antiphons honoring the Blessed Virgin (e.g., *Salve Regina*) which were eventually incorporated into the Divine Office as hymns.

ANTIPHONARY *(antiphonale, antiphonarium)*, a collection of hymns and liturgical songs that appeared in the Divine Office. The term might also refer to a missal hymnal which later acquired the name *Graduale*.

ANTIPOPE, one who claimed to be pope or was so hailed by his adherents, in opposition to a pontiff canonically elected or accepted by the historical church. It was difficult on occasion for the faithful to identify the legitimate pope as, for example, during the period of the Western Schism (1378–1415) when there were two and, for a number of years, three popes.

ANTITRINITARIANISM, term applied to different professedly Christian sects that rejected the doctrine of the Trinity: e.g., Ebionites and Modalists.

ANTONELLO DA MESSINA, d. 1479, Sicilian painter who introduced painting in oil from the Low Countries. His work reveals the influence of Jan van Eyck and represents, therefore, a blending of the Northern and Italian styles. Through Giovanni Bellini he exercised a good deal of influence on the Venetian school. His paintings are known for their delicate luminosity and sharp observation. Among his best known works are *Pietà, Annunciation, Calvary,* and *Madonna and Child*.

ANTONIANS, name given to several religious communities which claimed St. Anthony of Egypt (d. 356) as their founder. These included the original disciples of St. Anthony and a congregation founded by Gaston de Dauphiné in 1095 and known as the Hospital Brothers of St. Anthony.

ANTONIANS (Antonines), CROSS OF THE, a cross in the form of a T which, legend had it, St. Anthony of Egypt had used to drive away the plague. The Antonians used this cross as a symbol of their order.

ANTONIJ THE SAINT, d. 1073, founder of the Cave Monastery at Kiev, later archbishop of Minsk. He urged the union of the western Russians with the Greek church.

ANTONINES. *See* ANTONIANS.

ANTONINUS, ST., d. 1459, Dominican theologian and auditor general of the Rota under Pope Eugenius IV who took an active part in the discussions of the Council of Ferrara-Florence. He later became archbishop of Florence when he devoted himself to the cause of church reform, while at the same time undertaking diplomatic missions for the Florentine government. His writings include a major theological *summa (Summa Moralis)* which devoted much attention to commercial ethics and the morality of banking, and a general history of the world. He constructed the famed Convent of San Marco with funds provided by Cosimo de' Medici.

ANTONIUS ANDREAS, d. c. 1320, Franciscan scholastic who studied under Duns Scotus at

Paris. His works which were widely read reflect the influence of his mentor.

ANTONY OF EGYPT, ST. *See* ANTHONY OF EGYPT, ST.

ANTRUSTIONS *(Antrustiones),* attendants or retainers of the king especially during the Merovingian period.

ANTWERP, town on the Scheldt river in Flanders which was erected on the site of a fortress which the Northmen had destroyed in 836. By 1031 it had grown into an important port and flourished as a textile center from the early fourteenth century. The Hanseatic League planted a colony there in 1313. With the decline of Bruges and Ghent in the late Middle Ages, Antwerp gradually became the leading commercial and financial center of the Netherlands and western Europe. Among the city's most famous reminders of the Middle Ages are the Cathedral of Notre Dame (fourteenth-fifteenth century) and the old guild houses that line the Groote Markt (market place).

ANVARI (Auhad Al-Din Ali), d. c. 1190, Persian poet and panegyrist at the court of the Seljuk Turkish sultan Sanjar in Merv. He was unusually productive in the composition of poems, odes, and lyrics.

AON, God, according to the teaching of the cult of Mithras. The Manichaeans held Aon to have been an ancient god.

AOSTA, city in northwest Italy, near the junction of the Great and Little St. Bernard roads. In the eleventh century it passed to Humbert, the founder of the Savoy dynasty. Towers and an impressive cathedral (ninth-fifteenth century) remain from medieval times.

APELLES, second-century theologian, at first a disciple of Marcion, founder of a Gnostic sect that modified Marcion's position concerning the nature of Christ. He held that Christ had indeed come down from the good God but was not himself God but a body miraculously formed out of the elements.

APHRAATES (Afrahat), Syrian ascetic of the early fourth century who was known as the Persian Sage. His 23 homilies represent the most ancient literature dealing with the Christian church in Syria. They are important for the light they throw on fourth-century Christianity in Persia.

APHTHARTODOCETAE, a sect of Monophysites founded by Julian, bishop of Halicarnassus (d. after 518), which believed the body of Christ was rendered incorruptible, impassible, and immortal by virtue of his divine nature. The Byzantine emperor Justinian I (527–65) appears to have accepted this view during the closing years of his reign.

APHTHONIOS, a fourth-century Greek rhetorician of Antioch whose writings exerted great influence upon Byzantine education.

APIARIUS OF SICCA, a priest of the diocese of Sicca in north Africa whose appeal to the bishop of Rome, Pope Zosimus (417–8), against his local bishop's sentence of excommunication and the pope's subsequent order that he be reinstated provoked a famous exchange of arguments over the right of appeal to Rome in disciplinary matters. This right had been recognized by the Council of Sardica (342) but a Council of Carthage in 418 forbade such appeals beyond the sea (Mediterranean). The pope protested this canon.

APOCALYPSE. *See* APOCALYPTIC LITERATURE.

APOCALYPTIC LITERATURE. The word apocalypse means a "revelation" or "unveiling," so when joined to writings it refers to books that claim to reveal things that are normally hidden or only to come true in the future. Christian apocalyptic literature grew directly from the Jewish which found such subjects as the resurrection of the dead and the imminent coming of the Messiah quite in keeping with the church's hopes and expectations. It was, in fact, the acceptance of Jewish apocalyptic writings by the Christians that assured their preservation. In time Christian writers contributed their own share to the store of apocalyptic literature. Of a number of apocalypses that appeared in the first and second centuries, the most significant and popular was the *Book of Revelation* attributed to St. John the Evangelist. Its use of fantastic imagery and symbolic language, together with such themes as the overthrow of evil, final judgment, and the world to come which it introduces, are similar to those common to Jewish apocalyptic writings. When Christian expectation of an early return of Christ faded, apocalyptic writings, both Jewish and Christian, tended to lose their appeal.

APOCATASTASIS, the theological doctrine that maintains that no divine punishment is eternal and that all men, even the devil and the damned, will ultimately share the grace of salvation. The doctrine suffered formal condemnation at the Council of Constantinople in 543.

APOCRISIARIUS, the Byzantine name given to an envoy of one high ecclesiastical authority who was sent to another prelate or to a royal court. The term might also designate the senior court chaplains of the Frankish courts.

APOCRYPHA, term that when applied to Christian writings designated works whose authorship was attributed to Christ's apostles or disciples but that were considered spurious and not included in the New Testament: e.g., *Epistle of the Apostles, Protevangelium of James,* and *Gospel of Thomas.*

APOLLINARIANISM, a Christological heresy of the fourth century which held that Christ possessed a *Logos* in place of a human mind. By denying Christ complete manhood, he could not be held to have redeemed the whole of human nature, but only its spiritual elements. The heresy derived its name from Apollinaris, bishop of Laodicea (d. c. 390), who preached that doctrine. Several synods condemned the heresy,

above all the General Council of Constantinople I (381). It disappeared early in the fifth century.

APOLLINARIS (the Elder), grammarian of the fourth century, priest, and champion of the Nicene Creed. He translated the Pentateuch and other biblical writings into Greek hexameter verse in order to provide Christian instructors materials in the schools when Emperor Julian (361–3) forbade them the use of the pagan classics.

APOLLINARIS OF HIERAPOLIS, ST., bishop of Hierapolis (Phrygia), a Christian apologist of the second century who effectively attacked Montanism in his writings.

APOLLINARIS OF LAODICEA (the Younger), d. c. 390, bishop of Laodicea in Syria, son of Apollinaris the Elder. The younger Apollinaris opposed Arianism at the Council of Nicaea (325) but then advanced views of his own that were later condemned as heretical. These views provided the inspiration for Apollinarianism. [*See* APOLLINARIANISM.]

APOLLINARIS OF VALENCE, ST., d. c. 520, learned bishop of Valence (Burgundy) who proved himself a vigorous reformer and an active opponent of Arianism. His correspondence with Avitus is extant.

APOLLINARIS SIDONIUS. *See* SIDONIUS APOLLINARIS.

APOLLINARIS, ST., according to legend a companion of St. Peter who appointed him bishop of Ravenna. He suffered martyrdom and was buried, so it was believed, in the church of San Apollinare in Classe in Ravenna.

APOLLONIA OF ALEXANDRIA, ST., virgin who was martyred at Alexandria in 249. Her executioners broke out her teeth, for which reason the Middle Ages revered her as the patroness of dentists.

APOLLONIUS OF TYANA, possibly a first-century Pythagorean philosopher, ascetic, and wonder-worker, whose supposed sanctity and miraculous powers some pagans of the third and fourth century likened to those of Christ.

APOLLONIUS OF TYRE, Latin prose romance, probably based upon a Greek original of the third century A.D. This told of Apollonius and his wife who remained faithful to one another despite a variety of unusual adventures that had kept them apart for many years. Few stories matched its popularity in medieval literature.

APOLOGETICS, a term applied generally to theological literature of an expository character which was written for the purpose of explaining doctrine to non-Christians or of defending it against its critics. Much of the patristic writing of the second century goes by this classification. [See APOLOGISTS.]

APOLOGISTS, term used to identify especially the church fathers of the second and early third centuries who concerned themselves with defending Christianity against its critics and arguing the reasonableness and wholesomeness of its tenets and principles. Some of their writings were addressed to Roman emperors including Antoninus Pius (138–61) and Marcus Aurelius (161–80). Classified as apologists are Aristides, Justin Martyr, Tatian, Athenagoras, Theophilus, Minucius Felix, and Tertullian.

APOLYSIS, the dismissal blessing said or sung since the fourth century by the celebrant of the mass in the Greek church. It corresponded to the *Ite, Missa Est,* in the Latin church.

APOPHTHEGMATA PATRUM, literally the sayings of the fathers but referring more specifically to those of the desert fathers. A collection of their sayings made its appearance in the beginning of the fourth century.

APOSTLES, the twelve men specially selected by Christ to continue his teaching and to direct the work of the Christian church that he was establishing. They included Peter, Andrew, James (the Greater), John, Thomas, James (the Lesser), Jude (or Thaddeus), Philip, Bartholomew, Matthew, Simon, and Judas.

APOSTLES' CREED. *See* CREED, APOSTLES'.

APOSTLES SPOONS, a set of thirteen spoons, one for Christ, twelve for the Apostles, adorned with symbols which identified each, e.g., a key for Peter's spoon. They were often presented as baptismal gifts, either individually or as a set.

APOSTOLIC AGE, the first period of the church, that which fell approximately within the lifetime of the Apostles, roughly the first century.

APOSTOLIC CANONS, a series of 85 canons attributed to the Apostles which make up the concluding chapter of the *Apostolic Constitutions.* [See APOSTOLIC CONSTITUTIONS.] They are concerned principally with the conduct of the clergy. The first 50 were translated into Latin and became part of the canon law of the Western church.

APOSTOLIC CHURCHES, a term employed by Western writers of the early centuries to designate churches that were founded or administered by an Apostle, e.g., the church of Antioch founded by St. Peter.

APOSTOLIC CHURCH ORDER, an early Christian document concerning regulations on ecclesiastical practice and moral discipline. While the regulations were ascribed to different Apostles, it was probably composed in Egypt c. 300.

APOSTOLIC CONSTITUTIONS (Canons), a pseudo-apostolic collection of decrees, pertaining principally to the clergy, which were believed drawn up by the Apostles and given to the church by Clement I of Rome (d. 101). They appear to have been assembled in Syria about the year 380, probably by an Arian, although most of the canons were introduced to the Latin church by Dionysius Exiguus (fifth–sixth century). Despite the obscurity and dubiousness of their origins, many of the constitutions appear to be authentic. They furnish information of real importance about the history of the early church.

APOSTOLIC DECREE, a decree of the church in Jerusalem (Acts 15:22–29) that ordered converts from paganism in Syria and Cilicia to refrain from idolatry, fornication, and the shedding of blood, while releasing them from other requirements of Jewish law.

APOSTOLIC FATHERS, church fathers of the first and early second centuries, such as Clement of Rome (d. 101), Polycarp (d. 155?), and Ignatius of Antioch (d. 110), who may have known the Apostles or may have been associated with people who did.

APOSTOLICI, a sect centered in Syria and Asia Minor in the third century that claimed to live the poor, humble lives of the Apostles. The same name was used by a similar sect located in Italy and Spain in the thirteenth and fourteenth centuries which drew its inspiration from the Franciscan teaching on poverty, and by a group of Cathari in the twelfth century.

APOSTOLIC KING, title traditionally borne by the king of Hungary. It is believed to have been conferred on Stephen I, king of Hungary (d. 1038), by Pope Sylvester II in recognition of his apostolic zeal.

APOSTOLIC MONTHS, months of the year during which time any church benefice that became vacant was reserved to the papacy. In the fifteenth century these included the eight months of January, February, April, May, July, August, October, and November.

APOSTOLIC PENITENIARY. *See* PENITENTIARY.

APOSTOLIC PROTONOTARY, one of the notaries of the church in Rome who emerged from the general group in the fifth century.

APOSTOLIC SEE, a term first applied to any see founded by an Apostle, later reserved by Western writers to the see of Rome.

APOSTOLIC SIGNATURE, the highest court in the papal Curia. It appeared in the fourteenth century, then divided into two parts during the fifteenth.

APOSTOLIC TRADITION, a liturgical treatise, probably the work of Hippolytus (d. c. 236), which contains a description of the rites and practices presumably in use in Rome in the early third century.

APOSTOLIS, MICHAEL, d. c. 1486, Byzantine scholar who fled Constantinople for Crete when the city fell to the Turks in 1453. He later busied himself, upon the direction of Cardinal Bessarion, with searching the lands of the eastern Mediterranean for classical manuscripts. He left a collection of aphorisms which he had gathered from Greek classical writers.

APPANAGE (apanage), land or money given by kings and princes to their younger children to provide them means of support. They might be recovered, as in the case of the French crown, when the line failed to produce a male heir.

APPARITOR, an official of an ecclesiastical court who issued summons, arrested persons to be tried, and took possession of the property of the defendant when so ordered.

APPRENTICE, boy who lived with a master guildsman from about the age of twelve for five to seven years while he learned a trade. He became a journeyman at about the age of nineteen. [*See* GUILD.]

APSE, the semicircular extension of the nave which was ordinarily located at the east end of the church. Here were placed the main altar, the bishop's throne, and the seats of the clergy. Because of the location and function of the apse in church services, it was the part of the structure upon which the architect, sculptor, mosaicist, painter, and woodcarver expended their finest efforts.

APT, ULRICH, d. 1531 German painter whose artistry shows the influence of Holbein. One of his works is the *Matthäus Altarpiece*.

APULIA, region of southern Italy facing the Adriatic. After the fall of Rome, Ostrogoths occupied the area from the late fifth century until it was reconquered by the armies of the Byzantine emperor Justinian I (527–65). By the close of the sixth century most of the region was in the hands of the Lombards. Normans moved in during the eleventh and twelfth centuries, with Venetians and Turks later seizing control of scattered holdings along the coast. The feudal system which long prevailed in this poorly organized country hampered its economic and political development. Apulian architecture from the eleventh century reflected Greek, Arab, Norman, and Pisan influences.

AQUAMANILE, a medieval container of brass or bronze, usually richly ornamented, which contained water to be used to wash the priest's hands at Mass. It also referred to a bowl that might catch the water used in the washing of the hands of a bishop or other prelate.

AQUARIANS, name given to several sects in the early church, such as the Ebionites, who practiced an extreme, even idolatrous, veneration of water as the source of life.

AQUILEIA, city of ancient origin in northeastern Italy near the Adriatic, repeatedly destroyed by invaders including the Huns under Attila in 452. It was an early Christian center of learning and in the sixth century its bishops assumed the title of patriarch. The high point of Aquileia as an independent state came in the late eleventh and twelfth centuries when it acquired Friuli, Carniola, and Istria. In 1420 these provinces were lost to Venice, as was also lost the temporal power earlier possessed by the patriarch. From then on the patriarchs were Venetians.

AQUINAS, THOMAS, ST. *See* THOMAS AQUINAS, ST.

AQUITAINE, name given to southwestern France during the Merovingian period. The Visigoths overran the region in the early fifth century but lost it to the Franks in 507. Charlemagne gave Aquitaine as a kingdom to his son Louis (the Pious). Following the troubled times that accompanied the breakup of the Carolingian empire, Aquitaine emerged in the late ninth century as the duchy of William, count of Auvergne, and later as the possession of the count of Poitiers. Eleanor, the daughter and heiress of William X, the last of the Poitevin dukes, was first the wife of Louis VII of France, then of Henry II of England (1152), at which time the duchy became a possession of the king of England held as a fief of the king of France. France did not recover control of Aquitaine until the close of the Hundred Years' War.

ARABESQUE. *See* ISLAMIC ART AND ARCHITECTURE.

ARABIAN NIGHTS. *See* THOUSAND AND ONE NIGHTS.

ARABIC LITERATURE. Pre-Islamic literature existed among the Bedouins long before it was written down. It consisted of short poems and songs, for the most part about love, fighting, the stars, colors of the desert, Jinns, and Allah. Some of these poems have been preserved in such anthologies as the *Hamasah* of Abu Tammam (d. c. 845). The appearance of the Prophet proved no inspiration to poets, although the Koran was itself the first literary monument of Arabic prose and has always been considered the finest work of the language in terms of style and eloquence. The Abbasid caliphs Harun Al-Rashid and Al Ma'mun bestowed their patronage on poets as well as scholars, and among those who accepted their favor were Abu Nuwas and Abu-l-Atahiya. The most famous of the prose productions of the later period was the *Thousand and One Nights*. Mention might be made of the *Rubaiyat* of Omar Khayyam and the writings of Arabic geographers, astronomers, and philosophers. A full survey of Arabic literature would include a discussion of Persian and Turkish literature whose development was heavily affected by Arab influences.

ARABIC NUMERALS, numerals of ancient Hindu origin, knowledge of which came to Baghdad in the early ninth century when Al-Khwarizmi expounded their virtues. Spain learned of the numerals in the tenth century, although they did not come into general use in Western Europe until the fifteenth.

ARAGON, region just east of Navarre in the area of the Pyrenees which was largely under Frankish control until the middle of the ninth century when it was ruled by Navarre. It became an independent kingdom under Ramiro (d. 1063), expanded south toward the Ebro, then under Alfonso I (1104–34) captured Saragossa from the Almoravids. In 1150 it was united with Catalonia when the count of the latter country married the heiress of Aragon. Although Aragon lost its possessions in southern France following the Battle of Muret in 1213, it proved the most ambitious of the Christian Spanish states, acquiring the Balearic Islands in 1228, the kingdom of Valencia ten years later, then Sicily (1282), Sardinia (1320), and Naples (1442). The marriage of Ferdinand II of Aragon to Isabella of Castile in 1469 eventually led to the merging of these two countries into one Spain.

ARAGON, HOUSE OF, ruling family of Aragon, Catalonia, Majorca, Sicily, the kingdom of Naples, Sardinia, Roussillon, Athens, and other lands. It was founded by Ramiro I of Aragon (1035–63). Aragon and Catalonia were united after 1137 under one ruler, but the other territories were controlled by individual members of the dynasty. In the course of the eleventh century the house of Aragon acquired various fiefs in southern France, including Provence, Roussillon, and Montpellier, but lost most of these when Peter II intervened in the Albigensian Crusade and suffered defeat at Muret in 1213.

Alfonso V who conquered Naples in 1442, united all Aragonese dominions under his one rule. The marriage of Ferdinand II of Aragon with Isabella of Castile in 1469 led to the union of the two kingdoms and the establishment of Spain.

ARATOR, a sixth-century Christian Latin poet of Ligurian origin whose epic verses about the Apostles revealed meager talent although they made him quite popular.

ARBOGAST, a Frankish general in the Roman army, adviser to the youthful Valentinian II whom he later had murdered. Arbogast committed suicide in 394 after being defeated by Emperor Theodosius.

ARBROATH, ABBEY OF, Benedictine monastery founded by William the Lion in 1178 on the east coast of Scotland in honor of the recently murdered and canonized Thomas Becket. It was one of the wealthiest of Scottish monastic houses.

ARBUES, PEDRO DE, d. 1485, inquisitor for Aragon who was notorious for his harshness. He was murdered in the cathedral at Saragossa.

ARC, JOAN OF. *See* JOAN OF ARC.

ARCADIUS, Roman emperor, 395–408, succeeded to the emperorship in the eastern Roman empire upon the death of his father Theodosius in 395. It was actually his ministers Rufinus and Eutropius and his wife, Eudoxia, who directed the work of the government.

ARCHABBOT, abbot who held precedence or exercised authority over other abbots.

ARCHANGEL, an angel of the highest order of angels. The best known archangels were Michael, Gabriel, and Raphael.

ARCHBISHOP, a bishop who held rank above other bishops and might exercise a measure of jurisdiction over them. Although the archbishop did not appear before the sixth century, the metropolitan whose position paralleled that of the archbishop is heard of as early as the fourth.

ARCHCHAPLAIN, chief of the chaplains in the Frankish court, after 854 usually the chancellor as well.

ARCHDEACON, an ecclesiastical official who appeared in the fourth century and held a position of considerable importance in diocesan administration through the course of the Middle Ages. His was the highest post to which a clerk beneath the rank of priest might aspire.

ARCHDIOCESE, the province under the jurisdiction of an archbishop. This might include the dioceses of a number of suffragan bishops. The archdiocese as distinct from the diocese may have emerged as a jurisdictional area by the third century.

ARCHDUKE, title held since 1453 by princes of the royal family in Austria. It was first assumed by Rudolf IV, duke of Austria (d. 1365).

ARCHERS, a levy of troops under the rank of knight, usually crossbowmen, and largely limited to France from the reign of Charles VII (1422-61).

ARCHES, COURT OF THE, the ecclesiastical court of appeal for the province of Canterbury. It had its name from its location from the close of the thirteenth century in the church of St. Mary of the Arches in London.

ARCHIMANDRITE, in the Greek church the superior of one or more monasteries. His office corresponded to that of the abbot or abbot-general in the Latin church.

ARCHITECTURE, MEDIEVAL. See EARLY CHRISTIAN ART; BYZANTINE ART; ISLAMIC ART AND ARCHITECTURE; ROMANESQUE ART; GOTHIC ART; DECORATED GOTHIC; FLAMBOYANT; and RENAISSANCE ARCHITECTURE; as well as individual churches and architects.

ARCHPOET, a title given to several composers of

Goliardic verse. The best known of these was the versifier in the service of Archbishop Rainald of Dassel of Cologne (1159-67).

ARCHPRIEST, a priest who appeared in the fourth century and served as head of a college of presbyters in assisting or representing the bishop in the discharge of his liturgical and administrative responsibilities.

ARCOSOLIUM, term applied to a type of Christian tomb found in the catacombs built into a wall and surmounted with an arch. This type was common in Rome in the third century.

ARCULF, Frankish bishop of the late seventh century who gave a detailed account of the pilgrimage to the Holy Land to Adamnan, abbot of the monastery of Iona. Adamnan later incorporated this information into several of his own writings.

ARDENNES, WILD BOAR OF THE, William de la Marck, son of John I, count of La Marck and Aremberg, whom Emperor Maximilian ordered executed in 1485 for his many acts of brigandage.

ARDILLIERS, NOTRE DAME DES, a church and shrine at Saumur, France, near where Charlemagne founded a monastery. According to the story, the one monk who survived the destruction of the monastery by the Northmen fled to the spring of Ardilliers, carrying off with him a statue of Our Lady. A cult grew up around the statue.

ARDITI, ANDREA, a worker in gold and enamel who lived in Italy during the first half of the fourteenth century. He is best known for the bust of St. Zenobius and his miter in the cathedral of Florence.

ARENA-CHAPEL, a chapel erected in 1303-05 by Enrico Scrovegni in Padua on land that had once enclosed a Roman arena. One of Giotto's most renowned frescoes graces the structure.

AREOPAGITE, THE, the name given to the mystical writer Dionysius (fifth century?), so named because of an incorrect identification with the Dionysius converted by St. Paul's sermon on the Areopagus (Acts 17:34).

ARETHAS OF CAESAREA, d. c. 944, disciple of Photius, later archbishop of Caesarea. He ranked as one of the most distinguished of Greek theologians and exegetes. Contemporaries also considered him an authority on classical and patristic literature.

ARETINUS, GUIDO. *See* GUIDO OF AREZZO.

ARÉVALO, RODRIGUEZ SÁNCHEZ DE, d. 1470, studied law at Salamanca, served as secretary to the kings of Castile, then successively occupied several Spanish sees. He was a member of the Castilian delegation that attended the Council of Basel where he worked zealously for the cause of the papacy against that of the conciliarists. In his writings he discussed conciliarism and other ecclesiastical issues of the day.

AREZZO, city of north central Italy, the Roman Arretium, a flourishing center in the Middle Ages which fell to Florence in 1384. Medieval walls almost surround the city. Many fine structures from the fourteenth century enclose the splendid Piazza Grande, once the center of the city. The Gothic cathedral begun in 1286 is now completed. Of particular interest are the frescoes of Piero della Francesca (d. 1492) in the church of S. Francesco.

ARGENTEUIL, ABBEY OF, Benedictine abbey founded for women near Versailles some time between 650 and 675. Among its abbesses was Theotrade, a daughter of Charlemagne. Heloise studied at the abbey as a young girl. She later returned and became its abbess.

ARGYLL, county on the west coast of Scotland, invaded by Scots (Celts) from Ireland in the second century A.D. By the fourth century a kingdom known as Dalriada had emerged which continued until 844 when it was joined with the Picts of central Scotland. It was from this union that Scotland eventually evolved. The Vikings occupied the region from the tenth century until 1266 when they were expelled. Argyll then became part of the Scottish kingdom.

ARGYROPOULOS, JOHN, d. 1487, one of the most prominent Greek scholars to come to Italy from Constantinople. He first came as a member of the Greek delegation to the Council of Ferrara-Florence (1438–9). After the fall of Constantinople he made his home in Florence upon the invitation of Cosimo de' Medici. He later moved to Rome where he died. He made his principal contribution to the cause of humanism through his translation of Aristotle's works and his own eminence as a teacher.

ARGYROS, ISAAC, d. c. 1375, Greek monk, scientist, theologian, and religious polemicist. Besides theological works, he composed important astronomical treatises.

ARIALDO, ST., a courageous reformer who was slain in 1066 by agents of Bishop Guido of Milan because of his denunciation of simony and immorality among the clergy of the city.

ARIANISM, a heresy, originating with Arius (d. 336), priest of Alexandria, that denied the divinity of Christ and his co-eternity with the Father. In spite of its condemnation by the First Ecumenical Council of Nicaea in 325, the heresy remained a major threat to the church until the reign of Emperor Theodosius (d. 395). Constantine I was baptized by an Arian bishop, while several emperors openly endorsed its position regarding the nature of Christ. Through the efforts of Arian missionaries, above all those of Ulfilas (c. 340), several of the largest German tribes that entered the Roman empire, including the Visigoths, Vandals, and Ostrogoths, were Arians. Among these Germans, Arianism lived on until the close of the seventh century.

ARIBO, d. 1031, learned archbishop of Mainz and archchaplain of the empire. Because of the vigor with which he pushed the reform of the church, he often found himself involved in controversy with both ecclesiastical and imperial authorities. He was a learned and a prolific writer.

ARIBON, eleventh-century composer of music and musical theorist of the Netherlands. He composed a commentary on Guido of Arezzo's theories.

ARISTIDES OF ATHENS, Christian philosopher and apologist of the early second century who addressed an apology to Emperor Hadrian condemning him for his persecution of Christians. In this work he pointed out, first, the inadequacies of pagan religions and of Judaism as well, then praised the purity of Christian monotheism, and, finally, stressed the charity of Christians which alone preserved the world from the anger of God.

ARISTION, according to Papias as reported by Eusebius, a primary authority on the subject of traditions concerning Christ. He lived in the first century.

ARISTOBULUS, ST., presumably the recipient of greetings sent him by St. Paul (Rom. 16:10). A Spanish tradition says he became bishop of Britonia in Spain.

ARITHMETIC, one of the seven liberal arts which together with music, geometry, and astronomy made up the medieval quadrivium. This fourfold division of what the Middle Ages classified as mathematical sciences derived from the ancient Pythagoreans. The Middle Ages also retained the interest of Pythagoras in the theory and symbolism of numbers, as transmitted principally through the manuals which Boethius (d. c. 524) and Cassiodorus (d. c. 580) prepared on the subject.

ARI THORGILSSON, d. 1148, the earliest Icelandic writer of sagas. His only surviving work relates the history of Iceland from the appearance of the Norwegians c. 870 to 1120.

ARIUS, d. 336, learned and popular priest of Alexandria whose attack on the divine nature of Christ provoked such controversy among Christian theologians and prelates that the emperor Constantine I was constrained to convene the First Ecumenical Council at Nicaea (325) to resolve the matter. The council condemned the position taken by Arius and banished him to Illyricum, although influential supporters of his views, including Eusebius of Caesarea and Eusebius of Nicomedia, secured his reinstatement in 335.

ARLES, city in Provence situated on the Rhône delta, leading city of Gaul in the late Roman empire. Its first bishop was St. Trophimus (first century). In 417 the diocese became the primatial see of the province. Arles was the site of a number of church councils as well as a major center of Provençal culture. The famous Church of St. Trophime was begun in the eleventh century. In the tenth century the city became the capital of the kingdom of Arles.

ARLES, KINGDOM OF, name given to the state that appeared in 934 with the union of the kingdoms of Provence and Burgundy. As such the kingdom of Arles, also known as the kingdom of Burgundy, lay principally to the east of the Rhône river and extended as far north as Lorraine. In 1032, Rudolf III, its last independent ruler, bequeathed the kingdom to Conrad II of Germany although the German emperors never succeeded in fully establishing their authority over the country. French influence tended, instead, to replace the German, particularly from 1246 when Provence passed to Charles of Anjou, brother of Louis IX. Except for several eastern territories, which came into the hands of the counts of Savoy, all of the original kingdom had become subject to the French crown by 1378 when the emperor Charles IV relinquished his claim.

ARLES, SYNOD OF, first representative meeting of Christian bishops in the Western Roman empire. Constantine I convened the synod in 314 for the purpose of resolving the controversy over the date of Easter and, more important, to take a stand concerning the views of the Donatists. Bishops from 43 dioceses or their representatives attended the synod. The council confirmed the condemnation of Donatism that two earlier synods, one at Rome, the other in Africa, had pronounced. Another synod at Arles in 353 dealt with Arianism, that in 1234 with the Albigensian heresy, and a last in 1263 with the doctrines of Joachim of Fiore. In all three synods the doctrines before the council were condemned.

ARMAGH, county in north Ireland where tradition had it that St. Patrick erected a church and monastery c. 450. From this time Armagh was the religious center of the island. As was customary in early Ireland, abbots also served as bishops, which was probably the case with the abbot of the monastery at Armagh until c. 750. From 1152 Armagh was honored as one of the four metropolitan sees of Ireland. When Ireland passed under English control in 1215 and the archbishop of Canterbury was given jurisdiction over the Irish church, Armagh lost most of its independence and importance.

ARMAGH, THE BOOK OF, a codex from the eighth–ninth century which includes two lives of St. Patrick, the life of St. Martin of Tours by Sulpicius Severus, and a complete non-Vulgate text of the Latin New Testament.

ARMAGNAC, French county, once a part of Gascony, whose location in the frontier zone between Aquitaine, which the English possessed, and French-held Toulouse lent it special importance from the twelfth century during the long period of strife between England and France. In the tenth century its counts appeared as vassals of the dukes of Gascony. The greatest moment in the history of the county came during the years following the murder in 1407 of Louis duke of Orléans, the brother of the mad king Charles VI.

Louis's son married the daughter of Bernard VII of Armagnac, whereupon Bernard assumed the leadership of the Orléanist faction, now known as Armagnac, and made himself master of Paris and of the king until 1418 when the Burgundians gained control of the city and he was slain. The power of the Armagnacs declined rapidly after Bernard's death although the countship was not united with the French crown until 1497. Beyond being the name of the party that supported the cause of the dauphin (later Charles VII) against the English and Burgundians, the word "Armagnacs" also identified the rapacious Gascon mercenaries whom the count took into his service.

ARMAGNACS AND BURGUNDIANS. *See* ARMAGNAC.

ARMARIUM, also armadium, a small chest for sacred vessels in medieval churches which was suspended near the altar or kept in a recess in the wall. The word might also refer to a library or to the room where books were stored.

ARME HEINRICH, DER, poem by Hartmann von Aue (fl. 1190–1210), whose theme is that of a nobleman who was cured of his leprosy through the sacrifice of the daughter of one of his peasants. Her unselfishness brought home to him a realization of his own pride and general lack of virtue, whereupon he repented and eventually married the girl. The poem may have expressed Hartmann's own views concerning the shallowness of knightly ideals.

ARMENIA, kingdom of eastern Asia Minor over whose control the Byzantine empire and the Persians fought from the third century until the early seventh when the Arabs conquered the region. Persecution and martyrs came early to Armenia, said to be the oldest Christian state, and continued on through the greater part of its history as White Huns, Khazars, Arabs, Turks, and Mongols took up where Byzantium and Persia had left off. The country enjoyed a short period of autonomy under native rulers from

885 to 1046, was then briefly recovered by the Byzantine empire, but almost immediately lost to the Seljuk Turks. Many Armenians fled their country for Cilicia where they set up Little (Lesser) Armenia which enjoyed a troubled existence from 1080 until 1375 when it fell to the Mamluks of Egypt. A Little later Timur the Lame and his Mongols overran Greater Armenia and massacred a large part of the population. By the close of the Middle Ages, the entire region had fallen to the Ottoman Turks.

ARMENIA, CHRISTIANITY IN. The Armenians were converted to Christianity by Gregory the Illuminator who was consecrated bishop in 294. In the fifth century the Bible and liturgy were translated from Syriac to Armenian. While the Armenians took no part in the Council of Chalcedon (451), which condemned Monophysitism, some 50 years later they repudiated that council's action and adopted a Monophysite theology. The Armenians suffered severely at the hands of the country's many invaders, among these the Persians, Arabs, Mongols, and Turks, and much of their suffering was due to the steadfastness with which they clung to their faith. The church of Little Armenia recognized the authority of the Roman pope. In 1438 the Armenians sent representatives to the Council of Ferrara-Florence.

ARMENIAN LITERATURE. The Bible which was translated into Armenian in the fifth century established the standards for classical Armenian. The greater part of the country's literature consisted of lives of the saints and history, although the works of Aristotle appeared in translation as did the *Romance of Alexander*. The work by Moses of Khorni is the principal source for the history of pre-Christian Armenia. Of particular note is Catholicos Narses IV (d. 1172), prelate and poet of Little Armenia, whose literary style is unsurpassed in Armenian literature.

ARMORICA. *See* BRITTANY.

ARN (Arno), d. 821, Benedictine monk, abbot of a monastery in Flanders, who spent some years at Charlemagne's court in Aachen as a colleague of Alcuin. Charlemagne appointed him bishop of Salzburg (785), and for many years he constituted a major support of Carolingian power and diplomacy in Bavaria.

ARNALDUS AMALRICI (Arnaud-Amaury), d. 1225, Cistercian monk, abbot of several monasteries, the last that of Citeaux, a position that made him abbot general of the order. As papal legate he preached against the Albigenses in Languedoc and in 1209 led an army against members of the sect. Later as archbishop of Narbonne he came into bitter conflict with Simon de Montfort, principal leader of the Albigensian crusade. Again as papal legate in 1212, he commanded a contingent of French knights in the victory the Spanish won over the Moors at Las Navas de Tolosa.

ARNALDUS OF VILLANOVA (Arnaud de Vilanova), d. 1311, one of the leading physicians of the Middle Ages, studied at Montpellier and under Arabic scholars in Valencia. He taught at Montpellier, served as personal physician to several kings and popes, and left 70 medical treatises including some works he translated from the Arabic. Several of his mystical writings ran afoul of the inquisitorial tribunal.

ARNAUT DANIEL, Provençal troubadour of the twelfth century who lived in southern France but spent some time at the court of Richard I in England. Dante praised his talents (*Purgatorio*, XXVI, 117), as did Petrarch who called him "the great master of love."

ARNEBURG, powerful imperial fortress on the Elbe which the German kings began to use as early as the late tenth century as a bulwark against the westward movement of the Slavs.

ARNOBIUS, d. c. 327, a distinguished rhetorician, once a militant pagan and given to a licentious life, later converted to Christianity and became a leading apologist for that faith. His principal work, *Adversus Nationes,* supplies valuable information concerning ancient pagan beliefs and practices.

ARNOBIUS JUNIOR (the Younger), fifth-century African monk who attacked St. Augustine's doctrine of grace. His own writings suggest that his views were semi-Pelagian in character. They include commentaries on the Psalms, notes on the Gospels, and an anti-Monophysite treatise. The *Praedestinatus* has been attributed to him.

ARNOLD OF BONNEVAL (Marmoutier), d. after 1156, monk of Marmoutier, abbot of Bonneval in the diocese of Chartres, friend and acquaintance of many important personages including St. Bernard of Clairvaux of whom he left a biography. He also authored theological treatises and meditations.

ARNOLD OF BRESCIA, d. 1155, a student of Abelard's at Paris, canon regular of St. Augustine, and prior of the monastery in Brescia. His views that the church must return to the poverty of apostolic times, surrender its landholdings, and withdraw from secular affairs led to his banishment from Italy (1139), whence he made his way to France where he defended Abelard at the Council of Sens (1141). After this council had condemned Arnold, Pope Innocent II ordered him exiled and his writings burned. When the king, upon the insistence of St. Bernard of Clairvaux, expelled him from France, he went to Rome, made himself leader of a "republican" faction, seized control of the city, and for nine years governed it with the help of a senate organized after the ancient Roman model. In the end Pope Adrian IV excommunicated him and with the assistance of Frederick I Barbarossa, the Holy Roman emperor, had him condemned for heresy and executed.

ARNOLD OF LÜBECK, d. c. 1212, first abbot of the Benedictine monastery of St. John in Lübeck. He continued Helmold's *Chronicle of the Slavs* from 1172 to 1209 and, although inferior to Helmold as a historian, contributed valuable

information concerning the Third (1189–92) and Fourth (1202–4) Crusades as well as the struggle between Otto (IV) of Brunswick and Philip of Swabia over the German crown.

ARNOLFO DI CAMBIO, d. c. 1302, Italian architect and one of the greatest Italian sculptors, a pupil of Nicola Pisano whom he assisted with the sculpture on the pulpit in the cathedral of Siena. His most notable work as an architect, the design of the cathedral in Florence, marks him as a leading representative of the Gothic school in that city. He probably also designed the Baptistery and the Palazzo Vecchio. After 1296 he was occupied with the design and erection of the basic portion of Santa Maria del Fiore in Florence.

ARNULF OF CARINTHIA, d. 899, East Frankish king and last of the Carolingian emperors. He received Carinthia from his father, the king of Bavaria, whence his name. In 887 the East Frankish magnates who were disgusted with the weakness of Charles III (the Fat), renounced their allegiance to him and elected Arnulf. Arnulf retained control of Lorraine, defeated the Vikings, and, upon the plea of Pope Formosus, drove the duke of Spoleto from Rome. Pope Formosus crowned Arnulf in 896. Before Arnulf died, he had succeeded in persuading his magnates to accept the succession of his four-year-old son who is known in history as Louis the Child.

ARNULF OF GAP, ST., d. c. 1075, monk of Vêndome, for some years adviser to Pope Alexander II, later bishop of Gap (in Dauphiny) and a vigorous champion of Gregorian reform.

ARNULF OF LISIEUX, d. 1184, bishop of Lisieux who accompanied Louis VII on the Second Crusade (1147–49). He was successful in persuading French prelates to accept Alexander III as the legitimate pope following the death of Adrian IV, rather than Victor IV who had Frederick I Barbarossa's endorsement. In the controversy between Henry II and Thomas Becket, he favored the cause of the king. Arnulf left sermons, some poetry (epigrams), and letters, many of the latter being addressed to important people of the time.

ARNULF OF METZ, ST., d. 641, member of the Austrasian nobility, one of the principals who brought about the downfall of the Merovingian queen Brunhild, and a progenitor of the Carolingian dynasty through his son Ansegis. Ansegis married Begga, daughter of Pepin of Landen, and fathered Pepin of Heristal. Arnulf became bishop of Metz (c. 614) after his wife entered a convent. He eventually retired to an isolated place for the purpose of meditation and prayer.

ARNULF OF MILAN, d. 1077, a courageous ally of Pope Gregory VII in the pope's struggle with Henry IV of Germany over lay investiture. His scholarly history of the archbishops of Milan for the years 925 to 1077 constitutes a valuable source for the history of that troubled period.

ARPAD, d. 907, first grand prince of the Hungarians, who led his people in 895-6 to the region of Hungary when the Petchenegs drove them from lands they had earlier occupied in southern Russia. Arpad, who is called the founder of Hungary, established the dynasty of the Arpads which ruled Hungary in the male line until 1301.

ARQUEBUS, a firearm introduced in the fifteenth century. The weapon, a forerunner of the musket, was supported on a forked rest.

ARRAS, city in northern France, a bishop's seat in the sixth century, and a victim of Viking destruction in 880. About 900 it became a possession of Flanders, of the French crown in 1180, and served as the capital of Artois from 1237. In 1384 it passed to Philip the Bold, duke of Burgundy, after which date Burgundy and the kings of France and Germany quarreled for more than a century over its possession. Only in 1640 was it firmly reunited with France. Its wealth was based upon a textile industry which flourished especially during the twelfth and thir-

teenth centuries. Arras was famed for the splendor of its tapestries.

ARRAS, PEACE OF, treaty agreed to in 1435 by Charles VII of France and Philip the Good of Burgundy which severed the Anglo-Burgundian alliance and won Charles the neutrality of Burgundy during the closing years of the Hundred Years' War. The price which Charles paid for the treaty was the surrender to Philip of certain towns on the Somme (subject to redemption) and personal exemption of the duke from the obligation of giving the king homage.

ARRAS, TREATY OF, agreement in 1482 between Louis XI of France and representatives of the Netherlands regarding the status of Burgundy when its ruler, Mary of Burgundy, should die. It provided that Margaret of Austria, daughter of Archduke Maximilian (later Emperor Maximilian I), the widower of Mary, was to marry the dauphin (later Charles VIII), and bring to France as her dowry the provinces of Artois and Franche-Comté. When Charles VIII eventually married Anne of Brittany, the treaty became void.

ARS ANTIQUA (ancient art), term applied to polyphony of the period c. 1160 to 1325 when it was witnessing its early development. The term was first used by Philippe de Vitry (d. 1361) in a treatise entitled *Ars Nova* in which he described the "old technique" of composing which he and the disciples of the "new style" had abandoned. The center of this new musical trend was the cathedral of Notre Dame in Paris.

ARS DICTAMINIS, name given to the medieval art of epistolary composition which had its historical origin in the rhetoric of the trivium but which flourished during the eleventh and twelfth centuries in conjunction with a revival of classical studies. It encouraged the collection of letters, some of these of historical value, although the majority were purely stylistic models intended for notaries, scribes, and for teachers of rhetoric. Since the emphasis was almost exclusively on formal style, their literary value was negligible even though they contributed to the refinement of Latin as a language of scholarship and diplomacy.

ARSENIUS AUTORIANUS, d. 1273, monk, appointed patriarch of Constantinople in 1261 by Theodore II Lascaris, but removed by Michael VIII Palaeologus in 1266 when he excommunicated the emperor for blinding John IV Lascaris, Theodore's son, and seizing the throne. He died in exile. Adherents of Arsenius (Arsenites) were joined by others who objected to Michael's policy of seeking to end the schism with Rome. They eventually prevailed, and in 1310 the body of Arsenius was brought to Constantinople and buried in Hagia Sophia.

ARS MORIENDI, the art of dying, title given to a genre of late medieval literature and by extension to a related art whose theme was the struggle between angels and the evil spirits over the soul of a dying person. The purpose of the literature was usually devotional and was intended at least initially for the clergy, to instruct them in caring for the dying.

ARS NOVA (new art), the more diversified musical arrangements from the fourteenth century that had their name from a musical treatise by Philippe de Vitry (c. 1320) which bore that title. More narrowly, *ars nova* designated French music that was composed between c. 1320 and c. 1410. [*See* ARS ANTIQUA.]

ARS PRAEDICANDI (art of preaching), literary genre concerned with the art of preaching that grew in importance from the early thirteenth century as preaching came to assume a matter of greater importance in the work of the clergy. Manuals on the subject emphasized both the spiritual lessons the preacher might seek to impart to his flock as well as the means he might employ to improve his oratorical talents.

ARSUF, ancient town of Palestine on the coast a few miles north of Jerusalem. It was the site of a major victory which Richard I of England gained over Saladin in 1191 during the Third Crusade (1189-92). Though badly outnumbered, Richard here proved himself an able tactician in the use of infantry and knights.

ART, EARLY CHRISTIAN. *See* EARLY CHRISTIAN ART.

ARTEMON (Artemas), an Adoptionist heretic of the third century who preached that Christ was only a man although he excelled all the Prophets.

ARTEVELDE, JACOB VAN, d. 1345, burgher leader of Ghent and captain general of a league of Flemish cities which he dominated from 1338 until his death in an urban insurrection. After a brief attempt at neutrality in the Hundred Years' War, he concluded an alliance with England upon which country the Flemish textile industry depended for its wool. The other towns of Flanders accepted his leadership and the count fled to France. In time many Flemish began to object to Artevelde's despotic rule and to his apparent aim of replacing French sovereignty with that of the English. (He had Edward III recognized as king of France and thus suzerain of Flanders.) Artevelde was slain in the course of an insurrection that erupted in Ghent.

ARTEVELDE, PHILIP VAN, d. 1382, captain general of Ghent, the son of Jacob van Artevelde. In the struggle between the "Goods," that is, the aristocracy and propertied classes who supported the count of Flanders, and the "Bads," the textile workers led by the weavers, he put himself at the head of the latter, and was defeated and slain in the battle of Roosebeke by the French under Olivier de Clisson.

ARTHUR, duke of Brittany, son of Geoffrey, grandson of Henry II of England, married the heiress of Brittany and thus acquired the duchy. When after Richard I's death in 1199 Arthur's claim to the English throne was passed over in favor of that of his uncle John, he allied himself with Philip II Augustus of France who invested him with all of Richard's fiefs in France. The nobles of Anjou, Maine, and Touraine recognized Arthur as their lord, but he fell into the hands of John in 1202 and was probably murdered (1203). John's part in Arthur's murder led to a rapid deterioration of his position in Normandy and Anjou and the early loss of those provinces to Philip.

ARTHUR III, d. 1458, duke of Brittany, earlier earl of Richmond (Richemont), fought with Henry V at Agincourt (1415), then joined Charles VII (Dauphin) who made him constable of France and entrusted him with clearing the English from Normandy and Brittany. In 1436 Arthur captured Paris from the English and later had a major role in winning Normandy for France.

ARTHUR FESTIVALS, popular celebrations in honor of the legendary King Arthur which made their appearance in Wales toward the close of the eleventh century.

ARTHURIAN COURTS, festive gatherings of members of the aristocratic classes in the high Middle Ages commemorative of King Arthur and the Round Table. The term also applied to the halls where such gatherings took place.

ARTHURIAN LEGEND. A British King Arthur was mentioned by Nennius (c. 826), praised by Geoffrey of Monmouth (1136) in his history of the kings of Great Britain, and glorified by authors of courtly romance. If Arthur lived, he was a British warrior who successfully opposed the invading Angles and Saxons c. 500. Historical or not, King Arthur became the inspiration of one of the major cycles of romances in medieval literature. The source of the Arthurian legend, which has been traced to Wales, owed its dissemination from the eleventh century to the work of Bretons and to the appearance of Geoffrey's *Historia Regum Britanniae*. In 1155 the Norman poet Wace translated this work into French and added the story of the Round Table.

Arthur and the theme of the Round Table proved equally popular on the continent where the most famous versions were those of Chrétien de Troyes, Wolfram von Eschenbach, and Gottfried von Strassburg. Later in England appeared *Sir Gawain and the Green Knight* and the *Morte d'Arthur* of Sir Thomas Malory.

ARTICLES OF FAITH, revealed supernatural truths considered so fundamental as to require acceptance by all Christians, namely, those contained in the Apostles' Creed.

ARTOIS, ancient province of France, a possession of Flanders from 932 but acquired by Philip II of France in 1180 as part of his wife's dowry. Louis IX gave it to his son Robert as an appanage (1237), from whose descendants it passed to the county of Burgundy in the early fourteenth century. In 1477 it became the possession of the house of Hapsburg through the marriage of Maximilian to Mary, the daughter of Charles the Bold of Burgundy, who was its heiress.

ARTOKLASIA, a service in the Greek church that concluded vespers and involved the blessing of several loaves of bread and some wine. These were then distributed to the faithful who were in attendance.

ARTS, FACULTY OF THE, the instructors who composed the teaching staff in the division of the medieval university concerned with the arts; also these instructors when acting in an official capacity.

ARTS, LIBERAL, the seven branches of learning that traditionally made up the course of studies in medieval schools: grammar, rhetoric, dialectic, arithmetic, geometry, astronomy, and music. These seven were divided into the trivium and quadrivium. [*See* GRAMMAR; RHETORIC; DIALECTIC; ARITHMETIC; GEOMETRY; ASTRONOMY; MUSIC.]

ARUNDEL, EARLS OF. If the earldom of Arundel (in Sussex) was vested in the owner of the castle of Arundel, the first earl was Roger de Montgomery who came to England from France in 1067. In 1102 the honors and estates were forfeited to the crown, then in 1138 released to William D'Aubigny who married Adelaide, the widow of Henry I. In 1243 Arundel castle passed to John Fitzalan, but it appears that Richard Fitzalan was the first to be actually created earl of Arundel (c. 1289), instead of simply earl at Arundel. His son Edmund was executed in 1326 by partisans of Queen Isabella, Edward II's consort. His grandson Thomas became archbishop of Canterbury in 1396. His eldest grandson Richard, the earl, was involved in a conspiracy against Richard II and was executed (1397). Henry IV restored the family titles and estates to his son Thomas. In 1433 John Fitzalan secured the earldom and it continued as a possession of that family into the sixteenth century.

ARUNDEL, THOMAS, d. 1414, bishop of Ely (1374), archbishop of York (1388), and archbishop of Canterbury (1396), was banished in 1397 as royal chancellor by Richard II, then returned to England in 1399 to serve the new king Henry IV in the same capacity. He had joined the barons who opposed Richard. Arundel was among those instrumental in securing enactment of a statute in 1401 that authorized the execution of Lollards.

ASADI, the poetical name of perhaps two poets of Tus who lived in the eleventh century, the one Abu Nasr Ahmed ibn Mansur, the other his son Ali. The father may have composed poetry suggestive of Provençal *tensos,* while Ali composed an epic poem whose theme and style anticipated those of the later Persian epic.

ASAPH, ST., Welsh saint of the sixth century, head of the monastery of Llanelwy, later known as St. Asaph, and first bishop of that see.

ASBUKA (Azbuka), a word composed of the two initial letters of the Cyrillic alphabet and having a significance similar to the English ABC.

ASCANIANS, one of the powerful princely dynasties of Germany in the high Middle Ages. Its most renowned member was Albert the Bear (d. 1170), count of Ballenstädt, who founded the margravate of Brandenburg. The family's strength lay in Brandenburg and eastern Saxony.

ASCELLION (Asselino, Anselmo, Ascelin), d. 1254, Dominican scholar of Lombardy who headed a mission sent by Pope Innocent IV in 1245 to Persia in the hope of converting the Mongol khan Melik Saleh. Since the Tartars demanded the submission of the pope, the mission failed, although Ascellino did some preaching in Persia before returning to Europe in 1248.

ASCENSION, FEAST OF, a liturgical feast commemorating the ascension of the risen Christ into heaven which took place 40 days after Easter (Mark 16:19; Luke 24:51; Acts I:1–11). The feast was being celebrated as early as the close of the fourth century.

ASEITY, a term first employed by medieval theologians to refer to the property by which a being exists of and from itself *(a se),* without being dependent upon any outside cause. Only God, in their judgment, could possess such a power. Not only was he uncaused by any other, but he was all-sufficient in himself.

ASEN, ASEN AND PETER, Bulgarian lords who c. 1187 forced the Byzantine emperor Isaac II Angelus to recognize the autonomy of Bulgaria. [*See* BULGARIA.]

ASGAARD (Asgard), in Nordic folklore, the dwelling place of the gods. It was often identified with Valhalla.

A'SHA, AL-, d. after 625, blind Arab poet, active in political affairs in Persia and Arabia, and author of panegyrics, one in praise of Mohammed. Of some 300 works he is said to have written, only four or five are known to be extant. The most important of these examines Moslem sects and heresies and sets forth the orthodox doctrine.

ASH'ARITES, followers of the theologian-philosopher Abu'l Ali Al-Ash'ari (d. c. 935) who defended Sunnite doctrine with appeals to both revelation and reason. Their views, influenced by the teaching of Al-Ghazali, their most prominent member, provided the substance of Sunnite doctrine from the twelfth century.

ASHER BEN YEHIEL, d. 1327, Jewish rabbi and codifier, fled Germany to escape persecution and moved to Spain where he was made rabbi of Toledo. His primary interest was in the Talmud, and he was a determined opponent of the study of philosophy.

ASH WEDNESDAY (*dies cinerum,* day of ashes), the first day of Lent when the priest signed the foreheads of the faithful with ashes or sprinkled ashes on their heads in order to remind them of the penance God expected of sinners. The rite dates from at least the eighth century. The formula recited at the sprinkling of the ashes served to remind the recipient of the need to repent since death and judgment were inevitable.

ASKOLD (Hoskuldr), Swedish chieftain who captured Kiev c. 860 but failed in his attempt to take Constantinople in 864. He was slain by Prince Oleg in 882.

ASLAUG, according to the *Volsunga Saga,* the daughter of Sigurd (Siegfried) and Brynhild (Brunhild). She married Ragnar and became the mother of the royal family of Norway.

ASMA'I, AL-, d. 828, Arab philologist, grammarian, and lexicographer. He was a popular teacher and poet at the court of Harun al-Rashid. Most of the existing collections of pre-Islamic poetry were compiled by him.

ASPAR, d. 471, master of the soldiers, of Alan descent, in the service of the Eastern Roman emperors Marcian and Leo I. He failed to expel the Vandals from Africa, was more successful in fighting the Persians, but suffered defeat at the hands of Attila and the Huns before Constantinople in 443. In 457 he was chiefly responsible for the accession of Leo to the throne, but the emperor came to mistrust him and brought in Isaurians from Anatolia as a counterforce to the Gothic mercenaries under Aspar's command. He and his eldest son were treacherously assassinated in the palace.

ASPER, name given to various Byzantine and Balkan coins which were in use in the twelfth century.

ASPERGES, liturgical rite, dating from at least the tenth century, in which the priest sprinkled the faithful with holy water before the principal Mass on Sunday. During the Easter season the antiphon, instead of the usual *Asperges me,* opened with the words *Vidi aquam.*

ASPERSION, a rite involving the sprinkling with holy water which symbolized a cleansing from sin. The rite was a common one in the Christian church.

ASS, usually a picture or engraving depicting this animal with which critics of Christianity in the early centuries ridiculed its worship of God and Christ as that of an ass or one begotten from an ass. In Christian symbolism the ass appears as the symbol of ignorance or laziness.

ASSANDUN, BATTLE OF, battle fought some 50 miles northeast of London on October 18, 1016, in which the Danes under Canute (Cnut) defeated the English led by Edmund II Ironside.

ASSART, a tract of land cleared and added to the manor.

ASSASSINS, European name for the members of a politico-religious Moslem sect, a branch of the Ismalians, which was founded in the late eleventh century in Persia by Hasan ibn Sabbah (d. 1124) in the mountain fortress of Alamut. The order which was especially strong in Persia and Syria employed assassination as a means of preventing the rise of ambitious men to power. The Mongols destroyed the Persian Assassins in 1256, while the Mamluk sultan Baibars suppressed those in Egypt in 1272. The grand master of the order, Sheikh al-Jabal, was known in Western Europe as the Old Man of the Mountain.

ASSER (Asker), JOHN, d. 909, learned monk of St. David's, one of a group of scholars and churchmen whom Alfred the Great invited to his court for the purpose of raising the educational level of both court and country. Alfred rewarded Asser with several monasteries and some time before 900 appointed him bishop of Sherborne. Asser authored a valuable biography of Alfred and also assisted him with some of the translations which the king undertook.

ASSES, FEAST OF, a festival dating from the eleventh century when it consisted of a metrical dramatic dialogue during which Prophets of the Old Testament foretold the birth of Christ. The festival's name derived from the presence of Barlaam and his Ass in the procession of individuals which made up the *dramatis personae*. In time the role of Barlaam and the Ass developed into a separate episode of mystery play.

ASSESSORS, men trained in ecclesiastical law and theology who advised prelates or judges on giving judgment in causes concerning orthodoxy or in the trial of persons charged with heresy.

ASSISI, town of Umbria in central Italy, made famous as the home of St. Francis (d. 1226). Two Gothic churches, a lower and an upper structure, were erected above the saint's tomb. Frescoes by Cimabue, Giotto, and other artists decorate the churches. Two miles below Assisi is the late Renaissance church of Santa Maria degli Angeli which was built around the little chapel of Portiuncula which Francis used as his headquarters.

ASSIZE, name given to meetings of vassals with their feudal suzerain in twelfth-century England and Normandy. The name might also refer to the decrees that the king issued following such meetings; also, in the next century, to a court and its group of jurors.

ASSIZE OF CLARENDON. *See* CLARENDON, ASSIZE OF.

ASSIZE OF NORTHAMPTON. *See* NORTHAMPTON, ASSIZE OF.

ASSIZES OF JERUSALEM, a collection of laws and legal treatises compiled in the thirteenth century for the administration of the Crusading Kingdom of Jerusalem and of Cyprus. The laws attached particular importance to the court of the vassals, probably for the purpose of protecting the aristocratic class from the absolutist ambitions of Frederick II of Germany (d. 1250) and his agents in Cyprus.

ASSUMPTION OF THE BLESSED VIRGIN MARY, a liturgical feast commemorating the assumption of Mary's body into heaven. It may have originated in the fourth century since first mention of it appears in certain New Testament apocrypha from that time. By the end of the seventh century the feast had become widely known.

ASSYRIAN CHRISTIANS, a small group of Christians so called because of their supposed descent from the Assyrians of Nineveh. According to their tradition, they owed their conversion to the Apostle Thomas although the earliest firm reference to them dates from 431 when they gave refuge to Nestorius following his condemnation at the Council of Ephesus. They adopted, or already held, a Nestorian Christianity.

ASTERIUS OF AMASEA, d. c. 410, learned writer and lawyer of Pontus, later metropolitan of Amasea. His homilies have a historical value beyond their scriptural importance because of their numerous references to contemporary events and persons. His writings establish, for example, the fact that the early church venerated images.

ASTERIUS OF CAPPADOCIA, d. c. 341, Greek sophist, pupil of Lucian of Antioch, later a

Christian convert and a friend of Arius who drew upon Asterius's writings to support his own views concerning the nature of Christ. While Asterius's exegetical works have disappeared, his other writings, commentaries and homilies on the Psalms, serve to establish him as an influential preacher and theologian.

ASTRONOMY, one of the seven liberal arts and one of the four comprising the quadrivium. Knowledge of medieval astronomy continued to be based upon the geocentric system expounded by Ptolemy in the *Almagest* despite growing realization of its inadequacies. Until the thirteenth century when Western scholars assumed the lead in astronomical study, Moslem scholars such as Al-Battani (d. 929) achieved significant progress through observations of their own and the working out of new astronomical measurements and tables. The best known of these were the *Toledan Tables* edited by Al-Zarqali (d. c. 1087) which the *Alfonsine Tables* superseded c. 1270. What inspired continued search beyond normal human curiosity was the need for additional information to serve astrological and nautical purposes and for a reform of the calendar. Tangible results included a marked improvement of the astrolabe and the research of scholars such as Omar Khayyam (d. c. 1132), Robert Grosseteste (d. 1253), and Roger Bacon (d. c. 1292), which made possible the Gregorian Calendar (1582). Toward the close of the Middle Ages Nicole Oresme (d. 1382), among other scientists, was proposing the earth's diurnal rotation.

ASTURIAS, northwestern province of Spain whose name is derived from that of the Iberian people who occupied the region. The area fell to the Visigoths in the early fifth century, but the Moors were never able to conquer it. It served as a haven for refugee Christian nobles who there created the first Christian kingdom in Spain and from there organized an offensive drive against the Moors. The successors of King Alfonso I (739–57) succeeded in taking Galicia, Leon, and parts of Castile, Navarre, and Vizcaya from the Moors. In the tenth century the capital was moved from Oviedo to Leon, and three centuries later the country was united with the kingdom of Castile.

ASYLUM, RIGHT OF, a right of ancient Hebrew and pagan origin and recognized by most sects, including Islam, which invested churches, shrines, and their immediate vicinity with the character of places of refuge for criminals and for those pursued by officials of the state. [*See* SANCTUARY, RIGHT OF.]

ATABEG, originally a title used to address the teacher of a Turkish prince, later the title of a Persian emir of some importance; also, with the Mamluks of Egypt, a commander-in-chief.

ATAULF (Ataulphus), d. 415, Visigothic king (410–15), the brother-in-law of Alaric who took over as leader of the tribe when that great chieftain died. He led the Visigoths from Italy into southern Gaul. He had married Galla Placidia, the sister of the Western emperor Honorius whom the Goths had carried off captive from Rome when they sacked the city in 410. Ataulf was eventually forced out of Gaul into Spain and assassinated at Barcelona.

ATHANAGILD, d. 567, Visigothic king of Spain who ceded part of southern Spain to Justinian I, the Byzantine emperor, in return for the aid he had received in deposing his predecessor. He broke with the pro-Arian Christianity of the Visigoths and made peace with the Roman hierarchy. His court at Toledo was probably the most splendid in western Europe. His daughters Brunhild and Galswintha married grandsons of Clovis, king of the Franks, who were the rulers of Austrasia and Neustria.

ATHANARIC, d. 381, Visigothic chieftain who in 376 received permission from the Roman emperor Valens to take his people across the Danube in order to escape the oncoming Huns. He was a pagan and conducted a persecution of Christians. He died in Constantinople.

ATHANASIAN CREED, a doctrinal formula emphasizing the Trinity of God and the dual nature of Christ, laying stress on both his full and perfect divinity as well as his full and perfect humanity. It also introduced a list of the most important events in the life of Christ. The creed was once attributed to St. Athanasius (d. 373) but is now believed to have been the work of several authors of the fifth and sixth centuries.

ATHANASIUS I, patriarch of Constantinople, 1289–93, 1304–10, monk and priest who was advanced to the position of patriarch by Emperor Andronicus II. So severe did he show himself in matters of discipline that opposition eventually forced his resignation, although popular demand later had him restored.

ATHANASIUS, ST., d. 373, a leading church father of the Eastern church, came into prominence at the Council of Nicaea (325) as secretary to Alexander, patriarch of Alexandria, whom he assisted in defense of the doctrine of the Incarnation against Arius. Later as patriarch of Alexandria (328) he became the principal target of Arian persecution and was five times forced into exile by Arian prelates who had the ear of the emperor. He spent the first of these exiles in the West where he promoted the monastic ideal, a mission he further advanced through his *Life of St. Anthony*. The issue that evoked the bulk of his voluminous writings was the position of the Arians concerning the nature of Christ, namely, that of questioning his divine nature. His greatest doctrinal work is entitled *Discourses Against the Arians*.

ATHANASIUS, ST., d. 1003, the Athonite, a monk in Bithynia who migrated to Mount Athos where he founded in 961 the first of the monasteries located there. He eventually became abbot general of the communities on the Mount which at his death numbered 58.

ATHAULF. *See* ATAULF.

ATHELSTAN (Aethelstan), king of Wessex and England, 924–39, son of Edward the Elder, a favorite grandchild of Alfred the Great. He was one of the leading princes of western Europe, ruled over the greater part of England, and was recognized as overlord in Wales and southern Scotland. In 937 he defeated a powerful Scottish-Irish invasion at Brunanburh. He was generous to the church. Several of his sisters married French and German monarchs.

ATHENAGORAS, Christian apologist of the second century who founded a school of philosophy in Alexandria. He addressed an apology to the emperor Marcus Aurelius in which he denied as calumnies different charges brought against the Christians. His description of pagan ritual and worship provides valuable information concerning the nature of the paganism of the period.

ATHENS, was captured although not sacked by Alaric and the Visigoths in 395. It remained a provincial capital of the Byzantine empire until 1204 when, with the creation of the Latin Empire of Constantinople in the aftermath of the Fourth Crusade, it passed to a French noble from Franche-Comté. During the century of French rule that followed, the duchy of Athens enjoyed great prosperity while its institutions grew increasingly French. In 1311 the duchy fell to a band of Catalan adventurers who devastated the region, and Athens soon lost its importance as a cultural center and its prosperity as well. In 1388 Athens became the possession of the ruler of Corinth, a Florentine noble, and enjoyed a few years of relative prosperity before falling to the Ottoman Turks in 1458.

ATHIS AND PROPHILIAS, two close friends, the story of whose deep devotion to each other was carried from the Orient to the West where it reappeared in such places as the *Gesta Romanorum* and Boccaccio.

ATHOS, MOUNT, a desolate mountain at the

eastern end of the Chalcidic peninsula in the northern Aegean which began to attract hermits possibly as early as the fourth century. The first organized community, called Lavra, was established by St. Athanasius the Athonite in 963. His rule, based on those of St. Basil and St. Theodore the Studite, became uniform throughout the area. In 1045 women, even female animals, were ordered excluded from the mountain.

ATLAKVIDA, an ancient eddic song which contained much of the matter later presented in the *Nibelungenlied*.

ATLAMAL, an eddic song less ancient than the *Atlakvida* but handling the same theme although in a more general manner. [*See* ATLAKVIDA.]

ATLI, Nordic form of Etzel (Attila).

ATRIUM, also called paradise, an open place or court located in the entrance of a church. It might contain a fountain or well where the faithful could wash their hands before entering. Pilgrims and penitents might take their station in this area, and it was also used for a place of burial.

ATTAINDER, BILL OF, an act of Parliament which ordered the punishment, usually execution, of a person who had not been formally arraigned and tried. It was first employed in 1312 as a procedure intended to bypass the courts where it might be difficult to secure condemnation of the person charged because of his great influence or that of his aristocratic friends.

ATTALEIATES, MICHAEL, Byzantine statesman and historian who for many years occupied the highest judicial post in the empire. He left an account of the events that took place during the period 1034 to 1079.

ATTALUS, puppet Western Roman emperor whom Alaric I, leader of the Visigoths, appointed in 409 to replace Honorius who was holed up in Ravenna. When Attalus forbade Alaric to send an army to Africa, Alaric deposed him. In 414 Alaric's brother-in-law Ataulf again appointed him emperor, but later abandoned him. Honorius exiled him to Lipara.

ATTAR, FARID UD-DIN, d. c. 1230, Persian mystic and poet who busied himself for almost 40 years with collecting the verses and sayings of the Sufi saints. The most noted of his own poems, *Mantiq ut-Tair* (Language of the Birds), presents in allegory the seven stages of Sufism.

ATTICUS, d. 425, patriarch of Constantinople, a bitter opponent of St. John Chrysostom, although he relented after Chrysostom's death and readmitted his name to the diptychs. Emperor Theodosius II extended the patriarch's authority over the whole of Illyria and the "Provincia Orientalis."

ATTILA, d. 453, co-ruler of the Huns from 434 to 445 with his brother Bleda whom he then killed. Shortly after the Eastern Roman Emperor Marcian had cut off the tribute Constantinople had been paying the Huns, Attila led a huge army composed largely of German and Slavic mercenaries from his headquarters in Hungary westward into Gaul. There in 451 he suffered defeat on the Mauriac plain, several miles from Châlons-sur-Marne, at the hands of the Roman general Aetius and his army of Visigoths, Burgundians, and Franks. The following year he invaded Italy but returned to Hungary following a conference with Pope Leo I and a delegation of Roman senators, for what particular reasons no one knows. He died in his bed. [*See* HUNS.]

ATTO OF MILAN, d. c. 1085, canonist, cardinal, and archbishop (1072), at first a staunch supporter of Pope Gregory VII, later an adherent of Henry IV of Germany in their controversy over lay investiture. His collection of moral and canonical decrees (*Breviarium*), one of the first of its kind, was intended to provide Gregory's reform program with a legal foundation.

ATTO OF VERCELLI, d. 961, theologian and canonist, bishop of Vercelli, who for several years served as chancellor to Lothair II, king of France. He was a scholar of remarkable erudition. He left pastoral and exegetical writings, letters, and sermons.

AUBRY DE MONDIDIER, according to legend the name of a knight who was murdered c. 1371 by Richard de Macaire. In a contest with the knight's dog to ascertain whether he was guilty or not, Macaire was mortally wounded, whereupon he confessed his crime. The incident proved a popular theme in medieval literature.

AUBUSSON, PIERRE D', d. 1503, grand master of the Order of St. John of Jerusalem (1476) and cardinal (1489). In 1489 he valiantly defended Rhodes against a formidable attack by Sultan Mohammed II and the Turks. Despite the renown his exploits gained him, he failed in his efforts to arouse Europe to a crusade against the Turks. He was created a cardinal in 1489 by Pope Innocent VIII when he turned over to the pope Djem, brother of Sultan Bajazet II, who had fled to him for safety.

AUCASSIN AND NICOLETTE, Old French story of the late twelfth or early thirteenth century, partly prose, partly verse, which told of the love of a Christian count's son for a Saracen ex-slave who turned out in the end to be of aristocratic birth. It is preserved in a manuscript that contains the music to which the verses were to be sung.

AUCH, city of southwestern France, in Gascony, an important city of Roman Gaul, the see of a bishopric in the fourth century. A Benedictine abbey was founded there by Count Bernard Armagnac in the tenth century. Auch served as the capital of Armagnac.

AUDIANI, a Christian sect of the fourth century that withdrew from the church because it found the clergy too secularized and lacking in spiritual dedication.

AUDI BENIGNE CONDITOR, Lenten hymn, once attributed to Gregory the Great (590–604), but probably composed in the ninth century.

AUDIENTES, from the Latin meaning "hearers" and referring to those who wished to be baptized and were now at the first stage in their classification as catechumens.

AUDITOR, a clerk, trained in law and an official of a court, whose duty it was to hear causes before they were submitted to a regular court.

AUGSBURG, city of Swabia, provincial capital of the Roman province of Raetia, occupied by the Franks in 536 and a bishop's seat c. 600. Charlemagne invested the bishop with the power of a count. This authority was restricted in 1156, and in 1276 the city was created a free imperial city. Augsburg's prosperity was based on the trade, principally in linen and fustian cloth, that passed through it southward across the Alps to Milan and Venice.

AUGUSTALIS (Augustarius), gold coin minted by Frederick II of Germany in 1231. This was the first gold coin to be struck in Western Europe.

AUGUSTINE, ST., d. 430, leading Christian theologian of the Western world, was born at Tagaste in north Africa in 354 to the sainted Monica and a pagan father. According to his *Confessions* which he drew up at the age of 45, he wasted his restless youth in dissolute living, while his search for truth was taking him first to Manichaeism, next to skepticism, then to neo-Platonism, and finally, through the influence of St. Ambrose, to Christianity. He met Ambrose in Milan where he had taken employment as a rhetorician. He was baptized in 387, took up a monastic life for a short time, became a priest, then in 395 was consecrated bishop of Hippo. His death came about 35 years later as the Vandals were laying siege to Hippo.

Augustine's voluminous writings, which include 500 sermons and 200 letters, treat in definitive fashion almost every phase of Christian faith and morals although not in the systematic manner of Aquinas. Much of what he wrote he felt obliged to compose in order to defend orthodoxy against the views of such contemporary heretical groups as the Donatists, Manichaeans, and Pelagians. Perhaps a heritage of his earlier skepticism appeared in his distrust of sensory and material knowledge, which together with the influence of neo-Platonism and the miraculous nature of his own conversion left him convinced that all truth was spiritual, that it derived from God who was truth incarnate, and that the acceptance of truth (faith) was dependent upon God's grace. [*See* AUGUSTINIANISM.] For this reason Augustine devoted much attention to the study of God, to man's soul, knowledge of which would advance his knowledge of God since this was a reflection of the divine. (Augustine may be considered a founder of Christian mysticism.) For Augustine, therefore, truth was a good which the God-fearing man found within himself, in his soul, and this truth, a spark of the divine truth, would bring him in communion with his maker and provide him with peace and happiness. In the *City of God,* Augustine's best-known work, he presents the continuous struggle in history symbolically as between two cities, a city of those who do God's will, on the one hand, and a city of the forces of unbelief, on the other, intermingled and coexisting here on earth, but fated to be completely and irrevocably separated at the end of time. (For his influence upon monasticism, *see* AUGUSTINE, RULE OF.)

AUGUSTINE OF CANTERBURY, ST., d. 604, first archbishop of Canterbury, monk and prior of St. Andrews in Rome whom Pope Gregory the Great sent to Britain with some 30 companions to convert the pagan Angles and Saxons. Augustine reached Kent in 597, converted Ethelbert, king of Kent, and, contrary to Gregory's instructions, established his headquarters at Canterbury, Ethelbert's capital, rather than at London. He built Christ Church cathedral and an abbey outside the city wall later known as St. Augustine's. He failed in his efforts to persuade the leaders of the Celtic church in Britain to adopt Roman practices in matters of liturgy, discipline, and the date of Easter.

AUGUSTINE NOVELLUS, BL., d. 1309, jurist, served Manfred, king of Sicily, as chancellor. After Manfred's death (d. 1266), he became an Augustinian brother, later a priest, papal legate under Boniface VIII, and prior general of his order.

AUGUSTINE, RULE OF ST., a series of twelve chapters which St. Augustine drew up for his monastery at Hippo. In these treatises he placed special stress on the love of God and of neighbor, and recommended respect for authority, care of the sick, and self-discipline as virtues essential to community life. The Fourth Lateran Council (1215) declared this series of chapters to constitute the official Rule of St. Augustine. Some writers insist that Augustine expressed his views concerning monastic life in a letter to a community of nuns regarding virtues that women dedicated to the religious life should strive to attain. Other scholars trace his rule to two sermons in which he described and defended the monastic character of the life he and his clergy were living.

AUGUSTINIAN CANONESSES. *See* CANONESSES REGULAR OF ST. AUGUSTINE.

AUGUSTINIAN CANONS (Austin Canons or Canons Regular). *See* CANONS REGULAR OF ST. AUGUSTINE.

AUGUSTINIANISM, school of thought and theology that accepted the Christian neo-Platonism of St. Augustine and subscribed to his views concerning the primacy of faith and the supernatural nature of truth and reality. It recognized truth as inseparable from revelation and dependent upon God's grace for attainment. While reason was important, it performed the subordinate role of furnishing a fuller understanding of faith, as expressed in the formula made famous by St.

Anselm of Bec (d. 1109) but first employed by Augustine, namely, *credo ut intelligam* (I believe that I may understand). By means of his reason man can know the sensible world, but in order to bridge the gulf between this natural world and God he requires divine grace. This grace will motivate his will to seek a greater understanding of truth, attainment of which will ultimately come through divine illumination. Although Augustine did not accord philosophy a place apart from theology, later Augustinianism appealed to a philosophy based upon Plato as opposed to Thomism which had its foundation in Aristotle. Augustinianism dominated medieval thought until Aquinas (d. 1274), after whose appearance it continued chiefly in the writings of Franciscan scholastics.

AUGUSTINIANS (Austin Friars or Hermits), members of a mendicant religious order, also known as the Order of Hermits of St. Augustine, which honored St. Augustine as their spiritual father. Rather than claim a direct link to Augustine through the Canons Regular, they constituted a union of semi-eremetical communities in central Italy and Lombardy which, upon papal direction, accepted in 1244 (Little Union) and 1256 (Great Union) a constitution or rule similar to that of other mendicant orders, particularly that of the Dominicans. Although they called themselves friars, they retained something of their eremitical traditions.

AUGUSTINUS TRIUMPHUS OF ANCONA, d. 1328, Augustinian monk, teacher at Paris and Naples, and author of *Summa De Potestate Ecclesiastica*. In this work he argued the pope's right to depose monarchs *causa rationalis,* that is, for reasonable cause.

AULA, the forecourt in the early Christian basilica. The name later came to refer to that part of the church that was reserved for the laity, that is, the nave proper.

AUMALE, town in Normandy. Its first line of counts dates from Odo of Champagne, the brother-in-law of William the Conqueror. When Philip II Augustus annexed Normandy in 1204, the family retained possession of the title. In England the counts were known as earls of Albemarle.

AUMBRY, a recess in the wall near the main altar or in the sacristy where sacred vessels and books were kept; on occasion even the Sacrament was reserved there.

AUMONIÈRE, a belt pouch or wallet used from the twelfth to the fifteenth centuries by both men and women. It might serve as a place to keep alms or such objects of general use as coins and keys.

AUNGERVILLE (Aungervyle), RICHARD, d. 1345, commonly known as Richard de Bury, English bibliophile and author of *Philobiblon,* a treatise dealing with the care and study of books. He was keeper of the privy seal (1329–33), twice a delegate to the papal court at Avignon, bishop of Durham (1333), later lord treasurer and chancellor. He was a patron of scholars, a collector of books and letters, and a prose stylist.

AURAY, town in Brittany which grew up around the castle and priory of St. Gildas. The castle served as the residence of the dukes of Brittany. John of Montfort built a collegiate church near the town where he had defeated Charles of Blois in 1364 and taken over the dukedom. The church subsequently became a Carthusian monastery.

AURELIAN OF RÉOMÉ (France), ninth-century student of music, the first scholar to discuss Gregorian chant. His writings reveal a knowledge of theories inherited from the Greeks as well as a primitive notation and chironomy.

AURELIUS, ST., d. c. 430, bishop of Carthage who presided over a number of church councils. St. Augustine held him in high esteem for his learning and piety.

AURELIUS VICTOR, SEXTUS, Roman historian of

the fourth century whose *De Caesaribus* covers the lives of the emperors from Augustus (d. A.D. 14) to 360.

AUREOLE (nimbus), a radiance of light in the form of a disk, circle, or crown, employed in art to suggest divinity or sanctity. The aureole as a circle of light encircling the entire form was generally limited to figures of Christ and Mary.

AUREOLI (Aureolus, D'Auriol, Oriol), PETRUS, d. 1322, Franciscan philosopher and theologian, teacher at Toulouse and Paris, provincial of his order, and archbishop of Aix. His writings include commentaries on the *Sentences,* an introduction to Scripture, and a defense of the doctrine of the Immaculate Conception.

AURILLAC, ABBEY OF, Benedictine monastery founded c. 890 in the country of Auvergne. Gerbert (Pope Sylvester II) spent his youthful years at the abbey. The monastery took an active part in the Cluniac reform movement.

AURISPA, GIOVANNI, d. 1459, Italian humanist, taught Greek at Bologna and Florence, and served as secretary to Popes Eugenius IV and Nicholas V. He collected, translated, and edited Greek manuscripts and composed some Latin verse.

AURORA IAM SPARGIT POLUM, a hymn that hailed the dawn and with it the end of darkness as symbolic of the advent of the spiritual life with Christ. It may have been composed by Pope Gregory the Great (d. 604).

AURORA LUCIS RUTILAT, an Ambrosian hymn of unknown authorship which sang of the joys of Easter. It made its way into the Roman breviary.

AUSCULTA FILI, bull by Pope Boniface VIII and addressed to Philip IV in December 1301 in which he announced the summoning of a church council to Rome to consider means of correcting the situation in France where the king had subverted the church to serve his own ends. The bull prompted Philip to convene the first meeting of the Estates General (1302) before which a garbled version of the bull was presented. [*See* BONIFACE VIII, Pope.]

AUSONIUS, DECIMUS MAGNUS, d. c. 394, late Latin poet, a Christian, rhetorician at Bordeaux, and tutor of Gratian, the son of Emperor Valentinian I. When Gratian became emperor, he made Ausonius prefect of Gaul, Italy, and Africa, and finally consul. His best known poem is the *Mosella* in which he describes his journey on the Moselle river. His poetical writings represent academic exercises in versification rather than inspired or inspiring poetry.

AUSTIN CANONS. *See* CANONS REGULAR OF ST. AUGUSTINE.

AUSTIN FRIARS. *See* AUGUSTINIANS.

AUSTRASIA, in the Merovingian period the eastern portion of the Frankish realm which lay along the lower Rhine as opposed to Neustria which lay to the west. Austrasia usually included the county of Champagne. Its principal cities were Reims and Metz. Its existence dates from the partition of the kingdom of Clovis I in 511. As the power of the king declined, that of the mayor of the palace increased. In 687, Pepin II, the Austrasian mayor of the palace, defeated the Neustrian mayor of the palace, and took over that kingdom. His illegitimate son, Charles Martel, went on to reestablish the old kingdom of Clovis by extending his rule over Burgundy and Aquitaine. It was Charles Martel's son, Pépin III, who deposed the last of the Merovingian rulers of Austrasia and assumed the title of king of the new Frankish kingdom of what was to be known as that of the Carolingians.

AUSTRIA, region in the area of the upper Danube and Alps which the Bavarians occupied early in the sixth century. Charlemagne incorporated the area into his empire and upon the destruction of the Avars extended its frontiers to the east and southeast. Further expansion eastward came with the defeat of the Magyars at Lechfeld in

955. In 976 Otto II organized the region as the Ostmark (Ostarrichi). It was subsequently detached from Bavaria and given to the Babenbergs who retained it until 1246 when the family became extinct. Ottocar II of Bohemia then occupied the region but was deprived of it in 1278 when he fell in battle with Rudolf of Hapsburg. From that time Austria was destined to remain in the hands of the Hapsburgs until 1918. Rudolf extended his authority over Styria, Carniola, and Carinthia. His Hapsburg successors acquired Tyrol (1363) and Trieste (1382), while their influence was dominant in the ecclesiastical states of Salzburg, Trent, and Brixen.

AUSTRIANS, eastern branch of the Bavarian people which gradually developed a distinctive character of its own through absorption of tribes such as the Alemanni and the influence of the neighboring Slavic and Hungarian peoples.

AUTHARI, d. 590, Lombard king (584–90), elected by the Lombard dukes to succeed Alboin whose murder in 572(?) had ushered in a period of anarchy. Authari managed to consolidate Lombard control of northern Italy. He also repelled several Frankish invasions.

AUTOCEPHALI, churches whose bishops were subject to neither patriarch nor metropolitan, more particularly churches of the Greek rite which became autonomous or independent following Turkish capture of Constantinople in 1453. In the West the term also acquired the meaning of schismatic churches.

AUTODAFÉ, originally a public profession of faith in Spain and Portugal, later the public ceremony conducted in the presence of ecclesiastical and civil authorities and associated with the execution of the inquisition's judgment against heretics. Those persons who had been judged guilty of heresy were turned over to the secular authorities to be burned at the stake.

AUTOS SACRAMENTALES, that is, "sacramental plays," simple liturgical presentations, usually allegorical in character and concerned with the Eucharist. After their appearance in the thirteenth century, they grew more and more elaborate and frequently featured processions, floats, masqueraders, as well as performers.

AUTPERT, AMBROSE, d. 784, abbot of the Benedictine monastery of St. Vincent near Benevento in southern Italy whose knowledge of the Bible attracted the attention of Charlemagne. His voluminous writings included ascetical treatises, lives of the saints, sermons, and a commentary on the *Apocalypse*.

AUTUN, city southwest of Dijon, possibly a bishopric as early as 250 and site of several monasteries erected during the Merovingian period. The location of the abbey of Cluny within the diocese assured Autun a prominent role in the Cluniac reform movement. Autun was an early medieval center of learning. The Romanesque cathedral of St. Lazare (from the twelfth century) dominates the city.

AUVERGNE, province in east-central France, occupied by Visigoths and Franks, a county during the Carolingian period, and part of Aquitaine until 955 when it became a viscounty in the possession of the counts of Poitou. As a consequence of Eleanor of Aquitaine's marriage to Henry (II) in 1152, Auvergne became a fief of the kings of England until 1195 when Philip II Augustus acquired control of most of the area. In 1360 John II gave it to his son Jean as an appanage. At the close of the Middle Ages it was held by Charles, duc de Bourbon, constable of France.

AUXENTIUS, d. 373/4, bishop of Milan from 355. He was among the most prominent supporters of Arianism in the West. Although he suffered condemnation as a heretic by several councils (Ariminum, Paris, and Rome), he remained in possession of his see until he died.

AUXERRE, city from Roman times located on the river Yonne, a tributary of the Seine. It became a bishop's seat in the fourth century, remained a possession of the counts of Nevers until the French crown bought it in 1371, was surrendered to the duchy of Burgundy in 1435 but was recovered in 1477 by Louis XI. Several roads converged at the city, of which the most important was that running between Paris and the Mediterranean. The cathedral which was built from the thirteenth to the sixteenth century reveals the Gothic styles popular in Champagne.

AUXILIARY BISHOP, a bishop deputed to a diocesan to assist him in the discharge of his episcopal responsibilities, both spiritual and administrative. The auxiliary bishop may have appeared as early as the first century.

AUXILIARY SAINTS. *See* FOURTEEN HOLY HELPERS.

AVALON, in old Celtic or Welsh mythology, the Isle of the Saints, the happy otherworld of the dead and also the place to which legend had King Arthur retire in order to recuperate from his wounds. Since 1191 the site has been identified as Glastonbury in Somerset.

AVANZO, JACOPO, Italian painter of the North Italian school of the late fourteenth century, a disciple and assistant of Altichiero. He is known for his frescoes in the Oratory of St. George in Padua which reflect the influence of Giotto.

AVARS, mounted Asiatic nomads who swept into southern Russia and the Balkans during the second half of the sixth century, joined the Lombards in destroying the Gepids, then established a state of their own between the Danube and the Carpathians. In 626 they penetrated to the walls of Constantinople but failed to take the city. They held many Slavic groups in subjection and continued to carry on plundering raids into the Balkans, Italy, and Germany until Charlemagne destroyed them during the years 791 and 803. In the course of the centuries they spent in Europe, the Avars never rose appreciably above their ancient low cultural level. The loot they accumulated in the course of their depredations they simply hoarded. What remained of the nation was eventually absorbed into the Magyar people.

AVE, German poetess of the early twelfth century who composed poems on religious subjects such as the Seven Gifts of the Holy Spirit, St. John the Baptist, and the Antichrist. She was the first German poetess to be known by name.

AVELLANA COLLECTIO, a collection of letters that passed between the pope and the emperor in Constantinople during the period 368 to 553. The collection also contains a number of papal decrees as well as some apocryphal writings.

AVE MARIA. *See* HAIL MARY.

AVE MARIS STELLA (Hail, Star of the Sea), a popular poem honoring the Virgin Mary, of unknown authorship but generally dated to the ninth century. It was later incorporated into the Roman breviary.

AVEMPACE, IBN BADDSCHA, d. 1138, Arab Spanish philosopher, mathematician, and physician of Spain who has been called the first Aristotelian scholar of Islamic history. He authored works on medicine, mathematics, and philosophy, commentaries on several of Aristotle's scientific writings, and a treatise on the soul. His chief importance lies in the fact that he introduced Aristotelianism to Spain. He also influenced Averroës.

AVENZOAR (Abumeron), d. 1162, distinguished Spanish Moslem physician of Seville. He may have learned his medicine from Averroës. He was among the few who had the courage to disagree with Galen. He also attacked the superstitious remedies advocated by astrologers. His *Teisir* (*Rectification of Health*) was translated into Hebrew and into Latin.

AVE REGINA CAELORUM (Hail, Queen of Heaven), an antiphon in honor of the Virgin

Mary that was introduced into the divine office in the fourteenth century.

AVE VERUM CORPUS, a eucharistic hymn of unknown authorship but probably composed in north Italy in the thirteenth century.

AVERROËS (Ibn Rushd), d. 1198, was born in Córdoba, served as a judge in Seville, later as physician to the ruler of Morocco. Moslem theologians attacked him for his rationalistic views —he denied personal immortality and creation, and he considered God to be simply a first agent. He may have come to question these fundamental doctrines of Islam because of his inability to harmonize Greek philosophy with the Koran. [See AVERROISM, LATIN.] He was accused of heresy, his books were burned except those concerned with science, and he spent some time in prison. Perhaps his most important works are his commentaries on the writings of Aristotle, a philosopher whom he considered the supreme genius and one who never erred. The extensiveness of these commentaries and the considerable acclaim they enjoyed in the West, despite their errors, earned Averroës the title of Commentator. His work on medicine was used in medieval universities.

AVERROISM, LATIN, school of philosophy, with its center at the university of Paris, that based its views on those of Aristotle as interpreted by Averroës. It accepted the eternity of the world and of matter, stressed the present life as the ultimate end of man, and maintained the right to pursue philosophical thought apart from theological implications. Siger of Brabant, its leading representative, was charged with championing the doctrine of the double truth inasmuch as he insisted that the philosopher should be free to seek intellectual objectives even if these were contrary to faith. Despite repeated condemnation, the first in 1270 by the archbishop of Paris, Averroism continued to attract thinkers as late as the fourteenth century. [See MARSILIUS OF PADUA.]

AVIENUS (Avienius), composer of Latin fables who lived toward the close of the fourth century. His popular writings were used in the schools of the Middle Ages.

AVICEBROL (Avicebron). See IBN GABIROL.

AVICENNA (Ibn Sina), d. 1037, was born near Bukhara in 980 and when still in his teens was recognized by contemporaries as a prodigy. His encyclopedic writings (in Arabic and Persian) which embraced every field of intellectual endeavor exerted their greatest influence in the areas of medicine and philosophy. His enormous medical *Canon of Medicine* was held authoritative well into modern times. His rationalism which maintained the unlimited power of reason aroused much criticism among pious Moslems although the Sufis drew inspiration from his Platonic and neo-Platonic ideas, and he himself insisted that religion and philosophy were in accord. Because he incorporated a larger measure of Greek philosophy into his writings than any other Islamic thinker, his impact upon Western thought was perhaps foremost among Moslem scholars.

AVIGNON, city on the lower Rhône, a bishopric in the fifth century, and a commune in the twelfth under the suzerainty of the counts of Toulouse and Provence. The pope bought the city in 1348 and made it his residence for the greater part of the period from 1309 to 1377. [See AVIGNONESE RESIDENCE.] In 1475 the city became an archiepiscopal see. It was recognized as a leading cultural center in the late Middle Ages.

AVIGNONESE RESIDENCE, the period from 1309 to 1377, except for the years 1367–70, when the popes made their home at Avignon. The establishment of papal headquarters at Avignon came somewhat fortuitously. Contributing factors included the unstable conditions in Rome, the election of a French cardinal as pope (Clement V), who started to go to Rome but never left France, and continuing difficulties with

Philip IV over issues raised by Boniface VIII. The king's contemplated suppression of the Knights Templars also required papal attention which might be easier given in Avignon than in Rome. Although writers have emphasized the evils of the Residence, it is generally agreed that the popes themselves were reasonably qualified men and that much of the criticism heaped upon the Avignonese papacy for its alleged extravagance and corruption derived principally from the objections churchmen in foreign countries made to the growing centralization and expansion of papal government. [*See* PROVISIONS, PAPAL.] No doubt the most serious consequence for the church of the Residence was the Western Schism which it helped precipitate.

AVIGNON SCHOOL, fifteenth-century French school of painting that had its roots in the cultural development which Avignon experienced during the fourteenth century when it served as the residence of the pope. Italian artists, beginning with Simone Martini (d. 1344), made up the largest number of its visitors.

AVITUS, d. 456, Western Roman emperor, 455–6, member of a distinguished Gallic family, and father-in-law of Sidonius Apollinaris. He was instrumental in persuading the Visigoths of southwestern Gaul to support Aetius against Attila and his Huns at Chalons in 451. In 455 the Gallo-Romans hailed him as emperor at Arles, but it was not long after he reached Rome that Ricimer, the German chieftain in control there, forced him to abdicate. He became the bishop of Placentia.

AVITUS OF VIENNE (Alcimus Ecidicius), ST., d. c. 519, learned bishop of Vienne in Gaul and a foe of Arianism who was instrumental in converting the king of Burgundy. Avitus left letters, homilies, and some verse, including a long poem descriptive of the history of the Hebrews as based on the Old Testament.

AVIZ, ORDER OF, military-religious order of Portuguese knights which in 1147 came to be affiliated with the Castilian Order of Calatrava. In 1211 Alfonso II gave the knights the city of Aviz which they had helped capture from the Moors, whereupon they made the city their headquarters. The order was also known as the Knights of St. Benedict of Aviz because of their adoption of a modified version of the Rule of St. Benedict. The order played an important role in Portuguese history.

AVRANCHES, ancient town of Normandy on the Bay of Mont-Saint-Michel. It became an intellectual center in the early Middle Ages. The scholastic scholar Lanfranc (d. 1089) taught there before going to England. It was devastated in the course of the Hundred Years' War.

AYESHA. *See* AISHAH.

AYMER OF VALENCE, d. 1260, bishop of Winchester, son of King John's widow Isabella and Hugh X, count of La Marche, and half-brother of Henry III. When he came to England in 1247 Henry forced the chapter at Winchester to elect him bishop. Hostility toward him and his two brothers, Guy de Lusignan and William of Valence who also enjoyed Henry's favor, was an important factor in the Barons' War. He and his two brothers were later forced to flee back to the continent.

AYRSHIRE, region of southwestern Scotland occupied by the tribal kingdom of the Strathclyde Britons. In 1034 it became part of the early kingdom of Scotland with its king Duncan serving as the first king of all Scotland. Evidence of Norman penetration is confirmed by the great ruined castle at Dundonald (built in 1135). In 1244 the abbey of Crossraguel was founded. In 1263 a Norwegian invasion was thrown back by Alexander III. Robert Bruce, who was earl of Carrick, made his home in Turnberry castle.

AYYUBIDS, name of the Islamic dynasty founded by Saladin (Salah al-Din), son of Ayyub, which replaced the Atabeg house and ruled Egypt,

Moslem Syria, Palestine, Yemen, and the upper part of Mesopotamia from 1171 to 1260.

AZO (Azolinus), d. before 1235, known as *Procus* or *Soldanus,* teacher of law at Bologna after 1190 and author of a popular commentary on the *Codex* and *Institutes* of Justinian.

AZORES, islands west of Portugal which appear on a map of 1351. Portuguese sailors reached them in 1427 or 1431, with colonization beginning in 1445.

AZYMITES, a term of reproach by which Greek Christians referred to members of the Latin church after the schism of 1054 because of their use of unleavened bread in the eucharistic service. The word is derived from the Greek term for unleavened.

BAALZEBUB, god of Ekron; Satan.

BAANITES, a group of Paulicians whose name was derived from that of their leader Baanes (ninth century).

BABENBERG, ruling house of Austria, 976–1246. It may have descended from a powerful family of Franconia that derived its name from the fortress of that name (present-day site of the cathedral of Bamberg). Otto II (973–83) created Count Leopold of Babenberg margrave of the Eastern March (Austria). In 1192 the Babenbergs inherited Styria. It was Duke Leopold V who took part in the Third Crusade (1189–92) and waylaid Richard I of England on his return and held him captive. Frederick II of Babenberg died in 1246 without issue, and Austria passed (1251) to Ottocar II of Bohemia who had married Frederick's sister.

BABER (Babar, Babur), popular name of Zahir ud-din-Mohammed, d. 1530, a descendant of the Mongol khans and of Timur the Lame, founder of the Indian dynasty of the Great Moguls.

BABYLAS, ST., bishop of Antioch. According to the testimony of St. John Chrysostom, Babylas refused a Roman emperor, possibly Philip the Arabian, permission to be present at the celebration of the Easter vigil service because of an unrepented crime. Babylas died in prison from torture during the persecution of the emperor Decius (249–51).

BABYLONIAN CAPTIVITY, an opprobrious term applied by Petrarch and others to stigmatize the residence of the popes at Avignon, the implication being that the sin-ridden city of Avignon, together with its corrupt cardinals and pope, were holding the church captive much as the ancient Chaldeans had kept the Hebrews captive in their iniquitous capital of Babylon. [See AVIGNONESE RESIDENCE].

BACCALARIUS (Bakkalaureus, bachelor), a page; member of the lower clergy; lowest rank of graduates in the medieval university; inferior or younger member of a trade union.

BACCANCELD, SYNOD OF, a meeting in Kent in 694 of churchmen and lay lords, not unlike a *witenagemot,* which ordained that the church should retain in perpetuity all its rights, privileges, and properties. This enactment may represent the most ancient of English charters.

BACCARAT, a game of cards of French origin which may go back to the fifteenth century.

BACCHANTS, name given to students of the late Middle Ages who moved from one Latin school to another.

BACHELOR. *See* BACCALARIUS.

BACHELOR OF ARTS, degree that a university granted to a student after four years of study. The degree permitted him to do some preliminary teaching in the university while preparing himself to become a master, an achievement officially announced when he received a master of arts degree.

BACHIARIUS, fourth-century Spanish monk and theologian, author of a letter to the pope in which he defended himself against the charge of Priscillianism. Another work of his in which he pleaded for a repentant monk is valuable for the insight it affords into the character of the Spanish penitential system.

BACKGAMMON, ancient game of chance and skill, played by two people using dice, a special board, and pieces which they moved about the board according to a set of rules. The game became popular in Western Europe after the tenth century and particularly so in aristocratic circles.

BACKOFEN (Backoffen), JOHN, d. 1519, German sculptor of tombs and crucifixion groups. His work reflected the baroque tendencies of late Gothic sculpture.

BACON, JOHN. *See* BACONTHORPE, JOHN.

BACON, ROBERT, d. 1248, the first Dominican writer in England and a distinguished preacher. Matthew Paris praised him as a man most learned in theology and all other branches of knowledge.

BACON, ROGER. *See* ROGER BACON.

BACONTHORPE (Bacon), JOHN, d. c. 1348, English Carmelite, a student at Oxford and Paris, author of voluminous scholarly writings on theology (commentary on the *Sentences of Peter Lombard*), exegesis, canon law, and astronomy. Contemporaries considered him an Averroist, although his principal interest in Averroës was that of harmonizing that philosopher's views with Christianity. He was a sharp critic of St. Thomas Aquinas and Duns Scotus.

BADAJOZ, city of Estremadura in western Spain which became prominent under Moorish control and the seat of a powerful emirate (1022–94). It fell to Alfonso IX of Leon in 1228.

BADIA, an abbey church; also, among the Arabs, a fortress located in a desert.

BADR, BATTLE OF, bloody skirmish won by

Mohammed and Medina sympathizers in 624 when they attacked a Meccan caravan and its escort.

BADUIS, JODOCUS, d. 1535, scholar and printer of Paris, taught Greek and edited classics in Lyons before he became a printer. He published Greek and Latin classical works, also a life of Thomas à Kempis which he authored.

BAENA, JUAN ALFONSO DE, d. 1454, Spanish poet whose literary fame rests upon a collection of poems which he assembled and to which he gave his name (*Cancionero de Baena*).

BAGHDAD (Bagdad), city on the Tigris (initially on the west bank), erected on the site of a Nestorian monastery by Al-Mansur in 762 to serve as the capital of the newly established Abbasid caliphate. Because of the caliph's presence there and his patronage and its unsurpassed commercial advantages, Baghdad grew rapidly and within a century had become Islam's largest city and its principal industrial and cultural center. Perhaps its most illustrious period came during the reign of Harun al-Rashid who invited many scholars and artists to live in the city. This brilliant era frequently provided the setting for tales that appear in the *Thousand And One Nights*. The Mongol Hulagu destroyed the city in 1258, after which it was rebuilt, only to suffer later plunderings in 1393 and 1401 by Timur the Lame.

BAGRATUNES (Bagratides), an Armenian-Georgian family that claimed descent from David, threw off Moslem rule, and established itself as the ruling dynasty of Armenia (885–1079).

BAHA' AL-DIN (Beha Ud-din or Bahaddin), d. 1234, Arab scholar and statesman whom Saladin appointed judge of Jerusalem. He left a life of Saladin.

BAHA', AL-DIN ZUHAYR (Abu al-Fadl Zuhair ibn Muhammad al-Mukallabi), d. 1258, Arab poet and calligraphist at the court of the Ayyub sultans of Egypt. He was reputed to be the best writer of prose and verse and the best calligraphist of his day.

BAHIRA LEGEND, a story told in the principal biographies of Mohammed about a Christian monk or hermit by the name of Bahira who saw the Prophet when he was a boy of twelve and predicted a great future for him. The boy was accompanying a caravan led by Abu Bakr or Abu Talib.

BAHYA BEN JOSEPH IBN PAKUDA, Jewish religious philosopher of Spain in the second half of the eleventh century. His *Guidebook to the Duties of the Heart* which emphasized the importance of developing right attitudes and intentions as opposed to religious ritual and ethical practices, proved a popular and widely read classic of Jewish philosophic and devotional literature.

BAIBARS (Baybars, Beibars, Bibars) I, d. 1277, a slave, then general in the service of the Mamluk sultan Kutuz (Qutuz, Kotus), drove the Mongols from Syria, later slew the sultan and had himself proclaimed his successor in Cairo. He captured Antioch and Jaffa from Christian hands and made himself the leading power in the eastern Mediterranean.

BAIL, right of a feudal lord to administer the estates of a vassal when held by a minor or widow and to collect the revenues. The lord was expected to maintain the estates in good order and to provide for the needs of the ward or widow.

BAILEY, the outer enclosure consisting of ditch, hedge, later a wall, that protected the keep or motte. [*See* CASTLE].

BAILLI (bailiff), local royal administrative official in Normandy, England, and southern Italy, also employed later by the Hohenstaufens and by the French kings from the twelfth century. In France, where the *bailli* served in the central and northern parts of the county, he acquired supervisory authority over the prévôts and was as-

signed a bailliage to administer. His position corresponded roughly to that of the seneschal in southern France.

BAINBRIDGE, CHRISTOPHER, d. 1514, bishop of Durham, archbishop of York, cardinal, sent as a legate to Rome by Henry VII. He later championed the interests of Henry VIII.

BAITHEN, ST., d. c. 600, Irish monk who succeeded St. Columba as abbot of Iona. He wrote a life of Columba.

BAJAZET. *See* BAYAZID.

BAKER, GEOFFREY, fl. 1350, also known as Walter of Swinborn or Swinbroke, author of two chronicles, one from the Creation to 1326, a second, far more valuable, from 1303 to 1356.

BALADHURI, AL- (Ahmad Ibn Yahaya), d. 892, Arab historian whose writings are especially valuable for the early history of Islam. His major work, *Futuh al-Buldan,* describes the conquest of the different countries that made up the Islamic empire. Another work deals with the genealogies of early Arab aristocracy.

BALDACHINO (baldachin, baldachinium, baldachinum), canopy fixed on four poles and borne over a prelate or priest in a liturgical procession; also the domelike canopy above an altar or the canopy above a bishop's throne and over statues.

BALDER (Baldr, Baldur), god of the ancient Germans, a god of light, who appeared in the Eddas. He was the talented, brave, yet gentle son of Odin and Frigg. He was invulnerable to everything but mistletoe and was eventually killed by a mistletoe dart made by Loki but thrown by the blind god Hödr whom Loki had deceived.

BALDERIC (Baudry). *See* BAUDRY OF BOURGUEIL.

BALDOVINETTI, ALESSIO (Alesso), d. 1499, painter and mosaicist of Florence. He was one of the first Italian artists to experiment with the technique of oil painting. Among his surviving works is the *Nativity* which he painted for the cloister of Santa Annunziata. Little remains of his most ambitious undertaking, a series of frescoes representing scenes from the Old Testament accompanied by portraits of famous contemporaries which he painted for the Church of Santa Trinità in Rome.

BALDRIC, belt worn over one shoulder, diagonally across the chest and under the opposite arm, from which might hang a sword or horn; a waist girdle. It could also serve as an ornament.

BALDUS DE UBALDIS, d. 1400, distinguished jurist, canonist, and teacher of law at Bologna, Perugia, Pisa, Florence, and other Italian cities. His commentaries on the *Corpus Juris Civilis* and treatises on canon and feudal law gained him great renown, and he ranks with the leading jurists of the Middle Ages.

BALDWIN I, Latin Emperor of Constantinople, 1204–05, earlier count of Flanders and one of the leaders of the Fourth Crusade (1202–04). He was chosen to be the Latin empire's first ruler when the city fell to the Crusaders and Venetians. He was later captured in battle with the Bulgarians and died a captive.

BALDWIN II, Latin Emperor of Constantinople, 1228–61, began his own rule in 1237 upon the death of John of Brienne who had served as regent. He traveled about Western Europe in search of financial and military aid for his weakening realm, and in the end sold a large part of the True Cross and the Crown of Thorns to Louis IX of France. In 1261 Constantinople fell to the ruler of Nicaea and Baldwin escaped to Italy.

BALDWIN I, king of Jerusalem, 1100–18, one of the leaders of the First Crusade (1096–99), founder of the County of Edessa (1098), and elected king of Jerusalem in 1100 to succeed his brother Godfrey of Bouillon. On the strength of his success in expanding the frontiers of the kingdom by capturing Arsuf, Caesarea, Acre, and other cities, he has been called the real founder of the kingdom of Jerusalem.

BALDWIN II, king of Jerusalem, 1118–31, cousin of Baldwin I, strengthened and extended the frontiers of his kingdom with the help of the fleets of Genoa and Venice to whom he extended large commercial concessions. He also helped the rulers of the Crusading states of Antioch, Edessa, and Tripoli against the Moslems. He cooperated in the establishment of the Order of Knights Templars, militarized the Knights of St. John, and was recognized as suzerain by the heads of the other Crusading states.

BALDWIN III, king of Jerusalem, 1143–63, ruled with a large measure of success, with his mother until 1151, during the dangerous period of the Second Crusade (1147–9) and the rise of Nur ed-din who took over Damascus and north Syria. He succeeded in establishing friendly relations with Byzantium and married the niece of Emperor Manuel I Comnenus.

BALDWIN IV, king of Jerusalem, 1174–85, son and successor of Amalric I. For the greater part of his reign he was engaged in defending his endangered realm against the mounting strength of Saladin. His leprosy, the question of succession, and the contest for control between Guy de Lusignan and Raymond, count of Tripoli, threatened the survival of his kingdom.

BALDWIN, d. 1354, archbishop of Trier, member of the house of Luxemburg, whose powerful influence was instrumental in placing on the imperial throne of Germany first Henry VII, then Louis the Bavarian, and finally Charles IV.

BALDWIN OF CANTERBURY, d. 1190, Cistercian monk, abbot, bishop of Worcester, and archbishop of Canterbury (1184). He took part in the Third Crusade (1189–92) and bequeathed his fortune to the cause of the liberation of the Holy Land. He left sermons and theological works but earned his greatest prominence through his knowledge of canon law. In the dispute between Thomas Becket and Henry II, he sided with the prelate.

BÂLE. *See* BASEL.

BALEARIC ISLANDS, islands off the east coast of Spain in the Mediterranean. They fell to the Moors early in the eighth century, became an independent kingdom in the eleventh, and for a time served as a haven of pirates who preyed on ships and the coastal cities of the vicinity. They were taken over by James I of Aragon (1229–35), then from 1276 to 1343 were organized as an independent kingdom under the rule of Majorca, the largest of the islands. Later in 1343, they again reverted to Aragon.

BALL, JOHN, d. 1381, a vagrant priest, excommunicated for irregularities including heresy, joined the rebels in the Peasant Revolt of 1381, but was captured and executed. He is usually identified as an early Lollard.

BALLAD, a light, simple song, originally intended as the accompaniment to a dance; a narrative poem intended to be sung and preserved by an unsophisticated, culturally homogeneous folk.

BALLADE, the name given in medieval literature to strophic dance songs of Provençal origin.

BALLET, a form of theatrical performance which in its Western origins appeared in the late Middle Ages when pantomimes and dancing were introduced at festivals and banquets.

BALLIOL (Baliol), famous Scottish family of Norman ancestry that traced its rise to the reign of William II of England (1087–1100).

BALLIOL (Baliol), EDWARD, king of Scotland, 1332–56, son of John Balliol, seized the Scottish throne from David II, son of Robert Bruce, was crowned at Scone, but suffered exile in 1341 and spent most of his later years in England. There he lived on an English pension after 1356

when he resigned his crown. His cause never aroused much sympathy among the Scots.

BALLIOL, JOHN, king of Scotland, 1292–6, owed his accession to Edward I who preferred him to the rival candidate, Robert Bruce, when the Scottish royal line became extinct in 1290. (Edward had been recognized as feudal overlord of Scotland.) In 1296 when John refused to cooperate with Edward against the French, Edward forced him to resign his kingdom and imprisoned him in the Tower. There he remained until 1299 when he retired to his estates in Normandy where he died in 1314.

BALLIOL, JOHN, d. 1269, English baron, father of John Balliol, king of Scotland (1292–6), served as one of the regents for Alexander III until 1255 when he was charged with treason and his lands declared forfeit. He supported Henry III in the Barons' War and was captured with the king at Lewes in 1264.

BALLIOL COLLEGE, college of Oxford founded by John Balliol in 1263. John was the father of John Balliol, king of Scotland (1292–6).

BALLISTA, military machine that threw missiles. It was worked by tension on the order of the crossbow. [*See* CATAPULT.]

BALME (Balma), HENRY (Hugh), d. 1439, Franciscan theologian of Burgundy, author of a biography of St. Coletta which is no longer extant, also of *Theologia Mystica* which some scholars have attributed, probably in error, to St. Bonaventure.

BALMUNG, the sword which Siegfried won as his share of the horde of the Nibelungs.

BALSAM, an oily, aromatic substance found in certain plants which the Christian church mixed with olive oil for use as chrism.

BALSAMON, THEODORE, d. c. 1195, Greek canonist, legal adviser to the patriarch of Constantinople, and himself late in life patriarch of Antioch. His commentary on the *Nomocanon* of

Photius is valuable for the light it sheds on church (canon) law in the Byzantine empire.

BALTHASAR, according to legend, one of the three kings who visited the newly born Christ at Bethlehem (Matthew 2:1–12).

BALTS, peoples located along the south shore of the Baltic. They included the Lithuanians, Letts, and the now extinct Old Prussians. They were conquered by the Teutonic Knights and the Livonian Knights of the Sword and were forced to accept Christianity.

BALUE, JEAN, d. 1491, French statesman and cardinal, a trusted adviser of Louis XI who helped the king win his struggle with the League of Public Weal. He later turned against Louis and became the confidant of Charles the Bold of Burgundy. He arranged the meeting of the two men at Péronne in 1468 where Charles made Louis his prisoner. Louis later imprisoned Balue and released him only after the pope's intervention.

BAMBERG, city in Bavaria on the upper Main, first noted in 902 and made a bishop's seat in 1007 by Henry II of Germany who recognized its strategic location as a base of missionary operations among the Slavs to the east. In the thirteenth century its bishops were recognized as princes of the empire when they took their place in the diet immediately after the archbishops. A splendid thirteenth-century cathedral holds the tombs of Henry II and his wife, St. Kunigunde.

BAN, a proclamation, such as a call to arms; in general, the king's power to command and prohibit under pain of punishment; a sentence or decree of outlawry; an excommunication or condemnation by the church.

BAN (banus), at one time the highest official in Croatia ranking next to the princes; in the twelfth and thirteenth centuries the title of the governors of several frontier provinces in eastern Hungary. The area a ban administered was called a banat.

BANALITIES, exactions which the lord of the manor imposed upon his peasants for the use of his mill, oven, wine-press, and similar facilities. He might also require part of their fish-catch or warrens. What originally might have been reasonable exactions demanded in return for services rendered remained in time only taxes which in France continued until the French Revolution.

BANAT. *See* BAN (banus).

BANDES FRANÇAISES, French foot soldiers of the late fifteenth century who were modeled after the Swiss soldiers and intended to serve as a national infantry.

BANDINELLI. *See* ALEXANDER III, Pope.

BANDITS (Bandidi, Bravi), originally men who had become outlaws. In Italy in the thirteenth and fourteenth centuries they banded into associations when they had become quite numerous.

BANGOR, name of a number of places in Wales and Ireland: a) Bangor Fawr in north Wales whose see according to tradition was founded by St. Deiniol (d. c. 584). It later became the seat of the ancient see of Bangor. The cathedral burned down in 1402; b) Bangor, a seaport in north Ireland, whose abbey was founded in 555 or 559 by St. Comgall. It was the home of St. Columbanus and St. Gall. The Danes destroyed it in the ninth century. In 1120 St. Malachy rebuilt the abbey, and in 1460 the Franciscans took it over.

BANGOR, ANTIPHONARY OF, a Latin manuscript containing canticles, hymns, collects, and other prayers probably compiled in Bangor but taken to Bobbio in the early ninth century, perhaps by St. Dungal.

BANKING, as an established business or profession in the Middle Ages had no ancient origins since the banking of the Roman empire became a casualty of that empire's decline and barbarization. The forerunner of the medieval banker was, therefore, the perennial moneychanger and money-lender who in the early Middle Ages was usually a Jew since the church forbade the loaning of money by Christians (not by Jews). As the needs of industry and trade grew steadily from the tenth century onward, so did the demand for the financial facilities associated with banking. Gradually a special class of money-changers who had accumulated savings from their operations began to provide credit, and not Jews so much as Christians, once the latter had come to realize the financial profits that a growing capitalism could assure them. These Christian bankers became prominent first in north Italy, principally in Lombardy, where trade was first to revive. The term Lombard became synonymous with banker, even in non-Italian lands. [*See* MEDICI; BILL OF EXCHANGE; LETTER OF CREDIT.]

BAN MILE (banmeile, banlieue), the area within a mile, but more often three miles or more, of a city in the Middle Ages where foreigners were not permitted to engage in trade.

BANNOCKBURN, BATTLE OF, victory gained in 1314 by a small Scottish army under Robert Bruce near Stirling in Scotland over the English under Edward II. The Scottish foot soldiers exploited faulty English organization and overwhelmed the English army despite the latter's heavy preponderence in knights. The victory established Bruce firmly on the Scottish throne.

BANNS, formal announcements, normally three, of a coming marriage for the purpose of uncovering any impediment that might serve to bar the union. As a practice it may have first appeared in France about the close of the twelfth century.

BANSHEE, spirit in Celtic folklore whose mournful cry or screaming at night was believed to herald the death of one of the family visited.

BAPTISM, Christian rite and sacrament that involved the pouring of water on the head of the recipient of the sacrament. The rite, according to Christian belief, cleansed the person of original sin, qualified him for eternal salvation, and made him an official member of the church. In the early centuries baptism by immersion appears to have been the practice, although the pouring on of water was permissible when circumstances recommended this. Immersion of infants was a common practice as late as the thirteenth century. The administration of the sacrament for adults was originally restricted to Easter and the vigil of Pentecost. [*See* CATECHUMEN; BAPTISTERY.]

BAPTISMAL FONT, a basin containing water, usually on a pedestal, in which the person to be baptized was immersed or over which he was sprinkled. [*See* BAPTISTERY.]

BAPTISMAL WATER, water consecrated with a special rite on Holy Saturday or on the eve of Pentecost and reserved for use in baptism.

BAPTISTERY (*baptisterium*), first a room, then a building reserved for the administering of baptism, separate from but associated with the Christian church. It had already appeared by the fourth century. Perhaps the oldest still surviving is that in the Lateran basilica at Rome in which, according to tradition, the emperor Constantine was baptized (337). When immersion was no longer practiced, the larger area, often surrounded by columns with curtains to provide privacy, became unnecessary. Standing fonts came into common use and these were often richly decorated with sculptures and similar artistry. The separate baptistery continued on in such Italian cities as Florence, Pisa, Parma, and Siena. The baptistery at Florence is especially famous for the celebrated bronze doors of Pisano and Ghiberti.

BAPTIST OF MANTUA (Spagnoli), BL., d. 1516, Spanish Carmelite, prior general of the order, humanist, and poet. Although a zealous reformer and a sharp critic of abuses in the church, he gained fame as a humanist and on the strength of his *Eclogues* was referred to as the Christian Virgil.

BAR, the barrier in Anglo-Saxon courts that separated the judges and their assistants from the defendant, lawyer, and people.

BAR, DUCHY OF, principality on both sides of the upper Maas to the east of Champagne. With the extension of their control over areas in Lorraine and Champagne, the counts grew sufficiently powerful to contest the authority of their overlords, the dukes of Lorraine. In 1301 Philip IV forced the count to pay homage for the part of the county that lay west of the Meuse. In 1354 the count acquired the title duke of Bar. During the vicissitudes of the Hundred Years' War, Bar and Lorraine became united and generally remained so into modern times.

BARADAEUS, JACOB, d. 578, Syrian monk who became bishop of Edessa and exercised metropolitan authority over Syria and Asia Minor. His encouragement instilled new life into Monophysitism and it was from his name that the term Jacobites was derived, the name by which the Monophysites of the area are known.

BARBARA, ST., saint martyred in the third or fourth century and venerated from the seventh century although only legendary evidence supports the traditional story of her life and virtues. One tradition makes her the daughter of a pagan of Nicomedia who, on being converted to the Christian faith, was handed over by her father to the prefect and executed. The Middle Ages revered her as one of the Fourteen Holy Helpers, the patroness of firemen and of the makers and users of firearms. Her intercession was invoked for a happy death and against the danger of fire and thunderstorms.

BARBARO, ERMOLAO, d. 1493, humanist of Venice, taught philosophy at the University of Padua, and served as Venetian ambassador to Milan and the papal court. He translated the rhetorical and dialectical works of Aristotle, contributed a philological treatise on Pliny the Elder, and carried on important correspondence with the leading humanists of his day.

BARBARO, FRANCESCO, d. 1454, humanist and statesman of Venice whose writings and correspondence contain much information about contemporary affairs. He took an active part in the work of the Councils of Basel and Ferrara-Florence and labored for the reunion of Greek and Latin churches.

BARBARO, NICOLO, fifteenth-century Venetian ambassador to Constantinople who left an unusually accurate account of the city's capture by the Turks in 1453.

BARBAROSSA, FREDERICK. See FREDERICK I BARBAROSSA.

BARBAZAN, ARNAUD GUILLAUME, SEIGNEUR DE, d. 1431, French general in the Hundred Years' War, know as *le chevalier sans reproche,* the knight without blame. He was a member of the Armagnacs and a champion of the cause of the Dauphin (Charles VII). For ten years he was a prisoner of the English. He died fighting in Lorraine under René I.

BARBELITES, a name by which Gnostics were also known. They believed Barbelo was one of the female aeons, the mother of every living thing.

BARBER, JOHN. See BARBOUR, JOHN.

BARBERINO, ANDREA DA, d. after 1431, Italian poet and troubadour who was interested in the lore of Charlemagne. He also introduced themes or episodes from Tuscan and Venetian sources.

BARBERINO, FRANCESCO DA, d. 1348, Italian poet who composed poetry and wrote tracts about love and women after the *dolce stil nuova* of Dante and other lyric poets.

BARBER-SURGEONS, appeared in monastic communities after 1092 when monastic regulations required monks to be clean-shaven. From 1163, when the clergy were forbidden to shed blood, they practiced surgery, simple operations such as blood-letting for the most part. Although they rose to some eminence in their craft, they ranked beneath university-trained physicians and surgeons and to distinguish them from these might be identified as "doctors of the short robe."

BARBICAN, a defensive tower or outer fortification at a gate or bridge leading into a walled city or castle.

BARBOUR (Barber, Barbier), JOHN, d. 1395, first important poet of Scotland and author of a popular poem entitled *The Bruce*. This eulogized the exploits of Robert Bruce. Barbour studied at Oxford and Paris.

BARBUS, PAULUS, d. 1494, a Dominican, learned Italian philosopher, and theologian who taught at Milan, Bologna, and other Italian cities. He authored scholarly treatises in his fields of specialization.

BARBUTE, helmet worn by soldiers in the late Middle Ages. Its name derived from a chin-piece which covered the beard.

BARCELONA, city of northeastern Spain, from Roman origins, a bishopric in the fourth century, was captured by the Visigoths (415) and Moors (713), and in 801 became part of the Frankish kingdom of Charlemagne when it served as capital of the Spanish March. By the close of the tenth century the counts of Barcelona had gained their independence and ruled what came to be known as the principality of Catalonia. The marriage in 1137 of the count of Barcelona to the heiress of the kingdom of Aragon brought about the union of the two countries and heralded the emergence of the city as a powerful commercial rival of Venice and Genoa for control of Mediterranean trade. Its maritime code, the *Consolat del Mar,* which dates from the late thirteenth century, became accepted in western Mediterranean and Spanish waters. Barcelona was famed as a banking center in addition to being a major exporter of wool and metals.

BARCELONA, UNIVERSITY OF, a *studium generale* from 1430, was given a charter in 1450 by Alfonso V of Aragon and approved the same year by Pope Nicholas V.

BARD, minstrel or poet of Ireland, Wales, and Scotland whose verses glorified the virtues of his people and its chieftains. Bards were most numerous in Wales and Ireland where they were held in high esteem and might form separate orders or societies. In England an order was established in 940, then dissolved by Edward I. Toward the close of the Middle Ages their popularity declined, although formal gatherings of bards in Wales called *eisteddfodau* were held into modern times.

BARDAS, CAESAR, d. 865, brother of the empress Theodora who supported her in her efforts to restore the veneration of images. As regent for his nephew Michael III (842–67), he proved himself an able Caesar, helped defeat the Avars (863), encouraged Cyril and Methodius in their missionary work, and advanced the revival of profane studies in Constantinople. It was upon the urging of the imperial favorite Basil (I), a horse-groom, that Michael had Bardas murdered.

BARDESANES (Bar-Daisan), d. 222, native of Edessa, a poet, the "father of Syriac poetry." He composed some 150 hymns, together with many astrological and philosophical works. Gnosticism tinged his Christianity although he considered himself an enemy of that religious philosophy. His astrological and philosophical views were out of harmony with Christian teaching.

BARDI, the most powerful banking and business house in Florence in the thirteenth century. Anti-magnate ordinances enacted toward the close of the century as well as local wars hampered its activities, although the most serious setback came in 1345 when Edward III of England and other debtors defaulted on their loans. The family was nevertheless able to retain its place in Florentine economic life into modern times.

BARDO OF OPPERSHOFEN, ST., d. 1051, monk of Fulda and director of its school, abbot of Werden, later of Hersfeld, and from 1031 archbishop of Mainz. In 1049 he hosted an important reform synod in Mainz at which Pope Leo IX presided. Bardo gained fame for his piety and his eloquence as a preacher.

BARETT (barrett, birett, bret), head-covering worn by men and women in the fifteenth century. It was frequently brightly colored and decorated with feathers and jewels.

BARGELLO, a thirteenth-century palace in Florence, the residence of the leading city official. Today it serves as an art museum and houses works of such medieval artists as Giotto, Verocchio, and Donatello.

BAR-HEBRAEUS (Gregorius ibn Al-Ibri), d. 1286, son of a Jewish physician, was converted and became a Jacobite Syrian bishop, poet, and physician whose immense erudition stands revealed in his numerous exegetical, ascetical, theological, historical, and scientific writings. He was also the author of a grammar, an autobiography, and an encyclopedia of philosophy that considered every branch of knowledge in the Aristotelian tradition. Most of his many writings were in Syriac, a few in Arabic. Beyond his learning which earned him the respect of both Christians and Moslems, he took an active part in ecclesiastical affairs. On one occasion, when metropolitan of Aleppo, he negotiated unsuccessfully with the Mongol general Hulagu in an attempt to save the city from pillage.

BARI, seaport on the Adriatic in southern Italy, occupied first by the Visigoths, next by the Lombards, then recovered by Byzantium, only to be captured by the Normans in 1071. It was the principal city of Apulia and served as the port of embarkation for many Crusaders headed for the Holy Land. It became a fief of the kingdom of Naples and was ruled by powerful dukes. Its Romanesque basilica, with relics of St. Nicholas of Bari, attracted many pilgrims.

BARISANO DA TRANI (Barisanus of Trani), Italian sculptor of the late twelfth century, also a worker in brass. Among his works are the bronze doors of the cathedrals in Trani and Ravello in southern Italy and those of Monreale in Sicily. His art reflects Byzantine influence but is basically Romanesque in character.

BARKING ABBEY, Benedictine nunnery in Essex established c. 677 by the bishop of London and dedicated to the Virgin Mary and to St. Ethelburga.

BARLAAM AND JOSAPHAT (Joasaph), an edifying story of Indian origin and dealing with Buddha that was adapted to Christianity, possibly by John of Damascus, whence it passed into all European literatures. The Christian version told of the conversion of the Indian prince Joasaph by the monk Barlaam. Beyond that central theme, there are bits of fable, lives of the saints, and most of the apology of St. Aristides.

BARLAAM OF CALABRIA, d. 1350, learned Greek monk, abbot, theologian, and humanist whom the Byzantine emperor sent to Avignon in 1339 in the hope of bringing an end to the schism between the Greek and Latin churches. His attacks on Hesychasm brought him into difficulties in Constantinople, and he subsequently joined the Latin church. Through the influence of Petrarch to whom he taught Greek, he was appointed bishop of Gerace in Calabria.

BARLETIUS, MARINUS, d. c. 1512, priest of Scutari who fled to Venice when the Turks overran his country. He devoted his time to the writing of history, in particular that of Albania and its national hero, Scanderbeg.

BARMECIDE (Barmakid), patronymic of a family, the father Yahya and his two sons Al-Fadl and Jaffar (Djafar), to whom the caliph Harun al-Rashid entrusted the administration of the Abbasid empire fom 786 to 803. Without warning and for reasons that are not entirely clear, the caliph suddenly ordered Jaffar, his favorite, beheaded and the other two men imprisoned.

BARNABAS, a disciple of Christ who joined St. Paul on the first missionary apostolate outside of Palestine and Syria.

BARNABAS, EPISTLE OF, a theological tract of unknown authorship but ascribed to the Apostle Barnabas, probably of the early second century, that held the purpose of the Old Testament to be that of providing symbolic truths instructive to Christians. It contained a strong attack on Judaism.

BARNABAS, GOSPEL OF, a presumed gospel written in Italian and apparently fabricated not earlier than the fifteenth century. Its author was a Christian who became a Moslem.

BARNABAS OF TERNI, d. c. 1474, scholar learned in medicine, philosphy, and letters who became a Franciscan. He was also an eloquent preacher. He may have established the first *monti di pietà* or charitable loan institution.

BARNA DA SIENA, fl. 1330–60, Italian painter of the Sienese school who was famed for his frescoes in the Collegiata at San Gimignano showing scenes from the life of Christ. His art reflects the sensitive and poetic manner of his teacher Simone Martini.

BARNET, BATTLE OF, battle fought in April 1471 between the forces of Edward IV and Richard Neville, the earl of Warwick, who had broken with Edward and had thrown in his lot with Henry VI and Margaret (of Anjou). Warwick's death in this battle brought an end to the so-called Wars of the Roses.

BARON, in England and France a vassal who held directly from the crown and served as a member of the king's great council. The term, which derives from either a Germanic or Celtic root meaning man, was applied in the literature of the twelfth and thirteenth centuries to a person who distinguished himself by his nobility or by his bravery.

BARONS' WAR, in English history, the war between Henry III and many of his barons, 1263–67. What precipitated the hostilities was Henry's repudiation of the Provisions of Oxford (1258) and Provisions of Westminster (1259) which had deprived him of his royal supremacy and had vested all power in a council of barons. The barons, under the leadership of Simon de Montfort, earl of Leicester, defeated and captured Henry at the battle of Lewes (1264), but the following year, after the defection of some nobles, including the powerful Gilbert de Clare, earl of Gloucester, the barons suffered defeat at Evesham and Simon was slain.

BARRACK EMPERORS, Roman emperors who ruled during the semi-anarchical period from 235 to 285. Almost every short-lived emperor who reigned during these years owed his accession, and his murder, to his own soldiers or to those of imperial pretenders.

BARRIENTOS, LOPEZ DE, d. 1469, Spanish Dominican, professor of theology in the University of Salamanca, bishop of several Spanish sees, influential figure at the court of Castile and Leon, grand chancellor, and inquisitor general.

BARRIQUE (Oxhoft), early French wine measure of differing volume, of which the best known was that of Bordeaux.

BARRITUS (*barditus*), battle cry of the early Germans.

BAR-SALIBI, JACOB, d. 1171, metropolitan of Amid (Upper Mesopotamia), the leading Jacobite (Monophysite) theologian of the period, and author (in Syriac) of poems, prayers, homilies, liturgies, and commentaries on the Bible.

BAR SAUMA, RABBAN, d. 1294, Nestorian ecclesiastic whose diary of his extensive travels represents an important historical source for the period. He was born in Peking of a Christian family, spent some years in a monastery in China, then served in an ecclesiastical capacity in Armenia. The Mongol ruler of Persia sent him to western Europe to secure the alliance of Christian kings in a war against the Moslems in Syria and Palestine. Although favorably received in Rome, Paris, London, and Constantinople, nothing came of his trip.

BARSUMAS, d. 458, Monophysite archimandrite, a leading spokesman for the Eutychian group at the Synod of Constantinople (448), at the Latrocinium (449), and at the Council of Chalcedon (451).

BARSUMAS, d. c. 490, Nestorian bishop of Nisibis, founder of an important theological school at Nisibis.

BARTE (parte), medieval term for ax, in particular the short-handled ax which the knight used in fighting.

BARTHOLI, FRANCESCO DELLA ROSSA, d. c. 1272, Franciscan chronicler, the author of several treatises on theological subjects including one about the indulgence of St. Mary de Portiuncula.

BARTHOLOMAEUS ANGLICUS, also known as Bartholomew the Englishman, studied at Oxford and Paris, joined the Franciscans, and authored the first encyclopedia in Western Europe (*De Proprietatibus Rerum,* c. 1250). While he intended the work for students of theology and the Bible, he gave most attention to the natural sciences. It proved popular in learned circles although very little of the work could be called original.

BARTHOLOMEW, d. 1333, also known as Bartholomew the Little, patron of Armenia, Dominican missionary to Armenia where he was consecrated bishop. He translated some of the works of Augustine and Aquinas into Armenian.

BARTHOLOMEW FAIR, fair located near London (West Smithfield), chartered in 1133 by Henry I to his former jester, Rahere, who had become a monk and founded the Priory of St. Bartholomew. It was principally a cloth fair.

BARTHOLOMEW, GOSPEL OF, an apocryphal gospel known to Jerome and Bede. It may have been incorporated into the Gnostic "Questions of Bartholomew."

BARTHOLOMEW OF BRESCIA, d. 1258, teacher of canon law at Bologna and author of a widely used commentary on the *Decretum* of Gratian. This work, entitled *Glossa Ordinaria Decreti,* largely a revision of a commentary by Joannes Teutonicus, enjoyed such wide acceptance that it was usually appended to copies of the *Decretum.*

BARTHOLOMEW OF EXETER, d. 1184, learned English canonist, joined the household of Theobald, archbishop of Canterbury, and became a friend of John of Salisbury. As bishop of Exeter he supported Thomas Becket in his controversy with Henry II over church–state relations and after Becket's death labored with others to work out a solution of the problem. Pope Alexander III held him in high esteem and appointed him to a number of commissions.

BARTHOLOMEW (Ptolomeo, Tolomeo) OF LUCCA, d. 1327, Dominican, confessor of St. Thomas Aquinas, later of Pope John XXII, prior of several Dominican houses in Tuscany, finally bishop of Torcello. He was a political theorist, showed considerable interest in science, and authored several works on church history. The most noteworthy of these, *Historica Ecclesiastica,* in 24 books, covered the history of the church from the birth of Christ to 1314.

BARTHOLOMEW OF PISA, d. 1347, Dominican theologian, best known for his alphabetically arranged *Summa de Casibus Conscientiae.*

BARTHOLOMEW OF SAN CONCORDIO, d. 1347, learned Dominican theologian, famed preacher, lecturer at Lucca, Florence, and Pisa, and author of a collection of excerpts from the works of classical and ecclesiastical writers which he translated into Tuscan. He also drew up a compendium of moral theology, a popular volume dealing with the sacrament of penance, sermons, and treatises on Latin grammar and the tragedies of Seneca.

BARTHOLOMEW OF URBINO, d. 1350, student at Bologna and Paris, teacher at Bologna, and bishop of Urbino. He was a friend of Petrarch's and like him a collector of manuscripts. His most scholarly work was a compilation of the writings of Augustine.

BARTHOLOMEW, ST., one of the twelve apostles. The Latin church celebrated his feast on August 24, the Greek on June 11. He may have visited India.

BARTHOLOMITES, Armenian monks of Tarsus who fled to Italy in the early fourteenth century when Saracens overran their country. They were known as Bartholomites from the church in Genoa dedicated to St. Bartholomew which they occupied. They subsequently established communities in other Italian cities as well, adopted the Rule of St. Augustine, and wore a habit similar to that of the Dominicans.

BARTOLO DI FREDI, d. 1410, Italian painter of the Sienese school (fl. 1353–1410), much of whose work was in the abstract, a sharp departure from the realistic detail popular with most artists of the period. He may have been inspired by the sobering influence of the plague or by the Dominican spirituality that had attracted his interest. He painted frescoes in the Collegiata at San Gimignano.

BARTOLOMMEO, FRA, d. 1517, Italian painter of Florence who became a disciple of Savonarola and joined the Dominican order. Most of his work consisted of altarpieces, many of them executed with the help of Mariotto Albertinelli, his pupil and partner. His painting reveals the influence of Michelangelo and Raphael.

BARTOLO OF SASSOFERRATO, d. 1357, a distinguished jurist, studied at Bologna, then taught at Pisa where he gained great fame for his knowledge of law. He authored scholarly commentaries on the *Corpus Juris Civilis*.

BASARAB DYNASTY, Rumanian family, members of which ruled Walachia as woiwodes from the early fourteenth century. Its name derived from its founder, Basarab I (d. 1352), who had thrown off Hungarian rule.

BASEL (Basle), city on the Rhine in Switzerland, a Celtic settlement and a Roman military post, and episcopal see early in the fifth century. It was occupied by the Alemanni, then by the Franks who ruled it until 912 when it passed under the authority of the king of Burgundy. In 1006 it came under German control and remained so until the death of Frederick II in 1250 when it became virtually independent. In 1501 it joined the Swiss confederation.

BASEL, COUNCIL OF, general church council (Seventeenth Ecumenical), began its sessions in July 1431 with a reaffirmation of the principles of conciliar supremacy adopted by the Council of Constance (1414–8). Later that year Pope Eugenius IV prorogued the council because he feared its conciliarist mood, its aim to effect reforms in the papal Curia, and its talk of negotiating a compromise with the Hussites over their demands. Upon the refusal of the delegates at Basel to disband, the pope rescinded his order (1433) once it became clear they had the support of the great powers. In 1437, however, he ordered the council moved to Ferrara (in 1439 it moved to Florence upon an outbreak of the plague), ostensibly to accommodate an embassy from Constantinople that wished to discuss the possibility of ending the schism between the Greek and Latin churches. The sizable minority of prelates who heeded the pope's order continued to grow at Ferrara-Florence as the moderates abandoned Basel where radical conciliarism had gained the ascendancy. In 1439 the Basel group affirmed the supremacy of the general council, deposed the pope, and replaced him with one of their own members, Amadeus of Savoy, who took the name Felix V. These steps cost Basel the sympathy of the great powers who by this time had become convinced that they would have less difficulty forcing concessions from a harassed pope than from a divided council. In April 1449 the men at Basel finally rescinded their election of Felix, announced their submission to Rome, and adjourned. [*See* CONCILIARISM.]

BASEL, TREATY OF, treaty accepted by Emperor Maximilian in September 1499 which extended the Swiss de facto recognition as an independent state.

BASEL, UNIVERSITY OF, was founded in 1460 by Pope Pius II. It was the first university to appear in Switzerland.

BASHKIRS (Baschkurts), a Finnish-Hungarian people located in the southern Urals and first recorded in the tenth century. During the course of the thirteenth and fourteenth centuries this people passed under the sway of the Golden Horde and accepted the religion of Islam.

BASIL (the Great), ST., d. 379, a leading father of the church and a founder of Eastern monasticism. He was a member of an aristocratic family with a long history of loyalty to the church, acquired a classical education in Constantinople and Athens, lived for a time as a hermit, was later ordained, and in 370 became bishop of Caesarea. His own zeal in the cause of monasticism and the influence of his writings on that subject earned him recognition as the founder of cenobitic monasticism. Equally important to the cause of monasticism was his support of that institution since it convinced doubting ecclesiastical authorities of its worthiness. What contemporaries must have considered his greatest work, however, was his success, made possible through the cooperation of his brother Gregory of Nyssa and his friend Gregory of Nazianzen, in preventing the triumph of Arianism which at this time was about to overwhelm the church. Basil left numerous writings on exegetical, dogmatic,

and ascetical subjects, as well as homilies and a voluminous correspondence. It is difficult to overstate the achievement of this courageous, indefatigable church father.

BASIL I, Byzantine emperor, 867–86, founder of the Macedonian dynasty (867–1056). Basil came from a poor Armenian family, served as horse-groom in the imperial stables where he gained the favor of Michael III, murdered Michael's uncle Bardas who was regent, next murdered Michael (867), and took over the throne for himself. As emperor he instituted important administrative and fiscal reforms, introduced an improved code of laws, and reconquered southern Italy. He encouraged missionary work among the Slavic tribes and gained the good will of Rome by deposing Photius as patriarch. He later reinstated that prelate and entrusted him with the education of his sons.

BASIL II, Byzantine emperor, 976–1025, the most successful of the Macedonian emperors, established friendly relations with the Russians, while his victories over the Bulgarians (he was called the "Bulgarcide") and the Saracens in Armenia and north Syria gave the empire its greatest extent since the reign of Justinian I (d. 565). He proved himself a great general, an able administrator and statesman, and a match for the ambitious landed aristocracy which was seeking to submerge the free peasantry upon which the empire depended for its most loyal troops. Basil's alliance with Vladimir, the Russian prince of Kiev (c. 989), to whom he gave his sister Anna in marriage, opened the way to the conversion of the Russians.

BASILIAN MONKS, monks of the Greek church who followed the Rule of St. Basil the Great. The rule, in contrast to that of St. Benedict, did not establish any kind of organized community life, but restricted itself rather to principles proper to monastic living. The monasteries of these monks consisted of groups of small cells, the whole of which was known as a laura. The chief monastery was that of the Great Laura on Mount Athos. The most famous and venerated Basilian monk of the Middle Ages was the reformer St. Theodore the Studite (d. 826).

BASILIAN NUNS, officially the Order of the Basilians of St. Macrina, were religious communities of women, located principally in Italy, the eastern Mediterranean, and eastern Europe. They honored St. Basil the Great as their founder and inspiration.

BASILICA (Basilika), a collection of canon as well as of civil and public laws, for the most part the work of Basil I (867–86) and Leo VI (886–912) and constituting essentially a revision of the *Corpus Juris Civilis*. The work was undertaken in order to bring Justinian's legal work up to date and to correct certain major defects in the *Corpus*. So successfully did it accomplish these ends that it superseded the *Corpus*.

BASILICA, name given to the early Christian church which was modeled after ancient structures having the same general design, namely, a rectangular nave, flanking aisles on either side separated from it by rows of columns, and a semicircular apse usually at the eastern end. The windows in the clerestory area which could be large since the roof was of timber, introduced an abundance of light into the nave area.

BASILICA OF MAXENTIUS, last of the great pagan basilicas of ancient Rome. It was begun by Emperor Maxentius (d. 312) and completed by Constantine (d. 337).

BASILIDES, fl. 120–45, Gnostic teacher of Alexandria. His writings included poems and 24 books of commentary on a "Gospel" that he wrote. Much confusion remains concerning the nature of his real doctrine. The Basilidean sect of Gnosticism attracted many converts and still existed in Egypt in the fourth century.

BASILISCUS, Roman emperor, d. 477, usurped the Byzantine throne for a short time (475–6)

during the reign of Zeno who fled to Isauria. The incompetence of Basiliscus and his encouragement of Monophysitism led to his deposition and execution by Zeno who had returned.

BASILISK, serpent, lizard, or dragon, whose look, according to medieval bestiaries, was fatal. It frequently appeared in medieval art.

BASILISSA, name of various female martyrs whose existence and *vitae* were based upon legendary materials.

BASILIUS VALENTINUS, an obscure, possibly nonexistent, Benedictine monk of Erfurt of the fifteenth century to whom were attributed some 20 writings on the subject of alchemy. Basilius may have served as the writer's pseudonym.

BASIL OF ANCYRA, d. c. 364, Arian bishop, deposed by the Council of Sardica in 343 but reinstated by Emperor Constantius c. 348. His growing criticism of extreme Arian doctrines led later to his removal (360).

BASIL, RULE OF ST., monastic rule laid down by Basil the Great and the one adopted by most of the religious communities in the Greek church. It concerned itself more with principles of ascetic life than with matters of organization and routine. It was revised by St. Theodore the Studite (d. 826).

BASIN, THOMAS, d. 1491, bishop of Lisieux, adviser of Charles VII of France but sent into exile by his successor, Louis XI. Basin's history covers the reigns of these two kings. It represents a valuable historical source for the period but suffers for its want of objectivity concerning Louis.

BASOCHE (Bazoche), guild of clerks of the *parlement* of Paris, organized early in the fourteenth century as a miniature feudal state with king and other dignitaries. It had power to try minor cases among its members and cases brought by others against its members. Its mock trials were intended to provide practice and instruction in legal procedure. The basoche contributed indirectly to the development of the French stage.

BASQUES, ancient folk of northern Spain and southwestern France who were converted to Christianity from the third to the fifth centuries. Neither the Visigoths nor Franks were able to dominate them, and late in the sixth century they extended their rule over Gascony. In 778, after having been obliged to accept nominal vassalage to Charlemagne, they annihilated the rearguard of his army at Roncesvalles. In 824 the Basques founded the kingdom of Navarre at Pamplona which under Sancho III (1000–35) included almost all the territories occupied by that people. Several provinces had come under the rule of Castile by the end of the Middle Ages, while the kingdom of Navarre itself was annexed by Ferdinand II of Aragon in 1513.

BASSE DANSE, a dance that originated in courtly circles but became popular with the common people in the late Middle Ages. It retained something of its early grace and dignity.

BASSELIN, OLIVIER, d. c. 1450, French poet of Normandy, reputedly the author of French drinking songs popular in his native valley of *Vau-de-Vire*, the origin of the word "vaudeville."

BASTARD OF ORLÉANS. *See* DUNOIS, JEAN, COUNT OF.

BASTARNAE, a Germanic people that moved into the area between the Carpathians and the Black Sea in the third century B.C. When the Goths drove them from that region in A.D. 280, they were permitted to settle within the Roman empire in Thrace.

BASTIDE, name given to a fortified town in southwestern France from the twelfth to the fourteenth century. The function of *bastides* was not only military but political and economic as well, and for that reason they were endowed with charters of privileges in the hope of attracting inhabitants.

BASTILLE, initially a name given in France to fortified towers and castles, but later reserved to that of the castle that guarded the gate of St. Antoine at Paris, constructed between the years 1368 and 1382.

BATALHA, town in Portugal near which John I of Portugal defeated John I of Castile in 1385 and thus secured the independence of his country. A large Dominican convent of Santa Maria da Vitória ("St. Mary of the Victory") was founded there probably in 1388. It contains the tombs of a number of famous people and kings, including that of Prince Henry the Navigator.

BATH, city in Somerset, England, known for its warm springs since Roman times. A convent was founded there in 676 and a Benedictine abbey in the tenth century. In Chaucer's day Bath was a wool-marketing and cloth-making town.

BATH, ORDER OF THE, an English service order, probably founded by Henry IV in 1399, which had its name from the custom of the newly inducted members of taking a quasi-ceremonial bath.

BATHILDIS (Batilda), ST., d. c. 680, was stolen from her home in England and brought to Gaul (France) where she later married Clovis II, king of Neustria and Burgundy. She founded the monasteries of Corbie and Chelles.

BATHORY (Bathori, Battori), noted Hungarian family, members of which ruled portions of Transylvania and Hungary in the fifteenth century. Stephen II, woiwode of Siebenbürgen, won a major victory over the Turks at Kenyermezo in 1479.

BATTANI, MOHAMMED IBN JABIR AL- (Albategnius), d. 929, one of the most learned of Arab astronomers and mathematicians. His most important work, and the only one to survive, *Astronomical Treatise and Tables,* contributed significantly to the study of astronomy and the development of spherical trigonometry. With remarkable accuracy he was able to ascertain the obliquity of the ecliptic, the length of the year and the seasons, and the true orbit of the sun. His views helped destroy a number of Ptolemaic principles.

BATTLE, site northeast of Hastings where in 1066 Harold I, the Anglo-Saxon king of England, was slain and his army routed by William of Normandy who went on to become king. Ruins remain of Battle Abbey which William founded there to commemorate his victory. The authenticity of the Battle Abbey Roll, presumably a list of the noble companions of William in this battle, continues in doubt.

BATTLE OF THE SPURS, battle fought in 1302 near Courtrai, Belgium, between Flemish townsmen led by those of Bruges, and a French army sent there by Philip IV who had annexed Flanders in 1301. The French army, composed principally of knights, sustained a surprising and disastrous defeat. The enormous quantity of spurs taken from the fallen French knights gave the battle its name.

BATU KHAN, d. 1255, Mongol commander, grandson of Genghis Khan, conquered all of Russia (1235–46) except for Novgorod with the help of his general Sabutai, and ravaged Poland, Silesia, and Hungary. His return to Karakorum in Outer Mongolia in 1242 to take part in the election of a new khan may have saved western Europe from Mongol conquest. The splendid appearance of his camp of tents gave the name of Golden Horde to his army. He established his capital at Sarai on the Volga.

BATZEN, small silver coins, first known as Rollbatzen, used in south Germany and Switzerland at the close of the Middle Ages.

BAUDRY OF BOURGUEIL, d. 1130, Benedictine monk, abbot of Bourgueil-en-Vallée, and archbishop of Dol in Brittany. He composed secular verse, some of it in imitation of Ovid for whom he had a special admiration, and an account of the First Crusade (1096–99).

BAVARIA, duchy lying largely to the south of the upper Danube and to the east of Swabia. The Bavarians (Baiuoarii) who gave their name to the region were a branch of the Suevi and probably related to the Marcomanni who settled in the same general area. Boniface converted these people with the help of Celtic monks and during the rule of Duke Odilo (737–48) established several dioceses including Salzburg and Regensburg. Charlemagne deposed Tassilo III, the last of the Agilolfing dukes, and incorporated the region into his empire. In the division of this empire in 843 Bavaria fell to the kingdom of the East Franks of which it constituted the most powerful duchy and usually the most troublesome. For this reason it was stripped of the Ostmark (Austria) in 976 and of Styria in 1180, this last deprivation the work of Frederick I Barbarossa who then gave the duchy to Otto of Wittelsbach. This family continued to rule Bavaria until 1918.

BAYAZID (Bajesid, Bajezet, Bayazet) I, Ottoman Turkish sultan, 1389–1403, conquered the greater part of the Balkans and in 1396 crushed Sigismund and his Crusading army at Nicopolis. He himself suffered defeat at the hands of Timur the Lame in 1402 at Angora and died a prisoner.

BAYAZID II, Ottoman Turkish sultan, 1481–1512, successor of his father, Mohammed II. His younger brother Jem contested his succession but was defeated and fled to Europe where he died. Some territories were conquered along the Danube and Dniester which opened the way to the Crimea. Bayazid also seized parts of the Morea and cities along the Adriatic following a successful war against Venice (1499–1503).

BAYBARS. *See* BAIBARS.

BAYEUX TAPESTRY, a linen roll 231 feet long and 20 inches wide upon which was woven an account of the expedition of William, duke of Normandy, to Britain and his victory at Hastings. The tapestry was probably made on orders of Bishop Odo of Bayeux, William's half-brother. The tapestry with its 72 scenes possesses not only great value as a work of art but also contributes to the knowledge of warfare of the period.

BEANUS, name commonly given to the newly arrived student at the medieval university. The word derives from the French *béjoune,* meaning a very young bird, figuratively an ignorant, foolish fellow.

BÉARN, region in the Pyrenees in southwestern France. In 819 it became a viscounty of the duke of Aquitaine. In the thirteenth century, as one of the lordships of Gascony, it passed to the counts of Foix who later became kings of Navarre. In 1494 it came into the possession of the house of Albret and later it fell under control of the French crown.

BEATA NOBIS GAUDIA, hymn of unknown origin in honor of the Holy Spirit that was already popular in the tenth century.

BEATITUDES, eight blessings spoken by Christ at the opening of the Sermon on the Mount (Matthew 5:3–12).

BEATRICE, a Florentine woman, wife of Simone dei Bardi, who died in 1290 at the age of twenty-four. She served Dante as his inspiration in the *Vita Nuova* and as his guide in the *Paradiso.*

BEATRICE OF NAZARETH, d. 1268, was raised in a Beguine community in Brabant, became a Cistercian nun, later a prioress. Her mystical writings, which she composed in Flemish, provide an insight into the kind of spirituality the Beguines of the time practiced.

BEATRICE OF TUSCANY, d. 1076, daughter of the duke of Upper Lorraine, wife of the margrave of Tuscany, and regent for her son in 1052 when her husband died. In 1055 Henry III of Germany imprisoned her because she dared marry an enemy of the crown. Later released and again widowed, she assisted her daughter Matilda with the administration of the Canossan dominions. In the investiture struggle between Gregory VII and Henry IV her sympathies lay with the pope.

BEATRIX OF BURGUNDY, d. 1184, heiress of Count Rainald of Burgundy, second wife of Frederick I Barbarossa whom she married in 1156. Frederick chose her in order to strengthen his position in the region of Burgundy and to the south.

BEATUS, ST., d. 112, called the Apostle of Switzerland on the basis of a tenth-century legend which had St. Peter sending him there to convert the pagan Helvetians.

BEATUS OF LIÉBANA, d. 798, Spanish monk who fought the heresy of Adoptionism. His well-known commentary on the *Apocalypse* contained illustrations that revealed Celtic (or Coptic) influences and which in turn influenced Romanesque sculptors of Vézelay, Saint-Benoît-sur-Loire, and Moissac.

BEAUCHAMP, GUY DE. *See* WARWICK, EARLDOM OF.

BEAUCHAMP, RICHARD DE. *See* WARWICK, EARLDOM OF.

BEAUCHAMP, RICHARD, d. 1481, canonist, royal chaplain, bishop of Hereford (1448), later of Salisbury (1450). He served as an emissary in the Yorkist-Lancastrian struggle, also as an envoy to France. As dean of Windsor he had an important part in the erection of St. George's Chapel, which is considered an outstanding example of Perpendicular architecture.

BEAUCHAMP, THOMAS DE. *See* WARWICK, EARLDOM OF.

BEAUFORT, English aristocratic family which originated with John Beaufort, earl of Somerset (d. 1409), a natural son of John of Gaunt, duke of Lancaster, by Catherine Swynford. His younger brother, Henry Cardinal Beaufort, was the most distinguished member of the dynasty. The four children of John of Gaunt by Catherine were legitimized after their parents' subsequent marriage (1396), but they were expressly excluded from the succession to the throne by their half-brother Henry IV in 1407.

BEAUFORT, EDMUND. *See* SOMERSET.

BEAUFORT, HENRY, d. 1447, English prelate, statesman, and cardinal, natural son of John of Gaunt and a half-brother of Henry IV. His high connections brought him many benefices and in 1398 he became bishop of Lincoln, in 1404 that of Winchester. He held the office of lord chancellor for a few years under each of three Henrys (IV, V, VI). In 1417 he was created cardinal by Pope Martin V but Henry V forbade him to accept the honor. In 1426 he did so, however, and until 1431 served as papal legate to Germany, Hungary, and Bohemia where he commanded the pope's forces against the Hussites. His most powerful role came during the minority of Henry VI when as a member of the council of regency he led the opposition to Humphrey, duke of Gloucester, whom Henry V had assigned the management of affairs in England. Although enormously wealthy and ambitious, his death removed a major stabilizing influence from English political affairs.

BEAUFORT, LADY MARGARET, d. 1509, daughter of John Beaufort, duke of Somerset, descendant of John of Gaunt, the wife of Edmund Tudor (1455), the earl of Richmond, and the mother of Henry VII. She was known for her philanthropy and with the help of her confessor, John Fisher, founded Christ's College and St. John's College at Cambridge. She was a patron of many religious houses, also of Caxton.

BEAULIEU, ABBEY OF, Cistercian abbey in Hampshire founded by King John in 1204 for 30 monks from Citeaux. From its foundation it possessed rights of sanctuary.

BEAUMANOIR, PHILIPPE DE RÉMY (Rémi), SIRE

DE, d. 1296, well-known poet, a judge in the service of the French crown, and author of *Coutumes de Beauvaisis*. This work, which has been called the most popular French law book of the Middle Ages, describes with great understanding both the laws of Beauvaisis and the fundamental principles of the private law of the period.

BEAUNEVEU, ANDRÉ, d. 1403?, illuminator and sculptor in the employ of Charles V of France, the count of Flanders, and the duke of Berry. He carved several figures for the royal tombs at Saint-Denis. The influence he enjoyed with contemporaries enabled him to leave a deep mark on the art of France and of Flanders in the fourteenth century.

BEAUVAIS, city from Roman times located about 50 miles north of Paris which the Northmen ravaged and burned several times during the period of their depredations. In 1013 the bishop of Beauvais became the city's count, and around 1248 Louis IX asserted his royal authority over the region. It was the center of the Jacquerie in 1358. The city was in English hands for the greater part of the Hundred Years' War but remained loyal to Louis XI during the course of his troubles with the League of Public Weal. During the siege by the Burgundians in 1472, an enemy standard was captured by a girl, Jeanne Hachette. It was the bishop of Beauvais, Pierre Cauchon, who presided at the trial of Joan of Arc. The Gothic cathedral of St. Pierre boasts the loftiest choir ever built (157 feet). St. Etienne's church has a Romanesque nave and a Gothic choir.

BEBENBURG, LUPOLD OF, d. 1363, bishop of Bamberg, author of the legal treatise *De Juribus Regni Et Imperii* in which he maintained that the person whom the German princes elected as king automatically assumed the position of emperor without any action by the pope. This view reflected the force of the imperial ordinance *Licet Juris* which Louis IV had promulgated in 1338.

BEC, ABBEY OF, Benedictine monastery in Normandy, founded by Bl. Herluin in 1034, enjoyed considerable fame in the eleventh and twelfth centuries as a center of learning. It counted Lanfranc and Anselm among its most distinguished abbots.

BEC, COMPROMISE OF, an arrangement agreed to in 1106 by Henry I of England and Anselm, archbishop of Canterbury, who represented the church, over the selection and institution of bishops. The crown surrendered the practice of investing prelates with the symbols of their office although it retained a major voice in their selection. [*See* WORMS, CONCORDAT OF.]

BECKET, THOMAS, ST., d. 1170, archbishop of Canterbury, medieval England's most renowned martyr, his tomb at Canterbury its most popular shrine. Becket was the son of a Norman merchant, joined the household of Theobald, archbishop of Canterbury, became archdeacon, then in 1154 Henry II's chancellor in which office he proved himself an efficient, if worldly, administrator. In 1162 Henry secured Becket's election as archbishop of Canterbury, but instead of agreeing to a restriction of the church's authority in matters concerning justice and property which the king had expected, Becket resigned the office of chancellor, rejected the Constitutions of Clarendon in which the king had set down the new order in church–state relations, and fled to France (1164) to escape the king's anger. Pope Alexander III gave Becket his sympathetic support but urged him to adopt a conciliatory attitude, which Becket refused to do. The break continued until June 1170 when Henry and Becket agreed to a hollow reconciliation. Shortly after, Becket reopened the break when he excommunicated the English bishops who had taken part in the coronation of the young Henry, a ceremony which was his prerogative to perform. Upon hearing Henry's exasperated blast at Becket's action, four royal knights hurried to Canterbury and murdered the archbishop in his cathedral (29 December).

BED. When the poor had beds to sleep in, these consisted of large shallow chests with straw mattresses. The beds of the wealthier consisted of a frame constructed of turned wood, the main ornaments being the four balls that formed the lower terminals of the legs. The mattress or pallet was supported in an inclined position, which meant, given the use of head pillows, a semi-upright position for the sleeper. By the twelfth century beds of the wealthy might be inlaid with carving and painting, and graced with embroidered coverlets and mattresses. Curtains suspended from the ceiling served to keep out drafts. From about the thirteenth century until the sixteenth, people generally slept naked. Beds received more attention in construction and decoration than any other article of furniture and were invariably listed with other valuables in wills. The texter bed became common in the fifteenth century. A canopy above it was suspended from the ceiling or fastened to the wall, thereby creating a room within a room. Its curtains which provided privacy and protection from drafts during the night might be drawn in the daytime or looped in the form of a bag when the bed served as couch or seat. Fixed beds were introduced in the fifteenth century. They were held together with pegs which could be removed, thus allowing the bed to be transported with other baggage should the owners wish to travel. The support for the mattress was a trellis of leather straps nailed to the bed frame.

Louis XI (1461–83) is believed to have introduced the ceremony which had the king reclining on a bed known as the *lit de justice* when he was present at a meeting of *parlement*. The princes of the realm sat on stools, the greater officials stood, and the lesser ones knelt around about. On formal occasions the king and great nobles might possess a state bed or *lit de parade*.

BEDARESI (Bedersi), YEDAYAH BEN ABRAHAM, d. 1340, Jewish poet and philosopher born in Béziers. Many translations have been made of his didactic *Examination of the World*.

BEDE (Beda, Baeda), THE VENERABLE, d. 735, entered the Benedictine monastery at Jarrow as a youth and remained there his entire life, first as a student, then as teacher. Except for the translation of the Gospel of St. John into Anglo-Saxon, his voluminous writings are in Latin. (He knew Greek and possibly some Hebrew.) These writings include hymns, exegetical works, a life of St. Cuthbert, and manuals or treatises on the seven liberal arts and on a variety of scientific subjects. His study of chronology helped establish the birth of Christ as the base year in the Western calendar. His most important work, the *Ecclesiastical History of the English People*, has earned him recognition as the first modern historian, among other reasons because he stated that the first obligation of the historian was to tell the truth and because he cited the sources of his information. In his day he may have been the most learned man in Western Europe, and until the thirteenth century he was respected as the first authority in the field of theology.

BEDFORD, DUKES OF. The first duke of Bedford, John, was so created by his brother Henry V in 1414. Upon the king's death in 1422, he was designated protector for the young Henry VI, but since he felt that his first duty was to direct the war in France (Hundred Years' War), his brother Humphrey, duke of Gloucester, served in his stead at home. His administration of English possessions in France was efficient though severe, and his prosecution of the war was generally successful until the victories of Joan of Arc and the weakening of the English alliance with Burgundy led to eventual French victory. Bedford's reputation suffers from the fact that he authorized the execution of Joan of Arc. Until his death England was generally able to maintain its dominant position in western and northern France, while at the same time preventing factional strife in England from breaking out into civil war. He died in 1435, the year Burgundy repudiated its alliance with England. He left no legitimate issue.

George Neville (d. 1483), son of John, earl of Northumberland, was created duke of Bedford in 1470 but was degraded from the peerage in 1477 following his father's attainder and death at the battle of Barnet. Jasper Tudor (d. 1495), half-brother of Henry VI and uncle of Henry VII, was the next duke of Bedford.

BEDFORD, JOHN, DUKE OF. *See* BEDFORD, DUKES OF.

BEDLAM, English abbreviation for Bethlehem, once a priory (St. Mary of Bethlehem) founded in 1247 and situated in St. George's Field in Lambeth. The community maintained a hospital for the poor in the fourteenth century and appears to have extended its care to the mentally ill and insane (lunatics are recorded among its patients in 1402), whence the common term bedlam.

BEDOUINS (desert or tent dwellers), name originally given to members of pastoral, nomadic desert tribes in Arabia, then later, with the expansion of Islam, to those of Syria and North Africa. Camel breeding was the principal source of their livelihood.

BEELZEBUB. *See* BAALZEBUB.

BEGGA, ST., d. 693, daughter of Pepin of Landen, mother of Pepin (II) of Heristal, and foundress of a monastery at Andenne near Namur. The Beguines revered her as their patroness.

BEGHARD (Begard), member of any of a number of lay brotherhoods that appeared in the Rhineland, southern France, and Low Countries in the thirteenth century. The earliest such community may have been established as early as 1220 in Louvain. The brothers, often fullers, dyers, and weavers, especially in Flanders, dedicated themselves to prayer and social work but took no formal monastic vows. They were often identified with, if not influenced by, other semi-dissident groups such as the Spiritual Franciscans and Brethren of the Free Spirit.

BEGUINE (Beguin), member of any of several lay sisterhoods that appeared as early as the twelfth century and were most numerous in the Netherlands and Germany. They formed semireligious communities which in the more populous areas might be organized into a single *béguinage*. Although they engaged in works of charity and held to a routine of prayer, they took no formal vows, retained their property, and might withdraw from their communities at any time. Like the Beghards they occasionally suffered charges of heresy, not always unjustly, although they generally enjoyed the protection of the ecclesiastical authorities. In 1311 the Council of Vienne condemned some of their teaching as heretical.

BEHAIM (Böheim, Behem), MARTIN, d. 1507, a cartographer of Nuremberg. He studied astronomy, navigation, and mathematics possibly under Regiomontanus. His is the oldest globe still in existence although it is inaccurate and does not represent the best geographical knowledge of the late fifteenth century.

BEHAIM (Beham, Behem, Beheim), MICHEL, d. c. 1472, meistersinger who traveled about central Europe, now as a mercenary soldier, now as a poet. He sang of himself and of his times and also on religious and historical themes.

BEI (bej, beg, bek, bey), title given to higher officials among the Turks; also the title of the leader of certain Turkish tribes.

BEK, ANTHONY, d. 1311, chancellor under Edward I, one of his principal counselors and agents and, as bishop of Durham, a staunch and powerful aid to the king in his difficulties with the Scots. He led diplomatic missions to Scotland, Gascony, France, Germany, Italy, and Aragon. He ruled his palatinate diocese with semiregal power, arrogantly but with efficiency and courage.

BELA I, king of Hungary, 1060–3, a cousin of St. Stephen, seized the throne from his brother Andrew I, put down the last pagan revolt, then fell in battle with his nephew Salomo who had the support of Henry IV of Germany.

BELA III, king of Hungary, 1173–96, was reared in Constantinople and when king reorganized his government after the Byzantine administrative system. In 1180 he took Sirmium and Dalmatia from Byzantium.

BELA IV, king of Hungary, 1235–70, son of Andrew II and himself one of the leading monarchs of medieval Hungary. In 1241 he suffered a crushing defeat at the hands of the Mongols who then devastated the greater part of his country. When he returned after a year he devoted his efforts to reconstructing the economic life of the country and among other measures encouraged the immigration of German merchants and peasants. For most of his reign he had trouble with his neighbors. He lost Zara to Venice, managed to extend his authority over Styria and Bulgaria for a time, and in 1261 repelled a second invasion by the Mongols. His last years were disturbed by the rebellion of his son David who succeeded him.

BELESME (Bellême), ROBERT OF, d. c. 1131, earl of Shrewsbury, also a Norman baron with extensive holdings in that duchy. For a time he was the most powerful vassal of Henry I, king of England. Though cruel and irresponsible, he demonstrated a knowledge of military architecture in the construction of the castle of Gisors. He fought Henry I at the battle of Tinchebrai (1106), but when he came to England as the French ambassador, Henry had him put in prison where he died.

BELFROI (Belfried), tower, usually a bell tower. Such towers were particularly popular in the cities of Flanders.

BELGIUM, country whose name is derived from the Belgae, a people of ancient Gaul. The Roman province of Belgica was appreciably larger than modern Belgium. Franks began to move into the region in the third century. It was at Heristal that the Carolingian dynasty had its roots. When the Carolingian empire was divided in 843 Belgium became part of Lotharingia, later of the duchy of Lower Lorraine. This included all but the western part of the so-called Low Countries. When Lorraine disintegrated in the twelfth century, the duchies of Brabant and Luxemburg emerged, along with the bishopric of Liège. The history of these feudal states, together with that of Flanders and Hainaut, constitute the medieval history of Belgium. The most important development to take place in the region in the high and later Middle Ages was the rise of such great industrial and commercial centers as Ghent, Bruges, and Ypres. In the fifteenth century all of present-day Belgium came under control of the dukes of Burgundy. When Mary of Burgundy died in 1482, the general area of the Low Countries entered a period of foreign domination.

BELGRADE, city on the Danube, once a Roman military camp, a bishop's seat in the fourth century. Because of its strategic location, it was overrun or occupied successively by Avars, Slavs, Bulgars, Byzantium, Serbs, Hungarians, and Turks. In the twelfth century it became the capital of Serbia. It repelled a Turkish attack in 1456 but in 1521 fell to Suleiman I.

BELIAL, late Jewish name for Satan or the devil whom St. Paul identified as the antichrist. A book with that title appeared in Middle High German c. 1400 which contrasted Christ with the antichrist.

BELISARIUS, d. 565, Justinian's ablest general in his wars against the Persians, Vandals, and Ostrogoths. In a short campaign (533–4), he destroyed the Vandal kingdom in North Africa, then by 540 had all but reconquered Italy from the Ostrogoths. After his absence on a campaign against Chosres I, the Sassanid Persian monarch, he returned to Italy to find most of the peninsula under control of the Gothic chieftain Totila. Perhaps because Justinian did not trust him,

Belisarius did not receive sufficient supplies and forces to reconquer Italy and was eventually replaced by Narses. In 559 he came out of retirement to save Constantinople from a massive attack by the savage Kotrigurs.

BELLA GERANT ALII. TU, FELIX AUSTRIA, NUBE!, an observation in hexameter verse attributed to Matthias Corvinus, king of Hungary (1458–90), which commended the Hapsburgs for their good fortune in obtaining by marriage what others could only hope to achieve through war.

BELL, BOOK, AND CANDLE, a ceremony dating back possibly to the eighth century that was used when pronouncing the major excommunication. The bell is said to have represented the public character of the act, the book the authority of the words spoken by the bishop, and the candle to have symbolized the possibility that the ban might be lifted should the excommunicated person repent.

BELLECHOSE, HENRY, d. c. 1444, Flemish painter of Brabant who spent most of his active years as official painter to the Burgundian court. His more noteworthy paintings include a series of scenes from the life of Mary that he executed for the palace of the duke in Dijon.

BELLINI, GENTILE, d. 1507, Venetian painter, elder son of Jacopo, whose work revealed the influence of his father and his brother-in-law Mantegna. He is best known for a number of large paintings which depict miracles taking place before a Venetian background, as well as for portraits, pageants, and processional pictures which hold historical value since they succeed in representing contemporary Venetian life. In Venice he worked with his brother Giovanni on the great historic frescoes in the ducal palace. He also spent some time in Constantinople where he did a portrait of Sultan Mohammed II and the *Reception of a Venetian Ambassador at Constantinople*.

BELLINI, GIOVANNI, d. 1516, painter of Venice, younger son of Jacopo, and influenced by him and by Mantegna, his brother-in-law. His paintings, mostly Madonnas and altarpieces, rank with the most beautiful and intriguing of the Venetian Renaissance. His use of rich yet delicate coloring served to provide his compositions unity and a contemplative mood. A monumental quality, mastery of color, and an intensity of religious feeling mark his best work. He was reputed the greatest painter of his age, and it was his influence and achievement that transformed Venice from an artistically backward city into a major center of Renaissance art. Ruskin called his *The Madonna with Saints* one of the three most beautiful pictures in the world.

BELLINI, JACOPO, d. c. 1470, Venetian painter, pupil of Gentile da Fabriano and himself the father of Gentile and Giovanni who also became noted painters. By means of delicate coloring Jacopo succeeded in investing his subjects with repose and dignity in keeping with the grace of late Gothic. He worked principally in the churches and palaces of north Italy and maintained a studio in Padua where his sons received their early training. Many of his best paintings have perished, including the enormous *Crucifixion* in the cathedral at Verona.

BELLS. The tradition that Paulinus of Nola introduced the use of bells into the Christian worship (c. 420) may be legendary. They were in use in Scotland and Ireland as early as the sixth century and came into general use in the church during the eighth. They were used to summon the faithful to services, to announce the death of a member of the parish, and to sound the angelus.

BELLUNO, once a Lombard duchy, in the twelfth century a free city and a member of the Lombard League. It became subject to Venice in the fifteenth century.

BELVISIO, JACOBO, d. 1335, jurist, studied at Bologna, taught at Naples, Padua, Perugia, and Bologna. His legal writings show his knowledge of the ideas and methods of French jurisprudence which he was first to introduce into Italian law.

BEMA, in ecclesiastical architecture the end of a Christian church where the higher clergy sat and the altar was placed. It later took the form of a raised platform directly behind the altar in the apse.

BEN ASHER, name of a family of Masoretes who lived in Palestine in the ninth and tenth centuries. The most prominent members, Moses and his son Aaron, sought to establish the vocalization and accentuation of the consonantal text of the Hebrew Bible.

BENEDETTO DA MAJANO, d. 1497, sculptor and architect of the Florentine school, known especially for the great beauty of his pulpits, altarpieces, and other church furniture. His masterwork may be the altarpiece in the church of Monte Oliveto at Naples.

BENEDICAMUS DOMINO, Latin for *Let us bless the Lord*, a verse recited or sung as a conclusion to the Divine Office or the Mass service. The response is *Deo Gratias* ("Thanks be to God").

BENEDICITE, Latin for *Bless ye* [the Lord], the canticle of praise which Shadrach, Meshach, and Abednego sang as they stood in the fiery furnace (Daniel 3). It was in use in Christian liturgical worship from early times.

BENEDICT I, Pope, 575–9, probably a Roman whose short pontificate fell during the period of Lombard attacks on the city of Rome.

BENEDICT II, ST., Pope, June 26, 684, to May 8, 685, a Roman, among whose few actions as pope was that endorsing the decree of the Council of Constantinople III which condemned Monothelitism. It was during his pontificate that Emperor Constantine IV Pogonatus rescinded the decree that had required imperial ratification of papal elections.

BENEDICT III, Pope, 855–8, a Roman who with the aid of the clergy and people of Rome made good his election against the ambitions of Anastasius the Librarian who enjoyed the support of Louis II, king of Italy. When the emperor in Constantinople deposed Ignatius, the patriarch, Benedict refused to give his approval of the act before himself examining the validity of the charges brought against that prelate.

BENEDICT IV, Pope, 900–3, a Roman and the last pope for some fifty years who was able to act independently of the political factions that controlled the city. A Lateran synod which he summoned in 900 validated the acts of Pope Formosus (d. 896) whose election had been declared invalid.

BENEDICT V, Pope, May 22? to June 23, 964, a Roman, renounced his election when Otto I, king of Germany, who objected, came down across the Alps, laid siege to the city, and forced its surrender. Benedict was degraded to the rank of deacon and sent to Germany into the safekeeping of the archbishop of Hamburg where he died (966?).

BENEDICT VI, Pope, 973–4, a Roman, owed his election to Otto I, king of Germany. Upon Otto's death, the Roman aristocracy took over the city, chose Boniface VII (antipope) to be their pope, and murdered Benedict VI.

BENEDICT VII, Pope, 974–83, a Roman, bishop of Sutri, owed his selection to Otto II, king of Germany. (The antipope Boniface VII fled to Constantinople.) He took an interest in the conversion of the Slavs and granted monasteries exemption from episcopal control in the hope of expediting their reform.

BENEDICT VIII, Pope, 1012–24, member of the powerful Tusculani family, succeeded, in alliance with Genoa and Pisa, in driving the Saracens from Italy and Sardinia. He cooperated with Henry II of Germany in furthering the cause of the reform of the church.

BENEDICT IX, Pope, 1032–45, a nephew of Popes Benedict VIII and John XIX, owed his position to the Tusculani faction which controlled Rome. In 1044 a revolt drove him momentarily from the city. When he returned the following year, he sold his papal office to Gregory VI, but Henry III of Germany objected, whereupon a reform synod at Rome declared him deposed and acclaimed Clement II. Upon the death of Clement in 1047, Benedict made an attempt to reclaim the papal office but was driven from the city. He died c. 1055.

BENEDICT X, Pope (Antipope), 1058–9, a Roman, bishop of Velletri, whose election by the Romans was declared invalid by the reform party. He was confined to the monastery of Sant' Agnese and died c. 1080 during the pontificate of Gregory VII (1073–85).

BENEDICT XI, BL., Pope, Oct. 22, 1303, to July 7, 1304, an Italian, learned Dominican, master general of the order, cardinal, and adherent of Boniface VIII in his quarrel with Philip IV of France. He was one of the two cardinals who was with Boniface at Anagni when the French and their Colonna allies stormed the city and seized him. When Benedict was elected pope following the death of Boniface, he adopted a conciliatory policy toward Philip and modified the strong language concerning papal authority with which his predecessor had punctuated his bulls.

BENEDICT XII, Pope, 1334–42, a Frenchman, doctor of theology (Paris), Cistercian, bishop of Pamiers, papal inquisitor against the Waldenses and Albigenses, cardinal, and active in theological controversies over apostolic poverty and the doctrine of the beatific vision. In his constitution *Benedictus Deus* (1336) he defined this doctrine which held that the souls of the just who were without sins to expiate in purgatory enjoyed the beatific vision immediately after death. He actively supported curial and monastic reform and began the construction of a papal palace at Avignon.

BENEDICT XIII, Pope (Antipope), 1394–1417, as cardinal Petro de Luna took part in the election of Urban VI in 1378 but later threw his support to the Avignonese pope Clement VII. On Clement's death in 1394 he was elected by the Avignonese cardinals. Although the Council of Constance declared him deposed in 1417, he stoutly maintained the legitimacy of his position from Peniscola in Aragon where he had taken refuge. He died in 1423.

BENEDICT, ST., d. 547?, abbot of Monte Cassino and founder of Benedictine and Western monasticism. Benedict who was born c. 480 at Nursia (central Italy) was sent by his parents to Rome for an education but left the city because of its licentiousness and took up the life of a hermit near the ruins of Nero's palace above Subiaco (40 miles east of Rome). He organized the large number of disciples whom his sanctity attracted into a dozen monastic communities, then c. 530 moved with several monks to Monte Cassino, halfway on the road from Rome to Naples, where he established the mother house of the order that bears his name. The mark of Benedict's genius as an organizer of men dedicated to the spiritual life stands revealed in the rule he drew up for the management of the community at Monte Cassino. In this document (fewer then 50 pages in a modern format) he prescribed a year's probation for novices, required from the monks a vow of stability and their strict obedience to an abbot who would rule the community with their counsel, gave special emphasis to the practice of the virtues of humility and obedience, and set down an admirably balanced monastic day divided between prayer (public and private) and work (physical and intellectual). Central to the spiritual life was the recitation of the Divine Office (and the Rule), the temporal tranquillity of the community, the precise manner in which Benedict outlined the monk's activities during the day as well as the

measure of his food, drink, clothing, and sleep. It is to the Rule's careful attention to the daily life of the monk and the relative moderation of the regimen required of the members that scholars attribute the community's remarkable success.

BENEDICT BISCOP, ST., d. 690, a Northumbrian, scholarly monk of Lérins, moved to England where he founded the Benedictine abbeys of Wearmouth (674) and Jarrow (682), thereby establishing himself as the founder of Benedictine monachism in England. The Venerable Bede was his most famous pupil.

BENEDICTINES, members of the religious order founded c. 530 by St. Benedict, known simply as Black Monks until the fourteenth century when the identification of Benedictines came into use. What proved a turning point in the history of the order was the Lombard destruction of Monte Cassino in 577 and the flight of its community to Rome. To Pope Gregory the Great (590–604) the refugees appeared as godsends to staff the struggling church in the West and to carry the gospel to the heathen. It was Gregory's support, and later that of the Frankish kings, notably Charlemagne (d. 814), that assured the order such growth that by the year 800 it had supplanted other monastic observances on the continent. Louis the Pious, the son of Charlemagne, encouraged the reformer Benedict of Aniane in his efforts to establish greater uniformity among the monasteries in the Frankish empire, but all his work went for naught during the feudal period that followed when both church and monasticism dropped to their spiritual nadir.

The first step to defeudalize monasticism and give it new life was taken in 910 when William, duke of Aquitaine, established a Benedictine monastery at Cluny and surrendered any right to interfere in its administration. [See CLUNY, CONGREGATION OF.] A contemporary reform movement aimed at eliminating lay control emanated from the Benedictine monastery at

Gorze in Lorraine, while individual abbots, including Dunstan of Glastonbury in England, shared efforts in revitalizing monastic life throughout western Europe. The eleventh century witnessed the appearance of such monastic communities as the Camaldolese, the Vallombrosians, and the Cistercians, all of which groups departed from traditional Benedictine practice in the hope of recovering what they believed to have been the spiritual vigor of nascent Benedictine monasticism.

Until the rise of the popular mendicant orders of the thirteenth century Benedictine monasticism maintained its position of leadership in the religious and intellectual life of Western Europe. From the thirteenth century it shared that leadership with the newer orders, while all suffered a measure of decline in the late Middle Ages because of such disasters as the Black Death, the Hundred Years' War, and the Western Schism. [*See* BENEDICT, ST.; MONASTICISM.]

BENEDICTINES, OLIVETAN, an offshoot of the Benedictines which originated with Blessed Bernard Tolomei who founded the monastery of Mount Olivet near Siena c. 1313. He prescribed a monastic rule that combined the contemplative life with an active apostolate.

BENEDICTINES, SYLVESTRINE, a monastic congregation of Benedictines that adopted certain changes in the Benedictine Rule as proposed by St. Sylvester Guzzolini for his monastery at Montefano (near Ancona, Italy). For this community, which he founded in 1231, he prescribed a more ascetic life than what had become traditional with Benedictines and urged greater attention to the needs of the poor peasantry of the region.

BENEDICTION OF THE BLESSED SACRAMENT, a devotion honoring the eucharist in a liturgical rite during which the sacrament was exposed on the altar. The devotion, which had its origins in the evening service of the early thirteenth century, had acquired its modern character by the fifteenth century.

BENEDICTIONAL, book containing a collection of benedictions used in the Christian liturgy to serve different occasions, e.g., the blessing of a newly crowned monarch. The earliest such collection appeared in the eighth century.

BENEDICT OF ANIANE, ST., d. 821, monastic reformer, abbot of the monastery at Aniane in the diocese of Montpellier which he had founded on his own property. He was a leading councillor of Louis the Pious whose active assistance he enjoyed in his work of reforming both the court and the religious life of the Carolingian empire. Louis entrusted Benedict with supervisory authority over all the monasteries of the empire and in 817 summoned their abbots to a meeting at Aachen where a modification of the Benedictine rule was accepted as general code for all monasteries.

BENEDICT OF BENEVENTO, ST., d. 1003, monk of Calabria, then hermit, finally a missionary to Poland where he was murdered by the pagans.

BENEDICT OF PETERBOROUGH, d. 1193, abbot of Peterborough abbey and patron of learning. He proved himself an able administrator and left an account of the martyrdom of Thomas Becket of which only fragments survive.

BENEDICT, RULE OF ST. *See* BENEDICT, ST.

BENEDICTUS, opening word of the *Canticle of Zachary* (*Benedictus qui venit in nomine Domini,* or "Blessed is he who comes in the name of the Lord," Luke 1:68–79); also, one of the concluding verses of the *Sanctus* of the Mass, and a hymn included in the Lauds of the Divine Office. The verse *Benedictus qui venit in nomine Domini* was usually sung after the *Sanctus.*

BENEDIKTBEUERN, ABBEY OF, monastery in upper Bavaria founded c. 740 and consecrated by St. Boniface in 742. Despite suffering several disastrous raids and fires, its large library helped maintain its reputation as a center of learning while its store of precious relics assured its popularity as a shrine. [*See* CARMINA BURANA.]

BENEFICE, usually a tract of land or estate given by a king (lord), bishop, monastery, or nobleman to a member of the aristocracy (or bishop or monastery) or to a knight for limited or hereditary use in exchange for services. In ecclesiastical usage a benefice referred to an ecclesiastical living or office that returned a measure of revenue.

BENEFIT OF CLERGY, a privilege extended to members of the clergy, including tonsured clerks, that placed them beyond the jurisdiction of the secular courts. (Once a clerk married, he lost this benefit.) A man might establish his clerical status and, therefore, his right to benefit of clergy, by giving evidence of his ability to read. The privilege was established by the twelfth century when it extended only to the commission of felonies. The privilege aroused much criticism in England during the reign of Henry II (1154–89). [*See* CLARENDON, CONSTITUTIONS OF, and BECKET, THOMAS, ST.] The source of the criticism was the refusal of the church courts to inflict capital punishment. Their severest sentences were degradation and the imposition of penances. The fact that the privilege was enjoyed by clerks, in effect literate persons who were unmarried, led inevitably to misuse and abuse of the privilege.

BENEIT (Benoît, Beneeit), possibly the same as Benoît de Saint-More, an Anglo-Norman poet and chronicler of the late twelfth century who composed a life of Thomas Becket in verse.

BENET, ST., an older English form of the name of St. Benedict.

BENGLER: a) a knightly organization founded in Westphalia to oppose the landgrave of Hesse and the bishop of Paderborn; b) a group of Flagellants.

BENGTSSON, JOENS OXENSTJERNA (Joannes Benedicti), d. 1467, member of a powerful Swedish family, archbishop of Uppsala, and primate of Sweden. His own ambitions and the instability of the throne led to his enmeshment in political affairs and to his eventual exile from the country.

BENI ISRAEL, community of Jews in western India of uncertain origin who incorporated Christian and Islamic practices into their primitive Hebrew cult.

BENI SULEIM (Beni Soleim), warlike Arabic Bedouins who invaded Egypt in the tenth century and overran northwest Africa. They proved more successful than their predecessors in Arabizing the Berbers they found there.

BENIGNUS (Blenen), ST., d. 467, son of an Irish chieftain who was baptized by St. Patrick and consecrated bishop of Armagh.

BENITO, an Italian form of Benedict.

BENJAMIN OF TUDELA (Navarra), Spanish Jew who spent the years 1160 to 1173 on travels to Iraq, Iran, India, China, Tibet, and Egypt. The book of *Travels* which he drew up provides a valuable account of the impressions he gained on these travels. It also remains the best source for a knowledge of Jewish life in these lands, in Europe, and in north Africa in the twelfth century.

BEN NAPHTALI, name of a family of biblical scholars of Palestine of the ninth and tenth centuries who, like members of the contemporary Ben Asher family, were concerned with the standardization of the Hebrew Bible by establishing the vocalization and accentuation of the consonantal text. The most prominent representative of the Naphtali family engaged in this scholarly work was Moses Ben David.

BENNO OF MEISSEN, ST., d. c. 1106, son of a count who worked as a missionary among the pagan Wends, later became bishop of Meissen. The violence that attended the investiture controversy twice forced him from his see.

BENNO OF METZ, d. 940, canon of Strasbourg, hermit, then bishop of Metz, who returned to his hermitage when he was blinded by his enemies. The monastery of Einsiedeln traced its origins to this hermitage.

BENNO II OF OSNABRÜCK, BL., d. 1088, head of the cathedral school at Hildesheim, bishop of Osnabrück, and a central figure in the investiture conflict. Although Pope Gregory VII excommunicated him for his adherence to Henry IV of Germany to whom he owed his position, the two men were later reconciled. Benno enjoyed fame as an architect of churches and fortifications.

BENOÎT, French form for Benedict.

BENOÎT DE SAINT-MORE (Sainte-Maure), French poet of the twelfth century who left a chronicle of the dukes of Normandy. His *Roman de Troie,* a romance of 30,000 verses, traced the origins of the Franks back to the legendary Aeneas. It is possible that he was the same poet who on orders of Henry II of England undertook a rhymed *Chronique des ducs de Normandie.*

BENTIVOGLIO, an Italian family that dominated the city of Bologna during the second half of the fifteenth century. Under the guidance of its leading members, it succeeded in maintaining friendly relations with the powerful states in the vicinity, a policy which brought them wealth, lands, and titles. Like the Medici in Florence, they chose to rule Bologna simply as "first citizens." They did recognize the suzerainty of the pope.

BEOWULF, a folk epic composed probably in the late eighth century. It recounts in Old English the heroism of the valorous Beowulf. He slew the monster Grendel and his dam, reigned as ruler of the Geats, and killed a dragon that had been ravaging his kingdom, although Beowulf was mortally wounded. The author of the poem is believed to have been a monk or Christian court poet and the poem itself is thought to be a Christian allegory, Beowulf being the symbol of good, his enemies the personification of evil.

BERBERS, name given the aboriginal people of north Africa, for the most part those living west of Egypt and north of the Sahara who accepted the culture of Islam. It required several waves of Arab invaders from the east, the first in the seventh century, another in the tenth century [*See* BENI SULEIM], and a third in the twelfth, before the work of Arabization had been accomplished.

BERCEO, GONZALO DE, d. 1268?, Spanish poet born in Castile, the earliest known by name. He was a Benedictine monk, whose writings are devotional in character and deal for the most part with the lives of the saints. His *Milagros de Nuestra Señora* (miracles of Our Lady) consists of 25 poems dedicated to the Virgin.

BERCHEURE (Berchoire, Bersuire), PIERRE, d. 1362, Benedictine monk and prior at Maillezais, an eloquent preacher and the author of many homilies and of a dictionary of scriptural words and phrases to which he associated moral reflections.

BEREKHIAH BEN NATRONAI HA-NAKDAN, Jewish fabulist of the twelfth and thirteenth century, a biblical commentator, philosopher, grammarian, and translator. He is best known for a collection of fables in rhymed prose.

BERENGAR I, king of Italy, 888–924, grandson of Louis the Pious, who was crowned emperor in 915 by the pope following his successful campaign against the Saracens. His checkered career ended with assassination by an agent of Rudolf II of Burgundy whose army he had defeated.

BERENGAR II, king of Italy, 950–63. As marquis of Ivrea he succeeded in making himself king of Italy although he was obliged to recognize the suzerainty of Otto I of Germany. In 963 he repudiated that fealty, marched against Pope John XII, who appealed to Otto for assistance.

Otto hurried south and captured Berengar, who died in a German prison (966).

BERENGAR OF TOURS, d. 1088, archdeacon of Angers cathedral, pupil of Fulbert of Chartres, a noted scholastic and head of the cathedral school at Tours. He spent his last years in a hermitage. His views, based on those of Ratramnus of Corbie, questioned the doctrine of transubstantiation. He maintained that no distinction existed in the metaphysical order between substance and accident. He accepted the doctrine of the Real Presence but denied that any material change in the elements was required to explain it. Lanfranc's defense of transubstantiation, together with ecclesiastical pressure, led him to retract his views and he died at peace with the church.

BERENGARIA, d. c. 1230, queen consort of Richard I of England whom she married in 1191. She was the daughter of Sancho VI of Navarre. She bore no children.

BERGEN, city in Norway founded by King Olaf III c. 1070. It became a bishop's seat and coronation city in the twelfth century and from the mid-fourteenth served as one of the four major factories of the Hanseatic League. Its principal export consisted of codfish. The Black Death brought disaster to the city's population and trade, and in 1393 it was burned during the war betwen Stockholm and Margaret of Denmark, Norway's regent.

BERLIN, city in the valley of the Spree in Germany, founded c. 1230 by Margrave John I and Otto III of Brandenburg, probably on the site of an earlier Wendish settlement. Its location on the road from Magdeburg to Brandenburg, together with the privileges it received and its membership in the Hanseatic League, assured its rapid growth. By the fourteenth century it had become the leading city of the margravate of Brandenburg and from c. 1470 served as the residence of the elector of Brandenburg.

BERLINGHIERI (Berlinghiero), d. c. 1240, first Italian painter known by name, noted in particular for a crucifix he painted for the Church of S. Maria degli Angeli in Lucca and the panels of the Virgin and St. John that flank the cross. They reveal Tuscan Romanesque forms, also Byzantine influences, which he combined in a linear and lyrical manner. His three sons, Barone, Bonaventura, and Marco, were also painters.

BERME, the level area, roughly six to ten feet wide, that lay just beyond the walls of a medieval city and was reserved for graves.

BERNARD (Bernhard), d. 818, son of Pepin and grandson of Charlemagne, whom Louis the Pious, his uncle, appointed ruler of Italy. When Bernard was captured following his revolt, Louis commuted his death sentence to blinding, but he died of the effects.

BERNARD VII, d. 1418, count of Armagnac, constable of France, father-in-law of Charles d'Orleans. He was the actual leader of the Armagnacs against the Burgundians from 1415 to 1418 and the virtual ruler of that part of France not under English control. When Paris rebelled against his rule and welcomed John the Fearless of Burgundy, he was slain in the ensuing massacre.

BERNARD (Bernart) DE VENTADOUR, a troubadour of the twelfth century, perhaps the leading lyric poet of his day. He was a vassal of Eleanor of Aquitaine, the wife of Henry II of England, to whom he addressed many of his poems. He died a monk.

BERNARD GUI, d. 1331, Dominican, prior of several Dominican houses, inquisitor in Toulouse, bishop of Túy (Galicia), later of Lodève (Toulouse). He authored a universal chronicle and theological treatises, but he is best known for his description of the operations of the Court of the Inquisition.

BERNARDINE OF FELTRE, BL., d. 1494, an immensely popular Franciscan preacher of northern Italy who like his Dominican contemporary Savonarola attacked the low morals of the times. Despite strong opposition from bankers, he managed to establish a number of *montes pietatis* which provided loans to poor people at a low rate of interest.

BERNARDINE (Bernardino) OF SIENA, ST., d. 1444, a Franciscan, student of the classics as well as of scripture, canon law, and theology, the most eloquent preacher of his day and perhaps the most influential force for reform in Italy. He served as vicar general of the Friars of the Strict Observance in Tuscany, composed sermons and theological treatises, and enjoyed great success in spreading the devotion to the Holy Name of Jesus. His principal companion was St. John Capistran.

BERNARDINES, name occasionally given to the Cistercians because of the extraordinary achievement of St. Bernard of Clairvaux, the most distinguished member of the order.

BERNARDINE SISTERS OF THE THIRD ORDER OF ST. FRANCIS, a congregation of nuns founded in Poland in 1457. Although actually tertiaries of St. Francis, they came to be identified as Bernardine Sisters because they attended divine services in a church dedicated to St. Bernardine (of Siena).

BERNARDINO OF SIENA, ST. *See* BERNARDINE OF SIENA, ST.

BERNARDO DEL CARPIO, a hero of medieval Spanish legend and literature. He was believed to be the nephew of Alfonso II, king of the Asturias (791–842), who fought the king in order to secure the release of his father from prison. The Spanish accepted many stories about his supposed heroism and even made him the slayer of Roland at Roncesvalles. [*See* ROLAND, CHANSON DE.]

BERNARD OF AOSTA (Bernard of Menthon), ST., d. 1081?, an itinerant preacher in the region of Piedmont whose name is associated with the Little and the Great Saint Bernard Passes. He seems to have reestablished two earlier hospices in the passes that had disappeared and gave them his name. The men to whom he entrusted the care of the hospices later became Canons Regular of St. Augustine.

BERNARD OF BESSE, d. late thirteenth century, a Franciscan, secretary of Bonaventure, a chronicler of the Franciscan order and author of ascetical writings.

BERNARD OF CHARTRES (d. c. 1130), French scholastic philosopher, described by John of Salisbury as the "most perfect Platonist of our age." He served as head of the school at Chartres, later as chancellor of its cathedral. He was an extreme realist in the Platonic tradition. Gilbert de la Porrée and William of Conches were his pupils.

BERNARD OF CLAIRVAUX, ST., d. 1153, a Cistercian monk of aristocratic lineage who founded Clairvaux and other monasteries. He initially entered the monastery of Citeaux together with thirty other noblemen of Burgundy upon whom he had prevailed to accompany him. The force of his tremendous zeal and the impact of his personality breathed new vigor into the Cistercian order and made it the most popular and influential of the twelfth century. Although dedicated to the monastic ideal of worshipping God in the seclusion of a monastery, he lived a most active career: urging spiritual reform; attending church councils; ending a papal schism and securing recognition of Innocent II as canonically elected; preaching the Second Crusade; attacking the rationalism of Abelard and securing the condemnation of his writings on the Trinity at the Council of Sens (1140) which, under his prodding, also condemned Arnold of Brescia; carrying on a wide correspondence; even composing hymns. He may have drawn up the Rule of the Knights Templar. The popularity of the cult of the Virgin and the flowering of mysticism in the centuries following his death have been attributed to his influence. The eloquence and charm of his style of writing gained him the title "Mellifluous Doctor." Scholars consider him the most influential man of the first half of the twelfth century.

BERNARD OF CLUNY, also known as Bernard of Morlass or Morlass, a Benedictine monk of Cluny during the abbacy of Peter the Venerable (1122–57). He composed sermons and a well-known poem entitled *De Contemptu Mundi* that deplored the low morals of his day. His poem is the source of the hymn "Jerusalem the Golden."

BERNARD OF COMPOSTELLA THE ELDER, a thirteenth-century canonist of Spain who taught at Bologna, prepared a compilation of the decretals covering the first ten years of the pontificate of Innocent III (1198–1216), and left an apparatus of glosses on the *Decretum*.

BERNARD OF COMPOSTELLA THE YOUNGER, d. 1267, canonist, bishop, and author of commentaries on the decretals of Gregory IX (1227–41) and of Innocent IV (1243–54).

BERNARD OF MENTHON, ST., *See* BERNARD OF AOSTA, ST.

BERNARD OF PARMA, ST., d. 1133, abbot general of the Vallombrosian order who was considered its second founder because of the importance of his contribution to the well-being of the order. He became a cardinal, then bishop of Parma, and was appointed papal legate in Lombardy in order to organize resistance there to Henry IV of Germany during the investiture struggle. In this last work he enjoyed the cooperation of Countess Matilda of Tuscany.

BERNARD OF SAISSET, d. 1311, abbot of the Canons Regular of Saint-Antonin in Pamiers and the first bishop of the newly created diocese of that city. When Philip IV of France ordered the bishop arrested on charges of heresy and simony, he precipitated the final episode in the bitter dispute between himself and Pope Boniface VIII. Bernard fled to Rome in 1302 but in

1308 received a royal pardon and returned to France.

BERNARD OF TOLOMEI, BL., d. 1348, *podestà* of Siena, later Benedictine monk, and founder of the monastery of Our Lady of Monte Oliveto. This monastery became the mother house of the Olivetan Benedictine Congregation.

BERNARD PASS, GREAT ST. *See* SAINT BERNARD PASSES.

BERNARD PASS, LITTLE ST. *See* SAINT BERNARD PASSES.

BERNE (Bern), Swiss city, also the name of the canton of which it was the capital. It was founded in 1191 by Berchtold V, duke of Zähringen, as a military post to guard the passage over the Aare. In 1218 it became a free imperial city and in 1353 it proclaimed its independence when it joined the Swiss confederation. Within a short time it had assumed the leadership of the confederation.

BERNE, name of a woman's cloak of the late Middle Ages.

BERNER (Perner), small silver coins used in the Tyrol from the thirteenth century.

BERNERS (Bernes, Barnes), JULIANA, obscure English author of the early fifteenth century, according to tradition the prioress of Sopwell convent in Hertfordshire. No firm information exists about her. She has been credited with a popular treatise on hunting entitled *The Book of Saint Albans*.

BERNICIA, early Anglian kingdom established in 547 that was joined to Deira in the late sixth century to form Northumbria.

BERNLEF, blind Frisian poet of the eighth century who was converted by Liudger (d. 809). He is recognized as the oldest poet in the history of German literature. None of his verse remains extant.

BERNO OF REICHENAU, d. 1048, abbot of the

Benedictine monastery at Reichenau and a vigorous supporter of the political and ecclesiastical policies of Henry II of Germany to whom he owed his appointment. He was a student of music and the Christian liturgy and composed several works on these subjects.

BERNOLD OF CONSTANCE (Bernold of St. Blaise), d. 1100, a scholastic, canonist, and author of a chronicle of his times which was highly regarded despite its animosity toward Henry IV of Germany. He also composed several polemical tracts in support of Pope Gregory VII on the issue of investiture.

BERNWARD OF HILDESHEIM, ST., d. 1022, scion of a Saxon family, tutor and court chaplain of Otto III, and bishop of Hildesheim. He was a patron of goldsmiths and made a significant contribution to art with the construction and embellishment of the church of St. Michael at Hildesheim. This remains the leading church of the Ottonian period.

BEROL (Béroul), French poet of Brittany of the late twelfth century who composed verses on themes common to courtly romance, e.g., the Tristan story.

BERRY, duchy in central France lying just south of the Loire river, conquered by the Visigoths in the early fifth century, by the Franks in 507. It belonged to Aquitaine and was ruled by viscounts from the ninth century until Philip I bought it in 1101. King John the Good made it a duchy for his third son, Jean de France, in 1360.

BERRY, DUKE OF, JOHN (Jean de France), d. 1416, brother of Charles V of France, patron of the arts, especially the art of book illumination, and collector of paintings, jewelry, books, and illuminated manuscripts. His book of hours, the *Très Riches Heures,* provides an excellent record of his magnificent residences.

BERSERK, primitive men who, according to old Nordic superstition, possessed the power to assume the form of bears; also Viking warriors who banded usually in groups of twelve and accompanied chieftains on their voyages.

BERTHA, according to a Carolingian romance, a sister of Charlemagne (d. 814) and the mother of Roland.

BERTHA OF THE BIG FOOT, d. 783, wife of Pepin the Short, king of the Franks, the founder of the Carolingian dynasty. She was the mother of Charlemagne. She figures prominently in the legend of the Carolingian period.

BERTHARIUS, ST., d. 884, abbot of Monte Cassino. He encouraged the development of sacred studies and authored several medical treatises. Invading Saracens slew him and burned the monastery.

BERTHA, ST., daughter of a Frankish king who married Ethelbert of Kent in 588 and helped bring about his conversion to Christianity.

BERTHOLD OF REGENSBURG, d. 1272, a Franciscan who was considered the most renowned and accomplished preacher of medieval Germany. People referred to him as "Brother Berthold." In his extensive preaching which he did in both German and Latin, he traveled through most of Germany, Switzerland, Bohemia, and Hungary. In his sermons he laid more stress upon moral living than upon doctrine. His German sermons, which reflect the life of the people, constitute the principal monuments of Middle High German prose.

BERTINORO (Bartanura), OVADJA JARE, d. c. 1510, Jewish biblical scholar, also a banker in Italy. He spent some years traveling in the Near East, reorganized the Jewish community in Jerusalem, and left letters describing his travels. He is also the author of many liturgical poems.

BERTOLDO DI GIOVANNI, d. 1491, worker in bronze who studied under Donatello. He completed two pulpits in S. Lorenzo which Donatello had left unfinished. Among his best known works, which consisted principally of small pieces such as medallions, plaques, and statuettes, are likenesses of Mohammed II (1451–81). He was the first head of the Academy of Art which Lorenzo founded in Florence.

BERTRAND DE BORN, d. c. 1215, viscount of Hautefort, great knight, and a leading troubadour of Provence, author of some 40 extant poems. Although he died as a monk, Dante placed him in hell with the sowers of discord (*Inferno* XXVIII, 134) for turning the young Henry against his father, Henry II of England.

BERTRAND, PIERRE, d. 1349, teacher of law at Avignon, Montpellier, Paris, and Orléans, bishop of Autun, archbishop of Bourges, and cardinal. He authored several legal treatises and as a member of the council of state under Philip V carried out a number of diplomatic missions for the crown.

BERTRANT DE BAR-SUR-AUBE, French poet of the thirteenth century. The themes he chose for his *chansons* fall within the subject matter of the William of Orange cycle.

BESANÇON, city in the county of Burgundy which became a bishop's seat in the fourth century. It suffered destruction by the Alemanni in the fourth century and again by the Magyars in the tenth, but revived under Bishop Hugh of Salins (1031–67) who established it as a feudal principality and extended its authority over neighboring lords. In the twelfth century it became a commune under the nominal rule of the German emperor and managed to retain its independence, with some interruptions, until 1648. The university was founded c. 1422.

BÉSANT. *See* BEZANT.

BESSARABIA, region lying south of the Dniester and extending to the Black Sea, once part of the Roman province of Dacia. It was overrun by many peoples including the Goths, Petchenegs, Cumans, and Mongols. It received its name during the fourteenth century from the ruling

family Basarab. In 1367 it was joined to the province of Walachia and in 1455 it became a vassal state of the Ottoman Turks.

BESSARION, JOHN, d. 1472, Byzantine scholar and theologian, cardinal and humanist. As monk he took the name Bessarion, later became abbot of St. Basil's in Constantinople, then as archbishop of Nicaea accompanied the Greek delegation to the Council of Ferrara-Florence to plead the cause of union of the Latin and Greek churches. Pope Eugenius IV created him a cardinal in 1439, after which he remained in the papal service for five years. He taught Greek, authored elegies, panegyrics, and letters, translated Greek writings including Aristotle's *Metaphysics,* collected manuscripts, and showed his favor to other humanists, notably Lorenzo Valla. Most significant were his efforts in reconciling the thought of Plato and Aristotle and in demonstrating how the views of these two philosphers could be harmonized with Christianity. His collection of Greek manuscripts served as the nucleus of St. Mark's Library in Venice.

BESTIARY, a collection of descriptions of animals, birds, snakes, and similar creatures, usually with moral instructions based upon their presumed characteristics, which as a literary genre enjoyed considerable popularity in the thirteenth and fourteenth centuries. They were the source of a confusing array of strange beasts and animals and of many misconceptions concerning actual ones. Although traced to a Greek text of probably the second century entitled *Physiologus* which had incorporated materials from Aristotle and Pliny the Elder, the accretion of myths and superstitions over the centuries almost overwhelmed what scientific fact the descriptions of these creatures might originally have possessed. They did provide artists ideas and themes in religious building, painting, and sculpture.

BÉTHENCOURT, JEAN DE, d. 1422, Norman-French explorer who conquered the Canary Islands and ruled them in the name of the king of Castile. He undertook the first colonization of the islands with the help of Norman peasants.

BETHLEHEMITES, a hospital order of men and women, living under the Rule of St. Augustine, that maintained institutions for the care of the sick including the mentally ill. [*See* BEDLAM.]

BEUCKELSZ, WILLIAM, d. 1397, a Dutch fisherman who devised a method of packing and preserving herring which proved a source of great prosperity for Holland.

BEUNO, ST., d. c. 640, abbot of Clynnog, labored as a missionary in north Wales. He is said to have founded monasteries across the border in Herefordshire. His tomb at Clynnog Faur attracted many pilgrims.

BEVIS OF HAMPTON, English metrical romance of the thirteenth century. It also appeared in Anglo-French and Italian. Among other feats and adventures, Bevis, the hero, rescues and marries a princess and overcomes a dragon.

BEZANT (bésant, bisant, bezzant), Byzantine gold coin used in Europe from the fifth century to the close of the Middle Ages.

BHASCARA, called Acarija, the Learned, born in 1114, a Hindu mathematician and astronomer and head of the observatory of Oudjein. His work *Siddhantasiromani* offered chapters on arithmetic, algebra, and astronomy. He presents the first systematic exposition of the decimal system.

BIANCHI AND NERI, Whites and Blacks, factions that dominated Florence in the thirteenth and fourtenth centuries. The ascendancy of the Blacks in Dante's day led to his exile and that of other White leaders.

BIBLE MORALISÉE, an illustrated Bible, with commentary, that appeared in the thirteenth century and may have been dedicated to Louis IX of France. The 5,000 scenes that appear in the illustrations suggested parallelisms between events and figures of the Old and New Testaments and advanced different levels of interpretation for the text, namely, literal, allegorical, tropological, and anagogical.

BIBLIA PAUPERUM, Bible of the poor, an illustrated Bible with much of the text omitted but featuring pictures that served to illustrate the principal themes. It was used by the illiterate who could not read and by priests who could not afford a conventional Bible and found the illustrations a valuable aid in instructing the people. These Bibles first appeared in Bavaria toward the close of the thirteenth century.

BIBLIOTHÉQUE NATIONALE, French national library located in Paris whose origins may go back to Louis IX (1226–70) but whose first important acquisition was the *Librairie du Roi* of Charles V which he placed in the Louvre in 1367.

BID'A, new ideas and practices introduced in the religion of Islam that were not contained in the *Sunna*.

BIEL, GABRIEL, d. 1495, a scholastic philospher, theologian, and economist who studied at Heidelberg, Erfurt, and Cologne. He served as prior of a house of Brothers of the Common Life and as professor of philosophy and theology and rector at Tübingen. His commentry on the *Sentences* of Peter Lombard, which was used as a textbook, represented a classic presentation of late medieval nominalism. It exerted considerable influence upon Martin Luther. In addition to his treatises on theological subjects, he wrote a progressive work on economic theory.

BIGOD, English family noted for its opposition to the crown in the twelfth and thirteenth centuries. Hugh (d. 1177) joined the rebellion against King Stephen, then made peace with him and was given the title earl of Norfolk. He also took part in a revolt against Henry II in 1173–74. Roger (d. 1221), second earl, was among the barons opposed to John in 1215.

Roger (d. 1270), fourth earl, was prominent among the barons who fought Henry III although he eventually supported the king. Roger (d. 1306), fifth earl, refused to serve abroad until Edward I himself led the expedition, then later headed the movement that forced Edward to confirm the charters (1297). He was childless, and at his death his estates and titles passed to the crown.

BILLINGSGATE, the oldest market in London. It derived its name from Belin's gate where royal tolls were collected as early as A.D. 980.

BILL OF ATTAINDER. *See* ATTAINDER, BILL OF.

BILL OF EXCHANGE, a written order of one person to another to pay a sum of money to a third person or to his account. This device, which facilitated the settlement of the accounts of several persons living in different cities without the transportation of money had come into use in Italy by at least the thirteenth century.

BILLUNGS (Billings), the leading ruling dynasty in Saxony in the tenth and eleventh centuries. It had its name from Hermann Billung, duke of Saxony (d. 973), who received the region as a march to be held against the pagan Wends on the lower Elbe. The family died out in 1106.

BILWIS, according to a notion popular in the thirteenth century, a demon that caused illnes. In the following century, a sorceress or a magician might be called Bilwis.

BINCHOIS, GILLES (Egidius), d. 1460, chaplain and poet associated with the court of Philip the Good, duke of Burgundy. He composed sacred music including motets, hymns, parts of the mass, and *chansons*. He was recognized as one of the most distinguished musicians of his age. Some of his church music is related to English liturgical use. His secular *chansons* are excellent examples of that genre.

BINGEN, city on the Rhine that dates from pre-Roman times. It joined the Hanseatic League in 1254 and in 1281 passed under the rule of the archbishop of Mainz. On a rock near Bingen stood the famous Mäuseturm (mouse tower) where, legend had it, Archbishop Hatto of Mainz had been devoured by mice because of his mistreatment of his subjects.

BIONDO, FLAVIO, d. 1463, a leading humanist of the period who spent some years as a clerk in the papal Curia. He authored several works dealing with Roman antiquities, the archeological monuments of Italy, and a history of his times.

BIRD, a favorite symbol in medieval art: the dove to represent the Holy Spirit or Peace; the eagle as a symbol of Christ or of St. John the Evangelist; the pelican, a symbol of the Redeemer; the peacock, a symbol of the Resurrection.

BIRGER JARL (Magnusson), d. 1266, ancestor of the dynasty of the Folkungs and regent from 1250 for his son Waldemar whose election as king of Sweden he had managed to secure. He fought a successful war against Finland, negotiated treaties with the Hanse which proved of great value to Sweden, and, according to the testimony of the sagas, was the actual founder of Stockholm. It was due to his influence and accomplishments that Stockholm emerged as the administrative center of Sweden. In 1261 he married the Danish queen Mechthild.

BIRINUS, ST., d. 649/50, first bishop of Dorchester (near Oxford), a see given him by King Cynegils whom he had baptized in 635. He was the apostle of the West Saxons.

BIRKA, Viking trading post on the island of Björkö off the coast of Sweden, established in the early ninth century but destroyed by some catastrophe in 970. It was the oldest and most important of the early Swedish trading posts.

BIRMINGHAM, city some 100 miles northwest of London, probably first settled in Saxon times and listed as a small community in Domesday

Book (1085-6). Its first market charter was granted in 1166 although it was not before the early fourteenth century that the town had acquired any significance.

BIRTH OF MARY, FEAST OF THE, liturgical feast in the Greek church since the eighth century, in the Latin church since the eleventh. The feast was celebrated on September 9.

BIRUNI (Beruni), ABU-L-RAYHAN MUHAMMAD B. AHMAD, d. c. 1050, a native of Iran, one of the greatest of Islamic scholars. He was conversant in Turkish, Persian, Sanskrit, Hebrew, and Syriac. He wrote in Arabic. His 180 works reveal an encyclopedic learning which embraced the fields of astronomy, geography, the physical and natural sciences, mathematics, philosophy, theology, and history. In his astronomical works he discussed the theory of the earth's rotation on its axis and made accurate calculations of latitude and longitude. It may have been while on military campaigns as official astrologer to the sultan of Afghanistan that he acquired his extensive knowledge of India and of Hindu philosophy.

BISHOP, the director of a Christian administrative district or diocese who was assisted in his work by priests, deacons, and other ministers. The title, derived from the Greek meaning overseer or inspector, was held by the higher officials in the early church. As the successor of the apostles, the bishop was entrusted with the safeguarding of doctrinal orthodoxy. He also inherited the faculty of the laying on of hands which he employed in administering the sacraments of confirmation and holy orders.

BISHOP HATTO, an archbishop of Mainz who, according to legend, had a large number of poor people burned to death during a period of famine in order to leave more food for the use of the wealthy. An army of mice chased him to a town on the Rhine called Mäuseturm (Mouse Tower) and there killed him. [See MOUSE TOWER.]

BISHOP'S CHAIR, a seat used by the bishop that was ordinarily of stone and was placed in the apse, later on the north side of the choir.

BISHOP'S CROOK. See CROSIER.

BISHOPSGATE, the main gate on the north side of London.

BISHOP'S RING, ring placed on the right hand of a bishop during the ceremonies attending his consecration when he was invested with the symbols of his office. The ring symbolized his marriage with the church.

BISMARCK (Bismark), a family of burghers located in Stendal in Altmark. The first member of the family to receive notice was Herbord of Bismarck in 1270. He served as head of the guild of tailors.

BISMI'LLAH (Basmala, Tasmija), Arabic for *In the name of God,* an invocation Moslems used before undertaking any important business; also, a superscription appearing at the head of manuscripts or an ornamentation on a building.

BISTICCI, VESPASIANO DA, d. 1498, well-known bookseller of Florence, an agent of the Medici, whose shop was famed for its stock of precious manuscripts. Besides publishing copies of many manuscripts, he was the author of a work critical of contemporary personages.

BITEROLF AND DIETLEIB, poem of unknown Austrian authorship and grouped with German heroic sagas written shortly after the middle of the thirteenth century. Biterolf located his missing father Dietleib at Etzel's court, whence the two men accompanied Dietrich of Berne and other warriors to Worms where Dietrich and Siegfried engaged in an indecisive martial contest.

BITRUDJI, NUR AL-DIN ABU ISHAK AL-, twelfth-century Arab astronomer of Spain, known to the West as Alpetragius. His works, translated into Latin by Michael Scot, exerted considerable influence upon Western thought.

BL., abbreviation for Blessed, that is, a member of the faithful departed who has been beatified. Beatification allows only a restricted public veneration, in a particular diocese or country, for example, as opposed to canonization which permits veneration throughout the church. Such a distinction was probably unknown in the early centuries.

BLACK BOOK OF CARMARTHEN, Welsh manuscript of the twelfth century which contained many pieces of ancient Welsh poetry.

BLACK CANONS. See CANONS REGULAR OF ST. AUGUSTINE.

BLACK DEATH, name given to a deadly outbreak of the bubonic plague, called the Black Death from the dark color of the body after death, which made its way across Europe from Constantinople to Norway between the years 1347 and 1351. It reappeared several times thereafter although never with its initial virulence. Estimates of the number of deaths attributed to the Black Death range from a fourth to one third of the population.

BLACK FAST, THE, unusually rigorous regulations limiting the volume and quality of food to be consumed on days when fasting was required.

BLACK FRIARS. See DOMINICANS; CANONS AND CANONESSES REGULAR OF ST. AUGUSTINE; HERMITS OF ST. AUGUSTINE.

BLACKFRIARS, a district of London that took its name from the Dominican monastery established there in 1276. Parliament often met in Blackfriars.

BLACKHEATH, open common in London which served as a rallying ground for Wat Tyler (1381), Jack Cade (1450), and Lord Audley, leader of Cornish rebels who was captured there in 1497. It was here that the citizens of London greeted Henry V on his return from his magnificent victory at Agincourt (1415).

BLACK MASS, a Requiem Mass for the dead, so-called because of the black vestments worn by the celebrant. The term might also refer to a parody of the Mass celebrated for blasphemous intent.

BLACK MONKS. See BENEDICTINES.

BLACK PRINCE. See EDWARD, THE BLACK PRINCE.

BLACK STONE OF MECCA, stone reputed to have come from heaven and to have been revered by Abraham, built into the eastern wall of the Kaaba in Mecca. It dates from the pre-Islamic period and was the only sacred object that Mohammed left in the Kaaba when he occupied Mecca in 630.

BLACK SUNDAY. See PASSION SUNDAY.

BLAFFERT (blappart, blaphard, plappert), a variety of silver coins, so called for their dull coloring, which were used especially in Switzerland and southern Germany from the fourteenth century.

BLAISE OF SEBASTE, ST., d. c. 316, bishop of Sebaste in Armenia who, according to legend, healed a boy who had a fishbone stuck in his throat. Blaise came to be revered as the patron of throat diseases from the sixth century in the East and from the ninth in the West, and as one of the Fourteen Holy Helpers.

BLANC, a French groat in use since 1352.

BLANCA, an old Spanish coin of little value.

BLANCHE OF CASTILE, d. 1252, daughter of Alfonso VIII of Castile, wife of Louis VIII of France, and mother of Louis IX. She served as regent for her son from 1226 to 1234 during his minority and again when he was away on the first of his two Crusades (1248–52). With the help of the towns, she put down a revolt of French barons during her son's minority and threw back an invasion by Henry III of England. By means of judicious marriage treaties, she was able to secure the eventual absorption of Toulouse and Provence into the royal domain. Her son Louis always held his mother in the greatest esteem and reverence. He probably owed her not only his realm but also his deep devotion to Christianity.

BLANCHEFLUR (Blanescheflur): a) mother of the hero and lover of Rivalin in the story of Tristan and Isolde; b) the darling of Flore in *Flore and Blancheflur.*

BLASE, ST. *See* BLAISE OF SEBASTE, ST.

BLASTARES, MATTHEW, fourteenth-century canonist, monk of Mount Athos, later of Thessalonica, author of a popular compilation of ecclesiastical and civil laws to which he appended commentaries of his own and of earlier canonists. He also composed a number of theological tracts on controversial issues and may possibly have written five books against the Jews.

BLEDA, brother and co-ruler with Attila of the Huns until slain by him in 445.

BLEMMYDES (Blemmida), NICEPHORUS, d. 1272, learned monk and teacher, founder of a monastery near Ephesus, author of works on geographical, philosophical, and theological subjects, also of two autobiographies of lesser importance and some political verse. He devoted much effort to ending the schism between the Greek and Latin churches.

BLIAUD (Blialt), an outer garment suggestive of a blouse or shirt which served both men and women from the tenth to the fourteenth century. It also went by the name *cotte, robe,* or *roc,* although these garments were usually longer, reaching to the knees or ankles of men and to the feet of women.

BLIDE (Blyde, Bleide), a medieval catapult mention of which appears as early as the siege of Nicaea in 1097.

BLOCKBOOK, block of wood in the form of a book and ordinarily containing both picture and text which served to print a single page. These blocks appeared principally in Germany and the Netherlands from 1430.

BLOCK FLUTE, a flute that appeared at least as early as the eleventh century. It derived its name from a block inserted in the mouthpiece which channeled a blast of air against the lip of the incision.

BLÖDEL, the brother of Etzel in the *Nibelungenlied;* in history, Bleda, the brother of Attila.

BLOIS, capital city of the county of Blois and situated on the middle Loire in central France. The city's origins go back to Roman times although first mention of it is by Gregory of Tours in the sixth century. It was from its line of counts that the Capetian kings sprang. In 1152 its count became the count of Champagne. The last count of Blois, who was childless, sold his fief to Louis, duc d'Orléans, who took possession in 1397. His grandson, Louis XII, king of France, joined it to the royal domain in 1498.

BLONDEL DE NESLE, fl. late twelfth century, French troubadour, a favorite of Richard I of England whom he accompanied on the Third Crusade in 1190. According to a legendary story, Blondel, wandering about Germany in search of Richard whom Leopold II, margrave of Austria, had captured and imprisoned, located him by singing a song which only he and Richard knew. When Richard answered the song from his prison, Blondel rescued him.

BLUE MONDAY, the Monday before Ash Wednesday which the people in Switzerland and south Germany gave over to festivity.

BOABDIL, ABU 'ABD ALLAH, d. c. 1535, last Moorish ruler of Granada. In 1483 Ferdinand and Isabella of Spain forced him to become their vassal. In 1492 they conquered Granada and brought an end to Moorish power in the Iberian peninsula.

BOBADILLA, FRANCISCO DE, d. 1502, agent of Ferdinand and Isabella of Spain and governor of Córdoba who arrested Columbus in Santo Domingo in 1500 and brought him back to Spain in irons.

BOBBIO, ABBEY OF, monastery east of Genoa founded in 612 by St. Columban and his Irish monks. The abbey developed into a noted center of learning and was especially celebrated for its excellent library and for its manuscripts, notably the "Bobbio Missal," an important collection of liturgical texts going back to the eighth century. It benefited from generous patrons, among these the kings of Germany, and in 1014 became an episcopal see. Decline set in shortly after as a result of continued jurisdictional conflicts between bishops and monks.

BÖBLINGER, well-known fifteenth-century family of stonemasons and architects of Swabia. The family's most distinguished architects were Matthäus (d. 1505) and Hans (d. 1482).

BOCCACCIO, GIOVANNI, d. 1375, father of Italian prose and author of the *Decameron*. He was born in Paris in 1313 (his father was a Florentine merchant), served as a clerk in the Bardi banking house for some years, took up the study of canon law, then turned to literature. In 1340, after some years in Naples, he returned to Florence (he had grown up in Certaldo near Florence) where he spent the greater part of his life. Of his early literary efforts which he expended in the composition of love lyrics, those in honor of his beloved Fiametta were the most successful. It was fortunate that he was already busy with the *Decameron* when he met Petrarch in 1350 since, under that humanist's influence, he devoted most of his time thenceforth to a study of the classics. He was still revising his classical work on the genealogy of the gods when he died. The *Decameron,* first prose masterpiece of medieval literature, consists of a hundred tales exchanged by a group of young people who had isolated themselves from the Black Death. The literary style is new and inimitable; the themes old, drawn from classical sources and *fabliaux.*

BODEL, JEHAN, d. 1210, French lyric and epic poet, also the probable author of *fabliaux.* His *Jeu de Saint Nicolas* reveals marked dramatic qualities and expresses his Crusading fervor.

BODICE, closely fitting upper part of a woman's garment first worn in the thirteenth century.

BOECE (Boyce, Boethius), HECTOR, d. 1536, studied at Paris, later taught at the University of Aberdeen. His history of the Scots suffers from the author's lack of critical judgment in the use of his sources.

BOETHIUS, d. c. 524, Roman consul under Theodoric, king of the Ostrogoths, who had him executed on the charge of treason. While awaiting execution Boethius composed his renowned *Consolation of Philosophy* in which he argued the view that virtue is its own reward. As the first of the transmitters of classical and patristic learning during the period of the Dark Ages which was just settling upon the West, he contributed translations of several of Aristotle's logical works, a commentary on Porphyry's *Isagoge,* and manuals on the liberal arts. His *Consolation of Philosophy* was among the most widely read books of the Middle Ages. It was one of the few that Alfred the Great had translated into Anglo-Saxon.

BOGOMILS, members of a Manichaean sect that appeared in Bulgaria in the tenth century. Their name derived from an obscure priest by the name of Bogomil (Slavic for *Pleasing to God*) who introduced an element of Christian revivalism into their practices. They maintained that the physical world, including the human body, was the work of Satan, only the human soul being created by God. Despite persecution Bogomilism spread both in the Byzantine empire and to the west. In Italy its members were called Patarines or Cathari. [*See* ALBIGENSES.]

BOGORODZICA (Bogarodzica, Bogurodzica), the

oldest Polish hymn, a song addressed to Mary, the mother of God. Although it has been credited to St. Adalbert (d. 997), it is probably no older than the thirteenth or fourteenth century.

BOHAIRIC, a principal dialect of Coptic which originated in the northern part of the Nile delta and in time replaced the other dialects of Egypt. The Bohairic version of the Scriptures may date from the sixth-seventh centuries.

BOHEMIA, Slavic kingdom on the upper Elbe in east-central Europe in a region occupied by German tribes, notably the Marcomanni, until the close of the sixth century when the Slavs began to move in. These Slavs, called Czechs, were converted to Christianity by SS. Cyril and Methodius in the ninth century. Otto I of Germany (936–73) incorporated the land into his kingdom, after which time Bohemia remained a feudal fief of Germany throughout the medieval period. The first Bohemian ruler to secure the title of king was Ottocar I (d. 1230). In 1306 when the Premyslid dynasty became extinct, the crown fell to the house of Luxemburg whose most powerful representative, Charles IV, ruled as king of Germany and Holy Roman Emperor from 1346 to 1378. Heavy German immigration stimulated the economic and cultural development of the country but also aroused national consciousness which found a hero and martyr in John Hus who was burned at the stake in 1415 for heresy. Religious and civil warfare cursed the country through much of the fifteenth century.

BOHEMIAN BRETHREN, a religious community, members of the Unity of Brethren, which appeared about the middle of the fifteenth century in Bohemia and Moravia. The sect accepted the Bible as the sole source of truth, preached peace and the simple life, rejected transubstantiation, and denied the efficacy of sacraments when administered by unworthy priests.

BOHEMIAN COMPACTS, agreements made between the Council of Basel and the Calixtines (Utraquists) during the years 1433–6 which would have extended these moderate Hussites limited reception of communion in both bread and wine.

BOHEMIAN SCHOOL OF PAINTING, first school of painters to appear north of the Alps. It was firmly established by the mid-fourteenth century due chiefly to the patronage of Charles I (he became emperor in 1346). Since he invited painters from other countries to his court at Prague, the art works produced there were less native than international in character. A large proportion of the work of these artists was destroyed during the Hussite wars. Some paintings and frescoes survive.

BOHEMOND (Bohemund, Boëmund), d. 1111, one of the leaders of the First Crusade (1096–9) and founder of the Principality of Antioch (1099). He was the eldest son of Robert Guiscard. He led a force of Norman knights from southern Italy on this Crusade and was a principal in the capture of Antioch (1098). In 1108 Byzantium forced him to recognize its overlordship.

BOHM, HANS, d. 1476, a shepherd of Niklashausen in Baden, called Hansel the Piper, who was affected by Hussite teaching and was burned at the stake by the bishop of Würzburg for preaching violence and heresy.

BOHUN, English family of Marcher lords prominent in the thirteenth and fourteenth centuries. They came to England from Normandy in or soon after 1066.

BOHUN, HENRY DE, d. 1220, first earl of Hereford, grandson of Humphrey de Bohun, founder of a great Norman dynasty in England. Although King John had given Henry de Bohun the marcher lordship of Hereford (1199), Henry joined the other barons who forced the king to accept Magna Carta in 1215. He died on a pilgrimage to the Holy Land.

BOHUN, HUMPHREY V DE, d. 1274, second earl of Hereford, first earl of Essex, member of the household of Henry III. In 1258 he joined the baronial party which opposed the king and was one of the 24 men appointed by the parliament at Oxford to reform the government. In the Barons' War he led the barons of the Welsh Marches in support of the king and was captured at Lewes in 1264.

BOHUN, HUMPHREY VIII DE, d. 1322, fourth earl of Hereford, third earl of Essex, one of the lords ordainers who sought to curb Edward II. He helped bring about the execution of the king's favorite, Piers Gaveston. In 1314 he fought for Edward at the battle of Bannockburn, but was captured and exchanged. He lost his life fighting on the side of the barons against the king and the Despensers at Boroughbridge.

BOIARDO, MATTEO MARIA, d. 1494, count of Scandiano, poet, and humanist. He composed some Latin verse but won greatest fame for his epic poem *Orlando Innamorato* which glorified the virtues of knighthood and combined the military herosim of the Carolingian epic with the chivalrous love adventures of the Arthurian romance.

BOKE OF THE DUCHESSE, poem by Chaucer which he composed as a lament on the death of Blanche of Lancaster, wife of John of Gaunt.

BOKHARA. *See* BUKHARA.

BOLESLAW (Boleslaus, Boleslan) I (the Brave or the Great), duke of Poland, 992–1025, most powerful of the early Polish rulers, extended his authority over Slovakia, Silesia, Lusatia, Moravia, Pomerania, Ruthenia, and, for a time, over Bohemia. In 1000 he secured the elevation of Gniezno to the rank of a metropolitan see and thus freed the Polish church from German supervision. In 1018 he captured Kiev and in 1025 he was crowned king, the first Polish ruler to bear that title. He reorganized the country's administrative and tax systems, and created a large standing army. Although he left Poland one of the strongest states of Europe when he

died, his conquests melted away soon after his death.

BOLESLAW (Boleslaus, Boleslan) II (the Generous or the Bold), king of Poland, 1058–79, son and successor of Casimir I, took Slovakia from Hungary, held Kiev for a time, and in 1076 permitted himself to be chosen king (antiking) of Germany when some German princes deposed Henry IV. His murder of Stanislaus, the bishop of Cracow who had joined a revolt of his leading nobles against him, led to his excommunication by Pope Gregory VII and to his expulsion from the country. He fled to Hungary and died in exile.

BOLESLAW (Boleslaus, Boleslan) III (the Wry-Mouthed), king of Poland, 1102–38, reunited the Polish kingdom by defeating his half-brother who had been left half of it by their father. His half-brother had the assistance of the emperor and of other lords. After prolonged effort he managed to establish Polish authority over the south Baltic from the mouth of the Vistula to the Oder (Pomerania). He entrusted the Christianization of its people to the bishop of Bamberg. In 1135 he signed a treaty with Emperor Lothair II which invested him with Pomerania and Rügen as fiefs of the empire. Before he died he divided his realm among his four sons and left to the eldest the overlordship over the whole.

BOLOGNA, city south of the Po at the foot of the Apennines, a military colony in Roman times, came under papal rule in the eighth century. It was one of the first of the Lombard communes and joined the Lombard League in 1167. The presence of the university helped establish its reputation as a leading center of learning in Europe and, in particular, for the study of canon and civil law. After a long history of resistance to papal authority, Cardinal Egidio Albornoz asserted papal rule in 1360 but the city was not wholly incorporated into the Papal States until the pontificate of Pope Julius II (1503–13).

BOLOGNA, UNIVERSITY OF, was chartered by

Frederick I Barbarossa in 1158 although scholars believe it had acquired the character of a university some years before. It owed its high reputation as a center of legal learning principally to Gratian and Irnerius who taught there in the twelfth century and to the patronage of the popes.

BOMBARDE, a large-caliber, front-loading, siege gun, that was first noted in 1381. As missiles it used heavy stone balls.

BONANNO DA PISA, Italian sculptor and architect (fl. c. 1174–86) who made the bronze doors for the cathedrals of Monreale and Pisa. They are representative of the Italian Romanesque style, the doors of Monreale also revealing Byzantine influences.

BONAVENTURE (Bonaventura), ST., d. 1274, distinguished Franciscan scholastic known as the Seraphic Doctor. He studied at Paris under Alexander of Hales, taught there until 1257 when he became superior general of his order, and in 1265 was consecrated archbishop of Paris. So important was his work as administrator during what proved to be a most trying period in the history of the Franciscans that he has been honored as the second founder of the order. Although he ranked as a leading scholastic of the Augustinian school, he remained foremost a theogian rather than a metaphysician and insisted that faith must always lead reason in the search for truth, even in the natural order. His most influential work, *The Journey of the Soul to God,* won him recognition as the leading mystical theologian of the Middle Ages. Bonaventure felt the greatest reverence for St. Francis, the founder of his order, and authored what has been accepted as the official biography of the saint.

BONCOMPAGNO DA SIGNA, d. c. 1240, taught rhetoric at Bologna and left treatises on that subject and on the art of letter-writing. He is also the author of a description of the siege of Ancona.

BONDOL (Bandol, Bandolf), JEAN DE, also known as Jean de Bruges, fl. c. 1368–81, painter to Charles V of France who combined the elegant court style with Flemish realism in his depiction of figures and landscapes.

BÔNE. *See* HIPPO.

BONER (Bonerius), ULRICH, a fourteenth-century Dominican friar of Bern who composed 100 rhymed fables, pertaining principally to animals and plants, which he drew largely from Latin sources and published under the title *Der Edelstein.* It was the first book to be printed in German.

BONFINI, ANTONIO, d. c. 1505, Italian humanist and poet who spent the last years of his career as court historian in Hungary with King Matthias Corvinus. His history of Hungary covers the period from 363 to 1496.

BONHOMME (Jacques), nickname, meaning *good man,* which as a name for French peasants came into use in the fourteenth century.

BONIFACE I, ST., Pope, 418–22, a Roman, already advanced in years when he succeeded Pope Zosimus. He did little to assert papal authority and even left Emperor Honorius to deal with the Pelagians. He did secure the revocation by Theodosius II of his edict placing Illyricum under the jurisdiction of the patriarch of Constantinople.

BONIFACE II, Pope, 530–32, a German by descent who had difficulty establishing his right of succession following the death of Felix IV against the opposition of the clergy of Rome. Imperial and other opposition dissuaded him from issuing a decree that would have authorized the pope to appoint his successor.

BONIFACE III, Pope, February to November 607, a Roman who served as papal legate to the Byzantine court during the pontificate of Gregory the Great (I) (590–604).

BONIFACE IV, ST., Pope, 608–15, pious and

administratively active bishop of Rome. Monophysitism which remained strong in the eastern Mediterranean caused him his gravest problem. Boniface converted the Pantheon which the emperor Hadrian had completed, into a church and dedicated it to Our Lady of the Rotunda.

BONIFACE V, Pope 619–25?, a Neapolitan whose pontificate witnessed the further extension of Christianity into England, especially in Northumbria.

BONIFACE VI, Pope, 896, held the office of pope for approximately two weeks when he died. His election had been secured by Lambert of Spoleto who was contending for control of Rome with Arnulf, the German emperor. A synod summoned two years later by Pope John IX denounced the election of Boniface as that of an unworthy and suspended priest.

BONIFACE VII, Pope (Antipope), 974, 984–5, a Roman, cardinal deacon, owed his election to the influence of the Crescenti faction who seized and strangled the legitimate pope Benedict VI. Upon the appearance of Otto II of Germany, Boniface fled the city but returned after Otto's death, only to die a violent death after a year's pontificate.

BONIFACE VIII (Benedetto Gaetani), Pope, 1294–1303, learned jurist and a leading cardinal, succeeded to the papacy over the bitter opposition of the Colonna faction following the resignation of Pope Celestine V. In 1296 the financial demands which Edward I of England and Philip IV of France were making upon their clergy prompted Boniface to issue the bull *Clericis Laicos* which anathematized such taxation by the state, but the defiance of both monarchs forced him to rescind the decree. Boniface's difficulties continued with Philip, however, and in 1302 he issued the bull *Unam Sanctam* which has been called the most extreme statement of papal authority ever set forth. In this bull he declared that outside the church there could be no salvation and that all men, including Philip,

must submit themselves to his authority as Christ's vicar if they wished to be saved. Again Philip defied Boniface, sent Guillaume de Nogaret to Anagni where the pope was staying, and with the help of troops supplied by the Colonna faction seized him and held him prisoner for three days. Though the townspeople finally drove out Boniface's persecutors, the experience must have hastened his death which took place within a month. In 1300 Boniface instituted the custom of the Holy Year. He also expanded the *Corpus Juris Canonici* in 1298 with the publication of a third part, called the *Liber Sextus*. This addition included the most important papal canons issued since 1234.

BONIFACE IX, Pope, 1389–1404, a Neapolitan, successor of the Roman (as opposed to Avignonese) pope Urban VI. Although by nature peaceable, Boniface refused to consider any proposal by which the Western Schism might be resolved short of the Avignonese pope's unconditional submission. Apart from the problem of the schism, his principal difficulties were financial. These be sought to solve through practices that were scarcely better than simoniacal.

BONIFACE, d. 432, military governor of Africa, whose differences with the Western emperor opened the way to the conquest of the region by Gaiseric and his Vandals. In 432 Boniface returned to Italy and was appointed master of the soldiers by Placidia, regent for Valentinian III. He defeated Aetius whom she had dismissed from that office but died from a wound sustained in the battle.

BONIFACE OF MONTFERRAT, d. 1207, one of the leaders of the anti-Byzantine sentiment on the Fourth Crusade (1202–4) that led to the capture of Constantinople. He had hoped to become the first Latin emperor of Constantinople, but instead was given the kingdom of Thessalonica. He was slain fighting the Bulgarians.

BONIFACE OF SAVOY, BL., d. 1270, son of the count of Savoy, became a Carthusian, then bishop, and through the favor of Henry III who had married his niece, archbishop of Canterbury (1245). Despite his continuing interests in Savoy and diplomatic business, he proved himself a strong archbishop, asserted his metropolitan authority over his suffragan bishops, resisted royal demands for money from the English church, yet vigorously supported Henry III against his rebellious barons.

BONIFACE (Winfrid, Wynfrith), ST., d. 754, the Apostle of Germany, reformer of the Frankish church, missionary, and martyr. Boniface was born in Wessex c. 672, became a Benedictine monk, and in 716 crossed over to the continent to begin his long missionary labors in Frisia. In 717 he made the first of several trips to Rome, was consecrated bishop in 722, and was given broad episcopal authority over Germany by Pope Gregory II. With the encouragement and protection of Charles Martel, the ruler of the Frankish kingdom, he undertook a systematic reform and reorganization of the church principally with the assistance of monks and nuns whom he had invited over from England. (The local Merovingian church was hopelessly corrupt.) As metropolitan (732), papal legate, then after 744 as archbishop of Mainz, he continued his work, establishing a number of dioceses including Würzburg and Eichstädt and founding monasteries, the most renowed of these being Fulda. Early in 754 he surrendered his office as archbishop and returned to Frisia where he and his companions were massacred (June 5).

BONIFACE, ST. *See* BRUNO OF QUERFURT, ST.

BONI HOMINES *(bons hommes),* that is, good men, name popularly given to various religious communities such as the Monks of Grandmont and the Brothers of the Free Spirit, even to such sects as the Albigenses.

BONIZO (Bonitho), d. c. 1091, bishop of Sutri, then of Piacenza, who was driven from his see in 1089 because of his staunch support of Pope Gregory VII in his quarrel with Henry IV of Germany over investiture. He left a partisan, although useful, memoir of Pope Gregory.

BONO DA FERRARA, Italian painter of the fifteenth century who is best known for his *St. Jerome in a Landscape.*

BONVESIN DE LA RIVA, d. c. 1316, Italian writer who anticipated Dante's description of the other world in a poem of some 2,000 verses. He also left a work in Latin which extolled the glories of Milan.

BOOK, MEDIEVAL, usually a papyrus roll until the fourth century when a codex written on parchment came to be preferred since parchment was more readily available and could be reused. [*See* PALIMPSEST.] Until the twelfth century the production of books, at least in Western Europe, was limited to monastic scriptoria which also produced their own parchment. With the rise of universities and the increasing demand for books their production quickly became a secular craft in which poor students might become engaged either for a stipend or to procure manuscripts for themselves. Paper, which was introduced into Europe via Spain in the eleventh century, replaced parchment in the thirteenth. Foliation dates from the twelfth century although pagination remained rare. The scribe used a pen fashioned from the quill of a goose or swan or from the eleventh century he might prefer a reed. The black ink he used tended to change color with time, while he reserved red ink for rubrics. Bound books appeared from the ninth century, bound in covers of wood, less frequently of leather and parchment.

BOOK OF CEREMONIES, encyclopedia of information dealing with Byzantine history, archeology, government, robes, and ceremonies compiled under the direction of Constantine VII Porphyrogenitus (913–59).

BOOK OF KELLS. *See* KELLS, BOOK OF.

BOOK OF SENTENCES. *See* PETER LOMBARD.

BOOTH, LAWRENCE, d. 1480, chancellor of Queen Margaret (of Anjou), bishop of Durham (1457), and keeper of the privy seal (1456–60). He managed to gain the favor of Edward IV, served as his confessor, and in 1473, after some years when he was out of favor, served as his chancellor. In 1476 he was translated to York.

BORDEAUX, city on the Garonne in southwestern France, a commercial center already in Roman times and a bishopric in the fourth century, was occupied by the Visigoths in 418 and by the Franks in 507. Northmen destroyed the city in 848 but it was rebuilt. From the tenth century it served as the leading seaport of Gascony and from the eleventh as the seat of the dukes of Aquitaine. The bulk of its principal export, wine, went to England. For the greater part of the period from 1154 until 1453 it remained an English possession.

BORDEAUX PILGRIM, the earliest recorded pilgrim from the West to visit the Holy Land. He is said to have made his pilgrimage in 333–4.

BORGIA (Borja), a Spanish family which came into prominence in the fifteenth century because of its association with Peter IV of Aragon. Alfonso, cardinal-archbishop of Valencia, became Pope Callistus III (1455–8) and his nephew Rodrigo, Pope Alexander VI (1492–1503).

BORGIA, CESARE (Caesar), d. 1507, natural son of Cardinal Rodrigo (later Pope Alexander VI), archbishop of Valencia (he had received tonsure), and cardinal. In 1498 he renounced his cardinalate and married the sister of the king of Navarre. He obtained the duchy of Valentinois from Louis XII of France, then from 1499 was engaged in reestablishing papal authority in the provinces of Romagna and Umbria. After the death of Pope Alexander VI (1503), he was imprisoned for a time by Pope Julius II, then released only to be reimprisoned, this time in Spain on orders of Ferdinand, king of Spain. After two years he escaped (1506) but was slain the following year fighting in the service of his brother-in-law, the king of Navarre. Machiavelli considered him the model prince.

BORGIA, GIOVANNI (Joan, Juan), d. 1497, natural son of Cardinal Rodrigo (later Pope Alexander VI), duke of Gandia, driven from his duchy by Charles VIII of France. He fled to Rome where he was assassinated, possibly on orders of his brother Cesare.

BORGIA, LUCREZIA, d. 1519, daughter of Cardinal Rodrigo (later Pope Alexander VI), married, upon her father's insistence, to Giovanni Sforza (1493) in order to gain the friendship of Milan. This marriage was annulled in 1497 when a political realignment made Milan an enemy of Alexander's, whereupon she married a natural son of the king of Naples. In 1501, after the assassination of her husband had left her a widow, she married the son of the duke of Ferrara, to whom she bore seven children.

BORGIA, RODRIGO. *See* ALEXANDER VI, Pope.

BORIS I, Czar of Bulgaria, 852–89, who decided, after considerable controversy, that missionaries from Constantinople, rather than from the West, should convert his people. He extended his frontiers at the expense of the Macedonians and Serbs, and in 889 abdicated and became a monk. When his son Vladimir who had succeeded him joined in a pagan revolt, he returned to power long enough to replace him on the throne with his other son Symeon. Boris died in 907 and was canonized by the Eastern church.

BORIS AND GLEB, sons of Vladimir, prince of Kiev, who were slain by their half-brother Svyatopolk in 1015 in a quarrel over the succession. They were canonized by the Russian church and are listed as the first Russian saints.

BORNEIL, GIRAUD DE, French troubadour, known to his companions as the "Master of the Troubadours," sang at Spanish courts during the period 1175 to 1220. Among his patrons he counted Richard I of England whom he accompanied on the Third Crusade.

BOROUGH, a town in England with rights of self-government granted by royal charter. From the late thirteenth century a borough enjoyed the privilege of sending two representatives (burgesses) to meet with Parliament. The borough was originally simply a fortified settlement, whence its name which had the same root as burg.

BORRASSÁ, LUIS, d. c. 1425, Spanish Gothic painter active in Barcelona and Aragon from 1388 to 1424, and best known for the *Altarpiece of Sta Clara*. His works, which reveal French and Sienese influences, served to introduce Spain to the ornamental realism of Flemish painting.

BOSCH, HIERONYMUS (Hieronymus van Aeken), d. 1516, Flemish painter (fl. 1488–1515) whose themes of suffering, horror, and evil were unique for their portrayal of fantasy, realism, and the grotesque. They were at the same time alive with movement and color.

BOSNIA AND HERCEGOVINA, regions along the eastern coast of the Adriatic, settled by Serbs in the seventh century. It became an independent country by the twelfth, but later at times acknowledged the suzerainty of the kings of Hungary. Late in the fourteenth century Bosnia again became independent, when it annexed Hercegovina from Serbia. In 1463 it fell to the Turks. Religious strife among Catholics, Orthodox, and Bogomils tended to weaken the resistance of the country.

BOSO, d. 970, Benedictine monk whom Otto I appointed first bishop of Merseburg. He has been called the Apostle of the Wends.

BOSO, d. 887, count of Vienne and, in the aftermath of the death of Louis II (the Stammerer) of the West Franks in 879, founder of the kingdom of Arles (Lower Burgundy).

BOSTIUS, ARNOLD, d. 1499, also known as Arnold van Vaernewijck, a Carmelite of Ghent, composed a treatise in defense of the doctrine of the Immaculate Conception as well as works dealing with the history of his order. He encouraged classical studies and was the associate of the leading humanists of the period.

BOSWORTH FIELD, BATTLE OF, battle in central England (county of Leicester) on 22 August 1485 when Ricard III was defeated and slain. The victor, Henry (VII) Tudor, succeeded. Some scholars designate this battle as the closing engagement of the so-called Wars of the Roses.

BOTTICELLI, SANDRO (Alessandro Filipepi), d. 1510, Florentine painter whose work reflected the influence of his teachers Filippo Lippi and Verrochio and that of A. Pallaiuolo. The greater part of his painting was done in Florence where he enjoyed the patronage of Lorenzo the Magnificent, although he also executed several of the frescoes in the Sistine Chapel in Rome. A tender, spiritual beauty served to soften the element of medieval stiffness in his work. In later life when he came under the influence of Savonarola his work took on a mystic, intense, and ecstatic character. Among his best known paintings are his *Adoration of the Magi* and the *Birth of Venus*.

BOUCICAUT, JEAN LE MEINGRE, d. 1421, French soldier, an exponent of the ideals of chivalry, who distinguished himself fighting the Ottoman Turks at Nicopolis (1396) before being taken prisoner. In 1399 he defeated a Turkish fleet at Gallipoli, then was taken a prisoner by the English at Agincourt. He founded a society whose purpose was the protection of wives and daughters of absent knights.

BOUILLON, GODFRIED VON. *See* GODFREY OF BOUILLON.

BOURBON, French noble family, a branch of the Capetian, that traced its more immediate origins to Robert of Clermont, sixth son of Louis IX, who married (1272) the heiress of Stammburg

Bourbon l'Archambault with which the fief of Bourbonnais was joined. Their son, Louis I, was created duke of Bourbon in 1327.

BOURCHIER, THOMAS, d. 1486, chancellor of Oxford, bishop of Worcester, Ely, and archbishop of Canterbury (1454). He avoided identification with any of the factions during the difficult period of Henry VI's insanity which made him acceptable to all parties. To the neglect of his episcopal responsibilities, he gave his attention principally to political affairs and served as royal councillor under both Henry VI and Edward IV. In recognition of his staunch support of the Yorkist cause, Edward prevailed upon the pope to create him a cardinal (1467). He accepted the usurpation of Richard III and crowned both him and his successor, Henry VII.

BOURDEILLE, ELIAS OF, d. 1484, a Franciscan, bishop of Perigueux, confessor to Louis XI, archbishop of Tours, and cardinal. His writings include an attack on the Pragmatic Sanction of Bourges and a defense of the beatification of Joan of Arc.

BOURDICHON, JEAN, d. 1521, French painter and illuminator, best known for his *Book of the Hours of Anne of Brittany*. He did work for Louis XI and was court painter to Charles VIII.

BOURGEOIS DE PARIS, anonymous chronicler of the fifteenth century, author of *Le Journal d'un Bourgeois de Paris* which extends from 1405 to 1449. The chronicle concerns itself with developments of the period and not just events that took place in Paris. Despite such defects as evidence of Burgundian partisanship, it constitutes a valuable source for this period.

BOURGES, city of central France, site of a Celtic community, capital of Roman Aquitania, a diocese probably from A.D. 300, and the capital of the county (duchy) of Berry. It served as headquarters for Charles VII (1422–61) during the early part of his reign, whence the derisive title of "King of Bourges" given him by his enemies.

Louis XI founded the University of Bourges in 1463. The imposing palace of Jacques Coeur still graces the city as does also the Gothic cathedral of St. Etienne (thirteenth century).

BOUTS, DIRK (Dieric, Thierry), d. 1475, Dutch painter whose work reflects the influence of the Van Eyck brothers and that of Rogier van der Weyden. He broke with their symbolic style, however, and gave greater attention to psychological interpretation, as noted especially in the portrait he made of himself. His sense of color also distinguished his work — he was a master of harmonious color schemes — and he had a poetic feeling for his landscape backgrounds in which he placed his figures in three-dimensional spaces, correctly constructed in accordance with the rules of perspective.

BOUVINES, BATTLE OF, decisive battle fought in Flanders in July 1214 when Philip II Augustus won a great victory over the forces of Otto IV of Germany and the count of Flanders. This defeat cost Otto IV his throne, secured his replacement by Frederick II, and also confirmed Philip in his possession of Normandy and other French fiefs which he had already taken from John of England.

BOWER, WALTER, d. 1449, Scottish chronicler, abbot of Inchcolm monastery in the Firth of Forth. He is believed to have continued the work of John of Fordun. The original and his continuation (1153–1437) are together known as the *Scotichronicon*. This work is the source of much of the early history of Scotland.

BOYAR, name given to members of the Russian landed aristocracy of the twelfth and thirteenth centuries. Members of the Bulgarian aristocracy were referred to as boyars in the tenth century.

BOY BISHOP, title given to the leader of the choirboys who was elected "bishop" on St. Nicholas Day (December 6) to preside later on the feast of the Holy Innocents (December 28). On that day he and other choirboys occupied the important offices in the cathedral community. The practice whose origins have been traced to the tenth century spread from the cathedral to monasteries, schools, parishes, and continued on through the Middle Ages.

BOYD, name of a distinguished Scottish family. Robert Boyd (d. c. 1481) was created a peer c. 1454 and served as one of the regents of Scotland during the minority of James III. In 1466 he was appointed governor of the realm but three years later fled to England to escape execution. His eldest son Thomas, earl of Arran (d. c. 1473), who married Mary, sister of James III, made good his escape to Denmark.

BRABANÇONS, term given to mercenary soldiers of the twelfth and thirteenth centuries because so many of them hailed from Brabant.

BRABANT, DUCHY OF, originally a Frankish county lying between the Maas and Scheldt which became part of the kingdom of the East Franks in 870 when it was attached to Lower Lorraine. The counts of Löwen (Louvain) who acquired the principality in 1106 assumed the title of dukes of Brabant in 1190. In 1390 the county became a possession of Burgundy but in 1477 it fell to the Hapsburgs and Germany.

BRACCIO DA MONTONE, d. 1424, Italian *condottiere,* learned the profession of arms under Alberico da Barbiano, first of the great Italian war captains. In time he gave his name to a school of warfare. He seized holdings in the papal territories in Perugia and Umbria, and from 1420 until his death ruled these as vicar of Pope Martin V.

BRACTON (Bratton), HENRY DE, d. 1268, priest, chancellor of the diocese of Exeter, from 1248 a royal justice in the service of Henry III and a member of the king's council. His most important work, *On the Laws and Customs of England,* is considered the most informative and authoritative book on English law to appear in the Middle Ages.

BRADWARDINE, THOMAS, d. 1349, English philosopher, theologian, and mathematician, chancellor of Oxford, chaplain of Edward III, and archbishop of Canterbury (1349). His best known work was a controversial treatise on the problem of grace and free will in which he insisted on the necessity of grace and the "irresistible" efficacy of the Divine Will, which is the cause of all action. He also left treatises on mathematics, and he has been credited with awakening contemporary scholars to the principles of dynamics.

BRAGA, city in northern Portugal of Roman origin, capital of a Sueve state in the fifth century, occupied by the Visigoths in 485 and by the Moors in the early eighth century, and in 1040 taken from the Moors by Ferdinand I of Castile-Leon. From 1093 until 1147 it served as the residence of the king of Portugal and his court. The bishop of Braga rivaled the bishop of Toledo in influence. The city's twelfth-century cathedral reveals a blend of Moorish and Gothic styles.

BRAGA, RITE OF, the form of the Latin rite used in the cathedral of Braga in Portugal. It differed from the Roman rite only in details.

BRAGI, a) in ancient Nordic mythology, a son of Odin and the god of poetry; b) a bard who lived in Norway in the ninth century.

BRAKTEAT, a German silver penny, engraved on one side only, which came into use in the twelfth century; also a kind of gold necklace worn from the fifth and sixth centuries.

BRAMANTE, DONATO D'ANGELO, d. 1514, an Italian architect who specialized in the construction of domes. (His first artistic efforts were those of a painter.) He worked first in Milan (S. Maria presso S. Satiro), and in 1499 moved to Rome where his work established him as a leading architect of the High Renaissance. His original design of St. Peter's was greatly altered by his successors.

BRANCACCI CHAPEL, chapel in the church of Santa Maria del Carmine in Florence which was renowned for its superb frescoes. These included works by Masaccio and Filippino Lippi. The Brancacci family endowed the chapel.

BRANDENBURG, city of Germany on the banks of the Havel river, founded as Brennabor or Brennaburg by the west Slavonic Hevelli tribe. Henry I ("The Fowler") conquered the region in 928. In 948 it became the see of a diocese. Albert (the Bear) finally subdued the Hevelli and in 1153 rebuilt the town with Slavs occupying the settlement on the south bank ("old town"), the Germans the village on the north bank ("new town").

BRANDENBURG, MARGRAVATE OF, German principality located between the lower Elbe and the Oder. Slavs who occupied the region following the movement westward of the Germans were gradually brought into subjection through the efforts of Charlemagne, Henry I, Otto I, and particularly by Albert the Bear, count of Ballenstädt. Albert, the real founder of Brandenburg, invited many German peasants, reorganized the church, founded monasteries, and in 1140 assumed the title of margrave. Albert's descendants, the Ascanians, ruled Brandenburg until their extinction in 1320. By the middle of the thirteenth century the margrave had acquired the office of imperial chamberlain and was one of the secular electors, a rank confirmed by the Golden Bull of 1356 which designated him as one of the seven princes to cast a vote for the new emperor. In 1415 Emperor Sigismund invested Frederick of Hohenzollern with the margravate.

BRANDEUM, name of a cloth which was laid upon the grave of a martyr in the early church and then revered as a relic.

BRANDON, ST. See BRENDAN, ST.

BRANIMIR, Croatian prince of Dalmatia (879–92) who brought his people within the jurisdiction of the Roman church. He freed them from the jurisdiction of Venice.

BRANKOVICH, GEORGE, despot of Serbia, 1427–56, managed with the help of John Hunyadi, governor of Transylvania, to retain something of his country against Turkish attacks. Once the Serbian state received official recognition in the treaty of Szegedin (1444), he abandoned his alliance with Hunyadi and cultivated the friendship of the Turks as promising greater assurance of Serbia's independence.

BRANT (Brandt), SEBASTIAN, d. 1521, German poet and humanist who produced legal treatises and Latin poetry. He is best known for the *Narrenschiff* (Ship of Fools), a satire of the times.

BRASSES, MEMORIAL, inscribed plates of brass used as ornamental covers for tombs or simply as memorials. They appeared at least as early as the thirteenth century and proved especially popular in England.

BREASTPLATE OF ST. PATRICK, ancient Irish hymn that begins with the words, in translation, "I bind unto myself today the strong name of the Trinity." It is improbable that its traditional ascription to St. Patrick is historically accurate.

BREHAL, JEAN, d. c. 1479, French Dominican, theologian, and inquisitor general in France from 1452 to 1474. In 1466, after examining the acts and proceedings of the court that condemned Joan of Arc, he declared its judgment unjust and iniquitous.

BREHON LAWS, ancient laws of Ireland which were enacted as early as the eighth century if not earlier.

BRELAN, a board or table upon which dice or cards were played; also a French card game of chance.

BREMEN, city near the mouth of the Weser, first noted in 782, a bishop's seat in 787, and in 845 an archbishop's following the Viking destruction of Hamburg which had been the metropolitan see. It then included all Scandinavia, Iceland, and Greenland. Bremen became an imperial city in 1186, established a municipal government independent of episcopal control in 1225, and in 1358 joined the Hanseatic League.

BREMEN CITY MUSICIANS, actually domestic animals, under the direction of the ass, that went to Bremen or Amsterdam, so a tale of the twelfth century had it, in order to become musicians.

BRENDAN (Brandan, Brandon), ST., d. c. 578, abbot of the Irish monastery of Clonfert, one of the monasteries he founded during his missionary labors in Ireland and Wales. According to native legend, he came upon the island of the blessed on one of his many voyages, a discovery that provided the basis for the Latin romance entitled *Navigatio S. Brendani* (c. 950). This story, which proved extremely popular and was translated into many languages, combined much mythological matter with a measure of factual geography, or what was accepted as such, including a visit to the North American mainland.

BRENNER PASS, lowest pass, almost 4,500 feet high, over the Alps that was open the entire year and extended north from Trent to Augsburg. It was the most extensively traveled of the passes over the Alps.

BRESLAU, city of Silesia whose original castle was erected by Bratislaw (Bratislaus) I of Bohemia (894–921), whence its name. Poles and Bohemians fought for its possession, but heavy German immigration from the close of the twelfth century made it a German city, particularly after it was rebuilt following its destruction by the Mongols in 1241. In 1335 it passed to Bohemia and was the leading city of that country in the late Middle Ages. It reached the height of its prosperity during this period and in 1387 joined the Hanseatic League.

BRETAGNE. French for Brittany.

BRETHREN OF THE COMMON LIFE (Brethren of Good Will), a semimonastic community founded in Deventer c. 1376 by companions of Gerhard Groote (1340–84) and surely with his encouragement and guidance. The Brethren pursued an ascetic life either in communities or in their own homes, yet took no formal vows. They devoted themselves to prayer, engaged in social work, established some schools, and were especially active in copying religious literature (Bibles, missals, lives of the saints). Although most numerous in northern Germany and the Low Countries, their number was never large, partly because of the hostility of the mendicant orders, partly because of the suspicion of heterodoxy which left them suspect in the eyes of the ecclesiastical authorities.

BRETHREN OF THE CROSS, name of several religious communities that appeared during the period of the Crusades and engaged in missionary work. The best known of these was that composed of Canons Regular of St. Augustine, often identified as the Crosier Fathers, whose founder was Theodore of Celles (d. 1236). Similar orders included the Italian Cruciati, the Portuguese Canons Regular of the Holy Cross of Coimbra, the Bohemian Military Order of the Cross with a Red Star, and the Order of the Holy Cross with the Red Heart.

BRETHREN (and Sisters) OF THE FREE SPIRIT, name given to different communities of religiously motivated people, such as the Turlupini in Paris, who inclined to pantheism and rejected all external acts of religion. They preached that all creatures were identical with God and, in fact, became God when they rose above sin. In their way of life, even dress, they resembled the Beghards with whom they were frequently confused. They appeared in the Rhineland in the thirteenth century, somewhat later in Italy and France, and despite persecution managed to maintain an existence until the middle of the fifteenth century. Their views reappeared with the Anabaptists of the sixteenth century.

BRETHREN OF THE POOR LIFE. *See* APOSTOLICI.

BRETIGNY, TREATY OF, treaty agreed to in 1360 in this city just south of Paris in which the English, following their overwhelming victory over the French at Poitiers (1356), acquired Guienne in full sovereignty as well as the city of Calais. The ransom of King John who had been captured by the Black Prince was set at 3,000,000 gold pieces.

BRETON SUCCESSION, WAR OF THE, war (1341–64) fought between claimants for the duchy of Brittany following the death of John III in 1341. His younger brother, John de Montfort, one contestant, had the support of Edward III of England while the other contestant, Charles of Blois who had married a niece of the late duke, received that of Philip VI, John II, and Charles V of France. The war, an important aside during the period of the Hundred Years' War, ended in 1364 with the battle of Auray and the defeat and death of Charles.

BRETONS, Celtic peoples who fled Cornwall for Brittany during the fifth century in order to escape the invading Angles and Saxons. In sharp contrast to their neighbors, the Northmen (Normans), they clung tenaciously to their native ways and avoided those of the land to which they had come.

BRETWALDA, name given to eight Anglo-Saxon kings by the *Anglo-Saxon Chronicle*. These included Ethelbert of Kent (d. 616) and Oswiu, king of Northumbria (d. 670).

BREVE, a short apostolic letter that appeared in the late fourteenth century.

BREVIARY, name given to the single-volume collection of the different hymns, prayers, and scriptural readings that made up the Divine Office. The first such volumes appeared in the eleventh century when general agreement had established the substantial composition of the office. The mendicants of the thirteenth century were the first clerics to use portable breviaries.

BREVIARY OF ALARIC (*Breviarium Alaricianum, Lex Romana Visigothorum*), a collection of laws compiled by Alaric II, king of the Visigoths, which he promulgated for the use of his Roman subjects in 506. It consisted principally of Roman laws, constitutions, and the opinions of Roman jurists. In 654 when the division between Roman and Goth had become obscured, the *Breviary* was repealed. It proved influential in preserving some elements of Roman Law in the south and east of France.

BREVICOXA (Jean Courtecuisse), d. 1423, distinguished theologian of Paris, a conciliarist in his position concerning papal authority, who took part in the Council of Pisa (1409) and later played an important role at the Council of Constance in bringing the Western Schism to an end.

BREYDENBACH, BERNHARD OF, d. 1497, a traveler to the Holy Land who left an illustrated account of his journey, including sketches of the peoples, cities, and animals he saw on his trip. Up to this time no single volume had provided such information about foreign lands.

BRÉZÉ, Angevin noble family whose most prominent member, Pierre de Brézé, d. 1465, proved himself a trusted soldier and statesman in the service of Charles VII. Through the influence of Agnes Sorel, the king's mistress, he became the chief power in the state during the period 1444–50. He fell from power upon the accession of Louis XI (1461–83), but remained a loyal adviser to Margaret of Anjou, queen consort of Henry VI of England, when she returned to France after the death of her husband.

BRICTINIANS, a congregation of hermits that derived its name from the hill of Brettino near Fano, Italy, where its first monastery was erected early in the thirteenth century. The congregation which adopted the Rule of St. Augustine was combined in 1256 with other hermit congregations to form the one Order of Hermit Friars of St. Augustine. [*See* AUGUSTINIANS.]

BRIAN BORU (Brian Boroimhe), d. 1014, high king of Ireland, of the royal house of Munster, at first ruler only of the counties of Clare and Tipperary, later extended his authority over all Munster and Leinster and in 1002 was recognized high king of all Ireland. His relations with the Norse rulers along the coast worsened in time and in 1014 he annihilated a formidable alliance composed of Norse foes of Ireland, the Hebrides, Orkneys, and Iceland, as well as his Irish enemies. His victory ended Norse rule in Ireland.

BRIDE, ST. *See* BRIGIT, ST.

BRIDGE-BUILDING BROTHERHOODS, three societies, one organized at Avignon c. 1181, another at Lyons c. 1184, and a third at Pont-Saint-Esprit c. 1277, whose members, all laymen, dedicated their efforts toward erecting and maintaining bridges, less as artisans, however, than as solicitors for funds. The brotherhoods had disappeared by the early fourteenth century.

BRIDGET (Birgitta, Birgit, Birgida) OF SWEDEN, ST., d. 1373, patron saint of Sweden, a leading mystic of the Middle Ages, and foundress of the Brigittine Order. Bridget was the daughter of a Swedish provincial governor, served as lady in waiting to the queen of Sweden, married and had eight children, including St. Catherine of Sweden. When she became a widow, she entered the Cistercian order, founded in 1346 a new religious order known as the Brigittines, and in 1350 went to Rome to secure papal confirmation. Except for pilgrimages, she remained there for the remainder of her life, devoting her time to works of charity, to church reform, and to the cause of bringing the pope back to Rome from Avignon. [*See* AVIGNONESE RESIDENCE.] Papal confirmation of her order came in 1370. Her revelations which were considered of great importance have received intense theological study.

BRIDGET (Bridgit), ABBEY OF, mother house of the Brigittine Order which was erected c. 1371 on the royal estate of Vadstena that King

Magnus II Eriksson had given to St. Bridget in 1346. Its first abbess was Bridget's daughter, St. Catherine of Sweden.

BRIENNE, JOHN OF, d. 1237, king of Jerusalem by virtue of his marriage to the heiress of the kingdom, later lost the crown to Frederick II who married his daughter Isabella (Yolande). In 1228 he became Latin Emperor of Constantinople as regent for Baldwin II.

BRIGANDINE (Brigantine), corselet made of layers of metal used as protective armor in the late Middle Ages, especially by French troops serving under Louis XI.

BRIGANDS, name given to French soldiers during the early years of the Hundred Years' War. The term derived from the type of armor they wore. Because they often went unpaid and took to marauding, the term acquired its present meaning.

BRIGANTIA, a British goddess who was identified with the Irish goddess Brigit (Brighid), patroness of poets, physicians, and blacksmiths. Later tradition transformed her into a Christian saint.

BRIGIT (Brigid, Bridget, Brigida, Bride) OF IRELAND, ST., d. c. 528, abbess of Kildare and a patron saint of Ireland. The community at Kildare was a double monastery, the only such institution in Ireland. Much myth obscures the life of Brigit. She appears to have been active in founding other religious communities.

BRIGITTINES (Bridgettines), officially the Order of the Most Holy Savior, a semicloistered order of nuns founded by St. Bridget of Sweden (1346) and confirmed by Pope Urban V (1370). The constitution of the order provided that a convent for nuns and a monastery for monks be established in pairs with both houses being placed under the supervision of the abbess and both using the same chapel. The mother house of the order was the convent established c. 1371 at Vadstena. In keeping with the wish of

St. Bridget, the order paid special attention to the virtues of humility and simplicity of life.

BRINDISI, city of southeast Italy, of ancient origin, an embarkation port for many Crusaders on their way to the Holy Land. It was occupied by different conquerors during the period of the Germanic invasions, as well as by Moslems, and regained its importance only after the conquest of the area by the Normans in 1071. Its prosperity continued until the close of the fourteenth century when it suffered in the struggle over the succession to the throne of the kingdom of Naples. In 1456 a severe earthquake devastated the city.

BRISTOL, ancient seaport town of southwestern England, just below Wales. It was sufficiently important commercially in the tenth century to possess a mint. The Norman conquest brought more trade to the town and in 1155 it received its first charter. The manufacture of woolen cloth dates from the reign of Edward III (1327–77). The cathedral of Bristol, erected 1298–1330, is judged an excellent example of the Decorated Style.

BRITTANY, northwestern peninsula of France, known as Armorica until occupied by Britons (Bretons) from England in the fifth century. The immigrants maintained contact with the Celts of southwestern England and also clung to their own ways, a policy that might explain the success of Brittany in preserving a large measure of independence until the close of the Middle Ages. From c. 850 until 870 it was under Frankish rule, then became independent except for a brief period of Norman control in 919. In the tenth century its ruler assumed the title duke, a title held in the late twelfth century by Geoffrey, son of Henry II of England, who had married the heiress of Conan IV. It was Geoffrey's son Arthur whom King John of England is believed to have murdered in 1203. Arthur's brother-in-law Peter I secured the duchy with the blessing of Philip II Augustus. The extinction of the

direct line in 1341 led to the War of the Breton Succession (1341–64). Because England supported the claims of one contestant and France the other, Brittany was able to pursue a relatively neutral course during the period of the Hundred Years' War. In 1491 its heiress, Anne, married Charles VIII of France. When widowed, she married Louis XII in 1499, whereupon the province passed directly under royal authority.

BRÖDERLAM, MELCHIOR, artist of Ypres (fl. 1381–1409), served as court painter for the count of Flanders but principally for Duke Philip the Bold of Burgundy. His paintings include furniture, banners, and wings of the altarpiece for the Chartreuse de Champmol in Dijon. His work is representative of the Franco-Flemish style of the late fourteenth century.

BROTFELD, Hungarian Kenjermeza, site of a great victory the Hungarians gained over the Turks in 1479.

BRUCE, a distinguished Scottish family descended from Robert de Brus, an eleventh-century Norman duke who helped William I conquer England. William gave Robert lands in England, while Robert's son received fiefs in Scotland, which meant that the family rendered homage in both kingdoms. When Margaret, Maid of Norway, died in 1290, Robert the Bruce put in his claim for the throne against that of John Baliol. A grandson of this Robert was the famous Robert the Bruce who became Robert I of Scotland in 1306. Edward Bruce, the brother of Robert I, was crowned king of Ireland in 1316 but was killed in 1318 trying to make good his title. The younger son of Robert I, David II (1329–71), succeeded his father, and in turn was succeeded by his nephew Robert II, son of Robert I's daughter Marjory. This Robert was the first king of Scotland of the house of Stuart.

BRUCE, EDWARD, d. 1318, Scottish king of Ireland, brother of Robert I of Scotland. He helped his brother subdue Scotland and to defeat the English at Bannockburn. In 1315 when he was declared heir to Robert's throne in Scotland, he invaded Ulster with his brother's approval and was crowned king of Ireland (1316). He failed in his efforts to oust the Anglo-Irish rulers and was killed in battle.

BRUGES, city of Flanders, first noted in the seventh century, served as residence of the counts of Flanders from the close of the eleventh century. It developed into one of the first centers of the woolen industry and from the thirteenth century was the site of a major colony of the Hanseatic League. As a possession of the duke of Burgundy from 1382 it attained the height of its cultural splendor and was called the Venice of the north because of its canals and industrial activity. With the silting up of the Zwyn in the late fourteenth century, Bruges gradually lost its position as the leading wool-trading center of the Low Countries to Antwerp. Because of its wealth and the extensive political privileges it possessed, it played a decisive role in the chronic struggle between England, France, and Flanders. In 1302 it helped gain a great victory over Philip IV and the French at Courtrai. [See BATTLE OF THE SPURS.]

BRUIS (Bruys), PETER OF. See PETER DE BRUYES.

BRUNANBURH, BATTLE OF, battle won in 937 by Athelstan, king of Wessex, over Irish, Scots, and Strathclyde Britons at a site between Chester and Dumfries on the west coast of England. A famous poem in the *Anglo-Saxon Chronicle* celebrates this victory.

BRUNELLESCHI, FILIPPO, d. 1446, architect and sculptor of Florence who designed the dome of the cathedral in that city as well as the Pazzi Chapel which exhibits the first definite emergence of the Renaissance spirit in architecture. He was also a bronze founder and designed the doors for the baptistery in Florence. He made a study of the mathematical laws governing perspective although he must be considered an

engineer rather than a theorist. He is honored as the guiding influence in the revival of classical, as opposed to Gothic, art forms in the early fifteenth century.

BRUNFORTE, UGALINO, d. c. 1348, Franciscan friar of the monastery of Santa Maria in Monte Giorgio (south of Ancona), a chronicler and probable author of the *Little Flowers of St. Francis*.

BRUNHILD (Brünhild, Brunhilde, Brynhild), a heroic woman from Old Norse literature, in the *Nibelungenlied* the wife of King Gunther of Burgundy. In this epic she has Hagen slay Siegfried when she learns that it was Siegfried who bested her in a trial of strength and not Gunther whom she had married because of his supposed superior prowess. In the *Volsungasaga,* she is the chief of the Valkyries. Her identification with Brunhild, the Merovingian queen, is a matter of scholarly dispute.

BRUNHILD (Brynhild, Brunhilde, Brennehilde, Brunichilde), d. 613, daughter of King Athanagild of Spain, wife of Sigebert I, king of Austrasia, and sister of Galswintha, wife of Sigebert's brother Chilperic I, king of Neustria. Under the influence of his mistress Fredegunde, Chilperic had Galswintha and his brother Sigebert slain. Brunhild was at least so convinced, and for twenty years the ambitions and enmity of these two women were largely responsible for the bloody civil war that convulsed Merovingian France during the last quarter of the sixth century. Brunhild ruled Austrasia as regent for her son, grandsons, and finally her greatgrandson, until defeated and executed by Austrasian nobles in league with Chlotar II of Neustria.

BRUNI, LEONARDO, d. 1444, also called Aretino because of his birth in Arezzo, humanist and historian. He served as secretary to the papal chancery from 1405 until 1427, then as chancellor of Florence until his death. He is best known for his scholarly history of Florence (in Latin), next for his translations of many Greek works (Demosthenes, Plutarch, Aristotle), and for his biographies in Italian of Dante, Petrarch, and Boccaccio.

BRUNIA (burnie), mail-shirt of rings used by the Franks and other Germans.

BRUNO (Brun) OF COLOGNE, ST., d. 965, youngest son of Henry I of Germany and brother of Otto I (the Great) whom he served as chancellor from 940 in the direction of both imperial and ecclesiastical policies. About 940 he became abbot of Lorsch and Corvey, in 953 the archbishop of Cologne. Throughout his long career he proved himself a warm friend of learning and a champion of monastic reform.

BRUNO OF MAGDEBURG, d. after 1084, German chronicler, author of a partisan yet valuable account of the early part of the reign of Henry IV (1056–1106).

BRUNO (Brun, Bruns) OF QUERFURT, ST., d. 1009, was related to the Saxon ruling house and for a time was a member of the household of Otto III whom he accompanied to Italy in 997. In Rome he decided to take up the life of a missionary, labored among the pagan Petchenegs north of the Black Sea, then among the Prussians until massacred with his 18 companions. Bruno left a life of St. Adalbert, bishop of Prague (d. 997).

BRUNO THE CARTHUSIAN, ST., d. 1101, a student at Cologne, Reims, and Tours, teacher and head of the cathedral school of Reims. Following a brief period spent under the direction of St. Robert of Molesme, he and six companions retired to a mountainous district near Grenoble and there, at Chartreuse in the Alps, founded in 1084 the Carthusian order. He refused the archbishopric of Reggio and spent his last years in a desolate part of Calabria where he founded two other monasteries.

BRUNSWICK (Braunschweig), town chartered by Henry the Lion, duke of Saxony (1142–80), became an important member of the Hanseatic League in the fourteenth century. The cathedral, begun in 1173 by Henry the Lion, contains his tomb. Many churches and guild houses remain from the Middle Ages.

BRUNSWICK-LÜNEBURG, DUCHY OF, principality established by Frederick II of Germany in 1235 for Otto the Child from allodial lands remaining to Henry the Lion (Otto's grandfather) in 1180 when Frederick I Barbarossa had deprived him of Saxony and Bavaria.

BRUOCH (Bruch, Bruche), medieval term for the short, trunklike undergarment that covered the lower part of the body. Men wore this garment from the twelfth century.

BRUSSELS, city of Brabant, first noted in 966, took root at the fortress erected by the counts of Löwen (Louvain) (later dukes of Brabant) on an island in the Senne river. The history of its flourishing woolen industry dates from the twelfth century with completion of a major road through it which linked Cologne and Bruges. By the close of the fourteenth century it had become the principal city of Brabant; from the eleventh century it was the home of the dukes of Brabant.

BRUSSELS LACE, lace with floral motifs first made in Brussels in the fifteenth century.

BRUT (Brute, Brutus), a legendary hero whom Geoffrey of Monmouth declared was the grandson of Aeneas and the eponymous founder of Britain. His story also appears in Nennius. His name provided the title for long poems by Wace and Layamon.

BRUT, chronicle of English history by Layamon which extended from the legendary Brutus to Cadwalader (late seventh century). For his account Layamon drew principally upon the *Historia Regum Britanniae* of Geoffrey of Monmouth. In this history there appear for the first time in English the names of Arthur, Lear, and Cymbeline.

BRYENNIOS, JOSEPH, d. c. 1438, monk of the Studion monastery in Constantinople, a learned theologian and eloquent preacher, and a stout foe of union with Rome.

BRYENNIUS, NICEPHORUS, d. 1137, Byzantine general, statesman, and historian, the husband of Anna, daughter of Alexius I Comnenus. Although a successful general and in high favor at the court, he refused to take part in a conspiracy headed by Anna and her mother to depose John (II), the son of Alexius, and rule in his stead. His history chronicles the events of the years 1070-9, particularly the fortunes of the Comnenian family.

BUCCELLARII, private retainers maintained in the period of the late Roman empire by occasional generals, even by wealthy civilians. They were most common in the Eastern Roman or Byzantine empire.

BUCH, JEAN III DE GRAILLY, CAPTAL DE, d. 1376, leading vassal and officer of Gascony under Edward III and the Black Prince during the Hundred Years' War. His valor and chivalry drew frequent praise from the pen of Froissart. He was the principal agent of the Black Prince's victory at Poitiers in 1356. He took part in the battle of Nájera in Castile in 1367 when the Black Prince defeated Du Guesclin.

BUCHAREST, city of Rumania of obscure origins. It came into prominence in the fourteenth century as a residence of the princes of Wallachia.

BUCKINGHAM, an English earldom which may have appeared as early as the close of the eleventh century as the possession of Walter Giffard (d. 1102). It was later held by Richard de Clare, earl of Pembroke ("Strongbow"), but lapsed when he died in 1176. In 1377 the title of earl was revived and given to Thomas of Woodstock (duke of Gloucester) by his brother John of Gaunt, regent for the young Richard II. In 1438 the Stafford family came into possession of the earldom and held it until 1521.

BUCKINGHAM, HENRY STAFFORD, DUKE OF, d. 1483, one of the wealthiest English lords, a leading Yorkist and supporter of Edward IV. Upon Edward's death he declared for Richard III, whom he served as great chamberlain, and arranged the seizure of the boy Edward V. A few months later, for reasons not entirely clear, he threw in his lot with Henry (VII) Tudor. When the army he was bringing from Wales melted away, he was taken and beheaded.

BUDAI NAGY, ANTON, d. 1438, leader of Rumanian and Hungarian peasants who rose in revolt over the excessive exactions of their lord, the bishop of Lépes. Though at first victorious, he was eventually captured and executed.

BUDAPEST, capital city of Hungary, located on the Danube, whose modern origins reach back to the close of the ninth century when Magyar invaders planted a settlement on the ruins of what had been a major link (Aquincum) in the Roman *limes* protecting the Danubian frontier. The increasing flow of river traffic assured the settlement steady growth as an economic and cultural center until its destruction by the Mongols in 1241. In 1247 Bela IV erected a royal residence on Castle hill, and by the fourteenth Budapest had established itself as capital of the country.

BUEIL, JEAN DE, d. 1478, French captain, fought for Joan of Arc against the English and served as adviser to Charles VII. He left a treatise dealing with the military training of the aristocracy.

BUHTURI (Buchturi), ABU 'UBADA AL-WALID IBN 'UBAYD AL-, d. 897, Arab court poet and anthologist at Baghdad who eulogized the exploits of his patron, Caliph Al-Mutawakkil, and of other personages, even those of the city of Aleppo near where he had grown up. Apart from panegyrics he composed some love poetry, most of this directed to 'Alwa, a young woman of Aleppo.

BUKHARA (Bokhara), ancient city located east of the Oxus in the province of Transoxiana, already a thriving center when Moslems overran the country in the eighth century. After 999 when it fell to the Karakhanid Turks, it suffered from competition with nearby Samarkand. In 1220 Genghis Khan destroyed the city and slew or enslaved its population, but it was rebuilt and enjoyed considerable prominence in the fourteenth century as one of the leading cities of the empire of Timur the Lame.

BUKHARI, AL- (Muhammad Ibn Isma'il 'Abdallah Al-Ju'fi), d. 870, Arab scholar, considered by most Sunnites as the greatest of the Traditionists by virtue of the large number of acts and sayings of Mohammed that he collected and the extreme care he employed in judging their authenticity. It is said that he considered 600,000 traditions, of which he included 2,762, not counting repetitions, in his *Sahih*. Most Sunnites consider his work as second in importance only to the Koran itself as a source of doctrine and law.

BUKHTISHU, a Nestorian Christian family that produced a number of eminent physicians, several of whom were in attendance to Abbasid caliphs from the late eighth century to the late eleventh.

BULGAR. *See* BULGARIA.

BULGARIA, country in the west-central Balkans south of the Danube comprising largely the ancient Roman provinces of Moesia and Thrace. The first Bulgars, a Turko-Mongol people from Turkestan, appeared about the middle of the sixth century when they were still subject to the Avars. They overwhelmed the Slavic tribes that had preceded them. In 681 the Byzantine emperor Constantine IV recognized a Bulgar state in Moesia, although the first great Bulgarian ruler was Krum (802?–14) who defeated and slew Nicephorus I and even laid siege to Constantinople. Boris I (852–89) accepted Orthodox Christianity and had his people do the same.

Missionaries from both the Latin and Greek churches came to proselytize, but c. 870 Boris decided in favor of the Greek church. His son Simeon (893–927) assumed the title of czar, extended his empire to the Adriatic, and made Preslav, his capital, a rival of Constantinople in cultural brilliance. In the meantime the Bulgars had merged with the Slavs and had adopted their speech. Decline set in after Simeon's death. The eastern part of the country fell to the Byzantine emperor John Tzimisces in 971, the western part to Basil II in 1014. In the late twelfth century Bulgaria recovered its independence and enjoyed a new period of prominence under Ivan Asen II (1218–41) who extended his authority over Albania, Epirus, Macedonia, and Thrace. Mongol raids devastated northern Bulgaria shortly after his death. Portions of the empire were later lost to the Serbs, and in 1371 Bulgaria recognized Turkish suzerainty. In 1393 it was incorporated into the Ottoman empire.

BULGARIA (on the Volga), a loosely organized state composed of several backward peoples including the Bulgars, located in the middle Volga and Kama river basins. It maintained its existence from the ninth century until the close of the fifteenth when it was absorbed into rising Russia. Its capital city of Bulgar on the upper Volga fell to the Mongols in 1237 and was destroyed by Timur the Lame (d. 1405).

BULGARUS, d. 1166, Italian jurist, the most distinguished of the "four doctors" of the law school of the University of Bologna. He was regarded as the Chrysostom of the gloss writers, whence the name "Golden Mouth" frequently given him. He was a pupil of Irnerius and one of the most trusted advisers of the emperor Frederick I Barbarossa. He took the leading role among the lawyers at the diet of Roncaglia in 1158. His most scholarly work is his commentary *De Regulis Iuris,* a model specimen of the excellence of the method introduced by Irnerius.

BULLA, a lead seal, probably of Byzantine origin,

that was used as early as the sixth century to authenticate documents. From the thirteenth century documents bound with a lead seal were frequently referred to simply as bulls. For more important documents, such as royal decrees, silver or gold might replace the lead, whence the term golden bull.

BULLA AUREA (Golden Bull), name given to occasional bulls, such as that issued by Charles IV of Germany in 1356, from the fact that the seal attached to the document was placed in a golden case or that the seal itself was of gold.

BULLA CRUCIATA, name given to a papal bull or letter that granted special concessions or privileges to men fighting the Moslems. The first of these bulls was that issued by Pope Alexander II in 1063. Because the Crusades virtually ceased after the thirteenth century except in Spain, the term came to apply exclusively to papal bulls sent to that country.

BUONDELMONTI, CRISTOFORO, a Florentine of the late fourteenth century who visited Rhodes and the islands of the Aegean partly in search of ancient Greek manuscripts. He is the author of an informative description of the culture, history, and geography of the area.

BURCHARD (Burckard), JOHN, d. 1506, papal master of ceremonies from 1483, who left a diary that is the prime source for the history of the papacy in the late fifteenth and early sixteenth centuries. His principal work, entitled *Ordo Servandus,* consisted of a collection of rubrics with detailed instructions for the celebration of mass.

BURCHARD OF WORMS, d. 1025, bishop of Worms, reformer, builder, and canonist. He erected a number of monasteries and churches, including the cathedral of Worms, and left a scholarly collection of canons entitled *Decretum,* which Gratian and Ivo of Chartres used in the preparation of their own works.

BURCHIELLO, DOMENICO, d. 1449, Italian poet who satirized the times in ambiguous, often deliberately senseless verse. His humorous, nonsensical verse proved popular and had many imitators.

BURDA, the cloak that Mohammed is said to have given to the poet Ka'b ibn Suhair for composing a poem in his honor. It was also the title of a poem the Egyptian author al-Busiri (d. c. 1295) composed in honor of Mohammed who, he claimed, had cured him of his crippled condition in a dream with the help of this mantle.

BUREAU, JEAN (d. 1463) and GASPARD (d. 1469), French military engineers and mastergunners whose artillery destroyed English fortresses in short order during the closing years of the Hundred Years' War.

BURGAGE, a tenure in England by which townsmen or burgesses held lands or tenements of the king or another feudal lord, usually for a money rent.

BURGH (Bourke, Burke), historic Irish family that was long associated with Connaught. Its founder was William Burgh (d. 1206) who received grants of land from Prince John in 1185 and most of Connaught during Richard I's reign (1189-99). His grandson Walter (d. 1271) received the grant of Ulster and was known as the earl of Ulster. Walter's son Richard (d. 1326) was the greatest Irish noble of his day. The heiress of the Burgh estates and titles married Lionel, son of Edward III, and their descendant, the duke of York became King Edward IV in 1461.

BURGHER, the freeman of a borough, in general any commoner living in a town in the Middle Ages.

BURGH, HUBERT DE, d. 1243, earl of Kent, wealthy landowner, and chief justiciar under both John and Henry III whom he served loyally during their difficulties with their barons. He became particularly prominent during the minority of Henry III when he was probably the most powerful man in England next to the king. Shortly after Henry III announced his majority (1227), the enemies of Burgh brought charges against him that resulted in the deprivation of his offices and custodies, although he was able to retain his private lands and his earldom until his death. The office of justiciar lapsed with his death.

BURGOMASTER, head magistrate or chairman of a town government.

BURGOS, city in north-central Spain, founded in 884 as a fortified outpost in eastern Asturias against the Moors. Its early importance dates from c. 1000 when it served as the most ancient capital of Castile and a base for the Christian advance against the Moors. In 1087 the royal residence was moved to Toledo, and Burgos lost some of its cultural and economic importance. Burgos was the home and burial place of Rodrigo Diaz de Vivar, Spain's national hero. The cathedral of Burgos which was begun in 1220 reveals French Gothic influences.

BURGUNDIAN LAW, codes of law drawn up by Gundobad, king of the Burgundians (474–516). One code, the *Lex Romana Burgundiorum,* applied to the Romans under his rule, the *Lex Gundobada* to his own people.

BURGUNDIANS, an east German people, originally from Scandinavia, located in the valley of the Main early in the fourth century, whence it moved southward into the valley of the Rhône. There in 436 the Burgundians suffered a disastrous defeat at the hands of the Romans under Aetius who later permitted them to settle in the area of Savoy as *foederati.* Under their most powerful king, Gundobad (474–516), they occupied the entire Rhône valley including Provence. During the reign of Sigismund, the son of Gundobad, the Burgundians abandoned Arianism and accepted Christianity. In 534 their kingdom fell to the Franks.

BURGUNDY, COUNT OF. *See* FRANCHE-COMTÉ.

BURGUNDY, DUCHY OF, principality that in 936 comprised the territory between the upper Loire and Seine and included the cities of Autun, Troyes, and Langres. Capetian dukes ruled it until 1361 when it escheated to the crown, only to be given by John II two years later to his fourth son Philip (the Bold) as an appanage. A marriage which Charles V arranged for Philip with Margaret of Flanders added Nevers, Franche-Comté, Rethel, Artois, and Flanders to Burgundy. Upon the assassination of John the Fearless (1419), his son, Philip the Good, made an alliance with the English which endured until 1435 when Charles VII, by the Treaty of Arras, granted the duke of Burgundy an autonomous position within the kingdom. The ambition of Philip's son Charles (the Bold) to close the gap between the northern and southern parts of the Burgundian domains and establish a separate kingdom foundered before the statecraft of Louis XI. He was slain in 1477 by the Swiss at Nancy. In 1482 Louis was able to secure imperial confirmation of his claims to the duchy.

BURGUNDY, FREE COUNTY OF. *See* FRANCHE-COMTÉ.

BURGUNDY, KINGDOM OF, tribal state established early in the fifth century in the valley of the lower Rhône and conquered early in the sixth by the sons of Clovis. [*See* BURGUNDIANS.] As reestablished by Boso, ruler of Viennois (879–88), the kingdom of Burgundy included initially all the territory from Autun to the Mediterranean, although losses during his reign reduced it to Provence, whence the name kingdom of Provence or Lower (Cisjurane) Burgundy. In 934 Rudolf II, ruler of Trans- or Upper Burgundy, acquired possession of Provence and thus reestablished the whole of the kingdom of Burgundy. For its subsequent history, [*See* ARLES, KINGDOM OF.]

BURIDAN, JEAN. *See* JOHN BURIDAN.

BURNELL, ROBERT, d. 1292, chancellor of England, the most accomplished, successful, and trusted minister of Edward I. His control of the chancery and royal household largely accounts for the success of the first twenty years of Edward's reign. He helped secure Edward's succession after the death of Henry III (1272) and as Edward's chancellor reversed all the changes made by the baronial reformers. Edward made him bishop of Bath and Wells (1275) but failed to have him elected archbishop of Canterbury.

BURSE (bursa), a flat case, usually of silk, that came into use in the eleventh century. It held the corporal used at Mass.

BURY-SAINT-EDMUNDS, ABBEY OF, Benedictine abbey in the diocese of Norwich founded by King Canute near the shrine that marked the burial place of King Edmund (d. 869). The abbey was England's most popular shrine until the murder of Thomas Becket gave Canterbury its prominence. The monastery, one of the wealthiest and most influential in the Middle Ages, often received visits from kings. It was in the abbey church that the English barons in 1214 swore to compel King John to accept their demands which culminated in the Great Charter.

BUSCH, JAN, d. c. 1480, one of the leading members of the Brethren of the Common Life. He was prominent in the movement for monastic reform and for a time worked in cooperation with Nicholas of Cusa. He left a history of the Brethren's house at Windesheim.

BUSINE, a medieval trumpet of Saracen origin.

BUSNOIS (Busnoys), ANTOINE, d. 1492, well-known musician and composer of songs, motets, masses, and *chansons*. He lived as court chaplain at the Burgundian capital of Dijon, later in Bruges.

BUTLER, court official under the Merovingian and Carolingian kings who supervised the management of the royal cellar.

BUTTRESS. *See* FLYING BUTTRESS.

BUYL (Boyl), BERNAL, Benedictine monk of Spain whom King Ferdinand appointed the first vicar apostolic for the New World. Because of difficulties with Columbus he spent but a short time in America.

BYRHNOTH (Bryhtnoth), d. 991, ealdorman of the East Saxons, the leader of the English forces in the battle of Maldon. He was killed in the battle and buried at Ely.

BYRNIE, a defensive shirt of mail; hauberk.

BYZANTINE ART, one of the most distinctive and influential in Western history, its period extending roughly from the Christianizing of the Roman empire in the fourth century until the fall of Constantinople to the Turks in 1453. Its ancient components were principally Hellenistic and Roman, but both slipped into the background with the triumph of Christianity. Even the art of Western Europe in the Middle ages was never more a creature of the church. The man responsible for stabilizing the character of the new art was the emperor Justinian (527–65) who was both a dedicated Christian and an ambitious builder. During his reign great churches rose throughout the empire, the most renowned that of Hagia Sophia in Constantinople, which introduced to millions of the faithful the domed basilica with its interior resplendent with mosaics and wall paintings. A major break disturbed the course of Byzantine art in 726 when Emperor Leo III proclaimed the puritanical gospel of iconoclasm with its ban on the use of images. Until 843, the end of iconoclasm, Byzantine art marked time while iconoclasts "purified" churches, including Hagia Sophia, of their statues and mosaics. Once Byzantine art was again free to breathe, it scaled new heights of brilliance in creativity and craftsmanship in the fields of mosaics, wall paintings, ivory-carving, metalworking, enameling, silk-weaving, and illuminated manuscripts. This golden age paralleled a resurgence of imperial power which peaked under Basil II (d. 1025), then continued on, despite the decline of the empire, until 1204 when Crusaders (Fourth Crusade) sacked Constantinople and destroyed and dispersed its priceless art treasury. (Venice took the bronze horses from the Hippodrome to grace the facade of St. Mark's.) Although the Byzantine empire when reestablished in 1261 never regained its former political importance, Byzantine art did enjoy one last period of brilliance, less pretentious because of its straitened financial condition, yet properly proud of its beautifully constructed and artistically decorated churches. Constantinople became a Moslem capital in 1453.

BYZANTINE EMPIRE, name generally given to the later Roman empire in the east from the reign of Constantine I (the Great) (306–37) to the fall of Constantinople (1453). (Some scholars begin Byzantine history with Justinian I (527–65), a few with Heraclius (610–41). Two developments of the late third and early fourth centuries disrupted the flow of Western history and served to divide the Roman period proper from that of the Byzantine. One was the shifting of the capital from Rome to the eastern Mediterranean, first to Nicomedia, then to Constantinople; the second, more epochal in its consequences, was the triumph of Christianity. What confirmed the emergence of a separate Roman (Byzantine) empire in the east was the loss of the western half to German tribes, a loss largely accomplished by 476, the traditional date for the fall of the Roman empire. Factors contributing to the continued existence of the empire in the east were its large population and vast economic resources, the virtual impregnability of the city of Constantinople, and the movement of invading Germanic tribes to the west.

Upon the death of Emperor Theodosius in 395 and the accession of his two sons, Honorius to rule the western half and Arcadius the eastern, the two parts of the empire went their separate ways. Apart from the threat posed by Slavs and

Bulgars who spilled across the Danube and by the Sassanid Persians along the eastern frontier (the Ostrogoths had gone on to Italy), what occasioned the eastern emperors most concern during the fifth century was the controversy over the nature of Christ. They were convinced that the very stability of their regimes depended upon theological harmony, so seriously did their subjects take their religion. Until he had effected a compromise on this Christological problem that would satisfy both Rome and the Monophysites, the emperor Justinian (527–65) felt that his projected reconquest of the western provinces would be impossible. Although his efforts to bring religious peace to the empire proved no more successful than those of his predecessors, he did recover Italy, north Africa, and part of Spain from their German conquerors. His most enduring accomplishment was the codification of Roman law. [See CORPUS JURIS CIVILIS.]

Justinian's successors inherited his troubles along the Danube which Slavs and Hunnish tribes continued to cross, and those with the Persians. During the reign of Heraclius (610–41) these foes almost overwhelmed the empire. Almost miraculously Heraclius was able to avert disaster, inflicting a crippling defeat upon the Persians, only to have his own army destroyed at Yarmuk (636) by the Arabs. These Moslems went on to overrun Syria, Egypt, and north Africa and establish naval supremacy in the eastern Mediterranean. They almost succeeded in storming Constantinople itself in 674–78 and again in 717–18. To add to the empire's woes and to aggravate its perennial difficulties with Rome, the decree of Emperor Leo III in 726 condemned the cult of icons. The destruction of the Byzantine army by the Bulgars in 811 and the death of Emperor Nicephorus I emphasized the empire's grave peril. But the seizure of imperial power by the horsegroom Basil (I) in 867 not only preserved the empire but ushered in a period of renewed power and prosperity which peaked during the reign of Basil II (976–1025). His empire included the greater part of Syria, southern Italy, the Balkans, upper Mesopotamia, Armenia, and the islands of Crete and Cyprus. Basil also made an alliance with the Russian prince Vladimir whose conversion brought that vast country within the Christian orbit.

Decline set in anew following the death of Basil as incompetent rulers neglected the defense of the empire while permitting the landed aristocracy to subdue the free peasantry of Asia Minor. Since this peasantry had supplied the empire with its principal source of loyal native troops, their disappearance led to a greater dependence upon mercenaries, and its was the treachery of mercenaries, their pay in arrears, that enabled the Seljuk Turks to destroy the Byzantine army at Manzikert in 1071. That same year Normans captured Bari, the last Byzantine foothold in Italy, while Magyars and Cumans swept down across the Danube into the Balkans.

The disaster at Manzikert set the stage for the First Crusade (1096–9) which came in answer to the appeal of Emperor Alexius Comnenus to Pope Urban II for help. [See CRUSADES.] This and subsequent crusades proved more a curse than a blessing to Byzantium. Crusaders and Byzantine empire seldom cooperated, while the Italian cities, Venice and Genoa in particular, exploited empire and Christendom alike to advance their own commercial aims. Mutual suspicion and animosity reached their culmination in 1204 when Crusaders (Fourth Crusade) and Venice captured Constantinople and divided it and the empire among themselves.

From 1204 until 1261 the Byzantine empire ceased to exist [See CONSTANTINOPLE, LATIN EMPIRE OF], except for several small states that claimed to be its successors. Of these, the state founded by Theodore Lascaris, with its capital at Nicaea, regained possession of Constantinople in 1261 under the leadership of Michael Palaeologus (VIII). (The dynasty of the Palaeologi ruled the empire until its fall to the Turks in 1453.) The restored but weakened empire included part of northwest Asia Minor, most of Thrace and Macedonia, scattered islands, and Epirus, but not for long. Dynastic quarrels weakened the regime from within while a rising Serbian state threatened to overrun the whole of the Balkans. [See STEPHEN DUSHAN.] The real threat to the empire came from the Turks. In 1354 they crossed into Europe, destroyed Serbian power at Kossovo in 1389, and in 1396 annihilated a huge crusading army under Sigismund at Nicopolis. All that prevented Turkish capture of Constantinople at this time was the appearance of a Mongol army under Timur the Lame which overwhelmed the Turks at Angora (1402). Constantinople's final hope faded in 1444 with the defeat of a crusading army at Varna on the Black Sea. In April 1453 Sultan Mohammed II threw a blockade around the city and on May 29–30 the Turkish army stormed the walls. The last Byzantine emperor, Constantine XI, died fighting with his troops.

BYZANTIUM, ancient Greek city on the Bosphorus where Constantine established his new capital which he renamed Constantinople; the Byzantine empire.

C-M-B, abbreviation for Caspar, Melchior, and Balthasar, according to tradition the three wise men or kings who visited the newborn Christ child. A formulary composed of these three letters was placed on doors, especially in Germany and Austria, on the feast of the Epiphany (January 6).

CAABA. *See* KAABA.

CABALA (Cabbala, Kabbalah, Qabbala), system of theosophy based on a mystical interpretation of the Scriptures, originally only the non-Pentateuchal part of the Old Testament and the oral tradition of Judaism. It originated with Jewish rabbis of the late twelfth century in Provence, whence it passed to Spain. All the writings of the Scriptures were held to contain hidden divine mysteries, especially the names of God, which were themselves agencies by which to work miracles. Scholars consider the Cabala a product of Jewish Gnosticism. The cabala was supposed to accept such Christian doctrines as the Trinity and the atonement, for which reason some Christian scholars were attracted to it in the fifteenth century.

CABALLARIUS, heavily armed soldier in the Byzantine army of the seventh century. He wore a steel cap and a long mail-shirt that reached from the neck to the thighs.

CABALLERÍA (cavalleria), cavalry; the fief of a knight; the knightly order of Cabellería.

CABALLERO, Spanish knight and member of the lower aristocracy; a member of a military religious order.

CABASILAS, NICOLAS, d. before 1391, Byzantine theologian and author of sermons and treatises on liturgical and ascetical subjects. His *Commentary on the Divine Liturgy* influenced Western theologians as late as the Council of Trent (1545–63). In the Hesychast controversy he supported the position of the monks of Mount Athos. In his principal work, "Concerning the Life of Christ," he explained how through baptism, confirmation, and the eucharist, spiritual union with Christ was to be achieved.

CABOCHE, SIMON. *See* CABOCHIENS.

CABOCHIENS, burghers of Paris, including members of the butchers' and skinners' guilds, who in April 1413 joined John the Fearless, duke of Burgundy, in seizing control of the city and promulgating radical reforms in the city's government. They derived their name from their leader, Simon Caboche, a butcher, who fled Paris in August when Louis, duke of Orléans, and the Armagnacs took over the city.

CABOT, JOHN (Giovanni Caboto), d. 1498/99, English explorer, a native of Genoa, later a naturalized citizen of Venice, who received a patent from Henry VII of England in 1496 to search for a northwest passage around America which would take him to the Indies. His discovery of Labrador in 1497 helped establish English claims in North America.

CACCIA, musical setting for the description of a hunt or similar incident.

CADALOUS, d. 1072, bishop of Parma, was

elected pope in 1061 principally by German bishops despite the earlier election of Alexander II. He assumed the name of Honorius II and insisted upon the validity of his office although he was driven from Rome in 1064.

CADAMOSTO (Ca da Mosto, Cademosto), ALVISE (Luigi da), d. 1488 or 1511, Venetian explorer and mariner in the service of the king of Portugal and Prince Henry the Navigator who made two voyages in 1455 and 1456 down the west coast of Africa. He left a valuable account of Portuguese explorations in west Africa.

CADE, JACK (John), d. 1450, leader of a revolt of yeomen and other disgruntled men of Kent who marched on London in May 1450 to protest the misgovernment and extravagance of Henry VI and his ministers. Their grievances were chiefly political, not social, though the Statute of Laborers was listed among their complaints. They entered London on July 3 but were driven out a few days later. On July 12 the sheriff of Kent captured and executed Cade.

CADIZ, Spanish port city west of Gibraltar on the Atlantic coast which the Phoenicians colonized c. 1100 B.C. It was held by Carthage, then Rome, destroyed by the Visigoths in the early fifth century, and captured by the Moors in 711. In 1262 Alfonso X of Castile ousted the Moors and claimed the city for his country. A new period of prosperity opened for the city with the discovery of America and its designation as headquarters for the Spanish treasure fleets. It soon became the wealthiest port of western Europe.

CADOUIN, ABBEY OF, French Cistercian monastery near Périgueux founded in 1115. It became a popular shrine because of the Holy Shroud which Crusaders returning from Jerusalem had deposited there.

CADWALDR (Cadwallader), semilegendary British king who led the Britons against the Anglo-Saxons in the seventh century. Later bards made him into a national hero. According to Welsh tradition, he was the last king of the Cymry to wear the crown of Britain.

CAEDWALLA (Cadwallader), king of Wessex, c. 685–9, who conquered Sussex and Kent and died while on a pilgrimage to Rome.

CAEDMON (Cadmon), d. c. 680, a cowherd, lay brother and monk in the abbey of Whitby, the first English poet known by name, and author of the oldest Christian hymn in the English language, the Creation Hymn. The best account of Caedmon appears in Bede's *History*.

CAELESTIS URBS JERUSALEM, hymn of unknown authorship but probably composed in the eighth century. It was sung at the dedication of churches.

CAEN (Cadomum), capital city of lower Normandy which grew to importance during the rule of William the Conqueror. He constructed a castle there as well as the abbey church of St. Etienne *(aux hommes)* while his wife built the abbey church of La Trinité *(aux dames)*. William is buried in the abbey of St. Etienne.

CAERNARVON (Carnarvon), CASTLE OF, one of the strong fortresses Edward I erected in Wales, this one in northwest Wales c. 1284 on a peninsula between the estuary of the Saint (Seiont) river and the Cadnant stream. Caernarvon was itself named the capital of north Wales by Edward.

CAERULARIUS, MICHAEL, d. 1058, patriarch of Constantinople, 1043–58, whose aggressiveness, coupled with the intransigence of Cardinal Humbert, the pope's legate, precipitated the Schism of 1054. Caerularius was bitterly anti-Latin in outlook and fiercely attacked the *filioque* in the Latin creed and the use of unleavened bread in the Eucharist. The forceful Caerularius was able to repulse what he considered imperial intrusion into ecclesiastical affairs made by the weak Constantine IX Monomachus, but Isaac I Comnenus, whose accession he had supported, ordered him into exile (1058).

CAESAREA, name of several cities in the history of the early Christian church: Caesarea in Mauretania, Caesarea in Cappadocia, Caesarea in Samaria, and Caesarea Philippi in northern Galilee.

CAESAREA, SCHOOL OF, a theological school in Palestine which originated with Origen in the early third century when he moved there following his exile from the theological center in Alexandria. It was noted for its library.

CAESARIUS OF ARLES, ST., d. 542, monk of Lérins, abbot of a monastery near Arles, then archbishop of Arles (502). With the aid of Alaric II and Theodoric the Great, he succeeded in establishing the claim of Arles to be the primatial see in Gaul. He is best known for the monastic rules he drew up for the monks and nuns of his diocese. These were considered the best in the West prior to the appearance of the Rule of St. Benedict. His 238 sermons supply valuable information concerning the church in sixth-century France. [See ORANGE, COUNCILS OF.]

CAESARIUS OF HEISTERBACH, d. c. 1240, Cistercian monk, prior of the monastery at Heisterbach, and author of sermons, theological and exegetical works, and some historical writing including a life of St. Elizabeth. His most popular work, *Dialogue on Miracles,* was a collection of spiritual anecdotes intended for the edification of Cistercian novices.

CAESARIUS OF PRÜM, Benedictine monk of the early thirteenth century who served as abbot of Prüm, later resigned his office, and joined the Cistercian community at Heisterbach. He left a commentary dealing with the civilization of that region in the ninth century.

CAESAROPAPISM, position assumed by occasional Byzantine emperors which had them claiming the right to exercise supreme authority in the disposition of both civil and religious affairs. The origin of this claim may be traced to the ancient tradition that the Roman emperor was divine and his will was law, and to the failure of the bishops of Rome to advance claims of their prerogative to decide about spiritual matters until the fifth century after Christian emperors had already established precedent for doing so.

CAËTANI. *See* GAETANI.

CAGLIARI, town in Sardinia of Carthaginian origin which the Vandals captured in 454 and Byzantium in 533. After a period of Saracen rule, the city gained its independence for a short time but in 1052 passed under control of Pisa and under that of Aragon in 1326.

CAGNY (Caigny), PARCEVAL DE, d. after 1438, French chronicler, author of a history of the duchy of Alençon and of the part of the Hundred Years' War fought during the reign of Charles VII (1422–61). This last contains an account of the trial and execution of Joan of Arc.

CAGOTS (Agotak), a people living in the Pyrenees, especially in Navarre and the district of Bigoree, social outcasts for the most part, who were feared as much as they were despised. They were required to carry special marking on their clothes—a duck's foot of red cloth—to enable others to avoid them for fear of contagion.

CAHIER, a copy book in which members of the estates general set down grievances or requests of the voters and then presented it to the king. The practice of recording such grievances was first noted in 1468.

CAHORS, city in south-central France east of Bordeaux, a bishopric in the third century, occupied by the Visigoths in the fifth century and by the Saracens in the ninth. It came into the possession of the counts of Toulouse who held it until the close of the Albigensian crusade when it passed under the control of the crown. Its fame as a banking center dated from the thirteenth century. Its money lenders, called Cahorsins, rivaled the Jews and the Lombards. The University of Cahors received its charter in 1332. The city's Cathedral of St. Etienne, constructed in the twelfth–thirteenth centuries, has Byzantine cupolas.

CAHORSINS, name given to bankers and usurers in the Middle Ages. [*See* CAHORS.]

CAIAPHAS, Jewish high priest who presided at the arraignment and preliminary examination of Christ.

CAINITES, a Gnostic sect which held the God of the Old Testament responsible for the evil in the world and exalted all who had opposed him, including Cain, Esau, and Korah. They are believed to have had an apocryphal *Gospel of Judas Iscariot.*

CAIRO, city at the base of the Delta in Egypt which grew up near the military camp established there in 642 by Amr, Arab conqueror of Egypt. It was first known as Al Fustat. The present name originated with a settlement made nearby by the Fatimids in the tenth century which they called Al Kahira (the victorious). Cairo served as the capital city of the ruling dynasty of Egypt from the tenth century until 1517 when it fell to the Ottoman Turks.

CAIUS, ST., Pope. *See* GAIUS, ST. Pope.

CALAIS, city in northern France on the Channel, originally a fishing village but fortified in 1224 by the count of Boulogne. Shortly after the English victory at Crécy in 1346, Edward III occupied the city, after which it remained in English hands until 1558. By the opening of the fourteenth century Calais had become the leading center of wool trade in the Western world.

CALATAYUD, city of northeast Spain in Aragon, founded by the Moors in the eighth century and taken from them in 1120 by Alfonso I of Aragon. The collegiate Church of Santo Sepulcro, once the main church of the Knights Templars in Spain, still stands in the city, as does the Moorish castle.

CALATRAVA, ORDER OF, Spanish military-religious order founded in 1158 by King Sancho III of Castile to provide for the defense of Calatrava against the Moors. In 1195 the Moors captured the city but it was recaptured and the order reestablished there following the decisive Spanish victory at Las Navas de Tolosa in 1212. The order was affiliated with the neighboring Cistercian abbey of Morimond and was subject to an annual inquisitorial visit by its abbot. In 1489 Ferdinand and Isabella placed the order under control of the crown and in 1499 the title of grand master passed to the king.

CALCED (Calceati), members of religious orders such as Augustinians and Carmelites who wore shoes, as opposed to the discalced communities which wore sandals or went barefoot.

CALEDONIA, Celtic-Roman name for Scotland.

CALEFACTORY, Latin for "warming place," the room found most commonly in Cistercian monasteries where a fire or fires were maintained for the use or comfort of the monks.

CALENDAR, a catalog, index, martyrology; also a calendar in the modern use of the term.

CALEPINO, AMBROGIO (Ambrosio), d. 1511, Augustinian friar, Italian lexicographer, and humanist. His Latin dictionary greatly influenced the compilation of subsequent dictionaries.

CALIGAE, liturgical stockings worn by medieval bishops.

CALIPH, title derived from the Arabic meaning successor, lieutenant, or deputy, and held by the men who succeeded to Mohammed's position after his death. The first caliph was Abu Bakr (632–4), the father-in-law of the Prophet.

CALIPHATE, the headship of Islam dating from 632 when Mohammed died and Abu Bakr was chosen to be his successor, whence the title caliph. The so-called Orthodox caliphs were the first four: Abu Bakr, Omar, Othman, and Ali. Next followed a series of Omayyad caliphs who made Damascus their capital. In 750 this Omayyad caliphate was destroyed by the Abbasids who centered their caliphate at Baghdad. One of the Omayyads managed to escape to Spain where he founded the emirate of Córdoba which later became the Caliphate of Córdoba. This lasted until 1031. A third caliphate, established in Egypt by the Fatimids, endured from 909 to 1171. In 1258 when the Mongols captured Baghdad, the Abbasids fled to Egypt but since they were powerless there, the caliphate had, to all intents and purposes, come to an end. [For individual caliphs, *see,* e.g., HARUN AL-RASHID.]

CALIXTINES, a Christian sect, also known as Utraquists, which demanded the use of the chalice (Latin *calix*) for the laity. They constituted the more moderate and larger division of the Hussites. They drew their major support from the upper and middle classes and from the masters at the University of Prague. They received ecclesiastical recognition at the Prague Compacts of 1433. [*See* TABORITES.]

CALIXTUS. *See* CALLISTUS.

CALLINICUS, Syrian architect who is credited with the invention of Greek fire (c. 673).

CALLIOPIUS, grammarian of the Carolingian period who edited classical works including those of Terence.

CALLISTUS (Calixtus), I, ST., Pope, c. 217–22, a Roman, once a slave, who succeeded Pope Zephyrinus. As pope he favored a liberal policy toward lapsed Christians who had foresworn their faith under threat of execution, and toward those who had been guilty of adultery or fornication. He authorized the ordination of men who had been married more than once, and recognized marriages between free women and slaves. He was martyred during a local riot in Trastevere.

CALLISTUS (Calixtus) II, Pope, 1119–24, a descendant of the counts of Burgundy, archbishop of Vienne (1088), papal legate to France, and a principal in the negotiations that ultimately led to the Concordat of Worms (1122) and to the ending of the investiture controversy. At first he had taken a firm position on the issue of lay investiture and had excommunicated Henry V at the Council of Reims (1119). In 1123 he convoked the First Lateran Council which approved the Concordat and also voted decrees condemning simony and clerical concubinage.

CALLISTUS (Calixtus) III, Pope, 1455–8, a Spaniard, jurist of some renown, bishop of Valencia, and cardinal. His efforts to organize a crusade following the fall of Constantinople resulted in the Turks lifting the siege of Belgrade under pressure from the Hungarians and Bohemians and the preaching of St. John Capistran, and in the victory of a papal-Aragonese fleet over a Turkish fleet in 1457. Nepotism marred his pontificate, however, and among relatives he advanced was his nephrew Rodrigo de Borgia who later became Pope Alexander VI. His pontificate saw the revision of the trial of Joan of Arc by the annulment of the sentence and the declaration of her innocence.

CALMAR, UNION OF. *See* KALMAR, UNION OF.

CALZADA, SANTO DOMINGO DE LA, d. 1109, architect and engineer who constructed churches and hospices as well as roads to facilitate the travel of pilgrims to the shrine of St. James at Compostella in the western Pyrenees.

CAMALDOLESE, ORDER OF, or the Congregation of Monk Hermits of Camaldoli, a monastic community founded c. 1012 by Romuald at Camp Maldoli (Camaldoli), a valley in the Abruzzi. It observed the Rule of St. Benedict but modified this in the interest of greater isolation so as to permit more opportunity for contemplative prayer. Its ideal was the barest minimum of communal ties. This modification introduced an element of anchoritism into the order that was not traditional to Benedictine monasticism. Their regimen resembled that of the later Carthusians. Because Romuald left no written rule, practice diverged in different congregations.

CAMBIO, ARNOLFO DI. *See* ARNOLFO DI CAMBIO.

CAMBRAI (Cambray), city of Hainaut (Lower Lorraine) whose origins go back to Roman times when it was known as Camaracum. It became a diocese in the sixth century. Because of its strategic location, many states including Hainaut, Flanders, France, the Holy Roman Empire, and England fought over its possession. It was well known for its fine textiles and has given its name to cambric which was first manufactured there.

CAMBRIDGE, an ancient market town about 50 miles north of London, once a Roman fort. William the Conqueror built a castle there, but it began to attract attention only with the arrival of monks from neaby Ely who brought scholastic and ecclesiastical importance in the twelfth century and who represented the nucleus of the university foundations. Many churches survive from medieval times, including St. Benedict's (tenth century), St. Edward's (thirteenth), and Holy Sepulchre, one of four Norman round churches in England.

CAMBRIDGE, EARLS OF. Under the Norman and early Plantagenet kings of England the earldom of Cambridge was united with that of Huntingdon. As a separate dignity it dates from 1340 when Edward III bestowed the title on his brother-in-law, William, count of Jüliers (Jülich). In 1362, after William died, Edward created his son, Edward of Langley, earl of Cambridge. In 1415 the earl of Cambridge was executed for conspiring against Henry V. In 1461, the duke of York, who held the title of earl of Cambridge, became Edward IV.

CAMBRIDGE SONGS, the oldest collection of medieval Latin poems, consisting of some 50 pieces, mostly lyric, the majority from the tenth and eleventh centuries and probably of German origin. Some of the pieces were religious although the greater number were secular in theme and drawn from a variety of sources.

CAMBRIDGE, UNIVERSITY OF, university located some 50 miles northeast of London that may have originated in 1209 with a flight of scholars from Oxford. Mention of a chancellor appears in 1226, while in 1231 Henry III took note of the community and placed it under the jurisdiction of a master. Seven colleges, the first of which was Peterhouse (1284), made their appearance during the course of the next 70 years. In 1441 Henry VI founded the College of St. Mary and St. Nicholas (King's College); his consort, Margaret (of Anjou), established Queen's (1448).

CAM (Cão), DIOGO, fl. 1480–6, Portuguese navigator and explorer, the first European to discover the mouth of the Congo river. He made two voyages down the west coast of Africa in the service of John II of Portugal.

CAMELOT, in Arthurian legend, the place where King Arthur held court.

CAMENIATES, JOHN, Byzantine priest of the tenth century who left an eyewitness account of the sack of Thessalonica by the Arabs in 904.

CAMERA, APOSTOLIC (Romana), papal treasury that appeared in the late eleventh century when its principal official, the chamberlain *(camerarius, camerlengo),* assumed the position of chief financial official in the papal Curia. During the course of the thirteenth and fourteenth centuries he acquired juridical functions not directly related to fiscal matters.

CAMERA ROMANA. *See* CAMERA, APOSTOLIC.

CAMERLENGO, popular name for the papal chamberlain *(camerarius),* the officer in charge of the Apostolic Camera. The same title was held by the highest ranking financial official in the Italian city-state.

CAMERON, JOHN, d. 1446, bishop of Glasgow,

chancellor of Scotland, and Scottish representative at the Council of Basel. He was under sentence of excommunication for some time because of the support he gave to King James in his attack on the ecclesiastical courts in Scotland.

CAMINO, DA, an Italian feudal family, prominent during the thirteenth and early fourteenth centuries when, as counts, they possessed many fiefs—imperial, episcopal, and others—in the mark of Treviso, especially in the districts of Belluno, Cadore, and Ceneda.

CAMPANIA, region of southern Italy below Rome, occupied by the Ostrogoths in the late fifth century, recovered by Byzantium in the sixth, then claimed by the Lombards. In the seventh century, it became part of the duchy of Benevento. The Normans conquered it in the eleventh century, while in the twelfth it became part of the kingdom of Sicily. Its later history is associated with that of the kingdom of Naples.

CAMPANILE, bell tower which in Italy ordinarily stood near the church that it served, in contrast to central Europe where it was usually attached to the church. The first campaniles that may have appeared in Italy as early as the seventh century were plain, round structures with a few round-arched openings near the top. Among the earliest examples of bell towers are those of S. Apollinare in Classe and S. Apollinare Nuovo at Ravenna.

CAMPANUS, JOHN (Giovanni Campano), Italian mathematician of the thirteenth century who prepared commentaries on the works of astronomers, including Ptolemy, and published the first Latin translation of Euclid. His translation of Euclid was actually based on an earlier one made by Adelard of Bath.

CAMPEADOR, EL, Arabic for the warrior, the title given to Rodrigo Diaz de Vivar, the hero of *El Cid*. [*See* CID, EL.]

CAMPIN, ROBERT, d. 1444, painter of the school of Tournai, probably teacher of both Rogier van der Weyden and Jacques Daret. Some scholars identify Campin as the Master of Flémalle. One of Campin's best known pieces is the triptych of the *Annunciation* with the donors and St. Joseph on the wings. It has been difficult to distinguish his work from that of his more famous pupil Rogier van der Weyden.

CAMPOSANTO, cemetery in Italy that was customarily enclosed with arcades and whose walls were covered with frescoes. The most distinguished such cemetery was that erected near the cathedral of Pisa (1277 to c. 1350) whose walls were graced with frescoes by famous artists including Spinello Aretino and Benozzo Gozzoli.

CAMPOSANTO TEUTONICO, cemetery south of St. Peter's in Rome that was used as a burial place for Germans, possibly as early as the reign of Charlemagne.

CAMPSORES (Cambist, Cambio), medieval money-changers or bankers in the cities of northern Italy. They were generally referred to as Lombards.

CANARY ISLANDS, islands in the Atlantic about 70 miles west of North Africa which were once known to the Romans, then visited by the Arabs in 999 and by Genoese and other seamen from the thirteenth century. Castile laid claim to the islands in the early fifteenth century although they were not finally subjected to Spanish rule until 1496. Columbus stopped at the islands on his way to America.

CANCIÓN, a lyrical poem modeled after the Italian *canzone,* particularly after those composed by Petrarch.

CANCIONERO (Cancioneiro), collection of songs or song books used by singing groups in the region of the Pyrenees after the tradition of the Provençal troubadour.

CANDIA, city of Crete, founded by the Saracens in the ninth century, captured by the Byzantine emperor Nicephorus II in 961, and a Venetian colony in the thirteenth century. The Venetians fortified the city and improved its port.

CANDLEMAS, feast celebrated on February 2 with candles and a procession to commemorate the presentation of the child Jesus in the Temple and the purification of his mother Mary. The feast may have originated as early as the fourth century.

CANNON, mounted piece of artillery whose origins may be traced to the early fourteenth century but which did not become an effective weapon until about the middle of the fifteenth century. It was used to good effect in the closing years of the Hundred Years' War, in the Hussite Wars, and in the capture of Constantinople.

CANON, the list of inspired books which the church judged to compose Holy Scripture; that part of the mass which included the consecration; the rules governing the life and discipline of the church. In law, the word "canon" came in time to refer exclusively to ecclesiastical enactments. In the Middle Ages the law of the church came to be known as "canon law" as distinct from "civil law." In the councils of the early church the term was ordinarily reserved for disciplinary decisions. [*See* CORPUS JURIS CANONICI.]

CANON, in music, a kind of counterpoint that holds to the strictest form of imitation. All the voices of a canon have the same melody, beginning at different times and at the same or different pitches. One of the earliest is the thirteenth-century rondel *Sumer Is Icumen In*.

CANON, member of a chapter or of a group of clerks associated with a cathedral or collegiate church and living under some common rule. In the case of a cathedral the canons constituted a council which aided the bishop in the administration of the diocese. The term was applied as early as the fourth century to cenobites who lived together in a monastic community, although the historical origins of the word in the Western church go back no earlier than Chrodegang, bishop of Metz (766), who required the clerks living in his household to observe set regulations concerning prayer, silence, and confession.

CANONESS, name given in early centuries to any pious woman who performed some function in the church, later to virgins and widows not living in a convent who observed rules prescribed for their condition by bishops. From the eighth century a distinction was made between secular canonesses who lived in convents but retained the right to leave, and regular canonesses who took vows of celibacy and poverty. The majority of regular canonesses date from the eleventh and twelfth centuries when different congregations of canons regular, such as Saint-Victor in Paris, established double monasteries, one for men and one for women.

CANONESSES REGULAR OF ST. AUGUSTINE, nuns related to the Augustinian canons and observing essentially the same rules. They were a product of the Gregorian reform movement of the eleventh century which hoped to regularize the life of the clergy living in canonical communities.

CANONICAL HOURS. *See* HOURS, CANONICAL.

CANONISTS, experts in canon law.

CANONIZATION, defined as the definitive sentence by which the church (pope) declared a member of the faithful departed to be in heaven and worthy of veneration and intercession. In the early church, martyrs were the first to be publicly so honored. From the fourth century a cultus was extended to confessors, that is, to persons, now declared saints, who had not suffered martyrdom. Local bishops assumed responsibility for cults in their own dioceses. The first historically attested canonization, one intended to hold for all Christians, was that of Ulrich of Augsburg by Pope John XV in 993. The Decretals of Gregory IX (1227–41) restricted canonization to the official church.

CANON LAW, body of law that governed the Christian church. It was composed of laws drawn for the most part from Scripture, tradition, conciliar pronouncements, and papal decrees. [*See* CANON; CORPUS JURIS CANONICI.]

CANON OF THE HOLY SCRIPTURES, those books of the bible judged divinely inspired and therefore genuine.

CANON OF THE MASS, that part of the divine service that followed the Offertory, more immediately the Preface and Sanctus, and preceded the Communion, principally the Consecration. It was identified as a specific part of the mass as early as the fourth century and was modified by Gregory the Great (590–604), by whose time it had assumed virtually its present form.

CANONS, APOSTOLIC, collection of ecclesiastical decrees from the time of the Apostles. They concerned regulations and organization of the early church.

CANONS REGULAR OF ST. AUGUSTINE (Austin Canons), members of a semimonastic order who lived according to a rule based upon regulations which St. Augustine laid down for the clergy living at his cathedral in Hippo. The origin of these canons did not extend beyond the middle of the eleventh century. Their later popularity was due principally to the encouragement of Pope Gregory VII who urged all priests living in cathedrals or collegiate churches to observe monastic regulations concerning celibacy, obedience, and poverty.

CANOSSA, city in Tuscany whose origins extended to the tenth century. It was here that Henry IV of Germany made his submission to Pope Gregory VII in January of 1077 over the investiture issue. In doing so he freed himself from excommunication and left Gregory no alternative but to withdraw from his projected alliance with the German princes to bring about the king's deposition. At the time the city was a possession of Matilda, countess of Tuscany.

CANTATE SUNDAY, the fourth Sunday after Easter so named from the opening word of the Introit.

CANTERBURY, city in Kent whose origins went back to Roman times. The kings of Kent made the city their capital, while the archbishops of Canterbury traced their residence there to c. 600 when St. Augustine arrived with his band of monks. Together with St. Augustine's abbey, the city was a major religious and cultural center during the whole of the Saxon period. Phases of most of the major political and religious events of medieval England were enacted at Canterbury. In the twelfth century it was among the dozen or so economically most important boroughs in England. The tomb of Thomas Becket (d. 1170) made it the most popular shrine in England and the source of a flourishing tourist industry.

CANTERBURY CATHEDRAL, originally a Norman structure whose choir was rebuilt by William of Sens (fl. 1174–8) and its nave by Henry Yevelle in 1378–90. The crossing tower dates from 1494–7.

CANTERBURY, SEE OF, bishop's seat established by St. Augustine c. 600. As archbishop its prelate exercised jurisdiction over the southern province which included the greater part of England, leaving the northern province to the archbishop of York. The ancient rivalry between the two archbishops as to who was primate of England was resolved in the fourteenth century when the archbishop of Canterbury was authorized to designate himself primate of *all* England. (The title of the archbishop of York was primate of England.) The principal residence of the archbishop of Canterbury was Lambeth Palace in London.

CANTERBURY TALES. *See* CHAUCER, GEOFFREY.

CANTICLE OF THE SUN, a hymn of St. Francis in praise of the divine revelation in nature, traditionally supposed to have been composed in the garden of San Damiano at Assisi. It took its title from the second stanza in which Francis thanks God for "Brother Sun."

CANTICLES, BIBLICAL, term applied to songs from the Old Testament, exclusive of the Psalms themselves, and to several from the New (e.g., *Benedictus*) which found their way into the Christian liturgy.

CANTILUPE, THOMAS DE, ST., d. 1282, bishop of Hereford (1275), educated at Oxford, Paris, and Orléans, and chancellor of Oxford (1261). He supported Simon de Montfort and the barons against Henry III, went to Paris when Henry won out, later returned to his old post at Oxford, still later became the confidential adviser of Edward I. Although he died excommunicated by Archbishop Peckham over jurisdictional rights, he was canonized in 1320.

CANTOR, principal singer in an ecclesiastical choir, mention of whom appears in the Christian liturgical service as early as the fourth century. In the seventh century mention is made of a leader of cantors, suggesting the origins of the *schola cantorum*. From the eleventh century the title of cantor might be simply honorific and might have been given to members of a chapter who were entitled to prebends.

CANTUS (canto), term applied to the upper voice carrying the melody, also known as *cantus firmus*. Until the early fifteenth century this voice was normally that of the tenor.

CANTUS MENSURATUS (*mensurabilis*), music so written as to assign time values to the different notes.

CANTUS PLANUS, choral melody in early medieval music that assigned no specific time to the different notes.

CANUTE (Cnut, Knut), Danish king of England and Denmark, 1016–35. He completed the conquest of England which his father Sweyn Forkbeard, king of Denmark, had almost accomplished, married Emma (1017), the widow of Ethelred II, the last Anglo-Saxon king, and enjoyed a generally peaceful and popular reign. In 1028 he defeated Olaf II Haraldsson and made himself king of Norway. Canute proved himself a generous benefactor of the church and undertook a pilgrimage to Rome in 1026–7.

CANUTE (Cnut, Knut) VI, king of Denmark, 1182–1202, established Danish rule over Pomorze, Mecklenburg, and Holstein and received Lübeck's recognition of his suzerainty. His sister Ingeborg became the wife of Philip II Augustus of France. He died childless.

CANUTE THE SAINT, d. 1086, king (1080–6) and patron saint of Denmark. He erected churches and cathedrals and raised his bishops to the rank of princes. In 1085 he made an unsuccessful attempt to invade England.

CANZONE (*canzona*), a lyric poem that appeared in the twelfth century in Provence and was used by Italian poets in the thirteenth. It was accompanied by music. Petrarch wrote in this form.

CAPE, garment with attached hood, used in the early Middle Ages as an outer wrapper hung about the body.

CAPELLA, a small mantle, especially that of St. Martin of Tours (d. 397) which was kept as a relic in a room attached to the court of the Frankish kings, whence the term chapel.

CAPELLA, MARTIANUS. *See* MARTIANUS CAPELLA.

CAPET, HUGH, king of France, 987–96, eldest son of Hugh the Great, count of Paris, first of the Capetian kings of France. The founder of the dynasty was Robert the Strong, count of Anjou and Blois, whose two sons, Eudes and Robert I, ruled as kings of the West Franks. Hugh was the grandson of Robert I. Hugh, who reigned as king of France rather than ruled, managed to arrange the election of his son Robert (II) as king-designate.

CAPETIAN DYNASTY, royal family that ruled France from 987 (Hugh Capet) until 1328 through an unbroken line of fathers and sons. In 1328 upon the death of Charles IV, his cousin Philip (VI), son of Charles of Valois, succeeded. The earliest known ancestor of the Capetian family was Robert the Strong (d. 866), margrave of the Breton march, count of Anjou and Blois. The ablest and most famous members of the dynasty were Louis VI, Louis VII, Philip II, Louis IX, and Philip IV. [*See* CAPET, HUGH.]

CAPE VERDE ISLANDS, islands some 375 miles west of Africa which Portugal acquired in the late fifteenth century, probably on the strength of the voyages and explorations of Cadamosto.

CAPGRAVE, JOHN, d. 1464, Augustinian friar and theologian, author of exegetical works, a collection of lives of the saints believed to have been a rewriting of a work by a monk of Tynemouth, and a chronicle of English history that extends to 1417.

CAPISTRAN, JOHN, ST. *See* JOHN CAPISTRAN, ST.

CAPITULARE DE VILLIS, order that Charlemagne sent to the stewards of his villas containing detailed instructions concerning the administration and exploitation of the royal domain.

CAPITULARY, name given to acts of legislation, administration, or regulation, promulgated by Frankish kings of the eighth and ninth centuries. These capitularies might concern civil and judicial as well as ecclesiastical and monastic matters. The name is derived from *capitula*, that is, chapters or short articles dealing with particular matters. The setting for their promulgation by the king was frequently the assembly of the counts at the March Field. The term capitulary might also refer to the brief summary of the contents of individual books of the Bible.

CAPITULATIONS, term traditionally given to agreements entered into by the electors of popes or prelates for the purpose of limiting in advance of the election the authority of the man they would then proceed to choose for the office. In the case of papal electors (cardinals) of the fourteenth and fifteenth centuries, the aim of such capitulations was to protect their own strong position in the government of the church.

CAPPA (capa), outer vestment called a cope, originally hooded and made in the form of a long, semicircular cloak, which was worn by a priest or prelate at solemn liturgical functions.

CAPPADOCIAN FATHERS, THE, the leading church fathers of Cappadocia in the fourth century, namely, Basil the Great, bishop of Caesarea, Gregory, bishop of Nazianzus, and Gregory, bishop of Nyssa. They were largely responsible for the final defeat of Arianism at the Council of Constantinople in 381.

CAPRANICA, DOMENICO, d. 1458, humanist, bishop of Fermo, cardinal, and grand penitentiary in the papal Curia under Pope Nicholas V. At the Council of Ferrara-Florence (1438–9) he worked for an end to the schism and for the organization of a crusade against the Ottoman Turks.

CAPUTIATI (capuciati), members of a religious order of laymen that was organized c. 1182 in the area of Le Puy for the purpose of suppressing brigandage and the bands of mercenaries that were ravaging the countryside. Their name derived from the white hood they wore to which was attached a picture or image of Mary and the child Jesus.

CAPUT MORTUUM, term that alchemists gave to the worthless residue left after distillation or sublimation. The phrase also referred to a kind of iron that was considered worthless once it had been used.

CARAFA (Caraffa), OLIVIERO, d. 1511, jurist, humanist, diplomat, archbishop of Naples (1458), cardinal (1467), and dean of the sacred college. His efforts helped bring an end to the war between King Ferdinand of Naples and

Sixtus IV. He showed himself a generous patron of artists and writers.

CARAITES. *See* KARAITES.

CARAUSIUS, MARCUS AURELIUS, d. 293, Roman officer under Maximian in Gaul who in 286 proclaimed himself emperor in Britain. He defeated Maximian and for four years remained in control of Britain, then was murdered by one of his own officials as the army of Constantius I Chlorus began closing in on him.

CARAVEL (carvel), sailing ship, usually square-rigged, with three masts, a light ship generally with small displacement. The Portuguese employed this type of ship in the fifteenth century in exploring the west coast of Africa. Perhaps its principal excellence lay in its capacity for sailing windward and its greater speed.

CARCASSONNE, city in Languedoc west of Narbonne whose origins extended to pre-Roman times. It became a diocese in the sixth century, fell to the Saracens in 728, then to Pepin III (the Short) in 752. A series of counts and viscounts ruled the city from 819 until Simon de Montfort captured it in 1209 during the Albigensian crusade. In 1247 the French crown declared the city forfeit and annexed it.

CARCER MAMERTINUS, old Roman prison on the Capitoline hill. Legend had it that SS. Peter and Paul were incarcerated in this prison. It was here that the church of S. Pietro in Carcere was erected in the late fourteenth century.

CARDIFF, seaport city of southern Wales, the site of a Roman fort. Its castle was built in 1090. Some time before 1147 the town received a charter from its Norman lord. A Dominican friary was founded there in 1242 by Richard de Clare and a Franciscan house not long after. Owen Glendower partly destroyed it in 1404.

CARDINAL, term used perhaps for the first time in the sixth century to apply to deacons, priests, and bishops who served a church other than the one in which they had received orders. What created this situation were the wars of the period that had forced many bishops and clergy to flee their dioceses. From the pontificate of Leo IX (1049–54) cardinals served as the pope's principal advisers and administrative assistants. It appears that Urban II (1088–99) was the first pope to assemble the cardinals in formal session called a consistory, where they acted as an official body to advise him concerning matters of great importance, whence the origin of the college of cardinals. [*See* SACRED COLLEGE.] In 1059 cardinals assumed new importance when a papal decree designated them papal electors. From the close of the eleventh century the pope began to grant the cardinalate to prelates of foreign countries, a practice that continued until the schism of 1378 [*see* SCHISM, WESTERN] when Urban VI created only Italians for his new college of cardinals. Men created cardinals in foreign lands were required to make their residence in Rome.

CARENA. Lent.

CARILEFF, WILLIAM, ST., d. 1096, monk, abbot of the monastery of St. Vincent, bishop of Durham, and possibly justiciar under William II with whom he cooperated against Anselm, the archbishop of Canterbury. He began and completed the greater part of the cathedral of Durham.

CARINTHIA, region lying south of the upper Danube which was given its name by a Slavic people that occupied the area in the sixth century. Carinthia was under Avar rule from 590, in the eighth century under that of the dukes of Bavaria, and from the late eighth it was under Carolingian control. In 976 Otto II of Germany created it a duchy separate from Bavaria. It later became part of the state ruled by Ottocar II of Bohemia, then in 1276 passed under control of the house of Hapsburg and remained permanently there after 1335.

CARLISLE, city in northern Britain on the Scottish border. What was originally a Roman settlement (near Hadrian's Wall) was destroyed by the Danes in the ninth century and in the following century was given by Edmund I, grandson of Alfred the Great, to Malcolm I of Scotland. From that time England and Scotland fought over its possession until 1158 when Carlisle received a charter from Henry II and remained under British rule. The castle at Carlisle was built by William II (Rufus) in 1092.

CARLOMAN, d. 754, older brother of Pepin III (the Short) and the son of Charles Martel. The two brothers ruled jointly until 747 when Carloman retired to the monastery of Monte Cassino. From there Pepin had him transferred to the monastery at Vienne (on the Rhône) because of the encouragement he had given the Lombards.

CARLOMAN, d. 771, son of Pepin III and younger brother of Charles (Charlemagne). He ruled the eastern part of the Frankish kingdom from 768 until his death.

CARLOMAN, eldest son of Louis (II) the German, succeeded his father in 876 as king of the East Germans (Bavaria, Carinthia, Pannonia, and Moravia), and was recognized as king in northern Italy although the pope refused to grant him the imperial title. This went to his uncle Charles II (the Bald). When Carloman became ill, he renounced his lands and crown in favor of his brother Louis the Younger. His illegitimate son Arnulf became emperor in 896. Carloman was the first German king to become king of Italy.

CARMAGNOLA (Francesco Bussone), d. 1432, Italian *condottiere* in the service of Filippo Maria Visconti of Milan and later, in 1425, of Venice. His lack of success with the Venetians inspired a charge of treason and he was executed. His military prowess, together with his tragic end, made him a popular subject for poets, e.g., Alessandro Manzoni.

CARMARTHEN (Caerfyrddin), coastal town of south Wales that first attracted attention in the twelfth century under the Normans when it began to function as the administrative and economic center of southwestern Wales. Its first charter was granted by Henry III in 1227. In 1353 Edward III declared the town the sole staple (mart) for Wales. Its history in the Middle Ages was largely one of attacks, sieges, and burnings.

CARMATHIANS. *See* KARMATHIANS.

CARMELITES (Brothers of the Blessed Virgin Mary of Mount Carmel), a religious order originating with hermits living on Mt. Carmel in Palestine, probably as early as the twelfth century, and possibly founded c. 1154 by St. Berthold. The primitive rule laid down by Albert of Vercelli, patriarch of Jerusalem, in 1209 was one of extreme asceticism. In 1229 Pope Gregory IX approved the Carmelites as a mendicant order of friars. In 1247 the original rule was modified in order to enable the friars to engage in an active apostolate.

CARMELITE SISTERS, a religious order that appeared in the thirteenth century although it was not officially instituted until 1452 when Bl. John Soreth organized the Carmelite Second Order. It adopted the rule approved for the Carmelite Brothers. Some of the members of the order led cloistered lives as contemplatives.

CARMEL, MOUNT, mountain on the coast of north Palestine west of Galilee above Haifa, a sacred place and refuge in antiquity and a favorite haunt of early Christian anchorites. It was the home of the Carmelite Order.

CARMINA BURANA, collection of about 200 poems and songs, some in Middle High German, most of them in Latin, discovered in a thirteenth-century manuscript in the Benedictine abbey at Benediktbeuern (near Salzburg in Bavaria). The themes of the poems were typically Goliardic, that is, dealing for the most part with love, drinking, and the joy of living.

CARNARVON, CASTLE OF. *See* CAERNARVON, CASTLE OF.

CARNIOLA, region located just off the northeast end of the Adriatic. It was occupied by the Slovenes in the sixth century and became a duchy in 976. In later years it belonged successively to the Patriarchate of Aquileia, the dukes of Carinthia and Bohemia, the counts of Gorizia and Tyrol, and the Hapsburgs (1335).

CARNUNTUM, most powerful of the fortresses which Rome erected along the Danubian frontier, its location just below Vindobona (Vienna). It fell to barbarian invaders in 275, was rebuilt by the emperor Diocletian (284–305), then totally destroyed c. 400.

CAROCHA (coroza), a devil's cap worn by one condemned to death by the court of the Inquisition.

CAROL, song originally apparently associated with dancing and with the seasons of the year, especially Christmas. It made its appearance in England in the fourteenth century. Of a variety of themes that the carol might feature, the most common was religious.

CAROLE, name often given to chain and round dances in France and Italy.

CAROLINE BOOKS, documents probably drawn up by Theodulf of Orléans, not by Alcuin as once believed, and issued as formal decrees by Charlemagne, which condemned the position taken by the Seventh General Council at Nicaea (787) on the matter of images.

CAROLINGIAN DYNASTY, family of kings who ruled the Frankish empire from 751 beginning with Pepin III (the Short) and ending in France with Louis V (the Sluggard) in 987, in Germany with Louis the Child in 911. Its name derived from Charlemagne (Carolus, Charles the Great) who was its most renowned representative. Marked decline set in following the death of Charlemagne in 814 as the Northmen stepped up their attacks along the frontiers of the empire while the sons of Louis the Pious (814–40) fought over their inheritance within. In 843 at Verdun, the sons, Lothair, Louis, and Charles, agreed to a tripartite division of the empire [*see* VERDUN, TREATY OF], but this ended neither the wars within the empire nor the assaults of the Northmen from without. In 884–87 the entire empire was again united under Charles III (the Fat), but this unity was misleading since real authority at that time was held by the landed aristocracy, not by the king. The feudal age had dawned, a time when kings reigned, not ruled. [*See* FEUDALISM.]

CAROLINGIAN RENAISSANCE, a revival of learning, principally patristic and classical, that was centered at Aachen and supported by Charlemagne. Its origins may be credited to Pepin III (751–68) and to a monastic revival which was already under way, but without Charlemagne's genuine interest in learning and his grave concern over the low level of learning among the clergy of the empire, no substantial revival would have taken place at this time. The most dramatic facet of the revival was the coterie of scholars which Charlemagne gathered at Aachen to grace his palace, among them Alcuin, the most distinguished, Theodulf of Orléans, Peter of Pisa, and Paul the Deacon. Undoubtedly the most enduring accomplishment of the renaissance was the intellectual and religious stimulus it furnished such monastic schools of the period as Fulda, Reichenau, St. Gall, and Corbie. It could also boast among other achievements the evolution of a vastly improved script known as the Carolingian minuscule and a "purified" Latin which supplied the base for what is known as medieval Latin.

CARPACCIO, VITTORE, d. 1526, Italian painter of the Venetian school whose work was marked by exquisite detail and delicate coloring. His painting reveals the influence of Gentile Bellini. His best known work is the cycle of paintings with *Scenes from the Life of St. Ursula*.

CARPINI, GIOVANNI DE PLANO. *See* JOHN OF PLANO CARPINI.

CARPOCRATES, Gnostic teacher of the second century at Alexandria who is supposed to have given his name to the Carpocratians. This sect maintained that man, once united to the Absolute, had been corrupted, but by being reincarnated several times, could finally enter heaven. They held that Jesus was but one of several wise men who had achieved deliverance.

CARRARA, medieval Italian family, at first feudal lords of Padua, then in the fourteenth century ruling despots of the city. The Carrara court was one of the most brilliant of the period. Padua fell to Venice in 1405.

CARROCCIO, wagon, a kind of war chariot, used for transporting standards and flags and employed by the cities of north Italy, first by Milan. The loss of the carroccio in battle was regarded as an irretrievable humiliation.

CARROUSEL, kind of tournament staged from the late Middle Ages and featuring various exercises and events, including the throwing of lances at Turkish "heads."

CARTA CARITATIS or "Charter of Love," document that set down the constitution of the Cistercian Order and was presented to Pope Callistus II in 1119 for approval. It provided for autonomous houses, annual visitation of each house by the abbot of the house that had founded it, and an annual general chapter with legislative and judicial powers. It may have been largely the work of Stephen Harding.

CAR TEL EST NOTRE (BON) PLAISIR (for such is our will), formal conclusion used in French royal decrees since 1326 but only officially adopted by Louis XI in 1472.

CARTHAGE, ancient city of north Africa, taken by the Vandals (439–533), but recovered by Belisarius, Justinian's general, in 533. The Arabs in their sweep across north Africa in 698

practically destroyed it. It was there that Louis IX died in 1270 on the second of his crusades.

CARTHUSIANS, a contemplative order founded in 1084 by St. Bruno which was noted for the austerity of its semi-anchoritic rule and for the high level of spiritual life it managed to preserve throughout the Middle Ages. The monks, who took a vow of silence, lived each in his own cell within the monastery, working and devoting several hours to prayer and meditation, and meeting the other members for the divine office, the conventual mass, and for meals on feast days. The order had its name from the Chartreuse mountains in the French Alps north of Grenoble where St. Bruno located his monastery. The order maintained a system of visitation and chapters and, despite the harshness of its rule, numbered about 200 houses at the close of the medieval period.

CARUS, MARCUS AURELIUS, short-lived but able Roman emperor who in 282 was proclaimed Augustus by his troops in Pannonia but died the following year, probably murdered, after defeating the Persians and capturing their capital at Ctesiphon.

CASAQUE, piece of clothing worn over the cuirass and decorated with distinctive marks and coloring.

CASHEL, town in County Tipperary, Ireland, ancient capital of the kings of Munster and a stronghold of Brian Boru. The ruins of St. Patrick's Cathedral (fourteenth century) atop the lofty Rock of Cashel and below the Rock the ruins of Horre Abbey (1272) remain. St. Patrick visited the town in 450 and baptized its king.

CASHEL, SYNOD OF, a synod held in 1171 or 1172 under Henry II of England following his invasion of Ireland that brought the usages of the Celtic Church into conformity with those in England. This included a revision of the rite of baptism and of the system of tithes. The Irish chieftains gathered at Cashel acknowledged the suzerainty of Henry.

CASIMIR I (the Restorer), grand duke of Poland, 1038–58, son of Mieszko II, recovered his throne from which he had been deposed, reestablished order in Poland with the aid of Emperors Conrad II and Henry III of Germany, and regained possession of Mazovia and Silesia. In the achievement of these successes, however, he was obliged to extend numerous concessions to the nobility and the clergy.

CASIMIR II, Polish ruler, 1177–94, youngest son of Boleslaw III. He drove his brother Mieszko III from Cracow in 1177, thereby gaining the throne which went with that city and duchy. Although he was never crowned king, the nobility and clergy vested hereditary rights as rulers of Cracow in his descendants.

CASIMIR III (the Great), king of Poland, 1333–70, surrendered claims to Silesia and Pomerania in the interest of peace, but gained Galicia and late in his reign acquired control of Mazovia. He codified the laws, founded the University of Cracow (1364), encouraged the immigration of Germans and Jews, and alleviated the lot of the peasantry. His concessions to the Polish aristocracy threatened royal authority. He was the last of the Piast dynasty.

CASIMIR IV, king of Poland, 1447–92, also grand prince of Lithuania, secured possession of all of western Prussia from the Teutonic Order by the Peace of Torun (Thorn) in 1466, together with suzerainty rights over what remained of the Order's lands in east Prussia. (The Knights were to hold these lands as fiefs of the Polish crown.) Although he succeeded in reducing the power of the great magnates, he extended to the gentry the right to veto new taxes and a declaration of war. He placed his sons on the thrones of Bohemia (and Hungary) and Lithuania.

CASIMIR, ST., d. 1484, patron saint of Poland and Lithuania, third son of Casimir IV of Po-

land. Although heir apparent and regent for his father when the latter was away for two years in Poland, he chose to take a vow of celibacy and to devote himself to the religious life. He had a special devotion to the Virgin.

CASSIAN, JOHN, d. c. 435, a native of Gaul whose interest in monasticism took him to Palestine and Egypt. After some years in these lands he returned to Gaul and founded two monasteries at Marseilles, one for men, the other for women. The two books he composed on the subject of monasticism breathe the austerity of Eastern monastic life. The *Institutes* set down the ordinary rules for the monastic life and discussed the principal hindrances to a monk's perfection. In the *Conferences,* he recounted his conversations with the leaders of Eastern monasticism.

CASSIODORUS, FLAVIUS MAGNUS AURELIUS, d. c. 580, learned secretary of King Theodoric of the Ostrogoths, master of offices, and praetorian prefect. Shortly after Theodoric's death he retired to his villa in Calabria which he converted into a monastery (Vivarium) and where he spent some forty years in study and prayer. While encouraging his monks to copy classical and patristic manuscripts, he busied himself preparing spiritual instructions for his community, composing treatises on the seven liberal arts, and writing history. His history of the Goths is lost except for Jordanes's unscholarly compendium. Historians consider his correspondence as Theodoric's secretary most valuable. This includes twelve books of imperial edicts and decrees drawn up by himself. They served as a model for medieval chanceries. His *Institutiones Divinarum et Secularium Litterarum* which reveals the influence of St. Augustine, advocated the union of sacred and profane studies in Christian education.

CASSOCK, long garment, usually black, worn by the clergy and retained for use by the clergy after the sixth century when shorter garments became customary for secular garb. The cassock was already ordained as proper attire by the Council of Braga in 572.

CASSONE, term given a chest or coffer in late medieval Italy in which the bride-to-be kept her trousseau. No small piece of furniture of the Middle Ages received more lavish decoration.

CASTAGNO, ANDREA DEL, d. 1457, Florentine painter of frescoes whose work reveals the influence of Masaccio and Donatello. He was active in Venice and Florence. His monumental frescoes of Passion scenes and the *Last Supper* attracted wide acclaim for their vigorous design and their attention to movement and dramatic presentation.

CASTANETS, small, platelike or hollowed pieces of hard wood used in pairs and held in the hands to beat time with music. They appeared in Italy and Spain in the late Middle Ages.

CASTELLAN (chatelain), governor of a castle. In Poland an official by that name exercised judicial and military authority over the district served by a castle.

CASTELNAU, PIERRE DE. *See* PETER CASTEL-NAU.

CASTEL SANT'ANGELO, citadel on the Tiber, known as Hadrian's Tomb until 590 when, according to a contemporary story, its name was changed to "Castle of the Angel." From the fifth century it served both as a prison and a fortress. Popes used it as a place of refuge when enemy forces seized possession of Rome.

CASTILE, kingdom occupying the central tableland of the Spanish peninsula which the kings of the Asturias and Leon gradually recovered from Moorish rule. The history of Castile began with Fernán Gonzáles (d. 970), its first count, who made Burgos his capital and undertook attacks on Moorish holdings to the south. In 1029 Castile passed under the rule of Sancho III of Navarre whose son Ferdinand I (d. 1065) estab-lished it as a kingdom subject to Leon. Alfonso VIII ended Leon's suzerainty in 1188, and in 1230 Ferdinand III of Castile succeeded to the throne of the two kingdoms. The union of Castile with Aragon, promised by the marriage of Isabella and Ferdinand (1469), led to the establishment of modern Spain (1479).

CASTILLON, BATTLE OF, engagement near Bordeaux on July 17, 1453, ending in a French victory. It may be considered the closing battle of the Hundred Years' War. The surrender of Bordeaux the following October left no continental territory in English hands except for Calais. The successful employment of cannon by the French helped confirm the effectiveness of this new weapon of war.

CASTLE, a fortified structure, usually erected with thick walls of stone and surrounded by a moat. The standard type from which most such strongholds evolved was called the motte-and-bailey castle. The bailey consisted of a courtyard surrounded by a moat, palisade, or earthen embankment. Within this area was the motte, a mound or hill protected by another line of entrenchments and palisade and surmounted by a tower called a donjon or keep. This last, the lord's stronghold, was provided with well and stores to enable the garrison to hold out for some time after the outer works had fallen. A fortified tower called the barbican guarded the gateway, a heavy iron grating suspended by chains and called a portcullis, guarded the door itself, while a drawbridge denied ready access to any intruder once it had been lifted. Stone castles appeared in England with the Normans. They became universal throughout western Europe as a result of the experience gained in the Crusades. The virtual impregnability of the castle prior to the introduction of artillery in the first half of the fifteenth century enabled the landed aristocracy to maintain a powerful position vis-à-vis the king.

CASTRACANI, CASTRUCCIO, d. 1328, duke of

Lucca. Following a period of exile, he returned to Lucca and not only became its lord but also leader of the Ghibellines of Tuscany. He was successful in his wars against Florence and gained possession of Volterra, Pistoia, and Lunigiana. He died as he was threatening Florence itself.

CASTRIOTA, GEORGE. *See* SCANDERBEG.

CASTRO, INÉS DE, d. 1355, member of the Galician nobility, a beautiful lady-in-waiting at the Portuguese court, and mistress of Dom Pedro (later Peter I) by whom she had four children. Because King Alfonso IV did not approve of the influence she and her brothers had over Dom Pedro, he agreed to have her murdered. When Dom Pedro became king, he avenged her death. The tragic love story, with romantic accretions, became a favorite theme of Portuguese and Spanish writers.

CATACOMBS, subterranean cemeteries in Rome, Naples, and other Italian cities that the early Christians used for burial purposes. Since pagan Rome regarded every burial place as sacrosanct, Christians felt free to use the catacombs even in times of persecution. The bodies were placed in niches hewn in the side-walls. The stucco paintings that might cover the walls represent the first examples of Christian art. The principal services held in the catacombs were the eucharistic celebrations on the anniversaries of the martyrs.

CATAFALQUE, wooden frame used to support a coffin; a frame, simulating a coffin, draped in black and used to represent the dead in a service for his soul.

CATALAUNIAN FIELDS (*Campi Catalaunici*), site of Attila's defeat in 451 at the hands of Aetius and the Visigoths. [*See* CHÂLONS, BATTLE OF.]

CATALONIA, country of northeastern Spain, its name derived from its numerous castles, whose history in the Middle Ages began with that of the counts of Barcelona. They appeared in the ninth century as lords in the Spanish March that Charlemagne had established. In 1137 Catalonia was united with Aragon although it retained its own laws and culture. Catalan traders were rivals of those of Genoa and Venice and controlled most of the commerce of the western Mediterranean. Decline came in the fifteenth century as trade routes shifted to the Atlantic, but the spirit of autonomy grew stronger with the unification of all Spain under Ferdinand and Isabella.

CATAPHRACT, Byzantine horse-archer who carried lance, broadsword, bow, arrows, and dagger. He was the most formidable warrior of the sixth and seventh centuries.

CATAPULT, machine used in medieval warfare in the siege of castles and walled cities. It was employed to throw large stones against the walls or over them. A similar machine, the ballista, was used to hurl smaller stones but at a greater distance. Both machines disappeared with the introduction of gunpowder and artillery.

CATECHESIS, instruction given to Christian catechumens preparing for baptism, especially in the primitive church.

CATECHUMEN, term generally applied in the early church to persons seeking instruction in the faith before baptism. The catechumenate, which might last three years, was most popular in the fourth and fifth centuries because of the large number of adult men and women seeking baptism. The growing popularity of infant baptism in the seventh century led to its disappearance. Catechumens were assigned a place in church but were dismissed before the liturgy of the eucharist commenced.

CATENA, Latin for chain, a word applied to biblical commentaries in which successive verses of the Scriptural text were elucidated by "chains" of passages taken from previous commentators. The term might also apply to any collection of passages from different authors related to a single subject.

CATHARI, term meaning the "pure" that was applied to members of the Manichaean sect in France and Italy in the twelfth and thirteenth centuries. [See ALBIGENSES.]

CATHEDRA, meaning chair or seat, a term applied from the early church to the throne used by the bishop in his cathedral. In the early church it was first placed in the center of the apse behind the high altar, but in the medieval period it was often placed in the chancel.

CATHEDRAL, the church of a diocese, often the most imposing, where the bishop had his throne (*cathedra*) and where he presided. The word is actually an adjective in origin and modified the word church: i.e., cathedral church. As the responsibilities of the bishop grew more exacting, the administration of the cathedral was gradually given over to a separate body of clergy, a separate ecclesiastical corporation or chapter, with its own privileges and rights.

CATHEDRAL CHAPTER, the priests associated with a cathedral and organized into a corporation for the purpose of maintaining a higher level of dedication and of providing greater efficiency in the performance of their duties. They served as an advisory council, aided the bishop in the administration of the diocese, and from the early thirteenth century elected the bishop (subject to the approval of the pope). Although cathedral chapters existed before the late eleventh century, they appeared in increasing number from that time as a product of the religious reform movement which recommended that all priests, whenever possible, observe such monastic traditions as choir duty and a common residence.[See CHRODEGANG OF METZ.]

CATHEDRAL SCHOOL, school associated with a cathedral and intended principally for the education of the clergy of the diocese and for the choirboys of the cathedral church. These schools made their appearance in the sixth century when secular schools ceased to exist, either because they had been victims of the barbarian invasions or had been suppressed for their paganism. Until the eleventh century monastic schools dominated learning in the West, but from c. 1000 the cathedral schools of Reims, Paris, Chartres, Laon, and other cities assumed leadership. Cathedral schools in sufficient number to provide training for the diocesan clergy only came as a product of such reforms as that decreed by the Fourth Lateran Council in 1215.

CATHERINE OF ALEXANDRIA, ST., an obscure virgin who, according to a questionable tradition, was martyred at Alexandria in the early fourth century because she had protested to the emperor Maxentius against the persecution of Christians. She was tied to a wheel, tortured, then beheaded. Despite the obscurity attending her life, she was among the most widely venerated woman saints of the Middle Ages and honored as one of the Fourteen Holy Helpers. Her symbol is a spiked wheel.

CATHERINE OF GENOA, ST., d. c. 1510, and her husband took vows of celibacy, worked as nurses in a hospital, she later becoming an administrator of such an institution. Catherine is considered a major mystic of the period, and her views on purgatory have attracted considerable attention. It was her conviction that purgatory was less a place of suffering where souls were purged of their moral deficiences than a state where the love of God, as a purifying sea, transformed them into fit occupants of heaven.

CATHERINE OF SIENA, ST., d. 1380, tertiary of the Dominican order, the leading Italian mystic of the fourteenth century, and a woman who wielded great influence in ecclesiastical circles. Two major goals absorbed her energies: the return of the pope from Avignon to Rome where the good of the church demanded his presence; and the organization of a crusade under papal leadership against the Turks. It was partly the result of her pleading that Pope Gregory XI returned to Rome in 1377, thereby terminating the period of the Avignonese Residence. Yet scarcely had she blessed God for this happy event than the schism which divided Western Christendom into two churches, one supporting Urban VI, in her judgment the valid pope, and the other Clement VII, plunged her into deep sadness. Her writings (all dictated) include some prayers, about 380 letters, and *Dialogo* (*Il libro della divina dottrina*) which describes her mystical experiences.

CATHERINE OF SWEDEN, ST., d. 1381, daughter of St. Bridget of Sweden and the first superior of the convent of Bridgittines at Vadstena in Sweden which her mother had founded. Much of her life was spent in Italy where she had gone to secure confirmation of her order and the canonization of her mother.

CATHERINE OF VALOIS, d. 1437, daughter of Charles VI of France, wife of Henry V of England (1420), and mother of Henry VI. Some years after the death of her husband in 1422, she married Owen Tudor, a Welsh squire. An act of parliament had forbidden her to marry without the consent of the king and council, so Owen was imprisoned and she retired to Bermondsey abbey where she died. Their son Edmund, later created earl of Richmond, was the father of Henry VII.

CATHOLIC MAJESTY, title given to Ferdinand and Isabella, king and queen of Spain, by Pope Alexander VI in 1494 in recognition of their conquest of Granada. It was assumed by succeeding monarchs of that country.

CATHOLICOS, title, similar to patriarch, held by certain ecclesiastical superiors in the Eastern churches including archimandrites and metropolitans. The heads of the Armenian, Georgian, and Nestorian churches also bore this title.

CATTARO, small republic south of Dalmatia on the Adriatic which passed successively under Byzantine, Serbian, Hungarian, and Venetian rule.

CAUCHON (Calconeus), PIERRE, d. 1442, bishop of Beauvais, earlier rector of the University of Paris, who in 1431 presided at the trial of Joan of Arc in Rouen. He had served in the household of John, duke of Bedford, the brother of Henry V of England, who was in charge of the defense of English possessions in France during this period of the Hundred Years' War. Bedford was the man ultimately responsible for the decision to prosecute Joan for witchcraft. Cauchon later became bishop of Lisieux (1432) and attended the Council of Basel.

CAUDILLO, Spanish title for commander of an army.

CAULITES, an austere monastic order, founded in 1193 by a Carthusian lay brother, that observed strict silence and perpetual abstinence from meat. It spread from Burgundy to Spain, Portugal, and Scotland, and in the thirteenth century numbered about 30 houses.

CAVALCANTI, GUIDO, d. 1300, Italian poet, prominent member of the *dolce stil nuovo* school, a close friend of Dante's. He treated love not only as a source of joy but also of tragedy since by dulling reason it might bring death. As was true of many poets of this school, he excluded any consideration of moral and religious values in his handling of love. He is considered one of Italy's finest lyric poets.

CAVALLINI, PIETRO, d. c. 1330, Italian sculptor and mosaicist whose work suggested a departure from the traditional Byzantine forms toward naturalism. Some of his work survives in Rome in the mosaics of the *Life of the Virgin*. He influenced the paintings of Cimabue and Giotto.

CAVALLO, copper coin used in Naples at the close of the Middle Ages.

CAXTON, WILLIAM, d. 1491, first English printer. After being a wool merchant for 30 years and rising to the position of Governor of the English Merchant Adventurers, his interests shifted to literature and in 1470 he took up the life of a printer. He set up a press in Bruges in 1475 and the following year established the first to appear in England, near Westminster Abbey. The 100 or so items he published included romances, history, philosophy, devotional pieces, almost all writing that had appeared in English including *The Canterbury Tales*, and some translations from the French. Although kings, nobles, and wealthy merchants were counted among his friends, the products of his press reveal a practical concern about meeting the humbler tastes of a more numerous clientele. Although his work can make no claim to great originality or beauty, it enjoyed a deservedly high reputation for its accuracy and clarity.

CECCO D'ASCOLI, d. 1327, popular name of Francesco Degli Stabili, Italian poet, mathematician, physician, and astrologer. He taught mathematics and astrology at the University of Bologna and served as personal astrologer to Duke Charles of Calabria. His views incurred the charge of heresy and he died at the stake.

CECHY, Czech name for Bohemia.

CECILIA (Caecilia), ST., Roman virgin whose martyrdom has been assigned to a number of years including 177, 230, and 304. She was one of the most honored of medieval saints and in the fifteenth century came to be recognized as the patron saint of music. She is frequently represented as playing the organ.

CEDD (Cedda, Chad), ST., d. 664, Benedictine monk of Northumbria, a disciple of Aidan of Lindisfarne, and founder of several monasteries, notably that of Lastingham of which he became the first abbot. Although a member of the delegation of Celtic representatives at the synod of Whitby (664), he accepted its decision to adopt Roman usages and liturgy.

CEDRINUS, GEORGE, obscure Greek scholar of the eleventh century, perhaps a monk, whose chronicle of world history extends to 1057. This work is largely a compilation of extracts drawn from other chronicles, several of these, such as that of Scylitzes, being nowhere else to be found.

CELANO, THOMAS OF. *See* THOMAS OF CELANO.

CELESTINE I, ST., Pope, 422–32, a native of Campagna (south of Rome), asserted Rome's claim to primacy, condemned and deposed Nestorius, the archbishop of Constantinople, and in 431 sent Palladius to Ireland as that land's first bishop. He also sent a mission headed by Germanus of Auxerre to Britain to combat Pelagianism.

CELESTINE II, Pope, 1143–4, a disciple and friend of Abelard's, cardinal, and already an old man when elected pope.

CELESTINE III, Pope, 1191–8, a student of Abelard, whom he defended at the Council of Sens (1140), and active in the papal diplomatic service under Alexander III. When he became pope at the age of 85 he found himself caught up in the midst of the struggle Henry VI of Germany was waging to gain control of Sicily. Although demonstrating weakness or a lack of adequate information in opposing Henry's machinations, he showed firmness in refusing to accept the annulment of Philip II's marriage to Ingeborg which the French bishops had approved.

CELESTINE IV, Pope, October 25 to November 10, 1241, a nephew of Urban III, a Cistercian, cardinal-bishop of Sabina, and aged and infirm when hurriedly elected pope in order to block any interference on the part of Frederick II of Germany.

CELESTINE V (Peter of Morrone), ST., Pope, July 5 to December 13, 1294, Benedictine monk, founder of the Celestine Order, hermit on Mt. Morrone who was elected pope against his will when the cardinals found themselves deadlocked in their choice of pope. Celestine who quickly demonstrated his incompetence by filling the Curia and college of cardinals with protégés of Charles II of Anjou, the king of Naples, willingly resigned upon the suggestion of his cardinals. One of these, Benedict Gaetani, who succeeded him as Boniface VIII, abrogated his acts and kept him in honorable confinement lest he become the center of political intrigue.

CELESTINES, branch of the Benedictine order, also known as Hermits of St. Damian or Hermits of Morrone after their founder Peter of Morrone (Pope Celestine V). The order reached the height of its popularity in the fifteenth century when it counted 150 houses.

CELESTIUS, a heretic of the fifth century, a native of Britain, who met Pelagius in Rome and accepted his views, namely, that the free will of men enables them to overcome temptation without the need for divine grace, and that baptism was not necessary since there was no such thing as original sin. He was condemned by the Council of Carthage in 412, and his teachings were anathematized by the Council of Ephesus in 431.

CELIBACY OF THE CLERGY. Early councils of the Eastern church asserted or implied the right of the clergy to be married, although priests and deacons could not marry after ordination. The Latin church took a stricter position at least c. 306 when the Council of Elvira decreed all high clergy must be celibate, a position that a decretal of Pope Siricius confirmed in 386. Repeated canons were issued in the Middle Ages enforcing celibacy, while the Second Lateran Council of 1139 declared marriage of clerics to be not only unlawful but invalid. The suppression of clerical marriage and concubinage was a major objective of the Cluniac reform movement of the tenth and eleventh centuries. While much was accomplished toward attaining that objective, clerical concubinage remained a problem throughout the medieval period.

CELLA, name given to the small memorial chapel erected in early Christian cemeteries.

CELLARER, the monk placed in charge of the cellar or provisions. St. Benedict set down his responsibilities in his Rule. In practice the cellarer was usually responsible for most or all of the monastery's dealings with the outside tradesmen.

CELLE, in French law a little house, the home of a serf or commoner. Children who lived with their parents were classified as *en celle*. In the late Middle Ages the term might refer to an abbey, e.g., La Celle de Poitiers.

CELSUS, fl. last quarter of the second century, a Platonist, probably of Rome or Alexandria, who attacked Christianity as a threat to the Roman empire and to classical civilization. He praised the high moral code of the Christians but criticized them for accepting the miracles described in the New Testament and expressed repugnance for such doctrines as the Incarnation and Crucifixion. He demanded the suppression of Christianity because it proselytized, and was willing to tolerate the Jewish religion since it did not.

CELTIC CHURCH, the Christian church of the fourth, fifth, and sixth centuries in Ireland, Wales, England, Scotland, and Brittany, that is, wherever Celts constituted the dominant element in the population. Christianity was well established in England during the fourth century while monasticism was introduced from Gaul in the fifth. The invasions of the pagan Angles and Saxons extinguished Christianity throughout most of England. It did not extend to Ireland where St. Patrick (d. 461) and his successors had converted the natives and had established an unusually vigorous monasticism, so vigorous, indeed, that it provided the church an organization based upon monastic districts rather than episcopal dioceses. Irish monasticism also produced scores of missionaries, among the most influential St. Columba (d. 597) and St. Columban (d. 615), who carried the faith into Scotland, north England, and the continent. Meanwhile another source of evangelistic activity appeared in southeastern England following the landing there c. 597 of St. Augustine and his companions. The rivalry that resulted when these two streams of missionary endeavor, the Celtic and the Roman, encountered each other was resolved at the Synod of Whitby in 664 which declared in favor of Roman usage and liturgy. From this point Celtic missionary endeavor generally receded from both the continent and England, although the influence of monastic centers of Celtic origin such as Luxeuil and Bobbio was felt for many generations to come. A few memorials, including the Book of Kells and the Cross of Muiredach, continue to attest to the cultural achievement of the Irish or Celtic church. Only ruins mark the renowned centers of religious and intellectual activity at Armagh, Bangor, Iona, and Lindisfarne which flourished during the sixth and seventh centuries.

CELTIS (Celtes), CONRADUS, pseudonym of Konrad Pickel, d. 1508, German scholar, humanist, and poet. He lectured at various universities, taught rhetoric and poetry at the Universities of Ingolstadt and Vienna, and was created the first poet laureate of Germany. Among other manuscripts that he discovered were the plays of Hroswitha. He composed perhaps the finest Latin lyrical poetry of the Renaissance.

CENA DOMINI, term used to designate the Lord's meal or the eucharist.

CENIS PASS, MONT. *See* MONT CENIS PASS.

CENNINI, CENNINO, d. c. 1440, Italian painter of the fifteenth century who wrote a treatise on the art and technique of painting. In content and outlook it represents a transitional point between the medieval and modern periods. No authenticated paintings of his have been discovered.

CENOBITISM, monasticism as practiced by monks and nuns, cenobites, who lived as a community in monasteries or convents as opposed to anchorites and hermits who lived alone. Pachomius (d. 346) is considered the father of cenobitism.

CENS, any tax paid in money or kind that a lord collected from the commoners who lived on his lands.

CENSURE, ECCLESIASTICAL, spiritual sentence, such as excommunication, that the church pronounced against a person judged guilty of some serious offense.

CENT NOUVELLES NOUVELLES, a fifteenth-century collection of French stories, imitative of the *Decameron,* that were supposed to have been told at the Burgundian court.

CEOLWULF (Ceowulph, Ceolulph), d. 764, king of Northumbria, known for his piety and learning, who retired to Lindisfarne and there died as a monk. It was Ceolwulf to whom Bede dedicated his *History.* He reigned 729–37.

CEORL, in Anglo-Saxon England, a freeman who ranked above a slave and below a thegn (thane).

CEP (ceps, chep, sep), instrument of torture; also, by extension, chains, irons, and jail.

CERINTHUS, fl. c. 100, Gnostic heretic who may have had connections with the Ebionites and with Alexandrine Gnosticism. He maintained that the supreme God had not created the world, rather a Demiurge or angels, and that Christ was but a mere man until his baptism when a higher divine power descended upon him which left him before his crucifixion.

CERTOSA, name given a Carthusian monastery in Italy. It corresponded to the charterhouse in England.

CERTOSA DI PAVIA, an unusually magnificent Carthusian monastery at Pavia which has been maintained as a national monument. The church was begun in 1396 by Gian Galeazzo Visconti, duke of Milan. This early structure followed the norms of Italian Gothic, but the greater part of the structure, erected in the early sixteenth century, followed those of Renaissance architecture.

CERULARIUS, MICHAEL. *See* CAERULARIUS, MICHAEL.

CERVELIÈRE, round metal cap worn as a helmet by foot soldiers in the twelfth, thirteenth, and fourteenth centuries.

CESARINI, GIULIANO (Julian), d. 1444, member of an impoverished noble family of Rome, taught at Padua, was made a cardinal in 1426, and served as papal legate to the council of Basel and as its president until 1437 when he moved with the more moderate delegates to Ferrara. He was a friend of Nicholas of Cusa. He was among the Crusaders slain by the Turks in the battle of Varna.

CEUTA, Phoenician colony on the north coast of Morocco opposite Gibraltar, became first a Greek then a Roman city, was held by Vandals, Visigoths, and by the Byzantine empire before being captured by the Moslems in 711. Portugal took it from the Moors in 1415 and held it until 1580. The first paper mill to appear in the west is said to have been located in Ceuta.

CHABANNES, ANTOINE DE, d. 1488, a captain of *routiers,* fought with Joan of Arc at Orléans, and directed the crown's prosecution of Jacques Coeur. Although initially opposed to the centralizing policies of Louis XI, he later became one of his most trusted officials.

CHABANNES, JACQUES DE, d. 1453, French general, brother of Antoine who also served with Joan of Arc. He scored his greatest successes in expelling the English from Normandy and Guienne.

CHABHAM, THOMAS, English canonist of the early thirteenth century, author of sermons, a book on preaching, and a manual for confessors.

Two facts attest to the popularity of his *Summa De Arte Predicandi*, one, that it remains extant in 85 manuscripts, the other that it has been ascribed to St. Thomas Aquinas.

CHAD, ST. *See* CEDD, ST.

CHAISE D'OR (*florin à la chaise*), a large French gold coin first struck in 1303 by order of Philip IV.

CHALCEDON, COUNCIL OF, general church council (Fourth Ecumenical) convoked by Emperor Marcian in 451 at Chalcedon in Asia Minor which condemned Monophysitism and declared Christ was possessed of both a human and a divine nature. What had necessitated this council was Pope Leo I's denunciation of the so-called Robber Council at Ephesus (449) for having endorsed the Monophysite views of Dioscurus of Alexandria and Eutyches, and his insistence that the emperor convene another council to undo this heresy. The council at Chalcedon accepted Leo's position concerning the nature of Christ and condemned Eutyches, but the canon it had decreed giving primacy in the Eastern church to Constantinople evoked the pope's anathema.

CHALCONDYLES (Chalcocondylas), DEMETRIUS, d. 1511, Greek grammarian who fled Greece in 1447 and joined Cardinal Bessarion's circle of humanists in Italy. He edited several Greek works including Homer's poems, prepared a Greek grammar which served as a standard textbook, and taught Greek and Platonic philosophy in several Italian cities. Reuchlin, Poliziano, and Linacre were among his pupils.

CHALCONDYLES (Chalcocondylas), LAONICUS, d. c. 1490, Byzantine scholar who wrote a history covering the events of the years 1298 to 1463 in a style he hoped would be suggestive of Thucydides. He prefaced the central theme of his history, which was the rise of Ottoman power, with a survey of the role of the Greeks in world affairs. Despite inaccuracies and the interpolation of strange anecdotes, he is considered one of the most important of the late Greek historians.

CHALDEAN CHRISTIANS, name given to Nestorians who were reunited with the Latin church.

CHALICE, vessel used in the celebration of the Christian eucharistic service. In the early centuries ordinary drinking vessels were used, from the ninth century only precious metals were permitted.

CHALID IBN-WALID. *See* KHALID IBN AL-WALID.

CHÂLON-SUR-MARNE, city in the county of Champagne in northeastern France which became a bishop's seat in the third or fourth century and a flourishing trading center in the twelfth. It was ruled by its bishops who were peers of France. It was here, or near here, that Attila and the Huns suffered defeat in 451.

CHÂLONS, BATTLE OF, battle fought in 451 between Attila and an army composed of Romans, Visigoths, Franks, and Burgundians under command of Aetius at Mauriacus near Troyes. Attila and his Huns suffered a sharp though not disastrous reverse and withdrew back to Hungary.

CHALUMEAU, wooden wind instrument that may be considered the forerunner of the clarinet.

CHAMBER, KING'S, in Frankish and Anglo-Saxon countries the first royal financial office. It was originally simply the king's bedchamber where he kept his valuables, records, documents, and equipment. As the king's resources increased in volume and variety and the need for additional depositories arose, a central royal treasury, called exchequer in England, tended to assume major reponsibility for managing the realm's fiscal business. Where feudal traditions prevailed, as in England, the chamber might retain an identity of its own, acquire administrative and secretarial functions directly subject to

the king's discretion, and even a privy seal. In England, after periods of growth and decline, the chamber rose to a position of major importance during the reign of Henry VII when its treasurer became the leading financial officer of the crown.

CHAMBERLAIN, in Carolingian times a royal official in charge of the king's household who was usually his treasurer as well as one of his principal advisers. In France where the office of chamberlain (*grand chambrier de France*) was held by a great noble, its functions became purely honorary in time. Meanwhile the position of one of the chamberlains had grown so important by the thirteenth century that he was recognized as a great officer of the state. The chamberlain in England after the Norman conquest had charge of the administration of the royal household. When the office became hereditary it lost much of its importance.

CHAMBRE DES COMPTES, financial administrative branch of the French government which began to emerge during the thirteenth century and became an established institution during the reign of Philip IV (1285–1314). It was located in Paris.

CHAMPAGNE, French county that lay east of the Ile-de-France and north of the duchy of Burgundy. It derived its name from the great plains in the region of Reims, Châlon-sur-Marne, and Troyes, although Reims remained outside the jurisdiction of its count. The union of the countships of Meaux and Vermandois about the middle of the tenth century provided Champagne its nucleus, although its first count was Eudes II of Blois who assumed that title early in the eleventh century. The two following centuries saw Champagne at the height of its power and wealth, a period ushered in by Thibaut IV of Blois who became its count in 1125 and terminated by Louis X of France (1314–6). Louis inherited the county through his mother, its heiress, and joined it to the French crown upon his accession in 1314. What brought Champagne most fame, apart from its powerful counts, were its fairs (at Lagny, Bar-sur-Aube, Provins, Troyes) which met six times a year and enjoyed great popularity by virtue of the county's location on the roads connecting Germany, Flanders, Provence, and Italy. These fairs suffered sharp decline in the late thirteenth and early fourteenth centuries when trade, particularly that between Flanders and Italy, began to travel by different routes. Champagne was also known as one of the most cultured regions of France.

CHAMPART, right of the lord to a share in the fruit crops of his serfs' lands.

CHAMPION, in judicial parlance a knight who represented women or minors in trial by combat as well as men who lacked the means or skill to do their own fighting. A champion might also represent members of the clergy, even corporations.

CHANCA ÁLVAREZ, DIEGO, a Spanish physician who accompanied Columbus on his second voyage to America (1493–96) and left a description of the voyage and what he found in the new world.

CHANCEL, part of the church near the altar that was originally marked off by a screen (cancellus) or low railing that separated it from the nave or main part of the church.

CHANCELLOR, title held by various officials in the Middle Ages including the secretaries (notaries) of noblemen and kings in Frankish times, the head of the exchequer in England from the thirteenth century, and the principal administrator in certain universities. The chancellor who served the king was ordinarily a bishop selected for his knowledge of law and public affairs. [See CHANCERY.]

CHANCERY, area or place marked off by barriers (cancelli) in which official documents, judgements, rescripts, and similar judicial records were stored and processed. Chanceries or chancery courts were maintained by kings, popes, bishops, and members of the aristocracy, as well as by cities. In Germany the highest administrative and judicial bureau was called a chancery. In the Roman law court the cancellarius was the name of the official who stood at the bar or screen that separated the magistrate from the public. In time this official acquired the functions of a secretary or notary. [See CHANCELLOR.]

CHANCERY, APOSTOLIC (Papal), name given to the office in the papal Curia which was staffed by clerks who advised the pope, prepared documents, handled correspondence, and kept archives. Pope Gregory the Great (590–604) organized the members into a college.

CHANDOS, JOHN, d. 1370, English military captain, charter member of the Order of the Garter, who saved the life of the Black Prince at the battle of Poitiers (1356). In 1364 he captured Bertrand du Guesclin at the battle of Auray, and did so again later in 1367 at Navarete. In the end, he died of wounds sustained in a battle against the same Bertrand du Guesclin.

CHANNEL ISLANDS (Norman Isles), the islands of Jersey, Guernsey, Alderney, Sark, and others, off the coast of Normandy in the English Channel. The inhabitants accepted Christianity in the sixth century. In the tenth century the islands passed under the rule of the duke of Normandy and, therefore, were joined to England when William the Conqueror became king there in 1066. The French failed in several attempts during the period of the Hundred Years' War to reestablish control.

CHANSON, in Old French poetry an epic poem that was sung, such as the chansons de geste; in a more restricted use of the term a several-voiced French song generally about love or drinking.

CHANSON DE ROLAND. See ROLAND, CHANSON DE.

CHANSONS DE GESTE, Old French epics of the twelfth and thirteenth centuries which embodied legends that had grown up around heroic figures from the past such as Charlemagne and William of Orange. [*See* EPIC POETRY.]

CHANTELAGE, tax on wine levied by a lord or a town.

CHANTICLEER, the name of the cock in the *Roman de Renart* cycle and in the *Canterbury Tales.*

CHANT ROYAL, medieval French verse form that was employed especially when dealing with allegorical subjects. It consisted originally of a poem of 5 stanzas of 8 or 16 lines but had no refrain. The *chant royal* appeared in the fifteenth century.

CHANTRY, the endowment established to pay for the saying of masses usually for the benefit of the soul of the donor; a chapel or altar where such masses were said. While the erection of chantries and the endowment of chantry priests date from the early Middle Ages, it was only in the fourteenth and fifteenth centuries that chantries became common.

CHAPEL, place of worship or oratory in royal and episcopal residences. The name had its origin in *cappella,* diminutive of *cappa* (cloak), the term used to identify the shrine that enclosed the cloak of St. Martin of Tours. The name was given to any shrine that contained relics, e.g., Sainte Chapelle in Paris which Louis IX erected to enshrine the crown of thorns, and to places of worship that were not mother churches.

CHAPERON, a medieval cap worn by both sexes that enclosed head and neck; a jacket to which such a hood was attached.

CHAPLAIN, from the Latin *capellanus* or clerk who was in charge of the famous half-cloak of St. Martin of Tours. [*See* CHAPEL.] Relics were also given into the care of chaplains. During the Merovingian and Carolingian periods they acquired new importance by working with the royal notaries, keeping records, then serving as

advisers to the crown in both secular and ecclesiastical matters. They also rose to hold the highest offices in the government. Partly to reward chaplains for their services, partly to transfer the cost of their maintenance to the church, kings often had them appointed bishops.

CHAPTER, name given to corporate ecclesiastical bodies, principally assemblies of monks, who read a chapter of their particular monastic rule when they met in formal session before passing on to the business of the day. An assembly of representatives from the monasteries or a province was known as a provincial chapter, that composed of representatives of an entire order, a general chapter.

CHAPTER HOUSE, chamber or building attached to a monastery or cathedral where the chapter gathered to hold its meetings.

CHAPTER OF FAULTS, gathering of members of a religious community at regularly appointed times when individual members confessed transgressions of the rule. The practice that has been traced to the third century became traditional in Eastern monasteries from the fourth, in the West from the ninth.

CHARADRIUS, according to medieval bestiaries a white bird which healed a person of his malady by itself absorbing it and then taking it to the sun.

CHARLEMAGNE, name traditionally given to Charles (the Great), king of the Franks, 768–814, the son of Pepin III (the Short) and father of Louis the Pious. (His brother Carloman shared his rule of the Frankish kingdom from 768 until his death in 771.) Charlemagne's conquests which earned him his principal fame occupied him for the greater part of his career although from c. 800 he was content to defend, rather than extend, his frontiers. He subjugated the stubborn Saxons, destroyed the Lombard and Avar nations, secured the submission of the Slavs between the Elbe and Oder and the

Czechs, and extended his authority south of the Pyrenees over the Spanish March. It was the attack of the Basques on his baggage train as he was retreating north through the pass at Roncesvalles that furnished the historical germ for the *Chanson de Roland.*

In his wars Charlemagne considered himself the instrument of God in defending or advancing the faith, a responsibility he judged as much his as that of ruling his empire. For this reason he issued capitularies on religious reform, even on liturgy and theology, as freely as he did on judicial and military matters. Although he paid the pope the greatest reverence and in his behalf confirmed the Donation of Pepin, he considered the pope his subject, and for this reason some scholars believe Charlemagne was annoyed when Pope Leo III crowned him Roman emperor (Christmas Day 800). Charlemagne may have feared that subsequent popes would point to this act as establishing their right to crown, even to approve, the emperor. [*See* HOLY ROMAN EMPIRE.]

Charlemagne probably planned to adopt the title Roman (Holy) emperor as more suitable than "king of the Franks" in ruling so far-flung an empire. In the administration of this empire he introduced no major innovations. He standardized the use of *missi dominici* and through them and his own immense prestige and power succeeded in restraining the counts and margraves. Perhaps the most enduring phase of his work, since his empire disintegrated within a century of his death, was the encouragement he gave to learning. [*See* CAROLINGIAN RENAISSANCE.]

CHARLES (II) THE BALD, king of the West Franks, 843–77, son of Louis the Pious by his second wife Judith, who received the western third of the Carolingian empire in the tripartite division agreed to at Verdun in 843. Warfare cursed much of his reign. His magnates demanded lands and autonomy, Vikings harassed the northern and western frontiers, his brother Louis the German invaded his realm in 858, while his own ambitions seldom let him rest for long. He divided Lotharingia with Louis in 870 (Treaty of Mersen) and in 875 received the imperial crown from Pope John VIII. Most constructive was the support he lent the church and the considerable encouragement he gave to learning.

CHARLES (III) THE FAT, Frankish king and emperor, youngest son of Louis the German. Already king of Swabia and Italy, he was crowned emperor in 881 by Pope John VIII, became king of the East Franks in 882, then of the West Franks in 884, thereby reuniting the Carolingian empire (with the exception of Burgundy). But Charles was incompetent and weak, perhaps an epileptic as well. He fought unsuccessful campaigns against the Saracens in Italy and in 886 bought off the Vikings who were attacking Paris. This last show of weakness led the East Franks to repudiate his authority (887) and swear allegiance to Arnulf, his nephew, an act which marked the final dissolution of the Carolingian empire. Charles died in 888.

CHARLES IV, king of Germany, 1346–78, and Holy Roman Emperor, eldest son of John of Luxemburg, king of Bohemia. He fought at Crécy in 1346, that same year was chosen king of Germany by those princes who opposed Louis IV, then succeeded Louis IV when he died in 1347. (He was already king of Bohemia.) In 1355 he crossed into Italy and received the imperial crown from the pope. His most important act was the promulgation in 1356 of the Golden Bull which established the procedure to be observed in the election of the German king. Charles, who made Prague his capital, greatly enlarged Bohemia with the acquisition of Silesia, Brandenburg, and other lands. In 1348 he founded Charles University in Prague.

CHARLES (III) THE SIMPLE, king of France (West Franks), 893–923, ruled from Laon but with little actual authority. In 911 he granted

Rollo (Hrolf the Ganger), leader of the Vikings, possession of the territory near the mouth of the Seine which later became known as Normandy. A revolt of some of his magnates in 923 led to his capture and he died in prison (929).

CHARLES IV (the Fair), king of France, 1322–8, third son of Philip IV and the last Capetian ruler of the direct line. He succeeded his brother Philip V who had left only daughters. Troubles with England which filled his reign led shortly to the coming of the Hundred Years' War (1337–1453). His death without male issue brought his cousin Philip (VI) of Valois, a nephew of Philip IV, to the throne.

CHARLES V (the Wise), king of France, 1364–80, son of John II, agreed to the Treaty of Brétigny with England (1360) in the name of his father who had been captured in the disastrous defeat suffered at Poitiers (1356). During his reign Louis brought France from the threshold of anarchy and reestablished it as the leading power of Europe. He put down the *Jacquerie,* next a revolt of Parisian merchants led by Etienne Marcel, then with the help of captains like Bertrand du Guesclin expelled the English from the continent except for their footholds in the seaports of Bayonne, Bordeaux, and Calais. In order to strengthen France's eastern frontier he arranged a marriage between his brother Philip, duke of Burgundy, and the heiress of Flanders. It was his support of Clement VII, the Avignonese pope, that assured the coming of the Western Schism.

CHARLES VI (the Mad), king of France, 1380–1422, whose years of minority reign, followed by intermittent periods of insanity (from 1392), spawned a dangerous rivalry between two factions that sought control of the government, one headed by his brother Louis, duke of Orléans, and known as the Orléanist (later Armagnac), the other by his uncle Philip the Bold, duke of Burgundy. After the overwhelming defeat of the French at Agincourt

(1415), John the Fearless, the new duke of Burgundy, sought to reach an agreement with the Dauphin (later Charles VII), son of Charles VI, but was murdered in the act of making his obeisance. This crime prompted John's son, Philip the Good, to ratify the Treaty of Troyes (1420) with the English which disinherited the Dauphin and proclaimed Henry V of England the regent of France and the successor of Charles VI.

CHARLES VII (the Well-Served), king of France, 1422–61, son of Charles VI, who as dauphin was deprived of his right of succession by the Treaty of Troyes (1420). From his headquarters at Bourges he managed to maintain a measure of royal authority south of the Loire where he enjoyed the support of the Armagnacs. His own lack of resolution together with the conflicting advice of his counselors left him inactive and his cause became progressively more desperate until the appearance of Joan of Arc. She drove the English from Orléans which they had under siege and opened the way to Reims where the dauphin was crowned (Charles VII) on 17 July, 1429. In 1435 Charles weaned the Burgundians from their alliance with the English (Treaty of Arras), reorganized the army with financial help from Jacques Coeur and the Estates General, then proceeded to bring the Hundred Years' War to a successful conclusion. In 1438 he strained relations with the papacy by approving the Pragmatic Sanction of Bourges with its affirmation of the liberties of the Gallican Church.

CHARLES VIII, king of France, 1483–98, son of Louis XI, whose marriage to Anne of Brittany assured the absorption of that territory into the royal domain. Until 1492 his sister Anne and her husband Pierre de Bourbon, seigneur de Beaujeu, ruled in his name. Charles's expedition to Italy in 1494–5 which he undertook to make good his claim to the kingdom of Naples ended in his precipitate retreat.

CHARLES I, king of Naples and Sicily,

1268–85, brother of Louis IX of France, secured the countships of Anjou, Maine, and Provence, and in 1265, upon request of the pope, led an army into Italy for the purpose of extinguishing Hohenstaufen rule in the Italian peninsula and Sicily. This he accomplished with victories over Manfred, son of Frederick II, at Benevento (1266) and over Conradin, son of Conrad IV, at Tagliacozzo (1268). His dream of a Mediterranean empire faded, however, when the Sicilians revolted in 1282 (Sicilian Vespers) and drove him from the island. Peter III of Aragon, the husband of Manfred's daughter Constance, took over the rule of Sicily.

CHARLES D'ORLÉANS, d. 1465, son of Louis, duc d'Orléans, and nephew of Charles VI, the last and one of the greatest of the court poets of France. He was captured at the battle of Agincourt (1415) and spent 25 years in honorable imprisonment in England. He was the father of Louis XII.

CHARLES MARTEL (the Hammer), d. 741, son of Pepin of Heristal, succeeded as mayor of the palace of both Austrasia and Neustria in 714 despite his illegitimate birth. He gained victories over the Frisians, Saxons, Alemanni, Bavarians, and Aquitanians. His most renowned exploit was his defeat of the Moors at Tours in 732. His achievements prepared the foundations for the Carolingian empire of which his son Pepin III (the Short) was the first king. Charles encouraged St. Boniface and other missionaries in their efforts to convert the German tribes across the Rhine whom he had subjugated.

CHARLES THE BOLD (Rash), duke of Burgundy, 1467–77, son of Philip the Good, whose ambitious plan to establish a middle kingdom between France and Germany was thwarted by Louis XI with the help of the Swiss. For a time Charles appeared within reach of his objective after forcing Louis to return the towns on the Somme which his father had surrendered, and negotiating an alliance with Edward IV of England. His aggressions in the Rhineland, however, alienated Frederick III of Germany and also aroused Edward's suspicions who came to terms with Louis (Treaty of Picquigny). Following two earlier defeats, Charles was slain by the Swiss at the battle of Nancy. His daughter Mary married Maximilian who later became king of Germany and Holy Roman Emperor. [*See* BURGUNDY, DUCHY OF.]

CHARLES THE GREAT. *See* CHARLEMAGNE.

CHARNEL HOUSE, name given in the Middle Ages to a structure, often attached to a church and even serving as a chantry chapel, where bones were buried which the digging of new graves had uncovered.

CHARONTON (Quarton), ENGUERRAND, fl. c. 1447–61, Provençal painter of the late Gothic whose style reveals a uniting of Flemish and Italian influences. Among his paintings is *Virgin of Mercy*.

CHARRUAGE, tax imposed by the lord on his peasants for the use of his plows.

CHARTER, a grant or franchise of specified rights or privileges given by a king (lord) to an individual, corporation, or nation, e.g., Magna Carta.

CHARTERHOUSE, English corruption of Chartreuse or "House of the Carthusians," a term used to designate an English Carthusian monastery. The house founded in London in 1371 just west of Aldersgate was the best known of such houses. It was ordered dissolved in 1535.

CHARTIER, ALAIN, d. c. 1433, French poet, political writer, secretary to Charles VI and Charles VII, who composed verse in both French and Latin. For many years aspiring poets and prose writers used his style as a model. His poems consisted in the main of allegories in the courtly tradition; his prose reflected the broad interests of a historian, pamphleteer, and moralist.

CHARTRES, city some 50 miles southwest of

Paris whose site was occupied in both Celtic and Roman times. It became a bishopric in the fourth century, suffered sacking by the Burgundians c. 600 and by the Vikings in 858, but withstood a second assault in 911. Its counts ruled Blois and Champagne from the tenth century until 1286 when it passed under direct royal control and received a charter. Its cathedral, possibly the most distinguished of all Gothic churches and especially famed for its two lofty towers, stained glass, and sculpture, was begun in 1195 and completed c. 1230.

CHARTRES, SCHOOL OF, center of learning founded by Fulbert who was bishop of the city from 1006 to 1028. It gained fame first for the high character of its classical studies, then for its instruction in dialectic. Among its renowned teachers in the twelfth century were Bernard, his younger brother Thierry, and, above all, Gilbert de la Porrée.

CHARTREUSE, LA GRANDE, mother house of the Carthusian order, founded in a desolate valley of the Alps near Grenoble by Bruno in 1084. It took its name from the neighboring mountains of Chartreuse. When an avalanche destroyed the original monastery in 1132, a second was erected about a mile away.

CHARTULARY (cartulary), medieval register or volume containing muniments, deeds, and official documents relating to the foundation, property, rights, and privileges of an institution (college, monastery, municipal corporation).

CHASINI (Chazini), ABU-L-FATH 'ABD AR-RAHMAN AL-, Arab astronomer and student of physics of the early twelfth century who composed the most advanced work to appear in the Middle Ages on the subjects of mechanics, hydrostatics, and physics.

CHASTELLAIN (Chastelain, Châtelain), GEORGES, d. 1475, chronicler who was attached to the household of Philip the Good, duke of Burgundy. His history, which reveals a Burgundian bias, covers the years 1419–74.

CHASTITY BELT, a contrivance worn by wives between the upper thighs to which the husband kept the key. It was an invention of Francesco Carrarra (1395).

CHASUBLE, large outermost vestment worn since the ninth century by the priest or celebrant at mass.

CHATEAU, royal or seignorial residence and stronghold of medieval France. During the course of the fifteenth and sixteenth centuries, the chateau gradually sloughed off its defensive characteristics for those of a residence.

CHATEAU-GAILLARD, formidable castle built (1196–8) by Richard I of England that overlooked the Seine near Vexin. Its construction at that location became critical to the defense of Normandy once Vexin had been surrendered to the French. Its location on a high spur of rock overlooking the river left only the southern end open to attack. Philip II Augustus took it from King John in 1204 after a prolonged siege.

CHÂTELAINE, a chain attached to a woman's belt from which ornaments or such items as keys might be suspended. It was worn in the late Middle Ages.

CHATIB, title of the prayer leader who directed the Friday service in the mosque.

CHAUCER, GEOFFREY, d. 1400, medieval England's leading poet, the son of a prosperous London vintner, fought with Edward III's army in France and was captured and ransomed (1359). His marriage to Philippa, a sister of John of Gaunt's third wife Catherine Swynford, opened the door to a successful career as courtier, diplomat, even membership in parliament (1386). In a period politically unstable whose vicissitudes few men survived, he was a recipient of pensions from Edward III, Richard II, and Henry IV. He was buried in Westminster

Abbey. Apart from a few prose pieces, including a translation of Boethius's *Consolation of Philosophy,* his immense literary fame rests upon his poetry, above all on his *Canterbury Tales.* This literary masterpiece consisted of a Prologue (the most fascinating part of the poem) and the stories which twenty-four pilgrims exchanged when they stopped at Tabard Inn in Southwark on their way to the shrine of St. Thomas Becket in Canterbury. Those who had tales to tell included, among others, a knight, miller, prioress, monk, pardoner, friar, and wife of Bath.

CHAULIAC, GUY DE (Gui de Cauliaco), d. 1368, French surgeon, physician to the pope at Avignon, and author of a popular book on surgery. He was reputed to be one of the most learned men of his time.

CHELCICKY, PETER, d. c. 1460, lay Hussite theologian, political writer, and militant pacifist. He also condemned holding public office. His views, which he believed were those of John Wyclif and John Hus, helped inspire the doctrines of the Bohemian Brethren.

CHENOBOSKION, GNOSTIC TEXTS OF, a collection of 13 ancient Coptic manuscripts of the third and fourth centuries which throw valuable light on the Gnostic beliefs of that period. They were discovered c. 1945 near the site of Pachomius's monasteries.

CHERBOURG, channel port in Normandy which was occupied in Roman times. William the Conqueror contributed a hospital and a church to the community which Philip II Augustus later fortified to protect it from the English. The English did capture it in 1418 and held it until 1450.

CHERUBIM, in medieval Christian usage one of the highest orders of angelic spirits, ranked ordinarily after the seraphim. Theologians credited them with an intimate knowledge of God. In the *Apocalypse* they appear as celestial attendants.

CHESS, game involving a board and special pieces which probably originated in India in the seventh century whence it made its way to Europe by way of Persia and Islam.

CHESTER, English town on the Welsh border, fortified in Roman times and again from 907 during the Anglo-Saxon period. It was the last English city to yield to William the Conqueror. From 1071 to 1237 a series of powerful earls occupied Chester castle. Henry III took over the earldom and gave it to his son Edward (I) who used it in his conquest of Wales. The city was second in importance only to Bristol among the seaports on the west coast of Britain. Its trade was chiefly with Ireland. The town's earliest extant charter was that given to it by Henry II in 1176.

CHESTER, EARLDOM OF, English title first held by Hugh, viscount of Avranches (d. 1101), who received it from his kinsman William the Conqueror. Because of its vast holdings, the earldom was among the most powerful in England and enjoyed a semiregal status although it was not designated a county palatine until it came into possession of the crown. The most famous of the earls was Ranulf de Blundeville (d. 1232) who was duke of Brittany and earl of Richmond in right of his wife, Constance of Brittany. His loyalty to King John and to the young Henry III brought him the earldom of Lincoln. He took the cross in 1218. In 1254 Henry III conferred the earldom on his son Edward. Since 1301 the heir apparent to the English throne has held the title.

CHESTER PLAYS, a cycle of religious pageants presented at Chester, probably from the early fifteenth century.

CHEVAGE, personal tax which the serf (villein) owed his lord. His wife might pay a smaller tax.

CHEVALIER, originally the French word for horseman which acquired the meaning of knight with the evolution of chivalry. It was also a title given to members of the lower French nobility.

CHEVALIER SANS PEUR ET SANS REPROCHE, that is, knight without fear or reproach, a laudatory title bestowed upon several medieval knights.

CHEVET, an enlarged apse which contained a number of concentric chapels, a feature of the great Romanesque and Gothic churches. The term might also apply to the ambulatory to the rear and sides of the main altar in such a church, even to the entire choir. The chevet was most common to French cathedrals. Because of the problem of vaulting the apse when enlarged in this manner, the chevet provided an incentive toward the evolution of the ribbed and pointed vault.

CHEVY CHASE, a hunt in the Cheviot mountains described in an English ballad of the fifteenth century entitled *The Ballad of Chevy Chase*. The rivalry between the two families described in the ballad symbolized that between England and Scotland.

CHICHELE, HENRY, d. 1443, archbishop of Canterbury (1414) and cofounder with Henry VI of All Souls College, Oxford. He attended Oxford, served as royal proctor in Rome, was consecrated bishop of St. David's (1408), and represented the English bishops at the Council of Pisa (1409). As archbishop of Canterbury, he proved himself an efficient administrator and labored zealously to suppress the last traces of Lollardy in the southern province. His vicar general was the distinguished canonist William Lyndwood.

CHICHESTER, city in Sussex whose origins went back to Celtic times. The South Saxon kings had their mint in this city. In 1135 Chichester received a charter from King Stephen which authorized it to establish what may have been the oldest merchant guild in England. The wool trade made the town commercially important through the Middle Ages. The cathedral (twelfth-thirteenth century) has a detached bell tower.

CHICHESTER, DIOCESE OF, a suffragan diocese of the province of Canterbury, largely coterminous with Sussex, which became a see in 1082 when it replaced the old South Saxon see of Selsey. Selsey had become a diocese late in the seventh century.

CHIGI, AGOSTINO "IL MAGNIFICO," d. 1520, member of the Chigi banking house, patron of humanism, papal treasurer under Pope Alexander VI and his immediate successors, and owner of one of the richest business houses in Europe.

CHILDEBERT I, son of Clovis I, received the northern part of the Frankish realm upon the division of his father's Merovingian kingdom and ruled from Paris from 511 until his death in 558. He murdered the sons of his brother Clodomir and annexed Chartres and Orléans, and later increased his realm at the expense of Burgundy, the Visigoths, and Ostrogoths.

CHILDEBERT II, son of Sigibert I and Brunhild, reigned as king of Austrasia (575–95) after the death of his father, and of Burgundy (593–5) after the death of Guntram, his uncle, although largely under the guidance of his mother.

CHILDERIC I, d. 481, obscure Merovingian king of the Salian Franks, the father of Clovis I. He fought the Visigoths as an ally of the Roman general Aegidius, and later defeated the Saxons and Alemanni.

CHILDERIC II, son of Clovis II, reigned as king of Austrasia from 662 to 675 and for a time, from 673 to 675, over all the Franks and the entire Merovingian kingdom. Members of the aristocracy of Neustria resented his efforts to exercise real authority and murdered him.

CHILDERIC III, last of the Merovingian kings who already for a century had been simply *rois fainéants* (do-nothing kings). His reign extended from 743 to 751 when Pepin, the mayor of the palace, confined him in the monastery of

Sithiu and had himself elected king of the Franks.

CHILDERMAS, Old English name for the Feast of the Holy Innocents (Dec. 28), also for the day of the week throughout the year on which the feast fell. This was widely held to be a day of ill omen.

CHILDREN'S CRUSADE. *See* CRUSADE, CHILDREN'S.

CHILLENDEN, THOMAS, d. 1411, Benedictine monk, prior of Christ's Church in Canterbury, who proved himself an able administrator and gained renown as a builder. He employed Henry Yevele to rebuild the nave of the cathedral in Canterbury.

CHILPERIC I, king of Neustria (Merovingian France), 561–84, whom Gregory of Tours denounced as the Nero and Herod of the age. He murdered his brother Sigibert, king of Austrasia and husband of Brunhild, and his own wife Galswintha, the sister of Brunhild, probably upon the urging of his mistress Fredegund whom he then married. He showed a curious interest in poetry, grammar, and theology.

CHIMES, set of bells, suspended from a bar which were introduced into Europe in the ninth century. Tower chimes, usually controlled from a clock, made their appearance in Flanders and Holland in the fourteenth century.

CHIMNEY. Until the twelfth century the usual means of heating was the burning woodpile in the center of the room with an aperture in the roof to let out the smoke. The fireplace with hood and a flue to the outside appeared about the twelfth century. As fireplaces developed and steadily improved in efficiency and design, the visible part of the chimney often became an important architectural feature in the homes of the wealthy. Late medieval fireplaces might be of great size and richness. An example is the triple fireplace in the great hall of the Palais des Comtes at Poitiers.

CHINON, city in Touraine near Tours where the Dauphin, later Charles VII, made his residence after being disinherited by the Treaty of Troyes (1420). The castle there had earlier served as a favorite residence of Henry II of England and his wife Eleanor of Aquitaine.

CHIOGGIA, WAR OF, war (1378–81) between whose origins reached back to Roman times. It became a bishop's see in 1106 and from about the same time a commercial rival of Venice until the defeat of the Genoese fleet nearby in 1378–81. (Genoa was its ally.)

CHIOGGIA, WAR OF, war (1378–81) between Venice and Genoa, the two leading maritime powers of Europe at that time. The war, which took place near the small island of Chioggia at the southern end of the Venetian lagoons, ended with the surrender of the Genoese fleet and its some 4,000 men whom the Venetians had managed to trap at the mouth of a canal. Genoa never recovered from this defeat.

CHI RHO MONOGRAM, a symbolic representation of the name of Christ that consisted of the first two letters of the Greek word.

CHIROTHECAE, liturgical gloves used by bishops and abbots since the tenth century.

CHIVALRY, the institution of knighthood; the ideals and practices associated with medieval knighthood. The ideals to which knights were expected to aspire were prowess, loyalty to one's lord, generosity, courtesy, and service (to God, church, and society). Factors contributing to the evolution of these ideals included the preaching of the church, such decrees as the Peace and Truce of God, the Crusades, and the influence of courtly and troubadour literature.

CHLOTHAR (Clotaire) I, youngest son of Clovis I, ruled as king from Soissons over his part of the Frankish kingdom, roughly what came to be called Neustria, from 511, then, after the deaths of his brothers and their sons (c. 558), over all the realm until his own demise in 561. Wars cursed the greater part of his reign, now with his brothers and nephews, then principally with the Burgundians, Visigoths, Saxons, Bavarians, and Thuringians. Like the majority of these Merovingian rulers, he was cruel and treacherous.

CHLOTHAR (Clotaire) II, son of Chilperic I and Fredegund, ruled as king of Neustria from 584 and over the entire Frankish kingdom from 613 until his death in 629. It was he, in alliance with the Austrasian aristocracy, who captured and executed Brunhild. Chlothar reigned rather than ruled. His son Dagobert (d. 639) was the last Merovingian king who retained some semblance of power. The real ruler of the Frankish (Merovingian) kingdoms had become the mayor of the palace.

CHLOTILDA. See CLOTILDE.

CHODI, Czech peasants who were settled in the Bohemian forest in the eleventh and twelfth centuries for the purpose of protecting the frontier.

CHOIR, that part of the church where the stalls of the clergy were located, usually in the eastern end of the nave near the altar; a body of singers organized and trained for liturgical services. Congregational singing was probably common in Christian churches until about the sixth century when women were forbidden to participate. Gradually a select group of clerical singers emerged with the growth of monastic and cathedral communities, especially after the introduction of *organum* and counterpoint. The leader of the choir was the precentor, his assistant the succentor. [See SCHOLA CANTORUM.]

CHOIR BISHOP, a bishop of the Eastern church of the early centuries who administered a country district and was wholly subject to the authority of the diocesan bishop. They were numerous in the fourth century, especially so in Asia Minor. Their rights and functions were progressively restricted and by the thirteenth century they had disappeared. The name was also used in the Frankish kingdom from the eighth to the close of the tenth century for the bishop who assisted the diocesan bishop.

CHOIR CHAPEL, chapel located near the choir and provided with altars for the convenience of members of the community who wished to say mass. In time such chapels were reserved for the use of individual families and guilds.

CHOIR STOOL, originally a long bench, later an individual wooden seat arranged in rows on both sides of the choir and occupied by members of the clergy during liturgical services.

CHONIATES, MICHAEL, d. c. 1220, metropolitan of Athens whose homilies, correspondence, and poetry throw light on medieval Athens, also on the seriously weakened condition of the empire just before its collapse in the Fourth Crusade (1202–4).

CHONIATES, NICETAS, d. 1213, the most important Byzantine historian after Psellus. He served as imperial secretary, provincial governor, and grand logothete under Isaac II Angelus. Beyond his history, which covers the period from 1118 to 1206, he left speeches, poems, and some theological works.

CHORISANTES, name given to fanatical groups of wandering men and women who indulged in frenzied, often obscene, dances which they credited to spiritual inspiration. Such groups appeared intermittently throughout the Middle Ages.

CHOSROES (Khosrau) I ANUSHIRVAN, Persian emperor, 531–79, most powerful of the Sassanid rulers, encouraged industry and trade and was renowned for his sense of justice and for the magnificence of his capital at Ctesiphon. For more than twenty years his armies waged heavy but indecisive warfare with those of the Byzantine emperor Justinian.

CHOSROES (Khosrau) II PARVEZ, Persian emperor, 590–628, grandson of the great

Chosroes I, gained the throne with the assistance of the Byzantine emperor Maurice, then invaded Byzantium when Maurice was slain in order to avenge his death. After early successes, Chosroes suffered severe defeats at the hands of Heraclius, the Byzantine emperor. He was finally deposed and murdered.

CHOYSNET (Choinet), PIERRE, d. 1476, physician and astrologer of Louis XI of France and author of a manual on education which he composed for the instruction of the dauphin.

CHRÉTIEN DE TROYES, d. before 1190, author of five Arthurian romances including *Erec, Cligès,* and *Yvain*. His *Tristan* is lost. Chrétien is considered the principal representative, and perhaps inspiration, of the composers of the (courtly) romance.

CHRISM, mixture of olive oil and balsam which was blessed by a bishop and used in the administering of such sacraments as baptism and confirmation, and when the liturgy called for sacred anointing. It was not used in anointing the sick. Because of the strength-giving richness of the oil and the fragrance of the balsam, representing the fullness of sacramental grace and the gifts of the Holy Spirit, chrism was a favorite subject of allegorical interpretation.

CHRISMAL (chrismatory), the cloth covering in which relics were wrapped; the pall, altar cloth, or vessel that held the eucharist; the white-hooded robe worn by the newly baptized.

CHRISMATORY, small vessel used for keeping the three kinds of holy oils: oil for catechumens, oil for the sick, and chrism.

CHRISMON, a Greek monogram or symbol of the name of Christ or of the cross. It often appeared at the beginning of medieval documents.

CHRISTIAN I, king of Denmark, 1448–81, duke of Schleswig-Holstein, and founder of the house of Oldenburg. He ruled as king of Norway from 1450 and in Sweden from 1457 until 1471 although without any great measure of authority in the latter country. As a pledge of a dowry for his daughter Margaret who married James III of Scotland, he surrendered the Norwegian Orkneys and Shetlands as well as his sovereignty over the Hebrides and the Isle of Man. They were never redeemed. In 1479 he founded the University of Copenhagen.

CHRISTIAN KING, MOST (Most Christian Majesty), title used by French kings since 1464 and employed by popes in addressing them.

CHRISTIAN OF PRUSSIA, d. 1245, a Cistercian missionary bishop among the pagan Prussians. Because of the hostility of the Teutonic Knights who objected to his efforts in maintaining Prussian independence, he retired to a monastery in Poland.

CHRISTINE DE PISAN, d.c. 1430, French poetess of Italian descent who composed ballads in the courtly tradition, rondeaux, *complaintes,* a joyful poem about Joan of Arc, and a biography of Charles V. She grew up at the French court. When widowed, she took to composing poetry as a means of livelihood.

CHRISTMAS, feast commemorating the birth of Christ that came to be celebrated on December 25 at least as early as the year 336. It was on that day that pagans had honored the *Natalis Sol Invictus* and it may have been to neutralize that pagan feast that Christ's birth was assigned to it, the birth of the Sun of Righteousness. The Christological controversies of the fourth, fifth, and sixth centuries over the nature of Christ undoubtedly contributed to the growth of the importance of the feast.

CHRISTOPHER (Christophorus), Antipope, 903–4, a Roman who imprisoned Pope Leo V and had himself proclaimed pope, only to be seized and imprisoned by adherents of Bishop Sergius (later Pope Sergius III). Both Christopher and Leo were strangled in prison.

CHRISTOPHER III, king of Denmark and Sweden, 1440–8, and of Norway, 1442–8, who restored peace throughout Scandinavia while actively opposing the commercial penetration of the Hanseatic League. His death without issue brought the union of the three countries to an end.

CHRISTOPHER, ST., possibly a martyr during the persecution of Decius (249–51) to whom a church in Bithynia was dedicated in 452. He was one of the Fourteen Holy Helpers in need and honored as the patron of travelers. Of the many legends about Christopher, a favorite one tells how, being a veritable giant who made his living carrying travelers across a river, he found on one occasion that the weight of a small child forced him to his knees, the child being none other than the Christ Child.

CHRIST, ORDER OF THE KNIGHTS OF, papal order established in 1317 in Portugal and Spain and endowed with the wealth of the suppressed Knights Templars.

CHRISTUS, PETRUS, d. 1472 or 1473, Flemish painter, also known as Peter Christopher, a pupil of Jan van Eyck, who became the leader of the Bruges school after van Eyck's death. He painted with deep feeling and psychological insight, and with an interest in the accurate depiction of detail characteristic of van Eyck. The *Portrait of a Lady* is one of his best known pieces. Like Jan van Eyck, he added date and signature to some of his paintings.

CHRODEGANG OF METZ, d. 766, bishop (742) and archbishop (753) of Metz, chancellor to both Charles Martel and Pepin III, and papal legate to the kingdom of the Franks. He founded the monasteries of Gorze and Lorsch, two of the most renowned and influential in Germany. The daily gathering of his cathedral clergy for the purpose of reading a chapter of the monastic rule that he himself had drawn up, gave rise to the tradition of calling such a gathering a chapter.

CHROMATIUS, ST., d. 407, bishop of Aquileia, a learned scholar and a correspondent of such illustrious contemporaries as St. Jerome and Rufinus. He was a strong supporter of St. John Chrysostom but his earnest efforts to save that prelate from exile proved of no avail. He left homilies on the Scriptures.

CHRONICLE, a historical narrative of events, principally of political and ecclesiastical interest, arranged chronologically and often identified with a particular monastery, diocese, or town. Chronicles represented a more detailed and informative form of annals and, as opposed to history, avoided comment and analysis although at times expressing a high degree of independence in their treatment of personages and developments. Their compilers who were usually monks remained nameless for the most part until the twelfth century. Most influential in supplying the pattern that medieval chronicles followed, especially when beginning their narratives with the Creation and in viewing history as the story of man's salvation, were the historical works of Eusebius of Caesarea and Orosius and the *City of God* of St. Augustine. The wider horizon that the Crusades and the expansion of trade to Asia and into northern Europe brought within view of the monastic scribe made the period from the late twelfth century through the thirteenth the golden age of the medieval chronicle.

CHRONICLES AND MEMORIALS OF GREAT BRITAIN AND IRELAND DURING THE MIDDLE AGES, also known as the Rolls Series, a collection of source materials relating to the history of England in the Middle Ages. The first of some 250 volumes appeared in 1858.

CHRONICON EDESSENUM, a Syrian chronicle extending from 133 B.C. to A.D. 540 but with few entries prior to the third century A.D. It is concerned chiefly with Edessa but also supplies important incidental information pertinent to developments in both the Latin and Greek churches.

CHRONICON PASCHALE, Byzantine chronicle compiled in the early seventh century, so named from its having been based on the Easter reckoning. It covers in chronological order events from the Creation to 629. The last 27 years are most valuable since the author apparently lived during that period.

CHRONOGRAPHER OF A.D. 354, THE. The name by which Theodore Mommsen identified the unknown compiler of an almanac for use of the Christians in Rome in the fourth century. The document remains an invaluable source for the study of early ecclesiastical history.

CHRONOLOGY, CHRISTIAN, begins with the monk Dionysius Exiguus (fl. 496–540) who was the first writer to use the birth of Christ as the base year upon which to establish a calendar. What was most instrumental in spreading its use through the Christian world was the dating of Easter which proved a source of great controversy. Still it did not replace the use of the indiction in the papal chancery until the pontificate of John XIII (965–72). It was not adopted in most of Spain until the fourteenth century and in the Greek world not till the fifteenth. The most popular chronological unit used in the early Middle Ages was actually the indiction with its cycle of 15 years, reckoned from the accession of the emperor Constantine I in 312. Years were identified according to their place in the cycle of 15, although the number of the indiction itself was ignored. Kings and popes might supplement such dating with an indiction of the particular year of their reign or pontificate.

CHRYSOBERGES, ANDREW, d. 1451, a Greek who became a Roman Catholic and a Dominican friar and made his home in Padua where he taught philosophy. He served as papal legate to Constantinople and to the Council of Basel and was consecrated archbishop first of Rhodes, later of Nicosia.

CHRYSOLORAS, MANUEL, d. 1415, a leading humanist and founder of Greek studies in Italy. He made his first visit to Italy from Constantinople as an emissary of Emperor Manuel II Palaeologus to secure help for Byzantium against the Ottoman Turks. He was also interested in arranging a council of Latin and Greek theologians for the purpose of ending the schism. His principal achievement, however, was the knowledge of Greek that he brought to Italy and the immense enthusiasm he engendered there for Greek studies. He taught in Florence, Rome, and other Italian cities, drew up a Greek grammar, and translated Homer's works and Plato's *Republic* into Latin.

CHRYSOSTOM, LITURGY OF ST., the most popular liturgy used in the Eastern church and associated with the name of St. John Chrysostom.

CHRYSOSTOM, ST. JOHN. *See* JOHN CHRYSOSTOM, ST.

CHUMNUS NICEPHORUS, d. 1327, Byzantine scholar and statesman, principal minister of Emperor Andronicus II, and governor of Thessalonica. He left letters and orations on philosophical and religious subjects.

CHURCH AND STATE, the two institutions that dominated medieval society and were responsible for its spiritual and material advancement. Although strife frequently disrupted their relationship, they generally cooperated as partners in the work of God. The church consecrated the king and offered prayers for his well-being and that of the state; king and state protected churchmen and punished those who preached heresy.

The bitterness which on occasion disturbed relations between church and state rose not over the basic question whether one or the other was supreme. Most theologians and jurists subscribed to the principle laid down in the Gelasian Doctrine (494) that both church and state were divinely instituted, one to do God's work in the spiritual order, the order in the temporal. What did sow controversy was the difficulty in assigning precise limits to their respective jurisdictions, since rights and responsibilities did not fall in one or the other sphere as conveniently as implied in the Gelasian Doctrine.

By 494 when Pope Gelasius issued his doctrine, the position of the church had improved over what it had been under Constantine, the first Christian emperor (312–37). Constantine never admitted that in extending toleration to Christianity he was surrendering one tittle of the supreme and unlimited authority his pagan predecessors had exercised over men and affairs. His summons to Christian bishops to meet at Nicaea in 325 to resolve the issue raised by Arius was simply the act of a head of state anxious to allay strife. Constantine's successors in Constantinople generally adopted his position concerning the supremacy of the imperial authority in all matters, whether civil or spiritual. [See CAESAROPAPISM.]

The first firm voice to be raised in protest against this presumption to unlimited authority on the part of the state was that of St. Ambrose, bishop of Milan (d. 397), and he did so successfully, although a Roman emperor of a different sort than Theodosius would have ignored his pronouncement that in spiritual matters the church was supreme. Still it was circumstance, not Ambrose's protest, that in time invested the papacy with a position in the West somewhat akin to that outlined in the Gelasian Doctrine. The principal circumstance was the inability of the Byzantine emperor to enforce his will in Italy. Gregory the Great (590–604) was even obliged to assume the duties of a secular ruler in raising troops to defend Rome against the Lombards. Once popes had experienced this new independence from imperial authority, they sought to retain it, which they succeeded in doing with the assistance of the Franks [see DONATION OF PEPIN], although not without some uneasiness. Under Charlemagne (768–814), pope and church found themselves relegated to essentially the same position in the West as that held by patriarch and church in the Byzantine empire.

From the church's standpoint the situation improved under Louis the Pious (814–40), but shortly after both church and state succumbed before the destructive forces of feudalism. In the late tenth century, the state, in the person of the king of Germany, came to the church's rescue, reestablished the papacy, and supported a reform movement which, ironically, left a revitalized papacy under Gregory VII (1073–85) locked in fierce struggle with Henry IV over investiture. [See INVESTITURE CONTROVERSY.] This involved the most sensitive of all issues that aggravated church–state relations in the Middle Ages, namely, the question which of the two institutions should have the decisive voice in the selection of the bishop. A canonically elected bishop was the *sine qua non* of a healthy church, so reformers contended, while kings insisted quite as stoutly that their rule depended in large measure upon the loyalty of their ecclesiastical vassals. In 1122 both sides accepted the compromise hammered out at Worms, that while the election of the bishop was to be the church's prerogative, the man chosen must be acceptable to the king.

A century later, during the pontificate of Innocent III (1198–1216), the relationship between church and state again became a lively issue. Innocent who was an able and ambitious pope may have entertained the dream of welding Western Europe into a solid Christian commonwealth under his leadership. If he did, he did not press the plan; in fact, what limited success he experienced in dealing with the rulers of Europe came as a result of prudence on his part and of circumstance. Even he, the most powerful of medieval popes in the judgment of many scholars, found ecclesiastical weapons of excommunication and deposition ineffectual against John of England and Philip II Augustus of France until circumstances recommended to both men the wisdom of submitting to his demands.

The growing power of the state which Innocent III barely managed to contain revealed its true might at the turn of the fourteenth century. The issue that had Boniface VIII (1294–1303) fulminating against Edward I of England and Philip IV of France was the state's claim to the right to tax church property. Even a prudent and patient pope, which Boniface was not, could not have prevented these kings from establishing that claim. A broken Boniface, dying several weeks after his mistreatment at Anagni, symbolized the decisive defeat of the church in its thousand-year struggle with the state to maintain full jurisdiction over what it believed to be the spiritual sphere in human affairs. After 1300 there was no longer any contest.

Meanwhile jurists in the service of both church and state had been publishing treatises in support of the claims of their respective clients. These treatises supply an interesting backdrop to the contest between church and state, but little more. Even the arguments of William of Ockham and Marsilius of Padua, that the state assert its God-given right to supremacy over the church, passed kings by without comment. Later, when kings realized that a church dominated by a general council would prove less submissive than one guided by the pope, they washed their hands of conciliarism. By the close of the Middle Ages most kings were satisfied with their position vis-à-vis the church. What constituted a major obstacle to church reform in the late Middle Ages was, in fact, the powerful voice the state enjoyed in the affairs of the church.

CHURCHING OF WOMEN, a Christian ceremony, based upon the Mosaic rite of purification (Leviticus 12:6), which involved the blessing of women after childbirth. The ceremony is mentioned in a letter of St. Augustine of Canterbury to Pope Gregory the Great (590–604).

CHURCH YEAR, the organization of the year for the purpose of advancing and standardizing Christian worship. Basic to the division of the church year was the seven-day week beginning with Sunday, the Lord's day. The year itself was divided into five liturgical periods, that is, Advent, the beginning of the church year, Christmas-Epiphany season, Lent, Easter and Eastertide, and Pentecost and the period after Pentecost that extended to Advent. The major events in the life of Christ (Christmas, Easter, Ascension) and the descent of the Holy Spirit (Pentecost) provided the structure of the church year, but equally popular, if not more so, to the laity in particular, were the festivals dedicated to the commemoration of saints (angels), some of these universal such as Peter and Paul and the Fourteen Holy Helpers, others national or local in their appeal, e.g., George, Denis, Stanislaus.

CIBORIUM, a canopy of Byzantine origin that was placed over the altar; a chalice-shaped receptacle with lid for reserving the eucharist.

CID, EL, Arabic for "lord," Moorish name for the Spanish warrior and knight errant Rodrigo Diaz de Vivar. He is the central figure in the Spanish epic *Poema del Cid*. Rodrigo Diaz was born c. 1043, grew up at the court of Ferdinand I of Castile, and married a niece of Alfonso, king of Castile and Leon, who later exiled him for making an unauthorized attack on the Moorish kingdom of Toledo over which he had established a protectorate. For several years Rodrigo served the Moorish rulers of Saragossa, but in 1089 undertook his own conquest of the Moorish kingdom of Valencia. He died in Valencia in 1099. He was without question a military leader of remarkable ability as well as a shrewd and, at times, unprincipled, statesman. Despite their brilliance, his exploits had little impact on the course of Spanish history, although, coupled with his chivalry, courtesy, and generosity, they fired the popular imagination and made him a national hero.

CILICIA, mountainous region of southeast Asia Minor, part of the Byzantine empire and a bulwark against Arabic expansion northward. In

1080 Prince Reuben established a state generally known as Little Armenia. [*See* ARMENIA.] It cooperated with the neighboring Latin Kingdom of Jerusalem against the Turks but in 1375 fell to the Mamluks.

CILLI, ULRICH, COUNT OF, d. 1456, German magnate whom Emperor Sigismund made a prince of the empire in 1436. He served as regent of Bohemia in 1438 and was the virtual ruler of Hungary from 1453 until his murder.

CIMA, GIOVANNI BATTISTA, d. c. 1517, Venetian painter whose earlier works reflect the influence of Giovanni Bellini. A favorite subject of his was the Madonna.

CIMABUE, GIOVANNI (Cenni Di Pepi), d. after 1302, Italian painter of the Florentine school, mosaicist, and probably designer of stained glass windows. The frescoes that he and his assistants executed in the Upper Church of S. Francesco in Assisi are noteworthy for their scale and dramatic power. While respecting most of the old conventions in his work, he introduced a little naturalism in his treatment of heads and faces. His works mark a transition from the strictly formalized Byzantine style prevalent until then to the freer expression of the fourteenth century.

CINCTURE, kind of belt or cord that members of the clergy tied about their waists to confine the loose, flowing alb. It also bore the name of girdle.

CINGULUM MILITIAE (*militare*), belt that held the scabbard and with which the knight was girded on the occasion of his dubbing.

CINNAMUS, JOHN, fl. second half of the twelfth century, Byzantine historian who continued the *Alexiad* of Anna Comnena from 1118 to 1176. He was probably imperial secretary to Manuel I Comnenus (1143–80) and an eyewitness of the events that he recorded.

CINO DA PISTOIA (Cino Sigibuldi), d. 1336 or 1337, a lawyer of Pistoia and author of a number of legal treatises. He was also a poet and composed verse in the *dolce stil nuovo* genre which was suggestive of Petrarch. He was a friend of both Dante and Petrarch. Like Dante he entertained high hopes for Italian unification and peace following Henry VII's invasion of the peninsula.

CINQUE PORTS, a group of five port cities in Kent and Sussex (Sandwich, Dover, Hythe, Romney, Hastings) that were organized into an association during the reign of Edward the Confessor (1042–66) for the purpose of providing ships for the defense of the coast. Together with other towns in this area, they constituted the nucleus of the British royal navy until the fourteenth century. In return for this service, the towns enjoyed various privileges including exemption from taxation and freedom from certain laws governing other municipalities.

CINTRA, city of Portugal a few miles northwest of Lisbon which flourished as a Moorish center. After 1147 when Alfonso I captured the city, it became a favorite residence of the kings of Portugal. The ruins of the Moorish fortress remain, as well as those of an old royal palace and a monastery from the Middle Ages.

CIRCUMCELLIONS, militant bands of peasants of north Africa, especially of Numidia, in the fourth century, who vented their anger over social grievances on their Catholic neighbors. They were linked with the Donatists. Despite repressive measures taken against them, they survived into the fifth century.

CIRENCESTER, town near Gloucester of Roman origin which the Saxons captured in 577. Its fairs date from the early thirteenth century, from which time the town developed into an important center in the wool trade.

CISTER (sister), a stringed instrument which evolved from the earlier fiddle from the tenth to the twelfth century.

CISTERCIANS, monastic order founded by Robert of Molesme in 1098 at Citeaux (whence the name) in Burgundy. Because of the extensive administrative reorganization which Stephen Harding carried out while abbot (1109–33), he is honored as a second founder or co-founder. The aim of the order was to return to original Benedictine practice by introducing a greater degree of simplicity and eremitical solitude into traditional Benedictine monasticism. For this reason many Cistercian monasteries located themselves in unsettled regions where their presence encouraged the opening of extensive areas to settlement in western and eastern Europe. The Cistercians have also been credited with contributing to the advance of agricultural knowledge, particularly in the area of stock-raising. The order became the most popular of the twelfth century and counted some 500 houses by 1200 although it might well have foundered in its infancy but for the fame and prestige of St. Bernard of Clairvaux, its most distinguished member. Somewhat ironically, given Bernard's complete dedication to the monastic ideal, he influenced it by assuming a more active role in ecclesiastical and political affairs. In protest to the centralization of the Congregation of Cluny, the Cistercian rule left individual houses autonomous except for an annual visit by the abbot of the house that had founded them. Full legislative and judicial authority was vested in a general chapter, composed of the abbots of the order, which met annually at Citeaux.

CISTERCIAN NUNS, cloistered sisters who in general followed the monastic observances of Cistercian monks. The first community of nuns appeared c. 1120 at Tart, near Citeaux, although many such houses were simply Benedictine convents that had adopted Cistercian reforms.

CITEAUX, mother house of the Cistercian order located just south of Dijon in Burgundy. [See CISTERCIANS.]

CIVITATE DEI, De the *City of God*, title of St.

Augustine's best known work. Augustine opens the work with a defense of Christianity against its pagan critics, then presents with profound theological elaboration the history of God's plan for mankind. The book inspired most later medieval writers to propose a teleological approach in their analysis of history.

CIVITAVECCHIA, harbor city on the Tyrrhenian sea of Roman origin (Centumcellae), captured by the Saracens in 828, then given its medieval name by its inhabitants when they returned. It served as a base for the papal navy. Its arsenal was built by Bernini, the citadel by Bramante and Michelangelo.

CLAIRVAUX, ABBEY OF, monastery near Bar-sur-Aube in Champagne founded by St. Bernard in 1115. By the close of the Middle Ages there were 350 abbeys that owed their foundation to Clairvaux.

CLANVOWE, SIR THOMAS, fl. 1400, English courtier poet who is believed to have authored *The Boke of Cupide,* better known as *The Cuckoo and the Nightingale.* The two birds debate the power of love.

CLARE, the most powerful of the baronial families of England in the thirteenth century. Richard Fitz-Gilbert (d. c. 1090), who received some 170 lordships from William the Conqueror, was the founder of the house. One branch of the family, that headed by the earl of Pembroke, ended with Richard of Clare (Strongbow) (d. 1176) who had maintained a harsh rule over English-controlled Ireland. Richard de Clare, earl of Hertford and Gloucester, d. 1262, an extraordinarily wealthy and influential lord, shared with Simon de Montfort leadership of the baronial revolt against Henry III. His son Gilbert (Red Earl) married Joan, a daughter of Edward I. Their son, also a Gilbert, proved a moderating influence during the unstable reign of his uncle Edward II until slain in the battle of Bannockburn (1314). His death without issue led to the breakup of the vast holdings of the Clare family.

CLARENBAUD OF ARRAS, fl. 1130–70, French scholastic, representative of the school of Chartres, studied at Paris under Hugh of Saint-Victor and Thierry of Chartres, and taught at Laon and Arras. In his theological writings, notably that on the Trinity, he was critical of the views of Abelard and Gilbert de la Porrée. His works reveal extensive knowledge of Christian and non-Christian literature.

CLARENCE, DUKE OF, title reserved for younger sons of the English royal house. The first duke was Lionel, third son of Edward III, who received the title in 1362. His wife was a direct descendant of the Clares, whence the term Clarence.

CLARENCE, GEORGE, DUKE OF, d. 1478, son of Richard, duke of York. Against the order of his brother Edward IV, he married Isabella Neville and joined her father, Richard, earl of Warwick, in rebellion against him. In 1471 he deserted Warwick and received a pardon from Edward, but in 1478 Edward had him sent to the Tower where he was killed. [See ROSES, WARS OF THE.]

CLARENCE, LIONEL, DUKE OF, d. 1368, third son of Edward III who gained the title and lands of the earl of Ulster through his marriage to Elizabeth de Burgh. He served as governor of Ireland from 1361 to 1366. His daughter, Philippa, married Edmund Mortimer, earl of March. Richard, duke of York, derived his claim to the throne through his descent from Lionel.

CLARENDON, a royal manor near Salisbury and a favorite hunting lodge of Henry II.

CLARENDON, ASSIZE OF, order issued by Henry II in 1166 to the English sheriffs instructing them to summon a jury that would meet with the itinerant justices to try men accused of certain serious crimes (murder, larceny, robbery, harboring of criminals). The jury which was to be composed of twelve men from each hundred and four from each vill in the county, only presented the names of men under suspicion of having committed these crimes, whence the name jury of presentment. The jury did not pass judgment.

CLARENDON, CONSTITUTIONS OF, 16 articles or "customs" drawn up by Henry II of England in 1164 which were intended to define relations between church and state. Half of the articles served to place restrictions on the procedure of ecclesiastical judges and on the competence of church courts. The most famous of these was Article 3. This provided that criminous clerks be impleaded before the king's court, then tried before an ecclesiastical tribunal. If proved guilty, they were to be punished by the crown. The constitutions also prohibited members of the clergy to leave the realm without the king's permission and required royal approval of appeals made to Rome. The rejection of the constitutions by Thomas Becket, archbishop of Canterbury, precipitated a major break in the relations between Henry and the church and led eventually to the prelate's murder. [See BECKET, THOMAS, ST.]

CLARENI, a group of Spiritual Franciscans whom Pope Celestine V authorized in 1294 to withdraw from the regular order in order to live as hermits. After Pope Boniface VIII (1294–1303) had rescinded this permission, the Clareni, so called after one of their founders, suffered a checkered history. Several groups came under suspicion of heresy, while other communities received recognition as orthodox.

CLARE OF ASSISI, ST., d. 1253, founder of the order of the Poor Clares. Her friend, Francis of Assisi, had encouraged her to establish an order for women that would parallel his own. In 1212 she initiated the movement known as the Second Order of St. Francis. Shortly before she died she received papal approval of the rule she had composed. Many daughter houses were founded during the thirteenth century, almost 50 in Spain. [*See* POOR CLARES.]

CLARET, name the English in the twelfth century gave to the red wine they imported from Bordeaux. The word was the Middle English term for "clear."

CLAUDIANUS, CLAUDIUS, d. shortly after 404, last pagan Latin poet of significance. His poems, in both Greek and Latin, included political and mythological pieces, panegyrics, epistles, idylls, and epigrams. Though a master of rhetoric, his themes were shallow and lacked appeal.

CLAUDIUS, d. c. 840, bishop of Turin, a Spaniard by birth, author of attacks on image worship, relics, the adoration of the Cross, pilgrimages, and the intercession of saints. His views were refuted by Dungal and Jonas of Orléans. His biblical commentaries revealed an unusually wide knowledge of the works of St. Augustine.

CLAUSURA, that is, enclosure, the practice of barring part of a religious house to members of the opposite sex, also to the area so enclosed. The clausura, which was common to all religious orders, dates from the earliest monastic rules.

CLAVICHORD, a stringed musical instrument with keyboard, the predecessor of the piano. It came into use in the early fifteenth century.

CLAVUS, CLAUDIUS (Nicholas Niger), d. after 1424, Danish cartographer who influenced the development of cartography. His map of Europe was the first to show lines of latitude and longitude and included northern Europe, Greenland, and Iceland.

CLÉMANGES (Clamanges), MATHIEU-NICOLAS POILLEVILLAIN DE, d. c. 1435, French humanist and theologian, studied at Paris under Jean Gerson and Pierre d'Ailly, and took part in the Council of Constance. He contributed to the literature of conciliarism and the Western Schism.

CLEMENT I, ST., Pope, 92?–101, traditionally listed as the third bishop of Rome (pope). He is usually included with the Apostolic Fathers and credited with the authorship of the *First Epistle of Clement to the Corinthians*. Since he spoke with authority in this letter, it is regarded as a document of major importance by those scholars who maintain that the bishops of Rome, from St. Peter on, all claimed a position of primacy.

CLEMENT (Suidger) II, Pope, 1046–7, member of a noble Saxon family, chaplain at the imperial court, and bishop of Bamberg (1040), who owed his selection as pontiff to Henry III of Germany who had deposed Gregory VI. Clement crowned Henry III (Holy) Roman emperor and issued a series of reforms similar to those already in effect in Germany. He died after a pontificate of only nine months, probably from lead poisoning.

CLEMENT III, Pope, 1187–91, a Roman, who labored earnestly for the success of the Third Crusade. The efforts of Henry VI of Germany to establish his authority over southern Italy and Sicily filled his last years with anxiety. He removed the Scottish church from the jurisdiction of the archbishop of York.

CLEMENT IV, Pope, 1265–8, native of France, a lawyer in the service of the count of Toulouse, councillor of Louis IX, priest, bishop of Le Puy (1257), archbishop of Narbonne (1259), and cardinal bishop (1261). In order to extinguish the rule of the Hohenstaufens in Italy, he enthusiastically endorsed Charles of Anjou's occupation of Sicily and southern Italy and confirmed him as king of Naples. He actively encouraged a crusade against the pagan Slavs in Prussia and the Baltic regions, and another in Spain against the Moors.

CLEMENT V (Bertrand de Got), 1305–14, a Frenchman, canon lawyer, bishop of Comminges (1295), and archbishop of Bordeaux (1299). After his election as pope, he remained in France and in 1309 took up residence at Avignon. [*See* AVIGNONESE RESIDENCE.] Nine of the ten cardinals he created were French. He exculpated Philip IV of any misconduct in his harsh treatment of Pope Boniface VIII and, under pressure from Philip, ordered the suppression of the Order of the Templars (1312). He did much to advance scholarship, especially the study of medicine and Oriental languages, and he founded the Universities of Orléans (1306) and Perugia (1308).

CLEMENT VI, Pope, 1342–52, a Frenchman, Benedictine abbot, bishop of Arras, archbishop of Sens, then of Rouen, and cardinal priest (1338). As pope he continued papal residence at Avignon where he contributed to the growing centralization of the administration of the church, notably with his expansion of the practice of papal provisions. He also appointed a large number of French cardinals. Although guilty of nepotism and prodigality, he proved himself a generous benefactor to the poor and a protector of the Jews. Many were blaming the Jews for the Black Death.

CLEMENT VII (Robert of Geneva), Pope (antipope), 1378–94, bishop of Thérouanne (1361), archbishop of Cambrai (1368), and cardinal (1371). He was one of the principals in the move to declare invalid the election of Pope Urban VI and was himself elected by the other cardinals to replace Urban. Clement made his residence at Avignon where he received the adherence of France (except the part under English rule), Castile, Aragon, Navarre, Scotland, and parts of Italy. [See SCHISM, WESTERN.]

CLEMENTINAE (Clementine Decretals), title given to the collection of the decretals of Pope Clement V (1305–14) and the decrees of the Council of Vienne (1311–2). Pope John XXII extended them official confirmation in 1317.

CLEMENT OF ALEXANDRIA, d. c. 215, Eastern church father, a product of the early theological school of Alexandria and its principal representative after Origen. He was the author of exegetical, apologetical, moral, and mystical works. In his writings, which reveal the influence of Platonic metaphysics and Stoic ethics, he frequently stressed the value to Christianity of Greek learning and philosophy, while warning his readers against the theosophical ideas of Gnosticism. Although some of his views invited the charge of heresy, the Latin church reckoned him in the company of the saints until late in the sixteenth century.

CLEMENT THE BULGARIAN (Clement of Ochrida), ST., d. 916, pupil of Cyril (Constantine) and Methodius, who was expelled from Moravia and later became the bishop of Velitsa in Bulgaria. His writings, which included lives of the saints and homilies, established him as one of the fathers of Slavonic literature.

CLEMENT OF IRELAND, ST., d. after 828, Irish grammarian, member of the palace school at Aachen during the reigns of Charlemagne and Louis the Pious.

CLERESTORY, architectural term for the story above the arcade and triforium of a church whose walls were pierced with windows so as to permit light to enter the nave. It was characteristic of Gothic but not Romanesque churches.

CLERGY, a term derived from the Latin *clericus,* meaning clerk. The clergy included all orders from the episcopate down through the minor orders and tonsure, as well as all members of the religious orders. The official distinction between laity and clergy dated from the early fourth century when Constantine I (312–37) extended privileges and immunities to bishops, priests, and deacons. In general the clergy were exempted from the jurisdiction of the civil courts as well as from military service. They might enjoy additional privileges. [See BENEFIT OF CLERGY.]

CLERICIS LAICOS, bull issued by Pope Boniface VIII in 1296 which threatened with anathema any lay ruler who might tax members of the clergy or church property, and members of the clergy who might pay such a tax. When Edward I of England and Philip IV of France defied Boniface's decree, he in effect rescinded it by permitting kings to impose such a tax in times of emergency.

CLERK, a member of the clergy who had received tonsure but none of the minor nor major orders.

CLERMONT, COUNCIL OF, council summoned by Urban II which met in November 1095 to plan the First Crusade. Two hundred bishops attended the council, together with many members of the feudal aristocracy. The council confirmed the Truce of God and issued other regulations concerning the crusade. It issued 32 canons, one of which forbade kings from granting investiture of ecclesiastical honors.

CLETUS, pope. See ANACLETUS, Pope.

CLIFFORD, ROSAMOND (Fair Rosamond), d. 1176?, mistress of Henry II of England.

CLISSON, OLIVIER DE, d. 1407, French military commander who served England, France, and Brittany successively though not unselfishly. He amassed one of the largest fortunes of his day. In 1380 he succeeded du Guesclin as constable of France and shortly after defeated the Flemish at the battle of Roosebeke (1382). He did do much to keep Brittany within the French sphere of influence.

CLOCK. Boethius (d. 525) may have invented the first wheel clock. Pacificus, a ninth-century archdeacon of Verona, is credited with the first weight-driven clock. Gerbert, a leading scholar of the tenth century and later Pope Sylvester II, may have invented a mechanical clock (c. 996). Mechanical figures which struck a bell on the hour graced St. Paul's cathedral in London in 1286. Rouen was noted for the skill of its clockmakers and watchmakers. Mechanical clocks were almost exclusively limited to cathedral towns, monasteries, and public squares.

CLODOMIR, d. 524, eldest son of Clovis, shared with his three brothers in the division of the Frankish kingdom. His portion included Orléans which he made his capital. In 523 he defeated and killed the king of the Burgundians, but he lost his own life a year later. His brothers then murdered his children with the exception of Clodoal who managed to escape. He became a monk and founded the monastery of St. Cloud.

CLOISTER, term generally applied to those parts of a religious house reserved for the exclusive use of the members of the community. These did not include the church, sacristy, guest quarters, parlors, and public offices. The term might also apply to the covered walk or arcade around which the principal buildings were located, usually an open square or rectangular court which was reserved for the members' use.

CLOTAIRE. See CHLOTHAR.

CLOTILDE (Chlotilda, Chrodegilde, Chlothilde), ST., d. 545, Burgundian princess, daughter of Chilperic, king of Burgundy, and wife of Clovis I, founder of the Merovingian kingdom. According to Gregory of Tours (*History of the Franks*), the prayers of Clotilde were instrumental in bringing Clovis to accept baptism. After the death of her husband, she retired to the abbey of St. Martin at Tours.

CLOUD OF UNKNOWING, an anonymous treatise of the late fourteenth century in Middle English which outlined to the would-be contemplative the path he must follow to attain the blessedness of the mystic. It is considered the finest product of fourteenth-century English mysticism.

CLOVIS (Chlodwig, Chlodovech, Ludovicus) I, king of the Franks, 481–511, founder of the Merovingian kingdom. During his reign, which he began at the age of 15, he conquered the domain of Syagrius, an independent Roman governor at Soissons, subjugated the Ripuarian Franks, shattered the power of the Alemanni, and took Toulouse and Bordeaux from the Visigoths. He made Paris his capital and gave his name (Louis) to many of his successors. What many scholars believe proved a critical point in his career was his baptism as a Catholic Christian at Reims in 498. This assured him the support of the hierarchy against his neighbors who were principally Arians. This decision may have given proof of his sagacity, although Gregory of Tours in his *History of the Franks* attributes it to the miraculous victory which Clovis gained over the Alemanni at Tolbiac. This convinced Clovis of the almighty power of the god of his Christian wife Clotilde. He accepted the titles of consul and patrician from Emperor Anastasius I in Constantinople and left his realm to his four sons Clodomir, Childebert I, Chlothar I, and Theuderic.

CLUNY, CONGREGATION OF, organization of monastic houses affiliated with the Benedictine monastery of Cluny and subject to the authority of its abbot. The association had its origin in the monastery that William, duke of Aquitaine, founded at Cluny in Burgundy in 910, then declared it to be free of his (feudal) control. He also placed the other monasteries in his domain under the direction of Cluny. It was his hope, and that of Berno, Cluny's first abbot, that once free of the corrupting influence of secular interference, these monasteries could attain and maintain a high level of spiritual life and be better able to preserve this under the authority of a common abbot at Cluny rather than under their own separate superiors. The hope proved a popular if not correct one, and by the twelfth century some 300 houses scattered throughout Europe, most of them in Spain and France, had joined the congregation. The papacy encouraged the foundation by granting the affiliated monasteries exemption from episcopal control. Aside from the central supervision of the abbot of Cluny and a stricter observance of the Benedictine rule, what especially distinguished the Cluniac houses from other monastic communities was the larger amount of time allotted for

liturgical service. The Cluniac monk spent the greater part of his day at prayer in the abbey church. The Congregation of Cluny gave its name to the most famous and successful reform movement of the Middle Ages. This Cluniac reform movement had as its objectives the elimination of lay investiture, the marriage (concubinage) of the clergy, simony.

CNUT. *See* CANUTE.

COART (Couwaert, Cwaert), the hare in the *Roman de Renart,* whence the word "coward."

COBLENZ, a fortress on the Rhine from Roman times (*Castellum*), a Frankish capital in the sixth century, later a royal residence which Henry II of Germany gave to the archbishop of Trier in 1018 to serve as the archiepiscopal palace.

COCHE (concha, cogo, cogga, cocca, coqua, cocha), type of boat drawn by horses which was used from the thirteenth century.

COCKATRICE. *See* BASILISK.

CODEX, name given to a manuscript in leaf form, as opposed to one rolled. [*See* BOOK, MEDIEVAL.]

CODEX ALEXANDRINUS, ancient Greek manuscript of the Old and New Testaments, probably of the late fourth or early fifth century, so called because it was once the property of the see of Alexandria. It may have come from Mount Athos and it was probably written in Egypt.

CODEX AMIATINUS, ancient and superbly illuminated manuscript of the Latin Vulgate, probably made in Northumbria at either Wearmouth or Jarrow between c. 690 and 700. From the ninth or tenth century, the manuscript was in the monastery of Monte Amiata, hence its name.

CODEX ARGENTEUS, sixth-century manuscript in gold and silver writings which contains Ulfilas's translation of the gospels.

CODEX AUREUS, name given to medieval manuscripts which had golden letters or covers of gold.

CODEX EPHRAEMI RESCRIPTUS, ancient manuscript of the Greek Bible dating from the early fifth century. Its name derives from the fact that treatises by St. Ephraem the Syrian were written over the original text in the twelfth century.

CODEX SINAITICUS, a Greek manuscript of the Old and New Testaments probably from the fourth century. It was probably written in Egypt.

CODEX VATICANUS, the most important of the Greek manuscripts of the Bible. It has been assigned to the fourth century and was probably written in Alexandria. Its presence in the Vatican Library explains its name.

CODINUS, GEORGE, fl. late fifteenth century, author of several valuable works dealing with Byzantine topography, the buildings of Constantinople (*Patria*), court and higher ecclesiastical dignities and ceremonies (*De Officiis*), and history from the Creation to the fall of Constantinople to the Turks in 1453.

COENOBITE. *See* CENOBITISM.

COEUR, JACQUES, d. 1456, an immensely wealthy and influential French merchant prince, master of the mint in Paris in 1436, member of the king's council, and treasurer of the royal household under Charles VII. He was heavily engaged in Levantine trade and maintained factors in Barcelona, Lyons, Rouen, and other cities, with Marseilles as his principal port. It was partly through his heavy loans to the government that Charles VII was able to bring the Hundred Years' War to a successful conclusion. But prominent men including competitors and debtors had him charged with poisoning Agnes Sorel, the king's mistress, and with embezzlement and extortion, and he was convicted, imprisoned, and his vast wealth confiscated. He managed to escape prison and died in command of the papal navy. His palace in Bourges remains one of the finest monuments of domestic Gothic architecture.

COEUR DE LION. *See* RICHARD I.

COGGESHALL, RALPH OF, d. after 1227, abbot of the Cistercian abbey at Coggeshall in Essex. He contributed a chronicle covering the years 1187–1224 to the abbey's *Chronicon Anglicanum,* and a continuation of Ralph Niger's chronicle for the years 1162–78.

COIMBRA, the Roman city of *Aeminium,* a bishop's seat from the close of the ninth century, served as the residence of the kings of Portugal from 1064, when taken from the Moors, until 1260. In 1308 the university which King Diniz had founded in 1290 at Lisbon was moved to Coimbra. A fine cathedral survives from the twelfth century. The famous tragic heroine Inés de Castro was murdered here.

COLA DI RIENZO, d. 1354, Roman notary who went to Avignon to seek the pope's return, then returned to Rome where he assumed leadership of the popular party in 1347, gained dictatorial powers, and was crowned tribune. After a year of turbulent rule, he took refuge for a time with the Spiritual Franciscans in the Abruzzi, then went on to Prague to the court of Emperor Charles IV who sent him to Avignon. There he cleared himself of the charge of heresy and reestablished himself in the confidence of the pope who sent him to Rome to cooperate with Cardinal Albornoz in restoring papal authority. Although greeted enthusiastically by the people whom his eloquence and promises to bring back the ancient glories of Rome had captivated, violence broke out shortly over his arbitrary rule, and he was slain. This strange visionary still invites conflicting appraisals.

COLCHESTER, town in Essex from Roman times when it was known as Camulodunum, received its first charter in 1189 and permissions for fairs in that same year and in 1319. The castle keep, built c. 1070, is the largest of its kind in England. An Augustinian priory dedicated to St. Botolph was founded in the late eleventh century. Colchester flourished as a seaport in the thirteenth century.

COLETTE (Coletta), ST., d. 1447, born Nicolette Boylet (Boellet) in Picardy, lived as a recluse for a time, then as a Beguine, and finally became a Poor Clare. She eventually became abbess general of the order. She established a number of communities and insisted upon the observance of the Rule of St. Francis in its original austerity. She is honored as the founder of the Colettines.

COLETTINES. *See* ST. COLETTE.

COLLATION, a light meal permitted beyond the main meal on a fast day; a sermon based upon a passage from Scripture; the second step in securing a benefice, the first that of being presented, the second that of actual appointment or collation, the third the formal institution.

COLLECT, short prayer, suited to the time or occasion, recited or sung at mass and at times during the divine office. The writings of Pope Leo I show that such prayers as the collect, secret, and post-communion were familiar by the middle of the fifth century.

COLLECTION DE DOCUMENTS INEDITS SUR L'HISTOIRE DE FRANCE, a collection of unpublished materials dealing with the history of medieval France. The first of some 290 volumes made its appearance in 1836.

COLLEGE, term applied to a community, corporation, or other organized body engaged in some common pursuit or dedicated to some common purpose and possessing certain rights and privileges. In the thirteenth century the name might designate a hospice, a dormitory for students, a community or group of secular clergy living together in a foundation for religious, or a merchant guild.

COLLEGIATE CHURCH, a church, usually quite large, in which the resident clergy or canons were organized into a formal chapter not unlike a cathedral chapter. Unlike a cathedral church, it was not a bishop's see.

COLLEGIATI (*corporati*), merchants and artisans of the late Roman empire who were required to maintain membership in industrial corporations or colleges. The government thought it could better assure food and services for the army, for example, by negotiating with such colleges rather than with individuals.

COLLEONI, BARTOLOMMEO, d. 1475, Italian condottiere, fought in the wars of Venice and Milan, but changed sides so often he could not be trusted. In 1454 when he deserted Milan for the last time, he became generalissimo of Venice. The celebrated equestrian statue by Verrocchio in Venice has perpetuated his memory.

COLLYRIDIANS, a fourth-century sect whom St. Epiphanius mentions as originating in Thrace and consisting principally of women. The members constituted an idolatrous cult which sacrificed cakes to the Blessed Virgin Mary, then consumed them.

COLMAN, SS., name of a number of Irish saints of the sixth and seventh centuries, the best known being Colman of Lindisfarne (d. c. 670), a monk of Iona and bishop-abbot of Lindisfarne, who returned to Iona following the decision made at Whitby in 664 to adopt Roman usages and liturgy rather than those of the Celtic church. From Iona he led a group of some sixty monks, formerly of Lindisfarne, to the western coast of Ireland where he erected two monasteries, one in the province of Connaught for the Irish monks, a second at Mayo for the English. Colman had been the principal champion for the adoption of Celtic usages and liturgy at the Synod of Whitby.

COLMAR (Kolmar), city on the upper Rhine south of Strasbourg. It first appeared in 823 under the name *Columbarium*. In 1226 Frederick II fortified Colmar and granted it the status of an imperial city. It became one of the strongest cities in Germany and an important member of the Hanseatic League. St. Martin's Church in Colmar has the *Madonna of the Rose Arbor* by Martin Schongauer.

COLOGNE, city on the Rhine from Roman times when it was known as *Colonia*. It became a bishop's seat in the early fourth century. The Franks occupied the area c. 400 and in the division of the Merovingian kingdom following the death of Chlothar I (561), Cologne served as residence of the kings of Austrasia. The archbishop of Cologne who made his appearance in 785 remained in the forefront of political affairs in Germany throughout the Middle Ages and in 1356 became one of the seven imperial electors. Friction between the archbishop and the city merchants was fairly constant until 1288 when Cologne acquired a charter of self-government. The city's famous cathedral, constructed in the French Île de France style, was begun in 1248 and its choir completed in 1322. The work was interrupted in 1510 when Gothic fell into disrepute. It was only in 1880 that the church was finally completed. The cathedral contains the shrine of the Magi. The city's university, which received its charter from Pope Urban VI in 1388, grew rapidly since German students ceased attending French universities following the opening of the Western Schism in 1378. The four mendicant orders had already established *studia generalia* in the city.

COLOMAN (Calman) I, king of Hungary, 1095–1116, seized the throne upon the death of his uncle King Laszlo I and blinded his half-brother Almos who should have succeeded. Despite this brutal beginning, he proved himself an able legislator and administrator and acquired the greater part of Dalmatia in order to provide his country a seacoast.

COLOMAN, ST., d. 1012, Irish pilgrim who was seized near Vienna on his way to Jerusalem and executed as a spy. The report of miracles at his grave led to the transferral of his bones to Melk. Coloman, whose cult became popular in Austria, southern Germany, and Hungary, was honored as the patron saint of travelers.

COLOMBE, MICHEL, d. after 1512, French sculptor of Tours who was known for the white tomb he made for Francis II of Brittany and his consort in the cathedral of Nantes. He is considered the last Gothic sculptor of France.

COLOMBIER, right of the lord to erect a pigeon house.

COLOMBINI, GIOVANNI, BL., d. 1367, founder of the Gesuati, devoted himself to the service of the poor. With his friend Francisco Mini, he took up a life of evangelical poverty, prayer, and works of mercy. At first exiled by the city of Siena for attracting so many young men to take up his vocation, the city later recalled him when an epidemic broke out. In 1367 Urban V confirmed him and his disciples as the congregation of Gesuati.

COLONATE, type of land bondage common on the *latifundia* of the late Roman empire. Under this system tillers of the soil, called *coloni,* were bound to the estates on which they labored and their sons after them. This type of land holding had appeared prior to Diocletian's reign (284–305), but it was the system of taxation he introduced, based upon production and labor, that prompted the government to attach the *coloni* to the estates they worked in order to enable the landlords to meet their tax obligations.

COLONI. *See* COLONATE.

COLONNA, aristocratic family of Rome, descended from the counts of Tusculum, which came to notice c. 1100. Next to the Orsini, their hereditary enemies, the family was the most powerful and aggressive in Rome. It boasted a number of cardinals and one pope, Martin V (d. 1431), whose election as pope in 1417 heralded the end of the Western Schism. Giovanni (d. 1215), a cardinal, showed himself a strong friend of St. Francis of Assisi. Another Giovanni (d. 1244) served as papal legate on the Fifth Crusade. Two Colonna cardinals, Giacomo (d. 1318) and Pietro (d. 1326), among the bitterest foes of Pope Boniface VIII, took an active part in his humiliation at Anagni. In 1297 Boniface had deprived both cardinals of their dignity and excommunicated the entire family and seized their property.

COLOPHON, an inscription at the end of a manuscript or book that might supply information concerning the title, author, script, printer, place, and time of publication. They are sometimes found as early as the sixth century and continued to appear irregularly through the Middle Ages in manuscript texts and in early printed books.

COLORS, LITURGICAL, five colors — white, red, green, black, and violet — as prescribed for liturgical use by Pope Innocent III (1198–1216). Each color was intended to suggest a particular mood or ideal, suited to a particular feast or liturgical season: white symbolized purity and joy; black, sorrow and death; green, hope; violet, for the season of Lent. Red vestments were worn on Pentecost and the feasts of martyrs.

COLUCCIO, SALUTATO. *See* SALUTATI COLUCCIO.

COLUMBA OF IONA, ST., d. 597, born of a noble Irish family, learned monk of Clonard, established many monasteries in Ireland and Scotland of which the most renowned was the one he founded on the island of Iona (563). His erudition, religious zeal, and aristocratic birth fitted him for the extremely influential role he played in the political and ecclesiastical affairs of Scotland and Ireland. He may be called the founder of the Celtic Christian church in Scotland and North England.

COLUMBAN (Columbanus), ST., d. 615, learned

Irish monk, abbot, and missionary, taught many years at Bangor before moving to Burgundy in Gaul where he founded a monastery at Luxeuil. After his expulsion by King Theuderic II whom he had upraided for his dissolute life (many of the clergy of the area resented his attacks on their unworthy ways even more than they did the practices of the Celtic church he had brought with him), he made his way through east France and Switzerland to north Italy where he established a monastery at Bobbio (near Genoa). His letters, sermons, and poems reveal his acquaintance with Latin and Greek literature. The "Monastic Rule" and the "Penitential" are now held to be substantially his work.

COLUMBUS, CHRISTOPHER, d. 1506, a Genoese mariner, was born in 1451, took to the sea when he was fourteen, and almost lost his life in a sea battle between Portugal and Genoa off Cape St. Vincent (1476). He visited Iceland and spent some time in the Madeira Islands. His conviction that he could reach the Indies by sailing westward grew into an obsession. The king of Portugal remained unconvinced of the feasibility of his project, and so, at first, did Ferdinand and Isabella of Spain. They eventually met his demands, among these that he be knighted and appointed grand admiral and viceroy, and fitted out three ships for his epochal voyage of discovery. He left Palos on August 3 and, after reprovisioning in the Canary Islands, sailed west and landed on one of the Bahama Islands on October 12. He made three additional voyages (1493, 1498, and 1502) to the new world.

COMES, Latin for companion, a title held by a variety of higher military and civil officials from the fourth century. In Merovingian times the count (from the Latin *comes*) was a member of the aristocracy. He advised the king and administered a section (county) of the kingdom.

COMGALL, ST., d. c. 601, founder and first abbot of Bangor (in Ireland), a zealous propagator of monasticism. He is believed to have made a missionary expedition to Iona and other places in Scotland. St. Columban was his disciple.

COMITATUS, name given a warrior band among the early Germans. [*See* FEUDALISM.] The word might also identify the region administered by the Frankish count.

COMMENDAM. *See* COMMENDATION.

COMMENDATION, act by which a person placed himself under the protection of another to whom he surrendered the title to his property. Commendation became a general practice during the unstable seventh and eighth centuries when the need for protection was great, and it involved all levels of society from the peasantry to the aristocracy. The coalescing of commendation with other practices of the period such as vassalage and immunity contributed to the evolution of feudalism. [*See* FEUDALISM.]

In ecclesiastical usage commendation in the early centuries referred to benefices given in *commendam,* that is, assigned for a temporary period until a permanent appointment could be made. During the Carolingian and feudal periods laymen who received benefices *in commendam* held them for life. The practice of granting benefices *in commendam* to laymen or, in the case of monasteries, to secular clerks who enjoyed their revenues for life, even to bishops to hold with their sees, became common in the later Middle Ages. The practice invited much abuse.

COMMERCE, MEDIEVAL. *See* TRADE, REVIVAL OF.

COMMINES (Comines, Commynes), PHILLIPPE DE, d. 1511, Flemish chronicler of aristocratic birth who served as adviser to Charles the Bold of Burgundy and took part in the war of the League of the Public Weal. In 1472 he left Charles to become chamberlain and counselor of Louis XI of France. He was convinced that the astute, wily king would eventually destroy the imprudent duke, while Louis XI, on his part, recognized Commines's abilities as a diplomat.

His *Mémoires* which relate in vivid language the events that affected the lives of Charles and Louis from 1464 to 1498 show him to have been a perceptive judge of men and a writer of considerable detachment despite his admiration for Louis and contempt for the duke. He served as ambassador to Venice under Charles VIII.

COMMODIAN, obscure Christian Latin poet, probably of African origin, who lived in Gaul and whose life has been assigned to the third, fourth, or fifth century. He was probably a convert to Christianity, in any event surely a Christian since he assumed the role of teacher of Christian doctrine in most of his verse. Whether he chose to employ a vulgar Latin and an unrefined verse form to suit an unlettered audience or whether he could do no better is not known.

COMMON LAW, medieval term applied to the law and legal procedures that became common (universal) in England as a result of the legal reforms of Henry II (1154–89) and the influence of such legal treatises as that of Ralph Glanvill, Henry's justiciar. The sources of this law were partly custom, partly principles of Roman law which the Normans had brought with them, partly policies adopted by the crown. Surely a major force contributing to the evolution of a common law in England was the work of the itinerant (royal) justices. These men exercised jurisdiction over the same kinds of offenses and civil cases, observed procedures set down by the crown, and preserved records of their judgments for the instruction of other justices. Because these judges would modify legal principle and procedure, unconsciously for the most part, as passing years recommended, common law acquired and retained a measure of flexibility denied Roman law, which prevailed on the continent. An additional factor that helped insure this flexibility was the peculiar character of the school where the future justice received his instruction. This was not the English university which would have trained him in Roman law. Rather it was the Inns of the Court where professional lawyers gave him expert advice and instruction much as a master of a guild would provide this for his apprentice.

COMMON LIFE, BRETHREN OF THE. *See* BRETHREN OF THE COMMON LIFE.

COMMON PLEAS, COURT OF, English common law court which Henry II instituted in 1178 when he appointed five members of his council to entertain pleas involving disputes between individuals, as opposed to litigation in which the crown was a party. Almost all civil litigation came within its purview as well as the supervision of local and manorial courts. In 1272 it became a permanent court and received its own chief justice.

COMMON, RIGHTS OF, rights of the members of the manorial community to the use of such common property as waste lands, meadow, and woods.

COMMONS, HOUSE OF. *See* PARLIAMENT.

COMMUNE, term occasionally applied to cities in the Middle Ages that established municipal institutions and enjoyed a large measure of autonomy, appreciably larger than towns that had received charters from their lords. The first such commune was Venice. Venice emerged during the turbulent sixth century and, because of circumstances, chiefly its island position, was able to acquire and maintain its autonomy against the pretensions of Byzantium and the Holy Roman Empire. By the close of the eleventh century Genoa and Pisa had gained a similarly autonomous position, a status which many north Italian cities had achieved by the close of the thirteenth century. That they accomplished this at the expense of the Holy Roman Empire points up a critical factor in the rise of the commune, namely, the inability of the ruling state to block such a development. A similar situation prevailed in Flanders and north Germany where the weakness of the state also permitted the rise of Ghent, Bruges, and Hamburg. Whatever the circumstances that made possible the rise of these autonomous communities, the municipal government that generally emerged was oligarchic in character and was controlled by an aristocracy of birth.

COMMUNION IN BOTH KINDS. There was no one method of receiving Holy Communion in the Middle Ages. Church fathers of the third and fourth century speak of the laity taking the consecrated bread home with them for private communion. In the fifth century there is testimony that the host was given into the hands of the communicant. In general it was customary to receive Holy Communion under the two species of bread and wine until about the twelfth century, although receiving only the bread appears to have been the most common practice. Dipping the bread into the consecrated wine was also not uncommon. By the thirteenth century the practice of communicating under the species of wine had disappeared, which explains why the Hussites of the early fifteenth century insisted that the practice be restored. [*See* CALIXTINES.] The pope's refusal to permit communion under both species helped fuel the Hussite wars.

COMNENI, Byzantine family and ruling dynasty (1057–9, 1081–1185) whose first emperor, Isaac Comnenus, took over the throne in 1057. Members of the family ruled the Empire of Trebizond from 1204 until 1461 when Sultan Mohammed II deposed David, its last representative.

COMO, city located just north of Milan at the entrance to the St. Gotthard pass that linked Italy and Germany. After the construction of its walls in the twelfth century, it became a commune. It was generally leagued with the enemies of Milan until 1335 when it passed under that city's control. Como was an important center of the silk and woolen trade. The cathedral of Sta. Maria Maggiore presents a delightful example of the fusion of Gothic and Renaissance styles.

COMPACTS OF PRAGUE. *See* PRAGUE, COMPACTS OF.

COMPAGNI, DINO, d. 1324, Florentine statesman until exiled in 1301 with other members of the White faction. His valuable chronicle of Florence covered the years from 1280 to 1312.

COMPAGNIES D'ORDONNANCE, companies of cavalry created in 1445 by Charles VII of France and paid for by proceeds of the *taille*.

COMPASS, MARINER'S, instrument used to determine directions on the earth's surface by means of a magnetic needle. It may have originated in China where mention of it appears toward the close of the eleventh century, although it was not used in navigation before the early twelfth century when it was probably already known in the West. The first Western writer to make mention of the compass was Alexander Neckham in his *De Utensilibus* (1187). The earliest detailed description of the magnetic compass is by Petrus Peregrinus di Maricourt which he wrote in 1269.

COMPIÈGNE, town in northern France on the left bank of the Oise first mentioned in 557. It was the site of many assemblies and councils during the Merovingian period. Charles the Bald (d. 877) founded the Abbey of St. Corneille and extended it such privileges as acting for three days each year as lord of Compiègne. It became a commune in 1153. Joan of Arc was taken prisoner there by the Burgundians.

COMPLINE (complin), the last prayer of the day as recited or sung in the divine office. It may have originated with John Cassian (d. 435) who makes first mention of the prayer, although it received its liturgical form from St. Benedict who included it in his Rule.

COMPOSTELA, SANTIAGO DE, one of medieval Europe's most popular shrines, located in northwestern Galicia a few miles from the Atlantic. According to the traditional account, the body of St. James (the Greater) was brought there in the ninth century. About 1095 the ancient see of Iria was transferred to Compostela, after which that city became the center of the national and Christian crusade against the Moslem rulers of the peninsula.

COMPURGATION, method of ascertaining the guilt of a defendant used by the early Germans and employed well up into the Middle Ages, in ecclesiastical courts as late as the fourteenth century. It required an oath by the defendant denying the charge, then the oaths of a number of compurgators or "oath-helpers" who swore to the validity of the defendant's oath. The number of compurgators varied with their importance as well as with the social position of the defendant.

COMPUTUS, name given in the Middle Ages to the science of preparing a calendar, principally for the purpose of ascertaining the date of Easter. The earliest known computus to be used for determining the date of Easter was that made by Hippolytus (d. c. 236). Charlemagne directed the monastic schools of his kingdom to teach the science.

COMYN, JOHN, d. c. 1300, Scottish noble, known as Black Comyn to distinguish him from John Comyn the Red. In 1286 he was one of the six guardians to the Scottish throne. After the death of Margaret the Maid of Norway, he became a claimant to the throne but eventually gave his support to John Balliol who became king in 1292.

COMYN, JOHN, d. 1306, Scottish statesman, known as Red Comyn to distinguish him from John Comyn the Black, an ally of John Balliol, later appointed guardian of Scotland to succeed William Wallace. He finally made his submission to Edward I, but shortly after was murdered by supporters of Robert Bruce who feared him as a possible rival to the throne.

CONCEPTUALISM, a term used to identify the compromise proposed by Abelard in the controversy over universals, namely, that the idea was more than a mere word as claimed by the nominalists, although it did not exist apart from the thing it represented, a position maintained by the realists. The idea existed in the thing, *in re,* rather than *ante rem* (before the thing) as the realists insisted or *post rem* (after the thing) as did the nominalists and possessed intellectual reality.

CONCILIARISM, doctrine maintained by many theologians and canonists during the late Middle Ages that would have invested the general council, rather than the pope, with supreme authority in the church. Until the coming of the Western Schism (1378–1417), conciliarism remained an academic position, its rationale based on the argument that since it was the whole Christian community that constituted the church and it was through this body that the Holy Spirit guided the institution, then the people through a representative body, such as a general council, should exercise highest authority in matters concerning the faith and the general state of the church. Support for conciliarist theories came from such quarters as the Spiritual Franciscans who were convinced that a pope could teach heresy following John XXII's condemnation of their teaching regarding apostolic poverty. Still it was only with the refusal of the Roman, Avignonese, and Pisan popes to summon a council that would resolve the Western Schism that prompted moderate theologians such as Francesco Zabarella and Jean Gerson to endorse conciliarism. Conciliarism enjoyed its greatest day when the Council of Constance (1414–8) proclaimed the supreme authority of the general council *(Sacrosancta),* made provision for its regular convocation *(Frequens),* and deposed two popes (the third resigned). Popes Martin V and Eugenius IV bowed to conciliarism and summoned general councils at Pavia (1423) and Basel (1431). The action of the conciliarists at Basel in deposing Eugenius IV and electing another pope discredited them in the eyes of Europe and sounded the death knell of conciliarism. Few protested in 1460 when Pope Pius II anathematized conciliarism in the bull *Execrabilis.* [*See* OCKHAM, WILLIAM; MARSILIUS OF PADUA; CONSTANCE, COUNCIL OF; BASEL, COUNCIL OF.]

CONCLAVE, from the Latin *cum,* "together," and *clavis,* "key," a term applied either to the group of cardinals gathered together to elect a pope or to the room in which such an election was held. The conclave originated in 1274 with Gregory X who laid down procedures intended to prevent extended delays which occasionally held up the election of a new pope. In early times, the election of the bishop of Rome, like that of other bishops, was by the clergy, people, and neighboring bishops in their several capacities. The role of the people was largely one of approval though not always. In the case of St. Ambrose, bishop of Milan, the populace of the city may have been chiefly responsible for his election. During the years when Rome was part of the Byzantine empire, the emperor had exercised some voice in the selective process and so did Charlemagne (d. 814). With the death of Nicholas I in 867, the papacy had become largely a local institution, controlled by whatever group happened to be in the ascendancy at the time. From 962 until 1059, it was the German king who decided who would be pope. In 1059 a new electoral procedure called for the election of the pope by the cardinal clergy of Rome. In 1274, in the hope of eliminating the pressure that kings and political factions might be able to exert, an interference that could produce delays if no worse, Gregory X promulgated the constitution *Ubi Periculum* which outlined a new procedure, essentially that the cardinals were to meet within ten days of the death of a pope, in a closed conclave cut off from interference from the outer world, and remain so isolated until they could agree on a papal successor.

CONCORDAT, a public agreement between the papacy and a state concerning a matter of mutual concern, e.g., the Concordat of Worms in 1122 over the problem of lay investiture. This may have been the first occasion that the term concordat was employed.

CONDÉ, PIERRE DE, chaplain of Louis IX (1226–70), who accompanied the king on his last Crusade, the one to Tunis. Condé's letters furnish valuable information about this Crusade.

CONDOTTIERE (plural *condottieri*), captain of a band (often several thousand) of mercenary soldiers whom he recruited and paid. He was most typical of north Italy in the late Middle Ages when mercenary troops were in great demand since few Italian cities maintained armies of their own. The *condottieri* dealt directly with the cities and states and usually sold their services to the highest bidder. Among the most famous *condottieri* were the Attendolos, founders of the Sforza family, Colleoni, Carmagnola, and Sir John de Hawkwood.

CONDUCTUS, a medieval song that evolved from the liturgy and was normally presented by several voices. It proved popular in the twelfth and thirteenth centuries.

CONFESSIO, the resting place of a martyr, more generally that of any saint. It was also the term given to the vestibule or entrance to a crypt.

CONFESSIO AMANTIS. See GOWER, JOHN.

CONFESSION, the avowal of sin, made to a priest or to one empowered to grant absolution. The confession of sins appears early in the church's discipline of penance. Penance itself included the sinner's revealing his sins, the works of satisfaction imposed by the confessor, and the sinner's repentance. Much obscurity remains concerning the discipline of penance in the early centuries. Controversial issues such as whether such serious sins as adultery, murder, and apostasy could possibly be forgiven provoked much discussion. It remained for the Council of Nicaea in 325 to pass finally on this issue. It is still a matter of debate whether there was such a form of penance as private confession in the early church. It

appears that public confession and public penance were common until the close of the fourth century, and it was Celtic monks of the sixth century who introduced private confession as it came to be known. Still, even if the confession of sins was private, it was commonly put off until death was near, and it was for that reason that the Fourth Lateran Council in 1215, under the direction of Pope Innocent III, established the rule that all Christians must confess their sins, "in secret," at least once a year.

CONFESSIONAL, box, cabinet, or stall in which the priest sat to hear the confessions of penitents.

CONFESSION LETTER, papal dispensation that permitted the recipient free choice of confessor. The confessor might be authorized to pardon sins ordinarily reserved to the pope. The granting of this privilege, for which a fee was required, became common in the late Middle Ages.

CONFESSIONS OF ST. AUGUSTINE. See AUGUSTINE, ST.

CONFESSOR, title given to male saints who were not martyrs but whose sanctity proclaimed the intensity of their faith. Little distinction was made in the use of the terms confessor and martyr until after the third century when the era of actual martyrdom came to an end. King Edward of Anglo-Saxon England (1042–66) was declared a confessor by Pope Alexander III in 1161.

CONFIRMATION, a sacrament or rite administered some years after baptism that conferred the Holy Spirit and confirmed the faith received in baptism. It may not have been until the fifth century that this rite came to be clearly distinguishable from baptism. The Council of Lyons in 1274 officially defined confirmation as a sacrament necessary to salvation.

CONFITEOR, formal confession of sin made since the eleventh century by the priest and people at the beginning of mass. This confession was incorporated into the liturgy of the mass. It also served as part of the Compline.

CONGÉ D'ÉLIRE, Norman-French term for "permission to elect," in effect, an authorization by the king of England to the dean and chapter of a cathedral to proceed with the election of a bishop (archbishop). Henry II in the Constitutions of Clarendon (1164) laid down the procedure to be followed in the selection of bishops. In 1214 John agreed that while the dean and chapter of the cathedral should elect the bishop, royal permission to proceed with the election, that is, the *congé d'élire,* had first to be obtained from the king.

CONNAUGHT (Connacht), one of the five original kingdoms of Ireland. It lay along the west coast of the island between Donegal Bay to the north and Galway Bay to the south. Toirdelbach (Turloch) O'Connor (d. 1156) and his son Ruadri (Rory), who were its rulers in the early twelfth century, claimed lordship over all of Ireland. In 1227 Henry III granted the kingdom to Richard de Burgh, whose son Walter became the earl of Ulster as well as lord of Connaught. When he died without male issue, his daughter married Lionel, third son of Edward III, through whose daughter Philippa the title was transmitted to the Mortimer earls of March and ultimately to the crown (1461).

CONNÉTABLE. *See* CONSTABLE.

CONON, Pope, 686–7, a native of Sicily, priest of Rome, and already an old man and in feeble health when elected as a compromise choice. It was fortunate, given his naiveté and senility, that his pontificate lasted less than a year.

CONRAD I, king of Germany, 911–8, duke of Franconia who was elected king upon the death of Louis the Child, the last representative of the Carolingian dynasty. Most of Conrad's efforts as king were directed to halting Magyar raids and putting down revolts of his dukes. On his deathbed Conrad recommended the succession

of one of his sturdiest foes, Henry the Fowler, duke of Saxony.

CONRAD II, king of Germany, 1024–39, founder of the Salian or Franconian dynasty, was crowned Roman emperor by Pope John XIX in 1027. His vigorous policies, which included the use of *ministeriales,* bolstering the eastern frontier against the Slavs, and expanding the royal domain, contributed significantly to the strengthening of the German monarchy. In 1032 he secured possession of Burgundy (kingdom of Arles) when his empress Gisela inherited the country.

CONRAD III, king of Germany, 1137–52, duke of Franconia, the first of the Hohenstaufen kings of Germany. In 1127 he was elected antiking against Lothair who had succeeded Henry V (1106–25) but he failed in his bid for the crown although he did succeed upon Lothair's death in 1137. Four years of warfare followed with Lothair's son-in-law, Henry the Proud, duke of Bavaria, before peace returned to Germany. Conrad deprived Henry of his duchies, giving Saxony to Albert the Bear and Bavaria to Leopold of Austria. In 1147 Conrad joined Louis VII of France on the ill-fated Second Crusade (1147–9) and lost the bulk of his army to the Turks at Dorylaeum. Before he died, he designated as his successor his nephew Frederick III, duke of Swabia (Frederick I Barbarossa), rather than his own son Frederick who was too young.

CONRAD IV, king of Germany, 1250–4, duke of Swabia and through his mother Isabella (Yolande) de Brienne, heir to the kingdom of Jerusalem. Shortly after the death of his father Frederick II (d. 1250), Conrad left Germany which he had attempted to hold in the face of growing opposition from the papal party headed by the antiking William of Holland (successor to Henry Raspe), hurried to Italy, and occupied Sicily. When the pope remained deaf to his overtures to reach an understanding, he started for Germany to seek to improve his situation there but he died at Lavello (south of Foggia).

CONRAD, king of Jerusalem, 1192, marquis of Montferrat, a leading figure in the Third Crusade (1189–92). In 1187 he drove the Saracens from Tyre and became its lord. In the hope of reestablishing his claim to the throne, he married Isabella, daughter of Amalric I, and was acknowledged king in 1192. He was assassinated shortly after.

CONRADIN (Conradino), son of Conrad IV of Germany (1250–4) and grandson of Frederick II (1215–50), ruled Swabia as duke until Manfred, natural son of Frederick, met his death at the battle of Benevento (1266). Upon the urging of the Ghibellines, he came down to Italy but was captured by Charles of Anjou after the battle of Tagliacozzo (1268) and beheaded. With his death at the age of 15, the Hohenstaufen dynasty became extinct.

CONRAD OF GELNHAUSEN, d. 1390, German theologian, taught at Paris, later served as chancellor of the University of Heidelberg. He took an active part, both in negotiations and in writings (Epistola Brevis, Epistola Concordiae), in the efforts made to resolve the Western Schism. He may be credited with preparing the first systematic exposition of the conciliarist theory, namely, that the community of the faithful was superior in authority to the pope and the rightful judge of who might be the legitimate pope. Their instrument in reaching this judgment was the general council.

CONRAD OF LICHTENAU, d. 1240, Premonstratensian monk, later abbot of the monastery of Urseberg in Bavaria. He continued the Chronicon Ursbergense, a universal chronicle, from 1225 to 1229 and made the final redaction.

CONRAD OF MARBURG, d. 1233, papal inquisitor, may have studied at Paris or Bologna, zealous preacher of the Crusade, confessor of St. Elizabeth of Hungary, and a militant opponent of heretics. In 1231 he was appointed papal inquisitor in Germany. In the exercise of his authority he showed himself ruthless and on occasion willing to condemn on insufficient evidence. A court of bishops and priests at Mainz denounced him in 1233 and he was murdered on his way back to Marburg.

CONRAD OF MEGENBURG, d. 1374, learned and prolific scholar, teacher at Paris and Vienna, and author of some 24 works in Latin and German on scientific, theological, hagiographical, pastoral, and political subjects. It was by way of his translation of works on astronomy and on science in general that much of that knowledge came to Germany.

CONRAD OF WÜRZBURG, d. 1287, German poet, disciple of Gottfried von Strassburg and author of epics, narrative poetry, and romances in verse considered among the best in Middle High German.

CONRAD THE RED, d. 955, duke of Lotharingia, ancestor of the Salian dynasty of German kings, received the duchy of Lotharingia from Otto I whom he had supported against the king's rebellious dukes. Later, when he himself joined a revolt against Otto, he was deprived of his duchy. He lost his life at the battle of Lechfeld but not before helping Otto destroy the Magyar army.

CONSECRATION, the central ceremony during the liturgy of the mass when the celebrant spoke the words that the faithful believed changed the bread and wine into the body and blood of Christ. [See TRANSUBSTANTIATION.]

CONSISTORY. See CARDINAL.

CONSOLAT DEL MAR, "Consulate of the Sea," a collection of Spanish and French rules and practices pertaining to commerce that dated from the thirteenth century. They found general acceptance as rules of maritime law among the nations facing the Atlantic. Their official title was Libre de Consolat.

CONSORS PATERNI LUMINIS, a hymn sung at matins, once attributed to St. Ambrose (d. 397), which hailed Christ as the light of man's soul.

CONSTABLE (connétable), title of a great officer of state in many Western countries whose origins reach back to the count of the stable (comes stabuli) of late Roman times. Under Merovingian and Carolingian kings the constable had charge of the royal stables and might lead the army in the king's name. By the eleventh century he had become one of the five great officers of state in France and from the fourteenth he was the supreme commander in the army. In England, where the office became hereditary, the constable shared command of the army with the marshal and had duties at the king's court as well. Officers in charge of important garrisons also held the title, e.g., Constable of Dover. In England from the late thirteenth century, the petty officer in hundreds and villages who had responsibility for maintaining the peace was called a constable.

CONSTANCE, d. 1198, daughter of Roger II of Sicily, and, as it proved, heiress when her nephew, William II, designated her his successor. She married Henry (VI), son of Frederick I Barbarossa, and was the mother of Frederick (II). With the aid of Pope Innocent III she was able to retain Sicily for her infant son. She served as his regent until her death.

CONSTANCE, city located on the western end of Lake Constance on the site of an ancient Roman fortress. (The Rhine river flows from the lake at this point.) Alemanni occupied the area in the third century and Franks did so from the sixth. It became a bishopric in the sixth century, claimed the status of an imperial city in 1192, and enjoyed considerable prosperity as a center of the linen industry. Its bishops became powerful as princes of the Holy Roman Empire and holders of extensive territories.

CONSTANCE, COUNCIL OF, general church council (Sixteenth Ecumenical) which sat intermittently from November 1414 to April 1418. (Catholic theologians regard it as ecumenical only from July 1415 when Gregory XII officially convoked it.) The principal reason for calling the council was the resolution of the Western Schism which at that time was dividing Latin Christendom into three camps. John XXIII, the Pisan pope, convened the council under pressure from emperor-elect Sigismund who played a dominant role in its proceedings. In order to neutralize the preponderance of Italian prelates, votes were cast by individual nations, one vote each for the English, French, German, Italian, and Spanish delegations, and one vote for the cardinals acting as a group. In May 1415 the council deposed John XXIII, in July accepted the resignation of the Roman pope Gregory XII, and in July 1417 declared the intransigent Avignonese pope Benedict XIII deposed. In November 1417 an enlarged conclave elected Oddone Colonna pope, who took the name Martin V. In the spring of 1415 the council had enacted two decrees that established the principal of conciliar supremacy: the decree Sacrosancta which proclaimed the general council to be the supreme authority in the church, and the decree Frequens which provided for regular meetings of the council. The council also condemned John Wyclif and his writings and tried John Hus for heresy and ordered him burned at the stake. The council addressed itself, finally, to the problem of reform, although it could agree only on a few measures designed to reduce papal authority, viz., the matter of papal provisions.

CONSTANCE, PEACE OF, treaty agreed to in 1183 by Frederick I Barbarossa, king of Germany and Holy Roman Emperor, and the cities of Lombardy by which these cities accepted Frederick's imperial suzerainty in return for his extending them what amounted to an autonomous status.

CONSTANS I, Roman emperor, 337–50, co-emperor with his brothers Constantine II and

Constantius II. He ruled over the dioceses of Italy, Africa, and Illyricum, and after 340, after defeating and killing Constantine II at Aquileia, over Gaul and Britain as well. A conspiracy among his officers headed by Magnentius resulted in his assassination in 350.

CONSTANS II (Pogonatus), Byzantine emperor, 641–68, who lost Alexandria and Egypt to Islam. He lost naval supremacy in the Mediterranean as well. He ordered the exile of Pope Martin I (653) when he refused the imperial judgment in the controversy over Monothelitism. In 662 Constans took an army to Italy, then moved on to Syracuse, probably in the hope of bolstering the empire's defenses in that area against the Lombards and Arabs. He was assassinated there in 668.

CONSTANTINE I, Pope, 708–15, a Syrian who had a generally uneventful pontificate. He did have occasion to assert the authority of Rome over the exarch and metropolitan of Ravenna who had denied his right of jurisdiction. In 711 he visited Constantinople upon the invitation of Emperor Justinian II.

CONSTANTINE II, Antipope, 767–8, was elected pope on the death of Paul I but was driven out of Rome by Stephen IV who had the assistance of the Lombards.

CONSTANTINE I (the Great), Roman emperor, 306–37, extended Christians toleration and was himself the first Roman emperor to become a Christian. He was born c. 275 or later at Naissus in Moesia. His father, Constantius, was shortly to be appointed Caesar in the western empire; his mother was a tavern maid by the name of Helena. In 306 when Constantius died in Britain, his troops hailed Constantine Augustus, although dangerous years lay ahead before he finally emerged in 312 as co-emperor with Licinius. In 313 the two emperors met at Milan and agreed to extend Christians toleration, an event erroneously referred to as the Edict of Milan. Friction between the two emperors

ended only with Licinius's defeat in 324 and his execution the year following. Two decisions of epochal consequence stand out in Constantine's career: first, his benevolent policy toward Christianity and, second, the establishment of a new capital at Byzantium (Constantinople). The first decision, although probably inevitable, altered the entire course of history in the Western world. The selection of the well-nigh impregnable site of Byzantium for his "New Rome" assured the eastern half of the Roman empire a thousand years of existence after the western half had been lost.

CONSTANTINE II, Roman emperor, 337–40, son of Constantine I, shared the rule of the empire with his brothers Constans and Constantius when his father died until, dissatisfied with Britain, Gaul, and Spain which constituted his share, he invaded Italy and was slain at Aquileia by the army of Constans.

CONSTANTINE IV, Byzantine emperor, 668–85, eldest son of Constans II, managed with the aid of Greek fire to throw back a dangerous and extended assault Islam made on Constantinople (674–8). He also drove the Slav and Avar invaders from Thessalonica. But he could not prevent the Bulgars from crossing the Danube and was obliged to pay them tribute. In 680 he summoned a church council to Constantinople (Council of Constantinople III) which condemned Monothelitism.

CONSTANTINE V (Copronymus), Byzantine emperor, 741–75, vigorously pushed the iconoclastic policies of his father Leo III, won major victories over the Arabs and Bulgars, but lost Ravenna and central Italy to the Lombards. The "heretical" policy of Byzantium, coupled now with its inability to give Rome succor against the Lombards, prompted the popes to turn to the Franks for protection.

CONSTANTINE VI, Byzantine emperor, 780–97, succeeded his father Leo IV when he was ten although under the guardianship of his mother Irene. In 790 he managed to assert his authority, but Irene had no difficulty turning the people against him since he had divorced his wife and married his mistress. She had him blinded (797). He lived his last five years in virtual captivity.

CONSTANTINE VII (Porphyrogenitus), Byzantine emperor, 913–59, son of Leo VI, who assumed control of the empire only in 945 after the exile of Romanus I, his father-in-law. He proved himself a scholar rather than a statesman and is remembered principally for the *Book of Ceremonies,* a geographical and historical survey of the provinces of the empire, a treatise on foreign lands and peoples, and a biography of his grandfather, Basil I.

CONSTANTINE IX (Monomachus), Byzantine emperor, 1042–55, selected to marry and rule with Zoe when the incompetency of the two sisters, Zoe and Theodora, recommended such a move. Constantine brought no improvement. He neglected the defenses of the empire while squandering its wealth. During his reign Petchenegs and other barbarous tribes swarmed across the Danube into Macedonia and Thrace, while what proved a permanent schism drove a wedge in 1054 between Eastern and Western Christianity.

CONSTANTINE X (Ducas), Byzantine emperor, 1059–67, weak successor of Isaac I Comnenus, whose reign proved calamitous for the empire. His neglect of the frontier and army invited attacks from all quarters: Petchenegs and Cumans (Polovtsy) penetrated to Greece; Seljuk Turks overran Armenia and entered Asia Minor; Magyars occupied Belgrade; Normans all but extinguished the last of Byzantine holdings in Italy.

CONSTANTINE XI (Palaeologus), Byzantine emperor, 1449–53, the last ruler of Byzantium and, although able and courageous, unsuccessful in enlisting Western support against the overwhelming power of the Ottoman Turks. In the hope of securing Western aid, he had in 1452 proclaimed the union of the Greek with the Latin church. He fell fighting with his troops when the Turks captured Constantinople on May 29, 1453.

CONSTANTINE, d. 411, Roman general in Britain whose troops proclaimed him emperor in 407 against the Western emperor Honorius. Constantine succeeded in conquering Gaul and Spain and forced Honorius to recognize him as co-emperor. In the end he suffered defeat at the hands of Honorius's general Constantius (later Constantius III) and was beheaded. He had withdrawn the greater part of the Roman troops stationed in Britain and they were never replaced.

CONSTANTINE, DONATION OF, a fictitious transfer to Pope Sylvester I (314–335) by the emperor Constantine of the spiritual supremacy of the entire Christian world and temporal dominion over Rome and all the western provinces of the empire. The document which purported to make the pope this generous gift is believed to have been forged shortly after the middle of the eighth century, probably by a member of the papal Curia, for the purpose of blocking Byzantine efforts to reestablish imperial rule in Rome. Even though the justice of its claims drew early attacks, it was not until the fifteenth century that Lorenzo Valla and Nicholas of Cusa proved the document a forgery. Occasional popes had appealed to the document as validating their claim to a voice in the selection of the Holy Roman emperor.

CONSTANTINE III LEICHUDES, d. 1063, distinguished scholar and statesman and first minister of Constantine IX Monomachus, who in 1059 was raised to the position of patriarch of Constantinople by Isaac Comnenus upon the death of Michael Caerularius. Constantine Leichudes is credited with persuading his friend Psellus to write the *Chronographia.*

CONSTANTINE THE AFRICAN, d. c. 1087, merchant, physician, and scholar. He was born in north Africa, traveled widely in the Middle East, took service for some time with Robert Guiscard at Palermo, became a monk, then retired to Monte Cassino where he ended his days. At Monte Cassino he translated a number of Arabic works into Latin, the most important being medical writings that gave Western Europe its first general view of Greek medicine. These translations helped establish Salerno's reputation as a medical center.

CONSTANTINOPLE, the "New Rome" that Constantine I (the Great) established at Byzantium on the Bosphorus and made his capital. He dedicated the new capital in 330. What recommended the city to Constantine were its superb commercial and military advantages. No Western city boasted the volume of trade or approached it in population. None of a number of powerful assaults launched by a variety of foes including Arabs, Russians, and Bulgars succeeded until 1453 when it fell to the Ottoman Turks. Unusual circumstances explain the capture of the city in 1204 by Crusaders (Fourth Crusade).

CONSTANTINOPLE I, COUNCIL OF, general church council (Second Ecumenical), summoned by Emperor Theodosius I. It met in 381 and accepted the Nicene Creed although defining more precisely the natures of Christ and the Holy Spirit. In the process it repeated the condemnation of Arianism and Apollinarianism. This council, which was composed solely of Eastern bishops, also accorded Constantinople precedence of honor over all Eastern patriarchates. Pope Damasus (366–84) accepted the new Niceno-Constantinopolitan creed although not the canon that had awarded precedence in the east to Constantinople.

CONSTANTINOPLE II, COUNCIL OF, general church council (Fifth Ecumenical) summoned by Emperor Justinian I, which met in 553. It condemned any Nestorian interpretation of the

position taken by the Council of Chalcedon (451) as presented in the Three Chapters and confirmed the unity of the Person of Christ in the two natures. Lest the emperor force him to accept an intolerable compromise to satisfy the Monophysites, Pope Vigilius refused to heed Justinian's summons to appear, although he subsequently approved the work of the council.

CONSTANTINOPLE III, COUNCIL OF, general church council (Sixth Ecumenical) 680–81, summoned by Emperor Constantine IV. It condemned Monothelitism and specifically Pope Honorius I (625–38) for what it interpreted as his endorsement of that heresy. It affirmed the doctrine of two wills in Christ and two operations in each of the two natures of Christ. Because of its place of meeting, the council also goes by the name of First Trullan Council or Council *in Trullo*.

CONSTANTINOPLE IV, COUNCIL OF, general church council (Eighth Ecumenical), 869–70, convoked at the suggestion of Basil I, the new emperor, to confirm the restoration of St. Ignatius of Constantinople to the office of patriarch which Photius had resigned. The council condemned certain views attributed to Photius, announced 27 disciplinary canons, and reaffirmed the primacy of the bishop of Rome over the entire Christian world. The Eastern church did not recognize this council as ecumenical.

CONSTANTINOPLE, LATIN EMPIRE OF, 1204–61, was established by the Crusaders (Fourth Crusade) and Venice following their capture of Constantinople. Its jurisdiction was limited to Constantinople, the south Balkan peninsula, and the territory immediately across the Sea of Marmora in Asia Minor. From the beginning, the new state lacked a viable organization. Venice appropriated the most important harbors and islands of the former Byzantine empire as well as three-eighths of the city, while the remainder of the empire was parceled out as fiefs in accordance with Western feudal practice.

Another factor was the rise of principalities such as the French-controlled Achaia (Morea) over which the Latin emperor exercised purely nominal jurisdiction. What proved the principal threat to the Latin Empire was the emergence of what claimed to be the true Byzantine empire, namely, the Empire of Nicaea, under the rule of Theodore Lascaris, a son-in-law of Alexius III Angelus. While the latter state prospered, the Latin empire declined to the point where its authority was limited to the environs of Constantinople itself. In 1261 Michael VIII Palaeologus, who had usurped imperial authority from the ruling Lascarids in Nicaea, made an alliance with Genoa, then seized the city on 25 July when the Venetian fleet and most of the garrison were away. An armistice was presumably in effect.

CONSTANTIUS I (Chlorus), Roman emperor and father of Constantine I (the Great), who was appointed Caesar in 293 by Emperor Diocletian to maintain imperial rule in Gaul and Britain. Upon the abdication of Diocletian and his co-emperor Maximian in 305, Constantius rose to the position of Augustus with authority over the western half of the empire. He restored imperial rule in Britain which had been usurped by M. Aurelius Carausius, but died the next year (306) while campaigning against the Picts and Scots in the area about York. His troops hailed his son Constantine as Augustus.

CONSTANTIUS II, Roman emperor, 337–61, third son of Constantine I (the Great). He shared the rule of the empire with his brothers Constantine II and Constans, his part being the eastern provinces of Thrace, Macedonia, Greece, Asia, and Egypt. He ruled as sole emperor following the deaths of his brothers, Constantine II in 340 and Constans in 350. Fighting flared along the Rhine and Danubian frontiers during the greater part of his reign, and in the east against the Sassanid Persians. Within the empire his encouragement of Arianism, which approached persecution of Catholic Christians, occasioned consid-

erable unrest. In 355 he dispatched his cousin Julian to Gaul to drive back the Franks and Alemanni. Early in 360 he himself marched against the Persians who had invaded Roman Mesopotamia, then turned back when he learned that Julian's troops had saluted him as Augustus, but he died at Tarsus before the two armies met.

CONSTANTIUS III, FLAVIUS, d. 421, master of the soliders under the Roman emperor Honorius following the death of Stilicho (d. 408). He married the emperor's half-sister Placidia and by her was the father of Valentinian (III). Honorius recognized him as co-emperor in 421.

CONSTITUTIONS OF CLARENDON. *See* CLARENDON, CONSTITUTIONS OF.

CONSULATE OF THE SEA. *See* CONSOLAT DEL MAR.

CONTARINI, distinguished family of Venice, one of the twelve that elected the first doge in 697. The first member of the family to be chosen doge was Domenico (1043–70). Andrea was doge when Venice won the naval victory at Chioggia in 1381 which ended Genoese ambitions in the Adriatic.

CONTE, originally a story in verse, often moral and religious in theme, which appeared in the twelfth century. The influence of lays and *fabliaux* gradually caused it to become more varied in literary style and character.

CONTI, NICCOLÒ DEI, Venetian traveler of the fifteenth century who left Venice c. 1414 and visited Arabia, Persia, India, and Java. In 1444 he returned to Venice by way of Indo-China, the Red Sea, and Cairo. The papal secretary Poggio Bracciolini published an account of Conti's travels in his *Historiae de Varietate Fortunae*.

CONVENT, a term used instead of abbey or monastery by the mendicant orders. It ordinarily signified a house occupied by members of a religious community who maintained monastic observances.

CONVENTUALS, name generally given to those Franciscans who accepted a modification of the Rule of St. Francis which permitted them to hold corporate property, as opposed to the Observants who stayed with the original restriction.

CONVERSI, a term with several meanings: public penitents as in Spain; monks who assumed the monastic habit late in life; lay brothers belonging to a religious order.

CONVIVIO. *See* DANTE.

CONVOCATION, a meeting of the bishops of a province. On the continent only bishops attended such a meeting; in England (Canterbury and York) both bishops and representatives of the lower clergy took part. In England convocation had become a tax-granting assembly by the close of the fourteenth century when it usually met in conjunction with a session of parliament.

CONWAY, formerly Aberconwy, town in Caernarvonshire, Wales, whose walls and famous castle were constructed by Edward I (1272–1307) following his final conquest of Wales. To make room for the castle, Edward moved the Cistercian abbey of Aberconwy, the burial place of Llewelyn the Great. It was at Conway castle in 1399 that Richard II was betrayed by the earl of Northumberland to Henry Bolingbroke (Henry IV).

COPE, a liturgical cloak which came into use about the ninth century. It was usually worn by celebrants at liturgical functions other than the mass. It was used widely as a ceremonial choir habit by entire communities on feast days.

COPENHAGEN, capital city of Denmark, which grew from a fishing village called Havn (first noted in 1032). In 1167 Bishop Absalon of Roskilde erected a castle to protect the settlement from pirates, after which it enjoyed rapid growth. In the later Middle Ages it played an important role in wars with the Hanseatic League. It remained under rule of the bishop of Roskilde until 1417 when it passed under royal control. In 1445 Copenhagen replaced Roskilde as the Danish capital. Its university was founded by King Christian I in 1479.

COPTIC CHURCH, according to the testimony of Eusebius founded at Alexandria by St. Mark the Evangelist. Alexandria ranked with Antioch and Rome as one of the principal sees of the early church. In the fourth century, under the leadership of St. Athanasius (d. 373), its courageous patriarch, Alexandria was the most militant defender of the definition of the Council of Nicaea (325) regarding the nature of Christ against the threat of Arianism. In its defense of what it maintained to be orthodoxy against the attacks of Arianism, Alexandria tended to overemphasize Christ's divine nature, and after the condemnation of its patriarch Dioscurus by the Council of Chalcedon in 451, the Coptic church became formally Monophysite and increasingly isolated from the rest of Christendom. The conquest of Egypt by the Arabs in 642 ended any hope the Coptic church might have entertained of eventually winning Christendom to accept its position.

COPTIC LANGUAGE, language spoken by the natives of Egypt from the early Christian era until the tenth century. In essence, it was the language of ancient Egypt into which a large number of Greek words had been incorporated.

COPTIC RITE, the liturgical rite employed by the Monophysite Christians of Egypt from the fifth century.

COPTS, name given to the people of Egypt before the conquest of that country by the Arabs. The name usually carried a linguistic and religious connotation. The Copts were Monophysites.

COPYHOLDER, English peasant (serf, villein, not freeholder) who received a copy of the terms of his tenure from the lord of the manor. The servile obligations required of the unfree peasant gradually became fixed from the latter half of the fourteenth century when they might be inscribed on the court roll, of which the peasant could secure a copy. In time copyholder simply referred to the owner of farm lands that had originally been part of the manorial holdings of a lord.

CORACLE, a round, portable boat made of wickerwork and covered with leather.

CORBEIL, TREATY OF, agreement made in 1258 between Louis IX of France and James I of Aragon by which Louis surrendered claims to Barcelona and Roussillon, James those to Toulouse and Provence.

CORBIE, ABBEY OF, Benedictine monastery in northern France near Amiens founded in 662 by Queen Bathildis, the wife of Chlothar II. It attracted fame during the ninth century for the excellence of its school and library. Its scribes in the monastic scriptorium had an important role in the adoption of the Carolingian minuscule. A greater number of early manuscripts have survived from Corbie than from any other abbey.

CORDE, an old French wood measure, the ancestor of the modern measure of that name.

CÓRDOBA (Cordova), city in southern Spain, probably of Carthaginian origin, in Roman times the principal city of the province of Baetica. In the fourth century it became a bishopric, passed under Visigothic rule in the fifth, and in 711 was captured and largely destroyed by the Moors. In 756 it became the capital of an independent emirate which Abd al-Rahman I established, and in 929 it headed the caliphate of Córdoba under Abd al-Rahman III. During the period of Moorish rule, when it was perhaps the most populous and prosperous city in the Western world, it also ranked with the leading cultural centers of the Islamic world. Its library is said to have contained 400,000 volumes. In

1236 Ferdinand III of Castile took possession of the city. The caliphate itself had come to an end in 1031 with the deposition of the puppet ruler Hisham III. Its mosque, begun in the eighth century, remains one of the most celebrated monuments of Moslem architecture. In 1238 it was converted into a cathedral.

CORIPPUS, FLAVIUS CRESCONIUS, sixth-century Latin epic poet and panegyrist of African origin. He modeled his epic on the *Aeneid* of Virgil.

CORK, town located on the south coast of Ireland and site of a monastery erected there in the sixth or seventh century. On several occasions it suffered destruction during the period of Viking invasions. The present city, which was established by the Norse, remained a virtually independent state until 1172 when it accepted a charter from Henry II of England.

CORNARO, a patrician family of Venice. In 1489, Catherine (Caterina), queen of Cyprus, a very beautiful woman and the family's most prominent representative who had married James II of Cyprus, was forced to cede her kingdom to Venice.

CORNELIUS, Pope, 251–3, a Roman, was banished to Centumcellae (Civitavecchia) and probably martyred. In 251 he presided over a large synod which had gathered in Rome during a lull in the Decian persecution. The synod ordered the excommunication of Novatian who had objected to the relatively lenient policy adopted toward lapsed Christians who had foresworn their faith in order to escape death.

CORONAT, coin of Provence which was used from the twelfth century to the close of the Middle Ages.

CORONATO, a coin struck during the reign of Ferdinand I (1458–94) of Naples.

CORONER, English county official charged with safeguarding the king's property. He held inquests and assisted the sheriff in his judicial work, although it was as much the intent of the crown that he should serve as a check on the authority of the sheriff who had grown too powerful. The coroner appeared in the late twelfth century (1194) and always remained an elective officer.

CORPORAL, the white linen cloth upon which the wafers and the chalice were placed during the celebration of the mass. It was used as early as the fourth century although it was not distinguished before the ninth from the ordinary linen altar cloth used under the corporal.

CORPUS CHRISTI, a special feast in honor of the eucharist whose origins go back to the middle of the thirteenth century. In 1264 Pope Urban IV recommended the celebration of the eucharistic festival to the entire church, and in the fourteenth century the feast became universal in the Latin church.

CORPUS CHRISTI COLLEGE, college at Cambridge University founded in 1352 by a guild of Cambridge townspeople.

CORPUS JURIS CANONICI, body of laws that ecclesiastical authorities in the Western church employed in the government of the institution. The first compilation of laws to which appeal was made appeared shortly after the Council of Nicaea (325), to which in time were added the Apostolic Constitutions, papal decretals, and the canons of subsequent church councils. About the year 1140 Gratian prepared a scholarly compilation known as the *Decretum* which, because of its completeness and the excellence of its organization, superseded all other collections in the West. In 1234 the Decretals of Gregory IX were added to the Corpus, in 1298 the *Liber Sextus* of Boniface VIII, and in 1317 the *Clementinae* (Clement V). The *Extravagantes* of John XXII (1325) and the *Extravagantes Communes* of several later popes to Sixtus IV in 1484 were not added until after 1500.

CORPUS JURIS CIVILIS, title given the four parts of the codification of Roman law carried out by Emperor Justinian (527–65), namely the *Codex Constitutionum, Digest (Pandects), Institutes,* and *Novels.* The *Codex* included 4,652 enactments, many of them dating back to the reign of the emperor Hadrian (117–38). The *Digest* represented a compilation of the writings of the most eminent Roman jurists since the early second century A.D. The *Institutes,* based largely on the work by Gaius (c. 161), was a brief manual designed to introduce students to the elementary principles of Roman law, while the *Novels* constituted a collection of some 150 laws enacted during the reign of Justinian.

CORRODY, originally the right of a benefactor of a religious house to board and lodging for himself or for a nominee of his. The term also applied to pensions and similar allowances which the monastery made to persons who worked for it as well as to persons who, by payment of a lump sum, had secured a corrody as a kind of annuity for life. They were quite numerous in the late Middle Ages and contributed to the impoverishment of some monasteries.

CORSICA, island in the Mediterranean occupied by the Vandals in the fifth century, recovered by Byzantium in 552, taken over by the Lombards in 725, and subjected to Saracen attacks from the ninth to the early eleventh century until the combined fleets of Pisa and Genoa finally put a stop to them. In 1077 the pope, who claimed the island on the basis of the Donation of Pepin, turned its administration over to the bishop of Pisa, and in 1133 divided its jurisdiction between Pisa and Genoa. In 1284 the Genoese victory in the naval battle of Meloria ended Pisan influence. In 1296 Pope Boniface VIII invested the king of Aragon with the suzerainty of both Corsica and Sardinia, a move that ushered in a long period of rivalry and war.

CORTENUOVA, BATTLE OF, a decisive engagement in 1237 won by Frederick II of Germany against the Lombard (Milanese) army. He managed to trap the army at Cortenuova in Lombardy and destroyed it. It actually proved but another episode in the battle for Italy between Frederick and the Lombard cities and their ally, the pope.

CORTES, assembly consisting of nobles, clergy, and elected representatives of free municipalities that made its appearance in Spain, notably in Leon and Castile, as early as the late twelfth century. It convened when summoned by the king and considered royal proposals as well as petitions which it brought forward. Once accepted, these proposals became law.

CORVÉE, labor charges that the serf (villein) owed his manorial lord (seigneur). The most important charge, that of working the lord's demesne, might average three days a week. In theory corvée constituted the rent the peasant paid for the use of the lord's land. [See MANORIALISM.]

CORVEY, ABBEY OF, a Benedictine monastery situated just east of Paderborn in Saxony near the middle Weser which Louis the Pious founded in 815–6 with monks from the abbey of Corbie. It acquired fame as a center of learning and as a shrine by virtue of the relics of St. Stephen and St. Vitus.

COSMAS INDICOPLEUSTES, sixth-century geographer of Alexandria and the most important writer on geography of the period. After travels to India and Ceylon, he took up the life of a hermit and may have become a monk (Nestorian). The books which he wrote about his travels earned him the name of Indicopleustes or Indian navigator. His purpose in writing the *Topographia Christiana,* his principal surviving work, was to prove the accuracy of the biblical view of the universe.

COSMAS AND DAMIAN, SS., brothers, obscure Christian martyrs probably executed in Syria during the persecution of Diocletian (303–5).

These saints, the patrons of physicians, were honored not only for their medical knowledge but also for their refusal to accept fees for their services.

COSMAS OF PRAGUE, d. 1125, a Bohemian chronicler who studied at Liège and became dean of the cathedral chapter in Prague. His chronicle provides a reliable record of Bohemian history from 1038 to 1125.

COSMAS THE MELODIAN (Cosmas Melodus), ST., d. c. 760, monk, bishop of Maiuma (near Gaza), author of 14 canons or hymns in honor of the great Christian feasts, later incorporated into the liturgy of the Eastern church. Cosmas grew up in the household of John of Damascus. His poetry is brilliant in form and metrical design.

COSMATI, a name given to several families of Rome in the twelfth and thirteenth centuries who specialized in a colored marble and stone decorative inlay work. This kind of work was applied both to large surfaces such as bell towers and nave floors and to pulpits and tombs.

COSSA, FRANCESCO DEL, d. 1477–8, Italian painter of Ferrara who was influenced by Piero della Francesca and Mantegna. He, in turn, exercised a profound influence on the course of Bolognese painting. He earned fame for his frescoes including those of the *Months* (in the Palazzo Schifanoia at Ferrara) and altarpieces.

COSTER (Koster), LAURENS JANSZOON, d. 1484, a sacristan of Haarlem whom some scholars credit with the invention of the printing press.

COTTAR, a serf who possessed a dwelling and garden plot but had no land of his own to work. He worked for the lord of the manor, for free peasants, and for other serfs.

COTTE, a kind of shirt or blouse with long sleeves worn by both sexes as late as the fourteenth century.

COUCY, city near Soissons in northern France,

site of one of the most imposing castles of medieval France. The first castle, built in the tenth century by Hervé, the archbishop of Reims, was rebuilt by Enguerrand III in the thirteenth. The donjon of the castle rose to a height of 180 feet and was 103 feet in diameter. Coucy passed to the French crown in 1498.

COUNCIL, GENERAL (Ecumenical), gathering of members of the Christian hierarchy, summoned by Roman and Byzantine emperors, after 1054 by popes, for the purpose of defining major points of faith that had come into question and of considering questions of administration and discipline. Since a general council was viewed as representative of all Christians and under the guidance of the Holy Spirit, the canons it issued concerning faith and morals were considered binding upon all the faithful. The pope insisted upon his right to confirm or deny the validity of any canon a general council might announce, indeed of the council itself, and since the schism of 1054 reserved to himself the sole right of convoking such a council. Both the Eastern Orthodox and Latin churches recognized the first seven ecumenical councils. (The seventh was the Second Council of Nicaea in 787.) Western theologians have designated seventeen councils meeting during the Middle Ages as general or ecumenical. [See particular council by name, e.g., CHALCEDON, COUNCIL OF.]

COUNT, an official of the king, especially among the Franks and Anglo-Saxons, who served as his representative in administering an area (county). The term derived from the Latin *comes* (companion), a title which Constantine I (the Great) bestowed on senators and members of the imperial court who had special responsibilities, e.g., *comes stabuli* or count of the stable. The Germans adopted the title and assigned it to judges, military leaders, and men entrusted with the command of a city or county. During the feudal period the count ranked among the leaders of the aristocratic class. Within his county he exercised wide powers over law, finances, and de-

fense, officially in the name of the king, frequently as an autonomous lord. He might be the vassal of a duke, although counts like those of Toulouse and Anjou were as powerful as any French duke. In Germany a bishop might hold a countship as did the bishop of Würzburg.

COUNT-ABBOT, a layman who was invested with an abbey.

COUNTERPOINT, a term originating in the fourteenth century to describe an art already more than a century old, essentially that of composing one melody that would accompany another melody, note for note.

COUNTY PALATINE, English county of which the lord (earl) originally possessed royal privileges, including the right of exclusive civil and criminal jurisdiction. There were two such counties, those of Chester and Durham.

COURCI, JOHN DE, d. 1219, Anglo-Norman conqueror of Ulster, sent to Ireland by Henry II in 1176 with William FitzAldelm. Much of his career was embittered by a perennial feud with the de Lacys, another Anglo-Norman family in Ireland. In 1205 King John granted Ulster to Hugh de Lacy.

COURLAND, roughly the southwestern part of Latvia, occupied by a people called Curi and first mentioned c. 875. They raided Danish and Swedish shores and were not subjugated until the thirteenth century. This was accomplished by the Livonian Knights of the Sword.

COURTENAY, aristocratic family of France which supplied three emperors to the short-lived Latin Empire of Constantinople; an aristocratic family of Devonshire in England which acquired the earldom of Devon in 1335.

COURTENAY, WILLIAM, d. 1396, chancellor of Oxford, bishop of Hereford and London, and archbishop of Canterbury (1381). As bishop of London he directed the efforts which the church undertook to silence John Wyclif and probably arranged with John of Gaunt, acting regent for the youthful Richard II, the theologian's departure from Oxford and his retirement to Lutterworth. As archbishop, Courtenay secured the condemnation of 24 of the Reformer's propositions and the preaching of these views in England. It was his hope, vain as it proved, that this condemnation would lead to a rapid extinction of Lollardy. Despite the opposition of several of his suffragans, Courtenay managed to visit a large number of the dioceses of his province.

COURTLY LOVE, the love between man and woman which monopolized the talents of the troubadour from the close of the eleventh century until well into the thirteenth. Though the subject continues to be one of controversy, scholars generally agree that the nature of this love ran the gamut from the respect which a vassal might pay his Lady, the wife of his lord, to the carnal love which sought fulfillment; furthermore, that it did not include the love of husband for wife. In the judgment of the troubadour, love was the source of all true virtue and nobility. In time this literary genre, which emerged in the Provence and spread over Western Europe, developed a set of regulated schematizations of meters and rhymes, each to suit a particular mood, e.g., the *tenso* or debate; the *alba* or dawnsong, and the *pastourelle* that sang of the knight and the shepherdess.

COURTRAI, BATTLE OF, also know as the "Battle of the Spurs," a bloody engagement fought in 1302 between the army of Philip IV of France and the Flemish burghers. The Flemish infantry with their pikes and crossbows overwhelmed the army of French knights. The abundance of spurs collected after the victory gave its name to the engagement. The battle holds significance in the history of the art of war as one in which the foot soldier proved that the period of the supremacy of the knight was coming to an end.

COUVRE-CHEF, a tissue-like cloth made in

Reims from the fourteenth century. It was particularly popular with ladies.

COVENTRY, city in central England which grew up around a Benedictine monastery established there in 1043 by Leofric, earl of Mercia, and his wife Godgifu (Godiva). It was the seat of the ancient see of Coventry and Lichfield established c. 669. Following its devastation during the period of Viking invasions, the city was reestablished early in the twelfth century. Coventry, which was one of England's three most important towns outside of London, developed into a major center of the cloth industry. The Coventry plays, a cycle of religious pageants, dated from the fifteenth century.

COVILHÃO, PEDRO DE, d. after 1527, a Portuguese traveler whom King John II in 1487 sent to visit Cairo, Aden, East Africa, Calicut, and Goa to search for the kingdom of Prester John. On his return, Covilhao stopped in Abyssinia (c. 1490), where he married and received high honors from the king. This forced him to remain in that country.

COWL, a cloak used for outdoor wear to which was attached a hood that could be drawn over the head; the hood worn by members of many monastic orders; a choir robe like that worn by Benedictines during the recitation of the divine office.

CRACOW (Karkau, Krakow), city located on the upper Vistula in Poland which first received mention c. 1000 when Boleslaw I took it from the Czechs and made it a bishopric. The Mongols destroyed the city in 1241, but it was rebuilt in 1257, given the city law of Magdeburg, and shortly developed into one of the leading trade centers of eastern Europe. Since 1320 it served as the capital city of Poland. The University of Cracow, the second oldest in central Europe, was founded by Casimir the Great in 1364.

CRÉCELLE, a clacker used to summon the faithful to church service during times when it was not liturgically permissible to ring bells.

CRÈCHE, Christmas crib or manger in which was placed a figure or representation of the Christ Child, about which were figures of Mary and Joseph, shepherds with their sheep and cattle, and, with the coming of Epiphany (January 6), the Three Wise Men (Kings). The practice of displaying such cribs during the Christmas season may have originated with St. Francis of Assisi who fashioned such a crib in 1223 at Gréccio, Italy.

CRÉCY, BATTLE OF, battle fought in August 1346 in northern France near Ponthieu which ended in an overwhelming victory for the English under Edward III of England and against the army of Philip VI of France. It was the first major battle of the Hundred Years' War (1337–1453). Edward had marched an army up the Seine toward Paris, probably to do nothing more than devastate the countryside, then fell back upon the approach of the much larger French army. He owed his victory to the favorable position he had selected to make his stand, to his longbowmen who riddled the ranks of the French knights with their arrows, and to the overconfidence and lack of organization of the French.

CREDO, the opening word of the Nicene creed, meaning "I believe."

CREDO UT INTELLIGAM, a scholastic formula meaning "I believe that I may understand," that is, matters taken on faith still require the application of reason in order to advance understanding. It was a formula made famous by St. Anselm of Bec although he had drawn directly upon St. Augustine.

CREED, an official summary or statement of religious belief, e.g., the Apostles' Creed. Such a summary served as a practical guide in the instruction of catechumens who were preparing for baptism.

CREED, APOSTLES', a formula of Christian belief that may date from the close of the second century, called apostolic because its essential doctrines were believed taught in apostolic times. There was also a legend that the Apostles had met on one occasion when, inspired by the Holy Spirit, each had suggested a matter of faith which they then had incorporated into a creed.

CREED, NICENE, the confession of faith adopted by the Council of Nicaea in 325 and slightly reworded by the Council of Constantinople (Niceno-Constantinopolitan Creed) in 381 in order to confirm the doctrine concerning the divinity of the Holy Spirit. The dogma receiving pointed emphasis in the Nicene creed was that concerning the nature of the Son. The faithful were enjoined to believe that he was of one and the same substance with the Father. The Nicene Creed was introduced into the eucharistic liturgy in the fifth century.

CREMONA, city on the Po of Roman origin sacked by the Visigoths and Huns and rebuilt by the Lombards (seventh century). It became a commune in 1098 and joined the Lombard League in 1167 although its sympathies during the twelfth and thirteenth centuries usually lay with the Ghibellines. It passed under the control of Milan in 1499. [See GUELFS AND GHIBELLINES.]

CRENEL, embrasure in a wall or battlement which permitted the firing of weapons.

CRESCAS, HASDAI BEN ABRAHAM, d. 1412, distinguished Jewish scholar of Spain who went on several diplomatic missions for Peter IV of Aragon. His philosophic writings in defense of orthodoxy and against the rationalism of Maimonides and Gersonides influenced Spinoza. In 1391 he lost his son and his wealth in an outbreak of persecution against the Jews.

CRESCENTII (Crescenzi), a family prominent in Roman and papal affairs from c. 950 until the beginning of the eleventh century. In 974 Crescentius de Theodora led a revolt against Pope Benedict VI in favor of the antipope Boniface VII. Benedict was imprisoned in the Castel Sant'Angelo and there assassinated. Crescentius later received a pardon from Benedict VII who had prevailed against Boniface with the support of the German king, and he died a monk (d. 984). John Crescentius (II) Nomentanus, d. 998, ruled Rome as an autocrat, kept Pope John XV a prisoner in the Lateran palace, drove his successor Gregory from the city, but was captured and executed by Otto III who came to Gregory's rescue.

CRETE, large island off the southeast coast of Greece, part of the Byzantine empire until 826 when the Arabs seized control. In 961 Nicephorus II reconquered the island. In 1204 when the Byzantine empire fell to the Crusaders and Venice (Fourth Crusade), it became a possession of Venice, when it came to be generally known as Candia (after the duke's residence). The Turks captured the island in 1669.

CRISPIN AND CRISPINIAN, SS., two brothers, both shoemakers, who suffered martyrdom at Soissons in 287. Guilds of shoemakers, saddlers, and tanners honored the two as patron saints. In France solemn processions and merrymaking marked their feastday (October 25).

CRISPUS, FLAVIUS JULIUS, eldest son of Constantine I (the Great), who was given the title Caesar in 317 and won a decisive battle against Licinius, Constantine's co-emperor, in 324. In 326 his father ordered him executed on the charge of adultery although scholars reserve judgment as to the real explanation for Constantine's harsh action.

CRIVELLI, CARLO, d. before 1500, Italian painter of the Venetian School whose work reveals the influence of Francesco Squarcione and Donatello. Marked individuality characterizes his works — hard in form, sharp in outline, forceful and energetic, yet glowing with color and ornamentation. Noted works include the *Madonna* and *The Coronation of the Virgin.*

CROAGH PATRICK (Cruach Phadraig), a peak near Clew Bay on the west coast of Ireland where, according to tradition, St. Patrick fasted 40 days and 40 nights before beginning his Irish ministry.

CROATIA, roughly the ancient Roman province of Pannonia which took its name from the Croats, a south Slavic people that settled there in the seventh century. Croats also settled farther south in Dalmatia, then c. 850 joined those in Pannonia to form the first independent Croatian state. (The Croats in Pannonia had been under Frankish rule, those to the south under Byzantine.) They were converted to Christianity in the ninth century. In 925 Tomislav became the first king of Croatia when he received a royal crown from Pope John X. Emperor Basil II (976 – 1025) reestablished Byzantine authority over the Dalmatian Croats, but after his death Croatia was again independent and under Peter Kresimir (1058 – 74) attained the height of its power. Kresimir broke off relations with Constantinople and strengthened the country's ties with the papacy, which explains why the Croats remain an exception among the south Slavs in their adherence to the Roman rite. Civil war broke out when Kresimir died and ended with the Byzantine recovery of Dalmatia and with Hungary occupying most of the Pannonian Croatia. This latter part recognized the king of Hungary in 1102 and was associated with Hungary from then on although enjoying its own autonomous administration.

CROFTER, English peasant (serf) who usually had no more than a croft or garden for his own use. He worked by the day for the lord of the manor or for other peasants.

CRONACA, IL (Simone del Pollaiuolo), d. 1508, Italian master builder and representative of the neoclassical school of architects. He completed the monumental cornice of the Palazzo Strozzi in Florence.

CROSIER, a crook-shaped staff conferred on the bishop (or abbot) at his consecration. It symbolized the spiritual authority with which he would guide his human flock. It was first ordered as a liturgical ornament in the seventh century.

CROSIER FATHERS, officially Canons Regular of the Order of the Holy Cross, a monastic order that credited its founding c. 1210 to Theodore of Celles, a Crusader (Third Crusade). The impressions Theodore gained as a Crusader led him to abandon fighting the Infidel for the role of a missionary. According to the traditional account, he joined St. Dominic in southern France where he preached to the Albigenses, and later established a community near the village of Seyl (Celles) on the Meuse river in Belgium which practiced an apostolate of liturgical prayer and good works. In 1248, when Innocent IV gave the foundation his full approval, it added preaching to its apostolate. From 1410 the order came under the influence of the spiritual movement known as the *Devotio Moderna* with its greater emphasis upon prayer and the development of a personal devotional faith.

CROSS, a symbol used by Christians representative of the instrument upon which Christ was crucified. For them it served to recall Christ's crucifixion and the redemption of mankind. The Christian use of the sign of the cross in blessing oneself, others, or objects originated before 200 A.D. Constantine's mother, St. Helena, is traditionally credited by the Christian Church with finding the True Cross on Calvary in 327. Splinters of the True Cross were in great demand in the Middle Ages as relics. The use of the cross was among practices that drew the indignation of Iconoclasts in the eighth and ninth centuries.

The cross took many shapes. In the Latin cross the upright is longer than the transom. The cross with two transoms was called an archiepiscopal or patriarchial cross, with three, a papal cross. A cross popular with the Slavs had two transoms and a slanting crosspiece below. The Greek cross had arms of equal length. St. Andrew's cross was like an X; the Celtic, or Iona, cross had a circle at the crossing of the two arms.

CROSSBOW, or arbalest, a weapon consisting of a short bow fixed transversely on a wooden stock into which a groove was cut to guide the missle (quarrel). The weapon, which had a range of about 300 yards, made up in force what it lacked in accuracy. The army of the Lombard League used it effectively against Frederick I Barbarossa and his knights at Legnano (1176), as did Richard the Lion-Heart on the Third Crusade (1189–92).

CROWN OF THORNS, an instrument of torture used in Christ's Passion (John 19:2). First mention of it as a preserved relic comes in the fifth century. Cassiodorus (d. c. 580) refers to it as one of the glories of the earthly Jerusalem. It was apparently removed to Constantinople at some later date and in the thirteenth century was purchased from the impecunious Byzantine emperor by Louis IX of France who built Sainte-Chapelle in Paris to house it. The crowning of thorns was a popular art motif of the high and late Middle Ages.

CROZIER. *See* CROSIER.

CRUCIFIX, a model of a cross with the image of the crucified Lord. It was in common use in the Middle Ages, especially as the central ornament of the roodscreen. It came into general use as the central ornament of the altar in the fifteenth century.

CRUSADES, the term traditionally given to the military expeditions which Western Europe undertook between 1096 and 1270 for the purpose of driving the Moslems from, or keeping them out of, Palestine. During the eleventh century the Christian West had taken the offensive against Islam in Spain and in Italy. In 1085 Castile captured Toledo, while by 1091 Pisa,

Venice, and Genoa had forced the Moslems from Italian waters. Some scholars accordingly stress the factor of Western imperialism to explain the Crusades, namely, that it was simply the lure of fiefs, loot, and, in the case of the Italian cities, trade that led Christians to fight Moslems in the eastern Mediterranean by the close of the eleventh century. It was, nevertheless, the appeal that the Byzantine emperor Alexius Comnenus sent to Pope Urban II in 1094 for assistance against the Seljuk Turks that precipitated the First Crusade. (In 1071 the Turks had decimated the Byzantine army at Manzikert and shortly after occupied the greater part of Asia Minor.) Still another factor that calls for consideration in any explanation of the Crusades is the mistreatment suffered by pilgrims to and from Jerusalem. Peter the Hermit, one of the preachers of the First Crusade, had received rough handling in Syria and had been denied access to the holy places. Whatever the measure of mistreatment, the suffering of pilgrims supplied men like Peter the Hermit a stirring issue with which to arouse Western emotions. Without the cooperation of the rank-and-file Crusader who lacked material prospects to inspire him, there would have been no Crusades.

The impact of the Crusades upon Western Europe, given the tens of thousands of men engaged in operations that spanned almost two centuries, was surely of decisive importance, particularly in its influence upon economic developments. The Crusades provided a tremendous stimulus to the revival of trade and to the rise of towns, while the emergence of such Italian cities as Venice and Genoa to positions of commercial and maritime leadership in the West followed upon their ability to exploit their locations as carriers of knights and supplies. The appearance of these powerful city states in north Italy must be counted among the major political consequences of the Crusades, together with the grievous blow the capture of Constantinople in the Fourth Crusade dealt the Byzantine empire. Though reestablished in 1261, it never recov-

ered its former prominence. The position of leadership which the papacy generally assumed in the Crusading movement advanced its ambition to exercise spiritual dominion over Western Europe. In all probability interest in indulgences grew rapidly with its use during the Crusading period as a means of raising recruits.

Western Europe continued to organize crusades long after 1270. Since these had as their objective the blunting of the Turkish drive up through the Balkans to Vienna, tradition has not included them with the Crusades proper.

CRUSADE, CHILDREN'S, two movements of children, one from France, the other from Germany, which made their way in 1212 to French and Italian ports with Jerusalem as their objective. Several thousand children are believed to have boarded ships at Marseilles and Genoa and ended up in Moslem slave markets.

CRUSADE, PEASANT, an "army" composed of perhaps forty-thousand peasants and townspeople which started toward Jerusalem in the early summer of 1096. Most of them died or were dispersed before reaching Constantinople. The Turks annihilated the few that got beyond. Peter the Hermit was one of the leaders of this "crusade."

CRUSADE, FIRST, 1096–9, proclaimed by Pope Urban II at the Council of Clermont (1095). Several small armies led by feudal lords, including Raymond of Toulouse, Stephen of Blois, Robert of Flanders, Robert of Normandy, Godfrey of Bouillon, and Bohemond, began converging on Constantinople in the late summer of 1096 and won a major victory over the Turks at Dorylaeum in July 1097. They stormed Antioch in June 1098 and captured Jerusalem in July 1099. The victorious Christians carved out four feudal states for themselves: the Kingdom of Jerusalem, County of Tripoli, Principality of Antioch, and the County of Edessa.

CRUSADE, SECOND, 1147–9, proclaimed by Pope Eugenius III, preached by St. Bernard of

Clairvaux, and led by Louis VII of France and Conrad III of Germany. Conrad's army was decimated by the Turks near Dorylaeum, while the greater part of that of Louis never reached Palestine. The only success scored by the Crusaders was the capture of Lisbon by a group from England, Germany, and Scandinavia who stopped there on their way to Syria and aided the Portuguese in their attack on this Moorish stronghold.

CRUSADE, THIRD, 1189–92, precipitated by the success of Saladin in uniting the Moslem world, destroying a powerful Crusading army at Hattin (1187), and capturing Jerusalem shortly after. The kings of Germany, France, and England, Frederick I Barbarossa, Philip II Augustus, and Richard I (Lion-Heart), all able men, led armies on what might have proved the most successful of all Crusades had not Frederick drowned in Cilicia. The two young kings, Richard and Philip, stopped quarreling long enough to capture Acre, after which Philip returned to France, leaving Richard insufficient men and supplies to take Jerusalem. Richard did negotiate a truce with Saladin which opened the Holy Places to Christian pilgrims.

CRUSADE, FOURTH, 1202–4, sponsored by Pope Innocent III. When many Crusaders took ship at ports other than Venice, which had contracted for their passage, that city was able to persuade those who appeared to assist in the capture of the island of Zara which belonged to Christian Hungary. Subsequently the Crusaders permitted themselves to become enmeshed in a struggle for the throne in Constantinople, the upshot being their capture of the city and the establishment of the Latin Empire of Constantinople. From the point of view of Venice, this Crusade was an immense success since it took possession of about one-half of the city of Constantinople and most of the islands and ports once belonging to the Byzantine empire. The Crusaders never reached Palestine.

CRUSADE, FIFTH, 1218–21, had as its objective the capture of Jerusalem, not by way of Syria, the route the earlier crusades had followed, but by way of Egypt, thence northward. After several initial successes, including the capture of Damietta, the Egyptians, with the aid of the flooding Nile, trapped the entire Crusading host.

CRUSADE, SIXTH, 1228–9, organized and led by Frederick II of Germany who had married Isabella, heiress of the Kingdom of Jerusalem. It was Frederick's hope to secure Palestine through negotiation with the sultan of Egypt. By the Treaty of Jaffa he did gain possession of Jerusalem and the Holy Places. Many scholars have refused to designate this expedition as a Crusade since Frederick was an excommunicate at the time and, furthermore, won Jerusalem without any significant amount of fighting.

CRUSADE, SEVENTH, 1248–54, precipitated by the capture of Jerusalem in 1244 by the Khwarizmian Turks in alliance with Egypt. Louis IX of France undertook this Crusade, alone and without papal approval (the pope was fighting a crusade in Italy against Frederick II of Germany), and fitted out the largest crusading flotilla to attack Islam in the Middle Ages. A fatal military blunder on the part of Louis's brother Robert nullified a brilliant beginning, highlighted by the capture of Damietta, after which dysentery struck the Crusading army. All who remained alive, including Louis himself, were captured by the Turks.

CRUSADE, EIGHTH, 1270, was undertaken by Louis IX of France against the advice of his councillors and, strangely enough, with Tunis as his first objective. Louis's ambitious brother, Charles of Anjou, who was in possession of Naples and Sicily and also wanted Tunis, persuaded the king that a display of Christian power in Tunis would lead to the emir's conversion, who would then be willing to cooperate with the Christians against the Infidel in Syria.

Dysentery accomplished the destruction of the Crusading army and Louis was among those who succumbed.

CRUTCHED (Crouched, Crossed) FRIARS (Friars of the Cross), name generally given in England to members of military-religious orders, more particularly to members of the Order of the Holy Cross (Crosiers) or *Fratres Cruciferi* which was founded in 1211. In general the name was given to several religious congregations, notably canons regular, who had a custom of carrying a cross in their hands or having one sewn on the front of their habit.

CRUZADO (crusado), a gold and silver coin used in Portugal in the fifteenth century.

CRWTH (crewth, crotha, chrotta, crouth, crowd), an old Celtic stringed instrument which resembled the Greek lyre.

CRYPT, underground or basement area frequently found in churches and reserved for relics or for the tombs of important members of the community. They appeared in the earliest age of the church when Christian services sometimes took place in the catacombs or underground burial places in Rome.

CTESIPHON, ancient city on the Tigris, first mentioned by Polybius in 221 B.C. and sacked by the Romans in A.D. 165. It was rebuilt in the third century and served as the capital of the Sassanid Persian empire until its capture by the Arabs in 637.

CUBITIÈRE, metal piece of armor that protected the elbow.

CUCULLE, a long-hooded garment worn by Germans of the fourth and fifth centuries. It was also the garment which St. Benedict prescribed for use by his monks.

CUIRASS, close-fitting armor worn to protect the chest and back.

CUIRE, leather coat or similar garment worn under mail armor.

CUISSOT, protective covering of metal worn over the thigh.

CULDEES, from the Irish meaning "servants of God," religious ascetics found principally in Ireland and Scotland from at least the eighth century. Their attachment to traditional Celtic ways distinguished them from other ascetics. This group preserved old Irish rules, penitentials, and service books, as well as a mass of semilegendary accounts about the land of "saints and scholars." The Culdees frequently took the form of communities of secular clerics attached to regular monasteries. They declined from the twelfth century as Anglo-Norman influences penetrated these Celtic lands. Their decline might better be attributed to the extensive disciplinary reforms that St. Malachy (d. 1148) introduced in the Irish church.

CUMANS (Kumans), also known as Kipschaks and Polovtsi, a savage Turkish people that moved westward into the Ukraine in the eleventh century, ravaged Hungary, then as allies of Byzantium destroyed the Petchenegs. From roughly the region of Hungary they conducted raiding expeditions into Russia between 1061 and 1210. After the Mongols broke their power in 1239–40, they settled down and were eventually absorbed by the Magyars (Hungarians).

CUMBERLAND, county of northwestern England. St. Ninian introduced Christianity late in the fourth century. It suffered Danish and Irish raids and remained a battleground until 1068 when it was claimed by the king of Scotland. In 1092 William II (Rufus) captured Carlisle, the principal town, and erected a castle. In 1177 Henry II established it as a county. Because of its location on the border between England and Scotland, it witnessed much warfare during the period of the Edwards.

CURE OF SOULS, a clerical office carrying with it

the spiritual charge of people, usually the members of a parish.

CURFEW, regulation in medieval England that required homeowners to cover over or extinguish hearthfires at the ringing of a bell in the evening. The custom may have come to England with William the Conqueror.

CURIA, PAPAL, the papal government. Its personnel consisted at first of members of the clergy of Rome and environs who assisted the pope. An increasing number of clerks and cardinals appeared among its membership from the pontificates of Leo IX (1049–54) and Gregory VII (1073–85). [See CARDINAL.]

CURIAL STYLE, the literary or official style employed by clerks in the Roman Curia in the preparation of documents.

CURIALS, members of the city councils who administered the city state or municipality in Roman imperial times. The name might also apply to members of the papal Curia.

CURIA REGIS, the feudal king's court or government. The term might apply to the large assembly of king's vassals or tenants-in-chief that gathered with him in ceremonial session usually at Christmas, Easter, and Pentecost, or to the smaller group of officials who accompanied him and served as his advisers when the larger body was not in session. The *curia regis* performed in somewhat informal manner all the functions of a governing body. It might elect the king's successor; it met as a judicial body when the king dispensed justice to his vassals in their disputes with each other or in their claims against the crown; it handled the crown's finances; it advised with the king on legislative, military, and political matters, on anything, indeed, that touched the common weal. It was from this original governing body that judicial, legislative, administrative, and financial branches of governments emerged in the high and late Middle Ages.

CURSIVE SCRIPT, the formal bookhand, properly called "Greek minuscule," that employed small, rounded, lowercase letters, joined together in the interest of speed in writing. Its letter forms are first found in Egyptian manuscripts of the seventh and eighth centuries.

CURSOR MUNDI ("course of the world"), a Middle-English poem of unknown authorship that was probably composed early in the fourteenth century. The theme is the story of man's redemption told against the background of history. Although based on the Bible, it incorporated much material that was legendary.

CUSANUS, NICOLAUS. *See* NICHOLAS OF CUSA.

CUSTOMARY, a book containing the rites and ceremonies for liturgical services; also, the rules and customs of discipline of a particular monastery, cathedral, or religious order. In the Middle Ages, when there existed much diversity in practice, such books were of considerable importance. They retain great value as sourcebooks for the historian.

CUTHBERT OF LINDISFARNE, ST., d. 687, prior of Melrose abbey, later of Lindisfarne, who lived as a hermit for about sixteen years before assuming the office of bishop of Lindisfarne upon the urging of the king of Northumbria. Despite his Celtic birth, he endorsed the decision reached at Whitby (664) to adopt the Roman calendar and liturgical usages. Bede's biography of Cuthbert contributed to the great popularity this saint enjoyed in medieval England. His tomb is in the cathedral at Durham.

CYDONES, DEMETRIUS, d. 1397/8, Greek scholar of Thessalonica, imperial secretary of John V Palaeologus, and one of the most influential men of his day. He was one of the leaders in the development of philosophical thought (neo-Platonism), championed the cause of union with the Latin church, and established himself as a foe of the Hesychasts. His visits to Italy, together with his translation of some of the writings of SS. Augustine, Anselm, and Aquinas into Greek, promoted cultural understanding between East and West.

CYMBALS, name given to chimes, also to the shells used in monasteries to summon members of the community to meals.

CYMBELINE, a legendary king of Britain. Geoffrey of Monmouth introduced him in his *History of the Kings of Britain*.

CYNEWULF, English monk of the late eighth or ninth century, the author of four Old English religious poems. The poems are based upon Latin sources and display true metrical skill. Other poems of a similar character have been attributed to him but without sufficient evidence. The poems reveal the deep devotion of the author to the mysteries of the Christian faith and to the saints.

CYPRIAN OF CARTHAGE, ST., d. 258, pagan rhetorician, then a Christian and bishop of Carthage (249), author of many letters and treatises on moral subjects, Scripture, and the unity of the church. He urged a policy of sympathy toward lapsed Christians who had forsworn their faith in order to escape persecution but wished to be reconciled with the church, although he condemned Stephen, bishop of Rome, for accepting them back without rebaptism. His dedication to the unity of the church explains the bitterness he showed toward heretics. He suffered martyrdom under the emperor Valerian.

CYPRUS, large island in the eastern Mediterranean, a possession of the Byzantine empire until 1191 when Richard I of England conquered it. In 1192 it was given as a kingdom to Guy of Lusignan (he bought it). The Lusignan dynasty remained in possession of the island until 1489 when Venice annexed it.

CYRIACUS OF ANCONA, d. after 1449, a merchant by profession and humanist by avocation, who traveled extensively in Greece, Egypt, and the lands of the eastern Mediterranean in search of manuscripts, art objects, and inscriptions. He copied hundreds of inscriptions and prepared a systematic study of Roman ruins.

CYRIL (Constantine) AND METHODIUS, SS., two brothers, both scholars, theologians, and linguists, who in the ninth century labored as missionaries among the Slavs. To facilitate their work they invented a Slavic alphabet using Greek characters, translated the Scriptures into what came to be known as Old Church Slavonic, and introduced a Slavonic liturgy. They worked first among the Khazars, then moved into Moravia upon the invitation of its Slavic ruler who hoped to block the triumph of German influence in his country. When they encountered sharp hostility from the German hierarchy, they went to Rome to enlist papal support. Constantine died in Rome (869) after becoming a priest and monk and assuming the name of Cyril. Methodius resumed his labors in Pannonia and Moravia although he spent three years in prison in Bavaria despite his position as papal legate. Pope John VIII finally secured his release and installed him in the see of Greater Moravia. He died in 885. His disciples were later forced to leave Moravia, whence they transferred their labors to Bulgaria.

CYRIL OF ALEXANDRIA, ST., d. 444, learned theologian and patriarch of Alexandria (412), who held a dominant position in both spiritual and civil affairs in the city. He was not always scrupulous in the use of his power and was especially harsh in his treatment of Novatians, Nestorians, and Jews. During his patriarchate Hypathia was killed by an Alexandrine mob. His extensive writings included commentaries on the Pentateuch, the Prophets, and several gospels; dogmatic and polemical works; letters; and sermons. One of his best known works was his reply to Emperor Julian's *Against the Galilaeans*. Upon authorization of Pope Celestine I he presided at the Council of Ephesus (431) that condemned Nestorius, the archbishop of Constantinople, for his position concerning the nature of Christ.

CYRIL OF JERUSALEM, ST., d. 387, learned bishop of Jerusalem who was three times exiled from his see because of his anti-Arian views. He is best known for his *Catecheses,* a series of 24 catechetical lectures addressed to the catechumens of the city, which are believed to provide a valuable exposition of the ancient creed accepted in Jerusalem. He probably had a major part in the work of the Council of Constantinople I (381).

CYRIL OF SCYTHOPOLIS, Greek monk and hagiographer of the sixth century who lived for a time as an anchorite on the banks of the Jordan. He later attached himself first to the monastery of St. Euthymius, then to the neighboring mon-astery of St. Saba. His lives of seven Palestinian abbots are among the best of the Greek hagiographical works. Since they were written in popular Greek, they also possess considerable philological importance.

CYRILLIC SCRIPT, form of writing employed since the tenth century by Greek Orthodox Slavs. It is uncial as opposed to the cursive Glagolithic writing. Both scripts used letters taken from the Greek alphabet by Cyril (Constantine) (d. 869), missionary to the Slavs. [*See* CYRIL AND METHODIUS, SS.]

CZAR (tsar, zar), title assumed by several Slavonic rulers and by Mongol princes. The Bulgar prince Simeon assumed it in 917 and the Serb Stephen Dushan in 1346.

CZECHS. *See* BOHEMIA.

DACHERIANA COLLECTIO, a collection of Frankish canons compiled toward the close of the eighth century. They influenced the establishment of ecclesiastical discipline from the reign of Charlemagne (d. 814) to the appearance of Gratian's *Decretum* (c. 1140).

DADDI, BERNARDO, Italian painter active in Florence during the first half of the fourteenth century. His work consisted of frescoes, altarpieces, and devotional pictures.

DAFYDD AP GWILYM, d. c. 1380, the leading poet of Wales in the fourteenth century, in the judgment of many critics the greatest poet the Celts produced. His lyric poetry reveals his training in the Welsh bardic art and the presence of French influences. He introduced new themes and meters into Welsh poetry and used a diction free of archaisms. The themes of most of his verse were nature and love, themes which he treated with great sensitivity and wit.

DAGOBERT I, king of Austrasia, 623–8, and of all Merovingian Gaul from 629 to 639. He enjoyed a generally peaceful reign and earned a reputation for justice. His reign witnessed a remarkable increase in the number of monastic foundations. It is also noteworthy for its fine examples of the techniques of cloissonné ornamentation on gold and damascening on iron. Scholars consider him the last of the Merovingian kings who was king in more than name only. The most powerful of the mayors of the palace who would shortly take over complete control after his death was Pepin of Landen, a founder of the Carolingian dynasty.

DAGOBERT II, ST., reigned as king of Austrasia from 676 to 679 when he was murdered. He had earlier been exiled to an Irish monastery by Grimoald, mayor of the palace, then brought back and made king. Because he was murdered, contemporaries honored him as a saint.

D'AILLY, PIERRE. *See* AILLY, PIERRE D'.

DALBERG, JOHANN VON, d. 1503, bishop of Worms (1482). He studied law and Greek at Erfurt and in Italy and served as privy councillor to the elector of the Palatinate whom he assisted in establishing the fame of the University of Heidelberg as an institution of higher learning. He showed himself a patron of scholars, and it was largely through his efforts that Worms and Heidelberg became centers of German humanism.

DALMATIA, region lying along the eastern coast of the Adriatic, part of Illyria when a Roman province. Ostrogoths overran the area in the fifth century, but it was recovered by the Byzantine empire in the sixth and made a theme. In the seventh century most of its people were Slavs who had occupied the greater part of the region except for the coastal cities. By the tenth century the northern part constituted the kingdom of Croatia, the southern that of Serbia. Venice retained possession of several coastal cities and the neighboring islands and for several centuries contended with Hungary for control of Croatia.

DALMATIC, a loose outer vestment with short sleeves and open sides that reached to the knees. In the early centuries it was worn by bishops, and from the fourth century by deacons as well. From the twelfth century its public use was largely restricted to deacons, although bishops and other dignitaries continued to wear it under the chasuble.

DAMASCUS, one of the oldest cities of the world and a major commercial center on the route from Egypt to Mesopotamia. It fell to the Arabs in 635 and served as the capital of Islam during the rule of the Omayyad dynasty (661–750). The Seljuk Turks captured the city in 1076, and Nurredin added it to his Egyptian empire in 1154. In 1260 it fell to the Mongols under Hulagu and in 1401 it was sacked by Timur the Lame who carried most of its craftsmen off to Samarkand. In 1516 it passed under control of the Ottoman Turks.

DAMASCUS, JOHN, ST. *See* JOHN OF DAMASCUS, ST.

DAMASUS I, Pope, 366–84, a Roman of Spanish descent whose pontificate was troubled by factional strife because of the presence of such heretical groups as the Donatists, Macedonians, and Luciferians. He was the first pope to speak of Rome as the apostolic see. He also established Latin as the liturgical language of the Western church. In 377 he commissioned St. Jerome, his secretary, to prepare a new Latin translation of the Bible.

DAMASUS II, Pope, July 17, 1048, to August 9, 1048, a Bavarian, bishop of Brixen, who was advanced to the papacy by Henry III of Germany.

DAME, the wife of a knight in the courtly language of Old French.

DAMESPIEL (Damspiel, Dame), the ancestor of checkers which although not unknown in antiquity, experienced the greater part of its evolution during the course of the Middle Ages.

DAMIANI, PETER. *See* PETER DAMIAN.

DAMIAN, ST. *See* COSMAS AND DAMIAN, SS.

DAMIETTA (Dumjat, Tamiati, Tamiathis), city east of Alexandria which the Arabs fortified in order to control access to the Delta. It suffered attacks by Byzantium and the Normans, was captured by Crusaders on the Fifth Crusade (1218–21) and again by Louis IX on the first of his two Crusades (1249–50). Each time it remained in Christian hands only for a short time.

DAMIRI, MOHAMMED IBN MUSA, d. 1405, Arab scholar, theologian, and professor of tradition in Cairo. He was the author of works on canon law and of a dictionary of natural history which dealt principally with animals. He discussed their use in medicine and their lawfulness as food for Moslems.

DAMME, city near Bruges founded in 1178 that served as a port for Bruges and Ghent to which it was linked by canals. Philip II Augustus destroyed the city in 1213, but it was rebuilt. Its importance declined toward the close of the Middle Ages because of the sedimentation of its harbor.

DAMOISEAU, literally "little lord," that is, a boy who served at the court of a feudal lord as a page while acquiring some training in knighthood.

DAMOISELLE, wife of a squire in the knightly language of Old French; an unmarried daughter of a member of the aristocracy.

DANCE OF DEATH (*Totentanz, danse macabre*), a "death" motif found in the literature and art of the fifteenth century which may have had its inspiration in the ravages of the Black Death. The "dance" itself might have referred to the movements of the "corpse" as it led a living person away by hand to remind him of his inevitable fate. The best-known representations of the dance of death are the drawings of Holbein the Younger (d. 1543).

DANDAIN (dandin), bell hung around the neck of an animal out to pasture.

DANDOLO, an old patrician family of Venice which came to notice in the tenth century. Four of the family's members became doges. The two best known were Andrea (d. 1354), who authored two chronicles of Venice and ordered a compilation of the administrative regulations of the city and arranged a treaty with foreign powers, and Enrico (d. 1205), who directed Venice's exploitation of the Fourth Crusade to serve Venetian interests. He secured for Venice the lion's share in the division of the spoils. In 1205 he and Emperor Baldwin I of the Latin Empire of Constantinople suffered defeat at the hands of the Bulgars. He led the remnants of their army back to Constantinople and died shortly after.

DANEGELD, old English land tax, levied for the first time in 991 by King Aethelred II to buy off the Danish invaders. It was collected irregularly as an ordinary tax until 1162.

DANELAW, roughly that part of England which lay north of a line running from the mouth of the Thames, through London and Bedford, to Chester. According to the settlement agreed to by Alfred the Great and the Danish king Guthrum (d. 885), Danish law and custom were to prevail in this area. Actually the region was not occupied only by Danes, nor did Danish law submerge that which earlier prevailed there. King Edward the Elder (899–924) reestablished English authority over East Anglia and the Danish Midlands. The remainder of the Danelaw was reconquered by 954.

DANES. *See* VIKINGS.

DANEWERK (Dannevirke), a defensive wall erected in 808 by the Danish king Godfred (Gudfred, Goettrik) against Charlemagne and the threat of Frankish expansion from the south.

DANIA, medieval Latin word for Denmark.

DANIEL (Daniil), d. 1264, also called Daniel of Galicia, ruler of Volhynia, 1221–38, and of Galicia (Poland) from 1228. He founded a number of towns including Lemberg (Lvov, Lwiw, Lwow) and Chelm and sought to build up the land's economy by inviting foreign traders and craftsmen. He was obliged to accept the suzerainty of the Golden Horde (c. 1237), but in 1245 he won an important victory over Hungarian and Polish troops at Yaroslav.

DANIEL PALOMNIK, d. 1122, also known as Daniel of Kiev, a Russian abbot who left a generally reliable account in Russian of the pilgrimage he probably made to the Holy Land in 1106–7. His narrative begins with Constantinople and continues through Cyprus to Jerusalem where he was an interested observer of the Easter services.

DANIEL, ST., d. 493, a Stylite, the most famous of the disciples of St. Simeon Stylites. He spent his early years at Samosata and other monasteries in the east, then lived for 33 years on a pillar four miles from Constantinople.

DANSKER (Danziger, Danzker), lavatory or toilet in the shape of a tower located over the castle moat in towns belonging to the Teutonic Knights.

DANTE (Alighieri), 1265–1321, the greatest poet of the Middle Ages, a member of an aristocratic family of Florence. He entered public life and in 1301 found himself a leader of the Whites in their struggle for supremacy against the Blacks. To assure victory for themselves, the Blacks, with the approval of Pope Boniface VIII, invited in a French army, and it was while Dante was away on a desperate mission to Boniface to persuade him to alter his policy, that the French moved in. The upshot was exile for Dante, who spent the remaining twenty years of his life in different cities of Italy, the last of these in Ravenna where he died and was buried.

Few writers have matched Dante in the profundity of his thought and the variety of his literary efforts. Among his lesser works, two in Latin deserve mention. In the *Monarchia* he argued the need for a universal empire for the well-being of the world and pleaded for the revival of the Roman empire for which he believed God had intended a special mission. In the *De Vulgari Eloquentia* he remonstrated with scholars for their refusal to use the vernacular and recommended it as a thoroughly proper vehicle for the expression of their learning. Two minor works in Italian include the *Vita Nuova,* dedicated to Beatrice and displaying features of Provençal verse and the *dolce stil nuovo,* and the *Convivio,* that is, a banquet, in which he planned to introduce the reader to an encyclopedia of knowledge. (It was never finished.)

Dante's fame rests upon the *Commedia,* popularly known as the *Divine Comedy,* a sublime allegory in verse of unparalleled beauty, which tells the story of man's search for, and attainment of, God. The first part of the poem, the *Inferno,* shows Dante (sinful man) picking his way down the precipitous sides of hell under the guidance of Virgil (Reason) who explains why the souls they encounter there, the lustful, hypocrites, and suicides among others, are suffering the torments they do. At the pit of hell they find Lucifer who is gnawing in his three mouths the arch-traitors of society: Judas who betrayed Christ, the church; and Brutus and Cassius who betrayed Caesar, the state.

Dante and Virgil next slide down Lucifer's hairy legs and pass on through a tunnel to emerge at the base of Mount Purgatory (*Purgatorio*). Here gather those fortunate souls who died in God's grace, yet are still burdened with vices and sundry deficiencies which must be purged during the arduous climb up the mountain before qualifying them for admittance into heaven. As they proceed upward, not actual sins but the roots of sin, specifically the Seven Deadly Sins, are purged. Once this climb has been accomplished and Dante reaches the top of Mount Purgatory, the earthly paradise, he is ready to enter heaven though no longer with Virgil (Reason) as his guide but rather Beatrice who symbolizes divine faith and revelation. Beatrice guides him through the different spheres

that make up the heavens (*Paradiso*), from the unconstant moon on upward until the ninth heaven where the mystic St. Bernard of Clairvaux replaces her and introduces the poet to Mary who in turn brings him before the Beatific Vision. Despite the sublimity of his theme and the beauty of his imagery, Dante finds opportunity throughout the *Commedia* to express his views, frequently critical, of the church and of contemporary affairs.

DANZIG (Gdansk), seaport on the Baltic on the mouth of the Vistula, originally a Slavic settlement, first noted in 997 (Urbs Gyddanyzc) as a fishing village. A castle was erected there in 1148, while German immigration from the close of the twelfth century made it the largest city in the region of the south Baltic. In 1308 the Teutonic Knights took the city from the Poles, but Casimir IV recovered control in 1454 and granted the community autonomy.

DARK AGES, term often applied since the time of Petrarch (d. 1374) and until recent years to the period which elapsed between the decline of Rome and the early fourteenth century. When the term appears in modern usage it ordinarily identifies the period from c. 550 to 750. [*See* RENAISSANCE.]

DATARY, APOSTOLIC, office established within the papal chancery in the fourteenth century for the purpose of handling institutions to reserved benefices. Because of the large number of such benefices and the rapid expansion of the office, it stood in need of reform by the close of the fifteenth century.

DAUPHIN (Delphinus), surname of the counts of Albon from the eleventh century, then in the twelfth century that of the counts of Viennois. In 1349 the future Charles V purchased the lordship of Dauphiné and the following year was given the title *dauphin* as heir apparent to the French throne. From that time the eldest son of the king held that title.

DAUPHINÉ, province east of the Rhône and north of Provence which was sold to the future Charles V in 1349. Charles, when king, initiated the practice of ceding Dauphiné to the heir apparent, in this instance, to his son Charles (VI).

DAVID I, king of Scotland, 1124–53, son of Malcolm III and St. Margaret of Scotland, strengthened royal authority by erecting castles and placing sheriffs in charge, and by establishing a new Anglo-French aristocracy with the families of Bruce, Balliol, and Stewart whom he invited to come to Scotland. He also encouraged the growth of the Scottish church by founding at least a dozen major abbeys including Melrose and St. Andrews, reorganizing diocesan administration, and initiating the first steps to securing the independence of the Scottish church from York. During his reign a Scottish royal coinage made its appearance.

DAVID II, king of Scotland, 1329–71, son of Robert I Bruce. He married Joanna, sister of Edward III, suffered defeat at Halidon Hill (1333) at the hands of Edward III, then fled to France. He returned to Scotland in 1341, only to be defeated and captured at Neville's Cross (1346). After pledging to pay an enormous ransom, he secured his release in 1357, then ruled Scotland until his death. He showed little capacity for government and aroused considerable discontent by his extravagance.

DAVID, the name of three Welsh princes, all of whom ruled in Gwynedd, the principal lordship in north Wales. David I (d. c. 1203), son of Owen Gwynedd, married Emma, half-sister of Henry II of England, and died in exile in England where he had fled to escape irate kinsmen whose territorial claims he had ignored. David II (d. 1246), son of Llewelyn ap Iorwerth, through his mother a grandson of King John, repudiated English claims to suzerainty, assumed the title prince of Wales (1244), the first Welsh prince to do so, but died while his war with the English was in progress. David III (d. 1283), son of Gruffydd ap Llewelyn, the last Welsh prince to claim the title prince of Wales, revolted in 1282 over oppressive English administration in Welsh territories adjoining his own, but was betrayed into Edward's hands and executed. (His older brother Llewelyn had been slain in 1282.)

DAVID, GERARD, d. 1523, Flemish painter, the leading artist of Bruges following the death of Memling in 1494. Many of David's compositions, notably *The Virgin Feeding the Christ Child,* have attracted copiers. David was especially successful in painting landscapes.

DAVID OF AUGSBURG, d. 1272, Franciscan, theologian, mystic, and inquisitor against the Waldensians. His Latin and German writings —he was the first author to publish spiritual treatises in German, done in excellent prose— greatly influenced the growth of mysticism in Germany.

DAVID OF DINANT, d. after 1206, one of the leading spiritual writers of his day. His philosophical writings reveal the preponderant influence of Aristotle. His writings on mystical theology show the influence of John Scotus Erigena. These last were judged pantheistic in tone by the Council of Sens (1210) and ordered burned. David was exiled from France.

DAVID, ST., d. c. 601, patron saint of Wales, according to legend a member of a noble family who became a priest and founded monasteries and churches in southern Wales. Much obscurity and a superfluity of legend turn about this saint. His shrine at St. David's was a popular place of pilgrimage in the Middle Ages.

DEACON, title given in the early Christian centuries to anyone who provided service, later to men who assisted bishops at the eucharistic service. First mention of deacons appears in the Acts of the Apostles (6:1–7) which speaks of seven disciples being appointed to "serve at tables." From the eleventh century the deacon enjoyed a formal ranking in the hierarchy just below that of the priest.

DEACONESS, a woman appointed by the early Christian authorities to perform services similar to those of the deacon. Apart from social services, the deaconess might assist in the instruction of converts and in the performance of such rites as baptism by immersion. When adult baptism became rare, the office of deaconess lost most of its importance. Deaconesses appeared in greater number in the Eastern church and continued there after the eleventh century when they had already disappeared in the West.

DEADLY SINS, SEVEN. *See* SEVEN DEADLY SINS.

DEAN, title held by certain minor officials in the imperial household in the fourth century; official appointed by a bishop to administer distant parts of the diocese; the official who presided over a chapter; administrative head of a university faculty.

DECAMERON. *See* BOCCACCIO.

DECEMBRIO, PIER CANDIDO, d. 1477, Italian humanist who translated a number of Greek literary works into Latin. He also produced Latin biographies of several contemporary rulers.

DECIME, aid which the king could demand from the clergy.

DECIUS, GAIUS MESSIUS QUINTUS TRAIANUS, Roman emperor, 249–51, who was proclaimed Augustus by the troops the emperor Philip the Arabian had entrusted him with on the Danube. He defeated and slew Philip in a battle near Verona, then after a reign of about 18 months was himself slain in a battle with the Goths in the Dobruja. He is best known for the first systematic persecution of Christians to be conducted throughout the Roman empire. Among its victims were the bishops of Rome, Antioch, and Jerusalem.

DECORA LUX AETERNITATIS, hymn probably composed during the Carolingian period which made its way into the divine office and was assigned to the feasts of SS. Peter and Paul.

DECORATED GOTHIC, name given to English Gothic of the first three-quarters of the fourteenth century. This style featured large windows with curvilinear tracery, elaborate ribvaulting, and such decorative designs as naturalistically carved foliage. The period may be subdivided between the earlier Geometric period and the later Curvilinear. A fine example of the style is to be seen in Bristol Cathedral.

DECRETAL, a papal decree, of either limited or universal application, given in response to a question concerning doctrine or ecclesiastical law. The first decretal of which there is a record was issued by Pope Siricius in 385.

DECRETALIST, a canonist concerned principally with papal decretals that Pope Gregory IX promulgated in 1234, as opposed to decretists who studied the legal traditions of the church as presented in the *Decretum* (c. 1140) of Gratian. A major concern of both decretists and decretalists was the rights of the church vis-à-vis the state. Both groups of canonists assumed a strongly papalist position.

DECRETALS, FALSE. *See* PSEUDO-ISIDORIAN DECRETALS.

DECRETIST, student of canon law. The name derived from the study of Gratian's basic work, the *Decretum* (c. 1140).

DECRETUM. *See* GRATIAN.

DEER, BOOK OF, a ninth-century manuscript formerly at the monastery of Deer in Cuchan (Aberdeen) which contains a corrupt text of St. John's Gospel, parts of the other Gospels, the Apostles' Creed, and a series of grants to the monastery. These last cast light on the social structure of Scotland at that time.

DEFENSOR PACIS. *See* MARSILIUS OF PADUA.

DEFINITOR, RELIGIOUS, member of a religious community whose responsibilities were largely advisory, that is, to assist monastic superiors in the administration of their offices.

DE HERETICO COMBURENDO, English statute enacted in 1401 during the reign of Henry IV which authorized the execution of heretics (Lollards).

DEIRA, kingdom of Anglia which united with Bernicia to the north in the late sixth century to form Northumbria.

DELFT, town in southern Holland located on the Delft canal which took root in the eleventh century, received a charter from Count William II in 1246, and flourished as a brewery center from the thirteenth century.

DELLA ROBBIA. *See* ROBBIA, DELLA.

DELMEDIGO, ELIJAH, d. 1497, humanist and philosopher of Crete who taught in various Italian cities, and translated the works of Averroës into Latin. His principal work, which concerned religion (*Investigation of Religion*), attacked the scholastic position concerning the complementary nature of faith and reason.

DEMESNE, that part of the manorial lands which the lord reserved for his own use and did not give out to his serfs or villeins, although they worked it. [*See* MANORIALISM.]

DEMETRIUS, ST., d. 231 or 232, bishop of Alexandria from 189, whose importance as bishop turns about his treatment of Origen. He first supported Origen whom he appointed head of the Catechetical School in Alexandria. When the bishops of Jerusalem and Caesarea permitted Origen to preach even though he was a layman, Demetrius censured him for doing so. He later deprived him of his priesthood which he held to be irregular and banished him. Demetrius took part in the controveries with Gnosticism.

DEMICENT, a richly ornamented belt worn by women which was mentioned by Isidore of Seville (d. 636).

DE MONARCHIA, political treatise by Dante in which he urged the separation of church and state and the reestablishment of the Roman empire.

DENGA (dengi, deneschka), first Russian silver coin and the only one used during the period of Mongol rule.

DENIER (denar, denarius), French coin which originated during the ninth century. At first it was of silver, later of base silver and copper, and of varying value and form. Similar coins in Italy, Spain, and Portugal carried the names of *danaro* (*denaro*), *dinero,* and *dinheiro.*

DENIS OF PARIS, ST., patron of France, semilegendary first bishop of Paris who suffered martyrdom about 258. The Latin form of his name is Dionysius and he was long identified as Dionysius the Areopagite. His name was given to the great abbey church at St. Denis near Paris where his relics were translated in 626. The best hypothesis about this obscure saint is that he was sent to Gaul from Rome and there beheaded during the persecution of Valerian. Of the many legends told of him one has him being beheaded on Montmartre in Paris, after which he carried his head to a village northeast of the city where his extremely popular cult had its origin.

DENMARK, country north of Germany which derived its name from the role of its southern part during the Carolingian period when it served as the Danish march. Godfred (Gudfred), its first Viking ruler, threw up a great rampart known as the Danewerk (Dannevirke) to block penetration northward by Charlemagne (d. 814). During the Viking period the Danes joined other Northmen in conducting piratical raids along the west coast of Europe, and in establishing footholds in England (Danelaw) and France (Normandy). Harold Bluetooth (d. c. 985) accepted Christianity, unified the country, and conquered Norway. His son Sweyn Forkbeard conquered the greater part of England which his grandson Canute (d. 1035) incorporated into an empire comprising Denmark, England, and Norway. The empire dissolved after his death, then was reestablished by Waldemar I (1157–82) with the help of Absalon, bishop of Roskilde. In 1214 the German emperor recognized Danish suzerainty over German-Slav lands north of the Elbe and Elde. Another period of disunity after Waldemar's death continued until the accession of Waldemar IV (1340–75). His success in bringing the country under royal control led to war with some of his nobles who were aided by Sweden and certain Hanseatic towns. The coalition defeated Waldemar and forced upon him the Peace of Stralsund (1370) by which the Hanseatic League secured extensive commercial privileges throughout Danish waters.

Waldemar was succeeded by his daughter Margaret who ruled Denmark in the name of her son, then Norway when her husband, the king of that country, died, and, finally, Sweden in 1389 when the Swedish aristocracy expelled their Mecklenburger ruler. In 1397 Eric, her elder sister's grandson, was officially recognized as sovereign of all three countries, although Margaret continued in actual control until her death in 1412. (The proposed Union of Kalmar which would have formally joined the three countries into one empire never materialized.) Margaret's successors lacked her ability, and the union of Scandinavia came to an end in 1448 when Sweden withdrew.

DEO GRATIAS, Latin for "Thanks be to God," an expression frequently repeated in the Latin liturgy. The Rule of St. Benedict required its use by the doorkeeper when receiving a visitor (stranger, beggar).

DE PREDIS, AMBROGIO, d. c. 1506, portrait and miniature painter of Milan who worked with Leonardo da Vinci and adopted his style.

Among his portraits are those of Bianca Sforza and her husband Emperor Maximilian.

DE PROFUNDIS, Latin for "Out of the depths," opening words of Psalm 130 which often found their way into the liturgy during penitential seasons and on occasions of mourning.

DERBY, EARL OF, English title first held by Robert de Ferrers (d. 1139) who was made an earl by King Stephen in 1138. Robert's descendants held the earldom until 1266 when Robert, who had joined the baronial revolt against Henry III, was deprived of his lands. Henry III gave these estates to his son Edmund, earl of Lancaster, whose grandson Henry (d. 1361) passed on his titles of duke of Lancaster and earl of Derby to his son-in-law John of Gaunt, the son of Edward III. John of Gaunt's son Henry, earl of Derby, forced Richard II to abdicate in 1399, when the honor merged in the crown (Henry IV). In 1485 Henry VII created Thomas, Lord Stanley, earl of Derby. During the perilous period from the death of Edward IV in 1483 to his own death in 1504, Thomas barely managed to save himself from execution.

DE REGIMINE PRINCIPUM, political treatise by St. Thomas Aquinas in which he argued that government is necessary since man is by nature a social being; furthermore, that a king is a tyrant when he does not rule according to the moral law.

DERVISH, in general a pious Moslem or mystic, more particularly a member of a monastic community who dedicated himself to the spiritual life while providing material assistance and counsel to people in need. Dervishes made their appearance in 766.

DESCANT, name given the subordinate melody added above and accompanying the main melody. This variation upon the main melody which was introduced about the twelfth century was also referred to as a note-against-note movement.

DESCHAMPS, EUSTACHE, d. c. 1406, a leading French poet who composed *chants royaux, rondeaux, virolais, lais,* two comic plays, an allegorical presentation of the duties of a king, a satire on women, and a prose treatise on poetics. He saw considerable service with Charles V whom he accompanied on some of his campaigns and for whom he carried out several diplomatic missions.

DESIDERATA, daughter of Desiderius, king of the Lombards, who married Charlemagne in 770. The following year Charlemagne repudiated her preparatory to going to war against her father. [*See* DESIDERIUS.]

DESIDERIO DA SETTIGNANO, d. 1464, Italian sculptor of the Florentine school. His work, especially his carving in low relief, reveals the influence of Donatello. His marble carving, noted for its exquisite delicacy, is best seen in his church decorations and in his busts of women and children. One of his original touches is that of showing figures framed in a window, e.g., *Panciatichi Madonna.*

DESIDERIUS, d. after 774, last king of the Lombards, ruled from 757 until 774, when he was defeated and captured by Charlemagne at Pavia. Charlemagne had married Desiderata, the daughter of Desiderius, in 770, but then repudiated her a year later when he began his campaign against the Lombard king. Desiderius had supported Charlemagne's brother and his brother's children, then invaded the papal territories, action that provided Charlemagne additional cause for attacking him. Desiderius was confined to a monastery for the remainder of his life.

DESPENSER, HENRY, d. 1406, bishop of Norwich (1370), took an active part in suppressing the Peasants' Revolt (1381), then in 1382 undertook a "crusade" against Flanders because of its adherence to Clement VII, the pope at Avignon. After a few initial successes, the expedition foundered, and the bishop returned to England in disgrace. He was impeached and deprived of his temporalities, although these were later restored. He was one of the few peers who remained loyal to Richard II.

DESPENSER, HUGH LE, d. 1326, principal adviser of Edward II following the execution of Piers Gaveston in 1312. (He had been one of Gaveston's adherents.) In 1315 the opposition forced both Hugh and his son Hugh (the Younger) out of the government, and in 1321 both were exiled, but they returned to power the following year when Hugh was created earl of Winchester and his son given charge of the royal chamber. They were the real rulers of England until September 1326 when Queen Isabella and Roger Mortimer returned from France with the proclaimed purpose of driving them out of the government. Both Hughs fled with the king, the elder surrendering at Bristol and being promptly hanged in late October, the younger being taken and executed a month later.

DESPOT, title held in the twelfth century by the son-in-law of the Byzantine emperor and by the heir presumptive, later by all sons of the emperor, even by governors of autonomous provinces within the empire.

DESPRÉS, JOSQUIN (usually known as Josquin), d. 1521, Flemish composer, served as choirmaster at the Milan cathedral, then at the papal chapel, finally as provost of the collegiate church of Notre Dame in Condé. He composed masses, motets, and *chansons,* and brought to perfection the Franco-Flemish polyphonic style. He was the most renowed musical figure of his time.

DESTRIER, a war horse or charger.

DEUS IN ADJUTORIUM MEUM INTENDE, first verse of Psalm 69, a traditional introductory to the hours in the Roman and monastic breviaries.

DEUS, TUORUM MILITUM, Ambrosian hymn probably from the sixth century which was sung at matins and vespers on the feast of a martyr.

DEUSDEDIT (Adeodatus) I, ST., pope, 615–18, a Roman who as pope supported Byzantine authority in Italy against the Lombards.

DEUSDEDIT, CARDINAL, d. c. 1100, obscure monk in the Benedictine monastery of St. Martin (near Limoges) who has been identified as probably Anselm of Lucca. He vigorously endorsed the reform measures of Pope Gregory VII who created him a cardinal. To his authorship is credited a compilation of ecclesiastical canons which upheld the authority of the church and the papacy against the claims of the state.

DEVENTER, town located on the Yssel river in the Netherlands, founded in the eighth century, in the thirteenth century a member of the Hanseatic League. It was famed as a center of learning and of the mystical movement known as *Devotio Moderna*. Both Gerhard Groote and Thomas à Kempis are linked with the town. At the close of the Middle Ages it was also well known for its five annual fairs.

DEVOLUTION, RIGHT OF, right of collation of an ecclesiastical benefice that a higher official or extraordinary collator exercised upon failure of the ordinary collator to do so. The avowed purpose of exercising the right was that of preventing carelessness in the collation of benefices and of preventing extended vacancies.

DEVOTIO MODERNA, a term sometimes applied to the religous renewal of the late Middle Ages which had as its objective the achievement of an inner union with God through prayer and works of charity. It originated in the circle round Gerhard Groote, enjoyed its greatest popularity in Germany and the Low Countries, and found its best expression in the activities of such groups as the Brethren of the Common Life. What may be considered an excellent expression of the simple spirituality characteristic of the *devotio moderna* is that presented by Thomas à Kempis in his *Imitation of Christ*.

DE VULGARI ELOQUENTIA. *See* DANTE.

DIALECTIC, or logic, one of the seven liberal arts and a subject of the trivium. The discipline concerned itself with the science of correct reasoning. The growing interest which Western scholars showed in the subject from the late tenth century was the beginning of scholasticism.

DIAS (Diaz) DE NOVAIS, BARTHOLOMEU, d. 1500, Portuguese navigator who turned what he called the "stormy cape" in 1488, a name subsequently changed to Cape of Good Hope. His voyage confirmed the belief that one could reach India by circumnavigating Africa. He later accompanied Cabral on the voyage that resulted in the discovery of Brazil.

DIATESSARON, the edition of the four Gospels in a continuous narrative, compiled by Tatian c. 150–160. It remained the standard text of the Gospels in Syriac-speaking churches down to the fifth century when it was replaced by the four separate Gospels. Its original language may have been Syriac or Greek.

DICETO, RALPH DE, d. 1202, dean of St. Paul's in London and an associate of the prominent political and ecclesiastical figures in England of the time. He authored a chronicle covering the years 1149 to 1202.

DICTATUS PAPAE, list of 27 propositions or claims, attributed to Pope Gregory VII (1073–85) or prepared under his direction, which defined and affirmed the spiritual authority of the papacy over all Christians, including monarchs. The *Dictatus* maintained the superiority of the spiritual over secular authority and declared that the pope could depose a king although no earthly ruler might judge or depose a pope.

DIDACHE, that is, the teaching of the twelve Apostles, an anonymous Christian treatise in Greek, possibly the oldest extant, whose origin has been assigned to the early second century. Its sixteen short chapters concerned themselves with subjects of church practice and morals, e.g., baptism, the Eucharist, the responsibilities of ministers. The treatise holds much interest for students of early Christian liturgy. The author, date, and place of origin are unknown. It gives the Lord's Prayer in full.

DIDASCALIA APOSTOLORUM, series of instructions for Christians, both laity and clergy, concerning faith and morals, presumably drawn up by the Apostles but generally attributed to a Syrian of the early third century. It deals with a variety of subjects: the duties of the bishop, liturgical worship, penance, behavior during persecution, widows, and deaconesses. It is highly critical of Christians who continued to accept Jewish ceremonial law as binding.

DIDYMUS THE BLIND, d. c. 395, learned lay theologian of Alexandria whom St. Athanasius appointed head of the catechetical school. Among his pupils there were Gregory of Nazianzus, Jerome, and Rufinus. Although blind, he produced a large number of works dealing with dogma and exegesis. Although a staunch defender of the Nicene creed, he drew condemnation in 553 for Origenist views.

DIES IRAE, that is, "day of wrath," the opening words of a sequence whose theme is the last judgment. The hymn was probably already in use in the twelfth century although it has been customary to attribute its authorship to Thomas de Celano (d. c. 1260).

DIET, German assembly composed originally (c. 1100) of princes and princely bishops, later of counts and barons as well. From 1250 representatives of episcopal and imperial cities sat in the diet. It met when summoned by the king for the purpose of considering problems of general concern. Whatever resolutions it might agree upon would receive official proclamation as imperial decrees by the king, but since the diet lacked coercive authority it devolved upon the king to see to their enforcement. This he seldom had the power to do.

DIETRICH OF NIEHEIM (Niem), d. 1418, member of the papal Curia for almost 50 years, where he took an active part in discussions aimed at resolving the Western Schism. In his treatises on the subject he assumed a strongly conciliarist position and urged a sharp reduction in the authority of the pope. His *Dialogus de Schismate* represented the first comprehensive presentation of the theory of conciliarism. He published two treatises on curial administration.

DIETRICH VON BERN, heroic figure in German epic, notably in the *Nibelungenlied,* whose historical inspiration has been traced to Theodoric, king of the Ostrogoths (d. 526).

DIEU LE VEUT, late French for the Old French *Deus lo volt* ("God wills it"), the battlecry of Western knights on the First Crusade (1096–9).

DIFFIDATIO, formal repudiation by a vassal of his obligations to his feudal lord or suzerain.

DIGAMY, second marriage, an act which was generally disapproved of in the early church. Several heretical groups such as the Montanists and Novatians condemned it outright. The Council of Nicaea (325) provided that those who married twice were not to be excluded from Christian fellowship. The Eastern Church assumed a more severe position in the matter and since the tenth century officially forbade fourth marriages.

DIGENES AKRITAS, title of the best-known Byzantine epic, its name that of its hero, a half-Greek, half-Arab warrior who defended the Byzantine frontier along the upper Euphrates against brigands and wild beasts. The story, which appears to have been written about the middle of the eleventh century, may have had some basis in historical fact.

DIGEST, that part of Justinian's *Corpus Juris Civilis* that consisted of a condensation of the writings of eminent Roman jurists, most of these from the second and third centuries. Scholars consider it the most valuable part of the *Corpus.*

DIJON, capital of Burgundy from 1016, with origins that reached back into the Roman period. The monastery of St. Bénigne was founded there in 525. The city entered upon the most important period of its history in 1364 when a line of Valois dukes began their rule. Under Philip the Good (d. 1467) its court was probably the most brilliant in Western Europe.

DIMISSORIAL LETTERS, letters given by a bishop to members of the clergy of his diocese which extended them permission to be ordained by the bishop of another diocese.

DIMITRI DONSKOI (Demetrius Donskoj), grand prince of Moscow, 1359–89. He moved his residence from Vladimir to that city, established the supremacy of Moscow in central Russia against the threat of Lithuania, and dealt the Mongols a major defeat at Kulikovo on the Don in 1380. This victory assured him recognition as the national leader against the Mongols who until then had appeared invincible. In 1382 the Mongols again invaded Russia and sacked Moscow.

DINANT, city on the Meuse in the county of Namur, fortified from Merovingian times, a major copper-manufacturing center in the thirteenth century. It belonged to the bishop of Liège and was sacked in 1466 by Charles the Bold of Burgundy when it joined in a revolt against his rule.

DINAR, an Arab gold coin, corresponding to the Byzantine *solidus,* which came into use in all Arab countries and in the Crusading states of the eastern Mediterranean.

DING (English Thing), assembly among the early Germans and Scandinavians which functioned as an advisory body to the chieftain (king) and as a court of justice.

DINIZ (Dinis, Denis, Dines, Dionysius), king of Portugal, 1279–1325. He encouraged the development of agriculture and trade, reduced the power of the nobility and the church, and

founded the University of Lisbon (1290). He also encouraged the use of the vernacular and composed love poems in the Galician-Portuguese lyric style.

DIOCESE, territorial district subject to the jurisdiction of a bishop (archbishop). Both the term itself and the first districts actually organized as dioceses were taken over by the church from the administrative units established by Diocletian in his reorganization of the Roman empire.

DIOCLETIAN, Roman emperor, 284–305, who emerged as sole ruler following the murder of Carinus. From his accession he shared his rule with Maximian who administered the western half of the empire while he ruled the east from his new capital at Nicomedia. In 293 he appointed two Caesars, Galerius to assist him in the east, Constantius to assist Maximian in the west. The extensive reforms which Diocletian undertook in reorganizing the administration of the empire, army, economy, tax structure, and even imperial succession, although not all successful, served to restore the fabric of the empire and assure it a century or more of existence in the west. Most questionable of his reform measures was the persecution of Christians which he decreed in 303. In 305 he retired and forced the reluctant Maximian to do the same, while the two Caesars rose to the rank of Augusti. Diocletian died in 313.

DIODORUS OF TARSUS, d. c. 392, abbot of a monastery near Antioch, then bishop of Tarsus although several times forced into exile by emperors who sympathized with Arianism. He has been called the founder of the catechetical school at Antioch, and as teacher there, he insisted on literal and historical exegesis and on the complete humanity of Christ. His numerous writings include works on cosmology, astronomy, chronology, exegesis, and theology.

DIONYSIUS, ST., Pope, 259–68, a priest of Rome who as bishop of Rome reorganized the Christian community following the persecution of Emperor Valerian. Basil had occasion to commend Dionysius for the manner he handled the Christological controversy in Alexandria, and for his charity in assisting in the ransoming of captive Christians in Cappadocia.

DIONYSIUS OF ALEXANDRIA, ST. (The Great), bishop of Alexandria, 247–65, a disciple of Origen and head of the cathechetical school from 231. He went into hiding during the Decian persecution (250), but was exiled to Libya during the persecution of Valerian (257). Various heresies, including Novatianism and Sabellianism, aroused controversy during his episcopate. His writings are valuable since they were concerned with the many controversies of his time.

DIONYSIUS EXIGUUS (Denis the Little), monk and canonist of the late fifth and early sixth century, also exegete, mathematician, and astronomer. He was the first writer to use the birth of Christ as the base year from which to reckon the date of Easter. The most important of his works was the *Dionysiana Collectio,* a compilation of the canons of the councils of Nicaea, Constantinople, Chalcedon, and Sardica, of the Apostolic Canons whose authenticity he questioned, and of papal decretals. His principal objective was that of reconciling differences between the Eastern and Western churches and establishing the primacy of the bishop of Rome.

DIONYSIUS OF PARIS, ST. *See* DENIS, ST.

DIONYSIUS THE AREOPAGITE. *See* PSEUDO-DIONYSIUS.

DIONYSIUS THE CARTHUSIAN (Denys van Leeuwen, Denys Ryckel), d. 1471, theologian and mystic, member of the Carthusian monastery of Roermond. He was the author of extensive commentaries on the Old and New Testament and of treatises dealing with moral theology, ecclesiastical discipline, and homilies. His writings proved very popular, especially his *De Contemplatione* on the subject of mysticism, although they possessed little originality.

DIOSCORUS, Pope (Antipope), September 22 to October 14, 530, deacon of Alexandria who fled to Rome where he was elected pope following the death of Felix IV. The early death of Dioscorus resolved the schism in Rome brought about by members of the clergy who had opposed the election of Boniface II.

DIOSCORUS, d. 454, patriarch of Alexandria, 444–51, the successor of Cyril whose views on the nature of Christ he shared. He presided at the Robber Synod of Ephesus (449) and supported the heresy of Eutyches, for which reason he was ordered deposed by the Council of Chalcedon (451).

DIPTYCH, folding tablet of wood, ivory, or metal, usually secured by rings or hinges and richly ornamented or illuminated, upon which were inscribed the names of those persons who were to be remembered in the divine service. In the Byzantine church it was customary to list the names of successive bishops and to add or delete individual names depending upon the orthodoxy of the individual prelate.

DIRGE, from the Latin *Dirige,* the opening word of the antiphon which introduced the Office of the Dead. The office appears in early breviaries and early English primers.

DIRNITZ (Dürniz, Durnitz, Turnitz), a heated room in late medieval castles which was used for taking baths.

DISCALCED ORDERS, religious orders whose members went barefoot or wore only sandals, never shoes or similar foot-covering, e.g., Carmelites, Passionists. The practice was followed by early Eastern monks who went barefooted. It was introduced into the West by St. Francis of Assisi.

DISCIPLINA CLERICALIS, a collection of 34 fables, tales, poems, and proverbs from Oriental sources which the twelfth-century Spanish Jew Moses of Huesca (after baptism Petrus Alfonsi) translated into Latin.

DISENTIS (Dissentis), ABBEY OF, Benedictine monastery established in the Swiss Alps on the Lucmagn Pass between Germany and Italy. Saracens destroyed the monastery in 940, but it was rebuilt and especially favored by German kings, notably by Frederick I Barbarossa (d. 1190).

DISMAS, the name traditionally given to the Good Thief (Luke 23:39–43) who was crucified with Christ.

DIT, medieval verse whose subject matter was composed of sayings of a moral and serious as well as a satirical and humorous nature.

DIVES, name derived from the Latin word for rich which Christian writers used to identify the wealthy man spoken of in the parable of the rich man and Lazarus (Luke 16:19–31).

DIVINA COMMEDIA, LA. See DANTE.

DIVINE OFFICE, the Psalms, hymns, scriptural readings, as well as excerpts from patristic and hagiographical literature which the clergy, particularly members of the religious orders, sang, recited, or had read to them at different times during the day and night. By the eleventh century these prayers, hymns, and readings had become formularized in a compact form known as the breviary.

DIWAN (Divan), register of Islamic warriors with their titles and their entitlements to spoils, as that prepared by Caliph Omar (d. 644). Later, under the Abbasids, the term referred to a register of state financial operations, also to the principal departments of the government.

DJAFAR. See JAFFAR.

DJALAL-AL-DIN RUMI, d. 1273, mystic poet of Persia. His greatest work, *Mathnawi,* is a mixture of fables, anecdotes, and reflections whose purpose was the explanation of Sufi doctrines.

DLUGOSZ, JAN (John Longinus), d. 1480, Polish priest, a delegate to the Council of Basel, who wrote a monumental history of Poland in 12 volumes covering the years 1455 to 1480. His work describing the benefices belonging to the church of Cracow is a primary source for economic history. Casimir IV sent him on several diplomatic missions. He also served as tutor of the royal princes.

DOBRA, gold coin of Portugal first minted by Peter I (1357–67).

DOBRIN, KNIGHTS OF, military-religious order founded early in the thirteenth century whose rule was similar to that of the Order of the Knights of the Sword. In 1235 it was absorbed by the Teutonic Order.

DOBRUJA, region of eastern Europe between the lower Danube and the Black Sea, part of the Roman province of Moesia (Lower). It was repeatedly overrun by different peoples, including the Goths, Alans, Huns, and Bulgars. Byzantium recovered control in 1018, but in 1186 it was absorbed in the second Rumanian-Bulgarian empire. Soon after Petchenegs swarmed over the area, followed by Tatars in the thirteenth century. After a brief period under a local chieftain, it succumbed to the Ottoman Turks (1417).

DOBRZIN, ORDER OF, military-religious order established in Poland in 1230 for the purpose of blocking raids by the pagan Prussians.

DOCETISM, a heresy of the first century that denied Christ the material reality of a body and maintained that he only appeared to be a living creature and that his sufferings, therefore, were only apparent, not real. The heresy, which came to be identified with Gnosticism, harassed the Christian church during the first three centuries of its existence.

DOCTA IGNORANTIA, that is, learned ignorance, an idea proposed by late medieval mystics, including Nicholas of Cusa in his *De Docta Ignorantia,* as a proper approach to acquiring an understanding of God. It involved man's admission of the inadequacy of his knowledge as a necessary prerequisite to acquiring the true wisdom, which he might then accomplish with God's assistance.

DOCTOR, title generally synonymous with master and conferred upon scholars who had met all requirements at the university in the arts, medicine, law, or theology that qualified them for teaching. In the early Middle Ages the title might be given to any learned man. It was later used as an honorific title to identify some outstanding scholar, e.g., St. Thomas Aquinas as the Angelic Doctor.

DOCTOR LEGUM, doctor of laws, a title given principally in France and Italy to medieval scholars who taught law.

DOCTOR OF THE CHURCH, a man of eminent learning and sanctity whom the pope or church council officially proclaimed a doctor of the church. The first doctors so honored by the Western church (by Boniface VIII in 1298) were Ambrose, Augustine, Jerome, and Gregory the Great. The first four to be so designated in the Eastern church were John Chrysostom, Basil, Gregory of Nazianzen, and Athanasius.

DOGE, Byzantine official who ruled Venice from 697. In 1032 he lost most of his authority and retained only his position as commander of the army and navy.

DOGE'S PALACE, the Palazzo Ducale in Venice which was erected over a period of time. The principal external façade facing the water was built in 1309–40, that facing the Piazetta in 1423–38.

DOLCE STIL NUOVO, the "sweet new style," name given to the lyric themes and meters of the Provençal troubadours which Italian poets of the late thirteenth century began to adopt and to furnish with a content akin to that of metaphysical poetry.

DOLPHIN, figure of the aquatic animal which was used as an art symbol to represent Christians hurrying as it were toward Christ. Christ was usually represented by a sacred monogram.

DOMENICO VENEZIANO, d. 1461, Italian painter of the Florentine school. His best known work is the *St. Lucy Altarpiece*. Even though he did not introduce oil painting to Tuscany as Vasari declares, he did encourage interest in color and texture and the use of color instead of simple lines as the basis of perspective.

DOME OF THE ROCK. *See* OMAR, MOSQUE OF.

DOMESDAY BOOK, survey made in 1086 upon orders of William the Conqueror which recorded the names of all English landowners on the assumption that all held directly or indirectly from the king. The survey was to record the number of men living on these lands, the size of their holdings, as well as chattels, mills, fishponds, etc., with their value given in pounds. William's purpose in ordering the survey was to ascertain the extent and value of his own personal holdings as well as those of his tenants-in-chief. The survey represented a silent but convincing testimony to the strength and efficiency of William's rule.

DOMINICA, Latin word for Sunday.

DOMINICAL LETTER, one of the first seven letters of the alphabet as used in liturgical calendars to identify the Sundays of a particular year.

DOMINICAN NUNS, monastic order for women founded by St. Dominic in 1206 with the establishment of the convent of Notre Dame in Prouille (near Carcassonne). The object of this first community was that of receiving female converts from Albigensianism. The superiors of the Dominican first order exercised jurisdiction over the nuns who made up the second order, and also assumed responsibility for their spiritual development.

DOMINICANS, also known as Black Friars, Friars Preachers, and Order of Preachers, the order of mendicant friars founded by St. Dominic and approved by Pope Honorius III in 1216. Since canon law forbade the establishment of new orders, Dominic adopted the Rule of St. Augustine and reenforced this with the strict customs of the Premonstratensians. What emerged, nevertheless, was a monastic order substantially different not only from the traditional Benedictine order but also from the newly founded Franciscan organization. The Dominicans retained the divine office of traditional monasticism with its devotion to prayer and the liturgy. It shared with the Franciscans their poverty, although without quite the same emphasis, and their lay apostolate, but with greater concern for preaching and teaching than for works of charity. From the beginning the order readily granted dispensation from conventual observances in the interest of study and preaching. Unique, too, was the democratic organization of the order which provided for the representative principle in the affairs of both the individual community and the larger organization itself. A corollary to preaching was the order's insistence upon study and education. Each priory was required to have a resident teacher. The order spread rapidly in the Rhineland and western Germany where its members, both men and women, took the lead in the flowering of late medieval mysticism. It shared the intellectual leadership of western Europe with the Franciscans and through the thought of such eminent scholars as Albert the Great and St. Thomas Aquinas introduced Aristotelianism into Christian theology. The order's interest in learning and its concern for orthodoxy led to the use of many Dominican friars by the courts of the inquisition. Already in Dominic's lifetime (d. 1221), provision was made for a Second Order of nuns and a Third of laymen and laywomen. The traditional habit of the Dominicans consisted of a white tunic, scapular, and hood, with a black mantle added for formal occasion and for travel.

DOMINIC GUNDISALVI (Gundissalinus), a twelfth-century Spanish philosopher, probably an archdeacon of Toledo, who translated many Arabic works into Latin. (A learned Jew by the name of Avendauth translated the Arabic into Castilian, then Dominic the Castilian into Latin.) Although little of his work was original, he did seek to present the views of such scholars as Avicenna and Avicebrol in a manner that Christians could comprehend.

DOMINICI, JOHN, BL., d. 1419, Dominican scholar, reformer, and popular preacher in Florence and Venice. Pope Gregory XII appointed him archbishop of Ragusa (1407), created him a cardinal (1408), and appointed him papal legate to several countries and to the Council of Constance. He labored earnestly for the end of the Western Schism and left treatises on theological, exegetical, and ascetical subjects.

DOMINIC, ST., d. 1221, founder of the Dominicans or Order of Preachers, a canon of Osma (Castile) named Domingo de Gúzman, who with several other priests engaged in itinerant, mendicant preaching among the Cathari in southern France during the years 1206 to 1217. In 1214 he organized his company of preachers into a religious community and in 1216–17 secured papal approval of what came to represent in time a distinctly new order, although the prohibition against forming any new religious orders forced him to adopt the Rule of St. Augustine with the addition of the strict observances of Prémontré. What emerged was essentially the kind of community he had already established, namely, a monastic order that combined the spiritual-liturgical character of traditional monasticism with a lay apostolate of preaching. Dominic sent friars to different cities, including Paris and Bologna, to learn theology and canon law, also bands of preachers to form priories in England, Germany, Hungary, and Scandinavia. He also found several convents for women. [*See* DOMINICANS.]

DOMINO, a cape or cowl worn by monks for protection against the rain or cold.

DOMINUS VOBISCUM, a liturgical greeting in Latin meaning "The Lord be with you," which the principal in a religious service addressed on various occasions to his attendants and to the people. The answer these gave to the greeting was "Et cum spiritu tuo," that is, "and with thy spirit." The formula may be as old as Christianity itself.

DOMITILLA, FLAVIA, ST., late first century, niece of Emperor Domitian who exiled her and had her husband executed because of their Christian faith. Domitilla's niece of the same name may have suffered banishment.

DOMRÉMY (LA PUCELLE), village in Lorraine, the home of Joan of Arc. The house in which she was born (1412) and the church in which she was baptized are still standing.

DON, term derived from the Latin *dominus* meaning lord, a title first given to the pope, then to members of the upper clergy, and finally to all priests in Italy and even to many nobles.

DONAT, short for Donatus. *See* DONATUS.

DONATELLO, d. 1466, leading sculptor of the early fifteenth century and the most original and comprehensive genius of the group of contemporary sculptors, painters, and architects. He produced a revolution in art in Florence. His reliefs were the most advanced of the time, while his statues, despite their expression of aspects of classical sculpture, breathed the dramatic and emotional intensity of an original and sensitive artist. His best known works include *Lo Zuccone* and the equestrian statue of *Gattamelata*. His bronze *David* was one of the first large-scale, free-standing nudes of the Renaissance.

DONATION OF CONSTANTINE. *See* CONSTANTINE, DONATION OF.

DONATION OF PEPIN, the transfer in 756 to Pope Stephen II by Pepin III, king of the Franks (741–68), of Rome and the lands which he had taken from the Lombards, essentially the exarchate of Ravenna. Pepin retained the position of patrician or protector.

DONATISM, a "purist" schismatical movement of the fourth and fifth centuries, largely centered in north Africa, which denied the efficacy of sacraments administered by priests and bishops who were not in the state of grace. The Donatists also objected to receiving lapsed Christians back into the church without rebaptism. St. Augustine used his personal influence and his pen in combating the movement. Donatism declined during the fifth century from internal dissensions and from the repressive measures taken to suppress it by both church and state.

DONATISTS, students who had advanced beyond the elementary level in their study of Latin and had taken up the study of the grammar of Donatus.

DONATUS, bishop of Carthage, 313–47, founder of the schismatical movement to which he gave his name. He was ordered exiled to Spain where he died. [*See* DONATISM.]

DONATUS, a child marked for later admittance to a monastery; an adult who associated himself with a monastic or knightly order. [*See* OBLATE.]

DONATUS, AELIUS, Roman grammarian of the mid-fourth century whose Latin grammar was used throughout the Middle Ages. His name became, in fact, a metonymy for grammar in the forms *donat* and *donet*. He was the teacher of St. Jerome.

DONJON, inner tower or keep of a fortress (castle), usually rectangular and heavily fortified. [*See* CASTLE.]

DONUS, Pope, November 676 to April 678, a Roman, successor of Adeodatus (II), who had a short and uneventful pontificate.

DOOM, term which in Germanic languages

meant law, enactment, or a decision of a judge, particularly one that went against the defendant.

DOOMSDAY BOOK. *See* DOMESDAY BOOK.

DORDRECHT (Dordt), the oldest city of Holland, founded by Count Dirk III in 1008. It became a town c. 1200 and by 1400 had grown to be the largest in the country. It was the leading port on the mouth of the Rhine.

DÖRING, MATTHIAS, d. 1469, Franciscan, provincial of the order in Saxony. He attended the Council of Basel and subsequently suffered excommunication for his conciliarist views, whereupon he resigned his office and retired to a life of study. His writings attacked the doctrine of the supremacy of papal authority in the church.

DORLAND (Dorlant), PETER, d. 1507, Flemish Carthusian and author of some 60 Latin works which included sermons and treatises on ascetical, devotional, and historical subjects. Some scholars credit him with the authorship of the morality play *Elckerlyc* of which the English *Everyman* is probably a translation.

DORMITION OF THE VIRGIN, the falling asleep (death) of the Virgin, from the close of the fifth century a popular theme in the literature and art of the Christian church.

DORMITORIUM, the sleeping area or dormitory in which the monks slept until the later Middle Ages when the use of single rooms became the rule.

DORTMUND, city on the Rhine in Lower Lorraine which rose during the Carolingian period and soon grew into an industrial center on the strength of its excellent commercial location. It joined the Hanseatic League in the early thirteenth century, after which it developed extensive trade connections with England and Russia and prospered to such a degree that, on several occasions, it advanced loans to the English crown.

DOSSIÈRE, piece of armor, part of the cuirass, that protected the back of the knight.

DOUBLE MONASTERY, combination of two monastic establishments, one for men (monks), the other for women (nuns), one contiguous to the other and both administered by one superior. The superior might be either an abbot or an abbess. In the Brigittine order the abbess served as the superior of both houses. Double monasteries appeared early in the history of monasticism and were especially numerous in the East. Double monasteries declined in popularity from the tenth century.

DOUGLAS, ARCHIBALD, d. 1424, fourth earl of Douglas and first duke of Touraine. He took part in Scottish raids against the English and in the revolt of the Welsh under Owen Glendower against Henry IV. He supported the cause of the Dauphin (Charles VII) in France and met his death at the battle of Verneuil.

DOUGLAS, ARCHIBALD, d. 1514, fifth earl of Angus. He joined the revolt (1487–8) of Scottish nobles against James III when he earned his nickname "Bell-the-Cat" because of his capture of Robert Cochrane, the royal favorite whom the nobles hated. From 1493 to 1498 he served James IV as lord chancellor.

DOUGLAS, JAMES (the Good), d. 1330, first joined Robert Bruce, then attacked his own castle which was in English hands and destroyed it. His many raids across the border into England won him the name "Black Douglas" (he also had a dark complexion). In recognition of his heroism, including his bravery in the Scottish victory at Bannockburn, Bruce exempted him and his family from all feudal dues except military. He died fighting the Moors in Spain where he had stopped off on his way to the Holy Land. In his possession at the time was a silver casket containing Bruce's heart which he had promised to take to Palestine.

DOUGLAS, JAMES, d. 1491, ninth earl of Douglas. He led a revolt against James II of Scotland whom he accused of murdering his brother William. When deserted by his allies, he received aid from Edward IV but was later captured on a raid into southern Scotland and died a prisoner in the Lindores Abbey, Fife.

DOVE, in Christian liturgical art the symbol of the Holy Spirit, also of martyrdom, even of the church. A vessel fashioned in the form of a dove might serve as a container for the eucharist.

DOVER, town on the Channel of Celtic origin. Because of its location it became one of England's most important towns after 1066 when William, duke of Normandy, became king of England. It proved the easiest link with the possessions England held in France.

DRACHMA, an ancient Greek coin minted by the Crusaders in Syria.

DRACONTIUS, BLOSSIUS AEMILIUS, d. after 496, a lawyer of Carthage, the leading Christian Latin poet of north Africa. The best known of his works was a long epic poem on the goodness of God entitled *De Laudibus Dei*.

DRAMA, MEDIEVAL, had its origin in the trope which may be defined as a textual interpolation into the liturgy of the divine office or the mass for the purpose of dramatizing its meaning. One of the earliest tropes was the Easter play of the tenth century entitled *Quem Quaeritis* which enlarged on the gospel story about the holy women who came to the tomb on Easter morning. There gradually evolved from these efforts at dramatizing stories or incidents in the liturgy the dramatic performance known as the mystery play. From this mystery play which usually drew its theme from the Bible it was but a short step before the miracle play made its appearance with its much richer store of themes drawn from the lives of the saints. By the early thirteenth century the themes and associations of these mystery and miracle plays had departed so far from their liturgical origins that the Fourth Lateran Council (1215) forbade priests to take any further part in their presentation. In the fifteenth century medieval drama took an allegorical turn with the appearance of the morality play in which abstract virtues and vices were personified. The most popular of these in English-speaking lands was *Everyman*. The late Middle Ages also witnessed the birth of interludes or short, humorous plays which were presented between parts of miracle and morality plays, and of secular farces such as that of *Master Pierre Patelin*.

DREILING, a three-penny silver coin which was being minted in eastern Germany at the close of the Middle Ages.

DRESDEN, city of Saxony on the Elbe which probably grew out of an earlier Slav community that had located itself there because of its flood-free situation and the mines in the neighboring mountains. By 1216 when Margrave Dietrich provided its future growth along rectangular lines, it already boasted a church, a market, and a fortress. In 1287 a bridge was built across the Elbe. In 1270 it became the capital of the margraviate of Meissen.

DROGHEDA (Droichead Atha), town on the east coast of Ireland which served first the Norse, then the Anglo-Normans as a stronghold and trading post. What assured its continuous growth was its location within the English Pale, together with its commercial and military importance. Edward III granted it the right to coin money, several parliaments were held there, and it served as the seat of the primate of Ireland during the Middle Ages. During the reign of Edward III it was one of the four staple towns of Ireland.

DROGO OF METZ, d. 855, an illegitimate son of Charlemagne who became a monk, later bishop of Metz. He cooperated with Louis the Pious in reforming the church and from 843 served as the principal councillor of Emperor Lothair.

DROIT DE GÎTE. *See* PURVEYANCE, RIGHT OF.

DROIT DU SEIGNEUR. *See* JUS PRIMAE NOCTIS.

DRUZES (Druses), a Shiite sect which appeared at the beginning of the eleventh century. Its name derived from a certain al Darazi (d. 1019) who claimed that al-Hakim, the sixth Fatimite caliph (996–1020), was really the incarnation of God. Some Druzes continued to believe he was still alive.

DSCHAMI, MAULANA NUR OD-DIN 'ABD OR-RACHMAN, d. 1492, Persian poet and mystic, the author of some 50 works dealing with poetry, grammar, theology, and mysticism.

DUBLIN, city on the east coast of Ireland, settled possibly as early as the third century A.D. It was seized by the Norse in the ninth century and became the capital of a Viking kingdom in the tenth. Anglo-Norman invaders captured the town in 1170. Henry II came over in 1172 and held his court there and granted a charter. During the medieval period Dublin served as a capital city of the English Pale, a strip of territory on the eastern seaboard controlled by the English.

DUBLONE, an early Spanish gold coin.

DUBOIS, PIERRE (Petrus de Bosco), d. after 1321, French lawyer and polemicist who served as royal advocate from 1300 and supported Philip IV in his contest with Pope Boniface VIII and in his suppression of the Knights Templars. In *On the Recovery of the Holy Land* (c. 1306), his principal treatise dealing with political theory, he proposed that all western European rulers accept French hegemony as the only hope for a peaceful Europe and a necessary prelude to a successful crusade against Islam. He strongly opposed papal intervention in secular affairs.

DUCAS (Dukas, Doukas), Byzantine family which became prominent in the ninth century and supplied three rulers for the throne during the period 1059–78: Constantine X, Romanus IV, and Michael VII.

DUCAS, Byzantine historian of the fifteenth century whose work covers the period 1341 to 1462. His history, which is written in a journalistic style, suffers from inaccuracies. Ducas strongly urged the union of the Greek and Latin churches as a means of procuring Western aid for Byzantium against the Turks. After the fall of Constantinople, he was employed on diplomatic missions by the Genoese rulers of Lesbos.

DUCAT, a gold coin struck in Venice in 1284. The name came from the Latin legend on the reverse side which ended with the word *ducatus*. From the fourteenth century gold coins in Hungary and Bohemia were given the name ducat.

DUCCIO DI BUONINSEGNA, d. c. 1319, first great master of the Siena school. His earliest work of renown, and the only fully documented work of his that remains, is his altarpiece *Virgin in Majesty* on the high altar in the cathedral of Siena. His forte was pictorial narrative. He demonstrated remarkable skill in making the setting of a scene, such as figures and surroundings, a dramatic part of the action.

DUDO (Dudon), d. before 1043, author of a history of the first dukes of Normandy (to 996). His account, written in alternate prose and poetry, constitutes a useful source for the period despite its lack of objectivity and the introduction of clearly imaginative events.

DUFAY, GUILLAUME, d. 1474, considered by contemporaries and by modern scholars the greatest composer of his period of both religious (hymns, motets, masses) and secular (*ballades, rondeaux, virelais*) music. He was the founder and leading composer of the Burgundian school and served as director of music in the cathedral in Cambrai. His style combined Gothic and Italian elements with some influence from John Dunstable.

DUGUESCLIN (Du Guesclin), BERTRAND, d. 1380, a soldier of Brittany to whom Charles V entrusted the command of military operations against the English at a time when France appeared on the threshold of collapse following the defeat at Poitiers (1356). Although Duguesclin was captured three times by the English, the last time by the Black Prince in 1367 at the battle of Nájera, much of France's success against England during this period has been credited to his military talents as a tactician. In addition to fighting the English, he made it his responsibility to destroy the "Free Companies" of mercenary bands that were pillaging the countryside. In 1370 Charles appointed him constable of France. He died during a campaign in southern France.

DUKE, from the Latin *dux*, a title held from late Roman times by the ruler of a district or province known as a duchy. In England the title was reserved for members of the royal family until the reign of Richard II (1377–99). In France *duc* ranked just below royal prince.

DULCIMER, musical instrument related to the harp and psaltery which first appeared in Spain in the twelfth century. It was introduced by the Arabs.

DUNASH, name of two Jewish scholars of the tenth century: a) D. ben Labrat, grammarian and poet of Córdoba, and b) D. ibn Tamim, a student of the Hebrew language and a philologist.

DUNBAR, WILLIAM, d. c. 1530, a Franciscan of Scotland whom the king sent on various diplomatic missions. His verse earned him recognition as the first important Scottish poet.

DUNCAN I, king of Scotland, 1034–40, who reigned in, rather than ruled, that northern country. He was slain by Macbeth who usurped his throne.

DUNDEE, seaport north of Edinburgh, probably an ancient Pictish settlement, which first received mention c. 1200, shortly after which it became a royal burgh. Possession of the seaport passed between England and Scotland several times during the course of the fourteenth and fifteenth centuries.

DUNFERMLINE, ABBEY OF, Benedictine monastery in Fife founded by Queen Margaret of Scotland c. 1074. It became the leading monastery of Scotland and served as burial place for many Scottish rulers.

DUNGAL, Irish name held by several noteworthy persons including: a) D. of St. Denis, d. after 827, an Irishman who became a recluse at the abbey of St. Denis (near Paris) and whose letters reveal him to have been a man of considerable learning; and b) D. of Pavia, whom Lothair I (d. 855) appointed director of education in northern Italy.

DUNOIS, JEAN, COUNT OF, d. 1468, called the Bastard of Orléans, a natural son of Louis, duke of Orléans. He joined the Armagnacs in support of the Dauphin (Charles VII) and took an active part in the fighting in Normandy and Guienne against the English. He was in charge of the defense of Orléans when Joan of Arc arrived to relieve the city. Charles rewarded him for his services with the county of Dunois (1439) and appointed him grand chamberlain, although the count never abandoned his loyalty to the aristocracy. He joined the *Praguerie* against Charles VII and was a leader of the League of Public Weal against Louis XI.

DUNS SCOTUS, JOHN, d. 1308, the leading Franciscan scholastic and medieval England's greatest philosopher and theologian. Duns Scotus was born in Scotland, studied at Oxford and Paris, lectured in both cities, and received his doctorate at Paris in 1305. He was expelled shortly after with other Englishmen by Philip IV and went to Cologne where he died. Although he is best known for his highly critical mind — his honorific was the Subtle Doctor — he was a deeply religious man who never lost sight of the prime purpose of his studies, namely, the service of God. He shared with other scholastics the view that philosophy merited no direct study in itself but only as a useful discipline in the defense and explication of the signs of revelation. Even to theology he assigned a strictly practical, not speculative role, that of advancing man's love of God. Since God is love, everything has its origin in love, and it was only to manifest his love that God created man. Although God willed the Incarnation from all eternity, independent of any foreknowledge of Adam's fall, the primary purpose of that mystery was the manifestation of God's love for man. Duns Scotus assigned a major role to Mary in the redemption of man and was one of the first theologians to argue her immaculate conception.

Duns Scotus affirmed the absolute freedom of God's will even while insisting that God could not act contrary to reason. The supreme value of man is his freedom of will, and since knowledge comes before action, intellect has a priority of origin. Yet since it is the will that commands the intellect, and not the reverse, the will enjoys a superiority and primacy over the intellect even though both are interdependent. The will commands the intellect, while the will itself is motivated by God's grace. Duns Scotus in effect limited the role of reason in the pursuit of divine knowledge—this constitutes his most significant disagreement with St. Thomas Aquinas—and, furthermore, denied any complementary relationship between faith and reason. Since revelation was a matter of faith and was of divine origin, reason could contribute nothing to its confirmation. This first major objection of Duns Scotus to the basic scholastic premise of the complementary nature of faith and reason led in the following generation to the frontal attack another Franciscan, William of Ockham, made on this fundamental Thomistic position.

DUNSTABLE, JOHN, d. 1453, English mathematician and astronomer, although best known as a composer of motets and other ecclesiastical pieces. He was one of the very few English composers to exert any influence on the develop-

ment of European music. He accomplished this with the relaxation of harmony and rhythm. Some 60 of his works survive.

DUNSTAN, ST., d. 988, member of the household of the archbishop of Canterbury, abbot of the Benedictine monastery at Glastonbury, bishop of Worcester, and London, and archbishop of Canterbury (960). He enjoyed great influence with King Edgar (959–75) in whom he found a close collaborator in the reform and expansion of monasticism. His reform of English monasticism represented one of the three major monastic reform movements of the time, the other two being centered at Gorze in Lorraine and at Cluny in Burgundy.

DUFFING, a belt worn by men and women from the tenth century.

DUPPLIN, BATTLE OF, battle fought on August 12, 1332, between the supporters of Edward Balliol, who had the encouragement of Edward III, against Donald, earl of Mar, regent for the young David II, son of Robert I. Balliol won the battle and was crowned at Scone on September 24, 1332.

DURANDUS, GUILELMUS. See DURANTI, WILLIAM.

DURANDUS OF SAINT-POURÇAIN, d. 1334, Dominican philosopher and theologian who studied at Paris, taught at Avignon where he was held in high esteem by the popes, and later became bishop of Limoux, Le Puy, and Meaux. His major works include a commentary on the *Sentences* of Peter Lombard and a treatise concerning the respective authority of church and state. In his theological writings he leaned toward nominalism and was himself quite critical of Thomism, for which reason he came under frequent attack both from within and without the Dominican order.

DURAN, PROFIAT (Ephodi) (Isaac ben Moses Halevi), d. c. 1415, Jewish exegete and grammarian, probably born in Provence, who moved to Spain where he accepted baptism in order to escape persecution. He subsequently made his home in Palestine where he resumed the practice of Judaism. He was the author of biblical studies, a Hebrew grammar, and a commentary on Maimonides's *Guide of the Perplexed*.

DURAN, SIMON BEN ZEMAH, d. 1444, called Rashbaz, rabbi and physician of Algiers, author of a systematic study of theology but noted in particular for his *responsa* concerning contemporary social and religious problems. He was also a poet and an authority on the subject of Hebrew scholastic philosophy.

DURANTI (Durandus, Durantis), WILLIAM, d. 1296, a leading canonist who taught law at Bologna and Modena and served as papal auditor and as governor of Romagna. In 1285 he was consecrated bishop of Mende (France). He was the author of an influential treatise on judicial procedure in civil and ecclesiastical courts. His *Rationale Divinorum Officiorum* is recognized as the standard authority in the study of the liturgy of the thirteenth century.

DURAZZO, ancient city of Albania, captured by invading Goths, Serbs, Bulgars, and Normans, then by Crusaders of the Fourth Crusade (1202–4), when it became a possession of Venice. In 1267 it was made a duchy under the rule of the king of Naples. In 1392 Venice recovered control of the city and held it until 1501 when it passed to the Ottoman Turks.

DURENDAL (Durandart, Durandarte), the name of Roland's sword.

DURHAM, city in northeastern England whose origins went back to the Anglo-Saxon period. Durham became a bishop's seat in 995, the year that the remains of Cuthbert were brought there.

Its bishops were unusually powerful men in their role as prince-bishops of a county palatine whose remoteness from London and proximity to the Scottish border assured them an influential voice in Anglo-Scottish relations. They possessed such privileges as the right to hold courts of chancery and exchequer, the right to appoint justices of the peace and coroners, and the right to coin money. A castle was erected in 1072, and a Benedictine monastery was established in 1083, while the great Romanesque cathedral was constructed between 1093 and c. 1130. The cathedral is judged the finest example of Norman architecture in England.

DURROW, BOOK OF, a lavishly illuminated book containing the four gospels which was made in either Northumbria or Ireland about the year 675.

DUSHAN, STEPHEN. *See* STEPHEN DUSHAN.

DUSING (Duchsing, Dupfing, Dupsing), wide, loose belt worn by both sexes from the fourteenth century.

DWIN, city of Armenia established by Chosroes II (331–9) which served as a patriarchal seat from 465 to 931 and also as the capital of Armenia for the greater part of that time.

DWORJANE (Dvorjane, Dovorjanin), class of retainers who served members of the lowest aristocracy in Russia during the twelfth and thirteenth centuries. They began to acquire possessions of their own in the fourteenth century.

DYMPNA, ST., an Irish, British, or Armorican princess who, according to legend, fled to Antwerp where she lived as a recluse until slain by her father. Her cult became popular in Flanders in the thirteenth century. She was honored as the patroness of the insane.

EADMER (Edmer) OF CANTERBURY, d. c. 1130, chaplain and secretary of Anselm of Bec and his biographer. He also composed biographies of other saints, several devotional studies, the first theological defense of the doctrine of the Immaculate Conception, and a history of England (c. 1066 to 1122).

EALDORMAN, the Anglo-Saxon king's leading representative in the shire. He had command of the local militia and presided over the shire court. In the early eleventh century his title was changed to earl.

EARL, Anglo-Saxon nobleman who was know as an ealdorman until the reign of Canute (1016–35). The chieftains whom Canute brought with him from Denmark were called jarls, from which term the word earl is derived. The Norman kings retained the title, and it remained the highest in point of honor until 1337 when Edward III created the title of duke of Cornwall for his son Edward, the Black Prince. The two most powerful earls were those holding the great palatinate earldoms of Chester and Durham whose privileges included the right to maintain their own courts and to appoint their own justices of the peace and coroners. In time the title lost its earlier eminence and sank in prestige below that of marquis.

EARLY CHRISTIAN ART, a period in the history of art which reached from c. 300 to the tenth century. Until Emperor Constantine extended Christianity toleration, Christian artistic expression was limited for the most part to graffiti and casual drawings inscribed on the walls of catacombs. By the time Christians had emerged from the underground, their earlier hostility to the use of images, which they had inherited from their Jewish ancestors, had disappeared, although an explanation for the continued popularity of religious symbolism may be traced to this ancient aversion to the depiction of natural figures. Beyond paintings and mosaics which graced their churches, early Christian artists expended their talents on the production of ivories, silver reliquaries, oil lamps, gilded glass work, and carvings of sarcophagi. Christian iconography during this early period did not differ significantly from pagan art except in subject matter, and it declined, as did all the arts, with the decline of the Roman empire.

A major departure from pagan Roman usage appeared in the type of church the Christians selected for worship. They preferred a large enclosed space where they could conduct services away from the curious eyes of the uninitiated, and therefore chose a basilica-type structure rather than the shrine that had served pagan Greeks and Romans. The Christian church was a spacious, rectangular building, not unlike the civic hall the Romans used for their courts of justice. The enclosed area usually consisted of a central nave, flanked on either side by one or two aisles, which were separated from the nave by rows of columns that supported the entablature above. The light which lit the central area came through windows pierced in the clerestory walls. At one end of the nave, usually the eastern which faced Jerusalem, was the semicircular apse with its domed vault. The principal door was to the west. The roof of the main structure was made of timber whose rafters might be left visible or, in more pretentious structures, cased with richly gilded coffers. The most impressive features of the more splendid Christian basilicas were first their size, which the long perspective of oft-repeated columns made appear even greater than it was; the richness of wall, ceiling, and even floor decorations; and the abundance of light that flooded the interior.

In Italy where Byzantine influences continued strong in such places as Sicily and Ravenna, churches frequently revealed in their structural and decorative characteristics the fusing of Western and Byzantine elements, as in Saint' Appollinare in Classe. [See BYZANTINE ART.] The most striking departure from the early Christian basilica in the west was represented in Charlemagne's sixteen-sided church in Aachen.

EAST ANGLIA, kingdom in Anglo-Saxon England settled by Angles in the late fifth century. It comprised the present counties of Norfolk and Suffolk. Its history extended from the sixth to the ninth century. From about 650 it was subject for long periods to Mercia, then in 825 to Egbert of Wessex. The Danish invasions of 865–9 left most of the region in a state of destruction, after which it remained a part of the Danelaw until 917 when the Danes were finally expelled.

EASTER, feast commemorating the resurrection of Christ, probably the oldest Christian observance of its kind next to Sunday which was recognized as the weekly commemoration of the resurrection. The date of Easter proved a source of constant controversy in the early church. Some Christian communities observed Easter on the fourteenth day of the Jewish month of Nisan, the day the Jews celebrated Passover. As such it could be any day of the week. The Council of Nicaea (325) decreed a Sunday celebration, but disagreement continued as to which particular Sunday. Celtic usage which did not quite conform with the Quartodeciman (Easter on the same day as Passover) fell into disuse shortly after the decision reached at the Synod of

Whitby. in 664. From the eighth century the Latin church followed the Eastern cycle worked out by Dionysius Exiguus (d. after 525).

EASTER CYCLE, the sequence of dates by which the Sundays of Easter followed each other, from the earliest possible day of March 22 to April 25, the latest.

EASTERN ROMAN EMPIRE. See BYZANTINE EMPIRE.

EASTERN SCHISM, the renunciation in 1054 by the Greek church of its acceptance of the primacy and authority of the bishop of Rome. [See CAERULARIUS, MICHAEL.]

EAST MARK. See OSTMARK.

EAU D'AUGE, a medieval perfume.

EBEDJESUS. See ABDISHO BAR BERIKA.

EBENDORFER, THOMAS, d. 1464, Austrian theologian, diplomat, and historiographer. He studied at Vienna, served as the university's representative at the Council of Basel, and left an account of his activities there. He also composed several chronicles as well as treatises on philosophical and theological subjects.

EBERHARD IM BART, d. 1496, count and later duke of Württemberg, made a pilgrimage to Jerusalem in 1468 and founded the University of Tübingen in 1477. He established the law of primogeniture for his duchy and became a leading member of the Swabian League.

EBERHARD OF ROHRDORF, BL., d. 1245, monk and abbot of the Cistercian monastery of Salem (near Baden) who served as Pope Innocent III's emissary in Germany during the critical years following the death of Henry VI (1197). The *Codex Salemitanus* in which were recorded documents pertaining to the lands and legal titles held by the abbey during his abbacy constitutes an important source for the cultural and economic history of upper Swabia.

EBIONITES, name originally given to all Jews of

Palestine who accepted Christianity, later to a sect that fled Jerusalem and established its own community in Syria and Transjordan. They maintained that Christ had only a human nature until his baptism, condemned the theology of St. Paul, and dismissed his conversion as a demoniacal hallucination. The sect, which followed strict ascetical practices, flourished until the fourth century.

EBROIN, d. c. 683, powerful, cruel Frankish statesman, mayor of the palace of Neustria at a time when the Merovingian kings had lost most of their authority to these ambitious officials. His own vicious actions contributed to the general decadence of the times. Perhaps his most infamous deed was the mutilation and execution of Leger, bishop of Autun.

ECCE HOMO (Latin, "Behold the Man!"), words which Pilate addressed to the crowd when he showed them Christ after he had ordered him scourged and tortured (John 19:5). The incident proved a popular theme in the art of the late Middle Ages.

ECCE IAM NOCTIS TENUATUR UMBRA, hymn attributed to Alcuin (d. 804) which made its way into the divine office. It appeals to God for mercy and peace.

ECCLESIA AND SYNAGOGUE, symbols of the New and Old Covenants which were popular motifs in medieval art and literature.

ECCLESIA MILITANS, term referring to the church composed of those Christians who were still living and, therefore, fighting the forces of evil, as opposed to those who had already gone to their glory (*Ecclesia Triumphans*).

ECCLESIA NON SITIT SANGUINEM, that is, the church does not seek blood, a reference to the position assumed by the medieval church and perhaps first expressed by Pope Leo I (d. 461) when he declared that the church did not inflict the death penalty. While ecclesiastical tribunals never condemned any person, even heretics, to death, it was generally assumed that when the church turned such persons over to the civil authorities, their execution would follow.

ECCLESIA TRIUMPHANS, term referring to the church as composed of those who have already triumphed over evil and are enjoying the reward of the just in heaven. [*See* ECCLESIA MILITANS.]

ECHANSON, cup-bearer, one of the highest royal dignitaries in the French court at the close of the Middle Ages.

ECHAUGUETTE, small balcony which was added to fortified walls in order to facilitate the launching of projectiles. It was also used by sentinels.

ECHEVINS. *See* SCABINI.

ECHORCHEURS, that is, "Skinners," a name given to certain bands of soldiers during the latter decades of the Hundred Years' War for the merciless manner in which they ravaged the French countryside.

ECHTERNACH, MONASTERY OF, Benedictine abbey on the Moselle above Trier founded in 698 by Willibrord, bishop of Utrecht. It served as a port of entry for Irish and Anglo-Saxon missionaries and scholars coming to the continent, also as a missionary base for evangelizing efforts among the Frisians. From the eighth through the tenth century it enjoyed considerable renown for the excellence of its school and scriptorium.

ECKBERT OF SCHÖNAU, d. 1184, monk in the Benedictine monastery at Schönau (near Trier) who was famed for the eloquence of the sermons he preached against Catharism. He composed a biography of his saintly sister, Elizabeth of Schönau, and published her revelations.

ECKHART (Eckart, Eckehart), MEISTER, d. before 1328, a leading Dominican theologian and mystic, studied at Paris and Cologne, became provincial of his order in Saxony, and a teacher of theology at Paris and Strasbourg. He won most fame as a spiritual director and preacher at

Cologne where he expounded a message of personal piety, love of neighbor, and total detachment from the concerns of this life as the surest means of attaining union with God. Despite papal condemnation of many of his views, he is considered the leading mystic of the Rhineland and the founder of a new school of mystical theology. He counted John Tauler and Henry Suso among his devoted disciples.

ECRIN, chest in which jewels and other precious articles were kept.

ECTHESIS, a Monothelite profession of faith published by Emperor Heraclius in 638. It forbade the mention of "energies" in Christ, whether one or two, and asserted that the two natures were united in a single will.

ECU, almond-shaped shield.

ECU D'OR (Couronne d'or), principal French gold coin from the reign of Louis IX (1226–70).

ECUMENICAL COUNCIL. See COUNCIL, GENERAL.

ECUMENICAL PATRIARCH, title used by the patriarch of Constantinople despite protests of the pope, to signify his first position in the empire after the bishop of Rome.

EDDA, name given to two classes of old Icelandic literature. The Prose Edda, composed by Snorri Sturluson early in the thirteenth century, consists of quotations and excerpts from earlier poems and deals generally with mythology. The second, the Poetic Edda, consists of a collection (late thirteenth century) of some 30 songs with themes mythological and heroic written between c. 800 and c. 1200. Beyond legends concerning Sigurd (Siegfried), Brynhild (Brunhild), and the Norse gods, the Edda contains information pertinent to the history and literature of ancient Scandinavia. The preface to the Edda is a Christian essay on biblical history.

EDESSA, ancient city on the upper Euphrates, a center of Christianity from the third century. It was the home of the Nestorian "Persian School," and even after that center had been suppressed in 489, it continued to remain an important stronghold of Nestorianism. The city fell to the Arabs in 639 but returned to Christian rule in 1099 when conquered by Crusaders (First Crusade). It fell to the Turks in 1144. [See EDESSA, COUNTY OF.]

EDESSA, CHRONICLE OF, an anonymous chronicle of the city of Edessa which covered the years A.D. 201 to the sixth century, when it was composed.

EDESSA, COUNTY OF, the most northern in the tier of four states which the Crusaders established in the eastern Mediterranean during the period of the First Crusade (1096–99). It was located on the upper Euphrates in Mesopotamia and was claimed by Baldwin of Flanders, the brother of Godfrey of Bouillon, as his principality. Its capture by the Seljuk Turks in 1144 set Western Europe to organizing the Second Crusade.

EDESSA, SCHOOL OF, theological center east of the upper Euphrates which flourished from the early third century as a center of Oriental Christian culture until 489 when Emperor Zeno ordered its suppression because of its Nestorian tendencies. Its greatest period as a theological center dated from 363 when Ephrem the Syrian moved his school of theology there from Nisibis. Many of its students became bishops in Persia.

EDGAR, king of England, 959–75, son of Edmund I, died in his early thirties after a generally peaceful reign. He won for himself the title "the Peaceful." He enjoyed friendly relations with the Welsh and Scots, encouraged trade, and reformed the system of coinage. What probably proved his most enduring work was the support he gave to Dunstan whom he recalled from exile. He made him bishop of Worcester, then of London, and finally in 960 archbishop of Canterbury, and aided him in his efforts to reform the church, in particular monasticism.

EDGAR ATHELING, d. 1125?, grandson of Edmund Ironside, chosen to succeed to the throne after Harold's death at Hastings in 1066, but submitted to William the Conqueror. He fled to Scotland in 1068, took part in Scottish attacks on England, then joined Robert of Normandy on the First Crusade (1096–99). Upon his return, he joined Robert in his attempt to wrest the throne from Henry I and was taken prisoner at the battle of Tinchebrai (1106).

EDICT OF MILAN. *See* MILAN, EDICT OF.

EDINBURGH, city in southeastern Scotland whose firm history dates from the reign of Malcolm III (1058–93) who occasionally made his home at the castle there. The burgh grew up around the castle walls during the reign of David I (1124–53). Its first extant charter was granted by Robert I the Bruce in 1329. The city was twice destroyed by the English (1341 and 1385), and only emerged as clearly the capital of Scotland during the reign of James II (1437–60).

EDMUND I, king of England, 939–46, successor of his half-brother Aethelstan, recovered all of north England, including Northumbria, from its Norse rulers. He issued three law codes, one of these enjoining clerical celibacy for the clergy, no doubt upon the insistence of Dunstan, then abbot of Glastonbury. He died at the hands of an exiled robber.

EDMUND II IRONSIDE, son of Ethelred II, ruled northern England for a short time following the death of Swein Forkbeard (1015), the Danish conqueror, while his father held on to the southeastern part of the country. After early victories against Canute, the son of Swein, which earned him the title "Ironside," he was defeated although he retained control of Wessex until he died in 1016.

EDMUND RICH (of Abingdon), ST., d. 1240,

studied and taught at both Oxford and Paris and earned fame as a preacher and for the austere life he led. In 1233 he was consecrated archbishop of Canterbury, but in 1240 he returned to the Cistercian monastery at Pontigny following a quarrel with Henry III. He was among leading English ecclesiastics and barons who attacked the king for accepting the advice of his French councillors and for submitting to papal pressure to intervene in Sicily. His devotional treatise and sermons greatly influenced later English spiritual literature.

EDMUND THE MARTYR, ST., d. 869, king of East Anglia whose army was defeated by the Danes in that year. When he refused to share his kingdom with the pagan Danish leader Inguar, he was beheaded. His remains, transferred in the tenth century to Bury St. Edmunds, made the abbey a popular place of pilgrimage.

EDWARD I, king of England, 1272–1307, son of Henry III, had already assumed a major role in the government following the defeat and death of Simon de Montfort at Evesham in 1265. In 1270 he had undertaken to lead an army in support of the Crusade of Louis IX, and it was on his way home that he learned of the death of his father. Edward entertained great territorial ambitions which he partially satisifed with his conquest of Wales and the execution of David III in 1283, its last native prince. His efforts to establish his claim to suzerainty over Scotland cost him much effort since both John Balliol and William Wallace, who had earlier pledged him homage, refused to accord him the prerogatives this recognition entailed. He died on a third campaign into Scotland. What partly explained Edward's interest in Scotland was the support Scotland gave to and received from France, a relationship which he felt must be severed before he could expect any permanent success in defending his continental possessions, notably Gascony. His taxation of the clergy for the purpose of raising funds to pursue his wars precipitated a major clash with Pope Boniface VIII. [*See* BONIFACE VIII, POPE.] Without question Edward's greatest achievement was the extensive legislation he sponsored in the interest of reforming justice and local administration, his encouragement of foreign trade, and the strengthening of the crown. The most far-reaching development of his reign was the rise of Parliament which he encouraged by regularly summoning that body and, more important, inviting the shires and boroughs to send their representatives. [*See* PARLIAMENT.]

EDWARD II, king of England, 1307–27, son of Edward I, proved himself a weak monarch and the tool of ambitious and unpopular favorites. Baronial opposition to the crown, the scramble over the enormous holdings of Gilbert de Clare, earl of Gloucester, when he died without male issue, and factional divisions among the aristocracy kept the realm in turmoil. In 1311 the barons forced Edward to banish Piers Gaveston, earl of Cornwall, and accept the Ordinances which limited the royal prerogative particularly in the areas of finance and war. The renewal of the war with Scotland brought the realm further troubles, including the stunning defeat at Bannockburn (1314) and the ascendancy of Thomas, earl of Lancaster and the king's cousin. In 1319 Edward came under the influence of the Despensers who directed the government until 1326 when Queen Isabella returned from France with Roger Mortimer, her lover, and executed them. The following year she forced Edward to abdicate in favor of their son Edward (III). In all probability Edward II was murdered.

EDWARD III, king of England, 1327–77, son of Edward II, in 1330 seized and executed Roger Mortimer, his mother's paramour, and assumed direction of the government. In 1333 he "avenged" the English disaster at Bannockburn when he defeated the Scottish army at Halidon Hill, although the fruits of the magnificent victory he won over the French at Crecy (1346) and that gained by his son Edward, the Black Prince,

at Poitiers (1356), had been largely dissipated by the time of his death. [*See* BRETIGNY, TREATY OF.] Aside from the war with France which absorbed Edward's interest, the Black Death (1348), the enactment of the Statutes of Provisors (1351), Praemunire (1353), and Laborers (1351), as well as parliamentary developments made his a full and generally troubled reign.

EDWARD IV, king of England, 1461–83 (except for the period from October 1470 to April 1471), son of Richard, duke of York, who claimed the throne on the basis of his descent from Lionel and Edmund, two sons of Edward III, against that of the Lancastrian king Henry VI who claimed it through John of Gaunt, an older son of Edward. What ultimately secured the throne for Edward was the support of London together with his alliance with the powerful Neville family, headed by Richard, earl of Warwick, the richest lord in England. Warwick declared for Edward when Richard was slain in 1460. [*See* ROSES, WARS OF THE.] Warwick helped Edward defeat the Lancastrian army at Towton (1461), then broke with him in 1469, joined the Lancastrians, and went down to defeat with them in the spring of 1471. The last dozen years of Edward's reign were peaceful for the most part. Although something of a voluptuary, he appears to have been gifted with considerable administrative talent. His success in strengthening royal authority by improving the systems of royal finance and law enforcement prepared the way for the absolutism of the Tudors.

EDWARD V, d. 1483?, twelve-year-old son of Edward IV, reigned from April to June 1483 when his uncle Richard (III), duke of Gloucester, had him declared illegitimate and removed to the Tower. He and his younger brother Richard disappeared from view c. August 1483, very probably murdered on orders of Richard (III).

EDWARD (Duarte), I, king of Portugal, 1433–38, son of John I, a scholarly prince who promulgated a series of noteworthy reforms, one of which enabled the crown to recover alienated lands. He suffered a serious defeat at the hands of the Moors at Tangier in 1437, then left his brother Ferdinand (Fernando) in their hands as guarantee to his returning Ceuta. He never did this and Ferdinand died a prisoner.

EDWARD, THE BLACK PRINCE, d. 1376, eldest son of Edward III, duke of Cornwall, and prince of Wales. The overwhelming victory which he gained over the French at Poitiers (1356) brought him enormous fame and popularity in England of which he was not deserving. As prince of Aquitaine (1362–72) he demonstrated little statesmanship. In 1367 he permitted himself to be drawn into Castilian affairs in an effort to restore Peter (Pedro) the Cruel to his throne. Shortly after this venture, hostilities broke out again with the French, about which time his health began to deteriorate, and he returned to England a broken man. Disease carried him off a year before the death of his father.

EDWARD THE CONFESSOR, king of England, 1042–66, the last of the Anglo-Saxon kings to rule that country. He lived in exile in Normandy during the reign of Canute—he was the son of Ethelred II and Emma—and returned only in 1041 during the reign of his half-brother Hardicanute whom he succeeded. The friends he brought with him from Normandy and the Norman customs which he introduced, given the fact that his childless marriage promised a contest over the throne, caused the rise of two factions in England, a native Anglo-Saxon headed by Godwin, earl of the West Saxons, and a Norman. In 1051 he outlawed Godwin whose daughter Edith he had married (1045), but the following year he was obliged to restore him and his family and take back Edith whom he had sent away. Certain Norman lords, including Robert of Jumièges, the archbishop of Canterbury, thereupon fled to the continent. On his deathbed, Edward designated Harold, the son of Godwin, to be his successor. What may have principally marked the piety of Edward was the efforts he made in building Westminster Abbey. He was canonized in 1161.

EDWARD THE ELDER, king of West Saxons, 899–924, succeeded his father Alfred and continued his successes against the Danes. He proved himself an able military commander although it required the greater part of his reign and the erection of a series of powerful fortresses before he was finally able to subdue the whole of England south of the Humber.

EDWIN, ST., king of Northumbria, d. 632, accepted baptism by Paulinus following his victory over the West Saxons, as did many of his court. His wife was Ethelburga, daughter of Ethelbert, the Christian king of Kent, who had brought Paulinus with her. Edwin was slain in a battle with Penda, the pagan ruler of Mercia.

EGBERT, king of Wessex, 802–39, son of an underking of Kent. He spent some time before his accession in exile at the court of Charlemagne. When he became king, he managed to gain full control of Wessex and to conquer Cornwall. The people of Kent, Surrey, and Essex also acknowledged his rule, and for a time Northumbria submitted to his authority. In 838, at Hingston Down in Cornwall, he gained a great victory over the Danes.

EGBERT, ST., d. 729, hermit of Northumbria, monk of Lindisfarne, encouraged Celtic and Anglo-Saxon monks, including Willibrord, to do missionary work in Germany. He spent his last years at Iona where he persuaded the monks to accept the Roman method of calculating the date of Easter.

EGBERT (Ecgberht), d. 766, archbishop of York, a pupil of Bede, and founder of the cathedral school at York where he taught theology. He devoted much effort to the reform of the church and monasticism. He also prepared an epitome of ecclesiastical law, a pontifical, and a penitential manual. Alcuin was his pupil.

EGILL SKALLAGRIMSSON, a tenth-century Icelandic poet and adventurer whose stormy life is described in the thirteenth-century *Egils Saga*. He showed himself a master in the use of the highly complex scaldic measures and imagery.

EIKE (Eico, Heiko) OF REPGAU (Repgow, Repegouw), early thirteenth-century lawyer who served as councillor to the rulers of Saxony, Thuringia, and Brandenburg. He was the author of a world chronicle of Saxony and of the *Sachsenspiegel*.

EINHARD (Eginhard), d. 840, Frankish scholar and historian, reared and educated at Fulda. He moved c. 793 to Charlemagne's court at Aachen where he served as secretary to the emperor. He later became a trusted adviser of Louis the Pious who appointed him lay abbot of four monasteries. Einhard acquired great proficiency in Latin and became so knowledgeable in architecture that he was placed in charge of the royal building program. His best known work is the biography he left of Charlemagne *(Vita Caroli)*, for which he used Suetonius's *Lives of the Caesars* as a model.

EINSIEDELN, ABBEY OF, Benedictine monastery in Switzerland founded in 934 over what according to tradition was the cell of Meinrad (d. 861). The monastery enjoyed the patronage of the dukes of Swabia and the Ottos (kings of Germany). In 1274 the abbot was made a prince of the Holy Roman empire. The abbey was originally under the protection of the counts of Rapperswil, then of the Laufenburg Hapsburgs, after 1386 it belonged to Schwyz. The wooden statue of the Virgin, which Meinrad is supposed to have brought with him, known later as the "Black Madonna," helped make the abbey a popular pilgrimage center.

EISTEDDFOD, Welsh name for assembly. The word is also used as early as the fifteenth century to refer to sessions of bards and minstrels.

EKKEHARD (Ekkehart, Eckehart), name held by three monks of the abbey of St. Gaul in Switzerland: E. I, d. 973, author of sequences and hymns; E. II, d. 990, nephew of the first Ekkehard who also composed sequences and was prominent at the court of Otto I; E. IV, d. c. 1060, who taught in the monastery and contributed to the ancient chronicle of the institution, an important source for contemporary affairs and culture. His name appears in the history of early medieval music.

EKKEHARD II, d. 1046, margrave of Meissen, added Ostmark and Oberlausitz to his provinces. The figures in Naumburg cathedral are believed to be those of him and his wife Uta of Ballenstedt.

ELCKERLYC. *See* EVERYMAN.

ELDAD (Ben Mahli) HA-DANI, a Jewish traveler of the late ninth century, perhaps from south Arabia, whose accounts of Abyssinia, Mesopotamia, and China inspired stories concerning the abode of the "ten lost tribes of Israel" and the legend of Prester John. He himself claimed to be a descendant of the Danites (hence ha-Dani).

ELEANOR CROSSES. *See* ELEANOR OF CASTILE.

ELEANOR OF AQUITAINE, d. 1204, heiress of Aquitaine, wife of Louis VII of France to whom she bore two daughters, and of Henry II of England to whom she gave five sons and three daughters. She shared in the administration of Aquitaine until 1173 when her involvement in the revolt of her sons against Henry led to her confinement. She proved a powerful stabilizing force in England while Richard I was away on the Third Crusade (1189–92), and without her determined efforts the huge amount required to procure his ransom from Henry VI of Germany would never have been raised. She may also be credited with a major role in securing the crown for John when Richard died.

ELEANOR OF CASTILE, d. 1290, queen consort of Edward I, the daughter of Ferdinand III of Castile. With her marriage she brought Edward as dowry the territories of Ponthieu and Montreuil along with claims to Gascony. When she died, Edward had crosses erected at the places where the funeral cortège halted on its way from Lincoln to Westminster. One such place was Charing Cross.

ELEANOR OF PROVENCE, d. 1291, daughter of Raymond Berengar, count of Provence, wife of Henry III of England. A large number of Provençals and Savoyards who came to England after her marriage, seeking lands and positions, provided the barons both cause and rationale for their criticism of Henry's policies. She helped organize royal resistance following the capture of Henry at the battle of Lewes in 1264.

ELEASAR (Elasar) BEN JEHUDA, d. before 1230, a rabbi of Worms and principal spokesman of the German Cabala. He was the author of exegetical and ethical works, a prayer book, and liturgical poems.

ELECTORS, name given to the group of seven princes designated by Charles IV in his Golden Bull (1356) as the men who would cast a vote in the election of a new king of Germany. [See GOLDEN BULL OF 1356.]

ELEUTHERIUS, ST., Pope, c. 174–89, a Greek, who enjoyed a generally peaceful pontificate despite the existence of several heresies which disturbed the Christian church. He is said to have declared the propriety of all food for Christians, that is, including foods forbidden by Mosaic law.

ELIAS BAR SHINAYA, d. after 1049, Nestorian theologian and metropolitan of Nisibis in northern Mesopotamia. He was the author of treatises on canon and civil law, a Syriac grammar, an Arabic-Syriac dictionary, hymns, homilies, a dogmatic work in defense of Nestorianism, and a history of the church from A.D. 25 to 1018.

ELIAS OF CORTONA, d. 1253, a companion of St. Francis of Assisi and minister general of the Franciscan Order (1221–7, 1232–9). During the period of his rule, he completed the basilica in honor of Francis and encouraged the order to expand its missionary activities. In 1239 he was deposed at a general chapter presided over by Pope Gregory IX. While his imperiousness and extravagance had antagonized many members of the order, especially the Spiritual Franciscans toward whom he was quite harsh, his deposition may have been precipitated by his efforts to bring about a reconciliation between Emperor Frederick II and the papacy.

ELIAS, ST., d. 518, an Arab who spent some time as a hermit in Egypt and later became patriarch of Jerusalem (494). Emperor Anastasius I forced him into exile in 516 because of his strong defense of orthodoxy (as defined by the Council of Chalcedon in 451) against Monophysitism.

ELIGIUS, ST., d. 660, bishop of Noyon and patron saint of metalworkers. He served as master of the mint under Clothaire II and under his son, Dagobert I. Among his works of piety was the ransoming of captives and the founding of monasteries and churches. He worked as a missionary in Flanders and the Low Countries.

ELIPANDUS, d. 802, archbishop of Toledo, chief exponent of the Adoptionist heresy in Spain. In a council at Seville in 782 he directed the condemnation of Sabellianism. Although his own views concerning the relation of the Son to God the Father were condemned as heretical, he could not be removed from his office because of Arab occupation of the area.

ELIZABETH OF HUNGARY, ST., also known as Elizabeth of Thuringia, d. 1231, daughter of King Andrew II of Hungary and wife of Louis IV, the landgrave of Thuringia. When widowed and forced from her home by her brother-in-law Henry Raspe, she became a Franciscan tertiary and founded a hospital in Marburg where she tended the sick and the poor. In art she is portrayed carrying red roses. Legend has it that the food she was taking to the poor turned to roses when her husband, who disapproved of her almsgiving, demanded to see what she was carrying.

ELIZABETH OF PORTUGAL, ST., d. 1336, daughter of Peter (Pedro) III of Aragon and wife of King Diniz of Portugal. As queen she devoted herself to improving the well-being of her subjects and to preventing war with neighboring states. When her husband died she became a Franciscan tertiary.

ELIZABETH OF SCHÖNAU, ST., d. 1164, a mystic, abbess of the Benedictine (double) monastery at Schönau. She gave her support to Frederick I Barbarossa and his antipope Victor IV in their contest with Pope Alexander III. Some of her letters as well as the record her brother kept of her visions and ecstacies remain extant. Her visionary writings and her elaboration of the St. Ursula legend proved extremely popular.

ELIZABETH WOODVILLE, d. 1492, widow of John Grey of Groby and wife of Edward IV of England whom she bore two sons and five daughters. She was the mother of the tragic Edward V and of Elizabeth (of York) who married Henry VII.

ELMO, ST., also known as Erasmus, Rasmus, and Ermo, a semilegendary martyr of the early fourth century who was reputed to be the bishop of Formia (Campagna) and is so mentioned by Gregory the Great (d. 604). He is generally identified as St. Peter Gonzàlez (d. 1246), a famous Dominican preacher who devoted his life to working among the seafaring folk of the coasts of Spain. He was revered as one of the Holy Helpers in the cure of intestinal troubles. Seamen in Mediterranean countries also honored him as their patron, and they gave the name St. Elmo's Fire to the electrical discharges that appeared around mastheads.

ELY, a cathedral town north of Cambridge whose history goes back to 673 when Etheldreda, queen of Northumbria, founded a monastery there. In 870 the Danes destroyed the monastery but it was rebuilt a century later. In 1108–9 Ely was separated from Lincoln and made into a separate diocese. The foundation of the town's great cathedral was laid by Simeon, its first Norman abbot (1081–94). Much of the early structure is Norman in architecture, with additons and restorations in the Decorated and Perpendicular styles.

EMBER DAYS, twelve penitential days, three (Wednesday, Friday, and Saturday) assigned to each season of the year. The practice of observing these days as occasions of penance has been traced to the early church and may be of ancient Jewish origin. In their origin they might also have been associated with pagan religious observancies connected with harvest, vintage, and seeding.

EMERIC (Emerich, Imre) OF HUNGARY, ST., d. 1031, son of King Stephen I and canonized in 1083. America takes its name indirectly from this saint since Amerigo Vespucci was given his name in baptism.

EMINENCE, title of honor given to cardinals and to the three ecclesiastical electors of the king of Germany.

EMIR (amir), an Arab tribal leader; a title held by governors of provinces during the period of the caliphates.

EMPYREAN (Empyreum), the place of light or heaven as identified in the writings of certain Christian philosophers, theologians, and poets.

EMS, city near Coblenz, first noted in 880. It grew into an important city because of the lead and silver mines in the area.

EN CLARA VOX REDARGUIT, a hymn probably of the fifth century which made its way into the divine office. It was sung at Lauds during Advent.

ENCLOSURE (INCLOSURE), term applied to the practice of enclosing manorial lands that had been held in common or waste lands with hedges or fences and turning these over to the exclusive use of the lord of the manor. As a development in agriculture, it marked the first major step from the social, noncapitalistic character of the manor to the system of free and individual exploitation of the land. From the early thirteenth century protests raised in England against the practice produced legislation aimed at reducing the inevitable social dislocations such changes entailed. The expansion of the woolen industry in the late fourteenth century greatly accelerated the enclosure movement. Everywhere English landowners were converting, by purchase, force, or legal contrivance, the smaller holdings of their tenants (serfs) into large fields given over to sheep-raising. Hamlets and small villages disappeared in the process, while thousands of peasants became vagrants or charges of their communities. The practice of enclosure, together with its concomitant problems, carried over into the sixteenth century and beyond.

ENEA SILVIO DE PICCOLOMINI. *See* PIUS II, POPE.

ENGELBERT OF ADMONT, d. 1331, scholarly abbot of the Benedictine monastery at Admont and author of treatises on theological, philosophical, political, and scientific subjects. He also contributed translations of several of Aristotle's works.

ENGLAND. England's history during the medieval period began with the coming of the Angles, Saxons, and Jutes, and the collapse of Roman imperial rule in the early fifth century. That these invaders had long been harassing the island is clear from the name borne by one of the late Roman officials, namely, the count of the Saxon shore. The general obscurity which all of Western history shares during this period was even darker in the case of England. What appears to have happened is that the invaders made themselves masters of England by the close of the sixth century and extinguished in the process almost every trace of the higher culture that land had enjoyed during the centuries of Roman occupation.

At the very close of the sixth century St. Augustine arrived in Kent with his band of monks. They did not introduce Christianity. This had already been done by the Celtic sons of St. Patrick, notably by St. Columba and his missionaries from Iona, although they had limited their work principally to north and central England. Augustine's monks and their successors moved northward and in 664 at the synod of Whitby agreed with representatives of the Celtic church to accept Roman liturgical usages and calendar. The finest scholarly product of these two civilizing movements, one from the north and west, the other from the south, which brought England out of the barbarism into which the German invaders had plunged the island, was the Venerable Bede (d. 735).

The conversion of the native Anglo-Saxons usually started with the king, as was the case with Ethelbert, king of Kent, whom Augustine had baptized. Apart from the doings of churchmen and kings, little else remains recorded in the scattered annals of the period. Rulers of such kingdoms as Wessex, Mercia, and Northumbria fought over the possession of fluid frontiers, without accomplishing any really permanent success until Alfred the Great (871–99) who extended his rule over the greater part of south and central England. The authority that was left to rule the northeastern part of the country was not that of the Anglo-Saxons, however, but that of the Danes who had been raiding the country since the close of the eighth century. For a brief period, during the reign of Canute (1016–35), they even succeeded in making England part of a Danish empire. When Canute failed to establish a dynasty, this link with Denmark lapsed, only to be replaced shortly after in 1066, upon the death of Edward the Confessor, with an infinitely stronger tie to the continent as a result of the conquest of William, duke of Normandy.

William's conquest brought far-reaching changes to England. For centuries to come political affairs of England mingled with those of France; Anglo-Saxon culture, most noticeably its literature, submerged; the land's institutions became largely feudalized; and monarchs were usually strong men who extended their authority over the country. Shrewd man that William was, he appreciated the value of such Anglo-Saxon institutions as the sheriff and shire court and retained them. Because of these and other circumstances, England escaped in large measure the near-anarchy that marked the feudal period on the continent. By reason of the work of Henry II (1154–89) England secured a system of justice superior to that enjoyed by any other people of medieval Europe. In the face of deposition by his barons even the tyrannical King John acknowledged in the Magna Carta (1215) that his royal prerogatives were not unlimited, that he would respect the laws of the land in the administration of justice, and that he would seek the assistance of his barons should the royal revenues prove inadequate for the crown's needs.

It was this search for additional revenues that explains the rise of parliament during the fourteenth century when that body granted subsidies only in return for concessions. The thirteenth century had already witnessed parliament's birth when Simon de Montfort had established the precedent in 1265, during his civil war with Henry III, of directing the boroughs and shires to send representatives to meet with the great council. Prudence recommended to Edward I (1272–1307) that he continue the practice although he appreciated the importance of establishing closer associations with the squirearchy and burgher class to whom rising capitalism was bringing wealth and influence. Edward who was not unaware of the value of trade to the crown initiated legislation aimed at attracting foreign merchants and their wares. Already during his reign revenues realized from trade were exceeding those from all other sources, a development that would assist the king to establish royal absolutism at the close of the Middle Ages.

The most significant developments of late medieval England include this evolution of parliament, the decline of the manor and of serfdom, the expansion of trade and industry, the Hundred Years' War with France, and the growth of royal government, the latter at the expense of the church [see BONIFACE VIII, POPE; PROVISIONS, PAPAL] and, during the decades of the fifteenth century, at that of the landed aristocracy. The Black Death (1348–50) struck the country a serious, though not crippling, blow. Perhaps the only consequence that can be clearly established was the appearance of outlaws, peasants who had defied the Statute of Laborers (1351) and joined the rebels in the Peasant Revolt of 1381. This rebellion in turn marked the beginning of a century of instability whose basic source was not discontent among the lower classes so much as the ambition of members of the landed aristocracy to control the crown. In 1399 the aristocracy succeeded in forcing the abdication of Richard II who had not been content to rule with their consent. During the long reign of Henry VI (1422–61) the struggle between crown and aristocracy assumed new virulence because of the king's lack of ability, the loss of the Hundred Years' War and with it the magnificent empire Henry II had once ruled, and the ambitions of Richard of York whose blood-claim to the throne was as good as that of the Lancastrians. Because London and its merchants believed Richard's son Edward would bring peace to England, Edward (IV) won out over the Lancastrians in the Wars of the Roses, although not before the landed aristocracy had destroyed itself and thereby opened the door to the absolutism of Henry VII (1485) and the Tudors.

ENNODIUS, MAGNUS FELIX, d. 521, Christian Latin poet and rhetorician, bishop of Pavia, and twice papal emissary to Constantinople, his assignment being the reconciliation of the Greek church with Rome. His varied writings include poems, sermons, polemical works, an autobiography, a panegyric to Theodoric, king of the Ostrogoths, and *Dictiones* or model copies of speeches. His verse suffers from an excessive concern with form.

ENQUÊTEUR, royal official appointed in 1247 by Louis IX of France to investigate complaints concerning the misuse of royal authority on the part of *baillis* and seneschals.

ENZIO, d. 1272, natural son of Frederick II, who after marrying an heiress of Sardinia was made king of that island by his father. In 1249 he was captured while helping Modena against Bologna and spent the rest of his life in prison.

ÉON (Eons, Eudo, Euno, Evus) OF STELLA, d. c. 1148, a native of Brittany who claimed to be the son of God. He was convicted of heresy and died in prison. The sect he founded, known as the Eonites, which gained many adherents in Gascony and Brittany, attacked clerical wealth and advocated a system of communism.

EPARCH, governor of a Byzantine province known as an eparchy. The term eparchy might also apply to a diocese or ecclesiastical province in the Greek church.

EPHESUS, COUNCIL OF, general church council (Third Ecumenical) of 431, convoked by Emperor Theodosius II and presided over by Cyril of Alexandria as representative of Pope Celestine I. The council condemned the views of Nestorius concerning the nature of Christ and specifically proclaimed Mary to be the mother of God. The position of the Nestorians implied the separation of the two natures in Christ, a position which precluded Mary from being the mother of God.

EPHESUS, ROBBER COUNCIL OF (Latrocinium), name given by Pope Leo I to the church council (449) which Emperor Theodosius had summoned for the purpose of rehabilitating Eu-

tyches. He had been condemned for his Monophysite views. This council at Ephesus cleared Eutyches, at the same time condemning Nestorianism as well as the position held in Rome concerning the two natures in Christ.

EPHESUS, SEVEN SLEEPERS OF. *See* SEVEN SLEEPERS OF EPHESUS.

EPHREM (Ephraem, Afrem) THE SYRIAN, ST., d. 373, Syrian church father famed for the austerity and sanctity of his life as well as for his learning. He was the author of numerous exegetical, moral, dogmatic, and polemical (antiheretical) writings, and of sermons, discourses, and hymns. He had a special devotion to Mary and believed in her immaculate conception. If not the founder, he was one of the principal theologians whose name was associated with the exegetical school of Edessa. His liturgical poetry greatly influenced the development of both Syriac and Greek hymnography.

EPIC POETRY, oldest class of vernacular literature of medieval peoples. The themes of epic poetry were usually heroic and martial; their mood was dignified, even tragic, and their verse often a simple assonance. Scholars believe that the larger portion of this verse never passed beyond the recitative stage. Almost all that is extant bears the mark of Christian influence. It is likely, for example, that the author of the oldest of the Germanic epics, the Anglo-Saxon *Beowulf,* was a Christian priest, even though the matter of the poem is substantially pagan. The most advanced of the epic songs and poems were those of France, which flourished in the twelfth and thirteenth centuries. Many of these narrative poems embodied legends that had grown up around such heroic figures from the past as Charlemagne and William of Orange. Some, like the *Chanson de Roland,* contain a historical kernel. Controversy continues over their origin, one popular theory being that they evolved from stories told and retold along pilgrim routes. The most famous medieval epics, beyond those noted, include the *Nibelungenlied, Poema del Cid,* and the Icelandic sagas.

EPICIER (Epicière), a vase for holding spices; a servant whose responsibility it was to bring spices to the lord's table; a dealer in spices; an apothecary.

EPICLESIS, in ancient pagan and early Christian literature a term used to signify the invoking of a name in connection with God and, subsequently, with prayer in general. The earliest Christian liturgical epiclesis was that found in baptismal formulas where the names of the Three Persons of the Trinity were invoked over the catechumen. Similar invocations were expressed in the rites of confirmation and ordination, and in the eucharist liturgy.

EPICTETUS, d. c. 130, Stoic philosopher, probably born in Phrygia, a slave in the household of Nero, who studied under M. Rufus, a Stoic. He taught in Rome and with other philosophers but was exiled by Domitian. His disciple, Arrian, recorded his teaching in two treatises, the *Discourses of Epictetus* and the *Encheiridion.* There is no trace of Christian influence in his writing although his influence on Christian thought is believed to have been subtle and profound. Origen, Augustine, and Gregory of Nazianzus wrote commendably of him.

EPIGONATION (Hypogonation), liturgical garment, rectangular in shape and hanging from the waist to the knee, that was worn by leading members of the Greek church.

EPIPHANIUS OF CONSTANTIA (Salamis), d. 403, for thirty years abbot of a monastery near Eleutheropolis in Palestine and bishop of Constantia (Cyprus) from 367. His active participation in ecclesiastical affairs caused him to travel about a great deal, one trip taking him to Rome. His writings express both his hostility to such heresies as Origenism and Arianism as well as his suspicion of philosophy and speculative theol-ogy. He took an active part in the Apollinarian and Melitian controversies.

EPIPHANY, FEAST OF, from the Greek "showing," "manifesting," a feast commemorating the visit of the three magi to Bethlehem to adore the new-born Christ. The feast was celebrated on January 6 in the third century in the Eastern church where it commemorated the baptism of Christ. It was introduced to the West in the fourth century but there lost its initial character as a feast commemorating the baptism of Christ and instead was associated with the manifestation of Christ to the Gentiles in the persons of the three magi.

EPISCOPI VAGANTES, Latin for "wandering bishops," that is, bishops with no formal sees of their own who intruded into the jurisdiction of bishops with established dioceses. The Council of Antioch (341) addressed itself to this problem.

EREK (Erec), hero of courtly romances composed by Chrétien de Troyes and Hartmann von Aue.

ERGO BIBAMUS, that is, let us drink, a Latin phrase that frequently occurs in medieval drinking songs.

ERIC IX JEDVARDSSON (Erich), ST., d. c. 1160, king of Sweden, ancestor of a royal line of Swedish kings, who reigned from 1150 until his death. The zeal he showed in spreading Christianity there won him the title of patron saint of Sweden. Among other legends associated with him is one that tells of his crusade to Finland.

ERIC OF POMERANIA, d. 1459, great-nephew of Margaret of Denmark who was crowned king of Denmark, Norway, and Sweden in 1397, but assumed power only upon Margaret's death in 1412. (She had adopted him after the death of her own son.) Difficulties with the Hanseatic League and his territorial ambitions in Schleswig, both of which brought high taxes and a loss of trade, led to his deposition in 1439. He spent his last years in Gotland and Pomerania.

ERICSSON, LEIF. *See* LEIF ERICSSON.

ERIC (Erich) THE RED, d. c. 1007, actually Eric Thorvaldsson who discovered Greenland in 981 or 982 and established a colony there c. 986. He was the father of Leif Ericsson.

ERIGENA. *See* JOHN SCOTUS ERIGENA.

ERMANARIC, d. c. 375, king of the Ostrogoths, who extended his authority over a number of other German tribes in an area in eastern Europe north of the Danube. The Huns overran his country and probably slew him. He appears as a tyrant in Anglo-Saxon and Old Norse literature.

ERNEST (Ernst) II, duke of Swabia, d. 1030, revolted against his step-father Conrad II of Germany and was slain in battle near Falkenstein. The romance *Duke Ernst* has as its theme the story of his loyalty to his friend Count Werner of Thurgau.

ERNEST OF PARDUBICE (Pardubitz), d. 1364, a student of law at Bologna and Padua, bishop and first archbishop of Prague, and founder and first chancellor of Charles University (1348) in that city. He was a close friend of Charles IV, king of Germany, and on several occasions served as his emissary to the papal court.

ERNULF, d. 1124, Benedictine monk of Beauvais, prior of Christ Church in Canterbury, later abbot of Peterborough and bishop of Rochester. He rebuilt a part of Canterbury cathedral and wrote several canonical and theological treatises.

ERRARE HUMANUM EST, that is, to err is human, a statement which has been traced to St. Jerome's *errasse humanum est.*

ESCABEAU, portable stool popular in the Middle Ages.

ESCALIN, oldest silver money used in the Low Countries.

ESCAUFAILLE, container for coals used to warm the hands in a church.

ESCHEAT, RIGHT OF, right of the lord, according to feudal custom, to the property of his vassal or the holdings of a serf should either die without lawful heirs.

ESCOBAR, ANDRÉS DE, d. 1439 or 1440, canonist and theologian, abbot of the Benedictine abbey of Randuf in the diocese of Braga (Portugal), papal penitentiary, and papal representative at the councils of Constance, Basel, and Ferrara-Florence. His writings on the Eastern schism, on church reform, and on theological questions such as the sacrament gained him considerable fame.

ESCOFFION, woman's scarf which was worn over the temples.

ESKIL, d. 1181, bishop of Roskilde (1134), archbishop of Lund (1138), first primate of Sweden (1156), and papal legate for all of Scandinavia. He spent several years in exile because of his support of Pope Alexander III against Frederick I Barbarossa. In close cooperation with St. Bernard of Clairvaux he encouraged the growth of monasticism in his province. He spent his last years as a monk at Clairvaux.

ESPADA, large broadsword with two cutting edges which came into use in the fourteenth century. It was swung with both hands.

ESQUIRE, originally a shield-bearer or attendant of a knight. In the late Middle Ages the holder of a knight's fee who had not taken knighthood was referred to as an esquire.

ESSEX, EARLDOM OF. The title earl of Essex was first held by Geoffrey de Mandeville who received it from King Stephen in 1140. Upon the death of William de Mandeville, the title passed in 1236 to his nephew, Humphrey de Bohun, earl of Hereford. It remained in the Bohun family until 1373 when it passed to Thomas of Woodstock, duke of Gloucester, then to his grandson, Henry Bourchier, the treasurer of Edward IV.

ESSEX, KINGDOM OF, Anglo-Saxon kingdom located on the lower Thames with its principal town being London. At one time the kingdom may have included Middlesex. In the early seventh century its people accepted Christianity. St. Paul's church was erected at this time. During much of the seventh and eighth centuries it was subjected to Mercia. In 825 it was conquered by Egbert, king of Wessex, then after 878 passed under Danish control for a brief period following the treaty between Alfred the Great and Guthrum. In 917 Alfred's son Edward the Elder reconquered the area.

ESTAGE (estagium), obligation to do garrison duty.

ESTAMPE (estampie, istampita), a lively dance of the thirteenth and fourteenth centuries that featured the stamping of the feet.

ESTATES GENERAL (Etats Généraux), name given to the meeting of members of the aristocracy, clergy, and representatives of the towns that convened for the first time in 1302 when Philip IV of France summoned it for the purpose of securing for the crown the support of the three estates in his contest with Pope Boniface VIII. During the years following, the estates general met on occasion to consider problems of royal succession and finance. It might have aspired to a political role similar to that of the English parliament had it not voted the crown in 1439 the right to impose the *taille* whenever it felt this necessary. The English parliament never surrendered its control over taxation.

ESTE, HOUSE OF, aristocratic family of Ferrara of Lombard origin, the historical origin of the German Guelfs. The founder of the family was Alberto Azzo II (d. 1097) who made Este his home and was invested with Milan by the German emperor. He married the sister of Welf III, duke of Carinthia, who later adopted their son Welf as his heir. In 1070 the younger Welf became duke of Bavaria. The family controlled Ferrara from the thirteenth century and Modena and Reggio from the later Middle Ages. Members of the family, in particular Niccolò d'Este III (d. 1441), distinguished themselves as patrons of the arts during the Renaissance.

ESTONIA, country located south of the Gulf of Finland which the Estonians may have occupied from the first century A.D. when Tacitus makes mention of them. From the Vikings who raided the area c. 850, they learned about trade. Missionaries penetrated the country in the eleventh century and in 1186 Meinrad of Holstein was consecrated first bishop of Livonia (to the south). The man who took a prominent part in their pacification was Albert of Buxhoevden, bishop of Livonia, who helped organize the Knights of the Sword (1199) and moved his see to Riga (1201). In 1227 the conquest of Estonia was accomplished with the help of a Danish invasion. In 1237 the Teutonic Knights absorbed the Knights of the Sword and extended their rule over Livonia, then in 1346 purchased Danish rights to northern Estonia. They remained in control until 1561.

ESTRADIOTS (Stradiots), Greek and Albanian mercenaries who fought in the service of Venice in the fifteenth century.

ETHELBALD (Aethelbald), d. 757, king of Mercia (716–57), a strong ruler and in control of Britain south of the Humber. He made war on Northumbria and on the Welsh. It appears that he was generous to the church and encouraged missionary activity.

ETHELBERT (Aethelbert), ST., king of Kent, 560–616, first Anglo-Saxon king to accept Christianity. He married Bertha, daughter of the Merovingian king Charibert who was a Christian. In 597 he welcomed St. Augustine and his band of monks, was baptized, and later persuaded the kings of Essex and East Anglia to become Christian.

ETHELBURGA (Eathelburga), ST., d. c. 644, daughter of King Ethelbert and Queen Bertha of

Kent, the wife of the pagan King Edwin of Northumbria. Their daughter married Oswiu, king of Northumbria. Ethelburga converted her husband, then both cooperated with the bishop Paulinus in the conversion of the people of Northumbria. She died as abbess of Lymynge convent which she had founded.

ETHELRED (Aethelred) II (the Unready), king of England, 978–1016, son of King Edgar. He regularly paid tribute (the Danegeld) to the Danes from 991, then lost all of his country to Sweyn Forkbeard, king of Denmark, with the exception of southeast England which he managed to retain until his death. He was the father of Edward the Confessor (1042–66) by Emma, daughter of the duke of Normandy. After Ethelred's death, Emma married Canute.

ETHELREDA (Aethelreda), ST., d. 679, daughter of the king of East Anglia, lived as a religious before her marriage to Egfrid, later king of Northumbria, then after twelve years of married life returned to the convent with his permission. She was the founder and first abbess of the double monastery at Ely. From "St. Audrey," a variant of her name, is derived the word "tawdry" because of the cheap finery exposed for sale at St. Audrey's fair.

ETHELWOLD (Aethelwold), ST., d. 984, learned Anglo-Saxon Benedictine monk, later bishop of Winchester (963), who cooperated with Dunstan in the reform of the church. He founded or restored a number of monasteries, including Peterborough and Crowland, translated the Rule of St. Benedict into Anglo-Saxon, and composed a monk's customary entitled *Regularis Concordia*.

ETHELWULF (Aethelwulf), king of the West Saxons, 839–58, son of Egbert and father of Alfred the Great. His wife was Judith, a daughter of Charles the Bald, whom he married on his return from Rome where he had gone to seek God's help against the Danes. Shortly before he died, he relinquished his throne to his son Ethelbald in order to prevent war.

ETHERIA, PILGRIMAGE OF, a treatise of the late fourth century about the journey a Spanish abbess or nun made to Egypt, the Holy Land, Edessa, Asia Minor, and Constantinople. Not only does the author identify many biblical sites in her narrative, but she also describes liturgical matters such as services in Jerusalem, feastdays, and daily and Sunday offices.

ETHIOPIA, country of east central Africa whose Aksumite king accepted Christanity in the fourth century. This church became officially Monophysite after 451 when the patriarch of Alexandria refused to recognize the Council of Chalcedon's position regarding the nature of Christ. In the sixth century its king invaded Yemen in Arabia. The rise of Islam in the early seventh century cut the country off from the Red Sea and left it surrounded by hostile Moslem neighbors. Medieval Europe had little firm knowledge of this land-locked country except that its ruler was a Christian, whence the belief of many that he was the semilegendary Prester John. Several popes attempted to restore communion with the church there in the thirteenth century, but these failed, as did a Dominican mission. The delegates from Ethiopia who attended the Council of Florence (1438–9) did accept the decree of union, but this was rejected by their ruler.

ETIENNE MARCEL. *See* MARCEL, ETIENNE.

ETON COLLEGE, a school on the Thames near London which Henry VI founded in 1440.

ETUVE, name given to bathing establishments. These were relatively numerous in the thirteenth and fourteenth centuries.

ETZEL, Attila's name as it appears in old German and Norse literature.

EUCHARIST, the central rite of Christian worship, known also as the Lord's Supper, Holy Communion, the Mass, the Blessed Sacrament, and the Sacrament. From the earliest days of the church it constituted the indispensable component of the Christian service. Not only did it serve as a memorial action in which the eating of the bread and drinking of the wine reminded Christians of what Christ had said and done at the Last Supper, but for most medieval Christians, it also was the actual body and blood of Christ miraculously transubstantiated through the words spoken by the priest at the consecration.

EUDES (Odo). *See* ODO.

EUDOCIA, d. 460, beautiful daughter of the pagan philosopher Leontius whom Pulcheria selected as wife for her brother, the emperor Theodosius II. (The girl's pagan name was Athenais.) She enjoyed powerful influence in the government until 440 when she became estranged from her husband. She then made her home in Jerusalem and there devoted herself to charitable works and the founding of churches and monasteries. Her daughter Eudoxia became the wife of Valentinian III.

EUDOXIA, d. 404, daughter of the Frankish general Bauto and wife of Emperor Arcadius. Her influence over her weak husband became paramount after 400 and was partly responsible for the exile of St. John Chrysostom, archbishop of Constantinople, who had attacked the frivolity of the court. She was the mother of Theodosius II.

EUGENICUS, MARK, d. 1445, learned and pious monk who as metropolitan of Ephesus led the opposition at the Council of Ferrara-Florence (1438–9) to the proposed union of the Greek and Latin churches, then later aroused sentiment against the union among the monks and people back in Constantinople. His refusal to sign the decree of union led to his confinement for two years in the monastery of Lemnos. The Greek church revered him as a saint.

EUGENIUS I, ST., Pope, 654–7, member of an aristocratic Roman family, the successor of Martin I whom the Byzantine emperor had deposed. The heresy of Monothelitism occasioned the principal theological controversy during his pontificate.

EUGENIUS II, Pope, 824–7, the pope upon whose election Emperor Lothair I guaranteed free papal elections although requiring an oath of fidelity from the people of Rome. Iconoclasm provided the major doctrinal issue during his pontificate. In the fall of 826 Eugenius presided over a synod in Rome which enacted a large amount of disciplinary legislation.

EUGENIUS III, BL., Pope, 1145–53, a Cistercian of Clairvaux and abbot of the monastery of SS. Vincent and Anastasius in Rome. When pope he induced St. Bernard of Clairvaux to preach the Second Crusade to which the pope had summoned Europe. In 1148 he excommunicated Arnold of Brescia who had become the leader of the rebellious Roman Senate. In 1153 he concluded the Treaty of Constance with Frederick I Barbarossa. Despite the pressure of diplomatic and ecclesiastical affairs, Eugenius was able to lead a life of deep piety and to labor zealously for the reform of the church.

EUGENIUS IV, Pope, 1431–47, Augustinian monk, cardinal (1408), and governor of the march of Ancona and of Bologna. As pope he summoned the Council of Basel in 1431, then ordered it removed to Ferrara in 1438 (and to Florence in 1439), ostensibly to accommodate the Byzantine emperor and an embassy of Greek ecclesiastics who were coming to discuss reunion with the Latin church. If the pope's major motive in moving the council to Ferrara was to weaken the influence of the conciliarists, he succeeded. [*See* BASEL, COUNCIL OF.] He was also successful in persuading the Greek embassy to recognize papal primacy and to accept reunion, although most of the members repudiated the union once they returned to Constantinople. [*See* FERRARA-FLORENCE, COUNCIL OF.] Eugenius suffered further grievous disappointment in 1444 when the Turks destroyed a Crusading army at Varna. He was a man of deep piety as well as a patron of art and literature.

EULALIA, SONG OF, oldest monument of French literature, composed c. 880 after a Latin sequence in honor of St. Eulalia.

EULALIUS, Antipope, 418–9, Roman archdeacon who was elected after the death of Zosimus. Boniface I was considered to be the legitimate successor.

EULENSPIEGEL, TILL (Ulenspegel, Tyll), a German peasant buffoon or jester, said to have died in 1350, who was the hero of a tale composed in the late fifteenth century from a variety of anecdotes and bizarre stories told about him. The story persisted in one or more Low German versions. In north Britain he was called Howleglas.

EUNAPIUS (Ennapios), d. c. 420, pagan rhetorician, neo-Platonist, and historiographer of Sardis, also a priest of the cult of Eleusis, who showed himself hostile to Christianity. He was the author of *Lives of the Philosophers and Sophists* and of a history which covered the years A.D. 270 to 404. Only fragments of his history are extant.

EUNOMIUS, d. 393?, theologian of Cappadocia and exponent of extreme Arianism, that is, he rejected the moderate position of Semi-Arians that the Son was like the Father. For Eunomius, God had no origin, whereas the Son was begotten and created out of nothing, therefore had an origin and was quite unlike the Father. He became bishop of Cyzicus c. 361 but suffered exile on several occasions. His followers, known as Anomoeans, were never numerous.

EUPHEMIA, ST., Christian martyr of the third or fourth century, probably suffering death during the persecution of Diocletian (c. 303). Despite the obscurity of her life, she became a popular saint. In the basilica dedicated to her the Council of Chalcedon met in 451. This fact helped increase her fame still more; many churches were dedicated to her and several feastdays were established to commemorate her sanctity. Many miracles were attributed to her intercession.

EUSEBIUS, ST., Pope, April 18 to August 17, 309 or 310, suffered exile by Emperor Maxentius apparently for demanding harsh penances from *lapsi,* that is, from Christians who had forsworn their faith under threat of death. The emperor also exiled the leader of the group that had opposed Eusebius on this issue. Eusebius died in Sicily.

EUSEBIUS, bishop of Caesarea, d. c. 339, apologist, exegete and historian, author of a *Chronicle* and of an *Ecclesiastical History* that extended from the origins of Christianity to Constantine's victory over Licinius in 324. Despite its apologetic character the *History* constitutes a valuable source for the reign of Constantine. It contains extracts and paraphrased portions from other writings that are no longer extant and it greatly influenced the writing of history in the early Middle Ages. The *Chronicle* consists of an epitome of world history and a series of chronological tables. Eusebius also left a panegyric of Constantine and numerous exegetical and apologetical studies. As a biblical scholar he used both literal and allegorical exegesis. He came dangerously close to being identified as a semi-Arian.

EUSEBIUS, bishop of Dorylaeum (448), an opponent of Eutyches and Monophysitism who suffered condemnation by the Robber Council of Ephesus in 449 and was imprisoned. The Council of Chalcedon (451), in which he took a prominent part, ordered him restored to his see.

EUSEBIUS, bishop of Emesa, d. c. 359, semi-Arian theologian and exegete who resigned his see when accused of Sabellianism. He may have been a disciple of Eusebius of Caesarea. Most of his voluminous exegetical writings and homilies have been lost. St. Jerome judged them to be shallow.

EUSEBIUS, CHRONICLE OF. *See* EUSEBIUS, bishop of Caesarea.

EUSEBIUS OF NICOMEDIA, d. c. 341, bishop of Berytus (Beirut), Nicomedia (318), and Constantinople (339). He vigorously supported the views of Arius at the Council of Nicaea (325) and signed the final decree of condemnation only under imperial pressure. Several months later he was exiled for his Arian tendencies, then in 328 was recalled and restored to his see, when he helped bring about the exile of St. Athanasius, the bishop of Alexandria. In 337 he baptized Emperor Constantine on his deathbed.

EUSEBIUS OF SAMOSATA, ST., d. 380, bishop of Samosata (361) who for a time sympathized with Arianism but subsequently accepted the orthodox position through the influence of St. Basil of Caesarea and St. Gregory of Nazianzus, his friends. This led to his exile by the pro-Arian Emperor Valens in 374. He was recalled by Emperor Gratian and died from a wound inflicted by an Arian adherent.

EUSEBIUS OF VERCELLI, ST., d. 371, bishop of Vercelli (345) who suffered exile for protesting the exile of St. Athanasius but was restored to his see when the emperor Julian ordered the rescinding of all such condemnations. He devoted himself to the cause of orthodoxy and religious unity and left letters and probably a work on the Trinity. He is regarded as one of the founders of the Canons Regular.

EUSTACE (Eustachius) AND COMPANIONS, SS., semilegendary saint and companions who were believed to have suffered martyrdom c. 125. Eustace was believed to have been a Roman general under Hadrian when he was converted by a vision of a stag with a crucifix between its antlers. He was revered as one of the Fourteen Holy Helpers in need. He was the patron of hunters.

EUSTATHIUS OF ANTIOCH, d. before 337, sometimes known as the Great, bishop of Beroea (c. 320) and patriarch of Antioch (c. 324). He showed himself a sharp opponent of Arius at the Council of Nicaea (325), for which reason intriguing pro-Arian bishops later secured his exile by Emperor Constantine. Almost all of his voluminous writings, which he composed in an excellent literary style on a variety of exegetical, apologetical, and theological subjects, have been lost.

EUSTATHIUS OF THESSALONICA, d. c. 1194, Byzantine scholar and poet and archbishop of Thessalonica (1175). He lectured on classical Greek literature in Hagia Sophia and authored a treatise dealing with monastic reform. He also wrote a history of the capture of Thessalonica by the Normans in 1185, polemical works, and commentaries on various Greek classics including the *Iliad* and the *Odyssey*. Michael Acominatus was his disciple.

EUTHYMIOS (Ewtimij), d. c. 1402, patriarch of Tarnowo and a leading Bulgarian writer of the late Middle Ages. He translated religious works into Bulgarian and interested himself in improving the literary character of his people's language.

EUTHYMIUS I, patriarch of Constantinople, d. 917, abbot of the monastery of St. Theodora in Constantinople and confessor to Emperor Leo VI (886–912). When Nicholas I Mysticus, the patriarch, refused to sanction a fourth marriage for Emperor Leo, he was replaced by Euthymius, although the latter refused to enter the name of the emperor's new wife in the diptychs. When the emperor died, his successor Alexander banished Euthymius and reinstated Nicholas as patriarch.

EUTHYMIUS ZIGABENUS, Byzantine theologian of the early twelfth century whom the emperor Alexius Comnenus ordered to write a work against all heresies. Among the heresies he attacked was that of the Bogomils, and this work provides scholars most of what they know about this sect. He also composed extensive commentaries on the Psalms, Gospels, and the Pauline Epistles.

EUTROPIUS, Roman historian, author of a survey of Roman history which extended from the traditional founding of the city in 753 B.C. to the accession of Emperor Valens in 364. He accompanied the emperor Julian on his ill-fated Persian campaign (363), and later served as secretary to Emperor Valens in Constantinople. His history, which is reasonably impartial and accurate, is largely based on the works of other historians.

EUTROPIUS, d. 399, a eunuch, a favorite of the Eastern Roman emperor Arcadius and high in his counsels, who succeeded Rufinus as chief minister. He arranged the marriage of Arcadius to Eudoxia, daughter of a Frankish chieftain. His fall from power and execution were brought about by Eudoxia and Gainas, leader of the Gothic mercenaries in Constantinople.

EUTYCHES, d. c. 454, archimandrite of a monastery in Constantinople and for a time high in the favor of Emperor Theodosius II. What appears to have prompted him to place excessive emphasis upon the divine nature in Christ was his revulsion to Nestorianism with its extreme interest in Christ's humanity. He is considered the founder of Eutychianism, the purest form of Monophysitism, which maintained the complete absorption of Christ's human nature by his Godhead. The emperor ordered him deposed for his views and, although he was restored by the Robber Council of Ephesus in 449, he was condemned by the Council of Chalcedon in 451 and exiled by Emperor Marcian.

EUTYCHIAN, ST., Pope, 275–83, possibly a Tuscan although little is known of his pontificate. His Greek epitaph was discovered in the cemetery of Callistus.

EUTYCHIANISM. *See* EUTYCHES.

EUTYCHIOS OF ALEXANDRIA, d. 940, patriarch of Alexandria (933) and author of a history of the world to 938 which is valuable despite the inclusion of many legends. He may have been the author as well of a theological work in Arabic entitled *Book of Demonstration* which deals with the Creation, God, the Incarnation, and the destiny of man.

EVAGRIUS PONTICUS, d. 399, famed preacher and theologian of Constantinople who retired to Egypt in 383 where he lived as a hermit and supported himself by copying manuscripts. His mystical, ascetical, and theological writings, which enjoyed considerable popularity, established him as the founder of monastic mysticism. A synod in Constantinople in 553 judged his works tainted with Origenism and ordered them burned.

EVAGRIUS SCHOLASTICUS, d. after 594, Byzantine historian and author of *Ecclesiastical History* which extends from the Council of Ephesus (431) to 594. The work, written in excellent Greek, is of considerable importance for the history of dogma of the fifth and sixth centuries. It also incorporated documents from sources that are no longer extant. He was himself a poor theologian and inclined to accept legends as true. His *History* represents a continuation of the work of Eusebius, Socrates, Sozomenos, and Theodoret.

EVANGELISTS, SYMBOLS OF THE, figures which came into use as early as the fifth century to represent the four evangelists: a lion for Mark, a man or angel for Matthew, an ox for Luke, and an eagle for John. The supposed basis of these symbols is provided by the opening passages of their respective gospels, e.g., the man for Matthew since he opens his gospel with the genealogy and birth of Christ.

EVARD OF BÉTHUNE, obscure grammarian and polemicist of probably the late twelfth century. He was the author of a popular Latin grammar although his principal work was a criticism of the beliefs of the Cathari, Waldensians, and Jews.

EVARISTUS, ST., Pope, 97–107?, a Greek of Antioch who, according to the testimony of Irenaeus, succeeded Clement I. The tradition that he suffered martyrdom is generally discounted.

EVENSONG, name given to the canonical hour of Vespers in medieval England.

EVERARD OF YPRES, a late twelfth-century scholar and writer who studied under Gilbert de la Porrée. He was himself a teacher at Paris and wrote a compendium of canon law and a defense of the theological views of his mentor Gilbert. He lived his last years as a Cistercian at Clairvaux.

EVERYMAN, English morality play of the fifteenth century, probably a translation of the Dutch play entitled *Elckerlyc,* which appeared in a number of variant versions. It generally depicted a rich man who, despite the assurances of such friends as Wealth, Fellowship, and Pleasure, discovered that the only person who came to offer assistance when he died was Good Deeds.

EVESHAM ABBEY, Benedictine monastery founded in 702 by St. Egwin, bishop of Worcester. In 1206 the abbey, which became one of the wealthiest in England, won exemption from episcopal jurisdiction. The abbey suffered severely from the Black Death (1348–50) and was suppressed in 1540 when it was almost completely destroyed. The abbot exercised nearly complete control over the town of Evesham until 1482.

EVESHAM, BATTLE OF, battle won on August 4, 1265, by Edward (I), son of Henry III, over Simon de Montfort, leader of a baronial revolt who was slain in the fighting. This battle ended the short period of Montfort's rule which dated from his victory and capture of King Henry at Lewes in May 1264.

EVE'S UNEQUAL CHILDREN, a legendary tale of the fifteenth century with social application. It told how God had designated some of Eve's children as superior, others as deserving of only a lower station in life.

EVOCATION, RIGHT OF, right under Frankish and, generally, medieval law for the king to bring any lawsuit before his own tribunal. The pope assumed a similar prerogative with cases introduced to episcopal courts.

ÉVORA, city of Portugal whose origins extended back to Roman times. The city became a bishopric in the fifth century and, after being taken from the Moors in 1166, served on occasion as the capital of the country.

EXALTATION OF THE CROSS, THE, a feast in honor of the Cross of Christ which commemorated the exposition of the True Cross at Jerusalem in 629 by the emperor Heraclius after he had recovered it from the Persians. They had taken it back with them when they captured Jerusalem in 614. The feast may also have honored the earlier commemoration made in Jerusalem in 335 on the occasion of the dedication of the basilica built by the emperor Constantine on the site of the Holy Sepulchre.

EXARCH, title originally given to the administrator of a diocese in Emperor Diocletian's reorganization of the empire. In Byzantine times the title was held by provincial governors of the exarchates of Italy (Ravenna) and Africa, also by leading military and naval commanders. The title might also be given to an archbishop in the Greek church or to a superior who had charge of several monasteries.

EXARCHATE, name given to the Byzantine provinces of Africa and Italy (Ravenna) when these areas were reorganized following their recovery from the Vandals and Ostrogoths.

EXAUDI, name given to the sixth Sunday after Easter, from the opening words of the Introit.

EXCALIBUR, a corruption of "Caliburn," according to Geoffrey of Monmouth the name of King Arthur's sword.

EXCHEQUER, name of the financial department of the English royal government. The term derived from the checkerboard-type counting table which was employed in order to facilitate reckoning. Members of the *curia regis* who handled the business of the exchequer included the treasurer, the justiciar, and the chancellor who was responsible for all writs and summonses. The chief accountants were the sheriffs who presented their reports twice a year, at Easter and at Michaelmas. Beyond the fixed revenues from the farms of the king's demesne and payments from the boroughs for their liberties, the sheriffs reported what they had collected in aids and incidents, profits of justice, scutages, customs of ports, and gifts. The most valuable historical source concerning the early exchequer is the work by Richard, bishop of London, the royal treasurer, entitled *Dialogue of the Exchequer (Dialogus de Scaccario).*

EXCOMMUNICATION, exclusion of varying degree from membership in the church or from the communion of the faithful. Those whom the church declared *tolerati,* for example, might still mingle with the faithful, while the company of those judged *vitandi* was to be shunned. The first judgment might be referred to as minor, the second, as major excommunication.

EXECRABILIS, bull issued by Pope Pius II in 1460 which anathematized the principles of conciliarism and condemned any appeal from the authority of the pope.

EXEQUATUR, that is, let it be done, a statement referring to the order given by the king or his representative to ecclesiastical officials to proceed with some action, e.g., the election of a new bishop. [*See* PLACET AND CONGÉ D'ÉLIRE.]

EXERCITIA SPIRITUALIA, spiritual exercises usually of a contemplative nature, so organized as to advance the religious life of those observing them.

EX MORE DOCTI MYSTICO, hymn credited to Pope Gregory the Great (d. 604) whose theme concerned Lent. It found its way into the divine office.

EX OPERE OPERANTIS, a Latin phrase used by theologians to designate grace that followed from the work of the doer as opposed to *ex opere operato,* which referred to the grace-conferring power inherent in some rites.

EXORCISM, a solemn and official adjuration addressed to evil spirits ordering them to abandon a person of whom they had taken possession. In the early church the power to exorcise was restricted to persons believed to be favored with special powers. From about 250 the power was conferred on a special class of clergy called exorcists. Catechumens were regularly exorcised before baptism.

EXPECTANCIES (expectatives), benefices pledged ordinarily by the pope and usually secured by formal documents (*litterae expectativae*) which were to be conferred when they became vacant. The practice of promising expectancies dated from the twelfth century.

EXPLICIT, that is, here ends [the book or roll].

EXPOSITION OF THE BLESSED SACRAMENT, the exhibition of the consecrated eucharistic host for the purpose of devotion. The devotion originated in the fourteenth century.

EXSULTET IAM ANGELICA TURBA, opening words of the hymn of praise sung by the deacon in the Easter vigil service on Holy Saturday immediately following the *Lumen Christi* procession and the blessing of the Paschal Candle. The hymn, which appeared as early as the fourth century, was sung to one of the most beautiful chants in the Latin liturgy.

EXSULTET ORBIS GAUDIIS, hymn of unknown authorship which appeared in hymnals of the tenth century. It was included in the divine office on feasts of the apostles.

EXTRA ECCLESIAM NULLA SALUS, that is, outside the church there is no salvation, a dogmatic principle of the Christian church first enunciated by Cyprian of Carthage (d. 258) and Origen (d. c. 254) and reaffirmed in most positive language by Pope Boniface VIII in his bull *Unam Sanctam* (1302). The declaration has received varying interpretations.

EXTRAVAGANTES, term used to identify papal decrees not included in the *Decretum* (c. 1140) of Gratian chiefly for the reason that they were not issued until later.

EXTREME UNCTION, a sacrament or rite administered to the seriously ill to ask God to strengthen them in their last hour or, if it were the divine will, to restore them to health. Origen (d. c. 254) made mention of the rite although the name itself did not come into use before the twelfth century.

EXULTET. *See* EXSULTET IAM ANGELICA TURBA.

EYCK, HUBERT VAN, d. 1426 , Dutch painter who left no authenticated pictures of his own but appears to have collaborated with his younger brother Jan. He may have begun the famous altarpiece of Ghent which his brother finished after his death.

EYCK, JAN VAN, d. 1441, greatest artist of the early Netherlands school, court painter in the service of Philip the Good, duke of Burgundy. He painted alone, and with his older brother Hubert, the most famous of their joint efforts being the altarpiece of Ghent *(Adoration of the Lamb)*. His *Arnolfini and his Wife* reveals van Eyck the master of the art of oil painting in his ability to produce a naturalism of color and atmosphere to lend his work depth and perspective. His technical skill and artistic ingenuity, for example, in fitting a multitude of diverse objects into a simple theme, are unsurpassed.

EZZELINO DA ROMANO, d. 1259, son-in-law of Emperor Frederick II, lord of Verona, Vicenza, and Padua, the first Italian despot to hold power for any number of years (1236–59). After Frederick's victory over the Lombard League at Cortenuova (1237), he was the most powerful lord in northern Italy. In 1254 Pope Innocent IV excommunicated him. Dante placed him in hell with the tyrants *(Inferno* XII, 109).

FABER, FELIX, d. 1502, Dominican theologian and provincial of his order in Germany. He left descriptions of the pilgrimages he made to Palestine and is also the author of a history of the Swiss (to 1489).

FABIAN, ST., Pope, 236–50, a Roman known for his encouragement of the construction of church buildings and for his advancement of the church's administrative organization. He divided the city of Rome into seven ecclesiastical districts and placed a deacon in charge of each. He suffered martyrdom under the emperor Decius.

FABIOLA, ST., d. 399, wealthy and learned Roman noblewoman, friend and disciple of Jerome, and a generous benefactor of the poor and the sick, many of whom she attended in person. She is said to have founded the first public hospital in western Europe. She spent a number of years in Bethlehem, living an ascetic life, under the direction of St. Jerome.

FABLE, story about animals that retained their physical traits, yet took on the character of men. As was the case with the fables of Aesop and Phaedrus, those of the Middle Ages often contained a moral. The most prolific composer of fables was Marie de France (late twelfth century). Often classified with medieval fables is the *Romance of Renard the Fox,* although the stories about Renard held no moral, nor were they, in their origin, satirical. [*See* ROMAN DE RENART.]

FABLIAU, humorous tale in verse featuring a coarse but harmless satire at the expense of clerks, burghers, peasants, and women. Fabliaux were popular in the twelfth and thirteenth centuries and appealed particularly to the growing burgher class.

FABYAN, ROBERT, d. 1513, London clothier and alderman, author of a chronicle of English history that extended to the end of the reign of Richard III (1485). His writings on London are valuable. His narrative provided materials for later historians such as Raphael Holinshed.

FACETIAE, title of a collection of short stories written by Poggio Bracciolini (d. 1459) in Latin on themes humorous, satirical, and lascivious.

FACUNDUS OF HERMIANE, sixth-century bishop and theologian of north Africa who took an active part in the Christological controversies of the period, even daring to oppose the views of Emperor Justinian and Pope Vigilius I. His defense of the *Three Chapters* led to his expulsion in 547 from Constantinople where he had been participating in a synod attended by Pope Vigilius.

FAENZA (Faventia), town near Bologna where Totila defeated a Byzantine army in 542. The town gave its name to faience, a glazed earthenware of highly colored design, which came to be produced there in the late Middle Ages.

FAFNIR, the dragon slain by Siegfried (Sigurd) in the Norse version of the Nibelung legend.

FAIDITS, name given to men who lived as brigands or outcasts from society; inhabitants of Languedoc who fled in order to escape prosecution for heresy.

FAIR, essentially a market where buyers and sellers gathered at regular intervals, usually once or twice a year, to transact business. In contrast to the local products available in town markets, fairs offered prospective buyers a large variety of commodities, many of these from distant lands. The origin of the fair was ordinarily a local market which had succeeded in exploiting its location at a bridge, ford, or crossroad to attract a greater volume of business. Thus the most thriving fairs were those in the county of Champagne east of Paris whose location athwart trade routes connecting northern and southern Europe, and with the Seine offering access to the west, kept them humming with activity during the twelfth and thirteenth centuries. Although some fairs like those at Dresden, Nuremberg, Leipzig, and Stourbridge flourished up into modern times, for the majority decline set in during the fourteenth century when the rise of large cities deprived them of their function as the principal trading centers of western Europe. The medieval fair made a significant contribution to the evolution of standards of measure, weight (e.g., troy weight from the fair at Troyes in the county of Champagne), and quality, of mediums of financial exchange, and of commercial law.

FAIR ROSAMOND. *See* ROSAMOND, FAIR.

FAITHFUL, MASS OF THE, that part of the Mass which began with the Offertory. In the early church catechumens were dismissed before the beginning of the Offertory and only those already baptized were permitted to remain.

FAITH, ST., d. c. 287, virgin martyr. What were believed to be her relics were brought c. 855 to the abbey of Conques, which became a favorite pilgrimage place as a consequence. Her cult was very popular in the Middle Ages and many churches were dedicated to her honor.

FAKIR, a mendicant dervish.

FALCONRY, the sport of hunting birds with falcons, a popular pastime among the aristocracy. The most authoritative book on the subject was that written by Emperor Frederick II of Germany (d. 1250).

FALDSTOOL, movable folding chair used by a bishop in pontifical functions when he was away from his cathedral.

FALKAUNE (Falke, Falkonett), light field gun used in the late Middle Ages.

FALKENBERG, JOHN OF, d. c. 1435, Polish Dominican, polemicist, theologian, and inquisitor at Magdeburg. His treatise in support of tyrannicide led to his confinement in Rome by Pope Martin V. He also wrote in support of the legitimacy of the claims of Gregory XII against those of other popes during the Western Schism, and in behalf of the Teutonic Knights in their struggle with Poland.

FALKIRK, BATTLE OF, battle fought in 1298 between Edward I of England and William Wallace who had led a revolt against English claims to overlordship of Scotland. The Scots suffered defeat and Wallace went into exile.

FALS (fels, fils), copper coin used in the early centuries of Islam.

FALSE DECRETALS. *See* PSEUDO-ISIDORIAN DECRETALS.

FALSTAFF, SIR JOHN, d. 1459, actually Sir John Fastolf, an English captain who fought in the Hundred Years' War and served as governor of Anjou and Maine. He proved himself a solid soldier, quite unlike the braggart liar Shakespeare presents in his *Henry IV*. He became very wealthy by means perhaps not always above scrutiny. His neighbor, John Paston, inherited much of his fortune.

FAMILIA REGIS, name given the king's retinue or bodyguard, which was composed principally of knights, bannerets, and sergeants.

FAMILIARS, servants attached to a monastery.

FAMULUS, member of the unfree class who was privileged to serve a king or lord both in a personal and a military capacity.

FAN, LITURGICAL, a fan used at least from the fourth century at the Eucharist to keep flies and other insects away from the offerings. In the West the practice continued down to the fourteenth century, in the Eastern church considerably longer.

FANDANGO, early Spanish dance marked by the liveliness of its movements. It belonged to the class of flamencos.

FANEGA (fanegada, almuda, estajo), early Spanish linear measure; a measure used in handling grain.

FANON, liturgical garment similar to the amice which popes wore as early as the thirteenth century.

FAQUIN, term of Italian origin given to the dummy used by young men when practicing with the lance.

FARABI, AL-, d. 950, distinguished Moslem scholar and philosopher. He was born in Transoxiana of Turkish parentage and studied at Baghdad where he found Christian Arabic philosophers for teachers. He left voluminous writings on logic, ethics, mathematics, chemistry, politics, and music. In his metaphysical treatises, which reveal a blend of Aristotelian and Platonic influences, he advanced the position that the views of Plato and Aristotle could be brought into harmony.

FARANDOLE (farandoule), a lively French dance in six-eighths time which appeared in the fourteenth century.

FARGHANI (Ferghani), ABU-L-ABBAS ACHMED IBN MOHAMMED IBN KATHIRAL, d. after 861, Arabic astronomer whose writings, including one on the astrolabe, greatly influenced Western astronomers.

FARTHING, English silver coin of least value amounting to a quarter penny, from the reign of Edward I (1272–1307).

FASCICULUS, small bundle or packet.

FASTOLF, SIR JOHN. See FALSTAFF, SIR JOHN.

FATHERS OF THE CHURCH, Christian theologians of the early centuries of the church, often bishops and eminent teachers, whose writings and influence contributed significantly to the definition, defense, or spread of the faith. As a group they were conspicuous for their learning, orthodoxy, and the sanctity of their lives. It is traditional to extend the patristic period in the West to include Gregory the Great (d. 604) in view of his enormous influence upon the organization and character of the Latin church. (Some scholars extend the patristic period in the West to include the Venerable Bede (d. 735). In the Eastern church the patristic period may extend as far as John of Damascus (d. 749) who was perhaps the ranking theologian in the whole of the Greek medieval world. A popular grouping classifies the church fathers of the earliest period as apostolic (e.g., Clement of Rome) because they lived near the time of the Apostles; those of the second and early third centuries as apologists (e.g., Justin Martyr) because of their efforts to persuade the imperial authorities of the reasonableness of the Christian belief and the loyalty of its adherents; and those of the late second and third centuries as controversialists in view of their major concern with the heresies that were dividing the Christian community from within. What justifies the designation of the fourth and early fifth centuries as the golden age of the patristic period is the presence of Basil, Gregory of Nazianzus, John Chrysostom, and Athanasius, all representatives of the Greek church, and Ambrose, Jerome, and Augustine of the Latin church.

FATIMA, d. 632, daughter of Mohammed by Khadija and the only child to outlive the Prophet. She married his counsin Ali, whose two sons, Hasan and Husain, continued the line of the Prophet.

FATIMIDS, Moslem caliphate set up by Abu 'Abdallah al-Shi'i at Kairaman (below Tunis) in 909. They conquered Egypt in 969 and continued their hold on that country until 1171 when it was destroyed by Saladin. The Fatimids, who claimed descent from Fatima, the daughter of Mohammed, were the founders of the Isma'ili movement which was organized in the ninth century for the purpose of overthrowing the Abbasid caliphate.

FAUBOURG, an "outside burg" or suburb which grew up around the original settlement or burg.

FAUCHART (faussart), a weapon resembling a scythe or long-handled knife which was used from the eleventh century.

FAUSTA, FLAVIA MAXIMA, d. 326, daughter of Emperor Maximian who became the wife of Constantine in 307. She bore him three sons, Constantine, Constantius, and Constans. For reasons not entirely clear, possibly for adultery, Constantine had her executed.

FAUSTINUS AND JOVITA, SS., obscure martyrs of Brescia of the second century who were taken prisoner under Trajan, transported to Rome and Naples, on the way making innumerable converts, finally executed by Hadrian. That several cities claimed possession of their relics suggests the unreliability of the little information that remains about them.

FAUSTUS OF MILEVIS, late fourth-century Manichaean leader, a well-known rhetorician of Rome. Augustine tells in his *Confessions* how he went to Faustus when the latter came to Carthage to have him clear up some problems he was having as a Manichaean, only to find him nothing better than an eloquent fraud.

FAUSTUS OF RIEZ (Reji), d. c. 495, British monk, abbot of Lérins, later bishop of Riez in Provence. Although he was a celebrated theologian and a vigorous opponent of Arianism, his writings on the Holy Spirit and on grace revealed him to be an adherent of Semi-Pelagianism. In 477 the Visigothic king Euric expelled him from Gaul because of his opposition to Arianism. His teachings were condemned at the Second Council of Orange (529).

FAZENET (Fazelet, Fazilettlein), a fancy scarf or handkerchief used in Italy in the fifteenth century especially by upper class women.

FEALTY, OATH OF, oath of fidelity which the vassal took to his lord, usually on the relics of saints or the Bible. Its adoption in the Carolingian period when it was customarily given by the vassal after he had made the more ancient act of homage, has been credited to the growing influence of Christianity.

FEAST OF ASSES, also known as the Feast of Fools, celebrated on or about January 1, the feast of the Circumcision, or within the octave of the Epiphany (January 6) and commemorating the flight of the Holy Family into Egypt. By the thirteenth century the festival had drawn much criticism because of the buffoonery which its celebration had introduced into the liturgy which reformers sought to suppress. [*See* FOOLS, FEAST OF, and BOY BISHOP.]

FEAST OF FOOLS. *See* FOOLS, FEAST OF.

FEHM (Fehme, Feme, Veme). *See* VEHMGERICHT.

FELIX I, ST., Pope, 269–74, probably a Roman, about whom little reliable testimony remains. It is considered unlikely that he died a martyr.

FELIX II, Pope (Antipope), 355–8, who owed his pontificate to Emperor Constantius II who had exiled Pope Liberius. The Roman populace remained loyal to Liberius, however, and forced Felix into exile. He died in 365.

FELIX III, ST., Pope, 483–92, who was pontiff during the reign of Odoacer. His excommunication and deposition of Acacius, patriarch of Constantinople, in 484 on the charge of Monophysitism precipitated a schism (Acacian) that lasted for thirty-five years. Felix addressed a letter to Emperor Anastasius I in which he firmly asserted the supreme authority of the church in spiritual matters.

FELIX IV, ST., Pope, 526–30, Roman priest, who as pope presented a position on the problem of grace and free will, based upon the Bible and the writings of the Fathers, notably those of Augustine, that was given dogmatic recognition by the Second Council of Orange (529). It served to end the controversy over grace and led to the final suppression of Pelagianism. In the hope of averting factional strife in Rome, Felix designated the archdeacon Boniface as his successor, but the majority of the clergy chose the bishop Dioscorus. The latter's death after twenty-two days resolved the schism.

FELIX V, Pope (Antipope), 1440–9, was the choice of the conciliarists who remained at Basel after Eugenius IV had ordered the council removed to Ferrara. [See FERRARA-FLORENCE, COUNCIL OF.] They announced the deposition of Eugenius and selected as pope Amadeus VIII, duke of Savoy, a widower, who at the time had retired to a hermitage near Thonon, France, where he was directing a community of knights-hermits. In 1449 Felix made his submission to Pope Nicholas V and retired as a cardinal. Felix was the last of the antipopes.

FELIX CULPA, that is, "happy sin," a phrase in the Easter vigil service (*Exsultet*) in reference to the sin of Adam which was responsible in time for the appearance of Christ the Savior.

FELLAH, the peasant (plowman) in Arabic-speaking lands such as Syria and Egypt, as opposed to the nomadic herdsman or shepherd.

FELONY, treason, in feudal law any grave violation of the feudal contract by either the lord or vassal.

FERDINAND I, d. 1416, king of Aragon and Sicily and count of Barcelona. In 1410 he captured Antequera from the Moors and claimed the throne of Aragon. He managed to restore order in Sicily and Sardinia. In 1415 he agreed to withdraw support from Benedict XIII (Pedro de Luna), the Avignonese pope, in order to clear the way for the ending of the Western Schism.

FERDINAND II, d. 1516 (Ferdinand V of Castile), known as the Catholic, married Isabella of Castile in 1469. They ruled as joint sovereigns of Castile from 1474. In 1492 they extinguished Granada, the last Moorish state in Spain. The same year they expelled all Jews who refused to be baptized. In 1492 they financed Columbus's voyage to America. In 1494, by the Treaty of Tordesillas, Spain and Portugal divided the New World between themselves. In 1512 they annexed the greater part of Navarre, thus uniting under their rule not only Spain but also Sicily, Naples, Sardinia, and an overseas empire.

FERDINAND I (the Great), king of Castile, 1035–65. Son of Sancho III of Navarre, he inherited the throne of Leon in 1037 and added to his possessions at the expense of the Moors and the neighboring states of Navarre and Portugal. The rulers of Toledo, Saragossa, and Seville all recognized his suzerainty. He arranged that his kingdom should be divided among his three sons when he died.

FERDINAND III, ST., king of Castile, 1217–52, adopted a policy of tolerance toward Moslems and Jews although he took Córdoba and Seville from the Moors and reduced their power in Andalusia to Granada which he made a vassal state. In 1230 he added Leon to his domain and in 1239 chartered the University of Salamanca. He made efforts to advance legal studies and initiated the production of a uniform code of law.

FERDINAND (Ferrante) I, king of Naples, 1458–94, known in Italy as Don Ferrante, natural son of Alfonso V of Aragon. He suppressed a major revolt of his greater barons and extended his rule over southern Italy against the French who had the support of the lower aristocracy. His court became a center of humanism; he also promoted commerce and industry.

FERDINAND I, king of Portugal, 1367–83, known as the Handsome and the Inconstant, who made three unsuccessful and costly attempts to secure the Castilian throne. In 1373 he negotiated the historic alliance with England that helped preserve the integrity and independence of Portugal for centuries to come. (John of Gaunt, son of Edward III, had helped him in his war of 1373 against Henry II of Castile.) Ferdinand encouraged the development of agriculture, trade, and a merchant marine.

FERDINAND (Fernando), BL., d. 1443, pious son of John I of Portugal who was captured by the Moors in 1437 in an attack on Tangier. He remained a prisoner for the rest of his life as his brother Edward (Duarte), who succeeded his father on the throne, refused to give over Ceuta for his ransom.

FERIA, a weekday in Christian liturgical reckoning since the third century. The word was later joined with an ordinal number, e.g., *feria secunda,* that is, Monday.

FERID ED-DIN ATTAR, d. c. 1229, Persian poet, one of the leading mystic poets of Islam. He was converted to Sufism and in turn became a zealous expounder of that faith. His greatest work, entitled *Mantiq ut-Tair* (Language of the Birds), is a long allegory describing the philosophy and practice of the Sufis.

FERMENTUM, particle of the eucharistic bread which the bishop of Rome in the early church sent to other bishops as a symbol of unity. The practice fell into disuse shortly after the fourth century although it survived in a modified form on Maundy Thursday to the eighth century.

FERMOIR (fermouer), kind of clasp used to close books.

FERNANDES, ÁLVARO, Portuguese captain whom Prince Henry the Navigator sent to explore the coast of West Africa. In 1445 he sailed some 150 miles beyond the Cape Verde Islands, the following year some 300 miles, to a point near Sierra Leone. This represented the farthest Portuguese penetration southward until the 1460s.

FERNÁNDEZ DE CÓRDOBA, GONZALO, d. 1515, Spanish general, called the Great Captain, who had a leading role in the wars in Spain that cleared the way for the rule of Ferdinand and Isabella over the entire Iberian peninsula. He also aided Naples against Charles VIII of France and later served as governor of that Italian kingdom.

FERNANDEZ, JOÃO, Portuguese explorer who spent seven months in 1445–6 with nomadic tribes to the east and south of Río de Oro where he gained valuable information about the peoples and products of the western Sahara and Guinea. On the basis of this information the Portuguese began to depend upon trade agreements with Moorish and Negro chieftains for the slaves they had until then seized on raids of their own.

FERRARA, important city in the area of the Po delta, first noted in 753 when the Lombards captured it from the exarchate of Ravenna. It came under papal rule in 774 after the destruction of the Lombard kingdom by Charlemagne. In the tenth century it became a possession of the margrave of Tuscany. It joined the Lombard League against Frederick I Barbarossa in 1167, and in 1438 hosted a church council. A massive castle which the house of Este began building in 1385 (completed in 1472) dominated the city in the late Middle Ages.

FERRARA-FLORENCE, COUNCIL OF, general church council that opened early in 1438 at Ferrara. This represented less a new ecumenical assembly than a transfer to that city of the council that had been in session in Basel since 1431. Actually, only those ecclesiastics who supported the pope in his contest with the conciliarists heeded his instructions and came down to Ferrara. [*See* BASEL, COUNCIL OF.] Pope Eugenius IV justified his ordering the council to Ferrara on the grounds of economy since he had undertaken to defray the cost of the embassy Constantinople was sending west in the hope of ending the schism. This was a large embassy of some 700 persons and included Emperor John VIII Palaeologus and the patriarch of Constantinople. An outbreak of the plague, along with other considerations, led the council to move to Florence early in 1439. The following July, after extended and frequently bitter controversy over the principal issues — papal primacy, the *Filioque* in the Creed, and purgatory — the majority of the Byzantine representatives voted for acceptance, and Pope Eugenius solemnly proclaimed the reunion of the Latin and Greek churches. Although the majority of the Greek delegates repudiated their acceptance of reunion after their return to Constantinople, the promulgation at Florence of Christian unity in support of the doctrine of papal primacy greatly strengthened the cause of the pope against conciliarism. This proved its most significant achievement.

FERRARA, SCHOOL OF, center of art from 1440 that owed its existence to the patronage of the Este princes. Its principal artists included Pisanello, Piero della Francesca, Jacopo Bellini, Francesco del Cossa, Ercole de' Roberti, and Cosimo Tura. The center was famed for the richness of its manuscript illumination and for its fresco paintings.

FÈS (Fez), city in Morocco founded by the Idrisids in 790–898 as separate settlements on both sides of the Fès wadi riverbed which the Almoravids united as a single city in 1075. Refugees from Spain and Tunisia brought the settlement rapid growth and c. 1350 it is said to have had a population of 200,000. It developed into a major center of Islamic culture and learning (it possessed a university) and a thriving commercial city.

FESTUCA, usually a small piece of wood used in Frankish times to symbolize the transfer of property to another person, ordinarily to one who owed service.

FEUDALISM, a system of government in which a largely autonomous landed aristocracy assumed certain responsibilities to a king, principally military service (knights), in return for the use of land (fiefs) that it exploited with the labor of a semifree peasantry (serfs, villeins). As an institution feudalism emerged during the ninth century with the coalescing of such practices as commendation, immunity, and vassalage. [*See* COMMENDATION; IMMUNITY; VASSAL.] Major factors contributing to the evolution of these practices in particular and to the rise of feudalism in general were the poverty of the king which, combined with the obsolescence of the foot soldier, compelled the monarch to depend upon his landed aristocracy for officials and for fighting men. The incursions of the Vikings, Saracens, and Magyars during the ninth and tenth centuries completed the emasculation of the monarchy and the disintegration of the state.

Because of these developments the typical feudal monarch was a weak king who reigned but did not rule. Under ordinary circumstances he had no choice but to accept the possession of the greater part of his country by territorial princes (vassals) who administered it as fiefs in his name. For this reason the landed aristocracy dominated Western Europe during the feudal period, roughly from the middle of the ninth century into the twelfth. The introduction of new weapons in the late Middle Ages, including the crossbow, pike, and long bow, made the foot soldier again an effective fighter and reduced the king's dependence upon the aristocracy, particularly when he found himself able to tap the financial resources of a new and growing merchant class. By the close of the Middle Ages, therefore, several major factors that earlier had contributed to the rise of the landed aristocracy at the expense of the monarchy had been reversed, and Western Europe was preparing to enter an era of royal absolutism.

Certain misconceptions concerning feudalism have complicated what is itself a difficult subject because of the variety of twists it took in different parts of Europe. The most serious source of confusion is the mistake of considering feudalism and manorialism so intertwined as to defy any understanding when treated individually. [For an introduction to the social and economic organization of the peasantry during the feudal period, *see* MANORIALISM.] It has also been the wont of older scholars to blame feudalism for the unstable conditions that prevailed during the feudal period. Since feudalism is simply the name modern scholarship attaches to the form of political and social organization of western Europe during the period, however inadequate it proved, this is scarcely just. Feudal practices and principles that evolved at this time may deserve credit, indeed, for preventing the instability of the times from degenerating into anarchy. Foremost among these was the system of personal dependencies which members of the upper classes arranged among themselves. These personal ties supplied a measure of cohesiveness to a society in an age which knew nothing of national consciousness and also lacked the economic sinews that would come only with the expansion of trade. This personal relationship was formalized by the act of homage and oath of fealty which the vassal made to his lord (king). [*See* HOMAGE, ACT OF, and FEALTY, OATH OF.] By these acts he undertook to provide the lord (king) military service and counsel, to administer his fief in his name, and to make contributions or aids when a special need arose, e.g., when the lord was held for ransom. [*See* AID, FEUDAL; INCIDENTS.] Upon the lord (king) rested in return the obligation to protect his vassal, to leave him unmolested on his fief so long as he honored his obligations, and to accord him the

right of trial by his peers. From these mutual obligations of king and vassals stemmed feudalism's most precious contribution to Western society, namely, the principle of constitutional government.

FEZ (Fès), a head covering, usually red, worn in the city of Fès in Morocco. Its use spread to the Orient and even to Venice in the late fifteenth century.

FIALE, slender tower placed on the top of a flying buttress, perpendicular with the ground, which served as both decoration and ballast.

FIBONACCI, LEONARDO. *See* LEONARD OF PISA.

FICINO, MARSILIO, d. 1499, a leading Italian humanist and Platonist, student of Latin, Greek, philosophy, theology, and medicine. With the financial assistance of Cosimo de' Medici he founded the Platonic Academy in Florence which became the leading center of Greek studies and Platonic thought in Western Europe. Ficino sought to revive ancient Platonism which he believed could be brought into harmony with Christianity since the concern of both was the contemplation of God. He translated the works of Plato, Plotinus, and Dionysius the Areopagite, and left letters as well as treatises on philosophy, theology, medicine, and astrology.

FIDDLE, a musical instrument introduced into Europe from Asia in the ninth century.

FIDES QUAERENS INTELLECTUM, that is, faith seeking understanding, a scholastic principle which Anselm of Bec drew from Augustine. It expressed the position of the scholastic, that of finding substantiation in reason and philosophy for those doctrines which the church expected Christians to believe.

FIEF, heritable land (on occasion an official position or sum of money) held under feudal tenure by a vassal from a lord to whom he owed military and other services. [*See* FEUDALISM.]

FILARETE (Antonio Averlino), d. c. 1469,

sculptor and architect of Florence who executed bronze doors for St. Peter's (Rome) and began the hospital in Milan. He composed a treatise on architecture which proposed ambitious designs for palaces and for ideal cities.

FILELFO (Philelphus), FRANCESCO, d. 1481, Italian humanist who spent some years in Constantinople and brought back with him a knowledge of Greek and many classical manuscripts. He taught classical languages in several Italian cities, principally in Milan where he was in the service of the duke from c. 1440 to 1471, produced treatises on philosophy and literature, and translated many Greek works into Latin. His letters provide valuable information about the social history of his period.

FILIOQUE, Latin term meaning "and from the son," which referred to the theological view that the Holy Spirit proceeded from both the Father and the Son. The Latin church added the word to the Nicene Creed in the ninth century, although Spanish bishops had already adopted it in the seventh and Charlemagne had ordered its inclusion at Aachen in the eighth. The question of the procession of the Holy Spirit had been a matter of theological controversy from at least the fourth century. It proved a principal cause for the schism of 1054 and a stumbling block in subsequent efforts to induce the Greek church to accept unity with the Latin.

FILLASTRE (Fillâtre), GUILLAUME, d. 1428, French canonist, humanist, geographer, and cardinal. He endorsed conciliarism and left an informative account of the proceedings of the Council of Constance.

FILLASTRE (Fillâtre), GUILLAUME, d. 1473, probably a nephew of the older Fillastre, a Benedictine monk, abbot of Saint-Thierry of Reims, and bishop of Verdun, Toul, and later of Tournai. He served as councillor to Philip the Good of Burgundy and left a chronicle of French history.

FINALIS, a keynote in a musical mode, so called because it was the note on which a melody in the mode ended.

FINAN, ST., d. 661, Irish monk of Iona, successor of St. Aidan as bishop of Lindisfarne. He stoutly upheld the use of Celtic ecclesiastical customs in the liturgy against the Roman ones advanced by Augustine of Canterbury. Among those whom he converted to Christianity were Penda, ruler of the Middle Angles, and Sigebert, king of Essex.

FINIGUERRA, MASO (Tommaso), d. 1464, famed goldsmith of Florence and one of the first artists to engrave in copper. He may have introduced the copperplate engraving process into Italy.

FINLAND, country to the east and north of the Gulf of Bothnia which Balto-Finnic peoples occupied during the fifth and sixth centuries. Christian missionaries penetrated the country in the eleventh century although the monastery of Valamo claims foundation in 992. Sweden had annexed the greater part of the region by the middle of the thirteenth century but in 1362 extended the Finns the right to participate in the election of the king.

FIORETTI DI SAN FRANCESCO (I Fioretti de San Francesco), collection of legends about St. Francis of Assisi translated from a Latin work composed c. 1325 by Fra Ugolino Boniscambi. Its traditional English title is *The Little Flowers of St. Francis.*

FIRDAUSI (Firdusi), ABUL QASIM MANSUR, d. c. 1020, the leading poet of Persia, author of the *Shah-Nama* ("Book of Kings"), a national epic poem of almost 60,000 verses. This was based upon his own prose work which in large measure constituted a translation of a Pahlavi (Middle-Persian) history of the kings of Persia from ancient mythological times down to the reign of Chosroes II (590–628).

FIREPLACE. In early medieval times, a fire was

located upon a hearth or floor in the middle of the room, the smoke escaping through a hole(s) in the roof or eaves. By the thirteenth century, in structures of more than one story, the fireplace had been moved from the center of the room to an outer wall where the addition of a projecting hood and flue carried the smoke into a chimney and thence into the air outside. The essential features of the fireplace were, accordingly, known and used by the close of the Middle Ages. [*See* CHIMNEY.]

FIRMA BURGI, the annual fee farm which towns paid to the English crown in lieu of various tolls they owed the king.

FIRMICUS MATERNUS, JULIUS, d. after 350, pagan rhetorician, lawyer, and astrologer of Syracuse who after baptism became a Christian apologist and polemicist. As a pagan he wrote what is considered the most exhaustive study of astrology to appear in the Latin language. His Christian writings throw light on the nature of Oriental cults. In his most important work, *De Errore Profanarum Religionum,* he appealed to the co-emperors Constantius and Constans to destroy the pagan idols.

FIRST ORDER, the male branch of a monastic order. The second order was reserved for women, a third usually for lay men and lay women.

FIRUZABADI, ABU'L-TAHIR MAJD AL-DIN AL-, d. 1414, Arab lexicographer. He taught in Jerusalem for ten years, then traveled in Egypt and the lands of the Near East, after which he settled down in Mecca. He later served as chief cadi of Yemen and married the sultan's daughter. His famous dictionary, entitled *al-Qamus* (The Ocean), an enormous work of some 60 to 100 volumes, combined the contents of other dictionaries and served itself as the basis for later dictionaries.

FISH, symbol used in Christian art and literature to represent a believer, even Christ himself. It also served as an acrostic since the Greek word for fish corresponded in spelling with the first letters of the Greek phrase "Jesus Christ, Son of God, Savior." It came into use in the second century.

FITZ, a prefix of Anglo-Norman derivation meaning son that was attached to the father's name in Irish families of Anglo-Norman origin.

FITZGERALD, historic family of Ireland that sprang from Walter whom the Domesday Book (1086) listed as a large landowner. His son Gerald was the ancestor of the Fitzgeralds. He married the daughter of Griffith, prince of south Wales. In 1164 his son David established the fortunes of the family in Ireland when he acquired the barony of Naas from Richard Strongbow. In 1316 John, a scion of the family, was granted the earldom of Kildare. The other branch of the Fitzgerald line attained distinction in 1329 when Maurice, the greatest Irish noble of his day, was created earl of Desmond (southwest Ireland). The Fitzmaurice, also of Fitzgerald stock, were feudal lords of Kerry. Their dignity was recognized as a peerage in 1489 by Henry VII.

FITZHUGH, ROBERT, d. 1436, chancellor of Cambridge University, bishop of London (1431), and a noted pluralist. He took a vigorous stand against Lollardy and served as one of England's representatives at the Council of Basel.

FITZNEALE (Fitznigel), RICHARD, d. 1198, itinerant justice, judge of common pleas, bishop of London (1189), and royal treasurer under both Henry II and Richard I. His *Dialogue of the Exchequer* which he presented as a dialogue between himself and an anonymous pupil, furnishes a detailed description of the working of the financial department of the royal government. The exchequer was for the most part a creation of his own family since he was the son of Nigel, bishop of Ely, and great-nephew of Roger, bishop of Salisbury, both of whom had earlier served as royal treasurers.

FITZOSBERN, WILLIAM, d. 1071, earl of Hereford, one of the most loyal supporters of William the Conqueror. William gave Fitzosbern the Isle of Wight and the earldom of Hereford for his share of the spoils of the invasion. He commanded the army in the king's absence. The laws which he introduced to Hereford became a model for many western English, Welsh, and Irish boroughs.

FITZPETER, GEOFFREY, d. 1213, earl of Essex, justiciar under Richard I and John. He cooperated with Hubert Walter in the running of the government during Richard's absence on the Crusade and in 1198 succeeded him as chief justiciar. The writs which he left attest to the industry and justice with which he performed the duties of his office.

FITZRALPH, RICHARD, d. 1360, Oxford theologian and chancellor, archbishop of Armagh (1347), distinguished preacher, theologian, and polemicist. At the pope's request he composed a confutation of the views of the Armenians, but what attracted most notice were his sharp attacks on the privileges and wealth of the friars. His views on the friars may have influenced John Wyclif.

FITZSTEPHEN, WILLIAM, d. c. 1190, a member of the household of Thomas Becket, the archbishop of Canterbury, and author of the most valuable biography of that prelate. He was a witness to Becket's murder.

FITZTHEDMAR, ARNOLD, d. c. 1275, London merchant, author of a compilation of the laws of England and of a *Chronicle of the Mayors and Sheriffs of London* (1188–1274). He is the principal authority on the government of London and the political developments that took place in that city after 1239.

FITZWALTER, ROBERT, d. 1235, baronial leader against King John and "marshal" of the army that forced the king to accept the Magna Carta. He fled to France in 1212 after John had seized his lands, but these were later restored as part of John's settlement with Pope Innocent III. As leader of the Council of 25, he sought French aid when John failed to honor his promises and was given command of the baronial forces. The story, true or otherwise, that King John had designs on his daughter Matilda (Maud) became a popular subject of romance.

FIVE PILLARS OF ISLAM, the religious requirements that Mohammed placed upon the faithful. The first and most important obligation was faith, essentially the recognition of Allah as the one and only god and Mohammed as his prophet. A second duty was that of praying five times a day, at intervals spaced between sunrise and evening, with face turned toward Mecca. A third obligation was that of abstaining from food, drink, and anything pleasing to the senses during the daylight hours during the month of Ramadan. Almsgiving was a fourth obligation, while a fifth required all the faithful who could to make a pilgrimage to Mecca.

FLABELLUM, fan made of leather, silk, feathers, and other materials which was used in liturgical services.

FLAGELLANTS, fanatical groups or sects whose members scourged themselves or had themselves whipped in reparation for the sins of mankind and to secure God's mercy. Their popularity in the thirteenth and fourteenth centuries has been linked to the apocalyptic prophecies of Joachim of Fiore, the influence of the Spiritual Franciscans, and to the miseries attendant upon the Black Death and the Hundred Years' War. Although under censure during the second half of the thirteenth century and condemned by Pope Clement VI in 1349, they continued to attract adherents to the close of the medieval period.

FLAGEOLET, small wind instrument of the flute family that appeared in the thirteenth century.

FLAMBARD, RANULF, d. 1128, Norman bishop of Durham (1099) and leading minister of William II (Rufus). He served as chancellor under William I, became chaplain to William II and chief justiciar, and was given charge of the royal finances in which he proved himself an efficient although unscrupulous administrator. Henry I had him imprisoned, presumably blaming him for a share of William II's tyranny, but he escaped to Normandy. He was subsequently restored to royal favor although he devoted most of his later years to diocesan business including the completion of the great cathedral at Durham.

FLAMBERG, two-handed sword that appeared in the fifteenth century.

FLAMBOYANT GOTHIC, Gothic architecture of the late Middle Ages which was noted for its flamelike tracery and elaborate decoration. The style proved particularly popular in France, e.g., the Palace of Justice in Rouen.

FLAMENCA, Provençal courtly romance of the mid-thirteenth century which had as its theme the love of a married woman and a young nobleman.

FLAMENCO, Spanish gypsy style of dance and music that probably owed its distinctive character to Moorish influences.

FLANCART, small piece of armor plate designed to protect the thighs.

FLANÇOIS, the part of the armor of the charger that protected its flanks.

FLANDERS, name given to the marsh lands around Bruges in the eighth century, later to the entire Flemish coast. The principality traced its origins as a county to Baldwin I Iron-Arm who married Judith, daughter of Charles the Bald, in 862. Their son Baldwin II (879–918) enjoyed what amounted to independent rule over a large section of the coast along the North Sea. His successors extended their rule eastward to the Scheldt and westward to Normandy. In the early twelfth century the kings of France became interested in Flanders, and Philip II Augustus succeeded in annexing several of its possessions including Artois and Vermandois. But the ambition of Philip IV to establish direct control was thwarted with the bloody defeat of his army at the battle of Courtrai (Battle of the Spurs) in 1302. The threat in the fourteenth century that large towns such as Ghent would gain autonomy led the count of Flanders to draw closer to the king of France, whom he also supported at the outbreak of the Hundred Years' War. In 1369 the heiress of Flanders married Philip the Bold, duke of Burgundy, after which the county remained under Burgundian control until the death of Charles the Bold, when his daughter Mary, duchess and countess from 1477 to 1482, gave it with her hand to the Hapsburgs.

FLAVIAN I OF ANTIOCH, d. 404, bishop of Antioch (381) and foe of Arianism, who has been credited with initiating the practice of antiphonal singing in church services. He succeeded Meletius in 381 as bishop, but because of a dispute over who was rightful bishop [see MELETIUS OF ANTIOCH], the bishop of Rome delayed recognizing him as bishop until St. John Chrysostom, patriarch of Constantinople, appealed in his behalf.

FLAVIAN, ST., d. 449, patriarch of Constantinople from 446 until 449 when his active opposition to Monophysitism led to his condemnation and exile by the Robber Council of Ephesus. So cruelly did his foes mistreat him that he died three days after his condemnation. The Council of Chalcedon in 451 proclaimed him a martyr.

FLAVIO BIONDO, d. 1463, a leading Italian humanist and historian. He served as papal secretary under Pope Eugenius IV in 1434 and continued in the papal chancery for the greater part of his career. His most important writings include two encyclopedic works on Roman antiquities, a historical-geographical survey of

Italy, and a history of Rome from A.D. 410. The section in this history covering contemporary Italy is both comprehensive and reliable.

FLÉMALLE, MASTER OF. *See* MASTER OF FLÉMALLE.

FLEMING (Flemyng), RICHARD, d. 1431, bishop of Lincoln and founder of Lincoln College at Oxford. Early in his career he showed himself receptive to Wycliffite views which brought him into conflict with Thomas Arundel, archbishop of Canterbury. In 1420 he became bishop of Lincoln and shortly after represented England at the Councils of Pavia and Siena.

FLETE, WILLIAM, d. c. 1382, English hermit and mystic who spent the greater part of his life in an Augustinian monastery near Siena. He became a confidant of St. Catherine of Siena and was the author of *Spiritual Doctrine,* a volume of the conversations he had with her. He also wrote a treatise on the means of overcoming temptation.

FLEUR-DE-LIS, meaning lily flower, an emblem or device used in ornamentation and heraldry. Louis VI (1108–37) was perhaps the first French monarch to adopt this device. It showed a blue field adorned with an indefinite number of golden *fleurs-de-lis,* whose number was reduced to three in the fourteenth century. In time the *fleur-de-lis* came to be associated with the French royal arms.

FLEURON, ornamentation that often took its inspiration from plant forms and was used to decorate pinnacles and gables on Gothic structures.

FLIGHT TO EGYPT, flight to Egypt of Joseph, Mary, and the child Jesus to escape Herod (Matthew 2:13–14). The incident proved a favorite subject in medieval art.

FLODOARD (Frodoard) OF REIMS, d. 966, French priest and chronicler, author of a history of France and Germany for the years 919 to 966

and of the church at Reims. The volume is of particular value since the period is lacking in documentary evidence. He also prepared an abstract of the archiepiscopal archives at Reims which reproduced documents vital to the history of the eighth and ninth centuries. The excellence of Flodoard's Latin verse attests to the success of the cathedral school at Reims in maintaining its reputation as a center of learning.

FLORE AND BLANCHEFLEUR (Blancheflor), a love story of Byzantine, possibly Arabic origin, concerning the love of the Spanish Saracen king's son Flore for Blanchefleur, daughter of a Christian slave of noble birth. Some scholars believe the story may have the same source as the romance about Aucassin and Nicolette.

FLORENCE, city of north-central Italy of Roman origin which became the banking and humanistic center of Western Europe in the fifteenth century. The town suffered considerably in the course of successive captures by the Goths, the Byzantine empire, and the Lombards, and revived only during the reign of Charlemagne. In 1082 when Countess Matilda of Tuscany ruled the area, the city repelled a siege by the German emperor Henry IV. Along with other towns of the area it acquired increasing autonomy in the years following Matilda's death, and by the early twelfth century it had established its authority over the surrounding countryside, including the town of Prato. During the greater part of the thirteenth and fourteenth centuries Florence was kept in a state of turbulence by the struggle between Guelf and Ghibelline factions, shifting alliances of aristocratic families, disagreement over foreign policy, and the conflicting interests of guilds, banking houses, and even laboring classes. Only in 1434 when Cosimo de' Medici established himself as unofficial dictator did the city enjoy relative calm while he proceeded to make it a center of banking and, with his patronage of artists and scholars, of humanism. After the death of his grandson Lorenzo the Magnificent (1492), the Dominican friar, reformer, and demagogue Savonarola held sway in the city until his execution in 1498, whereupon the Medici returned to power. In 1252 the gold florin made its appearance and shortly established itself as Europe's most valuable and dependable currency. The city's cathedral was begun in 1294 according to plans drawn up by Arnolfo di Cambio. Brunelleschi designed the dome in 1421.

FLORENCE, COUNCIL OF. *See* FERRARA-FLORENCE, COUNCIL OF.

FLORENCE OF WORCESTER, d. 1118, monk of the Benedictine monastery at Worcester and generally recognized as the author of a world chronicle that is particularly valuable for the late Anglo-Saxon and early Norman period. John of Worcester continued the chronicle to 1131, when it was copied and extended at several other monasteries.

FLORENCE, SCHOOL OF, school of painting that came into prominence in the fifteenth century as a result of the work of Masaccio, Fra Angelico, Botticelli, and other artists. It was from Florence that the revival of ancient classical forms, particularly in architecture, spread through western Europe. In painting the school experimented with form and line, as opposed to the Venetian School's concern with color.

FLORIANS (Floriacenses), monastic community founded in 1189 by Joachim da Fiore, mystic and "prophet" of Calabria, and abbot of the Cistercian monastery at Corazzo. The community, which observed an unusually austere rule, believed in the early coming of the Holy Spirit who would initiate the third and last phase in the work of salvation. The order received approval of Pope Celestine III in 1196 and spread quickly in the thirteenth century although by the close of the Middle Ages it had become moribund.

FLORILEGIA, collections of excerpts from the writings of the church fathers that were compiled to present, or serve, some dogmatic (theological) or ethical (ascetical) purpose. They were often prepared by apologists or theologians in order to establish the orthodoxy or heterodoxy of individual theologians.

FLORIN, French name for the Italian fiorino, a gold coin of Florence issued for the first time in 1252. The coin proved the most popular currency of the period and made possible the leadership of Florence in European banking.

FLOR, ROGER DE, d. c. 1306, German commander of Spanish mercenaries. He fought at Acre in 1291 as a Knight Templar, entered the service of Frederick II of Sicily, then organized a band of Catalan adventurers and fought for Andronicus II against the Turks. When he was assassinated by imperial order, his followers migrated to Greece and established the duchy of Athens (1311).

FLOTTE, PIERRE, d. 1302, trusted adviser of Philip IV of France and a principal in the king's dispute with Pope Boniface VIII who persuaded the Estates General in 1302 to take the side of the crown. Flotte was slain in the battle of Courtrai.

FLYING BUTTRESS, a buttress supporting the wall of the nave in the Gothic church but raised above and outside the aisle roof and having its base anchored in the aisle wall. The flying buttress, the only strictly original feature of Gothic architecture, enabled the architect to raise the vault of the nave to impressive heights.

FOEDERATI (*federati*), that is, allies, usually barbarian soldiers who were granted the status of imperial allies by the late Roman emperors. Rome may have defeated them or purchased their support. Their principal responsibility as allies was that of defending the frontier.

FOIX, COUNTY OF, province in southwestern France bordering on Aragon that took its name from the town of Foix. Roger became the first count of Foix in the eleventh century when the region was detached from the countship of Carcassonne. Although his successors were allies of Raymond VI and VII of Toulouse in the Albigensian crusade, they managed to hold onto their possessions. The most famous of the counts of Foix was Gaston III. In 1479 the count of Foix inherited the kingdom of Navarre. The county, which controlled the pilgrim route to the shrine of the Virgin at Montserrat, succeeded in preserving an autonomous status until 1607 when it was incorporated into the French royal domain.

FOLIOT, GILBERT, d. 1187, English Cluniac monk, abbot of Gloucester, bishop of Hereford and of London (1163). Although genuinely dedicated to the reform of the church and himself a rigorist, his unsympathetic nature won him few admirers; modern scholars still disagree in their appraisal of the prelate. He regarded Thomas Becket as undeserving of the high post of archbishop and disagreed with his handling of the controversy with Henry II over the Constitutions of Clarendon. He left a valuable correspondence with the leading men of the period.

FOLKSTONE, seaport of Kent, a possession of Earl Godwin during the reign of Edward the Confessor (1042–66), then of Odo, bishop of Bayeux at the time of the Domesday survey (1086). It was a limb (member) of the Cinque Port of Dover and had to supply one of the 21 ships furnished by that port for the royal navy.

FOLKSTONE, ABBEY OF, the first nunnery in Anglo-Saxon England. It was founded c. 630 by Eadwald, king of Kent, for his daughter Eanswith who served as the institution's first abbess.

FOLKUNGER, the royal dynasty that ruled Sweden from 1250 to 1363 and Norway from 1250 to 1387.

FOLLARO (*follari*), copper coin used in the Byzantine empire, in Italy, and by the Crusaders in Syria.

FOLLIS, a bronze coin first minted during the

reign of Emperor Diocletian (284–305). It continued in use until the tenth century.

FOLQUET DE MARSEILLE, d. 1231, Provençal troubadour who took orders and rose to be archbishop of Toulouse. He earned dubious fame for the severity he showed as chief prosecutor of the Albigensian Crusade. Dante gave him a place in heaven (*Paradiso* IX, 67–142).

FOLZ (Foltz), HANS, d. 1515, a Meistersinger by avocation, a barber by profession. His verse, stories, and songs reveal both a religious and a satirical nature.

FONDACO, name given a merchant house in the Mediterranean area, such as that of Fondaco dei Tedeschi in Venice.

FONTAINEBLEAU, city some 50 km southeast of Paris which originated as a royal hunting-lodge. It was first noted in 1169. Louis VI erected a chapel there, Louis IX enlarged the buildings and fortified the community, and Charles VI established a library.

FONTENAY (Fontenoy), BATTLE OF, bloody but indecisive battle fought in 841 by the three sons of Louis the Pious—Lothair, Louis, and Charles. The emperor Lothair, in alliance with his nephew Pepin, ruler of Aquitaine, suffered a stunning defeat at the hands of Louis the German and Charles the Bald. In the spring of the following year at Strasbourg, Louis and Charles swore to continue their joint efforts against Lothair. [*See* STRASBOURG.]

FONTEVRAULT, MONASTERY OF, a double monastery, some 17 km southeast of Saumur, one of the largest and most famous in medieval France, founded c. 1101. The convent observed the Rule of St. Benedict while the male community lived under that of St. Augustine. Both were under the authority of the abbess. Henry II of England, who was a generous benefactor of the institution, his wife Eleanor, and their son Richard (I) were buried in the abbey. Fontevrault was the mother house of a number of dependent communities established in France, Spain, and England.

FOOLS, FEAST OF, a degeneration of the earlier tradition of having choir boys take over the important offices in the cathedral community for a day, either on December 28 (Holy Innocents) or January 1 (Circumcision). The feast became the occasion of much buffoonery and satire and was ordered suppressed by the Council of Basel in 1435. [*See* FEAST OF ASSES.]

FOPPA, VINCENZO, d. 1515, painter of Lombardy and Milan, founder of the Lombard school. His work reveals the influence of Jacopo Bellini and Mantegna. Among his better known works are *St. Francis Receiving the Stigmata, Madonna and Child,* and *Martyrdom of St. Sebastian.*

FORDUN, JOHN OF, d. after 1383, Scottish chronicler, perhaps a chantry priest in Aberdeen cathedral, and author of the *Gesta Annalia,* a history of Scotland to 1383. Despite the inclusion of legendary materials, the history is considered reasonably reliable.

FORFEITURE, RIGHT OF, right of the lord to recover a fief upon failure of the vassal to honor his obligations under the feudal contract. [*See* FEUDALISM.]

FORK, instrument used in eating known to the Germans already during the period of the migrations. It fell into disuse after 1000 particularly among the upper classes and was reintroduced from Byzantium through Italy and France in the later Middle Ages. The burgher class adopted it in the sixteenth century.

FORMARIAGE, known as *merchet* in England, the fee (fine) paid by the serf to the lord of the manor when the serf's daughter married a man from another manor.

FORMIGNY, BATTLE OF, battle won by the French in Normandy in 1450 over the English with the aid of field artillery. The victory announced the early expulsion of the English from that duchy.

FORMOSUS, Pope, 891–6, a Roman, papal legate, missionary in Bulgaria, bishop of Porto, whom Pope John VIII, who feared him as a rival, had exiled for several years to France. As pope, Formosus encouraged missionary activity in England and north Germany. When he died, Lambert, duke of Spoleto, whose dominance of Rome Formosus had opposed, ordered the pope's body exhumed and violated.

FORMULARIES, MEDIEVAL, samples of official letters, charters, and similar documents which secretaries and scribes used as models.

FORTESCUE, JOHN, d. c. 1476, chief justice of the king's bench, adviser to Henry VI and his wife Margaret (of Anjou) whom he followed into exile, and author of the *De Laudibus Legum,* a legal treatise he composed for the instruction of Prince Edward, the son of Henry VI. The treatise praises the English constitutional and legal systems.

FORTUNATUS, VENANTIUS HONORIUS CLEMENTIANUS, d. c. 600, a leading poet of the period, chaplain of a nunnery at Poitiers, and later bishop of that city. Although he composed several lives of the saints in prose, his principal fame rests upon his verse which included elegies, eulogies, panegyrics, and hymns. One of the best known of his hymns is the *Vexilla Regis Prodeunt.*

FORTUNE BOOKS, collections of oracular sayings of ancient origin made in the late Middle Ages.

FOSCARI, FRANCESCO, d. 1457, doge of Venice (1423) who added Brescia, Bergamo, Cremona, and other cities to the Venetian empire but at the cost of some 30 years of war with Milan. His concern with Italy caused him to neglect Venetian possessions in the eastern Mediterranean. Popular discontent over his policies, which also received blame for the fall of Constantinople, led to his resignation in 1457.

FOSSE (Fos) WAY, road that crossed Roman Britain from the southwest to the northeast, roughly from Exeter to Lincoln. It carried that name from at least the tenth century.

FOSSORS, Latin for gravediggers who in the early church were regarded as inferior clergy. In the fourth century they developed into powerful corporations that controlled the management of the catacombs and the decoration of the tombs.

FOUAGE, hearth tax levied annually by a feudal lord on each household.

FOUET D'ARMES, a kind of whip of chains or straps to which balls of metal were attached.

FOUNTAINS ABBEY, Cistercian abbey in Yorkshire founded in 1132 by a reform group of monks from the monastery of St. Mary's in York. Two years later, Hugh, dean of York, joined the community and brought with him his sizable fortune and library. In the twelfth century the abbey established seven daughter foundations, but extravagances and mismanagement brought decline in the thirteenth. The crown ordered the abbey dissolved in 1539.

FOUQUET (Focquet, Foucquet), JEAN, d. c. 1480, the leading painter of the period. His works include a portrait of *Charles VII* (he was court painter to Charles) and illuminations in the duc de Berry's *Book of Hours*. Both his miniatures and his panel paintings are distinguished for their precision in characterization and detail. He is considered the founder of the school of French painting which combined the art of the Van Eycks with that of the early Florentines.

FOUR FOREST CANTONS, THE, the cantons of Unterwalden, Schwyz, Uri, and Lucerne. These were the first Swiss cantons to gain their freedom from the Hapsburgs.

FOURTEEN HOLY HELPERS, a group of fourteen saints, honored especially in Germany in the late Middle Ages, whose cult was promoted by the Dominicans, Cistercians, and Benedictines. The aid of individual saints was invoked for particular needs: e.g., the intercession of St. Blaise for maladies of the throat.

FOWLER. *See* HENRY I (the Fowler), king of Germany.

FOXE (Fox), RICHARD, d. c. 1528, keeper of the privy seal under Henry VII, founder of Corpus Christi College at Oxford, and occupant of several sees including that of Winchester (1501). His continued absorption in political affairs left him little time for his episcopal responsibilities.

FRA ANGELICO. *See* ANGELICO, FRA.

FRANC, French gold coin first minted by King John the Good in 1360 in order to raise money for his ransom.

FRANCE, leading country of Western Europe from the early thirteenth century. Some scholars begin the history of France with the Treaty of Verdun (843) which divided the Carolingian empire into three parts and assigned the western section, the country of the West Franks, to Charles the Bald. Other scholars prefer to wait until 987 and the election of Hugh Capet as king of France, since it was only then that the West Frankish kingdom made a final break with the Carolingian dynasty which had once ruled western Europe from the Elbe to south of the Pyrenees. For the origins of their country's history French scholars reach back as far as Clovis (481–511), founder of the Merovingian dynasty, whom they designate as the first in a long line of Louises who ruled France. [For Clovis and his Merovingian and Carolingian successors, *see* MEROVINGIAN DYNASTY and CAROLINGIAN DYNASTY.]

Charles the Bald was not only the first king of the West Franks but also their only successful ruler. That his successors were less than competent is not to be implied. Conditions had become so turbulent as to render effective rule impossible. When Charles died in 877 western Europe had moved into the heart of the feudal period, a time when kings had little choice but reign at the will of their more powerful feudatories. This was surely true of France, and what assured Hugh Capet a majority of the votes of the French territorial princes in 987 was less the fact that an ancestor of his had achieved fame fighting the Vikings than that, given the modest extent of his wealth and possessions, he would not dare interfere in the princes' affairs. Hugh was a grandnephew of Odo (Eudes), count of Paris, who had saved Paris from the Vikings in 885. The western magnates had chosen Odo as their king after the deposition of Charles the Fat in 887, the last Carolingian to rule the whole of the former empire of Charlemagne. From Odo's death in 898, members of his family (called Robertians after his father, Robert the Strong) and Carolingians took turns reigning until the death of Louis V in 987 when Hugh Capet was elected.

Hugh Capet can claim no distinction beyond the accidental fact of initiating an unbroken sequence of father–son kings who continued an uninterrupted rule of France until 1316. Dynastic breaks did not disrupt the growth of the French monarchy as they did the German. Furthermore, since in almost all instances the son was a mature young man when his father died, the feudal principle of election had given way to hereditary succession by the close of the twelfth century. The consequence was a fairly steady growth of royal power from the reign of Louis VI (1108–37) until the close of the Middle Ages when it approached the level of absolutism. Louis's principal contribution to that end was the favorable policy he extended to towns by granting them charters and encouraging trade. This policy, continued by Louis's successors, assured the crown the support of the towns against the aristocracy and an increasing source of new revenues as industry and trade expanded.

A development of major import for France came during the reign of his son Louis VII (1137–80) when his divorced wife Eleanor of Aquitaine became the wife of Henry II of England. This marriage gave the English king possession of the western half of France, including Normandy, Anjou, and other French fiefs, a vast stretch of territory that extended from Flanders to the Pyrenees. This association with England might have permanently altered the course of French history had not Philip II Augustus (1180–1223), the son of Louis, succeeded in recovering for France the most important of the English-held possessions, Normandy and Anjou. His victory over Otto IV of Germany, the ally of King John of England, at Bouvines in 1214 assured French control of these provinces. It also marked the rise of France to the position of political leadership in Western Europe. To Philip II Augustus scholars also credit a significant expansion of the administrative machinery of the royal government when he appointed new officials, *baillis* and sensechals, to take the place of the hereditary *prévôts,* in the management of the king's judicial and financial affairs. The appearance of these officials reflected the growth of the central royal government and announced the early emergence from the traditional *curia regis* of two departments, the *chambre des comptes* and the *parlement de Paris,* the first to handle the crown's financial business, the second its judicial.

The growth of royal government continued without interruption during the reign of Louis IX (1226–70) despite the two Crusades he embarked upon and his concern with peace and justice rather than with conquests. It was, indeed, Louis's love of justice and his concern for the poor that gained him, and indirectly the French crown, a popular esteem unmatched in medieval history. This esteem became a casualty of the harsh methods his grandson Philip (IV) the Fair (1285–1314) employed in order to strengthen royal authority. These policies included the expansion of royal revenues which he accomplished by a variety of measures, the most reprehensible being the suppression of the Knights Templars and the subordination of the church which he achieved through his humiliation of Pope Boniface VIII. To assure himself the adherence of the clergy, aristocracy, and towns in his contests with the church and the Templars, Philip convened the Estates General in 1302 and again in 1308, a constitutional development that might have slowed or prevented the rise of royal absolutism had not this body in 1439 authorized the crown to impose taxes without its prior approval.

A succession of weak kings following Philip's death in 1314, together with the outbreak of the Hundred Years' War, halted any further consolidation of royal power. In fact, not only did the French crown almost succumb during the fifteenth century, but France itself came very close to being parceled out between England and Burgundy. [See HUNDRED YEARS' WAR.] Charles V (1364–80) succeeded in undoing the evil consequences for France of the overwhelming defeats suffered at the hands of the English at Crécy and Poitiers, although it was the outbreak of the *Jacquerie* that prevented a frightened aristocracy from cooperating with the Parisian burghers in emasculating the monarchy. Good fortune in the form of Joan of Arc, the death of Henry V of England, loans from Jacques Coeur, and an unexpected measure of statesmanship which Charles VII (1422–61) as dauphin had not displayed enabled him to undo the Treaty of Troyes (1420) and by 1453 force the English off the continent (save for Calais). Charles VII left the dangerous contest between crown and aristocracy to his unprepossessing but remarkably astute son Louis XI (1461–83), who thwarted the formidable bid Charles the Bold of Burgundy made for independence and in the process humbled the French aristocracy as well. All of France, with the exception of Brittany, was being ruled directly from Paris at the close of the Middle Ages.

FRANCESCA DA RIMINI, d. 1284, daughter of Guido da Polenta, the ruler of Ravenna, who became the wife of Gianciotto Malatesta of Rimini in 1275. For her liaison with Paolo, her brother-in-law, Dante placed her in the circle of the immoral. (*Inferno* V, 116ff.)

FRANCESCA, PIERO DELLA. *See* PIERO DELLA FRANCESCA.

FRANCESCO BARTHOLI, Franciscan preacher of the early fourteenth century, author of a book containing legends and traditions about the Franciscan order, a volume of sermons, and a concordance on the Passion.

FRANCESCO DI GIORGIO, d. 1501, Italian painter, sculptor, and architect of the Sienese school. His early works included manuscript illuminations, furniture panels, and altarpieces. He later produced bronze reliefs. His architectural masterpiece is S. Maria del Calcinaio in Cortona. In his book on architecture he took up the subjects of city planning and military architecture.

FRANCES D'AMBOISE, BL., d. 1485, wife of Peter II, count of Brittany, who devoted herself to the care of the sick and the poor. After the death of her husband she founded the first cloister of Carmelite nuns in France (1463) and later served as prioress of the convent of Our Lady of Couëts.

FRANCES OF ROME, ST., d. 1440, a noblewoman of Rome who administered to the poor and the sick of the city. She founded a religious community known as Oblates of Olivetan Benedictines, later called the Oblates of St. Frances. The order which did not require strict vows concerned itself more with the help of the poor than with prayer and the liturgy.

FRANCHE-COMTÉ, the Free or Imperial County of Burgundy, a province lodged between the upper Rhône and Switzerland. It was once part of the kingdom of Lothair (840–55) and was ruled after 888 by the kings of Burgundy. Although it became incorporated into the Holy Roman Empire in 1032, French influence grew steadily until in the early fourteenth century Philip V became its count and introduced direct

French rule. In 1384, Philip, duke of Burgundy, gained possession through his marriage to its heiress, after which it remained under Burgundian control until the death of Charles the Bold in 1477. Shortly after, it passed into the hands of the Hapsburgs when Mary, the daughter and heiress of Charles, married Maximilian I.

FRANCIA, d. 1517, Italian painter, goldsmith, and medalist of Bologna. His first paintings, including *Madonna Enthroned,* show the influence of Lorenzo Costa, his later works such as *Crucifixion* and *Madonna and Saints,* that of Perugino and Raphael.

FRANCIA, the land of the Franks, in particular the region north of the Seine and Marne rivers. The term is also employed when referring to the French royal domain prior to the additions made to it by Philip II Augustus (1180–1223).

FRANCISCAN SISTERS, members of the Second Order of St. Francis, founded by Clare, a close friend and associate of St. Francis of Assisi, who was invested in 1212. The order which was first known as Poor Ladies, then as Poor Clares, received final papal approval in 1253.

FRANCISCANS, mendicant order of friars, known as Friars Minor and in England as Grey Friars, founded by Francis of Assisi, given tentative approval by Pope Innocent III in 1209, and confirmed by Pope Honorius III in 1223. What proved to be the most popular and influential of the religious orders of the high and late Middle Ages had its origins in the decision of the young Francis to turn his back on the world and take up the life Christ had recommended to those who wished to be perfect (Luke 18:22). The first Franciscans were wandering evangelists who begged for their livelihood, preached a simple gospel of love of God and neighbor, and cared for the sick and needy. As the number of friars swelled, irregularities appeared which Francis, who objected to all formal organization, sought

to correct with annual chapters, later with "ministers" assigned to particular regions.

Further concession to organization could not have suppressed the source of most anguish for the Franciscans in the Middle Ages, namely, the order's extreme position on poverty. Already during the lifetime of Francis there were members who urged modification of the harsh rule which they felt impeded the order's apostolate. That Brother Elias of Cortona whom Francis appointed vicar-general in 1221 was deposed, then recalled, suggests something of the ferment that harassed the order. The able administration of Bonaventure (1257–74), a moderate on the issue of poverty, brought temporary peace. His success in convincing the order that study constituted a wholly commendable form of self-discipline also opened the way to the distinguished work Franciscan scholars achieved, notably in the fields of theology and science.

Still the issue of poverty would not down and time sharpened the cleavage between the Spirituals who resisted any modification of Francis's position and the majority of the friars, called Conventuals, who pleaded for some change. The intransigence of the Spirituals and the infection of some of their members with Joachimism led to papal condemnation and their eventual suppression. In the late fourteenth century a reform movement, known as the Observant, made its appearance, which had as its objective the return to the austerity and spiritual dedication that had characterized the order during the first decades of its existence. Although these Observants (or Friars Minor of the Observance) organized communities of their own, they remained within, were actually an autonomous branch of, the Franciscan order.

FRANCISCANS, THIRD ORDER REGULAR, a semireligious organization founded by Francis of Assisi in 1221 for lay men and women who wished to observe the principles of Franciscan monasticism. In time some tertiaries formed communities of their own and took the three traditional vows of chastity, obedience, and poverty. The first such community received papal recognition in 1447.

FRANCIS OF ASSISI (Giovanni Francesco Bernardone), ST., d. 1226, founder of the Franciscan Order and probably the most universally honored religious figure of the Middle Ages. He was born in 1181–82 at Assisi in Umbria of a wealthy cloth merchant and a French woman of some distinction. Following a carefree youth that ended in his capture in a skirmish with Perugia and a serious illness, he renounced his inheritance and dedicated himself to a life of poverty, prayer, and service to the sick (lepers) and poor. In 1209 Pope Innocent III gave a tentative approval to his Rule whose simple message of living as Christ did and heeding his admonitions mystified the great pope. In 1223 Honorius III who had been Francis's staunchest friend in the Curia, confirmed his Rule. Francis devoted his life to the direction of his order, to preaching, to the care of the sick, and, whenever possible, to prayer. In 1212 he founded the Second Order when Clare, a noble lady of Assisi, was invested, and in 1221 a Third Order for the laity. The desire to convert the Infidel, several times frustrated, led in 1219 to a futile visit to the sultan of Egypt. About the year 1224 when he received the stigmata, his sight had deteriorated to the point of near-blindness. In 1228 Gregory IX declared him a saint. Francis left a Rule, spiritual instructions, prayers, some letters, and the *Canticle of the Sun* which has been called the first expression of Italian national literature.

FRANCIS OF MEYRONNES (Mayronis), d. after 1328, a Franciscan, taught theology at Avignon, later became minister provincial of the order in Provence. Although he wrote treatises on political and theological subjects as well, his philosophical writings particularly attracted the attention of scholars. These established him as a leading representative of Scotism. (He was a pupil of Duns Scotus.) He was also known for his devotion to Mary and in his writing made

mention of her immaculate conception and assumption.

FRANCIS OF PAOLA (Paul), ST., d. 1507, founder of the order of the Minims. He lived as a recluse in the region of Paola where he gained the affection of the countryside for his love of the poor and the oppressed. He came to France to attend Louis XI on his deathbed—Louis hoped he would work a miracle and prolong his life—then remained in that country to tutor the future Charles VIII.

FRANCISQUE, a war hatchet used by the Franks.

FRANCO OF COLOGNE, obscure student of music of the late twelfth and early thirteenth centuries, possibly the prior of the Benedictine abbey in Cologne, whose treatise on the setting down of music dealt with rhythmical and metrical matters and contributed to the evolution of polyphonic music.

FRANCONIA, one of the five duchies that made up the kingdom of the East Franks as established by the Treaty of Verdun (843). The greater part of the province lay east of the middle Rhine. Because it embraced several powerful bishoprics, including Mainz, Worms, and Speyer, and because it had constituted royal demesne, no powerful duke emerged there as in Saxony and Bavaria. Western or Rhenish Franconia was absorbed by the Palatinate and by different bishoprics. The title duke of Franconia disappeared in 1152 when Frederick I Barbarossa, the titleholder, assumed the royal crown.

FRANCS-ARCHERS, kind of provincial militia organized by Charles VII of France (1422–61), the first attempt at the formation of regular infantry in France.

FRANGIPANI, prominent family of Rome from the eleventh through the thirteenth century. During the long struggle between papacy and empire, the family's loyalties shifted constantly, first allying itself with Robert Guiscard in 1084 when he came to the rescue of Gregory VII, later joining Henry V when he entered Rome. The family attained the height of its influence during the pontificate of Honorius II (1124–30) who had been its candidate.

FRANKALMOIN, meaning free alms, a feudal tenure by which a church (bishopric, monastery) might hold a fief. In lieu of military services or a reduction thereof, the king or lord would demand prayers for himself and his family and alms for the poor.

FRANKFURT AM MAIN, city on the Main near its confluence with the Rhine, an ancient settlement first mentioned in 793. The king of the East Franks made the town his capital after the division of the Carolingian empire in 843, but its real growth came only during the reign of the Hohenstaufens. The decline of the fairs in Champagne brought it new importance as a commercial and financial center and in 1372 it received the status of an imperial city. The Golden Bull of Charles IV (1356) designated Frankfurt as the place where the election of the king of Germany was to take place.

FRANKFURT AN DER ODER, town in Brandenburg on the Oder, founded in 1253 by Margrave John I with Franconian colonists. It joined the Hanseatic League in 1368. Its annual fair became one of the most important in Germany.

FRANKPLEDGE, a system employed in England during the Norman period (it has been traced to the laws of Canute) in which commoners were enrolled in groups of ten (frankpledge tithings) or twelve. Each member was held responsible for the good behavior of the others. He was also required to assist in the apprehension of anyone of the group accused of a crime.

FRANKS, German tribe first noted A.D. 258 when it was located between the lower Rhine and the Weser. Emperor Probus (276–82) forced the tribe back across the Rhine when it passed over at this time, although he and his successors could not prevent groups from ravaging Gaul. By the early fifth century the Franks on the lower Rhine came to be identified as the Salian branch of the tribe, those in the area of Cologne and above as the Ripuarian. In 358, Julian, to whom the emperor Constantius II had entrusted the Rhine frontier, granted the Salian Franks the status of *foederati*. This satisfied them until 428 when they revolted. They suffered defeat at the hands of Aetius, the Roman general. Aetius also defeated the Ripuarian Franks who had crossed the Rhine shortly after 406 and had captured Cologne and Trier, and forced them back across the river. After the death of Aetius in 454, the Franks became independent. [*See* MEROVINGIAN DYNASTY.]

FRANZISKA, kind of battle axe used by the Franks during the Merovingian period.

FRATER, Latin for brother, a term initially applied to any monk, later generally restricted to lay brothers and to members of the Mendicant orders, whence the word friar.

FRATICELLI, name given to extremist or heretical Franciscans of the fourteenth and fifteenth centuries, the successors of the Spirituals, who maintained that Pope John XXII had been guilty of heresy when he condemned their views concerning poverty. They held that Christ and his apostles had never possessed property and that it was sinful for churchmen to do so. Many of them suffered imprisonment, perhaps a hundred or so being burned as heretics. Despite such repressive measures, groups of Fraticelli persisted in their beliefs through the Middle Ages. Other groups of the Fraticelli known as Clareni returned to orthodoxy and received papal approbation of their views.

FRAUENLOB, that is, in praise of women, nickname of Heinrich von Meissen, German lyric poet and troubadour of the late thirteenth, early fourteenth century. He led the life of a wandering minstrel until 1312 when he settled in Mainz and founded the first Meistersinger school. His verse, on religious, moral, and didactic subjects, attests to his unusual knowledge of the refinements of rhetoric and prosody although he was inclined to sacrifice imagination and content to form.

FREDEGARIUS, probably the name of a Burgundian of the mid-seventh century who some scholars believe continued the *History of the Franks* by Gregory of Tours from 585 to 642. Other scholars ascribe the continuation to three different writers. Despite its unscholarly Latin and its partisanship to the Austrasian aristocracy, it represents a fairly original and dependable source for these years.

FREDEGUND (Fredegunde), d. 597, mistress, then after the murder of Galswintha, wife of Chilperic I, king of Neustria (Soissons). Gregory of Tours accuses both Fredegund and Chilperic of Galswintha's death. Because Galswintha was the sister of Brunhild, the wife of Sigebert, king of Austrasia, her death provoked a savage feud between Fredegund and Brunhild. Among the victims of this feud was Brunhild's husband Sigebert, killed by Fredegund's (and Chilperic's) assassins.

FREDERICK I BARBAROSSA, king of Germany, 1152–90, Holy Roman emperor (1155), a leader of the Third Crusade, and the greatest monarch of medieval Germany. Frederick's election as king of Germany in 1152 proved acceptable to the majority of German princes since his father was a Hohenstaufen, his mother a Guelf. [*See* GUELFS AND GHIBELLINES.] Despite his high ambitions and unusual talents as a statesman and general, he accomplished little in Germany toward strengthening his position because of the relative poverty of the crown and the powerful position held by the dukes. He did humble his principal rival, Henry the Lion, the duke of Bavaria and Saxony, although custom and the other German princes prevented him from seizing these duchies for himself. His hope of compelling the cities of north Italy to recognize his imperial authority led him to undertake six expeditions across the Alps. On the first of these he seized and executed Arnold of Brescia, for which he had the blessing of Pope Adrian IV who then crowned him emperor. In 1158, at the Diet of Roncaglia, he formally proclaimed his imperial rights. But the severe defeat dealt him at Legnano in 1176 by the Lombard League in alliance with Pope Alexander III forced him to content himself with a largely empty overlordship in Italy. In 1186 he arranged the marriage of his son Henry (VI) to Constance who shortly became the heiress of the kingdom of Sicily. The bright hopes of the Third Crusade went glimmering when Frederick drowned crossing the Saleph river in Cilicia.

FREDERICK II, king of Germany, 1215–50, Holy Roman emperor (1220), king of Sicily (1198), and king of Jerusalem (1229), one of the most brilliant monarchs of the Middle Ages. With the assistance of Pope Innocent III, the young Frederick, less than three years old when his father Henry VI of Germany died in 1197, managed to hold on to Sicily. Germany, the most important portion of his father's empire, fell to Otto (IV) of Brunswick after a long struggle with the Hohenstaufens. But Otto lost it again at the battle of Bouvines (1214) which was won by Philip II Augustus of France, the ally of Frederick. The misgivings with which Pope Innocent endorsed the election of Frederick as king of Germany proved well-founded. Never during the whole of the Middle Ages did the papacy encounter a more dangerous foe. In 1237 Frederick almost attained his objective of establishing his authority over Italy when he destroyed the Lombard army at Cortenuova. But he never succeeded and was still fighting in 1250 when dysentery carried him off. Partly because of his concentration on Italy, his reign witnessed the loss of most of what remained of imperial rights in Germany. He did establish an absolutist regime in Sicily, minted Europe's first gold coin, and gained possession of Jerusalem through negotiations with his friend, the sultan of Egypt. [*See* CRUSADE, SIXTH.] Frederick was a poet, linguist, statesman, scientist, and an authority on falconry.

FREDERICK III, king of Germany, 1440–93, senior member of the house of Hapsburg, son of Duke Ernest of Austria, elected king of Germany in 1440, and crowned Roman emperor by Pope Nicholas V in 1452. During his long reign conditions in many parts of Germany bordered on anarchy. For his failure to prevent this he has earned, perhaps unjustly, the criticism of historians, who also attack him for his lack of interest in Germany and his loss, for some years, of Austria and Bohemia to Hungary. His adherence to Pope Eugenius IV helped assure the papacy victory over the conciliarists at Basel [*see* BASEL, COUNCIL OF], while good fortune and his own ambitions bore fruit in the marriage of his son Maximilian to Mary of Burgundy, bringing the acquisition of the Low Countries for the Hapsburgs.

FREDERICK III (the Handsome), d. 1330, duke of Austria, head of the house of Hapsburg in 1308 upon the assassination of his father Albert I, king of Germany. When Emperor Henry VII died in 1313, Frederick, who had received the votes of several of the electors, challenged the succession of Louis (IV) of Bavaria but was defeated in 1322 and captured. In 1325 Louis released him and restored to him the rule of Austria.

FREDERICK III (II), king of Sicily, 1296–1337, son of Peter III of Aragon, regent for his brother James of Sicily until 1296 when the Sicilians acclaimed him king in order to block the transfer of their island to Charles II of Anjou. Frederick pursued an enlightened policy at home and conquered the duchy of Athens despite constant involvement in the wars in Italy between the Angevins and Ghibellines.

FREDERICK I, margrave and elector of Brandenburg, 1417–40, founder of the house of Hohenzollern. What ultimately brought him into prominence — he was the son of the burgrave of Nuremberg — was saving the life of Sigismund, king of Hungary, at the battle of Nicopolis in 1396. He also aided Sigismund in securing election as king of Germany (1410), whereupon Sigismund appointed him governor of Brandenburg the following year. Frederick had sufficiently pacified Brandenburg in 1417 to be formally invested with the province. He took an active part in imperial negotiations with the Hussites.

FREDERICK I (the Warlike), d. 1428, duke of Saxony, member of the house of Wettin, and margrave of Meissen. He received the electoral duchy of Saxony in 1423 from Emperor Sigismund in recognition of his zeal in fighting the Hussites. In 1408 Frederick and his brothers founded the University of Leipzig for the German students who had left Prague.

FRÉDOL, BERENGER (Berengarius Fredoli), d. 1323, canonist, teacher of canon law at Bologna, bishop of Béziers (1294), and cardinal (1305). He was active in papal diplomacy during the pontificates of Boniface VIII and Clement V. He was one of the canonists in charge of compiling the *Liber Sextus*.

FREE ALMS, TENURE BY. *See* FRANKALMOIN.

FREE CITIES, term applied to certain cities of Germany, usually episcopal cities like Cologne and Worms, that succeeded in throwing off the control of their lords during the thirteenth and fourteenth centuries. The classification was also given to cities in Hungary that enjoyed autonomy and the privilege of taking part in meetings of the Diet.

FREEHOLD, right to hold a piece of land or an office and to pass this on to one's heirs; an estate held in this manner.

FREE, JOHN, d. c. 1465, an early English humanist who studied at Oxford. He moved to Ferrara where he learned Greek and made his way into the circle of Italian humanists. He later earned a doctorate in medicine at Padua and spent his last years in Rome where he enjoyed the pope's patronage.

FREIA. *See* FRIGG.

FREIBERG, town established shortly after 1168 in the march of Meissen south of the upper Elbe when silver was discovered in the area. It became a leading commercial and financial center of upper Saxony in the late Middle Ages.

FREIBURG IM BREISGAU, town in the Black Forest founded in 1120 by Count Conrad of Zähringen on the crossroads between the upper Rhine and Danube and the North Sea and Italy. In 1218 it became a possession of the counts of Urach who assumed the title of counts of Freiburg. In 1368 it passed under Austrian rule. Archduke Albert VI of Austria founded the Albert Ludwig University in 1457.

FREIDANK, d. 1233, an unknown poet, probably a wandering minstrel, who accompanied Frederick II on his Crusade (1228–9). He authored a collection of didactic strophes and poetic aphorisms. Although the fables, proverbs, and related sources from which he drew his poems were common property, his verse retained its popularity until the late Middle Ages.

FREISING, town in upper Bavaria which was already settled in Roman times. Its castle was erected c. 700 when it became the home of the Agilolfing counts of Bavaria. In 739 Boniface made it a bishop's see. One of the world's oldest breweries was established there in 1040. The twelfth-century cathedral dominated the town.

FREQUENS, a decree issued by the Council of Constance in 1415 which required the pope to convene a general council at regular intervals, the first in five years, another in seven, and subsequent ones at ten-year intervals.

FREY AND FREYJA, Scandinavian deities, brother and sister, deities of love, fertility, and matrimony, also of light and peace. Uppsala in Sweden was the chief shrine of Frey. Freyja was easily confused with Frigg.

FRIAR, a term derived from the Latin and French for brother, which came to be applied in the thirteenth century to members of the Mendicant orders to distinguish them from monks. In England the four principal orders of friars were distinguished by their colors: the Grey Friars (Franciscans), the Black Friars (Dominicans) (black mantle over white tunic and scapular), the White Friars (Carmelites), and the Austin Friars (black).

FRIARS MINOR, ORDER OF. *See* FRANCISCANS.

FRIBOURG, town in western Switzerland, founded in 1157. In 1263 the town passed to the counts of Kyburg. In 1277 it was sold to the sons of Rudolf of Hapsburg. The Hapsburgs abandoned the town in 1452, when it accepted the overlordship of Saxony until 1481. It then joined the Swiss confederation.

FRIDESWIDE (Frideswida, Fredeswida) OF OXFORD, ST., d. 735, daughter of an Anglo-Saxon official who was believed to have founded a monastery of that name c. 727 at Oxford. The Danes burned the convent c. 1000, but Canons Regular of St. Augustine reestablished it in 1122. By the late twelfth century St. Frideswide was being honored as the patroness of the city and of the university.

FRIENDS OF GOD, a general term meaning pious, God-fearing people that took on new significance in the fourteenth century partly because of its frequent use by John Tauler and other mystics in referring to men and women who were making a special effort to live more Christ-like lives. The Friends pursued lives of prayer and self-renunciation, extended their assistance to the afflicted, and concerned themselves with the correction of abuses in the church. Despite their dedication to personal holiness, they remained orthodox and loyal to the hierarchy, and preserved a respect for formal religion.

The Friends were found in largest numbers in Bavaria, Switzerland, the Rhineland, and the Low Countries.

FRIGG (Frija, Frigga, Frea, Freia), Nordic goddess of beauty and love, the wife of Odin (Wotan, Wodan) and mother of Balder. Her name survives in Friday. She was confused with the Scandinavian goddess Freyja.

FRISIANS, German tribe first noted in 12 B.C. when it was located in the area of north Germany and Holland. Some Frisians may have joined the Angles and Saxons in their conquest of England. The nation attained the height of its power in the seventh century under King Radbod, but in the eighth it succumbed to Frankish rule. Anglo-Saxon missionaries, Willibrord among others, undertook the conversion of the tribe in the late seventh century. Boniface suffered martyrdom at their hands in 754.

FRITIGERN, d. after 382, one of the chiefs of the Visigoths who had a part in the defeat of Emperor Valens and the Roman army at Adrianople in 378. He subsequently made peace with Emperor Theodosius.

FRITZLAR, town in Hesse where Boniface established the abbey of St. Peter in 723 and a bishop's seat in 741. The town proved a favorite residence of the kings of Germany and a frequent meeting place for imperial assemblies.

FRIULI (Friaul), MARCH OF, district lying at the head of the Adriatic which the Lombards made into a duchy. During the Carolingian period it served as a march to protect the Slavonic frontier. It remained attached to Carinthia until 1077 when the greater part of it passed under the rule of the patriarch of Aquileia, who in turn lost it to Venice in 1419–20.

FROCK, long, loose gown with broad sleeves worn by monks, in particular by Benedictines, when they had occasion to leave the monastery precincts. The term might also refer to a coat of mail or to a long, loose coat worn by men.

FROG KING, the young man in a story popular in the Middle Ages who was turned into a frog, then rescued by a maiden whom he married.

FROISSART, JEAN, d. c. 1404, French chronicler whose *Chroniques* constitutes the principal source for the first part of the Hundred Years' War as well as a useful survey of the political events of western Europe, including Spain and Scotland, for the period 1325 to 1400. Because he wrote for patrons, including Edward III and the Black Prince, his account reveals on occasion a lack of objectivity. He traveled extensively through the area with which he was concerned, was a diligent researcher, and wrote with imagination and enthusiasm about the knightly virtues and chivalric splendor of the English and French aristocracy. He also composed allegorical and courtly poetry.

FROUMUND OF TEGERNSEE, d. c. 1008, monk, poet, and teacher in the Benedictine abbey of Tegernsee. He composed some verse but is best known for his collection of letters, which furnish considerable information about the monasticism of the period.

FRUMENTIUS, ST., d. c. 380, "Apostle of the Abyssinians," captured by Ethiopians on his way back from a voyage to India. He was brought to the king of Axum and later assisted him in the government while working as a missionary. About 340 he was consecrated bishop by Athanasius, bishop of Alexandria. He received the title "Abuna" meaning "Our Father," a title held by succeeding primates of the Abyssinian church.

FRUTOLF-EKKEHARD CHRONICLE, world chronicle that Frutolf of Michelsberg carried to 1101. Ekkehard of Aura and Burchard of Urseberg continued it to 1229.

FRUTOLF OF MICHELSBERG, d. 1103, monk of the Benedictine monastery in Michelsberg (near Bamberg), author of several treatises on music and a universal chronicle that extended to 1101.

The chronicle is accurate, comprehensive, and objective.

FUERO, a Spanish word that might refer to a charter or franchise which the crown granted to a municipality, also to a general body of law relating to a class or even to a kingdom, e.g., *Fuero de Léon* (c. 1020), that is, the laws applicable to the kingdom of Leon.

FUGGER, family of south Swabian merchants and bankers that owed the foundation of its wealth and influence to Ulrich Fugger and his son Hans (d. 1409), successful weavers of Augsburg. Jakob I (d. 1469) established the Fugger commercial house, while his sons, principally Jakob II (the Rich) (d. 1525), brought it worldwide prominence.

FULBERT OF CHARTRES, ST., d. 1028, pupil of Gerbert at Reims who taught in the cathedral school of Chartres, served as chancellor, and made it the leading center of learning in Western Europe. In 1006 he became bishop of the diocese. He was a leading classical scholar of the period and also took an active part in political and ecclesiastical affairs. He left poems, hymns, and letters.

FULCHER OF CHARTRES, d. c. 1127, priest, a chaplain of Stephen of Blois on the First Crusade, then of Baldwin, ruler of the county of Edessa, later king of Jerusalem. Fulcher's chronicle of the Crusade (*Historia Hierosolymitana*) is unusually reliable.

FULDA, MONASTERY OF, Benedictine abbey in Hesse founded in 744 by St. Sturmius, a disciple of Boniface. Fulda served Boniface as his headquarters and home, also as his burial place, a circumstance that caused it to develop into a great pilgrimage center. The abbey acquired a position of intellectual and cultural leadership during the abbacy of Rabanus Maurus (d. 856) and maintained this through the eleventh century. Its library contained 2,000 manuscripts and attracted fame for the excellence of its illu-

mination work and sculpture. The abbot of Fulda became a prince of the empire in the thirteenth century.

FULGENTIUS, FABIUS PLANCIADES, native of Roman Africa of the late fifth century who sought to give ancient myths an allegorical interpretation and ascribed to Virgil a mystical meaning in order to convince Christians of their usefulness.

FULGENTIUS OF RUSPE (Claudius Gordianus), d. 533, monk, bishop of Ruspe (below Carthage), and a leading theologian of the period. He suffered much persecution from the Vandal king who was an Arian. Fulgentius who was a great admirer of Augustine, left letters, sermons, and dogmatic and polemical writings.

FULK, king of Jerusalem, 1131–43, count of Anjou and father of the Geoffrey who married Matilda, daughter of Henry I of England. He twice visited the Holy Land, the second time in 1129 when he married the daughter of Baldwin II, king of Jerusalem, whom he succeeded. He erected a number of castles to strengthen his position in Syria and Palestine.

FULK NERRA, d. 1040, count of Anjou and unusually aggressive in his relations with his neighbors, Brittany, Blois, and Touraine. He built numerous castles to protect his borders from his enemies, so many, indeed, that he was called *le Grand Bâtisseur* ("the great builder"). He was the founder of the powerful Angevin dynasty. He made several pilgrimages to the Holy Land principally to atone for the monasteries he had burned and pillaged. To escape divine anger, he founded and restored several abbeys.

FURLONG, that is, a furrow long, the distance oxen could pull a plow without stopping to rest. In time this distance became standardized at 220 yards (200 m).

FUSTAT (Fostat), an Arab military encampment on the Nile, the origin of Cairo.

FUSTIAN, a fabric woven of cotton and linen cloth, usually coarse, which was popular during the Middle Ages.

FUST, JOHN, d. 1466, burgher and moneylender of Mainz and a partner of John Gutenberg. He advanced Gutenberg the money to set up his printing press, then foreclosed in 1455 just before Gutenberg had completed printing of the Bible in order to gain possession of his invention and equipment.

FYRD, Anglo-Saxon militia that the Norman kings retained.

GABAR, Arabic for non-Moslem or infidel, a term applied in particular to the Zoroastrians of Iran.

GABELLE, in France a tax on commodities. The first of these taxes was imposed during the reign of Philip IV in 1286. From the fifteenth century the term came to be restricted to the tax on salt.

GABIROL, SOLOMON BEN JUDAH IBN. *See* IBN GABIROL.

GABRIEL, an archangel mentioned in both the Old and the New Testament. He announced the coming birth of Christ to Mary (Luke 1:18ff). According to Christian tradition, Gabriel will be the trumpeter of the Last Judgment. The Koran was revealed to Mohammed by Gabriel.

GADDI, AGNOLO, fl., 1369–96, son of Taddeo Gaddi, known for his frescoes, which are so natural they suggest tapestrylike decorations. Like his father, he was a follower of Giotto. His works include *The True Cross* in the church of S. Croce, Florence.

GADDI, TADDEO, d. c. 1366, the father of Agnolo, for 24 years a disciple of Giotto and the leader of Florentine painting after the master's death. He is noted for his frescoes *Life of the Virgin* and *Last Supper*. He excelled as a narrative painter and liked to fill his pictures with episodes and details.

GADIFER DE LA SALLE, d. c. 1422, member of a noble Spanish family that settled in Poitou. He became a soldier and explorer and aided Jean de Béthencourt in his conquest of the Canary Islands (1402 and after). Earlier in his career he had fought in the Hundred Years' War against the English and in 1373 had captured Lusignan for the French.

GAETANI (Caetani), Italian family descended from the dukes of Gaeta which from the twelfth century had branches in Naples, Pisa, and Anagni. The most distinguished member of the family was Benedetto Gaetani who was elected pope in 1294 and took the name Boniface VIII.

GAFORIA, FRANCHINO, d. 1522, chapel master at the cathedral in Milan, a composer of masses, motets, and hymns, and a student of musical theory.

GAGUIN, ROBERT, d. 1501, general of the Trinitarians. He taught at the Sorbonne and authored several theological works. He was also a humanist, translated Caesar and Livy, and counted Erasmus and Reuchlin among his pupils.

GAILANI, AL-, family of Baghdad that gained prominence in religious circles because of the fame of 'Abdul Qadir al-Dijli (al-Gailani) (d. 1166). He professed and taught a Sunnite belief that combined elements of Sufism with orthodoxy.

GAISERIC (Genseric), d. c. 477, Vandal chieftain who led his people over to north Africa from Spain in 429 and accepted the status of *foederati* for them until 439 when he seized Carthage. He later gained naval supremacy in the western Mediterranean and extended his authority over Corsica, Sardinia, the Balearic Islands, and a part of Sicily. In 455 he sacked Rome.

GAIUS (Caius), ST., Pope, 283–96, possibly from Dalmatia and a relative of Emperor Diocletian. In all probability he did not die a martyr. Gaius is said to have ruled that a cleric must pass through all the lower ranks of the hierarchy before attaining the episcopacy.

GAIUS, noted Roman jurist of the second century whose *Institutes* provided the substance of a work of the same name which formed part of Justinian's *Corpus Juris Civilis*.

GALAHAD, SIR, son of Lancelot and Elaine who replaced Parzival in the late Arthurian legend of the Holy Grail. He was the purest knight of King Arthur's Round Table, for which reason he was vouchsafed a vision of the Holy Grail.

GALEERE (galley), the line ship used in the Mediterranean from the eleventh century. Although it carried sails, it depended principally upon oarsmen. The heavier *galeasse,* which made its appearance toward the close of the Middle Ages, was used only as a warship.

GALEN, d. c. 200, physician of Pergamon and Alexandria, founder of experimental physiology, and after Hippocrates the most renowned physician of the ancient world. He studied medicine in several cities of the eastern Mediterranean, including Alexandria. He moved to Rome in 164 where he attended both the emperor Marcus Aurelius and his son Commodus. His voluminous medical works of which 98 have been judged authentic, constituted a comprehensive corpus of ancient medical lore and were accepted as authoritative during the Middle Ages.

GALEOTTO (Galehaut, Galahot), a king in the romance of Lancelot who arranged a tryst between the hero and Queen Guinevere. In Dante and Boccaccio he appears as a messenger of love.

GALERIUS (Gaius Galerius Valerius Maximianus), Roman emperor, 305–11, appointed Caesar in 293 by Diocletian whose daughter he married, then senior Augustus following the retirement of his father-in-law in 305. He ruled the eastern empire with the assistance of his Caesar Maximinus whom he placed in charge of Syria and Egypt. On his deathbed he issued the first official decree of toleration to be extended to Christians. Ironically, it had been his encouragement to Diocletian that had led to the persecution of Christians by that emperor.

GALICIA, province in northwestern Spain, an independent Sueve kingdom from c. 410 to 585, then under Visigothic rule until the invasion of Spain by the Moors in the early eighth century when they overran much of the area. The king of the Asturias drove out the Moors, and from the close of the tenth century the region was under his rule. It later came under the rule of the king of Leon. Despite the remoteness of the area and the mountainous terrain, thousands of pilgrims came each year to visit the famous shrine of St. James at Compostella.

GALICIA, a province in southern Poland, conquered in 981 by Vladimir, the prince of Kiev. It was a largely independent principality from 1087 until 1200 when it was joined to Volhynia. In 1253 Daniel Romanovich was crowned king, but when his dynasty died out in 1323, Polish influence became dominant and in 1349 Casimir the Great annexed it to Poland.

GALLA PLACIDIA, d. 450, daughter of Theodosius I and carried off by Alaric, the king of the Visigoths, when he occupied Rome in 410. In 414 she married Athaulf, Alaric's brother-in-law, then in 416 joined her brother Honorius in Rome and acted as regent for her son Valentinian III. (After the death of Athaulf, she had married the general and co-emperor Constantius.) In the Eutychian controversy, she stoutly supported the position of Pope Leo I. She built several famous churches in Ravenna.

GALLEON, a large three-masted, square-rigged vessel that came into use as a warship and transport during the course of the fifteenth century.

GALLIARD, a lively dance of the fifteenth century. Together with the pavance, it was among the earliest of the court dances.

GALLICAN CHANTS, term applied to the pre-Gregorian chants of the ancient liturgies that were used in Gaul until suppressed in favor of the Roman liturgy.

GALLICANISM, a set of principles in support of the view that the church in France was an autonomous institution and largely independent of the jurisdiction of the pope in external affairs. As a policy endorsed by the French government, it can be traced to the ordinance issued in 1398 by Charles VI when he withdrew obedience to the Avignonese pope and claimed autonomy on the basis of France's ancient immunities and liberties. As an official policy it dated from the announcement of the Pragmatic Sanction of Bourges in 1438 which reaffirmed the principles of conciliarism and recognized papal jurisdiction only when conditioned by the will of the crown.

GALLICAN PSALTER, the revision of the Latin Psalter made by St. Jerome c. 392. The version became popular in Gaul, whence the name "Gallican." Under Alcuin's influence, it replaced the Hebrew Psalter in almost all subsequent biblical manuscripts.

GALLICAN RITES, term usually given to liturgical practices, however diversified, that prevailed in Gaul from early Christian centuries until the late eighth when Charlemagne ordered the adoption of Roman usage for his kingdom.

GALL, ST., d. after 615, a native of Bangor and a disciple of Columban whom he accompanied to Gaul and to Burgundy. When Columban moved down to Italy, Gall remained in the area of western Switzerland and labored as a missionary among the Alemanni. The monastery of St. Gall was established on the site of the hermitage in Switzerland that he had occupied.

GALLUS ANONYMUS (Martin?), oldest chronicler of Poland, probably a Benedictine monk, whose narrative extended to 1113. He composed his chronicle in Cracow between the years 1111 and 1116.

GALLUS CAESAR (Flavius Claudius Constantius), elder half-brother of the future Emperor Julian, who reigned as Caesar in Antioch, 351–4, where his harsh rule precipitated riots and led to his eventual execution by Emperor Constantius II. He put down revolts in Palestine and in Isauria and held the Persians in check.

GALSWINTHA, daughter of Athanagild, king of Visigothic Spain, and wife of Chilperic I, king of Neustria (561–84). Chilperic had her murdered, in all probability upon the urging of his lowborn mistress Fredegund.

GAMA, VASCO DA, d. 1524, Portuguese navigator who left Lisbon on 8 July 1497 with four vessels, circumnavigated Africa, and reached Calicut on 20 May 1498. He returned to Lisbon on 9 September 1499. His voyage opened up a way for Europe to tap the wealth of the Indies via a cheaper, all-water route and also made possible the establishment of the Portuguese empire in that part of the world.

GAMBACORTA, PETER, BL., d. 1435, also known as Peter of Pisa, member of an aristocratic family of Pisa who lived as a hermit near Urbino. He later founded the congregation of Poor Hermits of St. Jerome.

GAMBESON (gamboison), jacket worn by foot soldiers from the eleventh to the fifteenth centuries.

GAMBRINUS, legendary king of Flanders and traditionally hailed as the one who discovered the art of making beer. He was supposed to have been a contemporary of Charlemagne (d. 814).

GANA (GHANA, GANATA), Berber kingdom of Mauretania which was established c. A.D. 300. It endured to the thirteenth century.

GANDERSHEIM, CONVENT OF, Benedictine house in Lower Saxony which was founded as a house for canonesses in 852 in Brunshausen, then moved to Gandersheim in 856. It enjoyed royal favor from its foundation and in 1208 gained exemption from episcopal control.

GANELON (Gano), stepfather of Roland in the *Chanson de Roland* whose treason led to Roland's death.

GAON (pl. Geonim), title given from the sixth to the thirteenth centuries to the Jewish scholars who headed the Babylonian academies at Sura and Pumbeditha.

GARCIA, king of Leon, 910–4, who extended his kingdom toward the east and erected numerous castles along his eastern frontier, whence the name Castile.

GARGOYLE, stone spout projecting from the gutter of a building for the purpose of carrying off the rain water. It was often given the form of an animal or bird, either real, fanciful, or grotesque. They frequently marked Gothic structures, such as the Cathedral of Notre Dame in Paris.

GARLAND (Garlandia), JOHN, d. c. 1272, English grammarian and poet. He studied at Oxford and Paris and taught at Paris and Toulouse. His writings influenced the development of medieval Latin. He also composed a Latin vocabulary. One of his religious poems describes the Albigensian crusade.

GARNASCH, garment of Arab origin worn by men in the fourteenth century; in Germany, a long coat with half sleeves and belt; in France, a short coat without sleeves and belt.

GARTER, ORDER OF THE, the oldest and most exclusive of English chivalric orders. The original membership numbered but 26 knights, including the king, when it was instituted by Edward III in 1348.

GASCOIGNE, THOMAS, d. 1458, chancellor of Oxford, benefactor of college libraries, and author of a famous theological dictionary which is

an important guide to the political and religious history of the time. This volume reveals his deep concern over such abuses in the church as the practices of pluralities and nonresidence.

GASCOIGNE, SIR WILLIAM, d. 1419, English jurist, attorney to the duke of Hereford (later Henry IV), and chief justice from 1400. His reputation as an eminently just judge has been substantiated by the few facts about him accepted as trustworthy.

GASCONY, district in southwestern France, earlier occupied by Visigoths and Franks, but settled by Basques from the close of the seventh century. The Gascons gave all their would-be conquerors trouble, although Charlemagne forced them to accept his son Louis (the Pious) as their lord. The Gascons lived under their own dukes until the line became extinct in 1032. In 1058 the area became part of Aquitaine. For the greater part of the Middle Ages Gascony was a possession of England and the center of English power in that part of France.

GASTON III, d. 1391, count of Foix and viscount of Béarn, called Phoebus because of his handsome appearance. He maintained a brilliant court and extended warm hospitality to many famous visitors, among them the French chronicler Froissart. The count supported the kings of France against the English in the Hundred Years' War. He was a patron of art and literature as well as an enthusiastic huntsman.

GATES OF PARADISE, *See* GHIBERTI, LORENZO.

GATTAMELATA, d, 1443, a *condottiere* in the service of Venice who gained victories over Milan during the period 1434–41. Donatello executed an equestrian statue of the captain.

GAUDEAMUS IGITUR, Goliard song composed in 1267 whose theme encouraged young men to enjoy life while they were still young enough to do so.

GAUDENTIUS, ST., d. after 406, bishop of Brixia (Brescia), famed preacher and friend of Ambrose. His sermons, of which 21 are extant, reveal both his knowledge of theology and his acquaintance with Latin classical works.

GAUDETE SUNDAY, third Sunday of Lent, so named from the opening word of the Introit of the mass.

GAUNTLET, glove of leather covered with metal plates to protect the hand.

GAUTIER DE LILLE (Chatillon), Flemish poet of the late twelfth century and author of some Latin verse, several historical pieces, and treatises on theological subjects.

GAVESTON, PIERS, d. 1312, son of a Gascon knight, playmate of the future Edward II, but exiled by Edward I. Edward II recalled him, made him earl of Cornwall, and bestowed upon him other marks of royal favor. In 1308 he served as regent when Edward was away in France. Edward sent him to Ireland when the barons demanded his exile because of his greed and arrogance, but then recalled him (1309). Upon his return from Flanders where he had gone for a time, he was seized by the barons and executed. His was the first of many political executions in late medieval England.

GAWAIN (Gawan, Gawein, Gauvin), knight of the Round Table and a nephew of King Authur. He receives mention in both Geoffrey of Monmouth's *Historia Regum Britanniae* and the *Gesta Regum Anglorum* of William of Malmesbury.

GAZA (Gazes), THEODOROS, d. 1476, Greek scholar who taught Greek and philosophy in several cities of Italy. He also translated Greek works into Latin and composed a Greek grammar.

GEATS, Germanic tribe living in southern Sweden first mention of which appears in the *History of the Goths* of Jordanes (c. 551). Beowulf, the hero in the epic of *Beowulf,* was a nephew of the king of the Geats.

GEBENDE, a simple band worn by women in the twelfth century which extended from the head down over the chin and cheeks.

GEBER, Westernized form of the Arab-Persian Jabir ibn Hyyan (second half of the eighth century) who was once credited with more than 2,000 works on medicine, mathematics, music, astrology, and alchemy. It now appears that the name Jabir was used by a group of scholars of the ninth and tenth centuries who belonged to a Moslem sect of Ismal'iliya and produced these works. A writer of the early fourteenth century assumed the name Geber in order to give prominence to his work on alchemy and metallurgy.

GEDIMINAS, grand prince of Lithuania, 1316–41, to whom contemporary documents refer as "king of Lithuania and Russia." For a time his domain did include the Ukraine to the Dnieper as well as the principalities of Kiev and Novgorod. Because of the paganism of his subjects, he decided against becoming a Christian, which he had contemplated doing as a means of neutralizing the threat to his country posed by the Teutonic Knights. But he protected both the Latin and Greek clergy and encouraged them in their work of civilizing his people. He erected a series of fortresses and towns along his western frontier, of which one was Vilnius.

GEERTGEN VAN HAARLEM, d. c. 1493, Dutch painter of Haarlem. He was also known as Geertgen van Sint Jans because he lived with the Knights of St. John. He painted a triptych for them, the Crucifixion being the theme of the center panel, a *Pietà* and the *Legend of the Bones of St. John the Baptist* being those of the wings. His paintings show him to have been an artist of considerable power and imagination.

GEILER OF KAYSERSBERG, JOHN, d. 1510, theologian and humanist. He studied at Freiburg-im-Breisgau and Basel, taught at Freiburg, then became the university's rector. He later became the principal preacher in the cathedral in Strasbourg. Because the usual theme of his sermons was moral regeneration, they constitute an important source for a study of the social evils and clerical abuses of the time. Although he was referred to as the "German Savonarola" because of his attacks on abuses in the church, he never experienced any difficulties with the ecclesiastical authorities.

GELASIAN DOCTRINE, the position set forth by Pope Gelasius I concerning the relationship between the spiritual and secular authorities in a letter he addressed to Emperor Anastasius I in 494. He declared that while the spiritual authority was of its nature above the temporal, both institutions, church and state, were of divine origin and were essential to a well-ordered Christian society. For this reason, though each was supreme in its own domain, the church in the spiritual, the state in the secular, they should cooperate in the work of God which was their mutual responsibility.

GELASIUS I, Pope, 492–6, perhaps an African by birth and principal adviser to his predecessor Felix III. As pope he defined the relationship between church and state in letters to Emperor Anastasius I. [See GELASIAN DOCTRINE.] He continued the policy of his predecessor, Felix III, in maintaining the primacy of the Roman see against the claims of Constantinople during the Acacian Schism. Following a synod held in Rome in 494, he decreed that the revenues from church property be equally apportioned among bishop, clergy, the poor, and the maintenance of buildings.

GELASIUS II, Pope, 1118–9, an Italian, monk of Monte Cassino and cardinal, who as pope fled to France to escape capture by Henry V of Germany who had his own pope in Gregory VIII. He suffered much mistreatment at the hands of the pro-imperial faction of the Frangipani in Rome. Gelasius died at Cluny.

GELASIUS OF CAESAREA, d. c. 395, bishop of Caesarea (in Palestine) who spent some time in exile during the reign of Emperor Valens. Of his principal work, a continuation of Eusebius's history of the church, only fragments remain, although much of it was copied and used by subsequent church historians.

GELDERLAND (Guelderland), province of the Low Countries, east of Utrecht. The earliest rulers were counts of Gelre of the eleventh century who in time sought to exploit their location athwart the Rhine, Waal, Meuse, and IJssel rivers. Given the ambitions of England, France, and later Burgundy in the Low Countries, it was not an easy matter to expand. In 1473 the duchy of Gelderland was conquered by Charles the Bold of Burgundy. Shortly after his death it passed to the house of Hapsburg.

GELIMER (Geilamir), last Vandal king who seized the throne from Hilderich in 530 but was defeated and himself deposed in 533 by Belisarius, Emperor Justinian's general.

GELMÍREZ, DIEGO, d. c. 1139, archbishop of Santiago de Compostela (1120), papal legate in Spain. His driving ambition to advance the fame of the shrine he ruled as well as his own power and wealth involved him in many disputes, but he did much to develop the reputation of Santiago as a pilgrimage center. He also reformed the church in his province and caused the Peace and Truce of God to be proclaimed in Castile. He even organized a fleet which beat back a Moorish naval attack on Galicia.

GEMISTUS PLETHON, GEORGIUS, d. c. 1450, Renaissance scholar, a native of Constantinople, member of the Byzantine embassy to the Council of Florence (1438–9). He received a warm welcome from Italian humanists, notably Cosimo de' Medici. Because of his enthusiasm for the philosophy of Plato, he did much to redress the great reverence enjoyed by Aristotle in the West.

GENERAL CHAPTER, daily gathering of the members of a religious community for consideration of administrative and disciplinary matters; the regular meeting of superiors and representatives of a religious order belonging to a particular province. The Cistercian Order introduced the general chapter in 1119, and in 1215 the Fourth Lateran Council made such a chapter compulsory for all orders.

GENESIUS, JOSEPH, Byzantine historian of the mid-tenth century, the author of a history covering the years 813 to 886. The work possesses considerable historical value despite its strong sympathy for the Macedonian emperors.

GENEVA (Genève, Ginevra, Genf), Swiss city and canton whose site was occupied from Celtic times. Geneva became a bishop's seat in the fourth century and served as the residence of the kings of Burgundy in the fifth. The count of Geneva ruled the city until 1124 when Henry V of Germany placed the bishop in control. In 1162 the bishop of Geneva rose to the rank of prince of the empire. Growing opposition to episcopal control on the part of the citizenry led the count of Savoy to assume greater authority until finally in 1444 Count Felix V made himself the bishop.

GENEVIÈVE, ST., d. c. 500, a virgin who moved to Paris from Auxerre where she is said to have persuaded the citizens to defend their city against Attila and the Huns. Their defense proved successful. In 1129 the cessation of a serious pestilence in the city was attributed to her intercession. Paris revered her as its patroness.

GENGHIS KHAN (Chinghiz, Jenghiz, Tschingis, Dschingis), d. 1227, Mongol chieftain, probably born in 1167 and given the name of the Tatar chief Temujin (Temuchin) whom his father Yekusai had slain. In 1206, after extending his authority over the Turkish and Tungus tribes and the Tatars who occupied Mongolia, he, his sons, and his generals proceeded to conquer an enormous empire that stretched from China to the Caucasus and from the Arctic to the Himalayas. This empire included north China, Turkestan with its splendid cities of Samarkand and Bukhara which he razed, and parts of Persia and Afghanistan. Little remained in the wake of Genghis's armies save desolation and death. History has known no more ruthless conqueror. Genghis established his capital at Karakorum in Outer Mongolia.

GENNADIUS, d. c. 500, ecclesiastical historian and priest of Marseilles who continued Jerome's *De Viris Illustribus* and composed several tracts against Nestorius, Pelagius, and other heretics.

GENNADIUS I, patriarch of Constantinople, 458–71, learned theologian and exegete, a reformer, and author of numerous exegetical and dogmatic writings. In his exegesis he adopted the method of literal interpretation favored at the school of Antioch.

GENNADIUS II SCHOLARIUS, d. after 1472, patriarch of Constantinople and a leading theologian of the Eastern church. He served as secretary and adviser to Emperor John VIII Palaeologus at the Council of Ferrara-Florence where he endorsed reunion with the Latin church. Upon his return to Constantinople, he became a leader of anti-unionism. When the Turks captured the city, the sultan Mohammed appointed him patriarch, an office he held until 1466 when he retired to a monastery. His writings included sermons, pastoral letters, and prayers, as well as tracts opposing union with Rome. He was an ardent admirer of Aristotle and translated works of Thomas Aquinas into Greek.

GENOA, seaport in northwestern Italy which shared with Venice the maritime and commercial leadership of Italy from the twelfth century until the close of the Middle Ages. Although Genoa was a flourishing town in Roman times, successive captures by Ostrogoths and Lombards dropped it to the level of a fishing village. It revived during the tenth century, drove the Saracens from Corsica and Sardinia, and with the help of Pisa expelled them from Italian waters. The period of the Crusades brought rapid expansion, while the greatest era in its history followed after the reestablishment of the Byzantine empire in 1261 and its defeat of Pisa in the naval battle of Meloria (1284). It counted in its commercial and territorial empire possessions and trading concessions in areas scattered from Spain to the Crimea. But the fourteenth century brought decline, first through the Black Death, then by a major defeat at the hands of Venice (War of Chioggia), followed by the rise of Aragon and the Ottoman Turks. Genoa, which was a largely autonomous commune from the twelfth century, announced its independence when Frederick II of Germany died in 1250.

GENTILE DA FABRIANO, d. 1427, Italian painter of frescoes for the Doge's palace in Venice, the first great representative of the Umbrian school. His altarpiece entitled *Adoration of the Magi* is considered a masterpiece of the international Gothic school. In 1427 he decorated the Church of St. John the Baptist in Rome with frescoes depicting the life of that saint. He also painted the *Holy Family* for the Church of Santa Maria Maggiore. Most of his works are lost.

GENTILE DA FOLIGNO, d. 1348, Italian physician who practiced medicine in Bologna and Perugia. He went to Padua to treat its ruler Ubertino of Carrara and remained there to lecture at the university. He left tractates dealing with the Black Death, of which he was also a victim.

GEOFFREY OF CLAIRVAUX (of Auxerre), d. after 1188, student of Abelard, a Cistercian of Clairvaux and St. Bernard's secretary, later himself abbot of Clairvaux and other Cistercian abbeys. He collected Bernard's letters and completed the saint's biography begun by William of Saint-Thierry and Arnold of Bonneval. He also left sermons together with theological, exegetical, and mystical writings.

GEOFFREY OF MONMOUTH, d. 1155, bishop of Saint Asaph, Wales, but probably never resident there. His history of the kings of Great Britain *(Historia Regum Britanniae)* traced the history of that country from the fall of Troy through the settlement of Britain by Brutus, great-grandson of Aeneas. The history, which makes mention of Arthur, possesses little or no historical value although it enjoyed enormous popularity and influenced English chroniclers and writers of literature.

GEOFFREY OF VENDÔME, d. 1132, abbot of the Benedictine monastery of Sainte-Trinité at Vendôme, cardinal (1094), and author of hymns, sermons, theological tracts, and letters. He wrote in support of the papal cause in the investiture controversy.

GEOFFREY OF YORK, d. 1212, natural son of Henry II, bishop of Lincoln (1173), chancellor of England (1183), and archbishop of York (1189). He was the only son who attended Henry II on his deathbed. The other sons had taken up arms against their father. King John banished him in 1207 when he protested royal taxation of the clergy.

GEOFFREY PLANTAGENET, count of Anjou, 1129–51, son of Fulk, count of Anjou and king of Jerusalem. He married Matilda, the daughter of Henry I of England, and was the father by her of Henry (II) who became king in 1154. He was the ancestor of the Plantagenet kings of England and the first to bear that identification, allegedly because of the sprig of broom (*genista* or *genêt*) he carried in his helmet. After a considerable amount of fighting, he succeeded in conquering Normandy (1144). He took part in the Second Crusade (1147–9).

GEOMETRY, one of the seven liberal arts and one of the four that made up the quadrivium. It concerned itself principally with the measurement of land, supplemented with some knowledge of Euclid which Gerbert of Aurillac had brought from Spain.

GEORGE, d. 724, bishop of the Arabians in Mesopotamia (686) with his see at Akula. His writings constitute a major source for the history of Syriac Christianity and literature. He also composed translations and commentaries on a number of the works of Aristotle, as well as many letters on matters of doctrine, liturgy, and asceticism.

GEORGE CEDRENUS, probably a Byzantine monk of the late eleventh or early twelfth century who composed a world chronicle to 1057.

GEORGE OF CAPPADOCIA, d. 361, Arian bishop of Alexandria from 357 until his death by a rabble in 361. He was a grasping, violent person and a leader of the extreme Arian party. He has been confused with St. George, the patron of medieval England.

GEORGE OF PODEBRAD AND KUNSTAT. *See* PODIEBRAD, GEORGE OF.

GEORGE OF TREBIZOND, d. 1486, Greek scholar who settled in Venice where he taught Greek, philosophy, and rhetoric. In 1442 he went to Rome where he enjoyed the patronage of Pope Eugenius IV. He translated into Latin the works of both Plato and Aristotle as well as some Greek patristic writings.

GEORGE SCHOLARIUS. *See* GENNADIUS II SCHOLARIUS.

GEORGE, ST., obscure martyr, patron saint of England, Portugal, Aragon, Lithuania, as well as other countries and cities. He may have suffered martyrdom at or near Lydda (Palestine) in the early fourth century. His cult became popular in the sixth century, although the account of his slaying the dragon, a feat traditionally attributed to him, did not appear until the late twelfth. The *Golden Legend* of the late thirteenth century popularized the tale.

GEORGE SYNCELLUS, d. after 810, Byzantine monk, author of a world chronicle from the Creation to the accession of Diocletian (284).

The principal value of the chronicle consists of the fragments it contains of works that are no longer extant. Theophanes "the Confessor" wrote a continuation of the chronicle.

GEORGE THE MONK, also known as George Harmartolos ("sinner"), fl. middle of the ninth century, Byzantine historian whose world chronicle to the year 842 proved highly popular despite the author's strong prejudices and his edificatory motivation in writing it. He was unusually bitter toward the iconoclasts. The chronicle is especially useful for the years 813 to 842. A continuation of the chronicle to 948 goes by the title *Georgius Continuatus*.

GEORGE THE PISIDIAN (Georgios Pisides), Byzantine poet of the early seventh century, keeper of the records in the church of Hagia Sophia, and author of a history of the wars of Emperor Heraclius in verse, as well as of epigrams and poems on theological subjects. He contributed to the development of the Byzantine 12-syllable iambic verse.

GEORGIA, CHURCH OF. The origins of Christianity in Georgia reach back to the fourth century if not earlier. St. Nina, a Christian slave woman from Cappadocia, is said to have converted the royal family c. 330. The people then adopted the new religion and maintained the position on the nature of Christ declared at the Council of Chalcedon (451) and not the Monophysitism of neighboring Armenia. The Georgian church, dependent originally upon the patriarchate of Antioch, became autocephalous in the eighth century. The earliest version of the New Testament in the Georgian language dates from the sixth century.

GEPIDS, east German people that moved from Scandinavia to the lower Vistula, then settled south of the Carpathians (roughly Hungary) where they remained subject to the Huns until 453. During the second half of the sixth century they suffered destruction at the hands of the Cumans and the Lombards.

GERARD OF ABBÉVILLE, d. 1272, regent master in theology at Paris, one of the most outspoken critics of the friars, and a leader in the movement to secure their expulsion from the university. His attacks on the mendicant orders drew responses from both Thomas Aquinas and Bonaventure.

GERARD (Gerhard) OF CREMONA, d. 1187, studied at Toledo and translated many important philosophical and scientific works from Arabic into Latin. These included writings of Aristotle and those of his Arabic commentators, Euclid's geometrical studies, and Ptolemy's *Almagest*. It is probable that the more than 70 works credited to him actually represent the production of a school of translators whom he directed.

GERARD (Girard) OF YORK, d. 1108, royal chancellor under William II, bishop of Hereford (1096), and archbishop of York (1100). He found himself on the side of Henry I in the king's differences with Anselm, archbishop of Canterbury, but later cooperated with that prelate in the negotiations with the crown that led to the adoption of the Compromise of Bec (1106).

GERBERT OF AURILLAC. *See* SYLVESTER II, Pope.

GERHAERT VAN LEYDEN, NICOLAUS, d. 1473, German sculptor of Trier, Strasbourg, and Vienna. His work reflects the influence of Claus Sluter, although he succeeded in investing his religious figures with a warmth and naturalness unique among his contemporaries.

GERHOH OF REICHERSBERG, d. 1169, member of the monastery of Canons Regular of St. Augustine in Rottenbuch but for most of his career provost of the Austin monastery at Reichersberg. His writings include attacks on the views of Abelard and Gilbert de la Porrée, treatises on church reform and on relations between church and state, and a commentary on the Psalms. This last, his most important work, incorporated discussions on dogmatic and moral theology, church discipline, monastic life, canon law, and the liturgy. He was one of the principal agents of the Gregorian reform movement in Germany where his zeal brought him into conflict with such powerful personages as Frederick I Barbarossa.

GERMANIC LAWS, EARLY. Since the German tribes that overran the western half of the Roman empire had no script, they brought no written laws or law codes with them. Given the primitiveness of their culture and the dearth or absence of civil disputes, they required none. For them custom sufficed as a satisfactory means for determining the punishment of such crimes as theft and murder. Only after some years of acquaintance with the native Roman population and its higher ways and institutions did their kings have these customs compiled into written law codes. The Visigoths, Burgundians, and Salian Franks wrote down their laws about the year 500, the Lombards a century and a half later.

The oldest of these Germanic codes is the *Codex Euricianus* that King Euric (d. c. 484) had compiled for his Visigothic subjects. In 506 Alaric II had a code compiled, entitled *Lex Romana Visigothorum* or *Breviary of Alaric,* but this applied only to his Roman subjects. It is significant that the *Liber Visigothorum* (c. 654) which superseded these two codes related to Goths and Romans alike. By that time the two societies had become so intermingled that any distinction was no longer necessary. The *Lex Gundobada* issued by King Gundobad c. 501 applied to Burgundians but also covered disputes between Burgundians and Romans. The *Lex Romana Burgundiorum* (c. 506), despite its title, applied only to the Romans in his kingdom.

The most ancient of the Frankish codes, the *Lex Salica* of the Salian Franks, was compiled c. 508–11 by order of King Clovis I. This code made no distinction between Franks and Romans, partly because the Franks had permitted intermarriage with the native population from the beginning, partly perhaps, too, because the German element was as numerous as the Roman. By the middle of the seventh century, the Germanic states to the south of the Franks no longer made any distinction between Roman and German, so homogeneous had their society become. The most advanced Germanic code was the *Edictum Rotharis* that King Rothari promulgated in 643 at a diet at Pavia for his Lombard and Roman subjects.

In this assimilation of Roman and Germanic institutions, the simpler but inferior German usages generally prevailed. Even in Italy where Roman institutions were most deeply rooted, such crude Germanic devices as the ordeal and compurgation replaced the infinitely superior Roman judicial procedures.

GERMANUS, ST., d. 448, bishop of Auxerre who went to Britain in 429 on papal instructions to combat Pelagianism. In 447 he visited England for a second time, when, according to Bede, he led the Britons to a bloodless victory over the Picts and Scots. It is probable that both St. Patrick of Ireland and Illtyd of Wales were his pupils.

GERMANUS, ST., d. 576, bishop of Paris, earlier abbot of the monastery of St. Symphorian in Autun. He worked incessantly to bring an end to the constant fighting among the Frankish kings and appears to have enjoyed considerable influence with Childebert, son of Clovis. Two of the letters attributed to him throw important light on the history of the Gallican liturgy.

GERMANUS, ST., d. c. 733, patriarch of Constantinople (715), who shortly after his accession anathematized Monothelitism. He also attacked the iconoclastic decrees of Emperor Leo III, his opposition leading to his resignation of the see in 730. Among his few extant writings — most were destroyed by the iconoclasts — is a treatise against heresies and several homilies on the Virgin.

GERMANY. The history of medieval Germany may be said to begin with the tripartite division of the Carolingian empire effected by the Treaty of Verdun in 843 which assigned the eastern portion, the country of the East Franks, to Louis the German. Since the Carolingian empire was reunited once again under Charles the Fat (884–7), some scholars prefer to begin the history of the German monarchy with the election of Conrad I, duke of Franconia, in 911, when Louis the Child, the last of the East Frankish Carolingians, died.

A brief glance at the history of the East Franks after 843 reveals a realm floundering in the morass of feudal decentralization which characterized the greater part of central and western Europe from the mid-ninth century. In Germany the disintegration of the state did not proceed as far as in France, although the authority of Louis the German and his successors was no more compelling than that of the rulers of the West Franks. The ravaging inroads of Vikings and Magyars frustrated what royal ambitions they may have entertained. During this period of royal weakness local counts were apt to fare more successfully, which was also true of the men who made themselves dukes of such ethnic groups as the Bavarians, Swabians, Saxons, and Franconians (East Franks). These duchies acquired such vitality and cohesiveness during the ninth and tenth centuries that the German crown never found itself able during the Middle Ages to suppress their autonomy.

Conrad I (911–8), in a sense the first king of medieval Germany, was also the first to wrestle unsuccessfully with the rulers of these duchies. The futility of his efforts was not lost on his successor Henry I, duke of Saxony (919–36), who elected rather to devote his resources to strengthening his eastern frontiers against the Slavs and fighting the Magyars. His principal success was that of acquiring control of Lotharingia (Lorraine), the most populous and wealthiest of the German duchies. Under his son Otto I the Great (936–73) the early German monarchy attained the height of its power and influence. Otto broke Magyar power at the Lech river in 955, extended his rule over north Italy and Rome, deposed Pope John XII after he had received the imperial crown from his hands, and initiated almost a century of German control of the papacy. He pushed German influence eastward against the Slavs and established new dioceses there, including Magdeburg, to hold that territory. The most enduring phase of Otto's work was his enrichment of bishoprics with lands and privileges in order to use them as a counterweight against the secular princes. Since he controlled the appointment of these prelates, he and subsequent German kings could count on their financial and military support so long as the papacy could not protest that control.

This the reformed papacy of Gregory VII could no longer tolerate, and the result was a bitter clash between the pope and Henry IV (1056–1106) over the right of investiture. Because the German princes feared Henry might recover royal rights and properties they had seized during his minority, they sided with Gregory, which left Henry no alternative but to submit to the pope at Canossa (1077). Later, when Henry's fortunes had mended, he defied Gregory, but civil war ensued, and while the papacy salvaged the semblance of victory in the investiture controversy with the Concordat of Worms (1122), the real victors were the German princes who seized the lands of bishoprics and abbeys now that the king was powerless to prevent this. During the hundred years that elapsed between the accession of Henry IV in 1056 and that of Frederick I Barbarossa in 1152, the German crown suffered such losses in crown lands and royal prerogatives to the territorial princes that any hope of establishing a strong monarchy was extinguished.

For this reason the reigns of probably the three strongest and ablest kings of Germany in the Middle Ages, Frederick I Barbarossa (1152–90), Henry VI (1190–7), and Frederick II (1215–50), produced no significant growth of royal power. Frederick I Barbarossa did achieve some modest success through his extensive use of *miniteriales,* and he managed to deprive Henry the Lion, his most powerful adversary, of Bavaria and Saxony, but he could not retain these duchies for himself. Partly because of his inability to accomplish more in Germany, he kept expending his resources in Italy until 1176 when a stunning defeat suffered at Legnano shattered his dream of exercising real authority over the rich cities of Lombardy.

Frederick's son Henry VI married the heiress of Sicily and acquired a vast empire that stretched from the Mediterranean to the North Sea, but his death at the age of 33 deprived him of the opportunity of exploiting it. His death also precipitated another of the dynastic breaks which periodically interrupted the growth of the German monarchy and helped preserve its elective character. Otto IV emerged victorious from the contest for the throne which followed Henry's death, but at the battle of Bouvines in 1214 he lost the field to Phillip II Augustus of France and his crown to Frederick II. This young man, probably the most talented of the monarchs of medieval Germany, wasted all his efforts on the same dream of ruling Italy which his grandfather, Frederick I Barbarossa, had sufficient wit to abandon before it was too late.

The reign of Frederick II (1215–50) marks a major point of departure in the history of Germany. Prior to that reign there remained some hope for the establishment of a centralized state in Germany under the rule of a strong king; after that reign there remained none. Frederick's preoccupation with Italy led him to lose what remained of imperial rights in Germany. To make certain that no future king would attempt to reclaim these, the German princes in 1273 [*see* INTERREGNUM] selected for their monarch a minor Swabian count, Rudolf of Hapsburg, who they were certain would never cause them any difficulties. Rudolf knew his place. He concerned himself with advancing the fortunes of his family. No one cared any longer for the fortunes of the German monarchy. In Germany particularism and decentralization reigned triumphant. The rulers of some 1600 principalities — ecclesiastical states, imperial cities, the tiny domains of imperial knights, duchies — appropriated for themselves the powers a king should have exercised. As for this German king, he had no capital of his own, nor army, nor bureaucracy, only an impotent diet to advise him.

Rather than concern themselves with the depressing story of the late German monarchy, scholars have turned their attention to the Hanseatic League, to the rise of Switzerland, to the extension of German influence eastward through such agencies as the Teutonic Knights, and to the development of small but promising states like Bavaria, Saxony, and Brandenburg. An occasional monarch merits attention. Henry VII (1309–13) emulated his Hohenstaufen predecessors by marching an army into Italy where he received the commendation of Dante for his visionary ambition but nothing more. In 1338 Louis the Bavarian (IV) announced the decision of the German princes to repudiate the claims of the pope to a voice in the selection of a king of Germany. The matter of that king's election was regularized in 1356 by Charles IV in his Golden Bull which invested with the selection seven princes: the archbishops of Cologne, Mainz, and Trier, the count Palatine of the Rhine, the king of Bohemia, the duke of Saxony, and the margrave of Brandenburg. Sigismund, the son of Charles, brought momentary prestige to the imperial crown for the dominant role he played at the Council of Constance (1414–8) The marriage in 1438 of Albert of Hapsburg to the heiress of the Luxemburg domains united the two wealthiest and most influential families of Germany and assured Hapsburg possession of the throne for the future. During the long reign of Frederick III (1440–93) conditions in many parts of Germany approached the level of anarchy reminiscent of the worst of the feudal period. For the Hapsburgs, however, the Middle Ages closed on a happy note when Maximilian, the son of Frederick, married Mary of Burgundy and acquired through her possession of the rich Low Countries for his dynasty.

GERSHOM (Gerson) BEN JUDAH (Juhuda), d. 1040, French rabbi, also known as Rabbenu Gershom, rector of the rabbinical academy in Mainz and the founder of Talmudic studies in France and Germany. He was esteemed as the most distinguished rabbinical scholar in Western Europe. His legal decisions and counsels helped shape the organized life of European Jewry, while his *responsa* constitute an invaluable source for the history of the Jews in France during the tenth and eleventh centuries.

GERSON, JEAN, d. 1429, a student under Pierre d'Ailly, master of theology, chancellor of the University of Paris, a renowned orator, poet, humanist, and a master of the French language. His later theological writings, which reveal a turn toward mysticism, were admired by Nicholas of Cusa, the Brethren of the Common Life, and later by St. Ignatius Loyola, St. Robert Bellarmine, and St. Francis de Sales. He took an important part in the discussions aimed at ending the Western Schism and headed the French delegation at the Council of Constance (1414–8). His position was that of a moderate, for which reason he urged the different popes to resign in order to prevent the emergence of a radical conciliarist movement. He also had a major part in drawing up the Four Articles of Constance, the future charter of Gallicanism.

GERSONIDES (Levi Ben Gershon), d. c. 1344, Jewish mathematician, astronomer, philosopher, and biblical commentator of southern France. He is best known for his writings on exegesis and religious philosophy. What enhanced his influence was the charm of his literary style. Pope Clement VI requested him to translate into Latin his Hebrew treatise on astronomy. His inventions of astronomical instruments enabled him to correct the astronomical tables of the time. As a philosopher he carried further the synthesis of Aristotelianism and Judaism which Maimonides had initiated.

GERTRUDE, ST., d. 659, daughter of Pepin the Elder and Blessed Ida and abbess of a convent at Nivelles in Belgium which her mother had founded. Her cult was popular in the Low Countries and her intercession was invoked by travelers. For reasons unknown, her symbol is that of a mouse.

GERTRUDE, ST., d. 1302, nun and mystic in the Benedictine convent of Helfta in Saxony which she entered at the age of five. She worked as a copyist in the convent's scriptorium and composed several treatises on mysticism. She and her friend Mechtild of Hackborn, another mystic, helped popularize the devotion to the Sacred Heart of Jesus. Her *Legatus Divinae Pietatis* is judged one of the finest literary products of Christian mysticism. Her collection of prayers has appealed to many pious people.

GERVASE OF CANTERBURY, d. c. 1210, monk of Christ Church, Canterbury, author of a chronicle *(Chronica)* covering the period from 1100 to 1199, a continuation of the *Gesta Regum* to 1209, and a history of the archbishops of Canterbury from Augustine to Hubert Walter.

GERVASE OF TILBURY, d. c. 1220, studied and practiced law in Bologna and served under Henry III of England, William II of Sicily, and Otto IV of Germany who appointed him marshal of the kingdom of Arles. He composed the *Otia Imperiale* for Otto IV, purportedly an encyclopedia of universal knowledge but actually a miscellany of legend, history, and politics, and intended for instruction and entertainment.

GERVASIUS AND PROTASIUS, SS., obscure protomartyrs of Milan to whom Ambrose dedicated his new church in that city. Later tradition assigned their martyrdom to the latter half of the second century. What were believed to be their relics are under the main altar of the basilica in Milan.

GESTA, class of medieval historical writing popular in the tenth, eleventh, and early twelfth centuries. It was less factual than annals and chronicles, often interwoven with legend and anecdote, and generally concerned with an individual or a people.

GESTA FRANCORUM *(Gesta Francorum Et Aliorum Hierosolymitanorum),* an anonymous chronicle of the First Crusade (1096–9), written apparently by a Norman knight who accompanied Bohemund and was an eyewitness of the events he described. The chronicle served as a principal source for the work of Guibert of Nogent.

GESTA ROMANORUM, short tales on a wide variety of themes but possessing some moral application. They appeared in France and England c. 1300 when they often served the use of preachers. Poets, too, including Boccaccio, Chaucer, and Shakespeare *(Merchant of Venice)* drew upon them for episodes and ideas.

GESTE, CHANSONS DE, French epic poems principally of the twelfth and thirteenth centuries, usually by unknown authors who drew upon historical or pseudo-historical events of the eighth, ninth, and tenth centuries for the inspiration of their stories. [*See* EPIC POETRY.]

GESUATI. *See* JESUATI.

GEZA, grand prince of the Magyars, c. 972–97, who encouraged Christian missionaries to come to his country and permitted his son and successor Stephen (I) to be baptized.

GHASSANIDS, Arab ruling family of north Syria that controlled a large part of Palestine, east Jordan, and the Syrian desert under Byzantine suzerainty. They furnished mercenaries for the Byzantine armies. The area fell to Islam in 636.

GHAZALI, AL- (Algazel), d. 1111, Moslem theologian and mystic, a native of Khorasan. He abandoned a brilliant career as professor of law at Baghdad and took up the life of an ascetic and mystic. He had a profound distrust of speculation and of a philosophic approach in the study of the mysteries of religion and was one of the most influential opponents of Moslem rationalism. He composed his principal work, *The Revival of the Religious Sciences,* upon his return to Baghdad where he again became famous, this time as Islam's leading theologian. He is usually considered the father of Sufism.

GHENT (Gent, Gand), one of the leading cities of Flanders, located on the banks of the Lys, which grew up from the seventh-century village of Gandao and prospered under the protection of a castle which shielded it from Viking raids. It served as the residence of the counts of Flanders and by the thirteenth century had developed into the leading textile center of Europe and one of the largest cities of northern Europe. Its four major guilds, principally that of the weavers, vied with the count of Flanders for control of the city's policies. Under the leadership of Jacob and Philip van Artevelde the city sought to adhere to England during the Hundred Years' War because of the heavy imports of raw wool from that country upon which the prosperity of the community depended. (Ghent cloth, manufactured from English wool, enjoyed a reputation for high quality.) In 1384 Philip the Bold inherited Ghent and in 1453 Philip the Good sharply curtailed the city's privileges after putting down a revolt. In 1485 Archduke Maximilian (later Emperor Maximilian I), who had married Mary of Burgundy, made himself master of the rebellious city.

GHERARDESCA, DELLA, a leading family of Pisa from the tenth century. Ugolino della Gherardesca (d. 1289) attempted to establish a tyranny but ended up in a dungeon with his sons where they all starved to death. (See *Inferno,* XXXIII.) In 1317 Gaddo Gherardesca-Donoratico succeeded in restoring the family to its prominent position.

GHETTO, street or quarter of a city where Jews lived. Initially segregation in separate localities was voluntary and it was usual for Jews to live together. The Third (1179) and Fourth (1215) Lateran Councils prohibited Christians from lodging among Jews and required Jews to wear a distinctive badge. The rationale for such measures was the argument that the presence of Jews, given their own customs and ritualistic practices, would serve to cause scandal to Christians. The first compulsory ghettoes appeared in Spain and Portugal toward the close of the fourteenth century. [*See* JEWS, PERSECUTION OF.]

GHIBELLINES. *See* GUELFS AND GHIBELLINES.

GHIBERTI, LORENZO, d. 1455, sculptor of Florence, also goldsmith, painter, and architect. He is best known for the two pairs of bronze doors he made for the Baptistery in Florence, the last two being those which Michelangelo acclaimed as worthy to be the Gates of Paradise. The doors portray in their square panels scenes from the Old Testament. The doors occupied Ghiberti for the greater part of his career (1425–1452). Many of the most distinguished artists of the period, including Donatello and Michelangelo, received their training in his workshop. His artistry in the execution of relief sculpture has never been surpassed.

GHIRLANDAIO, DOMENICO, d. 1494, painter of Florence who won fame especially for his frescoes. Included among these are *St. Jerome, Last Supper,* and *Scenes from the Lives of the Virgin and St. John the Baptist.* Particularly well known are the frescoes he painted in the Sassetti Chapel in Santa Trinità in Florence, which depict scenes from the life of St. Francis with views of Florence serving as background. He often painted into his frescoes portraits of contemporaries he knew. Michelangelo learned some of his art in Ghirlandaio's workshop.

GHUSL, complete ritualistic washing which the

Moslem undertook in preparation for the Friday service.

GIAMBONO, MICHELE, d. 1462, painter and mosaicist of Venice whose work reveals the influence of the international Gothic style of Gentile da Fabriano and Pisanello. The most important of his mosaic works are probably the *Nativity* and *Presentation in the Temple.* Among his best known paintings are *The Redeemer with Saints, St. Peter,* and *Madonna.*

GIBRALTAR, meaning the hill of Tarik, the name given the rock at the entrance to the Mediterranean between Spain and Africa. It derived its name from the Berber chieftain Tarik who in 711 led his Moors into Spain at that point. In 1309 the Spanish captured the peninsula, lost it again in 1333, then recovered it for the last time in 1462.

GIFFARD, WALTER, d. 1279, bishop of Bath and Wells, chancellor of England, archbishop of York, and one of the three regents entrusted with the direction of the government between the death of Henry III (1272) and the return of Edward I from a Crusade (1274). He helped draw up the *Dictum de Kenilworth* (1266) which laid down relatively moderate terms by which the rebels who had supported Simon de Montfort in the Barons' War could recover their lands.

GIGLIATO, gold coin struck c. 1304 by King Charles II of Naples which was imitated in several countries of the eastern Mediterranean.

GIGUE, medieval stringed instrument similar to the rebec.

GIKATILLA, JOSEPH BEN ABRAHAM, d. after 1305, Jewish mystic of Spain whose writings sought to reconcile cabalism and philosophy. He maintained that the study of the mystic symbolisms of Hebrew letters and numbers would best explain biblical doctrines and prophetic concepts.

GILBERT CRISPIN, d. c. 1117, Benedictine monk of Bec, abbot of Westminister, and author of historical, exegetical, and doctrinal writings. His works, including his most important, *Disputatio Judaei et Christiani,* reveal the deep influence of Anselm of Bec.

GILBERT DE LA PORRÉE (Gilbert of Poitiers), d. 1154, noted philosopher and theologian, studied at Poitiers, then under Bernard of Chartres, later under Anselm of Laon. He served as chancellor of the cathedral of Chartres, taught at Paris, and in 1142 became bishop of Poitiers. His works, which still pose a problem of authenticity, include treatises on the Trinity and commentaries on the Psalms, Pauline Epistles, and the work of Boethius on the Trinity. When his writings on the Trinity drew the charge of heresy, he agreed to amend any view at variance with those of Bernard of Clairvaux. On the problem of universals, he attempted to effect a compromise between the positions of Plato and Aristotle.

GILBERT FOLIOT. *See* FOLIOT, GILBERT.

GILBERT OF SEMPRINGHAM, ST., d. 1189, founder of the English order of Gilbertines. In 1131 he organized a community consisting of seven young women and introduced a rule patterned after that of the Cistercians. When the Cistercians declined to assume the direction of the group, he turned to the Canons Regular of St. Augustine. In 1148 Eugenius III gave the order, called the Gilbertines, papal approval, and Gilbert was appointed master general. The Gilbertines who were organized in double monasteries, constituted the only exclusively English religious order of the Middle Ages.

GILBERTUS ANGLICUS, English canonist of the late twelfth, early thirteenth century, possibly a Dominican, the author of a collection of decretal letters for the years 1159 to 1202.

GILD. *See* GUILD.

GILDAS THE WISE (Gildas Sapiens, Gaildas

Badenicus), d. 570?, a native of Scotland, probably a monk, and author of a history of Britain from the Roman conquest *(De Excidio et Conquestu Britanniae)*. Because of the paucity of source materials concerning the Celts for this period, special importance attaches to his writing despite its errors and its moralistic rather than historical inspiration.

GILES OF ASSISI, BL., d. 1262, a companion of Francis of Assisi who accompanied him to Rome to secure papal approval for his order. Giles made pilgrimages to Jerusalem and Santiago de Compostella but spent the greater part of his life as a contemplative in remote hermitages. He was the author of a popular *Dicta,* a collection of pithy, moralistic sayings.

GILES (Gilles, Aegidius) OF CORBEIL, d. c. 1220, studied at Salerno, taught at Montpellier and Paris, and served as physician to Philip II Augustus of France. He was the author of medical treatises and of a satire on the higher clergy.

GILES (Aegidius) OF LESSINES, d. c. 1304, Dominican philosopher and scientist, a student of Albert the Great and possibly of Thomas Aquinas, and the author of treatises on philosophical and scientific subjects and of what is considered the most comprehensive work on usury to appear in the Middle Ages.

GILES (Aegidius) OF ROME, d. 1316, philosopher and theologian, a Hermit of St. Augustine, first Augustinian master in theology at Paris, vicar general of the order (1292), and archbishop of Bourges (1295). Although earlier the tutor of the young Philip (IV), for whom he wrote *De Regimine Principum,* he supported Boniface VIII in his controversy with the king and maintained that the pope must exercise political authority over all mankind. His treatise entitled *De Summi Pontificis Potestate* may have inspired Boniface's famous bull, the *Unam Sanctam.* His voluminous writings, which included commentaries on Aristotle and the *Sentences* of Peter Lombard, reveal the influence of

Augustinianism but also that of Thomas Aquinas under whom he may have studied.

GILES (Aegidius), ST., d. c. 720, a hermit who lived near the mouth of the Rhône and is supposed to have founded a monastery nearby known later as Saint-Gilles. He was revered as one of the Fourteen Holy Helpers, the patron of cripples, beggars, and blacksmiths. The town of St. Giles that sprang up near his grave became a popular place of pilgrimage. St. Giles proved an unusually popular saint and no fewer than 160 churches in England were dedicated to him.

GIOCONDO, FRA GIOVANNI DA VEROME (Fra Giovanni), d. 1515, Italian architect, engineer, and antiquary. He is credited with the design of the Palazzo del Consiglio in Verona. During his last years he served as one of three architects in charge of the construction of St. Peter's in Rome. Although a Franciscan friar and accomplished in philosophy, archeology, and classical literature, he is best known for his architectural and engineering works.

GIORGIO, FRANCESCO DI, d. 1502, Italian painter, sculptor, architect, and engineer. He fashioned the mines used in the siege of Naples in 1495. His paintings, which show the influence of Fra Filippo Lippi, include *Chess Players.* As an architect he made a model of the dome of the Milan cathedral. He was especially known for his bronze reliefs.

GIORGIONE (Giorgio da Castelfranco, Giorgio Barbarelli), d. 1510, Italian painter of the Venetian school and a disciple of Giovanni Bellini. His fame rests upon small paintings in oil such as *The Tempest* and *Sleeping Venus.* Considerable controversy continues over his proper place in the history of art since he left no signed and dated works. Many of his works, left unfinished because of his early death, were completed by other artists including Titian. He may be considered the major influence in Venetian painting.

GIOTTO DI BONDONE, d. 1337, Italian painter

and architect who has often been honored as the true founder of Florentine painting, even as the "father of modern painting." He worked in a number of Italian cities including Florence, Assisi, Rome, Padua, Naples, and Milan. His knowledge of the use of light and shadow and of colors enabled him to create an illusion of texture, expression, and depth not achieved by his contemporaries, and to invest his human figures with a naturalism unique for the times. His figures are graceful, dignified, natural, and quite individual. Faces and gestures are lifelike, movement is free and unconstrained. Some of his best known frescoes are those about Francis of Assisi. He exerted enormous influence on the painting of the succeeding century through his own works and those of his many pupils and imitators.

GIOVANNI CAPISTRANO. *See* JOHN CAPISTRAN, ST.

GIOVANNI DI PAOLO, d. 1482, Italian painter and illuminator of Siena, author of altarpieces and small devotional pictures. He was probably a pupil of Taddeo di Bartola and was influenced by Gentile da Fabriano. He was an artist of imagination and individualism though his expressionist style was little appreciated until modern times.

GIRALDA, the bell tower of the cathedral of Seville (100 m. high) which served as a minaret for the principal mosque of the city until the close of the twelfth century when the city fell to the Christians. The tower was built 1163–84.

GIRALDUS CAMBRENSIS (Gerald of Wales), d. 1223, a Welsh churchman, related to a princely family of south Wales. He served as royal chaplain to Henry II of England. He studied at Paris and Oxford and was twice elected bishop of St. David's but never consecrated since it was feared he would repudiate any obedience to Canterbury. He is the author of an autobiography, letters, poems, speeches, and, above all, of *Topographia Hibernica, Expugnatio Hibernica, Descriptio,* and *Itinerarium Cambriae.* These last volumes, despite the uncritical and emotional character of his writing, are indispensable to a study of Ireland and Wales.

GIRDLE, a sort of belt worn about the waist to hold in the loose-fitting alb. It was believed to symbolize chastity and spiritual watchfulness. [*See* CINCTURE.]

GIUDECCA (Judecca), lowest ring in the ninth circle of hell in Dante's *Inferno* (XXXIV) where Satan, together with the arch-traitors Judas Iscariot, Brutus, and Cassius, were imprisoned.

GIUSTINIANI, prominent Italian family of the fifteenth century which had branches in Venice, Genoa, Naples, and Corsica. Leonardo G., d. 1466, a state official of Venice, humanist, and poet, translated Greek and Latin classics into Italian and also composed amatory and religious verse in the vernacular. His son Bernardo, d. 1489, who served as amabassador to France and Rome and as a member of the Council of Ten in Venice, composed a history of Venice. [For Lorenzo Giustiniani, *see* LAWRENCE JUSTINIAN, ST.]

GJÖLL, in Nordic mythology the river separating the upper and lower worlds. The dead cross the bridge (Gjallarbu) over this river to enter the region of *Hel.*

GLAGOLITHIC SCRIPT, the cursive script consisting of uncial letters used in Slavic liturgical writing. It was devised by St. Cyril (d. 869), the Apostle of the Slavs.

GLAMORGAN, county in southern Wales. Monastic houses were founded at a number of places in the sixth century including Llandaff and Llancarfan. Normans under the leadership of Robert FitzHamon, lord of Gloucester, had conquered the area by the end of the eleventh century. Cistercian abbeys and Dominican and Franciscan houses sprang up in the twelfth and thirteenth centuries. In 1271 work was begun on the great castle of Caerphilly to protect the county from Llewelyn ap Gruffydd, the last Welsh prince of Wales.

GLANVILLE (Glanvil), RALPH (Randulf, Ranulph), d. 1190, justiciar and principal adviser of Henry II of England, also author of the first systematic treatise on English law *(Treatise Concerning the Laws and Customs of the Kingdom of England)*. It was based on the common law evolving in the courts of the itinerant justices and it did much to establish this law in competition with canon and feudal law. Glanville accompanied Richard I on the Third Crusade and died at Acre.

GLARUS, canton in east-central Switzerland, occupied largely by Alemanni who were converted in the sixth century by Fridolin and other missionaries. Glarus adhered to the Perpetual Compact in 1352 and won its independence from the Hapsburgs at the battle of Näfels in 1388.

GLASGOW, city in Scotland situated on the Clyde, 44 miles southwest of Edinburgh. It grew up around the church Mungo was believed to have erected there in the sixth century. About 1180 it was created a burgh of barony and c. 1188 it received the right to hold an annual fair. Glasgow became a bishopric before 1115 and a metropolitanate in 1492. Its university was founded in 1451 by a charter granted by Pope Nicholas V.

GLASTONBURY, ABBEY OF, Benedictine monastery in Somerset which, according to the *Anglo-Saxon Chronicle,* was founded by King Ine of Wessex c. 708 although Celtic monks had occupied the site in the fifth century. The monastery, probably the oldest and richest in England, was also one of the most influential. During the abbacy of Dunstan (943–55), it served as the center of a major monastic reform movement. During the thirteenth century, the abbey attained a position of intellectual leadership in English monastic life. Glastonbury became a famous place of pilgrimage since it was believed to contain the tombs of King Authur and St.

Dunstan. Many legends were also associated with it, an example being the one that had St. Joseph of Arimathea founding there the first church in England.

GLATZ, city on the eastern border of Bohemia where it served as a defense against the Poles in the tenth century. It was colonized by Germans in the twelfth century, acquired municipal rights, and became the principal city of the county of Glatz.

GLEBE, in general any farm or parcel of land, more narrowly land set aside for the maintenance of the priest.

GLENDOWER, OWEN (Owain Glyn Dŵr, Owain Ap Gruffydd), d. c. 1416, the last independent Welsh prince of Wales who assumed that title in 1400 when he led a major revolt against Henry IV of England. The revolt, which the Percies, the earl of Northumberland and his son Hotspur, joined, was initially successful and the year 1404 found Glendower in control of the greater part of Wales. By the end of 1408, however, the young Henry (V) had broken the back of the revolt although Glendower continued the struggle until he died.

GLEVE (Glefe, Gläve), smallest unit in the feudal army of the late Middle Ages. It consisted of the heavily armed knight with his squires, horses, and weapons. It might also refer to the staff, sword, or knife used by foot soldiers.

GLOCKENSPIEL, a percussion instrument, a sort of miniature carillon, that might be played mechanically by means of a rotating cylinder with pins stuck in it.

GLORIA IN EXCELSIS DEO, glory to God in the highest, the opening words of the song of praise recited or sung after the *Kyrie Eleison* of the Mass. This doxology may have appeared as early as the second century. It was first used in the divine office and not generally in the Mass until the eleventh century.

GLORIA, LAUS, ET HONOR, processional hymn for Palm Sunday which is usually credited to Theodulf of Orléans (d. 821).

GLORIA PATRI, glory [be] to the Father, opening words of the doxology to the Trinity which customarily concluded the singing or recitation of the Psalms. Its use at the end of the Psalms dates from the fourth century.

GLOSS, usually a glossary or collection of explanations and comments concerned with law, in particular with canon law. The term might also refer to words placed on the margin of a biblical text or between its lines in order to assist in its understanding. The first *Glossa Ordinaria* was the biblical commentary begun early in the twelfth century by Anselm of Laon. He was responsible for the gloss on the Psalter, the Pauline Epistles, and the Gospel of St. John. The entire Bible had been covered by about the middle of the twelfth century.

GLOSSATOR, person who prepared a gloss; a teacher or writer on Roman law in the high Middle Ages. As a professional group glossators first appeared in Bologna toward the close of the eleventh century.

GLOUCESTER, city on the Severn near the southeastern border of Wales on the site of an ancient Roman settlement. The abbey of St. Peter was founded there in 681 by the king of Mercia who made it his capital. The city became a borough in 1483.

GLOUCESTER, name of a prominent English family of earls and dukes. The first earl was Robert (d. 1147), a natural son of Henry I, who proved himself a powerful ally of Matilda and Henry (II) against King Stephen. Gilbert de Clare, eighth earl (d. 1295), was a leader of the baronial party under Simon de Montfort, earl of Leicester, in the Barons' War against Henry III. He captured the king at the battle of Lewes (1264), but then broke with Simon and joined Henry's son Edward in bringing about Simon's

defeat and death at Evesham in 1265. He also held the titles of earl of Clare and earl of Hertford and was probably the largest landowner in England. When his son Gilbert de Clare, ninth earl, was killed at the battle of Bannockburn (1314) and left no heirs, the mad scramble for his enormous holdings contributed significantly to the instability of Edward II's reign. Thomas of Woodstock (d. 1397), the youngest son of Edward III, became duke of Gloucester in 1385. He was the leading "Appellant" among the lords who sought to block Richard II from establishing personal rule. He may have been murdered by order of the king. Humphrey (d. 1447), youngest son of Henry IV, was created duke of Gloucester and earl of Cambridge in 1414 and served as a member of the regency during the minority of Henry VI. Because his older brother John, the duke of Bedford, who had been named "Protector," was away in France directing the war (Hundred Years' War) against France, Humphrey tended to assume a greater share in the government, the result being a serious clash with Henry Beaufort, his uncle. Humphrey's marriages and military expedition in Hainault brought him disgrace and he was under house arrest when he died. He was a patron of humanism and a friend of Oxford University, the recipient of much of his library. In 1461 Richard (III) acquired the title of duke of Gloucester.

GLOUCESTER, ABBEY OF, Benedictine monastery in the diocese of Worcester which was established on a site first occupied by a nunnery (c. 681). The period of its greatness dated from 1072 when William the Conqueror appointed Serle the abbey's abbot. Edward II was buried in the abbey.

GLOVE, covering for the hands, used by peasants of northern Europe from early times. Bishops used gloves from the first centuries of the church as part of their liturgical attire. In the eighth century the glove served as a symbol of authority in investiture ceremonies. A knight might send his right glove to challenge another to a duel.

GLUTTONY, one of the seven deadly or capital sins.

GLYCAS, MICHAEL, d. c. 1200, secretary to Emperor Manuel I Comnenus (1143–80), later monk and a leading theologian. He composed an important theological-exegetical work, letters, some political verse, and a chronicle from the Creation to 1118 possessing little original historical value.

GNIEZNO (Gnesen), city east of Poznan in Poland, established in the eighth century when it served as one of the oldest fortresses of the Polan tribe. In the eleventh century it was the capital of the Piast (Polish) state. In 1000 the town became the seat of the first Polish archdiocese and the place of coronation for Polish kings.

GNOSIS, Greek word for knowledge but applied more particularly to knowledge of God, of Christ, and of divine mysteries in general.

GNOSTICISM, a religious movement based upon a variety of mystical, religious, and philosophical doctrines, including Greek philosophies and Persian dualism. It became prominent in Christian circles in the second century and influenced such early Christian sects as the Docetists. Gnostics maintained that salvation could be achieved through knowledge *(gnosis)* since this would lead men to avoid evil. Some scholars speak of a distinct Christian Gnosticism, although it is not easy to distinguish this from Manichaeanism. "Christian" Gnosticism may simply have been a form of paganism that had adopted some of the language and images of Christianity. Characteristic of Gnostic teaching was the distinction between the Demiurge, a "creator god," and the supreme unknowable Divine Being. The Demiurge was the source of creation and ruled the world which was imperfect and antagonistic to what was truly spiritual. To Christian Gnostics the function of Christ had been to serve as the

emissary of the supreme God to bring *gnosis.* Irenaeus, Tertullian, and Hippolytus were the principal anti-Gnostic writers among the church fathers.

GOBELIN TAPESTRY, tapestry (scarlet) made in Paris by Jean (Jehan) Gobelin (d. 1476) and his family of dyers.

GODE, priest-owner of a temple in Iceland who shared with others of his class the jurisdiction of their region. Since 930, thirty-six of such priests constituted the law-making body of Iceland.

GODFREY OF BOUILLON, d. 1100, first Crusader king of Jerusalem, the son of the count of Boulogne, duke of Lower Lorraine (1087), and one of the leaders of the First Crusade. He had a major role in the siege and capture of Jerusalem (1099). In July 1099 he accepted the title of "Defender (Advocate) of the Church of the Holy Sepulchre" rather than the more pretentious "King of Jerusalem" which he felt only Christ deserved. The deeds of Godfrey, real and legendary, were glorified in the *chansons de geste.*

GODFREY (Gottfried) OF FONTAINES, d. 1306?, philosopher and theologian, taught at Paris where he was among those who opposed the presence of the friars at the university. Although he is classified as an independent thinker, his scholastic writings reveal a strongly Aristotelean-Thomistic bent.

GODFREY OF SAINT-VICTOR, d. after 1190, philosopher, theologian, canon of the Abbey of Saint-Victor, poet, and author of sermons, religious verse, and the *Microcosmus,* a work that presents man simply as a miniature of the universe, a microcosm.

GODFREY OF VITERBO, d. after 1191, chaplain and notary to Conrad III, Frederick I Barbarossa, and Henry VI. His historical writings, which were tremendously popular, are cluttered with fables and anecdotes and are principally concerned with the exploits of Frederick. His universal history, in prose and poetry, extends from the Creation to 1186.

GODIVA, d. 1080?, wife of Earl Leofric of Mercia and lord of Coventry, who was supposed to have secured remission of the heavy taxes her husband levied on Coventry by riding naked through the town. The story which is probably a legend first appeared in the chronicle of Roger of Wendover (d. 1236). Godiva and her husband did establish a monastery in Coventry.

GODWIN, d. 1053, powerful earl of Wessex and Kent, a favorite of King Canute, who was responsible for the accession of Edward the Confessor in 1042. Edward married Godwin's daughter Edith. As leader of the Anglo-Saxon faction and opposed to Norman influences, Godwin usually dominated Edward except for a brief period (1051-2) when he was forced into exile. He was the father of Harold who in 1066 contested the succession with William, duke of Normandy, and lost.

GOES, HUGO VAN DER, d. 1482, Flemish painter, best known for his *Portinari Altarpiece* (Uffizi) which presents the nativity of Christ in a landscape that spreads itself into the wings where appear the donor and his family. The artist proved himself a master of the problems of space by effectively relating the figure groups to the central theme. He handled his figures with complete confidence. It is said about Goes that his melancholy genius found expression in religious works of profound but often disturbing spirituality.

GOG AND MAGOG, nations which under the leadership of Satan will seek to destroy the kingdom of God (Revelation 20:8). To the Middle Ages they appeared as the barbarian peoples from the steppes of Asia.

GOLDEN BOOK, a Venetian record (from 1297) that contained the names of those patrician families who were members of the Great Council. The name also applied to richly decorated books

in which towns, universities, and guilds entered the names of honored guests.

GOLDEN BULL, document stamped with a seal impressed on gold because of its unusual importance; a document stamped with a seal kept in a golden case. Documents given that classification include the Golden Bull of Charles IV (1356), the Golden Bull of Eger which King Ottocar I received from Frederick II in 1213, and the Golden Bull of Hungary (1222).

GOLDEN BULL OF 1356, decree, consisting of 31 chapters, issued by Charles IV of Germany and providing for the election of future kings of Germany by seven formally designated electors (the archbishops of Mainz, Trier, and Cologne, the count palatine of the Rhine, the duke of Saxony, the margrave of Brandenburg, and the king of Bohemia). The bull also guaranteed the territorial integrity of these seven states and set down the procedure and ceremonials to be observed in the election process and in the coronation.

GOLDEN BULL OF ANDREW II, decree forced from King Andrew of Hungary in 1222 by his aristocracy and extending to the gentry and clergy tax exemption and the right of an annual assembly.

GOLDEN BULL OF EGER, decree issued by Frederick II of Germany in 1213 and extending to the church in Germany freedom of elections (episcopal and abbatial) and the right of appeal to Rome.

GOLDEN BULL OF RIMINI, decree issued by Frederick II of Germany in 1226 giving the Teutonic Order political and spiritual jurisdiction over the lands to the east that were occupied by pagan Prussians and Slavs.

GOLDEN FLEECE, ORDER OF THE *(Ordre de la Toison d'or, Toisón de Oro)*, chivalric order founded by Philip the Good, duke of Burgundy, in 1430 to commemorate his marriage to Isabella of Portugal. The duke's announced objective in founding the order was to defend Christianity and to uphold the ideals of knighthood.

GOLDEN GOOSE, the tale about the magic goose to which everyone adhered who touched it. The story, which is supposed to have made the sad daughter of a king finally laugh, may have first appeared c. 1220 in the *Edda*.

GOLDEN HORDE, initially the army camp of the Mongols, then the realm established by the Mongol chieftain Batu which extended over almost the whole of Russia and western Asia and had its capital at Sarai on the lower Volga. The magnificence of his camp was the source of the phrase "Golden Horde." The empire was at first tributary to the Great Khan at Karakorum, and its khan helped with Kublai Khan's conquest of south China. The victory gained by Dmitri Donskoi, grand duke of Moscow, in 1380 over the khan at Kulikovo signaled the beginning of the Golden Horde's decline. For a short time it passed under control of Timur the Lame. When he died in 1405 it broke up into a number of independent khanates. In 1430 Ivan III of Moscow established his independence and in 1502 he drove the last Mongols from Russia. The rule of the Golden Horde which cut Russia's ties with western Europe has been blamed for the "backwardness" of that country.

GOLDEN HORN, an arm of the Bosphorus which formed an excellent harbor-bay on the northern side of Constantinople.

GOLDEN LEGEND. *See* JACOBUS (Jacopo, James) DE VORAGINE.

GOLDEN ROSE, rose given by the pope on the fourth Sunday of Lent (*Laetare* Sunday) to a person considered most deserving because of his or her (customarily a woman) devotion to God. The practice can be traced back to Pope Leo IX in 1049 who already spoke of it as an ancient institution.

GOLF, sport played some time before 1457 in Scotland, the year it first drew the attention of contemporary writers. So popular had this sport become, together with "fute-ball," that the Scottish parliament that year ordered its suppression since it detracted from men's interest in archery. The country depended upon skilled archers for its defense.

GOLIARDS, composers of secular Latin lyrics of the twelfth and thirteenth centuries, principally of Germany, France, and England. They included wandering scholars and clerks as well as ecclesiastics of a higher station who composed light verse about wine, women, and song when they were not satirizing church and society. The most extensive collection of Goliardic poems is that known as *Carmina Burana*.

GOLIAS (Goliardus), name of the presumed author of occasional Latin poems of the twelfth and thirteenth centuries which were satirical and irreverent in tone, such as the *Confessio Goliae*. [*See* ARCHPOET.]

GOLUBAC (Taubersburg, Galambócz), fortress located at the pass Klisura on the right bank of the Danube in Serbia which served to block the advance of the Turks from the close of the fourteenth century. Once the Turks had captured this strong point, they used it as a base against the Hungarians.

GOMES, DIOGO, fl. 1440–82, Portuguese explorer who discovered the Cape Verde Islands and explored the Guinea coast.

GONDOLA, long narrow boat propelled by a pole or an oar at the stern. It appeared in Venice in the eleventh century and became common in Italy in the fourteenth.

GONFALON, battle standard used especially by the states of north Italy in the late Middle Ages.

GONFALONIER, one who carried the gonfalon; a military commander of the thirteenth century; a civic magistrate in Italy; an honorary title conferred by popes from the pontificate of Boniface VIII (1294–1303).

GONZAGA, an Italian princely dynasty that ruled the town of Mantua from the fourteenth century. The origins of the family appear in the twelfth century. It took its name from the village and castle of Gonzaga situated halfway between Mantua and Reggio. Like other aristocratic Italian families of the period, the Gonzagas were patrons of the arts while at the same time seeking to advance the family's territorial holdings.

GONZÁLEZ DE CLAVIJO, RUY, d. 1412, Spanish diplomat and traveler. He made a visit to the court of Timur the Lame in Samarkand as the ambassador of Henry III of Castile and Leon. The embassy left Spain in May 1403 and returned in March 1406. González de Clavijo's account of his visit provides a valuable description of Timur's court as seen through the eyes of a Westerner.

GONZALO DE CÓRDOBA, d. 1515, Spanish military leader who captured Granada from the Moors. He later gained even more fame as a warrior fighting in southern Italy against the French.

GOOD FRIDAY, the Friday before Easter when Christians commemorated the crucifixion and death of Christ.

GOOD SHEPHERD, popular theme in Christian art, that of Christ as the Good Shepherd, usually portrayed with a lamb on his shoulders.

GOOD THIEF. *See* DISMAS.

GORZE, ABBEY OF, Benedictine monastery in Lorraine founded in 749 by Bishop Chrodegang of Metz. Under Bishop Adalbero I, bishop of Metz (933), the monastery became the center of an important monastic reform movement. This worked for the most part within the traditions of St. Benedict of Aniane, a reforming abbot in the reign of Louis the Pious (814–40). Some 170 monastic houses, including such famous monasteries as Reichenau and St. Gall, adopted its customs.

GOSCELIN, d. after 1107, English hagiographer, member of the Benedictine monastery of St. Bertin at St. Omer. He came to England in 1058 and joined a number of monastic communities including Wilton, Peterborough, Ely, Ramsey, and, finally, St. Augustine's at Canterbury. He wrote the lives of many of the saints associated with the monasteries and their localities. He also left a book of spiritual direction for a nun at Wilton and a life of St. Edith.

GOSLAR, city in lower Saxony which was founded as a market in 922. The city grew rapidly because of the proximity of silver mines and because it served, on occasion, as the residence of the Salian kings of Germany. (The imperial palace was built c. 1040.) Goslar often served as the meeting place of the German Diet. The law of the city, which it acquired in the fourteenth century, was adopted as a model by other cities of the area. About the middle of the thirteenth century, Goslar became a member of the Hanseatic League.

GOTHIC ART, a period in the history of art that extends from the second half of the twelfth century to the close of the Middle Ages. Its birthplace was Paris and the region to the north and northeast of the city, whence it spread to all the countries of western Europe, less so to Italy than to England and Germany. It is customary to trace the origins of the Gothic to the reconstruction of the abbey church of Saint-Denis undertaken by Suger c. 1137, in particular to its façade of three portals, two towers, and round, central window. The salient factor that gave birth to Gothic was the use of ribbed vaulting over the nave. By pointing the arches of the crossvault which covered the square bays above the aisle areas in the Romanesque church, the Gothic architect discovered that he could use it to vault the oblong bays in the nave ceiling, an adaptation that enabled him to remove most of the clerestory walls and replace these with windows. Next he took the unprecedented step of moving the buttressing of the nave walls out above the aisle roof (flying buttresses), a step that permitted him to raise the nave vault to a most impressive height. The introduction of these two features, the pointed arch and the flying buttress, transformed the Romanesque church, with its massive pillars, blank walls, and generally low and dark interiors, into an edifice of soaring piers, lofty, brilliant naves, elaborate vaults, and extensive stained-glass windows. In place of the heavy walls which furnished the Romanesque church its air of stability and permanence, the Gothic architect employed a complex interplay of thrust and counter-thrust to hold his graceful structure together. [*See* DECORATED GOTHIC; FLAMBOYANT GOTHIC; PERPENDICULAR STYLE; PINNACLE; RAYONNANT STYLE.]

Gothic sculpture represents less a break with the Romanesque than Gothic architecture. A significant advance toward naturalism was inevitable as masons acquired greater ingenuity in their tasks. While saints and angels still remain part of the wall, they appear to be freer on their feet, to assume different poses, even to wear more cheerful countenances than their serious Romanesque predecessors. An interest in investing their figures with greater naturalism, as well as the ability to accomplish this, mark the work of the painters of illuminated manuscripts during the Gothic period.

GOTHIC SCRIPT, writing introduced by Ulfilas who mingled runic symbols with Greek uncials; Visigothic script, minuscule in form, used in Spain from c. 800 to the eleventh century; script that arose in north France in the eleventh century and attained its classical form in Textura; it prevailed north of the Alps from the thirteenth.

GOTHS, large Germanic tribe that moved from southern Scandinavia about the time of Christ to the lower Vistula, thence to the Black Sea which they reached by A.D. 200. During the third century they forced the Romans to surrender Dacia and conducted raids into the Balkans and Asia Minor. In the fourth century when they accepted Arian Christianity, they divided into the Ostrogoths (East Goths) who occupied the area east of the Dniester and the Visigoths (West Goths) who settled to the west. When the Huns subjugated the Ostrogoths in 375, the greater part of the Visigothic nation escaped across the Danube into the Roman empire. [*See* OSTROGOTHS; VISIGOTHS.]

GOTLAND, largest island in the Baltic Sea, located off the southeastern coast of Sweden. It was occupied by the Vikings and became an autonomous state under Swedish suzerainty c. 900. Wisby, its principal city, had developed into an important trading center by the twelfth century. Hanseatic merchants, especially those of Lübeck, began carrying the bulk of its trade from the mid-thirteenth century. In 1280 the Swedish king Magnus I conquered the island. In 1361 Waldemar IV Atterdag, king of Denmark, devastated the island and brought it under his control, but in 1370, by the Peace of Stralsund, he was obliged to cede it to the Hanseatic League. In 1398 it became a possession of the Teutonic Knights, and in 1408 it passed to Eric of Pomerania who held it until 1449 when it returned to Danish rule.

GOTTESFREUNDE. *See* FRIENDS OF GOD.

GOTTFRIED VON STRASSBURG, fl. 1210, leading Middle High German composer of courtly romances. His well-known *Tristan und Isolde* is considered the most successful version of the Tristan stories.

GOTTHARD (Godehard), ST., d. 1038, bishop of Hildesheim (1022), earlier a monk and abbot of the monastery at Nieder-Altaich. Henry, duke of Bavaria (later Emperor Henry I), commissioned him to reform the monasteries of Upper Germany. It is believed that the St. Gotthard Pass took its name from a chapel at the summit dedicated to him.

GOTTSCHALK OF LIMBURG, d. 1098, monk of

the Benedictine monastery at Limburg, composer of sacred music, a book of sermons, and some twenty sequences.

GOTTSCHALK (Godescale) OF ORBAIS, d. c. 867, theologian and poet, son of a Saxon count who became a member of the Benedictine monastery at Orbais (diocese of Soissons). It is said that his superior Rabanus Maurus forced him to remain and become a monk. His teachings concerning predestination — he believed that Christ died only for the elect — led to his excommunication, torture, and imprisonment by Hincmar, archbishop of Reims, who sent him to the monastery of Hautvillers. Gottschalk was able to continue his theological studies at this monastery as well as to voice his questionable views.

GOTTSCHALK, ST., d. 1066, prince of the Slavic Obotrites. He fled to England after the death of his father but later recovered his territory with the help of Archbishop Adalbert of Bremen. He was slain during the pagan uprising that followed Adalbert's death.

GOUVERNEUR, official in the French government who appeared in the fourteenth century and gradually assumed the civil and military responsibilities of the *bailli.*

GOWER, JOHN, d. 1408, English poet, a friend of Chaucer, author of two allegorical poems, one (in Latin) that expresses the fear and horror of the wealthy at the Peasants' Revolt (1381), the other (in French) furnishing a picture of his society. He was also the author of the English *Confessio Amantis,* a collection of stories illustrative of the Seven Deadly Sins. He composed in addition a series of *ballades* in French, and a Latin poem about the last years of Richard II.

GOZZOLI, BENOZZO DI LESE, d. 1497, Florentine painter who worked with both Ghiberti and Fra Angelico. All his works reveal the latter's influence. He is best known for the *Procession of the Magi* frescoes in the Medici-Riccardi Palace, Florence. These demonstrate his unique talents

as a decorative painter. He also produced a series of 24 frescoes for the walls of the Camposanto at Pisa with subjects drawn from the Old Testament.

GRACE OF GOD, BY THE, expression of dependence on God used by the church since the early centuries and given sanction by the Council of Ephesus in 431. Secular rulers began to employ the phrase from the Carolingian period.

GRADO, town situated on an island between Venice and Trieste, a place of refuge during the periods of Hunnic and Lombard invasions, and a patriarchate in 606. In 1451 the patriarch moved his see to Venice.

GRADUAL (*Graduale*), book containing the antiphons, usually from the Psalms, which were sung immediately after the first Scriptural lesson. The name may have been derived from the practice of singing it either on the altar steps, on which the deacon was ascending or on the steps of the ambo. By the ninth century this book with its chants had become separated from the *Responsiale* and *Antiphonarium.* The term gradual was also given to the chant sung after the first Scripture reading at mass.

GRAFFITI, ancient inscriptions that were merely scratched and not carved. Many Christian graffiti appear in the catacombs of Rome and other ancient holy places. They took the form of memorials of the dead and of prayers to God and to the saints commemorated there.

GRAIL (Holy), a sacred object, sometimes believed to be the cup used by Christ at the Last Supper, possession of which was believed to assure its owner earthly or heavenly happiness. Only the virtuous could expect to find it, however, and most of those whom the courtly romances mention as seeking it were members of King Arthur's Round Table. In Wolfram von Eschenbach's *Parzival* the grail appears as a precious stone. The legend first appeared in the *Perceval* of Chrétien of Troyes (1189/90).

GRAMMAR, one of the seven liberal arts and a subject of the trivium. It remained the most important of the liberal arts until the rise of scholasticism in the twelfth century which placed greatest emphasis upon dialectic. The most popular of the textbooks used in the study of grammar was that of Donatus (mid-fourth century).

GRAN (Esztergom), city on the Danube north of Budapest, one of the oldest cities of Hungary. Stephen I was born and crowned in Gran. According to the *Nibelungenlied,* Attila made his capital in that city.

GRANADA, city and province in southern Spain which was conquered by the Moslems in 711. Granada became an independent Moorish state in 1238, but from 1246 paid tribute to Castile, and in 1492 finally became a part of Spain. The city's renowned Alhambra, erected between 1238 and 1358, served its Moorish monarchs as palace and fortress. The city was known not only for its brilliant culture but also for its industry and commerce.

GRANDE CHARTREUSE, ABBEY OF LA. *See* CHARTREUSE, LA GRANDE.

GRANDEE *(Grande),* title held by members of the highest nobility of Castile from the thirteenth century.

GRAND INQUISITOR, the official who directed the work of the Court of the Inquisition, later of the Spanish Inquisition, in a given region or country.

GRAND MASTER, title held by the head of military-religious and chivalric orders.

GRAND PENITENTIARY, official who headed the apostolic penitentiary in Rome. He made his appearance in the fourteenth century.

GRAND PRINCE, title of the Russian prince from the close of the twelfth century who enjoyed precedence over other Russian princes. The Poles and Liths also used the title.

GRANDMONT, ORDER OF, known as Grandmontines, a religious order of men founded in 1077 by St. Stephen of Muret (d. 1124). He established his abbey, the mother house of the order, at Grandmont in Normandy. Although the Grandmontines were classified as members of the Benedictine order, they patterned their lives after the example of the Camaldolese. The monks, who lived in individual cells, followed an unusually austere rule, while lay brothers performed the necessary labor and administered the institution.

GRANO, unit of weight in Italy, Spain, and Portugal, its name derived from the latin *granum* (grain) and of varying value. The term also applied to a small copper coin used in Aragon from the reign of Ferdinand II (1479–1516).

GRATIAN (Flavius Gratianus), Roman emperor, 375–83, son of Valentinian I, who shared the rule of the western half of the empire with his younger half-brother Valentinian II while his uncle Valens ruled the east. After the death of Valens (d. 378), Gratian appointed Theodosius to administer the eastern half of the empire. Gratian was slain by Maximus, an imperial pretender from Britain. With the approval of St. Ambrose, bishop of Milan, Gratian adopted a harsh policy against what pagan elements remained in the empire.

GRATIAN, d. probably before 1159, renowned canonist and father of canon law, a Camaldolese monk in the monastery of SS. Nabor and Felix in Bologna, and author of the *Decretum,* its longer title being *Concordia Discordantium Canonum* (1140). This is a collection of decretals, conciliar decrees, apostolic constitutions, and patristic texts, supplemented with some commentary and explanatory introductions. The *Decretum* constituted the basic text in the study of canon law, first at Bologna, then, before the close of the twelfth century, at Oxford, Paris, and other medieval universities.

GRATZ (Graz), city in Austria that originated

with a fortress erected in the second half of the tenth century to defend the Carinthian march. Emperor Frederick III (1440–93) made the city his residence.

GRAVAMINA, in general, complaints, more particularly ecclesiastical protests brought officially to the attention of a superior authority.

GRAY, JOHN DE, d. 1214, bishop of Norwich (1200), a loyal supporter of King John of England and his choice to succeed to the see of Canterbury upon the death of Archbishop Hubert Walter in 1205. The disputed election that followed led to a long and bitter contest between the king and Pope Innocent III. [*See* LANGTON, STEPHEN.] In 1209 John sent De Gray to serve as his justiciar in Ireland.

GRAY'S INN, one of the Inns of the Court at London that flourished in the fifteenth century.

GRAY, WILLIAM, d. 1478, nephew of Humphrey, duke of Buckingham, chancellor of Oxford, prothonotary apostolic under Pope Nicholas V, bishop of Ely, royal treasurer, scholar, and diplomat. He collected an impressive library.

GREAT SAINT BERNARD HOSPICE, refuge on the pass that ran between Martigny in Switzerland and Aosta in Italy. It was established c. 1050 by Bernard of Aosta and staffed by brothers, then canons, later by the Augustinians of Martigny.

GREAT SCHISM. *See* SCHISM, WESTERN.

GREAVES, armor used to protect the lower legs.

GREECE, part of the Eastern Roman or Byzantine empire after the division of the Roman world following the death of Theodosius in 395. All or the greater part of the peninsula suffered severely from devastating raids by Goths, Huns, Avars, Slavs, and Bulgars. Most of the invaders left little trace with the exception of the Slavs. The Macedonian emperors of Byzantium recovered and ruled the entire area (867–1025). In

the eleventh century new invaders appeared with the Turks and Normans. In the early thirteenth century western Crusaders (Fourth Crusade, 1202–4) destroyed the Byzantine empire and left most of Greece under the rule of Venice and of French, Flemish, and Italian nobles. In 1261 the revived Byzantine empire recovered some parts of Greece but most remained under the control of Venice and other Italian rulers. In 1456 all of the peninsula fell to the Ottoman Turks.

GREEK CROSS, a cross whose four arms were all equal in length.

GREEK FIRE, incendiary material composed of sulphur, lime, and other ingredients and used for the first time in medieval warfare in 673 when it helped throw back a Moslem attack on Constantinople. The mixture which was thrown out in pots or projected from tubes caught fire spontaneously when it struck water. Its invention has been credited to Callinicus about the year 673.

GREEK (Byzantine) RITE, liturgy used by Greek-speaking Christians of the Byzantine empire and by peoples converted by Byzantine missionaries. After the schism of 1054, the Latin church considered most of these Christians schismatics.

GREENLAND, island in the north Atlantic discovered by Eric the Red in 982. (It may have been discovered by the Norwegian Gunnbjorn Ulfsson early in the tenth century.) Some Norse settled on the southwest coast in 986. From Greenland Leif Ericson proceeded on to North America in 1003. In 1126 a bishop's seat was established at Gardar and in 1261 Norway incorporated the island into its empire. A bull of Pope Alexander made mention in 1492 of the serious plight of the colony, by which time most if not all the settlers had abandoned the island.

GREGORAS, NICEPHORUS, d. 1359, learned Byzantine historian and theologian. Because of his strong advocacy of the reunion of the Greek church with the Latin he fell into disfavor. Later his opposition to the teachings of the Hesychasts brought him imprisonment. His scientific writings included a plan of calendar reform similar to that adopted in the sixteenth century (Gregorian Calendar). His Roman history covered the period 1204 to 1359. He also left funeral orations and treatises on philosophical and literary subjects.

GREGORIAN CHANT, a body of plain chant, unisonal and ecclesiastical, that the papal choir developed during the course of the fifth and sixth centuries. The music bears the name Gregorian for the codification that took place during the pontificate of Gregory the Great (590–604). Gregorian chant covered all the services of the Roman rite, principally the mass and the divine office. [See MUSIC.]

GREGORIAN MASSES, thirty masses said on successive days for the dead. The practice has been attributed to Pope Gregory I (the Great) (590–604).

GREGORIAN REFORM, reform of the church dramatized by Pope Gregory VII (1073–85) in his contest with Henry IV of Germany over investiture, but already well started on its way by Leo IX (1049–54) and succeeding popes. The prime objective of the reformers was the elimination of secular interference in the selection of bishops as the prerequisite to achieving the suppression of such abuses as simony and concubinage among the clergy.

GREGORIUS AKINDYNOS, d. c. 1349, Byzantine monk, priest, and theologian who attacked the views of Palamas in the controversy over Hesychasm. He was himself condemned as a heretic by synods in 1347 and 1351. He composed verse, letters, and writings on the subject of Hesychasm.

GREGORY I (the Great), ST., Pope, 590–604, a leading church father, member of a patrician family of Rome, and prefect of the city. About the year 575 he turned his back on a political career, became a monk (possibly Benedictine), and established a number of monasteries on his family's estates in Sicily. He entered the papal service with reluctance, served as ambassador at Constantinople (579–86), then became the principal adviser of Pope Pelagius II whom he succeeded. As pope he encouraged missionary activities—he sent Augustine with a band of monks to Britain—promoted the spread of monasticism, reformed the liturgy, and introduced a standard of practices in the church that continued to be observed through medieval times. Again with considerable reluctance he assumed the responsibility for protecting Rome from the Lombards, thereby initiating the role of the pope as temporal ruler. Despite his poor health and an extremely heavy burden of pastoral responsibilities, he found time to compose several highly influential books: *On Pastoral Rule,* which was to serve bishops as a guide in the direction of their dioceses; *Dialogues,* a collection of edifying stories about the saints, including Benedict; and *Moralia,* an introduction to Christian ethics based upon the *Book of Job.*

GREGORY II, ST., Pope, 715–31, a priest of Rome who as pope adopted a firm policy toward the Byzantine emperor Leo III on the issue of iconoclasm, and encouraged the work of Boniface and other missionaries in Germany. He had the walls about Rome repaired against the threat of Saracen attacks. His relations with the Lombards were, for the most part, friendly.

GREGORY III, ST., Pope, 731–41, a Syrian, clashed with the Byzantine emperor Leo III over iconoclasm and decreed the excommunication of any person who destroyed sacred images. Leo retaliated by removing Sicily, southern Italy, and Illyricum from papal control. Although Gregory was unsuccessful in enlisting the assistance of Charles Martel against the Lombards, he did have his cooperation in establishing new dioceses east of the Rhine.

GREGORY IV, Pope, 827–44, a Roman priest who as pope became deeply involved as would-be conciliator in the wars among Louis the Pious and his sons. He promulgated the observance of the Feast of All Saints.

GREGORY V, Pope, 996–9, chaplain of Otto III of Germany who arranged for his election as pope. The same year that Gregory was elected, he crowned Otto III Roman emperor. Otto seized John XVI, the pope (antipope) recognized by Constantinople, and imprisoned and blinded him.

GREGORY VI, Pope, May 1045 to December 1046, was elected upon the resignation of the unworthy Benedict IX but against the opposition of the Crescenti and Tusculani factions in Rome. On the charge of simony which could not be substantiated, Henry III of Germany ordered him exiled to Germany where Hildebrand, later Pope Gregory VII, accompanied him.

GREGORY VII, ST., Pope, 1073–85, born c. 1025 in Tuscany, as monk known as Hildebrand, accompanied Pope Gregory VI to exile in Germany (1046), then returned to Rome c. 1050 and rose to a position of great influence during the pontificates of Nicholas II (1058–61) and Alexander II (1061–73). Scholars believe that the decree entitled *Dictatus Pape,* which affirmed papal claims to supremacy over kings in matters of faith and morals, even to the point of deposing them, was drawn up by him. His decree in 1075 which condemned lay investiture precipitated a bitter contest with Henry IV of Germany. Because Gregory found the German princes equally hostile to Henry, he won the first round in the struggle, and the king made an abject submission at Canossa in January 1077. Gregory's subsequent excommunication of Henry, however, brought that king south of the Alps with an Army, followed by the pope's flight from Rome with Robert Guiscard and his Normans who had come to his defense.

GREGORY VIII, Pope, October 21 to December 17, 1187, Canon Regular of St. Augustine, cardinal, and chancellor. As pope he introduced some reforms in the Curia and initiated steps for a Crusade against the Moslems. He died before he reached Rome.

GREGORY VIII, Pope (antipope), 1118–21, Benedictine monk, bishop of Coimbra, and archbishop of Braga. Although he owed his election as pope to Henry V of Germany, Pope Callistus II who was considered the legitimate pope had him seized and imprisoned. He died in prison in 1137.

GREGORY IX, Pope, 1227–41, a nephew of Innocent III, student at Paris and Bologna. In 1233 he established the Court of the Inquisition in order to facilitate the eradication of heresy. In September 1227 he excommunicated Frederick II of Germany when he failed to leave on a promised Crusade. He agreed to a reconciliation with Frederick in 1230, then again broke with him in 1239, after which he remained in bitter conflict with him until his own death. In 1241 he summoned a general council to Rome with the intention of having it declare Frederick excommunicate, but the emperor intercepted the ships bringing the cardinals south and thus prevented the council from meeting.

GREGORY X, BL., Pope, 1271–6, was chosen pope after an interval of three years following the death of Clement IV. He encouraged the organization of a Crusade against the Turks, helped persuade the German princes to elect a king (Rudolf of Hapsburg), convened the Council of Lyons II in 1274 in the hope of terminating the schism with the Greek church, and provided new rules to govern the election of future popes. Among the reforms was the introduction of the conclave as a means of expediting the election of a new pope.

GREGORY XI, Pope, 1370–8, nephew of Clement VI. He fought a war with Florence over papal territories which had revolted, sought to bring an end to the Hundred Years' War, condemned Wyclif's theses, and terminated the period of the Avignonese Residence when he returned to Rome in 1377. He was contemplating returning to Avignon when he died.

GREGORY XII, Pope, 1406–15, bishop of Castello and cardinal, resigned as pope in July 1415 after formally summoning the Council of Constance (1414–8). The council, which was already in session, had agreed with Emperor Sigismund to accept his resignation, thereby clearing the path for the end of the Western Schism. Gregory retired to Porto as bishop and died there in 1417.

GREGORY III, patriarch of Constantinople, 1443–51, attended the Council of Ferrara-Florence (1438–39), accepted union with the Latin church, and composed two treatises in support of that union. The hostility to this union and to himself which he encountered in Constantinople led him to retire to Rome, where he died.

GREGORY IX, DECRETALS OF, a collection in one volume of papal decretals and constitutions promulgated by Pope Gregory IX in 1234. The collection embodied those issued by his papal predecessors since the appearance of Gratian's *Decretum* (c. 1140), together with his own constitutions. The Spanish Dominican Raymond of Penafort, who did most of the work of compiling, failed to correct errors and false ascriptions. The collection makes up the core of the *Corpus Iuris Canonici* of 1582.

GREGORY OF NAZIANZUS, ST., d. c. 390, father and doctor of the church, studied at Caesarea, Alexandria, and Athens, and became a friend and associate of Basil and Gregory of Nyssa (the three Cappadocians). Upon the urging of Basil, he accepted in 381 the office of archbishop of Constantinople but resigned that see after a few months and retired to Nazianzus. Although he gained fame as a preacher, he made his principal contribution to Christianity through his writings —sermons, letters, and theological orations—

which together with the efforts of Gregory of Nyssa and Basil proved successful in preventing the triumph of Arianism. He also composed some 16,000 lines of religious verse.

GREGORY OF NYSSA, ST., d. c. 395, father of the church, brother of Basil and friend of Gregory of Nazianzus. These three church fathers are known as the "Three Cappadocians." After the death of his wife, Gregory entered the monastery that Basil had established in Pontus, became bishop of Nyssa (371), and metropolitan of Caesarea (380). Gregory, who was a noted exegete and a vigorous foe of Arianism, possessed a thorough knowledge of Greek philosophy and is considered the most speculative of the Eastern church fathers.

GREGORY OF RIMINI, d. 1358, a member of the Hermits of St. Augustine and prior general of the order (1357). He taught at Bologna, Padua, Perugia, and Paris, and is considered a leading Augustinian philosopher and theologian. His thoroughly Augustinian writings reveal the influence of William of Ockham but without that scholar's tendency toward skepticism. Because he maintained that unbaptized infants were damned, he earned the title "tortor infantium."

GREGORY OF TOURS, d. 594, famous bishop of Tours (573) and author of a history of the Franks. He was a member of the Gallo-Roman aristocracy, proved himself an able and courageous prelate in that dangerous, unstable age, and left hagiographical writings and a treatise on church offices. His history, written in unadorned, if not unscholarly, Latin constitutes the most valuable source for his period.

GREGORY PALAMAS, ST., d. 1359, Greek theologian and a leading exponent of Hesychasm. With his two brothers he went to Mt. Athos where he learned about the Hesychast tradition of mystical prayer. He fled to Thessalonica to escape the Turks, was ordained a priest, then became a hermit. In 1331 he returned to Mt. Athos where he composed his most important work, *Triads in Defense of the Holy Hesychasts,* a defense of the contemplative practices of the Hesychasts. He was also the author of ascetical works, homilies, and letters.

GREGORY SINAITES, d. 1346, monk and mystic of Cyprus, Palestine, and Mt. Athos, and founder of a monastery on Mt. Paroria in Bulgaria. He composed theological and ascetical works, tropes, and hymns.

GREGORY THAUMATURGUS, ST., d. c. 270, church father, a disciple of Origen who converted him from paganism. He became bishop of Neo-Caesarea in Pontus and, according to contemporary accounts, was the worker of many miracles, hence his title of "wonder-worker." His writings include exegetical and theological works, also a panegyric of Origen. He was a practical churchman rather than a speculative theologian.

GREGORY THE ILLUMINATOR, ST., d. 332?, the "Apostle of Armenia," first metropolitan of Armenia and revered as the founder of the Armenian church. He converted King Tiridates who then proclaimed Armenia a Christian country. He lived his last years as a solitary in the desert.

GREMIALE, cloth which the bishop spread over his lap when seated on his throne while distributing blessed candles or engaged in similar activities, in order to protect his vestments.

GRENDEL, a monster slain by Beowulf.

GRENOBLE, city of southeastern France, the major city of Dauphiné. A bishopric was founded there in the fourth century. Its cathedral is from the twelfth-thirteenth century; the palace occupied by the dauphins dates from the late Middle Ages (Renaissance). The university was chartered in 1339. In 1349 Grenoble and all of Dauphiné were ceded to France.

GRIFFIN, legendary animal of the ancient and medieval world which was supposed to have the body of a lion, the head of an eagle, and wings.

GRIFFON (grijpen), Dutch coin of the late Middle Ages which bore the figure of a griffin.

GRISELDA, heroine who appeared in Petrarch, Boccaccio, and Chaucer as the long-suffering wife whose loyalty and humility finally convinced her husband of her fidelity and virtue. The model is supposed to have been the marquise of Saluzzo (eleventh century), whose husband subjected her to numerous tests of her loyalty and devotion.

GROAT, name of a coin small in value but thick, which was first noted in use in the Low Countries. It was issued in England by Edward I (1272–1307).

GROCYN, WILLIAM, d. 1519, English humanist, attended Oxford, later taught at Magdalen and Exeter Colleges. For two years he studied Greek and Latin in Italy, then returned to England where he was recognized as the leading scholar and teacher of the day. Colet, More, Linacre, and Erasmus were his friends.

GROOTE, GERHARD, d. 1384, member of a wealthy family of Deventer, studied at Cologne, Paris, and Prague, spent two years in a Carthusian monastery, then became a deacon and preacher in the diocese of Utrecht. His sermons which preached apostolic poverty and the simple life as necessary to a reform of the Christian community antagonized members of the higher clergy who had him silenced. His disciples at Deventer and Zwolle founded the Brethren of the Common Life, he himself the Sisters of the Common Life. His preaching, together with his mystical, ascetical writings, earned him recognition as the father of the *devotio moderna.* He was instrumental in making the spirituality of mysticism more practical, moderate, and methodical.

GROS, old French small silver coin first minted in 1266; a French unit of weight.

GROSSETESTE, ROBERT, d. 1253, a leading medieval scientist and scholar, probably studied at Oxford, then at Paris, taught theology at Oxford, and became the first chancellor of the university. In 1235 he was consecrated bishop of Lincoln. He composed a number of mathematical, scientific, and philosophical studies as well as allegories, sermons, and commentaries on the Bible. He urged the study of Arabic, Greek, and mathematics in order to advance the knowledge of science. He himself made a significant contribution in the realm of optics and calendar reform. His most famous pupil was Roger Bacon. Grosseteste, who was a zealous bishop, urged his priests to preach, invited Franciscans to come to Lincoln, and opposed papal appointments to benefices within his diocese. He also showed his courage in opposing the policies of Henry III although he never aligned himself with the king's political foes.

GROSSO, small Italian coin minted in Genoa since 1172, since 1182 in Florence.

GROS TURNOIS, a small coin or groat minted in Tours.

GROSZ, Polish coin similar to the English groat.

GROTEN (Grot, Grote), small silver coin of the Netherlands and northern Germany which was minted from the beginning of the fourteenth century.

GRUFFYDD AP LLEWELYN. See LLEWELYN AP GRUFFYDD.

GRUNWALD (Grünewald), BATTLE OF, a battle, also known as Tannenberg, fought on July 15, 1410, east of the Vistula, which ended in a major defeat of the Teutonic Knights at the hands of the Poles and Lithuanians. It heralded the rapid decline of the Teutonic order.

GUADELUPE, FRIARY OF, monastery near Cáceres, Spain, founded as a shrine for a statue of the Virgin which Pope Gregory was supposed to have sent to Leander of Seville. The statue was concealed when the Moors invaded Spain and discovered only c. 1300. Guadelupe became one of Spain's most popular shrines.

GUARDIAN, a superior of a Franciscan house, not designated a prior because of Francis of Assisi's dislike of that official. The superiors in the Franciscan order were expected to serve, not rule, their fellow friars.

GUARDIAN ANGEL, the angel, based on Jewish tradition and on Matthew 18:10 and Acts 12:15, which Christian theologians believed God had assigned each individual to guard him against the threat of spiritual and physical harm. Several theologians, including Basil, would have limited such angels to Christians. Thomas Aquinas held that only angels of the lowest order served as guardians.

GUARINO DA VERONA, d. 1460, Italian humanist and outstanding scholar of the classics, studied at Padua, Venice, and in Greece, and taught Graeco-Roman antiquities in several Italian cities including Venice, Verona, and Ferrara. He translated and edited a number of Greek and Latin classics.

GUDRUN (Kudrun), in the *Volsungasaga* the wife of Sigurd (Siegfried), then of Atli (Attila the Hun) whom she stabbed to death for his treachery. She corresponded to Kriemhild in the *Nibelungenlied* but was more savage.

GUELFS AND GHIBELLINES, two Italian parties which traced their origin to the contest between Otto IV and Frederick II for possession of Germany and the Holy Roman Empire (c. 1212–8), although they made their appearance in many cities of northern Italy only later, during the years when Frederick II was seeking to gain control of the peninsula (c. 1230–50). The term Guelf is derived from the family of the Welfs which ruled Bavaria, the term Ghibelline from Weibelungen (Waiblingen), the name of one of the Hohenstaufen castles in Swabia. Since members of the Hohenstaufen dynasty, that is,

Frederick I Barbarossa, Henry VI, and Frederick II, occupied the throne for the greater part of the century following 1152, they and their adherents became identified as advocates of a strong monarchy, while those who opposed them were assumed to champion the autonomy of feudal princes. Because the pope felt his own independence menaced by the ambitions of the Hohenstaufens, he traditionally placed himself in the camp of the Guelfs. After the death of Conradin in 1268 and the extinction of the Hohenstaufen dynasty, the identifications of Ghibelline and Guelf became mere political labels.

GUESCLIN, BERTRAND DU. *See* DUGUESCLIN, BERTRAND.

GUGEL (Gugele, Kogel, Kugel), hooded head-covering with neck-piece that was worn by the peasantry, also by members of the aristocracy when hunting or traveling

GUIBERT OF NOGENT, d. 1124, abbot of the Benedictine monastery of Nogent-sous-Coucy in the diocese of Laon, author of an autobiography, theological works, and a history of the First Crusade *(Gesta Dei per Francos)*. This history is useful although largely a paraphrase of the anonymous *Gesta Francorum.*

GUIBERT OF RAVENNA, d. 1100, imperial chancellor for Italy, appointed archbishop of Ravenna in 1072 by Henry IV of Germany, then chosen pope (Clement III) in June 1080 when so nominated by Henry. As archbishop he had shown himself one of the leading opponents of the Gregorian reform movement in Germany and its principal objective of eliminating lay interference in church appointments. With Henry's assistance, he took possession of Rome in 1084 and was recognized as pope by a majority of the cardinals and the greater part of Europe.

GUIBERT OF TOURNAI, d. 1284, Franciscan theologian, author of a history of the first Crusade of Louis IX (1248–54), sermons, a com-

mentary on the *Sentences,* and mystical, homiletic, and ascetical works.

GUIDO DE BAYSIO, d. 1313, teacher of canon law at Bologna and author of a work that supplemented Gratian's *Decretum.* Guido introduced materials from decretists and decretalists whom Gratian had not considered.

GUIDO DA SIENA, Italian painter of the second half of the thirteenth century and founder of the Sienese school. His human figures as they appear in the *Madonna and Child* in the Siena Town Hall assume a natural posture considered quite unusual for this early period (c. 1271).

GUIDO OF AREZZO, d. 1050, founder of the system of modern musical notation, a Benedictine monk, teacher at the cathedral school of Arezzo, and from 1047 prior of the Camaldolese monastery at Avellana. He is credited with introducing the four-line staff and square notes. His *Micrologus* is a major source of our knowledge of organum.

GUIENNE (Guyenne), duchy which first constituted roughly the northern half of Aquitaine but from the fourteenth century comprised the entire region of south-western France held by the English. It became an English possession in 1152 when Eleanor of Aquitaine married Henry (II) of England. The French recovered possession of Guienne by 1453, but the king secured direct control of the duchy only in 1472.

GUIGO (Guiguese du Chastel, de Castro), d. 1136, prior of the Carthusian monastery of La Grande Chartreuse and author of the *Consuetudines Cartusiae,* a codification of the customs regulating the lives of the monks in Carthusian houses. The *Consuetudines* were accepted as the rule of the order.

GUILD (gild), a term originally given to any association organized for mutual protection and aid, including a religious confraternity. The term applied more generally to trade associations, which appeared in Germany in the eighth century, in England in the tenth, and which flourished in western Europe during the twelfth and thirteenth centuries. Their aims included the protection of their members from the competition of foreign merchants and craftsmen and the maintenance of industrial and commercial standards. The first guilds were probably merchant guilds that, as industry expanded and grew more specialized, were replaced by craft guilds. A charter which the lord (king) granted the town customarily provided them this protection, while the guild itself assured the production of goods of reasonable quality by maintaining a system of industrial education [*see* APPRENTICE, JOURNEYMAN], and by enforcing guild regulations to that end. Although the guild was engaged in buying and selling, as an institution it was noncapitalistic. Members of the guild were forbidden to compete with one another, while all merchants sold their commodities at a "just price." [*See* JUST PRICE.] The expansion of capitalism, more particularly the impact of intra- and international trade, brought substantial alteration to the guild structure. Only in those industries that placed a premium upon skilled labor did that spirit of brotherhood which in the early guilds had prevailed among masters, journeymen, and apprentices outlive the Middle Ages.

GUILLAUME DE LORRIS. *See* ROMAN DE LA ROSE.

GUILLAUME D'ORANGE. *See* ORANGE, GUILLAUME D'.

GUINES, city and county in northern France directly across from Dover. It passed under English rule in 1352, was recovered by the French in 1413, then was inherited by Charles the Bold of Burgundy. After the death of Charles in 1477, it returned to French control.

GUINEVERE (Guanhamara, Ganievre, Ginevra, Ginover), the wife of King Arthur.

GUISCARD, ROBERT, d. 1085, son of Tancred of Hauteville and father of Bohemond, a leader of the First Crusade. Guiscard, one of the most ambitious and ruthless of Norman adventurers to come to southern Italy, conquered Apulia and Calabria, then accepted papal suzerainty after defeating Leo IX and his army. When he captured Bari in 1071, he extinguished the last Byzantine foothold in Italy. In 1084 he left Greece where he had been campaigning to come to Pope Gregory VII's rescue and drive Henry IV and his German army out of Rome. He died while directing the siege of Cephalonia.

GUITAR, musical stringed instrument used in the fifteenth century.

GUITMOND OF AVERSA, d. c. 1090, monk of the Benedictine monastery of La Croix-Saint-Leufroy (Evreux), then of Bec, later bishop of Aversa (southern Italy). The treatise he composed on the eucharist to confute the position of Berengar of Tours influenced subsequent thought despite its own lack of complete orthodoxy.

GUITTONE D'AREZZO, d. 1294, Italian lyric poet, founder of the school of Tuscan poetry and considered the inventor of the sacred ballad. He also composed letters in literary Italian prose.

GUNDOBAD (Gundibald, Gundebald), d. 516, king of Burgundy who fought with Clovis in 507 against the Visigoths. He ordered the preparation of the *Lex Romana Burgundionum* for the Roman population, the *Lex Gundobada* for his own people.

GUNNAR, in the *Edda,* Gunther, king of the Burgundians; in the *Volsungasaga,* the king of the Nibelungs; the central figure in *Njal's Saga.*

GUNPOWDER, a mixture of saltpeter, sulphur, and charcoal and capable of causing explosive effects. It was known in the West by the third quarter of the twelfth century. Its origins are obscure but it may have been known in China as early as the ninth century. The first gun to use gunpowder appeared c. 1325.

GUNTHER, king of Burgundy in the *Nibelungenlied,* the brother of Kriemhild and the husband of Brunhild. His name has been traced to Gundahar, king of Burgundy (c. 412–36).

GUNTHER OF PAIRIS, d. c. 1220, tutor of Conrad, the son of Frederick I Barbarossa, who joined the Cistercian community at Pairis. He composed narratives, largely in verse, about the First and Fourth Crusades, also a poetical version of Otto of Freising's *Gesta Frederici.*

GUNTRAM, d. 593, Frankish king of Burgundy and Orléans, son of Clotaire I. His principal objective was to bring stability to the Merovingian world by establishing a balance of power between his two warring brothers, Sigebert I and Chilperic I. Because of his orthodoxy and his interest in peace, he was revered as a saint.

GURDE, flask carried by medieval pilgrims and soldiers that was made of glass, clay, or metal. It might also be a dried gourd.

GUTENBERG, JOHN, d. 1468, in the opinion of most scholars the inventor of the printing press c. 1445. He did so with the help of money borrowed from John Fust who foreclosed and took over the press in 1455. Although no work bearing the name of Gutenberg as printer survives, it is believed that the so-called Gutenberg Bible and the Psalter were nearing completion before Gutenberg's break with Fust.

GUTHRUM (Guthrun, Godrum, Guthorm), d. 890, Danish king who accepted the peace of Wedmore from Alfred the Great in 878. The treaty extended him jurisdiction over the Danelaw, roughly northeastern England north of the Thames-Lea line. He also accepted baptism for himself and his people.

GUY OF BAZOCHES, d. 1203, author of a chronicle of the Third Crusade, a universal history from Constantine to 1199, and some writing on geography.

GUY OF LUSIGNAN. *See* LUSIGNAN.

GWYNEDD, Welsh princedom in northwest Wales founded in the fifth century by Cunedag. According to Nennius, this was the foundation of the early Welsh dynasty.

HAAKON I (the Good), king of Norway, c. 946–61, son of Harald Haarfager who sent him to England when he was one, where he grew up at the court of Athelstan. At the age of 15 he crossed to Norway and with the help of English arms seized the throne from his tyrannical half-brother Eric Bloodaxe. Haakon, who had been raised a Christian, failed in his efforts to establish Christianity in his land and was eventually forced to abandon his faith and adopt paganism. He died in battle with the sons of Eric who had the help of Danish forces.

HAAKON (the Great), d. 995, ruled the greater part of Norway for many years as jarl, not as king. He aided his suzerain Harald Gormsson, king of Denmark, against Otto II of Germany, and later repudiated Denmark's overlordship as well as his Christian faith. He grew unpopular in his last years and was murdered when Olaf I Tryggvason, son of a Norwegian jarl, invaded Norway and claimed the throne.

HAAKON IV (Haakonsson the Old), king of Norway, 1217–63, statesman and patron of letters, devoted his first years to putting down revolts, then stabilized his throne by having himself crowned by a papal legate in 1247 at Bergen. In 1261 he annexed Greenland, the following year Iceland, but he failed in his efforts to make good Norway's claims to the Hebrides. During his reign Old Norse literature flowered, and Snorri Sturluson spent some time at his court. Haakon is credited with carrying out important legal reforms.

HAARLEM (Harlem), town on the Spaarne river near its mouth on the North Sea, the residence of the counts of Holland and a prosperous community already by the twelfth century. It received its town charter in 1245.

HABSBURG. *See* HAPSBURG.

HADEWIJCH (Hedwig), BL., a mystic of the thirteenth century, probably of noble birth, born in Antwerp, who lived with a community of pious women similar to those of the Beguines which were soon to appear. She composed verse in the genre of the troubadours about her love of God. She wrote her letters and the account of her visions in the earliest prose in Dutch literature.

HADITH, that is, a saying or sacred tradition, based upon Mohammed's words (exclusive of those contained in the Koran) and actions. These traditions embody the *Sunna*. Perhaps most of the controversy engaged in by Moslem theologians during the early centuries following the Prophet's death was over the question which of the words and actions attributed to him were authentic and which were not.

HADRIAN I, Pope. *See* ADRIAN, I, Pope.

HADRIAN (the African)/(Hadrian of Canterbury), ST., d. 709, an African by birth, head of a monastery near Naples, who accompanied Theodore of Tarsus to England in 668. In England he became abbot of the monastery of SS. Peter and Paul at Canterbury and master of the school. During his 40 years in England he labored earnestly to bring that country's religious customs and practices in conformity with those of Rome. He was greatly interested in education and established schools in different parts of the country.

HADRIANA COLLECTIO, collection of church canons which Pope Adrian I gave to Charlemagne in 774. Most of these canons were taken from the *Dionysiana Collectio.*

HADSCHAR AL-ASWAD, the black stone enclosed in the southeastern corner of the Kaaba. Moslems believed Allah had given the stone to Abraham.

HAERETICO COMBURENDO, DE. *See* DE HERETICO COMBURENDO.

HAFIZ (Shamsuddin Muhammed), d. c. 1390, surname of the leading lyric Persian poet; a name designating anyone who had memorized the Koran. Hafiz, who lived his entire life in Shiraz, lectured on the Koran and other religious subjects and wrote commentaries on several religious classics. He was a dedicated Sufi.

HAGAR (Agar), concubine of Abraham, the mother of Ismael, from whom some Arabs traced their descent. Her supposed grave in Mecca became a Moslem shrine.

HAGEN OF TRONJE, in the *Nibelungenlied,* the vassal of Gunther who slew Siegfried in order to avenge the slight done to Brunhild, the wife of Gunther. In an older Norse tradition, Hagen did not murder Siegfried. In *Kudrum* he is the son of a king of Ireland who rescues three princesses, one of whom he marries. There is no link here with the Burgundian saga of the *Nibelungenlied.*

HAGGADAH (Hagada, Agada), nonlegal content of Jewish tradition as opposed to the Halakah. It consists of legends, proverbs, and exegetical writings of an allegorical character and provides matter of ethical, devotional, and historical interest.

HAGIA SOPHIA, the great domed basilica in Constantinople, dedicated to the Blessed Wisdom, which the emperor Justinian erected on the site of an earlier church of the same name which had been destroyed in the Nika riots of 532. The architects of the edifice were Anthemius of Tralles and Isidore of Miletus. The church's renowned dome which rests upon spherical pendentives rises 184 feet above the floor of the nave. The four minarets which rise at the different corners of the structure were added by the Turks when they transformed the church into a mosque. A lyrical description of the wonders of the building is found in Procopius's *Buildings.*

HAGIOS O THEOS. *See* AGIOS O THEOS.

HAGUE, THE, city in Holland that originated as a hunting lodge of the count of Holland. The town, which had grown into a prosperous settlement by 1370, took root around the castle erected there in 1248 by Count William II.

HAI BEN SHERIRA, d. 1038, *gaon* of the Pumbeditha academy in Baghdad. The academy enjoyed its greatest distinction during the period of his presidency. The 1,000 *responsa* that he prepared on points in the Talmud exceeded in number those offered by all the other *gaonim* combined.

HAIL MARY, popular prayer to Mary, the mother of God, which gradually acquired its form from the sixth to the sixteenth centuries. It represents a joining of the announcement of Christ's birth which Gabriel made to the Virgin (Luke 1:28) with Elizabeth's words when meeting Mary (Luke 1:42), and a concluding petition for assistance. Its devotional use dates from the eleventh century; the petition part came into general use only in the sixteenth.

HAIMON'S CHILDREN, the four sons of Count Haimon of Dordogne. They were Adelhart, Ritsart, Witsart, and Rainald. Haimon assumed the role of the hero in the best-known of the Carolingian sagas. The story of the children originated with St. Reinoldus and Charles Martel.

HAINAUT (Hainault, Hannegau, Henegouwen), country that appeared in the region of the upper

Scheldt from the late Carolingian period. The division of the Carolingian empire in 843 left it a fief of Lotharingia. It became the possession of the count of Flanders in the eleventh century, was joined to Holland and Zeeland in 1299, and passed under control of Philip the Good, the duke of Burgundy, in 1433. The Hapsburgs acquired it through the marriage in 1477 of the Archduke Maximilian to Mary of Burgundy.

HAIR SHIRT, penitential garment, woven usually from the hair of mountain goats or camels, which pious persons might wear next to the skin as a means of self-discipline. It also served as the garb of public penitents. In the late Middle Ages a strip of haircloth might be worn about the waist or as a scapular during the seasons of Lent and Advent.

HAITI, island in the Caribbean discovered by Columbus in December 1492 and given the name Española (Hispaniola). Here Columbus established the first Spanish colony in America. It comprised a group of 38 members of his crew, but all were killed by the Indians once he had left the island. A second colony founded in 1493 grew into the city of Santo Domingo.

HAKIM, in the Islamic world a learned man, judge, or doctor.

HAKIM, AL (Abu 'Ali Mansur Al-Hakim), sixth Fatimid caliph who became ruler in Cairo in 996 at the age of eleven. During his administration he appears to have encouraged the persecution of non-Moslems. Before he disappeared in 1021, some of the extreme followers of Isma'ilism hailed him as the incarnation of the divinity. [See DRUZES.]

HALBERD (halbert, halbard), combination spear, hook and battle-ax, approximately 8 feet long, which came into use in the fifteenth century. It was a favorite weapon with the Swiss.

HALES, ALEXANDER OF. See ALEXANDER OF HALES.

HALIDON HILL, BATTLE OF, battle fought in 1333 near Berwick where Edward III gained a smashing victory over a larger Scottish army. The English viewed the victory as avenging the destruction of their army by the Scots at Bannockburn in 1314.

HALLAJ, AL- (Abu Al-Mughith Al-Husain Ibn Mansur Ibn Mahamma Al-Baidawi), a celebrated Moslem mystic of Persia, usually known as Mansur, who served for some time as spiritual director of important functionaries at the Abbasid court in Baghdad. In 922 he was charged with heresy and executed, although leading mystics, including Al-Ghazali, insisted that the accusations brought against him were false.

HALLE, town in Germany about 20 miles northwest of Leipzig. First mention of it in 806 spoke of a fortress erected on the Saale. In 968 Otto I turned Halle and its valuable saltworks over to the newly founded archdiocese of Magdeburg and in 981 Otto II gave it a charter. In the thirteenth century it became a member of the Hanseatic League. In 1478 the town lost its liberties to the archbishop.

HALLELUJAH. See ALLELUIA.

HALLOWEEN. See ALL SAINTS, FEAST OF.

HALLUM, ROBERT, d. 1417, received a doctorate in law at Oxford, became chancellor of the university in 1403, and bishop of Salisbury in 1407. He attended the Council of Pisa (1409) and would have been created cardinal by Pope John XXIII had not Henry IV of England objected. At the Council of Constance (1414-8) he served as president of the English nation.

HALMWURF, a German phrase, meaning the throwing of a stalk (spear), which according to old German law sealed an agreement. It usually involved a transfer of land.

HALO (nimbus), a ring or disk of light about the head of a person symbolizing sanctity. It was already in use in Hellenistic art. It was conventional to use a triangular halo in representations of God or the Trinity, a round one for angels and saints, and a rectangular one to designate a living person who was considered holy.

HALSGERICHT, literally a throat or neck court, that is, a German court of the late Middle Ages that handled capital crimes.

HAMADHANI, AL- (Abu Al-Fadl Ahmad Ibn Al-Husain Al-Hamadhani), d. 1007, Arabic poet of Persia and Afghanistan whom contempories hailed as Badi' al-Zaman, the "Wonder of the Age." He introduced the *maqama* into Arabic poetry which was essentially an anecdote or short story that held a depth of meaning and was composed in ornate, rhythmic prose.

HAMASAH, an anthology of Arabic poems that extolled fortitude and patience, assembled by Abu Tammam (d. 845). The constancy that a man of patience and fortitude would develop was known as *hamasah*. One of the principal values of the *Hamasah* was its store of ancient legends.

HAMBURG, city on the lower Elbe some 68 miles from its mouth which took root at the fortress (Hammaburg) constructed there by Charlemagne against the Slavs and a church he had erected in 811. It served as a center of missionary work in the conversion of Scandinavia and of the lands to the east. In 831 Hamburg became a bishop's seat and three years later that of an archdiocese. Despite successive destructions by the Vikings, it managed to prosper, particularly from 1189 when it received a liberal grant of privileges from Frederick I Barbarossa in return for the financial assistance it had extended him for his crusade (Third Crusade). Its alliance with Lübeck helped prepare the foundations of the Hanseatic League of which Hamburg always remained a principal member.

HAMBURG-BREMEN, SEE OF, an archdiocese established in 847, shortly after the Northmen had destroyed Hamburg (845), when King Louis the German moved Ansgar, the archbishop of Hamburg, to the see of Bremen which was vacant. In 864 Pope Nicholas I confirmed Ansgar as archbishop of Hamburg and bishop of Bremen and made it independent of the archdiocese of Cologne. The archbishop made his home in Bremen. The archdiocese served as a center of Missionary activity in Scandinavia and claimed jurisdiction over that entire area until 1104 when the province of Lund was founded.

HAMDANI (Abu Mohammed Al-Hasan Ibn Ahmad Ibn Ya 'kub Al-Hamdani), d. 945, Arab geographer, grammarian, and poet of Yemen. His *Geography of the Arabian Peninsula* is the most valuable ancient work on the subject. He also wrote many volumes concerning the genealogies of the Himyarites and the wars of their kings.

HAMDANIDS, Arab dynasty that originated in northern Iraq and ruled Mosul and Aleppo c. 931 to 1003.

HAMELN (Hamelin), town in Lower Saxony which grew up in the eighth century near a monastery that monks from Fulda had founded on a crossing of the Weser. It served as a missionary and military center, became a market in the tenth century, and a city c. 1200. Until 1259 it was subject to the abbey of Fulda.

HAMMAD AL-RAWIYAH (Abu Al-Qasim Hammad Ibn Abi Laila Sabur), d. c. 772, Arab poet and genealogist who lived for many years in Damascus where he enjoyed the favor of the caliph. Contemporaries considered him the leading authority on ancient poetry, genealogies, and dialects.

HAMMUDS, Spanish-Arab dynasty established at Córdoba in 1016 by Ali ibn Hammud, member of the Idrisid ruling house in north Africa. It endured until 1058.

HANBALITES, an Islamic school of theology, law, and morality that accepted only the Koran and the *Hadith* as the basis for all legal cases, right conduct, and belief. Its founder, Ahmad Ibn Hanbal (d. 855), himself gathered about 80,000 *hadiths* that he judged to be genuine.

HANIFITES, followers of Abu Hanifa (d. 767), who subscribed to a liberal, if not wholly individual, interpretation of Moslem legal and ritualistic requirements.

HANNIBALDUS DE HANNIBALDIS, d. 1272, Dominican theologian and cardinal who studied under Thomas Aquinas at Paris and succeeded to his chair there. He was the author of a commentary on the *Sentences* which was once attributed to Aquinas.

HANNOVER, city in Lower Saxony, mentioned as a village c. 1100, which was destroyed in 1189 by Henry (VI), son of Frederick I Barbarossa, in a campaign against Henry the Lion. It was later restored and received city rights in 1241. In 1386 it joined the Hanseatic League.

HANSA (Hanse), medieval guild of merchants; the Hanseatic League.

HANSEATIC LEAGUE (Hansa, Hanse), an association of merchants and towns of north Germany organized for the purpose of advancing trade by providing mutual assistance against piracy and securing commercial privileges from foreign powers. Its origins reach back at least to 1157 when merchants of Cologne secured concessions from Henry II of England. During the twelfth and early thirteenth centuries Lübeck and other German towns gained mastery of the Baltic trade and with this a dominant position in the commerce of northern and western Europe. In 1210 Lübeck and Hamburg agreed to accept certain commercial principles as mutually binding, then in 1241 formally joined in an alliance against piracy. By 1265 all the towns which recognized the "Law of Lübeck" were cooperating in the suppression of piracy, while in 1293 different hansas, operating in London, Bruges, and the Baltic, joined together and formed a single association.

The principal objectives of the Hanseatic League included the suppression of piracy, the acquisition of commercial privileges in foreign countries, and the expediting of trade through the construction of devices such as lighthouses and buoys. During the fourteenth century the League assumed a more political character as resentment developed on the part of local mercantile interests in foreign countries against the monopolistic position it maintained. When such measures as boycott, embargo, and blockade failed to preserve its privileged position, the League undertook hostilities such as those against Waldemar, the ambitious king of Denmark. In the Peace of Stralsund (1370) the League forced him to grant its ships free passage through the Sound.

The membership of the Hanseatic League reached its high point about the middle of the fourteenth century when it numbered some 100 towns. The League suffered serious decline during the fifteenth century because of internal strife and competition, the rise of mercantilism, and the shifting of the herring fisheries from the Sound to the North Sea.

HAPSBURG (Habsburg), aristocratic family of Austria that derived its name from the castle of Habichtsburg ("hawk's castle") located in the Swiss canton of Aargau overlooking the Aar river. The family, which traced its origins to Guntram the Rich (d. 950), had become one of the most important in southwestern Germany by the early thirteenth century. In 1273 Rudolf IV, count of Hapsburg, was elected king of Germany, thereby bringing the Interregnum to an end. In 1282 he acquired the duchies of Austria and Styria for his sons Albert (I) and Rudolf. Albert ruled as king from 1298 until his murder in 1308, after which the royal title passed the family by until 1438. During this period the Swiss cantons were lost to the family, although Carinthia, Carniola, and Tyrol were acquired. In 1438 Albert of Austria succeeded to the territories of both the Hapsburg and the

Luxemburg families, a development that assured the Hapsburgs control of central Europe and the royal and imperial titles through to modern times. The marriage in 1477 of Maximilian to Mary, the daughter of Charles the Bold of Burgundy, added the Netherlands, Artois, and Franche-Comté to the Hapsburg domains.

HARALD BLUETOOTH, king of Denmark, c. 950–85, successor to his father, Gorm the Old. He extended his rule over Schleswig, the mouth of the Oder, and Norway. He recognized Otto I of Germany as his suzerain and was forced to accept Christianity.

HARALD I HAARFAGER (Fairhair), first king of Norway, c. 872–c. 933. He extended his authority over all the petty rulers of Norway with a great victory at Hafrs Fjord in 872. Some of the vanquished fled to Iceland and established the first Norwegian settlement in that island, while Rollo led a band of vikings to attack Normandy. Harald also extended his rule over the Shetland and Orkney Islands. Norwegian tradition preserved his memory as that of a ruler who brought peace to his country.

HARALD III HARDRAADE (Hardrada), king of Norway, 1045–66, son of a petty king of eastern Norway. He married a daughter of Yaroslav the Wise of Russia, spent some 10 years in the service of the Byzantine emperor Michael IV, then returned to Norway as king. In 1066 he joined Tostig, the disgruntled brother of Harold the Anglo-Saxon, in an attempt to make himself king of England but was slain at the battle of Stamford Bridge.

HARDING, ST. STEPHEN. See STEPHEN HARDING, ST.

HARDYNG, JOHN, d. c. 1465, English chronicler, author of a long rhymed chronicle of the fifteeth century. His writing reveals a measure of partisanship—favoring now the Lancastrians, now the Yorkists—and is not entirely trustworthy. He saw service with Henry V and took part in the battle of Agincourt.

HAREM, from the Arabic word meaning "forbidden," that part of a Moslem's residence (palace) reserved to women and accessible only to the husband; the women who lived in this area.

HARFLEUR, seaport of Normandy at the mouth of the Seine. It flourished during the late Middle Ages and played a major role in the Hundred Years' War. Henry V captured the city in 1415. The rise of Le Havre signaled the beginning of its decline.

HARIRI, AL- (Abu Muhammad Al-Qasim Al-Hariri), d. 1121, Arab scholar of Basra, author of treatises on literary style and syntax and of 50 maqamat or stories written in an ornate rhymed prose. His literary style is considered second in excellence after the Koran.

HARMARTOLOS, GEORGE. See GEORGE THE MONK.

HARMENOPULOS, CONSTANTINUS, d. 1383, high court official and adviser to the Byzantine emperor John VI Cantacuzenus. He was the author of an important compendium of civil law entitled Hexabiblos.

HARNOIS, a term applied in the fourteenth century to the full suit of armor which left no part of the body unprotected.

HAROLD II, Anglo-Saxon king of England, January 6 to October 14, 1066, the son of Earl Godwin, himself earl of Wessex and Kent. On September 25, 1066, he defeated his brother Tostig and Harald Hardraade at the battle of Stamford Bridge in the latter's bid for the throne following the death of Edward the Confessor, but was slain on October 14 at Hastings in a battle with William, duke of Normandy. Edward had designated Harold to be his successor.

HAROLD I (Harold Fairhair). See HARALD I HAARFAGER.

HAROLD BLUETOOTH. *See* HARALD BLUE-TOOTH.

HAROLD III HARDRAADE. *See* HARALD III HARDRAADE.

HARPSICHORD, a stringed musical instrument played from a keyboard. It came into use in the fourteenth century.

HARROWING OF HELL, English expression for the triumphant descent of Christ to hell following his death on the cross when he freed the souls of the virtuous and opened heaven to them. (Hell is used here in the sense of Limbo.) The term proclaimed the defeat of the powers of evil.

HARTMANN VON AUE, fl. 1190–1210, Middle High German poet of Swabia and author of the first Arthurian romance to appear in German literature. His secular romances *Erec* and *Iwein* are based on the works of Chrétien de Troyes. His best known poem, *Der Arme Heinrich,* tells of a lord who was cleansed of leprosy when a peasant girl offered her blood for his cure.

HARUN AL-RASHID, Abbasid caliph, 786–809, son of Al-Mahdi and father of Al-Ma'mun. He ruled Islam during what is traditionally considered its most brilliant era. He maintained a luxurious court at Baghdad, gave his patronage to scores of poets, artists, philosophers, and scientists, but until 803 left the administration of the empire to his guardian Yahya the Barmecide and his sons. Jaffar, the younger of the two sons, appears as the companion of his revels in the *Thousand and One Nights.* [*See* BARMECIDE.] He made ten pilgrimages to Mecca and was most generous in his almsgiving, but having seven wives (three more than the Koran permitted) and allowing graven images of beasts and men in the palace, and nightly revels with wine and music, scandalized good Moslems. The far-flung reaches of his empire, especially in Africa, had pretty well repudiated his authority by the time of his death.

HARVEY NEDELLEC (Hervaeus Natalis), d.

1323, Dominican theologian and master general of the order (1318). He was the author of numerous scholastic treatises, one of these a defense of Thomas Aquinas with whom he did not always agree.

HASAN, d. c. 669, son of Ali and grandson of Mohammed, who in 661 accepted a pension from Mu'awiya and surrendered any rights to the succession. Mu'awiya was one of the men who had opposed Ali although he may not have been directly involved in his murder. Hasan's act cleared the way for the establishment of the Omayyad dynasty by Mu'awiya.

HASDAI IBN SHAPRUT (Hasdai Abu Yusuf Ben Isaac Ben Ezra Ibn Shaprut), d. 975, Spanish Jew, court physician in Córdoba during the brilliant reign of Abd-al-Rahman III and his son al-Hakam II. He was a noted linguist and diplomat, also a patron of Hebrew literature and grammar. He employed his skills as a diplomat in negotiating treaties between the caliph and the Byzantine emperor and Spanish lords.

HASHIM, ancestor of the clan of which Mohammed was a member and, according to tradition, the Prophet's grandfather. Hashim gave his name to his clan. This was a subdivision of the Kuraish tribe.

HASSAN IBN THABIT, d. c. 674, court poet of Mohammed and Islam's first poet. He introduced many passages from the Koran in his verses.

HASTINGS, BATTLE OF, battle fought on 14 October 1066 between Harold the Anglo-Saxon, who had already been crowned king of England, and William, duke of Normandy, on the southeastern coast of England across from Flanders. Harold's death after a hard-fought battle opened the way to William's coronation and the Norman conquest of England.

HATFIELD, COUNCIL OF, council held in England in 680 at Hatfield (Heathfield) in response to Pope Agatho's wish to learn of the English church's position on the subject of Monothelitism. The papal representative was John, precentor of St. Peter's, who had accompanied Benedict Biscop to England. Under the presidency of Archbishop Theodore of Canterbury, the council repudiated Monothelitism and confirmed its acceptance of the Double Procession of the Holy Spirit.

HATTIN, BATTLE OF, decisive engagement between Saladin and a large Crusading army near Tiberias on the Sea of Galilee on 4 July 1187 which ended in the destruction of the Christian host. Saladin's occupation of Jerusalem on 2 October 1187 precipitated the Third Crusade.

HATTO I, d. 913, archbishop of Mainz, monk of Fulda, abbot of Reichenau, and an influential prelate during the reigns of Arnulf, Louis the Child whom he served as regent, and Conrad I.

HATTO OF REICHENAU, d. 836, monk of Reichenau and founder of its monastic school, a councillor of Charlemagne who appointed him bishop of Basel (802), then abbot of Reichenau (806), and later sent him to Constantinople to serve as his emissary. Hatto authored a number of theological and legal (canon law) treatises.

HAUBERK, coat of armor, usually of chain-mail, that reached below the knees. It was divided at the sides or in front and back to permit the knight to mount his steed.

HAUDRIETTES, religious congregation of women founded early in the fourteenth century by Jeanne Haudry of Paris. The members of the order dedicated themselves to the religious life and the service of the poor.

HAVELOK THE DANE, THE LAY OF, English verse romance of the early fourteenth century about the love of Havelok, son of the king of Denmark, for Goldborough, daughter of the king of England.

HAWKING. See FALCONRY.

HAWKWOOD, JOHN, d. 1394, famed English

condottiere who spent nearly 30 years fighting in the service of a number of Italian states including the Papal States, Florence, and Milan. He gained his first experience as a soldier with the Black Prince in the Hundred Years' War. Hawkwood had a reputation for maintaining an efficient, well-disciplined troop of mercenary soldiers.

HAYMO OF FAVERSHAM, d. 1244, English theologian and liturgist, a Franciscan and minister general of the order (1240), the only Englishman to hold that position. He helped reorganize the order and was principally responsible for ending the recruitment of lay brothers. Early in his career he had lectured at Paris. In 1233 he was sent to Constantinople to seek a reunion of the Greek church with Rome. At the request of Innocent IV, he revised the ordinals for the Roman Breviary, missal, and grace before and after meals.

HEARTH TAX, property tax on hearths levied occasionally in the Middle Ages.

HEBRIDES OR WESTERN ISLANDS, some 500 islands northwest of Scotland, occupied originally by Celts who were converted from Iona after Columba's visit there in 563. Norwegians conquered the islands in the tenth century and held them until 1266. From then native Scottish lords ruled the isles until 1346 when the Macdonalds established their control.

HEDWIG. See JADWIGA.

HEGESIPPUS, ST., church historian of the second century, a converted Jew and a probable native of Palestine. He wrote five books of "Memoirs" which constituted an attack on the Gnostics while providing much information about the early history of the church in Jerusalem. He is believed to have drawn up a "succession-list" of the early bishops of Rome.

HEGIRA. See HEJIRA.

HEGIUS, ALEXANDER, d. 1498, humanist, a pupil of Rudolf Agricola, and head of the monastic school in Emmerich, later in Deventer. He composed poetry, letters, and treatises on humanistic subjects, but gained greatest fame as a teacher of the classics. The best known of his pupils was Erasmus.

HEIDELBERG, city in Baden on the Neckar, site of an ancient Roman settlement first noted in 1196. It served as the residence of the Count Palatine of the Rhine from 1214 when Duke Louis I of Wittelsbach received that dignity from Frederick II of Germany. The university, the oldest in Germany, was founded in 1386 by Rupert I of Wittelsbach, Count Palatine of the Rhine.

HEIMSKRINGLA ("The round world"), history of the Norse kings from mythical times to 1177 by Snorri Sturluson. Its narrative of 16 sagas which relate the adventurous life of the Vikings is considered the finest example of Icelandic prose literature.

HEINRICH VON MORUNGEN, d. 1222, the leading poet of east central Germany of that period, spending the greater part of his life at the court of Duke Dietrich of Meissen. He treats the cult of love, the theme of his 33 poems, with both imagination and feeling.

HEIRIC OF AUXERRE, d. 876/7, hagiographer, abbot of the monastery of St. Germanus at Auxerre, then at Ferrières, next at Soissons. For a number of years he studied under Haymo of Auxerre and Servatus Lupus of Ferrières, and he had some association with John Scotus Erigena. He authored a metrical life of St. Germanus, the prose "Miracles of St. Germanus," and the *Collectanea,* a collection of notes drawn from classical and theological sources and based on the teaching of Haymo and Lupus.

HEJIRA (Hidjra, Hegira, Higra), the flight or emigration of Mohammed from Mecca to Medina (Yatrib) in September 622. Moslems adopted the incident as the base year in their calendar.

HEL, abode of the dead in German mythology; the goddess who rules under the earth and may bring men back to life.

HELENA, ST., d. 330, born in Bithynia of humble parentage, concubine of Constantius, the mother of Constantine I (the Great) who named her Augusta in 306 when he became an Augustus. (Constantius had abandoned her in 293 in order to marry the daughter of Emperor Maximian.) Helena encouraged Constantine in showing favor to the Christians and in his church-building program. She visited the Holy Land in 326 and founded the basilicas on the Mount of Olives and at Bethlehem. According to Eusebius, she discovered the cross at Jerusalem upon which Christ was crucified.

HELFTA, CONVENT OF, Cistercian community of women near Eisleben in Saxony founded in 1228 by Count Burchard of Mansfeld. (The community moved from Mansfeld to Helfta in 1258.) During the administration of Abbess Gertrude of Hackeborn (1251–92), the convent was recognized as the center of German mysticism.

HELIAND, Old Saxon alliterative poem of approximately 6,000 lines composed by an unknown poet of the ninth century, possibly a monk of Fulda. It is based on Tatian's harmony of the Gospels. The poem presents Christ against a Germanic background as a king, his apostles as warriors. Some scholars view the poem as the Gospel portion of a larger project which aimed to present the whole of the Bible in the vernacular. The poem represents all that remains of Old Saxon verse.

HÉLINAND OF FROIDMONT, d. after 1229, monk of the Cistercian monastery of Froidmont, later prior, author of sermons, poems in Old French on the theme of death, and a chronicle covering the years 634 to 1204. Only five of the 49 books of the chronicle remain extant.

HELL, the abode of the damned according to

Christian theologians. The word is derived from an Anglo-Saxon root meaning "concealed" or "covered," that is, hidden in the depths of the earth. The word Hel as it appears in German mythology refers to the abode of the dead. [*See* HEL.]

HELLEBARDE, cutting and stabbing weapon used by foot soldiers in the late Middle Ages. It was over six feet long.

HELLER (Häller, Haller, Händleinspfennig, Handelspfennig), penny struck in Swabia as early as 1200 and used after 1300 from the Rhine to Bohemia.

HELMOLD, d. after 1177, priest of Bosau in Holstein, author of a chronicle of the Slavs (*Cronica Slavorum*) which described the conquest, colonization, and conversion of Holstein, Mecklenburg, and Wagria from the time of Charlemagne until c. 1170. The chronicle, written in lucid Latin, is most valuable for the events contemporary to Helmold, specifically for the exploits of Henry the Lion of Saxony and Albert the Bear of Brandenburg.

HELOISE, d. 1164, niece of Canon Fulbert of Paris, pupil, mistress, then wife of Peter Abelard, the renowned scholastic. In the aftermath of a physical attack on Abelard, he became a monk, and she a nun. She was later prioress of the abbey of Argenteuil, eventually the first abbess of the Paraclete in the diocese of Troyes which Abelard had founded.

HELVIDIUS, theologian of the fourth century whom Jerome attacked for his denial of the perpetual virginity of Mary, the mother of Christ. Helvidius maintained that the "brothers" of the Lord (Matthew 12:46-50; Luke 8:9-21) were the natural sons of Joseph and Mary. His disciples, according to the testimony of Augustine, were known as Helvidians.

HEMMERLI(N), FELIX, d. 1458? Swiss lawyer, linguist, theologian, and reformer, who studied at Erfurt and Bologna. He took an active part in the Council of Basel and produced some 30 polemical works on the political and ecclesiastical controversies of the period. In his later years he actively supported Zürich's alliance with Austria against the Swiss Confederation.

HENGIST AND HORSA, according to tradition the first Anglo-Saxon chieftains to establish a solid foothold in England (c. 450). The British king Vortigern is said to have invited them over from Germany in order to get their help against the invading Picts from the north. They apparently turned on their host and in the fighting Horsa was slain but Hengist ruled Kent until his death in 488.

HENLEY, WALTER OF. *See* WALTER OF HENLEY.

HENNIN, the high, cone-shaped Burgundian cap for women with veil hanging down from the top or draped about it.

HENOTICON, decree issued by Emperor Zeno in 482 on the advice of Acacius, patriarch of Constantinople, in the hope of gaining Monophysite acceptance of the decisions of the Council of Chalcedon (451) by modifying that council's position concerning the nature of Christ. The decree not only failed to win the support of the Monophysite leaders but also alienated Rome which considered it a denial of Chalcedonian orthodoxy. It precipitated the Acacian Schism (484-519).

HENRI DE VALENCIENNES, historian of the early thirteenth century whose history of the Fourth Crusade (1202-04) supplemented the work of Villehardouin.

HENRICUS ARISTIPPUS, d. after 1162, scientist, master of the court school in Palermo, later ambassador to Constantinople whence he brought back valuable Greek manuscripts including a copy of Ptolemy's *Almagest*. He translated many Greek scientific works, including Aristotle's *Meteorologica,* into Latin.

HENRY (Enrique) II (Trastámara), king of Castile, 1369–79, natural son of Alfonso XI, who gained the throne from Peter the Cruel (Pedro I), his half-brother, whom he defeated and slew with his own hand. His first attempt to take the throne failed when Edward, the Black Prince, came to the aid of Peter. Later the combination of Peter's viciousness, which alienated many people, and help from Charles V of France brought him victory and the throne.

HENRY I, king of England, 1100–35, son of William I (the Conqueror). He succeeded his brother William II (Rufus) on the English throne, later took Normandy from his brother Robert. Upon his accession he issued a Charter of Liberties when he promised to correct the tyrannies of William Rufus, then ruled with a stern though efficient hand. He worked out the Compromise of Bec (1106) with Anselm, archbishop of Canterbury, over the investiture issue, and elicited oaths from his vassals that when he died they would accept his daughter Matilda as queen and regent for her son Henry (II). (Henry's only legitimate son, William, had drowned in the Channel.) At his death his vassals renounced their oaths in favor of Stephen of Blois.

HENRY II, king of England, 1154–89, probably medieval England's greatest monarch, succeeded Stephen of Blois and ruled an empire that included England, the English Pale, and the western provinces of France (Normandy, Anjou, Brittany, Aquitaine, among others) which he held as fiefs of the French king. He also claimed suzerainty over Scotland and Wales. His marriage to Eleanor, heiress of Aquitaine, whose first marriage to Louis VII of France had been annulled, brought him that large duchy, although he kept his wife confined from 1173 for her part in the revolt of their sons. So markedly did he increase royal revenues that by his death the exchequer had acquired the character of a separate branch of the government. Of a more fundamental nature was his contribution to the evolution of a system of royal courts whose efficiency and fairness were superior to those of any country of Western Europe. His efforts to reduce the autonomous character of the church and the jurisdiction of its courts were only partially successful because of the murder of Thomas Becket, the archbishop of Canterbury, for which he was held indirectly responsible. [See CLARENDON, CONSTITUTIONS OF; BECKET, THOMAS, ST.]

HENRY III, king of England, 1216–72, succeeded his father John and experienced a long but troubled reign, broken by a baronial revolt in 1264–65 which his lack of statesmanship helped precipitate. Most inept was his handling of foreign affairs. In 1258 he accepted the guidance of a privy council of 15 as provided by the Provisions of Oxford. When he renounced these Provisions in 1261, civil war broke out under the leadership of his brother-in-law Simon de Montfort. Simon captured Henry in the battle of Lewes (1264), but was himself slain the following year at Evesham. Thenceforth Henry's able son Edward (I) assumed a larger role in the government.

HENRY IV, king of England, 1399–1413, son of John of Gaunt and known as Henry Bolingbroke. He directed the revolt that culminated in the abdication and murder of Richard II. To many Englishmen he remained a usurper, a circumstance that deepened the cheerless character of his reign. He did put down a major revolt in Wales led by Owen Glendower who was abetted by the Percies, and parliament enacted the statute *De Haeretico Comburendo* which authorized the execution of convicted Lollards.

HENRY V, king of England, 1413–22, the son of Henry IV, reopened the war with France and gained an overwhelming victory over a much larger army at Agincourt in 1415. The Treaty of Troyes (1420) which he negotiated with the duke of Burgundy recognized him first as regent for the mentally sick Charles VI of France, then, after the death of Charles, as his successor on the strength of his marriage to Charles's daughter Catherine. He died of camp fever at the age of 35.

HENRY VI, king of England, 1422–61, 1470–1 son and successor of Henry V, pious, gentle, and, for intervals after 1453, mentally incapable. Factional strife and lawlessness cursed the greater part of his unhappy reign. Major contributing factors for these conditions included the king's weakness and poor health, the loss of the Hundred Years' War and Normandy, and a dynastic struggle with Richard of York and with Richard's son Edward, who had a claim to the throne. With the help of Richard Neville, the earl of Warwick, who later turned against Edward [See WARWICK, RICHARD NEVILLE, EARL OF], Edward eventually accomplished the defeat of the forces loyal to Henry (Lancastrians), and captured and murdered the king (1471). [See ROSES, WARS OF THE.] Margaret of Anjou, Henry's consort, assumed the principal role in directing the government and the Lancastrian war efforts during the period of the king's insanity.

HENRY VII, king of England, 1485–1509, son of Edmund Tudor, the earl of Richmond, and Margaret Beaufort, a great-granddaughter of John of Gaunt. He defeated Richard III at the battle of Bosworth Field (1485), married Elizabeth of York, the eldest daughter of Edward IV, and through such agencies as the Court of the Star Chamber ruled almost as an absolute monarch.

HENRY I, king of France, 1031–60, son of Robert II and grandson of Hugh Capet. He succeeded to the throne with the help of Robert, duke of Normandy. He ceded Burgundy to his younger brother Robert whom his mother had supported for the succession.

HENRY I (the Fowler), king of Germany, 919–936, duke of Saxony, whom Conrad I designated as his successor. He fought the Slavs and Magyars and erected fortresses to protect his eastern frontier. Although he was obliged to accept the autonomy of the powerful dukes of Swabia and Bavaria, he managed to reassert German authority over Lotharingia.

HENRY II, ST., king of Germany, 1002–24, duke of Bavaria who succeeded the childless Otto III largely because of the influence of Willigis, archbishop of Mainz. He was crowned Roman emperor in 1014, subdued the rulers of Capua and Salerno, secured the right of inheritance to Burgundy, and forced the Poles and Bohemians to recognize his suzerainty.

HENRY III, king of Germany, 1039–56, of the Salian dynasty, the son of Conrad II, was crowned emperor in 1046. He held the duchies of Swabia, Bavaria, and Franconia, and exercised the rights of suzerain over Poland, Bohemia, and Hungary. Some scholars consider him the most powerful of the medieval kings of Germany. His interest in church reform led him to remove three rival popes, then set up Clement II and, in sequence, three of his successors, including the great reforming pope Leo IX (1049–54).

HENRY IV, king of Germany, 1056–1106, of the Salian dynasty, the son of Henry III, aged six at his accession, devoted his efforts when he came of age to the task of recovering powers and possessions lost to his nobles during his minority. The steps he took drove his princes to ally themselves with Gregory VII in the pope's contest with Henry over investiture [see INVESTITURE CONTROVERSY], but he broke their common front against him by submitting to Gregory at Canossa (1077). He subsequently marched on Rome, put up his own pope, who crowned him emperor in 1084, and obliged Gregory to flee the city (with Robert Guiscard who had come to rescue him). Civil wars involving his own son cursed Henry's last years.

HENRY V, king of Germany, 1106–25, of the Salian dynasty, son of Henry IV. He had a generally unproductive reign except for the Concordat of Worms (1122) which provided a compromise on the issue of investiture. [*See* INVESTITURE CONTROVERSY.] Although he reasserted German suzerainty over Bohemia, he did nothing to strengthen the crown. He died without male issue.

HENRY VI, king of Germany, 1190–7, member of the Hohenstaufen dynasty, son of Frederick I Barbarossa. He established his authority over southern Italy and Sicily which he acquired through his marriage to Constance, aunt of William II. When he died in the course of preparations for a Crusade, he left a succession problem for Germany since his son Frederick (II) was not yet three years old. Henry kept Richard I of England prisoner from 1192 to 1194 and released him only on payment of a huge ransom. Richard had been captured returning from the Third Crusade.

HENRY VII, king of Germany, 1308–13, of the house of Luxemburg, succeeded to the throne following the murder of Albert I. Through the marriage of his son John to the sister of King Wenceslaus of Bohemia, he secured the addition of Bohemia to the Luxemburg possessions. He failed in his unrealistic ambition to establish imperial authority over Italy and died of the fever near Siena.

HENRY (VII), king of Germany, 1220–35, the son of Frederick II who had him elected king in 1220. He led a revolt against his father in 1234 but was defeated and deposed. He probably committed suicide.

HENRY, emperor of the Latin Empire of Constantinople, 1206–16, son of Baldwin, count of Flanders. He distinguished himself on the Fourth Crusade in the capture of Constantinople. When his brother Emperor Baldwin I was captured by the Bulgars, he was chosen to serve as regent. He proved himself the most capable and successful of the Latin emperors, restored Latin control over Thrace which the Bulgars had overrun, and even gained the grudging loyalty of many of his Greek subjects.

HENRY MURDAC, d. 1153, English Cistercian, abbot of a monastery at Vauclair (near Laon) which he founded, later of Fountains abbey in England which he brought to the peak of its spiritual influence. In 1153 he was consecrated archbishop of York. Despite his zeal, which contributed significantly to the growth of Cistercian monasticism in England, his somewhat contentious and intolerant nature involved him in long and fruitless disputes with the king and the bishop of Durham, among others. Through all his troubled career, he retained the confidence of St. Bernard of Clairvaux.

HENRY OF BLOIS, d. 1171, brother of Stephen who became king of England in 1135, abbot of Glastonbury (1126), and bishop of Winchester (1129). His influence proved an important factor in securing the throne for his brother. He had been brought up at Cluny and was imbued with high ideals concerning religious discipline and the rights of the church. During the dispute between Henry II and Thomas Becket he sought to find a solution both could accept. He was a great builder and left several castles in addition to the monastery of St. Cross at Winchester.

HENRY OF BURGUNDY, d. 1112 or 1114, count of Portugal, prepared the way for his son Alfonso I to become king of an independent Portugal. About 1095 he went to the aid of Alfonso VI against the Moors, married his daughter, and was made count of Coimbra (later Portugal).

HENRY OF GHENT, d. 1293, a respected philosopher and theologian and an independent thinker although in the Augustinian tradition and inclined toward neo-Platonism. He lectured at Paris and won esteem as the most distinguished teacher of the last quarter of the thirteenth century. His great learning is evident from his extensive writings, the most important of which were the *Quodlibeta* and the unfinished *Summa Theologica*.

HENRY OF HERP (Harphius van Erp), d. 1477, Dutch member of the Brethren of the Common Life, rector of the Brethren's house at Delft (1445), later a Franciscan Observant and vicar provincial of that religious order in the province of Cologne. He was the author of popular ascetical-mystical works and two volumes of treatises on the subject of oratory.

HENRY OF HUNTINGDON, d. 1155, English chronicler, priest, and archdeacon of Huntingdon. He composed several poems, a work on miracles, and, above all, a history of England which is a valuable source for the events of his period.

HENRY OF KALKAR, d. 1408, studied at Paris, became a Carthusian, was prior of several Carthusian communities and for 20 years a visitator of the Rhine province. He authored many sermons, letters, and ascetical and historical works and is credited with significantly influencing the development of the *Devotio Moderna.*

HENRY (Heinbuche) OF LANGENSTEIN, d. 1397, taught astronomy, philosophy, and theology at Paris where he joined other conciliarists in recommending the summoning of a general council for the purpose of ending the Western Schism. He was one of the founders of the University of Vienna (1384) and for several years served as its most distinguished teacher of theology. His writings include conciliar tracts, exegetical and devotional works, scientific treatises, hymns, and the first Hebrew grammar to appear in the German language.

HENRY OF LAUSANNE, d. c. 1145, a Benedictine monk who abandoned the monastic life for the role of preacher, prophet, and reformer, which took him to several cities of south and southwestern France. He attacked the worldliness of the clergy and insisted on the ideal of absolute poverty for all churchmen. A council of Toulouse (1119), the Lateran Council of 1139, and Bernard of Clairvaux condemned him for his anticlerical and antisacramental doctrines,

and he was eventually seized and imprisoned. A visionary sect known as the Henricians honored him as its patron. In some respects, he was a precursor of the Waldensians.

HENRY OF LIVONIA, d. after 1259, a chronicler, probably of Saxon origin, priest in the household of Albert I, the bishop of Riga, and a missionary among the Letts. He is the author of a chronicle relating the Saxon conquest of the Baltic area.

HENRY OF MEISSEN. *See* FRAUENLOB.

HENRY RASPE, d. 1247, landgrave of Thuringia, elected antiking in 1246 by those German princes who opposed Frederick II and his son Conrad (IV). Pope Innocent IV also endorsed Henry's election, but Henry's early death brought their efforts against Frederick to naught.

HENRYSON, ROBERT, fl. 1475, the leading Scottish poet of the period. His verse included a long poem containing 13 fables, a "complaint" of 86 stanzas with which he completed Chaucer's *Criseyde,* and shorter poems, one of these entitled *Orpheus and Eurydice.*

HENRY SUSO, BL., d. 1366, one of the Rhineland mystics. He was the son of a German count, joined the Dominican order in Constance, and studied at Cologne under Meister Eckhart. He dedicated himself to a career of preaching to nuns and Friends of God in Switzerland and the area of the Upper Rhine. Some critics consider his *Little Book of Eternal Wisdom* the finest product of German mysticism. Like the *Imitation of Christ,* it eschews theological speculation and mystical problems and contents itself with practical instruction for persons wishing to lead more devout lives. The work concludes with a hundred short meditations on the Passion.

HENRY THE LION, d. 1195, duke of Bavaria and Saxony (1142–80), the son of Henry the Proud, and leader of the Welf faction in Germany against the Hohenstaufens who had occupied the German throne beginning with Conrad

III in 1137. For more than 20 years he devoted his energies to extending his influence to the east against the Slavs. He encouraged the establishment of Saxon towns, reconstituted the dioceses of Mecklenburg and Oldenburg, and defeated the Obotrites. Partly because he failed to come to the aid of Frederick I Barbarossa against the Lombard League at Legnano (1176), the emperor declared his fiefs forfeit and deprived him of them. He was permitted to retain possession of his private lands of Brunswick and Lüneburg.

HENRY THE NAVIGATOR, d. 1460, third son of John I of Portugal, grand master of the Order of Christ (Portuguese successor of the Knights Templars), and director of a mariners' school at Cape St. Vincent during the period of its greatest activity. Among the achievements of his navigators were the rediscovery of the Madeira Islands, the exploration of the west coast of Africa to a point near Sierra Leone, and the development of the trade in gold and slaves. Henry encouraged the colonization of the Azores and met his death at the hands of the natives near the mouth of the Salum river.

HENRY THE PROUD, d. 1139, duke of Bavaria (1126–39) and Saxony (1137–9). His great wealth and his marriage to the daughter of Emperor Lothair II left him the most powerful noble in Germany and a strong candidate for the imperial succession. But Conrad III, a Hohenstaufen, was elected, who then proceeded to deprive Henry of Bavaria and Saxony. Henry managed to drive Albert the Bear from Saxony and was preparing to recover Bavaria when he died.

HEPTARCHY, term used since the sixteenth century for the kingdoms, presumably seven, which divided Anglo-Saxon England from roughly the sixth century to the second half of the ninth when the Danes absorbed several of them. The seven included Wessex, Sussex, Essex, Kent, East Anglia, Mercia, and Northumberland.

HERACLIUS, Byzantine emperor, 610–41, repelled Slav and Avar attacks on Constantinople, shattered Persian power at Nineveh in 628, and recovered Asia Minor, Armenia, and Syria from the Persians, but in 636 suffered a major defeat at the river Yarmuk at the hands of rising Islam. He is credited with introducing the system of themes in Asia Minor whose strong military character helped supply the empire with its best troops during the four centuries following. In 638 he issued the *Ecthesis*, a formula forbidding the mention of "energies," whether one or two, as present in Christ. [*See* ECTHESIS.]

HERALDRY, a system of personal recognition based upon the use of distinctive coats-of-arms and armorial bearing which made its appearance about the middle of the twelfth century in western Europe. In 1483 a heralds' college was founded which assumed jurisdiction over matters armorial.

HEREFORD, DIOCESE OF, a suffragan diocese of the province of Canterbury, founded probably in 676 although its jurisdictional limits were not precisely drawn until the ninth century. The tomb of the martyred Ethelbert, king of East Anglia (d. 794), caused Hereford to become a popular shrine. The cathedral dates from the eleventh century.

HEREFORD, NICHOLAS. *See* NICHOLAS OF HEREFORD.

HERESY, a religious view or doctrine judged inconsistent with what the church held to be orthodox. [*See* individual heresies, e.g., DONATISM.]

HEREWARD (The Wake), Anglo-Saxon rebel and outlaw who in 1070 joined a Danish force that had come to Ely, helped in the sacking of Peterborough Abbey, then held the island of Ely, until driven off by William I (the Conqueror). Little is known of his subsequent activities other than that he escaped William and continued his outlawry. His success against William and the Normans made him a folk hero to the Anglo-Saxons.

HERIGER OF LOBBES, d. 1007, monk, later abbot of the Benedictine monastery of Lobbes, and author of a history of the diocese of Liège from the fourth to the seventh century. He also composed some hagiography and several treatises on mathematical and theological subjects.

HERIOT (*mainmorte*), a payment in chattels or money which the lord of the manor might claim of the possessions of a deceased serf.

HERMANDAD (brotherhood), league of cities or municipalities that appeared in Castile in the twelfth century for the purpose of suppressing banditry and lawlessness. Such leagues generally supported the king against the aristocracy, and their decline paralleled the growth of royal authority which eventually made such organizations unnecessary. In 1476 Ferdinand and Isabella suppressed them in favor of a rural constabulary, known as the Santa Hermandad, which functioned throughout the kingdom.

HERMANN I, landgrave of Thuringia, 1190–1217, an honor he owed to Frederick I Barbarossa who earlier appointed him count palatine of Saxony. He was an ally of Frederick II against Otto IV. Walther von der Vogelweide and other minnesingers found him a generous patron at his castle, the Wartburg.

HERMANN OF ALTAICH (Niederaltaich), d. 1273, monk, then abbot of the Benedictine monastery of Niederaltaich, and author of several historical works. The most important of these, the *Annales Altahenses,* covered the years 1137 to 1273.

HERMANN OF SALZA, grand master of the Teutonic Order, 1209–39, and the most influential and successful of its administrators. In 1226 Frederick II assigned him and his order the region of the lower Vistula, including the area occupied by the Prussians, for conquest and conversion. He accompanied Frederick on his Crusade and in the bitter conflict between papacy and emperor worked earnestly to effect a reconciliation.

HERMANNUS (Herimannus) **CONTRACTUS** (Herman of Reichenau), d. 1054, Christian poet and chronicler, son of a count of Swabia, and educated in the monastery at Reichenau. Although crippled from birth, he gained considerable fame as an authority in theology, astronomy, mathematics, history, poetry, and languages, including Arabic. He composed a world chronicle (to 1054), hymns, sequences, and treatises on music, mathematics, and astronomy.

HERMAS, SHEPHERD OF, Christian apocalyptic work assigned to an obscure Christian of Rome of the mid-second century. It was a highly regarded book in the Eastern church and served as a textbook for catechumens. Its principal value is the light it throws on Christianity at Rome in this early period.

HERMIT, an early Christian recluse or anchorite who often retired to an isolated region the better to pray and practice mortifications. The first Christian hermits were probably those of Egypt who appeared in the third century. From there they spread to Palestine and Syria. Scattered hermits were also found in the medieval West but nothing like their number in the East.

HERMITS OF ST. AUGUSTINE, a religious order, not to be confused with Augustinian canons, which was formed in 1256 with the union of various anchoritic communities that had adopted the Augustinian rule. These included the Williamites and the Bonites.

HERMITS OF ST. PAUL (Paulists), religious order founded in 1250 with the union of two monasteries in Hungary, the one at Patach, the other at Pisilia. The order, which was popular in central and eastern Europe, adopted a strict observance of the Rule of St. Augustine. In 1382 the order founded what became the renowned shrine of the Black Madonna of Czestochowa.

HERRINGS, BATTLE OF THE, engagement in 1429 when the French attacked an English convoy under command of Sir John Falstaff that was bringing food, including herring, to the English army laying siege to Orléans. The French were driven off.

HERTFORD, COUNCIL OF, first general meeting of the Hierarchy and clergy of the English church (673). The council, which was summoned by Theodore of Tarsus, archbishop of Canterbury, adopted canons concerning reform, the liturgy, rights and duties of priests and monks, and the date of Easter. It also inaugurated a diocesan system based upon permanent sees and a stationary clergy.

HERTFORDSHIRE, English county east of Essex and north of London, included in the Anglo-Saxon kingdom of Essex. In 793 Offa of Mercia founded the abbey of St. Albans. In 1066 at Berkhamsted, William the Conqueror received the submission of the Saxon leaders. The area was the scene of two major battles of St. Albans (1455 and 1461) in the Wars of the Roses.

HERULIANS (Heruli), a Germanic people who were driven from their homeland in north Europe by the Danes. One part of the tribe moved into Gaul, the other south of the Carpathians, where it passed under Gothic and later Hunnic rule. After enjoying a brief period of independence following the collapse of the Huns, this southern group was destroyed by the Lombards.

HESSIANS, German tribe whom Tacitus called the Chatti located in the region between the Rhine and the Main. The tribe passed under Frankish rule during the fifth century. Many of its members were converted to Christianity by St. Boniface (d. 754).

HESYCHASM, a mystical doctrine, its aim spiritual tranquillity (Gr. *hesychia*), that maintained that the Holy Spirit was present in the pure of heart as an uncreated grace and that by virtue of that grace man can be saved. The goal of the hesychast was the vision of the divine light and interior tranquillity. These could be achieved through the suppression of all thought, the fixing of the eyes on a particular point (the place of the heart), and the repetition of a short prayer (the Jesus Prayer) containing the name of Jesus, the breathing, meanwhile being so controlled that it kept time with the recitation of the prayer. Hesychasm, which appeared at least as early as the fifth century, attained its fullest development and greatest popularity in the thirteenth and fourteenth centuries. It was associated above all with the monks of Mt. Athos. Its origins may extend as far back as St. Gregory of Nyssa (d. c. 395), while its most influential and controversial proponent was Gregory Palamas (d. 1359), a monk of Mt. Athos. Hesychasm was unique in producing both ardent champions and bitter critics. It was formally adopted by the Councils of Constantinople (1341, 1347, 1351), but it never spread to the West.

HESYCHIUS OF JERUSALEM, d. after 450, preacher and theologian of Jerusalem. He was the author of sermons, church history, and, above all, of exegetical treatises on the whole of the Bible whose scholarly character has only lately been recognized. He adopted the same principles that Origen had applied in his exegetical studies, in general, the Alexandrian method of exegesis.

HEUKE, cloak-type garment or shawl, with hood and buttoned on the shoulder. It was worn by men in central and northern Europe in the fourteenth century and by women well into modern times.

HEVELLIANS, Slavic people east of the Elbe whose capital, Brennabor, was captured by Henry I of Germany c. 928. Albert the Bear, margrave of Brandenburg (d. 1170), completed the conquest of this people.

HEXAPLA. *See* ORIGEN.

HEYNLIN OF STEIN, JOHN, d. 1496, rector of the University of Paris, an exponent of realism, teacher of theology at the Sorbonne, later at Tübingen, and one of the founders of the first printing press to be established in Paris (1470). He spent his last years as a Carthusian.

HIBERNENSIS COLLECTIO, a collection of canons concerning the church in Ireland. It was compiled c. 700 and drawn principally from the Bible, the church fathers, and Irish synods. The matter in the collection is arranged not chronologically but according to subject.

HIDALGO, Spanish term denoting a person who enjoyed the status of a knight. Such knights were assumed to be of ancient Christian descent and to be without Jewish or Moorish ancestors.

HIDE, Anglo-Saxon unit of land sufficiently large to support a family.

HIERONYMITES, name given to members of several religious congregations in late medieval Spain, Portugal, and Italy. Most popular was the Spanish Congregation of Hermits of St. Jerome which Pedro Fernandez Pecha organized in 1373. All the different orders observed the rule of St. Augustine.

HIERONYMUS, ST. *See* JEROME, ST.

HIGDEN (Higdon), RANULF, d. 1363 or 1364, monk of the Benedictine monastery of St. Warbury's, Chester, and author of the *Polychronicon,* a world chronicle from the Creation to 1352. What Higden wrote of the general culture of the fourteenth is useful, but more important are the chronicle's numerous continuations, above all, that of John of Malvern. In 1387 John de Trevisa translated the chronicle into English.

HIGH ALTAR, principal altar of the church. It usually occupied a central location in the sanctuary in the east end of the structure.

HIGH MASS, a mass in which much of the divine liturgy was sung and in which the deacon and subdeacon assisted the celebrant.

HIGH MIDDLE AGES, term frequently applied to the twelfth and thirteenth centuries.

HIGHWAY, a thoroughfare or principal way, usually under the protection of the king. It was raised above the surrounding terrain, whence the qualification high.

HILARION, ST., d. c. 371, founder of anchoritism in Palestine. Before coming to Palestine, he spent some years with St. Anthony in the Egyptian desert. St. Jerome was his biographer.

HILARIUS, fl. 1125, poet and wandering scholar, a pupil of Abelard. He composed light verse in Latin and three religious plays, also in Latin, the themes of the latter being the raising of Lazarus, Daniel, and St. Nicholas. They all show a variety of meter and dramatic power, and all have French refrains.

HILARY (Hilarius), ST., Pope, 461–8, born in Sardinia, the successor of Leo I (the Great). He left a reputation of a prudent and zealous administrator. The synod of 465 over which he presided is the most ancient for which the acts survive.

HILARY OF ARLES, ST., d. 449, monk of Lérins, bishop of Arles (429), who is usually classified as a Semi-Pelagian because of his views on grace and predestination. His zeal for reform led him to overstep his authority when he deposed the bishop of Besançon who was not subject to his metropolitan authority. Pope Leo I, to whom the bishop appealed, revoked Hilary's action and deprived him of his metropolitan rights although he did not remove him from his office.

HILARY OF CHICHESTER, d. 1169, learned canonist, advocate in the papal Curia, later employed by King Stephen of England on judicial business for the crown, and consecrated bishop of Chichester in 1147. He sided with Henry II in his controversy with Thomas Becket over the Constitutions of Clarendon.

HILARY OF POITIERS, ST., d. c. 367, bishop of Poitiers (c. 353), the most distinguished Western theologian before Augustine — he was referred to as the "Athanasius of the West" — and the first Latin church father to acquaint the West with the immense theological achievement of the Greek fathers. Because of his refusal to accept the condemnation of Athanasius by the pro-Arian Emperor Constantius, he was forced to spend several years in exile. His writings include hymns; polemical, theological, and exegetical treatises; and the first comprehensive study of the Trinity to appear in Latin.

HILDA OF WHITBY, ST., d. 680, superior of the monastery at Hartlepool and probably the most influential abbess of the Anglo-Saxon period. In the double monastery at Whitby which she founded, she taught many young scholars, five of whom later became bishops. She also encouraged Caedmon in his aspirations as a poet. At the Synod of Whitby (664), she sided with St. Colman in defense of the Celtic customs, although she accepted the decision to adopt Roman practices.

HILDEBERT OF LAVARDIN, d. 1133, archbishop of Tours. Earlier, when bishop of Le Mans, he was captured by William II (Rufus) and brought to England as a prisoner. In 1100 when William died, he returned to Le Mans and completed the cathedral there. In 1125 he was consecrated archbishop of Tours. The Latin of his literary works was superior to that of most of his contemporaries and served as models in the schools. He left letters, lives of several saints, and poetry on both sacred and secular subjects.

HILDEBRAND. See GREGORY VII, ST., pope.

HILDEBRANDSLIED, the oldest German epic poem, composed c. 810 – 20. In the story, Hildebrand, the faithful armorbearer of Dietrich of Bern, faces his son Hadubrand in battle. The son fails to recognize his father. A continuation of the story appeared in the thirteenth century.

HILDEGARD(E), ST., d. 1179, Benedictine abbess and mystic, founder of the abbey of Rupertsberg near Bingen. She composed a medical and scientific work, some hagiography, hymns, homilies, and a morality play. Her principal work, entitled *Scivias,* furnishes a record of her visions. Her learning and sanctity, together with her correspondence with the kings, popes, prelates, and saints, accounted for her great influence. Her missions carried her all over Germany.

HILDESHEIM, town in Lower Saxony, a trading post in the seventh or eighth century, and a bishop's seat in 815. Its most imposing structures included a cathedral dedicated in 1061 and St. Michael's abbey church built by Bishop Bernward (d. 1022). The bishops of Hildesheim later became princes of the Holy Roman Empire. The town was a member of the Hanseatic League.

HILTON, WALTER, d. 1395, English mystic, studied at Cambridge, took up the life of a recluse for some time, then became a Canon Regular of St. Augustine. He was the author of the *Ladder of Perfection,* the most systematic work on the subject of mysticism and the interior life to appear in medieval England. His volume enjoyed considerable popularity, especially among the Carthusians.

HINCMAR (Hinkmar) OF LAON, d. 879, nephew of Hincmar, archbishop of Reims. As bishop of Laon (858), the nephew challenged his uncle over his right to make an appeal directly to the pope, that is, over the head of his metropolitan. He also challenged Charles the Bald, king of the West Franks, over royal control of church property. He was eventually removed from his see and blinded.

HINCMAR OF REIMS, d. 882, powerful archbishop of Reims (845), a vigorous administrator who had earlier served in the court of Louis the Pious and Charles the Bald. After the death of King Lothair in 869, he helped secure the succession of Charles. In 870 when Hincmar's nephew insisted upon his right to make a direct appeal to the pope, the archbishop had him deposed. Hincmar became involved in several bitter disputes with Lothair II of Lorraine, one over his divorce of his wife which the archbishop condemned, another over the king's appointment of a friend as a bishop which the archbishop refused to accept. He imprisoned Gottschalk of Orléans when the latter's views on predestination led to his condemnation as a heretic by the council of Mainz (848). His writings include canonical, pastoral, political, philosophical, historical, and dogmatic subjects.

HIPPO, city west of Carthage, a bishop's seat under Augustine. It was captured by the Vandals in 431, by the Byzantine army in 533, and was destroyed by the Arabs in 697.

HIPPODROME, course for horse and chariot races, the best known being that in Constantinople begun by Emperor Septimius Severus in 203 and completed by Constantine I (the Great) in 330. Among the most renowned of the works of art that adorned the structure were the four bronze horses which Venice carried off to St. Mark's when the city fell to the Crusaders (Fourth Crusade) in 1204.

HIPPOLYTUS (Hippolyt) OF ROME, ST., d. c. 235, noted Roman theologian, a disciple of St. Irenaeus, and the most important student of theology in the West in his period. He was antipope during the pontificate of Pope Pontianus (230–5), although both men were exiled to Sardinia during the persecution of Emperor Maximinus. Hippolytus eventually renounced his office and was reconciled with the church. He died a martyr. His numerous writings, which reveal the author's militant nature, included dogmatic, exegetical, liturgical, canonical, and polemical works, as well as a world chronicle. His prinicipal work is his "Refutation of all Heresies," particularly those inconsistent with his philosophy.

HIRSAU, ABBEY OF, Benedictine monastery near Stuttgart founded in 830 near Calw in Würtemberg. In 1065 it was staffed by monks from Einsiedeln, after which it became one of the principal supports of the Cluniac reform movement.

HISHAM IBN AL-KALBI (Abu Al-Mundhir Hisham Ibn Muhammad Ibn Al-Sa'ib Al-Kalbi), d. c. 819, Arab historian and genealogist of the pre-Islamic tribes of Arabia. He spent most of his active life in Baghdad where he devoted his energies to collecting information about the early history of the Arabs. One of his surviving works describes the gods that the Arabs worshipped during the pre-Islamic period.

HISPANA COLLECTIO (Isidoriana), collection of conciliar canons and papal decretals from the earliest centuries of the Christian era. It was compiled in Gaul at the beginning of the eighth century and was widely used in the church until the eleventh century.

HISPERICA FAMINA, fragments of literary pieces from the fifth or sixth century written in a language composed of Latin, Greek, and Hebrew words. The language is believed to have been the invention of rhetoricians.

HOBILARS, English mounted infantry used in the fourteenth century in the fighting along the border between England and Scotland.

HOCCLEVE (Occleve), THOMAS, d. 1426, English poet and clerk in the office of the privy seal who dedicated his *Mirror (Regiment) of Princes* to Henry (V), the prince of Wales. It combined a lament over the corruption and evils of the times with instructions regarding the duties of a virtuous ruler. Hoccleve also composed moral and religious poems. His *La Male Regle* contains a description of life in London. He claimed Chaucer as his master and had a portrait of the poet painted in one of his manuscripts.

HOHENSTAUFEN, aristocratic family of Swabia that occupied the German throne from 1138 to 1254 except for the interval from 1208 to 1212.

The founder of the family was Count Frederick von Büren (d. 1105) who erected the castle of Staufen (whence the family's name) in the Jura mountains in Swabia. This Frederick received Swabia from Henry IV whose daughter Agnes he married. After the death of Henry V in 1125 without issue, the Salian possessions fell to the Hohenstaufens although the electors chose Lothair II, duke of Saxony, as his successor. Upon the death of Lothair in 1137, Conrad III, a Hohenstaufen, was elected. He in turn was succeeded by his nephew Frederick I Barbarossa (1152–90), and he by his son Henry VI (1190–7). Henry's brother Philip of Swabia maintained Hohenstaufen claims to the throne against the Welf faction until his murder in 1208. After the defeat of Otto IV at Bouvines in 1214, Frederick II, the son of Henry VI, who had already been elected king in 1212, ruled until his death in 1250, followed by his son Conrad IV to 1254. The capture and execution of Conradin, the son of Conrad, at Tagliacozzo in 1268 by Charles of Anjou brought an end to the dynasty. [See GUELFS AND GHIBELLINES.]

HOHENZOLLERN, aristocratic family of Swabia, first noted c. 1100, that probably derived its name from the castle Hohenzoller erected in the Zollern mountains south of Hechingen in the eleventh century. The family's first ancestor to receive mention was Burchard I, count of Zollern. The two sons of Frederick of Hohenzollern, who had become burgraves of Nuremberg in 1192, founded the two main lines of the house, the Swabian and the Franconian. The latter line was destined to have the more illustrious history chiefly because of the bestowal of the margravate of Brandenburg on the family by Emperor Sigismund in 1415.

HOKETUS (Hoquetus, Ochetus), multivoiced music of the late Middle Ages in which pauses and notes were so well blended as to give the impression of but one voice.

HOLSTEIN, territory at the base of the Danish peninsula, ruled in the eleventh century by counts who were vassals of the dukes of Saxony. In 1111 Holstein became a county of the Holy Roman Empire and Adolf of Schauenburg was invested with the countship. Early in the thirteenth century the Danes sought to occupy the region but were driven off. From 1432 the count of Holstein also ruled as duke of Schleswig. In 1474 the counties of Holstein, Wagria, and Dithmarschen were combined and accorded the rank of duchy by Frederick III, the Holy Roman emperor.

HOLY GRAIL. *See* GRAIL.

HOLY ISLAND. *See* LINDISFARNE, ABBEY OF.

HOLY OILS, oils, often a mixture of olive oil and balm, specially consecrated and used in liturgical services and in the anointment of kings, prelates, and the sick. [*See* CHRISM.]

HOLY ORDERS, the spiritual or sacred power or position conferred by means of external rites such as the imposition of hands. The major orders included those of priest, deacon, and subdeacon; the minor, those of porter, lector, exorcist, and acolyte. Tonsure was not classified as a minor order, only as a special rite preparing the individual for minor orders.

HOLY ROMAN EMPIRE, the medieval institution that originated on Christmas Day in the year 800 when Pope Leo III placed a crown on the head of Charlemagne as he knelt in St. Peter's and the assembled people hailed him "Emperor of the Romans." To contemporaries the pope's action constituted the formal reestablishment of the Roman empire in the west, a view which visionaries such as Arnold of Brescia and Dante continued to urge centuries later. (In 1157 the term "Holy Empire" appeared, that of "Holy Roman Empire" in 1254.)

Controversy continues over whether Charlemagne was annoyed by the pope's action, even though scholars generally agree that he appreciated the greater propriety of that title, as opposed to the simple "King of the Franks," in view of the extensiveness of his empire. If Charlemagne feared that Leo's action would set a precedent which subsequent popes would insist invested them with a voice in the selection of the emperor, he was correct. Popes in as late as the fourteenth century were asserting that claim despite the indifference the German electors customarily showed them. This reveals the weakness of the papal position. The German king who assumed that title did so only after his election as monarch by the German princes. Nevertheless, it was largely the fact that popes did the crowning of the emperor that lent the imperial title its character as the highest and most sublime in Western Christendom. This imperial title also served to justify the territorial ambitions of German kings in Italy and to explain their close association with the papacy.

The motive that had impelled Leo III to crown Charlemagne was that of formalizing the role of the king of the Franks as the protector of the papacy. Despite that hope, the title lapsed in 924, although when Otto I revived it in 962, his empire included north Italy and implied a protectorate over Rome and a dominant voice in papal affairs. The papacy found the paternalistic position that the German kings assumed from the time of Otto increasingly uncomfortable, but it required a century of bitter controversy and war with the Hohenstaufen emperors Frederick I Barbarossa, Henry VI, and Frederick II, before that association was terminated. Even after the German kings had turned their backs on Italy and the papacy in the later Middle Ages, their title of Holy Roman Emperor continued to assure them a position of leadership in European affairs. So Sigismund, by virtue of his imperial title, could still play the dominant role at the Council of Constance (1414–8), and Frederick III received with great pride and satisfaction the imperial crown from papal hands as late as 1452.

HOLY ROMAN EMPIRE OF THE GERMAN NA-TION, title traditionally assigned the Holy Roman Empire of which Otto I was crowned emperor in 962. It was referred to as *Sacrum Imperium* (Holy Empire) since 1157 when Frederick I Barbarossa first used that phrase, while the qualifying phrase "German Nation" came to be added in the fifteenth century to indicate its reduced, and largely German, character.

HOLY SEE (Apostolic Chair, *Sedes Apostolica*), term derived from the Latin *sedes* meaning seat or residence. It was applied to the papal office, to the pope himself, even to the papal Curia.

HOLY SEPULCHER, KNIGHTS OF THE, term generally applied to all knights who fought for, or in defense of, the Holy Sepulcher, after 1342 to those formally enrolled in a pious confraternity administered by the Franciscans.

HOLY THURSDAY, the Thursday before Easter on which day Christians commemorated the institution of the eucharist. In England the day was known as Maundy Thursday.

HOLY WATER. In ancient times water was often used as a symbol of purification. In the fourth century, the waters of the baptismal font or pool were exorcised with the sign of the cross. In general, holy water was simply water that had been blessed for use in the liturgy, the administering of the sacraments, and for pious private use.

HOLY WEEK, the week immediately preceding Easter and beginning with Palm Sunday. Within the week fell Holy Thursday, Good Friday, and Holy Saturday, the vigil of Easter.

HOLY YEAR, year specially designated by the pope for spiritual revival. The first year so honored was 1300 by order of Pope Boniface VIII who also decreed that a similar jubilee be observed every hundred years. Special indulgences were granted to members of the faithful who visited Rome during the year.

HOMAGE, ACT OF, formal ritual act by which a

person became the vassal of a lord. The vassal knelt before his lord, placed his hands between those of his lord, and swore to be his man (Latin *homo*). The ninth century saw the introduction of the oath of fealty which followed and, it was hoped, reenforced the act of homage.

HOMILIARY, a collection of homilies arranged according to the ecclesiastical calendar which were to be read at the office of Matins.

HOMINES INTELLIGENTIAE, sect centered at Brussels in the late Middle Ages. It was founded by Aegidius Cantoris (Sanghers), a lay mystic, and inclined toward pantheism and a rejection of the official church.

HOMOOUSIOS, Greek word meaning consubstantial, of the same substance, a term accepted by the Council of Nicaea in 325 to define Christ's nature as one of full equality with the Father, as opposed to *homoiousios,* a term meaning of like or similar substance.

HOMS (Hims, Hems, Humes), city of Syria, the ancient Emesa, on the caravan route between Damascus and Aleppo. The Arabs captured the city in 636 from the Byzantine empire and renamed it Hims. Timur the Lame and the Mongols occupied the city in 1401. It was one of the few cities that Timur did not destroy.

HONORATUS OF ARLES, ST., d. 430?, founder of a monastic community on the island of Lérins, in 426 bishop of Arles. His writings have been lost.

HONORIA, sister of Valentinian III, whose hand Attila the Hun is said to have demanded from the emperor in additon to half the western empire as her dowry. The historicity of the matter is very doubtful.

HONORIUS I, Pope, 625–38, a native of Campania, sent missionaries to England, also appealed to the Celtic Christians in Britain to adopt the Roman calendar and rite. The Council of Constantinople (681) condemned him as a here-

tic for having accepted Monothelitism, a judgment Pope Leo II confirmed in 682. Some modern scholars defend Honorius against the charge of heresy although admitting that the language he employed was gravely imprudent. In a letter to Sergius, the patriarch of Constantinople, he had used the unfortunate formula of "one will" in Christ.

HONORIUS II, Pope, 1124–30, Italian, cardinal, and papal representative during the negotiations in Germany with Henry V that led to the adoption of the Concordat of Worms (1122). As pope he recognized Roger II of Sicily as ruler of Apulia and confirmed the Premonstratensians and Templars. For a short time, Celestine II, antipope, the appointee of Conrad III of Germany, disputed the legitimacy of Honorius's papal office.

HONORIUS III, Pope, 1216–27, cardinal, administrator of the papal treasury, and already advanced in years when elected pope. He approved the Franciscan, Dominican, and Carmelite Orders and encouraged the growth of their Tertiary Orders. What occasioned him most anguish during his pontificate were the political ambitions of Emperor Frederick II in Italy. He had tutored the young Frederick, crowned him emperor in 1220, then urged him to lead a Crusade against the Turks, partly to take him out of the country.

HONORIUS IV, Pope, 1285–7, cardinal, who as pope became deeply involved in Italian and European political affairs after King Peter III of Aragon, who had seized Sicily in 1282, refused to recognize papal suzerainty over that island. His encouragement of French (Angevin) intervention in Sicily and Spain proved fruitless.

HONORIUS, FLAVIUS, Roman emperor, 395–423, son of Emperor Theodosius (d. 395). He ruled the western half of the empire, first from Milan, after 402 from Ravenna, while his brother Arcadius ruled the eastern half from Constantinople. His execution of Stilicho in

408, the Vandal general of the imperial army, removed the last obstacle in the path of Alaric and his Visigoths on their way into Italy. They sacked Rome in 410. In 421 Honorius was forced to accept Constantius, the husband of his sister Galla Placidia, as coemperor.

HONORIUS OF AUTUN, d. c. 1156, monk of the Benedictine monastery at Regensburg. He is the author of a work on the liturgy, commentaries on the Bible, a compendium of cosmology and geography, and a popular manual of theology, entitled *Elucidarium,* which was translated into several vernacular languages including Gaelic and Old Norse. He was a strong proponent of the doctrine of the Real Presence.

HORMISDAS, ST., Pope, 514–23, possibly of Persian origin, who was successful in ending the Acacian Schism (484–519). He persuaded the Byzantine emperor Justin I and his nephew Justinian to disavow the Monophysite policy of his predecessor Anastasius (d. 518) and accept the decision of the Council of Chalcedon and the Tome of Pope Leo I. Justin had strong political motives for recognizing the papal position.

HOSIUS (Ossius), d. c. 358, bishop of Córdoba, theologian, principal ecclesiastical adviser to Constantine I from 312 to 326, and an opponent of Donatism and Arianism. He presided at the Council of Nicaea (325) and also at the Council of Sardica (343). In 355 he was banished to Sirmium by the pro-Arian emperor Constantius.

HOSPITAL, as an institution maintained for the care of the sick, traced its origins in the medieval West to the responsibility placed upon deacons in the early Christian community of assisting brethren in need. With toleration and the encouragement of Constantine I, houses providing facilities for pilgrims, the sick, and the infirm quickly made their appearance. One of the first was established near Caesarea by Basil (d. 379). Although individual parishes and cathedrals and, in time, an increasing number of munici-

palities maintained hospitals, it was principally the monastic orders, more specifically those organized for nursing, that engaged most actively in eleemosynary work of this kind. During the twelfth century there appeared the St. Augustine nuns, the Order of the Holy Spirit, and the Antonines, while from the thirteenth Beguine and Beghard houses joined these older communities in caring for the sick, the poor, and the aged. The Knights Hospitallers cared for pilgrims from the late twelfth century.

HOSPITALLERS. *See* SAINT JOHN OF JERUSALEM, ORDER OF THE HOSPITAL OF.

HOSPITALLERS OF ST. LAZARUS OF JERUSALEM, religious order of knights and nurses founded c. 1120 in Jerusalem who followed the Rule of St. Augustine. It maintained hospitals for the care of pilgrims and for the sick and also engaged in missionary activities. In 1490 Pope Innocent VIII directed the order to unite with the Order of the Hospital of Saint John of Jerusalem (Hospitallers).

HOSTIENSIS (Henry of Segusio), d. 1271, noted canonist and decretalist who taught at Paris and Bologna. He became bishop of Sisteron (1243), archbishop of Embrun (1250), and cardinal (1262) when he carried out diplomatic missions for the pope. In his writing, which included a synthesis of canon law and commentaries on papal decretals, he revealed himself an advocate of the plentitude of papal power.

HOTELS AND INNS. Hotels and inns date from ancient times, although the medieval inn evolved from the practice of monasteries of providing lodging for travelers. Such hospitality, a requirement of the Rule of Benedict, was at first an informal service. With the increase of travelers, pilgrims, and Crusaders in the eleventh century, separate dormitories were often established with certain monks assigned to see to their administration. Since the location of monasteries was not dictated by the need to provide lodging for travelers, it was not long before hospices appeared on roads and near bridges as well as in the larger towns (e.g., Tabard Inn at Southwark, London). It appears that the wayfarer was at first expected to provide for his own food and bedding, even for his fuel.

HOTEL-DIEU, term given in France to any hospital, e.g., Hotel-Dieu de Paris, a hospital located near Notre Dame and a dependency of the cathedral chapter (1006).

HOTSPUR. *See* PERCY.

HOUPPELAND, long belted coat, with long, wide sleeves, worn by English soldiers in the mid-fourteenth century. It served as state apparel in Burgundy, France, and the Netherlands until 1450.

HOURI, beautiful young women who, according to the Koran, will gratify the blessed in paradise with their never-fading charms.

HOURS, BOOK OF, book containing the prayers prescribed for each of the canonical hours of the liturgical day.

HOURS, CANONICAL, the fixed parts of the divine office appointed to be recited or sung at specified hours of the day. They included matins, lauds, prime, terce, sext, none, vespers, and compline. [*See* DIVINE OFFICE.]

HOUSE MARK, mark similar to the heraldric figure made on the beam of a house. It indicated ownership.

HOVEDEN, ROGER OF. *See* ROGER OF HOVEDEN.

HOWARD, distinguished English family first noted in 1295 when William Howard (Haward) received a summons to parliament. The first lord of the family, John Howard, who was created duke in 1483 by Richard III, was slain at the battle of Bosworth Field (1485).

HOWEL DDA (the Good), d. 950, Welsh prince who ruled the greater part of Wales and gave his people a generally peaceful reign. In 918 he did homage to Edward the Elder and in 928 he paid a visit to Rome. He has been credited, perhaps without justification, with the codification of Welsh law.

HRABANUS MAURUS, BL. *See* RABANUS MAURUS, BL.

HROSWITHA. *See* ROSWITHA.

HUBERT DE BURGH, d. 1243, chief justiciar during the reigns of John and Henry III. Until 1227, when Henry was declared of age, he was the real ruler of England. Because of his criticism of the king for advancing the fortunes of the relatives of his foreign-born wife and of Peter des Roches, the Poitevin bishop of Winchester, and for his extravagance and his unwise foreign ventures, he was deprived of his office.

HUBERT, ST., d. c. 728, "Apostle of Ardennes," Frankish bishop of Liège, an especially popular saint in south Germany and northern France. He was revered as patron of the hunt and his intercession was invoked against hydrophobia. His symbol was that of a stag with head surmounted by a crucifix.

HUBERT WALTER. *See* WALTER, HUBERT.

HUCBALD (Hugbaldus) OF SAINT-AMAND, d. c. 930, Benedictine monk of Elnon sur la Scarpe, later director of the school at St. Amand (north France). He composed lives of the saints and divine offices. In his *De Institutione Harmonica* he sought to establish a relationship between Graeco-Boethian theories on music and Gregorian chant.

HUE AND CRY, term applied in Anglo-Saxon as well as in later England to the duty incumbent upon members of a community (village) to pursue a criminal with horn and voice.

HUGH, king of Italy, 926–45, count of Vienne. He forced Rudolf II of Burgundy out of Lombardy in 925, but was himself expelled from that area by Berengar II in 945. Hugh died two years later.

HUGH (THE GREAT), d. 956, count of Paris and duke of the Franks, the son of King Robert I and father of Hugh Capet. His attempt to secure the throne for himself failed, but he did win Burgundy for his family.

HUGH CAPET, d. 996, founder of the Capetian dynasty, eldest son of Hugh the Great, and duke of the Franks (956). He owed his election to the throne of France (987) partly to the influence of Gerbert, the abbot of Bobbio, and to Theophano, the widow of Otto II. In return for the support of Theophano, Hugh renounced all claims to Lorraine. He was the father of Robert II.

HUGH DESPENSER. *See* DESPENSER, HUGH LE.

HUGH OF BALMA, Carthusian of the late thirteenth century, prior of the Charterhouse of Meyriat, and author of an influential work on mystical theology (*De Theologia Mystica*). This was a systematic presentation of the interior life based partly on the writings of Pseudo-Dionysius.

HUGH OF CLUNY, ST., d. 1109, of noble Burgundian birth, monk, prior, and abbot of Cluny, and adviser to nine popes. During the sixty years of his abbacy he brought the monastery to the peak of its influence. He was a strong champion of Gregory VII's efforts to reform the church, and he took a leading part in organizing the First Crusade. Despite his deep involvement in ecclesiastical and political affairs—he attended numerous church councils and carried out diplomatic missions for the papacy—he remained a man of God.

HUGH OF DIGNE, d. c. 1255, Franciscan, provincial minister in Provence, and author of two treatises on poverty and the first systematic commentary on the Rule of St. Francis. He inspired the formation of the Order of Friars of the Sack and his sister's order of Beguines. The Spiritual Franciscans considered him one of their precursors.

HUGH OF FLEURY, d. after 1118, Benedictine of Saint-Bénoit-sur-Loire, author of an ecclesiastical history to 855, a chronicle of the kings of France from 842 to 1108, and a treatise on the investiture controversy.

HUGH OF LINCOLN, ST., d. 1200, Carthusian who came to England about 1176 to serve as prior of the Charterhouse at Whitham which Henry II had established. In 1186 he was consecrated bishop of Lincoln. Although he became involved in disputes with Henry II, Richard I, and John over the church's liberties, they all respected him for his zeal, his integrity, his love of the poor and oppressed, and his dedication to justice. Three kings helped bear his coffin to the tomb. His place of burial in the cathedral of Lincoln became a popular shrine.

HUGH OF SAINT-CHER, d. 1264, Dominican, twice provincial of his order in France, vicar general, first Dominican master of theology at the University of Paris, and also the first Dominican to be created a cardinal (1244). He produced several exegetical works but is best known for his part in correcting and indexing the Vulgate.

HUGH OF SAINT VICTOR, d. 1141, learned philosopher and theologian, according to the traditional account first a member of the community of Canons Regular of St. Augustine at Hammersleven, Saxony. Later (c. 1115) he moved to the newly founded abbey of St. Victor in Paris. From 1120 when he was the leading master at the abbey, he composed treatises on philosophical, theological, exegetical, and mystical subjects which were highly regarded by contemporaries. So important was the thought of Augustine in his own intellectual and spiritual development that he was known as "the second Augustine." He founded the tradition of mysticism for which the abbey gained distinction. He also wrote on grammar and geometry, and prepared biblical commentaries, and homilies.

HUGH TRIMBERG, d. after 1313, Middle High

German poet, composer of didactic and allegorical verse in both German and Latin. His most popular poem is *Der Renner,* a work of more than 24,000 verses, in which he satirized the different classes of society.

HUGUCCIO (Hugh of Pisa), d. 1210, probably the most influential of the decretists, teacher at Bologna, bishop of Ferrara (1190), and author of grammatical, theological, and legal writings. His commentary on the *Decretum* of Gratian was the most complete ever produced on that important work. Of special interest to students of linguistics is his *Liber Derivationum.*

HUGUET, JAIME, fl. 1448–92, Spanish painter of Barcelona and leading figure in the Catalan school in Sardinia. A large studio of followers who assisted him in the production of many large composite altarpieces helped spread his influence. Among his surviving works are the *Epiphany* and *Consecration of St. Augustine.*

HULAGU (Hülagü), d. 1265, grandson of Genghis Khan, who ruled over a Mongol empire that stretched from India to the Mediterranean. (The khan of the Golden Horde maintained a separate empire in Russia.) He overran Persia in 1256, practically exterminated the Assassins, and two years later captured Baghdad, executed Musta'sim, the last of the caliphs, and pillaged the city. His further penetration to the south toward Egypt was thrown back by the Mamluks in 1260.

HULK, a freighter with sails which appeared in north Europe in the thirteenth century.

HUMANISM. *See* RENAISSANCE.

HUMBERT OF ROMANS, d. 1277, Dominican friar, prior, provincial, and master general (1254–63) of the order. He revised the liturgy used by the order, reformed its administrative organization, and also composed several ascetical treatises.

HUMBERT OF SILVA-CANDIDA, d. 1061, Bene-dictine monk, cardinal bishop, and a figure of great influence in papal circles from 1050 until his death. He was in charge of the papal chancery from 1057 and was one of the principal advisers of Leo IX in his program of ecclesiastical reform. He is best known for his role in the schism with the Greek church in 1054 which his lack of prudence helped precipitate.

HUMERIAL VEIL, a silk shawl worn about the shoulders and covering the hands. It is mentioned in the Roman "Ordines" of the eighth century when the acolyte who held the paten wore it. From the eleventh century the subdeacon became the paten-bearer.

HUMILIATI, also known as Berettini, a religious lay movement which made its appearance in Lombardy in the twelfth century. Like the Patarines and Waldensians with whom they were often confused, the Humiliati practiced lives of self-denial, devoted themselves to the care of the sick and poor, and preached against corruption in the church. Although many suffered excommunication along with the Waldensians in 1184 when they ignored the papal prohibition to preach, others submitted to papal censure and were reorganized into semireligious communities by Pope Innocent III in 1201.

HUMPHREY OF GLOUCESTER. *See* GLOUCESTER, HUMPHREY, DUKE OF.

HUNDRED, a division of the county among the Franks, Alemanni, and Anglo-Saxons. In England it was intermediate between the village and the shire. It might have its own court as it did in England where it met once a month to handle both civil and criminal business.

HUNDRED YEARS' WAR, long period of conflict between France and England which extended from 1337 to 1453 and ended with the virtual expulsion of the English from the continent. The term Hundred Years' War is misleading since formal truces or simply the inability of either side to press the conflict reduced actual fighting to a relatively few years. Because England, a much smaller and poorer nation than France, won the major battles, largely because of French overconfidence in their heavy preponderance in knights, the war continued on until France was in a position to exploit its superior resources. English possession of Guienne as a fief of the French crown constituted the fundamental cause of the conflict. The English sought to gain sovereign control of this area, the French hoped to expel them before this could be accomplished.

England's overwhelming victories against larger French armies at Crécy (1346) and Poitiers (1356) left France no choice but to accept the Treaty of Brétigny (1360) which ceded Guienne, Calais, and Guines to the English. During the reign of Charles V (the Wise) (1364–80), success favored French arms, in part the result of the tactics Bertrand Duguesclin, the new constable of France, employed, in part due to the illness and death of the Black Prince and the senility of his father, Edward III. The war in fact languished until 1415 when Henry V reopened the conflict with a smashing victory at Agincourt. One of the factors in his victory was the insanity of Charles VI of France and the factional struggle between the Orleanists (Armagnacs) and Burgundians for control of the government. The murder of John the Fearless, duke of Burgundy, by an agent or adherent of the Dauphin (Charles VII), prompted Burgundy to conclude an alliance with the English and accept, in the name of France, the Treaty of Troyes (1420). This declared Henry V regent for the sick Charles and his successor after his death. He was to marry Catherine, Charles's daughter.

The desperate fortunes of the Dauphin whom the treaty had disinherited began to look up, however, early in 1429 with the appearance of Joan of Arc. She relieved the English siege of Orléans and opened the way to Reims where the Dauphin was crowned Charles VII in July. Two developments in 1435 assured ultimate victory for France. One was the death of John, duke of Bedford, the brother of Henry V, who had successfully maintained the English hold on most of their possessions in France. The other was the severance of the Anglo-Burgundian alliance. With money furnished by Jacques Coeur and the estates general, Charles VII modernized his army and by 1453 had cleared the English from the continent save for Calais.

HUNGARY, country located south and west of the Carpathians. The ancestors of the Hungarians were known as Magyars, a Finno-Ugric people that occupied the region between the Volga and Urals until the early Christian era when they were driven into the steppes near the mouth of the Don. There they were vassals of the Khazars. They were allies of Byzantium until the late ninth century when they moved into the region of the middle Danube south of the Carpathians. From there they directed their savage raids westward as far as France until 955 when Otto I put an end to their plundering with his victory at Lechfeld.

In 975 Geza, great-grandson of the Arpad who gave his name to the first ruling dynasty, was baptized. His son St. Stephen, who was crowned king in 1000, established the civil and ecclesiastical organization that was maintained for many centuries to come. Population and trade grew during the eleventh and twelfth centuries, as did the power of the aristocracy which forced new privileges from Andrew II in 1222. Mongols ravaged the country in 1241–2, but the following century brought industrial and territorial expansion notably during the reign of Louis I (the Great) who worked to "westernize" the land's economy and culture. Mary, the daughter of Louis, married Sigismund of Luxemburg, who ruled as king of Germany, Bohemia, Hungary, and as Holy Roman emperor. From the beginning of his reign the gravest concern for Hungary to the close of the Middle Ages and beyond was the rising threat of the Ottoman Turks. In 1396 the Turks annihilated the army of Sigismund at Nicopolis, which led to the loss of Serbia and Dalmatia together with

Hungary's suzerainty over Bosnia, Walachia, and Moldavia. Following another major defeat by the Turks at Varna in 1444, the estates appointed John (Janos) Hunyadi to serve as guardian of Laszlo V. His success against the Turks prompted the nobles to elect his son Matthias Corvinus their king (1458–90), the first national monarch to rule Hungary since the extinction of the Arpad dynasty in 1301. Matthias proved himself an enlightened despot, able administrator, and patron of arts, but his ambition to gain the imperial crown for himself along with Austrian and Czech possessions prevented him from undertaking any major offensive against Hungary's most dangerous enemy, the Ottoman Turks. His sudden death in 1490 left Hungary in turmoil.

HUNS, a nomadic people located at one time in north-central Asia, whence the Hunnic tribes to the east overran north China in the early fourth century, those to the west moved north of the Caspian Sea into the area above the Black Sea c. 375. There they found and subjugated the Alans and Ostrogoths, while the greater part of the Visigothic nation fled westward across the Danube to escape them. Until 450 the Huns appeared content to make their home in what later became Hungary where tribute from Byzantium kept them reasonably quiet. When this tribute ceased coming, they moved westward in 451 under their leader Attila, but were defeated at Châlons in Gaul by an army of Romans, Visigoths, and Franks under Aetius. In 452 Attila led his army into northern Italy but then abruptly returned to the Danube, possibly because of plague or restiveness among his troops. His death in 453 heralded an early end to Hunnic power. It was shattered in 455 in a general revolt of the German mercenaries in the Hunnic army at a battle on the Nedao river in Pannonia.

HUNYADI (Hunadi, Huniades), JOHN (Janos), d. 1456, Hungarian statesman and national hero. He saw service as a young man with Emperor Sigismund against the Hussites and Turks, and in 1439 was appointed woiwode of Transylvania. He drove the Turks from Serbia, Albania, and Bulgaria, but in 1444 suffered a disastrous defeat at Varna. In 1446 the nobles of Hungary appointed him regent for King Laszlo V, and in that capacity he achieved his greatest victory when he broke the Turkish siege of Belgrade in 1456. This victory saved Hungary from falling to the Turks; it also led the grateful Hungarian nobility to elect his son Matthias Corvinus as their king (1458–90).

HURDY-GURDY, musical instrument first mentioned in the tenth century when it required two men to play it. It generally had three strings which were made to vibrate by a wooden wheel turned by a crank. By the thirteenth century one man was able to handle the instrument. By that time it was also known as a symphonia.

HUS (Huss), JOHN, d. 1415, Bohemian religious reformer, national leader, and heretic. He studied at Prague and became identified with a national reform movement whose objectives included the reform of the church and the supremacy of Czech influences over foreign ones, mostly German, particularly in the University of Prague. Hus taught theology at the university and in 1409, when King Wenceslas IV deprived the Germans of their control there, was elected rector.

Hus meanwhile had become acquainted with the theological treatises of John Wyclif who influenced his thinking, although he did not deny the doctrine of transubstantiation, nor directly attack the primacy of the pope. But he did maintain that the faithful were not bound to obey the pope's directives when these conflicted with Christ's words. His views drew formal excommunication in 1412. Three years later he presented himself at Constance to defend them against the bishops and other prelates who had gathered there in general council. When he refused to disavow in their entirety the views of Wyclif and at the same time proclaimed the authoritative supremacy of the Bible, he was ordered burned as a heretic. His writings include a number of theological treatises in Czech, which are considered literary classics, and more numerous ones in Latin, including a series on indulgences and the church. His death at the stake made him a national martyr.

HUSAIN (Husayn, Husein), d. 680, son of Ali and grandson of Mohammed, revered by the Shi'ites as their imam and future caliph. When Mu'awiya died in 680, the supporters of Husain induced him to advance a claim to the succession against Yazid, the son of Mu'awiya, but he was slain near Kufa by the governor of Iraq. His followers commemorated the day of his death as a day of mourning.

HUSSARS, Hungarian term meaning adventurers or freebooters and applied in the fifteenth century to a body of light cavalry that served in the Hungarian army under Matthias Corvinus (1458-90).

HUSSE, outer garment without sleeves, open on the sides and reaching below the hips. It was worn by men in the fourteenth century.

HUSSITES, followers of John Hus who gave his name to a strong pre-Hussite reform and nationalistic movement in Bohemia which adopted him as their inspiration after his execution for heresy in 1415. The Hussites divided early into the more moderate Calixtines (Utraquists), who among other concessions demanded communion in both kinds for the laity, and the more revolutionary Taborites who would accept nothing short of what the more radical Protestant groups adopted for themselves in the sixteenth century. After the imperial armies had sustained a series of defeats at the hands of the Hussites and their able leaders John Zizka and Prokop the Great, Emperor Sigismund and members of the Council of Constance offered concessions called the Compacts of Prague which caused a split in their ranks. The Calixtines now helped the imperial troops defeat the Taborites (1434) and the Hus-

site movement came to an end. Some of the Hussites accepted reconciliation with the medieval church. More of them joined the Bohemian Brethren when these made their appearance about the middle of the century.

HYACINTH, ST., d. 1257, member of a noble Polish family, studied at Cracow, Prague, and Bologna. He met St. Dominic in Rome and joined his order, then labored as a missionary among the Slavs of Greece, Bohemia, Lithuania, Russia, and Poland. He was known as the apostle of the Slavs and the patron of Poland.

HYDE, ABBEY OF, Benedictine monastery in Winchester, also known as New Minster, founded by King Edward the Elder in 901. His father, King Alfred, was buried in the abbey church. In 965 the original secular canons were replaced by Benedictine monks from Abingdon. At the monastery's dissolution in 1538 all the monastic buildings were destroyed.

HYGINUS, ST., Pope, 138-42, obscure bishop of Rome about whom little reliable information remains. The *Liber Pontificalis* speaks of him as a philosopher from Athens.

HYMNARY, book containing the hymns of the divine office properly arranged according to the liturgical calendar. It was first appended to the Psalter or Antiphonary, and was later incorporated into the Breviary.

HYMNODY, LATIN, rooted in early Christian hymnody, in turn represented the product of Hellenizing influences upon the Hebrew hymns and traditions that the first Christians had inherited from Judaism. [For eminent Eastern hymnists, *see* GREGORY OF NAZIANZUS and ROMANUS MELODUS.] The earliest composer of hymns in the West was Hilary of Poitiers (d. c. 367) who had learned about hymns during his exile in the East. But the title "Father of Latin Hymnody" traditionally belongs to Ambrose, bishop of Milan (d. 397), who is said to have composed hymns in order to sustain the faithful in their struggle with the Arians. Ambrose also introduced the use of accentual verse, as opposed to the ancient classical measures based on quantity, as simpler and more readily memorized and sung. After Ambrose came a fairly constant stream of hymnists which peaked in the twelfth and thirteenth centuries, then dried up abruptly in the fifteenth when the rise of humanism interrupted its flow.

Among the more prominent hymnists were Prudentius (d. after 405), Sedulius (fifth century), Fortunatus (d. c. 600), Theodulf (d. 821) who was the most important of the Carolingian period, the late Carolingian Rabanus Maurus (d. 856), his pupil Walafrid Strabo (d. 849), and Gottschalk of Orbais (d. 868) who ran afoul of the authorities for his views on transubstantiation. The late ninth century witnessed the appearance of the sequence and Notker Balbulus (d. 912), one of its originators. It was probably the twelfth century that welcomed the *Dies Irae* that was once attributed to Thomas of Celano (d. c. 1260). Stephen Langton (d. 1228) is believed to have composed the *Veni, Sancte Spiritus,* and Thomas Aquinas (d. 1274) quite surely wrote the *Lauda, Sion, Salvatorem.* Pope Innocent III also composed hymns, as did Bernard of Clairvaux (d. 1153), Abelard (d. 1142),

and, in a most prolific and versatile manner, Adam of St. Victor (d. c. 1180). Among the late composers was Denis the Carthusian (d. 1471) who authored more than 120 hymns.

HYPATHIA, daughter of Theon, a mathematician and philosopher. She was a renowned neo-Platonic philosopher and mathematician in Alexandria and is said to have occupied the chair of philosophy in that city. She was famed not only for her learning and eloquence but also for her beauty. She was murdered by a Christian mob in 415. What mathematical and astronomical commentaries she composed are no longer extant. Her most distinguished pupil was Synesius of Cyrene who later became the bishop of Ptolemais.

HYPATIUS OF EPHESUS, d. after 536, bishop of Ephesus, theological adviser of Emperor Justinian I from 531 to 536, and an influential figure at the Council of Constantinople (536) which condemned Monophysitism.

HYPOSTATIC UNION, the union in the one person of Christ of both divine and human natures. The doctrine was elaborated by St. Cyril of Alexandria (d. 444) and accepted officially by the church in the Definition of Chalcedon (451).

IAMBLICHUS, d. c. 325, neo-Platonic philosopher, founder of the Syrian school of neo-Platonism, and a pupil of Porphyry. His commentaries on some of Plato's dialogues have not survived, but parts of his discussions of the philosophy of Pythagoras are extant. He was most responsible for transforming the neo-Platonism of Plotinus into a stiff pagan scholasticism capable of assimilating the magic and superstition of the ancient world. He maintained that human beings are subject to the influence of a multitude of beings of the spirit world, from whom a knowledge of the future may be secured. The emperor Julian drew his neo-Platonism from Iamblichus.

IAM CHRISTUS ASTRA ASCENDERAT, hymn composed in the fourth or fifth century, possibly by Ambrose, that made its way into the divine office for the feast of Pentecost.

IAM SOL RECEDIT IGNEUS, hymn by an unknown author, probably of the ninth century, that was incorporated into the divine office. It sang the praises of the Trinity.

IBN, Arabic for son.

IBN AL-FARID (Sharaf Al-Din Abu Hafs 'Umar), d. 1235, a leading Arab composer of verse on the theme of Sufi mysticism. He was born in Cairo, turned his back on a legal career, spent some years as a solitary in the desert, then moved to Mecca where he came under the influence of the Sufi mystic al-Suhrawardi. He expressed his deep religious feeling in odes that contained passages of exquisite beauty.

IBN 'ARABI (Muhyi Al-Din Ibn 'Arabi), d. 1240, Moslem theologian and mystic who proposed a vast theosophical synthesis that significantly influenced the development of both Moslem and Western mysticism. He was born in Spain, studied in Lisbon and Seville, later made his way to Arabia, and eventually settled in Damascus. His voluminous writings included love poems besides those concerned with mysticism.

IBN BATUTAH (Batuta) (Mohammad Ibn 'Abdallah Ibn Batutah), d. 1368, an Arab born in Tangier, considered the greatest Moslem traveler of the Middle Ages. He spent some 30 years traveling through much of Asia, eastern Africa, southern Russia, the Caucasus, and the East Indies. He spent almost eight years in India at the court of the sultan of Delhi, and about a quarter of his book is devoted to the people and civilization of India. Included in the vivid descriptions he left of his travels is his account of the visit of the Black Death to Syria and Egypt in 1348.

IBN EZRA, ABRAHAM BEN MEIR (Abenezra), d. 1167, Jewish scholar who was born in Toledo, spent some years in Córdoba, traveled to north Africa, Rome, Lucca, Mantua, London, and Narbonne, then probably returned to Spain where he died. He composed secular verse, liturgical poems, and treatises on grammatical, philosophical, astronomical, and mathematical subjects. His biblical commentaries, which are considered his most valuable works, reveal the mark of a meticulous and erudite scholar.

IBN EZRA, MOSES BEN JACOB, d. c. 1138, Jewish poet and philosopher of Spain who composed secular verse on the themes of love, nature, and youth, as well as penitential hymns for use in holiday liturgies. He was also an accomplished linguist and wrote on rhetoric and poetry.

IBN GABIROL (Solomon Ben Judah Ibn Gabirol), d. c. 1058, in the Western world usually referred to as Avincebrol or Avicebron, Jewish scholar of Spain, ethical writer, philosopher of note, and composer of some of the finest Hebrew poetry of the Middle Ages. Gloom and bitterness mark much of his secular verse, the result of his own tragic life. He composed on both secular and religious themes. His *Keter Malkhut* (The Royal Crown) on the nature of God and man's destiny was incorporated into the liturgy of the Day of the Atonement. His philosophical writings, which reflected a neo-Platonic position, influenced Western thinkers more so than Jewish. Franciscan scholastics generally accepted them, Dominicans rejected them.

IBN HANBAL (Ahmad Ibn Mohammed Ibn Hanbal), d. 855, Islamic theologian of Baghdad and founder (posthumously) of the law school of the Hanbalites which accepted the Koran and Sunna as the sole sources of the law. He rejected all reasoning, whether it led to orthodox or heretical conclusions, and insisted on the acceptance of tradition. His opposition to the introduction of the rationalistic Mu'tazilite doctrine that the Koran was created led to his imprisonment and torture. The caliph al-Mutawakkil reversed the position of his predecessors and declared the Koran uncreated, whereupon Ibn Hanbal was freed and thenceforth enjoyed immense popular acclaim as a saint. His son made a compilation of 30,000 traditions taken from his lectures which is entitled *Musnad*.

IBN ISHAQ (Muhammad Ibn Ishaq), d. c. 768, Arab historian, author of the most valuable source for the life of the Prophet, *Kitab Sirat Rasul Allah* or "Book of the Life of the Apostle of God."

IBN KHALDUN (Abu Zaid Abd Al-Rahman Ibn Muhammad Ibn Khaldun), d. 1406, the most renowned of Arab historians and founder of the sociological approach to history. He was born in Tunis of a patrician family and pursued a long and checkered career in the service of kings and rulers from Tunis, Fez, and Granada to Egypt where he served as Melikite cadi of Cairo. While on a military mission to Damascus he had several interviews with the dread Timur the Lame who had the city under siege. His epochal work, *Kitab al-'Ibar* ("Book of Examples"), consists of the *Muqaddimah* or introduction in which he presents his philosophy of history, followed by a survey of Islamic history. Except for what he offers concerning the Maghrib, this survey holds little value. In the *Muqaddimah* he discusses in most perceptive fashion, far in advance of his contemporaries, the pattern of history. In his analysis of the factors accounting for the rise and fall of civilizations, he gave attention to a great variety of physical, psychological, intellectual, and cultural conditions and elements.

IBN KHALLIKAN (Chillikan), d. 1282, Arab historian who served as a judge in Cairo and as chief cadi in Damascus. His valuable biographical dictionary of important men in Islamic history does not include a biography of Mohammed.

IBN QUTAYBAH (Kutaiba) (Abu Muhammad 'Abd-Allah Ibn Muslim Ibn Qutaybah), d. c. 899, Arab scholar who was born in Kufa, Iraq, but spent the greater part of his career in Baghdad as a teacher. He earned distinction especially in theology, philology, and literature. His *Secretary's Guide* is a compendium of Arabic usage and vocabulary, his *Book of Poetry and Poets* a study of the art of poetry which he illustrated with passages from early Arabic poetry. His theological works show him a conservative who maintained the *Hadith* as the only authoritative source for Islamic jurisprudence.

IBN TIBBON, Jewish family of southern France of the twelfth and thirteenth centuries, members of which translated Arabic scientific, philosophical, and linguistic works. Beyond making much information available to non-Arabic-speaking Jews, these translations served to enrich the Hebrew language with new words and to modernize its style. Prominent members of the family included Judah Ben Saul Ibn Tibbon, d. after 1190, who fled Spain and made his home in Lunel, southern France, where he practiced medicine; Samuel Ben Judah Ibn Tibbon, d. c. 1230, who translated several works of Maimonides, above all his *Guide of the Perplexed;* Moses Ben Samuel Ibn Tibbon, d. c. 1283, who translated many Arabic works together with those of Maimonides not yet rendered into Hebrew; and Jacob Ben Machir Ibn Tibbon, d. c. 1304, physician and astronomer, who translated Euclid's *Elements* and Ptolemy's *Almagest.*

IBN TUFAIL (Abu-Bakr Mohammed Ibn 'Abd-Al-Malik Ibn Tufail), d. 1185/86, *Latin* Abubacer, Moslem philosopher and physician of Spain who attended Abu Yaquk Yusuf, the Almohad ruler at Marrakech. He composed medical works in Arabic but is best known for his *Risalat Hayy ibn Yakzan (Treatise on Hayy ibn Yakzan),* a sort of philosophical novel about the intellectual and spiritual development of a man who lived an isolated life of 50 years on an uninhabited island. The man's development took place in accord with the principles of neo-Platonism.

IBN TUMART (Abu 'Abdullah Muhammad Ibn Tumart), d. 1130, a Berber, founder of the Almohad movement. From his youth he was interested in religion and was especially attracted by the doctrines of al-Ash'ari and al-Ghazali. He evolved a doctrine that combined certain Shi'ite practices with puritanical moral reform, and proclaimed himself the *mahdi,* the infallible

guide of a rejuvenated Islam. Although he failed to establish a theocratic state of his own, his favorite pupil Abd-al-Mumin succeeded. [*See* ALMOHADS.]

ICELAND, island in the north Atlantic, known by the fourth century A.D., but not settled before the ninth although visited by Irish hermits in the eighth. Ingolfur Arnarson, a Norwegian chieftain, brought his family there c. 875. By 1096 the island's population numbered c. 75,000, a figure not exceeded until 1900. Missionaries made their appearance during the tenth century and in 1000 the *althing* officially adopted Christianity in order to prevent trouble between pagans and Christians. The first bishop's seat was established in 1056 at Skalholt. When the island came under the jurisdiction of the archbishop of Nidaros (Trondheim) in 1152, it opened the door to increasing influence from Norway, culminating in the conquest of the island by Haakon IV (1204–63). Influential individuals called *Godhar* administered the affairs of local districts, general assemblies known as *things* ruled larger areas, while the national assembly, called the *althing,* made its appearance c. 930.

ICON, an image, figure, or, in general, a flat representation of someone or something held sacred in the Greek church, e.g., Christ, the Mother of God, or saints. They became popular in the East from the fifth century but much more so after the rise of iconoclasm in the eighth.

ICONOCLASM, the breaking of images, a policy initiated by Emperor Leo III in Constantinople in 726 when he sought to suppress the worship (veneration) of images. Iconoclasm expressed Eastern objection to the representation of the human figure as conducive to idolatry, that of Christ and of holy things as sacrilegious. It did not of necessity constitute an attack on the cult of saints, although the desire to reduce the powerful position of monasticism in the empire, the staunchest champion of the veneration of saints, may have been among Leo's motives. He also argued that the use of images posed a major obstacle to the conversion of Jews and Moslems. His son and successor, Constantine V Copronymos, pushed iconoclasm even more vigorously, but it was relaxed under Constantine's son Leo IV, and in 787, during the regency of Empress Irene who ruled in the name of her son Constantine VI, it was formally anathematized by the Council of Nicaea (II). Emperor Leo V the Armenian (813–20) revived iconoclasm, but in 843 it was finally suppressed by imperial decree. Iconoclasm not only strained relations with the Latin church but also worked a near-revolution in Byzantine art. In the aftermath of iconoclasm, Byzantine churches were usually decorated with flat pictures, mosaics, and bas-reliefs.

ICONODULE, one who honored icons, as against an iconoclast who favored their destruction.

ICONOSTATIS, a screen separating the sanctuary from the nave in the Byzantine church.

IDRISI (Abu 'Abdullah Mohammed Ibn Mohammed Ash-Sharif Al-Idrisi), d. c. 1166, Arab geographer, scientist, and poet. He was born in Ceuta, studied at Córdoba, spent some years traveling in Spain, north Africa, and Asia Minor, then found a patron and home with Roger II of Sicily. With Roger's encouragement he completed a volume entitled *Delight of him who wishes to traverse the regions of the world*, more popularly known as *The Book of Roger*, which purports to describe the geography of the world. Despite the inclusion of maps and sections such as that of Sicily which are quite detailed and reasonably accurate, the work contains legendary material and reveals a lack of acquaintance with several authorities, including al-Biruni, whom Idrisi might have consulted. He also made a silver celestial globe for Roger. His work on botany and *materia medica* also survives.

IDRISIDS, a Moslem dynasty which Idris I founded in northwest Africa in 788 with the help of Berbers. What prompted him and other Alids to flee Hejaz and revolt against the Abbasid caliphate was the policy of repression against non-Abbasid elements in the empire which the caliph al-Hadi (785–6) had adopted. The son of Idris, posthumously born and named Idris II, built a new capital at Fès. The state declined after reaching the peak of its prosperity c. 875, and was absorbed by the Fatimids of Egypt in 922.

IGNATIUS OF ANTIOCH, ST., d. c. 110, bishop of Antioch, author of seven famous epistles which he composed while being taken to Rome to be executed as a martyr. In these letters Ignatius urged the sacramental character of the church, supported the doctrine of the Real Presence, and attacked the views of the Docetists. He also sent letters to different Christian communities begging them to avoid heresy and to obey their ecclesiastical superiors, and thus preserve the unity of the church.

IGNATIUS (Nicetas), ST., patriarch of Constantinople, 847–58, 867–77, the son of the Byzantine emperor Michael I Rhangabe (811–3) who was castrated when his father was deposed and shut up in a monastery to prevent his succession. He became a monk, then abbot, and was appointed patriarch in 847 by Theodora, regent for the young Michael III, who approved of his hostility toward iconoclasm. In 858 her brother Bardas seized control, deposed Ignatius, and appointed Photius in his place. When Basil I assumed power in 867 he reinstated Ignatius.

IGOR, d. 945, grand prince of Kiev, the son of Prince Rurik of Novgorod. In 912 he succeeded to the Kievan throne, then embarked on a career of almost complete failure. His expedition into Transcaucasia as well as his two invasions of the Byzantine empire came to naught. He was slain by the Drevlyane (region of the Pripet river) who had rebelled against his rapaciousness.

IHS, monogram of the name of Jesus Christ, in use from the earliest centuries.

ILDEFONSUS, ST., d. 667, archbishop of Toledo, member of a noble family, usually regarded as a pupil of Isidore of Seville. He joined a Benedictine community near Toledo, became its abbot, and in 667 was appointed archbishop of Toledo. Of the many books attributed to him only four have survived: one in prose, to the Blessed Virgin, another on baptism and the discipline of catechumens, a third discussing the spiritual journey of the soul after baptism, and a history of the church in Spain in his century.

ILE-DE-FRANCE, under the Merovingian rulers of Gaul the territory between the Seine and Rhine. In the tenth and eleventh centuries it comprised the area of Paris and its environs, roughly the territory limited by the Seine, Marne, Beuvronne, Oise, and Nonette. This constituted the county of Paris as ruled by Hugh Capet when elected king of France in 987. The term itself came into use only in the fifteenth century.

ILE-DE-LA-CITÉ, the island in the Seine river at Paris on which the cathedral of Notre Dame was built.

IL-KHANS, Mongol dynasty of Iran founded by Hulagu that ruled that country from 1256 to 1335. It attained the height of its power under Ghazan (1295–1304) who introduced legal, fiscal, and administrative reforms while making Islam the official religion of the state and adopting a repressive policy toward other faiths.

ILLUMINATED MANUSCRIPTS. The illustration of manuscripts with miniature paintings and drawings represents a major phase of Christian art through the whole of the Middle Ages. From the sixth century to the eleventh illuminated manuscripts constitute the sole evidence of pictorial creation in the western world. After the eleventh they continued to be a highly popular art form until the very close of the Middle Ages when the invention of printing brought that era to an abrupt end. Given the inherent value of the manuscript, the parchment itself, the time, labor expended on its message, and the service of most manuscripts as Bibles, Psalters, or Gospel Books, it was to be expected that the monastic scriptoria which produced these illuminated manuscripts should have expended much thought on ornamenting them in a manner befitting their importance. The initial with which the writing began, sometimes the first initial of succeeding chapters, and occasionally the entire page was decorated with paintings, sketches, or linear designs of a fantastic variety.

The earliest Christian illuminated manuscripts are from the late Roman empire, more specifically the Byzantine half which had examples from the Hellenistic period to guide them in this technique. Byzantine manuscripts were often as richly illuminated as their churches. The Rabula Gospels contain one of the first representations of the Crucifixion. The earliest examples of manuscript illustration in Western Europe are also noted for their brilliance and their originality. Outstanding examples of Anglo-Irish art from the seventh and eighth centuries include the Books of Durrow, Kells, and Lindisfarne. Their interlaced patterns, curvilinear and geometric designs, and animal motifs are characteristic of the ornamentation of the illuminated manuscripts produced in this period.

The Carolingian period contributed its own rich share to the growing treasure of illuminated manuscripts, the products of scriptoria located in monasteries such as Regensburg, Hildesheim, Paris, Winchester, and Reims. The Utrecht Psalter may have been the most creative of the ninth century. The center of illuminated manuscript production in the Romanesque period (from A.D. 1000) was the monastery of Reichenau in Switzerland. Among the splendid examples of illumination from this period are the Evangeliary of Otto III and the Sacramentary of Henry II. As new developments may be counted the use of gold in decoration, the introduction of themes from the New Testament, and the appearance of grotesque and fabled monsters perhaps suggested by stories found in the bestiaries of the time.

The high Middle Ages or Gothic period witnessed a preference for small books, devotional for the most part and intended for personal and family use, and the Book of Hours, the most popular of all private devotional books, made its appearance. For the first time, too, secular works such as chronicles and romances were illustrated, a sign that the production of these ornamented manuscripts was slipping out of the monastic scriptoria and becoming an increasingly secular pursuit with wealthy patrons such as Charles V of France and his brothers, the dukes of Berry and Burgundy, anxious to reward their artists. Art critics generally consider the *Très riches Heures du duc de Berry,* executed by Pol of Limburg and his brothers, as the greatest of the miniature paintings of this era. The calendar, included with the prayers and lessons intended for the layman's edification, provides colorful evidence of the artist's ability to paint realistic landscapes, to show people of different walks of life engaged in their several occupations, and to depict contemporary life as it was. Such illustrated manuscripts inspired the Flemish masters of the fifteenth century, Hubert van Eyck and his brother Jan.

IMAM, the prayer leader or religious superior in the Islamic mosque. The word also served as an honorary title for distinguished Islamic scholars such as the caliph, who was referred to as the "Supreme Imam," and the sultan. The founders of the four principal schools of the Sunnites were also known as imams. [*See* IMAMITES.]

IMAMITES, a Shi'ite sect, also known as the "Twelvers," which believed in the hidden imam, al-Mahdi, the twelfth imam, who was believed to have entered a cave in 879 and disappeared from sight. They built their eschatology around his returning as their "messiah." The term Imamites came to be applied generally to all Moslems who maintained that the leadership of Islam belonged to the descendants of Ali and Fatima.

IMITATION OF CHRIST, devotional work generally attributed to Thomas à Kempis (d. 1471) and considered the most popular of the products of the *Devotio Moderna*. It is not a mystical work but rather a series of instructions in simple, lucid language directed to the ordinary person interested in pursuing a Christ-like life and in finding the peace of mind that came from the conviction that all material blessings are inconsequential before the promise of heaven.

IMMACULATE CONCEPTION, a Christian doctrine that Mary in view of her mission as mother of God was conceived without original sin. A feast celebrating Mary under that title was introduced in France in the twelfth century.

IMMUNITY, right of exemption from the jurisdiction of the Merovingian king's officials or count, a privilege monarchs extended first to high ecclesiastics as a mark of their favor, and later, without much choice on their part, to all their vassals. With immunity went the exercise of regalian rights which extended to the immunist the profits of justice, tolls, and military service. [*See* FEUDALISM.]

IMPERIAL CITIES, cities of Germany such as Mainz, Cologne, Lübeck, and Augsburg that were subject to no authority beyond that of the king or emperor. Some gained this status by gift, others by purchase, while others simply usurped it. From the thirteenth century they formed alliances and leagues for protection, and in 1489 they were formally recognized as members of the imperial diet.

IMPROPERIA, the reproaches addressed by Christ to the people in the liturgy of Good Friday.

IMRA (Imru) AL-KAIS (Amrilkais, Imrulkais), Arab poet of the sixth century whom Emperor Justinian appointed phylarch of Palestine. Mohammed among others considered him the leading poet of the pre-Islamic period.

INCARDINATION, canonical term applied to the juridical act by which a priest was attached to a particular diocese and subordinated to the authority of its ordinary. Excardination referred to the act by which a priest was released from the authority of his bishop and placed under the jurisdiction of another.

INCIDENTS, feudal perquisites governing the transfer of fiefs. They included relief, that is, the payment of a fee to the lord when the heir took over a fief upon the death of its vassal; wardship, the right of the lord to the income of a fief during the minority of the deceased vassal's son (or daughter) since the ward was unable to render the services required; and marriage, the right of the lord to select a husband for the fief's heiress if she chose to marry or if the lord wanted her to marry, on the theory that the husband of the heiress would have to be willing, and able, to render his lord the services, including military, that his position as vassal entailed. [*See* RELIEF; ESCHEAT; FORFEITURE; PURVEYANCE, RIGHT OF.]

INCIPIT, formulary placed at the beginning of texts in old manuscripts.

INCLOSURE. *See* ENCLOSURE.

IN COMMENDAM. *See* COMMENDATION.

INCUBUS, the devil-lover of a witch.

INCUNABULA, books printed before 1500.

I.N.D., that is, *In nomine Domini* (Dei) (In the name of the Lord(God)), a phrase introducing many ancient Christian documents.

INDICTION, a cycle of fifteen years used as a point of reference in the reckoning of time used from the time of Diocletian (284–305). Justinian I (527–65) ordered all legal documents to be dated by indiction, and it was a method employed in the papal Curia from the sixth century to 1087.

INDUCTION, the final stage, after nomination and institution, in the appointment of a new incumbent to a benefice.

INDULGENCE, remission in part (partial) or in full (plenary) of the temporal punishment due to sin, the guilt for which had itself been forgiven. The use of the indulgence in the accepted sense did not antedate the eleventh century when Pope Urban II at the Council of Clermont (1095) extended it to all persons who would take up arms against the Moslems.

INE (Ini, Ina), king of Wessex, 688–726, the successor of Caedwalla. He issued the first code of laws by a West Saxon king. He collected tribute from Kent and extended his rule over Sussex and Surrey and probably over Devon as well. When advanced in years, he made a pilgrimage to Rome and, it is said, founded the first English school there.

INEZ DE CASTRO. *See* CASTRO, INÉS DE.

INFANTE, title borne by the sons of the kings of Spain and Portugal from the thirteenth century.

INFERNO, title of the first part of Dante's *Divine Comedy*.

INFESSURA, STEFANO, d. c. 1500, teacher of law at Rome, a judge in Orte, and author of an uncritical history of Rome from 1303 to 1494. It is useful, however, for the pontificates of Martin V and Eugenius IV and for the popes from 1464 to 1492.

INFIDEL, a person who has a strong aversion to Christ and the Christian God, such as the Moslems.

INGEBORG, Danish princess who became the wife of Philip II Augustus of France in 1193. The king had the marriage annulled in 1195 on the ground of consanguinity, then married Agnes of Meran. In 1213, under pressure from Innocent III who had pressed Ingeborg's cause since 1198 when he became pope, Philip took her back.

INGOLSTADT, city in upper Bavaria, first noted in 806, and the residence of the dukes of Bavaria from 1392. The University of Ingolstadt was established in 1472 although authorization for a *studium generale,* composed of all four faculties, had already been issued by Pope Pius II in 1458.

IN HOC SIGNO VINCES, that is, In this sign you will conquer, a Latin version of the words which according to Lactantius Constantine I had seen in a vision prior to doing battle with Maxentius at the Milvian Bridge (312).

INNOCENT I, ST., Pope, 401–17, a vigorous champion of papal claims to the right of exercising authority over the entire church. He achieved greater success in attaining that objective than any of his predecessors. His intent to accomplish this found expression in several of the 36 letters of his that survive. In keeping with his claims, he refused to recognize the deposition of John Chrysostom by an Eastern synod. He also succeeded in bringing eastern Illyricum under his ecclesiastical jurisdiction.

INNOCENT II, Pope, 1130–43, as cardinal (1116) took an active part in the negotiations leading to the Concordat of Worms (1122). A schism vexed his pontificate until 1138 when it was resolved by the Second Lateran Council. First Anacletus II, then Victor IV, reigned as opposing popes (antipopes). They had enjoyed the support of Roger II of Sicily.

INNOCENT III, Pope, 1198–1216, traditionally considered the most powerful of medieval popes. He was born of a noble family in the Roman Campagna, studied at Bologna and Paris, achieved distinction as a canonist, was created cardinal in 1189, and was elected pope at the early age of 37. He composed several theological treatises and hymns and some 6,000 letters including many decretals. As pope he reorganized the Curia, sponsored the Fourth and Albigensian Crusades, and presided over the Fourth Lateran Council (1215) for whose

agenda and pronouncements he was principally responsible.

His claim to a supreme voice in all matters touching faith and morals as well as civil and political disputes not covered by civil law involved him in controversies with several kings. His patience, prudence, perhaps opportunism, together with circumstances over which he had no control, enabled him to persuade John of England (who was fearful of a pope-supported crusade from France) to accept Stephen Langton as archbishop of Canterbury and Philip II Augustus to take back his wife Ingeborg (Philip wished to lead the crusade against John). With less satisfaction he viewed the accession of his ward Frederick II as king of Germany. If Innocent envisaged a Christian commonwealth with all the kings of Western Europe accepting his position as suzerain, it was for the purpose of preventing wars among them and thus enhancing the success of a crusade against the Turks, which was one of his major goals.

INNOCENT IV, Pope, 1243–54, studied at Bologna and taught canon law there, served as papal auditor, was created cardinal (1227), and served as rector of the March of Ancona (1235–40). As pope he continued the bitter struggle of his predecessors against Frederick II of Germany and convoked a general council at Lyons in 1245 which excommunicated and deposed the emperor. He was largely responsible for the election of Henry Raspe, the landgrave of Thuringia, as German antiking in 1246, then prosecuted the war against Conrad IV and Manfred after Frederick's death. He sent several missions to Mongolia in the hope of enlisting the Mongol Khan's aid against the Moslems.

INNOCENT V, BL., Pope, January 21, 1276, to June 22, 1276, a Dominican, teacher of theology at Paris, twice provincial of his order in France, archbishop of Lyons (1272), and cardinal (1273). As pope he worked for union with the Greek church although his support of Charles of Anjou whose ambitions made Constantinople uneasy, did not advance that cause. His most important writing, done while teaching at Paris, was a popular commentary on the *Sentences.*

INNOCENT VI, Pope, 1352–62, professor of civil law at Toulouse, bishop of Noyons (1338) and Clermont (1340), and cardinal (1342). As pope he reorganized the Curia, advocated church reform, and directed Cardinal Gil Albornoz in the task of reestablishing order in the Papal States.

INNOCENT VII, Pope, 1404–6, taught law at Perugia and Padua, for ten years served as papal collector in England, was consecrated archbishop of Ravenna in 1387, and was created cardinal in 1389. His efforts as pope to resolve the Western Schism proved fruitless.

INNOCENT VIII, Pope, 1484–92, son of a Roman senator, became a priest after a dissolute youth, studied at Rome and Padua, was consecrated bishop of Savona (1467) and Molfetta (1472), and created cardinal (1473). As pope he involved himself deeply in Italian political affairs and left the *camera* depleted despite unscrupulous methods to raise revenues including the selling of offices and the creation of new ones to sell. In 1484 he issued the bull *Summis Desiderantes* which condemned witchcraft.

INNOCENTS, FEAST OF HOLY, feast commemorating the slaying of the male babies of Bethlehem and vicinity ordered by King Herod in an effort to bring about the death of the Christ child (Matthew 2:16–18). The feast, commemorated on December 28, was celebrated as early as the fifth century in the West.

INNS OF CHANCERY, groups of chancery clerks in the fourteenth century who occupied various inns where students might learn how to prepare writs and other legal documents in order to qualify for entrance to an Inn of Court. The Inns of Chancery were administered by the Inns of Court.

INNS OF COURT, private legal societies in London which enjoyed the exclusive right of admitting men to the bar. They included Lincoln's Inn, Gray's Inn, Middle Temple, and Inner Temple, all located between Westminster and the business district of London. They appear to have originated the late thirteenth century when legal apprentices began to take up residence in certain inns in order to acquire, under the supervision of prominent jurists, a knowledge of the principles and procedures of common law. The Inns also offered instruction for stewards and legal advisers.

INNSBRUCK, city of Austrian Tirol, originally a small market center whose location on the river Inn on the road leading to the Brenner pass assured its growth and prosperity. It was first noted in 1187, received city rights in 1239 when it was fortified, and became a possession of the Hapsburgs in 1363. It became the capital of Tirol in 1420.

IN PARTIBUS INFIDELIUM, that is, in the land of the unbelievers, phrase attached to titular or nonresidential sees.

INQUISITION, COURT OF THE, special tribunal established by Pope Gregory IX in 1233 for the purpose of eradicating the Waldensian and Albigensian heresies. The term inquisition denoted a judicial procedure aimed at ascertaining the orthodoxy of one accused of heresy. In the early church the usual punishment meted out to the heretic was excommunication although once Christianity became the official religion of the empire, civil authorities might consider heresy a crime against the state which merited confiscation of property and/or death. It was not until the rise of Catharism in the twelfth and thirteenth centuries that ecclesiastical authorities became willing to appeal to the civil authorities to suppress heretical movements and silence heretics with force.

Although the court of the inquisition was technically under the jurisdiction of the local bishop, it functioned as an arm of the papacy and was ordinarily staffed by Dominicans and Franciscans. The court imposed penances short of capital punishment. Persons who refused to retract their errors or who had relapsed were turned over to the civil authorities for execution. The court, which functioned only in France, Italy, and parts of Germany, reached the peak of its activity during the second half of the thirteenth century and generally ceased to operate in the early fourteenth. The court of the inquisition in Spain which Pope Sixtus authorized in 1478 should be viewed as distinct from the medieval court. [See SPANISH INQUISITION.]

I.N.R.I., the initial letters of the phrase *Iesus Nazarenus Rex Iudaeorum* which Pontius Pilate ordered placed above the crucified Christ on the cross (John 19:19).

INSCHALLAH, Arabic for "So God wills," a favorite expression of Moslems to express their submission to the will of God

INSTITUTES, one of the parts of the *Corpus Juris Civilis*. This work, largely based upon the work of Gaius, provided an introduction to the principles of Roman law.

INTERDICT, ecclesiastical order which might deprive a Christian community of all divine services and sacred rites with the exception of baptism and extreme unction. It generally did not extend to, or was suspended for, high feast-days such as Easter, Pentecost, and Christmas. Instances of interdicts appear from the sixth century. They were first imposed on churches in a single city, later on an entire diocese, and from the twelfth century on countries. Pope Innocent III placed England under an interdict from 1208 until 1213 in an effort to force King John to accept Stephen Langton as archbishop of Canterbury.

INTEREST. *See* USURY.

INTERREGNUM, the period between the death of

Conrad IV, king of Germany, in 1254 and the election of Rudolf of Hapsburg in 1273.

INTINCTION, the practice of dipping the Eucharistic bread into the consecrated wine prior to its distribution to the people. There is evidence that the consecrated bread might also be moistened with unconsecrated wine in order to make consumption easier for sick persons. Various methods of intinction had all disappeared in the Latin church by about 1200.

INTROIT, the antiphon with psalm and doxology sung or recited at the beginning of mass.

INVENTION OF THE CROSS, THE. According to the traditional account, St. Helena, the mother of Constantine I, uncovered three crosses on Golgotha, those of Christ and the two thieves crucified with him. By means of a miracle, the identity of the True Cross was established. St. Ambrose was the first Christian writer to speak of this event.

INVESTITURE, the act or ceremony by which a feudal lord granted a fief to a vassal. In the ceremony attending the consecration of a bishop, he was invested with ring and crozier, the symbols of his office.

INVESTITURE CONTROVERSY, controversy between church and state over the right of selecting the bishop (abbot) of a particular diocese (monastery) and of investing him with the insignia (staff and ring) of his office. The fact that the bishop was at once a high ecclesiastic and a vassal promised a struggle over his selection once the papacy had recovered a measure of authority following its near-collapse during the feudal period. That time had come by 1075 in the judgment of Pope Gregory VII when he issued a decree forbidding lay investiture, something reformers were demanding as the *sine qua non* of a reformed church. The person most culpable on the score of lay investiture and appointing his own bishops was the king of Germany who had long depended upon a loyal hierarchy for much of his authority. For this reason the investiture controversy traditionally conjures up the dramatic contest between Gregory VII and Henry IV of Germany, although a similar conflict of interests characterized the relations between church and state throughout the medieval period. For a partial resolution of the controversy, [*See* BEC, COMPROMISE OF, and WORMS, CONCORDAT OF.]

INVOCAVIT, first Sunday of Lent so called after the opening word of the introit.

IONA, ABBEY OF, monastery founded by Columba in 563 on an island in the Inner Hebrides off the west coast of Scotland. From Iona missionaries went out to Scotland and north England to convert the heathen and erect churches and monasteries. Iona maintained its position of leadership in the Celtic church in those parts of the British Isles until the Synod of Whitby (664) which voted in favor of the Roman liturgy and customs as opposed to the Celtic. Serious decline, however, came only with the Viking invasions which began in 795. Their final raid in 986 ended with the destruction of the abbey and the decimation of the community. In 1203 a Benedictine monastery and nunnery were established by the Scottish lord of the island.

IPSWICH, town in Suffolk, an ancient trading center which the Danish Vikings sacked in 991. The manufacture of Ipswich ware and later of Thetford ware apparently continued from the seventh century to the twelfth. The town received a charter c. 1200 and prospered as the export point for the cloth industry of East Anglia. In 1446 it was incorporated.

IRELAND, island to the west of Britain whose principal contact with Western culture during the early Christian era came through raiding parties to the east. The captive destined to be the most famous of those carried off by the Irish was Patrick who later escaped, returned as a monk in 432, and proceeded to convert the island. [*See* PATRICK, ST.] That Pope Celestine I (422–34)

sent Palladius to serve as the first bishop of the Irish suggests that there may have been Christians there before Patrick arrived. During this early period, clans and tribes, loosely organized under five provincial kingdoms, Ulster, Munster, Connaught, Leinster, and Meath, shared control of the island. Since these kings exercised little effective control over their own chieftains and in turn extended only nominal obedience to the high king of Tara, instability and petty wars for a long time were the bane of Ireland. Despite this political turbulence, however, Irish culture enjoyed a Golden Age from c. 500 to 800 through the work of the monasteries and through the instrumentality of dedicated missionaries such as Columba and Columban who carried Christianity and learning to Scotland, north England, and large sections of Gaul and Germany. (The abbey of Bobbio, east of Genoa, was founded by Columban and Irish monks.)

In the late eighth century (795) Norse Vikings made their first attacks on settlements along the east coast and by the middle of the ninth century had taken possession of Dublin, Waterford, and Limerick. Brian Boru, high king of Munster, defeated them in 1014 and ended the domination of Dublin. In the anarchy that followed his death, Dermot Mac Murrough, king of Leinster, fled to England to seek the intervention of Henry II. Henry, who had earlier secured authorization from Pope Adrian IV (the bull *Laudabiliter*) to extend English authority over Ireland, preferred to wait, but he permitted Dermot to recruit on his own. The most aggressive of the Norman lords along the Welsh border whom Dermot enlisted was Richard de Clare, earl of Pembroke, called "Strongbow." He married Dermot's daughter Eva and with other lords made such progress establishing his control that Henry, fearful he might erect an independent state, came over in person in 1171. He received homage from all the kings except those of Connaught and Ulster, and granted Strongbow the land of Leinster.

John, Henry's son, united the lordship of

Ireland (essentially the English Pale) with the English crown and established the first civil government. The growth of the number of English immigrants and their influence stirred increasing native resentment among the Irish, which was further aggravated by the efforts of Edward I to introduce English law and institutions. In 1315 many Irish lords and some Anglo-Normans joined Edward Bruce, brother of Robert I Bruce, king of Scotland, in a short-lived revolt. Lionel, duke of Clarence, the son of Edward III, sought to ensure English dominance with the Statute of Kilkenny (1366) which banned marriage with the Irish and enjoined the use of English as the speech of the colonists. Nevertheless, English influence weakened during the course of the fourteenth century though Richard II might have reversed that trend had the revolt that brought about his abdication not called him back to Britain. The Lancastrian kings paid little attention to Ireland and left its rule to the Anglo-Irish nobility for the most part, specifically to the earls of Desmond, Ormonde, and Kildare. At best the authority of these lords was limited to the eastern half of the island with Irish chieftains continuing in control of the west.

IRELAND, JOHN, d. c. 1500, Scottish literary figure, theologian, and diplomatist. He attended the universities of St. Andrews and Paris, remained in France, and was sent on several diplomatic missions by Louis XI. When Louis died, he returned to Scotland and served as chaplain to James III. It was for James's son, James IV, that he composed *The Meroure of Wyssdome,* a treatise on the importance of wisdom for temporal rulers.

IRENAEUS, ST., d. c. 202, early church father, the first great theologian of the West, a native of Asia Minor and a disciple of Polycarp of Smyrna. He came to Gaul to seek leniency for the Montanists and for those who did not observe the Roman date for Easter, remained there, became a priest, and was later appointed bishop of Lyons. His most important writings are two works in Greek attacking the views of the Gnostics. His is the strongest testimony among the early church fathers in support of the claims of the bishop of Rome to primacy in the church.

IRENE, Byzantine empress, d. 803, wife of Leo IV, who ruled as regent for her son Constantine VI from 780 until 797 when she had him deposed and blinded. She assumed control in her own right until deposed in 802 and exiled to Lesbos. In 787 she summoned the Council of Nicaea (II) which condemned iconoclasm and restored the worship (veneration) of images.

IRNERIUS, d. c. 1130, student of law, taught dialectic and rhetoric at Bologna, founded a school of law there in 1084, and drew up the first system of Roman jurisprudence in the Middle Ages. He was the first to introduce glosses to expound Roman law. Few of his writings are extant. His presence at Bologna contributed to that city's fame as a center of legal studies.

IRON CROWN OF LOMBARDY, a crown presumably made for Theodelinda, widow of Authoris, king of Lombardy, that was given to the duke of Turin in 594. When Charlemagne conquered Lombardy in 774, he acquired the crown for himself.

ISAAC I (Comnenus), Byzantine emperor, 1057–9, an officer who aided in the overthrow of the weak Michael VI and founded the dynasty of the Comneni. He introduced measures to restore a sound economy — the taxes he introduced cost him his popularity — strengthened the frontier defenses, and exiled Michael Caerularius, the patriarch, when he refused to recognize the superior authority of the crown. Ill health led him to abdicate in 1059, and he lived his last two years in a monastery.

ISAAC II (Angelus), Byzantine emperor, 1185–95, 1203–4, assumed power after the murder of Andronicus I Comnenus by a mob in Constantinople, made alliances with Hungary and Serbia, but was obliged to recognize the

Bulgarian empire. In 1195 his brother Alexius III dethroned and blinded him. For eight years he remained in prison until the Crusaders (Fourth Crusade) put him back on the throne (July 1203). Six months later he was again deposed.

ISAAC ISRAELI (Judaeus), d. c. 932, Jewish physician, a native of Egypt, who served as personal physician to the caliph at Kairouan (Tunisia). His medical and philosophical writings (in Arabic), which were translated into Hebrew and Latin, proved influential in both Jewish and Christian thought.

ISAAC (the Great) (of Antioch), ST., d. 439, Catholicos of the Armenian church. He studied at Constantinople and became Catholicos in 390. He succeeded in gaining patriarchal status for the church in Armenia, thus ending its dependence on Caesarea (Cappadocia). He helped in the translation of the Bible and many Greek works and in fostering the growth of a national Armenian literature. He may also have composed many Armenian hymns.

ISAAK (Yzaac), HEINRICH, d. 1517, Flemish composer who taught and composed music at the courts of Lorenzo the Magnificent and Maximilian I of Germany. He composed a collection of polyphonic masses for the Sundays of the year.

ISABEAU (Isabella), d. 1435, Bavarian princess, wife of Charles VI of France (1385). She endorsed the leadership of her brother-in-law Louis of Orléans when her husband became mentally ill, but subsequently threw her support to John the Fearless, duke of Burgundy, after he had murdered Louis. She accepted the disinheritance of her son, the future Charles VII, as provided by the terms of the Treaty of Troyes (1420). Her daughter Catherine became the wife of Henry V of England.

ISABELLA OF ANGOULÊME, d. 1246, married King John of England although already be-trothed to Hugh of Lusignan, thereby providing Philip II Augustus of France with the legal grounds upon which to seize Normandy and other fiefs held by John. She became the mother of Henry III.

ISABELLA I OF CASTILE, d. 1504, daughter of John II of Castile, married Ferdinand of Aragon in 1469, and in 1474 succeeded her step-brother Henry IV as ruler of Castile. In 1479 Ferdinand succeeded to the throne of Aragon and two years later proclaimed Isabella his co-ruler. From 1481 the "Catholic Kings" Ferdinand and Isabella ruled both kingdoms jointly. Isabella encouraged church reforms and was the principal patron of Columbus.

ISABELLA OF FRANCE, d. 1358, daughter of Philip IV, the wife of Edward II of England, and mother of Edward (III). In 1325 she went to France, there joined her lover Roger Mortimer, earl of March, invaded England in 1326, deposed Edward the year following and had him murdered. Three years later her son Edward seized control, had Mortimer executed, and forced her to retire from the court.

ISAURIANS, warlike tribesmen of the mountains of southern Anatolia whose chieftain, Zeno, became Byzantine emperor in 474. The emperor Justinian I (527–565) appears to have finally managed to tame their fierceness.

ISEGRIM (Isengrim), old German hero whose name came to be associated in Flanders with the wolf in the *Roman de Renart*.

ISEULT. *See* ISOLDE.

ISIDORE OF KIEV, d. 1464, monk and abbot of the convent of Demetrius in Constantinople, theologian, humanist, and scholar. As metropolitan of Kiev he attended the Council of Ferrara-Florence (1438) where he vigorously supported union with Rome. After his return to Moscow he was deprived of his office and imprisoned. He subsequently moved to Rome where he was

ISLAMIC ART AND ARCHITECTURE

appointed patriarch of Constantinople although he never occupied the see.

ISIDORE OF MILETUS, name of two architects from the reign of Justinian I. The first Isidore collaborated with Anthemius of Tralles in building the church of Hagia Sophia (532–7). The younger Isidore supervised the rebuilding of the dome after its destruction by an earthquake in 553.

ISIDORE OF PELUSIUM, ST., d. 435 or 449, church father, monk, and theologian of Alexandria, who endorsed the Christological views of Athanasius and John Chrysostom. For some 40 years he served as abbot of a monastery near Pelusium (Nile delta). The 2,000 letters he left reveal his knowledge of classical writers and patristic literature and his preference for the literal method of biblical interpretation pursued in Antioch.

ISIDORE OF SEVILLE, ST., d. 636, archbishop of Seville (600) and author of exegetical and theological writings, a universal chronicle, a collection of biographies of 86 figures from the Bible, a volume on heresies, and, above all, the *Etymologies (Origins),* an encyclopedia of religious and secular learning. Despite its deficiencies, it enjoyed great popularity as a reference work. Isidore's imperfect knowledge of Greek limited him in his examination of scholarly sources, while the ambitious scope of his undertaking left a critical examination of much of his information impossible. Isidore was a zealous prelate, founded schools and convents, and encouraged the conversion of Jews.

ISLAM, term that may be applied to the Moslem religion, to Moslems collectively, or to the empire ruled by the successors of Mohammed. The word means submission or resignation, that is, acceptance of the will of Allah. [For the history of Islam, *see* CALIPHATE, OMAYYADS, and ABBASIDS. For the religion of Islam, *see* MOHAMMED; FIVE PILLARS OF ISLAM; AND KORAN. For Islamic art, *see* ISLAMIC ART AND ARCHITECTURE.]

ISLAMIC ART AND ARCHITECTURE. Because the civilization of the Arabs in Mohammed's time was generally inferior to that of their neighbors, the Moslems often adopted the ways of the peoples they conquered, and this included their art forms as well, with one significant exception. Given the Koranic prohibition against depicting living forms, either human or animal, interior decoration remained abstract or so stylized as to obscure the geometric and plant forms from which it had originated. Elaborate designs of intertwined flowers, foliage, and geometrical patterns in either paint or low relief characterized the interior wall decoration of Islamic structures. This type of interior decoration was so characteristic of the Arab world that it acquired the identification of arabesque. In time, some of the Islamic sects permitted the painting of figures and pictures, provided these were not associated with religion, so that in Persia and India, for example, exquisitely drawn pictures appeared on walls and in manuscripts, illustrating romances, histories, and fables in an illusionistic but still thoroughly intelligible manner.

Moslem architecture was typified by the mosque, a word derived from the Arabic meaning "a place of prostration" (to God). At first, any place or almost any kind of building, even a former Christian church, might serve as a mosque. As Moslem liturgy matured and became standardized, the mosque acquired architectural and decorative characteristics. These included a central hall, often covered with a dome, such as the Mosque of Omar; the interior wall toward Mecca marked by a semicircular, recessed area called a *mihrab,* which was reserved for the imam who led the prayers and which pointed out the *qibla,* that is, the direction to Mecca toward which the faithful faced during prayer; an open courtyard surrounded by colonnaded or arcaded porticoes, with wells and fountains where the faithful performed their ablutions before prayer; and a minaret from which a muezzin summoned the faithful to prayer. Stucco carvings and brilliant polychrome ce-

389

ramics, often matching the arabesque decoration that illuminated the interiors of their mosques, adorned the exteriors. Because of the extensive destruction suffered from time to time by the cities of Syria and Iraq — the great mosque in Damascus was destroyed during Timur the Lame's occupation of the city — the most imposing and best preserved structures from the Middle Ages are found in Spain, including the largest of all mosques, that at Córdoba. [*See* ALHAMBRA.]

ISLIP, SIMON, d. 1366, royal clerk, member of the king's council, and archbishop of Canterbury (1349). He terminated the ancient controversy with the archbishop of York over precedence and also showed himself a generous benefactor of Oxford.

ISMA'ILISM, a Shi'ite sect, branch of the Shi'ah movement, that took its name from Isma'il (mid-eighth century). Isma'ili missionaries were active from the ninth century preaching the return of Mohammed, the son of Isma'il. The Karmatians, Fatimids, and Druzes represented offshoots from Isma'ilism. After the death of Caliph al-Mustansir in 1094, the main body split between the Musta'lis of Egypt and Yemen and the Nizaris of Persia and Syria. In 1171 Saladin deposed the last Fatimid caliph and extinguished Isma'ilism in Egypt. The Nizaris seized control of several fortresses in Persia and Syria where they employed war and assassination to expand their possessions, whence their nickname "Assassins."

ISOLDE (Iseult), the beloved of Tristan in the Tristan courtly romance; name of two characters in Arthurian legend.

ISTE CONFESSOR DOMINI COLENTES, breviary hymn honoring confessors and bishops. It has been credited to an unknown poet who lived in the eighth century or possibly somewhat earlier.

ITALY. Upon the death of Theodosius in 395, the western half of the Roman empire went its own way, officially under Emperor Honorius, son of Theodosius, and his imperial successors, more frequently under the direction of the German chieftain who happened to command the army. Stilicho, a Vandal, who held that position under Honorius, was able to prevent the Visigoths and their king Alaric from invading Italy. His execution in 408 opened the door, and in 410 the Visigoths sacked Rome. Men who bore the title Roman emperor but with ever diminishing authority continued to occupy the throne until 476 when Odoacer deposed Romulus Augustulus. He retained control of Italy until 493 when Theodoric, king of the Ostrogoths, slew him and established a kingdom that endured until c. 555 when the last of it fell to the armies of the Byzantine emperor Justinian. A tragic casualty of the twenty years of destructive warfare which this recovery of Italy entailed was classical culture.

In 568, three years after the death of Justinian, the Lombards under King Alboin invaded Italy, but his early death prevented their conquest of the entire peninsula. Italy remained a divided country from this time until 1870. In general the Lombards encountered no great difficulty in taking over the countryside and staking out a number of autonomous principalities for themselves. The larger cities, including Naples, Rome, and Ravenna, which the Byzantine navy could assist, together with Sicily, Apulia, and Calabria, remained under the authority of Constantinople. As Byzantine power waned during the seventh and eighth centuries, the Lombards made a last effort to complete their work. In 751 they seized Ravenna, then turned their attention to Rome. To save the city, the pope, who had fallen heir to Byzantine authority there, appealed to the Franks for assistance. In 754 Pepin III drove off the Lombards, and in 756 handed over to the pope the administration of Rome, the exarchate of Ravenna, and Pentapolis. [*See* DONATION OF PEPIN.] In 774 Charlemagne made an end to the Lombard kingdom and confirmed Pepin's Donation, although he retained its overlordship for himself. His title, (Holy) Roman emperor, served to preserve the notion for his German successors that they were entitled to the dominant position he had held in the peninsula.

The Treaty of Verdun (843) not only divided the empire of Charlemagne in three parts but also heralded the coming of the feudal age and an extended period of instability for Italy. Saracens, who had already attacked Sicily, now harassed cities along the west coast. Magyars carried their devastating raids down into the Po valley. Inside Italy Lombard margraves, dukes, and counts, even kings of Provence and Burgundy, together with a rejuvenated Byzantine empire, fought for control of the peninsula. A new era opened in 951 with the appearance of Otto I, king of Germany, who forced Berengar, king of Lombardy, to recognize his suzerainty, revived the title of Roman emperor for himself, and placed his own pope in Rome. His grandson, the visionary Otto III, even made Rome his home.

Two unexpected powers blocked the fruition of the dream of the German kings to rule Italy. One was a revitalized papacy, extricated from the mire of Roman factional strife by the German kings, whose pretensions to rule Italy it then blocked by allying itself, first with the princes of Germany against the crown (Henry IV), then with the cities of north Italy (Lombardy). The second power to thwart the German dream was that of the Normans under Robert Guiscard (d. 1085) and his brother Roger (I). They drove the Saracens from Sicily and southern Italy, captured Bari, the last Byzantine outpost in Italy, and in 1084 rescued Pope Gregory VII from Henry IV and his Germans who had him under attack in Rome. The Normans then proceeded to establish the first "modern" state in southern Italy and Sicily.

Difficulties in Germany kept its king out of Italian affairs until 1154 when Frederick I Barbarossa made the first of six expeditions south of the Alps. By this time the cities of north Italy, principally Milan, Florence, Pisa, Genoa, and Venice, had grown prosperous and powerful, in fact practically independent since for more than fifty years there had been no German king around to curb their aggressiveness. While the papacy wasted no love on these cities — many had run roughshod over the traditional rights of their episcopal lords — it had no choice but throw in its lot with the Lombard League and help it accomplish the defeat of Frederick at Legnano (1176). This did not close out the threat of German domination. Frederick's son Henry brought it even closer with his marriage to the heiress of Sicily and southern Italy, but his premature death in 1197 delayed the crisis. This came during the reign of Frederick II, son of Henry, who from c. 1230 until his death in 1250 battled the cities of Lombardy and the papacy for the mastery of the peninsula. For the papacy the situation appeared so desperate that it prevailed upon Louis IX of France to permit his brother Charles of Anjou to bring his army into Italy. While Charles did put an end to the threat of German domination when he executed Conradin, the grandson of Frederick II, in 1268, the situation for the papacy was scarcely any better. Instead of Germans, there were now the French, the cities of the north — Milan, Florence, Genoa, and Venice — more aggressive than ever, and from 1282 when they seized control of Sicily, the Aragonese to worry about. (For the history of Italy in the later Middle Ages, see individual states such as Milan, Naples, Venice, and the Papal States.)

ITE, MISSA EST, that is, "Go, it is the dismissal," the dismissal form used in the West from probably the third century to conclude the liturgy of the mass.

ITINERARIUM, guidebook providing information for the use of pilgrims who wished to visit certain shrines such as Jerusalem.

IUS: *ius curiae,* court law; *ius de non appellando et non evocando,* the exemption of German imperial electors from summonses to the imperial court; *ius primae noctis, see* JUS PRIMAE NOCTIS; *ius utrumque,* either of the two laws, civil or canon; *ius spolii,* right of the king to the movable property of a prelate upon his decease.

IVAIN (Iwein), hero in the Arthurian romance. He appears in the stories of Chrétien de Troyes and Hartmann von Aue.

IVAN II (Ivan Asen), d. 1241, czar of Bulgaria (1218–41), son of Kaloyan, who did not succeed immediately to the throne as his cousin usurped it. Ivan fled to Russia but returned in 1218, captured his cousin, and was crowned czar. Under Ivan the Bulgarian empire reached its greatest extent and was the strongest state in the Balkans.

IVAN I (Danilovich), grand prince of Vladimir (1328–41) and Moscow (1325–41), the son of Daniel of Moscow. He moved his own residence and that of the metropolitan from Vladimir to Moscow. He expanded his influence over neighboring principalities, appropriated the right to collect the tribute Russian princes paid to the khan of the Golden Horde, and made himself the richest and most powerful of the Russian lords. In 1331 he secured the title of grand prince.

IVAN III (Vasilievich), czar of Russia, 1462–1505, called the Great, as grand duke of Moscow conquered what Lithuanian lands lay east of the Dnieper, annexed Novgorod, forced out the Mongols, and united all of Russia under his rule. He also insisted that his marriage to Sophia, niece of Constantine XI, the last of the Byzantine emperors, gave him title to the position of Roman Caesar. Sophia helped introduce the customs of the Byzantine court. Ivan codified the laws, welcomed foreign artisans, and with the help of Italian architects erected churches and fortifications.

IVO OF CHARTRES, ST., d. 1115, the leading canonist of his day, studied at Paris and Bec, prior of the Canons Regular of St. Quentin in Beauvais, and bishop of Chartres (1090). He composed sermons, letters, and three collections of canons which may have been the most extensive before the appearance of Gratian's *Decretum*. His criticism of Philip I of France who wished to divorce his wife and marry another led to his imprisonment.

JACKE, outer garment worn by men and women from the fourteenth century. It consisted of a light, often sleeveless coat. It was also worn by soldiers to replace the earlier heavy leather jacket which had afforded them some protection against pointed missiles.

JACOBA VAN BEIEREN. *See* JACQUELINE.

JACOBINS, name given to Dominicans in Paris from their monastery of St. James which they occupied since 1218.

JACOBITES, name generally applied to the members of the Monophysite church in Syria which had broken communion with Rome during the Acacian Schism (484 – 519). The name derived from Jacobus Baradaeus (d. 578) who is said to have consecrated 30 bishops and ordained thousands of priests and deacons in the course of his missionary travels from Persia to Egypt. The Jacobites welcomed the invasion of the Arabs as promising them freedom from the repressive decrees issuing from Constantinople. The Jacobite patriarch of the twelfth century counted some two million souls scattered through Syria, Mesopotamia, and Cyprus.

JACOB OF VORAGINE. *See* JACOBUS DE VORAGINE.

JACOB OF SERUGH (Sarug), d. 521, Syrian church father, monk and bishop of Batan (Sarug). He was a prolific scholar and left hymns, homilies, funeral orations, biographies, exegetical works, and letters. He may have been inclined toward Monophysitism.

JACOBS'S SHELL, scallop carried by a pilgrim on his hatband on his way back from Jerusalem. It identified him as a pilgrim.

JACOBUS (Jacopo, James) DE VORAGINE, d. 1298, Italian hagiographer, Dominican preacher and theologian, provincial of the order in Lombardy, and archbishop of Genoa (1292). His fame rests upon his immensely popular *Legenda Aura* (Golden Legend), a collection of lives of the saints and of stories from the lives of Jesus and Mary, both authentic and legendary. His work was translated into all Western languages.

JACOB VAN MAERLANT. *See* MAERLANT, JACOB VAN.

JACOPONE DA TODI (Jacopo de' Beneditti), d. 1306, Franciscan lay brother and mystic who was imprisoned (1298 – 1303) by Boniface VIII for poems that had attacked the pope's position on poverty. (Jacopone adhered to the Spiritual Franciscans.) He also composed poems on ascetical and mystical themes, expressing deep fervor. Scholars no longer judge him the author of the *Stabat Mater*.

JACQUELINE (Jakobäa, Jacoba), d. 1436, countess of Holland, heiress of Bavaria, Holland, Zeeland, and Hainaut. She failed to secure possession of these lands for herself despite successive marriages to John of Brabant, Humphrey of Gloucester, and Frank of Borselen. Most of them went instead to Philip the Good, duke of Burgundy.

JACQUERIE, a peasant revolt that erupted in 1358 north of Paris near Compiègne shortly after the defeat of the French army at Poitiers

(1356). The uprising was triggered by the pillaging of French mercenaries, now without pay or direction, who roamed the countryside almost at will. The *Jacquerie* was directed against nobles because of their failure to protect the peasantry from these marauders while at the same time demanding the traditional rents and services. The uprising brought destruction to many castles and nobles, but many more of the peasantry died in the ruthless countermeasures taken against them toward the end of the summer of 1358. The term *Jacquerie* is derived from the name Jacques Bonhomme which was given to the French peasant by the nobility, often with a contemptuous connotation.

JACQUES DE MOLAY. *See* MOLAY, JACQUES DE. [*See* TEMPLARS, ORDER OF KNIGHTS.]

JACQUES (James) DE VITRY, d. 1240, theologian, hagiographer, bishop of Acre, and cardinal. He secured papal approval for the Beguines (1216) and preached against the Albigenses. His letters, sermons, and historical writings furnish information about monastic developments of the period and, in general, about conditions in France, Italy, and the Crusading states in the east.

JADWIGA (Hedwig), d. 1399, Polish queen, daughter of Louis I of Hungary. She married Jagiello of Lithuania, grand prince of Lithuania, in 1386 and through this alliance united the two countries in their struggle against the Teutonic Knights. She restored the regions of Lvov and Galich to Poland and founded a college of theology in Cracow.

JAFFAR (Djafar), the Barmecide, younger son of Yahya and a boon companion of Harun al-Rashid until 803 when the caliph suddenly ordered him beheaded. His name is linked with that of the caliph in the *Thousand and One Nights*.

JAGIELLO (Jagello, Jogaila), d. 1434, grand duke of Lithuania in 1377, king of Poland as Ladislaus II in 1386 upon his marriage to Jad-

wiga (Hedwig), queen of Poland. He accepted baptism before this marriage and took the name of Ladislaus. The alliance between the two countries enabled him to gain a decisive victory over the Teutonic Knights in the battle of Grunwald (Tannenberg) in 1410.

JALAL-UD-DIN RUMI (Mohammed Ibn Mohammed Moulavi Balkhi), d. 1273, one of the greatest mystical poets of Persia. He was born in Balkh but moved to Asia Minor where he abandoned his post as teacher of theology and philosophy for the pursuit of Sufi mysticism. He is considered the founder of the Mevlevi order of "dancing" dervishes.

JAMES I (the Conqueror), king of Aragon, 1213–76, count of Barcelona, proved himself an able administrator and legislator, and extended his favor to the schools and the Mendicant orders. He took the Balearic Islands and Valencia from the Moors and by the Treaty of Corbeil with Louis IX in 1258 agreed that Cerdana and Roussillon should mark the northernmost limit of Aragonese territorial ambitions. Louis relinquished all claims to Catalonia. James left a chronicle of his reign.

JAMES II, king of Aragon, 1291–1327, son of Peter III from whom he received Sicily in 1285. When his brother Alfonso III died in 1291, he became king of Aragon. In 1295 he surrendered Sicily to the Angevin rulers of Naples in exchange for Corsica and Sardinia. He managed to occupy only Sardinia. He showed himself a patron of letters and founded the University of Lérida (1300).

JAMES I, king of Scotland, 1424–37, son of Robert III. In 1406 when Robert sent him to France to protect him from assassins, he was captured by the English and held prisoner until 1424. Before returning to Scotland as king, he married Joan Beaufort, daughter of the earl of Somerset. As king he curbed the turbulent nobles and brought peace to Scotland. His legal reforms encountered much opposition, and he was murdered. If the poems attributed to him are his, he must be recognized as one of Scotland's leading poets.

JAMES II, king of Scotland, 1437–60, son of James I, succeeded in gaining the throne with the help of William, earl of Douglas. In 1452 he charged him with treason and slew him. He was an ally of the Lancastrians in the Wars of the Roses.

JAMES III, king of Scotland, 1460–88, son of James II, a man of culture but unequal to the task of ruling so unstable a country. In 1482 he invaded England against Edward IV who had befriended his rebellious brother Alexander, but was taken prisoner by the earl of Angus. Later a group of nobles murdered him.

JAMES OF THE MARCHES, ST., d. 1476, Franciscan Observant who preached against the Hussites, Bogomils, and Fraticelli. He established a number of *montes pietatis* in Italy.

JAMES OF VITERBO, d. 1308, joined the order of Hermits of St. Augustine, studied at Paris, and served there as the order's first master in theology. He became bishop of Benevento (1302) and archbishop of Naples (1303). His writings include commentaries on the Bible and the earliest known treatise on the church (*De Regimine Christiano*).

JAMES, SS., the name of two of the apostles: a) the Less, son of Alphaeus; b) the Greater, son of Zebedee.

JANE, a silver coin of Genoa introduced into England in the late fourteenth century.

JANIZARIES (Janissaries), meaning "new troops," a special corps of soldiers organized by Turkish sultans from 1329 and composed of slaves and prisoners. The children of subject Christian peoples began to be enrolled in the corps in 1360. The soldiers served on foot and constituted the sultan's guard. They were re-garded as almost his slaves and were completely subject to his will.

JANUARIUS (Gennaro), d. c. 305, bishop of Benevento, martyred at Pozzuoli, and honored as the patron saint of Naples where his remains were moved. Both Gregory of Tours and Bede make mention of him. Among other miracles associated with him was the liquefaction of his blood a number of times each year.

JARL, a Scandinavian chieftain or nobleman. He corresponded to the earl in Anglo-Saxon England.

JARROW, ABBEY OF, Benedictine monastery in Northumbria founded in 681 by Ceolfrid. It was considered a sister abbey of the house founded c. 673 by Benedict Biscop at Wearmouth, six miles away. The two houses were considered a joint foundation and were usually administered by one and the same abbot. The Norse sacked Jarrow in 794, the Danes in 867, and William the Conqueror in 1069.

JEAN DE MEUN. *See* ROMAN DE LA ROSE.

JEANNE D'ARC. *See* JOAN OF ARC.

JEANNE DE FRANCE. *See* JOAN OF FRANCE.

JENGHIZ KHAN. *See* GENGHIS KHAN.

JENSON, NICHOLAS, d. 1480, French publisher and printer who learned his skills in Mainz under John Gutenberg. He moved to Venice in 1470 where he published more than 150 titles. The *Antiqua* type he used encouraged the development of a newer Anglo-Saxon typography.

JEROME OF PRAGUE, d. 1416, a disciple of John Hus, attended the universities of Prague, Paris, and Oxford, and from the last university brought back to Prague some of Wyclif's doctrines. At Prague he took a major part in the struggle between Czech and foreign masters and was largely instrumental in persuading King Wenceslas to give the Czechs majority control. He was arrested at Constance where he had gone to help defend Hus and was there condemned as a heretic and burned at the stake. He died reciting hymns to the Blessed Virgin.

JEROME (Hieronymus), ST., d. 419 or 420, a leading church father of the West and author of the *Vulgate*. He was probably born in the vicinity of Aquileia, spent some time with an ascetic group in that city, then after a pilgrimage to Jerusalem took up the life of a hermit in the Syrian desert. After two years, he moved to Constantinople, next to Rome where he served as secretary to Pope Damasus. While in Rome he directed the spiritual instruction of a group of noble widows and virgins, some of whom followed him to Bethlehem where he retired shortly after the death of Damasus. The last 20 years of his life he spent in a monastery that Paula, one of these women, had built for him. He undertook his most celebrated work, the *Vulgate,* a translation of the Bible, upon the direction of Pope Damasus. While he might have employed a polished classical style — he was probably the leading classical scholar of the period — he chose a simpler Latin which a larger number of people would find more suitable. Its name, Vulgate, from the word for common, proved the wisdom of his choice. He left more than 100 letters, some history, hagiography, and biography, together with treatises on moral, exegetical, and dogmatic subjects. His militant nature comes through in the writings he leveled against Arianism, Pelagianism, and Origenism. He translated the *World Chronicle* of Eusebius of Caesarea and 14 of Origen's homilies. In art he is frequently represented with a lion at his feet. [*See* VULGATE.]

JERUSALEM, KINGDOM OF, Crusading state established after the capture of Jerusalem in July 1099. Godfrey of Bouillon, one of the leaders of the First Crusade, ruled the kingdom as Protector of the Holy Sepulcher. His brother Baldwin, who succeeded him in 1100, assumed the title king. In 1187 the city of Jerusalem fell to Saladin shortly after he had crushed a Crusading army at Hattin, but the kingdom maintained its existence and even recovered bits of territory by treaty in 1229 and 1241. In 1229 Emperor Frederick II secured possession of the city by treaty with the sultan of Egypt, after which it remained in Christian hands until 1244 when it fell to the Khwarismian Turks. From 1268 the kings of Cyprus assumed the title of kings of Jerusalem. The fall of Acre in 1291 extinguished what remained of the kingdom.

JERUSALEM, LITURGY OF, essentially the liturgy of Antioch although originally that of the Christian community in Jerusalem This liturgy had been brought to Antioch and from there spread throughout Syria and Asia Minor.

JERUSALEM, PATRIARCHATE OF, was recognized by the Council of Chalcedon (451) as having jurisdiction over 50 bishoprics and holding fifth place of honor after Rome, Constantinople, Alexandria, and Antioch.

JESUATI (Gesuati), lay congregation dedicated to the care of the sick and the burial of the dead. The order, which was founded by Blessed John Colombini about 1366, took its name from the frequent use of the name of Jesus by its members. In 1426 the order adopted the Rule of St. Augustine; it had earlier followed that of Benedict. The order spread throughout Italy and into southern France.

JESU, CORONA VIRGINUM, hymn, probably composed by Ambrose, that honored Christ as the heavenly bridegroom.

JESU, DULCIS MEMORIA, hymn honoring the holy name of Jesus. Its authorship was once ascribed to Bernard of Clairvaux but it is now believed to have been composed by an English Cistercian of the late twelfth century.

JESU, REDEMPTOR OMNIUM, hymn identified as Ambrosian although it was probably not composed until the eighth century. Its theme is that of Christ, the Redeemer.

JEWS, PERSECUTION OF. A number of Jewish revolts, which the Roman emperors put down with a ruthlessness that depopulated Judaea, left the Jews scattered about the Roman world with no common national or religious center. They retained their identity, however, wherever they migrated, because of their attachment to their ancestral traditions and laws. This loyalty prevented their absorption into the larger non-Jewish populations about them, but at the cost of discrimination minorities have generally suffered. Such was especially the case in the Middle Ages when Christianity, the religion that had triumphed, had as its founder Christ, the man whom the Jews were accused of crucifying. When conditions were bad or evils struck — pestilence, famine, war — it was easy, almost proper, to hold the Jews responsible.

In general no great change occurred in the condition of the Jews when the pagan Roman world became Christian. A number of legal enactments made their way into codes that limited their freedom of action and discriminated against them in their social life, although restrictions of this sort were not serious, and actual persecution, as in Visigothic Spain, was uncommon. Popes like Gregory I (the Great) forbade their persecution and forced conversion.

The rise of Islam served to improve the lot of Jews throughout that part of the Mediterranean world that came under Moslem control. True, like Christians, they were excluded from public office and paid a poll tax, but Islam permitted them to hold to their religious and social traditions without interference. In Moorish Spain, Jews enjoyed a freedom seldom accorded them in recent centuries. Jewish scholars and wealthy Jews moved into prominent positions in the government, while philosophers, mystics, scholars, and poets were free to develop their talents. The result was the most impressive flowering of Jewish culture in all the Middle Ages.

The Spanish situation worsened with the advent of the *Reconquista* in the eleventh century and as more and more Moorish territory was taken over by the Christian states of Leon, Castile, and Aragon. Only in the late fourteenth century, however, did repressive measures and persecution produce the first compulsory ghettoes in Europe, leading many Jews to accept baptism while continuing to honor their traditional loyalties in secret It was to root out this element, the Marranos, that the medieval inquisition was reinstituted in 1478. This resulted in the execution of many Jews and led in 1492 to the expulsion from Spain of all Jews still in the country.

The expulsion of Jews from Spain followed their expulsion from England in 1290, later from France, Portugal, and parts of Germany. Such harsh measures may be traced to the Crusades which began in 1096 and which sharpened and brought to the surface latent prejudices harbored against the Jews. Brutal massacres occurred in the Rhineland and elsewhere in central and eastern Europe, despite efforts of churchmen such as Bernard of Clairvaux to prevent them. During this period, vicious calumnies were propagated against the Jews, such as "ritual murders" that charged them with murdering Christians to obtain blood for the Passover and other rituals.

Beyond the prejudice against Jews almost inherent in medieval Christianity, the reputation of Jews as exorbitant money-lenders prepared a ready soil in which such vicious accusations took root. When the Jews left Palestine where many had engaged in agriculture and small industry, they moved into trade, and in time, by dint of industry and thrift, they found themselves among the few in the early Middle Ages who had money to lend. This role earned them the animosity many people bear toward money-lenders, particularly since the rates they charged were necessarily high in order to cover loans which influential creditors had repudiated. With the rise of trade and banking in the high Middle Ages, Jews found themselves elbowed out of the loan business by Lombards and Cahorsins and were left to content themselves with pawn operations, a type of activity that engendered neither sympathy nor respect.

Legislation of the Third and Fourth Lateran Councils (1179 and 1215) required Jews to wear a distinguishing badge and barred Christians from lodging in their streets. Such regulations were poorly enforced; they were intended not to be discriminatory but rather to protect Christians from possible scandal. [*See* GHETTO.] It is significant that Rome is the only major city of Europe where the Jewish community has been able to continue undisturbed from antiquity to the present. There were no persecutions of Jews in the Papal States or in Avignon. Apart from periodic pogroms, their lot in Germany was generally tolerable since they were under the protection of the emperor, a privileged status which cost them a heavy tax. Indeed, medieval kings often protected Jews from violent persecution, partly to prevent the disturbance of the peace, partly because they did not want the Jews to be robbed of the money they planned to take for themselves. Among the few monarchs who actually welcomed Jews was Casimir III (the Great) (1333–70) who invited them to help build up his country's economy.

JIHAD (Jehad), the "holy war" which some Moslems believed Mohammed had ordered them to wage against unbelievers.

JIMÉNEZ (Ximénes) DE CISNEROS, FRANCISCO, d. 1517, Spanish cardinal, grand inquisitor, and statesman. He studied at the University of Salamanca, became vicar general of the diocese of Sigüenza, then joined the Franciscan order. In 1492 Isabella of Castile appointed him her confessor. As archbishop of Toledo in 1495 he urged the government to force Moslems to become Christians, even to conquer north Africa, and he helped finance the capture of Oran and other ports. In 1507 he became a cardinal and was appointed grand inquisitor. In 1508 he founded the University of Alcala.

JINN (Djinn), lower spirits in Arabic and Moslem demonology.

JOACHIM, according to Christian apochryphal literature, the father of Mary who became the mother of Jesus.

JOACHIMITES, the followers of Joachim of Fiore.

JOACHIM OF FIORE (Floris, Flora), d. 1201 or 1202, a Cistercian mystic and a philosopher of history. He was born in Calabria, lived for some years the life of a lay preacher, then joined the Cistercians and in 1177 became abbot of the monastery at Corazzo. His zeal to lead a more austere life prompted him to found a monastic community of his own at San Giovanni in Fiore which received the approval of Pope Celestine III in 1196. His mystical views on the Trinity influenced the Spiritual Franciscans (Joachimites) although several of these doctrines suffered condemnation after his death. The practice of austerities and his apocalyptical preaching earned him the reputation of holy man and prophet. Dante placed him in Paradise.

JOAN (Joanna) I, queen of Naples, 1343–82, daughter of Charles, duke of Calabria, who succeeded her grandfather King Robert in 1343. She married her cousin Andrew, brother of Louis I of Hungary. When he died (1345), she was accused of his murder. When Louis invaded Naples she fled to Avignon to seek papal protection. There she was acquitted of the charge of murder and, perhaps to show her gratitude, sold Avignon to the papacy (1348). She repulsed a second Hungarian attack in 1350–2, but in 1382 she was captured when Naples fell to Charles of Durazzo and was executed.

JOAN (Joanna) II, queen of Naples, 1414–35, sister and successor of Lancelot. Her succession of favorites and their intrigues kept her court and Naples in turmoil. Her first husband died, her second she imprisoned when he attempted to seize power. Against Louis III, the Angevin claimant to her kingdom, she appealed to Alfonso V of Aragon for help, then when he sought to rule, repudiated him and switched to Louis who died in the process of driving out the Aragonese. Alfonso's brother René seized the throne when she died.

JOAN, "FAIR MAID OF KENT," d. 1385, heiress of the earldom of Kent, widow of Thomas de Holland (d. 1360), married Edward, the Black Prince, in 1361 and bore him the future Richard II. Her eldest son, Thomas de Holland, was designated earl of Kent in 1380.

JOAN OF ARC, d. 1431, peasant girl of Domrémy in Lorraine, called "La Pucelle," the "Maid of Orléans." She was born c. 1412 and as a young girl claimed to have had visions and to have spoken to SS. Michael, Catherine, and Margaret, who urged her to save France. In 1429 she went to Chinon and there convinced the Dauphin Charles (VII) that she was God's messenger sent to help him rescue France from the English. Her appearance and claims inspired the French with new courage. They drove the English army from Orléans which was under siege, then cleared the way to Reims where Charles was crowned July 17, 1429. In May of the year following, Joan fell into the hands of the Burgundians, who turned her over to the English. John of Bedford, uncle of Henry VI, had her tried before the episcopal court presided over by Pierre Cauchon, the bishop of Beauvais, on charges of witchcraft and heresy. She was found guilty and burned at the stake. An appellate court commissioned by Pope Callistus III in 1456 declared Joan innocent of all charges.

JOAN OF FRANCE (Valois) (Jeanne de France), ST., d. 1505, deformed daughter of Louis XI of France, who was forced to marry the duke of Orléans. He had the marriage annulled when Louis died, after which Joan devoted her life to works of charity. She was the foundress of the Franciscan Annunciades.

JOAN (Joanna), Pope, a wholly fictitious character whose existence derived from a story of the thirteenth century and a reference to her in a chronicle by the Dominican Martin of Troppau (d. 1278). According to the legend, she reigned as pope between Leo IV (d. 855) and Benedict III (d. 858). What may have provided the basis of the story was the powerful influence in papal affairs that Theodora, wife of Theophylact, and her daughters Theodora and Marozia enjoyed during the first half of the tenth century.

JOAN (Johanna) THE MAD, d. 1555, daughter of Ferdinand and Isabella of Spain, who married Philip, son of Emperor Maximilian I, in 1496. She was the mother of Charles V.

JOANNES ANDREAE, d. 1348, leading lay canonist of the Middle Ages. He studied at Bologna and taught canon law at Bologna and Padua. He composed commentaries on law and produced several canonical compilations. He is considered the first great historian of canon law.

JOANNES TEUTONICUS (Zemacke), d. 1245 or 1246, a leading glossator of the period, teacher at Bologna and noted for his *Glossa Ordinaria* on the *Decretum* of Gratian. The school of Bologna as well as juridical practice adopted it as the standard apparatus, and it remains a basic source in the study of the history of canon law.

JOCELIN OF BRAKELOND, fl. c. 1170–1215, monk of the Benedictine monastery of Bury-Saint-Edmonds and chronicler of the monastery for the period 1173–1202. His chronicle provides an admirable mirror of monastic life of the time.

JOGLAR, a minstrel, a name given him especially in Languedoc.

JOHANNES DE GROCHEO, fl. c. 1300, author of a treatise on musical theory *(De Musica),* a leading source for the history of the secular music of the period.

JOHANNITIUS (Hunayn Ibn Ishaq), d. 873, Nestorian Christian and physician at the caliph's court in Baghdad. He translated Greek works on medicine, science, and philosophy into Syriac and Arabic, and also contributed treatises of his own on medicine, light, and metaphysics.

JOHN I, ST., Pope, 523–6, went to Constantinople upon orders of Theodoric, king of the Ostrogoths, for the purpose of persuading Emperor Justin and his nephew Justinian to modify their anti-Arian policies. Upon his return, Theodoric imprisoned him for failing in his mission. He probably died of starvation.

JOHN II, Pope, 533–5, Roman priest, the first pope to change his name (Mercurius) upon his election. He excommunicated Scythian monks who had refused to accept the position of the Council of Chalcedon regarding the Trinity and who also objected to Mary's title as the "Mother of God."

JOHN III, Pope, 561–74, pope during the period of Lombard invasions. An indirect consequence of these invasions was the ending of the schism between Rome and the cities of north Italy.

JOHN IV, Pope, 640–2, a Dalmatian by birth who condemned Monothelitism, Pelagianism, and the Celtic manner of dating Easter. He upheld the position of Pope Honorius I on the question of the unity of Christ's will.

JOHN V, Pope, July 685 to August 686, Syrian who had served as Pope Agatho's legate to the Council of Constantinople III (680–1).

JOHN VI, Pope, 701–5, a Greek who quelled the revolt of the Italian militia against the imperial exarch Theophylact who had moved his residence from Sicily to Rome. He also succeeded in persuading Gisulf, the Lombard duke of Benevento, to withdraw from papal territory.

JOHN VII, Pope, 705–7, a Greek who enjoyed good relations with Aribert II, king of the Lombards, who restored to the church the estates it claimed in the Cottian Alps. He returned without comment the 102 canons adopted by the Trullan Council (692) which Justinian II had sent him for his judgment. Pope Sergius I (687–701) had rejected them. John's failure to pass judgment on these canons has received conflicting interpretations.

JOHN VIII, Pope, 872–82, a Roman, archdeacon of Rome, whose pontificate was concerned with problems of an Eastern schism, Saracen attacks on Italy, and factional intrigues in Rome. In order to defend the city from the Saracens he rebuilt its fortifications and established a navy. In 879 he confirmed the consecration of Photius as patriarch of Constantinople. He assured Methodius of his support in his missionary work among the Slavs and approved the use of the Slavonic language in their liturgy.

JOHN IX, Pope, 898–900, a Roman priest and abbot of the Benedictine monastery of Tivoli. Upon his accession he validated the acts of Pope Formosus (d. 896) with the exception of the coronation of Arnulf as German emperor. He also confirmed the rights of the emperor in the election of a pope.

JOHN X, Pope, 914–28, bishop of Bologna and archbishop of Ravenna who owed the papal office to the influence of the family of Theophylact. The latter's daughter Marozia later had him deposed and murdered when he allied himself with King Hugh of Italy. As pope John cooperated with the margrave of Spoleto in defeating the Saracens and driving them from their stronghold on the Garigliano River. He also brought an end to the schism with the Greek church.

JOHN XI, Pope, 931–35/36, son of Marozia, the daughter of Theophylact. As pope he was dominated by his mother who had arranged his election. When his brother Alberic took over the city, he proclaimed himself prince of Rome. Although incarcerated by Alberic, John continued to exercise his spiritual authority from prison.

JOHN XII, Pope, 955–64, son of Alberic II of Spoleto who had him elected pope when only eighteen years of age. He lacked experience and led a scandalous life. Against the threat of Berengar II, king of Italy, he appealed to Otto I of Germany for aid, crowned Otto emperor in 962 when he came to Rome, then conspired with Berengar against him once it became evident that Otto planned to retain a voice in Roman affairs. Otto promptly had John deposed on charges based upon his dissolute life, but once the emperor left Rome, John recovered his office and deprived Leo VIII whom Otto had appointed, of his position. He died when Otto was on his way back to Rome.

JOHN XIII, Pope, 965–72, pious and learned bishop of Narni who owed his election to Otto I of Germany. As pope he gave his encouragement to the Cluniac reform movement and appointed Adalbert archbishop of the newly established province of Magdeburg.

JOHN XIV, Pope, December 983 to August 984, bishop of Pavia who owed his election to the papacy to Otto II of Germany. When Otto II died in 983 and the Germans left Rome, the Crescentii who had been supporting the antipope Boniface VII seized John and put him in prison where he died.

JOHN XV, Pope, 985–96, owed his election to John Crescentius II, "Patrician of the Romans." He introduced the practice of formally canonizing saints, and he accepted the status of Poland as a fief of the papacy (990).

JOHN XVI (XVII), Antipope, 997–8, appointed pope by Crescentius II after Gregory V had been driven from Rome. Otto III of Germany seized and hanged Crescentius, forced John to flee Rome, then when John was captured, had him blinded and confined to a monastery. He died c. 1013.

JOHN XVII, Pope, June 16, 1003, to December 6, 1003, owed his election to Crescentius III, "Patrician of Rome." He succeeded Sylvester II (Gerbert).

JOHN XVIII, Pope, 1003–9, owed his election to the Crescenti family although he managed to administer the affairs of the church with relative freedom. He approved the foundation of the diocese of Bamberg. Some time before he died, he retired to a monastery outside of Rome.

JOHN XIX, Pope, 1024–32/33, member of the powerful Tusculani family which assumed control of the papacy, with the approval of Conrad II of Germany, after the death of Benedict VIII. John, who was the brother of Benedict, was still a layman when appointed pope. He received all the necessary orders in one day. At Easter in the year 1027 he crowned Conrad II emperor. He gave little support to the reform movement in the church.

JOHN XX, actually no pope although erroneously assumed to have reigned for four months between Boniface VII (d. 985) and John XV.

JOHN XXI, Pope, September 13, 1276, to May 20, 1277, a teacher of medicine at the University of Siena, later cardinal bishop of Tusculum (1273). He devoted the efforts of his short pontificate to the ending of the schism with the Greek church. He was the author of a popular work on logic and of treatises on philosophy, theology, and medicine. In the history of philosophy and medicine he is known as Petrus Hispanus (Peter of Spain).

JOHN XXII, Pope, 1316–34, studied at Paris and Orléans, taught canon law at Cahors and Toulouse, served as chancellor to Charles II of Naples, and was created cardinal in 1312. As pope—he was 72 when elected—he both expanded and centralized the papal government at Avignon, created a new financial system that vastly increased papal revenues, published the *Liber Septimus,* a collection of the decretals of

Clement V *(Clementinae),* and encouraged missionary work in distant lands. Most of his difficulties came from the Spiritual Franciscans whose extreme views on apostolic poverty he anathematized. Among others whom he excommunicated were the Fraticelli, Beguines, William of Ockham, and Michael Cesena, the provincial general of the Franciscan order. Louis IV of Germany, whose election John had protested, gave asylum to several Franciscans and encouraged William of Ockham, John of Jandun, and Marsilius of Padua in their attacks on papal power. In 1328 Louis IV promulgated the decree *Licet Juris* which excluded the pope from any voice in the election of the king of Germany or the coronation of the emperor. Louis IV occupied Rome in that same year and appointed a Spiritual Franciscan pope (antipope) who took the name Nicholas V. John's own views on the doctrine of the Beatific Vision drew charges of heresy. He opposed the general view that the souls of the blessed enjoyed the Beatific Vision before the Last Judgment.

JOHN XXIII, Pope (Antipope), 1410–5. As cardinal he had an important role at the Council of Pisa (1409) which declared both Roman and Avignonese popes deposed and chose Alexander V. John was unanimously elected to succeed Alexander on his death and in 1414 summoned the Council of Constance under the direction of Emperor Sigismund, only to find himself deposed by that body in May 1415. He fled Constance, was quickly apprehended, and was held in prison until 1419 when he made his peace with Pope Martin V and accepted the post of bishop of Frascati.

JOHN I (Tzimisces), Byzantine emperor, 969–76, a brilliant general and statesman of Armenian descent who conspired with Empress Theophano in the murder of her husband Nicephorus II Phocas, then ruled in the name of the young sons of Romanus II. He defeated the Bulgars, drove back the Russians, and from the Moslems recovered Damascus and the middle

reaches of the Euphrates. To assure himself of the good will of Otto I, king of Germany, he sent Theophano, probably his niece, to be the wife of Otto's son, Otto (II).

JOHN II (Comnenus), Byzantine emperor, 1118–43, son of Alexius I, crowned despite the intrigues of his sister Anna Comnena. He proved himself both an able diplomat and a good general. He recovered parts of Asia Minor (Cilicia) and Armenia from the Turkish Danishmends, extended his influence over the Crusading states of Syria, obliged Antioch to recognize his suzerainty, and destroyed the Petchenegs who had been ravaging the Balkans.

JOHN III (Ducas Vatatzes), Byzantine emperor at Nicaea, 1222–54, the ablest statesman in the history of the empire of Nicaea. Through skillful diplomacy he recovered significant territories from the Latin Empire of Constantinople, including the cities of Adrianople and Thessalonica (Saloniki), but failed to take Constantinople. He made allies of the Turks and an ally, too, of Frederick II of Germany whose daughter he married. He also revealed a genuine interest in learning and devoted efforts to improving his country's economy.

JOHN V (Palaeologus), Byzantine emperor, 1341–91. He reigned first as a minor under the regency of his father-in-law, John VI Cantacuzenus, who in 1347 seized the throne. In 1354 John Palaeologus managed to recover control with the aid of Genoa, but all his efforts to secure Western aid against the Turks, even to the extent of recognizing the authority of the pope, proved unavailing. In 1371 Sultan Murad I forced him to recognize Turkish suzerainty and to send his son Manuel as a hostage.

JOHN VI (Cantacuzenus), Byzantine emperor, 1347–54, regent for John V Palaeologus until 1347 when he seized the throne with the help of the Turks. On this occasion the Turks made their first appearance in Europe. In 1354 the threat of civil war, a Turkish invasion, and financial ruin drove him to abdicate. He spent his last years as a monk writing his memoirs.

JOHN VIII (Palaeologus), Byzantine emperor, 1425–48, successor of his father Manuel II. He attended the Council of Ferrara-Florence in 1439 and agreed to restore communion with the Latin church. But the Greek church and people of Constantinople refused to ratify reunion with the Latin church, and the last hope of military assistance from the West collapsed with the destruction of the Crusading army at Varna in 1444. When he died, little remained of the Byzantine empire beyond the city of Constantinople itself.

JOHN, king of Bohemia, 1310–46, son of the future Henry VII of Germany. In 1310 he became count of Luxemburg and king of Bohemia (he had married Elizabeth, sister of Wenceslas III), but failed of election to succeed his father when Henry died in 1313. He forced territorial concessions from Casimir III of Poland including the suzerainty of Silesia, acquired Tirol, but neglected Bohemia for the role of knight errant. He took up arms for various rulers from Toulouse to Prussia, and, although blind, died a hero's death fighting for the French at Crécy. His principal success was his part in securing the formal deposition of Louis IV (the Bavarian) as king of Germany and the succession of his son Charles (IV).

JOHN I, king of Castile, 1379–90, son of the future Henry II (1369–79). He announced his adherence to the Avignonese pope Clement VII upon his accession and renewed his country's alliance with France. To protect himself from English attack through Portugal, he married Beatriz, daughter of Ferdinand of Portugal, then invaded that country upon Ferdinand's death in 1383. His attempt to conquer Portugal failed, in fact, prompted John of Gaunt, uncle of Richard II of England, who had claims to the throne of Castile, to invade Leon. Here John was successful, and John of Gaunt withdrew upon payment of a huge indemnity (1388). Meanwhile, in order to raise the enormous sums his wars entailed, John was obliged to make important concessions to the *cortes*. He died of a riding accident.

JOHN, king of England, 1199–1216, youngest son of Henry II and brother of Richard I (Lion-Heart). Contemporary writers exaggerate his cruelty, rapacity, lechery, and faithlessness. He did plot with Philip II Augustus of France to deprive Richard of his throne while he was away on the Crusade and in prison in Germany. John's refusal to accept Stephen Langton as archbishop of Canterbury drew him into a long and acrimonious controversy with Pope Innocent III. [*See* STEPHEN LANGTON.] In 1213, when it appeared that the English barons with French assistance would depose him, he made his peace with Innocent and even recognized him as his feudal suzerain. The major source of baronial discontent which steadily mounted during his reign was the harsh, often cruel, methods he employed to force money from them for the purpose of recovering Normandy, Anjou, and other provinces. These had been seized by Philip II Augustus. Baronial opposition became more overt following Philip's victory at Bouvines (1214) over John's ally, Otto IV of Germany. In June 1215 John's barons forced him to accept *Magna Carta* (Great Charter) in which he acknowledged his subordination to the law of the land and promised to respect their feudal rights. [*See* MAGNA CARTA.]

JOHN II (The Good), king of France, 1350–64, son and successor of Philip VI. He was captured in 1356 and his army annihilated by the Black Prince at Poitiers. He subsequently accepted the Treaty of Bretigny (1360) which recognized English sovereignty over Guienne. He left England in 1360, but after the escape of the hostage who had taken his place as surety for the payment of a huge ransom, he returned.

JOHN I, king of Portugal, 1385–1433, an

illegitimate son of Peter I. He seized the throne when his half-brother Ferdinand died, beat back the invasion of John I of Castile, and was proclaimed king by the *cortes* of Coimbra. To protect himself against future attacks from Castile, he made an alliance with England in 1386 and married Philippa, the daughter of John of Gaunt. He encouraged the explorations undertaken by his third son, Henry the Navigator.

JOHN II, king of Portugal, 1481–95, son of Alfonso V. He proved himself an able statesman as well as a patron of learning and the arts. By means of ruthless measures, he succeeded in strengthening the crown at the expense of the aristocracy. In 1494 he agreed to the Treaty of Tordesillas with Spain which divided the New World between them. Although he encouraged Portuguese exploration down the west coast of Africa — Diaz rounded the Cape of Good Hope in 1488 — he turned a deaf ear to the proposals of Columbus.

JOHN XI BECCUS, patriarch of Constantinople, 1275–9 and 1280–2, first opposed union with the Latin church, then altered his position when convinced of the legitimacy of Rome's claims and subscribed to the union proclaimed at the Council of Lyons in 1274. Upon the patriarch's refusal to accept union, John was elected to replace him, but he failed in his efforts to secure ratification of the union in Constantinople. Most of the clergy, especially the monks, as well as members of the imperial family bitterly opposed union. He abdicated his office in 1279, was reinstated in 1280, then resigned again in 1282 when he was sent into exile. He died in 1297.

JOHN BURIDAN, d. after 1358, a scholastic at Paris who spent perhaps 50 years at the university as teacher and rector (1328–40). Although he was a leading nominalist of the time and a disciple of William of Ockham, his views were not so extreme as to invite censure. He composed commentaries on the *Physics, Ethics,* and *Politics* of Aristotle. His theories in the realm of physics

brought him most fame, in particular his explanation of locomotion by the theory of impetus. Some scholars consider him a precursor of Leonardo da Vinci, Copernicus, and Galileo on the strength of his theories concerning the nature of weight and falling bodies.

JOHN XIV CALECAS, patriarch of Constantinople, 1334–47. He presided over the synod that condemned the theologian Palamas and the doctrine of Hesychasm. He was later deposed and exiled for his part in this condemnation. His writings included polemical tracts and treatises on disciplinary, dogmatic, and canonical subjects.

JOHN X CAMATEROS, patriarch of Constantinople, 1198–1206, who fled to Bulgaria when the city fell to the Crusaders and Venice during the Fourth Crusade (1202–4). He repulsed the efforts of Pope Innocent III to effect a reconciliation, then resigned his office in 1206.

JOHN CAPISTRAN (Capestrano), ST., d. 1456, was born at Capistrano in the Abruzzi, studied law at Perugia, and for several years held office as a local judge. He then joined the Observant Franciscans, took an active part in the controversies regarding poverty that convulsed the order, served as vicar provincial and vicar general, founded several monasteries and convents, and preached unceasingly for the reform of the church and against groups such as the Fraticelli. From 1451 he devoted all his energies toward organizing crusades against the Hussites and the Turks, and he actually led part of Hunyadi's army in the great victory gained against the Turks at Belgrade (1456).

JOHN CASSIAN. *See* CASSIAN, JOHN.

JOHN CHRYSOSTOM, ST., d. 407, one of the four leading fathers of the Eastern church, called Chrysostom, the "Golden Mouthed," because of his eloquence as a preacher. He was reared in Antioch by his widowed mother, spent some years as an anchorite, then twelve as a priest in

Antioch where he established his fame as a brilliant preacher. In 398 Emperor Arcadius had him appointed archbishop of Constantinople. There his courageous attacks on corruption in high places in both church and lay society stirred sharp opposition. It appears that Queen Eudoxia considered his attacks on extravagance and immorality as aimed at herself. Theophilus, the patriarch of Alexandria, resented especially his refusal to accept the legitimacy of the Synod of the Oak (403) which was to consider charges brought against him. In 403 he was sent into exile but the order was almost immediately rescinded because of popular objection. The following year he was sent off to Armenia where he remained for three years, then was ordered moved to more remote Pityus but died on the way. He left numerous writings including letters, homilies, and exegetical works. In his exegetical writing he gave Scriptures the literal and grammatical interpretation taught in Antioch.

JOHN CLIMAX (Climacus), ST., d. 649, Syrian hermit of the monastery of St. Catherine on Mt. Sinai, then abbot there. His *The Ladder of Paradise,* a popular spiritual book, by means of 30 steps introduced the would-be ascetic to the teachings of the desert fathers concerning the road he must travel to reach his final goal.

JOHN DAMASCENE, ST. *See* JOHN OF DAMASCUS.

JOHN DE GRAY (Grey). *See* GRAY, JOHN DE.

JOHN DE SACROBOSCO. d. c. 1250, taught at Paris and authored three textbooks which were widely used in the schools of the late Middle Ages: an arithmetic entitled *Algorismus,* a *Computus* about the ecclesiastical calendar, and a *Sphere* which served as the most popular introductory work on the subject of astronomy into the seventeenth century.

JOHN VII GRAMMATICUS, patriarch of Constantinople, 837–43, called Grammaticus because of his literary accomplishments, was already a strong advocate of iconoclasm when he served as ecclesiastical counselor to the emperors Leo V and Theophilus. As patriarch he undertook a vigorous persecution of the bishops and monks who opposed iconoclasm. When Theophilus died and Empress Theodora succeeded, he was deposed and imprisoned. He died in prison some time before 863.

JOHN GUALBERT, ST., d. 1073, founder of the Vallombrosans. He joined the Benedictine community of S. Miniato in Florence, next moved to Camaldoli in order to pursue a more austere monastic regimen under St. Romuald (d. 1027), finally, c. 1038, founded a monastery at Vallombrosa under a modified Rule of St. Benedict, adapted to the conditions of a semihermitical way of life.

JOHN MALALAS. *See* MALALAS, JOHN.

JOHN MILIC, d. 1374, Bohemian ascetic, preacher, and reformer who introduced the *Devotio Moderna* to Bohemia. After studies at Prague, he became a canon at Prague, then in disgust over clerical laxity took up the life of an ascetic and preacher. In his preaching he urged daily communion and the use of the Bible in the vernacular. A charge of heresy led to a short period of imprisonment in Rome (1367–8), after which he returned to Prague to continue his preaching. A second charge of heresy brought him to Avignon where he was able to convince an assembly of cardinals of his orthodoxy.

JOHN OF DAMASCUS (John Damascene), ST., d. c. 750, a leading theologian of the Eastern church, was born at Damascus and became a monk in Jerusalem where he combined a life of asceticism with preaching. Contemporaries recognized him as the most courageous and unrelenting foe of iconoclasm. His enduring fame as the leading authority in the Greek church rests in large measure upon *The Fount of Knowledge* which for centuries served as the principal textbook in the education of the clergy. Others of his voluminous works included sermons; hymns;

writings of an ascetical, dogmatic, moral, and exegetical nature; and hagiography. Although his work lacks independence of thought, in authoritativeness its influence upon Greek theology has been compared with that of Aquinas in the west.

JOHN OF EPHESUS (of Asia, of Amida), d. 586, monk and missionary-bishop of Ephesus whose labors among pagans in the mountainous regions of Lydia and Caria were remarkably successful. Emperor Justin II had him imprisoned for his Monophysite views. His writings, all in Syriac, include lives of the Eastern saints and a history of the church to 585.

JOHN OF GAUNT. *See* LANCASTER, JOHN OF GAUNT, DUKE OF.

JOHN OF GORZE, BL., d. c. 975, monk of Gorze and for several years the legate of Otto I at the court of the caliph Abd-al-Rahman III in Córdoba. As abbot of the abbey of Gorze he continued to direct the powerful monastic reform movement that monastery had inspired.

JOHN OF HOVEDEN, d. after 1275, English poet, attended Oxford, served as a clerk in the household of Henry III, and composed religious-mystic poetry (in Latin of a high order). The theme of his best known poem, *Philomena,* is the birth, passion, and resurrection of Christ.

JOHN OF JANDUN, d. 1328, attended the University of Paris and taught there, authored commentaries on Aristotle and was a leading proponent of Latin Averroism. As such he maintained the eternity of the world and denied personal immortality. He may have influenced Marsilius of Padua in his composition of the *Defensor Pacis;* in any event, he found a haven with Marsilius at the court of Louis IV of Germany.

JOHN OF LANCASTER. *See* BEDFORD, DUKES OF.

JOHN OF LUXEMBURG, son of Emperor Henry VII of Germany, married the sister of King Wenceslas, and reigned as king of Bohemia from 1311 to 1346. He was the father of the future Charles IV of Germany to whom he turned over the administration of Bohemia in 1333.

JOHN OF MATHA, ST., d. 1213, founder of the Trinitarians, a religious order dedicated to the ransoming of Christians held captive in Moslem countries.

JOHN OF MONTE CORVINO, d. c. 1330, first Western missionary to visit China. As a Franciscan missionary he stopped a year in India on his way to Mongolia, then in that distant land served as archbishop (from 1307), converted some 6,000 souls, erected a number of churches, and prepared a translation of the New Testament in a native Mongolian dialect.

JOHN OF NEPOMUK (Pomuk), ST., d. 1393, ecclesiastical notary, student at Padua, and a doctor of canon law. In 1390 he served as vicar general of the archbishop of Prague. When the archbishop excommunicated one of the favorites of King Wenceslas IV, John was arrested as the prelate's chief agent and tortured to death. He was canonized presumably because, as the queen's confessor, he had refused to betray what she had confessed to him.

JOHN (Quidort) OF PARIS, d. 1306, Dominican theologian, probably a student at Paris, then a popular preacher in that city. He defended certain Thomistic views that had drawn attack and prepared a treatise on the subject of royal and papal authority. His support of consubstantiation (impanation) led to his permanent suspension from teaching and preaching.

JOHN OF PARMA, BL., d. 1289, Franciscan minister general. He became a Franciscan at Parma, studied at Paris, and earned a reputation as a teacher and preacher. In 1247 he was elected minister general of the order. In an effort to revive the discipline practiced by the early Franciscans, he traveled all over Europe and gained many enemies for those efforts and for his sympathy for the views of Joachim of Fiore. He was charged with heresy, cleared himself, but then retired from an active life to lead a solitary existence for the last 32 years of his life.

JOHN OF PLANO CARPINI (Giovanni de Plano Carpini), d. 1252, a Franciscan, provincial of his order in Germany, and member of one of the three embassies Pope Innocent IV sent to Mongolia early in 1245 in an effort to gain the Mongol khan's support against the Moslems. John left a valuable account of this mission, including a description of the country of the Mongols and their customs.

JOHN OF RAGUSA, d. c. 1443, Dominican theologian, master of theology at Paris (1420), and the pope's representative at the Councils of Pavia (1422) and Basel (1431). The pope sent him to Constantinople in an effort to persuade the Greeks to accept union with Rome, and the emperor John VIII Palaeologus responded by sending an embassy. He composed a treatise attacking the Hussites and a history of the Council of Basel. The many Greek manuscripts that he brought back with him from Constantinople he gave to the Dominican house in Basel.

JOHN OF SALISBURY, d. 1180, English humanist and philosopher, a pupil of Abelard, William of Conches, and Gilbert de la Porrée, and for 20 years a member of the household of Theobald, the archbishop of Canterbury. At Canterbury he became a friend of Thomas Becket. In 1176 he was consecrated bishop of Chartres. His writings include biographies of Anselm of Bec and Thomas Becket, letters, the *Policraticus* (*Statesman's Guide*) which dealt with political theory, the *Historica Pontificalis* which constitutes a valuable history of the papacy from 1148 to 1151, and the *Metalogicon*. In this last work he cautioned against the study of philosophy except as a literary subject. John was well acquainted with the Latin classics and Aristotle's *Organon*.

JOHN OF SEVILLE, d. 1157, a scholar of Seville who gained renown for his knowledge of astronomy and mathematics. Beyond translations of Arabic works into Latin, he composed treatises of his own on astrology, the astrolabe, and arithmetic.

JOHN OF THORESBY, d. 1373, keeper of the privy seal, royal chancellor, bishop first of Saint Davids, then of Worcester, and archbishop of York (1352). His willingness to be content with the title "Primate of England" and leave to the archbishop of Canterbury the more prestigious "Primate of All England," brought an end to a controversy that had embittered relations between the two provinces for many centuries.

JOHN, ORDER OF ST. *See* SAINT JOHN OF JERUSALEM, ORDER OF THE HOSPITAL OF.

JOHN PECKHAM (Pecham), d. 1292, English theologian and archbishop of Canterbury. He was a Franciscan, studied at Paris and Oxford, became minister provincial of the order in England, and was consecrated archbishop of Canterbury (1279). As a theologian he was recognized as a leading champion of Augustinianism against Thomism. As archbishop he proved himself a reformer. He attacked pluralities, encouraged preaching, and defended the rights of the church. He composed treatises on the subjects of philosophy and science (optics).

JOHN PHILOPONUS, also known as John the Grammarian, a sixth-century theologian and philosopher of Alexandria, author of treatises on astronomy, mathematics, grammar, philosophy, and theology. His theological writings reveal leanings toward Monophysitism.

JOHN III SCHOLASTICUS, patriarch of Constantinople, 565–77, appointed to that office by Emperor Justinian I. He became a friend and confidant of Emperor Justin II with whom he was in agreement concerning the condemnation of the Monophysites. He prepared the first systematic compilation of Byzantine canons. This included the principal *Novels* of Justinian I and the canons of St. Basil of Caesarea. His *Chronog-*

raphy is a primacy source for the religious and secular history of Antioch.

JOHN SCOTUS ERIGENA (Eriugena, John the Scot), d. c. 877, the foremost Western thinker of the ninth century. He was probably a native of Ireland who fled (c. 846) to the court of Charles the Bald, king of the West Franks, where he taught grammar and dialectic. Charles commissioned him to translate the works of the Pseudo-Dionysius and those of several Greek church fathers. He also composed commentaries on the *Gospel of St. John.* His principal claim to fame was his *De Divisione Naturae* in which he attempted to establish a harmony between neo-Platonism and Christianity. John found no conflict between rational and revealed truths and insisted that true philosophy does not differ from true theology. In 1210 the Council of Paris condemned his work for its pantheism.

JOHN'S FIRE, festival commemorated on the eve of June 24, the feast of St. John the Baptist. It grew out of an earlier pagan summer festival, but many Christians in the Middle Ages believed that nature underwent major changes on that day. If growing things were blessed at that time, they would produce crops.

JOHN, ST., one of the twelve apostles, the brother of James (the Greater).

JOHN THE BAPTIST, ST., son of Zachary and Elizabeth, the precursor of Christ.

JOHN IV THE FASTER, patriarch of Constantinople, 583–95, favored a policy of tolerance toward the Monophysites. Over the objections of the pope, he claimed for himself the title of "ecumenical patriarch" which gave him precedence over the other patriarchs of the East, a title which all his successors continued to use. His devotion to asceticism earned him the name "the Faster."

JOHN THE FEARLESS, duke of Burgundy, 1404–19, son of Philip the Bold, was among those captured by the Turks in their defeat of the Crusading army led by Sigismund at Nicopolis in 1396. In 1407 he murdered Louis of Orléans, brother of Charles VI of France, and replaced him as the dominant voice in the government until his own murder by an agent (?) of the Dauphin Charles (VII).

JOHN THE GRAMMARIAN. *See* JOHN PHILOPONUS.

JOINVILLE, JEAN (Jehan), SIRE DE, d. 1317, seneschal of Champagne who accompanied Louis IX of France on his first Crusade (1248–54) and was captured with the king by the Turks. He left a popular biography of the sainted monarch and was one of the major witnesses in the process leading to Louis's canonization.

JONAH MARINUS (Abul Walid Merwan Ibn Janah), d. c. 1050, Hebrew physician and grammarian. He was born in Córdoba but made his home in Saragossa. He wrote medical and exegetical treatises (in Arabic) although he is best remembered as the leading Hebrew grammarian and lexicographer of the Middle Ages.

JONGLEUR, name generally given to the minstrel of north France in the twelfth and thirteenth centuries. Some jongleurs also composed verse. The jongleur accompanied his songs with a fiddle or harp. He might also dance, do acrobatics, and perform the feats of a juggler.

JORDANES, a Goth of the sixth century and monk, author of an uncritical history of the Goths. How much of his work is based upon the twelve books Cassidorus wrote about the Goths remains a question. Jordanes declares he had but three days in which to examine Cassiodorus's manuscripts, which are no longer extant. Jordanes also wrote a chronicle of Roman history from Romulus to Justinian that has little value.

JORDAN OF SAXONY, ST., d. 1237, succeeded St. Dominic as master general of the Dominican order and prepared the way for its further expansion. He left a history of the order and a biography of Dominic. He also initiated the tradition of concluding the divine office of the day with the singing of the *Salve Regina*.

JORDANUS CATALANI, d. after 1330, French Dominican who visited India and China as missionary and explorer. In 1330 he was consecrated bishop of Columbum (Quilon) in Travancore. His letters and *Mirabilia* furnish valuable information about India.

JORDANUS DE NEMORE (Nemorarius), d. 1237, obscure mathematician and author of mathematical and geometrical writings. His school developed a number of mechanical ideas that were later adopted by Galileo and Descartes.

JOSAPHAT. *See* BARLAAM AND JOSAPHAT.

JOSEPH I, patriarch of Constantinople, 1267–75 and 1282–3, who resigned as patriarch over his opposition to the efforts Emperor Michael VIII Palaeologus made to reach an accord with the papacy and to the fruition of those efforts in the decree of union proclaimed by the Council of Lyons (1274). He was later reinstated as patriarch by Emperor Andronicus II.

JOSEPH OF EXETER, medieval Latin poet of the late twelfth century. His most ambitious poem concerned the Trojan war. Only fragments remain of his epic about King Richard and the Third Crusade (1189–92).

JOSEPH THE HYMNOGRAPHER, ST., d. 886, a prolific Greek hymn-writer. He was born in Sicily, fled upon the arrival of the Arabs, was captured by pirates, and served as a slave for several years in Crete. About 850, after he escaped, he established a monastery in Constantinople where his opposition to iconoclasm led to his exile. He is said to have composed 1,000 hymns.

JOSQUIN DES PRÉS. *See* PREZ, JOSQUIN DES.

JOURNEYMAN, name given to the member of a guild who had completed his apprenticeship and worked by the day (*journée*) in the shop of a master. He might continue to work indefinitely as a journeyman or rise to the position of master and have a shop of his own provided he could demonstrate to the leaders of the guild that he was a master at his trade and provided, too, that the guild had sufficient room for an additional master. [*See* GUILD.]

JOUST, a combat, real or mock, between two knights with lances on horseback.

JOVIAN, FLAVIUS, Roman emperor, 363–4, succeeded Julian whom he had accompanied on his Persian campaign. He made peace with the Persians by surrendering claims to Armenia and the territory east of the Tigris. He revoked Julian's anti-Christian policies and restored Athanasius to the see of Constantinople.

JOVINIAN, d. c. 405, a monk who suffered condemnation at Rome and Milan for his views concerning virginity which he denied was a higher state than marriage. He also attacked the belief in the perpetual virginity of Mary. These and other of his views drew attacks from both Jerome and Augustine.

JOYEUSE ENTRÉE, the ceremonial first visit a new ruler made to the cities and provinces of his country.

JUAN MANUEL, d. 1348 or 1349, grandson of Ferdinand III of Castile, an astute student of politics and himself politically active and ambitious. He served as regent during the minority of Alfonso XI (1321–5) and later twice revolted against Alfonso in an effort to advance his own political ambitions. Despite his involvement in public affairs, he achieved a distinguished literary record. His major work, a masterpiece of Spanish prose for which he drew upon Jewish, Arabic, and traditional sources, served with Boccaccio's *Decameron* to introduce the novel into Western literature. Other writings include a work on chivalry which was inspired by Ramon

Lull, a moral treatise on the education of princes, and a work on hunting.

JUBILATE SUNDAY, the third Sunday after Easter, so called from the opening word of the introit.

JUDA AL-CHARIZI (Harizi), d. before 1235, Jewish poet of Spain who translated Arabic works into Hebrew and composed poetry about God, nature, and the trials of human life.

JUDAH BEN SAMUEL HA-LEVI (Abu Al-Hasan Al-Lawi), d. c. 1145, Jewish physician of Spain who is considered the leading Hebrew poet of the Middle Ages. A popular theme of his religious verse was the virtues of God. The foibles and deficiencies of men and women provided the subject matter for his secular verse. He used Arabic prose in his discussion of philosophy and religion.

JUDAS ISCARIOT, one of the twelve apostles, the one who betrayed Christ.

JUDE, one of the apostles, possibly the author of the *Letter of St. Jude.*

JUDICA SUNDAY, second Sunday after Easter, the name being derived from the opening word of the introit.

JUGUM (*iugum*), unit of taxation used in the late Roman empire. It approximated the amount of land judged sufficient to maintain a household.

JULIANA OF LIÈGE, ST., d. 1258, Canoness Regular at Mont-Cornillon, later prioress of the convent, still later a recluse. Her visions are supposed to have led to the introduction of the feast of Corpus Christi, for the establishment of which feast she had devoted all her energies.

JULIANA OF NORWICH. *See* JULIAN OF NORWICH.

JULIAN, FLAVIUS CLAUDIUS, Roman emperor, 361–3, nephew of Constantine I (the Great), appointed Caesar by Constantius II in 355 and

given charge of maintaining the Rhine frontier against the Franks and Alemanni. His troops hailed him as emperor in 360, but before his army and that of Constantius II clashed to settle the issue, the emperor had died. As emperor Julian encouraged the establishment of a neo-Platonic paganism, ordered all instruction in the schools to be paganized, and subjected Christianity to some persecution. In the hope of weakening the church, he allowed all exiled bishops to return to their sees. (This included Athanasius.) He met his death on his retreat from Ctesiphon in a campaign against the Persians. He left orations, letters, satires, epigrams, and an attack on Christianity.

JULIAN OF HALICARNASSUS, d. after 527, bishop of Halicarnassus whose Monophysite sympathies caused him to be deposed c. 518 when he fled to Alexandria. There he became leader of the Aphtharto-Docetists, a sect which believed that Christ's body had remained incorruptible and had only appeared to die. He attacked Severus, patriarch of Antioch, in his writings, and also left some letters.

JULIAN OF NORWICH, d. after 1412, obscure English mystic and Benedictine who lived as an anchoress outside the walls of St. Julian's church in Norwich. In her *Revelations* she claimed to have received spiritual messages and instructions concerning the Passion and the Holy Trinity. She emphasized above all the importance of the love of God as providing the answer to all human problems.

JULIUS I, ST., Pope, 337–52, a Roman who as pope supported Athanasius against the emperor and Eastern bishops who favored Arianism and provided him a haven in Rome on his exile. He approved the decrees of the Council of Sardica (342–3) which cleared Athanasius, condemned certain Eastern bishops for their Monophysite views, and granted the papacy appellate powers. This last provision leaves Julius's name important in the history of the evolution of papal claims to primacy.

JULIUS AFRICANUS, SEXTUS, d. c. 240, Christian writer, probably born in Jerusalem, who enjoyed close relations with the royal house of Edessa and had interviews with two Roman emperors. His principal work was *History of the World* to A.D. 217. He maintained that the world would endure for 6,000 years and that Christ was born in the year 5500. He also composed an encyclopedic work dealing with a variety of subjects including history, medicine, and magic.

JUMIÈGES, ABBEY OF, monastery on the Seine in Normandy founded by Clovis II in 654 under the Luxeuil observance. It adopted the Rule of St. Benedict early in the eighth century. Missionaries from the monastery were active in England and Ireland. A series of Viking attacks about the middle of the ninth century brought an end to its first period of spiritual and intellectual eminence. A second period of cultural distinction extended from c. 1050 to c. 1350 when it was the richest monastery in Normandy.

JUPE, cloak worn by knights or men-at-arms from the twelfth century either as a castle coat or underneath their armor. Crusaders became acquainted with the cloak while fighting in Syria.

JURY, a judicial institution consisting of a body of local laymen summoned by a king or official to answer questions under oath (from the Latin *juro,* I swear). The origins of the jury may be traced back to late Roman times; its antecedents from the Carolingian period are less obscure. William the Conqueror brought the jury to England, but Henry II (1154–89) was the first ruler to introduce it as a regular step in legal procedure, first as a body that would bring forward names of men under suspicion of serious crimes [*see* CLARENDON, ASSIZE OF, and NORTHAMPTON, ASSIZE OF], then as a group

that would give judgment in certain kinds of civil disputes. The action of the Fourth Lateran Council (1215) to forbid the clergy to take part in the ordeal hastened the demise of that institution and led to the general adoption of the jury.

JUS (IUS) PRIMAE NOCTIS, right, which the seigneur may at one time have exercised in certain countries such as France, of sleeping the first night with the bride of a newly married serf, although references to the right usually appear in connection with the fee with which the serf redeemed this right.

JUSTICE OF THE PEACE, English magistrate, a conservator of the peace, who was empowered in 1327 to hear and determine felonies and trespasses. He might also supervise the collection of taxes and direct the local militia. His appointment may have represented an effort on the part of the king to reduce the authority and importance of the sheriff.

JUSTICIAR, chief adviser to the English king, head of the royal judicial system, and the monarch's viceroy when he was absent from the country. William the Conqueror introduced the official into the government where he remained until 1261 when the office lapsed. After Becket, who had retained the office of chancellor when elected archbishop of Canterbury, broke with Henry II (c. 1164), the justiciar became the principal minister in the kingdom.

JUSTIN I, Byzantine emperor, 518–27, an Illyrian peasant by birth, soldier in the service of the emperor, then commander of the imperial bodyguard. As emperor he depended heavily upon the counsels of his nephew and adopted son Justinian (I). He ended the Acacian Schism (484–519) with Rome and attempted to suppress Monophysitism which this rapprochement with papacy entailed, although not in Egypt where it was too firmly entrenched. His persecution of Arianism strained relations with Theodoric, king of Ostrogothic Italy.

JUSTIN II, Byzantine emperor, 565–78, nephew and successor of Justinian I, who proved himself a responsible ruler despite his failure to maintain the frontiers of the empire. Much of Italy was lost to the Lombards, he was obliged to buy peace with the Avars, and he also lacked success against the Persians. Tiberius I Constantine replaced him on the throne in 574 when he became insane.

JUSTINIAN I, Byzantine emperor, 527–65, the most important and influential ruler in the history of the Byzantine empire. His uncle Justin I (518–27) who had brought him from Thrace, left the management of public affairs largely to him during his own reign. Justinian's wife Theodora, once an actress, had an important role in imperial matters until her death in 548. What impressed contemporaries as Justinian's most noteworthy achievement was the recovery of large parts of the western empire which had been lost to the Germans. These included the whole of Italy, Dalmatia, north Africa, and a slice of southeastern Spain. While Justinian's generals, principally Belisarius and Narses, were engaged in the reconquest of these territories, their attention was regularly diverted to the Danubian frontier which Slavs and Hunnic tribes kept overrunning, and to Syria and Mesopotamia to meet the mighty threat of the army of the Sassanid Persians. Justinian's most enduring work was the codification of Roman law known as the *Corpus Juris Civilis*. The most imposing structure he erected was the church of Hagia Sophia in Constantinople. [*See* HAGIA SOPHIA.] His relations with the papacy followed a tortuous course because of his efforts, as fruitless as they were unending, to discover a solution to the mystery of Christ's nature that would satisfy both Rome and the Monophysites. [*See* CORPUS JURIS CIVILIS.]

JUSTINIAN II (Rhinotmetus), Byzantine emperor, 685–95, 705–11, succeeded his father Constantine IV, defeated the Slavs in Thrace but lost Armenia to the Arabs. His ruthlessness at home, principally in the measures employed to raise money for these campaigns and for a building program, led to his deposition and exile to Crimea. The Bulgars helped him recover his throne in 705, but a second revolt, provoked by the severity with which he punished those responsible for his exile, ended with his murder.

JUSTIN MARTYR, ST., philosopher, theologian, and the leading apologist of the second century. His studies gave him a wide acquaintance with and some sympathy for pagan philosophies. In his *Apologia* which he addressed to Emperor Antoninus Pius, he defended Christians against the charges of disloyalty and immorality. The work also gives an account of contemporary Christian baptismal ceremonies and eucharistic belief and practice. In the *Dialogue* he discussed the validity of the Christian belief with the Jew Trypho. Though no great philosopher, he was the first Christian thinker to seek to reconcile the claims of faith and reason. He and some of his disciples were scourged and beheaded in Rome c. 165.

JUST PRICE, the price which members of the guild could charge for their goods. This price permitted of no profit, that is, no money beyond what was required to maintain the merchant or craftsman in his station in life. It might fluctuate with such factors as the cost of materials.

JUS (Ius) UTRUMQUE, both laws, that is, both civil and canon law.

JUSTUS (Jodocus) OF GHENT (Joos van Wassenhove), active c. 1470–80, Flemish artist and portrait painter of Antwerp, Ghent, and Italy. He was noted for his quiet style and for his success in his later paintings of combining influences of the Netherlands with those of Italy. He may have been a pupil of the Van Eycks. One of his paintings is the *Communion of the Apostles*.

JUTES, a German people located in Jutland.

Members of the tribe who did not move into Flanders in the fifth century or cross the North Sea somewhat later to England south of the Thames (Kent) were eventually absorbed by the Danes.

JUVAINI, 'ALA UD-DIN 'ATA-MALIK, d. 1283, Persian historian whose narrative dealt extensively with the conquests of the Mongols. He twice visited Mongolia, then took service with the Mongol khan Hulagu in Baghdad.

KAABA (Ka'ba), a shrine in Mecca in the form of a cube, as the word suggests, which was sacred to Arabs from pre-Islamic times and remained the chief goal of the pilgrimages all Moslems were required to make to Mecca. Mohammed purged the shrine of several hundred idols when he gained control of Mecca (630), although he retained the Black Stone which was cemented into the eastern corner of the structure. The faithful believed Allah had given this stone to Abraham when he erected the shrine.

KADESIYA (Kadisiya, Qadisiya), BATTLE OF, decisive battle fought in 637 near Ctesiphon between the Arabs and Persians which ended in the destruction of the Persian army. Ctesiphon fell immediately thereafter, and with it the empire of the Sassanid Persians came to an end.

KADI (cadi). *See* QADI.

KAIROUAN (Kairawan, Kairwan), city south of Tunis founded by Okba, an Arab leader, in 670. It was revered as a sacred city of Islam and served as the seat of the governors of western North Africa and as the first capital of the Fatimites. In 1057 the city was largely destroyed and its position of prominence passed to Tunis. The most famous mosque in the city was the Grand Mosque which was started by Okba and was completed in the ninth century.

KAIS, originally the name of an ancient Arab god, later of a tribe that occupied much of central and northern Arabia, Syria, and Mesopotamia. Conflict between it and the tribe Kelb contributed to the overthrow of the Omayyad dynasty in 750.

KAISERSLAUTERN, city located on an ancient road between eastern Gaul and the Rhine, first noted in 882 by the name of Lustra. Frederick I Barbarossa built himself a palace in the town (1152–8). In 1276 Rudolf of Hapsburg gave the town the name of Lautern and declared it an imperial city.

KAKUBILLA (Cacucabilla, Cocucilla, Cucacilla), ST., probably a legendary saint whose name has been traced back to St. Columban (d. 615). His cult was popular in the fifteenth century when his aid was invoked against devils and natural evils.

KALANDS BRETHREN (*Fratres Calendarii*), members of lay and clerical associations whose name derived from the practice of holding divine services on the first day of the month. They appeared in the thirteenth century and were particularly popular in north Germany and the Netherlands where they engaged in works of charity and had Masses said for deceased members.

KALEVALA, national Finnish epic whose central theme was the conflict between the Finns and Lapps and which glorified the fabulous deeds of three semidivine brothers of gigantic stature. The matter had been passed on by folk singers for many centuries before being written down in the eighteenth century.

KALKA RIVER, BATTLE OF, battle fought near the Sea of Azov in 1223 which ended in a complete victory of the Mongols under Sabutai against a coalition of Russian princes and Cuman chieftains.

KALMAR, UNION OF, the union of the three Scandinavian countries of Denmark, Norway, and Sweden which was proposed at Kalmar in 1397 on the occasion of the coronation of Eric VII as king of these three countries. The proposal, largely the hope of Margaret, the actual ruler of all three countries at that time, was never ratified although Eric did reign as sovereign of the united realms until 1439 when he was deposed in Denmark and Sweden.

KALONYMOS, Jewish family that produced a number of poets, rabbis, and Talmudic scholars from the eighth century to the close of the Middle Ages. Members of the family lived in Italy, France, and Germany. Perhaps the most prominent was Kalonymos Ben Kalonymos Ben Meier, a fourteenth-century scholar of Provence, who translated scientific works of al-Farabi, al-Kindi, Galen, and other Arab and Greek writers into Hebrew. He translated a work by Averroës into Latin. Another member of the family was Samuel Ben Kalonymos, a twelfth-century Talmudist who lived in a mystical community in Germany. His writings included treatises on rabbinical laws, mysticism, and the Bible. He encouraged withdrawal from the world, an ascetic life, and a warm, personal love of God.

KALOTTE, a kind of skull cap worn since the thirteenth century by priests, also by soldiers under their helmets.

KALOYAN, czar of Bulgaria, 1197–1207, third of the Asen rulers. He took Nish from the Serbs, drove the Hungarians across the Danube, conquered western Macedonia, and soundly defeated an army of German Crusaders near Adrianople in 1205.

KAMIL, AL-, Ayyubid sultan of Egypt, 1218–38, granted Frederick II of Germany possession of Jerusalem and Bethlehem by the Treaty of Jaffa (1229). [See FREDERICK II, king of Germany, and CRUSADES, SIXTH.]

KAMILAVKION, head-covering in the form of a cylinder, with veil falling down behind, worn by bishops and members of the clergy of the Greek church.

KANON (Canon), one of the principal forms of Byzantine liturgical chant. It consisted of nine odes, based upon the nine biblical canticles of the Greek church. They originated in Jerusalem at the end of the seventh century. The greatest masters of this kind of chant were St. John of Damascus and his foster brother Cosmas "the Melodian." The monastery of St. Sabas in Jerusalem, where they lived, became the center of hymnography. About 800 the center shifted to Constantinople which boasted such famous hymnographers as St. Theodore the Studite and St. Joseph the Hymnographer.

KARAITES, a Jewish sect, originally called Ananites from their reputed founder Anan ben David (second half of the eighth century). They denied the rabbinical traditions contained in the Talmud and urged a return to the written word of Scripture which they claimed was self-explanatory and required no completion by Oral Law. Among other characteristics that marked their movement (Karaism) were a puritanical zeal, the practice of asceticism, and the encouragement of Messianic hopes. They derived many of their reformatory notions from the Islam school of Mu'tazilites. The sect flourished from the ninth to the twelfth century.

KARAKORUM, city in Mongolia (Outer) founded by Genghis Khan in 1220 to serve as the capital of his immense empire. In 1267 Kublai Khan destroyed the city when the local ruler, his younger brother, revolted and moved his court to Cambaluc (Peking).

KARELIANS, Finnish tribe which established itself on the isthmus west of Lake Ladoga in the ninth century. The Karelians accepted Christianity in the thirteenth century.

KARMATIANS (Karmathians, Carmathians), a Shiite sect of the Isma'ilis founded in the late ninth century in eastern Arabia with its capital at Bahrain. The sect may have derived its name from Hamdan Karmat, who was the leader of the movement in southern Iraq, or from the Aramaic word *karmat* meaning villager. The Karmatians who resembled the Assassin sect, maintained themselves to a large extent from plunder, and in 930 horrified Islam by sacking Mecca and carrying off the Black Stone from the Kaaba. The sect which apparently arose in Yemen ceased to be a political power after 1000.

KEEP. *See* DONJON.

KELLS, BOOK OF, illuminated book of the Gospels, in Latin, believed to have been done in part in the monastery at Iona (775–800). This book, which is considered the finest example of early Christian art of its kind, is presently at Trinity College, Dublin. [*See* ILLUMINATED MANUSCRIPTS.] According to tradition, it belonged to St. Columba (d. 597), but it clearly dates from c. 800.

KELLS, MONASTERY OF, monastic house founded in Meath in 550 by St. Columba.

KELLS, SYNOD OF, church council held in 1152. It established the diocesan system in Ireland and designated Armagh, Cashel, Tuam, and Dublin as archdioceses. Armagh was granted the honor of primacy.

KEMPE, MARGERY, d. after 1439, English mystic, author of *The Book of Margery Kempe,* a story of her pilgrimages, temptations, troubles, and mystical experiences. The daughter of the mayor of Lynn, she was married and had 14 children. After a period of madness, she and her husband went to Canterbury on a pilgrimage. She later visited the Holy Land and the shrine at Compostela. People often found her ways annoying and she was several times accused of being a Lollard although she was regularly cleared of the charge by the ecclesiastical authorities.

KEMPIS, THOMAS. *See* THOMAS À KEMPIS.

KEMP (Kempe), JOHN, d. 1454, cardinal and archbishop of Canterbury. After serving as chancellor and keeper of the privy seal in Normandy, he was consecrated bishop of Rochester, later of Chichester and London. He became archbishop of York in 1425 and of Canterbury in 1452. He carried out diplomatic missions for the crown during the period of Henry VI's minority, served as royal chancellor, and was a strong advocate of peace with France. In his later years he espoused the Lancastrian cause.

KENILWORTH, ancient town near Coventry whose twelfth-century castle was granted to Simon de Montfort by Henry III. The town gave its name to the Dictum of Kenilworth proclaimed in 1266 and it was there that Edward II surrendered his crown in 1327. It passed by marriage to John of Gaunt in the middle of the fourteenth century and through him to Henry IV. It remained in royal hands into the sixteenth.

KENNETH, name of two early kings of Scotland. Kenneth I MacAlpin, c. 834–58, the first king of the united Scots and Picts, ruled Scotland north of the Forth and Clyde. In order to save the remains of St. Columba from possible Viking plundering, he removed them from Iona to Dunkeld which then became the center of the Celtic church in Scotland. To provide greater protection to his court from Vikings from Ireland, he removed it to Scone. Kenneth II, 971–95, may have recognized the suzerainty of the Anglo-Saxon king Edgar in 973 from whom he received the land called Lothian.

KENSINGTON RUNE STONE, a stone with runic inscriptions found near Kensington, Minnesota, in 1898. The runes tell of a band of Norse explorers who camped there in 1362 after a journey of 14 days from the sea. The authenticity of the Stone continues as a matter of dispute among historians and archeologists.

KENT, Anglo-Saxon kingdom southeast of London in an area largely occupied by the Jutes. Their leaders Hengist and Horsa supposedly landed there c. 450 and Hengist ruled as the first king of Kent until his death in 488. Its history then becomes largely a blank until the reign of Ethelbert (560–616) who welcomed Augustine and his group of monks in 597 and aided them in the conversion of his people. Kent passed under control of Mercia during the eighth century and in 825 was conquered by Wessex. Although Kent suffered heavily from Viking raids, its location on the Channel, together with the archiepiscopal see of Canterbury, made it one of the most advanced of the Anglo-Saxon kingdoms.

KENT, EARLDOM OF, title first held by Odo, bishop of Bayeux, the half-brother of William the Conqueror. In 1321 the title was revived for Edmund of Woodstock, youngest son of Edward I. The title in 1352 passed to Joan, "Fair Maid of Kent," who married Edward the Black Prince and was the mother of Richard (II). Her eldest son Thomas de Holand by her first husband secured the title. In 1408 the title became extinct but was revived in 1461 for William Neville who died two years later without legitimate issue. In 1465 the title was bestowed upon Edmund Grey.

KENTIGERN (Mungo), ST., d. c. 612, bishop of Glasgow, labored as a missionary in the valley of the Clyde. When driven from Scotland, he made his way to Wales where he is said to have founded the monastery of St. Asaph. He later returned to Scotland.

KEVIN (Coemgen, Coemgenus), ST., d. 618 or 622, founder of the Irish monastery of Glendalough in southeastern Ireland. Tradition had it that he was a member of the royal race of Leinster. He lived for a time as a hermit, later founded Glendalough abbey.

KEYS, POWER OF THE, power given to St. Peter and the apostles to forgive sins (Matthew 16:19).

KHADIJA, d. c. 619, wealthy widow whom Mohammed married c. 595. She bore him seven children although only a daughter, Fatima, reached maturity.

KHALDUN, IBN. *See* IBN KHALDUN.

KHALID IBN AL-WALID, d. 642, unusually able Arab general who at one time helped the Meccans against Mohammed and Medina, later accepted the Prophet, distinguished himself in the Riddah Wars and in Islam's decisive victories in Iraq and Syria over the armies of Persia and Byzantium.

KHALIL (Al-Khali Ibn Ahmad Ibn 'Amr Ibn Tamin Al-Farahidi Al-Azdi), d. 786 or 791, Arab grammarian, philologist, and author of the first Arabic dictionary. He also discovered and codified the rules of Arabic prosody. He headed a school of philology at Basra.

KHAN (chan, chakan, kaghan, khaquan), a Mongolian word meaning lord or sovereign and used by Avars, Mongols, and Turks as a title for their rulers. Semi-independent lords in different parts of the Moslem world might also hold that title.

KHANSA, AL- (Tumadir Bint 'Amr), d. c. 645, Arab poet best known for her elegies. She is considered the most celebrated poet of her time.

KHAQANI (Ibrahim Ibn 'Ali Najjar), d. c. 1185, Persian poet, the author of court poems, satires, and epigrams. One of his poems gives a description of the pilgrimage he made to Mecca. On his return he was imprisoned. He used his suffering during this period for the theme of a "jail ballad," one of the best of its kind.

KHARIJITES, meaning "Seceders," an Islamic sect, at first devoted followers of Ali, the Prophet's son-in-law, later abandoning him when he agreed to arbitrate with Mu'awiya over the succession to the office of caliph. They then maintained the view that any person, even a slave, might be a caliph, and in their opposition to both Ali and Mu'awiya engaged in campaigns of terror. They were also known for their fanaticism and puritanism. Although Ali succeeded in putting down their revolt in 658, they survived through the Middle Ages, especially in north Africa.

KHAZARS, a Turkish people located in the region between the Caucasus Mountains, the lower Volga, and the Don from the second half of the sixth century. They conquered Crimea, levied tribute fom the eastern Slavs and from Kiev, and warred against the Arabs, Persians, and Armenians. The Byzantine empire usually found them valuable allies, not only against Islam whose penetration northward they served to block but also against other Turkish and Slavic tribes who threatened the Danubian frontier. Their assistance to Emperor Heraclius (610–41) probably prevented the destruction of Byzantium at that time. The eighth century found their power at its peak with a domain stretching from the north shores of the Black Sea to the Urals and Volga and up beyond Kazan to the north. Atil, the capital of the Khazar state in the Volga delta, was a major commercial center. The rise of Russia in the tenth century, coupled with Islamic expansion from the south, brought decline. After 1030 the tribe ceased to be important. The Khazars apparently accepted all religions although the majority of the ruling class converted to Judaism in 740.

KHOSRU (Khosrau) I. *See* CHOSROES I.

KHWARIZMI, AL-, d. 850, a leading Islamic mathematician and astronomer. He is the author of the oldest work on algebra, a treatise on Hindu numerals, and a set of astronomical tables. He gave his name to algorism, the term first used for arithmetic.

KIBLA. *See* QIBLA.

KIERSEY, CAPITULARY OF, decree issued in 877 by Charles the Bald, king of the West Franks, which declared all honors hereditary but limited the grant of lands to the life of the person receiving them.

KIEV, city on the middle Dnieper which, according to tradition, was founded in the eighth century by Kiy and his brothers. Varangians from Novgorod seized the city in 864, and in 882 it became the capital of the first major state in Russia. By the middle of the twelfth century Kiev is said to have had the largest population and the largest volume of trade of any Christian city after Constantinople. The Kievan state had a long history of wars with the nomadic peoples of the steppes including the Khazars, Petchenegs, and Cumans (Polovtsy). Decline set in during the late twelfth century. In 1169 a rival Russian prince sacked the city and in 1240 the Mongols left it in ruins. From that time until 1320 it paid tribute to the Golden Horde. In 1320 the city fell to Lithuania but in 1471 it was recovered for Russia by Ivan III.

KILDARE, county of south Ireland in Leinster. The city of Naas served as the capital of the ancient kingdom of Leinster. The town of Kildare originated as a religious foundation of St. Bridget in the fifth century. Kildare suffered severely during the period of Viking raids. Maurice Fitzgerald was among the earliest of the Anglo-Norman or Norman-Welsh adventurers who came to Ireland in the twelfth century. In Norman times more than 100 castles dotted the countryside. In 1296 Kildare was organized as a county. At the close of the Middle Ages the earls of Kildare were ruling the county.

KILIAN OF WÜRZBURG, ST., d. c. 689, "Apostle of Franconia," a native of Ireland who labored as a missionary-bishop in Thuringia and Franconia. He was put to death during the absence of the duke of Franconia whom he had converted.

KILKENNY, town of southeast Ireland. It took its name from the church or cell which St. Canice founded there in the sixth century. Strongbow built a castle there in the twelfth century. In

Kilkenny stands the great cathedral of St. Canice (thirteenth century).

KILKENNY, STATUTE OF, decree issued in 1366 by Edward III which forbade marriages between members of the Anglo-Norman colony in Ireland and the Irish. It also enjoined the use of English.

KILLARNEY, town of southwest Ireland (County of Kerry). Ruins of a sixth-century abbey founded by St. Finian, as well as those of the fifteenth-century Muckross Abbey, remain.

KILWARDBY, ROBERT, d. 1279, English Dominican, studied at Paris and Oxford, and taught theology at Oxford. He became provincial of the order in England, archbishop of Canterbury (1273), and cardinal (1278). In 1277 when he visited Oxford, he condemned 30 propositions in grammar, logic, and natural science which he traced to Aquinas's doctrine of the unity of form. He left a classification of knowledge based on Aristotle, as well as a commentary on the *Sentences*.

KIMCHI, DAVID, d. 1235, younger son of Joseph Kimchi, also known as Redak, the most famous member of this family of Hebrew grammarians. He produced commentaries on the Bible, a grammar, and a dictionary of the Hebrew language.

KIMCHI, JOSEPH, d. 1170, a native of southern Spain, moved to Provence to escape persecution. He composed the first Hebrew grammar available in Christian lands, and commentaries on a number of books of the Bible. In his exegetical writing he gave particular attention to grammatical and philological considerations. His two sons, David and Moses, were also grammarians.

KIMCHI, MOSES, d. c. 1190, elder son of Joseph, author of a guide to the use of the Hebrew language. His grammar became the most popular manual used by Christian humanists of the fifteenth and sixteenth centuries in their study of Hebrew.

KINDI, AL- (Yakub Ibn Ishak Al-Kindi), d. after 870, Arab mathematician, scientist, and philosopher. He was known as "the philosopher of the Arabs." He was born and lived his life in Baghdad where he enjoyed the patronage of the caliph Al-Ma'mun. He translated some of Aristotle's works into Arabic, prepared commentaries on several, and attempted to harmonize Islamic theology with Aristotelian and neo-Platonic thought. He maintained the righteousness as well as the unity of God. His writing on music, the first to appear in Arabic, and a treatise on swords suggest the variety of his interests. His work is more encyclopedic than original in character.

KING'S BENCH, COURT OF THE, royal court at Westminster which separated from the *coram rege* tribunal in 1268 when it became a distinct court with its own chief justice. It concerned itself principally with the adjudication of criminal or quasi-criminal cases.

KING'S COLLEGE, college at Cambridge University founded by Henry VI in 1441.

KING'S EVIL, TOUCHING FOR THE. The tradition that there existed some virtue in the king's touch which was effective in healing the "king's evil" or scrofula can be traced to the eleventh century. There is evidence that touching for scrofula was regarded as hereditary in the Capetians from the time of Philip I (1060–1108). The virtue was also attributed to Edward the Confessor (d. 1066). The custom of touching for the king's evil was practiced under Henry I and Henry II of England.

KINGSTON, town near London on the Thames which served as the coronation site of Anglo-Saxon kings from 900 to 979. The stone used at these functions is kept in the market place.

KISS OF PEACE, LITURGICAL, also PAX, kiss or embrace intended to express peace and fraternal good will, usually exchanged by members of the clergy in attendance at the eucharistic liturgy. It is first mentioned by Justin Martyr (second century) and may have been a usage from the Apostolic period.

KLOSTERNEUBURG, MONASTERY OF, house of Augustinian canons near Vienna established c. 1100 by Margrave Leopold III. It was first occupied by secular canons, but in 1133 it was transferred to the Augustinians. It possesses great art treasures as well as a large library of important manuscripts and incunabula.

KNIGHT, a retainer of a feudal lord who owed him military service; a landowner whose land (fief) owed his lord (king) the service of one fully equipped knight. [See CHIVALRY.]

KNIGHTHOOD. See CHIVALRY.

KNIGHTON (Cnitthon), HENRY, d. c. 1396, Austin canon of St. Mary's in Leicester, author of a valuable chronicle covering the years 1377 to 1395 which has much to say about the career of John of Gaunt, Wyclif, and the Lollards. Knighton also prepared a chronicle for the years 1066 to 1366 which was intended to provide a background for this earlier work.

KNIGHT'S FEE, the service, amounting to one fully equipped knight for forty days each year, which a knight owed his lord. [See SUBINFEUDATION.]

KNIGHTS HOSPITALLERS. See SAINT JOHN OF JERUSALEM, ORDER OF THE HOSPITAL OF.

KNIGHTS TEMPLARS. See TEMPLARS, ORDER OF KNIGHTS.

KOENIGSHOFEN, JACOB TWINGER DE, d. 1420, author of a chronicle which is important for the years 1382 to 1414. He paid particular attention to the city of Strasbourg.

KOGGE (Kocke), wide, bellied-shaped sailing ship of the late Middle Ages which was used in the North Sea. It also served as a warship.

KOL NIDRE, opening words of the Jewish prayer which began the divine service on the evening of Yom Kippur. The prayer was already in use in the ninth century.

KÖNIGSBERG (Kaliningrad), city on the Baltic in East Prussia founded by the Teutonic Order in 1255. It was named in honor of Ottocar II, king of Bohemia, who had undertaken a crusade in the area. In 1457 the grand master of the Teutonic Order made the city his residence. Königsberg became a town in 1286 and joined the Hanseatic League in 1340.

KONRAD OF MARBURG. See CONRAD OF MARBURG.

KONRAD OF WÜRZBURG. See CONRAD OF WÜRZBURG.

KONTAKION, Byzantine metrical sermon or poetical homily. Its greatest master was Romanus Melodus (d. c. 560).

KORAN (Qur'an), the holy book of Islam. The book, somewhat shorter than the New Testament, consists of revelations which Allah made to Mohammed between the years 610–31. These revelations, expressed directly by God to the reader in general or to Mohammed himself, contain instructions on every phase of life; social, intellectual, agricultural, legal, and, above all, moral and religious. Since the Koran is believed to be God's word, its teachings and requirements are accepted as true and literally applicable for all times. It is composed of 114 *suras* or chapters which appear to follow in no other order than one based upon length: the longest *suras* come first. It received this form c. 653 during the caliphate of Othman when it was given its present organization. The beauty of its rhythmic prose has never been surpassed in the history of Arabic literature; in fact, because of the Koran's popularity, it has exercised a powerful influence upon the development of Arabic language and literature. Two ideas receive constant emphasis in the Koran: first, that there is no god but the one, omniscient, almighty Allah whose laws men must observe or they will be damned; second, that all men must accept what happens as the will of Allah.

KOSSOVO, BATTLE OF, fought in 1389 between the Turks under their sultan Murad I and a large coalition of Balkan peoples including Serbs, Bosnians, Albanians, and Wallachians. Although Murad was slain (he was stabbed to death before the battle by a Serb who posed as a deserter), the battle ended in an overwhelming victory for the Turks. It brought an end both to Serbian hegemony in the Balkans and to its independence. Henceforth Serbia was a vassal state of the Turks. A second battle was fought at Kossovo in 1448 when Murad II defeated a Hungarian army led by John Hunyadi.

KOSTER, LAURENS JANSZOON. *See* COSTER, LAURENS JANSZOON.

KRAFT (Krafft), ADAM, d. 1509, German sculptor of the Nuremberg school. His figures were usually large and life-size. He made works for both public and private buildings, as well as relief sculpture and such decorative pieces as coats of arms. His masterpiece is probably the impressive tabernacle, 62 feet high, in the church of St. Laurence in Nuremberg.

KRAK DES CHEVALIERS, CASTLE OF, fortress built in 1131 by the Knights Hospitallers in Syria, one of the masterpieces of medieval military architecture. Saladin captured the fortress in 1188. The lordship of Krak and Montreal was one of the principal baronies of the Latin Kingdom of Jerusalem.

KREMLIN, the central fortress in medieval cities which was often separated from the surrounding parts of the city by wall, moat, and battlements. Inside the kremlin were located the cathedral, palaces, and provisions in case of siege. Several cities of Russia, including Moscow, Novgorod, and Vladimir, were built around an old kremlin.

KRIEMHILD, wife of Siegfried in the *Nibelungenlied*. She avenged his death by marrying Etzel (Attila), king of the Huns, who then destroyed Hagen, the murderer of Siegfried, and his entire clan.

KRUM, king (khan) of the Bulgars, 808–14, able statesman and administrator who subjugated and absorbed the last of the Avars north of the Danube, defeated the Byzantine emperor Nicephorus I in 811, and laid siege to Constantinople in 813. He failed in his attempt to take the city.

KUBLAI (Khubilai, Kubla) KHAN, grandson of Genghis Khan, last great Mongol ruler, who succeeded his brother Mangu in 1259 and ruled until 1294. He founded the Yüan dynasty of China after completing the conquest of China in 1279 and moving the Mongol capital from Karakorum in Mongolia to Peking (Cambaluc). Both his brother Hulagu in Persia and the ruler of the Golden Horde in Russia acknowledged his suzerainty. It was his court which Marco Polo visited and of which he left a famous account. Kublai was an able general and a capable and tolerant ruler; he showed an interest in learning and in religion. In time he became a convert to Lamaist Buddhism. His rule in China was characterized by a synthesis of traditional Chinese features and Mongol elements. He was the first non-Chinese to rule over the whole of China, and he was known in both the east and west as the Great Khan. He failed in his campaigns to add Japan, southeast Asia, and Indonesia to his empire.

KUMANS. *See* CUMANS.

KUNIGUNDE, BL., d. 1292, patroness of Poland and Lithuania, daughter of Bela IV of Hungary, and wife of Boleslaw V (the Chaste) of Poland. She showed much sympathy for the poor, built several hospitals, and, following the death of her husband, retired to the convent of the Poor Clares that she had founded.

KUNIGUNDE, ST., d. 1033 or 1039, wife of Henry IV, duke of Bavaria, who in 1002 became king (Henry II) of Germany. She counseled her husband in affairs of state and after his death retired to a convent that she had founded.

KURAISH (Quraysh), tribe that dominated Mecca at the time of Mohammed's birth. The Hashim clan of which the Prophet was a member belonged to this tribe.

KYRIE ELEISON, Greek phrase for "Lord, have mercy," prayer of supplication for mercy which made its appearance in the liturgy in the fourth century.

LABARUM, the sacred military standard of the Christian Roman emperors beginning with Constantine I (the Great) which incorporated the Chi Rho, the sacred monogram of Christ. According to Lactantius, Constantine in a dream had a vision of the first letters of Christ's name (Chi Rho) together with the words, "In this sign you will conquer." He is supposed to have ordered his soldiers to have the Chi Rho monogram put on their shields. The labarum was a Christianized version of a type of military standard used by Constantine's predecessors.

LACTANTIUS, LUCIUS CAE(CI)LIUS FIRMIANUS, d. c. 320, church father of north Africa, a pupil of Arnobius. He taught rhetoric in Nicomedia and Constantinople, and authored apologetical writings and some history *(De Mortibus Persecutorum)*. His principal work, *Divinae Institutiones,* which is a systematic presentation of Christian thought, also sought to defend it against the attacks of pagan philosophers. The flowing style of Lactantius's classical Latin won him the title of the Christian Cicero.

LADISLAS (Ladislaus, Wladislaw) I, ST., king of Hungary, 1077–95. He conquered the northern part of Croatia, defeated the Cumans, and began the "westernization" of his country. He built many churches, sided with Gregory VII in the investiture controversy with Henry IV of Germany, but refused to accept Urban II's claim to be suzerain of Hungary. He secured the canonization of Stephen I and his son Emeric. In Hungarian tradition, he was the model of chivalry.

LADISLAS (Ladislaus, Wladislaw) IV, king of Hungary, 1272–90, who supported Rudolf of Hapsburg against Ottocar of Bohemia. His mother was a Cuman and he adopted many Cuman customs and surrounded himself with Cuman followers. The powerful aristocracy grew more powerful during his reign. He was slain in battle with the Cumans.

LADISLAS (Lancelot), king of Naples, 1386–1414, son and successor of Charles III. He invaded Dalmatia and had himself crowned king of Hungary (1403). Almost his entire reign was consumed by his struggle with Louis II, the Angevin rival king of Naples, and with the claims of the different popes during the bitterest period of the Western Schism. In the course of his ambitious campaigns aimed at securing control of central Italy, he occupied Rome on several occasions and in 1413 sacked the city. He appeared on the point of gaining his goal when he died. He took an active part in the Western Schism and generally supported the claims of the Roman pope.

LADY CHAPEL, a chapel dedicated to the Virgin. The practice of adding such chapels dates from the thirteenth century and became popular in England, e.g., Henry VII's chapel to the Virgin in Westminster Abbey.

LAETARE SUNDAY, fourth Sunday of Lent, the name deriving from the opening words of the introit, *Laetare, Jerusalem* (Rejoice, Jerusalem).

LAETENTUR COELI (*Latin,* "Let the heavens rejoice"), title of the Greek Formulary of Union which Cyril, patriarch of Alexandria, sent to

John, bishop of Antioch in 433, and embodying the terms of reunion agreed upon by both prelates. The document was formally approved by the Council of Chalcedon (451). It expounds the orthodox doctrine of the Person of Christ, insisting upon the unity of person and distinction of natures, and honoring Mary as the Mother of God.

LAETUS, JULIUS POMPONIUS, d. 1498, humanist, pupil of Lorenzo Valla, and founder of the "pagan" Academia Romana. Pope Paul II imprisoned him for his efforts to revive pagan Roman practices, but Sixtus IV ordered him released and permitted him to reestablish the Academia. Laetus was the author of several humanist treatises on Roman antiquities and edited a number of classical works.

LA FAYETTE, GILBERT MOTIER DE, d. 1462, French marshal who fought for the Dauphin and Joan of Arc, became a member of the grand council of Charles VII, and introduced reforms in the army.

LAGOS, city on the southern coast of Portugal, the Roman Lacogriga, from which many ships sailed on voyages of exploration and discovery in the late Middle Ages.

LAKHMIDS (Lachmids), Arab people that dominated the lower Euphrates from the fourth century to 602 under Persian suzerainty. They fought as allies of the Sassanids while their rivals, the Ghassanids, took service with the Byzantine empire.

LA MARCHE, OLIVIER DE, d. 1502, Burgundian chronicler and poet who served as secretary to Charles the Bold of Burgundy and his daughter Mary. His writings, including the *Mémoires*, although somewhat partisan and lacking the perceptivity of those of his contemporary Philippe de Commines, possess considerable historical value. Like Jean Froissart, he proved himself an eloquent spokesman for the tradition of chivalry.

LAMB, popular Christian symbol which represented both the faithful — Christ shown as the Good Shepherd carrying a lamb on his shoulders — and Christ, as the Lamb of God.

LAMBERT (Lampbert) OF HERSFELD, d. c. 1085, Benedictine monk of Hersfeld who as abbot of Hasungen promoted the Cluniac reform movement. His writings include a valuable universal history *(Annals)* which begins with the Creation and extends to 1077. The first part of it is in annalistic form, the latter is more of a chronicle. He wrote with skill and used classical models.

LAMBERT OF MAASTRICHT, ST., d. 705 or 706, bishop of Maastricht who spent seven years in exile until restored to his see by Pepin (II) of Heristal. He labored in later life as a missionary in Brabant and was slain defending the rights of his church.

LAMBETH, a manor across the river from London which was the favorite residence of the archbishop of Canterbury from the thirteenth century. Archbishop Baldwin (1185–90) acquired the property. Archbishop Boniface built the chapel in 1245.

LAMMAS DAY, harvest festival observed by the church in England on 1 August. It is mentioned in a work of King Alfred's and was common in the Middle Ages. The word derives from "loaf-mass." On this day, loaves of bread were made from new grain.

LANCASTER, HOUSE OF, name of a branch of the Plantagenet family. It appeared as a title in 1267 when Henry III granted it to his son Edmund. Two of the sons of Edmund held the title of earl successively, his grandson Henry (d. 1361) being the first to receive the ducal title. Henry's daughter Blanche, his heiress, married John of Gaunt (d. 1399), third surviving son of Edward III, whose son Henry deposed Richard II and ruled as Henry IV. The duchy thus merged in the crown. The ruling dynasty of Lancastrians began with this Henry, continued through Henry V, and terminated with Henry VI (d. 1471). Its claims to the throne were taken up by the Tudors.

LANCASTER, EDMUND, EARL OF, d. 1296, fourth (second surviving) son of Henry III. He bore the nickname "Crouchback" ("Crossback," "Crusader"). His father secured the crown of Sicily for him from Innocent IV in 1254 but he never gained possession, and Pope Alexander IV quashed the arrangement. After the death of Simon de Montfort (d. 1265), Edmund received many of his estates including the earldom of Leicester. The newly created earldom of Lancaster became his in 1267. Altogether his titles and estates exceeded those of any English lord. For a time he governed Champagne as a vassal of Philip III of France through his marriage to its countess. He fought in the Welsh wars and against the French.

LANCASTER, JOHN OF GAUNT, DUKE OF, d. 1399, fourth (third surviving) son of Edward III and virtual regent during the last years of his father's reign and the minority of Richard II. (The Black Prince was in poor health and preceded his father in death by a year.) Gaunt's marriage to Blanche, heiress of the vast Lancastrian estates, brought him the title of duke and enormous wealth and influence. His protection of John Wyclif who, for a time, was a clerk in the service of the crown, preserved the Reformer from punishment although it brought down on his own head the ire of contemporary chroniclers. He campaigned without distinction in France (Hundred Years' War) and in Castile where he pressed claims to the throne on the strength of his (second) marriage to Constance, daughter of Pedro I. During the 1380s and 1390s when Richard II fought a powerful group of lords for control of the government, Gaunt held aloof for the most part or played the role of peacemaker. Without his loyalty it is doubtful whether Richard could have remained on the throne. His illegitimate children by his third wife, Catherine

Swynford, who were legitimized in 1397, included the later Cardinal Henry Beaufort.

LANCASTER, THOMAS, EARL OF, d. 1322, grandson of Henry III, one of the richest of the English lords and a principal in the baronial opposition to Edward II. His possessions included the earldoms of Lancaster, Derby, Leicester, Lincoln, and Salisbury. He was among those who brought about the banishment of Piers Gaveston (d. 1312), then led the opposition to the Despensers and secured their exile (1321). When some of his adherents abandoned him, he was defeated by the royalist forces, captured, and executed.

LANCELOT, a hero in the Arthurian romance, the lover of Guinevere and father of Galahad. Chrétien de Troyes introduced him to romance literature.

LANDFRIEDEN, imperial proclamations of peace which applied to all persons and places within the German empire. The first of these to be proclaimed, serving as a model for later ones, was that announced by Frederick II at the Diet of Mainz in 1235.

LANDGRAVE, German *Landgraf*, an official directly under the king who appeared in the twelfth century. His position was analogous to that of a count although he remained outside the authority of the duke and ranked with him.

LANDINI (Landino), FRANCESCO, d. 1397, a Florentine, the leading Italian composer of the fourteenth century. Although blind from his early youth, he gained fame for his knowledge of philosophy and astrology, and for his talents as an organ player and an improviser of music. He composed poetry, madrigals, and polyphonic pieces.

LANDO, Pope, July 913, to February 914, a Roman who owed his accession to the family of Theophylact. Nothing is known about his short pontificate.

LANDSKNECHT, a German foot-soldier ("man of the plains") of the late fifteenth century.

LANFRANC, d. 1089, scholastic theologian, a leading scholar and archbishop of Canterbury. In 1035 he left Pavia, where he had practiced law, for Tours where he studied under Berengar. In 1042 he left there for the monastery of Bec in Normandy. He became a monk and prior at Bec and a well-known teacher of dialectic. Among his pupils he counted Anselm of Bec and Ivo of Chartres. His writings include works on the trivium and biblical commentaries, although his theological fame rests principally on his criticism of the eucharistic teaching of Berengar. His principal achievement lay in raising Bec to the status of a great spiritual and intellectual center. He served William, duke of Normandy, as a trusted adviser and to him owed his appointment as archbishop of Canterbury (1070). He worked with William in advancing church reform in the matter of simony and concubinage, but agreed with him in ignoring Gregory VII's attack on lay investiture.

LANGENSTEIN, HENRY HEINBUCHE OF. *See* HENRY OF LANGENSTEIN.

LANGHAM, SIMON, d. 1376, abbot of Westminster Abbey, royal treasurer, bishop of Ely, royal chancellor (1363), and archbishop of Canterbury (1366). A dispute with Edward III led him to resign as archbishop. He went to Avignon where he was created cardinal (1368), and was on his way back to England when he died.

LANGLAND, WILLIAM, d. c. 1400, author of *The Vision Concerning Piers Plowman,* an alliterative poem considered in importance second only to Chaucer's *Canterbury Tales* in the literature of late medieval England. Little that is certain can be said about the author's life. He appears to have been a cleric in minor orders who later married. He was surely a most perceptive judge of human nature although more inclined to see what was wanting than what was good in men.

The theme of his poem is the journey of sinful —lazy, indifferent, selfish—men to their appointed ends, told in allegory that is both puzzling and profound. Human failing in all walks of life, but most especially in that of churchmen, continued to be the author's concern.

LANGTON, STEPHEN, d. 1228, noted English scholar, cardinal, and theologian. While studying at Paris, he became a close friend of Innocent III. In 1205, upon the death of Hubert Walter, as a compromise appointment in the disputed election of an archbishop of Canterbury, Innocent endorsed his election by the monks at Canterbury, but King John refused to accept him. After a long dispute, highlighted by an interdict the pope placed on England, John finally relented and permitted Langton to occupy the see (1213). Langton may have been the man most responsible for organizing baronial opposition to John which resulted in the granting of the Magna Carta. Langton's writings included commentaries on the Bible, on the *Sentences* of Peter Lombard, and on theological questions. He is credited with the division of the Books of the Bible into the chapters which is still in use.

LANGUE D'OC, the language spoken in Provence and used by the troubadours of southern France. The term is derived from the word *oc* (yes) as opposed to the corresponding *oui* used in northern France. Of the *langue d'oïl* dialects, that spoken in the Paris region gradually supplanted the others as the standard idiom and developed into modern French.

LANGUEDOC, French province on the Mediterranean which had its capital at Toulouse, its principal port at Narbonne. It was called Languedoc from the close of the thirteenth century after the *langue d'oc* spoken there. By 1271 it had become part of the French royal domain. The area which in Roman times constituted the province of Narbonese Gaul was occupied by the Visigoths from 412 to 507, then by the Franks except for Septimania which the Saracens held from c. 720 to 759. The counts of Toulouse ruled the region from the mid-eleventh century.

LAON, principal city of the county of Laon, a bishop's seat in 499 when it was detached from Reims, and a residence of the French Carolingian kings in the tenth century. The city's transitional Romanesque-Gothic cathedral was constructed during the period 1160 – 1230.

LAPIDARY, a story about the presumed powers and virtues of some precious stone or gem.

LAPPS, a people speaking a Finno-Ugric language which occupied parts of northern Scandinavia before the Finns moved in. They lived from hunting for the most part.

LAPSI, Christians of the third and fourth centuries who forswore their faith in order to escape persecution and death. It was probably not until the persecution of Emperor Decius (250 – 1) that the matter involved many people. Church fathers disagreed on how to treat such Christians when they wished to be readmitted, but the church followed the counsel of St. Cyprian of Carthage (d. 258) who urged sympathy. *Lapsi* were admitted to full membership after penance and a period of probation. The Novatians insisted on the unforgivable nature of such serious sins as that of forswearing the faith.

LA ROCHE-AUX-MOINES, BATTLE OF, battle fought near Angers in 1214 which ended in the victory of the French army led by the young Louis (VIII) over King John of England. The victory of Philip II Augustus of France over Otto IV of Germany, John's ally, at Bouvines shortly after in 1214 quashed all hope John had of recovering Normandy. The defeat helped precipitate the revolt of his barons which resulted in Magna Carta.

LA RUE, PIERRE DE, d. 1518, Franco-Flemish composer and singer at the courts of Burgundy and Spain. He composed 32 secular songs, 30 masses, and 45 motets. His work furnishes ex-

cellent examples of Franco-Flemish polyphonic music.

LA SALE, ANTOINE DE, d. c. 1464, French writer who gained an immense store of knowledge about the ways of the aristocracy while serving as tutor, counselor, and soldier in the service of the dukes of Anjou, the count of St. Pol, and other lords. His fame rests principally upon his *Jehan de Saintré,* a pseudo-biographical romance about the life of a knight at the court of Anjou. The work, which extols the ideals of chivalry, contributed in significant measure to the development of French prose fiction.

LASCARID DYNASTY, dynasty which ruled the empire of Nicaea from 1206 to 1261. Theodore I, its founder, the son-in-law of Alexius III Angelus, crowned emperor in 1208, was succeeded by his son-in-law John III Vatatzes (1222 – 54), and then by his grandson Theodore II (1254 – 8). The latter's son John IV was blinded and deposed by Michael VIII, founder of the dynasty of the Palaeologi.

LASCARIS, CONSTANTINE, d. 1501, Byzantine grammarian who taught Greek in several cities of Italy. His *Erotemata,* the first book printed in Greek characters, enjoyed a long popularity as an introductory grammar in the study of Greek.

LAS NAVAS DE TOLOSA, BATTLE OF, decisive battle fought in 1212 between Alfonso VIII of Castile, aided by the kings of Aragon, Navarre, and Portugal, and the Moors which ended in the overwhelming defeat of the latter. The defeat heralded the rapid decline of Almohad and Moorish power in Spain.

LAST SUPPER, the final meal which Christ took with his apostles on the eve of his passion and crucifixion (Matthew 26:17 – 29; Mark 14:12 – 25; Luke 22:7 – 38).

LÁSZLÓ IV THE KUMANIAN. *See* LADISLAS IV.

LATERAN I, COUNCIL OF, general church council (Ninth Ecumenical), convoked by Pope Callistus II, which in 1123 confirmed the settlement known as the Corcordat of Worms (1122) which officially ended the investiture controversy. The council forbade clerical marriage and concubinage.

LATERAN II, COUNCIL OF, general church council (Tenth Ecumenical), called by Pope Innocent II in 1139, which condemned the antipope Anacletus II. He had been chosen pope in 1130 in a closely contested election. The council also condemned the followers of Arnold of Brescia, usury, and the use of the crossbow.

LATERAN III, COUNCIL OF, general church council (Eleventh Ecumenical), summoned by Pope Alexander III in 1179, which ratified a treaty with Frederick I Barbarossa of Germany terminating a schism. It also decreed that subsequent popes must receive two-thirds of the votes cast by the cardinals to be elected. The council also ordered bishops to maintain schools for their clerics.

LATERAN IV, COUNCIL OF, general council (Twelfth Ecumenical), convoked by Pope Innocent III. It met in November 1215 and issued 70 canons dealing with a variety of doctrinal, disciplinary, and political matters. It stressed the obligation resting upon priests to preach, required bishops to maintain cathedral schools, took steps to suppress heresy (Catharism and Waldensianism), and defined the doctrine of transubstantiation. It ordained annual confession and communion during the Easter season. Priests were forbidden to take part in ordeals or in mystery plays, and arrangements were made for the organization of another Crusade against the Turks. The council ranks with the most important of church councils.

LATERAN PALACE, a building originally taken by Emperor Nero from the family of that name and turned over to the Christian church by Emperor Constantine in 312. It served as the residence of the popes until 1308 when it was destroyed by fire.

LATIFUNDIUM (pl. *latifundia*), a large landed estate in late Roman times.

LATIN EMPIRE. *See* CONSTANTINOPLE, LATIN EMPIRE OF.

LATINI, BRUNETTO, d. c. 1292, Florentine poet, statesman, Dante's teacher, and author of an encyclopedic work on Aristotle written in French.

LATINITAS CULINARIA, contemptuous term that the humanists of the late Middle Ages used in referring to the nonclassical Latin spoken in monasteries and universities.

LATIN, MEDIEVAL. *See* MEDIEVAL LATIN.

LATIN QUARTER, the left bank of the Seine in Paris where the University of Paris was located. Students at the cathedral school of Notre Dame situated on the Ile de la Cité had grown so numerous that they moved across to the left bank.

LA TRAPPE, ABBEY OF (Maison-Dieu Notre Dame de la Trappe), Cistercian monastery near Soligny in Normandy, founded as a Benedictine abbey in 1122 but adopting the Cistercian reform in 1148.

LATROCINIUM, "Robber Council," a church council that met in Ephesus in 449, summoned by Theodosius II to deal with difficulties stemming from the condemnation of Eutyches at the synod of Constantinople (448). Under the domination of Dioscorus, patriarch of Alexandria, who was a strong champion of Monophysitism, Eutyches was acquitted of heresy and reinstated in his monastery. The decrees of this council were reversed by the Council of Chalcedon in 451.

LAUDABILITER, bull issued by Pope Adrian IV c. 1155 extending the rights of a suzerain to Henry II of England over both the Irish people and their church.

LAUDANUM, a sedative used in the Middle Ages. Its quieting agent was usually opium.

LAUDA, SION, SALVATOREM, sequence composed by Thomas Aquinas for the feast of Corpus Christi.

LAUDES HINCMARI (*Laudes Regiae, Laudes Carolinae*), series of encomia honoring ecclesiastical or secular dignitaries probably used already in the late eighth century but once ascribed to Hincmar (d. 882).

LAUDS, the morning hour of the Divine Office. They followed after matins as the second of the offices of the canonical hours in the Roman breviary. They are one of the oldest parts of the Divine Office.

LAUENBURG, DUCHY OF, duchy located on the lower Elbe between the states of Holstein and Mecklenburg. The Slavic Polabians settled the area following the migration of the Germans to the west. When the Saxons moved back and pushed them out, the area became incorporated into the domain of Henry the Lion, duke of Saxony. When he was deprived of this duchy in 1180, it was turned over to the Ascanian Bernhard of Anhalt who then erected Lauenburg (1182). In 1260 it became a separate duchy of Saxe-Lauenburg.

LAURA (lavra), colony of anchorites who occupied separate cells but gathered together for the celebration of the liturgy. The oldest lauras were founded in Palestine in the early fourth century.

LAURANA, FRANCESCO DA, d. 1502, sculptor and medalist, active in Naples and at the court of René, duke of Anjou. His portraits of members of the Aragon and Sforza families express a detached dignity and reserve. His other works include medals, statues of the Madonna, tombs, and architectural sculpture.

LAURENTIAN CHRONICLE, oldest extant Russian chronicle, written c. 1377. The first portion of the narrative which extended to 1111 was known as the *Chronicle of Nestor*.

LAURENTIAN LIBRARY, library in Florence which consisted originally of the private collections of Cosimo and Lorenzo de' Medici.

LAVATER (lavator), the washer (launderer) in a monastery.

LAWRENCE JUSTINIAN, ST., d. 1456, Canon Regular of St. Augustine at San Giorgio near Venice, later superior of the house, general of the congregation, bishop of Castello (1433) and of Venice (1451). He was the first patriarch of Venice. His writings include a collection of sermons and doctrinal treatises.

LAWRENCE, ST., d. c. 258, Roman deacon and martyr who is said to have joked with his executioners while they were roasting him on a gridiron. He is listed among the saints in the canon of the mass.

LAY (lai), a short poem, usually narrative and sung by a minstrel, on a theme drawn from Celtic or Arthurian sources. The lay enjoyed great popularity in the late twelfth century.

LAY ABBOT, lay superior of a monastery. The appointment of lay abbots was not uncommon from the ninth to the eleventh centuries.

LAY ALTAR, an altar often found in abbey churches and located in front of the rood screen where it could be easily seen by the laity. The high altar in such churches was usually not visible from the nave.

LAYAMON, d. 1205, priest of Worcester, first prominent Middle English poet, author of the *Brut* which was in the main a translation into English verse of Wace's French *Brut* although appreciably longer. His is the first treatment in English of the Arthurian legend. Layamon also mentioned Lear and Cymbeline.

LAY BROTHER, member of a religious order who

professed but did not take formal vows. [*See* CONVERSI.] He was not required to recite the Divine Office, was usually not literate, and was occupied with manual labor. The practice of having lay brothers originated in the eleventh century when monks became literate and many of them became priests as well, and menial work was left to lay persons. A similar development took place in the religious orders of women.

LAY CONFESSION, confession to a member of the clergy who was not a priest, a practice that extended from the eighth to the fourteenth century.

LAZARUS, brother of Mary and Martha, the man Christ raised from the dead; the name given to the poor man covered with sores who sat at the entrance to the palatial residence of Dives (Luke 16:19–31).

LAZARUS, SAINT, ORDER OF, OF JERUSALEM, military-religious order founded in the twelfth century by Crusaders in Syria. Its first membership was composed of workers in a leper hospital.

LAZICA, small Christian state in northern Armenia bordering on the Black Sea. It controlled caravan trade with China and was fought over by Byzantium and the Sassanid kings of Persia.

LEAGUE OF PUBLIC WEAL, a coalition of French nobles organized in 1465 for the purpose of preserving their powerful position against the threat posed by the policies of Louis XI. Although they were initially able to force concessions from Louis, that wily monarch eventually destroyed the League, together with its principal creator, Charles the Bold, the duke of Burgundy.

LEAGUE OF UPPER GERMANY. *See* SWITZERLAND.

LEAR (Leir), legendary king of Britain, a descendant of Aeneas of Troy. Gregory of Monmouth, who speaks of Lear, claimed that he translated the story from old British records. The name Lear is also associated with a sea god of the ancient Britons.

LE BEL, JEAN, d. 1370, chronicler, probably of Hainaut, one of the first to write in French rather than in Latin. He was a soldier, then canon at the cathedral of Liège. His history treats the first campaigns of the Hundred Years' War, of which he was an eyewitness, with color and accuracy.

LECHFELD, BATTLE OF, decisive battle won by Otto I of Germany in 955 over the Magyars (Hungarians) in the vicinity of the Lech, a tributary of the Danube near Augsburg. After this defeat the Magyars ceased their marauding and accepted Christianity.

LECTIONARY, book containing the sacred readings (lessons) used in the liturgical services. The practice of assigning particular extracts from Scripture to particular days began in the fourth century.

LECTOR, a reader in the Latin church, that is, a clerk who had received the second of the four minor orders. In early times he read the Prophecies of the Old Testament, the Epistles, and, in some places, the Gospels.

LE DAIM, OLIVIER, d. 1484, court barber and valet to Louis XI of France, one of his favorite counselors. He became very wealthy but was promptly hanged when Louis died.

LEGATES, PAPAL, clerics or members of the hierarchy, seldom laymen, whom the pope sent to foreign countries to represent him in matters of common concern and who might be entrusted with his authority. The designation *legati missi* was extended to more formal legations which appeared about the ninth century. From the eleventh century *legati a latere* (legates from the pope's side) might be sent, usually cardinals who enjoyed a superior status and often superseded the authority of the local hierarchy. The term *legati nati* was applied to local bishops and archbishops who served as papal legates in matters concerning ecclesiastical jurisdiction.

LEGES ROMANAE BARBARORUM, a general designation given to law codes issued by Germanic kings for their subjects of Roman origin, e.g., *Lex Romana Visigothorum*.

LEGISTS, lawyers trained in Roman law as opposed to decretists who were specialists in canon law.

LEGNANO, BATTLE OF, battle fought 29 May 1176 near Milan in which the army of the Lombard League soundly defeated that of Frederick I Barbarossa of Germany. The League's foot soldiers, armed with crossbows, proved more than a match for Frederick's knights. The victory may have been the first major engagement won by the foot soldier over the horseman since the ninth century.

LEICESTER, EARLDOM OF, title created for Robert de Beaumont (d. 1118). It reverted to the crown in 1204 but was revived shortly after and given to Simon de Montfort. When Simon was slain in 1265, Henry III granted the title to his son Edmund, from which time it remained with the royal lineage until 1399 when it merged in the crown with the accession of Henry IV.

LEICESTER, SIMON, EARL OF. *See* MONTFORT, SIMON DE.

LEIDRADUS OF LYONS, d. 817, a disciple of Alcuin at Aachen whom Charlemagne appointed archbishop of Lyons in 797. Leidradus reformed the chant in his diocese and restored churches and monasteries.

LEIF ERICSSON (Eriksson), Norwegian seafarer, the son of Eric the Red. He spent his youth in Greenland and in 999 went to Norway. On his return the following year (1000), he was driven off course, according to one story, and discovered North America. He may have made his landfall on the coast of Labrador or Newfoundland. He called the place Vinland.

LEIPZIG, city of Saxony, first settled by the Lusatians, a site where Henry I (the Fowler) erected a fortress early in the tenth century. It became a possession of the margrave of Meissen in the twelfth century and was chartered in 1174 and acquired the city right of Magdeburg. Because of a number of highways that intersected there, and because of the encouragement given to trade by its rulers, it developed into an important commercial center. The University of Leipzig was founded in 1409 by German masters and students who left the University of Prague when a decree of King Wenceslas gave the Czechs a dominant position in that institution.

LENNOX, EARLDOM OF, Scottish title which probably originated with Alwyn (d. c. 1180), the first earl. Within a short time the earldom gained a prominent place in Scottish politics. Malcolm, fifth earl, an adherent of Robert I the Bruce, was slain at the battle of Halidon Hill (1333).

LENT, a forty-day period extending from Ash Wednesday to the eve of Easter during which time the faithful were required to observe certain regulations concerning fasting and abstinence. This penitential season of forty days has been traced to the canons of the Council of Nicaea (325). Before that time, the period of fasting in preparation for Easter did not, as a rule, exceed a few days.

LEO I (the Great), ST., Pope, 440–61, a vigorous champion of the primacy of the bishop of Rome. He acted firmly against the Pelagians, Manichaeans, and Priscillianists, supported the patriarch of Constantinople in the Eutychian controversy against the patriarch of Alexandria, and prepared the ground for the canons issued by the Council of Chalcedon (451) against Monophysitism. His Tome (449) was accepted by that council as a standard of Christological orthodoxy. He met the Hunnic chieftain Attila in 452 and may have had some part in his decision to spare Italy and return to Hungary.

Leo's writings include more than a hundred letters, also sermons for the entire liturgical cycle of feasts. Even though he was not a profound thinker and did not know Greek, his writings are distinguished by a clarity of thought and purity of language.

LEO II, ST., Pope, 682–3, a Sicilian who ratified the condemnation of Monothelitism decreed by the Council of Constantinople III (680–1).

LEO III, ST., Pope, 795–816, a Roman and cardinal priest. He fled to Charlemagne's court at Paderborn when attacked by the Roman faction that had opposed his election. Charlemagne came down to Rome and restored Leo after he had cleared himself of the charges brought against him by an oath of compurgation. On Christmas day 800 Leo crowned Charlemagne Roman emperor in St. Peter's. Leo took steps to suppress Adoptionism in Spain. Although he introduced the *Filioque* in the Nicene Creed upon the urging of Charlemagne, he would not permit it to be chanted in public liturgy lest this offend the Greeks.

LEO IV, ST., Pope, 847–55, native of Rome, a Benedictine monk. As pope he erected a wall that enclosed St. Peter's and the surrounding religious establishments against the threat of further Saracen attacks. The enclosed region became known as "the Leonine City." He forced Hincmar, the archbishop of Reims, to permit his suffragan bishops to make direct appeals to Rome. He was interested in liturgical chant, and the introduction of the *Asperges* has been ascribed to him.

LEO V, Pope, July to September 903, of obscure origins and murdered after three months in office. His murderer was Christopher, cardinal priest of S. Damasus, who succeeded him as pope (antipope?).

LEO VI, Pope, May to December 928, a priest of Rome who owed his election to Marozia and the family of Theophylact. He replaced Pope John X whom they had deposed and imprisoned.

LEO VII, Pope, 936–9, probably a Benedictine monk who was appointed pope by Alberic II of Spoleto. He actively cooperated with Henry I and Otto I of Germany in reforming the church.

LEO VIII, Pope, 963–5, appointed pope by Otto I of Germany while still a layman to succeed John XII whom the emperor had removed. No sooner had Otto left the city than John returned and deposed Leo. When John died the Romans elected Benedict V, but Otto returned to Rome and reinstated Leo.

LEO IX, ST., Pope, 1049–54, a native of Alsace of noble birth, bishop of Toul, who owed his appointment as pope to Henry III of Germany. In 1053 he was defeated and taken prisoner by the Normans of southern Italy who then accepted him as suzerain. Leo not only was a great reforming pope but he also worked successfully to reassert the papacy's position of leadership in Christendom by expanding the operations of the Roman Curia, by sending out legates to the different kings of Western Europe, and by extensive travels of his own. Among his able advisers were Hildebrand (Gregory VII), Humbert, and St. Peter Damian.

LEO I, Byzantine emperor, 457–74, a Thracian, the successor of Marcian, put on the throne by the patrician Aspar who expected him to be content with the role of a puppet. After about six years Leo pushed Aspar aside with the help of Isaurians from Anatolia and ruled in his own name. He gave his daughter Ariadne to one of the Isaurian chieftains who succeeded him under the name of Zeno. Leo supported the decisions of the Council of Chalcedon (451).

LEO III, Byzantine emperor, 717–41, usually referred to as "the Isaurian" but actually a Syrian peasant by birth, general under Anastasius II. He was raised to the throne after a successful revolt against Theodosius III. With the help of Greek fire he beat off a dangerous Arab attack on Constantinople in 717-8 and eventually drove the Moslems out of Asia Minor. He continued the provincial reorganization of the empire initiated by Heraclius (610-41) and established additional themes. In 726 he issued the *Ecloga* which came to replace the less "modern" *Corpus Juris Civilis* in the courts of the empire. Most controversial was the policy of iconoclasm that he introduced in 726 when he ordered the suppression of the veneration of icons. Because of papal opposition to his policy, he removed southern Italy, Greece, and parts of the Balkans from the pope's jurisdiction. In 740 he gained another major victory over the Arabs.

LEO V (the Armenian), Byzantine emperor, 813-20, succeeded in beating back a fierce Bulgar attack on the capital headed by their khan Krum. At home he revived the iconoclastic policies of Leo III and persecuted the orthodox party which was headed by Theodore the Studite. Leo was murdered by conspirators who proclaimed Michael II emperor.

LEO VI, Byzantine emperor, 886-912, also known as Leo the Wise or Leo the Philosopher, a weak ruler who lost Sicily to the Saracens and was obliged to pay the Bulgars tribute in order to keep them quiet. He put through the legal reforms, known as the *Basilica,* that his father Basil I had introduced. These represented a modernization of Justinian's Code and were intended to supersede the *Ecloga* of Leo III. While the pope confirmed the validity of his marriage which the patriarch had refused to do, Leo attacked the double procession of the Holy Ghost which was accepted in the Western church.

LEO I, king of Armenia, ruled Armenian Cilicia from 1129 until 1138 when the Byzantine emperor John II Comnenus captured him and kept him as an exile in Constantinople. He died after 1140.

LEO II, king of Armenia, ruler of Cilicia, 1199-1219, recognized the suzerainty of Henry VI of Germany and sought to advance his country by erecting schools, monasteries, and hospitals, and by negotiating trade treaties with other countries.

LEO DIACONUS (the Deacon), d. after 992, deacon of Constantinople who accompanied Basil II on his campaign against the Bulgarians. His history of the period 959 to 976, largely based on his own observations as an eyewitness, covers the military achievements of the emperors Nicephorus II Phocas and John Tzimisces.

LEO MARSICANUS (Ostiensis), d. 1115, monk of Monte Cassino, cardinal bishop, and author of a valuable history of Monte Cassino from its foundation by St. Benedict c. 529 until 1057.

LEÓN, kingdom of northwestern Spain that recognized the suzerainty of the caliphate of Córdoba during the greater part of the tenth century. Its rise dates from the reign of Garcia I (909-14) who moved his court from the Asturian capital of Oviedo to Leon. In 910 Leon was joined to the Asturias, in 1037 to Castile, then in 1157 gained its independence again and retained this until its final union with Castile in 1230. The location of Leon on the pilgrimage route to Santiago served to influence the country's cultural, economic, and political development.

LEÓN, MOSES BEN SHEM-TOB DE, d. 1305, Jewish mystic of Spain whose exegetical studies helped arrest the rise of rationalism among the Jews of Spain. His *Sefer ha-Zohar* is considered the leading work of Jewish mysticism.

LEONARD OF PISA (Leonardo Pisano, Fibonacci), d. 1230, mathematician credited with introducing the use of the Hindu-Arabic numerals and the zero to Western Europe. He also authored treatises on mathematics and geometry.

LEONARD, ST., sixth-century hermit, supposedly a nobleman at the court of Clovis, king of the Franks, whom St. Remigius converted and baptized. He lived in a cell at Noblac near Limoges and later founded a monastery there. Despite his obscurity, his cult proved very popular and numerous churches were dedicated to him.

LEONTIUS OF BYZANTIUM, d. 543, a leading theologian of the period. He became a monk of the New Laura in Palestine, went to Constantinople to defend Chalcedonian Christology against the Monophysites, later returned to Palestine where he defended Origenism against the Orthodox. He subsequently returned to Constantinople where his attack on the position of Theodore of Mopsuestia led ultimately to the condemnation of the Three Chapters by the Council of Constantinople (553).

LEONTIUS OF JERUSALEM, sixth-century monk and theologian. He endorsed the position of Cyril of Alexandria concerning the nature of Christ and attacked those maintained by the Monophysites and Nestorians.

LEOPARDI (Leopardo), ALESSANDRO, d. c. 1522, Italian goldsmith, engraver, architect, and sculptor, noted principally for his work in bronze. He completed Verrochio's unfinished equestrian statue of Colleoni. In architecture he is best known for the church of S. Giustina at Padua.

LEOPOLD III OF AUSTRIA, ST., d. 1136, margrave of Austria, married Agnes, daughter of Henry IV of Germany, and was by her the father of Bishop Otto of Freising and Archbishop Conrad II of Salzburg. He founded several monasteries and is credited with laying the foundations of Austria's future greatness.

LEO THE MATHEMATICIAN, one of the most distinguished scholars and mathematicians of the period. Caesar Bardas, regent for Michael III (d. 867), appointed him to head the galaxy of scholars who were gathered in Constantinople.

LÉRINS, ABBEY OF, monastery located on the isle of Saint-Honorat (originally *Lerinum*) off the southern coast of France (near Nice) which was founded by Honoratus of Arles c. 410. It became a center of intellectual activity and counted among its many pupils Augustine of Canterbury and possibly Patrick of Ireland. In 975 it was restored following its destruction by the Saracens c. 732. It attained the peak of its intellectual and spiritual influence in the eleventh century. The Rule of Lérins may have influenced Benedict in the preparation of his own rule.

LESSON, the reading or teaching lecture in the liturgy.

LETTER OF CREDIT, letter that a person (merchant) could purchase from a banking house, then cash in any city where an agent of that house might be located. Such financial transactions which became common in the thirteenth century greatly facilitated the buying and selling of goods and the exchange of money between distant places. [*See* BANKING.]

LEVI BEN GERSON. *See* GERSONIDES.

LEWES, BATTLE OF, battle fought in 1264 near the Channel south of London which ended in the capture of King Henry III and the young Edward (I) by Simon de Montfort, leader of the rebelling barons in the Barons' War.

LEWES, PRIORY OF, Benedictine house founded c. 1080 by William de Warenne, earl of Surrey. It was the first Cluniac house to be established in England.

LEX ROMANA BURGUNDIONUM, code of laws issued by Gundobad, king of Burgundy, c. 500, for his Roman subjects. [*See* GERMANIC LAWS, EARLY.]

LEX ROMANA VISIGOTHORUM. *See* BREVIARY OF ALARIC.

LEX SALICA, law code of the Franks issued by

Clovis c. 508–11 for his Frankish subjects. [*See* GERMANIC LAWS, EARLY.]

LIARD, French silver coin of the fifteenth century worth three *deniers*.

LIBANIUS, d. c. 393, leading rhetorician and sophist, a foe of Christianity and an admirer of Emperor Julian. His letters and orations contain valuable information about the political, cultural, and economic life of Antioch and the eastern provinces of the Roman empire.

LIBELLATICI (Libelli), Christians who held (purchased) *libelli,* that is, certificates stating that they had sacrificed to the cult of Augustus. In many instances no such sacrifice had been performed. The practice was condemned by church authorities.

LIBERAL ARTS. *See* ARTS, LIBERAL.

LIBER (*lex*) AUGUSTALIS. *See* MELFI, CONSTITUTIONS OF.

LIBER CENSUUM (*Romanae Ecclesiae*), register of tax reports and dues owed by individual churches during the period from 1188 to the pontificate of Pope Honorius III (d. 1227). This register, which was the work of Honorius when he served as papal chamberlain, constitutes a most useful source in the study of the financial history of the papacy for the period.

LIBER DE CAUSIS, a neo-Platonic treatise consisting principally of extracts from Proclus's *Elements of Theology*. The treatise, which was probably composed initially in Arabic, presented the neo-Platonic view of the universe and its hierarchical organization. In its Latin translation, made by Gerard of Cremona who proclaimed it a work of Aristotle, it greatly influenced scholastic thinkers of the twelfth and thirteenth centuries.

LIBER EXTRA (*Liber Decretalium Extra Decretum Gratiani Vagantium*), a collection of the decretals issued from the time of the publication of Gratian's *Decretum* (1140) to Pope Gregory IX (d. 1241). It was compiled by Raymond of Penaforte and published by Pope Gregory in 1234.

LIBERIUS, Pope, 352–66, the successor of Julius I, deposed by the pro-Arian emperor Constantius II in 355 and exiled to Thrace when he refused to accept the condemnation of St. Athanasius, patriarch of Alexandria. In 358, after having been brought to Milan, then Sirmium, and confronted by the emperor, he apparently shifted his position and was permitted to return to Rome. St. Jerome and Athanasius agreed that his submission was forced and that the formula to which he subscribed was indeed heretical in character. Scholars attribute his change of mind to a combination of old age, poor health, and fear.

LIBER PONTIFICALIS (*Book of the Popes*), a history of the popes to 1464. The first part consists of a chronicle of the popes from St. Peter to Stephen V (d. 891), followed by a cataloguing of the popes of the next two centuries, when the narrative resumes with Gregory VII (1073–85) and continues to 1464. The first section of part one, which was probably compiled by a priest of Rome, is the least reliable; the part from Anastasius II (496–8), on the other hand, is quite authentic. Despite its uneven quality, it constitutes an indispensable source for the history of the papacy and of Rome from the fifth to the fifteenth century.

LIBER SEXTUS, a codification of decretals and conciliar canons for the years 1234 to 1294. It takes up in 1234 where the *Liber Extra* of Pope Gregory IX leaves off.

LIBRARY, THE MEDIEVAL. The essential value of books was recognized from the early church as the most effective means of preserving learning and of passing this on to later generations. Although the learning churchmen were most interested in concerned the Christian faith, knowledge of that faith could not be imparted without the aid of a general education based on the ancient liberal arts. For this reason, not only the writings of the church fathers but also the Latin classics were treasured and copied. A vital link in the collection of books and the establishment of libraries were the monastic scriptoria where manuscripts were transcribed by monks who were convinced that their labor was pleasing to God. So Alcuin admonished his monks at Tours: "It is better to copy books than to cultivate vines." Even during the troubled centuries of Merovingian and Carolingian times, a constant exchange of books and manuscripts among monastic scriptoria enabled certain monasteries such as Fulda, Lorsch, Bobbio, Reichenau, St. Gall, and Monte Cassino to establish libraries that might boast holdings of a near-thousand or more volumes. In the eleventh century, when cathedral schools tended to outstrip monastic centers in the field of education, the libraries at Reims, Paris, Orléans, Chartres, Tours, and Laon compared favorably with those in the older monasteries.

With the rise of universities, the principal business of collecting books and establishing libraries shifted to these intellectual centers, to Bologna, Paris, Oxford, Cambridge, Cologne, Vienna, and Prague. At the same time, much of the learning of ancient Greece in the fields of science, philosophy, and medicine, as well as Roman law, together with the commentaries of Arabic scholars, became available through southern Italy and Spain. Also by the fifteenth century, private libraries of impressive size appeared, such as that of Humphrey, duke of Gloucester, whose gift of books to Oxford helped establish the foundations of the Bodleian Library. The most avid collectors of books in the late Middle Ages were the humanists of Italy, and it was by way of their enthusiasm and the generosity of patrons including the Medici that such famous libraries as the Vatican and Laurentian came into existence.

LIBRI CAROLINI, a work of four volumes consisting of polemical writings concerning the controversy over images as debated in the Latin church. The writings were probably collected by Theodulf of Orléans (some scholars say Alcuin) on instructions from Charlemagne.

LICENTIATE, the holder of a bachelor's degree who had permission (license) to teach.

LICET JURIS, title of a decree issued by Louis IV the Bavarian, Holy Roman emperor, in 1338 which announced that the man whom the German electors chose as king would also hold the title emperor. The document explicitly rejected any claim the pope might advance in the selection or coronation of the emperor.

LICINIUS, VALERIUS LICINIANUS, Roman emperor, ruled as Augustus in 308 over the Balkans, as co-Augustus of the eastern empire (Constantine ruled the west) from 313 until his defeat at the battle of Chrysopolis in 324. Constantine had him executed the following year. One factor leading to the estrangement of the two men, who in 313 had agreed to extend toleration to the Christians, was Licinius's resumption of persecution in the eastern provinces.

LIÈGE, city of the Low Countries, first noted in the eighth century when it became a bishopric. By the year 1000 it had gained fame as a center of learning largely through the efforts of its influential bishop Notger. It was an independent principality ruled by prince-bishops and subject to the Holy Roman emperor. In 1208 Philip, duke of Swabia, confirmed the charter granted its citizens by its bishop. In 1467 Charles the Bold, duke of Burgundy, sacked the city.

LIMBO, place or state certain theologians assigned to unbelieving souls who deserved neither the pains of hell nor the bliss of heaven or, in the case of believers, those who died before Christ's crucifixion. St. Augustine held that all unbaptized souls suffered some degree of punishment, even hell. St. Thomas Aquinas maintained that they were excluded from heavenly bliss although they enjoyed full natural happiness.

LIMBOURG (Limburg), BROTHERS OF, Pol

(Paul), Herment (Hermann), and Jean (Jan) Maluel, Dutch manuscript illuminators of the early fifteenth century who were employed by the duke of Berry in Bourges. Their most famous work is entitled the *Très Riches Heures.* Their style was essentially a court style, elegant, exquisite, and sophisticated, and their work is a supreme example of the International Gothic.

LIMERICK (Luimneach), city in Ireland located on the Shannon. The early settlement there was sacked by the Norse in 812 who then made it the principal town of their kingdom of Limerick. Brian Boru, the high king of Ireland, seized it near the close of the tenth century, after which it served as capital of the kings of Thomond or North Munster until 1174 when the English took possession. Richard I of England granted the town a charter in 1197. Limerick was often under siege in the thirteenth and fourteenth centuries.

LIMES, name given to the fortified frontier of the Roman Empire particularly in Britain and Germany. The *limes* extended from western Britain to the Black Sea. Earlier any military road might be termed *limes.*

LIMINA APOSTOLORUM, ecclesiastical term referring to Rome and more specifically to the tombs of SS. Peter and Paul. [*See* AD LIMINA VISIT.]

LIMOGES, city in west-central France whose original settlement was located there because of a ford across the Vienne river. St. Martial introduced the area to Christianity early in the third century, while later in that century it became a suffragan see of Bourges. It was the principal city of the county of Limousin which was generally held as a fief of the dukes of Aquitaine. The Black Prince sacked the city in 1370 early in the Hundred Years' War. Limoges was famous for the excellent work of its enamelers and goldsmiths.

LINACRE, THOMAS, d. 1524, English priest, court physician, and humanist. He composed works on grammar and medicine, translated Galen into Latin, and founded the College of Physicians in London.

LINCOLN, city in east-central England, the Roman *Lindum,* became a bishop's seat in the fourth century and served as residence of the kings of Mercia. The Danes occupied the city c. 877. Henry II granted it a charter c. 1157 although the first mention of the office of mayor appears only in 1206. The diocese of Lincoln was the largest and most populous in England. The construction of its early Gothic cathedral was begun in 1092.

LINDISFARNE, ABBEY OF, Celtic monastery founded in 635 on Lindisfarne Island (Holy Island) by monks from Iona under the direction of Aidan. (At low tide the island is connected with the shore by a stretch of sand.) After the decision reached in 664 at the Synod of Whitby against Celtic usages, the Scoto-Irish monks withdrew to Iona. Vikings destroyed the monastery in 793, while renewed raids c. 883 caused the monks to flee the area a second time. Lindisfarne served as a bishopric until 995 when Durham became the episcopal see. In the eleventh century the monastery adopted the Benedictine rule.

LINDISFARNE GOSPELS (Book of Durham), a volume of four gospels written at the Abbey of Lindisfarne probably between 695 and 698. The script is a noble Anglo-Saxon majuscule; the interlinear translation into Anglo-Saxon was added c. 970. The volume's splendid illuminations are well preserved.

LINE SYSTEM, the arrangement of musical notes on five parallel lines. Guido of Arezzo (d. 1050) is credited with having introduced the first fully developed system.

LINGUA ROMANA, a Romance language.

LINGUA TEUDESCA, a Germanic language.

LINUS, ST., Pope, 64? to 79?, obscure bishop of Rome, the immediate successor of St. Peter. He may have served as Peter's "coadjutor."

LIOBA, ST., d. c. 782, Benedictine nun of Wessex who accompanied St. Boniface, her relative, to Germany where she became the abbess of Tauberbischofsheim (near Mainz). She established several convents in Germany.

LION. The lion appears in early Christian art mainly in two connections: a) in the story of Daniel as a "type" of God's redemption of his chosen people; b) as a symbol of St. Mark. In late medieval art a lion often appears in pictures of St. Jerome.

LIPPI, FILIPPINO, d. 1504, painter of Florence, son of Fra Filippo Lippi. He is especially known for the altarpiece *The Vision of St. Bernard*. He served as an apprentice of Botticelli, later worked on the frescoed decoration of Lorenzo de Medici's villa at Spedaletto near Volterra. He also decorated the Caraffa Chapel in S. Maria sopra Minerva. Among his famous panel paintings is the *Adoration of the Magi*.

LIPPI, FRA FILIPPO, d. 1469, Italian painter, a Carmelite who was dispensed of his vows and married. His early work reveals the influence of Masaccio, his later that of Fra Angelico. Among his best-known paintings is the *Madonna with the Child Jesus*. Perhaps his finest panel painting is an altarpiece of the Annunciation in S. Lorenzo in Florence. He enjoyed the patronage of the Medici throughout his career.

LIRA: a) *L. Italiana,* a coin used in north Italy; b) *L. Tron,* coin minted during the reign of Doge Nicolo Tron (d. 1473).

LISBON (Lissabon, Lisboa), capital of Portugal which grew from pre-Roman origins. In the fourth century it became an episcopal see. The city fell successively to the Alans, Sueves, and Visigoths, then c. 712 to the Moors. Alfonso I of Portugal captured it in 1147 with the help of Crusaders (Second Crusade) and in 1256 Alfonso III moved his residence there from Coimbra. In 1390 it became a national metropolitan see. The University of Lisbon, founded by King Diniz in 1290, was moved to Coimbra in 1308–38 and 1354–77.

LITANY, a form of prayer in which the faithful responded to a series of petitions or invocations recited by a leader. Among the oldest responses were *Amen* and *Kyrie Eleison*. The term also applied to processions in which prayers of this kind were recited. The Litany of the Saints, possibly the oldest of the litanies, may reach back to the fourth century or beyond, to Antioch, whence the practice spread to Constantinople and then to Rome. There, late in the fifth century, Pope Gelasius (492–6) introduced a litany of intercessions of which the *Kyrie Eleison* is the sole surviving relic.

LITERATURE, MEDIEVAL. The literature of the Middle Ages falls into two classes, that written in Latin and that in the vernacular. Included in Latin prose literature is an enormous volume of hagiography, a variety of moralizing tales, the most popular of which were the *Gesta Romanorum,* annals, chronicles, patristic writings, in fact almost all writing on learned or serious subjects, together with letters, sermons, and the varied products of later medieval humanists. The Latin which the writers of this literature employed varied from the polished style of Boethius and John of Salisbury to the struggling passages of Gregory of Tours. [*See* MEDIEVAL LATIN.] Latin poetry was both religious and secular in theme. The first included hymns for the most part, composed by a steady stream of poets from St. Ambrose (d. 397) on down to the close of the Middle Ages. Secular verse consisted principally of the compositions of the Goliards. [*See* GOLIARDS.][For vernacular literature, *see* EPIC POETRY; ROMANCE, COURTLY; TROUBADOUR; FABLIAU; FABLE; DRAMA, MEDIEVAL; also, individual poems such as the ROMAN DE LA ROSE and poets such as DANTE.]

LITHUANIA, grand duchy from the thirteenth century when it comprised roughly the region between Poland and the Dnieper and stretched from the Baltic to the Black Sea. Its people, the Liths, who belonged to the Baltic group of nations, had located themselves c. 1000 on the south shore of the Baltic above the Niemen river. Missionaries and knights (Teutonic Knights and Knights of the Sword) from Germany began to move in among them c. 1200 to effect their conversion either by force or preaching. In 1251 the grand duke Mindaugas and many of his people accepted baptism, and in 1253 Pope Innocent IV recognized him as king. Upon his murder in 1263 a pagan reaction set in sired by the fear of eventual absorption into a state ruled by the Teutonic Knights. This fear led to an alliance with Poland cemented in 1386 by the marriage of Jagiello, grand duke of Lithuania, to Jadwiga, the heiress of Poland. The decisive victory gained by the united Liths and Poles over the Teutonic Knights at Grunwald (Tannenberg) in 1410 brought the return of Samogitia to Lithuania. Casimir IV (1447–92), king of Poland and grand prince of Lithuania, continued the war against the Teutonic Knights and by the Peace of Torun (Thorn) in 1466 forced them to cede Pomorze (Pomerania). As the power of the Teutonic Knights waned, Lithuania discovered a new threat to the east in the person of Ivan III, grand duke of Moscow (1462–1505), who deprived it of its lands east of the Dnieper.

LITTLE FLOWERS OF ST. FRANCIS. See FIORETTI DI SAN FRANCESCO.

LITTLE HOURS, an abbreviated Divine Office consisting of prime, terce, sext, and none. It did not include lauds and vespers.

LITTE OFFICE OF THE BLESSED VIRGIN MARY, an abridged version of the common office of the Blessed Virgin. It may have come into use before the tenth century, first among the religious orders and later among the secular clergy. Scenes suggested by the office often appeared reproduced and illuminated in the "Books of Hours" in the late Middle Ages.

LITTLETON, SIR THOMAS, d. 1481, English judge of common pleas, probably a member of the Inner Temple, and author of a celebrated legal treatise concerning property entitled *Littleton on Tenures*. The treatise, written in English, bears no mark of influence from Roman law.

LITURGICAL COLORS. See COLORS, LITURGICAL.

LIUDOLFINGER (*Ludolfinger*), aristocratic family of Saxony which came into prominence with Count Liudolf (d. 866). His son Otto (d. 912) acquired the duchy of Saxony. The German kings Henry I, Otto I, II, and III, and Henry II were members of the dynasty. It became extinct with the death of Henry II in 1024.

LIUDPRAND. See LIUTPRAND.

LIUTIZIANS, east Slavic people located between the lower Elbe and Oder rivers. In company with the Obotrites they secured their freedom from German rule with the help of Bohemia. Albert the Bear, margrave of Brandenburg, conquered them c. 1150 and encouraged German immigration.

LIUTPRAND, king of the Lombards, 712–44, extended his rule over the duchies of Benevento and Spoleto and brought the Lombard kingdom to the height of its power and influence. He introduced progressive legal and administrative reforms, modeled after Roman laws and institutions, which both improved the efficiency of his courts and enabled him to curb the power of local dukes and bishops.

LIUTPRAND (Liudprand, Luitprand) OF CREMONA, d. c. 972, Italian chronicler, member of a wealthy Lombard family, an emissary first of King Berengar II of Italy who sent him to Constantinople, then of Otto I of Germany who appointed him bishop of Cremona (c. 961). The mission Liutprand made to Constantinople for

Otto I to bring back a Byzantine wife for his son, the future Otto II, ended in failure. Liutprand left a valuable history of the times (*Antapodosis*), a chronicle of the reign of Otto I, and an account of his mission to Constantinople (*Relatio de Legatione Constantinopolitana*).

LIVERY, clothing with special markings worn by feudal retainers that identified them as vassals of a particular lord.

LIVERY COMPANIES, guilds of London that secured charters of incorporation in order to own property and enjoy a chartered monopoly over the purchase or sale of certain commodities. The companies, chartered largely from the reign of Edward III, regulated conditions of work, apprenticeship, and trade. They had the right to elect their own wardens as well as the common council of the city of London, which in turn elected the mayor and other officials of the city, even the city's representatives in parliament. They wore a distinctive livery or costume and a distinctive badge for ceremonial use and, thus attired, took part in municipal pageants and royal coronations.

LIVONIA, region between Estonia and Courland. The Livonians and the Letts who occupied this territory were subjugated and baptized during the course of the thirteenth century through the combined efforts of Bishop Albert of Riga, the Livonian Knights of the Swords, and the Teutonic Knights.

LIVONIAN KNIGHTS (Brothers) OF THE SWORD, military-religious order founded by Bishop Albert I of Riga in 1202 for the purpose of converting the pagan Balts and Slavs in the region south of the Baltic. In 1236 they were defeated by the Lithuanians and the following year merged with the Teutonic Knights. Their habit was a white robe with a red cross and sword.

LIVONIAN RHYMED CHRONICLE, a history composed by a member of the Teutonic Order toward the close of the thirteenth century. It described the wars which brought about the subjugation of Livonia.

LIVRE, French coin which evolved from the *libra gallica* of the Carolingian period.

LLANDAFF, ANCIENT SEE OF, one of the four oldest bishoprics of Wales. It lay in the neighborhood of Cardiff and was founded by Celtic monks in the fifth or sixth century. Urban, bishop of Llandaff, 1107–33, was the first of its ordinaries to take an oath of obedience to the archbishop of Canterbury.

LL.B. bachelor of laws; LL.D., doctor of laws; LL.M., master of laws.

LLEWELYN AP GRUFFYDD, d. 1282, grandson of Llewelyn the Great and recognized officially as the prince of Wales. He was the first ruler to use that title. Henry III empowered him to demand homage of all native lords and to do homage for the entire principality of Wales. In the Barons' War he was an ally of Simon de Montfort. His refusal to do homage to Edward I upon his coronation in 1272 led Edward to undertake two invasions of Wales. The first in 1277 cost Llewelyn all but a portion of north Wales. The second campaign ended with his death and the end of what remained of Welsh independence.

LLEWELYN AP IORWERTH, d. 1240, called the Great, married Joan, an illegitimate daughter of King John of England, and by 1202 had made himself actual ruler of the greater part of Wales. John invaded Wales in 1211 and defeated him, but in 1218 the regency under Henry III recognized him as a magnate of the realm. In 1238 he left his principality to his son Dafydd and retired to a Cistercian monastery. He showed himself a generous patron of Welsh bards.

LLULL, RAMON. *See* LULL, RAYMOND.

LOCHNER, STEPHAN, d. 1451, painter of Cologne, the leading representative of the school of

Cologne and director of a workshop in that city. His best known work, the altarpiece entitled *Adoration of the Magi,* is now in the cathedral at Cologne. Some of his works show the influence of the Van Eycks.

LOCUS, term used in the study of logic and rhetoric for the location of proofs or illustrations. *Locus dialecticus* was synonymous with proof. *Loci communes* could be defined as points of view useful in discovering and organizing materials.

LOCUS REGIT ACTUM, the legal principle that the place determines the kind of judicial procedure to be observed. This principle was based upon medieval customary law.

LODI, city near Milan and often its enemy. It suffered destruction on several occasions as in 1158 when it was razed by the Milanese. Although Emperor Frederick I Barbarossa rebuilt the city in 1160, it allied itself with the Lombard League in the next century against his grandson Frederick II. It eventually lost its independence to Milan.

LOGGIA, arcaded or roofed gallery built into the lower or upper floor of larger buildings or projecting from them. The Loggia della Signoria of Florence was built in 1376–82.

LOGIC, also known as dialectic, one of the seven liberal arts. The growing interest in logic in the eleventh century led to the rise of scholasticism. [*See* SCHOLASTICISM.]

LOGOS, Greek for "word" or "reason" and used in Christian theology with reference to Christ, the Second Person of the Trinity (John 1:1 and 14; 1 John 1:1; Revelation 19:13). The Apologists of the second century, notably St. Ignatius, pressed the idea of the Son as the Logos as a means of making Christian teaching compatible with Hellenistic philosophy which used that term and gave it several interpretations, such as the universal reason or the divine power in the world.

LOHENGRIN, son of Parzival in the story of the Holy Grail.

LOKI, German god of the underworld, agent of both mischief and evil among his fellow gods.

LOLLARDS, traditionally the followers of John Wyclif (d. 1384), although more properly applied to members of the lower classes who accepted the radical views of vagrant priests like John Ball (d. 1381) whose preaching antedated that of Wyclif. Ball and other preachers such as William Swinderby demanded not only a more popular church but a reform of society as well. A more intellectual group, sometimes called Lollards but better identified as Wycliffites, was composed of Wyclif's admirers at Oxford, including Nicholas Hereford and Philip Repington. As a major force, this wing of Lollardy was suppressed in 1382 by William Courtenay, archbishop of Canterbury, with the assistance of the government, who had already cooperated in forcing Wyclif to leave Oxford and retire to Lutterworth. The Lollard movement which never affected more than a small minority, and these mostly peasants and town workers, ebbed quickly following the enactment in 1401 of a statute that authorized the execution of heretics. It disappeared with little trace after the suppression of Sir John Oldcastle's abortive revolt in 1413, although it was not uncommon to hear of charges of Lollardy being brought against persons such as Margery Kempe who invited prosecution by their actions or beliefs.

LOMBARD LEAGUE, federation of north Italian cities organized in 1167 with the encouragement of Pope Alexander III for the purpose of thwarting the aim of Frederick I Barbarossa to establish his authority over Lombardy. The League's army defeated the emperor at Legnano in 1176. In 1226 the League was revived to meet the threat of Frederick II, again with the encouragement of the papacy.

LOMBARDO (Lombardi), Italian family of architects and sculptors of the fifteenth century. Pietro Lombardo, d. 1515, was active in Padua until 1467 when he made his home in Venice. He executed tombs and sepulchral monuments and was the architect of numerous churches and palaces. The church of S. Maria dei Miracoli in Venice is considered one of the most striking edifices erected in that city during the period of the Renaissance. His most famed sculpture is the Zanetti tomb in the cathedral at Treviso. The work of his sons Tullio and Antonio falls principally in the sixteenth century.

LOMBARDS (Langobards), a Germanic people, member of the Sueve nation, which was located east of the lower Elbe in the fifth century. From there they moved into southern Austria, destroyed the Gepids, then in 568 crossed the Alps into Italy under their king Alboin. Alboin's early death and the loss of unified control prevented their conquest of the entire peninsula. Cities and coastal areas, including Rome, Naples, Ravenna, Apulia, and Calabria, that could be supported from the sea remained under Byzantine control. The Lombard kingdom reached its height during the seventh and eighth centuries when it forced Spoleto and Benevento to recognize its suzerainty. In 751 the Lombards occupied Ravenna, but their threat to Rome prompted Pope Stephen II to appeal to Pepin the Short, king of the Franks, who drove off the Lombards and turned the exarchate of Ravenna over to the pope. [See DONATION OF PEPIN.] In 772 when the Lombard king Desiderius renewed his attack on Rome, Charlemagne came to the pope's rescue, captured Pavia, the Lombard capital, and brought an end to their kingdom (774). He kept the Iron Crown of the Lombards for himself.

LOMBARDS, banking firms in Italy; Italian bankers.

LOMBARDY, roughly the region of the Po valley west of Venice.

LONDON, city on the Thames, site of a Celtic community and given the name of *Londinium* when the Romans occupied the area c. A.D. 43. During the period of Anglo-Saxon invasions, it lost its earlier importance, including its bishop who had appeared in the fourth century, but it recovered somewhat under Ethelbert, king of Kent (d. 616), who founded St. Paul's cathedral. The Danes occupied the town in 871–2, but Alfred assured English possession in 886. By the eleventh century London had become the largest city in England and by 1180 it was the country's effective capital. In 1191 Richard granted the city a charter. London played an important role on several occasions, notably during the Peasant Revolt of 1381 and Cade's rebellion of 1450. The support it afforded Richard of York and his son Edward (IV) helped assure a Yorkist victory in the Wars of the Roses.

LONDON CHARTERHOUSE, Carthusian foundation established by Sir Walter Manny in 1371.

LONGBOW, a large bow drawn by hand, unusually accurate even at long distances, believed to have been developed in south Wales. The English used it from the twelfth century and employed it with great effectiveness against the French in the Hundred Years' War.

LONGCHAMP, WILLIAM, d. 1197, chancellor, bishop of Ely (1189), and justiciar (1190) under Richard I of England. His arrogance and arbitrary administration caused Englishmen to turn to John for help during Richard's absence on the Third Crusade. He was removed from office late in 1191 and returned to France, although Richard retained him as chancellor until his death.

LONGINUS, according to apochryphal biblical literature, the captain of the Roman company of soldiers present at Christ's crucifixion. Longinus is supposed to have been the one who opened Christ's side with a lance (Mark 15:39). He was honored as the first convert to Christianity and its first martyr.

LOPES, FERNÃO, d. c. 1460, court chronicler of Portugal, the first and greatest of Portuguese royal chroniclers, whose work covers the history of that country to 1411. His chronicles have special value since many of the documents he used and quoted are no longer extant. He wrote with considerable objectivity and in a prose style that ranks with the finest of the period. His search for historical truth was that employed by modern scholars, that is, through the examination of historical documents.

LÓPEZ DE AYALA, PEDRO, d. 1407, Spanish historian, poet, and satirist, and chancellor of Castile from 1398 during the reigns of four of the country's kings. He translated Boccaccio's *Decameron* into Portuguese. His most important works are the chronicles of the four kings he served (Peter I, Henry II, John I, Henry III).

LORDS APPELLANT, baronial faction which under the leadership of Thomas, duke of Gloucester, the brother of John of Gaunt, held a dominant position in England from 1386 until 1397 when Richard II gained the upper hand. He executed several leaders of the group and forced others into exile.

LORDS, HOUSE OF. *See* PARLIAMENT.

LORENZETTI, AMBROGIO (d. 1348) and PIETRO (d. 1348), brothers, painters of Siena, both apparently victims of the Black Death. Their paintings combined the harmonious color of Duccio with the realism of Giotto and the naturalism of Giovanni Pisano. Ambrogio's work possesses a realistic individualism and an ability to depict spatial depth. He was among the first painters to express an interest in classical antiquity. Among his works is an altarpiece showing scenes from the legend of St. Nicholas of Bari. Pietro painted frescoes and altarpieces, including the *Madonna and Child with Saints* and the *Nativity of the Virgin.*

LORENZO DI PIETRO, d. 1480, painter, sculptor, and goldsmith of Siena. His masterpiece is the altarpiece entitled *The Assumption of the Virgin.* He was one of the most important painters of the

Sienese school. The most important of his sculptures was *The Risen Christ* which he made for the high altar of the cathedral at Siena.

LORRAINE, DUCHY OF, also known as Lotharingia, the territory which lay between France to the west and the lower (Franconia) and middle Rhine (Swabia) to the east. It was originally the domain of Lothair II, son of Lothair I, whence its name. When Lothair II died, his uncles, Charles the Bald, king of the West Franks, and Louis, king of the East Franks, divided the area between them by the Treaty of Mersen (870). Now French, then German influence was dominant in the region. It became part of the empire of Otto I in 939 and was given the status of a duchy. In 959 it was divided into Upper (southern) and Lower (northern) Lorraine. Lower Lorraine, which included most of the Netherlands, separated in time into a number of countships including Hainaut, Louvain, and Namur and still later into the duchies of Brabant and Limburg. Upper Lorraine retained its name although several portions escaped the rule of its duke including the bishoprics of Metz, Toul, and Verdun. After the death of Frederick II of Germany in 1250, French influence gained the ascendancy. Charles the Bold, duke of Burgundy, had secured possession of the greater part of the duchy when he was slain at Nancy in 1477.

LORRAINE GESTE, five Old French courtly romances of the twelfth century whose themes concerned battles among the knights of Lorraine and Bordeaux.

LORRIS, GUILLAUME. *See* ROMAN DE LA ROSE.

LORSCH, ABBEY OF, Benedictine monastery on the Rhine above Mainz founded in 764 by Count Kankor and his mother Williswinda in Altenmünster. The monastery, which enjoyed the patronage of Charlemagne, was moved to Lorsch in 774. It enjoyed a position of intellectual and cultural leadership from the ninth to the twelfth centuries. In 1232 it became a Cistercian house and in 1244 it adopted the rule of the Premonstratensians.

LOTHAIR, king of France, 954–86, of the Carolingian dynasty, the son of Louis IV, ruled only what remained of Carolingian holdings in the vicinity of Laon. His repeated efforts to secure possession of Lorraine from the king of Germany proved unsuccessful.

LOTHAIR I, Holy Roman emperor, 840–55, son of Louis the Pious. In 841 at the battle of Fontenoy, his brothers Charles and Louis thwarted his attempt to take over the entire empire. The following year they renewed their alliance against Lothair in the so-called Oath of Strassburg. After considerable warfare, the three brothers finally agreed to the settlement known as the Treaty of Verdun (843). This agreement left Lothair the middle section of the empire which extended from Friesland and the mouth of the Rhine to below Rome. He also succeeded to the imperial dignity. In 844 he gave the administration of Italy to his eldest son Louis (II). Shortly before his death, he divided his kingdom between his sons Louis and Lothair and retired to a monastery.

LOTHAIR II, d. 869, son of Lothair I, received the northern part of his father's kingdom, the area between the Scheldt, Meuse, and Rhine, in 855 when his father died. It was called Lotharingia (Lorraine) after him. Only the firm opposition of Pope Nicholas I prevented him from divorcing his wife Theutberga and marrying again. When he died his uncles Charles the Bald and Louis the German divided his domain between themselves (Treaty of Mersen, 870).

LOTHAIR III, king of Germany, 1125–37, duke of Saxony (1106), was elected king following the death of Henry V who left no son. The marriage of Lothair's daughter Gertrude to Henry the Proud, the Welf duke of Bavaria, raised the Welf family to a powerful position in German affairs. The long struggle between the dukes of Saxony and the Hohenstaufens of Swabia who contested Lothair's rule dated from this time. In 1133 Pope Innocent II crowned him Roman emperor and invested him with the vast estate of the deceased Matilda of Tuscany.

LOTHAR, an older form of Chlotar. *See* LOTHAIR.

LOTHARINGIA. *See* LORRAINE.

LOUIS VI (the Fat), king of France, 1108–37, son of Philip I, subdued the barons of the Ile de France and extended his favor to towns, especially to those on the lands of his vassals. He founded Lorris, one of the first *villes neuves,* in his own territory. He was almost continuously at war with Henry I of England. His most trusted adviser was Suger, the abbot of St. Denis. He strongly favored the church, supported its enterprises, and selected churchmen as his ministers. At the close of his reign he arranged the marriage of his son Louis (VII) to Eleanor, heiress of Aquitaine. Louis may be credited with laying the foundation of the French monarchy.

LOUIS VII, king of France, 1137–80, son of Louis VI, one of the leaders of the ill-fated Second Crusade (1147–9). He had his marriage to Eleanor of Aquitaine annulled upon his return from Jerusalem, probably because she failed to bear him a son. Her marriage to Henry, count of Anjou and duke of Normandy, who was shortly to become king of England, deprived France of the possession of Aquitaine until the close of the Hundred Years' War. Louis continued the policy of his father of favoring towns and he also encouraged the sons of Henry II of England in their revolt 1173–4 against their father.

LOUIS VIII, king of France, 1223–6, son of Philip II Augustus, as crown prince defeated John of England at the battle of La Roche-aux-Moines (1214) and landed an army in England in 1216 to assist the barons in their revolt against John. He conquered Poitou and after his defeat of the Albigenses received the submission of Languedoc.

LOUIS IX, ST., king of France, 1226–70, son of

Louis VIII and Blanche of Castile, undertook two Crusades, 1248–54 and 1270, and died in Tunis on the second. During his minority, which extended to 1234, his mother put down a revolt with the help of the towns and forced the count of Toulouse to accept a marriage arrangement for his daughter which ultimately brought Toulouse into the royal domain. As king, Louis persuaded Henry III of England to abandon claims to Normandy and other lands north of the Loire and to do homage for Aquitaine. Except for his love of peace and justice, he might have forced the English completely off the continent. In the interest of peace, too, he agreed to a stabilization of France's frontier with Aragon, and, despite his profound love of the faith, refused to support the pope in his struggle with Frederick II of Germany. Beyond the continued expansion of the royal government, which was witnessing the emergence of the *Chambre des Comptes* and the *Parlement de Paris* during this period, Louis himself added a new official, the *enquêteur,* whose responsibility it was to seek out any evidence of abuse of royal authority on the part of the crown's officials. Louis's just rule and his manifest concern for the well-being of his people won him the affection of the French people.

LOUIS X, king of France, 1314–6, eldest son of Philip IV, earlier king of Navarre (1305–14), who surrendered that throne to his brother Philip (V) when he became king of France. Louis proved a weak administrator, quite a different person from his father.

LOUIS XI, king of France, 1461–83, son of Charles VII, who as Dauphin had shown himself a disloyal son, found himself in 1465 facing a revolt of his great feudatories who had organized the League of Public Weal. Rather than risk battle, the wily Louis bent to their demands, then during the years following gradually deprived them of what concessions he had extended them and many more of their traditional privileges as well. The most formidable obstacle

to his hope of establishing effective royal control over all of France was Charles the Bold, duke of Burgundy, who aimed to make his duchy independent. Louis prevented this by buying off Edward IV of England with the Treaty of Picquigny (1475), then paying the Swiss to destroy the Burgundian army. After Charles's death (1477), Louis retained the duchy of Burgundy, Picardy, Boulonnais, and Artois. By the time Louis died he had completed the extension of direct royal rule to the whole of France except for Brittany. His authority approached that of an absolute monarch.

LOUIS XII, king of France, 1498–1515, whose marriage to Anne of Brittany, widow of Charles VIII, achieved royal control of Brittany. His first marriage to the misshapen though pious Joan of France (Jeanne de France), daughter of Louis XI, was annulled.

LOUIS THE PIOUS, Holy Roman emperor, 814–40, son and successor of Charlemagne, a just monarch though lacking in firmness and administrative talents. For this reason, the practice of his father in sending out *missi dominici* to check on the powerful counts and margraves, fell into disuse. He showed great deference to the pope, supported Benedict of Aniane in his efforts to reform monasticism and the church, and sent missionaries to work among the Slavs and Scandinavians. His major mistake in assigning portions of the Carolingian empire to his sons, Lothair, Pepin, Louis, and Charles, and then failing to control them, brought on civil war, one time leading to his own temporary deposition, and heralded its early disintegration.

LOUIS II, Holy Roman emperor, 850–75, eldest son of Lothair I, in charge of Italy from 844. In 850 Pope Leo IV crowned him emperor. He had a good measure of success in halting the Saracen invasion of the peninsula, and with the cooperation of the Byzantine fleet destroyed Arab headquarters at Bari.

LOUIS III (the Blind), d. 928, the son of Boso,

king of Provence (Lower Burgundy). He became king of Lombardy in 900, was crowned Holy Roman emperor in 901, but in 905 was captured and blinded by Berengar who claimed Lombardy. From 890 Louis ruled Provence.

LOUIS IV (the Bavarian), king of Germany, 1314–47, Holy Roman emperor (1328), and duke of Bavaria (from 1294), member of the house of Wittelsbach, who succeeded to the throne following the death of Henry VII although his rival, Frederick (III) of Austria, held out until 1322. The refusal of Pope John XXII to confirm his election precipitated a sharp conflict with the Avignonese papacy, for which reason Louis provided a haven for such critics of the pope as Marsilius of Padua and William of Ockham. In 1328 he occupied Rome and had himself crowned emperor by Sciarra Colonna. Ten years later he issued the decree *Licet Juris* which repudiated any voice the pope might claim in the selection of any future king of Germany.

LOUIS THE GERMAN, king of the East Franks, 843–76, son of Louis I (the Pious). He ruled the lands east of the Rhine and Aare after the division of the Carolingian empire in 843 by the Treaty of Verdun. In 870 he secured eastern Lorraine by the Treaty of Mersen with his brother, Charles the Bald, king of the West Franks.

LOUIS IV, THE CHILD, king of the East Franks, 900–11, last of the Carolingians to rule in Germany. His reign witnessed increasing pressure from the Vikings, Magyars, and Slavs and the emergence of a number of German stem duchies including Franconia, Bavaria, Swabia, and Saxony.

LOUIS I (the Great), king of Hungary, 1342–82, and of Poland, 1370–82, son of Charles I. He took Ragusa (Dalmatia) from Venice and confirmed Hungarian rule over Bosnia, Wallachia, and Moldavia. He favored the church and the towns, maintained an efficient government, and showed himself a patron of art and learning. He was also successful in his campaigns against the Turks. Louis may be credited with bringing Hungarian power to its height.

LOUIS, duke of Orléans, d. 1407, brother of Charles VI of France, who sought to assume the direction of the government when the king became mentally ill in 1392. He was opposed first by Philip the Bold, duke of Burgundy, uncle of Charles VI, then by Philip's son, John the Fearless, who murdered him. Louis gave his name to the Orléanist faction which became the Armagnac after his death.

LOUIS D'ALEMAN (Allemand), BL., d. 1450, member of the papal Curia, cardinal archbishop of Arles, a leading prelate at the Council of Basel. His nomination of Amadeus VII of Savoy as pope brought papal excommunication, but he later submitted and was pardoned.

LOUVAIN (Leuven), city of Brabant first noted in the ninth century. It grew in importance in the eleventh century when the counts of Louvain made it their residence. These counts acquired the ducal title of Lower Lorraine in 1106 and from 1180 were known as dukes of Brabant. By the middle of the fourteenth century Louvain boasted a population of about 50,000 and a position of leadership in the cloth trade of the region. During the fifteenth century Louvain surrendered that leadership to Brussels. The University of Louvain was founded in 1425 by Pope Martin V upon the urging of John IV, the duke of Brabant.

LOUVRE, palace built in 1204 by Philip II Augustus (1180–1223) which Charles V (1364–80) converted to a royal treasury. The building also housed a library.

LOW MASS, simplified form of the Mass which appeared in the twelfth century when it became usual for all priests to say a daily Mass and when the more elaborate service with a number of assistants (deacon, subdeacon, etc.) and with chant was no longer practicable. Low Mass, except in cathedral and collegiate churches, became the usual form of celebration during the week, with a High Mass reserved for Sunday.

LOW SUNDAY, the first Sunday after Easter, probably deriving its name in contrast to the great solemnities of the preceding Easter Sunday.

LÜBECK, city located at the southern end of the Danish peninsula on the Baltic. It made its appearance as a Wendish fortress which was destroyed in 1138. Count Adolf II of Holstein rebuilt the community in 1143. Henry the Lion, duke of Saxony, did the same in 1158–59 after it had burned to the ground in 1157. The charter it received from Henry the Lion in 1158, which granted extensive communal rights, was copied by more than 100 other German cities. In 1226 it became an imperial city and a prime organizer of the Hanseatic League. Its excellent harbor proved a boon to trade, and from the fourteenth century it ranked with the largest and most influential cities of central Europe. Lübeck in 1160 became a diocese within the province of Hamburg-Bremen.

LUBLIN, city in Galicia (Poland), founded in the tenth century. It received a charter in 1317 and shortly after developed into the most important city between the Vistula and the Dnieper.

LUCCA, city from Roman times, located just north of Pisa on the principal road from Lombardy to Rome. The Lombards seized the city in 568 and a Lombard duke made it his residence. During the ninth and tenth centuries its dukes became margraves of Tuscany, a title held by Matilda, countess of Tuscany (d. 1115), who also made the city her home. In 1081 Henry IV of Germany granted the city a charter. Lucca had a long history of difficulties with the neighboring cities of Pisa and Florence and was seldom able to hold itself aloof from their interminable quarreling. Lucca's difficulties with Pisa stemmed from its desire to have a free outlet to the sea which Pisa denied her. This she never acquired,

although she was fortunate in not being absorbed by Florence after Florence had acquired Pisa (1406). Despite all its conflicts, Lucca prospered. Its bankers and merchants were noted all over Europe, as were its velvets and damasks.

LUCERNE, city located on Lake Lucerne in Switzerland which grew up around a Benedictine monastery established there by St. Leodegar in the eighth century. The opening of the St. Gotthard Pass c. 1230 brought it increased population and opened the way to its rapid commercial development. In 1291 it became a possession of the Hapsburgs but in 1332 it joined the Perpetual Compact as one of the Four Forest Cantons and secured its complete freedom with the defeat of the Hapsburgs at Sempach in 1386.

LUCIAN OF ANTIOCH, ST., a theologian of Antioch whose students included Arius, for which reason he has been called the father of Arianism. He helped establish Antioch as the principal center of exegetical study which favored the literal-historical interpretation of the Scripture. He suffered martyrdom at Nicomedia in 312.

LUCIAN OF SAMOSATA, d. c. 200, pagan satirist who made several references to Christianity in his writings. In his *De Morte Peregrini,* he writes of Peregrinus, a historical person, who converted to Christianity but later apostatized. In his account of Peregrinus's life, Lucian speaks of Christians as being kindly people but credulous.

LUCIFER, Latin for "light-bearer," name of the leader of the fallen angels (Luke 10:18).

LUCIFER OF CAGLIARI (Calaris), d. c. 370, bishop of Cagliari in Sardinia, a militant opponent of Arianism, whose encouragement of the exiled Athanasius led to his own exile by Emperor Constantius II. When the emperor Julian (361–3) ordered all exiled bishops to be free to return, he reoccupied his see, but then fell out with the pope when he consecrated a priest to be bishop of Antioch. He may have suffered excommunication. His followers, known as Luciferians, endorsed his rigorist views concerning Christian morality.

LUCIUS I, ST., Pope, June 253 to March 254, the successor of Pope Cornelius, banished from Rome by Emperor Gallus but permitted to return under Valerian. He continued the sympathetic policy Cornelius had adopted toward *lapsi*.

LUCIUS II, Pope, March 1144 to February 1145, successor of Celestine II, who served as a papal legate to Germany and as papal chancellor. He made peace with Roger II of Sicily and accepted Portugal as a papal fief. He died in the course of a revolt in Rome organized by adherents of the antipope Anacletus.

LUCIUS III, Pope, 1181–5, the trusted counselor of Pope Alexander III whom he succeeded. He was a Cistercian monk and in 1141 was created a cardinal. As pope he inherited his predecessor's difficulties with Frederick I Barbarossa although in the end he was successful in persuading the emperor to join the Crusade (Third) against the Turks.

LUCIUS, the legendary first Christian king of Britain. His existence was based apparently on a statement in the *Liber Pontificalis* about a British king by that name requesting Pope Eleutherius to send missionaries to Britain to convert him and his people. According to the story, Lucius and many of his subjects were baptized. Lucius died in 156. The legendary story grew with time and ended with Lucius being a son of Simon of Cyrene and being baptized by St. Timothy.

LUCY, RICHARD DE, d. 1179, chief justiciar of England under Henry II and one of his most trusted advisers. He deserves some credit for the progressive legislation enacted during this period and is considered the principal author of the Constitutions of Clarendon (1164). In 1179 he retired to Lesnes Abbey in Kent to do penance for his indirect part in the murder of Thomas Becket.

LUCY, ST., d. 303, a martyr of Syracuse during the persecution of Diocletian. Pope Gregory I (the Great) (590–604) added her name to the list of saints commemorated in the canon of the mass. She was quite popular in the early church.

LUDOLF OF SAXONY, d. 1378, obscure Carthusian of Strasbourg, in 1342 prior of the charterhouse at Coblenz who later resumed his status as an ordinary monk. His principal works are a commentary on the Psalms and a popular *Vita Christi*. This is not a biography of Christ, rather a meditation on Christ's life, accompanied by doctrinal, spiritual, and moral instructions as well as prayers.

LUDWIG from CHLODWIG. *See* LOUIS.

LUDWIGSLIED, Old German epic poem believed to be the earliest historical poem to appear in the German language. Its author was a priest of the ninth century, its theme the victory Louis III of France gained over the Normans at Saucourt in 881.

LUKE, EVANGELIST, ST., the author of one of the four Gospels and the *Acts of the Apostles*. In Christian iconography he was usually portrayed as an ox to symbolize the sacrificial role of Christ which his gospel appears to emphasize.

LULL (Llull, Lullus), RAYMOND (Ramón, Raimundus), BL., d. 1316, a mystic of Catalonia whose writings influenced both Franciscan and Sufi mysticism. He was trained as a knight, served as seneschal to the son of James I of Aragon, married, and probably became a member of the Third Order of St. Francis. On the advice of St. Raymond of Pénafort, he spent 9 years in Majorca in the study of Arabic and Christian thought. He was a student of Arabic language and culture and urged the study of Arabic and other languages in order to facilitate the conversion of non-Christians. His numerous writings included treatises on science, logic, education, and mystical theology. In his philosophical writings whose purpose was the defense of Christianity against Moslem thinkers, especially Averroës, he adhered to the Augustinian tradition. One of his most popular works was published by William Caxton in English translation under the title *The Booke of the Ordre of Chyualry.* His prose and his lyric poetry established the norms of literary Catalan.

LULLUS, ST., d. 786, bishop of Mainz, an Anglo-Saxon who was closely associated with St. Boniface whom he succeeded as bishop of Mainz. As bishop he became involved in a bitter and unsuccessful dispute with the monastery of Fulda which he wanted back under the jurisdiction of Mainz. (The monastery had earlier gained exemption.) Lullus founded a monastery at Hersfeld where he was buried. His large correspondence bears witness to his reputation for learning and to his wide acquaintance with important people.

LUMEN CHRISTI, versicle chanted by the deacon during the Easter vigil service while he lighted the Easter candle and bore it to the sanctuary. It was addressed to Christ as the "Light" of the world.

LUNA, PEDRO D. *See* BENEDICT XIII, POPE.

LUND, city located in south Sweden, founded c. 1020 by the Danish king Canute. It became a bishop's seat in 1060 and a metropolitanate in 1103. The city flourished as an ecclesiastical and commercial center.

LÜNEBURG, city in Lower Saxony west of the Elbe which grew up near a castle erected there c. 951 and the Benedictine monastery of St. Michael's founded some time before 956. It joined the Hanseatic League in the fourteenth century and served as the capital of the duchy of Lüneburg.

LUPOLD OF BEBENBURG, d. 1363, canonist, bishop of Bamberg, adviser to Emperor Charles IV (1346–78), and author of several treatises in which he attempted to define the relationship between the *sacerdotium,* the power of the church, and the *imperium,* the authority of the state.

LUPUS (Servatus) OF FERRIÈRES, d. c. 862, humanist and theologian, a pupil of Rabanus Maurus and abbot of Ferrières (840). He made the monastery a leading cultural center, carried on a wide correspondence with important people and scholars, and took an active part in the ecclesiastical synods and councils of the period. He was an avid collector of manuscripts and left a number which he himself copied and annotated. His principal theological work grew out of the dispute Gottschalk had opened over predestination.

LUSATIA, MARCH OF, region between the middle Elbe and Oder that took its name from the Lusatians, Slavic Wends or Sorbs, who had moved into the area in the ninth century. It came under German control in 1033. Upper Lusatia which was occupied by Slavic Milziensians, belonged from the eleventh century to the margravate of Meissen and in 1158 was given to Bohemia by Frederick I Barbarossa. Lower Lusatia which was occupied by the Slavic Lusatians belonged to Meissen after 1136 and to Bohemia after 1373.

LUSIGNAN, French aristocratic family which provided counts for La Marche, rulers for the kingdom of Jerusalem from 1186, and kings for Cyprus from 1192. Guy de Lusignan succeeded Baldwin V as king of Jerusalem in 1186 but was driven out by Saladin in 1187. He later bought Cyprus from Richard I of England and ruled it as king from 1193–4. His brother Amalric II reigned as king of both Jerusalem and Cyprus. In 1342 a member of a branch of the family became king of Armenia. In 1375 the titles of both king of Jerusalem and Armenia had become equally empty, and even the control of the Lusignan rulers over Cyprus was threatened by Egypt and Venice.

LUTE, a stringed instrument shaped like a pear which emerged about the tenth century in Europe. The modern lute, which appeared during the fifteenth century, evolved from this earlier instrument under influence of the Arab lute.

LUTTRELL PSALTER, famous illuminated psalter made c. 1340 by Sir Geoffrey Luttrell of Irnham, Lincolnshire.

LUXEMBURG, city west of the upper Moselle which grew up around the castle of Lucilinburhuc erected there after 963. It acquired city rights in 1244.

LUXEMBURG, DUCHY OF, principality located to the north of Lorraine which traced its name to the castle of Lucilinburhuc erected in that area some time after 963. Luxemburg became a county under Conrad (d. 1086) and in 1354 was made a duchy by Emperor Charles IV. Although the duchy gave four kings to Germany—Henry VII, Charles IV, Wenzel, and Sigismund—French influence continued to grow and during the fourteenth century gained the ascendancy. In 1441 Philip, duke of Burgundy, purchased the duchy, although it returned to the Hapsburgs and Germany with the marriage of Mary, its heiress, to Maximilian in 1477.

LUXEUIL, ABBEY OF, monastery located in east-central France and founded c. 590 by the Celtic missionary St. Columban. Early in the seventh century it adopted the Rule of St. Benedict. The monastery, which developed into an important spiritual and cultural center, suffered from Arab attack in 732, then was sacked by the Normans in 888 after Charlemagne had restored it.

LYDGATE, JOHN, d. 1449?, monk of the Benedictine monastery of Bury St. Edmunds, one of the most influential and greatly esteemed poets of his time even though his productivity was appreciably greater than his talents. He composed verse on a variety of themes: devotional, moral, scientific, historical, philosophical, and especially romantic. Among the best known of his works are *The Fall of Princes, The Siege of Thebes,* and *The Temple of Glass.* For a long time his reputation equaled that of Chaucer, and for a century he exercised great influence on budding poets.

LYNDWOOD, WILLIAM, d. 1446, canonist, keeper of the privy seal, and bishop of St. David's. He is known for the *Provinciale,* a digest of the constitutions issued by archbishops of Canterbury from Stephen Langton (1207–28) to Henry Chichele (1414–43). It remains a standard authority on English ecclesiastical law.

LYONS, city on the middle Rhône which became a bishop's seat in the second century. It was the place where Christianity was first introduced into Gaul. The Burgundians made it their capital in 470, while in the division of the Carolingian empire in 843 (Treaty of Verdun), it went to Lothair I. In 1032 Conrad II incorporated the city into the kingdom of Germany, but in 1312 Philip IV gained it for France. Its importance as a silk center dates from the fifteenth century. It hosted two ecumenical councils.

LYONS I, COUNCIL OF, general church council (Thirteenth Ecumenical), summoned by Pope Innocent IV in 1245 for the purpose of condemning Frederick II of Germany who was at war with the papacy and the cities of Lombardy. The council declared Frederick excommunicate and deposed him. The condemnation of the emperor proved of no consequence.

LYONS II, COUNCIL OF, general church council (Fourteenth Ecumenical), convoked by Pope Gregory X in 1274 (it ended in 1289). It adopted a number of reforms including one regulating the election of the pope, took steps toward organizing a Crusade against the Turks, and confirmed the union of the Latin and Greek churches. A Greek delegation which attended the council ratified this union, accepting the *Filioque,* the *Double Procession of the Holy Ghost,* and the primacy of the bishop of Rome, al-though it was rejected in Constantinople. St. Bonaventure died at the council; St. Thomas Aquinas died on his way there.

LYRA, a pear-shaped fiddle with but one string.

MABINOGION (Mabinogi), name given to a collection of eleven Welsh stories that were probably compiled from the eleventh to the thirteenth centuries. The themes of the stories drew on mythology, folklore, heroic traditions, and anonymous tales for their inspiration and matter.

MACARIUS, ST., d. c. 334, bishop of Jerusalem, attended the Council of Nicaea (325) where he proved himself a strong proponent of the orthodox position taken by the council against Arianism. The emperor Constantine commissioned Macarius to build the Church of the Holy Sepulchre in Jerusalem.

MACARIUS THE EGYPTIAN (the Elder, the Great), d. c. 389, hermit and spiritual director of fellow anchorites in Scete, one of the main centers of Egyptian monasticism. He was obliged to spend some years in exile because of his opposition to Arianism. Some fifty homilies together with other works have been traditionally ascribed to him.

MACBETH, king of Scotland, 1040–57, who slew his predecessor Duncan I in a battle near Elgin but was himself slain by Duncan's son Malcolm at the battle of Lumphanan. In 1050 Macbeth made a pilgrimage to Rome. He was buried at Iona which was regarded as a burial place for kings, not for usurpers.

MACCABEES, BOOKS OF, four books, found in some manuscripts of the Septuagint, the first two of which are included in the Canon of Scriptures as recognized by the Greek and Latin Churches. The first book, which covers the history of the Jews from 175 to 135 B.C. describes the efforts Antiochus IV Epiphanes of Syria made to suppress the Jewish religion and the resistance of Matthias and his sons. The second book records the history of the Maccabaean wars from 176 to 161 B.C. and the victories won by Judas Maccabaeus. It lacks the historical value of the first book. Contained in these books are important teaching on immortality and prayers for the dead.

MACE, heavy weapon similar to a sword but without cutting edge or point, and capable of breaking through armor. It came into use by at least the eleventh century. The use of the ceremonial mace as a symbol of royal authority dates from the late twelfth century.

MACEDONIA, a province first of the Roman, then of the Byzantine empire when the Roman empire was divided. Goths, Huns, and Avars overran the region as Roman power declined, but they left no permanent trace. The Slavs who began appearing in the sixth century gradually and permanently transformed the Hellenic culture into Slavonic. In the ninth century Bulgars conquered most of the province, but Basil II recovered it for Byzantium in 1018. After the fall of Constantinople to the Crusaders in 1204, its possession was contested by Bulgars, the emperors of Nicaea, the despots of Epirus, and the Latin emperor in Constantinople. The latter succeeded in regaining control in 1261, but it fell to the Serbs in the fourteenth century, who then lost it to the Turks with their defeat at the battle of Kossovo in 1389.

MACEDONIUS, d. c. 362, bishop of Constantinople from c. 342, who defended the Semi-Arian cause at the Council of Seleucia (359). In 360 he was deposed by the Arian Council of Constantinople. He has been regarded as the founder of the Pneumatomachians, a Christian division that denied the uncreated nature of the Holy Spirit. In 381 Pope Damasus anathematized Macedonius as a heretic.

MACHAUT, GUILLAUME DE, d. 1377, canon of Reims cathedral who enjoyed the esteem of his contemporaries and the patronage of kings and princes for his talents as poet and musician. He composed both secular and liturgical pieces, including masses, motets, *ballades, chants royaux, lais, rondeaux,* and *virelais.* He ranks as the leading French musician of the fourteenth century. He was the last great French poet to consider the lyric and its musical setting as a single entity.

MACMURCHADA, DIARMID (Dermot MacMurrough), d. 1171, king of Leinster, driven from Ireland because of his cruelty and aggressiveness, later recovered control of much of the eastern part of the island with the aid of English lords. These lords included Richard de Clare (Strongbow) to whom he gave his daughter Eva in marriage.

MACRINA, ST., d. c. 379, sister of Basil the Great and Gregory of Nyssa, also known as Macrina the Younger to distinguish her from Macrina the Elder, her paternal grandmother. She established a vigorous religious community on the family estate in Pontus.

MACROBIUS, AMBROSIUS THEODOSIUS, fl. 400, Latin grammarian, probably a pagan, who discussed grammatical, philosophical, and literary subjects in his *Saturnalia.* This work, which is in seven books, contains numerous quotations from earlier writers. Much of the work is devoted to a discussion of Virgil for whom the author had the highest respect. Macrobius's commentary on

Cicero's *Dream of Scipio* which was well-known in the Middle Ages, influenced Chaucer.

MADEIRA ISLANDS, group of islands off the coast of Morocco which Genoese adventurers may have explored before the middle of the fourteenth century. The Portuguese did explore the islands in 1419 and undertook their settlement upon the encouragement of Prince Henry the Navigator.

MADRID, a town that first made an appearance in the eighth century as a fortified settlement under the Arabic name Majrit. It served to bolster the defenses of Toledo. In 939 Ramiro II of Leon drove the Moors out of Madrid, as did Alfonso VI of Castile for a second time in 1083. Ferdinand and Isabella occupied the city in 1477 although it became the capital of Spain only in 1561.

MADRIGAL, form of poetry and also of music that flourished in northern Italy in the fourteenth century. It consisted of from one to four three-line stanzas of three iambic pentameters each, followed by a *ritornello* of two rhymed lines. Its introduction has been credited to Petrarch and his followers. The contemplation of nature was its usual theme and it was ordinarily provided a polyphonic musical setting. The greatest of the medieval composers of madrigals was the blind organist Francesco Landini (d. 1397).

MAERLANT, JACOB VAN, d. c. 1300, Flemish poet and earliest figure in the history of Dutch literature. His lyric poems and chivalric epic romances reflect French influences. He also composed long didactic poems which he intended for the rising class of commoners who wanted instructive reading in their own language. For his materials he drew principally upon Latin works. His best known didactic poem was modeled after the encyclopedic *Speculum Maius* of Vincent of Beauvais.

MAFTIR, name given to the last person to give a

453

reading of the Torah in a Jewish service; the selection read.

MAGDALEN COLLEGE, college at Oxford founded in 1458 by William Waynflete, bishop of Winchester and lord chancellor of England.

MAGDALENS, also known as Penitents (in reference to Mary Magdalene) or White Ladies, a religious order, initially Cistercian, then Dominican, founded by Rudolf of Worms c. 1227 at Metz for penitent women. Women of blameless life might also join these communities.

MAGDEBURG, city located on the middle Elbe. It first came to notice in 805. In 968 Otto I made it the see of an archdiocese which he established in order to advance his ambition of extending German rule to the east and converting the Slavic peoples of the area. The city became an important member of the Hanseatic League although it never entirely sloughed off the authority of its archbishops until the Protestant Reformation. The autonomous municipal administration which it established in the thirteenth century, known as the "Magdeburg Law," was widely adopted in Germany and eastern Europe.

MAGI, the wise men who visited the child Jesus in Bethlehem (Matthew 2:1–12). [See THREE KINGS.] They are traditionally credited with being the first Gentiles to believe in Christ. The first reference to their being kings appears in Tertullian (d. c. 230). Origen (d. c. 254) was the first to give their number as three. The names Caspar, Melchior, and Balthasar are first mentioned in the sixth century.

MAGISTER EQUITUM, master of the horse, the general placed in command of the imperial cavalry from the reign of Constantine I (the Great) (306–37).

MAGISTER MILITUM, master of the soldiers, an office created by Constantine I (the Great) (306–37). In the fourth and fifth centuries there were two masters of the soldiers in the western part of the empire, the one master of the horse, the other of the foot.

MAGISTER OFFICIORUM, master of offices, the head of the imperial chancery from the time of Constantine I (the Great) (306–37).

MAGNA CARTA, the Great Charter of rights and liberties upon which King John of England affixed his seal at Runnymede on June 15, 1215. The heavy financial demands he had been making on his barons, his acts of cruelty and oppression which all classes had suffered, and his apparent defiance of law and tradition created so universal a resentment to his misrule that a rebellious aristocracy left him no alternative except abdication.

In accepting the charter John formally acknowledged that as king, he, too, was subject to the law of the land. Of the some sixty promises he made, two stand out preeminent in their importance: first, that he would not interfere with the established laws and procedures pertaining to the administration of justice; second, that in the direction of the government he would limit himself to the use of those revenues that (feudal) custom permitted him, and appeal to his barons for what additional funds he might require. From the first guarantee emerged in time the principle of due process of law; from the second, Parliament's control of taxation. Provision number 61 set up a committee of 25 barons and entrusted them with the responsibility of deposing the king, by force if necessary, should he fail to honor any of his promises. The influence of the Great Charter on the constitutional development of medieval England has usually been exaggerated. Although it was reaffirmed on several occasions during the Middle Ages, its real impact came only in the seventeenth century in the course of the struggle between crown and parliament.

The idea of a charter was itself not new. Its most important English predecessor was the Charter of Liberties that Henry I had granted voluntarily to clergy and baronage upon his accession to the throne in 1100. In 1215, this document served as the prototype for the Great Charter which the barons demanded of John as a right. Stephen Langton, archbishop of Canterbury, is credited with assuming the lead in drawing up the provisions of the Great Charter and in persuading the barons to support it.

MAGNENTIUS, FLAVIUS MAGNUS, d. 353, a pretender who rose against Emperor Constans in Gaul in 350 but committed suicide following his defeat by Constantius II, the brother of Constans, in 353.

MAGNIFICAT, opening words of Mary's song of praise and thanksgiving over the sublime role God had destined for her when her cousin Elizabeth greeted her as the mother of the Lord (Luke 1:46–55). The prayer early became the most important canticle of the vesper service in the Latin church.

MAGNUS I (Olafsson the Good), king of Norway, 1035–47, the illegitimate son of Olaf the Saint who succeeded to the throne upon the death of Canute. In 1042, when Canute's son Hardicanute died, he also became king of Denmark. He annihilated the Wends (Slavs) who invaded Denmark and in 1046 agreed to share his kingdom with his uncle Harald Hardraade who had returned from Constantinople.

MAGNUS V (Lagaboeter), king of Norway, 1263–80, who created a common provincial law. However, it was the special law he drew up for Bergen that served as a model for other cities of his country. He made peace with the Scots by ceding them the Hebrides and the Isle of Man.

MAGNUS OF FÜSSEN, ST., d. 772, popularly known as St. Mang, missionary in Algau and a popular saint among the peasantry of south Germany and Switzerland.

MAGYARS. *See* HUNGARY.

MAHDI, AL-, the Deliverer, literally "the [divinely] guided one," whom the Shiites expected to appear just before the end of time to introduce peace and justice and to restore the true religion. Sunnite theologians did not share this belief since there is no mention of such a person in either the Koran or the *hadith*. The Shiites maintained that the Deliverer would be a descendant of Ali and Fatima and some of them acclaimed Mohammed ibn al-Hasan al-Askari (d. c. 874) as the Mahdi.

MAHDI, AL-, Abbasid caliph, 775–85, introduced administrative reforms in the government, improved the mail service, and took severe measures to suppress Zindiqism. He was the father of Harun al-Rashid.

MAHMUD OF GHAZNI, d. 1030, Turkish creator of a Ghaznavid empire and legendary hero of Islam in India. He deprived his brother of Afghanistan and Khurastan and later conquered the Punjab region of northwestern India. He adopted a strongly repressive campaign against people he judged to be heterodox or infidels and in north India destroyed Hindu temples including the temple to Siva at Somnath in Gujarat. Withal he proved himself a patron of poets and scholars and contributed to the flowering of Perso-Islamic literature that marked his reign. Many legends and anecdotes told of him as a martial hero and as a valiant defender of the faith.

MAID OF NORWAY. *See* MARGARET, queen of Scotland.

MAIDSTONE, town in Kent, England, a favorite residence of the archbishop of Canterbury. His palace, together with the Church of All Saints (late fourteenth century) and a hospital built c. 1260 for pilgrims visiting Canterbury, still grace the community.

MAIMONIDES (Moses Ben Maimon), d. 1204, Jewish scholar and philosopher, known to Jewish writers as "Rambam" (the initials of the words Rabbi Moses ben Maimon), born of an illustrious family in Córdoba. He fled following the fall of the city to the Almohads and eventually settled in Cairo. There he served as physician at the court of Saladin. He prepared a systematic study of rabbinical tradition (Mishna Torah) in an effort to organize the mass of Jewish oral law and make this more accessible and intelligible to rabbis and judges as well as to laymen. His best known work is his *Guide of the Perplexed* which he wrote in Arabic. In this work he discoursed on the existence and nature of God and wrestled with the nature of evil and other metaphysical and religious problems. He also composed a work on logic, a treatise on the calendar, and several medical writings including one on hygiene. His philosophical writings, in which he sought to harmonize faith and reason, exerted great influence upon Western thought.

MAINARDI, SEBASTIANO, d. 1513, Italian painter, pupil and collaborator of his brother-in-law Ghirlandio. He was noted principally for his frescoes and altarpieces.

MAINE, COUNTY OF, province between Normandy and Anjou that acquired a count of its own in the ninth century. It was a fief of Normandy from 1063 and of Anjou in 1110, and was joined to England through its count until 1205 when Philip II Augustus took it from John. Louis IX (1226–70) granted it as an appanage to his brother Charles of Anjou. It did not revert to the crown until 1481.

MAINMORTE. *See* HERIOT.

MAINO (Majano), BENEDETTO DA, d. 1497, sculptor and architect of Florence whose relief style and its use of narrative themes resembles that of Ghiberti and Donatello. Although he was noted for the naturalism of his work in ivory, he achieved greatest originality in the decorative architectural settings in which he placed his figures and reliefs.

MAINZ (Mayence), city on the middle Rhine, once a major roman military post, a bishop's see c. 200, but then ravaged successively from the fourth century by Alemanni, Vandals, and Slavs, and only returned to relative peace under the Franks (c. 500). As a result of the work of St. Boniface (d. 754) it became an archiepiscopal see c. 780. From the late ninth century the dignity of archchancellor of the German empire came to be associated with the city, and in the following century its archbishop secured the right to crown the German king. In 1244 Mainz received the status of a free city. The city is always linked with the name of John Gutenberg and the development of printing.

MAJORCA, largest of the Balearic Islands, taken from the Moors in 1230–5 by James I of Aragon who combined it with other islands, Roussillon, Cerdagne, and several fiefs in France to form an independent state. In 1343 Peter IV of Aragon took the kingdom from James II and reunited it with Aragon.

MAJORIAN (Maiorianus, Flavius Julianus), Roman emperor who owed his throne (457) to the German chieftain Ricimer whom he had helped overthrow his imperial predecessor Avitus. As emperor he repulsed a Vandal invasion of Campania in 457, but three years later, in alliance with the Visigothic king of southwestern Gaul, he suffered the loss of the larger part of his fleet to the Vandals in Spain and was forced to accept a humiliating peace. On his return to Italy he fell into the hands of Ricimer who had turned against him, and was executed. Majorian's efforts to restore Roman authority in the west, together with legislation which he enacted to improve imperial administration, mark him as the most capable of the Western emperors of the fifth century.

MAJOR ORDERS, the three highest ranking orders of the clergy. They included the subdeaconship, deaconship, and the priesthood.

MAJUSCULE SCRIPT, style of writing, similar to the use of modern capital letters, that was common for books in Greek and Latin from the fourth to the eighth century.

MAKRISI, d. 1442, Arab historian of Egypt who wrote a history of the Mamluk sultans and prepared a topographical history of Egypt.

MALABAR CHRISTIANS, a community of Christians in southwest India, also known as "Thomas Christians," who claimed their church was founded by the apostle Thomas. They may have come from eastern Syria, while the earliest reference to them, in the sixth century, regards them as Nestorians. They have had a continuous history up to today.

MALACHY (Malachias), ST., d. 1148, bishop of Connor and Down, abbot of Iveragh and archbishop of Armagh (1132). He served as papal legate for Ireland and was responsible for introducing the Roman liturgy to the island. In 1139 he visited Clairvaux where he became a close friend of St. Bernard who left a biography of him. The monastery of Mellifont which he founded in 1142 was the first Cisterian house to be established in Ireland.

MALALAS, JOHN, d. c. 578, Byzantine chronicler, author of the *Chronographia* which in 18 books covered the years from the Creation to perhaps 574 although it survives only to 563. His writing, which gives considerable attention to Antioch, reveals his Monophysite sympathies. Although his work is inaccurate and suffers from a lack of objectivity, it is of some value for the history of the first half of the sixth century. Some scholars identify John Malalas with "John Rhetor" or "Scholasticus," patriarch of Constantinople (565–77), who had earlier been a lawyer in Antioch.

MALANKAR RITE, liturgy used in Kerala, India, according to pious tradition since the time of the apostle Thomas. It was modified by Christian immigrants who moved in from Mesopotamia from the fourth to the ninth centuries. [*See* MALABAR CHRISTIANS.]

MALATESTA, prominent family of the Romagna that ruled Rimini for almost three centuries. In 1239 Malatesta da Verucchio, a Guelph leader, became *podestà* of the city. His hunchback grandson Giovanni, husband of Francesca da Rimini, killed her and her lover Paolo Malatesta (*Inferno* 5, 73–142). As the family's power and influence grew, it extended its rule over Pesaro, Cesana, and Fano. In the fourteenth and fifteenth centuries several members of the family acquired fame as condottieri in the service of various Italian states. The most famous of these condottieri was Sigismondo Pandolfo Malatesta (d. 1468) who as a typical Renaissance despot proved himself not only a warrior but also a patron of arts and letters. He eventually lost all his possessions with the exception of Rimini which the family sold to Venice in 1503.

MALCOLM, name held by several kings of Scotland, among them Malcolm III Canmore (1058–93) who slew Macbeth, the murderer of his father Duncan. As a youth he spent some years in exile at the court of Edward the Confessor. Although as king he did homage to William I (the Conqueror) for lands he held south of the Scottish border, he made frequent raids into northern England and on one of these lost his life.

MALDON, an old market town and port in Essex, England, to which Henry II granted a charter in 1171. Interesting structures include the thirteenth-century Church of All Saints with its triangular tower and the town hall (fifteenth century). A battle against Danish raiders fought near the town provided the theme for *The Battle of Maldon,* one of the last Anglo-Saxon heroic poems.

MALIK IBN ANAS, d. 795, Moslem jurist who lived most of his life in Medina. He was the founder of one of the four orthodox schools of Islamic law, the Malikite, which spread from Egypt to north Africa, parts of central and west Africa, and to Spain. His legal work consisted principally of organizing and systematizing older legal thought rather than that of giving this a new interpretation. Indicative of the high esteem he enjoyed was the visit Harun al-Rashid paid him on one of his pilgrimages to Mecca.

MALIK SHAH, d. 1092, son of Alp Arslan, the Turkish leader who brought Seljuk power to its height. He extended his rule over Syria and Palestine and even exercised a measure of control over Mecca and Medina. The caliph who married his daughter reigned as his puppet in Baghdad. Malik Shah pursued a tolerant policy in religious matters and showed himself a friend of writers, scientists, and artists. His generally peaceful reign could boast of splendid mosques that graced his capital Isfahan, the poetry of Omar Khayyam, and a reform of the calendar.

MALLEUS MALEFICARUM, the Witches' Hammer, a manual published in 1487 by two Dominicans, Jacob Sprenger and Henry Krämer, about witches and their nefarious deeds, with instructions concerning the methods to be employed in thwarting their machinations and bringing them to punishment.

MALLORCA. Spanish name of Majorca.

MALMESBURY, ABBEY OF, Benedictine house in Wiltshire which rose from a hermitage founded there c. 635 by Maildulf, an Irish or Scottish monk. It became a monastery c. 673, with Aldhelm, Maildulf's pupil, being its first abbot. It flourished as a center of learning during Anglo-Saxon times and continued to enjoy the patronage of English kings as late as Henry V (d. 1422). It was dissolved in 1539.

MALORY, THOMAS, SIR, d. 1471, author of a compilation of English Arthurian stories entitled *Morte D'Arthur*. This is the best-known prose account of King Arthur and the Round Table, and the first in modern English. Caxton who published the work in 1485 gave it its present title. (Malory entitled it *The Book of King Arthur and His Knights of the Round Table*.) That English writers drew on it almost exclusively for the Arthurian legend helps explain the significant influence Malory exerted on the development of the English prose style.

MALOUEL, JEAN, d. 1419, French-Flemish painter who worked in Paris and at the Burgundian court. The *Martyrdom of St. Denis* may be his work. He was among the earliest panel painters of northern Europe.

MALTA, island south of Sicily which was occupied successively by Vandals, Ostrogoths, Byzantium, and the Arabs (870). In 1091 the Normans conquered the island, and about 1249 Frederick II expelled the last of the Arab vassals still on the island. In 1266 Charles of Anjou took possession, but following the revolt of the Sicilian Vespers in 1282 the island became part of the kingdom of Aragon. In 1530 the emperor Charles V gave the island to the Hospitallers (Knights of St. John of Jerusalem).

MALTA, KNIGHTS OF. See SAINT JOHN OF JERUSALEM, ORDER OF THE HOSPITAL OF.

MAMLUKS (Mamelukes), originally white male slaves, mostly Turks and Circassians, taken from Russia, the Caucasus, and central Asia. They were recruited to serve as mercenaries first by the caliphs in Baghdad, then by the Fatimid sultans of Egypt who did not trust their north African and Sudanese troops. Saladin and his successors employed the Mamluks in their wars with the Crusaders. In 1250 the Mamluks seized control and continued their rule of Egypt until 1517 when that country fell to the Ottoman Turks. Perhaps their greatest military achievement was the victory Baibars (Baybars), Mamluk general, gained over the Mongols near Nazareth in 1260. This victory not only saved Cairo and Egypt for Islam but also ended the illusion of Mongol invincibility.

MAMMON, term used in the New Testament for riches when regarded as an object of avaricious pursuit (Matthew 6:24–28).

MA'MUN, AL- (Abu-Al-Abbas 'Abdullah Al-Ma'mun), Abbasid caliph, 813–33, son and successor of Harun al-Rashid although it required heavy fighting until 819 with his brother al-Amin before he was able to establish his sole rule. He showed himself a generous patron of scholars and artists and encouraged the study and translation of Greek writings on science and philosophy. The poet Abu Tamman, the historian Bukhari, and the jurist Ahmed ibn Hanbal flourished during his reign. A source of major trouble during his reign stemmed from the support he gave the Mu'tazilites who advocated a liberalization of Koranic regulations and a rationalization of the Moslem religion. Al Ma'mun adopted harsh policies toward the orthodox and compelled judges and other officials to profess publicly their belief that the Koran was the created, not the uncreated, word of God.

MANASSES, CONSTANTINE, d. 1187, metropolitan of Naupactus, author of political poems and a verse chronicle from the Creation to 1081. He also composed a number of orations including a funeral eulogy of the emperor Nicephorus Comnenus.

MANASSES, PRAYER OF, a short book, included with the Apochrypha of the Old Testament, that purports to be a penitential prayer recited by Manasseh, king of Judah (2 *Kings* 21:1–18; 2 Chronicles 33:1–20). Although used in the early church, it was never incorporated into the Vulgate Bible.

MANCHESTER, city in Lancashire, originally a Celtic settlement on a major road the Romans built from Chester to the north. Saxons controlled the town from the seventh century. In 870 the Danes destroyed the settlement, but in 920 Edward the Elder had it rebuilt. The Domesday Book (1086) lists the area as poor and sparsely populated. In 1229 Henry III granted the town an annual fair, and in 1330 Flemish immigrants introduced the textile industry that was to transform the economic life of the entire area.

MANDAEANS, a Gnostic sect first identified in the first and second centuries when it consisted of a small community east of the Jordan. The members believed that man's soul which demons kept imprisoned in the body (the "tomb of the soul") would be freed at death by the redeemer, the personified "Knowledge of Life." The origin of the sect's beliefs might have been Christian, even though it suffered persecution from the fourth century. The sect survives in southern Iraq and in Khuzistan. Medieval travelers spoke of the Mandaeans as "Christians of St. John" since the latter claimed John the Baptist as a member. Christ was the false Messiah and the practice of asceticism and celibacy were condemned as abominations.

MANDATUM, the rite of the washing of feet during the liturgy of Holy Thursday.

MANDEVILLE, GEOFFREY DE, d. 1144, earl of Essex, an honor he acquired, along with other offices and vast holdings, even control of the Tower of London, during the reign of the weak King Stephen. Stephen needed his help against Matilda, daughter of Henry I, who claimed the throne for her son Henry (II). In 1143 Mandeville saved himself from execution as a traitor by surrendering his offices and castles to Stephen, after which he seized the abbey of Ramsey and used it as the base from which to continue his depredations. To contemporary chroniclers he was the most infamous of the rapacious barons who plundered and robbed in that lawless age.

MANDEVILLE, SIR JOHN (Jehan de Mandeville), English writer of the mid-fourteenth century, author of a book in Norman French entitled *The Voyage and Travels of Sir John Mandeville, Knight,* which described travels he claimed to have made in Africa, the Near East, the Orient, even the Valley of the Devils, the realm of Prester John, and the country of the lost tribes of Israel. He is believed to have drawn the bulk of his material from accounts left by other travelers from which he extracted mostly the strange and bizarre. Despite, or because of, its patent imaginative character, the volume proved immensely popular, while its author enjoyed the dubious distinction of being the greatest traveler of the Middle Ages as well as its greatest liar.

MANDOLA (Mandora), a musical instrument, the forerunner of the mandolin, with four strings stretched over a rounded pear-shaped box. It came into use in the high Middle Ages.

MANEGOLD OF LAUTENBACH, d. after 1103, a monk of Lautenbach, later prior of the monastery of Marbach in Alsace. He composed commentaries on the Scriptures and on Plato and Ovid, and also drew up a polemic against Henry IV of Germany (1056–1106) which justified the deposing of any monarch who had forfeited the trust of his people.

MANES. *See* MANI.

MANETTI, GIANNOZZO, d. 1459, Florentine businessman, statesman, humanist, and secretary to Pope Nicholas V. He composed histories (e.g., of Genoa and Pistoia), biographies (e.g., of Dante and Petrarch), and orations, and translated portions of the Scriptures.

MANFRED, d. 1266, natural son of Frederick II of Germany who ruled the kingdom of Sicily from 1258 to 1266 as regent first for his half-brother Conrad IV, then for his nephew Conradin. In 1260, in a move to strengthen his position, he betrothed his daughter Constance to the *infante* Peter of Aragon. He continued the war his father had been waging against the papacy and certain cities of Lombardy, generally with success until the appearance of Charles of Anjou. He was slain at the battle of Benevento, and Dante placed him in purgatory with other excommunicates. (Purg. 3:105–144). Manfred shared his father's interest in philosophy and science.

MANGONEL, military machine used for hurling heavy stones and missiles.

MANI (Manes, Manichaeus), d. c. 276, a Persian or Median "prophet" whom persecution by the Zoroastrian regime drove to India where he labored as a missionary. In 242 he returned to Persia where he first enjoyed the encouragement of Sapor I. Later under Bahram I he was attacked by Zoroastrian priests and flayed to death. [*See* MANICHAEISM.]

MANIACES, GEORGE, brilliant Byzantine general who managed to win victories in Asia Minor and Sicily over the Arabs despite the general deterioration of Byzantine power. When Emperor Constantine IX (1042–55) ordered him replaced, he permitted his troops and a band of Norman adventurers to hail him as emperor, but he was slain (1043) before he could attack the imperial army. His death opened the way to the Norman conquest of southern Italy.

MANICHAEISM (Manicheism, Manichaeanism, Manicheanism), a dualistic Gnostic religion or religious philosophy based upon the principle of two contending forces in the universe, the one good (light), the other evil (darkness), the one spirit, the other material. Its author was the Persian "prophet" Mani (Manes, Manichaeus) who claimed to have drawn his ideas from the study of many prophets including Buddha, Zoroaster, and Jesus. According to Mani, the object of the practice of religion was to release the particles of light stolen by Satan from the world of Light and imprisoned in man's brain. Jesus, Buddha, the Prophets, and Mani himself had all been sent to assist man in this task. Man must cooperate by a practice of severe asceticism. Most of the tenets of Manichaeism were actually derived from Zoroastrian and Gnostic theories. Manichaeism was particularly strong during the third century but waned in strength from the fourth once Christianity had triumphed and had adopted vigorous measures to suppress it. Some of its views found acceptance with such later groups as the Bogomils and Cathari (Albigenses). St. Augustine for a time accepted Manichaean beliefs.

MANIPLE, originally an absorbent cloth that a priest used to wipe hand and mouth. It was accepted in time as a liturgical vestment when it took the form of a long thin strip of silk that the priest draped over his left forearm.

MAN, ISLE OF, island off the west coast of England (Northumbria) that the Vikings occupied. Although the Viking king Godred II recognized Henry II as his suzerain, the king of Norway claimed the island and in 1266 sold it to the king of Scotland. Edward I forced Scotland to recognize his suzerainty over the island, but Robert I (the Bruce) conquered it, only to have Edward III recover it and hold it permanently for England.

MANNA, the bread that fell from heaven to feed the Hebrews in the desert; in the Middle Ages a symbol of the eucharist.

MANNYNG, ROBERT, fl. 1283, also called Robert of Brunne, a Gilbertine canon at Sempringham priory in Lincolnshire, author of two poems, *Handlyng Synne,* a very popular and influential work dealing with sin and the sacraments and intended to serve as a manual for the layman, and *Story of England,* a chronicle of England of no value to historians. Scholars are attracted to *Handlyng Synne* because of the views presented there of the lower clergy and peasantry in the early fourteenth century.

MANORIALISM (Manorial, Seigneurial System), the social and economic organization of the peasantry of western Europe in the Middle Ages as based upon the manor. The manor was itself a district held by a feudal lord (seigneur) whose inhabitants were subject to the jurisdiction of his court. It generally comprised a village community and its supporting fields and woods, together with mills, barns, and granaries. All these belonged to the lord although it was the labor of the commoners that made the manor a source of value to him, while for them it furnished a means of livelihood. The peasants worked both their own plots of ground, the use of which they had inherited from their parents, and the lands which the seigneur had retained for his own use (*demesne*). (In France the *demesne* had disappeared by 1200, from which time the French peasant made a direct payment of grain (*taille*) to the lord.)

In addition to the labor (*corvée*) which the serf (or villein) expended on the lord's *demesne,* he owed him a number of charges and prestations including banalities and heriot. Such charges did not fall upon any freeman who happened to be living in the manorial village, and they might burden one serf more heavily than another, depending upon the contractual relationship each bore with the lord. Thus the cottar who had nothing but a hut for himself, that is, no lands to work, paid no banalities, as his economic status was far below that of the reasonably prosperous villein who paid a sizable amount.

Until the revival of trade and the rise of towns broke down the isolation of the village, the manorial system remained a fundamentally social institution. The rise of capitalism gradually altered this, so that by the close of the Middle Ages the manor had become, at least in the eyes of its lord, an economic investment to be exploited. The major development which transformed the manor from a social to an economic institution was the commutation of the labor charge to a money rent. As more money came into circulation from the fourteenth century, it made possible a gradual replacement of the labor rent with a money payment as a means of meeting the serf's obligations to his lord. And once the serf began paying his rent in money, it was but a short time before he purchased exemption from other servile obligations as well. By the close of the Middle Ages, he had in effect become a free man. [*See* SERF; TWO-, THREE-, OPEN-FIELD SYSTEM; BANALITIES; CORVEE; ENCLOSURE.]

MANRIQUE, GÓMEZ, d. c. 1490, Spanish poet, author of lyric and didactic verse and a nativity play. He is the earliest Spanish dramatist whose name is known to us. Gómez was also a politician and diplomat and, as governor of Toledo, won fame for his oratorical talents.

MANRIQUE, JORGE, d. 1479, Spanish soldier and poet, a nephew of Gómez Manrique. He composed amorous and satirical verse, as well as poetry on more serious themes, including a well-known elegy on the death of his father. It contains numerous references to the Bible and to Boethius, but it is the perfect technique of the versification and the sublimity of expression that have given it enduring fame. It was translated into Latin and English and also set to music.

MANS, LE, the Roman *Vindunum,* a bishop's seat since the fourth century and the principal city of the county of Maine (northwestern France). Portions of the walls erected at the close of the third century can still be seen. Normans occupied the town and province in 1063. It was joined to England through the person of its count until 1205 when it came under direct rule of Philip II Augustus of France. Its most noteworthy structure from the Middle Ages is the cathedral (eleventh-thirteenth centuries) whose choir is one of the most imposing in France and whose stained glass is among the most magnificent. Berengaria, the consort of Richard I Lion-Heart, is among the notables buried there.

MANSUR, AL- (Abu Ja'far 'Abdullah Al-Mansur), Abbasid caliph, 754–75, brother of Abu'l-Abbas, the founder of the Abbasid dynasty, although al-Mansur is generally considered the real founder of the new caliphate because of his success in extending Abbasid authority throughout the empire and his introduction of Persian practices and traditions of government. He rebuilt Baghdad (766) and made it his capital.

MANTEGNA, ANDREA, d. 1506, Italian painter of the Paduan school, whose frescoes, altar pieces, and portraits are considered the best of the period. What enabled him to achieve such success was his mastery of foreshortening. His work shows the influence of Donatello, while he in turn influenced that of his brother-in-law Giovanni Bellini. He is known for his *St. Sebastian* and the *Dead Christ,* perhaps above all for the ceiling of the *Camera degli sposi* of the ducal palace at Mantua through which a number of figures are represented looking down over a balustrade. He took great interest in the antique world and was one of the first artists to make an extensive collection of Greek and Roman works.

MANTELLETTA, a sleeveless vestment worn by certain dignitaries in the church. It reached to the knees and was open in front.

MANTLE, a rectangular or half-circular cape held loosely in front or on the right shoulder with strings, chains, or buttons.

MANTLET (mantelet), protective shield composed of branches wattled together with other branches or vines and often covered with hides. Under such a cover an attacking party might advance to the walls of a castle.

MANTUA, city of Lombardy of Etruscan origin, a fief of the rulers of Tuscany until 1115 when it secured the status of a free commune. Early in the fourteenth century the Gonzaga family gained possession of the city. Famous works of art grace the large ducal palace (begun c. 1302) and the court castle (built 1395–1406).

MANTUM, a red mantle, a ceremonial vestment worn by the pope. From the eleventh century to the fourteenth the mantum held special significance since its investiture symbolized the transfer to the pope of the right to govern the church.

MANUALE, book containing the forms that the priest was to observe in administering the sacraments. Its name derived from the Latin meaning a book of handy size.

MANUEL I COMNENUS, Byzantine emperor, 1143–80, conquered Serbia (1151), forced Raymond of Antioch to recognize his suzerainty (1159), and made Hungary a vassal state (1168). His career was filled with troubled negotiations with the Normans of southern Italy, with Conrad III and Frederick I Barbarossa of Germany, and with the papacy. In 1176 he suffered a major defeat at the hands of the Turks at Myriocephalum in Asia Minor, a defeat that heralded the decline of Byzantine power and the rapid expansion of Turkish influence in the Near East. His reign also saw the establishment in Constantinople of colonies of Genoese, Pisans, and Venetians. Their interference in imperial policy in the interest of their own commercial interests contributed significantly to the eventual destruction of Byzantium. Western writers blamed Manuel for the failure of the Second Crusade (1147–9) which he did not support. He refused to do so lest he anger his Turkish neighbors. He also realized that the Crusaders were intent only on protecting and advancing their own interests in Syria and Palestine.

MANUEL II (Palaeologus), Byzantine emperor, 1391–1425, who deposed his nephew John VII who had taken the throne from his father. He worked hard to hold on to what little remained of the Byzantine empire and made repeated visits to the west to enlist the aid of Latin Christendom against the Ottoman Turks who had all but surrounded his state. What promised to be a godsend to his cause, a formidable crusade organized by the Hungarian king Sigismund, vanished when the Turks destroyed the Christian host at Nicopolis in 1396. Had it not been for the disastrous defeat Timur the Lame inflicted on the Turkish army at Angora in 1402, Manuel's empire would not have lived on much longer. Manuel was an enlightened ruler and a patron of humanists. He composed poetry and treatises on theology and rhetoric.

MANUEL I, king of Portugal, 1495–1521, in keeping with his promise to Ferdinand and Isabella of Spain whose daughter Isabella he married, expelled all Jews and Moors who refused baptism from his realm. He continued the interest his predecessor had shown in overseas expansion and may be credited with the establishment of Portuguese influence in India. Vasco da Gama made his epochal trip around Africa (1497–8) during his reign.

MANUEL CALECAS, d. 1410, Byzantine theologian and rhetorician, an opponent of Hesychasm, and an active advocate of union with the Latin church. His theological writings reveal considerable Thomistic influence.

MANUSCRIPT, document written by hand. Most manuscripts of the Middle Ages prior to the thirteenth century were prepared and copied in monastic *scriptoria*. The usual writing material was parchment or vellum, the latter a fine variety of parchment made from the skins of lambs or kids. Such materials were expensive and were often beautifully decorated or illuminated. [*See* ILLUMINATED MANUSCRIPTS.] While paper may have been invented as early as the second century in China, it was only in the twelfth that the Arabs introduced it to the Mediterranean world and the West. With the invention of printing in the late fifteenth century, the era of manuscript-copying came to an end.

MANUSCRIPT ILLUMINATION. *See* ILLUMINATED MANUSCRIPTS.

MANUTIUS, ALDUS, d. 1515, printer of Venice who gave his name to the Aldine press. He gathered around him Greek scholars and compositors and published critical editions of Greek and Latin works including those of Aristotle. His most famous book, the *Hypnerotomachia Poliphili* of Francesco Colonna, with its superb woodcuts, appeared in 1499. Books produced by Aldus are called Aldine and carry his mark, a dolphin and an anchor.

MANZIKERT, BATTLE OF, battle fought in Armenia above Lake Van in 1071 between the Seljuk Turks under Alp Arslan and a large Byzantine army under Emperor Romanus IV. The desertion of some of the emperor's Turkish mercenaries contributed to his defeat and capture. This defeat opened Asia Minor to Turkish conquest and ultimately led to the organization of the First Crusade (1096–9).

MAP. Cartography, the art and science of map making, had advanced significantly during Roman times, notably through the study of such scholars as Strabo (d. A.D. 24?) and Ptolemy (second century A.D.). The principal departure made in the early Middle Ages was due to the influence of church fathers and other theologians who drew their ideas of the shape of the world from the Bible. An example of this type of map was the *Christian Topography* of Cosmas, a sixth-century merchant of Alexandria who became a monk. His world is surrounded by the ocean and surmounted by the heavens, the entire sketch being patterned after the Tabernacle as described in the Bible. Of greater value to travelers were the guidebooks of pilgrims. Some of these survive from the fourth century.

Medieval maps generally showed the earth as a flat disk containing the three continents of Europe, Asia, and Africa, with the center of the earth located at Jerusalem. This threefold division of the world accounted for the so-called T and O maps that were popular until the late Middle Ages. They showed the world as surrounded by a circular ocean, the O, the three continents of Europe, Asia, and Africa, divided by the perpendicular of the T representing the Mediterranean, and the top bar of the T consisting of the Nile, separating Africa and Asia, and the Dnieper, separating Europe and Asia.

Not until the fourteenth century did maps appear that attempted to incorporate information that travelers in particular had made available through their visits to different parts of the world. An example is the Catalan map of the world of 1375 prepared for the king of France.

The most important factor in the improvement of maps in the late Middle Ages was the availability of *portolani* or seamen's charts which plotted the best, and safest, courses ships could take between major seaports. Some 30 of such charts survive, all by Italians. They show the Mediterranean and Black Seas and the Atlantic (off the coast of Europe and Africa).

The fifteenth century produced two mapmakers of major importance: Fra Mauro, a monk of Venice, who completed his map in 1459 — it shows the world in the shape of a wheel — and Martin Behaim, a German who served as astronomer at the court of Portugal. His terrestrial globe, made in 1492, is the oldest in existence.

MAP (Mapes), WALTER, d. c. 1210, satirist and wit, probably of Wales, a clerk in the household of Henry II of England. He also served as itinerant justice and was a royal representative at the Third Lateran Council (1179). He composed light verse and courtly romances but is best known for the *De Nugis Curialium (Of Courtiers' Trifles)*, a volume of gossip, anecdotes, homilies, and homespun philosophy. Its numerous biblical, classical, and scholastic allusions bear witness to Map's great erudition and his excessive concern with literary precedent.

MAQDISI (Muqaddasi), AL-, d. c. 1000, Arab traveler and geographer, author of a work in Arabic describing the different lands that made up the Islamic world. The enormous amount of information about the lands, their people, and their culture he gathered during the 20 years he spent moving about these countries.

MARAVEDI (Marabotino, Almorabitino), Spanish coin, first of gold, later of silver, in circulation since 1170.

MARBACH ANNALS, historical narrative covering the years 631 to 1238 but of particular value for the years 1184 to 1200. It was composed about 1210 in the convent of Hohenburg.

MARBOD OF RENNES, d. 1123, pupil of Fulbert of Chartres, himself a teacher there, in 1096 bishop of Rennes in Brittany. He composed verse on both secular (*Upon a Beautiful Girl*) and religious (*On the Annunciation*) themes.

MARCEL, ETIENNE, d. 1358, French popular leader, provost of the merchants of Paris, who joined the Estates General in forcing the dauphin (later Charles V) to accept the direction of a council in levying and spending taxes, the authorization of military levies, and other extraordinary measures. This strange alliance of merchants and Estates (composed of clergy, nobles, and representatives of the towns) was brought about by the near-collapse of France following the shattering defeat suffered at Poitiers in 1356. But the revolt of the peasants (*Jacquerie*), together with Marcel's alliance with Charles II (the Bad) of Navarre, led the Estates to repudiate him. He was slain during a riot in Paris.

MARCELLA, ST., d. c. 410, Christian ascetic whose palace on the Aventine Hill in Rome served as a center of Christian influence. A group of noble Roman widows and virgins interested in pursuing the religious life constituted its core. St. Jerome gave the community guidance and instruction during the years he spent in Rome (382–5). Marcella was herself a student of the Scriptures and carried on a correspondence with Jerome concerning philological and exegetical problems. She sustained physical mistreatment at the hands of the Visigoths when they sacked Rome in 410 and died shortly after.

MARCELLINUS, ST., Pope, 296–304, a priest of Rome, successor of Gaius, said to have sacrificed to the gods when pope during the persecution of Diocletian in order to escape death. He later repented his lack of faith and suffered martyrdom. St. Augustine disputed the accuracy of the charge of apostasy, although there is also some question about his martyrdom.

MARCELLINUS COMES, d. c. 534, chancellor of Justinian I, author of *Annales,* a continuation to c. 543 of the *Chronicon* of Eusebius of Caesarea and Jerome.

MARCELLUS I, ST., Pope, May 308 to January 309. He reorganized the church of Rome and consecrated 21 bishops. Emperor Maxentius ordered him exiled because his policy of imposing severe penances upon *lapsi* had led to riots.

MARCELLUS OF ANCYRA, d. 374, bishop of Ancyra, a vigorous foe of Arianism, who was himself deposed on the charge of Sabellianism and was condemned by the Councils of Antioch (341) and Sardica (343). He maintained that in the Unity of the Godhead the Son and the Spirit emerged as independent entities only for the purposes of Creation and Redemption, and when once the work of redemption was completed, they would be resumed into the Divine Unity.

MARCH (German *Mark*), name given to a frontier county during the Carolingian period. It was administered by a margrave (*Markgraf*). Denmark was once the Danish march, whence its name. [*See* MARGRAVE.]

MARCH, AUSIÀS, d. 1459, leading Catalan poet of the period whose verse greatly influenced the development of Castilian poetry. His tormented verse reveals his inner struggle between sensuality and idealism. Except for Petrarch, the formative influences of his poetry were medieval: Provençal poetry, scholastic philosophy, and the *dolce stil nuovo*. What is modern about his verse is the expression he gives of his own often morbid feelings of despair and self-loathing.

MARCH, EARLDOM OF, title held by successive heads of the Mortimer family from 1328 to 1425. Richard Plantagenet, the duke of York, inherited the estates belonging to the family and acquired the title at that time and passed it on to his son Edward (IV).

MARCHE (La Marche), county in central France,

from 1199 the possession of the Lusignan family, and passed to the crown in 1308. It was detached from Limousin in the middle of the tenth century in order to protect Poitou (to the west) and the rest of the duchy of Aquitaine against invasion, either by the French king's troops from Berry or by Norman raiders from the north. It was held by the Bourbons as an appanage from 1327 until 1434, then by the Armagnacs to 1477, and after that by the house of Bourbon-Beaujeu.

MARCHES, THE, region of central Italy, noted by that name for the first time in the tenth century. It was included in the Donation of Pepin (756) but was never more than nominally under the authority of the pope. Powerful feudal families such as the Malatesta of Rimini and Montefeltro of Urbino dominated the greater part of the region. From the thirteenth century papal efforts to gain control of the region grew more persistent and finally suceeded in the sixteenth century.

MARCH FIELD, the annual gathering of Merovingian and Carolingian counts, crown officials, and other great men with the king in March when they met in the sight of the army to discuss laws and matters of war and peace. Pepin III (the Short) (751–68) postponed the meeting to May, whence the term May Field.

MARCIAN, Roman emperor in the East, 450–7, an officer in the army selected by and married to Pulcheria, sister of Theodosius, to be the successor of Theodosius II. He cut off tribute to the Huns, and after the death of Attila and the collapse of Hunnic power permitted the Ostrogoths to settle in Pannonia. In 451 he convoked the important Council of Chalcedon. Upon his death, the Theodosian dynasty came to an end in the East.

MARCION, d. c. 160, Christian Gnostic who condemned the Old Testament and demanded a life of rigorous asceticism from those who wished to be saved. He also insisted that the Gospel of the New Testament, a Gospel of Love, be disassociated from Judaism and the Law. As Canonical Scriptures he recognized only ten of the Epistles of St. Paul and an edited form of St. Luke's Gospel. His followers, known as Marcionites, established themselves in Rome in 144 but began to lose adherents during the third century. Scattered groups of them could be located in the east as late as the sixth century.

MARCOMANNI, German tribe that belonged to the nation of the Sueves and was located in the Main valley shortly after 100 B.C. From there they moved to Bohemia where in alliance with their neighbors, the Quadi, they battled the Romans along the upper Danube during the years 166–80. Some of them moved down into Italy during the reign of Marcus Aurelius (161–80). They later merged with the Bavarians.

MARCUS AURELIUS, Roman emperor, 161–80, the last of the so-called Good Emperors. His death and the accession of his worthless son Commodus announced the beginning of a marked and steady decline in the power and well-being of the empire. Aurelius had a high moral view of life and his guiding aim as an individual and emperor was to be good and to live in harmony with the Divine Reason. He set down his philosophy of life in his *Meditations,* a book less philosophical than practical in its approach. Despite the nobility of his character, he judged Christianity to be inimical to the state and continued the policy of persecution of his predecessors. Several "Apologies" which church fathers composed in efforts to convince him that Christians were not enemies of the state, but rather among its worthiest citizens, survive. It was his misfortune, and that of the empire, that fighting against dangerous enemies along the frontiers, against the Marcomanni and Quadi on the Danube and the Parthians in Mesopotamia, left him little time for works of peace.

MARGARET, d. 1412, queen of Denmark, Norway, and Sweden, the daughter of Waldemar IV of Denmark and wife of King Haakon VI of Norway. From 1376 she ruled Denmark in the name of her son Olaf; from 1380 when her husband died, she served as regent for her son in Norway; and from 1387 when her son died, she was queen of both Denmark and Norway. That same year she announced her claim to the throne of Sweden, and by 1398 had successfully completed the pacification of the country. In 1397 representatives of the three countries recognized her grandnephew and adopted son Eric (VII) of Pomerania as joint king of their countries, although Margaret continued to exercise royal authority until her death. She brought peace to Scandinavia and prepared those countries for the united rule which in the case of Denmark and Norway continued until 1814. [See KALMAR, UNION OF.]

MARGARET (Maid of Norway), queen of Scotland (1283–90), daughter of Eric II of Norway and of Margaret, daughter of Alexander III of Scotland. When Alexander died, Margaret became queen under a regency, and Edward I of England arranged a marriage between her and his son Edward (II). But Margaret died on her way south from Norway to Scotland and a period of civil war ensued in Scotland over the succession to the throne. [See SCOTLAND.]

MARGARET OF ANJOU, d. 1482, queen consort of Henry VI of England whose efforts to save the throne for her mentally ill husband and her son made her a central figure in the rivalry between the Yorkist and Lancastrian factions during the Wars of the Roses (1455–85). From 1459 she assumed leadership in organizing Lancastrian efforts to keep first Richard of York, then his son Edward (IV) off the throne. Her fortunes and those of her husband rose and fell during the turbulent course of the war. After the defeat at Towton (1461), she fled to Scotland, whence she went to France to enlist the aid of the wily Louis XI. For a moment in 1470 victory appeared within her grasp when she made peace with her bitter enemy, the powerful earl of

Warwick, known as the King-Maker, who had turned against Edward. Her son Edward was slain in the battle of Tewkesbury (1471), and she and her husband were captured. Henry was murdered shortly after in the Tower; she spent her last years in near-indigence in France.

MARGARET OF CARINTHIA, d. 1369, countess of Tyrol, known as the Ugly Duchess or Margaret Maultasch (from the German meaning pocket mouth). With the help of her loyal subjects and the assistance of the king of Bohemia, her husband's father, she thwarted the plan of Emperor Louis IV to deprive her of Tyrol. She subsequently had her marriage annulled, then married the son of Louis IV. Shortly after the death of her husband, she abdicated and retired to Vienna. Legend painted her as a woman of great power and even greater evil. A portrait of her, painted long after her death, served Tenniel as the model for the "Duchess" in his illustration of *Alice in Wonderland*.

MARGARET OF CORTONA, ST., d. 1297, Franciscan tertiary and founder of the Poverelle, a congregation of women who consecrated themselves to the care of the poor.

MARGARET OF PROVENCE, d. 1295, queen consort of Louis IX of France to whom she bore eleven children. She accompanied Louis on the first of his Crusades (1248–54) and worked hard to revive the spirits of the Crusaders following their disastrous defeat at Mansurah when her husband was captured.

MARGARET OF SCOTLAND, ST., d. 1093, wife of Malcolm III, brought up at the Hungarian court where her father, Edward Aetheling, son of King Edmund Ironside, was living in exile. After the battle of Hastings, she attempted to return to Hungary, but was shipwrecked and ended up in Scotland where she married the king, Malcolm III. She influenced her husband and his court in introducing reforms both in the government and in the church. Her principal adviser in the matter of ecclesiastical reform was Lanfranc. She restored the monastery at Iona and other Celtic churches.

MARGARET, ST., obscure saint of the third century, virgin martyr of Antioch, one of the Fourteen Holy Helpers. Her intercession was sought by women in childbirth. She may have been the St. Marina supposed to have been martyred during the persecution of Diocletian.

MARGRAVE, originally the title held by the count (*Graf*) who administered a frontier (*Mark*) province during the Carolingian period, e.g., the Spanish march. Because of the need to defend such frontier provinces against possible invasions, the margrave usually was expected to maintain greater military resources than the counts in the interior. The German kings of the Saxon dynasty employed a similar system to protect and extend their eastern frontier against the Slavs, e.g., Ostmark (Austria). Several later German princes who held the title of margrave had simply inherited it from an ancestor.

MARIAN ANTIPHONS, chants addressed to the Blessed Virgin. They included *Alma Redemptoris Mater, Ave Regina Caelorum, Regina Caeli,* and *Salve Regina.*

MARIANO, JACOPO, d. before 1458, an engineer of Siena whose sketches are of considerable importance in the study of late medieval technology.

MARIANUS SCOTUS, d. c. 1082, Irish monk and chronicler whose Gaelic name was Moel-Brigte, that is, "Servant of Bridget." He traveled to Germany and was ordained a priest, although he lived as a recluse most of his life. He is the author of a Latin chronicle that runs from the Creation to 1082 and which was used by Florence of Worcester and Sigebert of Gembloux.

MARIANUS SCOTUS, d. 1081, Irish monk whose Gaelic name was Muredach. In 1067 he left Ireland on a pilgrimage to Rome, then made his home in Regensburg where he became an abbot.

He is known for the fine calligraphic copies he made of portions of the Bible, most of which he accompanied with commentaries.

MARICOURT, PIERRE DE (Petrus Peregrinus), noble of Picardy of the thirteenth century who composed a treatise on the astrolabe and the first experimental textbook on magnetism.

MARIE DE FRANCE, d. c. 1190, earliest known French poetess, author of lays (*lais*) and fables. Her life remains largely a mystery. She was probably born in France but spent her literary years in England. Her *lais* belong to the genre of the courtly romance although they contain more about love and less about fighting than was ordinarily the case. Her fables reveal her interest in, and knowledge of, contemporary affairs and demonstrate real talent in her analyses of love which she presents against varying backgrounds of realism and fairy tale.

MARIGNOLLI, GIOVANNI DE', fl. 1338–57, Franciscan, member of the four-man embassy which Pope Benedict XII sent to the court of the great khan in China in 1338. On their way they visited the khan of the Golden Horde at Sarai on the Volga, built a church at Armalec, and finally reached Peking in May or June of 1342. Marignoli remained there three or four years, visited the shrine of St. Thomas the Apostle near Madras on his way back which took him through Ceylon, Baghdad, and Jerusalem. He reached Avignon in 1353. His *Annals of Bohemia* contain the notes he made on his travels.

MARIGNY, ENGUERRAND DE, d. 1315, leading financial minister at the court of Philip IV in 1313–4, when he had charge of the royal treasury and of the newly established auditing department, the *chambre des comptes.* Because of his position, the aristocracy and bourgeoisie held him responsible for the heavy taxation and the debasement of the coinage which Philip IV introduced. After Philip's death, his son Louis X listened to charges of financial irregularities, even of sorcery, which were brought against de Marigny and had him executed.

MARINIDS, Berber dynasty which ruled Morocco and other sections of north Africa from the thirteenth to the fifteenth century. The defeat of the Almohads and the capture of Marrakech in 1269 had enabled them to gain control of Morocco. They pursued the same policy in Spain as their predecessors in supporting the Moslem princes there, especially the ruler of Granada, in the hope of preventing Christian conquest of the entire peninsula. They were more successful in Africa and for a time managed to rule over much of Tunisia.

MARINUS I, Pope, 882–4, a priest of Rome, archdeacon and treasurer of the church in Rome, bishop of Caere (Tuscany), and successor of John VIII. As pope he pursued a conciliatory policy toward the ruling monarchs of Europe and conducted discussions with the Byzantine patriarch Photius. In all probability he did not condemn Photius for heresy nor deprive him of his office.

MARINUS II, Pope, 942–6, a priest of Rome, the successor of Stephen VIII, who owed his appointment as pope to Alberic II of Spoleto. He advanced the reform of the church in Rome, France, and Germany.

MARITIME LAW, legal rules concerning navigation and overseas commerce. In its origin it consisted of laws and customs from more ancient times that had undergone some development under the influence of Roman civil law. As trade and commerce expanded in the thirteenth and fourteenth centuries far beyond their importance in ancient times, several collections of maritime customs made their appearance. The best known were the *Consolat del Mar* or Consulate of the Sea, the Laws of Oléron, and the Laws of Visby (Wisby).

MARIUS OF AVENCHES (Aventicus), ST., d. 594, bishop of Avenches (574) who moved his see to Lausanne. He is the author of a chronicle

that continued from 455 to 581 the one undertaken earlier by Prosper of Aquitaine.

MARIUS MERCATOR, early fifth century Latin theologian, a disciple of St. Augustine, probably of north Africa, who attacked both Nestorius and Pelagius in his writings. His works represent a major source of our knowledge of Nestorianism.

MARIUS VICTORINUS, CAIUS, d. after 363, rhetorician of Rome whose theological writings, notably those attacking Arianism, reveal the influence of neo-Platonism. He composed the first Latin commentaries on the epistles of St. Paul.

MARK, monetary unit of 240 pennies which replaced the older pound after the twelfth century.

MARK, weight unit of eight ounces, usually of gold or silver, accepted in most of the countries of western Europe from the ninth century. In England it amounted at first to two-thirds of a pound in value, later to one-half a pound.

MARKET, place where goods were bought and sold, usually located in a village or town and ordinarily with authorization of the king or lord who, for a fee, extended the market his protection and its merchants certain economic and judicial privileges. Most markets offered only the products of the locality for sale. Those that could boast more than local commodities might develop into fairs.

MARKO (M. Kraljevic, Krali Marko), hero of Serbian (Croatian, Bulgarian) folk poetry who succored the oppressed and punished the wicked. He also appears in Bulgarian, Romanian, and Albanian folk songs. The historical Marko (d. 1395), a king of Serbia, was the son of King Vukasin of Macedonia and a vassal of the sultan of Turkey. The church near Skopje which his father had begun and which he completed is known as "Marko's Monastery."

MARK, ST., Pope, January to October 336, pope with a brief and uneventful pontificate.

MARK THE EVANGELIST, ST., the author of one of the four gospels. In Christian iconography he usually appears as a winged lion.

MARK THE HERMIT, d. after 430, Christian polemicist, a disciple of John Chrysostom, abbot of a monastery in Ancyra, and in his last years an anchorite. In his writings he attacked the Nestorians and Messalians. His position on human merit attracted the attention of certain older Protestant theologians.

MARKWART OF ANWEILER, d. 1202, imperial minister and adviser of Henry VI of Germany who appointed him margrave of Ancona and duke of Romagna. Markwart was unable to maintain German authority in Sicily after the death of Henry in 1197.

MARMION, SIMON, d. 1489, Flemish illuminator, best known for the altarpiece in the abbey of St. Omer. He delighted in the use of gay colors, small figures, and a light style.

MARMOUTIER, ABBEY OF, monastic house founded at Tours by St. Martin c. 372. The Northmen sacked the monastery in 853, but it was rebuilt in 986 and became a member of the Congregation of Cluny.

MARONITES, disciples of St. Maro of Cyr, a friend of John Chrysostom, to whom they traced their origin. They became distinguishable as a distinct community of Christians because of their adoption of Monothelite doctrines. Their monastery in northern Syria served as the center of their missionary activity. The Council of Constantinople (680) excommunicated the community; it returned to formal communion with latin Christianity only in 1182. The Syro-Antiochene rite they followed revealed a mixture of Latin and Greek usages and employed both Syriac and Arabic languages.

MAROZIA, member of the powerful Crescentii family, the daughter of Theophylact and Theodora. She ruled Rome, the papacy, and the Papal States during the first three decades of the tenth century until 932 when she was overthrown by her son Alberic II. Marozia was the wife successively of Alberic I of Spoleto, Guido of Tuscany, and of King Hugh of Italy.

MARQUIS (marquise, marchese, marchesa, marques, marquesa, marquess), French title which had its origin in the office of the Carolingian margrave. The marquis ranked between prince and count.

MARRAKESH, city of Morocco which in the eleventh century grew up from the campsite of the Almoravid leader Yusuf ibn Tashfin, and for two centuries served as the capital of that region. In 1269 it passed to the control of the Marinids who made Fès their capital. The city was the starting point for caravans setting out to the Sahara and Timbuktu. The 220-foot minaret (completed 1195) of the most important mosque dominated the city.

MARRANO, a derisive term meaning "swine," given to Spanish and Portuguese Jews who accepted baptism rather than go into exile or face death at the hands of the Inquisition. They often continued to practice their Judaism in secret and for that reason, but also because of their affluence and influence — they might occupy high positions in the government and even in the church's hierarchy — incurred the hatred of many Christians. Early in 1473 rioting and massacres took place in Córdoba and other cities. After 1480, when the Court of the Inquisition was established, this tribunal directed the suppression of the Marranos. Some 300 were burned at the stake during the first year of its operation. In 1492 all Jews, orthodox as well as Marranos, were ordered expelled from Spain.

MARSEILLES, seacoast city of southern France, of Phoenician or Greek origin, which was noted as a bishopric c. 314 and was captured by the

Ostrogoths in 481. It suffered periodic ravagings from different enemies and began a sustained growth only in the tenth century under the protection of its viscounts. The town gradually purchased the rights of self-government from these counts, only to have Charles of Anjou, count of Provence, establish his rule in 1252. In 1423 Alfonso V of Aragon sacked the city. In 1481 it passed under the authority of the French crown along with Provence, although it continued to enjoy an administration separate from that of the county.

MARSHAL, a master of the horse in early Frankish times, later in the Carolingian and imperial (Holy Roman Empire) periods a high court official in charge of military affairs and court ceremonials. The office was well established in England in the twelfth century and became hereditary the century following. Philip II Augustus introduced the office in France where it soon became one of the great offices of the court.

MARSHALL, WILLIAM, d.1219, earl of Pembroke and Striguil, councillor to Henry II, Richard I, and John, then, despite his ninety years, regent for Henry III during the first three critical years of the young king's reign.

MARSILIUS (Marsiglio) OF PADUA, d. 1342 or 1343, political philosopher and author of probably the most revolutionary political treatise to appear in the Middle Ages. He studied at Padua and Paris, served as rector of the University of Paris (1313), and taught there. In 1324 he published a treatise entitled *Defensor Pacis* in which he made the people, more precisely its responsible element, the ultimate authority in society. The people should not only elect their king but also depose him if he ruled unjustly. They should also exercise supreme authority in the church through the instrumentality of a general council. Marsilius would also deprive the church of all its temporal power and possessions and limit its functions to strictly spiritual matters, in the exercise of which it should never be

permitted to employ any coercive powers. When forced to flee Paris, Marsilius found a haven at the court of Louis IV of Germany, who appointed him vicar of the city of Rome in 1328 when he and his army occupied the city.

MARTHA, ST., sister of Lazarus and Mary and a friend of Jesus. From the incident related in Luke 10:38-42, when she complained to Christ that her sister Mary was leaving all the work of preparing for guests to her, she often appeared in medieval literature as symbolizing the "active" Christian life as contrasted with the "contemplative" life of her sister.

MARTIANUS CAPELLA, early fifth-century (pagan) author of the *Marriage of Mercury and Philology,* an introduction to the seven liberal arts. It proved one of the most popular textbooks of the Middle Ages.

MARTIN I, ST., Pope, 649–55, successor of Theodore I, presided over a Lateran synod in 649 which condemned Monothelitism. In 653 Emperor Constans II ordered him arrested for his opposition to Monothelitism, had him brought to Constantinople where he was publicly degraded after refusing to sign the *Typos* of the emperor, and exiled him to Cherson (Crimea) where he died. He is the last pope to be venerated as a martyr.

MARTIN II, Pope. *See* MARINUS I, Pope.

MARTIN III, Pope. *See* MARINUS II, Pope.

MARTIN IV, Pope, 1281–5, chancellor of Louis IX of France and keeper of the great seal, who owed his election as pope largely to the influence of Charles of Anjou, the king of Sicily. Martin's excommunication of the Byzantine emperor Michael VIII Palaeologus in 1281, a step he took to please Charles who had his eye on Constantinople, destroyed any immediate possibility of a reunion of the Latin and Greek churches. Martin permitted himself to become deeply involved in the French-Aragonese struggle over Sicily.

MARTIN V, Pope, 1417–31, a cardinal who was elected pope by the Council of Constance after the three popes, Roman, Avignonese, and Pisan, had either resigned or been deposed. His election ended the Western Schism. As pope he carried through a reorganization of the Curia in accord with the decrees adopted at Constance and also worked to rehabilitate papal authority in Rome and the Papal States. In deference to the conciliar decrees enacted at Constance, he convoked the Council of Pavia (1423) and the Council of Basel (1431). His energies were absorbed by the organization of crusades against the Hussites and Turks.

MARTINI, SIMONE, d. 1344, incorrectly called Simone Memmi by Vasari, Italian painter, a pupil of Duccio, who executed frescoes in a number of cities of Italy. His works helped spread the influence of the school of Siena. Noted paintings include *St. Louis of Toulouse Crowing the King* and his *Maestà* for the town hall of Siena. In Assisi he painted frescoes in the Chapel of San Martin in the Lower Church, and decorated the papal palace in Avignon.

MARTIN OF BRAGA (Cracara), ST., d. c. 580, bishop of Dumio and archbishop of Braga who labored as a missionary among the Sueves in Galicia (Spain) who still retained the Arian beliefs of their ancestors. His pastoral writings furnish an insight into the culture of the period. He also left a collection of canons.

MARTIN OF TOURS, ST., d. 397, member of the Roman cavalry, then monk, later founder of a monastery of hermits at Ligugé near Poitiers (c. 360), perhaps the first in Gaul, and a second at Marmoutier outside Tours. In 371 he became bishop of Tours. Because of the many miracles attributed to him and his missionary labors in Gaul, Merovingian kings honored him as the patron of their family. Martin was one of the first persons not a martyr to be publicly venerated as a saint. The most famous story told about him has to do with his conversion. As a soldier he gave half of his cloak to a beggar, and that night had a vision in which Christ appeared as the beggar. Martin's cloak lent its name to chapel (*cappella*), that is, a movable shrine containing his cloak (*cappa*). His cult was one of the most popular in the Middle Ages. [*See* MARTIN'S DAY, ST.]

MARTIN OF TROPPAU (Martinus Polonus), d. 1278, Dominican of Prague, papal chaplain, apostolic penitentiary, and archbishop of Gnesen. He was the author of an uncritical history of the popes and the German emperors.

MARTIN'S DAY, ST., November 11, also called Martinmas, the feastday of St. Martin of Tours. St. Martin's summer was the medieval equivalent of the modern Indian summer.

MARTYRIUM, building honoring the memory or the relics of a martyr; a monument in a cemetery in which a martyr was buried.

MARTYROLOGY, a history or register of martyrs or official calendar of martyrs arranged in order of their feast days. The earliest were simply calendars that merely named the martyr and gave place and date of martyrdom. The later historical martyrologies, such as that of Usard (d. c. 875), a Benedictine monk, supplemented this information with stories about the martyrs. The oldest surviving martyrologies are from the early fifth century.

MARULIC, MARKO, d. 1524, Croatian humanist, moralist, artist, and poet, author of moralistic and historical works as well as the first Croatian epic.

MARWAN II, Omayyad caliph, 744–50, a general who took over the rule of Islam following the abdication of Ibrahim. Revolts that broke out in different parts of the empire plagued his reign, that in 750 lead by the Abbasids resulting in his capture and execution. With his death the Omayyad dynasty came to an end.

MARY, the Blessed Virgin, mother of Christ,

received surprisingly little notice from the early church fathers; her name rarely comes up in early patristic literature. Although her perpetual virginity was probably assumed during the first centuries of the Christian era, it was not until the late fourth and early fifth centuries that it was preached and universally accepted. The major role that Mary was destined to occupy in the development of Christian theology and the first important step taken by the church that would make her devotion the most popular in the Middle Ages was the pronouncement made by the Council of Ephesus (431) which declared her to be the Mother of God (*Theotokos*). In the sixth century the doctrine of the corporeal assumption of Mary into heaven was formulated and shortly after the feast became widely observed. The view that Mary was conceived without original sin (Immaculate Conception) remained a matter of dispute during the medieval period. Documentary testimony to the belief in the efficacy of Mary's intercession and, therefore, direct prayers to her, date from the late third and early fourth century. The devotion to Mary was well established in Eastern Christendom from the sixth century, but it was only as a result of the immense influence of St. Bernard of Clairvaux, (d. 1153) who had a deep personal attachment to her, that it became widespread in the Latin West.

MARY, wife of Cleophas, one of the pious women who stood near the cross on Calvary (John 19:25).

MARY, duchess of Burgundy, d. 1482, daughter and heiress of Charles the Bold, duke of Burgundy, whose hand and possessions were eagerly sought after by France and the Holy Roman Empire. When Charles the Bold died (1477), Louis XI of France seized Burgundy and Picardy and prepared to take over the rest of the duke's possessions, above all the Low Countries. Mary prevented this by granting the estates of Brabant, Hainaut, and Holland the Great Privilege which restored to them the liberties her father

and grandfather had abrogated. She then felt free to spurn Louis's proposal that she marry the dauphin Charles and instead became the wife of Archduke Maximilian of Austria (1477), a marriage that ultimately gave the Low Countries, Artois, Flanders, and Franche-Comté, to the Hapsburgs.

MARY MAGDALEN(E), ST., once a sinner, then a follower of Christ and among the first to visit his tomb after his resurrection. She is not to be confused with Mary of Bethany.

MARY OF BETHANY, sister of Martha and Lazarus. *See* MARTHA, ST.

MARY OF EGYPT, d. c. 421, popular medieval saint who gave up a dissolute life in Alexandria and spent her last 47 years as a recluse in the desert beyond the Jordan.

MASACCIO, TOMMASO GIOVANNI DI, d.1428, one of the greatest of Italian painters whose ability to use light to define the construction of the body and its draperies enabled him to invest his figures with a high degree of naturalism. His works reveal the influence of Giotto, Brunelleschi, and Donatello. Like Donatello he gave less attention to surface appearances than to the portrayal of the human figure which he usually depicted as under stress of some particular emotion. His works include the *Virgin with St. Anne* and frescoes in the Brancacci Chapel of S. Maria del Carmine in Florence. Masaccio died at the early age of twenty-seven.

MASCHALLAH, Arabic for "What Allah wills," a common expression with Moslems. It may also express wonder at his work.

MASO DI BANCO, fl. 1341–6, painter of Florence and Naples whose work is noted for the expressiveness of his poses and for the treatment of draperies. His paintings, which reflect the influence of his teacher Giotto, include *St. Sylvester and the Emperor Constantine*.

MASOLINO DA PANICALE (Tommaso di Cristo-

473

foro Fini), d. c. 1447, Italian painter who worked with Masaccio on the frescoes in the Brancacci chapel of S. Maria del Carmine in Florence. His work has often been mistaken for that of Masaccio. After the death of Masaccio, Masolino's frescoes show a return to the decorative style of his early years.

MASORA (Masorah, Massora), the writings of the Masoretes, that is, Aramaic-speaking Jews of Babylonia and Palestine who sought to establish an authentic text of the Old Testament in Hebrew. Among the problems they faced was the absence of vowels and punctuation marks in the Hebrew texts. The Masoretes (Massoretes), keepers of the biblical text tradition (Masora), flourished in academies of Palestine and Babylonia from the eighth to the tenth centuries. The language of the Masora is mostly Aramaic, although some of the notes appear in Hebrew. Many scholars contributed their time to this work which ceased refinement only c. 1425.

MASS, the eucharistic rite of the Christian church. The word derives from the dismissal formula which ended the service: *ite, missa est,* that is, "Go, the Mass is ended." Although the liturgy and ceremonials of the mass or eucharistic service experienced considerable evolution during the course of the Middle Ages and even though the church was always willing to accept differences in ritual [*see* RITES, ENGLISH MEDIEVAL], the dual function of the mass, namely, that of paying honor to God and of sanctifying man, remained the same. In the opening prayers priest and people acknowledged their unworthiness to address the Almighty. Next they offered their gifts of bread and wine to God the Father, which the celebrant begged God to change into the body and blood of his son (transubstantiation). Finally, in the communion service that terminated the mass, the bread (and wine), now God the Father's gift to man, was partaken of by priest and faithful.

MASS, DRY, a service similar to the mass but with the principal parts omitted. First mention of such a mass appeared in the ninth century.

MASS, MUSIC OF THE. The origins of the music used for the mass service were undoubtedly Hebrew since the first Christians were Jews and the Gospels tell of Christ and his disciples singing a hymn at the Last Supper (Mark 14:26). Pliny the Younger (d. 113) attested to the singing of Christians at their eucharistic service. But the use of song in the liturgy long continued a matter of controversy among the church fathers. What emerged was a compromise that approved of singing but of a kind so simple and plain as to remain wholly subordinated to the liturgy, whence the term plain song or chant. This music held to a modest range of notes, lacked sharps and flats, and usually assigned a single note to each syllable. Because Pope Gregory I (d. 604) introduced a measure of uniformity into the manner this chant was being sung, this plain song often went by the name Gregorian chant.

This plain chant (monomelody) dominated the liturgy in the Latin church until the year 1000 when the first influences of polyphony began to be felt. As time passed and polyphony saw further development, the music of the liturgy by the close of the Middle Ages was offering two contrasting styles, the Gregorian or plain chant on the one hand, and the varied, harmonius polyphony on the other. The portions of the mass that lent themselves especially to the imagination of polyphonic composers were those common to most masses, that is, the *Kyrie Eleison, Gloria, Credo, Sanctus, Benedictus,* and *Agnus Dei.* It was these parts of the mass that in modern times evoked the magnificent renditions of Haydn, Bach, Mozart, and others. Even the plain song had by this time permitted some departure from its early simplicity, and there had come into use different tones, such as the solemn, joyous, and funereal tones, which suited the music to the atmosphere of the occasion. The starkness of the original Gregorian chant still persisted in the so-called propers of the mass, the Introit, Gradual, Offertory, and Communion verses.

MASS OF THE CATECHUMENS, the liturgy of the mass that preceded the offertory, a designation that went back no further than the eleventh century. Persons preparing for baptism were permitted to attend only this first part of the mass.

MASS, SOLEMN, high mass celebrated with the assistance of deacon and subdeacon.

MASTER, name given to various members of medieval society: a) member of the first rank in the guild organization, once a journeyman, who had proved himself a master at his trade and had met other requirements set down for admission to that rank; b) a teacher; c) a commoner poet as opposed to one who was a member of the aristocracy; d) an artist, unknown by name, but identified by the distinctiveness of his style.

MASTER FRANCKE, d. after 1424, a painter of Hamburg who was particularly successful in the art of book illumination.

MASTER OF ALTAR CLOTHS, a painter of Nuremberg known for his altar in the Frauenkirche in Nuremberg (c. 1445).

MASTER OF ARTS, degree granted by the medieval university to the student who had completed the entire arts course and had successfully defended his thesis. The degree formally admitted its recipient to membership in the guild of teachers of the arts and sciences. The titles master and doctor were used somewhat interchangeably with a preference of master being shown for teachers in the arts, doctor for those in theology, medicine, and law.

MASTER OF BARTHOLOMEW'S ALTAR, a Cologne painter active 1480–1510, and identified by his work on the altar of the Munich Pinakothek.

MASTER OF FLÉMALLE, obscure painter of the Low Countries known by no other name but believed to have been the Master of Mérode or Robert Campin (d. 1444). Some scholars maintain he was Rogier van der Weyden.

MASTER OF HOLY VERONICA, Cologne painter active 1410–20, but unknown except for the work that shows Veronica holding the veil with the imprint of Christ's face.

MASTER OF HOUSE BOOK (Hausbuch), German or Dutch painter of the late fifteenth century who made drawings of contemporary life.

MASTER OF KARLSRUHE PASSION, painter of the late fifteenth century known for three panels showing scenes of Christ's passion.

MASTER OF MOULINS. See MOULINS, LE MAÎTRE DE.

MASTER OF ST. GILES, artist of French or Netherlandish origin of the late fifteenth century who is known for two panels concerning the life of St. Giles.

MASTER OF TEGERNSEE, painter identified by his high altar (1445–6) in the abbey church in Tegernsee, Bavaria.

MASTER OF THE AIX ANNUNCIATION, probably a French artist who was influenced by Jan van Eyck in the production of his altarpiece in the Eglise des Prêcheurs in Aix-en-Provence (c. 1445).

MASTER OF THE DUKE OF BEDFORD, French artist who executed a breviary for the duke of Bedford while serving as regent of Henry VI in France.

MASTER OF THE LIFE OF THE VIRGIN, painter of Cologne, fl. 1463–80, known for an altarpiece and triptych depicting incidents in the life of the Virgin Mary.

MASTER OF THE ROHAN BOOK OF HOURS, French painter of the early fifteenth century who executed *Les Grandes Heures du Duc de Rohan*.

MASTER OF THE SACRED PALACE, the pope's theologian. The first person so designated, according to tradition, was St. Dominic (d. 1221).

MASTER OF THE ST. LUCY LEGEND, painter of Bruges of the late fifteenth century who painted scenes from the life of St. Lucy for the church of St. Jacques in Bruges.

MASTER OF THE ST. URSULA LEGEND, painter of Bruges of the late fifteenth century who painted scenes from the life of St. Ursula. His style followed that of Rogier van der Weyden.

MASTER OF TREBON (Wittingau), d. 1380, Bohemian painter of the altarpiece *The Resurrection*.

MASTERSINGER. *See* MEISTERSINGER.

MAS'UDI, AL (Abu Al-Hasan 'Ali Al-Masudi), d. c. 956, Arab historian referred to as the "Herodotus of the Arabs" because of the breadth and volume of his writings and the extensive travels upon which some of these were based. His travels took him through Persia, the Caucasus, India, Ceylon, the China seas, and Madagascar. His observations provide information about the geography of these lands, the mores of their peoples, and their literature and scholarship. He composed a thirty-volume *History of the Universe* of which only one volume survives. His *Golden Meadows* contains valuable information about several of the caliphs.

MATAPAN, Venetian silver coin that circulated between 1200 and the middle of the fourteenth century.

MATILDA (Maud), d. 1167, daughter of Henry I of England, wife of Henry V of Germany, and mother of Henry II of England. When she became a widow, her father prevailed upon her to marry Geoffrey Plantagenet, count of Anjou, in order to furnish the English throne with an heir. Not only did she give birth to the future Henry II but it was also her persistence and driving ambition that finally helped secure Henry's accession in 1154 after the death of Stephen. But for her arrogance, which alienated many would-be supporters, she might have achieved her son's accession in 1141 when her troops captured Stephen.

MATILDA, COUNTESS OF TUSCANY, d. 1115, friend and ally of Pope Gregory VII in his struggle with Henry IV of Germany over investiture. It was in her castle at Canossa that Henry made his submission to Gregory in 1077. On a second trip to Italy in 1081, Henry deposed Matilda, but she came to terms with his son Henry V in 1110 and made him heir of her allodial possessions. Because she had already promised these to the pope, they became and continued to be the source of endless controversy between empire and papacy.

MATINS (Mattins), the divine office recited during the "morning hours." The name was first applied to the office of the lauds which were recited at dawn. Matins were originally said or sung at midnight but moved to the eighth hour, i.e. 2:00 A.M. in the Rule of St. Benedict when it was known as vigils.

MATTEO DI GIOVANNI (da Siena), d. 1495, popular painter of the Sienese School. His madonnas bear witness to his reputation for unusual technical skill and decorative finesse. His paintings include the *Assumption of the Virgin* and the *Massacre of the Innocents*.

MATTHEW OF AQUASPARTA, d. 1302, Franciscan theologian who studied at Paris, taught at Bologna and Paris, and served as lector of the Sacred Palace in Rome. In 1287 he was elected minister general of the order and the year following was created a cardinal. He was a disciple of Bonaventure. His extensive scholastic writings reveal the influence of the Augustinian-Franciscan tradition. He also left sermons and biblical commentaries.

MATTHEW OF WESTMINSTER, name of the imaginary author of the chronicle of English history entitled *Flores Historiarum*. The chronicle, which covers the period from the Creation to 1326, was actually the work of several monks, while the part to 1265 is essentially a copy of the *Chronica Majora* of Matthew Paris.

MATTHEW PARIS, d. 1259, monk of St. Albans who is often considered the leading English chronicler of the Middle Ages. The first part of his *Chronica Majora* is largely an emended version of that of Roger of Wendover, but for the period from 1235 to 1259 his narrative is original and unusually valuable since it was based upon his own observations and the accounts of travelers, many of them from foreign countries, who accepted the hospitality offered by the monastery of St. Albans on their journeys to and from London. [*See* SAINT ALBANS.] His writing is lively and informative, although not consistently impartial, and he gives vent on occasion to the antipapal sentiment that the policy of the papacy aroused in England during the reign of Henry III. On occasion, too, he showed himself sharply critical of Henry III.

MATTHEW'S DAY, ST., February 24, popularly believed to be the first day of spring.

MATTHEW, ST., apostle and evangelist, a tax collector who became one of the twelve apostles and, it is believed, the author of one of the four gospels. In Christian iconography he appears as a winged man (angel).

MATTHIAS I CORVINUS, king of Hungary, 1458–90, statesman, general, administrator, and orator. Through his wife, the daughter of George of Podiebrad, he inherited the crown of Bohemia (1469–78). By way of war or purchase he gained Silesia, Moravia, Lausitz, Styria, Vienna, Carinthia, and Carniola. These possessions, together with alliances with the dukes of Bavaria and Saxony, made him the strongest ruler of central Europe. Much of his military success may be traced to the standing army he was able to maintain. In addition to pursuing his territorial ambitions, he reduced the position of the aristocracy in Hungary, encouraged industry, patronized scholars and artists, founded the first printing press in his country, and established the University of Bratislava (Pressburg, Pozsony). Since his achievements did not long outlive him, historians regret that he did not give his major attention to the menace posed by the Ottoman Turks who shortly after his death overran his country.

MATTHIAS, ST., one of the twelve apostles, the one chosen to replace Judas. His relics were believed to have been transported to Trier.

MAUNDY THURSDAY, Holy Thursday, the Thursday of Holy Week, the word Maundy being derived from the *mandatum novum* (new commandment), given on that day (John 13:34). From at least the fourth century Christ's institution of the Eucharist has been commemorated on that day.

MAURICE (Mauricius, Maurikios), Byzantine emperor, 582–602, a soldier of Cappadocia, then general, married the daughter of Tiberius II and became his successor. He fought the Avars and Slavs who were ravaging the Balkans, strengthened the frontiers of Italy and Syria, and established the exarchates of Ravenna and Africa. In return for aiding Chosroes II (Khosrau) to regain his throne in Persia, Maurice was ceded Persarmenia and East Mesopotamia. The economies he introduced in order to stave off bankruptcy and the military discipline he enforced instigated a mutiny in the army in Thrace, and he was murdered by its general Phocas.

MAURICE (Mauritius, Moritz), ST., d. c. 286, an early Christian martyr, according to a document of doubtful genuineness commander of a Theban legion (from the Thebaid in Egypt) which the emperor Maximian summoned to north Italy in order to aid the army in the suppression of Christianity. When the legion and Maurice refused the order, they were all executed. It is possible that the source of the story concerning

Maurice was the legend about St. Maurice of Apamea, also a military saint, who is supposed to have suffered martyrdom along with 70 soldiers under his command.

MAUROPUS, JOHN, eleventh-century archbishop of Euchaita in Asia Minor and a scholar who left sermons, poems in classical meter, letters, and a large collection of church hymns. For a time he worked as a private tutor in Constantinople, later was brought to the court of Constantine IX (1042–55) by the historian Michael Psellus, one of his pupils, and lectured in the university there. He later became a monk and archbishop.

MAXENTIUS, MARCUS AURELIUS VALERIUS, son of the emperor Maximian and ruler of Spain, Italy, and Africa or parts of those countries as one of several Augusti from 306 until his defeat by Constantine at the battle of Milvian Bridge in 312. He drowned in the Tiber along with thousands of his troops. Although a pagan, Maxentius put an end to the persecution of Christians in his part of the empire.

MAXIMIAN, MARCUS AURELIUS VALERIUS, d. 310, co-Augustus from 286 with Diocletian who assigned him the rule of the western half of the empire. When Diocletian resigned in 305, he obliged Maximian to do the same. But Maximian subsequently resumed the imperial authority in order to aid his son Maxentius and helped him defeat the armies of Severus and Galerius. Upon the insistence of Diocletian he abdicated for a second time. He gave his daughter in marriage to Constantine in order to gain his favor, but appears in the end to have betrayed his son-in-law. Whether Constantine spared his life or whether he forced him to commit suicide remains a question.

MAXIMILIAN I, king of Germany and Holy Roman emperor, 1493–1519, son of Frederick III of the house of Hapsburg, married Mary of Burgundy in 1477, and in 1486 was elected king of the Romans. He became de facto ruler of the empire at that time. In 1490 he drove the Hungarians from Austria and later arranged for the Hapsburgs to succeed to the throne of both Hungary and Bohemia. He surrendered Brittany to France but recovered Artois and Franche-Comté. In 1496 his son Philip married Joan, the daughter of Ferdinand and Isabella of Spain.

MAXIMINUS, GAIUS GALERIUS VALERIUS, called Daia, d. 313, the son of a shepherd, then soldier, and appointed Caesar by Diocletian in 305. He assumed the title of Augustus in 308 and ruled much of the eastern half of the empire including Egypt until 313 when he was defeated by Licinius. He died a fugitive. As emperor he undertook one of the last persecutions of the Christians and sought to revive paganism.

MAXIMINUS, GAIUS JULIUS VERUS, Roman emperor, 235–8, a Thracian, the first "barbarian" to gain the imperial throne. His enormous strength brought him to the attention of the emperor Septimius Severus. Under Alexander Severus he held a high command in the army on the Rhine. When Alexander was murdered, his army on the Rhine proclaimed him emperor. He maintained the Rhine and Danube frontiers against the pressure of Germans and Sarmatians, but at home he was guilty of exterminating many members of the upper classes. He was slain by his own troops.

MAXIMUS CONFESSOR (of Constantinople), ST., d. 662, monk, a leading Byzantine theologian of the period and an active opponent of Monophysitism and Monothelitism. His tongue and right hand were cut off when he refused to halt his attacks on these heresies. His writings include mystical treatises, together with polemical, exegetical, and ascetical works. He gave much attention to the Incarnation and summarized the teachings of the Cappadocian Fathers on the person of Christ. He maintained the procession of the Holy Spirit from the Father alone, a position that at that time was not a matter of controversy.

MAXIMUS, MAGNUS, d. 388, a Spaniard, commander of the Roman army in Britain, who proclaimed himself Roman emperor of Britain, Gaul, and Spain in 383 when Gratian was murdered. He was responsible for the withdrawal of Roman legions from the area of Hadrian's Wall which was never reoccupied. In 388 he was defeated by the emperor Theodosius and executed.

MAXIMUS, ST., d. between 408 and 423, a bishop of Turin. Over 100 of his sermons have survived. They contain much information concerning the history of the liturgy. They also throw light on the survival of paganism in north Italy.

MAY DAY, a festival widely spread throughout medieval Europe that probably had its origins in an ancient fertility feast or in pre-Christian agricultural rituals. Although much variation marked May Day celebrations in different places and countries, the festival usually witnessed the carrying in procession of shrubs, green branches, and flowers, the appointment of a May king and queen, and the setting up of the May tree or Maypole. One of the features of the celebration, that of dancing round the Maypole, has carried over into modern times.

MAY FIELD. *See* MARCH FIELD.

MAYOR OF THE PALACE, court official of the Merovingian kings who by the close of the seventh century had gained ascendancy over the king. The official can be traced back to Roman times when it was customary for great landowners to entrust a *major domus* or mayor of the household with supervisory authority over the managers or *majores* in charge of local or particular estates. The Merovingian kings took over this official who in time acquired new powers such as advising the king on the appointment of counts, protecting the king's *commendati,* and commanding the army. As the position of the Merovingian king weakened because of a number of factors, one that of debauchery, that of the

mayor of the palace grew correspondingly stronger. Finally, in 751, the mayor of the palace in the person of Pepin III (the Short) formally replaced the king and assumed the royal authority. He founded the next Frankish dynasty, the Carolingian.

MAZARIN BIBLE, also known as the Gutenberg Bible, the first printed Bible, probably the first book to be printed with movable type. It was printed by Gutenberg c. 1456.

MAZZOCCHIO, a turban-type cap worn by men in Italy in the fifteenth century.

MEA CULPA, Latin for "by my fault," a phrase taken from the confession of faults (*Confiteor*) recited at the beginning of mass.

MEAD, an alcoholic drink made by the fermentation of honey mixed with water. The drink was popular with the Anglo-Saxons both in Germany and in Britain, as it was with the Welsh. By the close of the Middle Ages, it had generally lost out to wine.

MEATH, county in east Ireland. The hill of Tara was from ancient times until the sixth century the traditional seat of the high kings of Ireland. At Kells the famous *Book of Kells* was inscribed during the eighth century. In 1172 Henry II gave Meath as an earldom to Hugh de Lacy, his viceroy in Ireland. The county came into existence in the thirteenth century. English rule weakened after the middle of the thirteenth century and by the close of the Middle Ages only part of Meath still remained under direct English rule (from Dublin).

MEATH, HUGH DE LACY, d. 1186, Anglo-Norman justiciar and First Lord of Meath, appointed in 1172 by Henry II of England whom he had accompanied to Ireland. For several years, he held the office of procurator general of Ireland. He succeeded in establishing English rule throughout the region. He erected numerous castles, organized the area into 18 baronies, and thereby created an English territorial aristocracy that carried over into modern times. While inspecting a new castle, whose building had necessitated the destruction of an ancient and venerated monastery, he was assassinated.

MECCA, birthplace of Mohammed, the Holy City of Islam, about 50 miles from the port of Jidda on the eastern shore of the Red Sea. Because of the location there of the Kaaba, a temple in which several hundred images of gods worshipped by the Arabs had been gathered, Mecca had become a holy city long before Mohammed made it the center of Islam. (He destroyed the idols but not the Kaaba.) It has remained the center of Islam largely because of the obligation resting upon Moslems of making a pilgrimage to the city once during their lifetime. Mohammed's flight from Mecca to Medina in 622, the *Hegira,* is reckoned as the base year of the Islamic era. Moslem tradition maintains that on the site of Mecca Hagar and her son Ishmael, the father of the Arab nation, nearly died of thirst.

MECHTHILD OF HACKEBORN, ST., d. c. 1299, Cistercian mystic in the convent of Helfta near Eisleben and a sister of Gertrude of Hackeborn, a nun of the monastery at Rodarsdorf who supervised her education. Her revelations have been preserved in the *Liber Specialis Gratiae.*

MECHTHILD OF MAGDEBURG, d. between 1282 and 1294, of noble Saxon parentage, Beguine mystic of Magdeburg who in her later years made her home in the Cistercian convent at Helfta. There she made friends with Mechthild of Hackeborn and Gertrude the Great. Her writings include a mystical work in Low German, spiritual poems, allegories, moral reflections and admonitions. Her poetry possesses high literary qualities.

MECKLENBURG, German duchy located on the south Baltic shore, the area first occupied by Germans but c. 600 taken over by Wends and Obotrites. Henry the Lion (d. 1195), duke of Saxony, reestablished German rule, although he

left most of the region to be held as a fief by the native prince. Missionaries moved into the area along with German immigrants, and shortly monasteries and towns arose together with the two newly erected dioceses of Ratzeburg and Schwerin. In 1348 Charles IV raised the princes of Mecklenburg to the rank of dukes.

MEDICI, wealthy family of Florence which dominated that city for the greater part of the fifteenth century. The family made its appearance in Florence early in the thirteenth century, gradually accumulated immense wealth through trade and money-lending but suffered mixed fortunes in the unstable era of Florentine politics until Giovanni di Bicci (d. 1429) established an alliance with the lower classes. These helped keep the family in power until 1494. Cosimo (d. 1464), the son of Giovanni di Bicci, secured the family's control of the city through a program of public works and a patronage of the arts which assured him the support of the common people and the encomia of the humanists. He founded the city's first public library and financed Marsilio Ficino's Platonic Academy, all the time ruling with absolute authority despite his avoidance of any extraordinary office. His son Piero the Gouty (d. 1469), though made of less stern stuff than his father, continued with the Medici role of "boss" and patron of the arts. Under the leadership of Piero's son Lorenzo the fame and prestige of the family attained its height. His title *magnifico signore,* whence the English Lorenzo the Magnificent, truly fitted the man who gathered about himself in Florence a galaxy of writers, artists, and scientists the like of which had never before been known in Western history. Like his predecessors he, too, ruled without benefit of official office; like them, he was able, although with increasing difficulty, to maintain a balance of power among Milan, Venice, Naples, and Florence. In 1494, shortly after he died, Charles VIII of France invaded Italy, and the people of Florence, under the prodding of the reformer Savonarola who denounced the Medici as a symbol of the city's general corruption, forced the family into exile. The family returned in 1512.

MEDICINE, MEDIEVAL. The principal authority in the field of medicine whom the Middle Ages inherited from ancient times was Galen (d. A.D. 200?) who left an encyclopedia of medical knowledge based upon Hippocrates, Hellenistic physicians, and his own experience as a physician and surgeon. The greatest advance over Galen made in the Middle Ages was the work of Islamic physicians who had immediate access to Galen. While barred by the Koran from dissecting the human body, they contributed significantly to the knowledge of disease since they were the best practitioners of the age and also boasted the most learned writers. The most prolific of the latter was Al Rhazes (d. 923 or 932) who contributed in his 140 books on medicine the most scientific treatise on smallpox to appear before the eighteenth century. The most eminent of all Islamic physicians was Avicenna, who has been called the greatest clinician of the Middle Ages. His *Canon* represented the most systematic and complete syllabus of medical knowledge available to the Middle Ages. Abul Kasim of Córdoba (d. c. 1013) wrote the first illustrated book on the subject of surgery.

The Christian West's contribution to medicine, by contrast to that of Islam, was relatively modest. No great names appear although a large amount of intensive study was carried on at Salerno, Montpellier, Bologna, Padua, and Paris. Salerno, the earliest medical center in the West, owed its repute to the presence there of Greek, Jewish, and Islamic physicians. Medieval physicians made considerable use of herbs and drugs, some of which such as castor oil and camphor still found useful in our modern age. The medieval physician also sought to induce a kind of anesthesia with the use of a liquid consisting principally of opium. His diagnoses were more successful than the means he fell back upon to heal the sick, and apart from such obstacles to progress as the absence of a micro-

scope and the church's ban on dissection, his acceptance of the view that the stars and planets influenced man's health did him no good. Yet Guy de Chauliac (d. 1368), physician and surgeon, merits mention for his writing which had a profound influence upon the progress of surgery.

To the credit of the medieval physician was the near-disappearance of leprosy by means of isolation of the infected. We hear of hernia operations, the grafting of skin, the use of gold leaf for dental cavities, but also of "blood-letting" which was judged an effective means of purging the body of impurities. What might be judged the most valuable single contribution of the medieval West in the field of medicine was the charitable hospital.

The Christian Middle Ages placed great reliance on the help of God and the saints in the cure of maladies. Cosmas and Damian, two brothers who suffered martyrdom (d. c. 303), were revered as the patron saints of the medical profession. More specialized in their concern about diseases and health problems were several of the Fourteen Holy Helpers, the assistance of St. Blaise being sought by persons suffering from throat troubles.

MEDIEVAL LATIN, the Latin employed in Western Europe by the church, schools, and governments from roughly the ninth century to the close of the Middle Ages. It traced its origins to the vulgar Latin spoken by the people of the declining Roman empire, essentially the language which St. Jerome had employed in his Vulgate, then more immediately to the Latin which Charlemagne and his scholars, bishops, and abbots had attempted to standardize as the language of the church and the educated. Medieval Latin lacked the literary grace of classical Latin, and it employed a simpler grammar and sentence structure. However, it could boast of an ever expanding vocabulary. It continued to enjoy general use among the educated until the humanists of the late Middle Ages, in their anxiety to purify the language of non-

Ciceronian words and constructions, brought it into disrepute.

MEDIEVAL LATIN LITERATURE. *See* LITERA-TURE, MEDIEVAL.

MEDINA (Medinet en-Nebbi), pre-Islamic community located in a large oasis about 250 miles north of Mecca to which Mohammed fled in 622. Medina served as the residence of the first three caliphs. Mohammed's tomb is in Medina.

MEINRAD OF EINSIEDELN, ST., d. 861, monk of the Benedictine monastery of Reichenau, later a hermit for seven years on the slope of Mount Etzel. The chapel he constructed there became the site of the monastery of Einsiedeln. He suffered death at the hands of two ruffians he had befriended.

MEINWERK (Meginwerk) OF PADERBORN, BL., d. 1036, chaplain of Otto III and Henry II, later bishop of Paderborn, a man of considerable influence in political affairs and a force in the ecclesiastical, intellectual, and cultural advancement of the church. He was a major figure in the Ottonian renaissance.

MEIR OF ROTHENBURG, d. 1293, opened a Talmudic school in Rothenburg where he gained fame as an authority on rabbinic law. For almost 50 years he served as the supreme court of appeals for Germany and surrounding countries. When Rudolf I in 1286 attempted to abrogate the political freedom of Jews, he became the principal figure in the struggle for Jewish freedom that followed. He eventually led a mass exodus out of Germany but was brought back and imprisoned. His glosses on the Talmud and his numerous *responsa,* that is, his answers to questions concerning law and ritual, possess considerable historical importance.

MEISTERSINGER, German poets and musicians of the late Middle Ages, members of artisan and trade guilds for the most part, who, at the cost of originality and spontaneousness, placed special emphasis upon the technical excellence of their verse. The consequence was a tendency for music, form, and subject matter to remain constant, fixed by an elaborate set of rules, a development that cost the Meistersinger the interest not only of the humanists but of the general public as well.

MELCHITES, Christians of Syria, Palestine, and Egypt who accepted the decrees of the Council of Chalcedon (451) which the Monophysites rejected. The term, which was pejorative in origin (from the Syriac meaning royalist), was used by Monophysites to designate those Christians whom fear had kept loyal to the decrees of the Byzantine emperors.

MELETIUS OF ANTIOCH, ST., d. 381, bishop of Sebaste, appointed patriarch of Antioch in 360 with the approval of both orthodox and Arian factions. When his essential orthodoxy on the question of Christ's nature became apparent, the Arian emperor Constans II ordered him into exile (360). The Arian bishop Euzoius replaced him, but when the orthodox Gratian became emperor, Meletius was restored to his see. He presided at the Council of Constantinople in 381, then shortly after died. But the Meletian Schism, the one to which he lends his name, continued for another 20 years. Perhaps never in the history of the Christian church were so many important personages — popes, emperors, and church fathers, notably Basil of Caesarea, a champion of Meletius — involved in such bitter controversy for so long a time.

MELFI, CONSTITUTIONS OF, name given to the legal and administrative enactments which the emperor Frederick II of Germany decreed for his kingdom of Sicily in 1231. They bore the title *Liber (Lex) Augustalis* although their common designation was Constitutions of Melfi for the place where Frederick promulgated them. They constituted the first systematic body of law possessed by any country in the West. What distinguished them so sharply from those in use in Western Europe was their incorporation of the principles of Roman jurisprudence as opposed to traditional law based upon custom.

MELITIAN SCHISMS. Name of two schisms of the fourth century. The first turned about St. Meletius of Antioch. [*See* MELITIUS OF ANTIOCH, ST.] A second Melitian Schism was caused by Melitius, bishop of Lycopolis in Egypt, whom Pater, bishop of Alexandria, excommunicated because of his refusal to abide by the moderate rules laid down for the reconciliation of Christians who had lapsed under pressure of persecution. Melitius formed his own schismatic church with clergy of his own ordination. His followers continued a rigorous monastic movement until the eighth century.

MELITO OF SARDIS, d. before 190, bishop of Sardis, apologist, theologian, and exegete. His writings, which were in Greek, exerted considerable influence upon the church fathers of his century and that following. The theme of the most important of his surviving works — the *Peri Pascha* ("On the Pascha") — is the new Pascha inaugurated by Christ. It contains polemics against Jews and Gnostics.

MELLITUS, ST., d. 624, first bishop of London and third archbishop of Canterbury. Pope Gregory the Great sent him to Britain in 601 where he served as a missionary bishop among the East Saxons. In 604 he baptized Saeberht, the pagan king of Essex, but in 616 was driven into exile to Gaul when Saeberht died and his three pagan sons succeeded. In 619 he returned and was consecrated archbishop of Canterbury.

MELORIA, rocky islet off the west coast of Italy, just below Pisa, the site of two major naval engagements in the thirteenth century. In the first battle, on 3 May 1241, the fleets of Emperor Frederick II of Germany and of Pisa attacked a Genoese flotilla and captured the French and Spanish prelates who were on their way to Rome where Pope Gregory IX had summoned them for a general council. (Gregory was at war with Frederick and the emperor

expected the council to excommunicate him.) The second battle was fought on 4 August 1284, between the Pisan and Genoese fleets. For two years Genoa and Pisa had been fighting over control of Corsica, although their ultimate objective was commercial control of that part of the Mediterranean. The larger Pisan fleet had engaged that of Genoa when a surprise flank attack by 30 ships from Sardinia resulted in a complete victory for the Genoese. Pisa was no longer able to dispute Genoa's control of that region.

MELOZZO DA FORLÌ, d. 1494, painter of Urbino, Rome, and other cities of Italy, and preeminent as a fresco painter in Rome. Much of his work was commissioned by the papacy, principally by Sixtus IV (1471–84). He is known for his picture of the court of Sixtus IV and the monumental fresco decorating the cupola of S.S. Apostoli. His frescoes demonstrate his ability in perspective and foreshortening.

MELROSE, ABBEY OF, the earliest Cistercian foundation in Scotland. It was founded in 1136 by King David I and was located on the Tweed, two miles from Old Melrose which had disappeared. At Old Melrose the earliest monastery of that region had been established by Columba in the seventh century. The *Chronicle of Melrose,* written by unidentified members of the monastic community, covers events for the years 735 to 1270.

MEMEL, city on the ice-free south shore of the Baltic located just north of the mouth of the Niemen which the Livonian Brothers of the Sword founded in 1253 and colonized with Low Germans. It served as an advance outpost for the German drive to the east. In 1258 it acquired the Law of Lübeck.

MEMENTO, opening word of a prayer said early in the canon of the mass for the living. A second *Memento* which followed the consecration asked God's mercy for the deceased.

MEMLING, HANS, d. 1494, Flemish painter who was born in Germany but spent most of his life in Bruges. His work shows the influence of the Van Eycks and of Rogier Van der Weyden. He was a most prolific painter, a director of a large workshop, and most of the leading galleries of Europe contain one or more of his works. His compositions are well-balanced and harmonious and in a quiet, restrained style. He was especially celebrated as a painter of portraits and altarpieces, e.g., *Portrait of a Young Man, Tommaso Portinari and his Wife, Last Judgment, Seven Griefs of Mary.*

MEMMI, LIPPO, painter of Siena, active 1317–47, who was noted for his extremely sensitive modeling. His works include *Madonna and Child* and *Virgin in Majesty.* He collaborated with Simone Martini, his brother-in-law, in the *Annunciation.*

MEMORANDUM, note, literally "let it be noted," a phrase often used to introduce formal documents.

MEMORARE, opening word meaning "remember" which lent its name to a special intercessory prayer addressed to the Virgin Mary. It has been ascribed to St. Bernard of Clairvaux (d. 1153) although some question remains regarding his authorship since it came into use only in the fifteenth century.

MENA, JUAN DE, d. 1456, Spanish poet and scholar. His verse was greatly influenced by Italian poets, and his masterpiece, a long allegorical poem entitled *El Laberinto de Fortuna,* also known as *Las Trezientas* (it contains 300 stanzas), was modeled upon Dante. His poetry reflects at the same time classical influences, especially from Virgil and Lucan.

MENANDER PROTECTOR, Byzantine historian of the second half of the sixth century, first studied law, then at the suggestion of Emperor Maurice (582–602) prepared a continuation of the history of Agathias which had ended in 558. His own history, which survives only in fragments, notes the invasion of the Kotrigur Huns in 558 and negotiations with the Avars at Sirmium in 582.

MENDICANT ORDERS, "begging orders," religious communities of the late twelfth and thirteenth centuries that adopted the practice of poverty, combined with begging, to voice their protest against the materialism in church and society. Their renunciation of worldly possessions forced them to depend upon begging and casual labor for their livelihood, although it was only the Franciscan order that hallowed poverty as the indispensable means to the fulfillment of its mission. The Council of Lyons in 1274 approved the four orders of Franciscans, Dominicans, Augustinians, and Carmelites. Their members came to be known as friars (from the Latin *frater*), rather than monks, since they chose to work among the people, especially in the towns, and minister to both their spiritual and material needs, combining the vocations of the contemplative with that of a priest. Their houses were called convents rather than monasteries. After some early hesitation, the papacy encouraged the rise of the Mendicants and, to further their activities, generally exempted them from episcopal jurisdiction and extended them broad faculties for preaching and hearing confessions. While these privileges, in combination with the zeal and dedication of the Mendicants, made them the most popular and spiritually active of the religious orders in the thirteenth and fourteenth centuries, they also aroused much hostility, not only from the secular clergy but also from the older monastic communities.

MENDOZA, PEDRO GONZÁLES DE, d. 1495, bishop of two Spanish sees, cardinal archbishop of Seville (1473) and archbishop of Toledo (1482). He was adviser to Ferdinand and Isabella, monarchs of Spain, a humanist, and a patron of scholars and authors. He left writings on political, theological, and legal subjects and translated some classical works into Castilian. Perhaps his greatest achievement was that of helping Isabella succeed her brother as queen of Castile.

MENNAS, d. 552, appointed patriarch of Constantinople in 536 by Pope Agapetus upon the recommendation of Emperor Justinian I to replace Anthimus who had been deposed for his Monophysitism. As patriarch Mennas found himself obliged to condemn the Three Chapters which the Monophysites had already rejected because of their implied support of Nestorianism. This drew upon him the censure of Pope Vigilius, but when the pope came to Constantinople to study the matter more closely, Mennas was able to convince him that the Chapters deserved condemnation, whereupon Vigilius added his own anathema. In general Mennas accepted the view, traditional in Constantinople, that the emperor should have a decisive voice in theological questions.

MENOLOGION, liturgical book containing lives of the saints, arranged by month, and used in the Greek church; a book containing selections from the divine office for the unchanging feasts of the year.

MENSA, that portion of the property of a church used for defraying the expenses of the clergy who lived there; the term applied in the early church to the large tables of stone set over or near a grave and apparently used for receiving food for meals in memory of the deceased.

MERCEDARIANS (Order of Our Lady of Mercy), religious order founded in 1218 by St. Peter Nolasco for the purpose of ransoming Christians held captive by Moslems.

MERCHANT ADVENTURERS, most powerful of the English merchant companies of the late Middle Ages which in 1407 received the monopoly of the woolen cloth trade with the Low Countries and Germany. The great expansion of the English woolen industry in the fifteenth century brought considerable wealth and influence to the Merchant Adventurers at the expense of the Merchant Staplers who exported wool.

MERCHANTS STAPLERS (Merchants of the Staple), an English trading company which enjoyed a monopoly of the trade in raw wool and leather from c. 1350. Its staple port across the Channel was Calais.

MERCHET. *See* FORMARIAGE.

MERCIA, Anglo-Saxon kingdom stretching from Wales to East Anglia and the North Sea. Angles probably moved into the area c. 500, and in the late sixth century it came under the rule of King Ethelbert of Kent. Penda (c. 632–54) brought the country into prominence by winning independence from Northumbria and extending his authority over both Wessex and East Anglia. The frontiers of Mercia expanded even farther during the strong rule of Ethelbald (716–57) and reached their greatest limits under Offa (757–96) whose authority extended over all England with the exception of Northumbria. Partly for reasons of defense, Offa erected a great dike to the west to define the frontier between his country and Wales. In the ninth century the Danes ravaged much of the eastern part of the country and made it part of their Danelaw. Wessex gained momentary control over the western part in 829 and permanent overlordship under Alfred in 885.

MERLIN, the magician and prophet in Arthurian literature, first mentioned by Geoffrey of Monmouth in his *History of the Kings of Britain*. Many political prophecies were ascribed to him throughout the Middle Ages.

MEROVINGIAN DYNASTY, Frankish ruling family, sprung from the semilegendary Merowech, first noted c. 430. The founder of the Merovingian kingdom was Clovis (481–511) who extended his rule over two-thirds of Gaul and made Paris his capital. His successors eventually pushed Merovingian authority to roughly the

485

traditional frontiers of France. Apart from Clovis's talents, a decisive factor in his success was the support of the church hierarchy which he gained by accepting baptism. A principal source of weakness to the Merovingians, on the other hand, was the practice of their kings of dividing the realm among their sons. During the civil wars, which almost invariably followed upon the death of a king, the surviving sons kept surrendering precious crown lands, their chief source of revenue, to buy the loyalty of their counts. The last Merovingian king who exercised some measure of royal authority was Dagobert (d. 639), after whose death his principal official, the mayor of the palace, became de facto ruler. This anomalous situation continued until 751 when Pepin secured the approval of the Frankish princes to depose Childerich III, the last of the Merovingians, and rule in his own name. This Pepin is considered the founder of the new Frankish dynasty, the Carolingian.

MERSEN, CAPITULARY OF, decree issued in 847 by Charles the Bald, king of the West Franks, which required every free man to be subject to some (feudal) lord.

MERSEN, TREATY OF, agreement reached in 870 by Louis the German, king of the East Franks, and Charles the Bald, king of the West Franks, to divide the possessions of their nephew Lothair II, essentially Lorraine, between themselves. This treaty reduced to two portions the tripartite division of the Carolingian empire agreed to in 843 by the Treaty of Verdun. It eliminated the last territories that still remained of the middle kingdom then assigned to Lothair, Charlemagne's grandson.

MERTON COLLEGE, college founded at Oxford in 1264 by Walter de Merton, chancellor of England and bishop of Rochester.

MESOPOTAMIA. Consequent upon the conquest of the region by the Arabs in 634, the culture of Mesopotamia became, and remained, essentially Moslem and Arabic, and its history for several centuries was intimately interwoven with that of Islam. Its capital, Baghdad, shortly grew to be one of the largest, most luxurious, and cultured cities of the world. The great period of the history of Mesopotamia, politically, economically, and culturally, came during the first century of Abbasid rule which began in 750. It reached its highest point, in terms of the brilliance and luxury of its civilization, during the reign of Harun al-Rashid (786–809). Even before the death of this caliph, outlying reaches of the empire were disputing his rule, and by the tenth century certain native dynasties, some as close by as Aleppo and Mosul, were governing their parts of the empire with little or no interference from Baghdad. In 1258 the Mongols under Hulagu overran the area and wreaked such devastation on Mesopotamia, destroying cities and massacring populations, that the region never recovered. Even the irrigation system that had functioned in the lower Euphrates from ancient times, was never restored. Mongol governors administered much of Mesopotamia for the next century, and in 1401 Timur the Lame brought perhaps as much destruction to the area as had Hulagu.

MESROP (Mesrob, Mashtotz), ST., d. 440, monk of Armenia, in 438 patriarch of that country. As part of his objective of eliminating all traces of Syrian institutions and culture from Armenian life, he invented an Armenian alphabet of 36 characters and began the translation of the Bible. He also translated several Greek and Syrian patristic writings into Armenian. He labored as a missionary among the Georgians and Albanians and founded schools and monasteries.

MESSALIANS, also known as Euchites, a Christian sect that appeared in Mesopotamia in the fourth century. The Messalians maintained that Christian baptism did not expel the demon with which all people were born as a result of Adam's sin. Only a life of unceasing prayer and mortification was able to accomplish this.

METAPHRASTES. *See* SYMEON LOGOTHETE.

METHODIUS OF OLYMPUS, ST., d. c. 311, bishop of Lycia (Asia Minor) who was probably martyred during the persecution initiated by Diocletian. Only a small part of his voluminous writings remain extant. His "Symposium" or "Banquet of the Ten Virgins" is the earliest work to extol Christian virginity. In his treatise on the Resurrection in which he attacked Origen, he maintained that a man's resurrected body was the same he had worn during his life.

METHODIUS, ST. *See* CYRIL AND METHODIUS, SS.

METHODIUS I, ST., patriarch of Constantinople, 843–7, who as monk suffered imprisonment for opposing iconoclasm. Later, upon the deposition of John the Grammarian, he assumed the office of patriarch and reestablished the cult of images. He composed several lives of the saints.

METOCHITES, GEORGE, d. c. 1328, archdeacon of Hagia Sophia who took an active part in the Council of Lyons (1274) and joined other members of the Byzantine mission in accepting reunion with the Latin church. When the emperor, who had the encouragement of most of the clergy and populace of Constantinople, refused to ratify this reunion, he was exiled (1283). He composed a number of devotional works, as well as treatises endorsing reunion with Rome.

METOCHITES, THEODORE, d. 1332, Byzantine scholar, patron of learning, author, and statesman. He served as grand logothete under Emperor Andronicus II (1282–1328), but lived his last years as a monk in the Chora monastery. He produced works on natural history, philosophy, and astronomy, rhetorical pieces, letters, and some verse.

METROPOLITAN, an archbishop who exercised authority over suffragan bishops. The earliest of these ecclesiastical prelates were located in the larger cities of the Roman province, whence the term metropolitan. The prelate is first referred to in conciliar documents which appeared in 325 in the decisions of the Council of Nicaea. The duties of a metropolitan included the summoning and presiding over of provincial synods, the visitation of the dioceses under his jurisdiction, and the care of vacant sees. At least in theory he had some voice in the election of his suffragan bishops and some disciplinary powers over them. Their authority varied sharply from country to country and from century to century. Metropolitans were usually archbishops and frequently also primates.

METZ, city in Upper Lorraine on the Moselle. It served as a strong point in the Roman defenses of the Rhine frontier, suffered sacking by Attila in 451, became a bishop's seat in 535 and about the same time the capital of Austrasia, and fell to Lothair in the division of the Carolingian empire. Lothair made Metz his capital. In the thirteenth century Metz received the status of an imperial city. Charles IV issued the Golden Bull from Metz in 1356. The Gothic cathedral of St. Etienne (thirteenth-sixteenth centuries) is noted for its huge pointed windows, slender columns, and the large number of flying buttresses. The church of St. Pierre-aux-Nonnains (fourth century) is the oldest in France.

MICHAEL I (Rhangabe), Byzantine emperor, 811–3, son-in-law and successor of Nicephorus I who supported orthodoxy against the attacks of the iconoclasts and recognized the imperial title of Charlemagne. Shortly after he had sustained a serious defeat near Adrianople at the hands of the Bulgars under Krum, caused partly by the desertion of his troops from Asia Minor, he was deposed and retired to a monastery.

MICHAEL II, Byzantine emperor, 820–9, founder of the Amorian dynasty, a native of Phrygia, a general, assisted Leo V to gain his throne, then joined the conspiracy that ended in Leo's assassination and his own accession. He pursued a policy of moderation on the issue of iconoclasm. During his reign Crete was lost to the Arabs while Saracens conducted deep raids into Sicily.

MICHAEL III (the Amorian or Phrygian), Byzantine emperor, 842–67, son and successor of Theophilus, in 856 wrested control of the empire from his mother Theodora who had been acting as regent. He followed a conciliatory policy toward iconoclasts although he continued to favor orthodoxy. He deposed Ignatius as patriarch and replaced him with Photius, thus precipitating a schism (Photian) with Rome. Wars with the Arabs, Slavs, and Russians disturbed his reign. In 866 he arranged for his groom Basil to murder his uncle and co-emperor Bardas, then shortly after was himself murdered by Basil.

MICHAEL IV (the Paphlagonian), Byzantine emperor, 1034–41, who owed the throne to his brother John the Orphanotrophus, a eunuch high in the counsels of Romanus III. John brought Michael to the court, and when Romanus conveniently died, the empress Zoe, who had fallen in love with him, made him emperor. Michael shortly after pushed Zoe aside and, although suffering from epilepsy, showed himself an eminently energetic and responsible monarch. He retired to a monastery just before he died.

MICHAEL VII (Ducas), Byzantine emperor, 1071–8, eldest son of Constantine X Ducas, more a student than an administrator. He was proclaimed emperor when Romanus IV Diogenes, who had married his mother, was captured by the Turks in the battle of Manzikert (1071). The initiative in the court party that was responsible for his accession was taken by his tutor, the historian Michael Psellus. Michael's weak reign was shaken by revolts and invasions (Turks), and he was finally forced to abdicate. He retired to a monastery.

MICHAEL VIII (Palaeologus), Byzantine emperor, 1259–82, who seized the throne of Ni-caea in 1259 from the Lascarid John IV whom he had served as regent and established the dynasty of the Palaeologi. In 1261 he captured Constantinople from the Latins and Venetians. He made peace with the papacy by accepting the reunion proclaimed by the Council of Lyons in 1274. He demonstrated real talent in preserving his throne and his endangered empire from a host of enemies including the rulers of Sicily, the Serbs, Bulgars, the despots of Epirus and Thessaly, and the Venetians. In all probability he helped arrange the overthrow of the Angevin rule in Sicily in 1282 (Sicilian Vespers) in order to thwart any designs Charles of Anjou might have had on Constantinople. During his reign the Turks overran the greater part of Asia Minor.

MICHAEL, ARCHANGEL, ST., archangel mentioned in the Old Testament, in the *Apocrypha,* and in the *Shepherd of Hermas*. He was venerated as early as the fourth century as patron of the sick in the East and as protector of soldiers in the West. His feast, "Michaelmas Day" (29 September), was associated with many traditions such as the beginning of autumn and the time for the fall meeting of the English parliament.

MICHAEL CAERULARIUS. *See* CAERULARIUS, MICHAEL.

MICHAEL DE NORTHBURGH, d. 1361, confessor to Edward III, keeper of the privy seal, bishop of London (1354), and co-founder of the London Charterhouse.

MICHAEL OF CESENA, d. 1342, Franciscan, a doctor of theology (Paris), and minister general of the order (1316). Together with William of Ockham, he fled to the court of Louis IV of Germany following Pope John XXII's condemnation of the views of the Spiritual Franciscans regarding the absolute poverty of Christ and the apostles. He composed a number of polemical and theological writings.

MICHAELMAS, feast of St. Michael on September 29. *See* MICHAEL, ARCHANGEL, ST.

MICHAEL SCOT. *See* SCOT, MICHAEL.

MICHAEL THE SYRIAN, Jacobite patriarch of Antioch, 1166–99. His chronicle, which extends from the Creation to 1194/5, contains many Syriac sources that are no longer extant. It furnishes information about the Jacobite Church and also about the Crusades.

MICHELOZZO DI BARTOLOMMEO, d. 1472, architect and sculptor of Florence who worked with Ghiberti, Donatello, and Luca della Robbia, after 1438 by himself. In 1446 he succeeded Brunelleschi as architect for the cathedral of Florence. His principal work in the field of architecture was executed for his patron, Cosimo de' Medici, for whom he erected the Medici-Riccardi Palace.

MICROLOGUS, a manual or epitome; an eleventh-century mass-book that throws light on the development of the Latin liturgy. It was probably the work of Bernold, a monk of Schaffhausen (d. 1100).

MIDDLE AGES, term ordinarily limited to Western history and identifying generally the centuries between the decline of Rome on the one hand (300–400) and the beginning of modern history (c. 1500) on the other. Some scholars prefer to introduce the period of the Middle Ages with the German migrations (c. 375) or the deposition of Romulus Augustulus (476) or with Charlemagne (c. 800). There are also scholars who include the period from c. 1350 with the Renaissance. In its broadest application the period of the Middle Ages includes the history of the Byzantine and Islamic worlds to 1500.

The term Middle Ages, in contrast to such traditionally accepted divisions of history as the History of Ancient Times or the History of the Modern World, for many years carried a note of disparagement. Its counterpart, the Dark Ages, was employed first by those scholars and literary figures of the late medieval period who possessed high admiration for the classical world of ancient Greece and Rome and who confidently felt that their literary achievements were bringing back to life the glorious era of Homer and Cicero. The man who first spoke disparagingly of the thousand years that had followed the collapse of Rome was Petrarch (d. 1374) who was inclined to dismiss the nonclassical millennium as the Dark Ages. Although the prejudiced neoclassicism of Petrarch and his successors would not of itself have long stigmatized the Middle Ages, the Protestant writers of early modern times were most ready to second that low judgment since it represented a time dominated by the church of Rome. It remained for the romanticists of the late eighteenth century to first disagree with this assessment of the Middle Ages as being a backward period since they discovered there the origins of their own glorious past. The art historians of the early nineteenth century came forward with their own encomia for the artistic achievements of that period—the term Gothic also possessed at one time a derogatory note—to be joined, finally, by historians in general who welcomed the medieval age as worthy to be studied and honored with any other era of history. Where earlier Protestant historians had emphasized certain defects in the medieval church, they credited that institution with having preserved much of the culture of the ancient world and passing this on to the semicivilized folks who had overrun the Roman empire. They came to view the medieval age as an institutional epoch when the modern state took form, when the university was born, when town life and modern representative government had their birth, when our present art forms were established, when trade, industry, and agriculture as we know them came into existence. These historians found the origins of modern capitalism in the Middle Ages, as well as the origins of most of the great nations of today and the moral and ethical criteria of modern civilization.

MIDDLE HIGH GERMAN, the German literary language of the twelfth to the fifteenth centuries.

MIDRASH, a term derived from the Hebrew meaning "investigation" and referring to certain methods of biblical exegesis and to a class of Jewish writings that employed those methods. The objective of such investigation or search was one of discovering the spirit of a passage, as opposed to its literal interpretation. Midrash made its appearance in the period of the scribes, although the earliest extant collection is from the second century A.D. With the passage of centuries, such a reinterpretation of the formulated law in the Pentateuch had become necessary, and there also existed disagreement between the Pharisees and Sadducees over the status of Oral Law.

MIESZKO I, prince or duke of Poland, c. 962–92, first important member of the house of Piast, who introduced Christianity to his country in 966 and placed his realm under the protection of the pope. He extended the frontiers of his domain to the Oder and Bug to include a large part of Pomerania. In 979 he repelled the invasion of the emperor Otto II, and between 989 and 992 acquired Silesia, Cracow, and Sandomierz from the Czechs.

MIESZKO II, king of Poland, 1025–34, son and successor of his father Boleslaw I. Considerable internal and external strife disturbed his reign. He lost Slovakia, Moravia, Ruthenia, and Pomerania to his neighbors, and in 1032 Conrad II, king of Germany, divided Poland itself between Mieszko and two of his relatives. His kingdom was in real jeopardy of disappearing when it passed to his son, Casimir I, the Restorer.

MIGRATION OF PEOPLES. It is better to classify the general movement of nations that took place in central Europe during the period from the late fourth to the sixth century as migration of peoples rather than Barbarian Invasions as this phenomenon is often described. These peoples moved slowly. There were no roads, and men, women, and children, together with possessions and stock, all moved together. To feed their growing numbers, these peoples were seeking to find homes in regions that were more productive. This took time, decades, sometimes centuries. Their level of civilization was also above that of barbarians. For several centuries German tribes north of the Roman frontier had had contact with the higher culture to the south. Even the mores of the Huns, the most important non-Germanic people on the move during this period, were above the level of barbarians.

German tribes had been bunched along the Rhine and Danube frontiers before the late fourth century when they began to cross over in large number. Many had already moved into the empire. Marcus Aurelius (d. 180) had settled thousands of Germans on depopulated lands and given them the status of allies (foederati). They were to help shore up the frontier. Many Germans had taken service in the Roman army. By the close of the fourth century that army, including its commanders, had become largely German. Roman army camps strung along the Rhine and Danube at Cologne, Coblenz, Mainz, Vienna, and Budapest, had grown into sizable German communities.

Despite this gradual Germanization of the frontier provinces south of the Rhine and Danube, pressure continued to grow steadily more critical as the strength of the empire weakened. About 375, Huns fell upon the Ostrogoths in the region of the lower Dnieper, causing their frightened cousins, the Visigoths, to hurry to the west and, with the permission of an uneasy emperor Valens, cross the Danube. They shortly after revolted, and when Valens attempted to pacify them, they destroyed his army at Adrianople (378).

Theodosius, the successor of Valens, was able to quiet the Visigoths, but they revolted when he died (395), and after plundering Greece, they moved west to Italy. In a desperate effort to keep the Visigoths out of Italy, Stilicho, the general in command of the imperial troops, called in the legions from Britain and the Rhine. This might have saved Rome, but the emperor Honorius had Stilicho executed for treason (408), and two years later Alaric and the Visigoths sacked Rome. From there they went on to carve out a state of their own in southern Gaul (France) and in Spain.

Now that the Rhine had been denuded of troops, a number of tribes crossed over without opposition. The most important of these were the Vandals who plundered their way across Gaul, through Spain, and, under Gaiseric, founded a kingdom in north Africa. The Burgundians had to content themselves with the greater part of the valley of the Rhone. The Franks, who had already moved across the lower Rhine, under Clovis (d. 511) extended their control to the Loire. Meanwhile Angles and Saxons had occupied most of England. After the defeat of Attila and his Huns at Châlons in 451, the Ostrogoths moved into Italy and Sicily under their greatest king Theodoric (d. 526). Finally in 568, the Lombards made their appearance south of the Alps and went on to occupy the greater part of north and central Italy. [*See* VISIGOTHS; VANDALS; BURGUNDIANS; FRANKS; ANGLES; SAXONS; OSTROGOTHS; LOMBARDS.]

MIHRAB, prayer niche in a mosque, located in the wall nearest Mecca.

MILAN, city of Celtic origin just north of the Po, an imperial capital from the time of Diocletian. It suffered severely from the Huns (452) and the Ostrogoths (493), but particularly during the conquest of Italy by the armies of Justinian (534–c. 562). During the early tenth century the town began to recover since its walls offered protection against the raids of the Magyars, but it profited principally from the revival of trade and the stimulation given this by the Crusades. In the early twelfth century a commune replaced the authority of the archbishop. When Frederick I Barbarossa marched down into Italy in 1162 he captured Milan and destroyed it, but it was quickly rebuilt, became the driving force behind the Lombard League, and took the lead in blocking the ambitions of both Frederick I Bar-

barossa and his grandson Frederick II in establishing imperial authority over north Italy. The rivalries of the Guelf and Ghibelline factions, together with the strife among the different classes in the city, kept Milan in some turmoil until 1277 when the family of the Visconti seized control. In 1395 Galeazzo Visconti was granted the title duke of Milan by the Holy Roman emperor. Francesco Sforza, who married the daughter of the last Visconti duke, assumed control in 1447. In 1499 the French army under Louis XII occupied the city. Milan's huge cathedral (Duomo), a late Gothic structure begun in 1386, required five centuries to complete. The church of S. Ambrogio, mostly from the eleventh and twelfth centuries, remains the outstanding Romanesque monument of the city.

MILAN, EDICT OF, an agreement rather than an edict between Constantine I and Licinius, Roman co-emperors, reached in Milan in February 313 and extending toleration to Christians. It was recorded in a rescript issued by Licinius in June 313 for his, the eastern, half of the empire. Eusebius and Lactantius preserved divergent records of the edict. It did not mark the end of all persecution. Licinius later reintroduced persecution in his part of the empire and the emperor Julian (361–3) also ordered repressive measures to be taken against Christianity.

MILCZ (Milic) OF KREMSIER, JAN, d. 1374, chancellor of Charles IV of Germany, a canon of Prague, whose preaching, including his attacks on the vices of the clergy, led him to run afoul of the inquisition at Rome in 1367. He had gone to Rome to preach the need for reform since he believed the world was coming to an end. While in prison he composed his *Libellus de Antichristo*. He has been classified as a pre-Hussite preacher.

MILITARY-RELIGIOUS ORDERS, a uniquely medieval institution that made its appearance in the early twelfth century initially to assist and protect pilgrims on their way to Jerusalem. In a sense the military-religious orders represented the combined ideals of monasticism and chivalry. Knights pledged themselves to observe canonical vows, to practice asceticism, and to recite the canonical hours, while at the same time defending Christendom from the Infidel (and pagans). The orders, which were particularly active in Syria, Spain, and Eastern Europe, enjoyed papal protection and were exempt from the jurisdiction of bishops. A prototype was the Order of the Temple (Order of Knights Templars) founded c. 1119 by Hugh de Payens for the protection of pilgrims going to the Holy Land. An earlier organization with similar inspiration was the Order of the Hospital of St. John of Jerusalem, known as the Hospitallers. Other military-religious orders included the Teutonic Knights, the Knights of the Sword, Knights of Calatrava, Leonese Knights of Alcantara, Portuguese Order of Aviz, and the Aragonese Knights of Montesa.

MILLENARIANISM, a belief, based upon Revelation 20:1 – 15, in a coming period of a thousand years when holiness will reign triumphant, usually with Christ returning and ruling the earth. In the early church millenarian views were found principally among Gnostics and Montanists, but also in the writings of some of the church fathers. Early in his life Augustine entertained millenarian views but he later subscribed to the orthodox position that the reference in the New Testament to the coming of Christ was primarily past rather than future and that the Kingdom of God on earth was embodied in the Christian Church.

MILTIADES, ST., Pope, c. 311–4, met with Western bishops at the Lateran in 313 and announced the excommunication of Donatus. He is listed as a martyr. During his pontificate Constantine gained his crucial victory over Maxentius at the Milvian Bridge. The Edict of Milan also dates from his pontificate.

MILTIADES, a second-century Christian apologist who according to the testimony of Tertullian and Eusebius wrote against the pagans and Jews and the Montanists and Valentinians. His writings are lost.

MILVIAN BRIDGE, BATTLE OF, battle won by Constantine in 312 at this bridge over the Tiber north of Rome against Maxentius and his army. Lactantius hailed Constantine's victory as the triumph of Christ and Christianity, and one that Constantine had gained with the help of God, since it was in accordance with a vision Constantine had had that he ordered the Chi Rho, a symbol of Christianity, to be inscribed on the shields of his soldiers before the battle.

MINARET, lofty tower attached to a mosque from which the muezzin summoned the faithful to prayer. The practice of having such towers originated with Mohammed who gave orders that the faithful should be called to prayer from the highest roof near the mosque.

MINIMS (Minimi), mendicant order founded in 1435 by St. Francis of Paola (Calabria). Its name expressed the aspiration of the members of the order to cultivate the virtue of humility and to live as the least of men and for God alone. They practiced extreme abstinence.

MINISTERIALS (Ministeriales), originally unfree servants holding such offices as butler and steward at the courts of German ecclesiastical and secular princes. Since their responsibilities involved expenses, they were given fiefs from which they derived the means of performing their duties. Such fiefs served in time to improve their social position, which in turn opened the way to greater administrative and political responsibilities. The most important group of ministerials was that in the service of the German kings. In general, they proved themselves loyal supporters of the crown against the ambitions of the aristocracy. By the fourteenth century they had joined the ranks of the lower aristocracy and formed the core of the lesser nobility. While an occasional ministerial might rise to the rank of prince of the empire, the class in general, because of its rapaciousness, constituted an unruly element in late medieval Germany.

MINNESINGER, the German troubadour or lyric poet of the twelfth and thirteenth centuries who sang of love (*Minne*). He was not unlike his counterpart in the Provence and northern France who preceded him in time and from whom he drew his inspiration. The Minnesinger's first theme was courtly love, the love of the knight for his lady. He eventually versed about romantic love as well. Like the troubadour, he usually composed both words and music and performed his songs in open court. The leading German representative of this class of lyric poets was Walther von der Vogelweide (d. c. 1230).

MINORCA, second largest of the Balearic Islands. It was taken from the Moors in 1286 by Alfonso III of Aragon and colonized principally by Catalans. [*See* MAJORCA.]

MINORITES. *See* FRANCISCANS.

MINOR ORDERS, ecclesiastical ranks that included those of porter, lector, exorcist, and acolyte. Before receiving any of these orders, the young man was tonsured, which officially made him a member of the clergy.

MINSTER (Münster), originally the monastery itself, from the high Middle Ages the church of a monastery or a collegiate church.

MINSTREL, a poet and singer, often known as a jongleur and most frequently associated with the twelfth and thirteenth centuries. He usually traveled about living off the largess of the aristocracy. He sang his verses to the accompaniment of a harp or lute, although bagpipe, tabor, and chimebells were not unknown. The themes he used were epic and romantic; the songs he sang were normally not his compositions but those of troubadours and trouvères. A forerunner of the minstrel of the high Middle Ages who

is noted among the Angles as early as the fourth century was the gleeman.

MINUCIUS FELIX, MARCUS, d. c. 250, Latin church father and apologist. His *Octavius* is considered to be among the most scholarly of Christian apologies, less because of its originality than because of its classical refinement. He wrote it in the form of a dialogue between Octavius, a Christian, and Caecilius, a pagan, who is converted in the end.

MINUSCULE, small cursive script that differed from the majuscule in that it consisted not of small letters of equal size, but of both upper and lower case. The Carolingian court adopted a minuscule script c. 780, later referred to as the Carolingian minuscule.

MIRACLE PLAY. *See* DRAMA, MEDIEVAL.

MIRKHOND (Mirkhwand; Mohammed Ibn Kwandshah Ibn Mahmud), d. 1498, Persian historian, author of the voluminous *Rauzat-us-Safa,* a seven-volume history of the Persian dynasties. Since the greater part of his history is based upon sources that have since been published in the original, only the books (V and VI) concerned with the Mongols and Timurids retain historical value.

MISERERE, name given to the penitential Psalm 50/51 which was frequently used in the Christian liturgy. Its opening words were *Miserere mei, Deus* ("Have mercy on me, O God.")

MISERICORD(E): a relaxation of a monastic regulation; monastic dining hall reserved for those who were dispensed from monastic regulations concerning food; a small bracket on the underside of a hinged seat of a choir stall which provided support when a person stood and leaned against it; a dagger used for giving the death stroke to one who was mortally wounded.

MISERICORDIAS DOMINI, second Sunday after Easter so named from the opening words of the Introit.

MISHNAH, term derived from the Hebrew meaning instruction, a collection of Jewish traditional laws completed early in the third century and constituting one of the two main parts of the Talmud. As opposed to Midrash in which exegetical material was attached to the biblical text, Mishnah consisted of exegetical commentaries collected on its own. That of the third century, attributed to Rabbi Judah ha-Nasi (d. c. 220), is considered the most authoritative.

MISSALE, book used for mass and containing all the prayers and readings for the liturgical year, as well as ceremonial directions for the celebration of the liturgy. These materials were once contained separately in the sacramentary, lectionary, and *graduale*. The *missale* appeared in the ninth century but came into general use only in the thirteenth.

MISSALE SPECIALE, a smaller version of the missal that contained only selections intended to serve particular needs. The best known is the *Missale Speciale Constantiense* (of Constance).

MISSI DOMINICI, Merovingian and Carolingian agents or commissaries sent out by the king to check on the loyalty and efficiency of counts and other officials. They also informed local communities of the nature of imperial decrees so that none could plead ignorance of the law. Under Charlemagne (768–814) who made them a regular part of his empire's administrative machinery they consisted of a bishop (abbot) and count who visited districts in which they were strangers. Under a strong ruler such as Charlemagne who had the power to remove or punish negligent or rebellious counts, the system of *missi* worked reasonably well. It broke down during the reign of his weak son Louis the Pious (814–40).

MISSIONS, MEDIEVAL. The spread of Christianity through missionary endeavor might be said to have begun with St. Paul and to have continued through and beyond the Middle Ages. By the end of ancient times and the beginning of the

Middle Ages (c. 400–500), most of the peoples who occupied the territories still, or once, belonging to the Roman Empire, had accepted Christianity. By that time occasional missionaries such as Ulfilas (d. 383) were already converting the semicivilized peoples along the frontiers, initiating a missionary movement that corresponded roughly with the spread of civilization. Although a number of the scores of missionaries who were active in the spread of Christianity gained fame because of the singular success of their efforts — Patrick, Columba, Columban, Boniface, Cyril and Methodius, Ansgar — missionary activity should best be viewed as the slow, persistent work carried on by numerous missionaries, first monks, then friars, who by the close of the Middle Ages had converted all of Europe to Christendom with the exception of Jews and of Moslems in Spain and those portions of southeastern Europe occupied by the Ottoman Turks. Mention should be made of the Christian missionaries, including the Nestorians, who carried the knowledge of Christ to Ethiopia, India, central Asia, and China. Persuasion and instruction were the ordinary tools missionaries employed in converting the heathen, but the key to the conversion of an entire nation was often the acceptance of Christianity by its ruler, and the use of force was not unknown as, for example, in the conversion of the Saxons by Charlemagne and in the activities of the Teutonic Knights in the Baltic region.

MITER (mitre), liturgical headdress of bishops and other ecclesiastical prelates. It was in general use from the twelfth century. In the Latin church it was shield-shaped with two lappets hanging down at the back. In the Greek church it took the form of a crown.

MITHRAISM, ancient Persian religious cult based on the worship of Mithra, the god of light. The cult was popular in the Roman empire of the second and third centuries. In contrast to other cults of that period which were inclined to be immoral and appeal to the sensuous, Mithraism placed emphasis upon such manly virtues as courage and honor. It was largely spread by the Roman army since soldiers often found its tenets appealing. It proved a major opponent of Christianity with which it shared several practices such as baptism and the eucharist.

MOAT, a deep, broad ditch dug around a fortress to impede attackers in their efforts to scale or demolish the walls. When possible the moat was filled with water. This further complicated the work of the enemy since it ruled out the use of movable towers, battering rams, and ladders until the moat had either been filled or a causeway constructed. The introduction of artillery in the fifteenth century virtually ended the era of the moat.

MOCHA (Mokka), principal seaport of Yemen in the fifteenth century. Its principal export was coffee.

MODALISM, heresy that denied the existence or permanence of three distinct persons in God and maintained rather the presence of only modes or aspects of three different persons. It was similar to Sabellianism, Patripassianism, and Monarchianism.

MODEL PARLIAMENT. *See* PARLIAMENT.

MODENA, city west of Bologna in the valley of the Po, the Roman Mutina, a bishop's seat in the fourth century, which was sacked by the Huns and Lombards and revived only in the course of the ninth century. Various factions, usually bearing the labels of Guelf and Ghibelline, kept the city in some turmoil until 1288 when it became a possession of the house of Este. Its cathedral, begun in 1099 in the Romanesque style, contains sculptures and paintings by a number of Renaissance artists. The detached campanile is among the finest in northern Italy.

MOECHIAN CONTROVERSY, dispute precipitated when the Byzantine emperor Constantine VI forced his wife to enter a convent in 795 and married his mistress. The Studite monks protested when Tarasius, patriarch of Constantinople, permitted Constantine to receive the sacrament. Some were imprisoned, others exiled. Peace returned in 797 when Irene, Constantine's mother, seized the throne, but trouble erupted again when she was deposed. It remained for Michael I (811–3) and Pope Leo III to end the controversy. The controversy derived its name from the Greek meaning adultery.

MOHAMMED (Muhammad) (Abu 'l-Kasim Muhammad ibn 'Abd Allah), d. 632, founder of Islam, born c. 570 into the Hashim clan and, being left an orphan, raised by his uncle Abu Talib. His marriage to the wealthy widow Khadija enabled him to devote his time to prayer and preaching. At about the age of forty he began to receive revelations, some from God directly, others through the instrumentality of the angel Gabriel. The ideas he wove into his religion were drawn principally from the Old Testament. They stressed the almighty power of God and his goodness; man's duty to worship and obey God; his duty, as well, to be generous to the poor since they were God's creatures; and, finally, man's obligation to avoid sin since God would punish in hell all who ignored his commandments. The monotheism he preached, his claim to be Allah's prophet, and his condemnation of their ancestors to hell antagonized the leaders of the Kuraish tribe that ruled Mecca, and after his wife and Abu Talib had died, Mohammed fled Mecca in 622 (*Hejira*) and found refuge in Medina. In 630 he returned with an army of Medinans, occupied Mecca, purged the Kaaba of its idols, and inaugurated a theocracy. By the time of his death two years later most Arabs had accepted him as Prophet. [*See* KORAN; HADITH; ISLAM; KAABA.]

MOHAMMED (Medmed) I, Turkish sultan, 1413–21, the son of Bayazid I. He dedicated himself to restoring the vitality of the Ottoman empire following the disastrous defeat the Turks had suffered in 1402 at Angora at the hands of Timur the Lame. He managed to reestablish

Ottoman rule over the greater part of Asia Minor.

MOHAMMED (Fatih) II, Turkish sultan, 1451–81, captured Constantinople in 1453 and conquered what remained of Byzantine possessions. He made the city his capital, settled there people from other captured cities, and extended privileges to the Greek and Armenian citizens of that city. He turned the great church of Hagia Sophia into a mosque. He conquered what lands in the Balkans still remained in Christian hands, seized several of the islands in the Aegean that Venice held, and extended his rule over all of Asia Minor. He is regarded as the founder of the Ottoman Empire.

MOHAMMED IBN TUMART, d. 1128 or 1129, Berber theologian and reformer and founder of the empire of the Muwahhids (Almohads). He spent some time in Baghdad where he came under the influence of Al-Ghazali. After his return to al-Maghrib, he preached religious reform based upon the doctrine of the oneness of God. After the warrior Abd Al-Mu'min had assumed military leadership of the Muwahhid movement which Tumart had initiated, they proceeded to destroy the Murabit (Almoravid) empire and established that of the Muwahhids or Almohads.

MOLAY, JACQUES DE, d. 1314, last grand master of the Knights Templars who distinguished himself fighting the Saracens in Syria. When the Crusaders were driven from Palestine, he moved to Cyprus. In 1306 he was summoned to France by Pope Clement V who did so under pressure from Philip IV, king of France, who wanted to suppress the order so he could confiscate its enormous wealth. In 1307 all the Templars in France including Molay were arrested and their property seized. A number of Templars, including Molay, confessed under torture that they were guilty of heresy. Still under pressure from Philip, Clement ordered the Templars suppressed and Molay and other dignitaries impris-

oned for life, whereupon Molay and the others retracted their confessions and were burned at the stake.

MOLDAVIA (Moldova, Moldau), principality west of the Dniester, part of the Roman province of Dacia which, despite being overrun by a series of invaders, managed to retain its Latinized speech. In the thirteenth century a Mongol invasion ended the rule of the Cumans, and in 1359 it passed under the rule of its native prince or woiwode Bogdan. At this time Moldavia included Bukovina and Bessarabia. In 1475 it reached the height of its power under Stephen the Great when he routed the Turks. In 1504 it became tributary to the Turks.

MOLINET, JEAN, d. 1507, court poet and chronicler in the service of Charles the Bold of Burgundy and after his death of his daughter Mary. He also composed a prose version of the *Roman de la Rose,* mysteries, and religious poems.

MOMBRITIUS (Mombrizio), BONINUS, d. c. 1500, humanist of Milan, teacher of the classics and a poet. He translated classical works, compiled a collection of legends of the saints, and left six books of his own poems in hexameter verse.

MONARCHIANISM, a heresy denying the distinctness of the three persons of the Trinity and affirming the sole deity of God the Father. It appeared in the second and third centuries when it usually took one of two forms: "Adoptionist" Monarchianism, which maintained that Christ was a mere man who had become the Son of God simply because of the high degree with which he was filled with divine power and wisdom at his baptism; and "Modalist" (Sabellian) Monarchianism, which held that the names Father and Son were simply different designations of the one and same God and that the only differentiation in the Godhead was a succession of modes or operations. They were also called Patripassians since it followed from their doctrine that the Father suffered with the Son.

MONASTERY, the home or dwelling(s) occupied by monks, clerics, or religious women living a common spiritual life; the community living in such a house. A monastery might consist of a gathering of simple huts grouped about a structure that served as chapel and assembly-room, such as that of the Camaldolese, or an elaborate establishment like the monastery of St. Gall whose buildings included a church, cloister, sacristies, novitiate, refectories, infirmary, dormitories, guest houses, cellar, workshops, scriptorium, library, kitchens, bake house, mill, kiln, barns, and stables.

MONASTERY, DOUBLE. *See* DOUBLE MONASTERY.

MONASTICISM, the way of life followed by ascetically minded men and women who withdrew from society in order to serve God more perfectly through prayer and self-denial. It took two general forms: anchoritism, which was the practice of monasticism by anchorites or hermits, and cenobitism, its practice by members of an organized community. The origins of monasticism become visible by the third century, especially in Egypt and Syria where the proximity of the desert invited men to take up a solitary life. Tradition honors Anthony (d. 356) as the father of monasticism. He gave counsel to other hermits whom the fame of his sanctity had attracted to the uninhabited oasis east of the Nile which he had made his home. His younger contemporary Pachomius (d. 346) introduced cenobitism near Tabennisi in upper Egypt where he organized communities of men who lived in cells of their own but gathered for prayer and instruction. Many of the Eastern church fathers spent some years as anchorites. Among these was Basil of Caesarea (d. 379), whose writings influenced the development of Eastern monasticism and whose influence served to convince dubious churchmen of the spiritual value of the institution.

Only with reluctance did monasticism move to the west. The climate there was less suited to the kind of monasticism practiced in the east nor was the level of religious maturity sufficiently high to induce men to accept the rigors of Eastern asceticism. The history of the early founders of western monasticism includes Jerome, Martin of Tours, Augustine of Hippo, John Cassian, and, above all, Benedict of Nursia (d. 547?). The monastic rule that Benedict introduced for the community he founded at Monte Cassino, by reason of its moderation and its insistence upon organization and obedience, assured the spread of Benedictine monasticism throughout western Europe. Except for Celtic monasticism, which traced its origins to St. Patrick (d. 461?) and produced zealous and learned missionaries like Columba and Columban, the work of converting and civilizing the pagans of western Europe became, and remained, the prime responsibility of the Benedictine monks.

Almost as constant a theme in the history of Western monasticism as its growth was the demand for reform. This goal was met in two ways: by modifying the Rule of Benedict to suit new circumstances, and by establishing new orders. New religious communities that made their appearance during the eleventh and twelfth centuries included the Camaldolese, Valombrosans, Carthusians, the Congregation of Cluny, Cistercians, and Premonstratensians. The Mendicant orders, especially the Franciscans and Dominicans, dominated the thirteenth century. They made a formal break with the traditional role of the monk as a contemplative by introducing the friar who combined the spirit of the cloister with an active apostolate. During the later Middle Ages, after the ardor inspired by the rise of the Mendicant orders had spent itself, new religious orders again made their appearance, presumably in answer to new needs. These included the Olivetans, Franciscan Observants, Minims, Brothers of the Common Life, and the semi-lay organizations of the Beguines and Beghards.

The contribution of monasticism to the

medieval church and society was inestimable. The monk and the friar converted and civilized the pagan Celt, German, and Slav. He preserved learning, continued its existence through the copying of manuscripts, maintained schools, and staffed universities. He dispensed most of the charity distributed during the medieval period. The papacy could not have achieved its position of leadership without the aid of monasticism, while the religious life of the secular clergy and lay society would have been infinitely poorer without its inspiration and leadership.

MONDINO DE' LUZZI, d. 1326, student of pharmacy and medicine at Bologna, then a teacher there of anatomy and surgery, and the author of *Anathomia,* an authoritative work on anatomy. He was instrumental in securing authorization for the dissection of human cadavers. In this work he depended principally upon the writings of Galen but he illustrated these on the basis of the human dissections he had performed. His dissections were almost the first undertaken since ancient times.

MONEY, MEDIEVAL. The rulers of the Germanic kingdoms that replaced the Roman empire inherited Rome's monetary system which Constantine the Great (I) had reformed, but because of unstable political conditions, along with a lack of administrative knowledge, they found it impossible to maintain. The consequence was reliance upon barter with monetary units serving at best as yardsticks of value rather than as means of payment. The situation in the eastern half of the Roman empire was quite different. There the Byzantine bezant, the old Roman *solidus,* and the Arabic dinar maintained their monetary integrity and thus gained universal acceptance, not only in the Mediterranean world but in western Europe as well.

In 755 Pepin, king of the Franks, struck a silver penny (*denarius*) which, although popular, did little to stabilize the money situation in western Europe since every lord during the feudal period which followed, enjoyed or usurped the right to coin money and to establish his own standards of weight and purity. A major breakthrough came in the twelfth century when Venice minted a highly respected silver penny. In the thirteenth century Florence and Venice began to mint gold coins (florins and ducats, respectively) which contributed significantly toward stabilizing the monetary system in western Europe and helped make possible a vast expansion of trade and industry in the later Middle Ages. In the late fifteenth century the discovery of great silver deposits in central Europe finally relieved the basic problem of a lack of bullion that had hampered the establishment of a monetary system. [*See* BANKING.]

MONGOLS, nomadic tribes of the steppes of eastern Asia, generally known as Tartars (corruption of Tatars). Their home lay southeast of Lake Baikal and they have been identified as descended from one of the Altaic or Turko-Mongolian ethnic groups. Little was heard of the Mongols before the emergence in 1206 of Temugin, son of a Mongol chieftain, who assumed the title Genghis Khan and welded the Mongols and related tribes of Turkish origin into a powerful confederation. He made the city of Karakorum his capital and through conquests attended by incredible cruelty and slaughter established an empire that stretched from north China and Korea to the Caspian and from the Danube to the Arctic. Although the Mongols possessed a lower culture than the majority of the peoples they conquered, their highly disciplined and mobile army proved irresistible. They also employed terror as a weapon, the result being that a number of cities surrendered before attack in the hope, usually vain, of escaping destruction and enslavement.

The Mongol empire of Genghis continued to expand during the reign of his son Ogadai. Sabutai, a general, and Batu, a grandson of Genghis, conquered Russia with the exception of Novgorod, then Hungary, and doubtless would have moved into central Europe had not Ogadai's death in 1241 necessitated a *kuraltai* (*quiriltai*). This involved the gathering of the members of the ruling family and the chief nobles in distant Karakorum where they would select a new khan. After some difficulties they agreed on Mangu (1251–9), a son of the youngest son of Genghis. His brothers Hulagu and Kublai thereupon proceeded to conquer the last important parts that ultimately made up the immense empire of the Mongols. Hulagu destroyed the Assassins in Persia, stormed and destroyed Baghdad (1258), and slew Musta'sim, the last of the Abbasid caliphs. From Iraq he moved into Syria, captured Damascus and Aleppo, and razed the huge city of Antioch. Further advance was halted when another *kuraltai* forced him to return to Mongolia. During his absence a Mamluk army from Egypt dealt his own army a major defeat, which probably saved Egypt and perhaps Greece as well from the Mongols. Kublai meantime was conquering south China and Burma although before he had accomplished this he had succeeded as great khan in 1260. Although the empire of Kublai was the most extensive in the history of the Mongols, it lacked the unity which only men of Genghis's fierce ambition and ruthlessness could provide it. The khanate of the Golden Horde with its capital at Sarai on the Volga became to all intents and purposes an independent country. Furthermore, as the Mongols settled down to live in the lands they had conquered, they gradually lost their primitive ferocity and with this their invincibility. Only in the steppes of Asia did they retain their native characteristics, but there they lacked the leadership of a genius such as Genghis to forge them into a united nation. [For a later resurgence of Mongol power, *see* TIMUR THE LAME.]

MONICA, ST., d. 387, wife of Patricius, a pagan official, and mother of St. Augustine of Hippo. Augustine's *Confessions* constitutes the principal source of information concerning Monica. He says it was her unceasing prayers that brought about his conversion.

MONK, male member of a monastic community who lived according to the religious rule adopted by that community, usually one that required vows of chastity, poverty, and obedience. The word is derived from the Greek meaning alone, which suggests the role of a solitary and contemplative to which the monk aspired. He is to be distinguished from a friar, the name given to members of religious communities who combined the life of the contemplative with an active apostolate (e.g., Franciscans).

MONOPHYSITISM, heresy of the fifth and sixth centuries which grew out of the reaction to Nestorianism. In its extreme form it admitted of but one nature in Christ, the divine, as against the orthodox teaching of a double nature, divine and human. This view has been traced to the teaching of Cyril (d. 444) and Dioscorus (d. 454), patriarchs of Alexandria, who overemphasized Christ's divine nature, and especially to Eutyches (d. 454), a monk of Constantinople. Although the position taken by the Monophysites suffered condemnation by the Council of Chalcedon in 451, Monophysitism remained a force in the Eastern church until the Council of Constantinople II (553) which also condemned it. Even then its influence within the Byzantine empire continued to be a major disturbing element until Islam's conquest of Syria and Egypt (635–42) where it had become most firmly entrenched. Monophysitism lived on in the Coptic, Jacobite, and Armenian churches. A major reason for the endurance of Monophysitism and for the great controversies in which it involved Eastern Christianity was the fact that the line dividing orthodoxy from moderate Monophysitism was not easy to define.

MONOTHELITISM, a heresy of the seventh century that accepted the existence of two natures in Christ but of only one will. It represented a seventh-century attempt to discover a position between Orthodoxy and Monophysitism that both groups could accept. [*See* MONOPHYSITISM.] It was condemned by the Sixth Ecumenical Council of Constantinople (III) in 681.

MONREALE, town in Sicily that grew up around a Benedictine monastery established in 1174 by William II of Sicily. Its abbot exercised episcopal and, from 1183, archiepiscopal rights. Its famed cathedral, a Romanesque basilican church begun in 1172 and substantially completed by 1189, reveals Byzantine, Saracen, Italian, and Norman influences.

MONSTRANCE. *See* OSTENSORIUM.

MONSTRELET, ENGUERRAND DE, d. 1453, French chronicler, member of a noble family of Picardy, who saw service in the court of John of Luxemburg. His *Chroniques,* whose concern was essentially France, covers roughly the years 1400 to 1444 and is especially valuable for the final stages of the Hundred Years' War.

MONTAGNA, BARTOLOMMEO, d. 1523, Italian painter, founder and most important representative of the school of Vicenza. He limited his painting to religious subjects who tend to be severe in design but dignified and beautifully colored. Among his most highly regarded works are the great altarpiece for S. Michele at Vicenza (*Madonna Enthroned*) and a series of frescoes illustrating the life of St. Blaise in the Church of San Nazaro in Verona.

MONTAGU, family name of the earls of Salisbury from the late Middle Ages. The ancestor of the family has been traced to the Domesday Book where he is listed as a large landholder in Somerset. His descendant, Simon de Montagu (d. 1316), was the first member of the family to achieve prominence. The first of the family to hold the title earl (of Salisbury in 1337) was William who was responsible for the conspiracy at Nottingham Castle in October 1330 that resulted in the overthrow of Roger Mortimer and Queen Isabella, and opened the way to the

accession of Edward III. He received rich rewards in lands, including the Isle of Man. The fortunes of the family fluctuated during the unstable late fourteenth and fifteenth centuries. Alice, the heiress of what remained of the family's lands, married Sir Richard Neville who became earl of Salisbury in her right. Their eldest son was Richard Neville (d. 1471), earl of Warwick, the "Kingmaker." [*See* WARWICK, RICHARD NEVILLE, EARL OF.]

MONTANISM, a second-century apocalyptic movement which originated with Montanus, a Christian of Phrygia (d. 175), who may once have been a priest of Cybele but later claimed to be the agent of the Holy Spirit. He was joined in his work by two women, Prisca (Priscilla) and Maximilla, who also claimed to possess the power of the Paraclete. The Montanists practiced a rigorous, almost fanatical, kind of Christianity. They disallowed second marriages, condemned existing fasting regulations as too lax, and forbade flight to escape persecution. They also believed in the imminent second coming of Christ. For a time Tertullian belonged to the sect. Montanism prospered until the close of the fourth century.

MONT CENIS PASS, pass located in Savoy, a historical invasion route, crossing the Western or French Alps between France and Italy. It proved of great importance to the revival of trade and the rise of towns in the high Middle Ages.

MONTE CASSINO, ABBEY OF, motherhouse of the Benedictine order located about halfway between Rome and Naples, founded c. 529 by St. Benedict when he moved there from Subiaco. The Lombards destroyed the abbey c. 581, the Saracens in 883, and an earthquake in 1349. Monte Cassino reached the height of its intellectual and spiritual influence in the eleventh century under Abbots Richer and Desiderius.

MONTE CORVINO, GIOVANNI DI, d. 1328, Franciscan missionary, founder of the earliest Christian missions in China, and first archbishop of Peking. In 1289, when working as a missionary in Armenia and Persia, he was sent as a papal legate to the court of the Great Khan at Tabriz, the chief city of Mongol Persia. From there he moved down into India, thence to Peking where he was created archbishop in 1307.

MONTEFELTRO (Montefeltre), name of a city and an aristocratic family located east of Florence. During the thirteenth and early fourteenth centuries members of the family were among the most prominent Ghibelline leaders in central Italy. At that time they were enemies of the papacy (and the Guelfs). In the late fourteenth century they served as vicars of the pope and enjoyed papal support against the Malatesta lords of Rimini. Frederigo III (d. 1482) captained the armies of Pope Pius II, and in 1474 Pope Sixtus IV made him duke of Urbino. Under him Urbino gained fame as a center of Renaissance culture.

MONTENEGRO, mountainous country of the Adriatic around Kotor and Scutari, known as the district of Zeta, part of the Serbian empire of Stephen Nemanja in the late twelfth century. When that empire disintegrated after 1355, the Balshich family ruled in Zeta until 1421. Many Serbs found refuge in Zeta after their disastrous defeat at the hands of the Turks at Kossovo in 1389. In the early fifteenth century Venice secured control of most of the Dalmatian coast, including Kotor. It was as vassals of Venice that the Crnojevich family succeeded to the Balshich. But the most formidable threat to Montenegro was not Venice but Turkey which had seized most of the country by the close of the Middle Ages.

MONTESA, KNIGHTS OF, military-religious order founded in 1317 by Pope John XXII at the request of James II of Aragon for the purpose of assuming possession of the properties belonging to the suppressed Templars.

MONTES PIETATIS, nonprofit credit organizations established by Franciscans about the mid-

dle of the fifteenth century to provide money for the poor at low rates of interest. The first of these appeared in Perugia. They drew criticism from the Dominicans on the ground that canon law forbade the charging of interest (usury). [*See* USURY.]

MONTFERRAT (Montferrato), MARQUESSATE OF, small principality in northwestern Italy, lodged between Savoy, Milan, and Genoa, which the Aleramici family ruled from the late tenth century until 1306 when the line became extinct. Margrave Boniface I, a poet, was one of the leaders of the Fourth Crusade (1202–4) and became king of Thessalonica. In 1310, a member of the imperial Byzantine family of the Palaeologi was invested with the march by the German emperor Henry VII.

MONTFORT, SIMON DE, d. 1218, count of Montfort and earl of Leicester, ambitious, able, and fanatically religious. He led the crusade in southern France against the Albigenses. In 1209 the papal legate invested him with the viscounties of Béziers and Carcassonne which he had seized from Raymond VI of Toulouse who was an ally of the Albigenses. He continued his war against Raymond and his ally Peter II of Aragon, and was slain in the siege of Toulouse. Through his mother he claimed the English earldom of Leicester which he passed on to his son Simon, the leader of the English barons in their war against Henry III.

MONTFORT, SIMON DE, d. 1265, son of Simon de Montfort, came to England in 1229 and two years later was recognized as earl of Leicester. He became influential at court and married Henry's sister Eleanor. In 1240 he distinguished himself in Palestine on a crusade led by Richard of Cornwall. In 1248 Henry III sent him to pacify Gascony which he accomplished so ruthlessly that he was recalled. In 1258 he joined other barons who were critical of Henry's administration and forced him to surrender most of his powers to a committee under the Provisions of

Oxford. Simon was a member of the committee. In 1263 he assumed leadership of the Barons' War against Henry and the year following defeated and captured the king at Lewes. But the next year he lost his life at the battle of Evesham. Simon's name is linked with the rise of parliament, as the great council he summoned in 1265 was the first to include members of both the shires and the boroughs, an innovation Edward I found prudent to adopt.

MONTPELLIER, city in southern France founded in 737. In 1204 it became a possession of Aragon, of the kingdom of Majorca in 1276, and of France in 1349. The University of Montpellier was founded in 1220 and was confirmed by the pope in 1289. It gained fame as a leading center in the study of medicine.

MONT-SAINT-MICHEL, ABBEY OF, Benedictine monastery on the southwestern coast of Normandy founded in 966 by Richard I, duke of Normandy. According to a legend, St. Aubert, bishop of Avranches, erected an oratory there c. 708 on instructions from St. Michael the Archangel. The abbey stands on the top of a rocky islet that at high tide is cut off from the continent. The abbey consists of a gigantic pile of structures rising three stories high and serves, together with the summit of the cone-shaped rock, as a base for the great abbey church that crowns them. The result is one of the most imposing achievements of Gothic architecture. The abbey was fortified in the thirteenth century and withstood English capture during the Hundred Years' War.

MONTSERRAT, ABBEY OF, Benedictine monastery located more than halfway up a mountain near Barcelona, founded as a priory by Oliva of Ripoll c. 1025. (Only ruins remain of the original monastery. The new monastery was built in the nineteenth century.) The shrine, dedicated to Our Lady of Montserrat, was founded early in the eleventh century and became a popular pilgrimage resort. It contains a wooden statue of the Virgin and Child, the faces of both mother and son blackened from the smoke of the lamps and candles burning through the centuries. In the Middle Ages the mountain was believed to have been the site of the castle of the Holy Grail.

MONUMENTA GERMANIAE HISTORICA, the first and most distinguished collection of source materials pertaining to the history of Germany in the Middle Ages. The first of more than 120 volumes was published in 1826.

MOORS, term applied by Christian writers of the Middle Ages to all Moslems, more narrowly to the Berbers of North Africa and the Moslems of Spain.

MORALITY PLAY. *See* DRAMA, MEDIEVAL.

MORAT, BATTLE OF, battle fought in 1476 which ended in an overwhelming defeat for Charles the Bold, duke of Burgundy, at the hands of the Swiss.

MORAVIA, region to the east of Bohemia, occupied first by Celtic tribes, then by Germans including the Quadi, followed c. 550 by the Moravians, a branch of the West Slavs, and by Avars in 567. Charlemagne extended his authority over the area but by the first half of the ninth century Moravia had become an independent state. In 863 the missionaries Cyril and Methodius came to Moravia in answer to an appeal sent by Duke Rostislav to the Byzantine emperor, and soon after the Moravians as a nation accepted Christianity. Magyars plundered the country early in the tenth century but were driven out by Otto I in 955. In 1029 Moravia was incorporated into Bohemia, after which its history was usually linked with that of its larger neighbor.

MORAVIAN CHURCH, a religious sect centered in Moravia whose nucleus consisted of moderate Hussites (Utraquists or Calixtines) who in 1457 became organized under the name *Fratres Legis Christi,* commonly known as Bohemian Brethren or simply as Brethren. They made the

Bible their sole rule of faith, observed an exemplary moral discipline, and accepted as a principle the priesthood of all believers. Despite continued persecution, they managed to survive until assured relative security with the coming of the Protestant Reformation.

MORAY (Murray), EARLDOM OF, title associated with one of the provinces of Scotland. The first known earl was Thomas Randolph (d. 1332) who was created earl (c. 1312) by his uncle, Robert I, the Bruce. After Robert's death, Thomas was regent for his son David II. He served on many embassies, one in 1323 when he went to Avignon and persuaded Pope John XXII to recognize Robert Bruce's right to the throne. He also proved himself a valiant warrior and played an important role in the Scottish victory over the English at Bannockburn (1314).

MORGARTEN, BATTLE OF, great victory won by the Swiss east of Lucerne in 1315 over the Austrian army commanded by Leopold I.

MORGEN, old German field measure approximating an acre, the amount of land that could be plowed in the course of a day's work.

MORGENGABE, German for morning gift, that is, the gift the husband made his bride at the end of the nuptials, later understood to constitute a payment for her virginity.

MORGENSTERN, a striking weapon, suggestive of a mace, with iron points often protruding from its head. It was used from the fourteenth century.

MORISCO, the name given to a Moslem in Spain who accepted Christianity.

MORIZ VON CRAUN (*Craon*), Middle High German poem composed about the beginning of the thirteenth century which told of the love adventures of a French minnesinger of the same name.

MOROCCO, country in northwestern Africa, fronting on the Atlantic and Mediterranean, in Roman times roughly coextensive with the province of Mauretania. Vandals passed through the country in the fifth century, and in 710 Arab Moslems established their rule. In 788 Morocco became an independent state under Idris I, whose son Idris II founded the town of Fès (808) to serve as his capital. In 974 the country lapsed into anarchy, but it revived, first under rule of the Fatimid caliphs of Egypt, then under two native Berber dynasties, the Almoravids and Almohads. These last two extended their rule into Spain. The Merinid dynasty governed the country from 1259 until 1550.

MOROSINI, aristocratic family of Venice that produced statesmen, generals, cardinals, and doges. Domenico M., d. 1156, doge in 1148, extended Venetian rule to Istria, Dalmatia, and the Adriatic. Antonio M., d. c. 1434, composed such an accurate history of Venice that the government ordered him to alter his account.

MORRIS DANCE (moriska, morrice, moresca, Moriskentanz), individual or group dance of the late Middle Ages which was possibly brought to Europe by the Crusaders as suggested by the occasional use of Moorish garb. It took various forms in different countries. In England it gave its name to a grotesque dance performed by persons in fancy costume, usually representing characters from the Robin Hood legend, e.g., Maid Marian.

MORSE (monile, fibula, firmale, pectorale), the rectangular decorated piece of material attached to the two front edges of the cope or cape to prevent it from slipping from the shoulders.

MORTIMER, name of a powerful Anglo-Norman aristocratic family located on the Welsh border which enjoyed great prominence in the thirteenth and fourteenth centuries usually as earls of March and Ulster. As marcher lords they were frequently engaged in warfare against the native Welsh, while their extensive landholdings and the large number of retainers they maintained usually involved them in political disputes over the throne. Roger Mortimer (d. 1282) had an important role in the final defeat of Simon de Montfort at Evesham (1265) but devoted most of his energies to fighting the Welsh. Another Roger (d. 1330) took a leading part in the troubled politics of the reign of Edward II. He opposed the Despensers and was captured in the wars of 1321–2, but he managed to escape to France where he became the paramour of Queen Isabella, the consort of Edward II. They returned to England in 1326, defeated and captured Edward, and forced him to abdicate. Mortimer was virtual ruler of England from 1327 until October 1330 when the young Edward III had him seized and hanged. Later Edward restored the Mortimer estates he had declared forfeit to Roger's grandson Roger (d. 1360), second earl of March who served with the king at the battle of Crécy (1346). Under Edmund Mortimer (d. 1425), fifth earl of March, the crown under Henry IV found the family a threat since many Englishmen judged Edmund the logical heir of the deposed Richard II. Owen Glendower, powerful Welsh chieftain, and the English marcher lords hoped to make Edmund king, but Henry IV kept a wary eye on him. He took part in Henry V's campaigns and in 1423 was appointed lieutenant of Ireland. In 1425 the family became extinct in the male line but a nephew, Richard, duke of York, assumed the title of earl of March and passed it on to his son Edward (IV).

MORTMAIN, term derived from the French meaning dead hand and referring in the Middle Ages to the ownership of land by a religious or ecclesiastical corporation. Since such an institution was an imperishable legal entity, it could hold property in perpetuity. To prevent the permanent alienation of lands to the church a provision in English law forbade such transfer of land without permission of the crown. The best known was the Statute of Mortmain promulgated by Edward I in 1279.

MORTON, JOHN, d. 1500, privy councillor, lord chancellor, archbishop of Canterbury (1486), and cardinal. An active supporter of the Lancastrian party, he went into exile after the Yorkist victory at Towton (1461). Edward IV granted him a pardon and made him master of the rolls and bishop of Ely (1479). He served as Henry VII's principal minister, became archbishop of Canterbury (1486), and lord chancellor in 1487. He is believed to have been the author of a Latin life of Richard III. The story about "Morton's Fork" which as wielded by this shrewd royal chancellor was supposed to exact benevolences or forced loans for the crown from those who lived extravagantly as well as those who did not—the latter saved their money, so Morton maintained—may have done him an injustice.

MOSCHUS, JOHN, d. 619, member of a monastery near Jerusalem, traveled widely and visited many monasteries. In his *Pratum Spirituale* he had many anecdotes to tell about monastic life.

MOSCOW, city of central Russia first noted in 1147, grew into an important trading center during the twelfth and thirteenth centuries. The first Kremlin (citadel) was erected in 1156. The Mongols burned the town in 1238 and again in 1293, but it recovered its earlier prosperity during the reign of Ivan I (1325–41) who made it the capital of the principality of Vladimir-Suzdal. In 1326 the metropolitan moved his see there from Vladimir. Although plundered again by the Mongols in 1382, it revived quickly and was recognized as the capital of Russia under Ivan III (1462–1505).

MOSCOW, GRAND PRINCE OF, line of rulers of Moscow that traced its origins to Daniel (c. 1280–1303), son of Alexander Nevski, the ruler of Novgorod. Ivan I Danilovich (1325–41) secured the title of grand prince of Vladimir from the khan of the Golden Horde, together with the right to collect the tribute owing to the khan from the other Russian princes. Ivan III ended Tartar dominion in 1480 and drove the Mongols from Russia.

MOSES BAR KEPHA, d. 903, Jacobite bishop of Mosul from c. 863. He is believed to have prepared commentaries on most of the books of the Bible, although only part of those on Genesis, the Gospels, and the Pauline Epistles survive.

MOSES OF CHORENE (Khoren, Movses Khorenatzi), known as the father of Armenian literature. He probably lived in the eighth century, although little firm knowledge of him remains. The most valuable part of his *History of Armenia* pertains to the pre-Christian Armenia, an otherwise largely unknown era. He also preserves many literary reminders of this pre-Christian period.

MOSLEM (Muslim), an adherent of Islam, more particularly, at least initially, a follower of Mohammed. [*See* ISLAM.]

MOSQUE. *See* ISLAMIC ART AND ARCHITECTURE.

MOSQUE OF OMAR. *See* OMAR. MOSQUE OF.

MOSUL, a city on the Tigris, opposite the ruins of Nineveh, an important Kurdish and Arab tribal center which had grown into a large, rich city by the eighth century and was the leading city of northern Mesopotamia. It prided itself on its markets, mosques, hostelries, gardens, baths, and Christian convents. It owed its commerical importance to its location on the main caravan route from Aleppo to Persia. It was the capital of independent dynasties in the tenth and eleventh centuries and the center of a generally prosperous and peaceful area until the coming of the Mongols in 1258 who destroyed the city and devastated the area. Ironically, what prosperity the city and region managed to recover, Timur the Lame spared, although neither city nor area has ever approached the level of prosperity they enjoyed before the coming of the Mongols.

MOTET, a polyphonic song of sacred music popular in the thirteenth century when it either followed or replaced the Offertory of the mass. It was also used at Vespers. Motets in vernacular languages and on secular themes appeared a little later.

MOTHER OF GOD, Greek *Theotokos,* the "God-bearer," a title given to Mary in the Eastern Church as early as the third century when Origen (d. 254?) was using the title. It was attacked by the Nestorians as incompatible with the full humanity of Christ, but was defended by St. Cyril of Alexandria and upheld by the Councils of Ephesus (431) and Chalcedon (451). It was then adopted by the Latin Church.

MOTTE (mound), a hillock or mound trenched and protected with a palisade. The medieval castle evolved from such a fortified place. [*See* CASTLE.]

MOULINS, LE MAÎTRE DE ("The Master of Moulins"), fl. c. 1480–c. 1500, French painter, miniaturist, and designer of stained-glass windows, one of the most important French painters of the fifteenth century. His name is derived from the triptych in the cathedral of Moulins, his masterpiece. He did most of his painting in the service of the Bourbon family. There has long persisted a question as to his identity, but it is now agreed that he was Jean Hey, a painter from the Low Countries best known for his *Ecce Homo* which he executed for a secretary of King Charles VIII.

MOUSE, a popular animal in medieval lore. Souls of unborn children might appear as mice; witches might take the form of mice; a mouse plague was represented as a punishment from heaven.

MOUSE TOWER (Mäuseturm), name given to the thirteenth-century tower on an island in the Rhine near Bingen where tolls were paid to the lord of the fortress of Ehrenfels which was in the vicinity. [*See* BINGEN.]

MOUTON D'OR (Agnel, Gouden Lam), gold

505

coin of the late Middle Ages which bore an engraving of the Lamb of God. It was popular in France and the Netherlands.

MOVABLE FEASTS, annual ecclesiastical feasts which, while always falling on certain days of the week, moved in the calendar with the incidence of Easter.

MOWBRAY, English baronial family founded by Geoffrey de Montbray, bishop of Coutances (1049–93), principal adviser to William I (the Conqueror). The fortunes of the family rose and fell during the reigns of William II, Henry I, Stephen, and Henry II. The best known member of the family in this early period was Roger, son of Nigel d'Aubigny and the Mowbray heiress, who took the Mowbray name and gained fame as a Crusader and as a patron of monasticism. By the late fourteenth century, Thomas, who had acquired the dignities of earl of Nottingham, earl marshal, and duke of Norfolk, ranked among the most influential magnates in England. The reign of Henry IV brought disaster, but Henry V restored the lands and titles his father had declared forfeit. The male line of the Mowbrays became extinct in 1476 and the family's titles and estates eventually passed to the Howards.

MOZARAB, Spanish Christian living under Moorish rule who had adapted his customs and even his religion to a degree to Moorish ways.

MOZARABIC CHANT, the music of the Mozarabic liturgy used in Spain up to the eleventh century. The oldest of the liturgical hymns may date from as early as the fourth century. Though most of the music has been preserved, the notation is in neumes of a type that remains indecipherable. It appears not to have been greatly different in style from the Gregorian, though perhaps more florid.

MOZARABIC STYLE, art forms used by the Mozarabs. It represented a fusing of Romanesque and Islamic elements.

MU'AWIYA (Muawiya Ibn Abi Sufyan) I, Moslem caliph, 661–80, founder of the dynasty of the Omayyads. His father was a wealthy merchant of Mecca who had once led the opposition to Mohammed. In 639 Omar I appointed Mu'awiya governor of Syria. When Othman was murdered in 656, Mu'awiya refused to recognize Ali, and even before Ali's assassination in January 661 had had himself proclaimed caliph (June 660). During Mu'awiya's reign and largely because of the strong, well-organized administration he introduced, Islamic expansion continued into central Asia and to the west across north Africa to the Atlantic. He made his capital at Damascus.

MUBARRAD, AL- (Abu-Al-'Abbas Muhammad Ibn Yazid Al-Thumali Al-Azdi), d. 898, Arab philologist whose principal work *Al-Kamil fi'l Adab* ("The Perfect in Literature") contains much information about traditions, proverbs, and history, and is particularly valuable as a storehouse of linguistic knowledge. It is also an important source for the study of Arabic.

MUDEJAR STYLE, Spanish style composed of Christian and Islamic elements which was popular in Toledo and Seville in the late Middle Ages. Its name was derived from the Mudejars, that is, the Moors who had been subjugated.

MUEZZIN (mu'eddhin), the man who summoned the Moslems to prayer at the appointed hours during the day and to public worship on Friday. He usually did so from a minaret or lofty platform outside the mosque.

MUFADDALIYAT (Mofaddaliyat), anthology of ancient Arabic poems composed by al-Mufaddal ibn Muhammad ibn Ya'la (d. 784). He compiled this anthology while serving as tutor to al-Mahdi, the son of the caliph al-Mansur. His anthology contains 126 poems, some complete odes, others fragmentary. They were products of the Golden Age of Arabic poetry (500–650) and represent the best collection of poems of that period. The collection is of the greatest importance as a record of the thought and poetic art of Arabia in the last pre-Islamic centuries.

MUMMERS, masked persons who paraded the streets during European winter festivals and entered houses to dance or dice in silence. Mumming was a popular, though frequently prohibited, amusement from the thirteenth to the sixteenth century.

MUNICH, settlement near the monastery of Tegernsee to which it owed its origin and its name (München, that is, home of the monks). Henry the Lion, duke of Bavaria, who may be considered its founder, granted the town city rights in 1158. The year previous he had destroyed the toll bridge at Freising in order to encourage the growth of Munich. From 1255 the Wittelsbach family made the town their home. It became the see of an archbishop at the close of the twelfth century. Its university was established in 1472.

MUNSTER (Mounster, Mumhu), large Irish province, one of the traditional "Fifths" of Ireland, that included all of southwestern Ireland. From about the year 400, a small people called the Eoganachta ruled the region. During the eighth and ninth centuries, they challenged the high-kings without success; neither could they prevent the Vikings from making settlements during the tenth century at Limerick and Waterford. After the Norman invasion, the feudal families of Fitzgerald and Butler dominated the province.

MÜNSTER (Munster), city in Westphalia which until 1068 was known as Mimigernaford. St. Ludger (d. 809), its first bishop, founded a Benedictine monastery in the town. In the thirteenth century Münster became an imperial city and during that century and the fourteenth it was a prominent member of the Hanseatic League.

MURAD I, sultan of Turkey, 1362–89, succeeded his father Orkhan, captured Adrianople in 1362, and made it his capital. He forced both Bulgaria and Constantinople to pay him tribute and in 1389, with a decisive victory at Kossovo, ended Serbian ambitions of establishing a Balkan empire. Murad was assassinated before the battle by a Serb who posed as a deserter.

MURAD II, sultan of Turkey, 1421–51, extended Turkish rule in the Balkans and in 1444 at Varna destroyed an army of Western Crusaders composed principally of Poles and Hungarians. Again in 1448 he inflicted another great defeat on the Hungarians at Kossovo. He reestablished Ottoman control over most of western Asia Minor, seized Thessalonica which a Byzantine emperor had sold to Venice in 1423, and forced Byzantium to pay tribute.

MURBACK, ABBEY OF, Benedictine monastery in Upper Alsace founded shortly before 728 by Count Eberhard and St. Pirmin of Reichenau. It was richly endowed and among other prerogatives was exempted from episcopal jurisdiction. Its school and library helped make it a leading center of learning during the Carolingian period. After a decline in the eleventh century, it revived in the high Middle Ages when its abbot took his place with the ranking imperial princes.

MURCIA, KINGDOM OF, independent Moorish state in southeastern Spain on the Mediterranean. The Moors seized the area in the early eighth century and after the collapse of the caliphate of Córdoba in the eleventh century, it established its independence. In the thirteenth century, after being subject to the Almoravid and Almohad rulers of Morocco during the periods of their ascendancy, it again became independent. In 1243 it became tributary to Castile, then in 1266 was annexed by that Spanish state.

MURET, BATTLE OF, battle fought in 1213 in southern France a few miles southwest of Toulouse between Crusaders led by Simon de Montfort and the armies of Raymond VI of Toulouse and King Peter II of Aragon. Peter's death in the battle led to a general flight of his army and

Raymond's defeat. Simon's victory opened the way to the surrender of Toulouse and to the extinction of Aragon's territorial pretensions north of the Pyrenees.

MURIS, JEAN, d. c. 1351, French philosopher and mathematician but best known for a musical treatise he composed entitled *Ars Novae Musicae*. He carried on a correspondence with many great composers of his day.

MURSA, BATTLE OF, fought on September 28, 351, between the armies of Constantius II and the imperial usurper Magnentius. The two armies converged at Mursa, a city on the Drava river in Pannonia, after Magnentius had failed in his attack on Sirmium. Constantius won the battle, said to have been the bloodiest of the century. His heavy cavalry proved the decisive factor in his victory.

MUSA IBN NUSAIR, d. 716 or 717, Arab general who completed the conquest of north Africa in the western Mediterranean area (698–710) and added a large part of Spain (712–4). He was recalled to Damascus by the envious Caliph Walid and died in indigence.

MUSCULUS, a shed or mantelet that shielded a battering ram used to penetrate or destroy the lower courses of a castle wall.

MUSIC, one of the seven liberal arts, one of the four making up the quadrivium. Medieval music had its origins in the plain song or chant which characterized liturgical singing from the early centuries of the Christian era. This plain song may be viewed as a compromise between the position of churchmen who questioned the propriety of music in the liturgy and those who encouraged it: music might be introduced, but it must always remain subordinate to the words and meaning of the liturgy. The absence of sharps and flats emphasized its unadorned melody. Early singing was in unison, often antiphonal, but from the fifth century when congre-

gational singing declined, it gradually became the responsibility of trained choirs (*scholae cantorum*). In the Carolingian period this song came to be classified Gregorian chant although some question remains whether the contribution of Pope Gregory I (590–604) extended beyond that of codifying it for general use in the Latin church.

The ninth and tenth centuries witnessed some advance beyond the monomelody which had persisted until then. The first step to be taken was called *organum* (organized melody), when a second voice, carrying a parallel melody but four or five tones below or above, accompanied the principal melody sung by the tenor. Free *organum* or descant which quickly followed permitted the accompanying voices greater freedom. The thirteenth century introduced counterpoint, essentially the harmonizing of two distinct melodies, a major and an accompanying one. From counterpoint it was a short and inevitable step to the evolution of many-melodied, many-voiced polyphony and harmony. No doubt the rich and varied tones of the organ provided a strong and constant incentive to the evolution of polyphony.

A significant aid to the development of music from the eleventh century was the system of musical notation that gradually evolved once advance beyond monomelody became desirable. Guido of Arezzo (d. 1050) is often credited with introducing the four-line staff and square notes although these and other symbols in musical notation, including sharps, flats, clefs, spaces, and rests, were either already in use or were about to appear. The enrichment of musical melodies made their introduction necessary.

MUSLIM IBN AL-HAJJAJ (Muslim Ibn Al-Hajjaj Abu'l Husain Al-Qushairi Al-Naisaburi), d. 875, Arab scholar who in the course of his extensive travels throughout the Middle Ages gathered some 300,000 traditions concerning the prophet Mohammed in his great work entitled *Sahih* ("The Genuine"). He was considered a leading authority on the *Hadith* and his work carried authority.

MUSSATO, ALBERTINO, d. 1329, Italian poet and historiographer. His Latin poems included a tragedy entitled *Ecerinis* which was modeled after Seneca's. His poetry established him as one of the earliest humanists of the dawning Renaissance. His historical writings are valuable for the history of Italy in the early fourteenth century.

MUTANABBI, AL- (Abu Al-Tayyib Ahmad Ibn Husain), d. 965, perhaps the greatest of all Arab poets. He was a professional poet who lived off the patronage of wealthy patrons whom he eulogized in his verse. He exerted considerable influence upon the development of Arabic poetry. His verse is mainly panegyric and ornately rhetorical.

MU'TASIM, AL-, Abbasid caliph, 833–42, organized a military corps composed of Turks who eventually stripped the caliphs of their power. In order to reduce friction between these Turkish mercenaries and the people of Baghdad, he established a new capital at Samarra farther up the Tigris north of Baghdad. The government returned to Baghdad in 889.

MUTAWAKKIL, AL-, Abbasid caliph, 847–61, managed for many years to maintain his authority despite increasing pressure from his Turkish mercenaries. Their leaders in the end brought about his assassination and assumed control.

MU'TAZILITES, Moslem intellectuals and theologians of the eighth and ninth centuries who subjected Islamic doctrines and traditions to rational examination. They maintained that impious Moslems held an intermediate position between true believers and infidels; that the Koran was not of the essence of God but had been created; that man was fully responsible for his actions. The caliph Al-Ma'mun (813–33) declared the doctrine of the Mu'tazilites the official theology of the empire. The Mu'tazilites represented the first important theological school in Islam. They were among the first Moslem theologians to use the categories and methods of Greek philosophy in expounding their faith.

MYRC, JOHN, fl. c. 1400, religious writer, prior of the canons regular of Lilleshall in Shropshire. He left a collection of sermons for the main festivals in the liturgical years. He was also the author of *Instructions for Parish Priests* which he put into English verse.

MYRIOBIBLON, an abridgment made by Photius (d. 891), Byzantine scholar and patriarch of Constantinople, of the writings of several hundred ancient and contemporary authors. [*See* PHOTIUS.]

MYSTERE D'ADAM, LE, oldest French dramatic piece (twelfth century). It was the first mystery play to be composed entirely in verse. The theme concerns the sin of Adam and Eve, Cain's murder of Abel, and the prophecies which foretold the birth of Christ the Savior.

MYSTERY PLAY. *See* DRAMA, MEDIEVAL.

MYSTICISM, the doctrine or practice of those who believe it is possible to achieve communion with God. Theologians of most religions have accepted the aims of mystics as legitimate and commendable, but no sect has witnessed so great a development of mysticism as Christianity. The institution of monasticism was especially responsible for encouraging mysticism, which explains why the majority of medieval mystics were associated with religious orders. Although the practice of mysticism and a formal mystical theology scarcely enjoyed a recognized place in Western spiritual endeavors before the thirteenth century, the writings of the obscure Dionysius the Areopagite (sixth century) were of utmost importance in their development. Other names of importance in the history of medieval mysticism include those of Augustine, Gregory the Great, Bernard of Clairvaux, Francis of Assisi, Bonaventure, the Rhineland Mystics, Catherine of Siena, and Walter Hilton.

NÄFELS, village in the canton of Glarus, Switzerland, where the Swiss won a decisive victory over the Hapsburg army in 1388. Here, as at Crécy and Poitiers, feudal cavalry found that it could not ride down well-disciplined infantry occupying a strong defensive position. This victory led first to a truce, then to independence for the Swiss.

NÁJERA, city of north Spain, founded in 1052, the capital of Navarre. In 1376 Peter the Cruel and the Black Prince defeated Henry of Trastamara and Duguesclin at this place.

NAMAS (namaz, nama). *See* SALAT.

NAMATIANUS, RUTILIUS CLAUDIUS, Latin poet of the early fifth century whose description of a trip he made from Rome to Gaul reveals the mind of a member of the old pagan aristocracy.

NAME DAY, feast day of the saint whose name one held from baptism.

NANCY, city of Lorraine which took root around a castle erected in the eleventh century by the duke of Lorraine. In the course of the twelfth century, the duke surrounded the town with a wall and made it his residence and capital. Charles the Bold, duke of Burgundy, was defeated and slain at Nancy in 1477 by the Swiss.

NANTES, city on the mouth of the Loire which had been a thriving commercial and administrative center in late Roman times. Christianity was introduced in the third century by St. Clair, and it became a bishop's see in the fourth. The town fell to the Bretons in 842, then to the Normans who kept possession of it until 936, after which

it became the residence of the counts of Brittany. In 1491 it was incorporated into the French royal domain.

NAPLES, city of Greek origin that changed hands during the wars between the Byzantine emperor Justinian I, and the Ostrogoths but never fell to the Lombards. It became a duchy under Byzantine rule, but by the ninth century, when that rule weakened, it gained its independence. During the tenth and eleventh centuries it cooperated with Pisa, Genoa, and Venice in the war against the Saracen invaders of Sicily and Italy, driving them from Italian waters (1087). In 1139 Roger II added Naples to his kingdom of Sicily. In 1194 Henry VI of Germany occupied the city, and it remained in German (Hohenstaufen) hands for most of the period until the death of Manfred in 1266, when Charles of Anjou captured the city. In 1282, when Sicily was lost to Aragon, Naples continued as the capital of the kingdom of Naples. In 1442 this kingdom passed under the rule of Aragon. The University of Naples, which Frederick II of Germany founded in 1224, may be classified as the first lay or state institution of higher learning in the Western world.

NAPLES, KINGDOM OF, the successor to the Norman kingdom of Sicily established by Robert Guiscard (d. 1085) and his brother Roger I (d. 1101). Roger II, the son of Roger I, conquered southern Italy and Sicily and in 1130 assumed the title of king of Sicily. Since the pope claimed suzerainty over southern Italy, he formally invested Roger II in 1139 with the kingdom of Sicily. When Roger's grandson William II died in 1189 without male issue, the succession, after some fighting, went to Henry VI of Germany who had married Roger's daughter Constance. Henry's son, Frederick II of Germany, eventually made good his claims to Naples and Sicily, and the Hohenstaufens remained in control there until 1266 when Manfred, son of Frederick, was slain in battle (Benevento) with Charles of Anjou. In 1282 the revolt in Sicily known as the Sicilian Vespers deprived Charles of Sicily, from which time the country of southern Italy came to be known as the kingdom of Naples. In 1442 Alfonso V of Aragon established his rule over Naples and southern Italy, after which he styled himself king of the Two Sicilies. Aragon retained control over Naples into the sixteenth century except for a brief moment after 1494 when Charles VIII, as heir of the Angevin claims, invaded Italy and captured Naples, only to be forced to return precipitately to France by threats from the League of Venice. The close of the Middle Ages did not terminate the turbulence of political life in southern Italy nor stay its drift toward economic and political bankruptcy. Once the first "modern" state of western Europe, southern Italy by the close of the Middle Ages had become one of the most backward.

NARBONNE, French seaport on the Mediterranean, a provincial capital in Roman times, a bishop's see c. 250, and a metropolitan see in 422. The Visigoths captured the city in 413 and made it their capital. In 719 the Saracens, after a siege of two years, captured the city but lost it to Pepin III in 759. In the thirteenth century Philip II Augustus granted the city to Simon de Montfort with the title of duke of Narbonne. Narbonne was an important center of a flourishing Jewish culture until the late thirteenth century when the Jews were expelled. This exodus of Jews, combined with the silting up of the harbor at the same time, brought about the city's rapid decline.

NARSAI (Narses), d. c. 503, one of the formative theologians of the Nestorian church, head of the school of Edessa (from 437?). About 471 he fled to Nisibis where he founded a school of theology. He produced many commentaries on the Old Testament and a large number of metrical homilies and some hymns.

NARSES, d. c. 573, slave and eunuch at the Byzantine court who became one of Emperor Justinian's most trusted generals. In 532 he played a major role in putting down the dangerous Nika riot. In 552 he completed the conquest of Italy which Belisarius had begun. Two years later he defeated an army of Franks and Alemanni that had crossed the Alps and had moved as far south as Capua.

NASIR-I-KHUSRAU, d. 1088, Persian mystic and poet. He composed didactic and devotional verse and more than a dozen treatises expounding the doctrine of the Isma'ilis. His most important prose work described his journey from his home in Balkh through Palestine to Egypt, where be became an Isma'ili convert, then back to Balkh again.

NASRIDS, ruling dynasty of Moorish Granada, 1238–1492. The dynasty rose to power following the collapse of Almohad power after the defeat suffered by the Almohads at Las Navas de Tolosa in 1212. Mohammed I (d. 1273), the first Nasrid ruler, recognized the suzerainty of the king of Castile as did all his successors. Mohammed began the construction of the Alhambra and followed the policy of welcoming refugees from other parts of Spain. Intermittent internal conflict and border fighting ended only with the conquest of Granada by Ferdinand and Isabella in 1492.

NASSAU, city and county east of the Rhine below Cologne where the counts of Laurenburg erected a castle c. 1100. The family divided into two branches in 1255, the Walram and Ottonian.

Adolf of Nassau, elected king of Germany in 1292, was a member of the Walram branch.

NATION, organization of university students from a given area under the guidance of a proctor who with other proctors might elect the rector of the institution. Nations appeared in Bologna in the twelfth century and somewhat later in Paris and a few other universities. Their first responsibility was that of providing instruction for their members, then of administering the examinations leading to a master's degree. They also defended the individual student's legal privileges and immunities.

NAUMBURG, city on the Saale in Saxony, established c. 1000 (Neuenburg), a bishop's seat c. 1030, and a thriving trading center until overshadowed by neighboring Leipzig in the early fifteenth century. The cathedral, built in the thirteenth and fourteenth centuries, contains some of the finest sculptures of the German Gothic period.

NAVARRE, KINGDOM OF, small state in the Pyrenees between Gascony to the northeast and the kingdom of Leon to the west, occupied largely by Basques, and traversed by the chief pilgrim roads from the north leading to Santiago de Compostela. Until the last half of the twelfth century it was known as the kingdom of Pamplona. It was once part of the Spanish march. At the pass of Roncesvalles which connected France to Navarre the Basques fell upon the rear guard of Charlemagne's army in 778, thus providing the theme for the *Chanson de Roland*. Sancho III (1005–35) extended the kingdom to both sides of the Pyrenees and, through his marriage to the heiress of Castile, ruled over nearly all of Christian Spain. In 1076 Aragon seized control of the principality and held it until 1134 when Garcia V, "the Restorer," reestablished Basque control. The Basque part of the country recognized the suzerainty of Castile c. 1200, while the remainder came under French influence in 1234. The best known of the rulers of French Navarre

was Charles II ("the Bad") (1349–87), who had an active role in the Hundred Years' War. Spanish Navarre encountered increasing difficulty in maintaining its autonomous position and finally lost it to Ferdinand of Spain in 1512. French Navarre was not absorbed into the French royal domain until the sixteenth century.

NAVAS DE TOLOSA. *See* LAS NAVAS DE TOLOSA.

NAVE, the central part of the church between the aisles which extended from the entrance (usually to the west) to the apse (usually to the east). [*See* EARLY CHRISTIAN ART.]

NAZZAM, AL- (Abu Ishaq Ibrahim Ibn Sayyar Ibn Hani' Ibn Ishaq), d. 846, Moslem scholar, jurist, theologian, and historian. He is said to have memorized the Koran, Pentateuch, the Gospels, and the Book of Psalms. He urged a rationalistic approach in the study of theology. Together with his teacher, Abu al Hudhayl, he led philosophic and theological thought in Islam during one of its formative periods.

NECKAM, ALEXANDER OF. *See* ALEXANDER NECKHAM.

NEDAD, BATTLE OF, battle fought on the Nedad river in Pannonia in 454 between the Huns and their German mercenaries, principally the Gepids, resulting in the final destruction of Hunnic power.

NEMANYIDS, ruling dynasty of Serbia founded by Stephen Nemanya I (1168–96). He expelled the Bogomils, extended his territories to the south, and established his independence from Constantinople. In 1196 he retired to a monastery. Stephen Nemanya II (1196–1223) managed to retain control of most of Serbia against Hungarian attacks with the help of an army of Cumans supplied him by Kaloyan, czar of Bulgaria. Kaloyan kept Belgrade and Nish for himself. The Nemanyid dynasty ended with Stephen Urosh V in 1371. [For its greatest representative, *see* STEPHEN DUSHAN.]

NENNIUS, d. c. 826, Celtic historian of North Wales who has been cited as the probable author of the *Historia Britonum*. He may only have compiled or revised the work. The first mention of Arthur to appear in literature is found in his *Historia*. The work, which presumes to trace the history of England to the eighth century, appeared in an Irish translation in the eleventh century.

NEO-PLATONISM, name given to the Platonism of the third to the sixth centuries as this was modified especially by Plotinus (d. 270) and his pupil Porphyry (d. c. 305). For Plato's Good they substituted the One, from whose self-knowledge emanated the first Intelligence (Logos or Word) which contained the abstract Ideas of all beings. From the Logos in turn there emanated a second Intelligence, the World Soul, from which the individual intelligences derived. Since neo-Platonism was popular during the period of Christianity's rise, it influenced many of the church fathers, including Basil and Gregory of Nyssa in the East and Ambrose and Augustine in the West. Through Augustine's writings especially it passed on to the early scholastics, almost all of whom subscribed to what is called Augustinianism. Through Pseudo-Dionysius (sixth century) neo-Platonism exerted significant influence upon Western mysticism. Among other Christian concepts which neo-Platonism influenced was the hierarchy of spiritual beings or Intelligences, with God standing at the summit; the spiritual nature of reality and the existence of universals; and the belief that the soul or being came from God or the One.

NEPOS, JULIUS, appointed by Emperor Leo I in 474 to govern the Western Empire as patrician. Orestes drove him out of Italy although he continued to be recognized in Gaul and by Constantinople until he was murdered in 480.

NERSES, ST., d. c. 373, sixth Catholicos of the Armenian Church (c. 363) who undertook a reform of his church and who at the Council of Ashtishat promulgated decrees against marriage between relatives and on fasting. He founded many hospitals and homes for orphans. His criticism of King Arshak III led to his exile, his attack on the immorality of the king's successor, to his own martyrdom.

NESTOR, d. c. 1114, monk of the Pecherskii Cave Monastery at Kiev, author of lives of the saints and the possible author of the *Russian Primary Chronicle*. (He may have compiled the basic version.) This chronicle, which is considered the most important historical work dealing with early Russia, was written partly in Old Church Slavonic, partly in Old Russian.

NESTORIANISM, the doctrine identified with Nestorius (d. after 451) which held that the two natures in Christ were not united metaphysically but only joined together in the psychological or moral order. For this reason the Nestorians denied Mary the title of mother of God. After the condemnation of Nestorius's position by the Council of Ephesus in 431, his followers at a synod held in Seleucia in 486 officially adopted his creed as formulated by Eustathius of Sebaste, Diodore of Tarsus, and Theodore of Mopsuestia. Persecution forced the Nestorians to leave the Byzantine empire, but missionaries carried their doctrine to Yemen, India, Ceylon, Persia, and Mongolia. The liturgical language of the Nestorian Church ("Church of the East") has remained Syriac.

NESTORIUS, d. after 451, a monk of Antioch who probably studied under Theodore of Mopsuestia. As patriarch of Constantinople (428–31) he proved himself a staunch opponent of Arianism and Pelagianism but he found himself condemned by the Council of Ephesus (431) for his views concerning the nature of Christ. He refused to recognize Mary as the mother of God nor would he attribute to the divine nature of Christ his human acts and sufferings. It was his fame as a preacher that had led to his appointment as patriarch by the emperor Theodosius II. The same emperor ordered him deposed and exiled, first to Arabia, later to Libya where he died.

NETTER, THOMAS, d. 1430, a Carmelite, studied at Oxford where he acquired a reputation for his knowledge of theology. He served as provincial of the English community and was their delegate to the Councils of Pisa and Constance. He served as confessor or spiritual adviser to Henry V and Henry VI. He was the author of the *Fasciculi Zizaniorum,* a collection of documents concerned with Wyclif and Lollardy.

NEUME (neum), symbol used in musical notation as early as the eighth century to indicate the rise or fall of the melody and the length of the note. It also indicated a prolonged group of notes sung to a single syllable, e.g., at the end of the Alleluia.

NEUSTRIA, northwestern part of the Merovingian kingdom as opposed to Austrasia, which lay to the east. Neustria included the cities of Paris, Soissons, Orléans, and Tours. The seventh century was marked by bitter rivalry and warfare between Neustria and Austrasia until 687 when Pepin of Heristal, mayor of the palace in Austrasia, gained a decisive victory over the mayor of the palace in Neustria. This victory assured the ultimate ascendancy of Austrasia. [*See* BRUNHILD.]

NEVERS, city on the Loire, capital city of the county of Nevers (east-central France), a bishop's seat since c. 500, a county c. 990, and a possession of Flanders until 1384 when its count became a vassal of the duke of Burgundy.

NEVILLE (Nevill), English aristocratic family closely related to the houses of York and Lancaster. It came into prominence in the twelfth century, although it was the marriage of Ralph Neville (d. 1425) to Joan Beaufort, daughter of John of Gaunt, that made the family powerful.

[For Ralph Neville, *see* WESTMORLAND, EARLDOM OF, and for Richard Neville, *see* WARWICK, RICHARD NEVILLE, EARL OF.]

NEVILLE, GEORGE, d. 1476, priest, brother of Richard, the earl of Warwick. He served as chancellor of Oxford, was consecrated bishop of Exeter, and became archbishop of York (1465). He occupied the post of royal lord chancellor for a number of years.

NEVILLE'S CROSS, BATTLE OF, battle fought in 1346 by King David II and his Scottish army against the English in order to force the latter to lift their siege of Calais against the French. The English defeated the Scots, captured David, and occupied a large part of southern Scotland.

NEWCASTLE UPON TYNE (Pons Aelii, Monk Chester), town in Northumberland, a Roman frontier post against the Scots, and a shrine in Anglo-Saxon times. It acquired its name from a castle built in 1080 by Robert, son of William I, that was rebuilt in the impressive style of late Norman architecture in 1172 by Henry II.

NEW TESTAMENT, the Christian portion of the Bible. It includes the four Gospels, the Acts of the Apostles, the Epistles (letters) of several apostles, and the Book of Revelations.

NEW TOWN. *See* VILLE NEUVE.

NIBELUNGENLIED, Middle High German epic written c. 1200, probably by an Austrian, that told of Siegfried's trick by which he gained the hand of Brunhild for Gunther, then Hagen's murder of Siegfried, followed by Kriemhild's avenging the death of her husband Siegfried with the assistance of Etzel (Attila the Hun) whom she married for that purpose.

NICAEA I, COUNCIL OF, general church council (First Ecumenical) convoked by Constantine I (the Great) which met in 325 to resolve the controversy raised by Arius concerning the nature of Christ. The council which Constantine, who was interested principally in religious peace, opened with a speech, was attended by about 300 bishops, almost all of whom came from the East. Hosius, bishop of Córdoba, and the delegates of Pope Sylvester presided at the council. The council declared that the Son, the Second Person of the Trinity, was of one and the same substance *(homoousios)* with the Father. The leading champion of the view that prevailed was Athanasius, deacon of Alexander, patriarch of Alexandria. The two bishops who refused to accept the decision of the council were deposed and banished.

NICAEA II, COUNCIL OF, general church council (Seventh Ecumenical), convoked by Empress Irene in 787 for the purpose of ending the controversy over iconoclasm. The council approved the veneration of the saints and of images and condemned the position of the iconoclasts. The Eastern Church recognized no subsequent councils as ecumenical.

NICAEA, EMPIRE OF, one of the successor states of the Byzantine empire following its destruction by the Crusaders (Fourth Crusade) in 1204. It was founded by Theodore I Lascaris, a son-in-law of Alexius III, and comprised a part of northwest Asia Minor with its capital at Nicaea. In 1259 Michael VIII Palaeologus usurped the throne. Two years later he captured Constantinople. [*See* LASCARID DYNASTY and MICHAEL VIII PALAEOLOGUS.]

NICCOLI, NICCOLO DE', d. 1437, Italian humanist who copied Greek and Latin classical works and collected a library of some 800 volumes of Greek and Latin manuscripts which became the foundation of the Laurentian Library in Florence. Niccolo enjoyed the patronage of Cosimo de' Medici.

NICE, French seaport on the Mediterranean, a bishop's see in the fourth century, which was pillaged by the Saracens in 859 and again in 880. It became independent in the eleventh century although it lost its freedom on several occasions to the counts of Provence. In 1388 it placed itself under the protection of the counts of Savoy, after which the city enjoyed considerable commercial growth.

NICENE CREED, more accurately the Niceno-Constantinople Creed, the profession of faith agreed to by the Council of Nicaea in 325, then defined more precisely by the Council of Constantinople in 381. The critical tenet of faith affirmed by this creed concerned the Trinity. It declared the Son was of one and the same substance with the Father.

NICEPHORUS I, Byzantine emperor, 802–11, minister of finance under Irene whom he deposed and succeeded. He continued the iconodule policy of Irene, introduced financial and military reforms, and extended the system of themes to the Balkans. He negotiated a treaty with Charlemagne that recognized Byzantine rule over Venice, Istria, the Dalmatian coast, and southern Italy. He was slain and his army destroyed in the battle with the Bulgars.

NICEPHORUS II (Phocas), Byzantine emperor, 963–9, successful general under Emperor Romanus II, married the empress Theophano after she had arranged the murder of Romanus. The criticism of the church of his marriage led him to pass repressive laws against monasticism. He failed to block the appropriation of small holdings by members of the landed aristocracy, but he did recover Cilicia, Cyprus, Crete, and a large part of Syria, including Antioch and Aleppo, from the Moslems. He was murdered in a plot which was probably instigated by his wife and her new lover, John Tzimisces.

NICEPHORUS III (Botaneiates), Byzantine emperor, 1078–81. He was able to maintain his throne and empire only because of the talents of his general Alexius Comnenus who in 1081 usurped the throne for himself.

NICEPHORUS, ST., d. 829, theologian and historian, patriarch of Constantinople (806), who was deposed and exiled in 815 because of his opposition to iconoclasm. Earlier, in 787, he had served as the representative of the Byzantine emperor Nicephorus at the Second Council of Nicaea. He composed several dogmatic works and a history covering the years 602 to 769 which drew high praise from Photius for its accuracy and literary excellence.

NICETAS CHONIATES (Akominates). *See* CHON-IATES, NICETAS.

NICHOLAS I, ST., Pope, 858–67, successor of Benedict III, member of a noble Roman family, who forced Lothair II, king of Lorraine, to take back his first wife whom he had divorced, and deposed the archbishops of Cologne and Trier for having endorsed that divorce. He affirmed the right of suffragan bishops against Arch-bishop Hincmar of Reims to bring their appeals directly to the papal court, encouraged SS. Cyril and Methodius in their missionary work in Bo-hemia, and engaged in bitter controversy with Photius, patriarch of Constantinople, over the latter's claims concerning the supremacy of his position in the Eastern Church.

NICHOLAS II, Pope, 1058–61, bishop of Flor-ence (1045), was elected by the reform group in Rome headed by Hildebrand (Gregory VII) who challenged the selection of Benedict X by the Tusculani cardinals. By means of synods and decretals, Nicholas helped prepare the ground-work for the Gregorian reform of the church. He issued the Papal Electoral Law of 1059 which regulated the election of the pope. He also gave his support to the Patarines in Milan against the lay and ecclesiastical aristocracy whom they had attacked for their corruption.

NICHOLAS III, Pope, 1277–80, member of the Orsini family, a cardinal (1244), and successor of John XXI. He initiated a reform of the papal Curia and established the Vatican as the perma-nent papal residence. Though he enjoyed some success in reconciling the Franciscan Conventuals and Spirituals, he failed in his efforts to arouse Europe to another Crusade against the Turks.

NICHOLAS IV, Pope, 1288–92, Italian Francis-can, minister general of the order (1274), cardi-nal (1278), bishop of Palestrina (1281), and successor of Honorius IV. As pope he supported Angevin claims in Sicily against Aragon and provided greater stability in the Papal States by allying the papacy with the Colonna faction. He also sent missionaries to Persia, China, and Ethiopia.

NICHOLAS V, Pope, 1447–55, Italian, student at Bologna, bishop of Bologna (1443), papal legate at the Diet of Frankfurt where he made a persuasive plea for the recognition of Eugenius IV by the German princes, and cardinal (1446). As pope, his conciliatory spirit and diplomatic skill enabled him to gain the good will of the princes of Western Europe against the conciliar-ist group at Basel. In 1449 the antipope Felix submitted. Nicholas patronized the arts, laid the foundation of the Vatican Library, and rebuilt churches, palaces, and fortifications in Rome. He also worked strenuously for the organization of a Crusade against the Turks following the fall of Constantinople. He is usually judged to have been the best of the Renaissance popes.

NICHOLAS V, Antipope, 1328–30, Franciscan, advanced to the papacy by Louis IV (the Bavar-ian) of Germany who had broken with Pope John XXII. Nicholas submitted to Pope John XXII in 1330.

NICHOLAS I, patriarch of Constantinople, 901–7, and c. 912–25, monk, friend of Pho-tius, and secretary to Emperor Leo VI. He was deposed as patriarch in 907 either for objecting to the emperor's fourth marriage or possibly for certain treasonable acts. He was later reinstated and headed the imperial regency for the young Constantine VII Porphyrogenitus.

NICHOLAS OF CLAIRVAUX, d. c. 1176, monk of Clairvaux, secretary to St. Bernard, later abbot of Montiéramey. He was the author of letters, sermons, sequences, and two offices.

NICHOLAS OF CLAMANGES (Clémanges), d. 1437, rector of the University of Paris, secretary to the Avignonese pope Benedict XIII, and author of writings dealing with the Western Schism and with the reform of the church. He left some 150 letters of correspondence with other humanists and also some verse.

NICHOLAS OF CUSA (Cues, Cusanus, Chrypffs, Krebs), d. 1464, theologian, mystic, philosopher, and humanist (he found some of the lost plays of Plautus). He studied at Deventer, Heidelberg, Padua, Rome, and Cologne, became a doctor of canon law, and played an active role at the Council of Basel (1431−8) where he joined other delegates in negotiations with the Hussites. He served as a member of the papal commission that went to Constantinople in 1437 to discuss the reunion of the Greek and Latin churches, became a cardinal (1448), bishop of Brixen (1450), and papal legate to Germany. His sympathies were initially with conciliarism *(De Concordantia Catholica)* although he later shifted his position and after 1437 became a firm advocate of papal supremacy. His sermons, writings on mathematics, geography, science, logic, humanism, and mysticism *(De Docta Ignorantia)* established him as one of the greatest thinkers of the century.

NICHOLAS OF DINKELSBÜHL, d. 1433, theologian of Vienna, rector of the university, and a German representative at the Council of Constance (1414−8). He left sermons, theological tracts, commentaries on the Scriptures, and writings on conciliarism and Hussitism.

NICHOLAS OF FLÜE, ST., d. 1487, also known as Brother Klaus, a native of Switzerland, a hermit who then married and served as a soldier and judge. He persuaded his wife to permit him to return to a solitary life in a hermitage nearby. Churchmen and statesmen sought his counsel, while to the people of the neighborhood he became an immensely popular figure for his advocacy of peace and brotherhood.

NICHOLAS OF HEREFORD, d. c. 1420, one of Wyclif's disciples at Oxford. He was condemned as a heretic in 1382, then fled to Rome to appeal his case to the pope. The pope had him imprisoned, but Nicholas subsequently made his escape back to England where he recanted. He later became a canon of Hereford and in 1417 a Carthusian monk. He probably had a prominent part, together with John Purvey, in the translation of the Bible into English.

NICHOLAS OF LYRA, d. 1349, Franciscan, a distinguished biblical scholar on the basis of his wide knowledge of Christian exegesis and his ability to read Hebrew. (He knew no Greek.) In his exegetical writings, his aim was to arrive at the exact and literal sense of the text. That his commentary on the Bible was the first to be printed is testimony to the reputation he enjoyed as a biblical scholar.

NICHOLAS OF MYRA, ST., bishop of Myra in Lycia who may have attended the Council of Nicaea (325) and who, despite his obscurity, had some 2,000 churches dedicated to his name. Of the many legends told of him, the most popular is that which eventually made him the original Santa Claus. He was honored as the patron saint of sailors and of children. The three balls which serve as a symbol of the pawnbroker were originally associated with him. Sailors brought his relics to Bari in 1087, which city then became a highly popular pilgrimage center.

NICHOLAS ORESME. *See* ORESME, NICHOLAS.

NICHOLAS TREVET, d. after 1334, Dominican theologian, a student at Oxford, later regent master, and author of commentaries on the Bible, the *City of God* of St. Augustine, and on several classical works, including the tragedies of Seneca. He also left annals covering English history from 1135 to 1307.

NICODEMUS, wealthy Jew, member of the Sanhedrin, and a secret follower of Christ, who helped Joseph of Arimathea to prepare his body for burial.

NICOPOLIS, BATTLE OF, decisive battle fought on the lower Danube in 1396 which ended in an overwhelming victory for the Turks over a huge Crusading army led by King Sigismund of Hungary. It was the overconfidence of the Western knights, chiefly French, who failed to heed the advice of Sigismund, that was the principal cause of the disaster.

NIDAROS. *See* TRONDHEIM.

NIDER, JOHN, d. 1438, Dominican theologian who preached against the Hussites. He attended the Councils of Constance and Basel. He taught theology at Vienna and left writings on moral, ascetical, and theological subjects. His principal work, entitled *Formicarius,* contains much information about the state of religion at that time.

NIEHEIM (Niem), DIETRICH OF. *See* DIETRICH OF NIEHEIM.

NIGEL WIREKER, d. before 1207, monk of Christ Church, Canterbury, author of *Speculum Stultorum* (Mirror of Fools), a poetical satire of the times. His satires proved quite popular in the fourteenth and fifteenth centuries. He also left a treatise in prose which attacked corruption in the church.

NIKA RIOT, riot that took place in Constantinople in 532 when the Blues and Greens, usually bitter opponents in the contests held in the Hippodrome, joined hands in an attack on the government of Emperor Justinian I. According to Procopius, the refusal of the empress Theodora to flee the city prompted the emperor and his generals, notably Narses and Belisarius, to make yet another and, as it proved, successful attempt to put down the revolt.

NÎMES, city of Celtic origin located just west of the lower Rhône. It had become a bishop's see by the end of the fourth century, suffered successive pillaging by Vandals, Visigoths, and Saracens, then in 1185 passed under control of the counts of Toulouse. In 1258 it became part of the French royal domain.

NIMWEGEN (Nijmegen), city in the Netherlands, originally a Celtic settlement and occupied in Roman times. It served as a Carolingian royal residence, became an imperial city in 1230, and shortly after joined the Hanseatic League.

NINIAN, ST., d. c. 432, Scottish missionary who went to Rome where he was consecrated bishop. On his way back to Scotland, he made the acquaintance of St. Martin of Tours and later dedicated to him a church he built at Whithorn. From this church, Ninian and his monks carried out missionary work among the Britons and Scots. His tomb became a popular place of pilgrimage.

NITHARD, d. 844, son of Angilbert and Bertha, the daughter of Charlemagne, and lay abbot of the abbey of Saint-Riquier. He served as a military adviser to Charles, one of the sons of Louis the Pious, and took part in the battle of Fontenoy (841). His history of the wars of the sons of Louis the Pious is quite valuable despite its strong prejudice against Lothair. It contains the full text of the Strasbourg oaths of 842.

NIVARD OF GHENT, fl. 1150, monk of the Benedictine monastery of Saint-Pierre-au-Mont-Blandin in Ghent, and author of *Ysengrimus,* a beast epic, and of a satirical allegory critical of pope, hierarchy, and clergy. His *Ysengrimus* may have provided the source for the *Roman de Renart.*

NIZAMI (Jamaluddin or Nizamuddin Abu Mohammed Elyas Ibn Yusuf), d. 1217?, a leading romantic and the first dramatic poet of Persia. He enjoyed the patronage of several princes although he never stooped to composing panegyrics in their honor. His writing attests to his deep insight into human psychology and to a broad acquaintance with historical, literary, and scientific subjects.

NIZARIS, a sect of Isma'ili or "Sevener" Shi'i division of Islam which upheld the right of Nizar, eldest son of Caliph al-Mustansir (d. 1094), to hold the office of *imam* rather than his younger brother whom the vizier had advanced to that position.

NJAL'S SAGA, leading saga of Iceland written by an unknown author of the late thirteenth century. The story tells of the wickedness of Hallgerd, wife of Gunnar, which resulted in the death of Gunnar and most of his family.

NOBLE, an English gold coin minted since 1344; it was worth 6 shillings 8 pence.

NOCTURN, early term applied to the night offices, more strictly to matins and their division into three parts or nocturns.

NOGARET, GUILLAUME DE, d. 1313, lawyer and councillor of Philip IV of France in his contest with Pope Boniface VIII. He was one of the most aggressive of the expositors of royal power; it was he who organized the Anagni affair which led to the seizure and humiliation of the pope. He also directed the crown's attack on the Knights Templars.

NOMINALISM, a philosophic view which held that universal or abstract terms had no real existence apart from the thing itself but were simply words (singular *nomen,* from which nominalism) or conveniences of language. Beyond that role, they possessed no significance. The first nominalists of the Middle Ages were scholastics of the twelfth century (see Roscelin), who disagreed with Plato and the realists in their contention that general ideas had existed from all eternity and preceded in time *(ante rem)* the appearance of physical things. The nominalists insisted that the general ideas came only after the thing *(post rem).* [*See* UNIVERSAL; REALISM; WILLIAM OF OCKHAM.]

NONES, the fifth of the seven canonical hours. They were sung or recited at the ninth hour or about three in the afternoon.

NORBERTINES. *See* PREMONSTRATENSIANS.

NORBERT OF XANTEN, ST., d. 1134, canon of the collegiate church of Xanten, then an itinerant preacher in north France. He founded a monastery in the valley of Prémontré near Laon in 1120 which served as the mother house of the Premonstratensian Order. In 1126 he was consecrated archbishop of Magdeburg, after which he took an active part in ecclesiastical and state affairs. He accompanied Emperor Lothair II to Rome in 1132–3 where he supported Innocent II against the antipope Anacletus. [*See* PREMONSTRATENSIANS.]

NORFOLK, central county on the east coast of England, occupied by Angles, Frisians, and Saxons and part of the kingdom of East Anglia. It became Christian in 631 and a bishop's see in 673. From the mid-ninth century Danes ravaged the land and in 869 it became a part of the Danelaw. By the time of the Domesday survey (1086), Norfolk was one of the most heavily populated and wealthiest regions of England. In 1094 the episcopal see was moved to Norwich from Thetford.

NORFOLK, EARLS AND DUKES OF. The title of earl of Norfolk originated c. 1067 when William the Conqueror granted it to Ralph the Staller. His son forfeited the title when he revolted against William, and it was not revived until 1141 when King Stephen conferred it on Hugh Bigod. Hugh later joined Henry (II) against Stephen, but in 1173, as a result of joining in a revolt against Henry, his lands were declared forfeit. In 1312 Edward II granted the title to his half-brother Thomas of Brotherton who later helped bring about his abdication. In 1397 Richard II created Thomas Mowbray duke of Norfolk. The title lapsed in 1476 and was granted to John Howard by Richard III in 1483. Howard was among those slain at Bosworth Field.

NORFOLK, THOMAS MOWBRAY, DUKE (First) OF, d. 1399, earl of Nottingham (1383), one of the lords appellant but among the more moderate in his opposition to Richard II. He eventually made his peace with the king, was appointed captain of Calais, and in 1394 accompanied the king to Ireland. His testimony helped incriminate several of the lords appellant when the king gained the upper hand in 1397. Richard created him duke of Norfolk in 1397, but the following year, not entirely trusting him, ordered him banished from the realm.

NORMANDY, region of northwest France that Charles (III) the Simple turned over to Rollo (Hrolf) and his Normans (Vikings) in 911. It was ruled by the king of England from the time of William I in 1066 until Philip II Augustus of France seized it in 1204. The English recovered Normandy early in the Hundred Years' War, surrendered it to France by the Treaty of Brétigny (1360) in exchange for sovereignty over Guienne, reoccupied it following Henry V's victory at Agincourt (1415), but lost it permanently in 1450. Normandy was the most important of the provinces in France held by the king of England.

NORMANS, name given to the Vikings who occupied Normandy in the tenth century where they accepted Christianity and adopted the language and many of the customs of the French. In 1066 Duke William defeated Harold, the Anglo-Saxon king of England, at the battle of Hastings and established his rule over Britain. Early in the eleventh century, bands of Norman pilgrims, on their way home from the Holy Land, stopped in southern Italy, where they served the local lords as mercenaries against Byzantine rule. Among the most ambitious of the Normans who followed these pilgrims from Normandy were the sons of Tancred de Hauteville, notably Robert Guiscard and Roger I, who conquered southern Italy and Sicily from their Byzantine, Saracen, papal, and feudal lords. In 1053, after defeating the army of Pope Leo IX, they were invested with all of southern Italy.

They established the foundations of the first "modern" state of western Europe.

NORMAN STYLE, in architecture the Romanesque style that was characteristic of construction in Normandy and England, also, to an extent, in southern Italy and Sicily, from c. 1066 to c. 1200. It featured heavier walls and buttressing than was generally true of traditional Romanesque; in England churches featured naves of impressive length and great round columns for the nave arcade, e.g., Durham cathedral. Norman churches were usually cruciform, while the larger ones might have a square tower placed over the crossing of the nave and transepts.

NORTHAMPTON, ASSIZE OF, decree issued by Henry II of England in 1176 that established the system of circuits to be followed by the itinerant justices. It also added arson and forgery to the list of crimes they could try. [See CLARENDON, ASSIZE OF.]

NORTHMEN (Norsemen, Normans). See VIKINGS.

NORTHUMBERLAND, EARLDOM OF, title that originated with the kings of Northumbria who were earls in the late Anglo-Saxon period. In 1066 William the Conqueror confirmed Morcar as holder of the title. After being alienated to the kings of Scotland in the twelfth century, the title was revived in 1377 and conferred upon Henry de Percy on the occasion of the coronation of Richard II. Percy later joined a revolt against Richard II and was largely instrumental in securing the throne for Henry IV. His son, Sir Henry Percy, known as Hotspur, was killed at the battle of Shrewsbury (1403); Northumberland himself was slain in 1408 after joining in the revolt of Owen Glendower, the Welsh rebel leader. The earldom was declared forfeit in 1461 by Edward IV after the third earl had been killed at Towton fighting with the Lancastrians. In 1470 Edward returned the title to the family in the person of Henry (d. 1489), the fourth earl, who acquiesced in the accession of Richard III but later submitted to Henry VII.

NORTHUMBRIA, northernmost Anglo-Saxon kingdom, established early in the seventh century when Aethelfrith (d. 616) united the two smaller kingdoms of Bernicia and Deira under his rule. Edwin, once ruler of Deira, succeeded him, introduced Christianity, and extended his authority into north Wales and south of the Humber. He was slain by Penda of Mercia in 632, but Northumbria managed to maintain its independence although with increasing difficulty. The position taken by King Oswiu (641–70) at the Synod of Whitby in 664 enabled Roman Christianity to win out over the Celtic. During the ninth century Danes overran the country and wreaked much destruction. It eventually fell to Canute who appointed a Danish earl, Siward by name (d. 1055), to rule.

NORWAY, a Viking state, was opened to Christianity by Harald I Haarfager (Fairhair) (d. c. 940), the first jarl able to unite a large part of the country. His son Eric Bloodaxe was forced to flee the country and Haakon I the Good (d. c. 960) seized control. Olaf I (d. c. 999) was slain in battle with Sweyn I of Denmark. Olaf II (1015–30) established royal authority over the entire country but was obliged to flee to Russia when attacked by Canute, king of Denmark and England. Olaf II, who was canonized a saint, is credited with completing the conversion of Norway. Magnus the Good, son of Olaf II, who succeeded in 1035, shared the kingdom with his uncle Harald III Hardraade from 1046 until 1066 when the latter, allied with Tostig, brother of Harold, king of England, was slain at Stamford Bridge in a bid for the English throne. Magnus II (1093–1103) subdued the Hebrides and the Isle of Man. Haakon (1217–63) reestablished royal authority, extended his rule over Greenland and Iceland, encouraged learning, and in 1217 negotiated a commercial treaty with Henry III of England.

The penetration of the Hanseatic League into the economic life of Norway dates from a commercial treaty negotiated in 1250 with Lübeck. The Hebrides and the Isle of Man were ceded to Scotland by Magnus V Lagaboeter (1263–80). The Black Death, which moved up into Norway in 1350, struck a severe blow at the population and economy of the country and left the door open to heavy Swedish immigration. Within a few years much of the land of Norway had been acquired by members of the Swedish aristocracy. In 1319, when the male line of the ruling family became extinct, Magnus Eriksson, grandson of the king of Sweden, was chosen king. His son Haakon VI, who ruled from 1343 to 1380, married Margaret, daughter of Waldemar IV of Denmark, who in turn served as regent for their son Olaf IV when he died. She eventually extended her authority over all three Scandinavian countries, a union which endured, in the case of Denmark and Norway, until 1814. [See MARGARET, queen of Denmark.]

NORWICH, city of Norfolk which in the eleventh century ranked with London, York, and Bristol in ecclesiastical and commercial importance. It was already a thriving community, with a mint, when sacked by the Danes in 1004. Its wool trade flourished from 1336 when Edward III induced Flemish weavers to settle there. In 1094 the episcopal see was moved from Thetford to Norwich. Its cathedral is largely twelfth-century with a distinctive Norman apse and nave and with Perpendicular additions.

NOTITIA DIGNITATUM, official list of civil and military offices in the Roman empire. The list was probably drawn up toward the close of the fourth century.

NOTKER BALBULUS (the Stammerer), d. 912, monk of St. Gall, librarian and master of the school, author of hymns and sequences and a chronicle of the reign of Charlemagne. He may also be the author of a collection of stories about Charlemagne which circulated under the identification of "a monk of St. Gall."

NOTKER LABEO, d. 1022, monk of St. Gall, one of the most learned men of his day. He taught in the monastic school, composed treatises on music and grammar, and translated classical and patristic works into German in order to make these accessible to his pupils. He is honored as one of the important founders of German literature.

NOTRE DAME DE PARIS, cathedral of Paris and a prime example of early French architecture. It stands on the Ile de la Cité, an island in the Seine. Pope Alexander III laid the cornerstone in 1163 and c. 1230 the building was finished except for the twin towers which remain unfinished. Perhaps most distinctive about the cathedral are the three sculptured portals deeply recessed in the majestic west front. A row of sculptures in niches extends above them across the façade, and over this, in the center, is the huge traceried wheel window.

NOTTINGHAM, town of central Mercia on the Trent River which became important during the Danish period and was known as a city in pre-Conquest times. It received its first charter in 1155. Fire destroyed much of the town in the twelfth century. Between 1330 and 1337 three parliaments met there. The town is linked with the folk legend about Robin Hood.

NOTTINGHAM, EARLDOM OF, title created in 1377 for John de Mowbray. It remained in the Mowbray family until 1476 when it was given to Richard, duke of York.

NOVATIANS, followers of an obscure bishop of the third century who appears to have been excommunicated by a Roman synod, after which he consecrated his own bishops and organized his own church. He died a martyr in 258. The Novatians supported his position concerning the unforgivable nature of certain serious sins.

NOVELLAE, name given to additions to law codes and to codicils of law. The term is derived from Novels, the name of the new laws added to the *Corpus Juris Civilis*.

NOVELS, compilation of some 150 laws issued by the Byzantine emperor Justinian I (527–65) which constituted a fourth part of the *Corpus Juris Civilis*. It casts no light on ancient Roman law, but it possesses special importance in a study of his reign.

NOVGOROD, ancient settlement on the left bank of the Volkhov river in northwest Russia. Earliest mention of the town appears in 862 when Varangians under Rurik occupied the site. In 882 Oleg, the successor of Rurik, captured Kiev and made it his headquarters. In 980 the prince of Novgorod captured Kiev, although Novgorod generally recognized the suzerainty of Kiev until c. 1150 when it became independent. By this time it had developed into a major trading center and a leading export point for such northern products as furs, amber, honey, and wax. Novgorod attained the height of its influence under Alexander Nevski (d. 1263), prince of Vladimir, whose aid it had sought against the Swedes and Teutonic Knights. During this period it enjoyed close associations with the Hanseatic League which maintained a major colony in the city. During the Mongol invasion of 1238–40, Batu Khan, the Mongol general, came within 60 miles of Novgorod but found the marshes of the region too treacherous for his horses. During the fourteenth century Novgorod enlisted the aid of Lithuania against the threat of Moscow, but c. 1456 it finally recognized the overlordship of the prince of Muscovy. In 1478 Ivan III captured the city and established full control.

NUMMUS, actually the copper coin *follis* which Constantine the Great (306–37) had struck and which Emperor Anastasius (491–518) stabilized by relating its value to gold.

NUN, a woman who dedicated herself to the religious life, usually as a member of an established monastic order.

NUNC DIMITTIS, opening words of the prayer of thanksgiving and resignation said by Simeon on the occasion of the Christ child's presentation in the temple (Luke 2:29–32). The prayer had been adopted into the liturgy by the fourth century and was incorporated into the compline of the divine office.

NUREDDIN (Abu'l Qasim Mahmud), d. 1174, Moslem ruler of Syria, the son of Zangi (Zengi), who captured Edessa, Damascus, and Egypt (1168). His successes prepared the way for Saladin's later unification of the Moslem-held lands of Egypt and of the eastern Mediterranean. He constructed mosques, schools, hospitals, and caravansaries, and also popularized the idea of conducting a "Crusade" against the unbelieving Christians.

NUREMBERG (Nürnberg), city of Bavaria, first noted in 1040 when Henry III, duke of Bavaria and emperor of Germany, erected a stronghold there. It grew quickly as a community of traders and artisans built their homes around the castle. It was destroyed in 1127, rebuilt, and in 1140–50 spread from the north to the south bank of the river Pegnitz. It became, with Augsburg, one of the great trade centers on the road from Italy to northern Europe. It was declared an imperial city in 1219, and it was there that Emperor Charles IV proclaimed his Golden Bull in 1356, announcing that the new king of Germany should hold his first diet in that city.

OAK, SYNOD OF THE, synod convoked by Emperor Arcadius in 403, probably at the urging of the empress Eudoxia who resented St. John Chrysostom's attacks on extravagance and immorality in high places. The purpose of the synod was to remove Chrysostom as patriarch of Constantinople, and this was accomplished with the help of such trumped up charges as that he favored Origenism. He was ordered exiled to Bithynia but was recalled after a few days because of popular indignation over the order. [*See* JOHN CHRYSOSTOM, ST.]

O ANTIPHONS, also known as the Greater Antiphons, the seven antiphons of the *Magnificat* that were sung in the Divine Office during the seven-day period before the vigil of Christmas. The antiphons all begin with the interjection O. They were in use in the liturgy from at least the eighth century.

OBEDIENTIARY, a minor official in a monastery who was appointed by the abbot. He might be a sacristan, cantor, cellarer, or other official.

OBIIT, that is, "he (she) died," an inscription appearing on many tombstones and gravemarkers.

OBLATE: a child who was dedicated to a monastery by his parents; an adult or lay brother who associated himself with a monastery; the lay member of a third order (monastic).

OBODRITES. *See* OBOTRITES.

OBOE, a reed instrument that entered Europe with the Arabs by way of Sicily.

OBOTRITES, Slavic people that occupied the country between the lower Elbe and the Baltic sea. Henry I of Germany (919–36) forced them to recognize his authority although they were not entirely subdued until the time of Henry the Lion, duke of Saxony (d. 1195). Their last ruler, Przbyslaw (d. 1178), who was recognized as a prince of the Holy Roman empire, was the ancestor of the dukes of Mecklenburg.

OBRECHT (Hobrecht), JACOB, d. 1505, a composer of the Netherlands, best known for his liturgical music and motets. He also wrote secular songs and served as choir master in Cambrai, Antwerp, and Ferrara.

OBSERVANTS (Observantines), Franciscans of the strict rule: they claimed they observed exactly the original Rule of St. Francis. [*See* FRANCISCANS.]

OCHRIDA (Okhrida), town of Macedonia, an important trading center in Roman times and an early episcopal see. In the ninth century it came under Bulgarian rule and in the tenth century it replaced Préslav as the seat of the Bulgarian patriarchate, when it flourished as the cultural and political center of Bulgaria. In the eleventh century it again came under Byzantine rule.

OCCAM, WILLIAM OF. *See* WILLIAM OF OCKHAM.

OCKHAMISM, school of thought based on the metaphysical views of William of Ockham. These included a denial of the existence of universals, the position that reality is a collection of independent singulars, and a rejection of the Thomistic premise that a harmony exists between faith and reason. This school of thought also accepted Ockham's position that there was no limitation to God's will other than that of contradiction: He could do whatever He wished, and whatever He did was good.

OCTAVE, from the Latin "eighth (day)," in liturgical usage, the eighth day after a feast, reckoned inclusively. The term also applied to the entire period of the eight days. In Christian usage, the practice has been traced to the order of Emperor Constantine I (d. 337) to celebrate for an octave the dedication of the basilicas at Jerusalem and Tyre. The first feasts to have an octave were Easter, Pentecost, and Epiphany.

OCULI, name given to the third Sunday of Lent. The word is the first of the introit for that day.

ODAL, heritable land in the possession of aristocratic families in Scandinavia which could not be alienated without consent of all the kinsmen.

ODILIA (Ottilia, Othilia), ST., d. c. 720, patroness of Alsace, born blind but miraculously cured when she was baptized. The nunnery she founded at Hohenburg in the Vosges Mountains became a favorite center of pilgrimage. Charlemagne and Pope Leo IX, and possibly Richard I of England, were among its famous visitors.

ODILO OF CLUNY, ST., d. 1049, fifth abbot of Cluny, a man of unusual administrative ability, and for 50 years the occupant of that office. During his abbacy the Congregation of Cluny experienced an enormous growth. Odilo showed a genuine interest in the poor, encouraged an extension of the Truce of God, and, because he was highly respected by popes and kings, was often engaged in diplomatic business. The observance of All Souls' Day (November 2) was introduced by him as a local feast at Cluny, whence it spread throughout the Christian world.

ODIN (Othin, Wuotan, Wotan, Wodan, Woden), supreme god of the Germans, a god of war, culture, and of the dead.

ODO (Eudes), count of Paris and son of Robert the Strong, elected king of the West Franks in 888 following the deposition of Charles III (the Fat) by the East Franks. Odo reigned, although with no great authority, until his death in 898. In 893 some magnates hailed Charles III (the Simple) as king at Reims, which led to several battles between him and Odo. Despite the decisive victory Odo gained over the Normans in 888, they continued to harass his country throughout his reign.

ODOACER (Odovacar, Odoaker, Odowakar), barbarian "king" of Italy, a Scirian chieftain, who with his companions served Rome as mercenaries until 476 when he slew Orestes and deposed his son Romulus Augustulus, the last "Roman emperor" in the west. Although Odoacer established himself as ruler of Italy, he recognized the overlordship of the emperor Zeno in Constantinople and ruled officially as patrician. In 493 he was treacherously slain by Theodoric, king of the Ostrogoths, who had been delegated by Zeno to get rid of him.

O'DONNELL, Irish family consisting of five clans or septs which was prominent from the thirteenth to the sixteenth century. The most powerful of the clans was that of Tir Conaill (Tyrconnell) which controlled the county of Donegal.

ODO OF BAYEUX, d. 1097, half-brother of William the Conqueror and bishop of Bayeaux. He took part in the battle of Hastings, became earl of Kent, and later served as William's viceroy. He was apparently imprisoned by William for having planned to lead a military expedition to Italy, and was released only when William was on his deathbed. He later joined a revolt that aimed to replace William II (Rufus) with his brother Robert. Odo died on the First Crusade.

ODO OF CLUNY, ST., d. 942, monk at Baume (a Cluniac monastery), abbot of Cluny from 927, and one of the organizers of the Cluniac reform movement. He was chiefy responsible for the position of leadership which the monastery enjoyed during the next centuries. His writings include a number of moral essays and sermons, hymns, and lives of the saints.

ODORIC OF PORDENONE, BL., d. 1331, a Franciscan who labored for some 35 years as a missionary in the Balkans, Persia, Trebizond, Peking, and among the Mongols of southern Russia. The description of his extensive travels in India, China, and the East Indies enjoyed considerable popularity in the late Middle Ages. Sir John Mandeville appropriated extensive excerpts and presented them as his own.

ODOVACAR. *See* ODOACER.

OECUMENICAL COUNCILS. *See* COUNCIL, GENERAL.

OENGUS, ST., called the Culdee, fl. eighth-ninth centuries, obscure Irish monk and reformer of Clonenagh in Leix. He is believed to have been the author of an Irish "devotional" calendar (*Félire*). The calendar consisted of 365 quatrains, one for each day of the year, each quatrain listing for the day the names of Irish and foreign saints honored on that day. Some historical or legendary detail might accompany the name of the saint.

OFFA, king of Mercia, 757–96, who called himself "rex Anglorum," that is, king of the English. He is considered England's leading monarch before Alfred the Great (d. 899) and perhaps the most powerful English sovereign before the tenth century. He extended his authority over Sussex, Wessex, Kent, and Northumbria, and seized territory along the Welsh border. To protect his western frontier against the Welsh he then threw up a great earthwork called Offa's Dyke. He introduced a system of coinage based on the silver penny which endured for 500 years, while his code of laws drew praise from Alfred. The first recorded commercial treaty in English history is the one he negotiated with Charlemagne. It is possible that the annual payment he agreed to send to Rome in 787 may

have been the origin of Peter's Pence. He showed himself generous to monasteries, and St. Albans honored him as its founder.

OFFA'S DYKE. *See* OFFA.

OFFERTORY, the early part of the Mass during which offerings of bread and wine were made to God. The term also applied to the short anthem or antiphon sung at the time of offering.

OFFICE, DIVINE. *See* DIVINE OFFICE.

OFFICIAL, the representative in the diocese of the bishop in legal matters.

OGADAI (Ogodai, Ogatai, Ugedai), third son and successor of Genghis Khan who ruled the Mongol empire from 1229 to 1241. He was the first of the Mongol leaders to style himself khagan (chief khan). By conquest he added north China and Korea to his empire. He caused much destruction in Russia and marched through Hungary to the Adriatic.

OGHAM (Ogam) **SCRIPT**, ancient Irish script used in inscriptions in Ireland and England from the fifth century.

OGIER THE DANE, semilegendary Danish hero who appears in the *Chanson de Roland* as one of Charlemagne's most valiant warriors. The many adventures attributed to him furnished materials for writers from the thirteenth century to the close of the Middle Ages. Ogier's historical prototype was Autcharius, a vassal of Pepin III (the Short), then of Carloman, Charlemagne's brother.

OHM (Aam, Ahm, Aime, Äm), liquid measure of varying size used by several peoples of central and northeastern Europe.

OKEGHEM, JAN VAN, d. c. 1495, Flemish composer, singer, and chaplain at the court of the French kings Charles VII, Louis XI, and Charles VIII. He composed some 20 *chansons*, 14 masses, and a number of motets including several Marian hymns.

OLAF, name of two kings of the Norse kingdoms of Northumbria and Dublin. Olaf Guthfrithson, d. 941, king of Dublin, engaged in plundering throughout his life. In 937 he and his Scottish allies were defeated by Aethelstan at Brunanburh. He later seized York, then was given Northumbria and part of Danish Mercia by Edmund I. Olaf Sihtricson, d. 981, succeeded Olaf Guthfrithson, his father, as king of Northumbria, while his brother received Dublin. After Edmund I had defeated him, he was deposed in 943 by the Northumbrians. He later fled to Ireland where he became king of Dublin. Still later, from 949 to 952, he ruled Northumbria. After suffering a defeat in Ireland he withdrew to Iona where he died.

OLAF I (Tryggvesson), king of Norway, 995–c. 999, great-grandson of Harald I Haarfager (Fairhair), who may have been with the Vikings who defeated the Anglo-Saxons at the battle of Maldon in 991. He left England in 995 for Norway, overthrew Haakon, and was proclaimed king. By persuasion and force, he converted most of the people living along the coast as well as those in Ireland to Christianity where it became the official religion of the land. He was slain in battle with Sweyn I, the king of Denmark.

OLAF (Olave) II, ST., king of Norway, 1015–30, also known as Olaf the Fat, a descendant of Harald I Haarfager (Fairhair) who accompanied Viking raiders possibly as far as Spain, was baptized at Rouen in Normandy, and in 1015 returned to Norway to claim the throne. When Canute proclaimed himself king of Norway in 1028, Olaf, who had antagonized his jarls by his policy of appointing commoners as royal officials and encouraging Icelandic influences, fled to Russia, then was slain in 1030 when he returned to Norway to recover his throne. His piety and his efforts to bring his subjects to accept Christianity earned him the title of patron saint of Norway. His shrine at Nidaros (Trondheim) became a popular place of pilgrimage.

OLD CHURCH SLAVONIC, language created by St. Cyril (Constantine) (d. 869) for the south and west Slavs. He provided them with an alphabet and founded the first Slavonic literary language.

OLDCASTLE, SIR JOHN, d. 1417, knight of Herefordshire, Lord Cobham through marriage, the most prominent Englishman to accept Lollardy. He fought with the young Henry (V) against the Welsh and became his friend. (Henry sought earnestly to prevent his execution.) In 1413 Oldcastle escaped from the Tower where he had been confined to wait trial for heresy, organized a forlorn revolt, then fled to the Welsh marches where he was captured and executed.

OLDENBURG (Schleswig-Holstein), principal community of the Obotrites in the ninth century. In 948 Otto I established an episcopal seat there, the first one among the Wends. It received a charter in 1345. Christian of Oldenburg became king of Denmark in 1448.

OLD MAN OF THE MOUNTAIN, name by which some Western writers referred to the grand master of the Assassins. No one actually knew his true identity and he may have been confused with Prester John, also a legendary figure. [See PRESTER JOHN.]

OLD SARUM. See SALISBURY, DIOCESE OF.

OLEG, d. c. 912, first grand prince of Kiev. He left Novgorod after the death of his kinsman Rurik and seized Kiev (882). From Kiev as his capital he extended his rule over a number of Slavic and Finnish tribes. About 905 he made an attack on Constantinople, which, although unsuccessful, led to a trade agreement with Byzantium (907). Some scholars consider him the founder of the Russian state.

OLÉRON, LAW OF, a maritime code promulgated by Louis IX of France (d. 1270). It took its name from an island in the Bay of Biscay. Seamen in the waters west of France and Spain usually observed its code.

OLGERD (Olgierd, Algirdas), grand prince of Lithuania, 1345–77, successfully defended his country from the attacks of the Teutonic Knights and extended the frontiers of his realm eastward at the expense of the Russians and south toward the Black Sea (1368) after defeating the Tatars. Perhaps the greater share of his success was owed to the ability of his brother and co-ruler Keistut.

OLIFANT, horn of Byzantine origin which was often decorated with hunting and battle scenes. It was the name given to Roland's horn in the *Chanson de Roland*.

OLIVETANS, Order of Our Lady of Mount Olivet, a branch of the Benedictines founded in 1319 by Giovanni Tolomei (St. Bernard Ptolomei) at Monte Oliveto near Siena. The Olivetans who observed a strict interpretation of the Rule of Benedict, soon attracted fame for the saintliness of their lives and the rigor of their observance.

OLIVIER (Oliver), the companion of Roland in the *Chanson de Roland*.

OLMÜTZ (Olomouc), principal city of Moravia, first noted in the tenth century. It became a bishop's see in 1063. The Mongols failed in their attempt to storm the city in 1242 and were driven off by Wenceslas II. The city served as a strong point of the Catholic party during the Hussite wars. In 1478, Moravia was ceded to the king of Hungary.

OLYMPIODORUS, name of several Greek writers. Olympiodorus of Thebes was sent as an emissary to Attila, the Hunnic king, by Honorius, the Western Roman emperor, in 412. His history covers events in the west from 407 to 425. Olympiodorus of Alexandria (sixth century), a neo-Platonist, appears to have maintained the Platonic tradition in Alexandria after Justinian

had suppressed the Athenian school. He left commentaries on several of Plato's dialogues, a life of Plato, commentaries on Aristotle's *Categories* and *Meteora,* and an introduction to his philosophy.

OMAR ('Umar Ibn Al-Khattab) I, caliph from 634 to 644, the first of the successors of Mohammed to call himself "Commander of the Faithful." He was responsible for the selection of Abu Bakr as the Prophet's successor, who, in turn, nominated Omar as his successor. Omar, who proved himself a stern though just ruler, established the administrative and legal structure of the Islamic state and in effect changed it from an Arabic principality to a world power. During his reign Islamic power spread over Mesopotamia, Syria, Palestine, Egypt, and the greater part of Iran.

OMAR ('Umar Ibn 'Abd-al-'Aziz) II, caliph from 717 to 720, whose reign witnessed a massive, though unsuccessful, assault on Constantinople (717–8). He encouraged conversions by exempting converts from poll taxes and he also sought to extend equality to non-Arab Moslems. Because of his piety and his concern for the "pious opposition," he was the only Omayyad caliph whose tomb was not destroyed by the victorious Abbasids.

OMAR KHAYYAM (Chajjam), d. c. 1132, eminent mathematician and astronomer, also an authority on philosophy, jurisprudence, and history. The Western world knows him best as the author of the *Rubaiyat,* part of which he composed. This first came to the notice of the Western world c. 1700, although it was not actually admired until the appearance of Edward Fitz-Gerald's paraphrased English translation.

OMAR, MOSQUE OF, mosque more properly known as Dome of the Rock. Caliph Abd al-Malik (685–705) had it erected in Jerusalem at the place where the temple of Solomon was believed to have stood. Moslems venerated the site as that from which Mohammed ascended to heaven. For the Jews it was the place on which Abraham was prepared to sacrifice Isaac.

OMAYYADS (Umayyads, Ommiads), the first of the two great dynasties to rule Islam. Its rule extended from 660 to 750. The founder of the dynasty was Mu'awiya, governor of Syria, who refused to recognize Ali as caliph following the murder of Othman in 656, although he did not formally assume authority until 660. Mu'awiya made Damascus his capital and staffed the administration principally with Arabs although he patterned its organization and operation after those of Byzantium. A source of discontent during the period of Omayyad rule was its policy of discrimination against non-Arab Moslems (*mawali*), although the major source of opposition came from the hostility of the Shiites. The Omayyads were Sunnites. The *mawali* joined the followers of Ali, as did also those Moslems who believed that the succession should have been through Abbas, the uncle of Mohammed, in overthrowing the Omayyad dynasty in 750. Abd ar-Rahman, the only surviving member of the dynasty, managed to escape to Spain where he set up an independent Moslem state in 756. [*See* CÓRDOBA.] During the period of Ommayad rule, Islam had continued to expand — into Transoxiana, India, north Africa, Spain, and southwestern France.

ONTOLOGICAL ARGUMENT, THE, an argument first developed by St. Anselm of Bec (d. 1109) which established the existence of God on the basis of the assumption that the very notion of God contains, by implication, the idea that nothing greater can be conceived. If one were to suppose God did not exist, this would involve a contradiction since an entity greater than a non-existing God, could be conceived, namely, a God who existed. St. Thomas Aquinas denied the validity of the argument.

OPEN FIELD, the arable acres that belonged to a manor and divided into two or three large fields, with neither fences nor hedges to set off the individual holdings of the lord, serfs, and freemen. What made the use of fences impractical was the tradition of dividing the land possessed by each peasant into strips of an acre or half-acre in size and scattering these about the two (or three) fields, presumably for the purpose that all share alike in the poor and better soil.

OPHITES AND NAASENES, Gnostic sects, notorious for their immorality and worship of the serpent. They adopted the teaching of Marcion that a hostility existed between the God of the Old Testament and the God of the New. For this reason, they revered the "villains" of the Old Testament, including Cain, the Sodomites, the Egyptians, and the serpent of Eden.

OPORTO, seaport of northwest Portugal from Roman times, occupied by the Visigoths in 540, by the Moors in 716, and taken from the Moors in 997 by Alfonso I of the Asturias. In the eleventh century Henry of Burgundy secured the title of duke of Portucalense. It was an episcopal see ruled by its bishop until 1254.

OPUS ANGLICANUM, name given to English ecclesiastical embroidery.

OPUS DEI, literally the "work of God," more particularly the name given to the Divine Office by the Benedictines.

ORA ET LABORA, Latin for "pray and work," an old monastic principle usually associated with the Benedictine order.

ORANGE, COUNCILS OF: a) council held at Orange in south France in 441, under the presidency of St. Hilary of Arles, which issued 30 canons dealing mainly with disciplinary matters; b) council held in 529 which issued 25 dogmatic *capitula* which served to endorse Augustine's doctrines on the nature of grace against the views of the Semi-Pelagians.

ORANGE, GUILLAUME D', hero of Old French courtly romances of the twelfth and thirteenth centuries and a central figure in the cycle of

Narbonne. He was supposedly a loyal vassal of Louis the Pious (814–40).

ORA PRO NOBIS, Latin for "pray for us," the response said by the laity when invoking the intercession of saints in litanies.

ORATION, prayer introduced by *Oremus* ("let us pray"). It appeared frequently in the Mass and the Divine Office.

ORATORY, term loosely used for both churches and private chapels but better reserved for places of worship other than parish churches. They were usually located in country districts where there were no churches. The origin of oratories may have been the chapels built over the tombs of martyrs.

ORATRES FRATRES, the exhortation "Pray, Brethren," addressed to the faithful by the priest after the offertory and before the secret in the Roman Mass. It appeared more frequently in the Greek than in the Latin liturgy, although it seems to have originated in Italy in the eleventh century.

ORCAGNA, ANDREA (Andrea di Cione), d. c. 1368, the leading Florentine artist of his age, a painter, sculptor, and architect. His best known work is the altarpiece of *The Redeemer* in the Strozzi Chapel of S. Maria Novella. He was the first great artist after Giotto although he rejected Giotto's innovations and returned to Gothic, even to Byzantine, practices in his pictorial style.

ORDEAL, method of trial in which the accused person was subjected to a physical test (e.g., hot iron, boiling water, ordeal by battle) which he could meet successfully only if he were innocent since God (the gods) would determine the outcome. The origins of the medieval ordeal were Germanic and pagan. Although the church sought to improve its effectiveness by accompanying it with a solemn ritual, society had in general recognized its futility before 1215 when the Fourth Lateran Council forbade the clergy to participate any longer in ordeals. In England, the

legal procedures introduced by Henry II (1154–89) almost eliminated the use of the ordeal in that country.

ORDER OF PREACHERS. *See* DOMINICANS.

ORDERICUS VITALIS, d. c. 1142, monk of the Benedictine abbey of St. Evroul in Normandy, the author of the *Historia Ecclesiastica,* a history of Christianity to 1141. His narrative, which is the work of a critical scholar, is quite valuable for the political and ecclesiastical history of Normandy, England, and France for the period 1082–1141.

ORDERS, SACRAMENT OF HOLY, rite by which the recipient was raised to an ecclesiastical order, namely, that of subdeacon, deacon, or priest, through the imposition of hands by the bishop.

ORDINAL, a manual of instructions for priests concerning the office to be recited in accordance with variations in the ecclesiastical year.

ORDINARY, official in the church whose authority or jurisdiction was original and not that of a deputy. As an identification it was usually applied to bishops, abbots, and generals and provincials of religious orders.

ORDINES ROMANI, document concerned with the liturgy in the Middle Ages, from the singular *ordo,* a term applied to directive documents describing in some detail the procedure to be followed in liturgical functions, e.g., the celebration of mass.

OREMUS, "let us pray," said or sung before collects and other short prayers in the Roman rite.

ORESME, NICHOLAS (Nicole), d. 1382, a founder of modern science and mathematics. He studied theology at Paris and was consecrated bishop of Lisieux (1377). In addition to several works of Aristotle which he translated into French, he left writings of his own on theology, science, mathematics, economics, politics, and geometry. He prepared the first scientific study of money. In his *De Coelo et Mundo* he discussed the movement of the earth in terms that anticipated Copernicus, while his writings on analytical geometry anticipated the ideas of Descartes and Galileo.

ORESTES, master of the soldiers in the western empire in 475. He overthrew Julius Nepos whom Emperor Leo in Constantinople had appointed emperor in the west, and placed his own son Romulus (Augustulus) on the throne. He was slain by Odoacer in 476.

ORGAN. The use of organs is recorded at Malmesbury as well as on the Continent in the early eighth century, while in the tenth century such places as Glastonbury and Winchester prided themselves on having one. By the thirteenth century organs were common in the larger parish churches and they were almost universal by the close of the Middle Ages. The organ in the cathedral at Halberstadt, Germany, had three chromatic keyboards and pedals. In north Germany by 1500, all the important features of the modern organ had been introduced.

ORGANUM, two-voice harmony in which the single tone of the Gregorian chant was accompanied by another at an interval of a fourth or fifth. It made its appearance in the ninth century.

ORIFLAMME, royal banner of the kings of France used from the reign of Louis VI and associated, at least in literature, with that of Charlemagne (d. 814).

ORIGEN, d. c. 254, a leading church father of the Eastern church and the most prolific writer of all the church fathers. He was a native of Alexandria. For some years he was head of the city's catechetical school but later moved to Caesarea where he was ordained a priest. He was imprisoned and tortured during the persecution of the emperor Decius (249–51) and died in broken health a few years later. The *Hexapla* in which he arranged the Hebrew version of the Bible with four Greek texts in six parallel columns represented the first systematic study of the Scriptures. In his *On First Principles* he attempted to formulate a Christian theology into which he had assimilated some of the principles of neo-Platonism. He was the first church father to introduce some clarity into the terminology of the Trinitarian doctrine. In his commentaries on the Bible he paid particular attention to the spiritual (moral and mystical) meaning of the text. Even though few of his writings have survived, their influence upon the development of Christian theology was not exceeded by that of any other Eastern church father. Because of the prodigious scope of his writing and the pioneering character of much of it, his work was not free of error nor above misinterpretation, and a heresy called Origenism harassed the church from the late second century through the sixth. Its adherents preached such views as the preexistence of souls and universal salvation which they attributed to Origen.

ORIGENISM. *See* ORIGEN.

ORIGINAL SIN, the sin of Adam which deprived mankind of sanctifying grace and ultimate salvation. Christians believed that the sacrament of baptism removed the most serious consequences of this sin, and that, with the grace of God, the faithful could attain heaven.

ORKHAN (Orchan), d. 1362, son and successor of Osman I, and ruler (*beg*) of the Ottoman Turks from 1326 to 1362. He captured Nicaea and Nicomedia, crossed into the Balkans in 1345 to assist John VI Cantacuzenus in what proved a successful bid for the Byzantine throne, and in 1354 seized Gallipoli (Callipolis) for himself. His Turks were the first to make their appearance on the European mainland.

ORKNEY, EARLDOM OF, Scottish title created for Sir Henry Sinclair in 1379. His mother was Isabella, daughter of Malise, the last of the ancient line of earls or jarls who had ruled the Orkney Islands from the ninth century. Sir

Henry Sinclair ruled the islands as virtual king. His grandson William, who became chancellor of Scotland, resigned the title to James III of Scotland in 1470. James had acquired sovereignty over the Orkneys by virtue of his marriage to the daughter of the king of Denmark and Norway who had claimed overlordship.

ORKNEY ISLANDS, some 90 islands off the north coast of Scotland, claimed in 875 for Norway by Harald I (Harald Fairhair). They remained under the nominal control of Norway until 1468 when Christian I of Norway and Denmark pledged them as security for his daughter, Margaret, who married James III of Scotland. The pledge was never redeemed.

ORLEANISTS, group of French noblemen who supported the right of Louis, duke of Orléans, the younger brother of Charles VI of France, to take over the direction of the government when the king became mentally ill in 1392. They were opposed by the Burgundian faction headed by Charles's uncle Philip, the duke of Burgundy. After the murder of Louis in 1407, leadership of the Orleanist faction fell to the count of Armagnac, the father-in-law of the duke's son, whence the name Armagnacs to replace that of the Orleanists.

ORLÉANS, city located on the middle Loire whose site was occupied from Celtic times. It became as episcopal see in the fourth century and in 451 withstood the attack of Attila and his Huns. During the reign of Charlemagne, Orléans enjoyed a reputation as an intellectual center largely because of the nearby abbey of Fleury. The schools established by Bishop Theodulf, abbot of Fleury, formed the beginnings of the University of Orléans, founded by Pope Clement V in 1305. The early Capetians often made the city their residence, and in the tenth and eleventh centuries it served as the real capital of France. The city's chief episode in the late Middle Ages was the driving off of the English by Joan of Arc in 1429 after a siege of seven months.

ORLÉANS, DUKE OF, as a ducal title originated in 1344 when King Philip VI gave the duchy to his younger son Philip. When Philip died without heirs in 1375, it reverted to the crown, a contingency that enabled Charles VI to grant the title and duchy to his brother Louis in 1392. [For Louis, see LOUIS, duke of Orléans.] Upon the murder of Louis in 1407, his son Charles inherited the title, although his marriage to the daughter of Bernard VII, count of Armagnac, gave the count leadership of the Orleanist faction, which thenceforth was known as the Armagnac. The younger Charles spent 25 years as a prisoner in England after his capture at the battle of Agincourt (1415). His verse which he composed in both French and English established him as one of the leading court poets of the period.

ORMULUM, THE, poem in Middle English composed during the first half of the thirteenth century by Orm (Ormin), an Augustinian monk. It consists of paraphrases of the Gospels with accompanying homilies.

OROSIUS, PAULUS, d. after 418, a native of Spain who served as a priest at Hippo. He became a disciple of Augustine who encouraged him to write his *Seven Books of History Against the Pagans*. Although this proved a popular history in the Middle Ages, its value is limited to the years 377 to 417. Orosius paid particular attention to disasters and catastrophes that had taken place in ancient times in order to disprove the charge made by some pagans of the time that if Rome had remained faithful to the pagan gods, it would not have fallen to the Visigoths in 410. His history was among the "great books" which Alfred the Great had translated into English. Upon Augustine's urging, Orosius also produced a summary of the errors of Priscillian and Origen.

ORSINI, prominent family of Rome after 1100, leaders of the Guelf faction and generally staunch supporters of the papacy. The family claimed a number of cardinals and two popes, Celestine III (1191–8) and Nicholas III (1277–80).

ORTLIBARII, members of an ascetic group that originated with Ortlieb of Strasbourg (c. 1200). They accepted in substance the dualism of the Cathari and rejected such fundamental tenets of Christianity as the doctrine of the Trinity, the Eucharist, and the creation of the universe. It appears that most of them were eventually absorbed by the Brothers and Sisters of the Free Spirit.

ORVIETO, city in central Italy in the Apennines that was ruled as a free commune by consuls from the close of the tenth century. The city often served the medieval popes as a place of refuge. It passed officially under their control in 1450. The city's beautiful cathedral, begun in 1290 and completed in the sixteenth century, contains sculptures, mosaics, and frescoes by some of Italy's greatest artists.

O SALUTARIS HOSTIA, the first line of the penultimate stanza of the hymn *Verum Supernum Prodiens* that Thomas Aquinas (d. 1274) composed for the feast of *Corpus Christi*.

OSEBERG, site along the Oslo Fjord in Norway where a burial-ship was discovered in 1903. The tomb, possibly that of the grandmother of Harald I Haarfager (Fairhair), may have been placed there in the ninth century.

OSLO, town on the southeast coast of Norway founded c. 1048 by King Harald III. In the fourteenth century it became a bishop's see and the de facto capital of the country. It was generally under control of the Hanseatic League. One of the reasons it flourished was the ice-free character of its harbor.

OSMAN. *See* OTHMAN.

OSMUND OF SALISBURY, ST., d. 1099, a Norman who accompanied his uncle William the Conqueror to England where he served him as chancellor. As bishop of Salisbury (1078) he took an active part in civil and ecclesiastical affairs. His organization of the liturgical service in his diocese may have provided the basis for the Sarum rite. His constitution of the cathedral chapter became the model of many similar foundations.

OSSIAN (Oisin, Oisean), supposedly the son of Finn mac Cumhail, warrior of the third century and hero of the Irish Ossian saga. Ossian kept alive the story of his father's exploits in both song and verse. He is generally represented as the venerable, blind singer who appears occasionally in early medieval literature.

OSTENSORIUM, sacred vessel, also known as monstrance, designed for the exhibition of the consecrated host. It probably came into use no earlier than the thirteenth century.

OSTIARY, the order of porter, the first and lowest of the minor orders. His responsibilities included those of opening and locking the door of the church and ringing the bell to summon the faithful to services. In the early centuries of Christendom it was his responsibility to bar entrance to the church to persons not authorized to participate in the service.

OSTMARK, roughly the nucleus of Austria which Charlemagne organized as a march to block an invasion of the Avars. Otto I (936–73) gave the province the name of Ostmark (east march).

OSTRAKA, inscribed potsherds, more specifically Christian inscriptions on clay, wood, metal, and other hard materials from the early centuries.

OSTROGOTHS, east branch of the Goths located north of the Black Sea which retained its independence until subjugated by the Huns in 375. Upon the collapse of Hunnic power in 453, the Ostrogoths moved into Pannonia and settled there as *foederati* of the Roman empire. In 488 their King Theodoric (the Great) led them to Italy upon the suggestion of Emperor Zeno who feared their proximity, overthrew the regime of

Odoacer, and took possession of the peninsula. After the death of Theodoric in 526, his grandson Athalaric succeeded under the regency of Theodoric's daughter Amalasuntha who put herself under the protection of the Byzantine emperor Justinian. Upon the murder of Amalasuntha, Justinian moved his armies into Italy and c. 560 finally accomplished the destruction of the Ostrogothic kingdom. What remnants remained of the nation disappeared across the Alps. [*See* BELISARIUS; TOTILA.]

OSWALD OF YORK, ST., d. 992, a Dane, nephew of Odo, the archbishop of Canterbury. He became a Benedictine monk, was consecrated bishop of Worcester and in 972 became archbishop of York. He assisted Dunstan in his efforts to reform the church in England. He left several theological treatises and synodal decrees.

OSWALD, ST., king of Northumbria, d. 641, the son of King Ethelfrith, who was obliged to flee the land when his uncle Edwin usurped the throne upon his father's death. Oswald, who grew up in Iona, returned to Northumbria in 633, defeated Cadwallon, who had killed his uncle Edwin, and recovered his throne. The missonaries whom he invited in from Iona included Aidan who became the first bishop of Northumbria with his see at Lindisfarne. Oswald made himself master of Wessex but not of Mercia and was slain in battle with Penda, Mercia's heathen king. Oswald was honored as a martyr.

OSWIU (Oswy), king of Northumbria, 641–70, son of Ethelfrith. He extended his authority over all of Northumbria after defeating and killing Penda, king of Mercia, at the battle of Winwaed. For the greater part of his reign he was recognized as overlord of all the kingdoms south of the Humber. His vote in favor of Roman usages and liturgy at the Synod of Whitby in 664 proved decisive and the Celtic clergy withdrew from the area.

OTFRID (Otfried) OF WEISSENBURG, fl. ninth century, studied at Fulda under Rabanus Maurus, became a monk in the Benedictine monastery of Weissenburg (Alsace), and was later head of the monastic school there. His principal work, entitled *Evangelienbuch,* composed between 863 and 871, represents the first poem in German to use rhyme rather than alliteration. The poem possesses linguistic importance as an early example of the South Rhenish Franconian dialect. The work deals with the life of Christ, combining the narrative in small chapters with a commentary.

OTHLO (Othoh) OF ST. EMMERAM, d. 1072 or 1073, Benedictine monk of St. Emmeram (for a time at Fulda) and author of treatises on scriptural and theological subjects, a life of St. Boniface, sermons, hymns, and a collection of proverbs.

OTHMAN ('Uthman), Islamic caliph (third), 644–56, a son-in-law of Mohammed, member of the Omayyad family, the successor of Omar. Although he was not a strong ruler, the spread of Islamic power continued on without interruption. An expanded fleet defeated the Byzantine navy and captured Cyprus. During Othman's caliphate the standard text of the Koran was established. He was murdered by one of the groups, apparently not the followers of Ali, whom his high-handed methods had antagonized.

OTHMAN (Osman) I, d. 1326, founder of the Ottoman Turkish state which he ruled from 1288 to 1326. He had at first served as a vassal of the Seljuk Turks, but when their rule crumbled, he declared his independence. In 1300 he assumed the title of sultan.

OTOKAR. *See* OTTOCAR.

OTTO I (the Great), king of Germany, 936–73, the son of the future Henry I and his successor. Otto succeeded after a struggle in forcing his dukes to accept his authority, broke the power of the Magyars at the battle of the Lech (955), and pushed German influence to the Oder against the Slavs. There, along the eastern frontier, he erected a number of dioceses including Brandenburg and Magdeburg for the purpose of advancing the Germanization and Christianization of that region. He extended his rule to Italy, including Rome, where he was crowned emperor in 962 by Pope John XII. When John later challenged his authority, he deposed him, set up a new pope, and initiated almost a century of German control of the papacy. He had already achieved effective control of the German hierarchy whose lands he expanded and protected, a policy that assured him the loyalty of a large part of Germany. He also secured the hand of Theophano, a Byzantine princess, for his son Otto (II).

OTTO II, king of Germany, 973–83, put down a revolt in Bavaria, detached Carinthia and the Ostmark (later Austria) from that powerful duchy, then gave it to the house of Babenberg. A shattering defeat at the hands of the Saracens in 982 at Cape Colonne thwarted his hope of conquering southern Italy.

OTTO III, king of Germany, 983–1002, and Roman emperor (996), was tutored by Gerbert whom he later raised to the papal throne in 999 as Sylvester II. His mother Theophano, served as regent until her death in 991. Otto supported monastic reform and erected Gniezno as the metropolitan see of Poland. In 998 he made his home in Rome as a preliminary step to reestablising the ancient empire of the Roman Caesars.

OTTO IV, king of Germany, 1208–15, and Roman emperor (1209), won election as king of Germany when the opposing candidate, Philip of Swabia, was murdered. His invasion of Tuscany, then of southern Italy, cost him the support of Pope Innocent III who had earlier championed his selection as king over Philip, who was a Hohenstaufen. Innocent, after Otto's invasion of Italy, had no difficulty arousing some German princes as well as Philip II Augustus of France against him. His defeat at the battle of Bouvines in 1214 cost him his crown. He died in 1218.

OTTO I OF WITTELSBACH, duke of Bavaria, 1180–3, owed his duchy to Frederick I Barbarossa who gave it to him in recognition of the assistance he had tendered the emperor in Italy. Frederick had deprived Henry the Lion of the duchy.

OTTOCAR (Ottokar, Premysl Ottocar) I, first king of Bohemia, 1198–1230, who was recognized as such by Henry VI in 1192, then in 1216 gained imperial recognition of the hereditary character of his kingship from Emperor Frederick II of Germany.

OTTOCAR (Ottokar, Premysl Ottocar) II, king of Bohemia, 1253–78, seized control of Austria, Styria, Carinthia, and Carniola, partly by force, partly through trickery. Because these acquisitions made him the most powerful prince in the empire, the electors chose Rudolf of Hapsburg to be king of Germany and gave him their blessing to regain these territories, which he did. Ottocar's attempt to recover them cost him his life at the battle of Marchfeld. He had a leading part in a crusade against the pagan Slavs in East Prussia, where the castle of Königsberg ("King's Mountain") was founded and named after him. This Ottocar may be considered the greatest of the native kings of Bohemia after George of Podiebrad.

OTTOMAN TURKS. *See* TURKEY.

OTTONIAN RENAISSANCE, the cultural revival during the reigns of Otto I, II, and III of Germany, that is, roughly during the period from 936 to 1002. Much of the inspiration for the revival came from the imperial court. The monastic and cathedral schools of Passau, Regensburg, Magdeburg, Corvey, and Gandersheim constituted its principal centers. Among the prominent figures associated with the renaissance are Widukind of Corvey, Roswitha of

Gandersheim, Liutprand of Cremona, and Bernward of Hildesheim. The period witnessed not only significant advances in the field of learning but also in those of book illumination, sculpture, and miniatures.

OTTO OF BAMBERG, ST., d. 1139, born of a noble family of Swabia, chancellor of Henry IV of Germany, and bishop of Bamberg (1102). He had a major role in the discussions leading to the acceptance of the Concordat of Worms in 1122. He was also active in his diocese, reforming the clergy and founding more than 20 monasteries. His extensive missionary labors earned him the title of Apostle of Pomerania.

OTTO OF FREISING, d. 1158, son of Leopold III of Austria and grandson of Henry IV of Germany. He studied at Paris under Hugh of St. Victor and possibly Abelard, also at Reims and Chartres. In 1138 he became abbot of the Cistercian abbey of Morimond (eastern Champagne) and shortly after bishop of Freising. He accompanied his half-brother Conrad III on the Second Crusade. His principal work, entitled *History of Two Cities,* which is a chronicle from the Creation to 1146, shows the influence of St. Augustine's *City of God.* It is a reflective work, not a profound study of the course of events, in which he constantly warns his reader of the transitoriness of this life. His other work, *Deeds of Frederick Barbarossa,* who was his nephew, was left unfinished.

OUEN (Audoin, Owen), ST., d. 684, archbishop of Rouen. He earlier served at the courts of Clothaire II and Dagobert I. In 641 he was consecrated archbishop of Rouen. He founded many monasteries, supported reform in the church, encouraged scholarship, and was employed on several political missions by the Merovingian kings.

OUR LADY OF THE SNOW, title given to Mary on the basis of a legend concerning a Roman couple who had promised their wealth to the Virgin but wished her to give a sign how she wanted it spent. When snow fell during the summer on the Esquiline Hill, they chose that site for the basilica of Santa Maria Maggiore. [*See* S. MARIA MAGGIORE.]

OVIEDO, town in the Asturias, founded c. 760 around a monastery built by Fruela I, flourished as the capital of that country into the ninth century, then declined when the capital was moved to Leon. The cathedral, begun in 1388, contains the tombs of the Asturian kings.

OWEN GLENDOWER. *See* GLENDOWER, OWEN.

OWL AND THE NIGHTINGALE, THE, a twelfth-thirteenth-century poem in Middle English, probably by Nicholas de Guildford, which tells of a debate between two birds. They discuss many subjects, including moral and intellectual questions. The nightingale, which has a positive, optimistic bent, argues in favor of the new secular poetry, while the owl, who takes a more sober view of life supports the older didactic verse.

OXFORD, city on the upper Thames where St. Frideswide is said to have founded a convent as early as the eighth century. In 912 when the site was fortified against the Danes it went by the name of Oxenford. Parliament met in Oxford on several occasions in the thirteenth century. The University of Oxford sprang from obscure origins during the second half of the twelfth century. Some scholars associate its founding with the expulsion of English students from Paris in 1167. Its first chancellor was Robert Grosseteste, scientist and mathematician, who held the post from c. 1215 until 1235 when he was consecrated bishop of Lincoln. The bishop of Lincoln retained some authority over the institution until 1368. Colleges established at Oxford during the Middle Ages included University, Balliol, Merton, St. Edmund Hall, Exeter, Oriel, Queen's, New, Lincoln, All Souls, and Magdalen.

OXFORD, EARLDOM OF, title created by Empress Matilda for Aubrey III de Vere in 1142 and later recognized by King Stephen. Robert de Vere, ninth earl (d. 1392), was created marquess of Dublin and duke of Ireland by Richard II. These honors aroused the anger of the lords appellant, and when they gained the ascendancy over Richard in 1388, Robert thought it prudent to flee to the Netherlands where he died. John de Vere, thirteenth earl, a staunch adherent of the Lancastrians in the Wars of the Roses, fled to France after the defeat of Warwick's army at Barnet (1471), later joined Henry Tudor (VII), and commanded the right wing of his army at Bosworth Field (1485).

OXFORD, PROVISIONS OF, a constitution, sometimes called the first written constitution in English history, which Henry III accepted in 1258 under pressure from his rebellious barons. The constitution provided for a Council of Fifteen which would advise the king in all important matters, appoint his chief officers including the justiciar, chancellor, and treasurer, and exercise control over sheriffs and lesser officials. Papal annulment of the Provisions (1261–2), its condemnation by Louis IX of France in the Mise of Amiens (1264), and Henry's repudiation of the document precipitated the Barons' War.

PACHER, MICHAEL, d. 1498, a painter and woodcarver of Tyrol. His best known work is the *St. Wolfgang Altarpiece* in upper Austria, painted with scenes from the lives of Christ and St. Wolfgang. Although the style is the late Gothic then popular in Germany, it reflects strong Italian influences, notably that of the painter Mantegna.

PACHOMIUS, ST., d. 346, founder of cenobitism who established and directed a number of monastic communities of men and of women in the Thebaid near the Nile. He is honored as the father of cenobitism, as opposed to anchoritism, since he was the first monastic figure to preside as superior general over a large number of monks who lived together in a closely knit congregation. His monks occupied individual cells but gathered for prayer and meals. They also engaged in such activities as basket-making in order to provide for the material well-being of the community. The rule of Pachomius influenced St. Benedict, Basil, and John Cassian.

PACHYMERES, GEORGE, d. c. 1310, Byzantine theologian and historian who occupied high civil and ecclesiastical posts in Constantinople. He composed a number of theological treatises and a history of the reigns of Michael VIII Palaeologus (1259–82) and Andronicus II Palaeologus (1282–1328).

PACIOLI (Paciuoli), LUCA, d. after 1514, a Franciscan, taught mathematics in several Italian cities and produced a systematic presentation of mathematics which showed its association with general truths and principles.

PADERBORN, Saxon settlement east of the Rhine near the source of the Lippe. Charlemagne captured the town and made it a missionary center and a bishop's see (806). The cathedral was built during the eleventh-thirteenth centuries. Later the city belonged to the Hanseatic League.

PADUA, city in northeast Italy, a leading city of Italy during Roman times. It was destroyed by the Lombards in 601 but it recovered quickly, and for the greater part of the period from the twelfth to the fourteenth century was a free commune. It enjoyed some fame as a cultural center. The university, the oldest in Italy after Bologna, was founded in 1222 by masters and students who migrated from Bologna. The archbishop of Padua held jurisdiction over the university.

PADUA, SCHOOL OF, school of Italian painting that originated with Francesco Squarcione (d. c. 1468) and his pupils Mantegna, Tura, and Crivelli. Other artists associated with the school were Giorgio Schiavone and Marco Zoppo.

PADUA, UNIVERSITY OF. *See* PADUA.

PAGE, young man of free birth who attended a knight in his home, on the hunt, and, on occasion, in battle, in order to prepare himself for his future life as a knight (lord). In extended usage the name page might be given to the helper or apprentice of a master-workman.

PAINTING. The most impressive painting of the early Middle Ages, perhaps the only painting that interests students of art, is that of manuscript illumination. [*See* ILLUMINATED MANU-

SCRIPTS.] Many wall paintings and frescoes remain, but their figures are lifeless and stiff and bear the stamp of the impersonal art of Byzantium. Yet it was his careful study of these seemingly dull, flat Byzantine paintings and mosaics that enabled Giotto (d. 1337), the "father of modern painting," to rediscover the art of creating the illusion of depth on a flat surface. While flat and rigid in its appearance, Byzantine art furnished him with an introduction to the principles of foreshortening and revealed a shading and mixture of colors far superior to anything known in the West. With this knowledge Giotto was able to use light to define the construction of the body and its draperies and to invest his figures with a high degree of naturalism, as, e.g., in *Faith* and *Lamentation*.

About a century later Masaccio (d. 1428), a veritable genius who died in his 28th year, brought about a revolution in painting by placing his figures in a perspective frame, employing space to give his scene unity. By means of his knowledge of anatomy and the laws of foreshortening, his people comported themselves as human beings. Leonardo da Vinci, Michelangelo, and Raphael studied his *Tribute Money* to learn how to invest their own work with the quiet simplicity that marked this genius's artistry.

The next major departure in late medieval painting was the work of the Flemish artist Jan Van Eyck (d. 1441) who broke with Italian painters in their dependence upon the principles of foreshortening and perspective in order to create the illusion of space and to invest his figures with life. He achieved his astonishing success by adding detail upon detail until the picture he painted became a mirror of the visible world. To accomplish this he introduced the use of oil paints that dried more slowly than the traditional tempera. Oil paint left him to work more slowly and accurately. By means of delicate shading of colors and elaborate detail — fabric, furniture, flowers, jewelry, all carefully arranged as to proper spacial relationships — he was able to give his subjects the illusion of depth, as in *Arnolfini and his Wife*. A new era in painting opened next with men and women sitting for their portraits, and so Hans Memling (d. 1494) could paint them as they looked (e.g., *Tommaso Portinari and his Wife*).

PALACE, official residence of a king or bishop.

PALACE SCHOOL, name given to the court school maintained by some Frankish kings in the later Merovingian and Carolingian periods usually for members of the court and for children of the aristocracy. It is unlikely that any palace school approached the intellectual level of the school at Aachen during the reign of Charlemagne (d. 814).

PALAEOLOGUS, HOUSE OF, ruling dynasty of the Byzantine empire from its restoration in 1261 to the fall of Constantinople in 1453. The emperors included Michael VIII (1261–82), the founder of the dynasty and the restorer of the empire, Andronicus II (1282–1328), Andronicus III (1328–41), and John V who succeeded in 1341 but who was kept from the throne until 1355 by John VI Cantacuzenus, Andronicus IV Palaeologus (1376–9), and by John VII (1390). When John V died in 1391, Manuel II Palaeologus succeeded but shared the throne with John VII Palaeologus after 1399. His sons John VIII (1425–48) and Constantine XI (1448–1453) completed the series. Constantine was killed by the Turks when the city of Constantinople was captured.

PALAMAS, GREGORY. *See* GREGORY PALAMAS, ST.

PALATINATE, county on both sides of the middle Rhine north of Strasbourg which grew out of the jurisdiction of the count palatine of Lotharingia (Lorraine). In 1155 Frederick I Barbarossa granted the office of count palatine to his half-brother Conrad who had possessions in the area and who made Heidelberg his capital. In 1214 Frederick II enfeoffed Louis I, duke of Bavaria, of the house of Wittelsbach, with the office of palatine. The Wittelsbachs enlarged their holdings along the Bohemian frontier, a region that was organized as the Upper Palatinate. The count palatine of the Rhine was the foremost secular prince of the empire and the supreme judge in matters concerning the royal domain. The Golden Bull of 1356 confirmed him in his right to share in the election of the king of Germany, a right he had already exercised as early as 1198. In 1400 the elector Rupert became emperor.

PALATINE, COUNT, an official of the Frankish and German kings who supervised crown lands and revenues; the count of the Palatinate; a representative of the king of Hungary; in England, the lord or bishop who exercised powers normally reserved to the crown in counties such as Cheshire and Lancashire. The bishop of Durham was a count palatine.

PALAZZO VECCHIO, palace in Florence whose construction began c. 1300. Arnolfo di Cambio was the principal architect.

PALE, THE ENGLISH, region extending some 30 miles around Dublin which English lords conquered in the twelfth century and which became part of the empire of Henry II (d. 1189). Henry made a trip to Ireland 1171–2 to confirm his rights to the area.

PALENCIA, city in north-central Spain, originally a Roman settlement, which was almost destroyed in the course of the wars between the Sueves and Visigoths. It probably served as a bishop's see in the third century. Its university, the oldest in Spain, was founded in 1208 by Alfonso VIII of Leon. The Gothic cathedral was begun in 1321.

PALERMO, ancient Phoenician settlement, held successively by Vandals, Ostrogoths, the Byzantine empire, and Saracens (831–1071). In 1071 when the Normans expelled the Saracens, they made Palermo the capital of their kingdom of Sicily. In 1194 the Hohenstaufen emperors of Germany established their authority in Sicily, relinquished it to the Angevins (Charles of Anjou) in 1266, from whom it was taken by the Aragonese following the Sicilian Vespers in 1282. During the twelfth and thirteenth centuries, Palermo ranked with the most advanced cities of Europe in terms of population, industry, trade, and cultural beauty and attainments. The cathedral holds the tombs of six kings and emperors.

PALIMPSEST, a manuscript of leather or parchment from which the original writing has been largely erased although still partly visible under a second or later writing.

PALL, a square-shaped cloth or cardboard covered with cloth that was used to cover the chalice.

PALLADIUS OF HELENOPOLIS, d. before 431, monk of Egypt and Palestine, bishop of Helenopolis, later of Asuna (both in Asia Minor), who was exiled in 406 by Emperor Arcadius because of his staunch support of St. John Chrysostom. His writings include treatises on theology and monasticism and, above all, the *Lausiac History,* the single most valuable surviving work concerning the history of early monasteries. St. Jerome accused Palladius of Origenism although the charge has not been confirmed.

PALLADIUS, ST., early fifth-century Irish missionary. According to Prosper of Aquitaine, Palladius persuaded Pope Celestine I (422–32) to send St. Germanus, the bishop of Auxerre, to Britain to eradicate Pelagianism there. Pope Celestine later consecrated Palladius and sent him to Ireland as that land's first bishop. The natives appear to have received him with suspicion, so he moved to Scotland where he died.

PALLIUM, liturgical vestment consisting of a circular band of white wool worn over the chasuble and about the neck, having generally two pendants, one hanging down in front, the other behind. Eastern bishops wore the pallium from the fourth century, metropolitans in the Latin church from the ninth. Archbishops were not permitted to exercise certain metropolitan powers until the pallium had been received from Rome. It constituted a check that the pope might employ in determining the choice of prelate.

PALM, leaf of the palm tree blessed on Palm Sunday when it was carried as a symbol of joy and triumph to commemorate Christ's entry into Jerusalem. Christians kept sprigs of the palm in their homes to ward off evil. The first Palm Sunday procession may have been that recorded as taking place in Jerusalem in the fourth century.

PALM DONKEY, wooden donkey that represented the beast that Christ rode when entering Jerusalem. It might be dragged along in the procession on Palm Sunday.

PALM SUNDAY, the first day of Holy Week, the Sunday before Easter, so named from the gospel reading about Christ coming to Jerusalem when he was greeted by people carrying palms (Mark 11:1-10).

PALOMAR, JOHN OF, fl. 1431-8, Spanish theologian, chaplain to Pope Eugenius IV, and opponent of conciliarism. He assumed a leading role during the proceedings of the Council of Basel (1431-38).

PAMPHILUS, d. 310, official of Berytus, studied at the catechetical school in Alexandria, then reopened the school in Caesarea which Origen had founded. Contemporaries referred to him as Origen the Younger because of his unusual talents and his deep veneration for Origen. He left an apology in defense of Origen. He was martyred in Caesarea.

PAMPLONA, ancient city of the Basques in north Spain, captured by the Visigoths, Charlemagne, and Moors, but never held very long by any outsider. The Basque kingdom of Pamplona, which was founded in 824, later came to be known as the kingdom of Navarre, with the city of Pamplona remaining its capital until 1512. The Gothic cathedral in Pamplona was built in the fourteenth-fifteenth centuries.

PANDECTS. *See* DIGEST.

PANDULF, d. 1226, Italian papal legate who handled negotiations leading to King John of England's acceptance of Stephen Langton as archbishop of Canterbury. He supported John during his troubles with his barons and served as a member of the regency during the minority of Henry III until 1221 when the pope recalled him to Rome. In 1222 he was consecrated bishop of Norwich.

PANGE LINGUA GLORIOSI, the opening words of two liturgical hymns: a) *Pange lingua gloriosi lauream certaminis* which Fortunatus composed (c. 569) on the theme of the Cross; b) *Pange lingua gloriosi corporis mysterium,* a hymn in honor of the Blessed Sacrament which has been credited to St. Thomas Aquinas.

PANIS ANGELICUS. *See* SACRIS SOLEMNIS.

PANNAGE, fee paid by a serf or peasant to the lord of the manor for permission to let his hogs feed on the roots and mast in the woods.

PANNONIA, ancient Roman province lying between the upper Danube and the Save and comprising the upper section of Illyricum. The Romans abandoned the province after the death of Theodosius in 395 when the Visigoths seized control. The province included the cities of Vindobona (Vienna), Aquincum (Budapest), and Sirmium.

PANORMITANUS, d. 1445, also known as Abbas Modernus and Siculus, a canonist and Benedictine monk who taught at Parma, Siena, and Bologna. He was consecrated archbishop of Palermo in 1435. He attended the Council of Basel as the representative of Alfonso of Aragon, where he supported the antipope Felix V against

Eugenius IV. He left a tractate in support of conciliarism and commentaries on canon law.

PANTALEON, ST., d. c. 305, a physician who attended the Emperor Galerius at Nicomedia, an early Christian who apostasized, then reconverted, and suffered martyrdom during the persecution of Diocletian. His cult was especially popular in the Eastern church. He was venerated as one of the patron saints of physicians and was listed with the Fourteen Holy Helpers.

PANTOCRATOR, Greek for ruler of all, a title generally reserved to God the Father. In Eastern iconography he may appear as the throned and ruling Christ.

PAPACY, HISTORY OF THE MEDIEVAL. Conventionally the history of the papacy begins with the apostle Peter whom Christ chose as the rock upon which he would build his church (Matthew 16:18–19). The tradition that Peter served as the first bishop of Rome provided the basis of the argument pressed by the champions of the primacy of Rome that Peter's successors there fell heir to his high position. Bishops of Rome as early as Clement I appear to have advanced that claim. Clement reminded the Christians of Corinth in 95 to respect his admonitions since they were divinely inspired. This primacy, which earlier bishops of Rome had urged, became an accomplished fact during the pontificate of Leo I (440–61). [See POPE.]

Perhaps of greater concern to the papacy of these early centuries than the question of primacy were persecution by a hostile state and heresy. The history of persecution of Christians began in the year 64 with the emperor Nero and ended only with the death of Julian in 363. A number of popes suffered martyrdom, while all had difficulty administering an institution which the state sought to suppress. The situation changed with Constantine I (306–37) who not only halted persecution but also granted the church a privileged status in the empire. Then in a series of decrees issued in 391–2, the emperor Theodosius proscribed paganism and made Christianity the religion of the empire. [See PERSECUTIONS, EARLY CHRISTIAN.]

Meanwhile heresy was proving as much of a problem to the papacy and the church as persecution. Not only did heresy threaten the integrity of Christendom, it also constituted a direct attack on the authority of the papacy. The most dangerous and long-lived heresies were Arianism, Monophysitism, and Nestorianism. They were especially dangerous because they concerned the very heart of Christianity, the nature of Christ, its founder. The emperor in Constantinople, either out of personal conviction or out of fear that religious disharmony would bring down his state, wanted to dictate a settlement. Justinian I deposed Pope Silverius in 537 when the latter refused to bend to his wishes and summoned his successor Vigilius to come to Constantinople, while in 726 Emperor Leo III condemned the veneration of images. [See ICONOCLASM.] As Byzantine authority weakened in Italy and with it the emperor's ability to influence the papacy, the relationship between Rome and Constantinople assumed a more inflexible character. In 1054, a series of schisms that had periodically disrupted that relationship became final. [See CAERULARIUS, MICHAEL.]

Long before this last schism, Byzantine authority had disappeared from central and north Italy. In 568, a few years after Justinian's death, Lombards began moving down across the Alps into Italy and soon had much of the central part of the peninsula under their control. With Byzantine power no longer there to provide protection, the pope, in the face of Lombard threats to Rome, turned to the Franks. In 754 Pepin III (the Short) answered Pope Stephen II's appeal for help, drove back the Lombards from Rome and turned the city and the exarchate of Ravenna over to the pope. This development, called the Donation of Pepin, later confirmed by Pepin's son Charlemagne, established the pope as a secular ruler, and from that time until the latter half of the nineteenth century, historians spoke of the temporal power of the papacy.

While the papacy appreciated Charlemagne's protection, it found his paternalistic attitude uncomfortably assertive. Charlemagne's son, Louis the Pious, however, deferred to the papacy at every turn. This happy age for the papacy ended abruptly with the death of Nicholas I (d. 867), after which the Carolingian state disintegrated before the disruptive forces that ushered in the feudal age. Now there was no king about who might be willing, or able, to lend the papacy protection. The result was that the papacy became the football of Roman factional politics, and people such as Theophylact, his wife Theodora, and daughters Theodora and Marozia made and unmade popes as they chose. The papacy fell to the lowest level in its history and came very close to disappearing as an ecclesiastical institution.

In 962 when Otto I of Germany marched into Rome upon the plea of Pope John XII, his coming ushered in a new era for the papacy. For almost a century, Otto and his successors decided who would be pope and, fortunately for the papacy, they appointed men of high caliber, among them such an outstanding pontiff as Leo IX (1049–54). Once the papacy, with the help of the German monarchy, was back on its feet, it turned against its savior since the selection of the pope by any secular ruler, saint or otherwise, was intolerable to reformers. In their judgment, no real reform of the church could be carried out until kings and aristocracy were deprived of their power to control the selection of popes and bishops.

The upshot was a violent struggle between the papacy and the kings of Germany over the issue of lay investiture, in essence, the practice of secular authorities to select members of the hierarchy. The opening salvo was the Papal Electoral Law of 1059 which eliminated the German king's voice in the selection of the pope and turned this over to the cardinal clergy of Rome. In 1075 Gregory VII forced the issue when he condemned lay investiture, the same year that Henry IV of Germany filled the see of Milan with his own archbishop. Much bitterness and passionate polemics on both sides marked the investiture controversy until 1122 when a compromise on the issue was hammered out in the Concordat of Worms. The church would possess the right to select bishops, although the prelate chosen would have to be acceptable to the king. [*See* INVESTITURE CONTROVERSY.]

At the close of the century, in 1198, Innocent III was chosen pope, a man many scholars believe was the church's greatest medieval pope at a time when the papacy was at the peak of its influence and strength. Several developments had contributed to enhancing the papacy's position in the twelfth century. The pope had assumed the initiative in proclaiming the Crusades, and nothing moved more people nor stirred them more deeply than the Crusades. Several reform movements, the most famous that of Cluny, and the rise of new monastic orders such as the Cistercians, all contributed to strengthening the pope's position of leadership in the church. Innocent, a man of unusual talents in the field of diplomacy, succeeded in accomplishing what most popes might have failed to do or even contemplate. He forced John of England to accept Stephen Langton as archbishop of Canterbury and Philip II Augustus to take back the wife he had repudiated, and he placed his ward, Frederick of Sicily, on the German throne.

Still it required all the skill of an Innocent and favorable circumstances to enable the papacy to contend on reasonably equal terms with the monarchs of western Europe in 1200 for they, like the popes, had also grown stronger and more ambitious. A century later the papacy found this no longer possible. Even Innocent III would probably not have been any more successful than Boniface VIII in preventing the state from taxing church property. Innocent might have saved himself the humiliation that Boniface suffered at Anagni, but kings like Philip II of France and Edward I of England would have had their way in the end. It was, indeed, fortunate for the papacy that medieval monarchs of the fourteenth century still had an arrogant aristocracy to humble, or the position of the papacy vis-à-vis the state would have fallen to what it became in the sixteenth century.

If the thirteenth century was one of the brightest for the papacy, the fourteenth was among the most disastrous, and the trouble did not stem wholly from kings who wanted to tax church wealth. It also emanated from within. First, there was the period of nearly 70 years when the popes made their home in Avignon, the Babylonian Captivity as Petrarch denounced it, when the papacy appeared under the thumb of the French king. This was not entirely the case, although the "international" image of the papacy suffered. So much had the papacy been identified with Rome, that many, unconsciously if not openly, wondered about the legitimacy of the Avignonese popes. [See AVIGNONESE RESIDENCE.] A painful clash within the Franciscan order with John XXII, who had anathematized the Spiritual Franciscans for insisting that the church must return to the absolute poverty of apostolic times, further undermined the papacy. Critics of the papacy appeared in growing numbers, William of Ockham and Marsilius of Padua among them, and kings like Louis IV of Bavaria provided them with encouragement.

The greatest evil of the fourteenth century, the Western Schism, followed when first two, then three popes, claimed to be the vicar of Christ, and a puzzled Christendom turned to conciliarism as the only means of resolving the problem. In 1414, under the leadership of Emperor Sigismund, bishops and cardinals, as well as representatives of the kings of western Europe, met at Constance to heal the schism. This the council accomplished. It accepted the resignation of the Roman pope and deposed the Pisan and

Avignonese popes. Then it adopted measures establishing the supremacy of the general council in the church and investing it with an authority above that of the papacy. The new pope Martin V prudently bent to the unfavorable winds of triumphant conciliarism and, in accordance with the decisions made at Constance, called a general council at Pavia and at Basel. When Pope Eugenius IV moved the council from Basel to Ferrara, the conciliarists refused to leave Basel, grew increasingly antipapal, and in the end elected a new pope of their own (Felix V). A new schism and a church controlled by an intractable general council was undesirable to Europe's kings, and conciliarism met a sudden death. After 1450 the papacy gave most effort to organizing a crusade to stem the spread of Turkish power in the Balkans, at the same time seeking to establish a balance of power among the aggressive despots of north Italy. Several popes had time for humanism.

PAPAL ELECTORAL DECREE OF 1059, decree issued by Pope Nicholas II which provided for the election of future popes by the cardinal clergy of Rome. The clergy and laity of the city were to accord their approval after having been informed of the choice made by the cardinals. Although the king of Germany was not mentioned in the decree, the chief purpose of the pronouncement was probably that of excluding him from the selection process.

PAPAL REGISTERS, volumes containing copies of official papal letters and documents. They exist from the pontificate of Innocent III (1198–1216).

PAPAL STATES, the state consisting of territories in central Italy, stretching from below Rome to the mouth of the Po, which was ruled by the popes. The origins of papal political power may be traced to the estates acquired by the church beginning in the fourth century, called the Patrimony of St. Peter, inasmuch as possession of land at that time usually invested the proprietor with broad authority over the people who occupied his lands. That authority grew perceptibly from the late sixth century as Byzantine authority waned in Italy, and the pope was already exercising the de facto powers of a political lord long before 756 when the Donation of Pepin invested him with control over Rome, the exarchate of Ravenna, and the Pentapolis. In 774 Charlemagne confirmed the pope to be in possession of these territories which increased in the early twelfth century with the acquisition of parts of the vast holdings of Countess Matilda of Tuscany (d. 1115). Still papal authority over these territories became sovereign only after the death of Frederick II in 1250 who, like his predecessors, had claimed suzerainty as Holy Roman emperor, and then only in a strictly legal sense. Because of the elective character of the papal office, it was a rare medieval pope who actually succeeded in forcing the aristocratic factions in Rome and the ambitious vassals in The Marches and Romagna, not to mention communal groups inside the city and German kings north of the Alps, to respect his voice. The work of pacification undertaken by Cardinal Albornoz in the 1350s and 1360s was successful but short-lived, and it was not until the pontificate of Alexander VI (1492–1503) that papal authority approached that of a hereditary monarch.

PAPIAS OF HIERAPOLIS, d. c. 125, bishop of Hierapolis (western Asia Minor), author of an influential although no longer extant collection of interpretations of the sayings of Christ. His exegesis was used by Origen and by Irenaeus. He apparently held millenarian views and believed that there would be a period of a thousand years after the Resurrection during which time the Kingdom of Christ would be established on earth in a material form.

PARACLETE, the Holy Spirit.

PARADISE, the Garden of Eden, also referred to symbolically as heaven; the name given to the vestibule or atrium of the early Christian church.

PARADISE RIVERS, four rivers, Pison, Gichon, Euphrates, and Tigris, all represented in Christian art as flowing from Paradise.

PARADISO. *See* DANTE.

PARAPHONY, parallel singing at intervals of a fourth or fifth introduced to add greater depth to Gregorian chant.

PARASCEVE, name given to Good Friday in the Christian liturgy.

PARIS, a Celtic settlement on the Seine, known as Lutetia in Roman times. The name Paris appears only in the fifth century. A tradition, recorded by St. Gregory of Tours, has it that St. Denis (d. 258) and his companions brought Christianity to the area. During the period of Hunnic invasions (450–1), Paris followed the counsel of St. Geneviève and managed to escape capture and destruction. In 508 Clovis made Paris his capital although some of his successors did not reside there. During the second half of the ninth century the town suffered occasional sackings by the Vikings. It was not until the Capetians made Paris their capital and residence, beginning with Hugh in 987, that the town began to grow in importance. As royal power advanced, so did the population and influence of Paris, so that by the close of the Middle Ages no medieval capital approached the importance of Paris to its country and people. Construction on the cathedral of Notre Dame, located on an island in the Seine called the Ile de la Cité, began in 1163 and continued for a century. The University of Paris was formally chartered in 1200 although it had already been in existence for a number of decades as a *studium generale*.

PARIS, MATTHEW. *See* MATTHEW PARIS.

PARIS, UNIVERSITY OF, the leading university of the Middle Ages, emerged from the cathedral school of Notre Dame but the presence of the abbey of St. Victor and the collegiate church of Ste. Geneviève contributed to Paris's reputation in the twelfth century as the leading center of learning in western Europe. A *studium generale* existed in Paris some decades before 1200, but the founding of the university is traditionally assigned to 1200 during which year Philip II Augustus granted the masters and students a charter. Early in the thirteenth century, the four nations, the Gallican, Norman, Picard, and English, as well as the four faculties of theology, law, medicine, and the arts, appeared. The university was recognized as the theological arbiter of Europe until the Western Schism (1378–1415) deprived it of some of its international character. The first college to be established at Paris was founded c. 1257 by Robert of Sorbon, confessor of St. Louis. He founded a house to provide lodging and food for sixteen needy theological students.

PARISH, territorial district within a diocese that had its own church and usually a priest of its own who attended to its spiritual needs. As such it appeared late in the fourth century.

PARLEMENT DE PARIS, French royal court for judicial matters and the highest court of appeal. It emerged from the *curia regis* during the reign of Louis IX (1226–70) when it was referred to as *curia regis in parlamento* or *parlement*. It received official recognition as an independent unit of royal government only in the fourteenth century.

PARLIAMENT, English legislative (and to an extent judicial) body that emerged from the *curia regis,* more accurately from the great council which the king ordinarily convened two or three times a year to advise him on matters of state. At one time all feudal tenants-in-chief attended the meetings of the great council. In time, because of the expense and difficulties of travel, only those vassals who received a personal summons attended. Those who received a general summons issued by the sheriff were inclined to ignore it. The introduction in 1265 of members of the shires and boroughs broadened the representa-

tion of the body. Its composition in 1295, when it comprised both commoners and peers of the realm, struck contemporaries as proper, whence the term Model Parliament.

The principal factor that assured the further development of parliament — this term gradually replaced that of the great council — was the crown's need for subsidies to prosecute the Hundred Years' War against France. Parliament made its willingness to consider financial aid contingent upon the king's harkening to its petitions concerning grievances and concessions, and it limited its grants to a year. It was this practice of voting aid in return for concessions on the part of the crown and then only for a limited period that enabled parliament to assume its first major function, that of checking the authority of the king. A second function, which it acquired during the course of the fourteenth century, was that of sharing the crown's responsibility for enacting legislation. During this same century it became customary for lords and commoners to meet separately, whence the two Houses of Lords and Commons. The move to meet separately originated with the burgesses and knights who felt ill at ease in the presence of their social betters. Of the two houses, that of the Lords remained by far the more important into early modern times. Still, despite its impressive growth from the original great council, parliament at the close of the Middle Ages could be entirely ignored by the king, as it was by Edward IV (1461–83), unless he needed money.

PARLIAMENT, MODEL. *See* PARLIAMENT.

PAROUSIA, from the Greek meaning presence, a term employed to denote the second coming of Christ when he would return to judge the living and the dead. Such a belief, and that his coming was imminent, appears to have been a conviction with many in the first century of Christianity.

PARTICULAR JUDGMENT, the judgment which each individual soul received when he or she died. This was prior to and distinct from the

General Judgment on the Last Day. Justin, Tertullian, and Ambrose, among other theologians, maintained that an intermediate state of sleep intervened between the day of death and the final judgment. Controversy on the issue continued until 1336 when Benedict XII, in the bull *Benedictus Deus,* declared that the Particular Judgment admitted the soul at once to heaven, purgatory, or hell. The Eastern Church retained the older position.

PARZIVAL (Parsifal, Parseval), hero of the courtly romance of the same name composed by Wolfram von Eschenbach. The central theme was Parzival's search for the Holy Grail.

PASCHA, medieval Latin term for Easter.

PASCHAL I, ST., Pope, 817–24, a Roman, member of the papal Curia, the successor of Stephen IV. He secured from Louis the Pious recognition of papal sovereignty over Rome and the freedom of papal elections. In 823 he crowned Louis's son Lothair I as co-emperor.

PASCHAL II, Pope, 1099–1118, Benedictine abbot and cardinal (c. 1080), the successor of Urban II. As pope he became involved in the controversy over investiture with Henry IV and Henry V of Germany and for a time was held a prisoner by the latter. In 1111 he agreed that bishops should renounce all regalia (lands, privileges, honors) acquired since Charlemagne in return for Henry's renunciation of investiture, but the aristocracy, both lay and secular, would not hear of it. The settlement which Paschal accepted in the case of England in 1106, known as the Compromise of Bec, prepared the way for the subsequent agreement ratified in the Concordat of Worms (1122).

PASCHAL CANDLE, candle blessed during the Easter vigil service on Holy Saturday. It symbolized the risen Christ.

PASCHASIUS RADBERTUS, ST., d. c. 860, Benedictine theologian, abbot of Corbie, who resigned over opposition to his reform measures.

He prepared commentaries on the Scriptures, composed poems, wrote lives of the saints, and, most important, produced the first extended doctrinal treatment of the Eucharist. He maintained the real presence of Christ in the Eucharist and appears to have accepted what later came to be the church's doctrine of transubstantiation.

PASHA, Turkish title of honor which was used by the Seljuk Turks. At first it was reserved for close relatives of the sultan, although later the title was extended to provincial governors and viziers.

PASSAU, city on the confluence of the Danube and Inn in Bavaria which grew up from Celtic origins. It was made a bishop's see in 739 by St. Boniface. In later years it developed into a thriving center of trade.

PASSION PLAYS, a branch of mystery plays that made their appearance during the thirteenth century and had as their subject the passion and death of Christ. [*See* DRAMA, MEDIEVAL.]

PASSION SUNDAY, the fifth Sunday of Lent, the Sunday immediately preceding Palm Sunday.

PASTON LETTERS, a noted collection of letters consisting of both personal and business correspondence carried on by members of the Paston family of Norfolk. The letters, which fall within the period from 1422 to 1509, constitute an invaluable source for the study of the manners, morals, customs, and practices of the times. They provide a particularly vivid picture of the turbulence that afflicted England during the period of the Wars of the Roses (1455–85).

PASTOR (Papa) ANGELICUS, the "Angelic Shepherd" spoken of by visionaries such as Joachim of Fiore and the Spiritual Franciscans. They predicted that such a person would appear some day and reestablish the holiness of the early Christian church.

PASTOREAUX, CRUSADE OF THE, bands of peasants (some townspeople) who marched through France in 1251, their goal Egypt where they hoped to free Louis IX who was being held a prisoner by the Moslems. [*See* CRUSADE, SEVENTH.] Because of their growing violence, the government, headed by Blanche of Castile, Louis's mother, which was at first sympathetic, eventually took steps to suppress them. They hailed their semimystic leader the "Master of Hungary." A similar popular movement during the reign of Philip V, which also had as its aim a crusade, turned to violence and pillage, and was destroyed in Languedoc by the seneschal of Carcassonne.

PASTOURELLE, old Provençal lyric poem whose theme was usually that of a dialogue between a knight and a shepherdess.

PATARINES (Patarenes), a reform movement composed principally of members of the laity which appeared during the second half of the eleventh century in a number of cities of north Italy. It centered in Milan, which suggests a possible source of its name, that is, the *Pataria,* a quarter of Milan where the group was especially active. The more moderate Patarines sought to raise moral standards among the clergy and to suppress simony. They also welcomed papal intervention in the largely autonomous Ambrosian church and supported Gregory VII against Henry IV over the king's appointment of the new archbishop. The more radical Patarines refused to recognize the validity of sacraments or masses administered or said by unworthy priests. The enthusiasm stirred by the First Crusade (1096–9) absorbed the attention of these reformers and the movement disappeared. The name reappeared in the late twelfth century when it was given to heretics in general and more particularly to the Cathari in Italy.

PATEN, metal plate or dish that held the Eucharist during the Mass.

PATER NOSTER, the Lord's Prayer; a kind of rosary used for counting Our Fathers.

PATRIARCH, title of honor given at first to any bishop of advanced age, later to bishops who occupied sees of special dignity. These included Rome, Alexandria, Antioch, Jerusalem, and Constantinople. The Council of Nicaea (325) recognized the bishops of Rome, Alexandria, and Antioch as patriarchs, and the Council of Chalcedon (451), those of Jerusalem and Constantinople. The jurisdiction of patriarchs extended over the adjoining territories and included the right to consecrate bishops, to try those accused of heresy and to hear appeals from their judgments.

PATRIARCH, ECUMENICAL, title claimed by the patriarch of Constantinople as the one holding precedence over the other patriarchs of the Eastern Church. The patriarch of Constantinople used the title from the time of the Acacian Schism (484–519) despite Rome's refusal to recognize it.

PATRICIUS ROMANORUM, honorary title given by Emperor Constantine I to his chief judicial and military officers. In the fifth and sixth centuries it was granted to barbarian chieftains and kings, and by Pope Stephen II in 754 to Pepin III and to his sons Charlemagne and Carloman.

PATRICK, ST., d. c. 461, "Apostle of the Irish," born in Roman Britain where he was captured as a youth of sixteen by Irish raiders and sold into slavery in Ireland. After six years, he escaped to Britain and may have received his education there. That he studied at Lérins cannot be confirmed, as is the case with many other stories told about him. In 432 he returned to Ireland to succeed Bishop Palladius. It is believed he made his see at Armagh. Patrick left a *Confessio* in which he told of his spiritual development and acknowledged the goodness of God in helping him to become a missionary. He is honored as the founder of Celtic monasticism and the man to whom the conversion of much of Ireland is credited.

PATRIMONY OF SAINT PETER, originally the private property belonging to the church in

Rome, Illyria, Gaul, Corsica, Sardinia, and near Hippo; later, the territories, principally those in central Italy, taken from the Lombards [see DONATION OF PEPIN] and the districts of Venetia and Istria, over which the pope exercised political authority.

PATRIPASSIANISM, heresy of the second century, a form of Monarchianism, which denied a subsistence to the Logos or Christ but which maintained rather that it was the Father who was born, suffered, and died in the guise of the Son. The heresy also went by the name of Sabellianism.

PATROCINIUM, institution of the late Roman empire through which men of wealth and influence, usually members of the senatorial aristocracy, exercised almost exclusive economic and political control over the people who lived on their estates. These people, peasants for the most part and semifree, usually went by the name *coloni*.

PATRON SAINT, saint or angel honored by an individual, church, group, even town or country, as its intercessor in heaven. The custom of having patron saints for churches has been traced to the practice of building churches over the tombs of martyrs.

PAUL I, ST., Pope, 757–67, a Roman, member of the papal Curia, and brother of Pope Stephen II. As pope he enjoyed the assistance of Pepin III against the Lombards. His principal problem with Byzantium concerned the issue of iconoclasm which the emperor favored.

PAUL II, Pope, 1464–71, nephew of Pope Eugenius IV who made him a cardinal at the age of 23. He was a person of considerable influence in the Curia during the pontificates of Nicholas V (1447–55) and Callistus III (1455–8). As pope he showed himself a patron of scholars and artists although he dissolved the Roman Academy because of its "paganism." He involved himself in the political affairs of Bohemia and what efforts he put forth to arouse Europe to a Crusade against the Turks went for naught.

PAULA, ST., d. 404, wealthy Roman widow, member of a group of pious women whom St. Jerome served as spiritual adviser. She followed him to Bethlehem where she founded several monasteries and devoted her life to the practice of asceticism and good works.

PAULICIANS, Armenian sect of the seventh century which derived its name from either St. Paul, the Apostle, or from Paul of Samosata. The Paulicians accepted a dualistic view of the universe based on the belief in a god of evil and one of good. They rejected the Old Testament, baptism, eucharist, marriage, and the doctrine of the redemption. Persecution from the second half of the seventh century and military measures taken against them by Emperor Basil I in 872 finally broke their power although their ideas continued to live on among the Bogomils of Bulgaria.

PAULINE PRIVILEGE, privilege of a person married to a heathen to contract a new marriage on becoming a Christian should the non-Christian partner wish to separate or impede the convert in his or her practice of the faith. The privilege is mentioned by St. Jerome and Ambrosiaster.

PAULINUS OF AQUILEIA, ST., d. 802, member of Charlemagne's circle of scholars at Aachen, later appointed patriarch of Aquileia. He left theological writings, letters, poems, and hymns. He attended a number of church councils, took a prominent part in relations between the Eastern and Western churches, and worked actively for the suppression of Adoptionism.

PAULINUS OF NOLA, ST., d. 431, a pupil of Ausonius, a Roman senator, consul, and governor of Campania. He became a priest, gave his fortune to the poor and the church, founded a home for monks and the poor at Nola, and was consecrated bishop of that city in 409. He left a valuable collection of letters, many to famous contemporaries such as Augustine and Jerome, and poems that led critics to rank him with Prudentius as the leading Latin poets of the patristic age.

PAULINUS OF VENICE, d. 1344, a Franciscan, served as apostolic penitentiary, inquisitor, and papal legate, and from 1324 as bishop of Pozzuoli. He prepared a catalog of Franciscan communities and a universal chronicle from the Creation to 1313 (death of Henry VII) which has little historical value.

PAULINUS OF YORK, ST., d. 644, a monk whom Pope Gregory I sent to England in 601 to assist St. Augustine in the conversion of the Anglo-Saxons. He served as chaplain of Ethelburga, the queen of King Edwin of Northumbria, and eventually converted him. In 625 he was consecrated bishop of the newly established diocese of York, and c. 632 that of Rochester.

PAUL OF AEGINA, d. 690, physician, born on the island of Aegina, who practiced in Alexandria where his obstetrical skill placed him in great demand. From the many writings that he left on the subject of medicine, it is clear he depended heavily on Galen, Oribasius, and Aëtius. His *Epitome* contains practically everything known in his day in the field of medicine.

PAUL OF SAMOSATA, third-century bishop of Antioch (260–8) and an official in the court of Zenobia, queen of Palmyra. His teachings on the Person of Christ, which were condemned several times, led to his deposition in 268. He taught that the Logos came to dwell in Christ when he was baptized, but that Jesus possessed no extraordinary virtues above those of other men. In Christology he was a precursor of Nestorius in drawing a sharp line between the two natures in Christ.

PAUL, ST., one of the Apostles, first a bitter persecutor of the Christians, then a convert and the most active and militant of missionaries in spreading and explaining Christ's doctrines. He is believed to have suffered martyrdom at Rome in either the year 64 or 67 during the persecution of the emperor Nero.

PAUL, ST., the Hermit, d. c. 341, an anchorite of Thebes in Egypt whom St. Jerome called the first Christian hermit. St. Anthony, who is usually given that honor, is supposed to have visited Paul when he was 90, Paul 113.

PAUL I, ST., patriarch of Constantinople, d. 350, a close associate of St. Athanasius who succeeded Alexander in the see of Constantinople in 336. The emperor Constantius shortly after replaced him with the Arian Macedonius. After recovering his see twice again and being twice removed depending on who happened to be emperor and what his position on Arianism was, he was eventually exiled to Armenia where he was strangled.

PAUL II, patriarch of Constantinople, d. 653, appointed by Emperor Constans II in 641 and excommunicated by Pope Martin I in 649 for his Monothelitism. The emperor took Paul's part and in 653 sent the pope into exile to Cherson (Crimea).

PAUL IV, ST., patriarch of Constantinople, d. 784, appointed patriarch by the iconoclastic emperor Leo IV but forced to resign in 780 when Leo died and Irene became regent for her son Constantine VI. Paul renounced iconoclasm and retired to a monastery.

PAUL THE DEACON, d. 799?, a member of a noble Lombard family and educated at the Lombard court at Pavia. When Charlemagne captured Pavia and destroyed the Lombard kingdom (774), Paul fled to Monte Cassino and later spent a number of years as a member of the circle of scholars at Aachen. He was a grammarian, poet, hagiographer, and author of some liturgical works and homilies, but he is best known for his *History of the Lombards* (568–744). His history of the diocese of Metz and a *Historia Romana* are of appreciably less value.

PAULUS SILENTIARIUS, sixth-century Christian poet whose principal work is a hymn marking the consecration of Hagia Sophia in Constantinople (562). It provides a full description of the church in hexameter verse and is of interest to students of Byzantine art. He was also the author of some 80 epigrams.

PAVIA, city south of Milan on the Po, known as Ticinum in Roman times, later as Papia. Attila pillaged the city in 452 and Odoacer in 476. Theodoric, king of the Ostrogoths (493–526), made Pavia his capital, and it continued to serve the Lombard kings as such until the conquest of the Lombard kingdom in 774 by Charlemagne. From the eleventh century it had a long history of hostilities with Milan which continued until 1361 when Duke Galeazzo Visconti finally forced it to accept his rule. That same year he founded the University of Pavia.

PAX BREDE (pax, osculatorium), a small plate of ivory, metal, or wood, with a representation of some religious subject on its face and a projecting handle. It was used at mass for conveying the kiss of peace to the laity and to those in the choir. It was first kissed by the celebrant, then by the others in turn. It came into use in the late Middle Ages.

PAX ROMANA, the period of relative peace that obtained throughout the Roman empire from the accession of Augustus (c. 31 B.C.) to the death of Marcus Aurelius (180).

PEACE OF GOD, immunity from violence for holy places, the clergy, peasantry, travelers, and pilgrims, as proclaimed by several church councils of the tenth and eleventh centuries. Men who violated such immunity incurred the church's anathema. Neither the Peace of God nor the church's anathema proved especially effective.

PEARL, THE, Middle English alliterative poem of the late fourteenth century which has as its general theme the acceptance of God's will in times of adversity. It has been explained as an elegy for the poet's little daughter whom he sees in paradise, when he becomes reconciled to her death.

PEASANT CRUSADE. *See* CRUSADE, PEASANT.

PEASANT REVOLT OF 1381, a peasant uprising in England which broke out in June, lasted about six weeks, and was limited for the most part to southeastern England. The rebels managed to gain entrance to London where their leaders, including Wat Tyler, met with the young king Richard II, then dispersed after his promise to abolish serfdom and fix land rents. Most of the rebellious peasants were subsequently hunted down and executed. The most prominent casualty in the uprising was Archbishop Sudbury, the chancellor, whom the peasants held responsible for the hated poll tax. The revolt had little or no influence on the course of English history.

PECIA, sections consisting of a few pages of manuscript which bookstores loaned to students in the thirteenth and fourteenth centuries. They might copy these for their own use or simply for remuneration.

PECKHAM, JOHN, d. 1292, archbishop of Canterbury. He studied at Paris and Oxford, joined the Franciscans, later occupied the Franciscan chair of theology, still later taught at Oxford and Rome. Consecrated archbishop in 1279, he showed himself a dedicated reformer and took vigorous measures to suppress abuses such as pluralism and nonresidence, and he visited all the dioceses in his province. In his theology he upheld the Franciscan tradition. His writings include commentaries on the *Sentences* and on several books of the Bible, and a treatise on optics. He was also a gifted poet.

PECOCK, REGINALD, d. 1460 or 1461, a Welshman, studied at Oxford, became bishop of St. Asaph, later of Chichester. His writings, which he hoped would win back Lollards to orthodoxy, evoked charges of heresy, and he was obliged to resign his see and retire to the monastery of Thorney. Perhaps most of his difficulties stemmed from the fact that he sympathized strongly with the Lancastrians, thereby making enemies among the Yorkists. His best-known work, *The Repressor of Overmuch Blaming of the Clergy,* provides a perceptive analysis of the doctrines of the Lollards while defending the church against their criticisms.

PECTORALE, ornament worn on the breast; breast cross; clasp to fasten the choir cloak; and breastpiece in a suit of armor.

PECTORIUS, EPITAPH OF, an inscription in verse, located near Autun, France, probably from the second half of the fourth century. The inscription sheds light on early Christian practices concerning baptism and the eucharist.

PECULIAR, a place exempt from the jurisdiction of the bishop of a diocese, such as a monastery or similar religious house.

PEDRO. *See* PETER.

PEDUM, a bishop's staff. The *pedum rectum,* which lacked the crook, was included with the papal insignia although never used.

PEERS, a classification which in England included members of the upper nobility by virtue of their feudal holdings, together with other lords who received a personal summons from the king to attend a meeting of parliament. In the fourteenth century they constituted the House of Lords.

PEGAU, MONASTERY OF, Benedictine abbey near Leipzig founded in 1091. Monks there kept the *Annales Pegavienses,* an important source for the history of the years 1000 to 1227.

PEGOLOTTI, FRANCESCO BALDUCCI, fl. 1315–40, a factor in the service of the mercantile house of the Bardi, whose *Practica* furnishes valuable insight into trade and travel of his day. The manuscript contains a glossary of foreign terms for taxes and for payments made for goods, as well as the location of shops in different cities and the commodities bought and sold there. It also notes some of the major trade routes of the period, the imports and exports of different regions, and the comparative value of the leading currencies and of weights and measures.

PEIRE VIDAL, widely traveled Provençal troubadour of the late twelfth and early thirteenth century. He traveled to Spain, Cyprus, and Malta, and had among his patrons Richard I of England. His poems are among the finest examples of troubadour love poetry.

PELAGIANISM. *See* PELAGIUS.

PELAGIUS I, Pope, 556–61, theological adviser of Pope Vigilius and for some years papal legate to Constantinople. When the emperor Justinian learned of the death of Vigilius, he immediately appointed Pelagius to succeed him. Certain western bishops, including the bishops of Milan and Istria, refused to recognize him as pope on the assumption, erroneous as it proved, that Pelagius, as an imperial appointee, must have endorsed Justinian's condemnation of the Three Chapters. [*See* THREE CHAPTERS.]

PELAGIUS II, Pope, 579–90, a Goth by birth whose election as successor of Benedict I failed to gain the support of the bishops in the area of Venice and Istria (Aquileian Schism). As pope he refused to recognize the title of "ecumenical patriarch" which the patriarch of Constantinople had been using since the Acacian Schism (484–519).

PELAGIUS, a British monk who traveled to Rome c. 380 where he was highly regarded as a spiritual director, thence to Africa and Palestine where he disappeared from view (c. 418). He denied the doctrine of original sin and maintained rather that man was quite free in his choice between good and evil and that he could gain heaven without the assistance of divine grace. His views sired Pelagianism, a troublesome heresy during the first half of the fifth century. It drew attacks from St. Augustine and was condemned by Pope Innocent I in 417 and by the Council of Ephesus in 431. Controversy over the issues raised by Pelagius continued in Gaul until the Second Council of Orange in 529 came up with a satisfactory theological formula.

PELICAN, symbol of Christ the Redeemer and a popular subject in Christian art. The pelican was supposed to have revived its dead young from its own blood.

PEMBROKE, EARLDOM OF, title created in 1138 by King Stephen of England and granted to Gilbert de Clare. The earldom reverted to the crown in 1245 when Henry III gave it to William de Valence, his favorite half-brother, who remained loyal to him in the Barons' War with Simon de Montfort. William's son Aymer de Valence was virtual head of the royal administration from 1318 to 1321 during the reign of Edward II. In 1414 Humphrey, fourth son of Henry IV, received the title. When he died in 1447 it went to William de la Pole, first duke of Suffolk. In 1452, after Suffolk's execution, Jasper Tudor was created earl, but then forfeited the title in 1461 when he was attainted. When Henry Tudor triumphed at Bosworth Field in 1485 he regranted the title to Jasper, who then held it until his death in 1495. It then reverted to the crown.

PEMBROKE, RICHARD DE CLARE. See CLARE.

PEMBROKE, WILLIAM MARSHALL. See MARSHALL, WILLIAM.

PENANCE, SACRAMENT OF, the sacrament by which the penitent received remission of his sins from a priest authorized to forgive sins. The early history of the sacrament is obscure. By the third century, a system of public penance had come into use in the case of serious sins that occasioned scandal. Private confession is generally traced to Celtic and Anglo-Saxon missionaries. It received its traditional character when the Fourth Lateran Council (1215) required all

Christians to confess at least once a year. [See CONFESSION.]

PENDA, king of Mercia, 632–54, who claimed descent from Wodan, gained independence for his kingdom in 641 when he defeated and killed King Oswald of Northumbria. In time he extended his authority over most of the kingdom south of the Humber, but when he invaded Northumbria in 654 he was slain by King Oswiu. Several of his children were later honored as saints although he himself remained a pagan.

PENDENTIVE, name given to the four spandrels that supported a dome over a square area. The use of pendentives was the principal engineering feature incorporated into the construction of the great church of Hagia Sophia in Constantinople by Justinian (527–65).

PENITENTIALS (Penitential Books), manuals used by confessors to assist them in determining suitable penance for penitents who confessed to them. They were apparently of Celtic origin and brought to the Continent by Celtic and Anglo-Saxon missionaries. The best-known is that ascribed to Archbishop Theodore (d. 690).

PENITENTIARY, office or tribunal in the papal Curia which handled matters of penance, dispensation, and absolution. The office took form in the thirteenth century.

PENNY, a small coin which first appeared in the eighth century in the Frankish kingdom of Pepin III. Its use spread over western Europe.

PENTAGRAM, a magical sign having five lines.

PENTAPOLIS, the area covered by the five cities of Arminium (Rimini), Pisarum (Pesaro), Fanum (Fano), Senagellica (Senigallia), and Ancona, all situated on the east coast of Italy. Pepin III (the Short) turned these cities over to the pope in 756 with his Donation of Pepin.

PENTECOST (Whitsunday), that is, the "fiftieth" day after Easter (ten days after Christ's ascension into heaven) when Christians celebrated the coming of the Holy Spirit to the apostles. In early times the word "Pentecost" also applied to the entire period between Easter and Pentecost.

PEPIN I (of Landen), d. c. 640, mayor of the palace of Austrasia and one of the leaders in the revolt that ended with the death of Brunhild. Through his daughter Begga who married the son of Arnulf, bishop of Metz, Pepin may be counted the founder of the Carolingian dynasty.

PEPIN II (of Heristal), d. 714, grandson of Pepin I, ruled Austrasia, Neustria, and Burgundy as mayor of the palace. He defeated the Frisians, the Alemanni, and the Bavarians, and was able to maintain an unusually strong government in those difficult times.

PEPIN III (the Short), king of the Franks, 751–68, son of Charles Martel. He established the new Carolingian dynasty in 751 when the German princes authorized him to depose Childerich III, the Merovingian king and puppet. He was anointed by St. Boniface, then again in 754 by Pope Stephen II when he received the title "patrician." In 756 he forced the Lombards to surrender the exarchate of Ravenna and Pentapolis which he then transferred to the pope in the so-called Donation of Pepin. He took Septimania from the Moors and drove them across the Pyrenees. In his interest in learning and the support he gave to Christian missionaries, he anticipated the work of his famous son Charlemagne.

PERCY, prominent family founded by William de Percy (d. 1096), a vassal of William the Conqueror who granted him extensive estates in Yorkshire and Lincolnshire. Henry de Percy (d. 1314) served Edward I in the Scottish wars and purchased the lordship of Alnwick in Northumberland which thenceforth constituted the principal center of the family's power. From this time the Percys were the most powerful landowners in Northumberland and the principal guardians of the Scottish border. The most colorful of these ambitious lords was Sir Henry Percy, called Hotspur because of his military aggressiveness in the fighting along the Scottish and Welsh frontiers. Although he and his father Henry, first earl of Northumberland, were among the first to join Henry Bolingbroke (Henry IV) when he landed in 1399 to overthrow Richard II, later in 1403 they joined the Welsh in their revolt, their objective being to dethrone Henry and place Edmund, earl of March, the nephew of Hotspur's wife, on the throne. Hotspur was slain at the battle of Shrewsbury in 1403, his father in 1408 at Bramham Moor.

PEREGRINATIO AETHERIAE. *See* ETHERIA, PILGRIMAGE OF.

PEREIRA, BEATO NUNO ÁLVARES, d. 1431, Portuguese national hero who helped win the battle of Aljubarrota in 1385 against the Castilians and took Ceuta from the Moors. Late in life he retired to live as a Carmelite lay brother in Lisbon.

PÉREZ, JUAN, d. c. 1515, Franciscan vicar provincial of Castile and confessor of Queen Isabella who befriended Columbus and besought the queen to give him assistance.

PERICOPE, from the Greek meaning a section, that is, a passage from the Scriptures, usually one appointed to be read in the church service. The use of such prescribed portions of the Scriptures appeared as early as the fourth century.

PÉROTIN, gifted musical composer of the early thirteenth century, a member of the school of Notre Dame in Paris. He was probably the first musician to compose in as many as four parts.

PERPENDICULAR STYLE, the final phase of the Gothic style in England so named because of the popular use of straight, vertical lines in tracery and in the decorative work in windows and wall paneling. Timber-trussed ceilings and roofs also characterized the style, as in Westminster Hall, London.

PERPETUAL COMPACT, an agreement made in 1291 by the three forest cantons of Uri, Schwyz, and Unterwalden, when they pledged to assist each other in blocking the efforts of the Hapsburgs to establish direct rule over the region.

PERRERS, ALICE, d. 1400, mistress of Edward III of England, possibly as early as 1366, who wielded great influence over him, much to the indignation of contemporary chroniclers. She also enjoyed some favor and acquired much wealth during the reign of Richard II.

PERSECUTIONS, EARLY CHRISTIAN. The first persecution of Christians by the Roman state was that of the emperor Nero in 64 who may have used them as a scapegoat to escape the charge of having himself put the city of Rome on fire. From the reign of Domitian (81–96), Christians suffered some form of persecution even during the era of the Good Emperors (Nerva, Trajan, Hadrian, Antoninus Pius, Marcus Aurelius) (96–180). It was Trajan who in his letter to Pliny the Younger, a governor of Bithynia, probably laid down the general policy of the empire toward Christians, namely, that while the state would not ferret them out, any person proved guilty of being a Christian would be executed. The most famous of the Good Emperors, Marcus Aurelius, had a personal dislike for Christians and sanctioned a severe persecution in Lyons (177). The first empire-wide persecution was that of Decius (249–51). The severity of persecutions varied with the emperors and from province to province. Constantius ignored Diocletian's decree in Britain and Gaul, provinces under his administration. From the reign of Gallienus in 260 there came a lull that carried until 303 when Diocletian instituted the severest of all persecutions. For most Christians, persecution entailed the loss of civic privileges and the imposition of civil disabilities. Ordinar-

ily the Christian leaders stood in greatest danger of execution.

That Rome persecuted Christians is something of an anomaly since few states have shown themselves more tolerant toward alien creeds and cults. Rome's strange hostility toward Christians may be explained by their refusal to recognize the cult of Augustus. (Jews, also, refused to pay homage to this cult, although the state felt it could safely ignore them in view of their limited number.) In the eyes of the state, Christian refusal to recognize this cult was tantamount to treason.

Toleration first came in 311 when Galerius, on his deathbed, signed such a decree. He confessed the state's inability to suppress the superstition and expressed the hope that the Christians, now free to practice their religion, would enlist the favor of their god for the well-being of the state. In 313 Constantine and Licinius, in a decree known somewhat incorrectly as the Edict of Milan, ordered the end of all persecution. Licinius later reintroduced persecution in his half of the empire. With his defeat by Constantine in 324, persecution ceased except for the repressive measures taken against Christians by the emperor Julian (361–3).

PER SE . . . PER ACCIDENS, a scholastic distinction between that which follows from its own nature and that which is determined by something outside itself.

PERTH, city in central Scotland, initially a Roman settlement, which became a town in 1106 and served as the royal residence from 1210 to 1437. Robert the Bruce failed in several attempts to take the city, then finally succeeded in 1311. It changed hands again during the period 1335–9. Many parliaments assembled in Perth.

PERUZZI and BARDI, the leading banking houses of the fourteenth century. They made the mistake of lending large sums to Edward III and both went bankrupt, in 1343 and 1344 respectively, when he repudiated his obligation.

PESELLINO, IL, FRANCESCO DI STEFANO, d. 1457, painter of the Florentine school, a disciple and associate of Filippo Lippi. He is best known as a painter of romantic and flowery *cassone* pictures, that is, decorative panels for chests, e.g., *Judgment Scene*.

PETCHENEGS (Pechenegs, Petzinaks), barbarous Turkish nomads first encountered in 834. They overran southern Russia in 969 and repeatedly invaded Thrace during the tenth and eleventh centuries. In 1090−1 they penetrated to the very walls of Constantinople. Alexius I succeeded in defeating them with the help of the Cumans. In 1122 John II Comnenus finally destroyed them as a nation.

PETER (Pedro) II, king of Aragon, 1196−1213, count of Barcelona, was crowned at Rome by Pope Innocent III whom he accepted as his overlord. In 1212 he joined Alfonso VIII of Castile in winning a decisive victory over the Moors at the battle of Las Navas de Tolosa. He found himself an ally of Raymond VI of Toulouse against Simon de Montfort, leader of the Albigensian Crusade. Peter was slain in the battle of Muret, a defeat that marked the end of Catalan influence in southern France.

PETER (Pedro) (the Great) III, king of Aragon, 1276−85, successor of his father James I, married Constance, the daughter of Manfred, king of Sicily, and through her claimed Sicily which he seized in 1282 following the revolt of the Sicilians (Sicilian Vespers). In 1280 he succeeded in establishing Aragonese influence in north Africa. In 1283 he was constrained to extend to the nobles and the towns of Aragon privileges that paralleled those King John of England granted in the Magna Carta. He founded the first university in Aragon in Huesca.

PETER (Pedro) IV, king of Aragon, 1336−87,

son of Alfonso IV, recovered control of Majorca, secured possession of Sardinia, and sharply reduced the privileges his predecessors had extended to the nobility. The intermittent war that he carried on against Peter I of Castile proved disastrous to the economy of Aragon.

PETER (Pedro) (the Cruel), king of Castile, 1350−69, son of Alfonso XI, concluded an alliance with John II of France in 1352 but then antagonized John when he repudiated the French princess he had married. From 1356 he was involved in meeting revolts organized by his bastard half-brothers led by Henry of Trastamara and assisted by Peter, king of Aragon. Once he was forced to flee to Gascony, but in the end he emerged victorious, thanks to the assistance that John of Gaunt, whose daughter Constance he had married, and the English army gave him against the Trastamarians and their French allies at the battle of Nájera (1367). He was assassinated by his brother.

PETER (Orseolo), king of Hungary, 1038−41 and 1044−6, son of the doge of Venice, was driven from Hungary in 1041 but did homage to Henry III of Germany who then helped him recover his throne. In 1046 he was forced into exile a second time when pagan elements gained control of the country.

PETER, APOSTLE, ST., designated by Christ to be the first of the Apostles. According to ancient tradition, he became the first bishop of Rome and suffered martyrdom during the persecution of Nero (64 or 65).

PETER ALFONSI, d. c. 1140, Aragonese Jew who served Alfonso I of Aragon and Henry I of England as physician. He subsequently converted to Christianity. He composed a collection of Oriental tales and also acquired some fame as an astronomer.

PETER AUREOLI, d. 1322, learned Franciscan theologian and archbishop. He lectured at Bologna, Toulouse, and Paris, served as provincial of his order in Aquitaine (1320), and in 1321 was consecrated archbishop of Aix-en-Provence. His theological writings, of which his commentary on the *Sentences* of Peter Lombard is the most important, reveal an original and highly speculative thinker. Despite his reverence for Aristotle and Averroës, he attached appreciably less importance to their work than did Thomas Aquinas.

PETERBOROUGH, ABBEY OF, Benedictine monastery, first known as Medeshamstede, was founded c. 655 by King Penda of Mercia. It was destroyed by the Danes in 870 but rebuilt c. 970 by Ethelwold of Winchester who dedicated it to St. Peter, hence the village's name Peterborough. The abbey was one of the wealthiest and most influential in Anglo-Norman England. The cathedral, a Norman church, was begun in 1118 and completed and consecrated in 1237.

PETER CASTELNAU, BL., d. 1208, a Cistercian who was sent as papal legate to Languedoc by Pope Innocent III to enlist the cooperation of Raymond VI, count of Toulouse, against the Albigenses. His murder, possibly by an agent of the count's, prompted Innocent to proclaim the Albigensian Crusade.

PETER COMESTOR, d. c. 1180, chancellor of the cathedral school in Paris, canon regular of Saint Victor, and author of a church history that extended from the Creation to the end of the period covered by the Acts of the Apostles. This became the standard work on the history of the Bible, and Peter was known as the "Magister Historiarum." He also left commentaries on the Scriptures and on the *Sentences* of Peter Lombard, as well as numerous sermons.

PETER DAMIAN, ST., d. 1072, prior of the Benedictine community at Fonte Avellana which had incorporated into its rule the extreme asceticism of St. Romuald, the founder of the Camaldolese order. In 1057 he was made cardinal bishop of Ostia and sent by the pope on several diplomatic missions to France and Ger-

many. Peter was dedicated to the reform of the church which he believed could be best accomplished through the joint efforts of church and emperor. He left many letters, sermons, hymns, and treatises on scriptural, legal, theological, and ascetical subjects. His was one of the most polished Latin styles in the Middle Ages.

PETER DE BRUYES, d. c. 1140, heretical priest of Provence and Dauphine who rejected baptism, the mass, a large part of the Scriptures, as well as the authority of the church. His followers, and they were many, were known as "Petrobrusians." His teachings were condemned by the Second Lateran Council in 1139. He was apparently burned to death by people infuriated by his burning of crosses.

PETER DES ROCHES, d. 1238, loyal councillor of John, king of England, to whom he owed his appointment in 1205 as bishop of Winchester. Peter was an influential figure in court circles during the early years of Henry III's reign and the source of much baronial resentment because of the foreigners he brought over with him from Poitou. Despite a full political career, he founded a number of churches and religious houses.

PETER JOHN OLIVI, d. 1298, Franciscan philosopher and theologian. He studied at Paris under Bonaventure and composed many treatises on philosophical, theological, scriptural, and ascetical subjects. Because of his preference for a strict observance of the Rule of St. Francis concerning poverty, he found himself caught up in the fierce struggle that was convulsing the order. Although a commission in 1282 judged some of his writings to be heretical, a judgment confirmed by a general chapter three years later, subsequent chapters rehabilitated him and cleared his name.

PETER LOMBARD, d. 1160, teacher of theology and author of a standard text used in most schools of theology in the Middle Ages. He taught at the cathedral school of Notre Dame in

Paris and in 1159 was consecrated bishop of Paris. His *Book of Sentences* constituted a one-volume synthesis of Christian doctrine based upon the Scriptures, tradition, and the writings of the church fathers. He placed only a moderate reliance upon dialectic. What may help explain the popularity of the *Sentences* was the author's lack of identification with either Thomism or Augustinianism. The work came under attack by the followers of Joachim of Fiore but was declared orthodox by the Fourth Lateran Council (1215). It was eventually superseded by Aquinas's *Summa Theologiae*.

PETER MARTYR, ST., d. 1252, inquisitor, born at Verona of parents who were Cathari, became a Dominican, was prior of several houses, and was appointed inquisitor for north Italy (1125). He forced some Cathari into exile and brought many others back to the faith. He gained a reputation as a preacher and a worker of miracles. He was murdered by the Cathari.

PETER NIGRI (Schwarz), d. 1483, Dominican philosopher, theologian, and Hebraist. He served as rector of the University of Budapest and composed a number of theological and exegetical works. His *Tractatus* was probably the first book to be printed in Hebrew characters.

PETER NOLASCO, ST., d. 1249 or 1256, devoted his life to the ransoming of Christians from the Moors and, with St. Raymond of Peñafort, founded the Order of Our Lady of Ransom (Mercedarians) to expedite that work. Many legends were told of the saint. He may have taken part in the Crusade against the Albigensians.

PETER OF ABANO. *See* ABANO, PETER OF.

PETER OF AILLY. *See* AILLY, PIERRE D'.

PETER OF ARGENTERIA (Argillata), well-known surgeon of the fourteenth century who left several works on the subject of surgery.

PETER OF AUVERGNE (Alvernia), d. 1304, taught philosophy and theology at Paris, served as rector of the university, and composed commentaries on the works of Aristotle. He also completed those that Aquinas had undertaken on that philosopher. He closed out his career as bishop of Clermont (from 1302).

PETER OF BLOIS, d. 1212?, humanist and political thinker. He studied at Bologna and Paris, served as tutor to the future William II, king of Sicily, and as secretary to two archbishops of Canterbury. He was a popular figure at the court of Henry II of England and on occasion served him in a diplomatic capacity. In addition to poems, he composed sermons, satires, and treatises on history, political theory, and theology. Because of the many important people he knew, his letters possess considerable value.

PETER OF CANDIA. *See* ALEXANDER V.

PETER OF LA PALU (Paludanus), d. 1342, learned Dominican theologian who lectured at Paris and who several times was appointed to commissions to judge writings whose orthodoxy had come into question, e.g., those of Durandus and Pope John XXII's writings concerning the Beatific Vision. He composed two works on ecclesiology. His appointment in 1392 as patriarch of Jerusalem led him to devote his labors to the organization of a Crusade.

PETER OF LUNA. *See* BENEDICT XIII.

PETER OF MARICOURT. *See* MARICOURT, PIERRE DE.

PETER OF PISA, d. before 799, a deacon, grammarian, and poet who spent some years with the circle of scholars at Aachen. He may have instructed Charlemagne in Latin grammar.

PETER OF POITIERS, d. 1205, taught theology at Paris and was chancellor of the university from 1193 until his death. Through his teaching and writing he contributed to the development of Paris as the leading theological center in Europe.

His *Sentences,* a systematic exposition of dogmatic and moral theology, has been likened to that of Peter Lombard, his teacher.

PETER OF TARANTAISE, ST., d. 1175, a native of Dauphiné, became a Cistercian and in 1142 was consecrated archbishop of Tarantaise (Savoy). He founded many hospitals. His practice of distributing free bread and soup in the weeks before harvest was the origin of the "May Bread" which may have survived until the French Revolution. He fled his high office but was discovered as a lay brother in a Swiss monastery and was forced to return.

PETER OF VAUX-DE-CERNAY, d. after 1218, Cistercian monk at Vaux-de-Cernay near Paris who took part in the Fourth and Albigensian Crusades. He left a valuable history of the Albigensian Crusade.

PETER OF VINEA, d. 1249, notary and judge in the service of Frederick II, king of Germany and Sicily, who rose to become his chief councillor or logothete. When the emperor had him blinded in 1249 for treason, he committed suicide.

PETER'S PENCE, a tax paid to the papacy by each household in England. The tax may have originated with Offa, king of Mercia (757-96), or with Alfred the Great (871-99). It became an annual tax during the reign of Edward the Confessor (1042-66). After the twelfth century the tax was also collected in Poland, Hungary, Denmark, Norway, and Sweden.

PETER THE CHANTER, d. 1197, theologian, studied at Reims and Paris, taught at Paris, and in 1197 became dean of Reims. He produced glosses on all the books of the Bible, treatises on the sacraments, and a work on virtues and vices. He was one of the most influential theologians of the late twelfth century. His views are believed to have influenced the Fourth Lateran Council's decision to bar priests from taking part in ordeals. He also condemned the death penalty for heretics.

PETER THE HERMIT (of Amiens), d. 1115, called the Hermit because of his attire, the most eloquent of the preachers of the First Crusade. He led one of the groups that made up the Peasants' Crusade (1096), later joined the regular Crusading army when his following was scattered by the Turks in Asia Minor. During the siege of Antioch (1098), he tried to escape but was brought back, although he entered Jerusalem with the victorious Crusaders in July 1099. He closed out his life as prior of a community of Canons Regular of St. Augustine at Neufmoûtier (Belgium).

PETER THE VENERABLE, d. 1156, abbot of Cluny from 1122 and director of some 2,000 Cluniac houses in western Europe. Already during his life, his saintly, peace-loving nature earned him the title "Venerable." Despite the extensive traveling he undertook in the interest of reforming monastic life, he found time for study and meditation. He had the Koran translated into Latin in order to further the conversion of Moslems. He secured the reconciliation of Peter Abelard with the ecclesiastical authorities following the condemnation of that scholastic's writings at the Council of Sens (1140). He left a number of sermons, some poetry, and treatises attacking Peter de Bruyes and the Jews. He lived in the shadow cast by his great contemporary Bernard of Clairvaux.

PETER WALDO. *See* WALDENSES.

PETRARCH, FRANCESCO, 1374, one of the greatest lyric poets in the history of literature. Petrarch, the son of a Florentine exile, studied at Montpellier and Bologna, but abandoned all thought of a legal career when his father died. Although he was a man of deep faith and a sharp critic of the Avignonese papacy, he earned his renown, both with contemporaries and with posterity, with the Italian sonnets he composed in honor of Laura, the wife of another man. His lyric poetry, which ranks with the finest ever composed, drew the earnest attention of would-be poets in the West for centuries to come. Despite the manifest genius he revealed in the composition of verse in the vernacular, he derived most gratification from the letters, biographies, and verse he composed in classical Latin. His dedication to the study of the classics and his success in encouraging others to do the same earned him the title of father of humanism. Petrarch was probably most responsible for the name of "Dark Ages" being given to the centuries that intervened between the decline of Roman civilization and his own century.

PETRINE DOCTRINE, the position maintained by the proponents of the primacy of the bishop of Rome (pope), namely, that as bishop of Rome he inherited the position of primacy among all bishops of Christendom which St. Peter, the first bishop of Rome, had held among the apostles. This position was based in turn upon a sympathetic interpretation of three scriptural passages, known as the Petrine Texts (Matthew 16:17–19; Luke 33:31–32; John 21:15–17), which describe Christ as investing Peter with a position of primacy. [*See* POPE.]

PETROBRUSIANS, followers of Peter de Bruyes (d. c. 1130) who endorsed his criticism of the clergy, his attacks on the mass and sacraments, and his demands for reform. They were most numerous in the twelfth century. [*See* PETER DE BRUYES.]

PEW. Because of the scarcity of furniture until the late Middle Ages, it was customary for worshippers to stand and kneel, with no seats provided. In time, as a concession to the aged and infirm, stone seats were attached to the walls or to the piers of the nave. By the close of the thirteenth century many English churches appear to have provided a number of fixed wooden benches, often known as "pews," meaning seats raised above the floor.

PHILIP I, king of France, 1060–1108, engaged in intermittent warfare with William I and II of England while making some modest additions to the royal domain. His attempt to divorce his wife involved him in difficulties with the papacy which for a time left him an excommunicate and France under an interdict.

PHILIP II AUGUSTUS, king of France, 1180–1223, probably France's leading monarch of the Middle Ages. His principal achievement was the immense expansion of the royal domain which he accomplished. Territories which he added included Maine, Touraine, Anjou, Brittany, and Normandy, all of which he seized from King John of England. His decisive defeat of John's ally, Otto IV of Germany, at Bouvines (1214) confirmed him in the possession of these territories. He also added Artois, Vermandois, and Valois, and by permitting his vassals to undertake a crusade against the Albigenses in Languedoc, he prepared the way for the eventual absorption of Toulouse into the royal domain. Everywhere in France he enhanced the royal authority with the introduction of *baillis* and *seneschaux* whom he appointed to do justice in his name, to collect revenues, and to call up the armed forces. He beautified Paris, chartered the University of Paris, accompanied Richard I of England and Frederick I Barbarossa of Germany on the Third Crusade (1189–92), but invited a long struggle with Pope Innocent III when he divorced his wife Ingeborg, sister of the Danish king, and married Agnes of Meran. He eventually made his peace with the church, after Agnes had died, in order to qualify for leadership of a projected crusade against John across the channel.

PHILIP III, king of France, 1270–85, managed to absorb Poitou and the greater part of Languedoc into the royal domain, although his venture into Aragon in support of papal and French policy in Sicily proved unsuccessful.

PHILIP IV (the Fair), king of France, 1285–1314, a strong, if not unscrupulous, monarch whose harsh measures effected a significant increase in the power and revenues of the

French crown. His humiliation of Pope Boniface VIII gave him greater control of the church in France than that enjoyed by any of his predecessors. His new taxes, including impositions on the sale of wheat, wine, and salt, together with the monies he confiscated from Jews and bankers whom he expelled and the Knights of the Temple whom he suppressed, enabled him to pursue aggressive policies against the English, whom he wanted out of Guienne, and in Flanders, which he wished to appropriate. To bolster his attack on the papacy, he summoned the estates general (1302) for the first time in the history of that body.

PHILIP V, king of France, 1316–22, second son of Philip IV, younger brother and successor of Louis X who put down a baronial revolt in Champagne. Since Louis left only a daughter when he died, France faced the question whether a woman could succeed to the throne. Philip, who had the support of the officers of the crown and of the bourgeois, declared himself king and was crowned.

PHILIP VI, king of France, 1328–50, nephew of Philip IV, the son of Charles of Valois and the first king of the Valois dynasty to rule France. Philip precipitated the Hundred Years' War when he declared Guienne forfeit in May 1337. Nine years later, in 1346, he suffered a humiliating defeat at the hands of the English at Crécy. He purchased Montpellier from James III of Majorca and arranged the sale of Dauphiné to his grandson, the future Charles V.

PHILIP, APOSTLE, ST., one of the twelve apostles.

PHILIP (the Bold), duke of Burgundy, 1364–1404, son of John II of France, who gained Flanders, Franche-Comté, Artois, Nevers, and Rethel through his marriage to Margaret of Flanders. In 1392 when Charles VI, his nephew, became insane, he clashed with Louis, duke of Orléans, brother of Charles, over the right to control the government. Philip

showed himself a patron of the arts and a most avid collector of manuscripts and illuminated books.

PHILIP (the Good), duke of Burgundy, 1419–67, supported the English following the murder of his father, John the Fearless, in 1419, against the Dauphin (Charles VII) whom he held responsible for the deed. He recognized Henry VI of England as king of France by the Treaty of Troyes (1420) but later, by the Treaty of Arras (1435) with Charles VII, withdrew from the English alliance in return for the cession of the "Somme towns" and virtual autonomy for Burgundy. He showed himself a patron of artists, musicians, and writers, and founded the Order of the Golden Fleece.

PHILIP (the Handsome), duke of Burgundy, d. 1506, son of Maximilian and Mary of Burgundy, married Joanna, daughter of Ferdinand of Aragon and Isabella of Castile. He was the father of Charles V and of Ferdinand I, Holy Roman emperors.

PHILIP OF SWABIA, brother of Henry VI and the choice of the Hohenstaufen supporters to succeed him in 1197 when he died. He was opposed by Otto of Brunswick, the Guelf candidate, who had the support of a number of German princes as well as that of Pope Innocent III. The murder of Philip in 1208 resolved the issue and Otto was elected king of Germany.

PHILOTHEUS COCCINUS, d. 1379, patriarch of Constantinople, 1353–4 and 1364–76, monk of Mt. Sinai and Mt. Athos, bishop of Heraclea, who in 1353 was raised by the emperor John VI to the office of patriarch. He was deposed when the emperor lost his throne, but was restored in 1364. His writings include polemical works, hagiography, homilies, hymns, and commentaries on the Scriptures.

PHILOXENUS OF MABBUGH, d. 523, bishop of Mabbugh in Syria who was exiled by Emperor Justin I in 519 for his strong Monophysite views, first to Thrace, then to Paphlagonia where he was murdered. He was the author of numerous exegetical, dogmatic, ascetical, and homiletic writings. His most influential work was probably his revised Syriac version of the Bible.

PHOCAS, Byzantine emperor, 602–10, a rough Thracian soldier who was acclaimed emperor after Maurice had been deposed and executed. He instituted a reign of terror which he directed principally at the leading families of the city. He also persecuted Monophysites and Jews. One friend he made was Pope Gregory I (the Great) whose primacy he recognized. As Persians were overrunning Asia Minor and Slavs and Avars the Balkans, Heraclius, son of the exarch of Carthage, entered the city and executed Phocas whom a mob had already seized. Heraclius succeeded as emperor.

PHOENIX, legendary bird that lived for 500 years, then died, only to be reborn from its own ashes. In Christian iconography the phoenix symbolized the Resurrection.

PHOTIUS, patriarch of Constantinople, 858–67 and 877–86, reputedly the most learned man of his age, a "second Aristotle." He was a teacher of philosophy in Constantinople, director for a time of the imperial chancery, and in 858, when still a layman, appointed to replace Ignatius as patriarch. Pope Nicholas I excommunicated Photius in 863 on the basis of inaccurate information and ordered Ignatius restored. The papal order was ignored until 867 when Basil murdered Michael III, seized the throne, and sent Photius into exile. Photius meanwhile had denounced the presence of Latin missionaries in Bulgaria and had also made clear his objection to the *Filioque* clause in the creed. Basil later called Photius back to Constantinople and appointed him to tutor his sons. In 877 when Ignatius died, Photius was again appointed patriarch and this time received papal confirmation (from John VIII). He later resigned his see or was deposed. Photius's voluminous writings included theolog-

ical works, letters, homilies, philosophical treatises, and the *Myriobiblon*. The latter consisted of a review of some 280 books, many of them no longer in existence. Photius's writings, especially his *Treatise on the Holy Ghost*, furnished subsequent Byzantine theologians with their objections to the Latin dogma concerning the Third Person.

PHYSIOLOGUS, a collection of stories about animals composed in the second century A.D., probably in or near Egypt. Beyond legendary animals, the collection included descriptions of those known in the ancient world, India, and Africa. The stories supplemented a description of each animal with a moral lesson based upon a study of its supposed traits and habits. [*See* BESTIARY.]

PIACENZA, city of north central Italy on the Po, occupied successively by Goths, Lombards, and Franks. By the twelfth century it had become a free commune and joined the Lombard League. The thirteenth-century cathedral is graced with famous frescoes, while the town hall of the same period is one of the finest in Italy.

PIAN CARPINE, GIOVANNI. *See* JOHN OF PLANO CARPINI.

PIAST DYNASTY, Polish ruling dynasty of semimythical origin whose first historical leader was Mieszko I (963–92). The first male line ended with the death of Casimir III in 1370. [*See* POLAND.]

PICARDS, a heretical group not unlike the Beghards in their emphasis upon individual piety although they denied the priesthood, the eucharist, and the role of the Holy Spirit. They appeared in Bohemia in the late fourteenth century. The term Picard was occasionally used to designate Bohemian Brethren, the Brethren of the Free Spirit, and the Adamites.

PICARDY, province in northern France between Normandy and the Low Countries. It had its capital at Amiens. The upper portion of the province came under royal control in 1213, that of the south in 1369. From 1279 the countship of Ponthieu was held by the English as a fief. The entire region fell under the rule of the duke of Burgundy from 1435 to 1477. The term Picardy did not appear before the thirteenth century.

PICCOLOMINI, aristocratic family of Siena first noted in the late eleventh century which became an important house in the thirteenth. It maintained banking houses in Italy, France, and England. The family produced many bishops, several cardinals, and one pope, Pius II (1458–64).

PICO DELLA MIRANDOLA, GIOVANNI, d. 1494, humanist, mystical writer, and philosopher, a member of the Academy of Florence, who sought to construct a single system of truth based upon Aristotelianism, Platonism, Christianity, Judaism, and Oriental religions. In his *Oration on the Dignity of Man* he discoursed on the ability of man, who, because he was the master of his fate, was able to rise to a dignity denied to all other earthly creatures. He was known for his great learning, his urbanity, his piety, as well as his handsome figure. He died clothed in the Dominican habit of Savonarola.

PICQUIGNY, TREATY OF, treaty agreed to by Edward IV of England and Louis XI of France in 1475. Edward renounced his alliance with Charles the Bold of Burgundy and returned to England with his army upon promise of a large amount of money and an annual pension. The treaty isolated Charles and led to his early destruction (1477).

PICTS, pre-Celtic or Celtic people of Scotland who harassed the northern frontier of Britain during late Roman times. Those of the south accepted Christianity from St. Ninian (d. 432), those in the north from St. Columba (d. 597). The two parts were united into one nation with the Scots by Kenneth I MacAlpin c. 843.

PIED (piede, pe), a foot, measure of variable length used especially in Romance countries.

PIEDMONT, region of northwest Italy, the upper Po valley, that came to be known as Piedmont by the thirteenth century. It then consisted of the two Western Lombard marches of Turin and Ivrea which had come under the rule of Savoy in the eleventh. Free communes maintained themselves within the region, as did powerful feudal lords such as the marquises of Saluzzo and Montferrat. In the fifteenth century Savoy gained control of the entire area.

PIED PIPER OF HAMELIN, a musician who, legend had it, led the children away from Hamelin, Germany, in 1284, with his flute playing charming music. He had done this because the town had refused to pay him for ridding the community of rats.

PIERO DELLA FRANCESCA (Piero dei Franceschi), d. 1492, Italian painter and mathematician who was active in different cities of Italy although his style shows heavy Florentine influence. (He grew up in Florence.) His knowledge of mathematics is reflected in the rigid framework of geometry in which he constructed his paintings. Another unique mark of his art was his ability to present a synthesis of the natural with the artificial in his painting and of the rustic with the sophisticated, as in the fresco of the *Legend of the Holy Cross.* Some art historians regard him as the greatest of the Quattrocento painters.

PIERRE D'AILLY. *See* AILLY, PIERRE D'.

PIERS THE PLOWMAN, THE VISION OF WILLIAM CONCERNING. *See* LANGLAND, WILLIAM.

PIETÀ, a word derived from the Italian meaning pity and applied to a representation of the sorrowing Mary holding the dead Christ. The representation was of thirteenth-century German origin.

PIETRO D'ABANO. *See* ABANO, PETER OF.

PIETRO DELLA VIGNA. *See* PETER OF VINEA.

563

PIKEMAN, foot soldier armed with a weapon consisting of a long wooden shaft (some 20 feet in length) topped with a barb. Pikemen appeared in the Low Countries as early as the eleventh century. They proved of decisive importance at the battle of Courtrai (1302) and in the Swiss victories over Charles the Bold of Burgundy (d. 1477).

PILATE, PONTIUS, Roman procurator of Judaea who condemned Jesus to death.

PILEOLUS (Kalotte, Soli-Deo), kind of skull cap worn under another headcovering by popes and other prelates while saying mass.

PILGRIMAGES. The practice of making pilgrimages to holy places antedates the Christian era but did not attain popularity until the Middle Ages. The history of Christian pilgrimages begins with the reign of Constantine I (the Great) who halted persecutions, and with his mother Helena who visited Jerusalem in 326 where she is believed to have discovered the True Cross. Jerusalem and Bethlehem remained the most popular places of pilgrimage with the eleventh century witnessing a trek of 7,000 pilgrims from Germany alone. The most popular shrines in western Europe were Rome which was believed to hold the tombs of SS. Peter and Paul, Santiago de Compostella in northwestern Galicia, which was believed to have the body of St. James, and Canterbury after the murder there of Thomas Becket (d. 1170). But most regions could count on a fairly constant flow of pilgrims to the tombs of local saints where the presence of relics was believed to have worked miracles. Another factor contributing to the large number of pilgrims in the Middle Ages was the practice of assigning a pilgrimage as penance to persons guilty of serious or public sins. Moslem interference, real or alleged, with pilgrims visiting the Holy Places in Palestine aroused Christians of western Europe to undertake the Crusades. Still the most popular of all pilgrimages was that which countless Moslems made to visit the Kaaba in Mecca and the tomb of the Prophet in Medina.

PILLAR SAINTS. *See* STYLITES.

PINNACLE, a small turret or spire, in a subordinate architectural role, usually crowning a pier, buttress, or gable. Pinnacles appeared in late Romanesque churches but became particularly prominent in Gothic churches where they were used to provide vertical emphasis and break up hard outlines, to fill major corners and flanking gables, and to rest atop parapets and buttresses. Those that crowned flying buttresses served both a decorative and a practical function since their weight added stability to the buttress. With the advance of Gothic, pinnacles appeared in ever increasing numbers, with their multiplication leading to Decorated Gothic in England and the Flamboyant style in France, e.g., Salisbury cathedral and the choir of Notre Dame in Paris.

PINTURICCHIO (Bernardino di Betto), d. 1513, painter of Umbria who was known for his lavish use of gold and brilliant colors. He assisted Perugino in the execution of the frescoes in the Sistine Chapel.

PINZÓN, MARTIN ALONSO, d. 1493, Spanish navigator, commander of the Pinta on Columbus's first voyage to the New World. His brother Vicente Yañez commanded the Niña. Both brothers contributed to the success of Columbus's voyage.

PIPE ROLLS, rolls of records kept by the office of the English exchequer of revenues and expenditures. The extant series begins in 1156 with the reign of Henry II although one important roll remains from the year 1130. Their name probably derived from the pipelike form of the rolled parchments on which the records were kept.

PIRENNE THESIS, the revolutionary position taken by the distinguished Belgian historian Henri Pirenne, who in the 1920s proposed the view that it was not the semicivilized German invaders who had brought about a rapid decline in the civilization of the western half of the Roman empire — the traditional view — but rather that the rise of Islam must be held responsible./Arab conquest of Syria, Egypt, north Africa, and later of Spain had cut the jugular vein of the Mediterranean world, thus disrupting the unity of the Roman empire and expediting its decline. Most scholars dispute Pirenne's thesis although they are willing to reduce the extent of damage to Roman institutions and trade traditionally attributed to the Germans.

PISA, city in Italy west of Florence near the Tyrrhenian Sea (it was once on the coast). Although its origins go back to Roman times and beyond, it developed into a major industrial and commercial center only in the twelfth and thirteenth centuries when its trade and political importance rivaled those of Genoa and Venice. Rivalry with Genoa over control of the commerce of the area, and over Corsica and Sardinia, continued until 1284 when Pisa's naval power was crushed by Genoa in the sea battle of Meloria. The Black Death brought further decline in the fourteenth century, and in 1406 the city fell to Florence. Its cathedral, a Romanesque structure, was begun in 1063. The university was recognized as a *studium generale* in 1343 and so confirmed by Emperor Charles IV in 1355.

PISA, COUNCIL OF, convened in 1409 in response to the demands of Christians everywhere for an end to the Western Schism. The council was attended by cardinals of both Roman and Avignonese obediences and by representatives of most European princes. The council formally deposed the two popes, Benedict XIII and Gregory XII, and elected Peter of Candia, the cardinal of Milan, who took the name of Alexander V. Instead of terminating the schism, as the cardinals had hoped, it simply saddled Western Christendom with still another pope.

PISAN, CHRISTINE DE, d. between 1429 and 1431, French poet of Italian descent, author of a large number of romances in verse, and of lyric poems and works in prose. She was highly regarded as a woman of remarkable character and virtue.

PISANELLO (Pisano), ANTONIO, d. c. 1455, Italian medalist and painter of frescoes, portraits, birds, animals, and medallions. His works show the influence of Gentile da Fabriano. Many of his drawings survive. One of his best known frescoes is *The Annunciation,* one of his finest medallions that of John VIII Palaeologus.

PISANO, GIOVANNI, d. after 1314, son of Nicola, Tuscan architect and sculptor whose work reveals French influences. He was one of the first artists to incorporate monumental statuary into architecture as seen in his work on the façade of the cathedral in Siena. He also did some Madonnas and the tomb of Margaret, wife of Henry VII of Germany.

PISANO, ANDREA, d. c. 1348, Tuscan goldsmith and sculptor, founder of the Florentine school of sculpture. His work reveals the influence of Giotto. His work, especially the bronze doors for the Baptistery at Florence, in turn influenced Ghiberti.

PISANO, NICOLA, d. c. 1283, architect and first great Italian sculptor, best known for the sculptured reliefs he made for the baptistery of Pisa. He combined Gothic and classical influences as, for example, in his *Presentation of Jesus in the Temple* for the pulpit in the Pisa baptistery, in which the pagan Dionysus serves as the high priest Simeon. He designed the great fountain for Perugia.

PISANO, NINO, d. 1368, son of Andrea and like his father a sculptor, architect, and goldsmith. Only his sculpture in marble survives, including the *Madonna* in S. Maria Novella in Florence.

PISCINA, baptismal font or the cistern into which water flowed from the head of the person being baptized; basin in which the priest at mass washed his hands and the chalice.

PISTOL, single-handed firearm which came into use in the fifteenth century.

PITTI, PALAZZO, Florentine palace whose construction got under way in 1458 according to plans drawn up by Brunelleschi.

PIUS I, ST., Pope, 142–55, probably an Italian from Aquileia and possibly a brother of Hermas, the author of the *Shepherd*. Gnosticism posed a problem during his pontificate.

PIUS II, Pope, 1458–64, Enea Silvio de' Piccolomini, one of the leading humanists of his age, author of love poems, and later ashamed of the dissolute youth he had led. He attended the Council of Basel where he supported conciliarism and eventually served as secretary to Pope Felix V (antipope), then entered the service of Emperor Frederick III as court poet and secretary to the chancery in Vienna. In 1445 he altered his position on conciliarism, repudiated Felix, and was reconciled to Pope Eugenius IV, then won over the emperor. Next he became a priest, was consecrated bishop (Trieste, then Siena), and created cardinal (1456). As pope he anathematized conciliarism with the bull *Execrabilis* (1460), then devoted his greatest efforts to organizing a Crusade against the Turks. His memoirs represent the only autobiography left by a pope.

PLACET, vote of assent or agreement formula used at councils.

PLACIDIA, GALLA. *See* GALLA, PLACIDIA.

PLACITUM REGIUM. *See* EXEQUATUR.

PLAIN CHANT or SONG. *See* MASS, MUSIC OF THE.

PLAGUE. *See* BLACK DEATH.

PLANTAGENET, ruling family of England from the reign of Henry II (1154–89) to the abdication of Richard II in 1399. The name may have been derived from the nickname given to Geoffrey, count of Anjou (1129–51), the father of Henry II, because of his habit of wearing a sprig of broom (plan-taj unet) in his helmet.

PLANUDES, MAXIMUS, d. c. 1310, monk, founder of a monastery for laymen in Constantinople and of a school near the imperial palace. His writings include translations of Latin classical and patristic works into Greek, letters, and theological treatises. Among his most important works were his prose collection of Aesop's *Fables* and his Greek Anthology. He was a proponent of union with the Latin church.

PLATINA, BARTOLOMEO, d. 1481, Italian humanist, patronized by Pius II, imprisoned by Paul II, then back in papal favor under Sixtus IV who made him librarian of the Vatican (1475). While holding that office he produced his *Lives of the Popes*, a readable but not especially scholarly work. His mention of the anathema of Callistus III leveled against the Turks, in the context of his reference to Halley's comet, was the source of the charge that the pope had excommunicated the comet.

PLEGMUND OF CANTERBURY, d. 914, hermit of Cheshire who served as tutor and adviser of Alfred the Great. In 890 he was consecrated archbishop of Canterbury.

PLETHON, GEORGIOS GEMISTOS, d. 1452, the leading philosopher of late Byzantine times. As director of a theological and Platonic center in southern Greece he contributed, through his associations with Italian humanists, to the foundation of the Platonic Academy in Florence. His principal work, *Nomon Syngraphe*, proposed a political utopia based on an idealized paganism.

PLINY THE YOUNGER, d. c. 113, governor of Bithynia. His correspondence with the emperor Trajan throws significant light on the persecution of Christians by the Roman government. Trajan, in his reply to Pliny's inquiry as to what he should do about Christians, instructed him to execute all persons duly convicted of being Christians, but not to ferret them out. This policy was probably the one adopted by the majority of Roman emperors.

PLOTINUS, d. 270, a philosopher, born in Egypt, who studied in Alexandria and in Mesopotamia, and made his home in Rome where he opened a school. He has been called the father of neo-Platonism in that he was more successful than others in establishing a philosophy of life based upon the idealism of Plato and the mysticism of the eastern Mediterranean. He taught that man can identify himself with the Mind of the universe through mystical contemplation although complete identification with God can come only when death frees the soul from the physical bonds of the body. His disciple Porphyry drew upon the ideas of Plotinus to fashion a kind of pagan religion which proved quite popular in the fourth century. [*See* NEO-PLATONISM.]

PLUTARCH OF ATHENS, Greek philosopher of the fourth or fifth century who headed the Platonic School in Athens. He prepared commentaries on several of the works of Plato and Aristotle.

PNEUMATOMACHIANS, a fourth-century Christian sect that denied the divinity of the Holy Spirit. The sect was condemned by Pope Damasus in 374 and by the Council of Constantinople in 381.

PODESTÀ, imperial governor, the highest magistrate, appointed for Italian cities by the German emperors of the twelfth century, later elected by the communes themselves. The importance of the office declined after the thirteenth century.

PODIEBRAD, GEORGE OF (Jiri of Podebrady), king of Bohemia, 1458–71, who served as regent for Ladislas V from 1451 to 1453, then was elected king by the Bohemian estates in 1458 when Ladislas died. As a Bohemian nobleman he had become a leader of the Utraquists or moderate Hussites against the Taborites whom he succeeded in crushing. As regent he brought peace to Bohemia, strengthened the royal government, and established its authority throughout Bohemia and its dependencies (Moravia, Silesia, and Lusatia). His success was made possible largely because of the continued loyalty of the moderate Hussites. When he refused to abolish the Compacts of Prague which recognized their privileged status, Pope Paul II excommunicated him and called on Matthias I Corvinus, king of Hungary, to depose him. Podiebrad was able to defeat Matthias although to strengthen himself made an alliance with Casimir IV of Poland which provided for the latter's son to succeed Podiebrad as king of Bohemia.

POEMA DEL CID, Spanish national epic of the twelfth century which glorified the exploits of Rodrigo de Vivar. [*See* CID, EL.]

POETA SAXO, medieval Latin poet of the late ninth century, known as the Saxon Poet, whose best known poem deals with the reign of Charlemagne. He was a monk of Corvey.

POGGIO BRACCIOLINI, GIOVANNI FRANCESCO, d. 1459, humanist, *scriptor* for almost 50 years in the papal Curia, chancellor of the Republic of Florence. He collected classical manuscripts, a great many of which he found in monastic libraries, translated Greek works into Latin, and acquired an excellent knowledge of classical Latin, as evident in his letters, anecdotes, and a history of Florence. He was also the author of moral dialogues and of polemical and satirical poems — these at the expense of individuals including rival scholars — all in Latin but ranging in style from Ciceronian to idiomatic.

POITIERS, city in west-central France whose origins go back to Roman times. It became a bishop's see about the middle of the fourth century when St. Hilary (d. c. 367) served as its first bishop. It was occupied by the Visigoths, then in 507 by the Franks. Near the city took place the famous battle between Charles Martel and the Moors in 732 which ended in a decisive victory for the Franks. Poitiers was also the site of the tremendous victory gained in 1356 by the Black Prince over the French. Poitiers served as the capital of the county of Poitou.

POITOU, province of France on the Atlantic just south of Brittany, occupied first by the Visigoths, then by the Franks (507), whose counts acquired possession of Aquitaine in the ninth century. When Aquitaine became part of the empire of Henry II, Poitou went along, but early in the thirteenth century it was separated from Aquitaine. This was done by Philip II Augustus who took over all the provinces north of the Loire as well as Poitou from John of England. During the course of the Hundred Years' War, Poitou was now under French control, now under English. It was ceded to the English by the Treaty of Brétigny (1360), but recovered for France by Duguesclin c. 1370.

POKAL, goblet with lid and frequently adorned with precious stones. Such goblets became popular in the fifteenth century.

POLABIANS (Polabs), westernmost group of Slavic tribes located to the east of the lower Elbe. In Charlemagne's time they divided between the Obotrites in the west and the Lutycy or Wilcy in the east. The latter became subject to the dukes of Saxony in the twelfth century. [See OBOTRITES.]

POLAND, state in east-central Europe whose historical origins reach back to the ninth and tenth centuries when the Piast dynasty established its leadership. The first prince to reign over a united Poland was Mieszko I (d. 992) who recognized the suzerainty of Otto I of Germany and became a Christian. (Bohemian missionaries were already at work converting the Poles.) Mieszko's son Boleslaw the Brave (992–1025) was the first Polish ruler to hold the title of king. A major obstacle to the political development of Poland was the practice of Polish kings of dividing their realms among their sons. Equally disastrous was the occasional need of the king to grant generous privileges to his demanding aristocracy. Casimir III (d. 1370), for example, Poland's greatest monarch in the medieval period, extended his rule over Galicia and advanced Poland's population and economic growth by encouraging the immigration of Germans and Jews, yet made concessions to the aristocracy that impeded the emergence of strong royal government. A permanent obstacle to Poland's future as a great power lay in the absence of natural frontiers to block the aggressiveness of powerful neighbors. To ward off attacks from Prussians, Lithuanians, and Mongols the Polish prince of Mazovia invited the Teutonic Order to come into the area early in the thirteenth century. The Knights accomplished their purpose and more, for they proceeded to erect a state that stretched from Pomerania to the Gulf of Finland and effectively blocked Poland's access to the Baltic. To counter this new enemy, the Poles allied themselves in 1386 with the Lithuanians who were equally menaced by Teutonic expansion, and cemented this alliance with the marriage of Hedwiga, heiress of Poland, to Jagiello, grand prince of Lithuania. In 1410 the united Poles and Lithuanians inflicted a crushing defeat on the Knights at Grunwald (Tannenberg) and by 1466 (Peace of Torun) were able to force the Teutonic Order to cede Pomerania and West Prussia, while retaining East Prussia as a fief of Poland.

POLE, WILLIAM DE LA. See SUFFOLK, EARLS AND DUKES OF.

POLITIAN (Angelo Ambrogini Poliziano), d. 1494, a leading humanist, philologist, and poet. He served as tutor to the sons of Lorenzo de' Medici, and taught classics at the University of Florence. His translation of part of the *Iliad* into Latin hexameters first brought him to the attention of the humanist world. Besides elegies, odes, and epigrams in Latin, he composed songs and verse in Italian. Together with Lorenzo de' Medici, he was chiefly responsible for the new interest in, and appreciation of, vernacular literature.

POLIZIANO. *See* POLITIAN.

POLLAIUOLO, ANTONIO, d. 1498, goldsmith, worker in bronze, painter, engraver, and sculptor. Some of his work, especially the engraving entitled *Battle of the Naked Men,* stimulated interest in anatomy. His brother Piero (d. 1496) practiced the same arts. He is best known for the bronze tombs he made for Popes Sixtus IV and Innocent VIII.

POLO, MARCO, d. 1324, accompanied his father Niccolo and uncle Maffeo, Venetian merchants, in 1271, when he was 17 years old, on their journey through Persia, Balkh, across the Gobi Desert, to the court of Kublai Khan at Shang-tu near Peking. The khan took a liking to Marco, entrusted him with several missions, and may even have appointed him governor of Yangchow as Marco claims. Marco also declared that he visited Burma, Malaya, and India. In 1292, with considerable reluctance, Kublai permitted the Polos to leave his court. Their return trip took them by way of south China, Singapore, Ceylon, Persia, Armenia, and Trebizond, and finally, after an absence of 25 years, to Venice. Marco dictated the account of his travels to a French companion in a prison in Genoa. The story represented the first extended account of China and significantly encouraged the study of scientific geography.

POLOVTSI. *See* CUMANS.

POLTON, THOMAS, d. 1433, English curialist and abbreviator, papal envoy under Henry V, and a member of the English delegation to the Council of Constance (1414–18). He was bishop successively of Hereford, Chichester, and Worcester.

POLYCARP, ST., bishop of Smyrna, probably the leading Christian figure of Asia Minor in his day. He suffered martyrdom at the age of 86 at Smyrna in the year 155, 156, 164, or even later. The account of his death constituted the first martyrology. He devoted much of his time and energy to combating heresies. It is unlikely that he was a disciple of St. John the Evangelist, as some scholars have claimed, but he was a close friend of St. Ignatius of Antioch.

POMERANIA, duchy located on both sides of the lower Oder which had been occupied by Slavs (Pomorane or Pomorzanie and Polabs) about the year 500. In 1000 a diocese was established with Kolobrzeg as its see. The local duke recognized Polish suzerainty during the reign of Boleslaw III (1102–38), but in 1181 western and central Pomerania passed under the authority of the German king. At the same time this area was transferred from the jurisdiction of the archbishop of Gniezno and placed under the authority of the archbishop of Magdeburg. Eastern Pomerania (Pomerelia) remained under Polish rule until 1308 when the Teutonic Order occupied the area. It was returned to Polish control in 1466. Western and central Pomerania remained under German control.

POMERELIA, province to the west of the lower Vistula with as principal city Danzig which the Germans colonized in the thirteenth century. In 1308 the Teutonic Order, Pomerania, and Brandenburg divided the province among themselves.

POMPONIUS LAETUS (Julio Pomponio Leto, Giulio Sanseverino), d. c. 1497, Italian humanist who studied under Lorenzo Valla and founded the Roman academy. His writings reveal an interest in grammar, history, and archeology.

PONTANO, GIOVANNI, d. 1503, poet, historian, and statesman, secretary and counselor to Ferdinand (Ferrante) I of Naples, and director of the humanist academy in Naples (known later as the Accademia Pontaniana, after him). He was the author of Latin poems and treatises on a variety of historical and moral subjects. The breadth of his knowledge combined with lack of originality was characteristic of most of the humanists of the period.

PONTIANUS, ST., Pope, 230–5, a Roman who was exiled by Emperor Maximinus Thrax to Sardinia in 235 where he died of maltreatment.

PONTIFICAL, ROMAN, book containing the prayers and ceremonies for rites to be used for ordinations and consecrations, for the consecration of churches, etc. The first such volume appeared in the eighth century.

PONTIFICALS, a prelate's vestments and insignia (e.g., buskins, sandals, gloves, miter) worn by a prelate when celebrating a pontifical mass; liturgical functions in which a bishop presided with staff and miter.

POOR CLARES, order of contemplative nuns, originally known as Poor Ladies, later as the Second Order of St. Francis. St. Clare of Assisi founded the community in 1212. The order was thoroughly reformed in the fifteenth century by St. Colette who restored the practice of strict poverty in her houses. Pope Urban IV in 1263 had approved a modification of the original austerity of the rule.

POOR MEN OF LYONS. *See* WALDENSES.

POPE, from the Latin and Greek colloquial word for father. It was a title generally given to bishops and occasionally to abbots from the third century. It was probably not reserved to the bishop of Rome before the eleventh century, surely not before the fifth. During this century, the fifth, the bishop of Rome established his claim to primacy among the bishops of Christendom. The basis for that claim was the so-called Petrine Doctrine, namely, that inasmuch as Peter was the first bishop of Rome, his successor in that city fell heir to his position of leadership in the church. Although the evidence is not conclusive, it appears that a number of Roman bishops, beginning with Clement I (d. 101), did advance such a claim and on occasion sought to

implement it. Victor I (189–99) excommunicated the bishops of Asia Minor for their refusal to follow Roman usage in celebrating Easter on Sunday, a use of authority, however, that many bishops at the time condemned as unauthorized. It may be significant that emperors, not popes, convoked the first seven ecumenical councils, although the Council of Sardica (343) accorded the pope appellate powers while the Council of Constantinople I (381) granted him primacy. This primacy became fully established during the forceful pontificates of Innocent I (401–17) and Leo I (440–61). Surely a major factor that contributed to the emergence of the bishop of Rome as head of the medieval church was the location of his see in the imperial capital. Apart from the prestige the Eternal City afforded him, his aloofness from the bitter theological controversies which periodically convulsed eastern Christendom enabled him to assume a more objective, and historically more acceptable, position. [*See* PAPACY, HISTORY OF THE MEDIEVAL.]

PORPHYRY, d. after 301, neo-Platonic philosopher, a disciple of Plotinus and his successor as head of his school in Rome. While he served as the principal exponent of Plotinus's doctrines, he went far beyond his mentor in his concern over moral and religious questions. A major concern of his was, in fact, the establishment of a religious cult. This brought him into conflict with Christianity which he attacked in fifteen books. Porphyry's best known work is the *Isagoge,* an introduction to Aristotle's *Organon,* which served to introduce the Middle Ages to the problem of universals.

PORTER. *See* OSTIARY.

PORTIUNCULA, chapel near Assisi and the favorite church of St. Francis. It was probably constructed in the tenth or eleventh century.

PORTOLANI (portulane, portolane), navigational charts describing the course which ships might best follow when sailing from one port to another. They came into extensive use in the late Middle Ages.

PORTUGAL, once a province of the Roman empire, was overrun by Sueves and Visigoths during the period of Germanic migrations, and in the early eighth century was conquered by the Moslems. Its reconquest by the Christians was initiated by Ferdinand I of Castile who captured the town of Coimbra in 1064. Alfonso VI of Castile (1072–1109) sought French aid to bolster his efforts against the Moors. Among those who responded was Henry of Burgundy who married an illegitimate daughter of Alfonso's and established a dynasty that endured to 1385. His son Alfonso Henriques (d. 1185) acclaimed himself king in 1139, and to protect himself against his Christian enemies became a vassal of the pope. In 1147 knights participating in the Second Crusade aided him in wresting Lisbon from the Moors. When he died in 1185 Portugal was an independent state.

Credit for establishing Portugal's traditional frontiers goes to Alfonso III (1248–79) who also affirmed royal authority over the church and incorporated commoners for the first time in the Cortes (1254). His son Diniz (1279–1325) founded the University of Coimbra in 1290 (at first located in Lisbon), encouraged the construction of a navy, and gave so much attention to agriculture that he gained the name of Farmer. To strengthen the country against Castile, Ferdinand I (1367–83) made an alliance in 1372 with John of Gaunt who had claims of his own to the Castilian throne. In 1386 this Anglo-Portuguese understanding was formalized by the Treaty of Windsor.

In 1385 a new dynasty under John I inaugurated a most active period in the history of Portugal. The principal interest which precipitated a century and more of ambitious expansion was that of colonial discovery and exploration. Portugal's appetite for expansion was whetted by the capture in 1415 of Ceuta, the pirate stronghold across from Gibraltar in Africa.

Leadership in directing Portuguese expeditions down southward along the west coast of Africa was taken by Henry the Navigator (d. 1460), third son of John I, who headed a mariners' school at Cape St. Vincent and who also undertook several voyages of his own. Madeira and the Azores were colonized, Tangier was taken from Morocco (1471), Bartholomew Diaz turned the Cape of Good Hope in 1488, and in 1498 Vasco da Gama finally completed the long-sought all-water route to India when he dropped anchor in the harbor of Calicut.

POSAUNE, wind instrument similar to the trombone which had evolved from the trumpet by the fifteenth century.

POSTCOMMUNION, oration generally expressing thanksgiving which concluded the eucharistic service of the mass.

PRAEMUNIRE, STATUTE OF, law enacted in 1353 and confirmed in 1393 which enjoined appeals outside England, that is, to the papal Curia, in all disputes concerning the appointment to benefices. The purpose of the statute was that of enforcing the provisions of the Statute of Provisors enacted in 1351 and confirmed in 1390. It did not receive the broader application that Henry VIII (1509–47) gave it in his struggle with the papacy. [See PROVISORS, STATUTE OF.]

PRAETORIAN PREFECT, civil administrator of each of the four prefectures established by Emperor Diocletian (284–305) in his reorganization of the Roman empire. A prefect administered each of the prefectures of Gaul, Italy, Illyricum, and the East.

PRAGMATIC SANCTION OF BOURGES, pronouncement made by the French clergy in 1438, under the direction of Charles VII, which affirmed the superiority of the general council (as opposed to papal supremacy), and invested the French crown with control over appointments to ecclesiastical offices, the reception of papal bulls, judicial appeals to Rome, and financial payments to the papal Curia.

PRAGUE, the leading city of Bohemia whose origins may go back to the eighth century although first mention of the community appears only in 928. Prague became a diocesan see in 973, the capital of Bohemia in that same century, and a metropolitan see in 1344. Its location on trade routes passing to the north, south, east, and west assured it continuous industrial growth. In 1348 Emperor Charles IV founded Charles University and made the city one of the leading cultural centers of Europe.

PRAGUE, COMPACTS OF, concessions, particularly that of receiving communion in both species, which the Council of Basel granted the Hussites in 1436. The papacy's refusal to endorse the concession contributed to the coming of the Hussite wars.

PRAGUE, FOUR ARTICLES OF, Hussite demands put forward in 1420 which included the chalice for the laity, freedom for laymen to preach the word of God, the confiscation of church property, and the proper punishment of mortal sin and violations of the divine law.

PRAGUERIE, a revolt of princes and nobles against Charles VII of France in February 1440 that grew out of opposition to the king's ordinance forbidding the raising or maintenance of troops without his permission. Charles had already given clear evidence of his intention to reduce the power of the princes, so this new ordinance led to what proved a short-lived revolt. The crown and the Constable de Richemont succeeded in suppressing it in July.

PRAGUE, SCHOOL OF, Bohemian school of painting that was centered at the court of Emperor Charles IV at Prague. It flourished during the period of his reign when king of Bohemia (1346–78).

PRAGUE, UNIVERSITY OF, also known as Charles University, was founded in 1348 by Charles IV, king of Germany and Holy Roman emperor. The four nations that composed the faculty were the Czech, Saxon, Bavarian, and Polish. It acquired prominence after the Western Schism led German students to leave the University of Paris. The struggle between the German and Czech masters and students for control of the institution raged until 1409 when Emperor Wenceslas granted the Czech element a dominant position. The Germans then left Prague and founded the University of Leipzig. During the Hussite wars, the university was a center of Utraquist influence.

PREBEND, the part of the revenue of a cathedral or collegiate church that was given to a priest. The prebend ordinarily consisted of the revenue from one manor belonging to the particular church. The term might also apply to the property that yielded such an income.

PRECARIA (*precarium*), grant of land by a proprietor to one who offered his service in exchange for protection. Such land was held in precarious tenure which might be terminated at the will of the lord although it generally extended to the death of the grantee. It was not hereditary.

PRECENTOR, the leading chanter, also choir director, in a monastery. In the later Middle Ages the precentor's duties might include those of librarian and registrar.

PREDELLA, the base of an altarpiece that might serve as a kneeler.

PREDESTINATION, the foreordaining by God, before the beginning of time, that certain souls will be saved, others damned. The doctrine posed a profoundly difficult question since it was intimately linked with the problem of divine grace and the will of the incomprehensible deity. The issue became especially controversial in the early fifth century when Pelagius preached his views on the subject and St. Augustine took up the cudgels in defense of what was the traditional teaching of the church.

PREFACE, prayer introducing the Canon from which it was separated by the Sanctus.

PREMONSTRATENSIANS, Canons Regular of Prémontré, also known as Norbertines from their founder St. Norbert of Xanten, who established this monastic order at Prémontré (near Laon) in 1120. Pope Honorius II confirmed the order in 1126. The Premonstratensians combined the contemplative life with an active apostolate of teaching and preaching. They also maintained a second and a third order. In England the Premonstratensians were known as White Canons from the color of their habit. The order was especially popular in Hungary where it took an active part in converting the Slavs located between the Elbe and the Oder.

PREMYSL, early dynasty of Bohemia. [*See* BOHEMIA.]

PRESBYTER, a term derived from the Greek meaning *older* in the sense of an *elder,* an official in the early church who might perform both sacerdotal and episcopal functions. From the second century, the title of bishop was normally restricted to the presidents of councils of presbyters (elders), and it was from such bishops that the presbyters derived their authority by delegation.

PRESTER JOHN, legendary ruler of a Christian kingdom believed located either in eastern Asia, the Indies, or Ethiopia. First mention of his name appeared in 1145 in the chronicle of Otto of Freising. A letter addressed to various kings in 1165 referred to him as the king of the Indies and guardian of the tomb of the Apostle Thomas in Mylapore. Some people claimed he was the son of Genghis Khan, others that he was Gor Khan, a Chinese prince, who defeated the Sultan of Persia in 1141. After the mid-fourteenth century, most references to him made him out to be the king of Ethiopia. The traditions concerning Prester John persisted into the seventeenth century.

PRÉVÔT, French royal official stationed in different parts of France whose responsibility it was to administer the royal estates. His office was usually hereditary. From the early thirteenth century he found most of his authority taken over by the *bailli* or seneschal.

PREZ, JOSQUIN DES (de Près, Deprez, Jodocus Pratensis, Josquinus a Prato), d. 1521, chapel singer and music director in several cities of Italy and at the court of Louis XII of France. He composed masses, motets, and *chansons* and contributed to the further development of polyphonic music.

PRIEST, from the Greek meaning *elder,* an early Christian official, later a clergyman who ministered to the spiritual needs of the people under the jurisdiction of a bishop.

PRIMACY OF THE BISHOP OF ROME. *See* POPE.

PRIMATE, an archbishop, usually the highest ranking bishop, in a province or country.

PRIME, that part of the Divine Office traditionally appointed for the first hour, i.e., 6 A.M. It was at first recited in the dormitory, later was transferred to the choir, and from there to the office said by the secular clergy.

PRIMOGENITURE, in law, the right of the eldest son to inherit the estate or office of his father. Its adoption by the major powers of western Europe, first by France and England, represented a decisive step forward in the evolution of royal authority. It replaced the principle of election based upon feudal custom.

PRINCE-BISHOP, name given to bishops in the Holy Roman empire who governed territories as secular princes, e.g., the archbishop of Cologne.

PRINCE OF WALES, title held by a native Welsh chieftain until the death in 1282 of Llewellyn, then assigned in 1301 by Edward I to his son Edward (II). The title has since been borne by the eldest son (heir apparent) of the king or queen of England.

PRINTING. Printing was invented in China although the use of movable types made from molds has traditionally been credited to John Gutenberg of Mainz (c. 1445). Movable wood characters were in use in China in the eleventh century and cast metal characters in Korea in the fourteenth. But Gutenberg was the first person to invent a satisfactory method of printing books by using metal type cast in molds. The first experimental printing was done in his workshop in 1444–7. The earliest dated piece of printing, made in 1454, consisted of a collection of papal indulgences. The first complete book was the Gutenberg or Forty-Two-Line Bible, which was completed in 1456.

PRIORY, any religious house administered by a prior or prioress. If the prior was subject to a resident abbot, the house was called an abbey or monastery. The title prioress was held by the female superior of certain religious houses for women.

PRISCIAN, Latin grammarian of the late fifth or early sixth century who taught in Constantinople. His most important work bore the title *Institutiones grammaticae.* Priscian shared with Donatus the authorship of the most popular Latin grammars used in the Middle Ages. Their works had a profound influence on the teaching of Latin and of grammar in western Europe.

PRISCILLIAN, d. 386, bishop of Avila whose insistence upon a more ascetic kind of Christianity led to the charge of Manichaeism and his execution by the usurper Emperor Maximus. Neither the pope nor a church council had condemned him. He gave his name to Priscillianism, a mystical, ascetical movement that was particularly strong in Spain. While claiming to derive its doctrine from the Bible, it showed a marked preference for the apocryphal books. Among other of their views, the Priscillianists believed that the devil was not a fallen angel, rather the principle of evil, and the human body was his creation. Hence marriage and the procreation of children, as well as the use of meat, were condemned. The sect was condemned by Pope Leo I in 447 but lived on until the latter half of the sixth century.

PRISCILLIANISM. *See* PRISCILLIAN.

PRIVATEER, an armed ship, privately owned and operated, but commissioned by a state. Privateers appeared in the fifteenth century.

PRIVY COUNCIL, group of household officials and ministers, appointed by the king of England, who advised him on the affairs of state. The council evolved from the *curia regis* of the Norman kings and became important in the fourteenth century. By the close of the Middle Ages, it had become the principal instrument of the crown.

PROCLUS, ST., d. 446, patriarch of Constantinople (434–46), popular preacher, and author of homilies, epistles, and the *Tome of St. Proclus.* The Tome presented the doctrine of one Christ in two natures, to refute the position of Theodore of Mopsuestia.

PROCLUS, d. 485, often called Diadochus, a neo-Platonist who was head of the Platonic Academy in Athens. He was the author of voluminous writings on literary, scientific, religious, and philosophical subjects. His writings exerted great influence on medieval thought.

PROCOPIUS OF CAESAREA, d. after 562, secretary of the general Belisarius and author of *History of the Wars, On Buildings,* and *Secret History.* His reputation as the leading Greek historian since Polybius is based upon his excellent work in *Wars* which records the military history of the reign of Justinian. In *Buildings* Procopius assumed the garb of a sycophant in praising Justinian for the construction of countless structures — churches, fortresses, spas — including the magnificent Hagia Sophia. In his *Secret History* he stoops to assassinate the characters of Justinian, his wife Theodora, and Belisarius, the emperor's most famous general, and his wife. [*See* JUSTINIAN I.]

PROCOPIUS THE GREATER. *See* PROKOP.

PRODROMOS, THEODOROS, d. c. 1160, Byzantine poet who composed poetry in the tradition of the courtly romance as well as satirical verse. His writings are of value to the historian for the sidelights they provide on everyday social and economic life. The poet ended his life as a monk.

PROFESSOR, DEGREE OF, a university degree largely synonymous with doctor and master. [*See* MASTER OF ARTS.]

PROKOP, the name of two Hussite leaders. Prokop the Greater, a Utraquist priest, led the Hussite armies to several victories (Ustinad-Labem and Domazlice) over the imperial armies. After he had rejected the Compacts of Prague which the Utraquists had accepted, he found himself facing the now united Utraquists and Catholics and was defeated and slain in the battle at Lipany in 1434. He had joined the Taborites when the Utraquists made peace with the emperor, then when Jan Ziska died (1424), took over the leadership of their army. Prokop the Lesser, also a priest, joined Prokop the Greater and was slain with him at Lipany.

PROPRIETARY CHURCHES, churches (and monasteries) whose structure and temporal possessions, as well as the right to nominate the priest or other incumbent, were owned privately, either by a layman who might have founded the institution or by a monastery or bishop.

PROPRIUM. *Proprium de tempore* or common of the season, included those parts of the breviary and missal appointed for the days of the year that had special offices or masses; *proprium sanctorum* or common of the saints, was composed of the offices recited on days honoring particular saints.

PROSPER OF AQUITAINE, ST., d. after 455, learned lay theologian, a friend of St. Hilary and secretary of Pope Leo I. He was the author of hymns, epigrams, a chronicle, and a number of works in defense of Augustine's views on grace and predestination. His history, which until 398 is largely taken from Eusebius and Jerome, is of value for his own time (425–55).

PROVENÇALS, inhabitants of southeastern France, of the old district of Languedoc, more narrowly of Provence.

PROVENCE, the oldest possession of ancient Rome north of the Alps to which they gave the name *Provincia,* the province. It formed part of Narbonese Gaul. Burgundians occupied the area in the early fifth century, then Visigoths, Ostrogoths, and Franks, while Arab raids proved a constant problem from the eighth to the eleventh century. Despite these vicissitudes the vestiges remaining of the deeply rooted Roman heritage later combined with other influences, including Arabic, to give Provence a distinct culture. The language spoken there, the Provençal, served as the vehicle of lyric poetry for most of western Europe until the late Middle Ages. The Treaty of Verdun (843) assigned the region to Lothair I, but Charles the Bald, king of the West Franks, seized it in 875. From 879 to 934 it served as the center of the kingdom of Arles. Part of it was absorbed into the dominion of the count of Toulouse and with it became royal domain in 1271. The larger part of Provence passed under control of the Angevin dynasty of Naples in 1246 and came under the direct authority of the French crown only in 1481. The University of Provence was chartered in 1409.

PROVINCIAL, a monastic officer serving under a superior general and exercising general supervision over local superiors in a division of the order known as a province.

PROVINS, town of north-central France, from Roman times, the lower town founded in the ninth century by refugees fleeing the Vikings. Later it belonged to the counts of Vermandois, still later it became the residence of the counts of Champagne, a flourishing wool center, and one of the major fairs of the county. The name "city of roses" was given to Provins because of the roses cultivated there with seeds brought from the east by the crusader Thibaut IV (d. 1253).

PROVISIONS OF OXFORD. *See* OXFORD, PROVISIONS OF.

PROVISIONS, PAPAL, appointments by the pope to benefices defined as reserved to the papacy. The practice expanded markedly during the fourteenth century and did so at the expense, and to the annoyance, of local patrons, including bishops, monasteries, and members of the aristocracy. In England legislation had pretty well suppressed the practice of papal provisions by the close of the fourteenth century. [*See* PROVISORS, STATUTE OF.] In France the Pragmatic Sanction of Bourges of 1438 accomplished essentially the same result.

PROVISORS, STATUTE OF, law enacted in 1351 and reissued in 1390 which confirmed English patrons in their right to present to church offices. In the event of a dispute with the Roman Curia over the right of presentation, that right devolved upon the king. As supplemented with the Statutes of Praemunire, the legislation had all but ended the problem of papal provisions by the close of the fourteenth century. [*See* PRAEMUNIRE, STATUTE OF.]

PRUDENTIUS (Aurelius Prudentius Clemens), d. after 405, Spanish lay composer of hymns and religious poems, considered the leading Christian Latin poet of the early church. His poems contain many classical echoes of Virgil, Horace, Lucretius, Juvenal, and others. His *Psychomachia,* a description of Christian asceticism presented under the allegory of a spiritual warfare, exercised great influence upon medieval poetry.

PRUSSIA, region between the Vistula and the Memel which was given that name by the Prussians (Prusi, Pruzzi, Borussi), a people belonging to the Baltic family of Indo-European peoples. Missionaries achieved no success in their efforts to convert this fiercely pagan people. The most famous of the missionaries they martyred was St. Adalbert of Prague (d. 997). In 1230 the Polish duke of Mazovia invited the Teutonic Order to subjugate the people and conquer the area. The Teutonic Order obliged and held the region until forced to cede the greater part of it to Poland in 1466 (Treaty of Torun). They retained only what came to be called East Prussia as a fief of the Polish crown.

PSALTER, a book of Psalms containing most of the prayers that made up the Divine Office. Such books or collections were used from the first centuries of Christianity, the earliest being translations from the *Septuagint.*

PSALTERY, ancient stringed musical instrument played by plucking the strings with the fingers or a plectrum. It made its appearance in western Europe in the twelfth century.

PSELLUS, MICHAEL (Constantine), d. c. 1078, Byzantine polymath, member of the imperial secretariat for most of the period from 1042 (Michael V and Constantine IX) until his death, and one of the most influential men in the government. He was the author of the *Chronographia,* a valuable and reasonably authoritative history of Byzantium from 976 to 1077. Psellus was much interested in the revival of classical learning and of Platonic philosophy, and he was the first professor of philosophy in the newly founded University of Constantinople. He wrote on many subjects, produced speeches, letters, and poetry, biblical commentaries, as well as commentaries on some of Plato's and Aristotle's works.

PSEUDO-CLEMENTINES, collection of early Christian writings, including homilies and epistles, once attributed to Clement of Rome (d. 101), but now generally assigned to the third century.

PSEUDO-DIONYSIUS (Dionysius the Areopagite), name used by the author of four Greek treatises on liturgical and mystical theology that appeared at the beginning of the sixth century. The author affirmed the treatises to be the work of Dionysius, the Areopagite, who was baptized after hearing a sermon preached by St. Paul in the Areopagus of Athens (Acts 17:34). The treatises, which are strongly neo-Platonist in concept and terminology, provide a symbolic and mystical explanation of the universe and all that is in it. They became available in Latin translations made by Abbot Hilduin of Saint-Denis (d. 855) and by John Scotus Erigena (d. c. 877) and exerted a significant influence upon the development of Western mysticism.

PSEUDO-ISIDORIAN DECRETALS, a collection of documents published in the ninth century consisting of papal briefs from the pontificates of Clement I (97?–101) to Gregory II (715–31). Most are fictitious. They had as their object the elimination of state interference in what were considered the affairs of the church and the protection of the rights of the bishop against the encroachments of metropolitans and the secular authority. They also affirmed the supreme authority of the pope over the entire church. Popes from the time of Leo IX (1049–54) appealed to them, especially Popes Gregory VII (1073–85) and Urban II (1088–99).

PTOLEMY (Claudius Ptolemaeus), d. between 161 and 180, astronomer, mathematician, geometrician, and geographer whose most influential work, called *Almagest* ("the greatest [book]") by the Arabs and commonly known by that name, preserved much of the astronomical knowledge of the ancient world. Ptolemy was an astronomer in his own right and added several hundred stars not previously identified. The Western world continued to accept his geocentric theory of the universe until the time of Copernicus.

PULCHERIA, ST., d. 453, daughter of Emperor Arcadius, regent for her brother Theodosius II (408–50), and wife of Emperor Marcian who succeeded. Pulcheria was a person of marked administrative ability and took an active part in political and ecclesiastical affairs. She persuaded Theodosius to condemn Nestorius and sought the support of Pope Leo I against Monophysitism. She and her husband Marcian convoked the Council of Chalcedon (451).

PULCI, LUIGI, d. 1484, Italian poet who enjoyed the patronage of Lorenzo the Magnificent. His *Morgante Maggiore* represented a semicomic rendition of the Charlemagne epic.

PURBACH (Peuerbach), GEORGE, d. 1461, mathematician and astronomer, tutor of Regiomontanus (Johann Müller), and author of treatises dealing with trigonometry and astronomy.

PURGATORY, place, state, or condition of the souls who died in a state of grace but with satisfaction owing divine justice for offenses still unexpiated. The doctrine of purgatory evolved during the early centuries of the church and was based largely on the position taken by St. Augustine, namely, that the fate of the individual soul was decided at death and that subsequent to death, there would come purifying pains in the next life. Gregory the Great maintained that one of the purgatorial pains was the deprivation of the vision of God, a view endorsed by Bede who left lurid descriptions of the horrors of purgatory. Thomas Aquinas, too, maintained that the smallest pain in purgatory was greater than the greatest on earth. The doctrine of purgatory received most attention from theologians after the eleventh century partly because of the growing popularity of indulgences which the Crusades had encouraged.

PURGATORY, ST. PATRICK'S, place of pilgrimage on the island of Lough Derg, County Donegal, Ireland. Some scholars question its association with St. Patrick.

PURIFICATION OF MARY, the symbolic purification of Mary 40 days after the birth of Jesus as required by the law of Moses. (Luke 2:34–35).

PURVEY, JOHN, d. c. 1428, priest and associate of John Wyclif at Oxford who probably translated those works of Wyclif that appeared in English. He may also have revised the almost unreadable English version of the Bible some times attributed to John Wyclif and Nicholas Hereford. In 1401 he was arrested on charges of Lollardy, imprisoned, and forced to recant. It appears he never really abandoned some of his Lollard views.

PURVEYANCE, RIGHT OF, right of hospitality, known as *droit de gîte* in France, which the lord received from his vassal. The vassal was required to provide his lord and his retinue with both food and lodging should the lord stop by in his travels about his domain. It also permitted the king to purchase goods and horses and carts to convey goods at the "king's price," a price lower than the usual figure. At great fairs, the king might take a customary levy of the wine.

PUZZLE-JUG, pitcher or jug that permitted drinking by means of a small hole located under the handle or in the spout.

PYX, container for the eucharist (reserved host). It was kept in people's houses, later in the church.

QADI (kadi, cadi), Moslem judge who based the judgments which he rendered on canon law which, in turn, was founded on the Koran and the *hadith*. The second caliph Omar was the first to appoint a qadi to relieve himself of having to judge every dispute brought forward by the people.

QIBLA, the "direction of prayer" for Moslems. At first this was toward Jerusalem, but soon after 622 toward Mecca.

QUADRAGESIMA, Latin term for the forty days of Lent.

QUADRIVIUM, the second group of subjects constituting the liberal arts, as opposed to the trivium. The quadrivium included arithmetic, geometry, music, and astronomy.

QUARTODECIMAN, one who adhered to the practice of the early church of celebrating Easter on the fourteenth of the month of Nisan, the day of the Jewish Passover. St. Polycarp (d. 155?) accepted this date for Easter, and it was not until Pope Victor I (d. 199) that the practice of doing so was condemned. A sect, known as the Quartodecimans, survived to the fifth century.

QUASIMODO SUNDAY, the first Sunday after Easter, the term derived from the opening word of the introit.

QUATTRINO, Italian silver coin minted from the middle of the fifteenth century. It was especially popular in Venice.

QUATTROCENTO, the fifteenth century, a term usually employed in discussions concerning Italian art and literature.

QUEM TERRA, PONTUS, SIDERA, hymn honoring Mary which may have been composed by Fortunatus (d. 600). It made its way into the breviary.

QUERCIA, JACOPO DELLA, d. 1438, leading sculptor of Siena, also a woodcarver and worker in bronze. He collaborated with Ghiberti and Donatello on the reliefs for the baptistery at Siena. His reliefs on the portal of S. Petronio, Bologna, with their figures drawn from *Genesis* and the nativity of Christ, won the admiration of Michelangelo. He was one of the most original sculptors of his time.

QUICUMQUE CHRISTUM QUAERITIS, hymn taken from Prudentius's *Hymnus Epiphaniae*. It was incorporated into the breviary for the feast of the Transfiguration.

QUIDDITY, the Anglicized scholastic term *quidditas* meaning essence or "whatness."

QUINISEXT SYNOD. *See* TRULLAN SYNOD.

QUINQUAGESIMA, third and last Sunday of the pre-Lenten period.

QUINQUE COMPLICATIONES ANTIQUAE, five collections of decretals made between the publication of Gratian's *Decretum* (c. 1140) and the Gregorian Decretals in 1234.

QUODLIBET, a question, an academic exercise, often subtle, discussed in scholastic disputations, particularly at the University of Paris in the late thirteenth and early fourteenth centuries. The writings left by many scholastic theologians included *quodlibeta*.

QUO VADIS, or "Domine, quo vadis?", a question which, according to the apocryphal Acts of Peter, St. Peter, fleeing from Rome to escape persecution, is supposed to have addressed to Christ when he met him on the Appian Way. Upon Christ's answer that he was coming there to be crucified again, Peter turned back to Rome and was martyred.

RABANUS (Hrabanus, Rhabanus) MAURUS, BL., d. 856, Benedictine monk, one of the leading theologians of his age. He studied at Tours under Alcuin, became head of the monastic school at Fulda, then abbot, and in 847 was appointed archbishop of Mainz. During his 30 years at Fulda, the abbey progressed markedly in all respects, material, spiritual, and intellectual. His voluminous writings included a study of grammar, homilies, some Latin hymns — the *Veni Creator Spiritus* has been attributed to him — and commentaries on the Bible. He prepared his *De Clericorum Institutione,* a manual dealing with the sacraments, public prayer, and other subjects, as a guide to his clergy. Walafrid Strabo was among his pupils. He has been called the preceptor of Germany.

RABBULA (Rabulas), d. 435 or 436, Syrian theologian, bishop of Edessa, a great admirer of Cyril of Alexandria (d. 444), and one of the foremost opponents of Nestorianism. He devoted himself to the reform of the church.

RACHIMBURGI, prominent landowners who rendered judgment in the local Merovingian court.

RACHIS, king of the Lombards, 744–9 and 756–7, the successor of Luitprand, who was deposed in 749 because of his conciliatory policy toward the papacy but later regained his throne although for only a short time. When forced out a second time by his brother Aistulf, he retired to Monte Cassino.

RADEGUNDA, ST., d. 587, daughter of the Thuringian king, taken prisoner and forced to marry Clothaire I, a rough Merovingian monarch, whom she left when he murdered her brother. She was ordained a deaconess and founded a community of nuns near Poitiers which adopted the rule of Caesarius of Arles. Here she spent the last 30 years of her life in study, prayer, and good works.

RADULPH OF RIVO (of Tongres) (Radulph van der Beeke), d. 1403, rector of the University of Cologne, author of grammatical and liturgical writings and of a chronicle of the bishops of Liège.

RAGUSA, JOHN OF, d. 1443, Dominican theologian, procurator-general of the order, who left an account of the Council of Basel (1431–1438/9) which he attended. He eventually joined the ranks of the conciliarists and was created a cardinal by Felix V (antipope).

RAINALD OF DASSEL, d. 1167, chancellor and principal adviser of Frederick I Barbarossa who appointed him archbishop of Cologne (1159). He maintained that the pope was subject to the German emperor in the same way that French bishops were responsible to the French king. For this reason he recognized Victor IV and Paschal III, the two popes (antipopes) whom Frederick appointed.

RAINALDUCCI (Rainallucci), PIETRO, d. 1333, a Franciscan, appointed pope (Nicholas V) by Emperor Louis IV in 1328 when he occupied Rome and declared John XXII at Avignon deposed. In 1330 Pietro made his peace with John XXII and was kept in honorable confinement in Avignon where he died.

RAIS, GILLES DE. *See* RETZ, GILLES DE LAVAL.

RALPH HIGDEN. *See* HIGDEN, RANULF.

RALPH OF COGGESHALL, d. c. 1227, abbot of the Cistercian abbey of Coggeshall in Essex who continued the *Chronicon Anglicanum* from 1187 to 1224 and the chronicle of Ralph Niger from 1162 to 1178. His extension of the first chronicle is of considerable importance for a study of the reigns of Richard I and John.

RALPH OF DICETO, d. 1202, English chronicler, probably of French origin, dean of St. Paul's cathedral in London, and author of several historical works that are quite valuable for his period.

RAMADAN, the ninth month in the Islamic calendar. During this month Moslems were required to eschew food, drink, and sensual satisfaction during the daylight hours. The first revelation of the Koran was commemorated in this month.

RAMIRO I, first king of Aragon, 1035–63, an illegitimate son of Sancho III of Navarre. He conquered a few adjoining territories held by the Moors and forced several Moorish rulers to recognize his suzerainty.

RAMIRO II, king of Aragon, 1134–37, first a monk, then bishop-elect, who was chosen to succeed his brother Alfonso I. Shortly after his daughter married Ramón Berenguer IV, count of Barcelona, who had aided him against his rebellious nobles, he abdicated in favor of his son-in-law, thus preparing the way for the union of the crowns of Aragon and Catalonia. Ramiro retired to a priory where he died in 1157.

RAMÓN LULL. *See* LULL, RAYMOND.

RAPHAEL, ST., archangel whose name appears in the Book of Tobit (Tobias). The Middle Ages honored him as the patron of apothecaries and travelers.

RASHI (Rabbi Solomon Ben Isaac), d. 1105, Jewish scholar, founder of a Talmudic school at Troyes, and author of highly erudite and popular commentaries on the Bible and the Talmud. He made Troyes the leading center of rabbinic scholarship in central Europe.

RASHID AL-DIN TABIB, d. 1318, Persian statesman and historian, a convert from Judaism to Islam. He served as physician to one Mongol ruler of Persia and vizier to another, but was put to death on the charge of poisoning the latter. His universal history contains valuable information about China and the Mongol tribes.

RASPE, HENRY. *See* HENRY RASPE.

RATHERIUS (Rather) OF VERONA, d. 974, Benedictine monk, bishop of Verona and later of Liège, whose critical tongue usually kept him in exile from his sees. His writings include sermons, letters, and a guide to right living. This last he composed in a prison near Pavia where Hugh of Provence, king of Italy, had ordered him confined for daring to criticize him for meddling in church affairs.

RATISBON. *See* REGENSBURG.

RATRAMNUS OF CORBIE, d. after 868, teacher in the Benedictine monastery of Corbie, whose writings on the eucharist, predestination, and the *Filioque* controversy drew attack on grounds of heresy. In his treatise on the eucharist he emphasized the figurative and symbolic aspects of the sacrament in order to correct what he judged an excessively realistic interpretation. For him the bread and wine were mystic symbols commemorative of Christ's body and blood but retaining their physical characters.

RAVENNA, city of Etruscan origin located on islands near the mouth of the Po. Because of the marshes which protected it from attack, it served as residence for Emperor Honorius (from 402), the German chieftain Odoacer, the Ostrogothic kings, and the exarch of Ravenna from 584 until its capture by the Lombards in 751. In 756 Pepin III, king of the Franks, forced the Lombards to surrender Ravenna to the Pope. [*See* DONATION OF PEPIN.] The archbishop of Ravenna ruled the city until the thirteenth century when the house of Da Polenta seized control. In 1441 it passed under Venetian rule. The city is famed for its treasures of early Christian art. Its most noted churches are S. Apollinare Nuovo, S. Vitale, and S. Apollinare in Classe.

RAVENNA, EXARCHATE OF, created by the Byzantine emperor Maurice (582–602) to serve as an administrative province comprising all the empire's possessions in Italy with the exception of Sicily. At the beginning of the seventh century these included the greater part of central and southern Italy, the march of Istria, and maritime Venetia. During the course of the seventh century, territories were lost to the Lombard kings and dukes (Benevento). In 751 King Aistulf captured Ravenna but in 756 Pepin III, king of the Franks, forced him to turn it over to the papacy. Venice and Istria in the north became independent to all intents and purposes long before Byzantium lost Bari, its last foothold on the peninsula, to the Normans in 1071.

RAYMOND (Raynald of Châtillon), d. 1187, count of Tripoli, 1152–87, who had a major role in the last years of the Latin Kingdom of Jerusalem. He served as regent first for King Baldwin IV (1174–6), then for Baldwin V (1183–5). He bitterly opposed Guy of Lusignan who became king in 1186 and was accused of having made an alliance with Saladin. But he joined Guy and all the forces the Christians could muster in the great battle of Hattin in 1187 which ended in the annihilation of the Crusading army by Saladin. Raymond was among the few who escaped death or capture. He died shortly after at Tyre.

RAYMOND IV, d. 1105, count of Toulouse and marquis of Provence. He was one of the leaders of the First Crusade (1096–9) with an army recruited from Provence, and the real leader of the Crusade after the capture of Antioch where many Crusaders terminated their campaigning. It appears that he was offered, but refused, the crown of king of Jerusalem. He died during the siege of Tripoli which his descendants established as the capital of the County of Tripoli.

RAYMOND VI, d. 1222, count of Toulouse and a principal in the Albigensian Crusade. His failure to take measures against the Albigenses prompted Pope Innocent III to send his legate Peter de Castelnau to remonstrate with him. Upon Peter's murder in 1208, Innocent launched a crusade which almost brought about Raymond's ruin. He and his ally Peter II of Aragon suffered defeat at the hands of Simon de Montfort at the battle of Muret (1213), and two years later he was deprived of his countship by the Fourth Lateran Council. He managed to fight his way back, however, and when he died he had recovered the bulk of his lands.

RAYMOND VII, count of Toulouse, d. 1249, supported his father Raymond (VI) during the Albigensian Crusade, was later reconciled to the church. When Catharism again appeared to thrive in Toulouse, he was excommunicated and his countship declared forfeit. In 1229 he agreed to a treaty with Louis IX of France (actually with Blanche of Castile, Louis's mother) by which he gave his daughter in marriage to Alphonse of Poitiers, the king's brother. An attempt to extricate himself from this treaty by revolting against Louis in 1242 failed and he bought peace by promising to destroy the Albigenses, which he did. When he died in 1249 Toulouse passed under the direct authority of the French crown.

RAYMOND, LULL. *See* LULL, RAYMOND.

RAYMOND NONNATUS, ST., d. 1240, Mercedarian missionary. He joined the Mercedarians at Barcelona under St. Peter Nolasco and worked in north Africa, ransoming Christian slaves and converting many Moslems. He returned to Spain in 1239, was nominated cardinal, but died on his way to Rome. He was the patron saint of midwives.

RAYMOND OF AGILES (Aguiliers), chronicler of the First Crusade (1096–9). He accompanied Bishop Adhemar, the papal deputy, on this crusade and later served as chaplain to Raymond of Toulouse. The inclusion of uncritical episodes in his chronicle does not seriously detract from its importance.

RAYMOND OF PENAFORT (Penaforte), ST., d. 1275, Dominican canonist, papal penitentiary, master general of the Dominican order (1238–40). He drew up a revision of the Dominican constitution which remained in effect until recently. He was the author of two important works, one a collection of the *Decretals of Gregory IX,* the other a manual of canon law for use by confessors. He studied law and lectured at Bologna and for a time maintained a school of Arabic and Hebrew studies in Spain in order to further the conversion of Jews and Moors. Upon his suggestion Thomas Aquinas undertook the *Summa contra Gentiles* which Aquinas intended primarily for Moslem and Jewish theologians.

RAYMOND OF SEBONDE, d. 1432/6, Spanish philosopher, taught that subject and theology and medicine at the University of Barcelona. His most important work, *Liber Naturae sive Creaturarum,* received great attention after his death. The most controversial position taken by the author was that it was possible for human reason to discover the substance of Christian revelation through a study of nature.

RAYONNANT STYLE, term applied to French Gothic of the late thirteenth and fourteenth centuries. This featured the radiating tracery of the rose window, a large number of mullions combined with elaborate geometrical patterns based on circles, and an accentuation of vertical lines. In essence, rayonnant style represented a shift on the part of the architects from emphasis on structural development to decoration. The cathedral of Amiens and the Sainte-Chapelle in Paris were constructed during this period.

RAZI, AL- (Fakhr Al-Din Abu 'Abdullah Mo-

hammed Ibn 'Umar Ibn Al-Husain Al-Razi), d. 1209, Moslem theologian and scholar of Persia who gained recognition as an authority on mysticism but above all as a champion of orthodoxy against doctrinal innovation. So sharp was his criticism of the Mu'tazilites that he was obliged to leave his home. His writings included legal and dogmatic works and, most important, an extensive commentary on the Koran entitled *Mafatih al-Ghaib (Keys of the Hidden).*

READING, a passage, usually from the Bible, from the divine office, or from the church fathers, which was read at a liturgical service.

REALISM, the philosophic doctrine that universal ideas and concepts possess objective reality apart from individuals ("particulars") in which they are embodied. It was opposed to nominalism which dismissed these universal ideas as simply terms or words. According to Plato who might be called the father of realism, these ideas had existed from all eternity; they preceded in time the appearance of physical things. Since Plato's influence dominated philosophical thought in the Middle Ages prior to the thirteenth century through the writings of Plotinus, Porphyry, and Augustine, most scholastics of the twelfth century were realists. [*See* NOMINALISM; UNIVERSAL.]

REBEC, a bowed stringed instrument which originated in the Middle East and became popular in medieval Europe.

REBUS, a mode of expressing a word or phrase by means of a picture or symbol that had a name similar to the word which it represented, e.g., canting arms in medieval heraldry.

RECONQUISTA, the reconquest of Spain from the Moslems which got under way in 1064 when Ferdinand I, king of Castile, captured Coimbra and forced the emir of Badajoz to recognize his suzerainty. The *Reconquista* was completed in 1492 with the conquest of Granada by Ferdinand and Isabella of Spain.

RECTOR, the head of a faculty or a university.

RECTOR POTENS, VERAX DEUS, breviary hymn probably composed by St. Ambrose (d. 397). The theme is God as the ruler of the universe.

RED MASS, mass in honor of the Holy Spirit celebrated at the opening of the judicial year and at which the celebrant wore red vestments. The justices and university faculty also wore scarlet and red robes. The liturgical color of red symbolized the Holy Spirit who should guide justices in making proper judgments. The practice dates from the thirteenth century.

RED STAR, MILITARY ORDER OF THE CROSS WITH A (Knights of the Cross with a Red Star), a Crusading order established early in the thirteenth century and centered in Bohemia. Its members devoted themselves principally to the care of the sick. A group of the same name but more military in its activities was organized at Cracow in 1250.

REEVE, the chief royal officer of a shire or district in Anglo-Saxon England; the steward or overseer of a manor; a representative of a higher governmental authority.

REFERENDARIUS: a) a Byzantine official who brought petitions to the emperor and then carried his decision to the judges; b) a Frankish official, later the chancellor, who had similar duties; c) an officer in the papal Curia who performed a similar function and also counseled the pope concerning the disposition of petitions and carried out his judgment.

REGALE, JUS (Ius), right claimed by medieval kings to appropriate the temporalities of vacant sees and abbeys. It was founded on the position of the king as feudal overlord. The claim was rejected by the church and became involved in the investiture controversy. In more general usage, *iura regalia* included the king's rights over customs, the mint, markets, escort, forest, the hunt, fisheries, mountains, salt, the Jews, and escheat.

REGALIA, royal possessions or rights; temporalities held by bishops and abbots of feudal lords for which they owed feudal services.

REGENSBURG (Ratisbon), city located on the right bank of the upper Danube in Bavaria, of Celtic origin. It was known as Regina Castra in Roman times when it served as a military stronghold. From 530 it was the residence of the dukes of Bavaria. St. Boniface made it a bishop's see in 739. From 827 Louis the German used it as his capital. In 1245 it became an imperial free city and flourished as the principal commercial center of southern Germany during the late Middle Ages. The cathedral of St. Peter (1275–1530) is the most important Gothic church in Bavaria.

REGESTA, copies of letters, decrees, and other official documents preserved in papal, imperial, or royal archives.

REGINA COELI LAETARE, Marian antiphon used to introduce the *Magnificat* and to conclude the compline. It also served as the Eastertide anthem to the Blessed Virgin. It probably dates from the twelfth century; its author is unknown.

REGINALD (Raynald) OF CHÂTILLON, d. 1187, Crusader, lord of the fortresses of Krak and Montreal in the Latin Kingdom of Jerusalem. He came to the Holy Land on the Second Crusade (1147–9), and married Constance, daughter of Bohemond II of Antioch. His ambitious, somewhat irresponsible character involved him in constant disputes with other Crusading leaders. For 15 years he was held a prisoner by the Saracens. In 1182–3 he raided the Arabian coast of the Red Sea, while his attack in 1187 on a Moslem caravan violated the truce with Saladin and led to the decisive battle of Hattin and the annihilation of the Crusading army. Reginald was captured and immediately executed, perhaps by Saladin himself.

REGINO OF PRÜM, d. 915, abbot of the Benedictine monastery at Prüm, later of that of St.

Martin at Trier. He left a collection of canonical texts, a treatise on church music, and a history of the church from the birth of Christ to 906. He gave his name to a valuable collection of canonical texts which he compiled for the use of bishops in the administration of their dioceses.

REGIOMONTANUS (Johann Müller), d. 1476, astronomer and mathematician. He studied at Leipzig and at Vienna, and in Rome learned Greek from Cardinal Bessarion. He established an observatory and a printing press at Nuremberg. His mathematical studies served to establish trigonometry as a study independent of astronomy. Included with his astronomical treatises were tables of solar declination which navigators found most useful. He is considered the greatest of the predecessors of Copernicus. In 1472 Pope Sixtus IV summoned him to Rome to assist in reforming the calendar. There he was made bishop of Regensburg.

REGULARS, members of the regular clergy, that is, monks who observed a monastic rule (Latin: regula), e.g., Rule of St. Benedict.

REICHENAU, ABBEY OF, Benedictine monastery located on the island of Reichenau in Lake Constance which was founded by Charles Martel in 724. St. Pirmin was its first abbot. Among its distinguished scholars were Walafrid Strabo (d. 848) and Hermannus Contractus (d. 1054). Under Abbot Berno (1008–48) the abbey gained distinction in the art of book illumination.

REICHSTAG. See DIET.

REIMS (Rheims), city northeast of Paris which originated as a Celtic settlement. During the period of Roman rule it functioned as the hub of the road system in northern Gaul. It served as a bishop's see in the second half of the third century and as the residence of the rulers of Austrasia during Merovingian times. Its archbishop, who appeared in 743, gained the right in 1179 to crown the kings of France. No doubt

the tradition that Clovis was baptized in Reims in 496 by St. Remigius, its bishop, helped gain the archbishop that privilege. The city's famed cathedral, a Gothic edifice, was constructed from 1211 to 1311.

REINMAR OF HAGENAU (R. der Alte), d. before 1210, Alsatian minnesinger of the twelfth century at Vienna where he became court poet of the Babenberg dukes. Walther von der Vogelweide praised him as his teacher. To his contemporaries, he was the "nightingale" of his day.

RELIEF, fee paid by the heir of a deceased vassal on securing possession of a fief. Although tradition determined the amount the lord might demand by way of relief, there was always the temptation to impose a heavier payment than customary since only a single vassal was involved at any given time and the danger of a revolt therefore minimal.

RELIGIOUS-MILITARY ORDERS. See MILITARY RELIGIOUS ORDERS.

RELIQUARY, small box or casket of various materials in which a relic was stored or exhibited.

REMEMBRANCER, an English official whose duties included the compilation of memoranda rolls which would remind the barons of the exchequer of pending business.

REMIGIUS (Remi) OF AUXERE, d. 908, medieval philosopher, Benedictine monk of the abbey of Saint-Germain at Auxerre who taught there, at Reims, and at Paris. He was the author of commentaries on the liberal arts, on the writings of classical authors, and on Boethius's *Consolation of Philosophy,* as well as on some books of the Bible.

REMIGIUS (Rémi, Rémy) OF REIMS, ST., d. c. 533, the "Apostle of the Franks," a bishop of Reims who was distinguished for both his learning and his piety. He baptized Clovis, king of the Franks, in 496, and is supposed to have conferred upon him the power of touching for the king's evil. [*See* KING'S EVIL, TOUCHING FOR THE.]

RENAISSANCE, a term applied to the transitional centuries covering the late Middle Ages and the beginning of modern times, more specifically the cultural developments of the fourteenth, fifteenth, and sixteenth centuries. In the judgment of certain scholars, the rise of humanism led thinkers and artists to view the world differently. The first scholar to introduce humanism was Petrarch (d. 1374) whose passionate interest in classical antiquities prompted him to brand the preceding millennium as the Dark Ages and to identify his own world as a neoclassic period when the Muses were again able to be about their tasks. His break with the cultural past could not have come at a more propitious time since scholasticism was in decline and intellectuals were on the search for new interests. They found these in the study of classical antiquity. They also discovered wealthy and influential patrons, among them the Medici and several popes, who were willing to finance their activities and advance their interests.

These activities took a variety of forms, although all aimed at reviving the glories of ancient Greece and Rome. Many humanists became avid manuscript-hunters and a good number of manuscripts turned up as a result of their search; the majority of these were found in monastic libraries where they had remained largely unused since the rise of scholasticism. Others gathered coins and statuary or, like Pope Pius II (1458–64), sought to preserve the hallowed architectural ruins of the ancient past. A favorite avocation was that of composing essays, letters, and verse, even history, in a style reminiscent of Cicero, Horace, and Livy. When Manuel Chrysoloras arrived in Florence in 1397, men of affairs hurried there to learn the ancient Greek of Homer and Sophocles. Artists and architects in Italy shared this interest in the past. Their new structures featured engaged columns and pilasters, cornices, barrel vaults, coffered ceilings, rosettes, and medallions. A product of a more scientific approach in the study of manuscripts was Lorenzo Valla's discovery that the Donation of Constantine was a forgery. On the other hand, in ridding Latin of its postclassical accretions, these humanists left it incapable of serving the needs of a living language, and it died. Present opinion faults this revival of the classical past with exerting little or no influence upon science, vernacular literature, industry, government, or religion. Humanism did have an impact upon education, and in a short time theology was yielding its dominant place in the curriculum to literature and history.

RENAISSANCE ARCHITECTURE, the neoclassic style of construction which became popular in Italy in the late Middle Ages. It featured classical columns, entablatures, barrel vaults, round arches, pilasters, and coffered panels and ceilings.

RENARD THE FOX. *See* ROMAN DE RENART.

RENART, JEAN, early thirteenth-century French poet whose romances of adventure contained much information about contemporary life and manners.

RENAUD DE MONTAUBAN, or *Les Quatre Fils Aymon,* title of an Old French *chanson de geste.* According to the story, Renaud slew Bertolai, a nephew of Charlemagne, after a quarrel over chess. He and his friends were then besieged in the fortress of Montessor, later in Montauban. He subsequently became a monk and helped in the building of the cathedral of Cologne.

RENAUD OF CHÂTILLON. *See* REGINALD OF CHÂTILLON.

RENÉ D'ANJOU, d. 1480, duke of Anjou and count of Provence who was known as Good King René. (He was also titular king of Naples, Sicily, and Jerusalem.) His daughter Margaret (of Anjou) became the wife of Henry VI of England. Despite his checkered fortunes — he was prisoner of Philip the Good, duke of Burgundy, from 1431 to 1437 — he showed himself a genuine patron of poets and musicians and was something of a poet in his own right. He was one of the last champions of medieval chivalry and culture.

RENSE, DECLARATION OF, proclamation made by the German electors in 1338 that the election of a German king by a majority of electors required no papal confirmation to be valid.

REPINGTON (Repyngton, Repyngdon), PHILIP, d. 1424, Canon Regular of St. Augustine, an Oxford theologian and disciple of John Wyclif, who was excommunicated for his Wycliffite views in 1382 but recanted. In 1397 he became chancellor of the University of Oxford, served Henry IV as chaplain, was consecrated bishop of Lincoln in 1404, and in 1408 was created cardinal.

REPROACHES, THE. *See* IMPROPERIA.

REQUIEM, a mass for the dead, so named from the first word of the introit. While several of the prayers which eventually made up the Requiem service appeared quite early, the complete set of propers was not in use before the tenth century.

REREDOS, any decoration placed above or behind an altar. It might be a painting or a symbol, a silken hanging or a piece of jeweled metal work. A painted altarpiece was often in the form of a triptych.

RERUM CREATOR OPTIME, hymn honoring God as the creator of the world which has been ascribed to Pope Gregory I (590–604). It was incorporated into the breviary.

RERUM DEUS TENAX VIGOR, breviary hymn possibly composed by St. Ambrose (d. 397) and dedicated to God as the director of the universe and of man's destiny therein.

RESPONSORY, in liturgical chant the answer or refrain with which a choir or group of monks responded to the verses of the psalms sung by a cantor. The practice goes back to the worship of the Synagogue and is mentioned in use by Ter-

tullian (d. after 220). St. Benedict (d. c. 547) prescribed the use of responsories in the Divine Office.

RETABLE, a screen, usually carved or painted and placed behind the altar. Altarpieces tended to replace them in the fifteenth century.

RETZ (Rais), GILLES DE LAVAL, d. 1440, marshal of France, a noted soldier who was with Joan of Arc at Orléans. He was a patron of music, literature, and other arts. After his retirement he was charged with, and he confessed to, having kidnapped and murdered more than 100 children. He was executed after having been tried by an ecclesiastical court.

REVAL (Tallinn, Rewel), city located on the Gulf of Finland which rose at a castle erected in 1219 by King Waldemar II of Denmark. It became a member of the Hanseatic League in 1285 and a possession of the Teutonic Order in 1346.

REX GLORIOSE MARTYRUM, breviary hymn probably of sixth-century composition which invoked Christ's assistance in the name of the martyrs.

REX SEMPITERNE CAELITUM, breviary hymn probably composed in the fifth or sixth century. It celebrated the redemptive work of Christ.

REYNARD THE FOX. *See* ROMAN DE RENART.

RHADAGUNDE, ST. *See* RADEGUNDE, ST.

RHAZES (Rasis, Razes, Al-Razi) (Abu-Bakr Mohammed Ibn Zakariyya Ar-Razi), d. 923 or 932, greatest physician of the Islamic world, philosopher, alchemist, and scientist. He served as chief physician in the hospital at Rayy (near Teheran), later in Baghdad. Perhaps the best known of his more than 100 works is his "Treatise on Small Pox and Measles." His prinicipal medical works, which included the *Kitab al-Mansuri* and *Al-Hawi* (The Comprehensive Book), were translated into Latin during the twelfth century and significantly influenced the study of medicine in medieval universities. His philosophical writings show him a Platonist, his cosmology suggests an acquaintance with Democritus.

RHETORIC, one of the subjects of the trivium. Cassiodorus (d. c. 580) defined the discipline as the art of speaking and writing effectively, especially on "civil questions." Perhaps its chief value in the early Middle Ages was the knowledge it afforded in the proper drafting of letters and documents.

RHINELAND MYSTICS, name given to John Eckhart and his disciples John Tauler and Henry Suso.

RHODES, island off the southwest coast of Asia Minor, a possession of the Byzantine (Eastern Roman) empire, occupied briefly by Arabs (653–8, 717–8), then progressively influenced and controlled by Venice. After the fall of the Byzantine empire (1204) it was forced at times to acknowledge the overlordship of the emperors of Nicaea. In 1309 it was conquered by the Knights Hospitallers of St. John of Jerusalem who built it into a powerful fortress. Rhodes managed to repel a tremendous Turkish siege in 1480 but in 1522 it surrendered the island to the Turks.

RHODES, KNIGHTS OF. See SAINT JOHN OF JERUSALEM, ORDER OF THE HOSPITAL OF.

RIBAULD, a kind of cart also known as *ribauldequin,* on which small tubes of gunpowder were attached which could be discharged simultaneously. It was used as a defensive weapon.

RICHARD (Coeur de Lion, Lion-Heart) I, king of England, 1189–99, son of Henry II and one of the leaders of the Third Crusade (1189–92). He was an undutiful son toward his father but was devoted to his mother, Eleanor (of Aquitaine). No sooner did he become king than he set off on the Crusade. After the fall of Acre and the return of Philip II Augustus to France, Richard continued the war against Saladin until Sep-

tember 1192 when the two men agreed to a settlement which opened the Holy Places to Christian pilgrims. On his return Richard was captured by Duke Leopold of Austria who turned him over to Henry VI, the Holy Roman emperor, who did not release him until early 1194 and the payment of a huge ransom. Within a short time after his return, Richard recovered the possessions in France that Philip II Augustus had seized, then erected the formidable Château Gaillard on the Seine to protect the approaches to Normandy. He died of a wound sustained while laying siege to the castle of a petty vassal in Aquitaine. Richard spent but ten months of his ten-year reign in England.

RICHARD II, king of England, 1377–99, son of Edward, the Black Prince, and grandson of Edward III whom he succeeded. During his minority his uncle John of Gaunt, duke of Lancaster, served as unofficial regent but in fact maintained a dominant position in the government until c. 1386. Five years earlier, in 1381, Richard made a brief appearance when he demonstrated his courage and prudence in negotiating with the rebel leaders in the Peasant Revolt. In 1388 an aristocratic group opposed to the rise of the court party which Richard was organizing forced the issue in the Merciless Parliament and ordered the execution of the king's "evil" advisers. But in 1397 it came Richard's turn. He executed the leaders of the opposition or forced them into exile and instituted personal rule. His confiscation in 1399 of the huge Lancastrian estates precipitated a revolt that ended with his abdication and the accession of Henry Bolingbroke, Gaunt's son. Richard was murdered. [For the principal religious developments of his reign, *see* WYCLIF, JOHN, and LOLLARDS.]

RICHARD III, king of England, 1483–5, brother of Edward IV and duke of Gloucester. He served Edward loyally and efficiently, and Edward named him protector of his son Edward (V), but two months after his brother's death he seized the throne. Edward V and his brother Richard, who had been placed in the Tower, disappeared from view two months later, probably murdered on Richard's orders. In 1485 Henry Tudor (VII) defeated Richard at the battle of Bosworth Field where he died.

RICHARD DE MORES (Ricardus Anglicus), d. 1242, English Augustinian and canonist, the first Englishman to teach at Bologna. From 1202 until his death he served as prior of the Augustinian canons at Dunstable. He authored several influential works on canon law and papal decretals and was also responsible for a large portion of the *Dunstable Annals.*

RICHARD OF CORNWALL, d. 1272, earl of Cornwall, son of King John and brother of Henry III, probably the richest magnate in England. He led an English force to the Holy Land, accompanied Henry on several military ventures in France, revealed his prudence by refusing Pope Innocent IV's offer of the crown of Sicily, then his lack of prudence by wasting money and effort on a vain quest for the crown of Germany. Although at times critical of Henry III, he remained loyal to him and was captured with him by Simon de Montfort at the battle of Lewes (1264).

RICHARD OF DEVIZES, d. after 1192, English Benedictine monk, author of the *Chronicle* which sheds light on the reign of Richard I. He may also have been the author of the *Annals of Winchester.*

RICHARD OF SAINT-VICTOR, d. 1173, Scottish theologian and exegete, from 1162 prior of the abbey of Saint-Victor in Paris. His most important work, *De Trinitate,* contains his principal philosophical doctrines. His exegetical, theological, and mystical writings reveal his independence as a thinker, although he had strong links with Hugh of St. Victor (d. 1141). Of particular importance were his writings on mystical theology because of their influence upon St. Bonaventure and the Franciscan mystics. While he

stressed the need of an empirical basis for proof of God's existence, he maintained that it was possible to arrive at the essentials of the doctrine of the Trinity by the process of speculative reasoning.

RICHARD OF WALLINGFORD, d. 1336, abbot of St. Albans, inventor of an astronomical clock and author of treatises on mathematical and astronomical subjects.

RICHARD PLANTAGENET. *See* YORK, HOUSE OF.

RICHARD SWYNESHED (Swineshead, Suisseth), fl. 1340–55, Oxford scholastic and author of the *Liber Calculationum.* This book, which won him the name of The Calculator, established him as one of the foremost mathematicians of the Middle Ages.

RICHMOND, EARLDOM OF, title held by the counts and dukes of Brittany from the eleventh century to the close of the fourteenth. Important people who held the title included Arthur (d. 1203), son of Geoffrey and grandson of Henry II [*see* ARTHUR]; John (d. 1435), duke of Bedford, third son of Henry IV [*see* BEDFORD, DUKES OF]; Edmund Tudor (d. 1456), son of Owen Tudor and Catherine, widow of Henry V, and father of Henry VII [*see* TUDOR].

RICIMER, FLAVIUS, d. 472, son of a Sueve chieftain and the daughter of the Visigothic king Wallia. As patrician, he won a naval victory over the Vandals in 456. In the same year he deposed the western emperor Avitus and ruled that half of the empire either through puppets or in his own person until his death.

RIDDAH (Ridda) WARS, military campaign undertaken in 633–4 by Abu Bakr, the successor of Mohammed, to bring back to the fold certain tribes who had repudiated Mecca's control when the Prophet died (632). These tribes were forced to submit, and so were other tribes inside Arabia who had not previously accepted the faith of the Prophet.

RIENZI, COLA DI. *See* COLA DI RIENZO.

RIEVAULX, MONASTERY OF, Cistercian foundation, located about 20 miles north of York and dedicated to the Blessed Virgin. It was founded in 1131 by Abbot William Espec who had been sent to England by St. Bernard of Clairvaux. The community grew rapidly and within 25 years of its founding numbered some 600 members. It was known as a center of learning and spirituality and also attracted notice for its contribution to agriculture. The fourteenth century witnessed destructive raids from across the Scottish border.

RIGA, city located on the Gulf of Riga, its shores already used by Bremen merchants when Meinhard established his monastery there in 1190. It became a bishop's see in 1201 and an archbishop's in 1253 and served as a missionary center for the Livonian Knights. In 1282 it became a member of the Hanseatic League and shortly developed into a major commercial center.

RIMINI, seaport city of north-central Italy on the Adriatic, in Romagna, member of Pentapolis under Byzantine rule. It was included in the Donation of Pepin (754) and was governed by dukes and counts in the name of the pope until the tenth century when the German emperor's authority became dominant. For a short time it became an independent commune following the death of Frederick II, king of Germany, in 1250, but in 1295 the Malatesta family secured control and held it until 1508 when it passed to the Papal States.

RITES, ENGLISH MEDIEVAL, variants of the Roman rite. They included the Use of Sarum, Use of York, Use of Hereford, and the Use of Bangor. [*See* SALISBURY or SARUM, USE OF.]

RIVERS, ANTHONY WOODVILLE (Wydeville), EARL, d. 1483, brother-in-law of Edward IV who joined him on his campaigns and accompanied him into exile. In his later years his interests became more spiritual and he made pilgrimages to Santiago de Compostella and Rome. Shortly after Richard III seized the throne, he had Rivers arrested and executed.

RIVERS, RICHARD WOODVILLE (Wydeville), EARL, d. 1469, father of Elizabeth, the Lancastrian heiress whom Edward IV married in 1464. He served as a squire in the Hundred Years' War, was created Baron Rivers in 1448, and fought with the Lancastrians against the Yorkists. He made his peace with Edward IV following the latter's victory at Towton (March 1461), but was later captured by Warwick after the latter had broken with Edward, and was executed.

ROBBIA, LUCA DELLA, d. 1482, sculptor of Florence who was considered the peer of Donatello by his contemporaries. Some of his best work can be seen in the marble reliefs of the Singing Gallery in the cathedral in Florence. Although his figures lack the dramatic grandeur of Donatello's, they reflect a highly appealing, cheerful humanity. Robbia also developed a technique for applying pottery glazes, in different colors, to terracotta figures.

ROBERT I, king of France, 922-3, a younger son of Robert the Strong. As count of Paris he swore fealty to Charles III (the Simple), but in 922 he joined in a revolt against Charles and was elected king at Reims. The following year he was slain in battle with Charles.

ROBERT II (the Pious), king of France, 996-1031, son of Hugh Capet and his successor, conquered the duchy of Burgundy (1015), supported monastic reform, and labored for the adoption and observance of the Truce of God.

ROBERT I, The Bruce, king of Scotland, 1306-29, a descendant of a Norman family that came to Scotland in the twelfth century, and grandson of the first Robert Bruce (d. 1295). This last Robert's claim to the Scottish throne was denied by Edward I, king of England, Scotland's overlord, when Margaret died in

1290, and he gave the crown instead to John Balliol. In 1306, after the capture and execution of William Wallace who had won out over Balliol, Robert seized the throne but suffered defeat by the English under Edward I and became a fugitive off the north Irish coast. In 1307 he returned to Scotland, strengthened his position by exploiting Edward II's domestic difficulties in England, and in 1314 inflicted an overwhelming defeat on a much larger English army at Bannockburn. The victory assured Scottish independence. The best known of the popular tales about Robert the Bruce is the story of the spider.

ROBERT II, king of Scotland, 1371–90, first sovereign of the house of Stuart, who served as regent of the exiled David II from c. 1334 to 1341, and then again during David's captivity, 1346–57. Robert was among those who escaped the defeat of the Scottish army at the battle of Neville's Cross in 1346. He proved a weak king.

ROBERT (the Magnificent, the Devil), duke of Normandy, 1027–35, father of William the Conqueror. He gained fame as a warrior and died on his return from a pilgrimage to Jerusalem. His memory lived on in sagas and romances in which he was confused with a legendary son of a duke of Normandy, the central figure in the late twelfth-century romance entitled *Robert Le Diable*.

ROBERT II, duke of Normandy, c. 1054–1134, eldest son of William I (the Conqueror), who supported a revolt against his father with the help of Philip I of France. He was later exiled, then was assigned to Normandy while his younger brother William (II) (Rufus) received England. He fought William II intermittently, then joined the First Crusade (1096–9). On his return he was defeated by Henry I, his younger brother, at the battle of Tinchebrai (1106) and imprisoned.

ROBERT BACON. *See* BACON, ROBERT.

ROBERT GROSSETESTE. *See* GROSSETESTE, ROBERT.

ROBERT GUISCARD. *See* GUISCARD, ROBERT.

ROBERT KILWARDBY. *See* KILWARDBY, ROBERT.

ROBERT OF ARBRISSEL, BL., d. 1117, lived as a recluse in the Anjou forest, later took up a life of preaching. He founded a number of monastic communities including the double monastery at Fontevrault. This house became the center of the Order of Fontevrault which he founded.

ROBERT OF CORUÇON, d. 1219, theologian at Paris who reorganized the studies in the university and drew up a series of statutes governing the institution. He died on the Fifth Crusade (1218–21) during the siege of Damietta.

ROBERT OF GENEVA. *See* CLEMENT VII.

ROBERT OF JUMIÈGES, d. 1055, abbot of the Benedictine monastery of Jumièges, later bishop of London and archbishop of Canterbury (1051). In 1052 when Earl Godwin and his sons, the leaders of the Anglo-Saxon opposition to the policies of Edward the Confessor, gained the ascendancy, they forced Robert into exile. He returned to Jumièges. His exile enabled William, duke of Normandy, to secure the papacy's blessing for his invasion of England in 1066.

ROBERT OF MELUN, d. 1167, scholastic theologian, an Englishman by birth, who studied at Paris and succeeded Abelard as head of the school of Mont Ste. Geneviève. In 1142 he became director of the school at Melun, then in 1163 returned to England and was consecrated bishop of Hereford. He left theological treatises, those on the Trinity being of particular importance since he had wide knowledge of the literature on that subject.

ROBERT OF MOLESME, ST., d. 1110, member of a noble family of Champagne and prior of two different Benedictine monasteries before becoming superior of a community of hermits at Molesme. When the monks there refused to accept a strict observance of the rule of St. Benedict, Robert organized a separate group with which he established a new order at Citeaux in 1098, later known as the Cistercians. He later returned to Molesme. He shares with Stephen Harding the distinction of founding the Cistercian order.

ROBERT THE STRONG, d. 866, margrave of the Breton march and duke of Francia, father of Odo, king of the West Franks (d. 889), and progenitor of the Capetians. He was killed fighting the Normans.

ROBIN HOOD, hero of English folk ballads of the late Middle Ages. He was a legendary outlaw, his name probably belonging originally to a mythical elf of the forest and applied by writers from the twelfth century to any robber-leader who lived in the forest. The Pipe Roll of 1230 makes mention of a "Robert Hood, fugitive," and William Langland refers to the "rymes of Robyn Hood."

ROCH (Rock, Rocco), ST., d. c. 1378, native of Montpellier who cured many stricken by the plague in the town of Aquapendente as well as in other towns and cities. He was regularly invoked against plague, cholera, and skin diseases, as in the outbreak of the plague in 1414 during the sessions of the Council of Constance.

ROCHESTER, city in Kent, located on the Roman way from Kentish ports to London. It was the oldest, and smallest, suffragan see of Canterbury, and was founded in 604 by St. Augustine of Canterbury. William I erected a castle there and in 1227 Henry III granted the town a charter. A Norman cathedral consecrated in 1130 replaced an earlier one which had been destroyed by the Mercians and Danes. The Norman cathedral has the oldest nave in England.

RODERIC (Ruadri, Rory O'Connor), d. 1198, king of Connaught, the last high king of Ireland. His attack on Dermot MacMurrough, king of

Leinster, led the latter to appeal to Henry II of England for help, an appeal that opened the way to the Anglo-Norman invasion of 1166. By the Treaty of Windsor, Roderic recognized the suzerainty of Henry. In 1191 he retired to a monastery.

RODERICK, d. 713?, last Visigothic king of Spain. He was fighting Franks and Burgundians in the north when Tarik, leader of the Moors, crossed over from north Africa in 711. Roderick hurried south and was defeated by Tarik at a battle mistakenly known as that of Guadalete. Whether Roderick was slain in this battle or later in 713, his name as the "last of the Goths," lived on in Spanish literature.

RODRIGO DIAZ DE VIVAR. *See* CID, EL.

ROGATION DAYS, name given originally to what were known as the Minor Litanies and Major Litany. The Minor Litanies or Rogations, which appeared in the late fifth century, were celebrated on the three days preceding the feast of the Ascension. The Major Litany or Rogation, which dated from the pontificate of Gregory the Great (590–604), was celebrated on April 25. This last Rogation Day supplanted a pagan celebration when sacrifice was made to the gods for good crops.

ROGER I, king of Sicily, d. 1101, count of Sicily and Calabria, born in Normandy, the son of Tancred of Hauteville and the youngest brother of Robert Guiscard. He aided his brother in driving the Saracens from Apulia and Sicily and in 1085 succeeded him as ruler of southern Italy. To confirm his control of the church, which he reorganized, he had Pope Urban II appoint him apostolic legate in his domains. Toward Jews and Moslems he adopted a policy of complete toleration.

ROGER II, king of Sicily, 1130–54, son of Roger I. He extended his authority over the whole of southern Italy with the capture of Naples and Capua, established a foothold in

Arabic-held Tunisia and Tripoli, and attacked Byzantine possessions in Greece (he captured Corfu). He centralized the government, issued a new code of laws, and despite a full career of hostilities with the papacy, Byzantine empire, Venice, and Pisa, not to mention internal difficulties, showed himself a patron of science, literature, and art. By reason of his strong, efficient rule, he has been referred to as the "first modern ruler."

ROGER BACON, d. c. 1292, English scholar, scientist, and Franciscan. He appears to have studied at Paris where he received a master's degree, then in 1247 moved to Oxford where he devoted himself to the study of languages, mathematics, and the sciences. The man most responsible for Bacon's new interests was Robert Grosseteste, bishop of Lincoln, for whom he had the highest respect. Bacon advocated the study of Greek, Arabic, mathematics, and the sciences, and made a significant contribution to the study of optics and the advance of experimental sciences. In the *Opus Maius,* a work which he produced upon the request of Pope Clement IV, he discussed the scientific method and drew up a prospectus of what a knowledge of science would in time accomplish. His prediction of marvels that the development of science would one day bring, together with his confinement (1277–9) over certain eschatological views considered heretical (he appears to have been influenced by Joachim of Fiore), have perhaps earned him a greater reputation as a scholar and scientist than he deserves.

ROGER OF HOVEDEN (Howden), d. 1201 or 1202, royal justice under Henry II and chronicler of the reigns of Henry II and Richard I (to 1201). He accompanied Richard on the Third Crusade (1189–92). Some of his writings have been mistakenly attributed to Benedict of Peterborough.

ROGER OF SALISBURY, d. 1139, bishop of Salisbury (1101), chancellor and justiciar under Henry I and his principal councillor. He supported Stephen of Blois in seizing the throne after Henry's death, but in 1139 was deprived of his castles when he lost Stephen's confidence.

ROGER OF WENDOVER, d. 1236, monk of the Benedictine abbey of St. Albans and author of *Chronica sive Flores Historiarum,* a chronicle that stretched from the Creation to 1235. For the material from 1192 to 1201 he depended heavily on Roger of Hoveden. His chronicle is of considerable value for the early part of the reign of Henry III.

ROIS FAINÉANTS, that is, "do-nothing kings," Merovingian monarchs who were kings in name only. Their period of rule extended from the death in 639 of Dagobert, considered the last Merovingian monarch to exercise any measure of effective authority, to 751 when Pepin the Short, mayor of the palace, deposed Childerich III. Pepin (III) who was then crowned king of the Franks, was the founder of the Carolingian dynasty.

ROLAND, CHANSON DE (*Song of Roland*), the most famous of the *chansons de geste* or medieval epics. Its theme is the heroism and death of Roland, according to the story the nephew of Charlemagne. (Roland appears as a prefect of the Breton march.) Roland was the commander of the rear guard of the Frankish army. Because of the treachery of Roland's step-father Ganelon, the Moors, actually the Basques, attacked his company as it was making its way to France through the defile in the Pyrenees at Roncesvalles, and all were slain, that is, all except Roland. Roland died from the effects of a tremendous blast he blew on his horn to summon Charlemagne to his aid. When Charlemagne heard the horn, he turned his army about and shortly destroyed the Moorish enemy. The Roland story was a popular one with French, Spanish, and Italian poets. The oldest surviving manuscript of the poem dates from c. 1100.

ROLLE DE HAMPOLE, RICHARD, d. 1349, English hermit of Yorkshire, a contemplative, author of commentaries on the Bible and translator of several books of the Bible. He is known principally for his mystical works. Most of his works are in Latin, although his English works, written in a clear, lyrical prose, are important for the study of the language.

ROLLO (Hrolf), Viking chieftain who in 911 received the greater part of what later was known as Normandy from Charles (III) the Simple, king of the West Franks. Rollo agreed to hold Normandy as a fief although he and his men were in full possession of the region.

ROLLS SERIES. *See* CHRONICLES AND MEMORIALS OF GREAT BRITAIN AND IRELAND DURING THE MIDDLE AGES.

ROMAGNA, region east of Florence on the Adriatic which was usually part of the Papal States. San Marino was an enclave within the Romagna. While under Byzantine control (540–751), Romagna constituted part of the exarchate of Ravenna. In 1209 Otto IV recognized papal rights to the territory, although it did not come under effective papal authority until the pontificate of Julius II (1503–13).

ROMANCE, COURTLY, a literary genre, particularly popular in Western Europe during the twelfth and thirteenth centuries, whose wholly imaginative themes usually combined the martial heroism of the epic with love and romantic adventure.

ROMAN D'ALEXANDRE, LE, a twelfth-century French verse romance whose theme was drawn from the legends concerning Alexander the Great.

ROMAN DE LA ROSE, allegorical poem in Old French of some 22,000 lines composed by two poets, the first part by Guillaume de Lorris between 1225 and 1230, the second by Jean de Meun who completed the work 40 years later. The story of the poem is that of a youth who falls asleep and dreams of a rose enclosed in a garden, the symbol of the young woman he desires and whom he finally possesses. In his efforts to reach the girl, obstacles constantly obstruct his way, usually in the guise of personified vices such as Danger, Evil Tongue, and Jealousy, while virtues, Delight, Nature, and others help open a path for him. Lorris's part constitutes a psychological study of love in the tradition of troubadour literature. Jean de Meun reveals a deep and perceptive interest in people, in their foibles and deficiencies for the most part and especially in those of women and members of the clergy. He also reveals an impressive interest in, even knowledge of, science, classical literature, and mythology.

ROMAN DE RENART, a collection of tales of the late twelfth century, found principally in Latin, French, German, Dutch, and English, which in time came to be organized in a series of 27 branches. The characters in the stories are animals who comport themselves partly as animals should, partly as identifiable human types. They included King Noble the Lion, Reynard the Fox, Isengrim the Wolf, Bernard the Ass, and a number of other animals. French sources contributed most to the original story. The cycle may have appeared in Lorraine as early as the tenth century. Their intent, at least initially, was simply entertainment: no satire was intended. Later favorite butts of the satire were the upper classes and the clergy.

ROMANESQUE ART, term applied in general to the art of Western Europe during the eleventh and twelfth centuries. Architecturally the Romanesque church featured round arches, thick columns or composite piers, massive walls, heavy proportions, small windows, and barrel vaults. Since the enormous weight of the barrel vault of the nave forced the elimination of the clerestory or a severe reduction in the number and size of its windows, the interior of the Romanesque building was apt to be dark. Partly for this reason interior walls were left unadorned, although relief sculpture graced the capitals and the tympana. Romanesque sculpture lacked naturalism and human warmth. Its figures were often distorted and elongated and the vegetation was stylized, with geometric and interlacing patterns providing a popular background. It possessed nonetheless strength, grandeur, and serenity, qualities that conformed to the general impression of power and permanence that characterized the Romanesque structure. [See NORMAN STYLE; TRIFORIUM.]

ROMAN RITE, the ceremonials, prayers, and liturgical practices that came into use in Rome and generally throughout Western Europe in the celebration of the mass, the administering of the sacraments, and the recitation of the divine office.

ROMANS, KING OF THE, title given to the son of the king of Germany and Holy Roman emperor in the hope of assuring his succession. The son could not be crowned emperor until his father's death. This became a practice from 1125.

ROMANUS, Pope, August to November 897, Roman priest and cardinal, the successor of the murdered Stephen VI. He had the body of Pope Formosus rescued from the Tiber but he died before he was able to revalidate the orders that Formosus had conferred.

ROMANUS (Romanos) MELODUS, ST., d. c. 560, a Syrian, possibly of Jewish origin, the greatest hymnist and poet of the Eastern church. He moved to Constantinople where he achieved his fame. Of the thousand poems (metrical sermons chanted to music) attributed to him, only 85 have survived; none of the music is extant. The verse he employed was based upon stress-accent rather than on quantity.

ROME. When Diocletian (284–305) divided the administration of the Roman empire and took up his residence in Nicomedia, he announced the end of Rome's history as the capital and center of the Western world. The population of the city, a half-million in his day, sank to one-tenth that figure, where it remained until the late Middle Ages. The Western emperor, rather than reside in Rome which could not be defended, made his headquarters in Milan or Ravenna. If the successors of St. Peter had not made Rome their home, that city might have taken its place alongside such other ancient capitals as Nineveh and Babylon and passed into oblivion.

In 410 Rome suffered its first sacking, this by Alaric and the Visigoths. In 455 the Vandals looted the city. In 476 the Scirian Odoacer deposed Romulus Augustulus, the last "Roman emperor," while he remained in Ravenna. There he was slain by Theodoric, king of the Ostrogoths, whose nation ruled Rome and Italy until c. 550 when Justinian's generals, after years of destructive warfare, managed to restore the peninsula to imperial rule. No sooner were the Ostrogoths gone, than the Lombards appeared and so reduced Byzantium's power in Italy that Pope Gregory I (590–604) found that the defense of the city of Rome had become his responsibility. By the middle of the eighth century Lombard threat to the city had become so great that the pope turned to the Frankish kings who destroyed the Lombard kingdom and assumed a protectorate over Rome and the papacy. This served until the last quarter of the ninth century when the Carolingian empire disintegrated and Rome and the papacy came under the dominance of aristocratic factions. [See THEOPHYLACT.]

In 962 the situation improved when Otto I of Germany came down to protect the pope and Rome against Berengar, a petty Italian ruler. For about a century, Rome and the papacy enjoyed relative peace under the tutelage of German kings who, when occasion demanded, were ready to come down across the Alps. In 1084 Henry IV, Gregory VII's archenemy in the investiture controversy, did so, and Gregory appealed to Robert Guiscard and his Normans who proceeded to loot the city and left one-third of it in ashes. During the twelfth century the

Frangipani and Pierleone families competed for control, and for a short time (1144–55), a visionary, Arnold of Brescia, ruled the city. Still instability and factional strife were never far removed, and even so powerful a pope as Innocent III (1198–1216) twice had to flee the city.

In the thirteenth century, the powerful families of the Orsini, Colonna, and Gaetani fought for control, with the leader of the Colonna faction sharing in the humiliation of the Gaetani Pope Boniface VIII in 1303. During much of the fourteenth century the popes made their home in Avignon [see AVIGNONESE RESIDENCE], partly because of the semi-anarchy that prevailed in Rome. A Roman demagogue, Cola di Rienzo, led a revolution in 1347 which aimed to restore the ancient republic of Rome. At first the pope had hopes Rienzo might be the answer, but he then turned to Cardinal Gil Albornoz, commander of the papal army in Italy, who succeeded in establishing sufficient quiet to permit Gregory XI to leave Avignon and return to Rome. The fifteenth century proved the most stable in the history of medieval Rome, which enabled the papacy to vie with the despots of north Italy for its share of the troubled peninsula and in the promotion of humanism.

ROMUALD II OF SALERNO, d. 1182 or 1183, archbishop of Salerno and a friend of William I of Sicily and of Robert Guiscard. He was influential in court and papal affairs. He was learned in medicine, a patron of the arts, and the author of a universal history to 1178.

ROMUALD, ST., d. 1027, a nobleman of Ravenna, monk of the monastery of San Apollinaris near Ravenna, but for the greater part of his life a hermit near the monastery of Cuxa in the Pyrenees. He later returned to Italy to Pareum near Ravenna. Among the eremetical congregations that he established in northern Italy and southern France was that of the Camaldolese which he founded c. 1012 near Arezzo in Tuscany.

ROMULUS AUGUSTULUS, son of the patrician Orestes, who reigned as the last of the western Roman emperors from 475 until 476 when the German chieftain Odoacer deposed him. Odoacer slew Orestes but spared Romulus because of his youth. Only in a narrowly theoretical sense does the deposition of Romulus mark the end of the Roman empire in the west.

RONCESVALLES (French: Roncevaux), town near Pamplona located on the pass in the western Pyrenees where the Basques destroyed the rear guard of Charlemagne's army in 778 as it was leaving Spain and returning to France. In 1130 an Augustinian abbey was founded there by the bishop of Pamplona to minister to pilgrims on their way to Santiago de Compostella. [See ROLAND, CHANSON DE.]

RONDEAU (rondo, rondel), name given to several related medieval verse and musical forms not unlike the *virelay* and *ballade*. They were characterized by the use of a refrain. The rondeau developed in France and had already become popular by the thirteenth century.

ROOD, term used to signify the True Cross (Holy Rood), more generally a large crucifix placed over the entrance to the choir.

ROSAMOND, FAIR, d. 1176?, mistress of Henry II of England. Almost all that is told of her is legend.

ROSARY, a string of beads used to keep count of fifteen decades, each consisting of one Pater Noster, ten Ave Marias, and Gloria Patri. The practice of counting repeated prayers on beads dated from the pre-Christian era and was also known in Islam. The Christian rosary used in the West may have appeared as early as the ninth century. Its development has been credited to Dominican and Cistercian influence.

ROSATE (Rosciate), ALBERICO DE, d. 1354, lawyer of Bergamo and author of commentaries on the *Corpus Juris Civilis*.

ROSCELIN (Roscellinus) OF COMPIÈGNE, d. c. 1125, dialectician and nominalist, taught at several schools, including Loches where he had Abelard as a pupil. His theories are known principally through the attacks of his critics including Anselm of Bec, Abelard, and John of Salisbury. He was one of the first leading defenders of nominalism. He was obliged to retract his views on the Trinity which were judged to approach the heresy of tritheism.

ROSES, WARS OF THE, name traditionally given to the conflict between the houses of Lancaster and York for possession of the English throne and extending roughly from 1455 to 1485. After 1471 conditions were reasonably quiet except for the battle of Bosworth Field (1485) when Richard III was slain and Henry VII succeeded. Of a variety of factors that contributed to this period of violence and bloodshed, three may be considered fundamental: first, the long minority of Henry VI, his gentle nature, and his mental illness that produced a situation conducive to the rise of factions; second, the claim of Richard of York, then of his son Edward, to the succession; and third, the loss of the Hundred Years' War which left the English in a bitter mood. Most of the battles were minor engagements, although that fought at Towton (1461) is said to have left more than 25,000 dead on the field of battle. The Wars of the Roses dealt a crushing blow to the position of the landed aristocracy. Many were among the slain, many others had their lands declared forfeit, thus clearing the way for the emergence of Tudor absolutism. Probably the principal reason for the eventual victory of Edward IV and the Yorkists was the support of London which felt that faction held the greater promise for peace. [See MARGARET OF ANJOU; WARWICK, RICHARD NEVILLE, EARL OF; YORK, HOUSE OF.]

ROSE WINDOW, large circular stone-traceried window usually centrally located in the façade or transept. It was most popular in French Gothic cathedrals.

ROSKILDE, Danish city on the island of Seeland that served as the royal residence until 1443 and as a bishop's see from the tenth century. Many Danish kings are buried in its magnificent cathedral (eleventh-twelfth century).

ROSSELLINO, ANTONIO, d. c. 1478, Florentine sculptor whose work is noted for its religious sentiment and grace of style. His St. Sebastian is considered one of the finest statues of the period.

ROSSELLINO, BERNARDO, d. 1464, Florentine architect and sculptor. He operated a workshop with his four brothers in Florence. He built structures in several Italian cities including the Rucellai Palace in Florence. He also did reconstruction work in Rome and prepared a design for St. Peter's. His most famous sculpture is the tomb of Leonardo Bruni in the church of Santa Croce, Florence.

ROSTOCK, town located just to the east of Lübeck, a Wendish fortress in the twelfth century. It was founded as a German community c. 1208. In 1270 a Cistercian monastery was established there. It became a leading member of the Hanseatic League in the fourteenth century, a possession of Mecklenburg in 1323, and that of the dukes of Schwerin in 1352. The duke of Mecklenburg founded the city's university in 1419.

ROSWITHA (Rosvitha, Hrosvitha) OF GANDERSHEIM, d. after 1000, canoness of the monastery of Gandersheim, born of a noble Saxon family, author of legends in verse, two verse chronicles, one about the deeds of Otto the Great, the other a history of the convent of Gandersheim, and six dramas or comedies based on pious legends, with the ancient classical poet Terence serving as her model. Her purpose in composing the dramas was to deny Terence's portrayal of women as frail and to present to readers stories of Christian virgins and penitents. Her knowledge of Scriptures, the church fathers, and classical literature was most unusual for that period.

ROTA, ROMAN, papal tribunal for judging cases brought before the Holy See which developed into an independent institution early in the thirteenth century. Its name apparently derived from the circular table used by the judges at Avignon when its business witnessed an enormous expansion.

ROTTA, musical instrument of the early Middle Ages related to the lyre and zither.

ROTTERDAM, city of Holland which grew up at the site of a dike on the Rotte river. It received a charter in 1299 and in 1340 had permission from Count William IV of Holland to build a canal to the river Schie. This canal provided Rotterdam a link with the towns of Delft, Leiden, and The Hague, and assured its rapid growth.

ROTULI, Latin for rolls, that is, strips of parchment or papyrus, written on one side, which were then rolled up and secured.

ROUEN, city located on the Seine in Normandy which sprang from Celtic origins. The Normans captured the town in 841 and again in 876, then in 912 made it their capital. It was an English possession from 1066 to 1204 and again from 1418 to 1449, after which time it remained in French hands. It had gained fame as a center of art and culture by the late fifteenth century. Its cathedral, most of it from the first half of the thirteenth century, is one of the finest Gothic churches in France. The Palais de Justice is in the late Gothic style.

ROUND TABLE, THE, a table in the Arthurian legend around which King Arthur's knights sat and where all places held equal dignity. The poet Wace was the first to make mention of the table (c. 1154).

ROUSSILLON, county in southern France just north of the Pyrenees and fronting on the Mediterranean. It was overrun by the Visigoths early in the fifth century, by the Saracens c. 720, and by the Franks in 759. Aragon extended its

authority over the region in 1177 and in 1258 Louis IX of France surrendered all claims to the territory. From 1461 to 1472 it was again under French control, but in 1493 Charles VIII receded it to Ferdinand II of Aragon.

ROUTIERS, French professional men-at-arms who were organized into companies and usually fought for a lord (king) for pay. They were notorious for the brutal manner with which they ravaged the countryside during the Hundred Years' War.

RUBAIYAT. *See* OMAR KHAYYAM.

RUBEL, silver coin first noted in Novgorod in the fourteenth century.

RUBRIC, title or chapter heading in medieval manuscripts written in red (Latin: *ruber*) ink to distinguish it from the text. Rubrics also consisted of instructions introduced at the beginning of a document or liturgical prayer.

RUBRUQUIS (Ruysbroeck, Rubrouck), WILLIAM OF, d. after 1295, a Franciscan, born in a village near Saint-Omer whom Louis IX of France sent to Mongolia in the hope of enlisting the aid of the Mongols against the Moslems. In 1253 Rubruquis set out for the court of Batu Khan on the Volga, from there went on to Karakorum to the court of Mangu Khan, and in 1254 started on his return journey. His is the best extant eyewitness description of the Mongol realm and its people. Roger Bacon, a brother Franciscan, made extensive use of Rubruquis's account in the geographical section of his *Opus Maius*.

RUDOLF I, king of Germany, 1273–91, son of Albert IV, the count of Hapsburg and landgrave of Alsace, whose election in 1273 brought an end to the period of the Interregnum (1254–73). By surrendering imperial claims to the Papal States and to Sicily, Rudolf won the approval of the pope although the pope refused to crown him Roman emperor. Rudolf's major achievement was his defeat of Ottocar II, king of

Bohemia, at Marchfeld in 1278, and his recovery of the imperial fiefs of Austria, Styria, Carinthia, and Carniola which Ottocar had usurped. Rudolf made Vienna his capital. Because of the manner in which Rudolf had succeeded in expanding the power of his family, the imperial electors passed over his son Albert when Rudolf died and chose Adolf of Nassau.

RUDOLF OF EMS (Hohenems), d. c. 1250, the most prolific Middle High German poet of the Middle Ages. His poems, which include *Der guote Gerhart* and *Barlaam und Josaphat* show the author to have been a man of great learning with a high sense of moral responsibility. His works also reveal considerable originality.

RUFINUS, d. 395, praetorian prefect of Illyricum, minister of Theodosius I and of his son Arcadius. Because of his ambition and his rapacity he was universally hated. After the death of Theodosius, he was virtual ruler of the eastern empire and he entertained hope of becoming co-emperor by marrying his daughter to Arcadius. He failed in this and was assassinated by Gothic mercenaries at the order of their commander Gaïnas.

RUFINUS OF AQUILEIA, d. 410, monk, historian, and scholar who spent some time as a hermit in Egypt; he later founded a monastery in Jerusalem. In addition to writing theological treatises, a commentary on the Apostles' Creed, some exegetical works, and a continuation of Eusebius's *Ecclesiastical History,* he translated many patristic writings from the Greek into Latin. These last may have represented his most important contributions since the knowledge of Greek had almost disappeared in the West. His deep interest in Origen evoked accusations of Origenism from St. Jerome who had earlier been his friend.

RUGIANS, east German tribe located near the mouth of the Vistula. After the collapse of Hunnic power they moved into lower Austria

where they were destroyed by Odoacer c. 488. A remnant of the tribe joined the Ostrogoths.

RUIZ, JUAN, d. c. 1350, a priest, perhaps Spain's leading medieval poet. He composed on both religious and profane themes, while his best-known poem is a sort of autobiography entitled *Libro de buen amor (The book of Good Love)* which offers a satirical panorama of medieval society against the background of Christian and Moorish views of life.

RUMANIANS, a people of mixed ethnic origins, the descendants of Dacians, other tribes from late Roman times, and colonists whom the emperor Trajan (98–117) settled in the province of Dacia. The area was overrun by Slavs, Gepids, Avars, Petchenegs, Cumans, Turks, and Magyars. The history of Rumania begins in the fourteenth century with the rise of the principality of Wallachia. Christianity was introduced by the fourth century, if not earlier, by Roman soldiers and other colonists.

RUNE, a character of an alphabet used in the oldest form of Germanic writing. Runes may date from the third century A.D. when they were used in Scandinavia.

RUNNYMEDE (Runnimede), a meadow, 20 miles from medieval London, on the south bank of the Thames where King John is believed to have placed his seal on the Magna Carta (1215).

RUPERT (Ruprecht) III, d. 1410, count of the Palatinate, a member of the house of Wittelsbach, who reigned as king of Germany from 1400 to 1410 following the deposition of King Wenceslas, although his support was limited largely to the Rhineland. He did enjoy the recognition of Pope Boniface IX. In 1386 Rupert founded the University of Heidelberg.

RURIK (Rjurik, Rörik, Hrorekr), d. c. 879, a Viking (Varangian) chieftain who with his two brothers, according to tradition, established the first Russian principality at Novgorod in 862.

RUS, a term probably of Finnish origin which the Slavs gave to the Swedish Vikings who penetrated Russia about the middle of the eighth century.

RUSSIA, name given to the vast eastern European plain which was occupied for the most part by Slavs who began entering the region in the third century A.D. The productivity of the land, the relative peacefulness of the Slavs, and the absence of formidable physical barriers attracted many warlike tribes to the country. Among these were the Goths, Huns, Avars, Bulgars, Hungarians (Magyars), Khazars, Petchenegs, and Cumans. Invaders from the northwest, the Swedish Vikings or Varangians whom the Slavs called Rus, introduced the country to history. According to the traditional account the Swede Rurik established the first Russian principality at Novgorod in 862. Shortly after Oleg took some of Rurik's followers and founded Kiev, the state that was to dominate Russia until 1169. Soon the south-flowing waters of the Dnieper and the Don transported these Swedish-Russians to the Black Sea, then to Constantinople. When attacks failed to open the city, commercial agreements succeeded. The most far-reaching in its cultural consequences was the treaty negotiated by Vladimir, prince of Kiev, c. 989, when he promised to accept Christianity for himself and his people. Under Yaroslav the Wise (1019–54), the greatest ruler of the Kievan period, Kiev prospered economically and culturally. Few cities of Europe could boast so large a population or so thriving an economy. But then more Petchenegs and Cumans appeared, and in 1169 the prince of Suzdal sacked Kiev and brought an end to medieval Russia's first great state.

Kiev's complete destruction came in 1240 at the hands of the Mongols who made their first invasion of Russia in 1223. In 1237 they returned under Batu Khan, conquered all of Russia except Novgorod, and demanded tribute and military contingents from all the native princes. Russia was slow to recover from the extensive destruction it suffered from the Mongols. Leadership in the post-Kievan period gradually fell to Moscow, a city that first came to notice in 1147. What contributed to Moscow's emergence was first its location at the center of the continental river trade, then the permanent acquisition of the title of grand prince by its rulers. With this title went the right to collect tribute from the Russian princes, even to settle their disputes, prerogatives which ambitious grand princes were quick to exploit. Alexander Nevski, prince of Novgorod, became grand prince of Vladimir in 1252. His son Daniel was the first to hold the title of prince of Moscow. Daniel's son Ivan I (d. 1341) was the first grand prince of Moscow. By purchase and force Ivan extended his authority over the entire province of Moscow and also induced the metropolitan to move his see there from Kiev. An attempt in 1380 to slough off Mongol rule proved premature, but a century later Ivan III (1462–1505) managed to accomplish this. He also captured Novgorod, expelled the Hanseatic merchants, and drove the Lithuanians west of the Dnieper. He had already married the niece of the last Byzantine emperor Constantine XI Palaeologus and on that basis claimed to be successor of the Roman Caesars when Constantinople fell in 1453. Ivan was the founder of the modern Russian state.

RUTEBEUF (Rutebuff, Rustebuff), d. c. 1285, leading French lyric poet before Villon. His works include satirical and polemical pieces which he directed at almost every order of society including individuals such as Louis IX and the pope. He also composed Crusading poems, saints' lives, hymns, and a miracle play. His verse, like that of Villon, expresses the views of a sensitive individual of broad experience who had a sharp eye for contemporary society.

RUTILIUS CLAUDIUS NAMATIANUS, fl. 417, Roman poet, at one time prefect of Rome, author of an elegiac poem which told of his journey from Rome to his home in southern Gaul (Provence?). He was a pagan and a member of the wealthy landowning class, and his writings reveal the mind of the non-Christian aristocrat who found himself a member of a declining culture. His narrative, which has much the character of a diary, is written in beautiful Latin.

RUTLAND, EARLDOM OF, title first granted in 1390 to Edward Plantagenet, a grandson of Edward III. The second earl, Edmund, the son of Richard, duke of York, was slain at the battle of Wakefield (1460) in the Wars of the Roses.

RUYSBROECK (Ruisbroeck, Rusbroek, Ruus-broec), JAN VAN, BL., d. 1381, Flemish mystic, founder of the Augustinian abbey at Groenen-dael near Brussels. John Tauler and Gerard Groote were among his most distinguished friends. Of the mystical and devotional works which he composed the most important and influential was *The Spiritual Espousals*. This work, written with unusual lucidity for books on the difficult subject of mysticism, served to present the views of mystics in a manner that made them acceptable to ecclesiastical authorities.

RUYSBROECK, WILLIAM. *See* RUBRUQUIS, WILLIAM OF.

SAADI. *See* SA'DI.

SA'ADIA BEN JOSEPH, GAON, d. 942, eminent Jewish biblical scholar, philosopher, and polemicist, head of the great Jewish academy at Sura in Babylonia, which during his rule ranked as the leading center of learning among Jews. His writings include an exposition of the Jewish religion, biblical commentaries, a Hebrew dictionary, poems, and a translation of the Old Testament into Arabic. This translation became the standard version for all Arabic-speaking Jews. He was outspoken in his hostility to the validity of oral tradition and the authority of the Talmud. His *Book of Language* laid the foundation of Hebrew grammar, while his *Book of Beliefs and Opinions* exerted far-reaching influence on the development of Jewish thought in the Middle Ages. In this work he presented a religious system based upon revelation and reason (he shows a thorough knowledge of Aristotle) which he held to be mutually complementary. He is considered the most important figure in the literary and political history of medieval Judaism.

SABA (Sabas), SS. Saba, d. 532, a native of Cappadocia and a leading figure in the history of eastern monasticism. He founded monasteries and hospices in Judaea, notably the monastery of Great Laura of Mar Saba which is still in existence. In 492 he was given charge of all the hermits in Palestine. He was also active in the defense of orthodoxy against the attacks of the Monophysites.

Saba the Goth, a fourth-century martyr of Cappadocia who is said to have chosen death rather than eat meat that had been sacrificed to the gods.

Saba the Younger, d. 990, member of the monastery of St. Philip of Agira in Sicily who fled to Calabria when the Saracens overran the island. He erected a number of churches and monasteries in both Sicily and in Lucania.

SABAOTH, word derived from the Hebrew meaning armies and used in the New Testament, in medieval hymns, and in the liturgy (*Sanctus* and *Te Deum*) together with the title of God: *Deus Sabaoth* or "Lord of Hosts."

SABBATH, the last day of the week in the Jewish calendar and observed by Jews from ancient times as a day of rest as suggested in Genesis 2:1–2 and prescribed in Deuteronomy 5:14, as well as a day set aside especially for the worship of God (Exodus 31:13–17). Jewish Christians continued to observe the Sabbath although not for long since the belief that Christ's Resurrection took place on a Sunday led to an early replacement of that day for the Jewish Sabbath.

SABBATINE PRIVILEGE, a privilege extended to the members of the Carmelite Order, on the basis of a bull ascribed to Pope John XXII (1322), that promised them, under certain conditions, unfailing salvation and early release from purgatory.

SABELLIANISM, a Trinitarian or Monarchian heresy named after Sabellius (fl. c. 220), a Christian theologian who moved from north Africa to Rome where he preached the doctrine of the "economic Trinity," that is, a unity of the deity so indivisible that it denied the Son a subsistence or personality distinct from that of the Father. God simply appeared successively as the Father, Son, and Holy Spirit. Pope Callistus I, perhaps himself once tainted with Sabellianism, excommunicated Sabellius in 220. The heresy appeared later in Spain in the form of Priscillianism. Actually the name Sabellianism was used to distinguish different varieties of related sects and in the East it included all forms of Monarchianism. Sabellianism aroused much controversy in the fourth century when Arian sympathizers customarily leveled the charge of that heresy at the advocates of Nicene orthodoxy.

SABELLIUS. *See* SABELLIANISM.

SABINA OF ROME, ST., presumably a widow of Umbria who owed her conversion to her servant. She suffered martyrdom c. 126. It is believed that the *acta* which tell of her martyrdom were fabricated in order to explain the existence of the church of St. Sabina which is located on the Aventine Hill in Rome.

SABINIAN, Pope, 604–6, papal legate to Byzantium under Pope Gregory the Great who held him in great esteem. Although obscurity shrouds much of the man and his pontificate, his policies are believed to have been more conservative than those of his predecessor Gregory the Great.

SABUTAI (Subutai), d. 1246, Mongol commander who conquered Korea for Genghis Khan, then helped him with the subjugation of Iran and Afghanistan. He later collaborated with Batu Khan in the conquest of Russia and Hungary.

SACCHETI, FRANCO, d. 1400, Florentine merchant, statesman *(podesta),* and composer of *canzoni* and madrigals, also of short stories in prose, based upon humorous incidents and anecdotes somewhat after the manner of Boccaccio's *Decameron.* These writings with their colorful description of people and places give evidence of his wide travels, while his views on political and moral subjects find expression in his letters.

SACCHONI, RAINERIO (Reiner), d. c. 1263, a Catharist bishop who converted and became a Dominican friar. As preacher and inquisitor he worked to suppress Catharism in central and northern Italy. He left a description of contemporary heretical beliefs and practices.

SACK, FRIARS OF THE, mendicant order established in Provence and confirmed by Pope Alexander IV in 1255. It disappeared in the early fourteenth century.

SACRAMENT, one of a number of rites that Christians believed were instituted by Christ for the sanctification of men. Augustine defined a sacrament as "the visible form of an invisible grace," Thomas Aquinas as the "sign of a sacred thing in so far as it sanctifies men." Before the appearance of Peter Lombard's *Sentences* (c. 1151), the classification of sacrament might be given to as many as thirty rites, but Peter's reduction of these to seven received the approval of Aquinas and the late medieval church. The seven sacraments are baptism, confirmation, Eucharist, penance, extreme unction, holy orders, and matrimony. Christians believed that all seven owed their institution to Christ and that they actually bestowed grace, the grace that enabled men to become sanctified.

SACRAMENTALS, religious practices and objects, such as holy water, vestments, ashes, incense, and the sign of the cross that were usually employed in conjunction with the administering of the sacraments. Of themselves they did not convey grace, nor were they founded by Christ but instead were introduced by the church. Through the church's intercession they produced spiritual effects, however, and such practices as the sign of the cross served as a means of obtaining grace.

SACRAMENTARY, liturgical book used at mass from the fourth to the thirteenth century when it was replaced by the missal. It contained the collects, prefaces, and canons of the mass, also ordination formularies and blessings, but not the epistles, gospels, or those parts of the service that were sung.

SACRAMENT HOUSE, shrinelike receptacle that appeared in the late Middle Ages when it became customary to reserve the Blessed Sacrament (Eucharist). They usually took the form of a small tower, the central part of which might be done in open work. Tabernacles began to displace these "houses" from the close of the Middle Ages.

SACRED COLLEGE, term applied to the college of cardinals whose principal responsibilities were those of electing the pope and serving as his privy council. Technically the college included rectors of certain parish churches in Rome, seven deacons of the city, and bishops of surrounding dioceses. Because of political pressures and vicissitudes both inside and outside of Italy, the number of cardinals who actually cast a vote for a new pope tended to fluctuate sharply during much of the Middle Ages.

SACRIS SOLEMNIS, breviary hymn composed by St. Thomas Aquinas (d. 1274) to celebrate the newly established feast of Corpus Christi.

SACRISTAN, an official, usually a member of the clergy, who had charge of the contents of a church, more particularly those associated with the sacristy and sanctuary.

SACRISTY, a room in, or annexed to, a church or chapel where vestments, sacred vessels, and other articles used for liturgical services were kept; also the place where priests and other clerics might vest.

SACROSANCTA, decree, also known as *Haec Sancta,* adopted in 1415 by the Council of Constance (1414–8), that proclaimed the general council to be the highest authority in the Christian church and one, therefore, to which the pope himself was subject. It has been called the most revolutionary pronouncement of the Middle Ages. [*See* CONSTANCE, COUNCIL OF.]

SA'DI (Mushariff-Ud-Din), d. c. 1291, a Persian poet and prose writer, author of two classics of Persian literature, the *Bustan* ("Orchard") and the *Gulistan* ("Rose Garden"). The *Bustan,* entirely in verse, consists of stories that recommend the traditional virtues of Moslem life (hospitality, justice, contentment); the *Gulistan,* which is principally in prose, also offers moral considerations for the entertainment and instruction of its readers, together with charming aphorisms and personal recollections. Sa'di was also the author of a number of celebrated odes.

SAEMUND SIGFÚSSON, d. 1133, Icelandic priest and historian whose writings are known only through references by later historians.

SAGA, an epic narrative in prose or verse in Old Norse literature, particularly the Icelandic and Norwegian, usually centering on some historical or legendary figure. Although the saga interweaves legend with historical fact, scholars base much of their knowledge of the customs and institutions of medieval Scandinavia upon such writings. The most persistent theme of these sagas is violence and war. Among the best known sagas are the *Heimskringla* and the *Starlunga Saga* by Snorri Sturluson, the *Laxdaela,* the *Njala,* and the *Frithjof.* The saga, long preserved by word of mouth, began to appear in writing in the twelfth century.

SAGRA DI SAN MICHELE, ABBEY OF, Benedictine monastery in Piedmont founded by St. John Vincentius (d. 1012), a disciple of St. Romuald. It acquired vast holdings in time and enjoyed great political importance because of its wealth and its location which commanded the valley of Mt. Cenis Pass. Its spiritual health declined with the increase of its wealth and influence.

SAGRES, village-port of Portugal east of Cape St. Vincent whence Portuguese explorers often set sail in the fifteenth century.

SAHAGÚN, JOHN OF, ST., d. 1479, Augustinian preacher and reformer of Salamanca, also popular preacher and confessor, who is said to have been poisoned because of his criticism of oppressive landlords.

SAINT, designation that the Christian church gave to those individuals (angels) whom it recognized to be in heaven and whose heroic virtues made them worthy of honor and intercession, that is, the saint could be asked to intercede with God for a special favor. Saints were usually accorded special days in the liturgical calendar, at which time they were commemorated and their intercession requested. Although major saints such as Mary, Peter, Paul, and Joseph were universally venerated in the Middle Ages, individual countries and dioceses might reserve places in their calendars for strictly national or local saints. The general criteria for recognition of sainthood were martyrdom, an exemplary life, miracles in life and after death, and a popular cult. Many local saints of the earlier Middle Ages owed their canonization to popular acclaim, ordinarily confirmed by a bishop, but from the thirteenth century the process of canonization remained largely under the jurisdiction of the papacy. [See PATRON SAINT.]

SAINT ALBANS, a cathedral city approximately twenty miles northwest of London. It grew up around a Benedictine monastery that King Offa of Mercia founded there c. 794. Pope Adrian IV (1154–9), the only English pope of the Middle Ages, granted the abbey episcopal exemption and gave it precedence over all monastic houses in England. Because of its location on the road leading north of London, kings and nobles as well as friars and ordinary travelers put up at the abbey where some brought with them valuable information that contributed to the high quality of the chronicles recorded there. Among the most noted chronicles were those of Roger of Wendover, Matthew Paris, William Rishanger, and Thomas Walsingham.

The town and abbey took their name from St. Alban, England's first martyr, the abbey church itself standing on the hill traditionally believed to be the site of his martyrdom. The abbey has seen much reconstruction over the centuries, and of the church, which had the longest Gothic nave in Christendom (292 ft.), only the tower, transepts, and the east end of the nave remain. Much history was made at St. Albans. Stephen Langton read his first draft of the Magna Carta to an assembly of clergy and nobles at the abbey; King John of France was kept there after his capture at the Battle of Poitiers (1356); John Ball, famous Lollard preacher, was executed there; and two critical battles of the Wars of the Roses were fought there.

SAINT-AMPOULE, vessel in which a dove was believed to have brought the holy oils for the baptism of Clovis. The legend served to establish Reims as the coronation city of French kings. [See AMPULLA.]

SAINT ANDREWS, university town and seaport of Fife, Scotland, its bishopric the most important in Scotland in the early twelfth century. The origins of Saint Andrews reach back to the Celtic ecclesiastical community of the early sixth century. King Angus I of the Picts (731–61) established a Celtic house of Culdees there and dedicated the church to St. Andrew, who became recognized as the patron saint of the Scottish nation. In 1472 the archbishop of Saint Andrews was proclaimed primate of Scotland. The priory of St. Andrews, a foundation of Canons Regular of St. Augustine, owed its foundation between 1127 and 1144 to Bishop Robert, who also organized the local residents into a burgh which became one of the largest in medieval Scotland. The university of Saint Andrews, the oldest in Scotland, received its charter from the bishop in 1412.

SAINT-ASAPH, a cathedral village in north Wales, one of the four ancient dioceses of Wales, founded c. 560 by St. Kentigern, bishop of Glasgow. Asaph, to whom the cathedral is dedicated, was a bishop (abbot?) there in the sixth century.

SAINT AUGUSTINE, ABBEY OF, monastery, probably the first to be established in Canterbury, founded by King Ethelbert of Kent (d. 616). About the year 980 it became a Benedictine house. The abbey had a long history of difficulties with the archbishop of Canterbury from whose jurisdiction it claimed exemption.

SAINT BERNARD PASSES. The Great Saint Bernard, 8,110 ft. high, runs from Aosta in Italy northward to Martigny situated just south of Lake Geneva in Switzerland. The hospice on the pass, which was founded (refounded?) by St. Bernard of Menthon c. 1081, has been in charge of Augustinian (Austin) friars since the twelfth century. Famous medieval monarchs including Charlemagne, Henry IV of Germany, and Frederick I Barbarossa are known to have used the pass. The Little Saint Bernard, 7,178 ft. high, runs from Aosta in Italy westward to Bourg-Saint-Maurice in the valley of the Isère (Savoy). A hospice there has also been attributed to St. Bernard of Menthon. Saint Bernard dogs, largest of domestic dogs, which took their name after this St. Bernard, were perhaps not used in the pass until the seventeenth century.

SAINT DAVID'S, cathedral village of Pembrokeshire in south Wales. Traces of ancient settlements may still be seen, together with the ruins of early Celtic chapels (e.g., St. Justinian and St. Non). These last, along with the imposing cathedral, the most famous and architecturally the most attractive in Wales — it is principally Transitional Norman in style and built of red-violet sandstone — served to make St. David's the most popular place of pilgrimage in medieval Wales. Natives judged two pilgrimages to St. David's the equal of one to Rome, three the equal of one to Jerusalem. In 1115 St. David's became a suffragan see of Canterbury.

SAINT-DENIS, ABBEY OF, a monastery in Paris founded by Dagobert I in 626 and dedicated to St. Denis (d. c. 258) who was believed to be buried there. Medieval France honored this saint as its patron. Benedictines took charge of the house in 656. The basilica which greatly influenced the evolution of Gothic architecture was the work of Suger (d. 1151) who in his rebuilding of the abbey introduced principles of Gothic architecture to western Europe. Louis VI, whom Suger served as adviser, selected the abbey's banner, the oriflamme, as the royal standard. Many French monarchs are buried in the abbey.

SAINTE-CHAPELLE, unusually attractive chapel constructed (1242–8) by Louis IX of France to house the Crown of Thorns that he had purchased from the Byzantine emperor. The architect, Pierre de Montreil, was one of the most distinguished of the thirteenth century. It remains one of the purest examples of Gothic architecture. The extensiveness of its 15 stained glass windows, which extend from the ceiling almost to the floor, seemingly eliminate the structural portions of the building. It consists of two chapels, one above the other, and a spire. In Louis's day it was part of the royal palace and served as his library.

SAINT ELMO'S FIRE, name which Neapolitan seamen gave to the blue, electrical discharges that might appear on the masts of their ships during stormy weather. They believed these flames assured them of the protection of St. Elmo, his name actually a corruption of St. Erasmus, the patron saint of Mediterranean seamen.

SAINT GALL (Sankt Gallen), ABBEY OF, monastery located south of Lake Constance, founded in 612 by the Irish monk St. Gall, a companion of St. Columban. It suffered repeated destruction during the wars between the Franks and the Alemanni, but from the time of Othmar, who served as the first Benedictine abbot (c. 720), it gained importance as a center of learning and of missionary activity. Until the eleventh century it ranked as the leading educational center north of the Alps, while the fame of its library and the skill of the monks in the art of manuscript illumination continued well into the late Middle Ages. In 1204 its abbots became princes of the Holy Roman empire. In 1454 the town of St. Gall joined the Swiss Confederation.

ST. GEORGE, ORDER OF, name given to several military-religious orders including the Constantinian Order of St. George which was founded c. 1191 and survived the fall of Constantinople, and the Order of St. George which James II of Aragon organized in 1316. The latter recruited its members principally from former Templars who were without a home following the dissolution of their order in 1312.

SAINT-GERMAIN-DES-PRÉS, historic abbey and church of Paris, founded c. 543 by Childebert I (d. 558), son of Clovis. Several Merovingian kings were buried there. Both abbey and church suffered repeated destructions. The present church, a Romanesque structure from the eleventh century, is noted for its imposing façade.

SAINT GOTTHARD PASS, Alpine pass, 6,916 feet high, which links Italy (Milan) through Switzerland (Lucerne) to south Germany and the Rhineland. It may not have come into general use until the thirteenth century. Its name probably derives from a hospice built at its summit by the dukes of Bavaria and dedicated to St. Godehard (Gotthard) (d. 1038), a bishop of Hildesheim.

SAINT-HUBERT, ORDER OF, name given to a number of knightly and hunting orders of the fifteenth century, including that of Bavaria which Gerard V, duke of Jülich and Berg, founded in 1444.

SAINT IVES, fishing town of Cornwall, England, on the west shore of St. Ives Bay. Its name is that of St. Eia, a fifth-century woman missionary who, according to tradition, floated over from Ireland on a leaf (coracle) and was subsequently martyred. Perkin Warbeck was proclaimed Richard IV when his ship anchored at St. Ives in 1497.

SAINT JAMES OF COMPOSTELLA, ORDER OF, military-religious order founded in the twelfth century for the purpose of driving the Moslems from Spain. Its headquarters were located in the province of Cuenca. The rule it observed was patterned after that of the Canons of St. Augustine.

ST. JOHN LATERAN. *See* LATERAN PALACE.

SAINT JOHN OF JERUSALEM, ORDER OF THE HOSPITAL OF, military-religious order, also known as the Knights of St. John or the Hospitallers. It was established c. 1070 by merchants of Amalfi to administer to the sick in the Hospital of St. John in Jerusalem. With the coming of the Crusades, the order assumed a military character, and for more than 150 years it proved a major bastion of Christian power in Syria. After the fall of Acre in 1291, the order moved its headquarters to Cyprus, and in 1309, after the acquisition of Rhodes, it moved to that island, from which time the order was known as the Knights of Rhodes. The order retained its interest in the sick and maintained hospitals and hospices in both Europe and the Levant. Its members wore a black mantle surmounted by a white cross.

SAINT-MALO, town in Brittany on the English Channel, settled in the ninth century by refugees from Norman raids on Saint-Servan which lay on the opposite bank of the Rance estuary. In the twelfth century the see was moved to Saint-Malo, soon after which privileges from the dukes of Brittany and the kings of France contributed to its growth into an important seaport.

S. MARIA MAGGIORE (Saint Mary Major), one of the largest churches of Rome, built by Pope Sixtus III in 432. Scholars believe that the stately Ionic columns of the nave, constructed of Hymettian marble, are from an earlier pagan temple that may have stood on that site. The transept was added in 1290, the coffered ceiling of the nave in 1500. The interior remains the most beautiful of the early Christian basilicas. [*See* ST. MARY OF THE SNOWS, FEAST OF.]

SAINT MARK'S, famous cathedral in Venice which originated with the Romanesque structure erected there in the ninth century as a shrine for the relics of St. Mark. This earlier structure was destroyed by fire and rebuilt c. 1071 with the help of architects from Constantinople. They incorporated Byzantine influences which came to be accentuated in the course of the twelfth and later centuries with the addition of further alterations and adornments. These have left the cathedral one of the most celebrated examples of Byzantine art in the world. Gothic additions were made to the façade in the fifteenth century. Marble slabs grace the lower walls of the interior, while vaults and domes are completely covered with exquisitely colored mosaics spread over a golden background. Of particular historical interest are the four bronze horses that stand upon the gallery over the main entrance. They may first have adorned Nero's triumphal arch in Rome, then from the fourth century the Hippodrome in Constantinople, whence they were brought to Venice when Constantinople was looted during the course of the Fourth Crusade (1202-4).

ST. MARY OF THE SNOWS, FEAST OF, feast commemorating the dedication of the church of S. Maria Maggiore in Rome which was erected c. 432. Legend had it that the site upon which the structure was erected was miraculously pointed out by a snowfall. The Virgin is supposed to have left her footprints in the snow. [*See* S. MARIA MAGGIORE.]

SAINT MICHAEL'S MOUNT, a lofty, pyramidal island off the shore of Mounts Bay in Cornwall, England. A castle and a chapel dedicated to St. Michael stand on its summit. Edward the Confessor gave the Mount to Mont-Saint-Michel in Normandy, which monastery held it as a priory until Henry V terminated the link and turned it over to the convent of Syon in Middlesex. It was a popular pilgrimage resort from the eleventh century.

SAINT-OMER, city of Flanders that took its name from a monastery founded there by St. Omer in the seventh century. In the ninth century the counts of Flanders fortified the town with a fortress and enclosed it with walls. Saint-Omer flourished as a major textile center from the eleventh century until 1336 when Edward III banned the export of English wool upon which the city depended for its raw material. The city is noted for its many reminders of the art and architecture of the Middle Ages, notably the magnificent paintings and sculpture in the Gothic basilica of Notre Dame (thirteenth-fourteenth century).

SAINT-OUEN, ABBEY OF, Benedictine monastery in Rouen, Normandy, dedicated to St. Ouen, the name of the bishop buried there in 684. It suffered destruction by the Vikings but revived in the early eleventh century and took a leading part in the revival of Norman monasticism. It gained distinction in the thirteenth century as a theological center.

ST. PATRICK'S PURGATORY, place of pilgrimage on Station Island in Donegal where according to tradition St. Patrick saw a vision that promised all pious visitors a plenary indulgence, a sight of the torments of the damned, and the joys of the blessed. It has been a place of pilgrimage since the early Middle Ages. Scholars doubt its connection with St. Patrick.

ST. PAUL'S OUTSIDE THE WALLS, famous five-aisled transeptal basilica outside Rome whose original structure was erected over the relics of St. Paul by the Emperor Constantine in 324. It may have been the largest and most magnificent of early churches (390 feet long). Later that century the basilica was rebuilt but it was destroyed by fire in 1823.

SAINT PETER PORT, town located on Guernsey, Channel Islands, that owed its importance as a commercial center to its excellent harbor, the protection of two neighboring castles, and the thriving wine trade between Gascony and England for which it proved an ideal port. In 1329 it was visited by more than 500 ships.

ST. PETER'S, BASILICA OF, church begun by Emperor Constantine c. 324 and completed by his son Constantius c. 354. Its site was Nero's circus and according to tradition it was erected over the grave of the Apostle Peter. In 1506 Pope Julius II had the church razed in order to make room for the present St. Peter's. Recent excavations have uncovered the remains of a shrine which may date from the third century or earlier.

SAINT-QUENTIN, city on the Somme of Roman origin which served as capital of the counts of Vermandois. It took its name from St. Quentin, a bishop who was beheaded there in 287. The Gothic collegiate church (twelfth-fifteenth century), dedicated to him, remains as does the city hall. The town, a popular pilgrimage resort, also became important as a major center of the cloth industry.

SAINT-RIQUIER, ABBEY OF, Benedictine monastery near Abbéville in northern France founded probably in the seventh century and named in honor of St. Riquier who was buried there. In Carolingian times, when Angilbert (d. 814) was abbot, the monastery counted some 400 monks and was noted for the activity of its monks in copying manuscripts.

ST. VICTOR, ABBEY OF. *See* VICTORINES.

SAINT VINCENT, CAPE, a promontory off the southwestern extremity of Portugal. Strabo referred to it as "the most westerly point not only of Europe, but of all the inhabited world." It was here that Henry the Navigator established a naval observatory and a school for navigators c. 1420. The center's location, together with other factors, helped Portugal take the lead in the exploration of the south Atlantic and the coast of Africa.

SAISSET, BERNARD. *See* BERNARD OF SAISSET.

SALADIN (Salah Al-Din), d. 1193, a Kurd, general in the service of Nureddin of Damascus, who in 1171 ended the rule of the Fatimids in Egypt and founded the dynasty of the Ayyubids. In 1174, upon the death of Nureddin, he assumed the title of sultan of Egypt and Syria. In 1187 at Hattin (west of the Sea of Galilee) he destroyed the largest Crusading army ever assembled, captured Jerusalem, and held it despite the valiant efforts undertaken by the Christian West in the Third Crusade (1189–92) to recover the city. The treaty he negotiated with Richard I (Lion-Heart) of England permitted Christians the privilege of visiting the Holy Places without molestation. The most enduring evidence of the high esteen Saladin enjoyed in the Christian world is found in Dante's *Inferno* (IV, 129) where the Moslem chieftain appears in the circle the poet reserved for the great men of the past who, though unbelievers, had lived virtuous lives.

SALAMANCA, city of Leon in west-central Spain whose origins reach back into Roman times. It became a diocesan see in the seventh century, was conquered by the Moors early in the eighth century, and was recovered by the Christians after 1087. Alfonso IX c. 1227 founded its university which in 1255 received extensive privileges from Pope Alexander IV. With the help of Arabic and Jewish scholars the university succeeded in establishing itself as a major center of learning, especially in the fields of philosophy and science. The Old Cathedral, begun c. 1140, is a fine example of late Romanesque.

SALAT, the prayer requirement resting upon Moslems, one of the so-called Pillars of Islam. Moslems must pray five times a day with faces turned toward the holy city of Mecca, the first prayer at sunrise, the last late in the evening.

SALERNO, seaport of Campania, Italy, and the principal city of the province of Salerno. The area became part of the duchy of Benevento after the sixth century, an independent principality in the ninth century. In 1076 Robert Guiscard and his Normans conquered the province. Guiscard is credited with rebuilding the city's chief monument, the Cathedral of St. Matteo. (The crypt of the cathedral is said to hold the bones of St. Matthew.) Because of the mingling there of Latin, Greek, Arabic, and Jewish influences, Salerno gained fame as early as the ninth century as the leading center of medical learning in western Europe. In 1221 Frederick II designated it the only institution in his realm authorized to license teachers and practitioners of medicine. Some scholars refer to this center as medieval Europe's first university.

SALIC LAW, the ancient folk law of the Salian Franks which Clovis, founder of the Merovingian dynasty, ordered to be issued in Latin (c. 507–11). Despite its having been written down in Latin, the law reveals but slight Roman and Christian influence. As with most early law codes, this is preeminently a penal code. For the most part it enumerates crimes and offenses, together with their respective fines and punishments. The most famous of its civil law enactments was that which barred daughters from inheriting lands. On the strength of this principle French lawyers of the early fourteenth century argued successfully that a woman should not succeed to the crown, and neither could males descended from the female line. Certain noble families have adhered to the principle into modern times. [See GERMANIC LAWS, EARLY.]

SALIMBENE, d. after 1288, Italian Franciscan and author of a chronicle that extended from c. 1261 to c. 1288. The chronicle, which reveals the author as a loquacious, boastful, yet pious friar, contains much biographical material concerning important people of the period, including Frederick II, the Holy Roman emperor.

SALISBURY or NEW SARUM, a city of Wiltshire, England, which grew up around the stately Gothic cathedral that commands the town. [See SALISBURY, DIOCESE OF.] Peculiar to Salisbury is the checkered arrangement of its streets. A number of its timber-framed structures, the palace of the bishop, and several churches have survived the Middle Ages. In 1269 the town received a charter licensing it to hold a fair, and from the early fourteenth century it flourished as a center of the wool and cloth trades.

SALISBURY, DIOCESE OF, founded in 1058 with the union of the sees of Sherborne (then including only the county of Dorset) and Ramsbury. In 1075 the see was moved from Sherborne to Old Sarum, then c. 1220 to New Sarum which later came to be known as Salisbury. Salisbury's Gothic cathedral was constructed between 1220 and c. 1260. The tower and spire, the highest in England (404 ft.), were built in the Decorated Style in the fourteenth century.

SALISBURY or SARUM, USE OF, a modification of the Roman rite followed in the diocese of Salisbury. St. Osmund, bishop of Salisbury (1078–99), is credited with having instituted the Sarum liturgical use, although a complete directory of the services as well as statutes and customs of the cathedral were the work of Richard Poore (d. 1237). The Salisbury rite, the most copied of a number used in England in the Middle Ages, included deviations from the Roman in the liturgy, ceremonials, and the breviary. [See RITES, ENGLISH MEDIEVAL.]

SALMAN AL-FARISI, a companion of Mohammed, a Christian in his youth but eventually joining the Prophet in Medina. He has been credited with suggesting to Mohammed the digging of a ditch about the city in a desperate move to withstand a powerful army from Mecca, a device that saved the city and Mohammed's life. Several Moslem mystical orders honor him as an important link in their chains of spiritual authority.

SALOMO, king of Hungary (d. c. 1087), son of Andrew I, who was driven from the country by his uncle Bela but returned in 1063 with the help of his brother-in-law Henry IV of Germany. He was finally overthrown and exiled in 1074 by his nephew Geza.

SALONIKA (Salonica, Thessalonica), seaport city of northern Greece at the neck of the Chalcidice Peninsula, founded c. 315, capital of the prefecture of Illyricum under the emperor Constantine (d. 337), a major center of trade and second only to Constantinople throughout the life of the Byzantine empire. It suffered attacks from a number of powerful foes including Goths, Avars, Slavs, Bulgarians, Arabs, Normans, and finally Turks who devastated the city in 1430 and massacred thousands of its inhabitants.

SALTARELLO, a lively Italian dance known since the fourteenth century.

SALUT, French gold coin struck by King Charles VI (1380–1422). Its name is derived from the *Ave* inscribed on its face. This was the salutation that the Angel Gabriel addressed to Mary (Luke 1:28).

SALUTATI COLUCCIO, d. 1406, humanist and statesman of Florence whose numerous writings included poems and essays composed in classical Latin. He had a major role in inducing Manuel Chrysoloras to come to Florence (1396) and is considered the principal influence in the development of Florentine humanism. His private letters express his views on philosophy and on literary and textual criticism.

SALVE MUNDI SALUTARE, hymn honoring Christ's suffering. The hymn has been credited to St. Bernard of Clairvaux (d. 1153).

SALVE REGINA, one of the oldest and most popular Marian antiphons, often recited or sung at the end of the canonical hours. Its authorship is unknown although it is usually assigned to the end of the eleventh century.

SALVIAN, d. after 480, monk and prior of Lérins, a renowned preacher, teacher of rhetoric, and author of homilies and sacramentaries. His best known work, *On the Government of God,* attributed the capture of Rome by the Visigoths in 410 to God's judgment upon the city's low morals.

SALZBURG, city and province of Austria which originated with the monastery of St. Peter erected c. 690 by St. Rupert on the ruins of a Roman settlement. In 739 St. Boniface made it a bishop's seat. It became an archiepiscopal see in 798 and acquired a charter in 996. The fortress of Hohensalzburg, erected in 1077, provided the monastery and town powerful protection. In 1278 Rudolf I raised its ecclesiastical ruler to the dignity of a prince of the Holy Roman Empire.

SAMARKAND, ancient city beyond the Oxus in Turkestan whose origins reach back at least to the fourth century B.C. The oldest city of central Asia, it long served as the meeting point of Western and Chinese cultures. In 712 the Arabs captured the city. During the ninth and tenth centuries the Samanid dynasty exercised control, but in 1220 it fell to Genghis Khan and was destroyed. It later revived and in 1369 Timur the Lame made it his capital. As a result of his policy of transporting all captured persons who had technical skills to Samarkand, that city soon gained fame as the most magnificent capital of the world. Several remarkable monuments to this fabled era survive, including Timur's mausoleum. Samarkand's palaces, gardens, and paved streets brought it great renown, and caravans from India, Persia, and China combined to make it one of the busiest trading centers of the world.

SAMO, d. c. 660, a Frankish merchant whom Dagobert I, king of the Franks, sent to the Slavs to arrange an alliance with them against the Avars. The Slavs made Samo their king, who then established a regime centered in Bohemia and Moravia.

SAMUEL HA-NAGID, d. 1056, Spanish Jew, statesman, warrior, grammarian, calligrapher, linguist, and poet. He served King Habbus of Malaga and his son Badis as vizier and from 1016 was the virtual ruler of Granada, directing all its military campaigns. He was also a student of Jewish law and the reputed author of a popular introduction to the Talmud.

SANCHO III GARCÉS, d. 1035, called "the Great," began his career in 1005 as king of Pamplona, but through diplomacy, some questionable, and marriage, he managed to establish himself as ruler of the greater part of Spain. His realm included the states of Navarre, Leon, Aragon, and Castile. Unfortunately, this promising move toward establishing the unity of the Iberian peninsula was nipped in the bud when he divided his realm among his four sons. He took no interest in advancing the Crusade against the Moors, but he did encourage the spread of the Cluniac reform movement.

SANCHO VII (d. 1234), called "the Strong," king of Navarre from 1194 to 1234, at first enraged the Christian world by taking service with the Almohads in north Africa — he was something of a swashbuckler — but later he helped crush these same Almohads in the decisive battle of Las Navas de Tolosa (1212). He encouraged the growth of towns and trade by granting many municipal *fueros*.

SANCTORUM MERITIS, breviary hymn of unknown authorship that sings the praises of the saints and the power of their intercession. It appeared for the first time in manuscripts of the ninth century and has been attributed to Rabanus Maurus (d. 856).

SANCTUARY, the area in the church usually reserved for the high altar and the clergy. A communion rail or rood screen might separate it from the nave.

SANCTUARY, RIGHT OF, in Christian Europe the right of the bishop, recognized by Roman law, to protect a fugitive from justice, presumably to intercede in his behalf. In the Germanic kingdoms the church would relinquish protection of a fugitive once the authorities had sworn not to execute him. In England all churches enjoyed the right of sanctuary and a fugitive from the law could take refuge there. He might not be removed, but would take an oath of abjuration before the coroner never to return to the realm, after which he would proceed to a seaport. Should he return without the crown's permission, he would be treated as an outlaw. If the fugitive refused to abjure the realm, he was starved into submission after 40 days. Beyond churches there existed at least 22 places in England in which criminals might find refuge from the royal officials. The fugitive might remain there for life. [*See* ASYLUM, RIGHT OF.]

SANCTUS, a prayer (doxology) or hymn of adoration that opened with the words *Sanctus, Sanctus, Sanctus* (Holy, Holy, Holy). The phrase appeared in a number of hymns, but its most common appearance came in the mass where it concluded the preface and introduced the canon.

SANDWICH, seaport of Kent, one of the Cinque Ports, and the principal naval and military port in England under Henry VII (1485–1509). A number of structures from the Middle Ages remain including St. Bartholomew's hospital which was founded in 1217(?).

SANGALLO, GIULIANO DA, d. 1516, architect and sculptor of Florence whose work reveals him to have been a follower of Brunelleschi. His importance as showing the transition from the Quattrocento to the High Renaissance is best seen in his projects for St. Peter's where he succeeded Bramante as architect in 1514. He also designed a church at Prato and palaces in Florence.

SAN MARINO, a small, poor, largely inaccessible county in the Apennines near the Adriatic and located between Emilia and the Marches. It enjoyed an almost unbroken independent status from the ninth century. Its name came from St. Marinus, a stonecutter from Dalmatia, who erected a monastery there in the fourth century.

SANO DI PIETRO (Ansano Di Pietro Di Mencio), d. 1481, Italian painter, a pupil of Sassetta. He directed a large workshop in Siena which was the principal source of the altarpieces made for that area.

SANTA SOPHIA. *See* HAGIA SOPHIA.

SANTIAGO DE COMPOSTELA, one of medieval Europe's most popular shrines, located in northwestern Galicia a few miles from the Atlantic coast. According to the traditional account, the body of St. James (the Greater) was discovered in a tomb at Padrón in the first half of the ninth century. (Santiago is Spanish for St. James.) A city grew up around the shrine which in the Middle Ages ranked next to Jerusalem and Rome as the most famous and respected place of pilgrimage. Though the military commander of the Caliphate of Córdoba destroyed the town, but not the tomb, in 997, the region remained in Christian hands. The most striking structure from the Middle Ages is the Romanesque cathedral, erected during the eleventh and twelfth centuries, its exterior transformed later by baroque and plateresque additions.

SANTILLANA, IÑIGO LÓPEZ DE MENDOZA, MARQUÉS DE, d. 1458, leading Spanish poet of the period, a scholar and author of sonnets, pastoral poems, and a collection of proverbs. He also translated several Greek and Latin works into Castilian. He is perhaps best known for his ten *serranillas,* charming love lyrics.

SAPPHIRA (Saphira), wife of Ananias. Both husband and wife fell dead when they attempted to defraud the early Christian community in Jerusalem (Acts 5:1–10).

SARACENS, the ancient Arab inhabitants of the northwestern Arabian desert. Christian writers of the Middle Ages might apply the name to all Arabs, or to the Seljuk Turks whom they encountered on the Crusades.

SARAGOSSA, city on the Ebro, whose origins go back to Roman times. It became a bishop's see in the third century. Sueves occupied the city in the early fifth century, then Visigoths, followed by Moors who captured it in 712, when it became the capital of an independent emirate. Charlemagne laid siege to the city in 778 but withdrew when trouble developed back in Saxony. After 1118 when Alfonso I of Aragon took the city from its Almoravid rulers, it served as the capital of the kingdom of Aragon. Abundant works of art, many showing Moorish influence, survive, together with a Gothic cathedral (twelfth-sixteenth centuries) and several churches.

SARAI (Seria), name of two cities on the lower Volga, the one ancient, the other erected by Batu Khan (d. 1255) to serve as the capital of his Khanate of the Golden Horde. It flourished as a center of trade between Europe and central Asia until 1395 when Timur the Lame destroyed it.

SARDICA, COUNCIL OF, summoned by Emperors Constans I and Constantius II at the request of Pope Julius I and convened in 342 (343?). (Sardica is modern Sofia.) The council cleared St. Athanasius of the charge of heresy which the Arians had brought against him, condemned certain eastern bishops as Arians, set the date of Easter for the next 50 years, and approved the right of appeal to Rome, thereby contributing significantly to the principle of papal primacy.

SARDINIA, large island to the west of Italy, occupied by the Vandals c. 456, but restored to Roman (Byzantine) rule in 533–4. Arab attacks began in 711 and endured until 1016, after which Pisa and Genoa vied for control of the island. In 1323–4 Aragon extended its authority over the greater part of the island and by the close of the fifteenth century had completed its conquest. While Aragon rule brought peace, it also entailed heavier taxation, and the economy of the island, which had earlier flourished, now began to decline.

SARMATIANS, a Ural-Altaic nation of pastoral nomads which occupied the region north of the Black Sea from the fourth century B.C. to the fourth A.D. By the close of the fourth century those Sarmatians who had not been assimilated by the Goths, who had come into the area c. 200 A.D., were conquered by the Huns c. 375 and disappeared into history.

SARUM USE. *See* SALISBURY or SARUM, USE OF.

SASSANIDS (Sassanidae, Sassanians), Persian dynasty that ruled from 224 A.D. until 642. It replaced the Parthian empire which Roman armies had destroyed during the reign of Septimius Severus (193–211). At its height, Sassanid rule extended over all of Persia, Mesopotamia, and Armenia, and vigorously contested Byzantine control in Syria and the eastern provinces of Asia Minor. For a short time even Egypt was part of their empire, but by 642 it had disappeared before the rising power of Islam. The most successful and ambitious of the Sassanid rulers was Chosroes I "Nushirwan" (531–79). He brought the empire to the peak of its power and might have forced Byzantine power completely out of Syria and Asia Minor but for resistance offered by Justinian, the greatest of the Byzantine emperors.

SASSETTA, STEFANO DI GIOVANNI, d. 1450, probably the most original artist of Siena in the fifteenth century. He was unusually successful in combining simplicity and courtly sophistication in his painting. His best known work is the altarpiece for the church of S. Francesco at Borgo San Sepulcro with its eight panels showing scenes from the life of St. Francis of Assisi.

SATAN, in the Judaeo-Christian tradition, as well as in Islam, the supreme embodiment of evil. He is called the devil, Lucifer, the prince of the angels, whom God drove out of heaven because of his pride. All three monotheistic religions commonly ascribe the origin of much of the world's evil to the machinations of Satan and his fellow demons, the principal concern of these devils being the destruction of souls.

SATANISM, the cult of Satan or the worship of Satan, in part a survival from ancient times of the worship of demons. It surfaced during the twelfth century and aroused most concern in the fifteenth century when it became associated with witchcraft. [*See* WITCHCRAFT.]

SAVA (Sabas), ST., d. 1236, youngest son of the grand zhupan of Serbia, who left his father's court and became a monk on Mt. Athos. His father later joined him there, then both returned to Serbia where they founded the monastery of Chilandari (Khilandar) which became the center of theological learning in that country. Sava worked so successfully for the political and ecclesiastical unity of Serbia that he is principally responsible for the permanent adherence of the Serbian Church to Constantinople rather than to Rome. His description of his father's last years represents the first original piece of Serbian literature.

SAVONAROLA, GIROLAMO, d. 1498, born in Ferrara, joined the Dominican order, and in 1491 became superior of San Marco priory in Florence. He appears to have been a genuine reformer and during the period of his ascendancy was so recognized by most citizens of the city. The flaming eloquence with which he delivered his attacks on the city, the Medici, the church, the papacy, even the people themselves, won him the enthusiastic acclaim of the populace. From 1495 his autocratic position in Florence resembled that which Calvin would hold in Geneva in the following century. Pope Alexander VI sought to silence the friar, perhaps less because of the attacks he had made upon the pope's own morals than because the papacy was allied with Milan and Naples in an effort to block the invasion of Charles VIII of France which Savonarola had welcomed. Alexander ordered Savonarola to cease his preaching, and when the friar persisted, excommunicated him (1497). The miscarriage of an ordeal which a disciple had agreed to and which would have confirmed the divine inspiration of Savonarola's mission supplied the spark to the opposition that had been building against him. Almost overnight the populace abandoned the saintly demagogue, whereupon he was tried, found guilty of heresy and schism, and executed.

SAVOY, region between Lake Geneva and the Rhône that included the greater part of Piedmont. Burgundians moved into the region in the early fifth century. Early in the tenth century it became part of the kingdom of Arles, and in 1033 of the Holy Roman empire. Because its location gave it control of the approaches to Italy through the Mount Cenis, Little St. Bernard, and Great St. Bernard passes, Savoy found itself continuously entangled in the political affairs and ambitions of the empire, France, and the Lombard League. In 1416 Amadaeus VIII, until then a count, took the title of duke. His jurisdiction, the most extensive Savoy ever enjoyed, included Piedmont, provinces in Switzerland, and several in France, including Nice.

SAXO GRAMMATICUS, fl. 1188–1201, probably a priest, a notary in the service of Absalon, archbishop of Lund, who encouraged him to write the *Gesta Danorum*. This is a chronicle of Danish history that extends from a legendary King Dan to the conquest of Pomerania by Canute VI in 1185. The first nine books drew principally on legend and oral tradition for its material—Hamlet, giants, and national gods are mentioned—, but the last seven, which deal principally with contemporary events, are quite valuable. The first part proved a source of inspiration to Danish romantic poets of the nine-teenth century. Saxo's ornate Latin was the source of his title "Grammaticus."

SAXONS, powerful German tribe located during the first and second centuries A.D. roughly between the lower Rhine and the Elbe. From this area c. 450 they conducted raids against the Franks to the west and against the Romans and Celts in Britain across the North Sea. Occasional Merovingian kings were able to force them to accept their authority for brief periods, but it remained for Charlemagne (768–814) after 35 years of campaigning to finally break the power of this stubborn nation and bring them into submission. He also forced them to accept Christianity.

SAXONY, region in Germany between the lower Rhine and Elbe which went to Louis the German in the partition of the Carolingian empire by the Treaty of Verdun in 843. One of Louis's counts, Liudolf, was recognized as duke of the East Saxons. He gave his name to the Liudolfings who controlled the duchy until 961 when Otto I gave it to Hermann Billung. In 1106 the daughter of the last Billung married Welf, duke of Bavaria, but Henry V granted the duchy to Lothair of Supplinburg who succeeded him as king in 1125. The Welf leader Henry the Lion secured the duchy in 1139 and ruled it, together with Bavaria, until 1180 when Frederick I Barbarossa deprived him of it and the duchy was broken up into numerous fiefs. Extensive territories passed under the control of ecclesiastical rulers, notably the archbishops of Bremen, Magdeburg, and Cologne. Several counties became immediate fiefs of the empire. In 1356 the Golden Bull raised the dukes of Saxe-Wittenberg to the rank of elector—this was a branch of the Ascanian lines of dukes who had received parts of the original Saxony—and this part was afterward known as Electoral Saxony. Ironically this territory had never lain within the frontiers of the original stem duchy of Saxony, so, in effect, Saxony had moved from northwest Germany to east Germany. In 1423 Emperor Sigismund gave Saxony to Frederick the Warlike, margrave of Meissen. In 1485 this Saxony suffered further partition.

SCABINI (French: *échevins*), prominent men from each county whom Charlemagne (768–814) appointed to assist the count in the adjudication of civil disputes and the trial of criminals. It was their responsibility to determine which law, e.g., Lombard, Saxon, or Burgundian, should be enforced.

SCALA SANCTA, that is, Holy Stairs, steps believed to have led to the praetorium of Pilate at Jerusalem and used by Christ at his trial. Helena, the mother of Emperor Constantine (306–37), is supposed to have had the stairs brought to Rome c. 326 and placed in the Lateran Palace.

SCALLOP-SHELL, shell carried by a pilgrim for the purpose of identifying him as such. Recognition as a pilgrim might ensure him certain privileges and protection. Because of this association the scallop figured prominently in ecclesiastical art of the Middle Ages and in the coats of arms of important families. Its presence would indicate that some member of the family had made a religious pilgrimage.

SCANDERBEG (George Castriota), d. 1467, an Albanian or Serb who was reared as a hostage and Moslem, at the court of the Turkish sultan Murad II. The Turks gave him the name Iskender beg (Prince Alexander) in recognition of his prowess in campaigns against the Mongols. In 1442 he abjured Islam, abandoned his friendship with the Turks, and escaped to Albania where he proclaimed himself prince. He managed to hold out against the Turks, in the end virtually alone, in his fortress of Kroia. He remains a national hero of that country.

SCAPULAR, a sleeveless outer garment falling from the shoulders in both front and back and worn by members of the monastic orders. An abbreviated scapular, composed of two pieces of cloth connected by a cord, one worn on the chest, the other on the back, served as a mark of membership in the third orders and was worn by people living in the world.

SCHILTBERGER, JOHANN (or Hans), d. 1440?, Bavarian nobleman and author of the *Reisebuch,* an interesting record of late medieval European history and topography. In 1396 he joined the Hungarian king Sigismund's Crusade against the Turks and was captured at Nicopolis and enslaved. As the sultan's slave he visited Asia Minor and Egypt. Enslaved by the Mongols of Timur the Lame when these defeated the Turks at the battle of Angora (1402), he spent some time in Armenia, Georgia, Samarkand, and southeastern and central Russia. He finally escaped his captors and returned to Bavaria by way of Constantinople and the Carpathians. In his *Reisebuch* he describes his experiences and the countries he saw.

SCHISM, formal and willful separation of a group of believers from the communion and jurisdiction of the Church. It is to be distinguished from heresy since it does not involve doctrine or a dogma of faith, hence the formulation, "heresy is sin against truth, schism sin against charity." Schismatic bishops may continue to ordain and confirm, schismatic priests to say mass and administer the sacraments. The medieval church suffered a number of schisms, the most enduring and serious in its consequences that which severed the unity of the Latin and Greek halves of Christendom in 1054.

SCHISM, WESTERN, a division of obedience among Christians of Western Europe which was precipitated when the cardinals repudiated Pope Urban VI in September 1378 and chose Robert of Geneva, who took the name Clement VII. What inspired this grave step on the part of the cardinals was the domineering, almost abusive, attitude Urban had assumed toward them and his manifest intention of reducing their importance in the governance of the church. They justified their action on the plea that the violence of the Roman populace when they met in conclave had left them no choice but to select Urban VI, an Italian. Clement made his residence in Avignon, Urban remained in Rome, while the countries of Europe permitted political considerations to determine their allegiances. The empire, England, Hungary, Scandinavia, and the greater part of Italy adhered to Urban, while France, Savoy, Scotland, Spain, and Sicily recognized Clement. The refusal of both popes to resign or call a general council to resolve the situation prompted the cardinals to call their own council, which met at Pisa in 1409. There they elected a third pope who took the name Alexander V. Meantime the intransigence of the popes had so encouraged the acceptance of conciliarist ideas that Western Europe readily endorsed the action of Emperor Sigismund who persuaded John XXIII, the successor of Alexander V, to call a general council to meet at Constance (1414–8). The council ended the schism by accepting the resignation of Gregory XII, the Roman pope, and deposing John XXIII, the Pisan pope, and Benedict XIII, the Avignonese pope. [*See* CONSTANCE, COUNCIL OF.]

SCHLESWIG-HOLSTEIN, two provinces located at the base of the Danish peninsula. Schleswig was created a duchy in 1115 by the king of Denmark. Early in the thirteenth century Waldemar II, duke of Schleswig, expelled the German and Slavic lords from Holstein and took possession. A little later (1227) Denmark established its claims to suzerainty over Holstein. From 1386 the county of Holstein exercised jurisdiction over both provinces and in 1460 received recognition of its authority from Christian I, king of Denmark, whom it recognized as suzerain. Still, both duchies were connected with the Danish crown only through personal union

and could not be incorporated into the Danish crownlands.

SCHOLA CANTORUM, a group of singers, composed of boys, young women, lectors, and members of the clergy, that took the lead in antiphonal singing. Some evidence suggests that this organization of singers grew out of reforms instituted by Pope Gregory I (590–604). The first notice of the existence of a separate group of singers in Rome appears in the *Vita (Liber Pontificalis)* of Pope Sergius I (687–701). In the course of time most important churches came to maintain a *schola cantorum*.

SCHOLASTICA, ST., d. c. 543, sister of St. Benedict and founder of the order of Benedictine nuns. She established a convent at Plombariola, a few miles from Monte Cassino.

SCHOLASTICISM, in a broad understanding of the term, the system of Christian theology and thought that accepted the existence of God as a fundamental truth. Other truths concomitant with this basic premise included the existence of a supernatural order of beings, man's ultimate destiny as a full member of that order, and the objectivity of human knowledge. A more precise definition of scholasticism in the medieval context would be the system of thought that dominated the schools of Western Europe from the eleventh to the fifteenth century which had as its objective the clarification of Christian faith through the instrumentality of reason. The origins of this endeavor to apply reason to matters of faith may be traced to the revival of interest in dialectic which took place during the eleventh century. Scholasticism justified its efforts to apply reason to faith on the assumption that a harmony existed between faith and reason since both were the products of God's omniscience. Furthermore, in the judgment of theologians such as Anselm of Bec (d. 1109), the "father" of scholasticism, it was God's wish that man whom he had made in his own image should seek to understand, as far as humanly possible, the truths which the church required him to accept. The scholar most successful in incorporating reason (philosophy) into Christian theology was St. Thomas Aquinas (d. 1274). His success in so doing was in large measure due to his knowledge of Aristotle and to his ability to assimilate that pagan philosopher's thought into the system of Christian theology.

But the emphasis which Aquinas placed upon knowledge, supplemented by faith, as the proper means in the attainment of truth was not shared by all theologians. His contemporary St. Bonaventure (d. 1274) assigned greatest importance to God's grace which must motivate man's will if he is to believe theological truths. Duns Scotus (d. 1308) went even further in disputing the assumptions of Aquinas. He questioned the utility to faith of knowledge based upon experience and natural theology, while William of Ockham (d. 1349) bluntly denied the basic assumption of the Thomists that a necessary harmony existed between faith and reason. The attacks of scholars like Duns Scotus and William of Ockham hastened the decline of scholasticism which was already under way.

SCHOLIUM (Scholia), an explanatory note or comment on a difficult passage in Scripture, usually found in the margins of ancient manuscripts. Its difficulty might rise from such circumstances as variant readings, obscure allusions, or grammatical problems.

SCHONGAUER, MARTIN, d. 1491, German painter and engraver, known also as Martin Schön, whose altarpieces, including the *Madonna of the Rose Bower* in St. Martin's church, Colmar, reveal the influence of Rogier van der Weyden. Only in this work did he approach the genius of van der Weyden, but as an engraver he had no rival in northern Europe. His subjects were usually religious — he shunned the gross or uninspiring — and many survive, including *Madonna in the Courtyard, St. Sebastian, Adoration of the Magi,* and *The Wise and Foolish Virgins.* Until his success in expanding the range of contrasts and textures in engraving, this art had been primarily the domain of the goldsmith.

SCHOOLMEN, teachers of philosophy and theology in the medieval universities.

SCHWARZ, BERTHOLD, probably a German monk who lived in southwest Germany c. 1380. He was an alchemist and for a time was credited with the invention of gunpowder. It is possible that he was the first to manufacture bronze canons, in a foundry he maintained in Venice.

SCHWYZ, Swiss canton east of Lake Lucerne, one of the Four Forest Cantons, which received a grant of imperial autonomy from Frederick II in 1240. Rudolf I of Hapsburg's revocation of this charter in 1274 prompted Schwyz to join Uri and Unterwalden in 1291 in proclaiming the Perpetual Compact. This became the basis for Swiss liberty. [*See* PERPETUAL COMPACT.] The word Schwyz is the English Switzerland.

SCIRI, German tribe located on the lower Vistula in the third century A.D., later moved into Galicia where it became subject to the Huns. Shortly after the death of Attila (d. 453), ruler of the Huns, they suffered attacks by the Ostrogoths, and to protect themselves they took service with the Romans. Odoacer who deposed Romulus Augustulus in 476 is believed to have been a member of this tribe.

SCONE, parish in the county of Perth, Scotland, that contains Old Scone, the site of the royal residence of Scottish kings (1157–1488). Scottish kings may have been crowned on the Stone of Scone or Coronation Stone as early as the tenth century, a tradition that continued until Edward I had it taken to Westminster Abbey (1296), this to remind the Scots that as suzerain of Scotland it was his right to decide who was to serve as king in that northern realm. An Augustinian house, founded by Alexander I c. 1115, superseded a Culdee foundation that had existed there much earlier.

SCOTISM. *See* DUNS SCOTUS, JOHN.

SCOTLAND, country north of England, occupied by the Picts and Scots, and never a part of the Roman empire. Credit for having converted the people is given to St. Columba who founded a monastery on the island of Iona in 563 and many others on the mainland. During the course of the eighth and ninth centuries, Northmen raided the Scottish shores and occupied the Orkney and Shetland Islands, the Western Isles, and the Isle of Man. Kenneth I MacAlpin (d. 858) was the first king to rule over both the Scots and the Picts. The victory that Malcolm II gained over the Northumbrians in 1016 (or 1018) assured Scotland possession of Lothian, while the dynasty that he founded ruled Scotland until the death of Alexander III in 1286. Four years later his granddaughter Margaret the "Maid of Norway," died; she had been betrothed to Edward (II). Edward I who claimed the rights of overlord now came forward and gave the succession to John Balliol (1292–6) over a dozen other aspirants to the throne including Robert the Bruce. But the demands that Edward made upon Balliol led him to revolt and to negotiate an alliance with France. Edward managed to force the resignation of Balliol, but hostilities continued, first against William Wallace, Balliol's regent, whom Edward seized and executed in 1305, then against Robert the Bruce who was crowned king in 1306. The decisive victory that Bruce gained against the English at Bannockburn in 1314 ended any possibility that Scotland could be conquered although the war continued for another 30 years. Edward III defeated the Scots at the battle of Halidon Hill in 1333, then again in 1346 at the battle of Neville's Cross when he captured David II. The principal victors during these years of warfare were the Scottish nobles, several of whom became so powerful that they could defy the king. This was surely true of the Douglas family which controlled a large part of southern Scotland. James I (1406–37) and James II (1437–60) succeeded in humbling the Douglas family, while James III (1460–88)

recovered possession of the Orkney and Shetland Islands from Norway.

SCOT, MICHAEL, d. 1235?, astronomer, mathematician, and astrologer, studied at the leading universities of Europe and took service with Frederick II, king of Sicily and Holy Roman emperor, whom he advised about matters of science and astrology. In 1230 he visited Oxford and introduced there the study of Aristotle. He translated some Arabic texts on astronomy, Averroës's commentaries on Aristotle, and several of Aristotle's own works (e.g., *On Animals*). He also contributed treatises on astrology and astronomy and perhaps some on the subject of alchemy. In Dante's *Inferno* (XX: 115–7), he appears as a magician.

SCOTS, an old Irish folk who had moved into the region of Argyle by the early sixth century. They joined the Picts in carrying on raids against Roman Britain to the south and about the middle of the ninth century united with them under one monarch.

SCOT, THOMAS, d. 1500, born Thomas Rotherhan, chancellor of Cambridge University, chaplain of Edward IV, keeper of the privy seal, bishop first of Rochester, then of Lincoln, in 1480 archbishop of York. He served both Richard III and Henry VII as councillor. He showed himself a generous benefactor of Cambridge University.

SCOTTISH DIALECT, English dialect of the Lowlands, used in the eleventh-century courts, and the official language of Scotland when Malcolm III (1058–93) abandoned Scottish Gaelic and adopted it. The oldest literary monument of the Scottish dialect is *The Bruce* (fourteenth century) by John Barbour. In vocabulary the Scottish dialect retained more archaic terms from earlier centuries than did standard English. The golden age of the dialect as a medium for literary expression came in the fifteenth and sixteenth centuries.

SCOTUS, DUNS. *See* DUNS SCOTUS, JOHN.

SCOTUS (Erigena), JOHN. *See* JOHN SCOTUS ERIGENA.

SCRIBE, a teacher and interpreter of Jewish law, originally a Jewish scholar who knew the art of writing.

SCRIPTORES HISTORIAE AUGUSTAE (Historia Augusta), collection of biographies of Roman emperors from Hadrian to Carus (117–285). It is the work of different writers and lacks both literary grace and reliability.

SCRIPTORIUM, a room, usually in a monastery, where manuscripts were copied. It might also serve as a library.

SCROFULA. *See* KING'S EVIL, TOUCHING FOR THE.

SCROPE, RICHARD LE, archbishop of York, 1398–1405, who joined the opposition to Richard II and helped force his abdication. Though at first a strong adherent of Henry IV, he took part in a revolt headed by the earl of Northumberland in 1405 and led an army against the royal troops. He was tricked into surrendering, then tried, and executed for treason. His reputation for sanctity, together with his execution which some judged a martyrdom, led to the popular belief that miracles took place at his tomb.

SCULPTURE. As the might of Rome declined, so did the work of its sculptors. As late as the second century A.D., the Roman sculptor could prove his excellence in the fields of portraiture and historical relief. How quickly he lost his skill as a craftsman is painfully visible in the squat, stolid figures that adorn the entablature of Constantine's arch of triumph. Only by removing sculptures from earlier structures were Constantine's artists able to lend his arch an attractiveness approaching that of earlier triumphal monuments. The rise of Christianity breathed new life into the art of the sculptor, not so much in terms of the skill he had lost but in new subjects and ideas. It opened to him the rich, imaginative world of symbolism that he had almost forgotten. In the Byzantine empire, the rise of Christianity brought significant change in architecture and wall-covering [*see* BYZANTINE ART], but little in the field of sculpture. Iconoclasm with its fear of images eliminated three-dimensional figures and limited the artist to ivory carving and the products of the goldsmith. [*See* EARLY CHRISTIAN ART.]

With the coming of semicivilized Germans and Celts into the falling Roman empire in the fourth century and the instability of the succeeding centuries, little could be expected in the world of sculpture. Perhaps the best that can still be seen are the figures and ornaments adorning the large stone crosses in Ireland and Britain. The most ambitious of these include panels of figures from the Bible. This kind of sculpture must also have been produced on the continent during the Carolingian period, although none has survived. The most impressive sculpture, at the very end of the troubled period, the early eleventh century, is that which adorns the bronze doors of the cathedral at Hildesheim in Germany. Here panels draw their inspiration from incidents in the Old and New Testaments.

The sculpture of the Romanesque period, roughly the eleventh and twelfth centuries, is as distinctly Romanesque as the heavy walls of the Romanesque church. It had, in fact, lost its identity as an art apart from architecture. Its principal function was that of serving architecture, to decorate the capitals of columns and the areas to the sides and above entrances to churches. Its figures, for this reason, might be elongated, almost columnar, in order to conform to the vertical lines of the structure. The figures tend to be stereotyped and clothed in heavy garments which served to conceal the artist's inability to do more natural work but at the same time enhancing the solemn, almost somber, atmosphere of the building. Subjects and themes are almost wholly from the Bible. Among the most attractive are the figures that appear in the tympanum above the lintel of the twelfth-century church of St. Trophime at Arles. There the seated Christ is shown surrounded by his evangelists, each in the guise of his traditional symbol, e.g., an ox representing Luke.

Gothic sculpture represents a slight though significant advance beyond the function Romanesque set for itself. It still serves architecture though its figures begin to move a bit away from the masonry; they are more lifelike and less stereotyped than the Romanesque; they are inclined to reflect a more enjoyable world than their somber predecessors. The Gothic saint may venture a smile, and the folds of his garment may be looser and more flowing than in the Romanesque, but he still retains the element of the abstract and spiritual, the principal characteristics of medieval art. The *Beau-Dieu* of Amiens cathedral is Christ the man, but he is also God, and the lines of the figure and expression of the face, while sufficiently lifelike to show his humanity, are not so natural as to obscure his godliness.

By the late Middle Ages or Renaissance, the sculptor had moved his figures completely away from the walls of the churches. They were freestanding; they had an existence and an appeal all their own. They were no longer subordinated to architecture. By this time the sculptor had learned his art so well that he could carve and shape figures as natural and lifelike as any from the ancient world. He could present figures of men and women exactly as nature had made them and in whatever pose he chose. To make manifest his skill in portraying the human body in all its natural beauty, he might leave it unclothed. Claus Sluter's *Moses* is the living image of the venerable patriarch of the ancient Hebrews; Donatello's *David,* the still undeveloped young shepherd who slew Goliath.

SCUTAGE, sum that the holder of a knight's fee paid his lord in lieu of military service. This pecuniary commutation of military service which came into use in the twelfth century was most highly developed in England. An impecunious king like John of England might levy the fee more frequently than tradition permitted, so his barons included a check on its use in the Magna Carta (1215) which they forced him to accept.

SCUTARI, a seaport city on the coast of Albania in Roman times which was taken from the Byzantine empire by the Serbs in the seventh century. Until the defeat of the Serbs by the Turks in 1389 at the battle of Kossovo, Scutari served as the seat of the princes of Zeta (Montenegro), who promised it to Venice in return for a subsidy to continue the war against the Turks. In 1479 it was lost to the Turks.

SCYLITZES, JOHN, a Byzantine historian of the second half of the eleventh century whose writings covered the years 811 to 1057. He was a contemporary of Michael Psellus and like him the holder of a high post at the court.

SEBASTIAN, ST., a Christian, possibly of Milan, captain of a cohort of soldiers, who suffered martyrdom at Rome during the persecution of Diocletian (303 – 5). He was shot by arrows, left for dead, then nursed back to health, after which he is said to have presented himself before the emperor Diocletian who had him clubbed to death. His intercession was invoked against the plague. He was a favorite of medieval artists who represented him as a handsome youth pierced by arrows.

SECOND ORDER, the female branch of several mendicant orders in which the members took formal vows and lived in organized communities similar to those of the friars.

SECRET, prayer similar in content to the collect and postcommunion which was recited in silence by the priest. It concluded the offertory part of the mass.

SECULAR ARM, the authority of the state as opposed to that of the church. It was a term used especially in canon law to describe the state or any lay authority that might be concerned in ecclesiastical cases. The most frequent of such cases in the Middle Ages had to do with heresy, when the ecclesiastical court, after having tried and convicted a person of heresy, would turn him over to the secular authority to be punished. Sentences that carried punishments not involving blood, imprisonment, for example, were handled by the church. Punishments involving blood, such as mutilation or execution, were left to the secular authorities.

SECULAR CLERGY, the clergy, principally parish priests, who administered to the spiritual needs of the people under the jurisdiction of a bishop. They were not members of any monastic order. The word *secular* derived from the fact that they lived in the *world* (Latin: *saeculum*) as opposed to monks who remained in their monasteries.

SEDILIA, a set of seats, usually three, located on the south side of the sanctuary where they were used by the officiating clergy (celebrant, deacon, and subdeacon). In medieval England they were often stone benches built into a niche in the wall. On the continent wooden seats were more common.

SEDULIUS SCOTUS, fl. 848–58, Latin scholar of Irish origin, who taught in Liège and Cologne. He composed poems mostly in classical Latin meters, a grammar, and commentaries on the Bible—he took considerable interest in the Greek text of the Bible. His *Collectaneum* consists of moral maxims which he drew from the writings of the church fathers and from such classical authors as Cicero and Seneca.

SEELING, WILLIAM, d. 1494, Benedictine monk and priest, student at Oxford, Padua, and Bologna, and prior of Christ Church, Canterbury. He proved himself a patron of humanism.

SEGOVIA, city of central Spain in Old Castile.

The town was repeatedly taken and lost by the Moors from 714 until Alfonso VI captured it in 1083. It was the favorite residence of the kings of Castile. The aqueduct built by the Romans which was used during the Middle Ages continues to bring water into the city. The principal monument from medieval times is the alcázar, a stronghold built mainly in the fourteenth and fifteenth centuries but since then extensively restored.

SEGOVIA, JOHN OF, d. after 1456, Spanish theologian, a leading conciliarist at the Council of Basel who was created a cardinal by the antipope Felix V. Following his reconciliation with Rome, which cost him his cardinalship, he served as bishop of several sees. He left an account of the proceedings that took place at Basel.

SEIGNEUR, feudal lord to whom the vassal owed knightly service and to whom the serf or peasant owed servile service.

SEIGNORIAL SYSTEM. *See* MANORIALISM.

SELJUK (Saljuk, Salchuk, Selchuk) TURKS, Turkish people of central Asia which under their chieftain Seljuk moved into the region of Bukhara during the second half of the tenth century where they embraced the religion of Islam. With Tughril Beg as their leader they captured Baghdad in 1055 and reduced the caliph to the position of a puppet. Under his nephew Alp Arslan (1063–72) they overran Georgia and Armenia and defeated the Byzantine army led by Emperor Romanus IV Diogenes at Manzikert in 1071. Within a short time they had conquered the greater part of Asia Minor and had established their capital at Nicaea. Their successes precipitated the First Crusade (1096–9). The Seljuk Sultanate of Roum (Rum) in western Asia Minor survived until 1243.

SEMI-PELAGIANISM. *See* PELAGIUS.

SENESCHAL, a Frankish official who was given

charge of the royal estates; an official who administered a manor in the name of his lord; a French royal official from the thirteenth century, often a member of the nobility, who exercised both judicial and military authority over a district or province.

SENLIS, city northeast of Paris, a royal residence from the time of Clovis (d. 511). Vestiges remain of walls from both Roman and medieval times. Notable structures from the Middle Ages are the twelfth-century Gothic cathedral of Notre Dame and a town hall (fifteenth century). Here in 1493 Charles VIII signed a treaty that ceded Franche-Comté, Artois, and Charolais to Maximilian I of Germany.

SENS, town of north-central France, leading city of the Roman province of Lugdunensis, and an archiepiscopal see in the fourth century. Several important church councils were held in Sens, including the one in 1140 which condemned some of the writings of Abelard as heretical. Its principal monument from the Middle Ages is the famous cathedral of Saint-Etienne (c. 1130-sixteenth century), one of the earliest of Gothic churches. Carvings from the twelfth – thirteenth centuries embellish the three portals to the west. The magnificent stained glass windows date from the twelfth to the seventeenth century. The cathedral's treasury, one of the richest in France, contains ancient fabrics and liturgical vestments, among the latter some worn by St. Thomas Becket.

SENTENCES, short reasoned expositions of Christian doctrine. The term is derived from the Latin word *sententia* which originally meant any exposition of thought. In the Middle Ages it acquired the new technical meaning that limited it to exegesis. The most famous collection of *Sentences* was that of Peter Lombard (d. 1160) which served as the standard text in theology until the adoption of Aquinas's *Summa Theologiae*.

SENTENTIARY, a student learned in the *Sentences* of Peter Lombard.

SEPTUAGESIMA, the third Sunday before Ash Wednesday and therefore the ninth Sunday before Easter. It marked the beginning of the penitential season which would shortly move into Lent and was introduced liturgically with the use of purple vestments and the omission of the *Gloria* and *Alleluia*.

SEPTUAGINT, the earliest and most influential extant Greek translation of the Old Testament. This was prepared during the third and second centuries B.C. from the original Hebrew. In the third century A.D. Origen compared a number of Greek and Hebrew versions of the Old Testament in an effort to halt further degeneration of the text and to establish one which would become standard. The Septuagint served as the basis for the Old Latin, Coptic, Ethiopic, Armenian, Georgian, Slavonic, and part of the Arabic translations of the Old Testament. Jerome's Vulgate (fourth century), which that church father based principally on the ancient Hebrew, ultimately emerged as the accepted version of the Old Testament in the Latin church. [*See* VULGATE.]

SEQUENCE, a Latin hymn introduced into the mass on special occasions or on feastdays in a musical setting following the *Alleluia* and before the singing of the gospel. The best known of the sequences, the *Dies Irae,* was incorporated into the liturgy of masses said for the dead. Sequences made their appearance in the ninth century and some 50 have been credited to Notker Balbulus (d. 912) of the monastery of St. Gall who may have been their originator.

SERAPHIC DOCTOR. *See* BONAVENTURE, ST.

SERAPHIM, members of the highest order of angels, ranked above the cherubim and the other seven "choirs" of angels. Their earliest appearance is in Isaiah 6:2–6, where the prophet tells of a vision in which he beheld them as six-winged creatures standing before the throne of God and singing his praises.

SERBIA, land of the Serbs, a South Slavic people that moved into the Balkans during the seventh century A.D. The first *zhupan* or chieftain to come to view was Viseslav (c. 780). The evangelization of the Serbs was largely accomplished during the tenth century by the disciples of SS. Cyril and Methodius. Until 1167 the Serbs generally lived under Byzantine rule or that of the Bulgars. In that year Stephen Nemanja (Nemanya), grand *zhupan*, established the independence of his people from Byzantine rule. In 1217 Pope Honorius III crowned Stephen I, son of Nemanja, king of the Serbs. During the interval between the decline of Byzantine power after the death of Basil II (d. 1025) and the rise of the Ottoman Turks, Serbian power reached its height. The most successful and ambitious of the Serbian kings was Stephen Dushan (Dusan) (1331–55). He conquered all of Macedonia, founded the Serbian church as an independent patriarchate, assumed the title "Czar of the Serbs and Greeks," and was leading an army against Constantinople when he died. Almost immediately followed defeats suffered at the hands of the Ottoman Turks, including a crushing disaster at Kossovo in 1389 which left the Serbs no alternative but to accept Turkish suzerainty. What they retained of autonomy the Turks took from them in 1459.

SERBIAN ORTHODOX CHURCH, established in the latter part of the ninth century when disciples of St. Methodius (d. 885), with the help of Slavonic translations of the Scripture and liturgical books, succeeded in converting the pagan Serbs. In 891 the king recognized Christianity as his country's official religion. Because of the location of Serbia on the line dividing Latin and Greek influences, its ultimate adherence to the Greek Orthodox church was not finally assured until the early thirteenth century. St. Sava established an independent Serbian church in 1219 and in 1375 the Serbian patriarchate received recognition from Constantinople. In 1459 Turks overran the country and abolished the patriarchate which was not revived until 1557.

SERF, the semifree peasant who worked his lord's land (demesne) and paid him certain dues, usually in kind, in return for the use of acres, the possession (not ownership) of which he had inherited from his father. The serf was representative of the majority of peasants in western Europe from the eighth to the fourteenth century when serfdom began to decline. From the thirteenth century, the terms serf and villein were largely synonymous, whereas earlier, especially in France, the villein was free even though saddled with rents and services. The variations in the degree of subjection among serfs were as numerous as they were confusing. The serf in France, for example, ceased working his lord's land in the thirteenth century, but paid instead a heavier *taille* (tallage) than his cousin in England who enjoyed quite as much freedom despite the *corvée* charge his lord continued to exact.

Serfdom emerged as an institution in a period of natural economy during the unstable sixth, seventh, and eighth centuries when men either lost their freedom (and lands) to their stronger neighbors or surrendered them voluntarily in return for protection. The major factor in the decline of serfdom in the later Middle Ages was the rise of a money economy which enabled the serf to substitute a fixed money rent for his labor charge. Not long after he ceased working the lord's land the serf gained his freedom. [See MANORIALISM.]

SERGEANT (Serjeant), a servant who accompanied his lord to battle; a horseman of lower status who was used in the light cavalry. In England the term sergeanty or serjeanty was applied to a type of tenure in which a man owed service to the king or lord, usually of a nonknightly character. He might be expected to make bows and arrows, serve in his lord's winecellar, or carry the lord's banner. Still he paid the feudal dues of wardship, marriage, and relief but no scutage since he performed no knight's service. The practice of granting land in return for such services dated from the Norman Conquest and had all but ceased by the late twelfth century.

SERGIUS I, ST., Pope, 687–701, a priest of Rome who was born in Palermo of Syrian parents. As pope he defied the Byzantine emperor and rejected those decrees of the Trullo Council (692) that were contrary to Roman practice, such as the canon that sanctioned married clergy. He introduced the *Agnus Dei* to the mass and encouraged Willibrord's missionary work among the Frisians.

SERGIUS II, Pope, 844–7, member of the Roman aristocracy who, although consecrated without informing Lothair I, subsequently had the Romans swear an oath of loyalty to the emperor. The bulk of the construction undertaken in Rome during his pontificate was the work of his brother Benedict. During his pontificate Saracens ravaged Rome and plundered the churches of St. Peter and St. Paul.

SERGIUS III, Pope, 904–11, a Roman deacon and bishop of Cere. His approval of a fourth marriage for the Byzantine emperor Leo VI lowered the prestige that the Latin church had been enjoying in the East. He worked in close alliance with the family of Theophylact who headed one of the factions in Rome. He may have had a son by Theophylact's daughter Marozia, the future Pope John XI. He declared a number of his papal predecessors, including Formosus, John IX, Benedict IV, and Leo V, to have been antipopes and refused to recognize any of their official acts.

SERGIUS IV, Pope, 1009–12, a Roman, bishop of Albano, and a partisan of the Crescentii against the Tusculani. These were the leading factions in Rome at the time and between the two of them, Sergius was helpless.

SERGIUS I, d. 638, patriarch of Constantinople from 610 and an exponent of Monothelitism. This was the name given to his analysis of the nature of Christ, namely, that Christ possessed two natures but only one will. [*See* MONOTHELITISM.] He proposed this interpretation in an effort to reconcile the views of the Monophysites with those of the adherents of Chalcedonian orthodoxy. His position satisfied no one and was condemned by the pope and by the Sixth Ecumenical Council of Constantinople (681).

SERGIUS AND BACCHUS, SS., two fourth-century martyrs who suffered martyrdom during the persecution of Diocletian. According to legend, both were officers of the Roman army on the Syrian frontier. When they refused to offer sacrifice to Jupiter they were sent to Rosafa in Mesopotamia, where they were scourged so brutally that Bacchus died. Sergius was later beheaded. The two saints were honored as protectors of the Byzantine army.

SERGIUS OF RADONEZH, ST., d. 1392, Russian spiritual leader, monastic reformer, and mystic, to whom the monastery of the Holy Trinity (Troitse-Sergiyevo) near Moscow owed its fame as a center of the religious and social life of the nation. Of noble birth, he lived for a time as a hermit, took monastic vows in 1337, and in the course of his life founded some 40 monasteries including the famous monastery of the Holy Trinity, thereby reviving the religious life of Russia which the Tartars had all but destroyed. He refused the office of metropolitan and remained a humble, hard-working member of his monastic community despite the widespread renown his sanctity won him and the many people, noble and peasant, who came to seek his counsel and blessing.

SERJEANT. *See* SERGEANT.

SERVITES, also known as Order of Friar Servants of St. Mary, founded in 1233 by seven wealthy Florentines, St. Bonfilius and six companions (the Seven Founders). They adopted the Rule of St. Augustine, wore a black habit, and observed the strict poverty of a mendicant order. The order which in its constitutions shows heavy Dominican influence, combined the principles of monastic and eremetical life. It practiced great devotion to the Blessed Virgin.

SERVIUS, fl. c. 400, Latin grammarian of Rome, teacher and author of a valuable commentary on Virgil. He had such great respect for Virgil that he judged his thought to be the highest truth. His commentary is extant in two versions, the first and longer one paying special attention to grammatical and stylistic points.

SERVUS SERVORUM DEI, "servant of the servants of God," a title first used by Gregory I (590–614) in his official documents and in general use since Gregory VII (1073–85).

SEVEN DEADLY (CAPITAL) SINS, seminal sins which are the fountainheads from which actual sins are sprung. They include pride, avarice, lust, envy, anger, gluttony, and sloth.

SEVEN LIBERAL ARTS. *See* LIBERAL ARTS.

SEVEN SLEEPERS OF EPHESUS, seven young Christian soldiers who according to a famous legend fell asleep in a mountain cave near Ephesus where they had gone to pray in preparation for their execution during the persecution of Decius (c. 250). When they awakened a century or more later, they found that the people of the area had become Christians. The legend enjoyed wide acceptance in the Christian world and even in Islam since it appeared to affirm belief in the resurrection of the dead, and the supposed cave long attracted both Christian and Moslem pilgrims.

SEVENTY-FOUR TITLES, COLLECTION OF, a compilation of some 300 ordinances, principally papal, which were organized under 74 titles. The work was probably that of Bernold of Constance (d. 1090). Among other matters included in the ordinances were the rights of the papacy as against those claimed by the secular authority.

SEVERINUS, Pope, May 28, 640, to August 2, 640, a Roman who defined the Latin position concerning the nature of Christ. He had been elected shortly after the death of Honorius I in October 638, but was not consecrated until May 640 because the emperor Heraclius refused to ratify his election pending his acceptance of the *Ecthesis*. [*See* MONOTHELITISM.]

SEVERUS, FLAVIUS VALERIUS, Roman emperor, 306–7, officially the Western Caesar under Constantius I who invested him with authority over Italy, Africa, and Pannonia. When Constantius died in July 306, Galerius, the Augustus in the East, made him Augustus of the West, but a revolt broke out precipitated by discontent over Severus's moves to disband the praetorian guards and impose a poll tax on the citizens of Rome. Maxentius, son of Emperor Maximian who had abdicated, headed the revolt and eventually captured Severus and had him beheaded.

SEVERUS IBN AL-MUKAFFA, late tenth-century bishop of Ushmunein (Upper Egypt), the author of numerous theological writings and a *History of the Patriarchs of Alexandria*. This last work contains much information about the church in Egypt, Nubia, and Ethiopia.

SEVERUS OF ANTIOCH, d. 538, monk and hermit who founded his own monastery near Gaza. While patriarch of Antioch (512–8) he was twice forced to flee to Egypt when his Monophysitism aroused imperial hostility in Constantinople. He left many sermons, 4,000 letters, and numerous theological treatises on the subject of Christ's nature. Some scholars consider him the father of Monophysitism. [*See* MONOPHYSITISM.]

SEVERUS SANCTUS ENDELECHUS, Christian rhetorician and poet of the fourth century.

SEVILLE, city in southwestern Spain (Andalusia) that rose from Roman origins. It served as a Vandal capital in the early fifth century, fell to the Visigoths a little later, and in 712 to the Moors. From 1023 to 1091 it was the capital of an Abbadid dynasty, then of the Almoravids and Almohads. During the period of Moslem rule Seville was one of the leading cultural centers of western Europe and a flourishing exporter of olive oil. In 1248 Ferdinand III, king of Castile and Leon, captured the city, after which it remained in Christian hands. The finest structure from the Moorish period is the Alcázar palace which was begun in 1181. Another famous reminder of Moorish art is the tower of the Church of San Marcos, once the minaret of a mosque. The cathedral, one of the world's largest Gothic structures, was begun in 1402 and completed by 1519. It contains the tomb of Columbus.

SEXAGESIMA, the second Sunday before Lent, the eighth before Easter. It fell within the semi-penitential period which began with Septuagesima, the preceding Sunday.

SEXT, the part of the divine office that was recited at the sixth hour, that is, at noon; also the title in canon law of the sixth book of decretals which Pope Boniface VIII promulgated in 1298. It contained the decretals that had been issued since the publication of five books by Gregory IX (1234).

SFORZA, ruling family of Milan, 1450–1535, during the period when France and the rulers of Germany and the Holy Roman empire fought for control of north Italy. Muzio Attendolo, d. 1424, the first prominent member of the family, was the son of a peasant of Romagna and served a number of *condottieri*, including Alberico da Barbiano who gave him the nickname of Sforza because of his great strength. Muzio was successful in acquiring lands and titles in Romagna and Naples but lost his life when he became involved in the wars over the Neapolitan succession. His son Alessandro, d. 1473, acquired possession of Pesaro in the Papal States. His natural son Francesco, d. 1466, the most powerful *condot-*

tiere of his day, held the March of Ancona in the Papal States for 14 years, lost it, but then married the illegitimate daughter of the last Visconti duke of Milan, Filippo Maria. He overthrew the republic, which had been proclaimed when his father-in-law died, with the help of the Medici and in 1450 made himself duke. For 16 years he gave Milan a despotic but enlightened government. Francesco's son Ascanio became a cardinal but was more a credit to humanism than to the church. Another son, Galeazzo Maria, d. 1476, who succeeded his father as ruler of Milan, though dissolute and cruel, was a patron of letters and the arts. He was cut down in the church of San Stefano in Milan by republican conspirators. Galeazzo's power passed after a period of violence to his brother Ludovico il Moro (the Moor), so called because of his swarthy complexion. (He was the youngest son of Francesco.) Ludovico is remembered for his patronage of such artists as Leonardo da Vinci and for his part in having Charles VIII of France invade north Italy. He had concluded an alliance with the French king in order to protect himself from the king of Naples. In 1495 he turned against Charles and helped drive him from Italy. In 1499 Louis XII of France marched into Italy and drove Ludovico from his duchy. He was eventually captured and died in a French prison (1508). Ludovico was typical of many of the Renaissance princes of Italy—powerful, wealthy, a wily diplomat, and an unscrupulous intriguer.

SHAFI'I, AL- (Abu 'Abdallah Mohammed Ibn Idris Al-Shafi'i), d. 820, one of the greatest of Islamic jurists, the founder of the Shafi'i school of canon law. This school accepted only solid analogy with the Koran or *hadith*, not extended parallelisms, as a valid basis in the application of Islamic law. Shafi'i also gained fame for his knowledge of classical Arabic and old Arabian poetry.

SHAPUR (Sapor) II, d. 379, king of Persia during the Sassanid period, called the Great for his generally successful efforts in maintaining (actually expanding) the frontiers of his realm and the measures he took to advance the unity and prosperity of his people. He recovered territories the Arabs had seized during his minority, strengthened his hold on provinces along his eastern frontier, and gained possession of upper Mesopotamia and suzerainty over Armenia. These last two accomplishments were at the expense of Rome against which empire he reopened hostilities in 337. He defeated the armies of Constantius II, while that of Julian which was heading toward the capital of Ctesiphon was forced to retreat and the emperor was slain. Less successful were his efforts to force all his people to accept Zoroastrian orthodoxy despite his harsh persecution of all dissidents including Christians.

SHARAF AL-DIN, 'ALI YAZDI, d. c. 1435, Persian poet and historian whose book *Zafar-Name* constitutes the principal source for the history of the reign of Timur the Lame.

SHENOUTE OF ATRIPE, d. 466, abbot of the White Monastery (Deir Auba Chenouda) in Egypt for more than 80 years. During his administration this community of monks and nuns observed a monastic rule even more austere than that adopted by St. Pachomius. In 431 he accompanied St. Cyril, the archbishop of Alexandria, to the Council of Ephesus where he helped refute the views of Nestorius. Shenoute left many letters, sermons, and spiritual exhortations.

SHERIFF, Anglo-Saxon official who was the chief administrative and judicial officer of the shire. The Norman kings retained him, entrusted him with protecting the crown's judicial and military rights in the shire, and invested him with authority to execute all royal writs. The subsequent introduction of the itinerant justice, coroner, and justice of the peace progressively reduced the importance of his office.

SHIITES, Moslems who drew away from the majority Sunnites and insisted that the succession (caliphate) in Islam should descend through Ali (d. 661), the Prophet's cousin and the husband of his daughter Fatima, and the father of Hasan and Husain. They had never accepted the succession of Mu'awiya who after the assassination of Ali had made himself caliph. They maintained that their *imams* (religious leaders) were all descendants of Ali through his son Husain, that these *imams* were infallible, and that they were Allah's appointed rulers over the Islamic community in spite of the fact that few of them attained the office of caliph.

SHILLING, silver coin used originally by the Carolingians and introduced into England in the fourteenth century.

SHIPS. An important departure from the type of ships used in Roman times came with the introduction of the lateen sail. Byzantine and Moslem seamen found this more satisfactory than the square sail since, on its long sloping yard, it could be carried so as to receive the wind on either side. In the West the most efficient ship was that which the Vikings sailed on their plundering expeditions along the western shores of Europe and the British Isles. These ships might carry a mast as high as 40 feet, although they also depended on oars projected through holes in the bulwarks. The ships that William the Conqueror used in his invasion of Britain were long and double-ended, with a rectangular sail placed athwart the middle. The introduction of the rudder c. 1200 heralded a major change in the history of shipping. The rudder added to the efficiency and maneuverability of the ship and led necessarily to a differentiation between bow and stern. About this time Venetians and Genoese were building ships that had two and three decks and were a hundred feet in length and almost half that in width. By the closing centuries of the Middle Ages when seamen had learned to tack and greater reliance could be placed on sails, the use of oars disappeared, a development that permitted the greater part of the hold to be reserved for cargo. By the close of the Middle Ages ships of three and four masts were being used, the largest presenting eight sails to the wind. The smooth, carvel-type surface of the ships used in southern Europe had pretty well displaced the clinker-built kind used in the north.

SHIRE, the English county. The shire court conducted the administrative, financial, and judicial business of the people living in the county. It dates from at least the middle of the tenth century, therefore, from Anglo-Saxon times, and it represented one of the few institutions the Normans judged useful enough to preserve. Through the sheriff whom the king appointed, the crown could expect to exercise more authority in the provinces than was possible where feudalism prevailed as in France.

SHORE, JANE, d. 1527, mistress of Edward IV from c. 1470. Although she wielded considerable influence over the king, according to the testimony of Thomas More in *Richard III,* it was never to any man's hurt. Richard III had her accused of sorcery and forced her to do public penance as a harlot. She died in penury.

SHREWSBURY, town northwest of Birmingham, once a Saxon and Norman stronghold. Ruins remain of an eleventh-century castle and abbey, as well as a number of old bridges and churches. Some of the oak-timbered, black-and-white houses are from the fifteenth century. In 1403 Henry IV defeated Henry Percy (Hotspur) on a plain near Shrewsbury and had the rebel's body displayed in the town to convince the townspeople of his death.

SHREWSBURY, EARL OF, title first held by Roger de Montgomery (d. 1094), a Norman baron. The title lapsed in 1102, but was revived in 1442 for John, Lord Talbot, who served against the Welsh and from 1419 in the Hundred Years' War against the French. He was present at the siege of Orléans, was later captured at

Patay and held a prisoner for four years. His defeat and death at Castillon in Aquitaine in 1453 terminated English rule in that province.

SHROUD, HOLY, the Shroud of Turin, according to pious tradition, a linen cloth about 14 ft., 3 in. long and 3 ft., 7 in. wide, which was the burial cloth of Christ. It has been preserved in Turin, Italy.

SHROVETIDE, the three days before Ash Wednesday, that is Shrove Sunday, Monday, and Tuesday. The term Shrove Tuesday was the most common since the faithful went to confession (they were "shriven") on that day in preparation for Lent.

SIBERT OF BEKA, d. 1332, Carmelite of Cologne, regent of theology at Paris and provincial prior of the order in Germany. He was the author of an ordinal used by the Carmelites, several theological treatises, and a refutation of Marsilius of Padua's *Defensor Pacis.*

SICARD OF CREMONA, d. 1215, teacher of canon law and theology at Paris, bishop of Cremona, and papal legate to Germany. He was the author of a universal chronicle (to 1213) which is a major source for the history of the Crusade of Frederick I Barbarossa [*see* CRUSADES], an important treatise dealing with the liturgy, and an important *Summa* on the *Decretum* of Gratian.

SICILIAN VESPERS, revolt of the Sicilians against the French rule of Charles I of Anjou in 1282 which began at the hour of vespers on Easter Monday in a church outside Palermo. It led to the expulsion of the French and the conquest of the island by Peter III of Aragon who had married the daughter of Manfred. (Manfred had ruled Sicily from 1258 to 1266.) The Sicilians had appealed to Aragon for assistance against King Charles when he transferred his capital from Palermo to Naples, a move which left Sicily to be governed by French officials whom they hated. The uprising resulted in a massacre of the 2,000 French men, women, and children. The War of the Sicilian Vespers followed.

SICILY, largest and most populous island of the Mediterranean. Its medieval period began with the weakening of Roman rule and Vandal raids in the fifth century, followed by its conquest by the Ostrogoths. The island returned to Byzantine rule under the emperor Justinian in 535, and for the following two centuries many Greeks migrated to the island from the eastern Mediterranean. Arab conquest of the island in the ninth century brought in many Arabs from north Africa, and this mingling of Latin, Greek, and Arabic influences made Sicily one of the leading cultural centers of western Europe. In 1060 Normans from Normandy invaded the island, and in 1130 Roger II became its first king. Though he held Sicily only nominally under papal suzerainty, the link with Rome kept Sicily enmeshed in the affairs of the papacy and the great powers until the close of the Middle Ages. The most critical period came during the reign of Frederick II, king of Sicily and king of Germany, whose ambition to rule not only Germany and Sicily but also all of Italy involved him in a death struggle with the papacy. In order to prevent Frederick's successors from attaining this ambition, the pope invited Charles of Anjou, brother of Louis IX of France, who ended German rule in Sicily and established his own regime (1266). This French period ended in 1282 with the Sicilian Vespers after which followed several centuries during which Sicily was part of the kingdom of Aragon. Decline set in almost immediately and where Sicily had once been a leader in the economic, political, and cultural developments of Europe, it now took on the character of a backward state.

SIDONIUS APOLLINARIS, d. c. 488, Roman official in Gaul, bishop of Clermont, and author of poems, panegyrics, and letters, the latter a valuable source for the history of the period. He is regarded as the last representative of classical culture.

SIEGFRIED (Seyfrid, Seifried, Sigurd), hero of the *Nibelungenlied*. He was considered the personification of all manly virtues. In the German epic he is the conqueror of Brunhild and the husband of Kriemhild, but he was murdered by Hagen at the instigation of the vengeful Brunhild.

SIENA, city of Etruscan origin and a bishop's see in the fifth century. Early in the twelfth century a free commune replaced a government run by counts and bishops. Later that century, because of its traditional rivalry with Florence, it became the center of Tuscan Ghibellinism in opposition to the Guelf interests which controlled Florence. From about 1277, shortly after the death of Manfred who had been the leader of the Ghibellines, a Guelf oligarchy in Siena allied itself with Florence. The fourteenth century ushered in a period of economic decline. Siena's university dates from the thirteenth century. Its cathedral, begun as a Romanesque structure in the twelfth century, was later transformed into one of the finest examples of Italian Gothic. Siena flourished as a center of art from the thirteenth century until the close of the Middle Ages.

SIENA, SCHOOL OF, flourished from the thirteenth century until the close of the Middle Ages and was characterized by a preference for the decorative beauty and grace of late Gothic. It was also noted for its polychromed wooden sculpture and the popularity of religious themes which it presented with a unique, gentle charm. Representatives of the school included Duccio di Buoninsegna, his pupil Simone Martini, Sassetta, Matteo di Giovanni, and Bartolo di Fredi.

SIGEBERT I, d. 575, Frankish king of Austrasia during the Merovingian period. He married Brunhild, daughter of the Visigothic king of Spain, while his half-brother Chilperic I of Neustria married her sister Galswintha. At the instigation of his mistress Fredegund, Chilperic had Galswintha murdered and then married Fredegund. Some time later Chilperic attacked

Austrasia but was defeated by Sigebert who succeeded in overrunning Neustria and was on the point of being proclaimed its king when he was murdered by Fredegund.

SIGEBERT OF GEMBLOUX, d. 1112, monk of the Benedictine monastery of Gembloux (near Brussels), the author of polemical tracts that disputed the claims of Pope Gregory VII in the political world, some hagiography, and a world chronicle to 1111. This chronicle offers valuable historical information from the year 1024.

SIGER OF BRABANT, d. c. 1282, considered a leading representative of "Latin Averroism." (Some scholars dispute the justice of that identification.) His views, which he revealed in the course of teaching theology at Paris, drew attack from both St. Thomas Aquinas and St. Bonaventure. What drew their fire were his commentaries on Aristotle in which he examined tenets of that pagan philosophy that could not be reconciled with Christianity, e.g., the eternity of the world. His critics charged Siger with holding to the position that some of Aristotle's principles, while inconsistent with Christian theology, could be true in the realm of philosophy. When the bishop of Paris condemned several of Siger's opinions, he fled to Rome where he died. Dante placed him in paradise (*Paradiso* X, 133-8).

SIGISMUND (Sigmund), Holy Roman Emperor, 1433-7, king of Hungary (1387), king of Germany (1411), and king of Bohemia (1436), a member of the house of Luxemburg, and the son of Emperor Charles IV. He was persuaded to take the initiative in convening the Council of Constance (1414-8). In 1396 he and his Crusading army suffered an overwhelming defeat at Nicopolis at the hands of the Ottoman Turks. Although unsuccessful in his campaigns against the Hussites, his approval of the Compacts of Prague in 1436 brought peace to Bohemia. He granted Brandenburg to the house of Hohenzollern and the electorate of Saxony to the Wettins. The marriage of his daughter to Albert V of Austria, of the house of Hapsburg (the future Albert II), united the two most powerful families of central Europe.

SIGNATURA, APOSTOLIC, supreme tribunal of the church which was concerned with questions of procedure and rights. It evolved from the practice of the referendarius of the twelfth century who received petitions and presented them to the pope for his disposition.

SIGNORELLI, LUCA, d. 1523, Italian painter whose work featured a sculptural rendering of figures and a representation of action with emphasis upon muscular development. The fresco series he did for the cathedral of Orvieto with its scenes of *The End of the World* and *The Last Judgment* illustrate his artistry.

SIGURD I, king of Norway, 1103-30, called Jorsalafar (Jerusalem-farer). He set sail for the Holy Land c. 1107 but stopped to visit England, France, Spain, and Sicily on the way. Baldwin I, king of Jerusalem, gave him a cordial welcome when he arrived. When he reached Constantinople, he left his ships there as a gift to the emperor Alexius I and returned overland to Norway. During his reign he strengthened the defenses and worked to stabilize the administration of the church by introducing tithes.

SIGURD. *See* SIEGFRIED.

SILESIA, district to the east of the upper Oder. It was occupied by the Siling branch of the Vandals until they moved west about the middle of the fourth century and the Slavs moved in. The Polish Piasts controlled the area from the tenth century until 1163 when Frederick I Barbarossa organized the region into two duchies and encouraged the immigration of German merchants, peasants, and artisans. The king of Bohemia claimed the province from the fourteenth century although with limited success. Silesia supported Emperor Sigismund in the Hussite wars, while Matthias I Corvinus, king of Hungary, ruled the province from 1469 to 1490. When he died Bohemia recovered control.

SILVERIUS, ST., Pope, June 536 to November 537, the son of Pope Hormisdas (born before his father became a priest). He incurred the anger of Theodora, Emperor Justinian's consort, because of his opposition to Monophysitism and to the patriarch Anthimus. Although the evidence is not wholly dependable, it appears that she secured his exile to the island of Palmaria (Ponza) where he died.

SILVESTER GUZZOLINI, ST., d. 1267, studied law at Bologna and Padua, became a regular canon, then a hermit. In 1231 he founded a monastery at Montefano near Fabriano, Italy, which observed the Rule of St. Benedict although it practiced greater austerity than the Rule required. His order, known as the Sylvestrine Benedictines, was approved by Pope Innocent IV in 1247.

SIMEON, ruler of the Bulgars, 893–927, the first such leader to call himself czar. He proved himself a more dangerous threat to Byzantium than his rough predecessor Krum (d. 814). Thrace and Adrianople fell to him, as did all of Greece to the Gulf of Corinth. He also extended his rule over the Serbs and might have made himself master of Constantinople but for the rise of Romanus Lecapenus to the imperial throne.

SIMEON METAPHRASTES, ST., d. c. 984, also known as Logothetes and Magistros, the most famous of the Byzantine hagiographers. His *Menologion* in ten volumes contains the lives of 148 saints based on information that he took from various older collections. He acquired his name from the fact that he revised the narratives stylistically in order to make them more readable to his contemporaries. So popular did his *Menologion* prove that older collections of saints ceased to be read or copied, resulting in the disappearance of many pre-Metaphrastean lives. Simeon also left letters, religious poetry, and a universal chronicle.

SIMEON OF DURHAM, d. c. 1130, Benedictine monk and chronicler. His best known work is a history of the see of Durham from its establishment in 635 at Lindisfarne to 1096. In all probability he is also the author of a general chronicle of English history for the years 848–1118 which is based on the writings of Asser and Florence of Worcester. His name is also linked with a narrative of the years 1119–29 that is partly Eadmer's.

SIMEON STYLITES (the Elder), **ST.** *See* STYLITES.

SIMOCATTES, THEOPHYLACT, fl. sixth or seventh century, Byzantine historian, author of a valuable history covering the reign of Emperor Maurice (582–602). Among the sources that he was able to consult were official documents of the imperial government. He was also the author of a work dealing with natural history and a number of literary exercises in epistolary form.

SIMON DE MONTFORT. *See* MONTFORT, SIMON DE.

SIMON ISLIP, d. 1366, member of the ecclesiastical courts in Lincoln and London, keeper of the privy seal, archbishop of Canterbury (1349), and founder of Canterbury Hall at Oxford.

SIMON LANGHAM. *See* LANGHAM, SIMON.

SIMON MAGUS, a sorcerer according to Acts 8:9–24, who was converted to Christianity but rebuked by St. Peter when he sought to purchase spiritual power to work miracles. He gave his name to simony. [*See* SIMONY.]

SIMON MEPHAM, d. 1333, doctor of theology, archbishop of Canterbury (1328), and active politically during the early years of the reign of Edward III. He suffered papal excommunication when he insisted upon his right to visit the Abbey of St. Augustine in Canterbury.

SIMON, ST., one of the 12 apostles.

SIMONY, the buying or selling of spiritual things including church offices. The term derived from

Simon Magus who attempted to purchase the gift of the Holy Spirit from SS. Peter and Paul (Acts 8:9–24). The first legislation aimed at curbing the buying of church offices was enacted by the Council of Chalcedon in 451. From the feudal period (c. ninth century) to the close of the Middle Ages, the principal target of legislation intended to suppress simony was the traffic in benefices. This traffic became common throughout western Europe because of the prevalence of regalian and other proprietary rights over prelacies and churches.

SIMPLICIUS, ST., Pope, 468–83, pope who had an uneventful pontificate despite continued controversy in the East between the Monophysites and the Orthodox. It was during his pontificate in 476 that Odoacer deposed Romulus Augustulus.

SIMPLICIUS, sixth-century Greek philosopher of Cilicia and author of commentaries on several of Aristotle's works. After the closing of the Platonic School in Athens, he spent some time in Persia. He believed that Plato and Aristotle were in essential agreement with one another.

SIN, defined as the deliberate disobedience of a creature to the known will of God. Its acceptance as a constant factor in the experience of the people of God and of the world stems from the sin of Adam, an explanation that Jews, Christians, and Moslems in general endorse. The prophets of the Old Testament constantly warned the Hebrews of the punishments that the anger of God over their sins would bring upon them whether in this life or in the life to come. Christianity found little to quarrel with in this ancient view of sin although much thought was devoted to the subject by the church fathers and the theologians of the high Middle Ages. Neither orthodox Hebrews nor Christians ever subscribed to the Manichaean view that evil was a substance and that the created universe, including man's body, was inherently evil, although

heretical movements such as Catharism did find many adherents in Christian Europe.

SINBAD, hero of a collection of tales of sea adventures collected by a Persian of the first half of the tenth century. The tales were later incorporated into the *Thousand and One Nights.*

SINTRA. *See* CINTRA.

SIRICIUS, POPE, 384–99, a Roman who is credited with issuing the oldest surviving papal decree (decretal). In this decree, to Himerius, bishop of Tarragona, he proposed relatively lenient treatment of penitents. Several of his letters affect a tone of authority as for example in the one he addressed to the bishops of Gaul, Spain, and Africa concerning the disciplinary canons reached by a Roman synod. His pontificate marked a significant stage in the development of papal authority.

SIRVENTE, Provençal verse form employed in the treatment of serious subjects.

SISINNIUS, Pope, January 15 to February 4, 708, a native of Syria, who ordered the walls of Rome strengthened against the threat posed by the Lombards and the Saracens.

SISTINE CHAPEL, private chapel in the Vatican palace erected by Pope Sixtus IV in 1473, whence the name. It is famous for its decorations, above all Michelangelo's frescoes of scenes from the Old Testament and his *Last Judgment.* Frescoes by other artists, including Botticelli, also adorn the chapel. The origin of the group of singers associated with the chapel, known as the Sistine Choir, has been traced to the *Schola Cantorum* that Pope Gregory I (590–604) inaugurated.

SIXTUS I, ST., Pope, 116? to 125?, probably a Roman although in all probability not a martyr. He was the successor of Alexander I and thus the sixth bishop of Rome.

SIXTUS II, ST., Pope, 257–58, successor of Stephen I. He upheld the validity of baptism when administered by heretics and thereby restored relations with St. Cyprian and the churches of Africa and Asia Minor which had supported that position. Sixtus's predecessor had rejected their judgment.

SIXTUS III, ST., Pope, 432–40, a Roman priest who was known to St. Augustine. As pope he became involved in controversies over Pelagianism and the nature of Christ. He rebuilt the Lateran baptistery and directed the reconstruction of the Liberian Basilica of Saint Mary Major on the Esquiline Hill.

SIXTUS IV, Pope, 1471–84, Francesco Della Rovere by name, a Franciscan, general of his order (1464), and cardinal (1467). He succeeded Paul II and was expected to be a reformer, but he permitted himself to become so embroiled in political ambitions that he proved a disappointment on that score. He was an excellent administrator, improved and beautified Rome, built the Sistine Chapel, supported humanism, but failed in his efforts to organize a Crusade against the Turks. His greatest failing was the excessive interest he showed in advancing the fortunes of his nephews, while his choice of cardinals was dictated more by political considerations than merit. He became involved in a struggle with Louis XI over control of the church in France, sought to block that king's ambitions in Naples, and undertook a war against Florence. He consented to the establishment of the Spanish Inquisition, but all efforts he made to suppress its illegal procedures and to mitigate the severity of its judgments were ignored. Jews expelled from Spain found a haven in the Papal States.

SKALD, name given to ancient Scandinavian poets, principally those of Norway and Iceland, during the ninth and tenth centuries.

SKELTON, JOHN, d. 1529, English poet, rhetorician, and priest, tutor of the princes at the court of Henry VII. He translated several classical works (Cicero's *Letters* and Diodorus Siculus's *Historical Library*), but he is best known for his satires against the clergy such as *Bowge of Courte* (1499). A form of verse he frequently used — short lines, alliterative verse with insistent rhymes, sometimes repeated through several sets of couplets (Skeltonics) — influenced several later poets. In 1499 Erasmus referred to Skelton as "the incomparable light and glory of English letters."

SLAVS, a prolific people, an eastern branch of the Indo-European family which about the fourth century A.D. was located in the area between the Vistula and Dnieper rivers and north of the Carpathians. In the course of the fifth century, following the collapse of the Hunnish empire (455), several tribes of Slavs, including the Czechs, Poles, Moravians, and Slovaks moved westward, while the Serbs, Slovenes, and Croats moved to the south. These last made their first attack on Constantinople in 540. During this century and those immediately succeeding, they occupied the greater part of the Balkans and, less by conquest than by force of numbers, eventually absorbed most of the other peoples of the area.

SLOTH, one of the seven capital sins. Theologians defined sloth as an indifference in spiritual matters.

SLOVAKS, a west Slavic folk of central Europe. The Slovaks moved into the land to which they gave their name from Silesia during the sixth or seventh century. They were first subject to the Avars, then in the ninth century became part of a Moravian state and were converted by SS. Cyril and Methodius. In the early tenth century, when the Magyars destroyed the Moravian state, they became subject to Hungarian rule.

SLOVENES, a south Slavic people that moved into the region of the eastern Alps from western Russia around the close of the sixth century.

SLUTER, CLAUS, d. 1406, Dutch sculptor who did much of his work in the employ of Philip the

Bold, duke of Burgundy, in the Carthusian monastery at Champmol near Dijon. Sluter was considerably ahead of his time in his ability to individualize his subjects. A distinctive mark of his art was the heavy folds with which he draped his figures. His best known work, the *Well of Moses,* presents Old Testament prophets as powerful individuals, each a psychological study.

SMOLENSK, city on the upper Dnieper which was captured by Oleg, prince of the Varangians, in 882. It became a member of the Hanseatic League in the thirteenth century and fell to the Lithuanians in 1404.

SMYRNA, great and famous seaport city of Turkey on the Aegean Sea, an early center of Christianity, and one of the Seven Churches of Asia Minor (Revelation 2:8). It fell to the Seljuks in the eleventh century but was restored to Byzantine rule during the First Crusade (1096–9). When the Byzantine empire fell in 1204 it became part of the empire of Nicaea. In 1261 Constantinople recovered the city but in return for the assistance it had received from Genoa it surrendered virtual possession of Smyrna's economic and political life to that Italian state. Smyrna again fell to the Seljuks c. 1300, and in 1402 Timur the Lame sacked the city. In 1424 it fell to the Ottoman Turks.

SNORRI STURLUSON, d. 1241, Icelandic poet, historian, and statesman, the author of the *Prose Edda,* a treatise on poetry, the *Heimskringla,* and probably the *Egils Saga.* The *Heimskringla* traces the history of the kings of Norway from mythological origins to 1184. In the *Prose Edda* the author describes and interprets the heroic legends of Norway.

SOCAGE, a kind of tenure in feudal England by which free men, usually farmers but below the level of knights, held land. The socager owed services similar to the aids and incidents exacted from knights.

SOCRATES (Scholasticus), d. c. 450, a lawyer of

Constantinople who continued Eusebius's *Ecclesiastical History* to 439. It is generally objective.

SOFIA, city of Bulgaria, once a Roman settlement. It suffered destruction by the Goths and the Huns. During the period of Byzantine control, it served as a strategic point in the defense of the area from the reign of Justinian (527–65) until the Bulgars captured it in 810. The city fell to the Turks in 1382, then in 1443 was burned by western Crusaders.

SOISSONS, city of France located on the Aisne river; it served as the capital of the Roman province of Belgica. St. Crispin and St. Crispinian were martyred there c. 286. Clovis and his Franks defeated Syagrius in a decisive battle in 486, thereby ending all vestige of Rome's authority. The city served as capital for several Merovingian kings. It was one of the towns in that part of France that the Vikings could not take. The communal charter of the town dates from 1131. At a synod held at Soissons in 1121 some of Abelard's views suffered condemnation. The town suffered severely during the Hundred Years' War. The cathedral, begun in the twelfth century, survives, as do extensive remains of the magnificent Abbey of Saint-Jean-des-Vignes where Thomas Becket spent some of his exile, and the abbey church of Saint-Léger. The wealthiest of all abbeys in Soissons, that of Saint-Médard, served as a burial place of Merovingian kings.

SOLIDUS, gold coin struck by Emperor Constantine I c. 312. It continued in use in the Byzantine empire until 1453.

SOLOTHURN, Swiss canton on the upper Aar, occupied by the Alemanni in the fifth century. In 888 it passed under the rule of the king of Burgundy. It was incorporated into the German empire in 1032 but in 1481 became a member of the League of Upper Germany (Switzerland).

SOMERSET, English ducal title held by the Beaufort family from 1397, when Richard II granted it to John Beaufort, eldest son of John of Gaunt by Catherine Swynford, until 1471, when Edmund, the last of the male line, was executed following the battle of Tewkesbury. The most eminent of the dukes was Edmund, son of the first duke John, who was one of the most powerful political figures in the country from the 1440s until his death at the battle of St. Albans in 1455.

SONG OF ROLAND. *See* ROLAND, CHANSON DE.

SONNET, a poem normally of fourteen lines and with rhymes arranged according to some definite scheme such as that employed by Petrarch. It appeared in Italy in the thirteenth century.

SORBON, ROBERT DE, d. 1274, theologian at the University of Paris, confessor of Louis IX, author of sermons and of treatises on moral and spiritual subjects. In 1257 he founded the home (college) for poor students of theology which gave its name to the present Sorbonne.

SORBONNE. *See* SORBON, ROBERT DE.

SORDELLO DI GOITO, d. 1270, the most famous troubadour of Italy to compose in Provençal. On his travels, which took him to Verona, Spain, and southern France, he found Charles of Anjou (Charles I of Naples and Sicily) his most generous host.

SOREL, AGNES. *See* AGNES SOREL.

SOTER, ST., Pope, 166? to 174?, obscure bishop of Rome, probably from Campania.

SOTTIE, a farce that satirized social and political life. It proved popular in northern France from the middle of the fifteenth century.

SOUTHWARK, one of the oldest sections of London. Chaucer had his pilgrims gather at the Tabard Inn in Southwark preparatory to continuing on to Canterbury. It lay south of the Thames at the end of London Bridge.

SOZOMENOS (Sozomen, Salaminius Hermias), d. c. 450, Byzantine church historian who continued Eusebius's *Ecclesiastical History* from 324 to 439. He wrote in an elegant style.

SPAIN, a country that embraced the whole of the Iberian peninsula except for Portugal, and achieved unification in 1479 after the marriage in 1469 of Ferdinand (II) of Aragon and Isabella of Castile. The country, which had been Romanized to a considerable degree, particularly in the south and southeast, retained a good measure of its classical culture despite the waves of Vandals, Sueves, Alans, and Visigoths that swept into the peninsula during the first half of the fifth century. The kingdom established by the Visigoths ruled the greater part of the country until the appearance of the Moors in 711. By 719 the Moors had conquered the entire peninsula with the exception of Galicia in the northwest. In 756 Abd ar-Rahman, the only member of the Omayyad dynasty to survive the purge carried out by the triumphant Abbasids in 750, founded an emirate with Córdoba as his capital. In 929 the ablest representative of these Spanish Omayyads, Abd ar-Rahman III (912–61), proclaimed himself caliph. During his reign and the century following, Córdoba ranked as the most populous and culturally advanced city west of Constantinople. In 1031 the caliphate, which was already in decline, disintegrated into a number of petty Moorish kingdoms of which the most important was that of the Abbadids. In 1086, in response to the plea of the Abbadids for aid against Alfonso VI of Castile, the Almoravids came in from north Africa and extended their rule over all Moorish-held Spain. In 1147 another Berber dynasty, the Almohads, overwhelmed the Almoravids, and ruled the southern half of Spain until 1212 when they suffered a decisive defeat at the battle of Las Navas de Tolosa. From this defeat Moslem power never recovered. The sole Moorish principality able for long to preserve its autonomy was Granada which succumbed to the armies of Ferdinand and Isabella in 1492.

Meanwhile Christian states had undertaken

the long task of reconquering the peninsula from the Moors. The process began in Galicia in the northwest which had managed to retain its independence. The first loss of territory which the Moors sustained was to Charlemagne (d. 814) who carved out the territory between the Pyrenees and the Ebro, known as the Spanish March, to add to his empire. During the tenth and eleventh centuries the kingdoms of the Asturias, Leon, Navarre, Castile, and the county of Barcelona (Spanish March) undertook the crusade against the Infidel although they were never hesitant about seizing territories from their Christian neighbors when the opportunity arose. Ferdinand I of Castile (1035–65) extended his authority over Leon, drove the Moors south of the Tagus, and forced the kings of Seville and Toledo to recognize his suzerainty. His son Alfonso VI (1065–1109) captured Toledo, then managed to hold what he had conquered with the valiant assistance of Rodrigo Diaz de Vivar, "El Cid." His grandson, Alfonso VII (1126–57), even anticipated for a brief moment the ultimate unification of Spain by extending his influence over the county of Barcelona and forcing the rulers of Aragon and Navarre to recognize his title of "Emperor of all Spain." The thirteenth and fourteenth centuries brought only trouble to Castile, as the crown involved itself first in wars with Portugal, Aragon, and Navarre, then in the Hundred Years' War as a result of the dynastic struggle between Peter (Pedro) the Cruel (1350–69) and his half-brother Henry of Trastamara. Henry (II) eventually won out, but repeated concessions to the feudal aristocracy by the kings of Castile had meantime made its power so formidable that the very existence of the monarchy was threatened. Had it not been for the support of the towns and their brotherhoods (*hermandades*), Castile might have disappeared. The monarchy reached its nadir during the reign of Henry IV (1454–74), then revived somewhat under his half-sister Isabella (1474–1504), whose marriage in 1469 to Ferdinand of Aragon heralded the early unification of the peninsula.

Aragon, which showed itself the most aggressive of the Spanish states during these later Middle Ages, started unobtrusively as a small kingdom in the Pyrenees. About 1051 it won its independence from Navarre, and later under Alfonso I (1104–34) it captured Saragossa from the Almoravids. The marriage of its heiress in 1150 to the count of Barcelona (Catalonia) led to the union of the two states under the leadership of the more industrially advanced Barcelona. In 1235 the Balearic Islands were occupied and in 1238 Valencia was captured from the Moors. Aragon's most ambitious acquisition came in 1282 when the Sicilians invited Peter (Pedro) III to be their king. He had married Constance, daughter of Manfred, the natural son of Emperor Frederick II, and was, therefore, the heir to the Hohenstaufen claims to Sicily. In 1297 Aragon gained Sardinia, even the duchy of Athens for the period 1311–88, while Alfonso V (1416–58) secured the crown of Naples for himself. As his viceroy in Aragon he appointed his brother John, and it was John's son Ferdinand (II) who ascended the throne in 1479. In 1469 he had married Isabella of Castile. As joint rulers of Castile and Aragon, these "Catholic Kings" as they had been entitled by the pope, proceeded to deprive the feudal aristocracy of many of their traditional rights and possessions, instituted the Inquisition (1478) to establish religious uniformity throughout their lands, and in 1492, the year Columbus discovered the New World for them, extinguished Granada, the last of the Moorish states.

SPANISH INQUISITION, an entirely new tribunal, not to be associated with the medieval inquisition, which Pope Sixtus IV created in 1478 upon the request of Ferdinand and Isabella of Spain. Its purpose, the establishment of complete religious uniformity in Spain, was aimed initially at Jews and Moslems who had failed to leave the country but had accepted baptism simply to escape punishment. It later rigorously suppressed any deviation from what was judged orthodox doctrine. The Spanish monarchs organized a Supreme Council of the Inquisition and placed it under the direction of the Dominican Tomás de Torquemada, who served as inquisitor general until his death in 1498.

SPANISH MARCH, region between the Pyrenees and the Ebro over which Charlemagne (d. 814) extended his authority. [See BARCELONA.]

SPEYER, city on the left bank of the Rhine in the Lower Palatinate which had earlier been a Celtic and then a Roman settlement. It was destroyed by the Huns (c. 450), was rebuilt, and became a bishop's see in the seventh century and a royal residence during the Carolingian period (after 800). In 1111 it was made a free imperial city, but its ruler, a bishop and prince of the Holy Roman Empire, held substantial territories on both sides of the Rhine. Its Romanesque cathedral (tenth century), one of the finest in Germany, contains the tombs of eight emperors.

SPHRANTZES, GEORGE, d. close of the fifteenth century, Byzantine historian and logothete whose writing covers the years 1413–77. A later edition of his chronicle extended the narrative to the accession of the Palaeologi in 1261.

SPINA, ALFONSO DE, d. c. 1491, a convert from Judaism who became a Franciscan, then superior of the Franciscan house of studies at Salamanca, and finally bishop of Thermopylae. He was an eloquent preacher and the author of sermons and apologetical writings.

SPINELLO ARETINO, d. 1410, Italian painter, probably trained in Florence, whose altarpieces and frescoes made him the most popular narrative painter of his day. In order to expedite his work the artist did not hesitate to borrow scenes and characters from the masters.

SPIRITUAL FRANCISCANS, name given to those members of the Franciscan order who demanded a strict observance of the Rule of St. Francis regarding the possession of property. The controversy over poverty proved a most disruptive issue during the late thirteenth and fourteenth centuries. Most of the Spirituals eventually accepted the modified rule adopted by the order under papal direction. Some later joined the Clareni or the Observants. Several hundred suffered imprisonment or death as a result of the harsh measures undertaken by Pope John XXII (1316–34). The most extreme who repudiated papal authority were known as Fraticelli. [See FRANCISCANS; CLARENI; FRATICELLI.]

SPLIT, a seaport city of Dalmatia from ancient times and possessing the best harbor on the Adriatic coast. The huge, extensive palace which the emperor Diocletian built there (295–305), provided the nucleus of the town that grew up in the seventh century. The inhabitants of nearby Salona found refuge from the Avars within the tremendous walls of the palace. Diocletian's mausoleum has served as a cathedral since that same century. Given its excellent location Split soon became a flourishing commercial port and its possession was much sought after by its neighbors. It remained under Byzantine rule until 1068 when it fell to Croatia, then was fought over principally by Hungary and Venice until 1420 when the latter prevailed.

SPOLETO, city in Umbria, just above Rome, whose origins reach to Etruscan times. It became an episcopal see in the fourth century and the capital of a major Lombard duchy c. 570, when it included the greater part of Umbria, the Marches, and the Abruzzi. In 1155 Frederick I Barbarossa destroyed the city but it was rebuilt. It remained under the formal overlordship of the Holy Roman emperor until 1201 and soon after came under direct papal rule. Spoleto boasted a local school of painters in the late Middle Ages. Many fine churches remain from medieval times, the most important the twelfth-century cathedral which has a magnificent fresco by Fra Filippo Lippi *(Coronation of the Virgin)*. The massive Rocca (fortress) built for Cardinal Albornoz in 1364 dominated the city.

SPY WEDNESDAY, in Irish use, the Wednesday before Good Friday, the term derived from Judas's betrayal of Christ on that day.

SQUARCIONE, FRANCESCO, d. 1468, painter and sculptor, sometimes called the founder of the School of Padua because of the many artists, including Mantegna, Zoppo, and Schiavone, who served their apprenticeship in his workshop. He showed a taste for antique art and spent much effort in the collection of art pieces from the classical period.

STABAT MATER, hymn (sequence) honoring the Sorrowful Mother at the cross. The hymn is probably of thirteenth-century origin although its former ascription to Jacopone da Todi (d. 1306) is now questioned.

STAINED GLASS. *See* GOTHIC ART.

STALL, in church architecture, a fixed seat enclosed at the back and separated from adjacent stalls by high projecting arms. Stalls were often placed in one or more rows along the sides of the chancel in cathedral, monastic, and collegiate churches where they were occupied by the clergy. They were often richly carved and generally surmounted by canopies. The seats could usually be folded back so as to permit the occupant to stand or kneel. Beneath the seat might be fixed a small bracket, the *miserere* or misericord, which afforded a slight rest for the person while standing.

STALLAGE, fee paid by merchants for the privilege of displaying their goods in stalls at a fair.

STAMFORD BRIDGE, BATTLE OF, battle fought in northern England in 1066 and won by Harold the Anglo-Saxon against the forces led by his brother Tostig and by Harald III Hardraade, king of Norway. The latter had advanced a claim to the English throne left vacant by the death of Edward the Confessor. Both Tostig and Hardraade were among the slain.

STANISLAUS, ST., d. 1079, bishop of Cracow from 1072, the first Pole to be canonized (1253), and the patron saint of Poland. He was accused of joining in a Bohemian-German plot to unseat King Boleslaw II, was found guilty by the royal court, and was sentenced to death by dismemberment. When the knights hesitated to carry out the sentence, the king himself slew the bishop in St. Michael's church. The tragedy remains an unsolved mystery since Polish historians exculpate the bishop. Poles consider him a saintly bishop who was murdered simply because he excommunicated a cruel and licentious king. His body lies beneath the main altar of the cathedral church in Cracow.

STAPELDON, WALTER DE, d. 1326, bishop of Exeter from 1308. He helped rebuild Exeter cathedral and founded Stapeldon (Exeter) Hall at Oxford. While lord treasurer (from 1320) he worked to reform the royal exchequer. He was murdered by a London mob because of his association with the misgovernment of Edward II.

STAR CHAMBER, a court set up by Henry VII in 1487 for the purpose of suppressing the widespread lawlessness of the times and ending such practices as that of arrogant lords maintaining bands of retainers with which they browbeat judges and seized what estates they might covet. The court itself was really an older court which was now commissioned to handle criminal cases without any common-law precedents to hamper its actions. The name derived from the starred ceiling of the room in which it met. Although the history of this special court is principally that of the sixteenth century, within a dozen years of its establishment it had succeeded in bringing to England a measure of tranquillity it had not enjoyed in more than a century.

STATUTE, a legal enactment of particular importance which the king of England promulgated after consulting parliament and securing its assent. Its force was expected to be permanent, as opposed to the more temporary character of the royal ordinance.

STATUTE OF LABORERS, law enacted in 1351 which fixed wages and prices in an effort to prevent laborers from exploiting the shortage of labor created by the Black Death in 1348.

STEELYARD, MERCHANTS OF THE, merchants of the Hanseatic League who were in residence at the League's headquarters in London. They secured wide privileges from Henry II (1157) who was anxious to promote commerce, but their success, often at the expense of local merchants, made them unpopular. They remained in London until the reign of Elizabeth (1558–1603).

STEPHEN I, Pope, 254–7, the first bishop of Rome after Victor I (189? to 198/9) who exercised authority over the entire Christian church. He was probably the first bishop of Rome to refer explicitly to the Petrine doctrine. The question concerning the validity of baptism when administered by heretics disturbed his pontificate.

STEPHEN II, Pope, March 23 to 25, 752, a Roman priest who had so brief a pontificate that he is frequently omitted from the list of popes. He died before his episcopal consecration.

STEPHEN II, Pope, 752–7. He appealed to Pepin III, king of the Franks, in 754 against the Lombards who had invaded papal territory. Pepin undertook two campaigns against the Lombards, then in 756 turned over the disputed territory, essentially the exarchate of Ravenna, to the pope. [See DONATION OF PEPIN.]

STEPHEN III, Pope, 768–72, owed his office to the intervention of Desiderius, king of the Lombards, who came to his assistance against an aristocratic faction in Rome which had put up its own pope. He later came to fear the Lombards and for that reason objected to the marriage of

Charlemagne to Desiderata, daughter of Desiderius.

STEPHEN IV, Pope, June 816 to January 817, a member of the Roman aristocracy. He crowned Louis the Pious in Reims in 817. He established as a principle the superiority of the spiritual authority over the secular in all matters concerning faith and morals.

STEPHEN V, Pope, 885–91, a priest of Rome. He was pope during the period of instability that attended the disintegration of the Carolingian empire. He supported the German hierarchy in its efforts to block the introduction of a Slavonic liturgy into Moravia.

STEPHEN VI, Pope, 896–7, bishop of Anagni who as pope presided at the posthumous trial of his predecessor, Pope Formosus (891–6), and declared his acts invalid. A subsequent revolt led to his deposition and murder.

STEPHEN VII, Pope, 928–31, cardinal priest who owed his appointment to Marozia who had arranged the murder of his predecessor John X (914–28). He lent his support to the Cluniac reform movement.

STEPHEN VIII, Pope, 939–42, cardinal priest, a protégé of Alberic of Spoleto, the ruler of Rome. He supported the Cluniac reform movement.

STEPHEN IX, Pope, August 1057 to March 1058, brother of Godfrey, duke of Lorraine, a leading adviser of Pope Leo IX (1049–54), abbot of Monte Cassino, and cardinal priest. As pope he advanced the work of the reformers Peter Damian and Humbert of Silva Candida and consulted with Hildebrand (Gregory VII) over problems of church reform.

STEPHEN, king of England, 1135–54, count of Blois, nephew of Henry I, and grandson of William I. Henry I had required his barons to swear that they would recognize his daughter Matilda as regent for her son Henry (II) when he died, but they repudiated their oaths, partly because of their hatred of the Angevins (the young Henry's father was the count of Anjou), partly because they were confident Stephen would prove an easy-going monarch. Stephen's long but weak reign was marked by feudal turbulence and by attempts by Matilda to place her son Henry on the throne. In 1153 Stephen agreed that Henry should succeed when he died.

STEPHEN I, ST., king of Hungary, 997–1038, the first king of Hungary who assumed that title in the year 1000. Tradition has it that he received the crown from Pope Sylvester II. He completed the conversion of his people and organized his country and government after the manner of the Germans. In the course of accomplishing these objectives, he put down revolts by his pagan nobles who opposed his pro-German policy. The crown that Pope Sylvester II sent to him for his coronation became the sacred symbol of the Hungarian national state.

STEPHEN DUSHAN (Dusan), king of Serbia, 1331–55, the most powerful and successful of the rulers of medieval Serbia. He conquered Macedonia, Albania, Epirus, and Thessaly, and in 1345 proclaimed himself "Czar of the Serbs and the Greeks." He issued a code of laws and established an independent Serbian patriarchate. His dream of conquering all the Balkans died with him as he was leading his army toward Constantinople. [See SERBIA.]

STEPHEN HARDING, ST., d. 1134, English monastic reformer. He entered the abbey at Sherborne, later joined the community in Molesme, Burgundy, then with 20 other monks moved to Citeaux because of its more austere rule. In 1109 he became the abbot at Citeaux, but the community there had all but reached the point of extinction when Bernard (of Clairvaux) and his 30 companions arrived. Much of the organization of the Cistercian order may be credited to Harding, at least the regulations governing the relations between the abbey at Citeaux and its many filiations.

STEPHEN OF MURET, ST., d. 1124, founder of the Order of Grandmont, a semi-eremetical institution. He established its mother house in the mountains at Muret north of Limoges.

STEPHEN, ST., d. c. 36, one of the seven deacons selected by the apostles to serve the growing Christian community in Jerusalem. He was the first Christian to suffer martyrdom (Acts 7:59).

STEWARD, official appointed by a feudal lord (king) to administer the affairs of his household or of a manor. He was ordinarily a freeman and served as the lord's representative.

STIGAND OF CANTERBURY, d. 1072, bishop of Elmham and of Winchester, then translated to Canterbury (1052) after Earl Godwin regained his powerful position at the court of Edward the Confessor and the Norman archbishop, Robert of Jumièges, had fled. William the Conqueror waited until 1070 before deposing the Saxon Stigand.

STIGMATIZATION, defined as the reproduction on or in the human body of the wounds that Christ suffered during his Passion. These might include wounds in the hands, feet, head, shoulders, and side. They were considered a visible sign of participation in Christ's Passion. The first person believed to have received the stigmata was St. Francis of Assisi (on his hands, feet, and side). From that time the number of persons with the stigmata has increased. The Church has reserved judgment concerning the genuineness of such stigmata.

STILICHO, FLAVIUS, a Vandal, master of the troops under Emperor Honorius who was his son-in-law. By calling in troops from the northern frontier, Stilicho managed to keep Alaric and the Visigoths out of Italy, but in 408 his enemies gained the ear of Honorius and he was executed on the charge of treason.

STOCKHOLM, leading city of Sweden, first noted in 1252, that owed its rapid growth to its extensive trade with the Hanseatic League.

STOLE, long strip of cloth worn about the neck with ends falling in front or crossed over the breast. Members of the clergy wore a stole when taking part in liturgical functions.

STOSS, VEIT, d. 1533, German sculptor, engraver, and woodcarver whose earliest work was the altar and massive altarpiece he made for St. Mary's church in Cracow between the years 1477 and 1489. His style, which tended to be dramatic and monumental, showed some indifference to matters of detail, even for the correct proportions of the human body.

STRALSUND, PEACE OF, treaty of 1370 that ended the war between Waldemar IV of Denmark and the Hanseatic League. Waldemar agreed to permit the Hansa free trade throughout Danish territory, free passage through Danish waters, and possession of four castles in Scania which would assure them control of the Sound.

STRASBOURG (Strasburg), city located on the left bank of the Rhine in Alsace, of Celtic origin. It probably became a bishop's see in the fourth century. It was destroyed by the Huns but was revived by the Franks who occupied the site toward the close of the fifth century and gave the town its name. In 842 it served as a meeting place for Charles (the Bald) and Louis (the German) when they confirmed their alliance against their brother Lothair in the so-called Strasbourg Oaths. Charles took his oath in Old High German, Louis in Old French. In the thirteenth century it received the status of a free imperial city. The city was the home of Gottfried von Strasburg (fl. 1210), one of the leading poets of medieval Germany, and it may have been in Strasbourg that Gutenberg invented the printing press.

STRASBOURG OATHS. *See* STRASBOURG.

STROZZI, aristocratic family of Florence, prominent from the second half of the thirteenth century. Its leaders, who were usually opponents of the Medici, spent long intervals in exile. Filippo Strozzi, d. 1491, a merchant and banker of Naples, built the famed Palazzo Strozzi after the Medici permitted him to return to Florence in 1461.

STUDION (Studiu, Studios) MONASTERY, famous monastic community in Constantinople founded 462 or 463. Its members, called Studites, exercised powerful influence in the Eastern church in matters of both theology and ecclesiastical policy. They represented the most unyielding foes of Monophysitism and iconoclasm. The Crusaders (Fourth Crusade) destroyed the monastery in 1204. It was rebuilt in 1290 only to be destroyed a second time by the Turks when they captured Constantinople in 1453. The monastery served as the model and center of Eastern monasticism. Its most famous abbot was St. Theodore the Studite.

STUDIUM GENERALE, a cathedral school that offered instruction in one or more of the faculties of the arts, law, theology, and medicine, and whose fame attracted students from other dioceses. It was the term by which the first medieval universities were known.

STYLITES, anchorites of Syria and Palestine for the most part, but also known in Mesopotamia, Egypt, and Greece, who lived on the top of pillars, whence the name "pillar saints." Their appearance, which was a phenomenon of the fifth century, never spread to the West although it endured in the East into the twelfth century. The most famous of these men was Simeon Stylites (the Elder), d. 459, who lived for 36 years on a tower some miles east of Antioch.

STYRIA, region between the upper Save and Drave rivers which comprised essentially the ancient Roman province of Pannonia. It passed under Avar control in the late sixth century, in the seventh under that of the Slavs (Slovenes), in

772 under the dukes of Bavaria, later under the authority of the Carolingians, and finally under the authority of the Holy Roman emperor.

SUBDEACON, member of the clergy who held the lowest of the two major orders leading to the priesthood. Until the thirteenth century the subdeaconship was considered a minor order.

SUBIACO, a community 50 miles east of Rome where St. Benedict (d. 547?) founded a number of monasteries before moving on to Monte Cassino. St. Scholastica, the sister of St. Benedict, established here the first monastic community for women. A church built in 981 and dedicated to St. Scholastica was destroyed by an earthquake (1228) and rebuilt in Gothic style. It was in Subiaco that the first printing press in Italy was set up.

SUBINFEUDATION, the division of a fief by its lord into one or more fiefs which he then handed over to a subtenant(s) properly known as his vassal(s). In theory a fief could be subdivided as long as the portion given in fee did not fall in value below what was required to fit out a knight with horse and armor, a knight's fee.

SUBUTAI. *See* SABUTAI.

SUEVES, a west German people which included the Semnones, Chatti, Quadi, and Marcomanni. One branch established itself in Galicia (Spain), the other, known as the Alemanni, in the area later known as Swabia.

SUFFOLK, county in eastern England, in the Anglo-Saxon period a part of the kingdom of East Anglia. It was ravaged by the Danes in the late ninth and late tenth centuries although apparently not seriously since, together with Norfolk, it formed the most populous and prosperous region of England before 1066. The Normans organized Suffolk as a shire. Its most famous and influential abbey was that of Bury St. Edmunds whose ruins may still be seen, together with those of a number of castles erected after the Norman invasion. By the four-

teenth century Suffolk had developed into a flourishing center of the cloth industry.

SUFFOLK, EARLS AND DUKES OF, the first earl of Suffolk was one of six new earls created by Edward III in 1337. The title lapsed in 1382 but was regranted to Michael de la Pole by Richard II in 1385. Michael, who was a trusted adviser of the king, escaped with his life to France when parliament seized control in 1387–8. The most influential bearer of the title was William de la Pole, fourth earl and, from 1448, duke, a general during the closing years of the Hundred Years' War and a leading member of the Beaufort faction. His greed and ambition made him many enemies, and he was also blamed for English losses in France. When Henry VI ordered him banished in a move to save his life, William's enemies seized and slew him (1450).

SUFISM, essentially Moslem mysticism, the term being derived from the word *sufi,* meaning a wearer of wool. As a means of self-mortification, then as a mark of their vocation, the *sufis* wore coarse woolen garments. Sufism was largely a Persian creation which emerged among the Shiites in the late tenth and early eleventh centuries, and its principal apostle was the Persian al-Ghazali (d. 1111). Like the mystics of the Christian world, the Sufis believed in the immediate personal union of the soul with God.

SUGER, d. 1151, abbot of Saint-Denis in Paris, counselor of Louis VI and Louis VII, and regent for the latter during the period of the Second Crusade (1147–9). He was the author of a life of Louis VI, and he is also credited with introducing principles of Gothic architecture to western Europe in his rebuilding of the abbey church of Saint-Denis.

SUIDAS, the name given to the most comprehensive Byzantine compendium of information pertaining to historical, biographical, geographical, theological, and literary matters. The work, which made its appearance late in the tenth century, proved a popular book of reference.

SULPICIUS SEVERUS, d. c. 420, monk of Aquitaine who lived as a hermit for some years and became a close friend of St. Martin of Tours. He is the author of a universal chronicle which extended from the Creation to 403, and of a life of St. Martin of Tours.

SULTAN, title first held by the Moslem caliph, then by the Turkish conquerors when these assumed control of Islam in the twelfth century.

SUMMA, systematic presentation of some subject; a compendium of theology, philosophy, or canon law used as a textbook or book of reference.

SUNNA, traditions concerning the life, words, and actions of Mohammed which were not recorded in the Koran but were based upon *hadith* or "sayings" found elsewhere.

SUNNITES, Moslems who accepted the Sunna and Koran as well as the legitimacy of the Omayyad caliphs. The Sunnites shunned membership in any Moslem sect, accepted a literal interpretation of the Koran, and proclaimed the almighty and absolute power of Allah.

SURPLICE, white liturgical garment which came into use in the eleventh century. It resembled the alb although it had large sleeves and was worn loose at the waist.

SUSO, HENRY. *See* HENRY SUSO, BL.

SUSSEX, small Saxon kingdom on the Channel west of Kent which, according to tradition, was established by the Saxon Aella (Aelle) who landed there in 477. The history of Sussex is unusually obscure. Its people may have been the last of the Saxons to abandon paganism. In 825 the country became subject to Egbert, king of Wessex. William of Normandy landed in Sussex, at Pevensey, in 1066 whence he moved to Hastings.

SUTTON HOO SHIP, early Anglo-Saxon king's grave containing a ship apparently fully equipped to serve in the afterlife. It was discovered in Suffolk in 1939. The ship and its contents throw light on the equipment, furnishings, weapons, and, since many of the items are from foreign countries, contacts of early Anglo-Saxon kings. Items of solid gold and rich ceremonial regalia suggest a relatively high level of culture and wealth. Because it was clearly a burial ship, there remains a strong possibility of hitherto unsuspected Swedish origin for the East Anglian royal dynasty.

SUYUTI, AL- (Abu Al-Fadl Abd Al-Rahman Ibn Abi Bakr Jalal Al-Din Suyuti), d. 1505, Arab scholar of Cairo whose voluminous writings included a commentary on the Koran, a history of the caliphs, and a biographical dictionary of grammarians and lexicographers. He wrote, in fact, on almost every subject, giving special attention to religion, and because he had talent for compiling and abridging, his writings are of particular value.

SVYATOSLAV I, d. 972, grand prince of Kiev from 945, the son of Igor and of St. Olga. Military campaigns filled most of his reign which ushered in the most brilliant period of Kievan Russia. He destroyed the empire of the Khazars on the lower Don, subjugated the Ossetians and the Circassians in the northern Caucasus, and aided the Byzantine emperor John I Tzimisces to conquer the Danubian Bulgars. But the might of Byzantium blocked his ambition to establish his capital on the Danube. In 972 he was ambushed by the Petchenegs and slain.

SWABIA, duchy located east of the upper Rhine in southwestern Germany which took its name from the Sueves who occupied the region in the fourth and fifth centuries. (It was actually the Alemanni, a branch of the Sueves, who had settled there, whence the use of the term Alemannia until the eleventh century.) The people of the area accepted baptism from the hands of

Celtic missionaries. The abbeys of St. Gall and Reichenau were located in Swabia, as well as the dioceses of Basel, Constance, and Augsburg. Swabia constituted one of the five great duchies that comprised the kingdom of the East Franks. In 1079 Henry IV enfiefed his son-in-law, Frederick of Hohenstaufen, as duke of Swabia, from which time the duchy remained in the Hohenstaufen family until the line became extinct in 1268. In 1313 the title fell out of use.

SWABIAN CITY LEAGUE (Swabian League), association of Swabian cities and other states in southwestern Germany for the general purpose of protecting trade and establishing peace. Such associations appeared as early as 1331, but none proved so successful as that organized in 1488. This was the largest up to that time and included more than 26 cities together with a number of ecclesiastical and temporal states; it also had the support of the emperor. It had a formal constitution, boasted a court, and maintained an army. Since its principal opposition came from the powerful territorial princes, the league, in effect, was an ally of the emperor in the cause of imperial reform. It helped rescue Frederick III's son, the future emperor Maximilian I, from captivity in the Netherlands and was the chief mainstay of Hapsburg authority in southwestern Germany during Maximilian's reign. It played an even more important role in German affairs in the early sixteenth century.

SWEDEN, a Viking state that entered European history in the ninth century through the raids its people conducted along the rivers east of the Baltic into Russia. Honor as the country's oldest town traditionally goes to Birka which was founded c. 800. In the ninth century Frankish missionaries began penetrating the unfriendly land, although little progress was made prior to the reign of Olaf Skutkonung (993–1024), the country's first Christian ruler. The Christian church marked its final triumph over paganism in 1164 when it assigned an archbishop to Uppsala, the ancient center of pagan worship.

During this period wars among the different aristocratic families of Sweden contributed to the obscurity and unstable character of its history. Relative calm came with Sverker (1134–50), while St. Eric IX (1150–60) even undertook a Crusade against the pagan Finns. From 1248 until his death in 1266, Birger Magnusson, who as jarl held the highest position in the state under the king, actually directed Swedish affairs. He encouraged German immigration and trade, issued the first national laws, checked the power of the aristocracy, and, through his nephew Waldemar whose election as king he arranged in 1250, founded the Folkung dynasty. Still Sweden could point to little national progress during the next century. A common law was adopted in 1347, but the Hanseatic League was establishing a hold over Swedish commerce that would not loosen before the fifteenth century. In 1359 Magnus II (1319–65) arranged the marriage of his son Haakon to Margaret, daughter and heiress of Waldemar IV, king of Denmark. Lest Haakon, who was already king of Norway, grow too formidable as ruler of Denmark and Sweden as well, the Swedish aristocracy invited in Albert of Mecklenburg (1363–88) whom they knew they could manage. Yet in 1389 they were ready to accept Margaret as regent even though she had been ruling Norway and Denmark since 1380, the year Haakon died. In 1397 at Kalmar Swedish representatives joined those of Norway and Denmark in recognizing Margaret's greatnephew, Eric of Pomerania, as their common king. After his deposition in 1439, the Swedes accepted a joint king with Norway and Denmark until 1448 when they chose Karl Knutsson, one of their fellow nobles, to reign (Charles VIII). Since the position of the aristocracy continued dominant, the throne remained unstable into the sixteenth century.

SWEYN (Swein) I, "Forkbeard," king of Denmark from c. 987 to 1014, son of Harald Bluetooth. In 994, in alliance with Olaf Tryggvason, an exiled prince of Norway, he attacked

England and after doing much destruction, accepted a payment of 16,000 pounds (Danegeld). Olaf then established himself as king of Norway but was defeated and slain in battle with Sweyn and the king of Sweden (1000), who divided his kingdom. In 1003 Sweyn made a second attack on England but suffered defeat in East Anglia. He returned for a third time in 1013 and had all but conquered the entire country when he died.

SWEYN (Swein) II, king of Denmark (1043–1074), the nephew of King Canute of England. When Canute had Sweyn's father murdered, Sweyn fled to Sweden and a few years later, through treachery, made himself king of Denmark. He encouraged rebellious English lords in their revolt against William I (the Conqueror), then permitted himself to be bought off. It is said that Sweyn furnished Adam of Bremen much information which that monk incorporated into his history of northwestern Europe.

SWITHIN (Swithun), ST., d. 862, bishop of Winchester, and possibly adviser of Egbert, king of Wessex. Little firm knowledge but much legend exists concerning this obscure saint. Upon reports of miracles attributed to him, his body was translated to the cathedral of Winchester. His cult became so popular that his name replaced those of St. Peter and St. Paul in the dedication of the cathedral. One of the superstitions associated with St. Swithin is the belief that should rain fall on his feastday (July 15), it will rain on the 40 days following.

SWITZERLAND, Alpine state whose political origins date from the Perpetual Compact entered into by the three forest cantons of Uri, Schwyz, and Unterwalden in 1291 in the hope of blocking the attempt of the Hapsburgs to bring them under direct rule. In 1315 Leopold I of Hapsburg determined to humble these cantons, but they routed his army at the battle of Morgarten. Shortly after more cantons joined the league, among these Lucerne, Zürich, and Berne. In

1386 the Swiss gained a second decisive victory over the Hapsburgs at Sempach and two years later another victory at Näfels. Internal friction among the cantons, even hostilities, slowed the evolution of a centralized federal state, but the rising threat of Burgundy in the second half of the fifteenth century led Germany to accept the existence of a Swiss state as a lesser evil. The new state gained indirect recognition at the Peace of Basel in 1499. Meantime the original compact of three cantons had swelled to thirteen, to which a number of towns, districts, and other cantons adhered in a federal union known as the League of Upper Germany.

SWORD, KNIGHTS OF THE. *See* LIVONIAN KNIGHTS OF THE SWORD.

SYAGRIUS, a Gallo-Roman general who claimed to represent Roman imperial authority in the region about Soissons. He was defeated and executed by Clovis in 486.

SYLVESTER I, ST., Pope, 314–35, a Roman priest whose career as pope was almost wholly overshadowed by the prestige and vigor of the emperor Constantine I. It was Constantine, not Sylvester, who summoned the bishops to Arles in 314 to deal with the problem of Donatism. Constantine also had them assemble at Nicaea in 325 to decide about Arianism. Of the many legends told about Sylvester the best known is that which furnished the basis for the Donation of Constantine.

SYLVESTER II, Pope, 999–1003, known before his pontificate as Gerbert of Aurillac, the "most learned man of his century." As head of the cathedral school at Reims he earned fame for his knowledge of Latin, astronomy, mathematics, and dialectic, and for his talents as a teacher. He authored an influential work on the abacus and was one of the first scholars in the West to use Arabic numerals. Otto II had him elected abbot of Bobbio. He served as tutor of Otto III who had him consecrated archbishop of Ravenna and later raised him to the papacy. Sylvester was the first Frenchman to rise to that high office. As pope he devoted his efforts to suppressing simony and concubinage and to establishing the freedom of election for abbots.

SYLVESTER III, antipope for three months in 1045 during the pontificate of Benedict IX.

SYLVESTER IV, antipope, 1105–11, during the pontificate of Paschal II.

SYLVESTRINES. *See* SILVESTER GUZZOLINI, ST.

SYMEON THE NEW THEOLOGIAN, d. 1022, monk of the Studion monastery at Constantinople, abbot of the monastery of St. Marina. He left sermons, short rules called chapters, hymns, and letters. He has been called the most important mystic of the Greek Church.

SYMMACHUS, ST., Pope, 498–514, a deacon of Sardinia, the successor of Anastasius II. His pontificate was troubled by two schisms, the Acacian and the Laurentian. Laurentius had been elected pope by a pro-Byzantine minority among the Roman clergy. He defended orthodoxy against the supporters of *Henoticon* [*see* ACACIAN SCHISM] and expelled the Manichaeans from Rome. He also introduced the singing of the *Gloria in excelsis* in the mass on Sundays.

SYMMACHUS, QUINTUS AURELIUS, d. c. 402, Roman consul and prefect of the city, an eloquent orator and one of the last champions of Roman paganism. He is best known for his *De Ara Victoriae,* a brilliant oration which he delivered in a plea to have the statue of *Victory* restored to its place in the senate house at Rome. St. Ambrose had persuaded the emperor to have it removed.

SYNCELLI, monks or members of the secular clergy who lived with their bishops, performed daily spiritual exercises with them, and in the Eastern church also served as their counselors.

SYNESIUS OF CYRENE, d. c. 414, neo-Platonist of Alexandria and Cyrene, and a devoted disciple of Hypathia. He became a Christian and, despite being married and over his protests, was appointed bishop of Ptolemais. His writings, all from the period before his conversion, include hymns, homilies, letters, and philosophical tracts.

SYNOPTIC GOSPELS, the gospels of Matthew, Luke, and Mark. The term synoptic suggests that the writers presented their gospel narratives from the same general point of view.

SYRACUSE, city of southeastern Sicily whose history in the Christian era may have dated from the three days St. Paul spent there on his way to Rome. Its first bishop was said to have been Marcianus. Lucy, patron saint of the city, was martyred c. 305 during the reign of Diocletian. The Byzantine emperor Constans II planned to move his capital to Syracuse as more secure than Constantinople but he was murdered (668). Arabs seized the city in 878, and the emir of Syracuse encouraged the Normans to invade the island in 1060. Syracuse ranked second to Palermo as a seaport.

SYRIA, state located on the western littoral of Asia above Egypt, part of the Byzantine empire until 636 when the destruction of the imperial army by the Arabs at Yarmuk led to the collapse of Byzantine authority. During the period of the Omayyad caliphate (661–750) that followed, Syria prospered under the generally benevolent rule of Islam which both Christians and Jews accepted. Damascus served as the capital of the Islamic world, while Syria proved itself an ideal base from which Islam continued its offensive against the Christian world to the west. In 750 when the Abbasid caliphate replaced the Omayyad, the center of Islam shifted eastward to Baghdad on the Tigris, and Damascus and Syria lost their preeminent position. One of the consequences for Syria was the increase of Egyptian influence from the south. The second half of the eleventh century saw the conquest of Syria by the Seljuk Turks and soon after the beginning of the Crusading period (1096–1270). The Christians managed to conquer and hold much of Syria until 1187 when Saladin, the sultan of Egypt, destroyed a huge Crusading army at Hattin. In 1260 the Mamluk rulers of Egypt drove Mongol invaders from the north out of Syria, but in 1401 they found themselves no match for the ruthless Mongol khan, Timur the Lame, who ravaged much of the area, destroyed several of its major cities including Damascus, massacred a large part of the population, and carried off many craftsmen to Samarkand. Economic decline that then set in continued into the sixteenth century when Syria fell to the Ottoman Turks.

SYRIAC, a branch of the Aramaic language spoken in Edessa and vicinity shortly before the beginning of the Christian era. Because of the activity of the Christian communities in this area, Syriac was in extensive use in the early Church. Most of the literature that survives is Christian, while a number of Greek patristic works remain only in Syriac translations. The triumph of Islam in the seventh century restricted in time the use of Syriac to the liturgy of the Nestorians and Jacobites.

SYRIAN RITE, the rite used in the church of Antioch in the fourth century. After the condemnation of Monophysitism by the Council of Chalcedon in 451, the rite was usually identified as that adopted by the Jacobite church. [See JACOBITES.]

TABARI, AL- (ʿAbu Jaʿfar Muhammad Ibn Jarir Al-Tabari), d. 923, Persian historian and theologian who spent most of his life in Baghdad where he was a teacher of law and tradition. He was especially proud of his legal works of which only fragments have survived. He is best known for his annalistic history, entitled *Annals of the Prophets and Kings,* which extended from the Creation to 915. This is largely a collection of writings of earlier historians which al-Tabari recorded with little or no analysis on his part. He also prepared a commentary on the Koran. He remains the first important Moslem historian.

TABERNA, a wine cellar.

TABERNACLE, a receptacle, often near or attached to the altar, where the consecrated hosts were reserved. The modern tabernacle located in the middle of the altar probably did not appear before the sixteenth century.

TABORITES, the radical wing of the Hussites as opposed to the Calixtines or Utraquists. The Taborites — they derived their name from the biblical Mount Tabor — maintained the Bible to be the sole source of faith, condemned the veneration of saints, demanded the confiscation of church property, and retained only the sacraments of baptism and eucharist. They also demanded the abolition of oaths, courts of justice, and all worldly dignities. John Zizka (d. 1424) welded them into a powerful military force which repeatedly defeated the imperial armies. In 1433 the moderate wing of the Hussites accepted the Compacts of Prague and joined the Catholics, the following year inflicting a decisive defeat on the Taborites at Lipany.

TACITUS, CORNELIUS, d. 120, major Roman historian whose *Germania* furnishes the best description of the early Germans. He also makes one of the few references to Christians found in classical authors when he mentions how Nero made them a scapegoat in the aftermath of the great fire in Rome.

TAGLIACOZZO, BATTLE OF, battle won by Charles of Anjou in 1268 over the Ghibelline forces in Italy. After his victory he seized and executed the fifteen-year-old Conradin. With the death of Conradin the line of the Hohenstaufens became extinct. The pope, who had permitted Louis IX to let his brother lead his army into Italy now found that the French were as much a threat to his position as the Germans had been.

TAILLE, a tax usually levied on property which the serf paid his lord somewhat irregularly except in France where in 1439 it became a regular tax on property or income. The tax was paid by all nonprivileged classes.

TALLAGE, tax levied in England upon boroughs and upon the tenants living on the king's estates. It was probably instituted by Henry I (1100–35) to replace the Danegeld and became a common source of revenue during the reigns of Richard I and John. It corresponded roughly to the French taille.

TALMUD, compilation of the Oral Law of the Hebrews with commentaries, as opposed to the

Scriptures and Written Laws. Its two divisions are the Mishna (in Hebrew) and the Gemara (in Aramaic), the latter a kind of commentary on the former. Both the Palestinian and the Babylonian schools produced Talmuds (fifth and sixth centuries, respectively).

TAMMERLANE. *See* TIMUR THE LAME.

TANCRED, d. 1112, a Norman Crusader, nephew of Bohemond whom he accompanied on the First Crusade (1096–9). He played a major role in the capture of Antioch. He later served as regent of Antioch during periods when Bohemond was away and of Edessa when Baldwin II was a captive of the Moslems. While there he made extensive conquests in Cilicia and northern Syria. Tancred was probably the most successful of the Crusaders in the campaign against the Moslems during the years immediately following the First Crusade.

TANCRED, d. 1234/6, noted canonist of Bologna, author of a compilation of the decretals of Pope Honorius III (1216–27) and of a volume dealing with procedure in ecclesiastical courts.

TANGIER, city of Morocco, the ancient Tingis, which the Arabs captured in the latter half of the seventh century. Tangier served as the leading port of Morocco before the rise of Fès in the early ninth century. From 951 until the collapse of the Caliphate of Córdoba (1236), it was subject to Moslem Spanish rule. The Portuguese captured the city in 1471.

TANNENBERG, BATTLE OF. *See* GRUNWALD, BATTLE OF.

TANNHÄUSER (Tannhuser), d. c. 1270, Middle High German lyric poet of Bavaria who traveled widely and even accompanied the Crusade undertaken by Frederick II in 1238. Contemporary events and legendary materials provide the themes of his poems.

TANTUM ERGO, title given to the last two stanzas of the *Pange Lingua Gloriosi,* a hymn composed by St. Thomas Aquinas in commemoration of the Blessed Sacrament.

TARANTO, ancient Roman Tarentum, seaport of Apulia, taken from Byzantium by the Goths, then recovered, next occupied by the Lombards, destroyed by the Arabs (927), again recovered by Byzantium (967), finally captured by Robert Guiscard (c. 1060). It was one of the popular embarkation ports for Crusaders going to Syria. [For its later history, *see* NAPLES, KINGDOM OF.]

TARASIUS, ST., d. 806, patriarch of Constantinople (784), secretary of the empress Irene I. He worked for the restoration of good relations with Rome and persuaded the empress to convoke the Seventh Ecumenical Council at Nicaea in 787 which condemned iconoclasm and restored the veneration of images. In 802 he crowned Nicephorus emperor after Irene had been dethroned.

TARIK, Berber lieutenant of Musa, the governor of North Africa, who invaded Spain in 711, defeated Roderick, the last Visigothic king of Spain, and captured Córdoba and Toledo, at which point the envious Musa recalled him. Tarik gave his name to Gibraltar (*Jebel-al-Tarik,* that is, Tarik's mountain).

TARSICIUS, ST., obscure martyr of the third or early fourth century, who, according to tradition, was killed by a mob while carrying the eucharist to Christian prisoners. He refused to reveal to the crowd what he was carrying under his cloak.

TARSUS, seaport of Cilicia (southern Turkey), one of the leading cities of the Byzantine empire. Soon after 660 the Arabs destroyed the city, but Harun al-Rashid had it rebuilt, after which it served as a military base to raid Byzantine shipping. In 965 Nicephorus II Phocas recovered control of the city for Byzantium, and in the twelfth century it was incorporated into the Christian kingdom of Little Armenia. In 1359 it fell to the Mamluks and in the late fifteenth century to the Ottoman Turks.

TARTARS (Taters). *See* MONGOLS.

TATIAN, second-century Christian theologian of eastern Syria, a pupil of Justin Martyr, later head of a Gnostic sect. His principal work was a harmony of the four Gospels entitled *Diatessaron.* He preached a strict asceticism on the principle that matter had been corrupted by sin.

TAULER, JOHN, d. 1361, Dominican mystic, studied at Strasbourg, later became a pupil of Meister Eckhart at Cologne. He devoted his active years to preaching and pastoral work in the Rhineland. During the Black Death he labored zealously among the stricken. In his letters and sermons he urged Christians to lead humble, simple lives while accepting suffering with joy as faithful followers of Christ. Like other mystics, he emphasized the indwelling of God in the human soul. His sermons received praise from Martin Luther.

TE DEUM (Laudamus), hymn of praise directed to the Father and Son, in rhythmical prose, perhaps a composite of excerpts taken from earlier hymns, whose date of composition has been assigned to the beginning of the fifth century. It was apparently referred to in the Rules of St. Caesarius of Arles and of St. Benedict. By the sixth century it had been adopted for liturgical use.

TELESPHORUS, ST., Pope, 125? to 138?, probably a Greek, martyred under the emperor Hadrian. Irenaeus says he was the first Roman bishop to be honored as a martyr. He also notes that Telesphorus observed Easter on Sunday, as against the Quartodeciman practice.

TELL, WILLIAM, legendary Swiss hero, supposedly a peasant of Uri of the late thirteenth or early fourteenth century, who was forced to shoot an apple from the head of his son by the harsh provincial governor Gessler. The earliest manuscript of the story appeared c. 1470.

TE LUCIS ANTE TERMINUM, breviary hymn honoring God. The hymn, probably from the eighth century, was sung especially during the summer and on great feast days.

TEMPLARS, ORDER OF KNIGHTS (Knights Templar), military-religious order, also known as "Poor Fellow-Soldiers of Christ and the Temple of Solomon," founded in 1119 by Hugh des Payens, a knight of Champagne, and Godfrey of Saint-Omer. The order derived its name from the site given it by Baldwin, king of Jerusalem, which was near the place where Solomon's temple was believed to have stood. It adopted the rule of the Augustinian canons and its members took vows of poverty and chastity. They were divided into four classes: knights and sergeants who did the fighting, and chaplains and servants. The order enjoyed most renown in the twelfth century as its members fought the Moslems in the Kingdom of Jerusalem where they maintained a number of fortresses. Their grand master was among the slain at the fall of Acre in 1291, the last Christian foothold in Palestine. Pope Clement V ordered the suppression of the order at the Council of Vienne in 1312, under pressure from Philip IV of France who coveted the order's enormous wealth and who had trumped up charges of blasphemy, heresy, and gross immorality against its members. The Templars wore a white mantle adorned with an eight-pointed red cross. [*See* MOLAY, JACQUES DE.]

TENEBRAE, term given to the matins and lauds sung in anticipation of the following day on the evening before Holy Thursday, Good Friday, and Holy Saturday. The term derived from the darkness of the sanctuary as lights were extinguished and the candles on the altar put out until only one remained lit.

TENOR, musical term for the part or voice that held the plainsong.

TERCE, SECT, AND NONES, together with Prime, the "Little Hours," recited at the third, sixth, and ninth hours respectively.

TERTIARY, member of a Third Order as distinguished from the First Order, which was reserved for monks, and the Second for women. Tertiaries were lay people who strove after Christian perfection under the guidance of, and in harmony with, the spirit of some religious order. [*See* THIRD ORDERS.]

TERTULLIAN, QUINTUS SEPTIMIUS FLORENS, d. after 220, a leading father of the Latin church and the author of much of its theological terminology. He was a convert from paganism, married, and never became a priest. For a time he served as instructor of catechumens in Carthage. From the time of his conversion he adopted a rigorist position concerning faith and morals. When he found Christianity too moderate, he joined the Montanists (c. 207), and in the end established his own extremist sect. He was the author of numerous apologetic, theological, polemical, and ascetical works, most of these in Latin. His treatises on dogmatic and moral subjects exercised considerable influence on other church fathers. Probably no Christian writer matched his literary and rhetorical skill as a writer and a polemicist. In his attack on Roman paganism he argued that Christians were worthy citizens and that the "blood of martyrs was the seed of the church."

TESTONE (teston, testoon), an Italian coin in use from the middle of the fifteenth century.

TEUTONIC KNIGHTS, ORDER OF, a military-religious order, also known as the German Order, which first appeared as a hospital that merchants of Lübeck and Bremen established in Acre in 1190. Pope Innocent III approved it as a military-religious order in 1199. It was composed of knights, priests, and lay brothers. They first fought in Syria and Palestine against the Saracens, then in the early thirteenth century moved most of their activities to eastern Europe, against the pagan Slavs in Hungary, then against the pagan Prussians along the south Baltic coast. In the course of destroying paganism in this area, the order established a state of its own which stretched from Pomerania to the Gulf of Finland. The threat which the Knights posed for Poland and Lithuania led these countries to form an alliance in 1386 which by 1466 had deprived the order of its possessions except for East Prussia which the Knights were permitted to retain as a fief of Poland.

TEWKESBURY, BATTLE OF, engagement won by Edward IV over the Lancastrian army in 1471 which resulted in the death of Henry VI's son Edward and the capture of Queen Margaret (of Anjou). Shortly after the battle Henry VI was murdered in the Tower. [*See* ROSES, WARS OF THE.]

THECLA, a supposed pupil of St. Paul who had converted her. She is the heroine of the apocryphal *Acta Pauli et Theclae*. She was greatly venerated in both the East and the West though apparently not in Rome.

THEGN, among the Anglo-Saxons a freeman who held land of the king or a lord. Thegns played an important role in local jurisdiction and administration. Ealdormen were generally chosen from among them.

THE HAGUE. *See* HAGUE, THE.

THEME, name given to large military districts established first by Emperor Heraclius (610–41) and administered by generals who exercised full military and civil authority. Much of the land in these themes was turned over to soldiers to whom the Byzantine state guaranteed possession of their holdings in return for military service. Territories in the Balkans were later organized in the same manner.

THEOBALD, d. 1161, monk, prior, and abbot at Bec, archbishop of Canterbury in 1138. He gave his support to Stephen of Blois against Matilda, the daughter of Henry I, who strove to have her son Henry (II) succeed to the throne when her father died. When Theobald attended the Council of Reims in 1148 against Stephen's orders, he was exiled, but an interdict placed on England by Pope Eugenius III induced Stephen to withdraw his order. In 1152 Theobald fled to Flanders rather than crown Stephen's son Eustace. After the death of Eustace, he helped Stephen and Henry reach an agreement in the Treaty of Winchester, and he himself crowned Henry when Stephen died. Finally, he recommended his secretary Thomas Becket to Henry as an able chancellor.

THEODORA, Byzantine empress, d. 548, lowborn wife of the emperor Justinian whom he married in 525(?). It was Theodora's courage, according to the historian Procopius, that saved the emperor his crown on the occasion of the Nika riot in 532. Procopius is also responsible in his *Secret History* for giving her the image of a depraved, vicious woman, which most scholars believe she was not. Theodora enjoyed Justinian's confidence and appears to have shared his counsel in many matters, both political and ecclesiastical. She may have sympathized with the Monophysites, perhaps one of the reasons why the emperor worked hard to find a compromise between them and Rome.

THEODORA, Byzantine empress, d. 862, wife of Emperor Theophilus (829–42) and mother of Michael III (842–67). As regent with her brother, the Caesar Bardas, she convoked a synod in 843 which condemned iconoclasm and restored the veneration of images. She was honored as a saint by the Greek Church.

THEODORA THE ELDER, wife of the Roman consul and senator Theophylact. She controlled Rome and the papacy c. 900–26. Her daughter, Theodora the Younger, d. c. 950, was a woman of great influence in Roman affairs and the mother of Pope John XIII and of Crescentius I.

THEODORE I, Pope, 642–9, a Greek, who as pope opposed the Monothelitic position of Emperor Heraclius as set forth in the *Ecthesis*. This was a document drawn up by Sergius I, the patriarch of Constantinople, and promulgated by Heraclius in 638 which affirmed the existence of but one will in Christ.

THEODORE II, Pope, whose pontificate lasted but 20 days in November 897. He upheld the validity of the acts of his predecessor Pope Formosus and gave his mutilated corpse proper burial.

THEODORE, bishop of Mopsuestia, d. 428, priest and bishop of Mopsuestia in Cilicia and a leading representative of the theological school in Antioch. In his biblical commentaries he adopted the literal, historical interpretation as opposed to the allegorical of the school of Alexandria. The Councils of Ephesus (431) and Constantinople II (553) condemned several of his writings for the Nestorian views they contained. Cyril of Alexandria (d. 444) had already attacked them for the same reason.

THEODORE OF TARSUS, d. 690, a Greek who studied at Tarsus and Athens, left Asia Minor for Rome, then accompanied Benedict Biscop and Hadrian to England where he was consecrated archbishop of Canterbury (after 669). In 672 he summoned and presided over the first important synod of the English church in Hertford. Theodore provided the English church with a solid foundation and helped establish Canterbury both as the metropolitan authority of the province and as a center of learning.

THEODORE THE STUDITE (Studion, of Studios), St., d. 826, learned and zealous theologian of Constantinople and abbot of the Studite monastery in that city. He made the monastery a model of Byzantine monasticism and the center of the monastic life of the East. His vigorous stand against the iconoclastic policies of the emperor led twice to his exile. He proved himself a man of austere sanctity and iron determination, a valiant defender of the rights of the church, and a militant reformer of monasticism. His writings included letters, liturgical and ascetical studies, and hymns.

THEODORET OF CYR, d. c. 460, monk, bishop of Cyr (Cyrrhus), near Antioch. He was a personal friend of Nestorius and initially sided with him against Cyril of Alexandria in their Christological controversy over the nature of Christ and the title of *Theotokos* for Mary. In 449 the Council of Ephesus ordered him deposed and exiled, but two years later at the Council of Chalcedon he shifted his position and agreed to the anathematization of Nestorius. His writings included theological, exegetical, and apologetical works, sermons, biographies of monks, letters, and a continuation to 428 of the church history of Eusebius.

THEODORIC (Dietrich) OF FREIBERG, d. c. 1310, Dominican provincial of Germany whose preaching exerted considerable influence upon German mystics. His writings include works on logic, psychology, science, and theology.

THEODORIC (the Great), king of the Ostrogoths, 471–526, as a youth a hostage for several years at Constantinople. As king he led his people from the area of Pannonia, where they had settled as *foederati*, to Italy, commissioned to do so by the emperor Zeno. He slew Odoacer at Ravenna in 493 and assumed control of the peninsula. His kingdom in time included all of Italy, Sicily, and the territory north and east of the upper Adriatic. Despite his attachment to the traditions of his people, he worked to preserve Roman culture and institutions and employed the scholars Boethius and Cassiodorus as councillors in the business of government and education. Although Theodoric was an Arian, his relations with the pope remained satisfactory until the close of his reign when he feared the church would cooperate with the Byzantine emperor in an attempt to recover Italy. During this last period he had Boethius executed (c. 524). Theodoric appears as Dietrich von Bern in the *Nibelungenlied*.

THEODORIC I, king of the Visigoths, 419–51, who renounced the authority of Rome in 425

although joining Aetius at Châlons where his army proved of decisive importance in defeating Attila and his Huns. He was slain in the fighting.

THEODOSIAN CODE, a codification of the constitutions (laws) of Constantine I (306–37) and his successors which was ordered compiled by Emperor Theodosius II. He promulgated the code in 438. It contained laws that proscribed paganism and penalized heresy, and others that regulated the position of the clergy and the relationship between church and state.

THEODOSIUS I (the Great), Roman emperor, 379–95, a Spaniard, son of Count Theodosius, a Roman general in Spain, whom Gratian appointed co-emperor following the death of Valens at the battle of Adrianople (378). Theodosius succeeded in pacifying the Visigoths, then ruled as sole emperor when Gratian (d. 383) and Valentinian II (d. 392) died. Theodosius dispensed with the title of Pontifex Maximus, proscribed paganism, Arianism, and other heresies, and proclaimed Christianity the official religion of the empire. He did public penance on orders of St. Ambrose, bishop of Milan, for the massacre of several thousand Thessalonians. His incompetent sons, Arcadius and Honorius, succeeded him as emperors, Arcadius ruling from Constantinople and Honorius from Ravenna.

THEODOSIUS II, Byzantine emperor, 408–50, son and successor of Arcadius. He issued the Theodosian Code in 438, summoned the Council of Ephesus (431), and rebuilt the fortifications of Constantinople. Principal credit for the achievements of his reign should go to his sister Pulcheria, his wife Eudocia, and his other advisers. [*See* THEODOSIAN CODE.]

THEODULF OF ORLEANS, d. 821, theologian and poet, a native of Spain of Gothic descent. He served as abbot of Fleury, then as bishop and archbishop of Orleans (800) until deposed on the charge of conspiracy by Louis the Pious in 818. Among his theological treatises is one in which he defended the addition of the *Filioque* to the Nicene creed. Theodulf, who is considered the most accomplished poet of his day in the West, spent some time as a member of the circle of scholars Charlemagne had gathered at Aachen. His hymn, *Gloria, Laus, et Honor,* became the Palm Sunday processional in the Western Church. Theodulf was a reformer, introduced parish schools, and made a contribution to ecclesiastical art and architecture.

THEODURUS (Theodore) ABU QURRA, d. c. 825, Melchite bishop of Harran (east of Aleppo) who engaged in discussions with Jews, Moslems, and Sabaeans. He showed himself a vocal champion of the teaching authority and primacy of the bishop of Rome. His theological treatises, written in Greek, Arabic, and Syriac, devoted much attention to Christological problems.

THEOPHANES THE CONFESSOR, ST., d. c. 818, a monk, author of a chronicle *(Chronographia)* from 284 A.D. to 813 which is the best historical source for the history of Byzantium during the seventh and eighth centuries. He suffered exile to Samothrace for opposing the iconoclastic policy of Emperor Leo V.

THEOPHANO, the beautiful, unprincipled wife of Emperor Romanus II (959–963) who married the able general Nicephorus Phocas following the death of Romanus. He ruled as emperor until 969 when she arranged his murder with the assistance of John Tzimisces, another great general, whom she planned to marry. But the patriarch protested in the name of the church and the people, whereupon Tzimisces was obliged to send her into exile.

THEOPHANO (Theophanu), d. 991, Byzantine princess who became the wife of Otto (II) of Germany in 972. She served as regent during the early years of the reign of her son Otto III. Some scholars suggest that the appearance of Byzantine influences in the art of the Ottonian period may be traced to her.

THEOPHILUS, Byzantine emperor, 829–42, son of Michael II, co-emperor from 820 and sole ruler after 829. He encouraged the revival of iconoclasm and showed a genuine interest in learning and art. During his reign Sicily as well as extensive areas of Asia Minor, including the powerful fortress of Amorium, were lost to the Moslems.

THEOPHILUS OF ANTIOCH, second-century bishop of Antioch, author of apologetical tracts, exegetical works, and a harmony of the gospels. Only his "Apology" has survived. He was the first writer to proclaim the divine inspiration of the New Testament, and the first to use the word "Triad" when referring to the Godhead.

THEOPHYLACT, d. c. 926, Tusculani count, husband of Theodora (the Elder) and father of Marozia and Theodora (the Younger). He enjoyed a commanding influence in both Roman and papal affairs.

THEOPHYLACT, eleventh-century Byzantine exegete, a pupil of Michael Psellus and tutor of Constantine VII Porphyrogenitus, the son of Michael VII. About the year 1078 he was made archbishop of Ochryda in the country of the Bulgarians. Despite the backwardness of the region and its lack of books and scholars, he prepared commentaries on several books of the Old Testament and all of the New except Revelation. His approach was an insistence upon practical morality in the tradition of St. John Chrysostom whom he admired. He sympathized with the Western Church's position on images and the use of unleavened bread.

THEOTOKOS, Greek for "Mother of God" or "God-bearer," a title given to Mary by Greek Fathers from Origen (d. 254) onward. In 429 Nestorius attacked the use of the title as incompatible with the full humanity of Christ. The position of St. Cyril of Alexandria, who took the opposite view, was upheld at the councils of Ephesus (431) and Chalcedon (451).

THIBAUT IV, d. 1253, count of Champagne and king of Navarre (from 1234), the best known of the aristocratic *trouvères*. He led a Crusade in 1239 and recovered Ascalon from the Moslems. He left 60 lyrics, principally love songs and *tensos* (debates), and nine religious poems.

THIERRY (Theodoric) OF CHARTRES, d. c. 1156, also known as Thierry the Breton, a brother of Bernard of Chartres. He was head of the school of Chartres and later taught at Paris where John of Salisbury attended his lectures on rhetoric. He was one of the leading exponents of the Platonist tendencies of the school at Chartres. He composed a work on the seven liberal arts, a number of theological treatises, a commentary on Genesis, and one on Cicero's *De Inventione*. His realism carried him close to pantheism.

THIETMAR (Dietmar) OF MERSEBURG, d. 1018, son of a Saxon count, bishop of Merseburg, and author of a chronicle of his diocese and of Germany from the accession of Henry I (919) to 1018.

THIRD ESTATE, term applied in the high and late Middle Ages to commoners, that is, to the class below the clergy (first estate) and the aristocracy (second estate).

THIRD ORDERS (Tertiaries), informal organizations of lay people whose members continued their activities in the world while devoting themselves to the ideals of some religious order, usually one of the Mendicants, as far as their secular responsibilities would permit. The first tertiaries remained in their homes. The "Regular Tertiaries" who lived in communities made their appearance in the late thirteenth and fourteenth centuries. Many of these took formal vows.

THOMAS À KEMPIS, d. 1471, a leading representative of the *Devotio Moderna*. He was born at Kempen near Düsseldorf, studied at Deventer, and entered the monastery of Canons Regular of St. Augustine at Mt. St. Agnes where he spent the greater part of his life writing, preaching, copying manuscripts, and serving as spiritual adviser. His writings include sermons, lives of the saints, devotional works, chronicles, and, above all, the *Imitation of Christ*. Some question remains concerning his authorship of this work. [*See* IMITATION OF CHRIST.]

THOMAS AQUINAS, ST., d. 1274, a Dominican who attended the abbey school of Monte Cassino which was near his home of Aquino, then the universities of Naples and Paris. He later accompanied his mentor, Albert the Great, to Cologne. He was the first Dominican to occupy the chair of theology at the University of Paris. The erudition and piety of Aquinas won universal acclaim. A summons from Pope Gregory X found him on his way to attend the Council of Lyons when he died. The factors that explain his eminence as a scholar and theologian were his brilliance of mind, his industry, and his deep appreciation of Aristotle upon whose thought he constantly drew. A central premise of Aquinas's theology was the existence of a harmony between faith and reason. Of nothing he was more convinced than that the universe was as much a manifestation of God's intelligence as it was an expression of his will. He accepted the natural goodness of men which drew them toward God, an inclination which, when favored with supernatural grace, would also bring them blessedness and happiness.

Aquinas placed far greater emphasis than preceding schoolmen on the role of sense experience in the attainment of truth, although he was willing to admit that the "five ways" he proposed for demonstrating the existence of God might require some assistance from God before man would come to believe. The most influential of his voluminous writings — he had the assistance of secretaries in his later years — was the *Summa Theologiae*. This stands preeminent as the most scholarly and systematic presentation of Christian theology till then attempted. The *Summa Contra Gentiles* represents an introduction to Christian theology based upon rational principles for its verification in the hope that it might convince Moslems and Jews who refused to accept the evidence of the Bible. In the *De Regimine Principum,* one of a number of monographs, he argued that since man was a social being, government was necessary, although a king who failed to observe the moral law was a tyrant. Among his other works are commentaries on the Bible, on Aristotle, and several beautiful eucharistic hymns, e.g., *Pange Lingua Gloriosi.*

THOMAS BECKET. *See* BECKET, THOMAS, ST.

THOMAS BRADWARDINE. *See* BRADWARDINE, THOMAS.

THOMAS, CHRISTIANS OF ST., ancient communities of Christians on the east and west coasts of India which traced their spiritual descent back to a visit made to that country by St. Thomas, the Apostle.

THOMAS OF CELANO, d. c. 1260, a Franciscan, biographer of St. Francis, who until recent years was credited with the composition of the *Dies Irae.*

THOMAS, ST., one of the twelve Apostles, the one who at first doubted the resurrection of Christ (John 20:24–29).

THOR (Thunar, Donar), one of the principal gods of the Germans, in Nordic mythology the god of thunder and war. He was a son of Odin (Woden). He gives his name to Thursday.

THORFINN KARLSEFNI, fl. 1002–7, the leader of the first Scandinavian expedition to colonize North America. The expedition, which included women, spent some time (1004–6?) on the mainland south of the Gulf of St. Lawrence in the region known as Vinland.

THORN, PEACE OF. *See* TORUN, PEACE OF.

THOUSAND AND ONE NIGHTS, also known as the *Arabian Nights,* a collection of tales, romances, and adventures of uncertain date and authorship written originally in Arabic. The ear-

liest known version dates from the ninth century. The chief elements of the stories have been traced to India, Iran, Iraq, Egypt, and Turkey, although the setting of many of the tales is Baghdad during the reign of Harun al-Rashid (786–809).

THREE CHAPTERS, chapters from the writings of three theologians of Antioch, Theodore of Mopsuestia, Theodoret of Cyr, and Ibas of Edessa, which Emperor Justinian ordered condemned in 544 because of their implied support of Nestorianism. The Council of Ephesus (431) had earlier condemned the writings of these three theologians. Justinian hoped his action would conciliate the Monophysites and effect a compromise between them and Rome, but his hope proved vain. [*See* VIGILIUS, POPE, for the West's position.]

THREE-FIELD SYSTEM, the practice of dividing the arable soil pertaining to a manor into three large fields and cropping two of these each year on a rotating basis. This method of crop rotation tended to replace the two-field system in those areas of France, England, and Germany from the eleventh century where the quality of the soil permitted more intensive cultivation. [*See* MANORIALISM.]

THREE KINGS, originally the Magi or Wise Men spoken of by the Evangelist Matthew (2:1–12), but presented as three kings from the fifth century. By approximately the sixth century the three men had acquired the names of Caspar, Melchior, and Balthasar.

THURINGIA, region of Germany along the upper Weser which received its name from the Thuringians, a German tribe first noted in the second half of the fourth century A.D. The Thuringians were subject to the Huns, and when the Hunnish empire collapsed they established a kingdom of their own between the Harz Mountains and the Danube. The Franks extended their rule over the area in the early sixth century, while Charlemagne founded the Thuringian march in 804 to contain the pressure of the Slavs to the east. They were converted to Christianity by St. Boniface (d. 754). In 908 the duke of Saxony seized the march, after which it remained under Saxon rule until the extinction of the line in 1024. During the next two centuries members of the Ludowing family ruled it as landgraves until 1247. In 1264, after several years of dispute, the Wettins acquired it. They held the greater part of Thuringia into the sixteenth century.

TIARA, beehive-shaped, triple-crowned headdress of the pope which he used on festive, extraliturgical, occasions. It was first mentioned in a life of Pope Constantine I (708–15), but it was not until the fifteenth century that a second and third coronet had been added to take its modern shape.

TIBERIAS, BATTLE OF. *See* HATTIN, BATTLE OF.

TIBERIUS III, Byzantine emperor, 698–705, a general whom the city militia acclaimed emperor. He deposed Leontius (695–8), but was himself captured by Justinian II, an earlier refugee emperor, and executed.

TIMOTHEUS, Nestorian patriarch, 780–823, bishop of Beth-Baghash, then patriarch. He enjoyed the favor of Islamic caliphs (al-Mahdi and Harun al-Rashid) and undertook missionary trips to India, China, and Yemen. His writings include many letters and works on canon law, theology, and astronomy.

TIMUR THE LAME (Timur Leng, Tamerlane), d. 1405, one of the greatest conquerors of history. He was of Turkish stock, claimed descent from Genghis Khan through his wife, and was born near Samarkand in Transoxiana which he conquered c. 1370 when he proclaimed himself khan of the Mongol empire. In the course of his conquests, which he carried out with a savagery paralleled only by that of Genghis Khan, he extended his rule over Afghanistan, Persia, Mesopotamia, a large part of India, the khanate of the Golden Horde in Russia, Syria, and Anato-

lia. In 1402 he routed the Ottoman Turkish army at Angora and carried off the sultan Bayazid I into captivity. He returned to Samarkand (1403) and died two years later on his way to conquer China. During his reign he brought thousands of craftsmen from the countries he conquered to his capital at Samarkand which they helped make into one of the most brilliant cities of the world.

TITHE, one-tenth of a person's income paid as a tax to support the church. The practice which was based on the law of Moses appears to have been adopted in the Christian West in the sixth century. A synod held in England in 788 enjoined the payment of tithes.

TITIVIL (Tutivillus), name of a devil said to collect words skipped or mumbled during the recitation of the Divine Office and to give a report of these to God.

TIU (Tyr, Teiwas, Tiwas, Ziu, Tiv), ancient German god of war and the sky who gave his name to Tuesday.

TLEMCEN, town of northwest Algeria, a commercial center from ancient times, located on roads connecting Algeria and Morocco and the Mediterranean with the lands south of the Sahara. It flourished especially during the period of the thirteenth to the fifteenth centuries as the capital of a Moslem Berber dynasty. The famous Arab historian Ibn Khaldun included an account of Tlemcen and that part of Africa, roughly the Maghrib, in his universal history.

TOLEDO, city in central Spain on the Tagus River which the Visigoths made their capital in the seventh century. It fell to the Moslems in 711 and served as capital of a Moorish state from 1036. In 1085 Alfonso VI of Castile captured the city, from which time it enjoyed a position of leadership in the political and cultural life of Castile. It was known for its silk and woolen textiles but was most famous for its sword blades which were highly prized throughout the world. Toledo may have been a bishop's see by the close of the first century; it was that of a metropolitan in the fourth and acquired primatial rank in 1088.

TOME OF LEO, THE, letter sent by Pope Leo I to Flavian, patriarch of Constantinople, in 449 in which he presented the Christological doctrine of the Latin Church. The letter, directed against the heresy of Eutyches, was formally accepted by the Council of Chalcedon (451) as the classic statement of the Christian doctrine of the Incarnation, namely, that Christ is One Person, possessed of two natures, the Divine and the human, united though distinct, each exercising its own particular faculties but within the unity of the Person.

TONDO, round picture or medallion, a popular art form in Italy in the fourteenth and fifteenth centuries.

TONNAGE AND POUNDAGE, a tax on each pound's worth of merchandise and on each tun or cask of wine. It was imposed for the first time during the reign of Edward I (1272–1307).

TONSURE, rite of shaving the head (usually the crown) of the person joining a monastic order or becoming a member of the secular clergy. The practice originated in Eastern monastic communities in the fourth and fifth centuries and was not introduced until the sixth and seventh in the West where it symbolized the admission of the person to the clerical state. The rite preceded the minor orders.

TORDESILLAS, TREATY OF, agreement between Spain and Portugal in 1494 which moved the line of demarcation dividing their spheres of discovery and exploration in the New World, established by Pope Alexander VI in 1493, 370 leagues to the west of the Cape Verde Islands. This treaty enabled Portugal to lay claim to Brazil after its discovery by Cabral in 1500.

TORQUEMADA, JUAN DE (John de Turrecremata), d. 1468, Spanish Dominican, distin-

guished theologian, canonist, and cardinal (1439). He served as the papal theologian at the Council of Basel in 1433 and took an active part in discussions with the Greeks at the Council of Ferrara-Florence (1438–9). In his principal work, *Summa de Ecclesia,* he defended the authority of the church and the primacy of the pope against the attacks of conciliarists and heretics.

TORQUEMADA, TOMÁS DE, d. 1498, Spanish Dominican theologian, confessor to Ferdinand and Isabella of Spain, whom they appointed grand inquisitor in 1483. He set up tribunals in various cities of Spain and laid down directions for the guidance of inquisitors. He was largely responsible for the efficient and ruthless operation of the Spanish inquisition. Perhaps as many as 2,000 persons were burned at the stake during his term of office. He was also principally responsible for the expulsion of the Jews in 1492.

TORUN (Thorn), PEACE OF: a) the first treaty of Torun was agreed to in 1411 between the defeated Teutonic Knights and the victorious Poles and Liths. Despite their disastrous defeat, the Knights surrendered only Samogitia and paid an indemnity; b) the second treaty in 1466 cost the Teutonic Knights West Prussia which was ceded to Poland. They continued to hold East Prussia as a fief of Poland.

TOSTIG, d. 1066, son of Earl Godwin of Wessex, banished with his father to Flanders in 1051 but made earl of Northumbria in 1055. In 1065 the Northumbrians drove him out because of his harsh rule. He fled to Flanders, then joined Harald Hardraade, king of Norway, in his attempt to take over England. His brother Harold, king of England, defeated Hardraade's army at Stamford Bridge where Tostig was killed.

TOTILA (Badwila), d. 552, valiant Ostrogothic chieftain who succeeded in reconquering the greater part of Italy after its recovery by Belisarius, Justinian's general. In 552 Justinian replaced Belisarius with Narses and entrusted him with forces sufficient to defeat Totila in a battle in Umbria where the Gothic chieftain was slain. Procopius, the Byzantine historian, had high praise for the valor and high sense of honor of Totila.

TOULOUSE, city in southern France on the Garonne which became a bishop's see in the third century, an archbishop's in 1317. In the tenth century its counts claimed the title of dukes of Aquitaine. They were known for their tolerant rule, and many Jews settled in the area, while the brilliant court they maintained and their generous patronage attracted leading troubadours to that part of France. But their ambivalent if not sympathetic attitude toward Catharism led to the Albigensian Crusade (1208–29), which cost Toulouse its autonomous position. In 1271 it became part of the French royal domain. The University of Toulouse was chartered in 1229, partly for the purpose of combating Catharism. [*See* RAYMOND VI and RAYMOND VII; ALBIGENSES.]

TOURAINE, a county located on both sides of the lower Loire. Its capital city was Tours. Clovis drove the Visigoths from the area in 507. During the Carolingian period it constituted a county, and in 1044 it became a possession of the count of Anjou. It came under English rule in 1152 but was recovered by Philip II Augustus in 1204 and incorporated into the royal domain.

TOURNAI (Doornik), city in Flanders on the Scheldt, already settled in Roman times, the birthplace of Clovis. It served as a Merovingian capital in the sixth century. Northmen destroyed the town in 881. In 1477 it became part of the Holy Roman empire.

TOURNAMENT. *See* TOURNEY.

TOURNEY (tournament), an organized encounter among knights, a kind of mock warfare, in which the contestants sought to best their opponents. It originated in France probably in the late tenth century and initially served as a proving place for knights until the late Middle Ages when it remained little more than pageantry.

TOURS, city of the lower Loire which grew from Roman origins and became the capital city of Touraine. The tomb of St. Martin (d. 397?) brought it great popularity as a shrine. It was at Tours that Charles Martel and the Franks defeated the Moors in 732. Vikings pillaged the town in 853 and 903. It served Louis XI of France (1461–83) as his favorite residence.

TOWER OF LONDON, fortress erected by William the Conqueror — he began construction immediately after his coronation late in 1066 — on the north bank of the Thames. Additions to the fortress were made in the twelfth and thirteenth centuries. The Tower served variously as a royal residence, a prison, and a royal fortress.

TOWN AIR IS FREE AIR, a principle expressed in many town charters that proclaimed the freedom of any serf who had sojourned there for a year and a day without being claimed by his lord.

TOWNS, RISE OF. The rise of towns coincided with the revival of trade in the late tenth century. By definition, the medieval town was a commercial center, a community that stood in sharp contrast to the manorial village. Members of its population engaged in buying and selling, in trade; the village was an agricultural community. True, a measure of buying and selling went on in many villages [*see* MARKET], and farmers must surely have lived in towns, either while still active or retired. Yet in a legal sense, a town did not acquire that particular status until it had received a charter from its lord which accorded it privileges denied the inhabitants of the manorial village.

The rise of towns was brought about by a rising population from the late tenth and eleventh centuries, the relative stability of western Europe at that time, and, of course, the revival of trade itself. That trade was the usual factor in the rise of towns is evident from a look at the sites of these towns. Almost invariably the location enjoyed some advantage to trade such as crossroads, a bridge (Bruges), or ford across a stream (Oxford), or it provided a measure of protection as a castle (Hamburg, Burgos) or as an administrative center. The one exception was the so-called new town *(ville neuve)* that a king or lord might establish in order to bring trade into that area or encourage immigration; e.g. Lorris, Berlin, Dresden, Breslau. The most populous and commercially active towns were the industrial centers of Flanders and the Low Countries, the cities of Ghent, Ypres, Arras, Bruges, and Saint Omer, where many people found employment in the various processes involved in the manufacture of textiles, also in such cities of Italy as Florence, Milan, Pisa, Genoa, and Venice.

Although the people of towns engaged in activities other than those found in the manorial village, their legal status remained no different until they had secured a charter from their lord. This charter officially created the town. The initiative in securing a charter came from the merchants. They objected to paying the lord the traditional obligations of *corvée* and banalities [*see* CORVEE; BANALITIES]; they wanted magistrates of their own choice and the right to maintain their own courts; and they wished to control the buying and selling in their community, more specifically the right to organize guilds. If the lord needed the money or appreciated the increased revenue a thriving town would mean for him, and many of them did, he granted the town a charter, for which he demanded a handsome fee.

The town represented a revolutionary development in the world of the Middle Ages. Until the rise of this mercantile element, there were three clearly established classes: the first estate, the clergy; the second, the aristocracy; and the third, the common class. Now there appeared a fourth element, still composed of commoners but free since "town air was free air." A serf (villein) who fled to a town won his freedom

after living there for a year and a day. [*See* COMMUNE.]

TOWTON, BATTLE OF, bloodiest battle ever fought in England when more than 25,000 men died on the battlefield near York in March 1461. The battle was won by Edward (IV) over the Lancastrians. King Henry VI, his wife Margaret (of Anjou), and their son managed to escape to Scotland. [*See* ROSES, WARS OF THE.]

TRACT: a) a prayer taken from the Psalms or other part of the Scriptures that was substituted for the *Alleluia* during the penitential season of Lent. It followed the gradual of the mass; b) a pamphlet, usually one issued with a religious or moral purpose. Its origins are obscure. Many medieval works, such as the English writings of Wyclif, were classified as tracts.

TRADE, REVIVAL OF. Trade within the Roman empire declined with the decline of that empire and did not revive in western Europe until the close of the tenth century. Even during the centuries of Rome's greatness, trade had never constituted an important phase of its civilization, and what did exist suffered significant decline as the economy of the late empire grew increasingly agrarian in character. The advent of the invading Germans, who did not possess any tradition of trade, did not help. In the seventh century the expansion of Islam ruptured the economic unity of the Mediterranean world, a disaster to trade that the destructive raids of Vikings, Magyars, and Saracens (from north Africa) further aggravated. [*See* PIRENNE THESIS.]

From what might be considered the nadir reached by western European trade in the ninth and early tenth centuries, historians have suggested several developments that contributed to its gradual revival. By the close of the tenth century the worst of the political turmoil that had marked the feudal period was past. By that time the Magyars had been pacified and so had the Vikings. A little later, by 1002, Venice had managed to clear the Adriatic of Moslem ships, and by 1087, with the help of Genoa and Pisa, it had forced them completely out of Italian waters. This relative stability brought with it a significant increase in population. Between 1000 and 1300, population grew from 10 million to twice that figure. The rise of towns and industrial centers that had sprung up as trade revived assured the continuation of that revival. Once under way, the Crusades constituted the most powerful factor in the further expansion of trade.

The rising towns of north Italy and particularly Venice took the lead in the revival of trade. Venice was closest to Constantinople and had received valuable concessions from its emperors for the help it had given against the Normans. Other cities of Italy, Brindisi, Pisa, Genoa, Amalfi, soon joined Venice in establishing commercial relations with the cities of the eastern Mediterranean. They brought back to the affluent classes in Italy luxury commodities such as silks, brocades, rugs, mirrors, precious stones, perfumes, dates, sugar, and spices from Africa, Persia, Turkestan, India, and from worlds as faraway as China and the East Indies.

This trade with the cities of the eastern Mediterranean and in commodities from Asia and Africa would of itself not have produced the remarkable expansion of trade that shortly took place in western Europe. Those imports were expensive and the purchasing power of most Europeans was low. This early trade did serve as a catalyst, however, and within a few years the ripples of trade that had first been felt in Italy moved up through the Alpine passes to the network of rivers—the Rhine, Weser, Elbe, Oder—that served central Europe, then to the Channel, the North Sea, and the Baltic. Once trade had expanded to most of the areas of western and northern Europe, it had taken on a new character. Instead of the luxury commodities from the eastern world, it was now products of Europe—timber, wine, fish, salt, grain, textiles, tin, copper, leather—that bulked largest in the trade that moved about that continent.

Meanwhile, this revival and expansion of trade had transformed the economy of Europe. In place of or alongside of the static, agrarian life that had centered in the manorial village, there had risen bustling towns and industrial centers, and with these a new class of society, the burghers, merchants who were new to western Europe, new almost to the western half of the Mediterranean world. This new merchant class gradually introduced Europe to a kind of activity hitherto unknown, an industrial, commercial society engaged in capitalistic endeavor. [*See* COMMUNE; CRUSADES; FAIRS; GUILD; TOWNS, RISE OF.]

TRANSEPT, the part of a cross- or T-shaped church that was set at right angles to the nave. The transept appeared in the early Christian basilica although it was most popular during the Romanesque period as a means of accommodating the large number of clergy in abbey churches and cathedrals.

TRANSFIGURATION, FEAST OF THE, feast celebrated on August 6 to commemorate the manifestation of Christ's divine glory as described in Matthew 17 and Mark 9. The feast originated in the Eastern Church where it had become widely adopted by the year 1000. It was only later introduced to the West where Pope Callistus III ordered its universal observance in commemoration of the victory won over the Turks at Belgrade in 1456.

TRANSUBSTANTIATION, the doctrine of the Christian church that the substance of the bread and wine become the body and blood of Christ during the consecration of the mass. The word was widely used in the latter part of the twelfth century and was officially defined by the Fourth Lateran Council in 1215. Still, the doctrine received its classic formulation only as a result of the work of the scholastic theologians of the thirteenth century, principally St. Thomas Aquinas.

TRAPPISTS. *See* CISTERCIANS.

TREBIZOND, EMPIRE OF, a state organized by Alexius and David Comnenus in northeastern Anatolia on the shore of the Black Sea following the capture of Constantinople in 1204 by the Venetians and Crusaders (Fourth Crusade) and the destruction of the Byzantine empire. The state of Trebizond managed to maintain its existence, even to prosper, during the reigns of Alexius II (1297–1330) and Alexius III (1349–90). The city of Trebizond which flourished as one of the leading commercial centers of the world, was famed for its wealth and beauty. The empire fell to the Ottoman Turks in 1461.

TREBUCHET, a machine used to hurl large stones against walls and fortifications or over the walls into the city. This engine of war, which was developed during the Middle Ages, gradually replaced the ballista. It was also known as a perrier or petrary.

TREE OF JESSE, a popular art form which represented the genealogy of Christ from Jesse, the father of David.

TRÈS RICHES HEURES DU DUC DE BERRY, an illuminated manuscript of the fifteenth century illustrated by the Limbourg brothers. [See LIM-BOURG, BROTHERS OF.]

TREUGA DEI. See TRUCE OF GOD.

TRÈVES. See TRIER.

TRIBONIAN, d. 543/5, legist whom Emperor Justinian I appointed to head the commission entrusted with the codification of Roman law. Earlier Justinian had removed him from his high position as master of the offices to placate the mob during the Nika riot. The emperor later restored him to that office and Tribonian remained his principal adviser until his death.

TRIER (Trèves), city located west of the middle Rhine which served as an imperial capital after Diocletian's reorganization of the Roman empire. It was a bishop's see by the second century and a metropolitanate in the sixth. During the period of Frankish rule it served as the capital of Austrasia. The Treaty of Verdun (843) assigned the city to Lothair, but Louis, king of the East Franks, acquired it by the Treaty of Mersen (870). Its archbishops established their authority over the city in the late ninth century and were invested with the right of imperial election by the Golden Bull of 1356, a right they had already been exercising from the end of the twelfth century.

TRIFORIUM, gallery in the wall above the arches on either side of the nave and under the clerestory. The triforium became an integral part of interior architectural design during the Romanesque period. During the Gothic period the large windows of the clerestory tended to reduce its prominence.

TRINITARIANS, members of the Order of the Most Holy Trinity for the Redemption of Captives, founded by John of Matha and approved by Pope Innocent III in 1198. The order, which combined the contemplative with the active life, devoted its activities principally to the ransoming of Christians held captive by the Moslems.

TRINITY SUNDAY, the Sunday following Pentecost (Whitsunday) which was dedicated to the Holy Trinity. Its observance as marking the conclusion of the Easter season and the descent of the Holy Spirit was universally enjoined by Pope John XXII in 1334.

TRIPOLI, COUNTY OF, the smallest of the Crusading states established following the success of the First Crusade (1096–9). It lay on the coast to the south of Antioch and above the northern frontier of the kingdom of Jerusalem. About the year 1200 it was united with the principality of Antioch. [See RAYMOND IV, count of Toulouse.]

TRISTAN AND ISOLDE (Tristam, Iseult), the two leading characters in a popular romance probably of Celtic origin. By some misadventure the two young people drink a love potion that should have been shared by King Mark of

Cornwall, Tristan's lord, and by Isolde. Chrétien de Troyes, Gottfried von Strasburg, and Sir Thomas Mallory, among other poets, composed versions of the story.

TRITHEISM, a heresy that denied the unity of substance in the Three Divine Persons. The doctrine is associated with a group of sixth-century Monophysites who maintained the existence of three Divine substances in the Trinity. In the Middle Ages the extreme nominalism of Roscelin as well as the extreme realism of Gilbert de la Porrée caused both theologians to be accused of tritheism. Joachim of Fiore was influenced by the latter's views.

TRIVIUM, the three arts included in the upper division of the seven liberal arts, namely, grammar, rhetoric, and dialectic. This designation, as opposed to that of the quadrivium, came into use during the Carolingian period. The subjects which comprised the trivium might be classified as the arts. Their function was that of furnishing the student the tools of learning. [See DIALECTIC, GRAMMAR, RHETORIC.]

TROILUS AND CRESSIDA, a medieval love story remotely related to the characters in the ancient Greek legend. The first version of the story appeared in the twelfth century. Both Boccaccio and Chaucer dealt with the theme.

TROLL, in Nordic folklore a supernatural being that might take the form of a giant or a dwarf.

TRONDHEIM, the medieval Nidaros, a city located on the west central coast of Norway and founded by Olaf I in 997. It became a bishop's see in 1029 and until c. 1200 served as the royal capital. In 1152 its bishop received the rank of an archbishop. It prospered as a commercial center until the fourteenth century when the Hanseatic League diverted the bulk of its trade to Bergen. The tomb of St. Olaf II made Nidaros a popular place of pilgrimage.

TROPE. See DRAMA, MEDIEVAL.

TROUBADOUR, a poet of Provence who composed lyric verse in the language known as Provençal. He wrote on the general theme of love but this could run the gamut of the sentiments a knight felt for his Lady or the wife of his feudal lord to the carnal love which hoped for reciprocation and fulfillment. William IX, duke of Aquitaine (d. 1127), who may have been the first troubadour, emphasized the ennobling influence the love of woman had upon man. The troubadour also employed different verse forms to suit a variety of moods: the formal love lyric (canzone, chanso); tenso or debate over questions concerning love; pastourelle, a song about a knight and a shepherdess; and the alba or dawn song, about the nightingale that warned lovers of approaching day. The troubadour and his verses enjoyed greatest popularity during the twelfth and thirteenth centuries. Among the best known troubadours were Bernard de Ventadour, Bertrand de Born, and Peire Vidal. The minnesinger may be considered a troubadour of Germany although until the late Middle Ages poets generally employed Provençal, whatever their national dialect, when they wrote about love. The leading German minnesinger was Walther von der Vogelweide (d. c. 1230).

TROUVÈRE, poet of north and central France who composed on lyric, satiric, even humorous themes during the Old French period, as opposed to the troubadour of southern France who sang principally of love.

TROYES, city on the Seine in northeast France, a Roman town, which became an episcopal see in the fourth century. In the eleventh century it served as the capital of the county of Champagne. Its fair, held twice a year, was among the most famous of the Middle Ages. The fine Gothic cathedral of St. Pierre (thirteenth-sixteenth century) graces the city.

TROYES, TREATY OF, treaty agreed to in 1420 by Philip the Good, duke of Burgundy, Isabella [see ISABEAU], wife of the mentally ill Charles VI of France, and Henry V of England, which declared the dauphin Charles to be illegitimate, named Henry heir and regent of France, and arranged for his marriage to Catherine, daughter of Charles VI. Henry was to rule as king when Charles died, while England was to retain all its possessions as far south as the Loire.

TRUCE OF GOD, a proclamation similar in origin and intent to the Peace of God but appearing a little later (early eleventh century). It banned fighting on certain days of the week and during specified periods, such as Saturdays, Sundays, and Lent. In time the entire interval from Wednesday evening to Monday morning was declared a period of peace. The Truce of God enjoyed but limited success.

TRULLAN SYNOD, also called the Quinisext or Fifth-Sixth Council, since it was intended to complete the work of the Fifth (553) and Sixth (680) General Councils. It met in 692 and was attended by Eastern bishops, and sat in the domed room ("trullus") of Justinian II's palace in Constantinople. Its disciplinary decrees, which concerned such matters as clerical marriage and impediments to matrimony, were rejected by the pope.

TUDOR, ruling dynasty of England from 1485 to 1603. It traced its claim to the throne to Owen Tudor (d. 1461), a member of an old Welsh aristocratic family who had married Catherine, the widow of Henry V. Their eldest son Edmund (d. 1456), earl of Richmond, married Margaret Beaufort, the daughter of John Beaufort, who was the grandson of John of Gaunt by Catherine Swynford. (Gaunt's children by Catherine had been declared legitimate.) Henry (VII), the son of Edmund and Margaret, gained the throne after his victory over Richard III in 1485 at the battle of Bosworth Field.

TUGHRIL BEG, leader of the Seljuk Turks who captured Baghdad in 1055 and was proclaimed sultan with the title "King of the East and the West."

TUNIC, generally any vestment shaped like a sack, with closed upper part except for a slit for putting the garment over the head, and with sleeves or mere slits on the sides to accommodate the arms.

TURA, COSIMO (Cosmè), d. 1495, court painter to the d'Este family, the first major representative of the Ferrara School. His preference for the sculptured figure style suggests the influence of Mantegna. Despite their feeling for monumentality, his compositions are full of pattern and gaiety. Included among his works are *Allegorical Figure* and *St. Jerome*.

TURKEY, country that straddled the Bosphorus from 1453 when the Ottoman Turks captured the Byzantine capital of Constantinople. This branch of the Turkish family took its name from Osman (Othman) I (d. 1326) who established an independent principality in Bithynia (northwest Anatolia) called Osmanli. His son Orkhan I (1326–62) captured Nicaea and Nicomedia. In 1345 the first Turks crossed over to Europe, this time, and again in 1352, as allies of the Byzantine emperor John Cantacuzenus. But in 1354 a Turkish army came over on its own and seized Gallipoli. In 1362 Murad I captured Adrianople and made it his capital. From here Ottoman power spread over Thrace, destroyed the Serbian state at the battle of Kossovo (1389), and subjugated Bulgaria (1392). In 1396 the Christian West attempted to stop the Turkish march, but a large Crusading army under Sigismund, king of Hungary, suffered an overwhelming defeat at Nicopolis. The sultan Bayazid I (1389–1402) might have gone on to capture Constantinople which was under siege had not Timur appeared with his Mongols and captured him instead and destroyed his army at Angora (1402). This defeat and the subsequent struggle over the succession interrupted the seemingly irresistible advance of Turkish arms. In 1444 Murad II (1421–51) defeated another Crusading army under Ladislas III of Poland and Hungary and John Hunyadi, governor of Transylvania, at Varna and four years later dealt Hunyadi a final defeat at Kossovo. By this time Turkish rule had engulfed the Balkans except for Belgrade which remained in Christian hands and, of course, Constantinople. Finally, Turkish artillery breached the walls of Constantinople in 1453 and in April the city fell to Mohammed II (1451–81). Hostilities with Venice continued until 1479 when that maritime state agreed to pay a handsome sum for the privilege of trading in the Black Sea. [*See* SELJUK TURKS.]

TURPIN (Tilpin) OF REIMS, d. 794, monk and archbishop of Reims (753) who, legend had it, died with Roland at Roncesvalles. The *Chanson de Roland* presents him as a mighty warrior even though he was a thoroughly dedicated bishop.

TUSCANY, region of central Italy, a Lombard duchy, conquered by Charlemagne in the late eighth century, after which it became a march governed by the counts of Lucca. In the tenth century the house of Attoni of Canossa was invested with the margravate, of which Matilda was the most famous member (d. 1115). She bequeathed her extensive territories to the church, which precipitated a long struggle over her estates between church and German emperors. In the twelfth and thirteenth centuries Pisa and Florence contended for control, a contest which Florence won after 1284.

TUSCULANI, prominent family of Rome of the eleventh century when it boasted three popes, Benedict VIII, John XIX, and Benedict IX. The first two popes were brothers, the third their nephew.

TUSI, NASIR AL-DIN, d. 1274, Persian philosopher, scientist, and mathematician. He served as adviser to Hulagu Khan and was a member of his retinue when he destroyed Baghdad in 1258. He translated the works of Euclid, Ptolemy, and other Greek scientists, and made contributions of his own in mathematics and astronomy. One of his most learned works was a treatise on ethics in the Greek tradition.

TVER, PRINCES OF, rulers of a principality in northeast Russia who vied with Moscow for the leadership of that region. Moscow secured the advantage during the second half of the fourteenth century, although the principality of Tver did not fall to Ivan III until 1485.

TWO-FIELD SYSTEM, the practice, inherited from ancient times, of dividing the arable soil belonging to an agricultural community (village or manor) into two large fields and cropping these in alternate years. The three-field system tended to replace it from the eleventh century in many parts of France, England, and western Germany.

TWO SICILIES, KINGDOM OF THE. *See* NAPLES, KINGDOM OF.

TYLER, WAT, d. 1381, probably a disbanded soldier of Kent who was one of the principal rebel leaders in the Peasant Revolt of 1381. He was stabbed and seriously wounded by the mayor of London in the course of their meeting with the young Richard II. Later he was seized and beheaded on order of the mayor.

TZETZES, JOHN, Byzantine polymath and poet of the twelfth century. He was a prodigious writer. Even though his work suffered from pedantry and abounded in inaccuracies, he deserves credit for preserving much useful information about ancient Greek literature and scholarship.

TZIMISCES, JOHN. *See* JOHN I (Tzimisces).

UBERTINO OF CASALE, d. c. 1329–41, a leader of the Franciscan Spirituals who was imbued by the ideas of Joachim of Fiore and was also influenced by John of Parma and Peter John Olivi. In 1310 he came to Avignon at the request of Clement V to present the views of the Spirituals, and in 1322 he was consulted by John XXII on the question of theological poverty. He was permitted to transfer to the Benedictine order, but when new difficulties arose, he fled Avignon, possibly fearing a charge of heresy. Obscurity hides his last years. He was the author of a mystical work on the life and passion of Christ which included meditations on St. Francis and poverty, attacks on the Conventual Franciscans, and criticism of Popes Boniface VIII and Benedict XI.

UCCELLO, PAOLO (Paolo di Dono), d. 1475, painter, mosaicist, and craftsman of Florence whose work shows the influence of Donatello. His works reveal a preoccupation with linear perspective and geometry, although he succeeded in blending this with a poetical interpretation of reality and a highly imaginative approach. His works include the painting *The Flood* and tapestries for the Medici entitled *The Rout of San Romano*.

UGOLINO OF ORVIETO, d. after 1457, author of treatises dealing with musical theory in which he considered the mathematical and philosophical aspects of music. He also composed music of his own.

ULFILAS (Ulphilas, Wulfila), d. 382/3, Arian missionary-bishop, consecrated by the Arian Eu-sebius of Nicomedia. He labored for 40 years among the Goths both to the north and the south of the Danube. He translated the Bible into Gothic and may have invented the alphabet he used. He omitted the Book of Kings lest its account of warlike deeds encourage the militaristic tendencies of the Goths.

ULM, city on the upper Danube in Wurtemberg, first noted in 854. It received city rights c. 1163 and was declared an imperial city about the middle of the fourteenth century. It ruled an extensive area north of the Danube and was one of the most powerful cities of Germany in the fifteenth century.

ULRIC (Ulrich) OF AUGSBURG, ST., d. 973, bishop of Augsburg who encouraged a reform of the liturgy and lent strong support to Otto I in his efforts to reform the church in general. He organized the defenses of Augsburg against the Magyars and was the first German bishop to receive the right to mint money. He was also the first person to be formally canonized by the pope.

ULRICH OF LICHTENSTEIN, d. c. 1276, Middle High German poet, one of the late minnesingers, a knight of Styria, who composed love and dance songs as well as a lament over the decline of chivalry. This last carried the title *Frauendienst* (service of women).

ULSTER, EARLDOM OF, the first title of honor in Ireland that was of English creation. King John conferred the title on Hugh de Lacy in 1205. Lionel (d. 1368), third son of Edward III, acquired the title by right of his wife. Their daughter Philippa married Edmund de Mortimer (d. 1381), third earl of March, through whom the title eventually passed to Richard of York (d. 1460), leader of the Yorkists, who passed it on to his son Edward (IV).

ULUGH (Ulug) BEG, d. 1449, a grandson of Timur the Lame who succeeded to the Timurid domain in 1447 and brought its culture to its peak. He made Samarkand the center of Moslem culture. Among other writings (in Arabic), he produced a history of the sons of Genghis Khan. To advance his study of the stars and planets, he erected an observatory at Samarkand. His own astronomical calculations did not always agree with those of Ptolemy.

'UMAR IBN ABI RABI'AH ('Umar Ibn 'Abdallah Ibn Abi Rabi 'Ah Al-Makhzumi), d. 712 or 719, reputedly the greatest amatory poet of early Arabic literature. He lived in Mecca and was a member of the ruling Kuraish tribe. His poetry furnishes a good picture of the social life of the aristocracy of the Hedjaz in his time.

UMAYYADS. See OMAYYADS.

UMBRIA, SCHOOL OF, school of painting that gained prominence as a result of the work of Perugino and Raphael.

UNAM SANCTAM, bull issued by Pope Boniface VIII in 1302 at the height of his controversy with Philip IV of France. In this document Boniface solemnly declared that the pope was the head of the one universal church which Christ had founded; that outside of that church there was no salvation; and that all men must accept the pope's authority if they wished to be saved. The bull declared that both the temporal and spiritual swords were committed to the church. The purpose of the bull was to block Philip in his efforts to gain greater control of the church in France. It failed and ultimately led to Boniface's humiliation at Anagni. [See BONIFACE VIII, Pope.]

UNCIAL SCRIPT, a form of majuscule script used for books in Greek and Latin from about the fourth to the eighth century, e.g., *Codex Sinaiticus* (Greek), *Codex Amiatinus* (Latin).

UNICORN, fabled horse of the Middle Ages that was believed to have a sharp horn in the middle of its forehead. The unicorn had already appeared in ancient art and literature, and in the *Physiologus* (second century A.D.).

UNION OF KALMAR. *See* KALMAR, UNION OF.

UNIVERSAL, a general term, idea, or concept that enables one to identify a particular thing (e.g., tree). The realist maintained that such ideas existed before the individual thing *(ante rem)*, the nominalist the reverse, namely, that it was only after the mind had perceived similar objects and had abstracted what qualities they shared, that the idea itself came into being *(post rem)*. The problem antedated the Middle Ages and as a philosophical question originated with Plato who maintained that these general ideas had existence from all eternity. Since Plato's position dominated philosophical thinking in the Middle Ages until the thirteenth century through the media of the writings of Plotinus, Porphyry, and Augustine, most scholastics of the twelfth century were inclined to agree with the Greek philosopher. [*See* REALISM AND NOMINALISM.]

UNIVERSITY, THE MEDIEVAL, an institution of higher learning that emerged from the cathedral school in the twelfth century. The principal factor that gave rise to the university was the introduction of philosophical and scientific works from the Islamic and Byzantine worlds. These included the *Corpus Juris Civilis*, the works of Aristotle, Galen, and Ptolemy as well as those of other Greek scholars and scientists, together with the writings of such Arabic commentators as Avicenna and Averroës. A second factor was the intellectual ferment among Western scholars for which the rise of scholasticism was principally responsible. Western scholars in increasing numbers applied themselves to the assimilation of this knowledge from the ancient past into Christian thought. A third factor in the appearance of some universities was the tradition of scholarship cathedral schools had enjoyed or the renown which the presence of famous lecturers had brought them, as was the case with Bologna where Irnerius and Gratian had lectured.

The initial term employed to designate the university was *studium generale*, which might be defined as a cathedral school whose scholarly reputation had attracted students from beyond the confines of the diocese in which it was located. What principally attracted such students was the school's ability to provide instruction in several fields. A *studium generale* might have functioned as a true university some time before pope or king had granted it a charter, at which time it became a university. The term university was itself nothing more than another word for guild. In the case of the university, it referred to a guild of masters and/or students, a legal entity that ordinarily received the grant of a charter and handled relations with the local authorities. It was some time before the university received the respect its masters and students demanded. Failing to get satisfaction in the inevitable clashes with the town officials, faculty and students might at first have simply migrated to some other location. Almost half of the medieval universities owed their foundation to such migrations. Oxford was founded by English scholars who left the *studium generale* at Paris in 1167. Migration or its threat became unnecessary once church and state came to appreciate the importance of these new institutions, at which time they were quite ready to accord them an autonomous status.

The chancellor of the cathedral chapter who had directed the cathedral school early lost his authority to a rector or proctor. This official was usually the dean of the arts faculty since all students ordinarily enrolled in that school before proceeding to the professional schools. The authority of the rector was, however, carefully controlled by the faculty, the ultimate source of power in most universities. (In Italy the guild of students generally had charge of the administration of the institution.) The larger universities were organized into the four faculties of arts, law, medicine, and theology; also at the larger universities, as at Paris, the students divided into nations. [*See* NATION.] The first colleges were simply dormitories which in time might assume much of the responsibility of teaching, as at Oxford. [*See* SORBON, ROBERT DE.]

Medieval Latin was the language used in the medieval university. The subject matter studied in what today would pass as the college of the liberal arts were the traditional seven liberal arts but with more attention given the trivium than the quadrivium and more to logic than to grammar and rhetoric. Aristotle provided the substance of the subject matter, more specifically his ethics, metaphysics, logic, and natural sciences. In theology the *Sentences* of Peter Lombard constituted the standard textbook, supplemented with commentaries on the Bible and the writings of the church fathers. In law the student concentrated on Gratian's *Decretum* if he sought a career in the church, on the *Digest* if he hoped to be a civil lawyer. The subject matter in the field of medicine was provided by Galen, Hippocrates, and the commentaries of Avicenna and other Islamic scholars.

After four years of study in the arts curriculum the student received a bachelor's degree, at which time the majority left the university. Two additional years were required of those who continued for a master's degree. This was granted them after they successfully defended a thesis and convinced their examiners that they were masters at that trade. Professional faculties normally granted the doctor's degree.

UNTERWALDEN, one of the three forest cantons of Switzerland that formed the Perpetual Compact in 1291. The Hapsburgs were the counts and chief landowners of the canton. [*See* SWITZERLAND.]

UPPSALA, city to the northwest of Stockholm, a center of pagan religious rites. It became an episcopal see in 1130 (Old Uppsala) and the seat of a metropolitanate at its modern site in the late thirteenth century. The cathedral of Uppsala (1287–1435) served as the usual coronation place of the Swedish kings. It remains the largest church in Sweden. Its university was founded by Archbishop Jakob Ulfsson in 1477.

URBAN I, ST., Pope, 222–30, about whom there remains little firm information. It is improbable that he suffered martyrdom since Alexander Severus, the emperor at the time, was favorably disposed toward Christianity.

URBAN II, BL., Pope, 1088–99, monk and prior of Cluny, cardinal bishop, and a vigorous supporter of the Gregorian reform movement with its objective of suppressing the practice of lay investiture, simony, and clerical concubinage. He succeeded Victor III, but since Henry IV of Germany refused to abandon Clement III, the antipope, it was some time before Urban could move into Rome. Urban is best known for calling a council at Clermont in 1095 and there proclaiming the First Crusade.

URBAN III, Pope, 1185–7, archbishop of Milan, whose short pontificate was filled with controversy with Emperor Federick I Barbarossa. Among other problems there was the dispute over the lands of Countess Matilda of Tuscany which both pope and emperor claimed.

URBAN IV, Pope, 1261–4, bishop of Verdun (1253) and patriarch of Jerusalem (1255). As pope he prevailed upon Louis IX of France to permit his brother Charles of Anjou to bring an army into Italy to oppose the Hohenstaufens and their Ghibelline allies. Urban introduced the feast of Corpus Christi into the liturgical calendar.

URBAN V, BL., Pope, 1362–70, studied at Paris and Avignon, then taught canon law at Montpellier and Avignon, later became abbot first of Saint-Germain in Auxerre, then of Saint-Victor in Marseilles. As pope at Avignon he introduced financial economies. In 1367 he returned to Rome where he met the Byzantine emperor John V Palaeologus. The reunion of the Greek and Latin churches to which they agreed later failed to find acceptance in Constantinople. While in Rome Urban made efforts to restore the city which was in need of much reconstruction after almost 70 years of neglect. Despite the warning of St. Bridget that he would die should he return to Avignon, he did so in 1370 and promptly died.

URBAN VI, Pope, 1378–89, archbishop of Bari (1377), elected pope by cardinals who were under some pressure from the Roman populace to elect an Italian. (The Romans feared that a French pope would return to Avignon and continue the Avignonese Residence.). Immediately following his election, Urban assumed a domineering, even insulting, attitude toward the cardinals, whereupon they repudiated him as having been invalidly elected and chose Robert of Geneva (Clement VII) in his stead. Their action precipitated the Western schism which endured until 1415. [See SCHISM, WESTERN.] Urban meanwhile created a new college of cardinals that was Italian in character and remained so into modern times. Urban in his later years personally led an army against the ruler of Naples in an effort to conquer that country.

URBS BEATA JERUSALEM DICTA PACIS VISIO, hymn of unknown authorship composed c. 700 which celebrated the Heavenly Jerusalem in terms suggested in Revelation 21. The hymn was introduced into the liturgy for the dedication of a church.

URI, one of three forest cantons of Switzerland that entered into the Perpetual Compact of 1291. [See SWITZERLAND.]

URSULA, ST., perhaps a legendary saint who according to tradition was martyred together with 11,000 other virgins at Cologne. In time the name of Ursula was given to the leader of this army of virgins and identified as a British princess who had taken the virgins to Rome on a pilgrimage, then on their return were massacred by the Huns. The legend proved a popular one in the Middle Ages.

USUARD, MARTYROLOGY OF, the most popular martyrology of the Middle Ages and the basis of the modern "Roman Martyrology." Its compiler was a Benedictine monk of the abbey of St. Germain-des-Prés at Paris called Usuard (d. c. 875) who was commissioned to do the work by Charles the Bald, king of the West Franks.

USURY, term generally employed to connote interest until the late Middle Ages when a distinction came to be made between excessive interest, that is, usury in the modern sense, and the reasonable return an investor could expect for the use of his money. This last came to be designated interest. Until the late Middle Ages theologians condemned the charging of any kind of interest on the theory that money was a measure of wealth, not a means of creating more wealth. In their judgment loans were consumptive in character, not capitalistic, wherefore the laws of justice and charity forbade the charging of interest. It was condemned by the Councils of Arles (314), Nicaea (325), Third Lateran (1179), and Second Council of Lyons (1274), although the charging of interest was allowed to Jews by the Fourth Lateran Council (1215). Medieval theologians were not alone in their condemnation of interest. The Old Testament, the Koran, Plato, Aristotle, and Cicero all condemned interest.

UTICA, MARTYRS OF, African Christians martyred during the persecution of Valerian (c. 258) by being thrown alive into slaking quicklime which reduced their bodies to a white mass of powder. According to the testimony of St. Augustine, there were 153 Christians so martyred at Utica, 35 miles from Carthage. The Roman Martyrology increased the number to 300 and assigned the incident to Carthage.

UTRAQUISTS. *See* CALIXTINES.

UTRECHT, city in the Netherlands which was a military post in Roman times. Franks moved into the area in the fourth century. They were converted by the Anglo-Saxon missionary Willibrord who served as first bishop of Utrecht (695). The bishops of Utrecht ruled as princes of the Holy Roman Empire. Utrecht was one of the first cities of the Low Countries to develop into a flourishing textile center.

UTRECHT PSALTER, a psalter manuscript of the ninth century, a product of the school of Reims.

UTRIUSQUE IURIS, of both laws, that is, of both canon and civil law.

VACARIUS, d. 1200?, Italian scholar of civil and canon law, the first known teacher of Roman law in England. He may have been brought to Canterbury by Thomas Becket. He prepared a compendium of the *Digest* and *Codex* of Justinian. This book became the leading law textbook in early Oxford where Vacarius himself possibly taught from 1149. In 1154 he became the legal adviser to the archbishop of York.

VADSTENA, ABBEY OF, monastic house on Lake Wetter in Sweden, founded in 1346 by St. Bridget. It served as the mother house of the Brigittine order.

VALDEMAR. *See* WALDEMAR.

VALENCIA, the Roman Valentia, city located on the east coast of Spain. It fell to the Visigoths in 413 and to the Moors in 714. In 1021 when the Caliphate of Córdoba collapsed, it became an independent emirate. From 1089 until 1099, it was largely under control of The Cid, then returned to Moorish rule in 1102. In 1238 James of Aragon incorporated it into his kingdom. During the fourteenth and fifteenth centuries the city and province of Valencia enjoyed the height of their economic prosperity and cultural flowering. The University of Valencia was founded in 1411 principally through the efforts of St. Vincent Ferrer.

VALENS, FLAVIUS, Roman emperor, 364–78, raised to the emperorship by his brother, Valentinian I, and assigned the administration of the eastern empire. In 375 he permitted the Visigoths to cross the Danube into Moesia in order to escape the Huns, but they revolted and at Adrianople in 378 killed him and destroyed the Roman army. Valens was an Arian and banished bishops who were orthodox in their views. He was succeeded by Theodosius I.

VALENTINE, Pope, August to September 827, a Roman, cardinal deacon, and successor of Eugenius II.

VALENTINE, ST., a name that may commemorate two saints, the one an obscure priest of Rome who suffered martyrdom c. 269, the other a bishop of Terni (Interamna) who was martyred about the same time. The origins of the late medieval custom of sending love missives on St. Valentine's Day should probably be traced to the ancient Roman festival of Lupercalia which was celebrated in mid-February.

VALENTINIAN I, FLAVIUS, Roman emperor, 364–75, ablest of the Roman rulers who succeeded Constantine I. He reestablished the imperial frontiers along the Rhine and Danube and sent his general Theodosius to Britain to halt the invasions of the Picts and Scots. He appointed his brother Valens to administer the eastern part of the empire. An Orthodox Christian, he showed himself tolerant in matters of religion.

VALENTINIAN II, FLAVIUS, Roman emperor, 375–92, son of Valentinian I, appointed co-augustus for Italy and Illyricum by his half-brother Gratian. In 383 Maximus, who was in command in Britain, revolted and killed Gratian. When he moved into Italy, Valentinian fled, but he was reinstated by Theodosius, emperor in the east, who appointed his general Arbogast to advise and protect Valentinian. Shortly after

Valentinian dismissed Arbogast, he was found dead, probably slain by followers of Arbogast.

VALENTINIAN III, FLAVIUS PLACIDUS, Roman emperor, 425–55, son of Constantius III and Placidia and nephew of Honorius. His mother and later his general Aetius ruled the western empire in his name. Valentinian cooperated with Pope Leo I in enforcing ecclesiastical regulations in the west. In 454 he arranged the murder of Aetius, the general who had defeated Attila and the Huns at Châlons in 451, and the following year he was himself slain by officers of Aetius.

VALENTINUS, Gnostic theologian of the second century, founder of the Valentinians. He was a native of Egypt, lived for a time in Rome, then moved to Cyprus. His most influential writing was a systematic theology that incorporated Platonic and Pythagorean elements. He was probably the most influential of the Gnostic leaders. Only a few fragments of his numerous works remain.

VALERIAN, PUBLIUS LICINIUS, Roman emperor, 253–60. He appointed his son Gallienus co-augustus in the west while he administered the east. He continued with greater vigor the persecution of Christians which Decius had initiated. In a campaign against the Persians, he was captured and died their prisoner.

VALHALLA, in Nordic mythology the realm of the dead that was reserved for heroes and kings. The Valkyries brought the dead warriors to this "martial paradise."

VALKYRIE, any of the maidens or daughters of Odin who were believed to bring the souls of slain heroes to Valhalla where they tended them. Chief among the Valkyries was Brynhild (Brunhild).

VALLA, LORENZO, d. 1457, a leading humanist, born in Rome. He became a priest and lectured in several cities of Italy before serving as secretary to King Alfonso V of Aragon and Naples. When he lost the king's favor in 1448, Pope Nicholas V befriended him despite his materialist views and gave him a papal secretaryship. Valla had earlier written the *De Voluptate* in which he applauded the pleasures of the senses as the greatest good. The pope commissioned him to translate a number of Greek classics, including the *Iliad*. Valla also composed a popular classical Latin grammar and made a significant contribution to the development of textual criticism by proving the Donation of Constantine to be a forgery.

VALLOMBROSANS (Vallumbrosans), congregation of monks founded by John Gualbert c. 1038 for the purpose of reviving the Rule of St. Benedict in all its original austerity. The congregation took its name from the Tuscan mountains near Florence where Gualbert founded the mother house. In keeping with Benedict's rule, the monasteries that joined the congregation remained wholly autonomous. The Vallombrosans spread rapidly and numbered more than 50 communities by the end of the twelfth century. The Vallombrosan monks wore habits of coarse gray wool.

VALOIS, county to the northeast of Paris which escheated to the crown in 1213. In 1285 Philip III gave the county to his younger son Charles. Charles's son Philip (VI) succeeded to the throne in 1328 when Charles IV, the last of the direct Capetian kings, died without male issue. With Philip VI began the Valois line of French kings. They ruled France until 1589.

VANDALS, German tribe located along the middle Oder where they divided into two branches, the Asding and the Siling. Both groups crossed the Rhine late in 406, the Asding branch joining the Sueves and occupying Galicia in Spain, the Siling branch moving to southern Spain, thence over to Africa under Gaiseric in 429 when they were attacked by the Visigoths. They captured Carthage in 435 and proceeded to establish an independent state which included Sardinia and Corsica. By means of their navy — they were the only Germanic people to have ships—they secured effective control of the entire western half of the Mediterranean. In 455 they sacked Rome and carried off the Empress Eudoxia and her daughter as hostages. The Vandals were Arians and persecuted the native Orthodox Christian population. After the death of Gaiseric in 477, the Vandal kingdom began to decline and in 534 it fell to the army of Belisarius, the general of the Byzantine emperor Justinian I.

VAN EYCK, HUBERT AND JAN. *See* EYCK, HUBERT AND JAN VAN.

VARANGIAN GUARD, name given to the Russian contingent of 6,000 troops that came to the aid of the Byzantine emperor Basil II in 988 and served as an imperial guard. They remained in Constantinople until the eleventh century when they were largely replaced by soldiers from England.

VARANGIANS, the name employed by Russian chroniclers when referring to the Scandinavian Vikings who penetrated their country in the ninth century. The term became synonymous with Russians. [*See* KIEV.]

VARNA, BATTLE OF, battle fought in 1444 on the Bulgarian coast of the Black Sea between the Turks under Murad II and Western Crusaders, principally Hungarians and Wallachians led by Ladislas of Poland and Hungary and John Hunyadi, governor of Transylvania. The destruction of the Crusading army all but ended the final hope Constantinople entertained of holding off its capture by the Turks.

VASCO DA GAMA. *See* GAMA, VASCO DA.

VASSAL, in the feudal period the free man who held land, called a fief, from a lord to whom he paid homage and swore fealty. As vassal he owed his lord various services, the most important of which was military. Other services included that of advising the lord and paying him the traditional aids. [*See* AID, FEUDAL.] The term vassal was first applied in the late Merovingian

period to servants in the king's household. Since they proved more trustworthy than his regular officials and counts, the king began to assign them more duties and to grant them lands from which they drew the revenues to enable them to perform these services. The term vassal gradually lost its earlier servile meaning during the eighth and ninth centuries when members of the aristocracy voluntarily accepted the status of vassal in order to qualify as recipients of royal lands. The king required them to give him in return an act of homage, which in time came to be confirmed with an oath of fealty.

VATICAN, the buildings that made up the papal capital located on Vatican hill in Rome. The central structure was Old St. Peter's, on either side of which Pope Symmachus (498–514) erected two small residences. About 1200 Pope Innocent III rebuilt one of these. After a fire had seriously damaged the Lateran palace in 1309, the Vatican became the principal papal residence except for the period of the Avignonese Residence.

VATICAN LIBRARY, the collection of books and manuscripts in the Vatican. It traced its origin to the efforts of Nicholas V (1447–55) to gather these holdings. He erected the structure to house them c. 1450. The library was enlarged by Sixtus IV (1471–84) and opened to scholars.

VEGETIUS (Flavius Vegetius Renatus), military writer of the fourth century whose treatise, *De Re Militari*, was accepted as an important tactical manual in the late Middle Ages.

VEGIUS (Vegio), MAPHEUS (Maffeo), d. 1458, an Augustinian, teacher of poetry and law at Pavia, papal secretary, humanist, and educator. He stressed moral training as the prime objective in the education of children

VEHMGERICHT (Vehme, Vehmic Court, Fehm), tribunals appearing in the aftermath of the disintegration of the Carolingian empire and the feudalization of western Europe, first and especially in Westphalia, which attempted to put an end to the lawlessness of the period. These tribunals constituted "holy bands," sworn to secrecy, which administered a summary kind of justice, often more feared than just. They were most numerous in the fifteenth century when conditions in many parts of Germany bordered on anarchy. Once the states of Germany became consolidated under the growing power of their lords, these tribunals were suppressed.

VENANTIUS FORTUNATUS. *See* FORTUNATUS, VENANTIUS HONORIUS CLEMENTIANUS.

VENI CREATOR SPIRITUS, breviary hymn honoring the Holy Spirit generally assigned to the ninth century. Rabanus Maurus (d. 856) has been suggested as a possible author.

VENI SANCTE SPIRITUS, sequence assigned to the feast of Pentecost. Some scholars have attributed its composition to Pope Innocent III (1198–1216) but Stephen Langton (d. 1228) seems more probable as its author.

VENICE, city built on islands at the northern end of the Adriatic whose origins reach back to refugees who fled there upon the advance of Attila and his Huns in 452. The invasion of the Lombards in 568 swelled this refugee population and turned it into a permanent settlement. Venice was officially subject to the jurisdiction of the exarch of Ravenna, even though its insular position and the weakness of Byzantium left it virtually autonomous. In 810 Charlemagne and Emperor Nicephorus I agreed that Venice should not be incorporated into the Carolingian empire, but that it could continue to trade with the neighboring lands. Venice's location enabled it to assume the lead in the revival of trade which began to affect the economy of western Europe during the second half of the tenth century. By the close of the eleventh century it had secured control of the waters of the Adriatic, while its ships, by treaty or tacit agreement, were moving to and from Constantinople and Syrian ports. In 1082 Alexius I Comnenus extended to the city

the right of free trade in the empire in acknowledgment of Venice's assistance against Robert Guiscard and the Normans.

The Crusades brought Venice an enormous volume of trade but they also benefited that city's rivals, of whom the most aggressive was Genoa. Bitter rivalry and hostility marked the relations between the two city-states to the close of the Middle Ages. Venice stole a march on Genoa when it diverted the Fourth Crusade (1202-4) to serve its own ends and netted a large share of the loot of Constantinople and its possessions when the great city was captured. The rivalry continued, now in Venice's favor, now against it, although its victory over Genoa in the War of Chioggia (1378–81) gave it unquestioned supremacy thenceforth in the eastern Mediterranean. Still no sooner were the Genoese disposed of than there were the Turks to cause trouble and, as the fortunes of Turkey rose, so those of Venice fell. The fall of Constantinople to the Turks in 1453 which struck a major blow at Venetian maritime supremacy was followed by warfare that extended to 1479 when Venice agreed to surrender Scutari and pay a heavy annual sum for the privilege of trading in the Black Sea. Venice's position was struck a permanent blow, one from which that state never recovered, by the discovery in 1498 by Vasco da Gama of an all-water route to India. With cheap water trade to the Indies Venice could not compete.

VENTADOUR, BERNARD DE. *See* BERNARD DE VENTADOUR.

VERBUM SUPERNUM PRODIENS, the opening line of two hymns: a) hymn about the Incarnation composed between the fifth and eighth centuries; b) hymn honoring the eucharist and generally ascribed to St. Thomas Aquinas.

VERDUN (Verdun-sur-Meuse), originally a Celtic settlement, a bishop's seat in the fourth century. It was assigned to Lothair in the division of the Carolingian empire agreed to in the Treaty of Verdun (843). In the eleventh century it served as the center of the reform movement in Lorraine.

VERDUN, TREATY OF, agreement reached in 843 among the sons of Louis the Pious, namely, Lothair, Louis, and Charles, over a tripartite division of the Carolingian empire. Charles (the Bald) secured the western third of the empire, Louis (the German) received the eastern section, while Lothair was assigned the central portion which included the Rhineland and Italy. He was also to hold the title Roman emperor.

VERGERIO, PIETRO PAOLO, d. 1444, teacher of Latin in several cities of Italy, chronicler at the court of the princes of Carrara and Padua, papal secretary, secretary to Emperor Sigismund following the sessions of the Council of Constance (1414–8), and humanist. In his famous treatise *On the Manners of a Gentleman and Liberal Studies* he urged that most attention in the schools be given to the liberal arts and especially to the study of Latin literature.

VERGIL. *See* VIRGIL.

VERONA, city on the Adige in northern Italy which was used as a residence by the Ostrogothic ruler Theodoric, the Lombard king Alboin, and Charlemagne. After the tenth century the march of Verona became the possession of Bavaria, later of Carinthia. In the eleventh century it became a free commune, in the twelfth it joined the Lombard League, and from 1262 until 1386 it was controlled by the Scaliger (della Scala) family. In 1387 it fell to Milan, and in 1405 it passed under control of Venice.

VERONICA, ST., the woman of Jerusalem popularly identified in medieval legend as the one who gave Christ the cloth on his way to Calvary to wipe his face. A portrait, presumably the original imprint, seems to have been at Rome since the eighth century. The relic was greatly revered in the Middle Ages.

VERROCCHIO, ANDREA DEL, d. 1488, Italian sculptor, painter, engineer, and silver and goldsmith of the Florentine school. He was probably a pupil of Donatello. Among the pupils who attended his workship was Leonardo da Vinci. His own work reveals his interest in naturalism and the depiction of psychological traits. His equestrian statue of the *condottiere* Bartolomeo Colleoni and the nude bronze of David illustrate his curious interest in executing contrasting subjects.

VESPERS, the last divine office of the day before compline. It was recited an hour before sunset or somewhat earlier from the time of St. Benedict, and since the late Middle Ages in the afternoon.

VESPERS, SICILIAN. *See* SICILIAN VESPERS.

VESPUCCI, AMERIGO, d. 1512, Italian explorer who made four voyages to the New World. His descriptions of the new continent led to the adoption of his name for that world.

VEXILLA REGIS PRODEUNT, hymn composed by Fortunatus (d. c. 600) and honoring Christ as triumphant upon the tree of the Cross. The hymn served as a processional on Good Friday.

VICAR OF CHRIST, a title employed by prelates as early as the third century but whose use came to be limited to that of the popes from the pontificate of Innocent III (1198–1216). It expressed the papal claim to universal jurisdiction over the church.

VICAR GENERAL, prelate who assisted the bishop in the administration of a diocese. His appearance in the twelfth century tended to reduce the authority of the archdeacon.

VICENZA, the Roman Vicetia, located to the west of Venice, which served as the residence of the duke of Lombardy. It became a free commune and joined the Lombard League in the twelfth century. The city later passed under the control successively of Verona (1314), Milan (1387), and Venice (1404).

VICOMTE. *See* VISCOUNT.

VICTIMAE PASCHALI LAUDES, Easter sequence celebrating Christ's triumphant conquest of death, composed by Wipo (d. after 1046), a hymn-writer of Burgundy or Swabia.

VICTOR I, ST., Pope, 189? to 198 or 199, an African by birth, whose effort to establish as universal practice the Roman observance of the date of Easter may have constituted the first attempt by a bishop of Rome to extend his jurisdiction over the Eastern patriarchs. His excommunication of those bishops, all in the east, who refused to accept his instruction, evoked criticism from St. Irenaeus and other western bishops.

VICTOR II, Pope, 1055–7, bishop of Eichstätt (1042) and chancellor of Henry III of Germany who arranged for his election as pope. Victor is classified as a reforming pope.

VICTOR III, BL., Pope, May 1086 to September 1087, monk and abbot of Monte Cassino who in 1058 helped bring about an understanding between the papacy and Robert Guiscard, the Norman ruler of southern Italy. Victor succeeded Gregory VII.

VICTOR IV, two Antipopes: a) Cardinal Gregory Conti who was elected in opposition to Innocent II in 1138; b) Octavius, a cardinal, who was elected in 1159 following the death of Adrian IV, in opposition to Alexander III. He enjoyed the support of Frederick I Barbarossa.

VICTORINES, Canons Regular of St. Victor at Paris, a house founded by William of Champeaux and built in 1113 by King Louis VI. St. Bernard of Clairvaux drew up the "customs" for the house. Although the Victorines never became numerous, they counted many scholars, mystics, and poets in their ranks, among them Adam, Hugh, and Richard of St. Victor.

VICTORINUS AFER, CAIUS (or Fabius) MARIUS, rhetorician and theologian of the fourth century who gained a great reputation as a teacher in Rome. In 362 he resigned his teaching position and became a Christian. He left writings against the Arians, some exegetical works, and hymns. When still a pagan he produced commentaries on Cicero and translated some of the writings of Aristotle, Porphyry, and Plotinus.

VIDAL, PEIRE. *See* PEIRE VIDAL.

VIENNA, originally a Celtic town whose name Vindobona was retained by the Romans. The town served as a major *castrum* along the northern frontier but disappeared from view during the period of the Germanic invasions. When it reappeared in 880 it was with the name of Venia. About the year 1000 it became a possession of the Babenberg family and in 1156 it became the residence of the count of Austria. The town grew rapidly and in 1137 received a charter. In 1276, Rudolf of Hapsburg, newly elected king of Germany, took the city from Ottocar II, king of Bohemia, after which it remained in the possession of the Hapsburgs until 1918. The University of Vienna was founded in 1365 by Archduke Rudolf IV.

VIENNE, the Roman Vienna, a city located on the left bank of the Rhône. It became a bishop's see in the third century, that of an archbishop in 450. It was captured by Burgundians, Franks, Lombards, and Saracens. In 879 it served as capital of the kingdom of Lower Burgundy. It remained within the Holy Roman Empire until 1448 when France acquired possession.

VIENNE, COUNCIL OF, general church council (Fifteenth Ecumenical), 1311–2, convoked by Pope Clement V under pressure from Philip IV of France who coveted the wealth of the Templars. The council ordered the suppression of the military-religious order. It also voted measures for the reform of the church, condemned the Beghards, and provided for *studia* in Oriental languages (Arabic, Chaldaic, Hebrew, and probably Greek) to be established at five different universities.

VIERER, a silver coin of Tyrol which was first minted in 1360.

VIERLANDER, name of a coin struck by Philip the Good of Burgundy (d. 1467) for Flanders, Brabant, Hainaut, and Holland.

VIGILIUS, Pope, 537–55, successor of Pope Silverius in whose deposition he may have had a hand. He had served as apocrisarius at the court of the Byzantine emperor in Constantinople where he had come under the influence of Theodora, the empress; he may have promised her to support Monophysitism and condemn the decisions of the Council of Chalcedon. The emperor Justinian summoned him to Constantinople to secure his acceptance of a compromise on the issue raised by the Three Chapters. Vigilius, to protect himself, persuaded Justinian to convoke a general council [See CONSTANTINOPLE II, COUNCIL OF] in 553. Under pressure from the emperor he made concessions to the Monophysite leaders of the Eastern church that outraged Western bishops and led to his excommunication by a synod at Carthage. He died on his return journey to Rome.

VIKINGS, seafarers of Scandinavia, also known as Northmen, who conducted raiding expeditions from the close of the eighth century along the coastlines and up the rivers of the greater part of western Europe, even into the Mediterranean and to Constantinople. During the ninth century they began to establish settlements and in time occupied areas including Normandy (to which they gave their name), the Danelaw in England, Iceland, Greenland, and the Orkneys. Among other factors that led to this exodus from Scandinavia was surely the pressure of overpopulation. In general the Danes moved southward through the North Sea and the English Channel. The proximity and vastness of Russia absorbed the energies of the Swedes, while the Norwegians made settlements in Ireland, Greenland, Vinland, and the islands to the north of Scotland.

Their settlements in these islands proved the most permanent.

VILLANI, GIOVANNI, d. 1348, author of the *Florentine Chronicle* which approaches the character of a world chronicle (he starts with the Tower of Babel) while furnishing considerable information about the administration and economy of Florence. His brother Matteo added ten books to the *Chronicle* and extended it from 1348 to 1363. The history is one of the early monuments of Italian prose and, with Dante's works, helped establish the Tuscan language as the standard for Italy.

VILLARD DE HONNECOURT, noted French engineer and architect of Picardy whose *Sketchbook* of architectural drawings has been preserved. Scholars suggest the year 1244 as the date of its appearance. The book demonstrates the construction of ground plans and elevations of Gothic buildings, furniture, and engines. His reputation led him to visit a number of cities and countries.

VILLE NEUVE, a "new town," a settlement which was founded as opposed to one that simply took root because of natural circumstances. Perhaps most of them were founded by German lords along their eastern frontiers.

VILLEHARDOUIN, GEOFFROY (Geoffroi) DE, d. 1213, marshal of Champagne who took part in the Fourth Crusade (1202–4) and left a valuable and detailed description of its history in his *Conquête de Constantinople*. His work is one of the early masterpieces of French prose.

VILLEIN. See SERF.

VILLON, FRANÇOIS (Montcorbier), d. after 1463, the leading lyric poet of medieval France. As an orphan he was adopted by Guillaume Villon who sent him to the University of Paris where he took up a life of vice and crime. In 1455 he killed a man in a fight and was banished. The following year his protectors succeeded in having his banishment revoked, but he continued his criminal activities and was last seen hurrying from Paris to escape the gallows. His poems, which include the *Grand Testament, Petit Testament,* and miscellaneous ballads, contain much autobiographical material and express the author's unusually perceptive and poignant views of human life. His life was a mixture of misery, remorse, and moral degradation.

VINCENNES, hunting lodge on the edge of the forest near Paris which Louis VII (1137–80) had constructed for his use. A castle rose there early in the fourteenth century.

VINCENT FERRER, ST., d. 1419, Dominican of Valencia, author of treatises dealing with logic as well as with the spiritual life. He taught theology at Valencia, but was preeminently a preacher of penance and moral reform. On travels that took him for some 20 years through Spain, north Italy, Switzerland, and the Low Countries his preaching led many people to reform their lives, while others turned to such severe forms of penance as flagellation. A matter that occasioned him as much concern as the need for moral reform was the schism in the church. For a time he was a strong supporter of the Avignonese papacy.

VINCENT OF BEAUVAIS, d. c. 1264, Dominican scholar, author of the *Speculum Maius,* the most pretentious encyclopedia of knowledge undertaken in the Middle Ages. It was divided into three parts: *Speculum Naturale* (natural sciences), *Speculum Doctrinale* (scholastic knowledge), and *Speculum Historiale* (from the Creation to the Crusade of Louis IX in 1248), and consisted of 80 books and 9,885 chapters. It drew heavily upon Latin, Greek, Arabic, and Hebrew authors. The part that Vincent devoted to the natural sciences is of most interest to scholars.

VINCENT OF LÉRINS, ST., d. before 450, learned priest, monk, and theologian, and author of a number of writings in defense of orthodoxy. While emphasizing the importance of tradition and the authority of the Church, he maintained that the final source of Christian truth was Holy Scripture. He disagreed with St. Augustine concerning grace and may have been judged a Semi-Pelagian.

VINCENT OF SPAIN, d. after 1234, a leading canonist of the Middle Ages, teacher of canon law at Bologna, bishop of Saragossa (or of Idanha in Portugal), and author of influential works on canon law.

VINE, a popular symbol in Christian art, suggestive of several lessons, the one most frequently proposed being that of Christ as the vine, the faithful as the branches (John 15:1–2).

VINLAND (Wineland), term once used to designate the east coast of North America, variously identified as Labrador, Newfoundland, Nova Scotia, or Maine, that Björn Herjulfsson sighted in 986 and Leif Eriksson explored c. 1000.

VIRELAY (Virelai, Vireli), French dance and love song of the late Middle Ages.

VIRGIL (Vergil), d. 19 B.C., classical poet whose poems served the Middle Ages as exemplars in the study of grammar. Some of Virgil's popularity in the Middle Ages derived from the reference in the poet's fourth *Eclogue* to a child whose birth would usher in an era of peace, a prophetic reference, Christians believed, to the birth of Christ. Virgil served as Dante's guide in the *Inferno.*

VIRGINIS PROLES OPIFEXQUE MATRIS, breviary hymn of unknown authorship but probably from the eighth century. Its theme honored virgin martyrs.

VISBY (Wisby), seaport located on the Swedish island of Gotland which controlled the trade of the Baltic until the early fourteenth century. The influx of many German merchants almost made it a German city. During the thirteenth century it issued a code of laws and minted its own coins.

Waldemar IV of Denmark gained possession of the city in 1361.

VISCONTI, aristocratic family of Lombardy which ruled Milan from 1277 until 1447. Ottone V., d. 1295, archbishop of Milan (1262), established the prominence of the family. Matteo V., d. 1322, exercised an overlordship over the cities of Lombardy with the blessing of the emperor Henry VII whom he served as imperial vicar. Giovanni V., d. 1354, archbishop of Milan, ruled the city from 1349 and was instrumental in acquiring Bologna. Gian Galeazzo V., d. 1402, became duke of Milan in 1395 and ruled the greater part of northern Italy. Bianca Maria, the illegitimate daughter of his son Filippo Maria (d. 1447), married Francesco Sforza who inherited the family's position in 1450.

VISCOUNT, English title which first appeared in 1440 during the reign of Henry VI. In Carolingian times *vicecomites* (viscounts) served as agents of the court. Countships in general became hereditary, and by the end of the eleventh century it had become customary for viscounts to qualify their titles with the name of their most important fief. Others remained simply minor feudatories and lost their judicial functions.

VISIGOTHS or West Goths, a tribe located to the west of the Dniester river north of the Black Sea, whence they moved across the Danube in 375 in order to escape the approaching Huns who had already subjugated the Ostrogoths. They had been granted permission to cross the Danube by the reluctant Roman emperor Valens who did not dare to deny them asylum, while he could charge them with the responsibility of blocking the Huns from crossing the river. Trouble shortly developed between the Goths and the Roman officials, whereupon the Goths revolted and destroyed the imperial army at Adrianople (378). Later their king Alaric led them to Italy where they sacked Rome in 410. Under Athaulf, the brother-in-law of Alaric, they moved westward and eventually established a kingdom that stretched from southern France to Gibraltar. The Franks drove them across the Pyrenees in the sixth century, while the Moors moved in from Gibraltar in 711 and shortly after extinguished their kingdom.

VISITATION, ARCHIEPISCOPAL, the visitation by an archbishop of the dioceses of his province for the purpose of investigating their spiritual wellbeing and the worthiness and efficiency of those members of the church, notably his suffragan bishops, who were under his jurisdiction. It was a right to which most bishops objected and which they quite frequently contested and successfully so.

VISITATION, CANONICAL, an official visit, usually inquisitorial, by superiors of religious houses and persons under their jurisdiction.

VISITATION, EPISCOPAL, the visitation by a bishop of his diocese for the purpose of inspecting and examining the activities of his clergy and others under his jurisdiction.

VISITATION, FEAST OF THE, liturgical feast commemorating the visit of Mary to Elizabeth (Luke 1:39–56). It was introduced into the Latin church's liturgical calendar from the Greek in the thirteenth century.

VITAL DU FOUR (Vidal, Vitalis de Furno), d. 1327, Franciscan theologian, minister provincial of the order in Aquitaine, cardinal, bishop of Albano, and author of several philosophical and theological treatises.

VITALIAN, ST., Pope, 657–72, the successor of Eugenius I. Vitalian's election terminated a schism with the Eastern church and Byzantium over Monothelitism. As pope, Vitalian helped secure the acceptance of the Roman liturgy in Britain, which was accomplished at the Synod of Whitby in 664. Vitalian consecrated Theodore of Tarsus archbishop of Canterbury.

VITERBO, city of Tuscany in central Italy, a possession of Matilda (d. 1115), countess of

Tuscany, who bequeathed it along with her other possessions to the papacy. Her action precipitated a long struggle between the papacy and the German emperor who claimed her estates, a struggle that grew particularly bitter during the reign of Frederick II (1215–50). Viterbo became an episcopal see in 1193 and on occasion served as a papal residence.

VITRY, PHILIPPE DE, d. 1361, bishop of Meaux and secretary to Charles IV and Philip VI, kings of France. He gained fame as a philosopher, mathematician, and musician, and as the author of treatises on musical theory and the composer of motets.

VITTORINO DA FELTRE (Dei Ramboldoni), d. 1446, humanist and teacher, taught rhetoric in several cities of Italy. At Padua he tutored the Gonzaga children, while at Mantua he cooperated in the establishment of the first important school of the "new learning." This learning placed emphasis upon the humanities and upon moral, physical, and vocational training. He wrote little but he has been called the first modern schoolmaster.

VIVARINI, ANTONIO, d. between 1476 and 1484, founder of a family studio near Venice. There he was joined by his brother-in-law Giovanni d'Alemagna in making altarpieces. Although their styles are similar, Antonio is judged the ranking partner; he is in fact considered the most important and productive Venetian artist of the first half of the fifteenth century. Bartolomeo, d. 1499, his younger brother, first worked with him; he later came under the influence of Mantegna when he did his most distinguished altarpieces.

VLADIMIR I, ST., grand duke of Kiev, 980–1015, and prince of Novgorod from 970. He negotiated a treaty with Byzantium that established trade relations between the two countries and provided for the conversion of Russia. He was successful in his wars with the Lithuanians, Bulgars, and Greeks (in the Cri-

mea). In 988 he was baptized and married Anna, the sister of Emperor Basil II. He erected many churches and monasteries and used both persuasion and force to bring his people to accept Christianity.

VLADIMIR II, grand duke of Kiev, 1113–25, pacified his country, waged successful wars against the Livonians, Finns, Bulgars, and Cumans, and even marched against Constantinople. He established towns and opened up areas of his country to colonization. His "testament" which he left for his sons represents the earliest known example of Russian "literature" written by a layman.

VLADIMIR (Wladimir), city east of Moscow, founded in the tenth or eleventh century. By the twelfth century it had developed into the leading city of central Russia by virtue of the residence there of the grand prince Andrei Bogoliubski. In 1299 the metropolitan moved his see there from Kiev. In 1238 and again in 1293 the city suffered destruction by the Mongols, and after 1320 it surrendered its position of leadership to Moscow.

VOIVODE. *See* WOIWODE.

VOJTECH RANKUV Z JEZOVA, d. 1388, Czech theologian, rector of the University of Paris, and exponent of the *Devotio Moderna* in Bohemia. Despite his orthodoxy and his loyalty to the Roman church, the Hussites honored him as one of their founders.

VÖLKERWANDERUNG, in terms of Europe, the migration of peoples, most of these Germans — Goths, Burgundians, Franks, Vandals, Angles, Saxons, and Lombards — across the frontiers of the Roman empire during the period from the late fourth to the late sixth century. [*See* MIGRATION OF PEOPLES.]

VOLSUNGA SAGA, prose version of heroic songs concerning the families of the Volsungs and Nibelungs of which fragments survive in the poetic *Edda*. It was probably assembled in the twelfth and thirtenth centuries. Volsung was considered a descendant of Odin and the father of Sigurd (Siegfried). The Brunhild of the *Nibelungenlied* appears here as Brynhild.

VULGATE, the Latin translation of the Bible which St. Jerome (d. 420) prepared from the oldest Greek, Hebrew, and Chaldaic manuscripts during the last quarter of the fourth century (completed c. 405) upon the direction of Pope Damasus. It was the hope of the pope that the new text would resolve some of the problems growing out of the discrepancies among the different texts then in use. By the thirteenth century Jerome's edition had become the popularly accepted version of the Bible, whence its name (Lt. *vulgarus* meaning common). [*See* JEROME, ST.]

WACE, ROBERT, d. c. 1183, Anglo-Norman poet who added the theme of the Knights of the Round Table to the matter of King Arthur in his *Roman de Brut*. His chronicle is based on Geoffrey of Monmouth's history. Wace's *Roman de Rou* gives a description of the battle of Hastings.

WAKEFIELD, BATTLE OF, battle fought in 1460 which ended in the rout of the Yorkists and the death of Richard, duke of York. [*See* ROSES, WARS OF THE.]

WALACHIA (Wallachia) region between the southern Carpathians and the lower Danube, part of the Roman province of Dacia, which was successively overrun and occupied by the Goths, the Lombards, the Avars, the Bulgarians, the Cumans, and the Mongols (1240). After the Mongols had left, the native leaders organized the principality of Walachia. The woiwode Basarab (d. 1352) united the various states in the fourteenth century and founded a dynasty that endured until the seventeenth. In 1460 the land passed under Turkish control. The early Rumanians often went by the name of Walachians.

WALAFRID (Walahfrid) STRABO, d. 849, known as Walafrid the Squinter, a monk of Reichenau, pupil of Rabanus Maurus at Fulda, a tutor of Charles the Bald, and abbot of Reichenau (838). During his abbacy he brought fame to Reichenau for its library and scriptorium. He was a biblical scholar of note as well as a composer of secular and religious verse. His most important work is a handbook on matters of liturgical and archeological interest which throws valuable light on the religious practices of his time.

WALBURGA, ST., d. c. 780, Anglo-Saxon nun, sister of Willibald and Wynnebald, both missionaries in Germany. Wynnebald established a double monastery at Heidenheim and had Walburga, who at the time was at St. Boniface's mission at Bischofsheim, to serve as superioress of the convent. When he died in 761, she became abbess of both the male and female communities. The coincidence of her feast day of May 1 being on the same day as an old pagan feast commemorating the beginning of summer with rites to protect the people from witchcraft gave the name of "Walpurgis" to May 1.

WALDEMAR (Valdemar) I, king of Denmark, 1157–82, who united the country under his authority. With the help of Henry the Lion of Saxony and Albert the Bear of Brandenburg, he conducted a crusade against the pagan Wends in Rügen and Pomerania. Later he erected a wall (Wall of Waldemar or Dannevirke) to protect his people from Saxony to the south and swore homage to Frederick I Barbarossa as added protection against the aggressiveness of Henry the Lion.

WALDEMAR (Valdemar) II, king of Denmark, 1202–41, second son of Waldemar I, conquered Holstein and Hamburg, and forced Lübeck to acknowledge his suzerainty. In 1214 Frederick II of Germany recognized him as lord of all German territory north of the Elbe and Elde. In alliance with the German Knights of the Sword, he led a crusade against the Wends in

Estonia and brought that country under his control. Fortune deserted him, and a revolt of his north German allies and his own disgruntled nobles left him only Denmark in the end.

WALDEMAR (Valdemar) IV, king of Denmark, 1340–75, known as Atterdag, brought up at the court of Louis IV the Bavarian, gained possession of the throne with the help of certain Hanseatic towns. He took measures to strengthen royal authority such as introducing a form of general enlistment and building numerous castles. He also arranged the marriage of his daughter Margaret to Haakon, son of Magnus II, king of Sweden. But his seizure of Gotland and its important city of Visby brought on war with the Hanseatic League and his eventual defeat. Although he lost no territory at the Peace of Stralsund (1370), he was forced to recognize Hanseatic hegemony in the Baltic area. [See STRALSUND, PEACE OF.]

WALDENSES (Waldensians), followers of Peter Waldo (Valdes), a wealthy merchant of Lyons, who gave away his wealth to the poor, dedicated himself to the care of the needy, and took up the life of a mendicant preacher. His first preaching was directed at the worldliness of the clergy and the heresy of the Catharists. In 1179 Pope Alexander III granted him and his companions reluctant permission to carry on their social work, even to preach, provided they received the approval of their bishop. In 1184 their anticlericalism and heterodoxy evoked papal condemnation, after which many submitted and remained in the church, while others organized their own church. This became in time quite similar in terms of tenets and practices to the Protestant communities of the sixteenth century. They questioned the validity of sacraments administered by unworthy priests and the veneration of saints and relics, and denounced the taking of oaths and all forms of killing, including in war and as capital punishment. They spread to southern France, Spain, Germany, and north

Italy but declined after the repressive measures introduced by Pope Innocent III (1198–1216).

WALES, Celtic land which boasted three bishops and monastic communities as early as the fourth century. The Welsh credited their conversion to Celtic monks, above all to St. David whom they later revered as their patron saint. So broken was the land by mountains that no one ruler succeeded in establishing his authority over the entire country. The land suffered from attacks by the Mercians, later by the Vikings. During the time of Alfred the Great (871–99), the Welsh chieftain Rhodri Mawr managed to extend his authority over a large part of the land. In 1063 Harold of England invaded the region and in a battle with the Welsh, their leader Llewelyn ap Gruffydd was slain. William the Conqueror supported Welsh chieftains against the aggressions of the English Marcher lords, while Owen Gwynedd (d. 1170) succeeded in thwarting the attempt which Henry II made to conquer the country. Llewelyn the Great (d. 1240) who married Joan, an illegitimate daughter of King John of England, made himself the most powerful of the Welsh chieftains although he was careful to do homage to Henry III. This homage Llewelyn Ap Gruffydd, the first "Prince of Wales," refused to give to Edward I in 1276, which gave the ambitious young English king an excuse to invade Wales. Two campaigns ended in the conquest of the country and the death of Llewelyn (d. 1282). As a conciliatory gesture Edward had his son Edward (II), who was born in the great castle of Caernarvon which he had erected, declared prince of Wales (1301). From the death of Llewelyn, Wales remained reasonably quiet until 1402 when Owen Glendower headed a dangerous revolt which was not quashed until 1409.

WALLACE, WILLIAM, d. 1305, Scottish hero who served as regent for John Balliol whom Edward I had sent into exile. Edward managed to defeat Wallace when he led a revolt in 1297 but he did not capture him until 1305 when he had him executed. Wallace remained one of Scotland's medieval heroes.

WALLIA (Walja), d. 418, king of the Visigoths, 415–8. As an ally of Rome he drove the Vandals (the Siling branch) out of Spain, then ruled Spain, western Aquitaine, and Toulouse under Roman suzerainty.

WALSINGHAM, MONASTERY OF, house of Canons Regular of St. Augustine established in northern Norfolk in 1153 and assigned the care of the shrine of Our Lady of Walsingham. This contained what was believed to be a replica of the Holy House of Nazareth which had been built there c. 1061. The monastery achieved prominence in the thirteenth century when both Henry III and Edward I paid it a number of visits. It was one of England's most popular medieval shrines.

WALSINGHAM, THOMAS, d. c. 1422, monk and chronicler of St. Albans. He continued the chronicle of Matthew Paris from 1259 to 1422. The portion covering the years after 1392, including the reigns of Richard II, Henry IV, and Henry V, was largely original. Walsingham was outspoken in his judgments, and, like his great predecessor at St. Albans, felt no reluctance in expressing them.

WALTER DE STAPELDON. *See* STAPELDON, WALTER DE.

WALTER, HUBERT, d. 1205, a nephew of the eminent lawyer Ranulf de Glanville in whose household he was reared. In 1189 he was consecrated bishop of Salisbury, then accompanied Richard I on the Third Crusade (1189–92), during which he had the responsibility of securing supplies and of directing the return of the Crusaders to England. In 1193, upon Richard's recommendation, he was translated to Canterbury. As justiciar while Richard was absent from England and later as chancellor under John, he gave England a strong, statesmanlike government. He may be credited with making a major contribution to the development of royal administrative machinery.

WALTER MAP. *See* MAP WALTER.

WALTER OF CHÂTILLON, d. c. 1200, teacher at Paris, Laon, and Châtillon, canon at Reims and Amiens, and composer of some lyric verse and a long courtly romance about Alexander the Great.

WALTER OF HENLEY (Walter de Henley), English writer of the thirteenth century on the subject of agriculture. He wrote his treatise, *Husbandry*, in Norman French. England considered him the leading authority for the next 200 years on matters dealing with agriculture and with rural economy in general.

WALTER THE PENNILESS (Sansavoir), poor French knight who led one of the bands that made up the so-called Peasant Crusade (1096). Before the regular Crusading contingents got on their way, he led his band through the Balkans where they pillaged as they went, meanwhile suffering severely at the hands of the Bulgarians. They finally joined Peter the Hermit and his band, only to be decimated by the Turks when they reached Asia Minor.

WALTHARIUS (Waltarilied), Latin heroic poem in hexameter verse composed at the close of the ninth or the early tenth century by a canon named Gerald (or by Ekkehard I of St. Gall, d. 973). The theme concerned the adventures of Walther of Aquitaine and his fiancée, Hiltgund of Burgundy. The two young people grew up as hostages at the court of Attila, the Hunnic king, but later returned to Aquitaine.

WALTHER VON DER VOGELWEIDE, d. c. 1230, the leading German minnesinger of the Middle Ages and the greatest lyric poet of medieval Germany. Beyond the usual love themes that inspired the troubador, his verse included moral, religious, political (antipapal), and satirical poems. He counted Leopold V, duke of Austria, and Hermann, landgrave of Thuringia, among his patrons, and in the end he received a small fief from Frederick II of Germany.

WANDERING JEW, a legendary Jew, said to have been Pontius Pilate's doorkeeper, who reproached Christ for his tardiness on the way to Calvary. Christ reproved him for his lack of charity and told him he would remain on earth until he (Christ) would return. The legend took many twists and turns before continuing into modern times.

WAQIDI, AL- (Abu 'Abdallah Mohammed Ibn 'Omar Al-Waqidi), d. 823, Arab historian who left a valuable account of the campaigns undertaken by Mohammed. He was a friend of the caliph Al-Ma'mun.

WARBECK, PERKIN, d. 1499, a Flemish apprentice who was persuaded to impersonate an heir to the house of York in a conspiracy to unseat Henry VII (Tudor). The foes of Henry threw their support behind Warbeck, including Maximilian, king of Germany, the king of Scotland, and the duke of Burgundy, as well as thousands of Englishmen. The threat to Henry petered out for lack of organization and he had little difficulty capturing Warbeck and having him executed.

WARDSHIP, feudal perquisite that granted the lord the right to the income of a fief during the minority of its heir, on the theory that the latter was incapable of rendering the services required of him (her). The lord was required to maintain the buildings on the fief and to see to the material needs of his ward. When his ward came of age, the lord was to release the fief to him (her) in the condition in which he had received it.

WARSAW (Warschau, Warazawa), capital city of Poland situated on the east bank of the Vistula. It was founded about the middle of the thirteenth century, probably on the site of an old Slavic fishing village. By the close of the Middle Ages it had developed into an important trade center by reason of its location on the Vistula and on crossroads leading from Lithuania, Ruthenia, Pomerania, and Silesia. Early in the fifteenth century, the New City of Warsaw was founded to the north of the Old City.

WARWICK, EARLDOM OF, English title created in 1088 and granted to Henry, son of Roger de Beaumont, by William II. The Beauchamp family came into possession of the title in 1268. Its most important representatives to hold the title were Guy, Thomas, and Richard Beauchamp. Guy (d. 1315) took an active part in Edward I's campaigns in Scotland but vigorously opposed Edward II's misrule and served as one of the Lords Ordainers. Thomas (d. 1401) was one of the leading lords appellant who opposed Richard II's ministers and sought to curb the king's power. When Richard gained full control in 1389, Thomas retired to his estates where he was arrested in 1397 and lodged in the Tower (Beauchamp Tower). There he remained until the accession of Henry IV who restored his titles. Richard (d. 1439), a loyal adherent of Henry IV, was appointed captain of Calais by Henry V and from 1437 served as one of the king's lieutenants in the conquest of Normandy. He was a man of piety and was famed throughout Europe as a true knight of chivalry. His son Henry, who was made earl in 1444, died without male issue, but Richard's daughter Anne married Richard Neville who inherited the title by right of his wife. [See WARWICK, RICHARD NEVILLE, EARL OF.] After the death of Richard Neville, the earldom went to George, duke of Clarence, the brother of Edward IV, then to Clarence's son Edward whom Henry VII executed in 1499 for his part in the plot of Perkin Warbeck. With the death of Edward, the title became extinct.

WARWICK, RICHARD NEVILLE, EARL OF, d. 1471, called the king-maker for putting Edward IV on the throne in 1461 and restoring Henry VI late in 1470. In 1450 he was created earl of

Warwick by reason of his marriage to Anne, daughter and heiress of Richard Beauchamp, duke and earl of Warwick. Without the financial assistance of Warwick, the richest landowner in England, and his shrewd counsel, it is doubtful that Edward would have become king. But Edward's marriage to Elizabeth Woodville in 1464 which aborted Warwick's efforts to secure an understanding with Louis XI of France (Warwick was planning a French marriage for Edward), followed by the policy of Edward of advancing members of the Woodville family, alienated the earl. Fearing the loss of his powerful position in the government, he broke with Edward, joined fortunes with his hated rival Margaret (of Anjou), Henry VI's consort, and succeeded momentarily in restoring Henry VI to the throne (1470–1). In April, at the battle of Barnet, he was among the slain. [*See* ROSES, WARS OF THE.].

WATERMARK, a mark developed in Italy in the late thirteenth century which left a translucent design on paper. Papermakers used the process to identify their work.

WAT TYLER. *See* TYLER, WAT.

WAY OF THE CROSS, also known as Stations of the Cross, a Christian devotion consisting of the recitation of special prayers at different stations, usually marked by tableaux depicting incidents attending Christ's passion and death. The practice came to Europe from Jerusalem in the twelfth century and by the close of the Middle Ages had grown quite popular, principally through the encouragement of the Franciscans who had been given custody of the Holy Places in Palestine.

WEARMOUTH, ABBEY OF. *See* JARROW, ABBEY OF.

WEDMORE, PEACE OF, treaty agreed to by Alfred the Great and Guthrum, the Danish king, at Wedmore in Somerset in 878 which left the Danes the possession of that part of England roughly northeast of a line drawn from London to Chester on the Welsh border. This region came to be known as the Danelaw.

WELF, aristocratic family of Bavaria that derived its name from a Count Welf (d. c. 825). The family came into prominence in 1070 when it acquired the duchy of Bavaria. The most illustrious member of the family was Henry the Lion, duke of both Bavaria and Saxony, whom Frederick I Barbarossa deprived of both duchies in 1180. When Henry V, king of Germany, died in 1125 without male issue, the contest over the succession between Frederick of Swabia, who was of the house of Hohenstaufen, and Lothair of Saxony, who was a Welf, gave birth to the long, bitter struggle between the Welfs and Hohenstaufens in Germany. Their adherents and allies in Italy were known respectively as Guelfs and Ghibellines. [*See* GUELFS AND GHIBELLINES.]

WENCESLAS (Wenzel), king of Germany (1378–1400), king of Bohemia (1363–1419), son and successor of Emperor Charles IV. Because he was a Bohemian and had little interest in Germany and at times acted imprudently, his was not a successful reign. His sale of Milan as a hereditary fief to Gian Galeazzo Visconti in 1395 led to his deposition from the throne of Germany and his replacement by Rupert of the Palatinate. When Rupert died, Wenceslas surrendered his claim to the throne to his brother Sigismund. In Bohemia his quarrels twice led to his imprisonment by his nobles, although he remained popular with the commoners. While initially sympathetic to John Hus, he changed his position upon the outbreak of the Hussite wars.

WENCESLAS (Wenzel), St., d. 929, duke of Bohemia (c. 922). He recognized the overlordship of Germany partly to bring his people into closer association with the religion and culture of western Europe. His sympathy for Christianity led to a pagan, nativist movement under the leadership of his brother, and he was slain. He is the Wenceslas of the Christmas carol. The crown of St. Wenceslas came to be the symbol of Czech independence.

WENDS, a tribe of west Slavs located during the eighth and ninth centuries in central and eastern Germany. First Charlemagne fought them, and in 1147 Henry the Lion and Albert the Bear of Brandenburg conducted a crusade against them. By the end of the twelfth century nearly the entire region east of the Elbe, with the exception of East Prussia, had been Christianized and made subject to the rulers of Germany. The name Wends was often applied to all Slavs east of the Elbe.

WEREWOLF, according to medieval superstition a person who had been transformed into a wolf or was able to change himself into one.

WERGELD (Wergild), payment required by old German law as a fine or compensation to be given by the family of the murderer to the family of the person slain. The amount varied with the importance of the man slain.

WESSEL, d. 1489, Dutch theologian, also known as Gansfort, educated by the Brethren of the Common Life at Deventer. He spent 16 years studying and teaching at Paris, then visited Italy where he made his acquaintance with humanism. His attitude toward the papacy, the teaching authority of the church, and the superstitious tendencies of the times later earned him the name of one of the "Reformers before the Reformation."

WESSEX, Anglo-Saxon kingdom which comprised all of southwestern England south of Mercia. Recurrent hostilities with Mercia are among the few firm facts remaining from this early period. In 825 Egbert defeated the Mercians and won for his kingdom the hegemony of England south of the Humber. Egbert faced a new enemy in the Danes who finally met their master in Alfred the Great (871–99), the most

illustrious of all the kings of Anglo-Saxon England. By the Peace of Wedmore (878), Alfred forced the Danes to accept baptism and to restrict themselves to the Danelaw, roughly the northeastern half of England. Alfred's son, Edward the Elder, and his grandson, Athelstan, completed the conquest of this region by 927, which made the kings of Wessex also the kings of England.

WESTERN SCHISM. *See* SCHISM, WESTERN.

WESTMINSTER ABBEY, monastery in London, founded in the seventh century (616?) and reformed by St. Dunstan (d. 988). Edward the Confessor (1042–66) devoted much effort to the rebuilding of the abbey church which was later reconstructed by Henry III (1216–72) in the French style. Henry VII added an imposing chapel (begun in 1503) to replace an earlier Lady Chapel. The abbey became one of the richest in England and enjoyed a special position in relation to the crown because of its proximity and its traditions.

WESTMORLAND, EARLDOM OF, an English title held from 1397 by members of the Neville family, probably the most powerful family in fifteenth-century England. Although Ralph Neville owed his earldom to Richard II, he joined his brother-in-law, Henry Bolingbroke, duke of Lancaster (later Henry IV), in forcing the abdication of Richard. Henry IV granted him honors and estates in northwestern England in order to establish a counterpoise there to the strength of the Percy family. The wisdom of this policy was revealed in 1403–5 when the earl helped suppress the rebellion of the Percys. The title of earl went to Ralph's grandson, also a Ralph (c. 1406–84), although the larger share of the family's estates was settled upon Richard Neville, earl of Salisbury, and his brothers, who were offspring of Ralph Neville's second marriage to Joan Beaufort.

WETTIN, German aristocratic family that traced its name to its castle in a small town near Halle, its origin to Bucco (Burkhard) (d. 908), margrave of the Serbian march, but whose real founder was Conrad I of Meissen (d. 1157). The family acquired Saxony and the electorate from the German king Sigismund in 1423. In 1425 Frederick I was made elector of Saxony.

WEYDEN, ROGIER (Roger) VAN DER, d. 1464, leading Flemish painter of the mid-fifteenth century who was appointed official painter to the city of Brussels. In time he executed many famous works for the churches, guilds, and private donors of that city. The influence of Jan van Eyck and especially that of his master Robert Campin is revealed in his work. He in turn exercised great influence upon other artists because of the large workshop he maintained and the many assistants in his employ. Stylistically his most important work is the *Descent from the Cross*. His other works include *Madonna with Four Saints* and *Entombment*. His religious paintings are inclined to be somber if not tragic.

WHEEL OF FORTUNE, disk seen in art forms from the twelfth century to describe the fortuitous character of fortune and the inevitability of the Last Judgment.

WHITBY, SYNOD OF, meeting in 664 at Whitby (east coast of Northumbria) where representatives of the Celtic church agreed to accept certain liturgical and desciplinary practices common to the Roman church, above all the date of Easter. SS. Colman and Cedd argued for the Celtic position, but, according to Bede who is the principal authority for the proceedings, it was the decision of Oswiu, king of Northumbria, to go with Rome whose St. Peter held the keys to heaven, that finally ended the controversy.

WHITE CANONS. *See* PREMONSTRATENSIANS.

WHITE FRIARS. *See* CARMELITES.

WHITSUNDAY. *See* PENTECOST.

WHITTINGTON, RICHARD, d. 1423, English merchant, three times mayor of London, and a generous benefactor of the city.

WICLIF, JOHN. *See* WYCLIF, JOHN.

WIDOW, Christian woman in the early church who after the death of her husband dedicated herself to a life of prayer and good works. Such women enjoyed what approached a clerical status.

WIDUKIND (Wittekind), d. after 785, Saxon chieftain who fought Charlemagne for many years but finally submitted in 785 and accepted baptism. His Saxons followed his lead in being baptized, either willingly or by force.

WIDUKIND OF CORVEY, d. after 976, monk of Corvey and author of the *Deeds of the Saxons*. This is an important source for the history of tenth-century Germany.

WILFRID, ST., d.c. 709, son of a Northumbrian thegn and abbot of Ripon. He spent some years in Lyons and in Rome and at the synod of Whitby (664) successfully pleaded the acceptance of Roman customs and liturgy by the church in England. He succeeded Colman as bishop of York, later was driven from his see, and spent six years as a missionary among the South Saxons. He subsequently became bishop of Hexham although he spent his last years in his monastery at Ripon.

WILLIAM I (the Conqueror), king of England, 1066–87, son of Robert I, duke of Normandy, whom he succeeded as duke with the help of his suzerain, Henry I, king of France. He made good his claim to the English throne following the death of Edward the Confessor by his victory over Harold the Anglo-Saxon at Hastings in 1066. Although he introduced feudal institutions and customs from Normandy, he retained the Anglo-Saxon fyrd, sheriff, and shire court. Evidence of his great authority which belied that of the traditionally weak feudal monarch, was the survey he ordered made in 1086, called the Domesday Book, which provided him with an inventory of the property held in England by his vassals. (He claimed all of England for himself.) He cooperated with Lanfranc, archbishop of Canterbury, in the work of reorganizing the English church and approved the establishment of a separate system of ecclesiastical courts.

WILLIAM II (Rufus), king of England, 1087–1100, son and successor of William I (the Conqueror), who had his father's sternness but lacked his sense of justice. He drove the saintly Anselm, archbishop of Canterbury, into exile. He ruled with an iron if not cruel hand, put down several revolts, and held Normandy as mortgage for the loan he gave his brother Robert to enable him to accompany the First Crusade. No doubt he intended to keep Normandy but he was killed by an arrow before Robert returned. He forced Malcolm III, king of Scotland, to pay him homage and he took over the city of Carlisle for settlement by Englishmen.

WILLIAM DE LA MARE, d. c. 1290, English Franciscan who taught theology at Paris. His scholastic writings express his admiration for St. Bonaventure and his occasional disagreement with St. Thomas Aquinas. His exegetical works mark him as a leading biblical scholar of the period.

WILLIAMITES, name identifying several religious orders and sects: a) Benedictine congregation of monks and nuns founded by William of Vercelli in 1119; b) Hermits of St. William, founded by William of Maleval (d. 1157) and two companions; c) followers of William of Saint-Amour (d. 1272) who opposed the presence of Mendicants at the University of Paris; d) sect founded by Wilhelmine of Milan (d. 1282) who claimed to be the incarnation of the Holy Spirit; e) followers of the late fourteenth-century Aegidius Cantoris of Brussels, a Carmelite priest, who called himself the "Savior of Man."

WILLIAM OF ALNWICK, d. 1333, English Franciscan, a student of Duns Scotus, who taught theology in several cities including Paris, Ox-

ford, and Bologna. In 1330 he was consecrated bishop of Giovinazzo. His philosophical and theological writings shed considerable light on the views of Scotus and other contemporary scholars. William did not always agree with Scotus.

WILLIAM OF AUXERRE, d. 1231, scholastic theologian, taught at Paris and authored a *Summa*. In 1231 Gregory IX appointed him to a commission to examine and amend the physical treatises of Aristotle whose study had been suppressed at Paris in 1210. He was among the first to make use of the learning of the newly discovered Aristotle.

WILLIAM OF CHAMPEAUX, d. 1122, scholastic philosopher, a disciple of Anselm of Laon and Roscelin of Compiègne. He taught dialectic and theology at the cathedral school of Notre Dame and later at the Abbey of Saint-Victor where he laid the foundation of the Victorine school. His views on universals drew attack from his pupil Abelard and he was obliged to modify his realism. In 1113 he was consecrated bishop of Châlons-sur-Marne. His writings included several works on logic and theology.

WILLIAM OF CONCHES, d. c. 1160, philosopher and theologian of the school of Chartres, a disciple of Bernard of Chartres. He taught at Chartres where his interest in classical studies provoked criticism from the Cistercians and from the "Cornificians," a group who objected to what they considered an excessive concern with the pagan classics. His scholastic writings, which included glosses on Boethius and on Plato's *Timaeus*, reveal him to have been a Platonist whose realism approached that of a pantheist.

WILLIAM OF JUMIÈGES, fl. c. 1070, monk of the Benedictine monastery of Jumièges in Normandy and author of a history of Normandy to 1066. This was perhaps more popular than it was trustworthy.

WILLIAM OF MALMESBURY, d. 1143, monk, precentor, and librarian of the Benedictine monastery at Malmesbury and the most notable English historian since Bede. He composed a history of England from the Anglo-Saxon period (*Gesta Regum Anglorum*), a history of English bishops, dioceses, and monasteries, as well as several theological, devotional, and hagiographical works. In his historical writings he departed from the annalistic form in favor of a more narrative style.

WILLIAM OF MELITONA (Middleton), d. c. 1260, English Franciscan, theologian, and author of a work on the sacraments. He collaborated with other scholars in the completion of Alexander of Hales's *Summa Theologica*.

WILLIAM OF MOERBEKE, d. 1286, Dominican of Ghent, studied at Cologne possibly under Albert the Great, later collaborated with St. Thomas Aquinas particularly in the translation of Greek philosophical writings, including those of Aristotle as well as commentaries on the philosopher's works. He served as papal penitentiary to several popes, was consecrated archbishop of Thebes (1278), and devoted much effort to the cause of the reunion of the Greek and Latin churches.

WILLIAM OF NEWBURGH, d. c. 1200, Austin canon of Newburgh in Yorkshire, author of a commentary on the *Canticle of Canticles* and of a valuable history of England from 1066 to 1198 (*Historia Rerum Anglicarum*). His historical writing is both unusually accurate and impartial.

WILLIAM OF NORWICH, ST., d. 1144, supposed victim of a Jewish ritual murder who had been enticed from his home during Holy Week; his body was discovered on Holy Saturday. According to the testimony of Thomas of Monmouth, a monk of Norwich, the only authority for the story, William had been crucified by Jews. Since the local authorities took no action in the matter, the story is open to much suspicion. In any event,

the tomb of William in Norwich became a popular place of pilgrimage.

WILLIAM OF OCKHAM, d. 1349, English Franciscan, studied at Oxford, lectured on the *Sentences*, and in 1326 went to Avignon (the pope was living there at the time) to defend himself against the charge of heresy. Pope John XXII had ordered several of his writings scrutinized for possible heresy, but none was actually condemned. In 1328 Ockham fled Avignon for the court of Louis of Bavaria in the company of Michael of Cesena, the general of the Franciscan order, whose sympathies for the Spiritual Franciscans he shared. He apparently died unreconciled with the papacy.

Ockham was an extreme nominalist. He denied the existence of universals, even to the extent of rejecting the church's teaching authority as that of an institution that had no real being. He also rejected the usefulness of metaphysics and natural theology to faith since he dismissed the position of St. Thomas Aquinas that a necessary harmony existed between faith and reason. He also disagreed with Aquinas in maintaining that the will, not the intellect, was the primary faculty of the soul. Safely out of the reach of the papacy, he also attacked the wealth of the church and the temporal authority of the papacy, accepted the fallibility of the pope, and argued for the supremacy of the general council in matters of faith. His three treatises on logic represented a significant contribution to that subject.

WILLIAM OF RUBRUQUIS. *See* RUBRUQUIS, WILLIAM OF.

WILLIAM OF SAINT-THIERRY, d. c. 1148, theologian and mystical writer, a disciple of Anselm of Laon, abbot of Saint-Thierry (near Reims), and a friend of St. Bernard of Clairvaux. He resigned his abbacy in 1135 and joined a group of Cistercians in the forest of the Ardennes. He was the author of commentaries on the Bible, theological works, and treatises on the spiritual life. He also attacked Abelard for his views on the Trinity and Redemption and urged Bernard to press his criticism. His writings reveal a wide knowledge of the Bible and the Fathers, both Greek and Latin.

WILLIAM OF TYRE, d. c. 1187, born in Palestine of Frankish parents, studied at Paris and Bologna, served as chancellor of the Latin kingdom of Jerusalem in 1174, and the year following was consecrated archbishop of Tyre. His fame rests upon his scholarly chronicle of the history of Palestine from 614 and in particular upon his description of the events of the Crusading period from 1095 to 1184. In contrast to most medieval chroniclers, William presented his material as topics rather than in chronological order.

WILLIAM OF VERCELLI, ST., d. 1142, founder of an order of Benedictine hermits known as Williamites. He also founded the abbey and shrine of our Lady of Monte Vergine near Avellino (south Italy) as well as other monasteries.

WILLIAM OF WAYNFLETE, d. 1486, bishop of Winchester (1447), studied at Oxford, served as provost of Eton College, and founded Magdalen College at Oxford for the purpose of fostering the study of theology and philosophy. He took an active part in the turbulent political affairs of Henry VI's reign, served as his chancellor from 1456 to 1460, and in 1450 conducted negotiations with the rebel leader Jack Cade.

WILLIAM OF WYKEHAM, d. 1404, bishop of Winchester (1367), entered the royal service as a clerk c. 1349, after which he was presented to an unusually large number of benefices. In 1364 he served as Keeper of the Privy Seal and in 1367 as royal chancellor. In 1371 he was forced out of office; he was later accused of malversation. He was eventually cleared of this charge and served as chancellor again from 1389 to 1391. He founded New College at Oxford and a school for 70 poor scholars at Winchester.

WISBY. See VISBY.

WITAN, council composed of high ecclesiastics and nobles that advised the king in Anglo-Saxon times. It would also elect the successor to the throne upon the death of the king. When it met in formal session it was called a *witenagemot*.

WITCHCRAFT. As early as the reign of Charlemagne (d. 814), there is evidence of the persecution of witches. Bishops of the tenth and eleventh centuries took measures against them, although Pope Gregory VII (1073–85) forbade the killing of women for presumably causing such evils as storms and epidemics. The period of the Crusades served to increase western Europe's fear of witches as Arabic and Jewish magic was imported from the eastern Mediterranean. The Court of the Inquisition, established in 1233, was authorized to deal with witchcraft if this was connected with heresy. Secular courts in Germany punished many witches for their alleged crimes. The widespread persecution of men and women accused of being witches dates from the late fifteenth century. The extent of the belief in witches and their ability to do harm is revealed by the action of Pope Innocent VIII in 1484 when he encouraged the courts of the inquisition to take severe measures against them. The most famous book on the subject of witchcraft made its appearance in 1487 under the title *Malleus Maleficarum (Hammer of Witches)*. Its authors were two Dominican inquisitors, Jacob Sprenger and Henry Krämer.

WITELO (Wito, Wido, Guido), d. c. 1275, Polish philosopher, scientist, and mathematician, and author of one of the leading treatises on optics to appear in the Middle Ages. It held much in common with the views of Robert Grosseteste and Roger Bacon. His *Perspectiva,* which is based in large measure on the work of the Arabic scholar Alhazen, is of interest because of its psychological doctrines. Its metaphysical teaching is neo-Platonist.

WITENAGEMOT. *See* WITAN.

WITTELSBACH, ruling family of Bavaria that

traced its origin to Margrave Liutpold of Scheyern (d. 907) who assumed the title duke of Bavaria. The family adopted the name of Wittelsbach in 1115 from their castle near Aichach. In 1180 Frederick I Barbarossa invested Otto VI, count of Wittelsbach, with Bavaria. In 1214 Otto's grandson Otto II received the Rhenish Palatinate. The Wittelsbach fortunes reached their peak when Duke Louis I became Emperor Louis IV (1314–47). The Wittelsbach possessions suffered several divisions. The Palatinate branch secured the right of imperial election by the Golden Bull of 1356.

WITTEN, silver penny of Lübeck that was used since 1325.

WLADYSLAW II JAGIELLO. *See* JAGIELLO.

WODAN. *See* ODIN.

WOHLGEMUTH (Wolgemut), MICHAEL (Michel), d. 1519, painter, woodcarver, engraver of Nüremberg, and director of a flourishing workshop. Albrecht Dürer was his pupil. He produced a number of altarpieces and portraits, also wood engravings for books.

WOIWODE (voivode), title given to the commanding general in Poland, the Seven Mountains, and Walachia.

WOLFRAM VON ESCHENBACH, d. c. 1220, a Bavarian knight, the leading German composer of courtly romances. He established his reputation with *Parzival,* a poem of 25,000 lines in short rhyming couplets, which presents one of the most appealing versions of the Grail story. He developed the theme as an allegory of man's spiritual evolution from one of innocence, through a period of moral corruption, to final purification by means of atonement.

WOOLSACK, THE, seat of the lord chancellor in the House of Lords; it may have been adopted as early as the reign of Edward III (1327–77). It served to symbolize the importance to England of the wool trade.

WORCESTER, WILLIAM (Botoner), d. c. 1480, English scholar and antiquary, secretary to Sir John Fastolf, and author of the *Itinerarium,* the first topographical study of England. His authorship of annals covering the years 1324 to 1468, which have been traditionally attributed to him, has been questioned.

WORMS, city located on the Rhine in the Palatinate whose origins reach back to Celtic times. It became a bishopric in the fourth century and was a leading Burgundian community in the fifth. Its destruction by the Huns in 436 found an echo in the *Nibelungenlied.* During the investiture conflict it gave its support to Henry IV who in return accorded it the status of an imperial city.

WORMS, CONCORDAT OF, an agreement concerning rights of investiture accepted in 1122 by Henry V of Germany and legates of Pope Callistus II. The king agreed to abandon the practice of investing prelates with the spiritual insignia of their office. He insisted, however, that in case of disagreement he could interpose and decide the matter. In Germany the electee was to receive the temporalities of the see from the king before his consecration, in Italy and Burgundy six months after his consecration.

WOTAN. *See* ODIN.

WRIT, in England a formal legal document issued in the name of the king that ordered, or prohibited, the execution of some contemplated action.

WULFSTAN (Wulstan) OF WORCESTER, ST., d. 1095, monk and prior of the cathedral of Worcester who was consecrated bishop of Worcester in 1062. Despite his earlier support of Harold the Anglo-Saxon, he made his peace with William I (the Conqueror) and became one of his most trusted advisers. He was known for his asceticism and sanctity.

WULFSTAN, ST., d. 1023, bishop of London (996), archbishop of York (1002), counselor to the king, distinguished writer in Old English, and author of numerous homilies. His largest work, *Institutes of Polity, Civil and Ecclesiastical,* presents what the author judges to be the duties of the different classes of society. Wulfstan is credited with much of the legislation issued after 1008 by Kings Ethelred II and Canute. He also drafted or influenced various private law codes.

WÜRTEMBERG (Württemberg), part of the old tribal duchy of Swabia. It was ruled by a dynasty that originated with Conradus de Wirinisberc c. 1080 and was administered by an unbroken line of counts beginning with Ulrich I (d. 1265). In 1495 it attained the rank of a duchy.

WÜRZBURG, city of Franconia, created an episcopal see by St. Boniface in 741. After the disintegration of Franconia in the tenth century, the bishop of Würzburg ruled an extensive territory on both sides of the Main as a prince of the Holy Roman empire. In the fifteenth century the bishop acquired the title duke of Eastern Franconia.

WYCLIF (Wiclif, Wycliffe, Wyclyf), JOHN, d. 1384, Oxford theologian and royal clerk whose views on dominion led to efforts in 1377–8 on the part of the ecclesiastical authorities, including Pope Gregory IX, to discipline him. John of Gaunt, the son of Edward III and the uncle of the young Richard II, who dominated the government following the death of the Black Prince in 1376, gave Wyclif his protection, although Wyclif was ordered to cease his attacks on the church. These included assaults on vows, indulgences, the sacramental system, transubstantiation, and the papacy. While Wyclif died as a priest in good standing, the Council of Constance (1414–8) ordered his writings burned and his bones removed from consecrated ground. His voluminous writings included philosophical treatises that reveal his extreme realism, but above all theological works concerning many practices and doctrines of the medieval church that drew his criticism. Some question remains regarding his part in the English Bible often credited to him. He may have done little more than encourage his disciples in their work of translation. [*See* LOLLARDS.]

WYCLIFFITES, the disciples of Wyclif at Oxford, including Philip Repingdon and Nicholas Hereford. They might be viewed as a separate branch of the Lollards with little in common with men like John Ball and William Swinderby who were as much interested in social and economic as in religious reform.

WYKEHAM, WILLIAM OF. *See* WILLIAM OF WYKEHAM.

WYNTOUN, ANDREW OF, d. before 1425, canon regular of the Augustinian cathedral priory of Saint Andrews, later prior. He was the author of a metrical history of Scotland which extended to 1420, a prime source for the late fourteenth and early fifteenth century. The chronicle has philological value as an extended example of Middle Scots.

XANTEN, city on the Rhine in lower Lorraine, initially a Roman camp, which was noted again in 838. In the *Nibelungenlied* it served as Siegfried's home.

XANTHOPULUS, NICEPHORUS CALLISTUS, d. c. 1335, teacher in the patriarchal school at Hagia Sophia, author of works on liturgy, exegesis, and rhetoric, as well as religious verse, prayers, and a history of Christianity to 618.

XIMÉNES (JIMÉNEZ) DE CISNEROS, FRANCISCO. *See* JIMENEZ DE CISNEROS, FRANCISCO.

XIMÉNEZ DE RADA, RODRIGO, d. 1247, archbishop of Toledo (1208), chief adviser of Ferdinand III of Castile, a protector of the Jews, but a vigorous advocate of war against the Moors. He was the author of a chronicle of Spanish history.

XIPHILINUS, JOHN, d. 1075, Byzantine jurist, theologian, abbot of the monastery of the Holy Spirit on Mt. Olympus in Bithynia, and patriarch of Constantinople. He was the author of philosophical writings. He counted among his friends the historian Michael Psellus.

YA'QUBI (Ahmad Ibn Ya'qub Ibn Ja'far Ibn Wahb Ibn Wadih), d. 897, Arab historian and geographer. His universal history extended from the pre-Islamic period to 872 and included an account of Greece, Egypt, and India. In his geographical work he described the cities of Iraq, Iran, India, China, Syria, Egypt, the Maghreb, and the Byzantine empire.

YARMUK, BATTLE OF, battle fought in 636 on a tributary of the Jordan river that ended in an overwhelming victory for the Arabs over the Byzantine army. Shortly after the victory both Damascus and Jerusalem fell to the Moslems, and the loss of most of Syria and Egypt and north Africa was just a matter of time.

YEOMAN, in Britain a freeholder below the class of the gentry who worked his own land.

YEOMEN OF THE GUARD, a guard composed of yeomen who served as a personal guard for the English king. Henry VII established the guard following his victory at the battle of Bosworth Field in 1485.

YESIRAH, BOOK OF, Hebrew work probably of the seventh century which, together with the Zohar, provided the substance for the Cabala and helped inspire Jewish Gnosticism.

YIDDISH, a language that evolved from a fusion of the Hebrew with dialects of medieval Germany and was subsequently influenced by contact with Slavic languages.

YORK, city about 200 miles north of London. It served as military headquarters in late Roman times. It was first mentioned as a see in 314 when its bishop attended the Council of Arles. Saxons destroyed the Christian community which was restored in the seventh century when Paulinus was consecrated bishop (625). In 735 the see was raised to archiepiscopal rank and its prelate, Egbert, a pupil of Bede, made primate of the northern province. Egbert also founded the cathedral school which became one of the leading centers of learning in the West. Its most distinguished scholar, Alcuin (d. 804), joined the circle of learned men Charlemagne gathered at Aachen. Monasticism, which had suffered from the Danish invasions, revived with the Norman conquest. The dispute over questions of precedence with the archbishop of Canterbury began with the consecration of the first Norman archbishop and was finally resolved by Innocent VI (1352–62). As resolved, it granted the archbishop of Canterbury precedence and the title of "Primate of all England" while according the archbishop of York the title of "Primate of England." The York Plays, which represented the most extensive cycle of miracle plays in England, reached the height of their popularity in the fifteenth century. The city of York was one of the two largest provincial towns in medieval England.

YORK, HOUSE OF, branch of the Plantagenet family which ruled England from 1461 to 1485 in the persons of Edward IV, Edward V, and Richard III. The first duke of York was Edmund of Langley (d. 1402), fourth surviving son of Edward III. His son Edward (d. 1415), second earl of York, was the author of *The Master of Game*, the oldest book on hunting in English. (It was largely a translation of a French work on the subject.) This Edward died at the battle of Agincourt. The most famous member of the Yorkist family who did not ascend the throne was his nephew Richard (d. 1460), the third duke of York, who from 1447 was heir presumptive to the throne. Richard could claim descent from two sons of Edward III, a claim that was better than that of Henry VI himself. He served as lieutenant general and governor of France and Normandy but attained real prominence as leader of the opposition to the government following the loss of Normandy in 1453. When Henry became mentally ill that summer, he demanded and received the position of protector. But the birth of a son (Edward) to Henry's queen Margaret threatened Richard's succession, so he forced the issue by attacking the royal forces at St. Albans in 1455. Victorious here, he suffered defeat in 1459 at Ludlow Bridge and won a victory at Northampton in July 1460, whereupon Parliament proclaimed him the successor to Henry. In December of that year he lost his life at the battle of Wakefield. His son Edward (IV) went on to win the throne. [*See* ROSES, WARS OF THE.]

YULE, originally the principal pagan winter festival in Gemanic lands, later the name given to Christmas. The tradition of burning the Yule log at Christmas went back at least to 1184 when first mention of the practice appears.

YVES (YVO) OF CHARTRES. *See* IVO OF CHARTRES, ST.

ZABARELLA, FRANCESCO, d. 1417, a leading canonist, teacher of canon law at Florence and Padua, and bishop of Florence. He took part in the Council of Pisa in 1409 and was created cardinal deacon by the Pisan pope John XXIII. He collaborated with Emperor Sigismund in arranging for the summoning of the Council of Constance (1414–8). Although Zabarella was initially a papalist in his views concerning the supreme authority of the pope, he eventually joined the conciliarists as offering the only practical means whereby the Western Schism might be resolved. His principal work on the subject of supreme authority in the church is entitled *De Schismate*. His writings on canon law long remained standard works.

ZACHARY (Zacharias), Pope, 741–52, a Greek who as pope conducted generally successful diplomatic negotiations with Byzantium, the Lombards, and the Franks. He persuaded Liutprand, the king of the Lombards, to return the cities and other possessions he had taken from the duchy of Rome and in 751 authorized Pepin the Short to assume the Frankish crown. What encouragement he could give he extended to St. Boniface and other missionaries active in Gaul and Germany. He vigorously condemned the iconoclastic policy of the Byzantine emperor Constantine Copronymus.

ZACHARY (Zacharias) THE RHETOR, d. after 536, metropolitan of Mytilene on the island of Lesbos, author of biographies of several contemporary churchmen and of an ecclesiastical history of Egypt and Palestine covering the years 450 to 491.

ZAGORSK, town in central Russia that grew up around the fortified walls of the famous monastery founded in 1337–40 by St. Sergius of Radonezh. He dedicated the monastery to the Trinity, hence its double name Troitsa-Sergiyev. The Troitsa cathedral (1427) contains the tomb of St. Sergius. [*See* SERGIUS, ST.]

ZAKAT, Arabic for alms. The giving of alms was one of the major requirements placed upon Moslems by the Prophet in the Koran.

ZANGI (Zengi), d. 1146, atabeg of Mosul. He captured Edessa in 1144 which had been in the hands of the Christians since the First Crusade (1096–9). He extended his rule over various districts in Iraq and Syria including the cities of Aleppo and Hama. His capture of Edessa marked the extinction of one of the most important states established by the Crusaders and the turning point in the history of the Crusades.

ZENO, Roman emperor, 474–91, an Isaurian chieftain who was placed in command of the imperial troops by Emperor Leo I, married his daughter Ariadne, then succeeded to the throne upon Leo's death. He rid himself of the problem posed by the proximity of the Ostrogoths in Pannonia by persuading their king Theodoric to lead them to Italy and there destroy the usurper Odoacer. In 482 he issued the decree *Henoticon* which he hoped would satisfy both Rome and the Monophysites on the problem of Christ's nature but which did neither. [*See* HENOTICON.]

ZEPHYRINUS, ST., Pope, 198–217, successor of Victor I, whose pontificate was troubled by the heresies of Montanism and Monarchianism as well as by the persecution of the Roman emperor Septimius Severus.

ZHUPAN (zupan), the head or leader of a Slavic community or state, a title used by the Croats and Slovenes.

ZIRIDS, Moslem Berbers who ruled north Africa as allies of the Fatimids from the tenth century, then in 1050 announced their independence. In 1152 they were conquered by the Almoravids.

ZIZKA (Ziska), JOHN, d. 1424, Bohemian general, member of the lesser gentry, and a follower of John Hus. He first gained fame fighting with the Poles against the Teutonic Knights in the battle of Grunwald. As leader of the Hussites he gained a number of victories over the imperial armies. Toward the end of his career he adhered to the Calixtine group as opposed to the more radical Taborites and accepted the moderate position set forth in the Four Articles of Prague. Zizka proved himself one of the great military innovators of the times. The bulk of his army was composed of peasants and townspeople, but the combination of their religious enthusiasm, Zizka's skillful strategy, and his use of primitive "tanks" which carried small cannons, gave them the victory over the best knightly armies of the day.

ZOE, Byzantine empress, 1028–50, daughter of Constantine VIII, and wife successively of Romanus III, Michael IV, and Constantine IX. For a short time in 1042 she shared the imperial authority with her sister Theodora. Her extravagance and lack of responsibility contributed to a serious decline of the empire.

ZOHAR, a product of the Jewish Cabala. It consisted principally of commentaries on different passages in the Hebrew Bible.

ZONARAS, JOHN, d. after 1160, Byzantine historian, monk, and author of an important world chronicle (to 1118), homilies, lives of the saints, and a massive commentary on the canons of the apostles, councils, and synods. The first 21 books of Dio Cassius's history are preserved with his writings.

ZOSIMUS (Sosimus), ST., Pope, 417–8, of Greek or Jewish ancestry. He experienced a stormy pontificate because of Pelagianism and the powerful position he assigned to Patroclus, the bishop of Arles, which angered the other bishops of Gaul. He may have been forced by St. Augustine to retract his earlier judgment favoring Pelagianism.

ZOSIMUS, fl. 450, Greek historian who authored a valuable history of Rome to the year 410. Though writing in the fifth century, he held to a pagan, anti-Christian interpretation of history, and so attributed the fall of the city of Rome to Alaric and the Visigoths in 410 to Rome's abandonment of the pagan gods.

ZURARA, GOMES EANES DE, d. 1474, Portuguese chronicler who left an account, not entirely trustworthy, of the Portuguese explorations along the west coast of Africa. His works include a history of Tangier.

ZÜRICH, city in Switzerland, originally a Roman settlement. It became an Alemanni community in the fifth century and a Frankish in the sixth. In the ninth century it served as a residence of a Carolingian king, received the status of an imperial city in 1218, and in 1351 joined the League of Upper Germany. In 1400 it bought its freedom from the German emperor.